TO THE STUDENT   A Study Guide for the textbook is available through your college bookstore under the title Study Guide to accompany Business Law: Text and Cases by John W. Collins, Patrick J. Cihon, Mary Ann Donnelly, Richard Hartzler, James P. Karp, Frederick J. Naffziger, and Arthur D. Wolfe. The Study Guide can help you with course material by acting as a tutorial, review and study aid. If the Study Guide is not in stock, ask the bookstore manager to order a copy for you.

BUSINESS
LAW
TEXT AND CASES

BUSINESS LAW TEXTBOOKS FROM JOHN WILEY & SONS

BUSINESS LAW

TEXT AND CASES

John W. Collins
Syracuse University

Patrick J. Cihon
Syracuse University

Mary Ann Donnelly
Le Moyne College

Richard Hartzler
Clarkson University

James P. Karp
Syracuse University

Frederick J. Naffziger
Indiana University at South Bend

Arthur D. Wolfe
Michigan State University

John Wiley & Sons

New York   Chichester   Brisbane   Toronto   Singapore

Library of Congress Cataloging in Publication Data:

Main entry under title:
Business law.

    Includes index.
    1. Business law—United States. 2. Trade regulation
—United States. I. Collins, John W., 1938–

KF889.B86 1986	346.73'07	85-20391
ISBN 0-471-04075-4	347.3067	

Printed in the United States of America

10 9 8 7 6 5 4 3 2

ABOUT THE AUTHORS

JOHN W. COLLINS   received an A.B. from Hamilton College and a J.D. from Harvard Law School. His published articles include "Improving the Relationship Between Lawyers and Business Clients," "Law in the Business Curriculum," and "Creative Analysis of Judicial Decisions." He is presently a staff editor of the American Business Law Journal and professor of Law and Public Policy in the Syracuse University School of Management.

PATRICK J. CIHON   received a B.A. in political science from Pennsylvania State University, an LL.B. from Osgoode Hall Law School of York University, and an LL.M. from Yale Law School. His areas of interest are labor relations and government regulation of business. He is currently an assistant professor of law and public policy at the Syracuse University School of Management.

MARY ANN DONNELLY   received a B.A. in English from Le Moyne College in Syracuse, New York, and a J.D. from Harvard Law School. She is a coauthor of *Bankruptcy, Arrangements and Reorganizations.* For the past 14 years she has coauthored "Commercial Law" in the *Annual Survey of New York Law* published by the Syracuse Law Review. She is a member of the New York State Bar and is currently an associate professor in the Business Administration Department at Le Moyne College.

H. RICHARD HARTZLER   received an A.B. degree in government and a J.D. from Indiana University. He has specialized in Uniform Commercial Code and small business management subjects as well as in legal history, philosophy, and justice. He has served many years as an administrator in Schools of Management and was most recently Dean of the School of Management and Public Affairs at the University of Alaska, Anchorage, before returning to full-time teaching and research. Presently, Hartzler is editor of the *North Country Business and Economic Report for Entrepreneurs* published by the

School of Management, Clarkson University, Potsdam, New York, where he holds the rank of professor.

JAMES P. KARP   received a B.S. from Pennsylvania State University and a J.D. from Villanova University. He has written numerous articles on environmental law and land use law. He has been an advisor to several government agencies and private corporations on environmental and land use matters. He is coauthor of a text on real estate law. He has served as a staff editor for the *American Business Law Journal.* Currently, James P. Karp is a professor of law and public policy at Syracuse University.

FRED J. NAFFZIGER   received both his B.A. and J.D. from the University of Illinois. He is a coauthor of *A Basic Guide to Federal Labor Law* and *The Law of American Business Organizations.* He has served as a staff editor of the *American Business Law Journal* and is a past president of the Tri-State Business Law Association. He has been a U.S. Department of State Scholar-Diplomat and has also taught in Saudi Arabia. He is a member of the Illinois, District of Columbia, and Texas Bars and currently is a professor of business law at Indiana University, South Bend.

ARTHUR D. WOLFE   received a B.A. in history and a J.D. from Ohio State University and an M.A. in economics from the University of Illinois. He has written numerous articles, including "Undergraduate Legal Instruction and the Development of Cognitive Behaviors" and "A Legal and Ethical Critique of the Use of Cost Benefit Analysis in the Public Law System," and he is the coauthor of four books on business law and the legal environment of business. He has served on the editorial board of the *American Business Law Journal* for 10 years and was editor-in-chief in 1984–1985. He is a member of the Indiana, Ohio, and U.S. Virgin Islands Bars and is professor of business law at Michigan State University.

PREFACE

This book is about law. Our intention, however, is not that it be used by lawyers. Instead, this book has been written for people who are not lawyers but who nevertheless recognize that a basic understanding of the law and the legal system is indispensable in contemporary society. We expect that most, although not all, of our readers will be instructors and students in universities and colleges throughout the United States. We hope that they and others who use this book will find it enjoyable and useful.

THE PURPOSE OF THIS BOOK

The purpose of this book is to help the reader to learn about business law and the legal environment of business. The book has been designed to be a teaching tool that will help instructors to convey their knowledge of law to their students, and it has been written with an eye to avoiding the pitfalls common to many business law books. Thus, students who use this book should develop a thorough knowledge of law and a firm understanding of its effects on business and society.

The book's accurate and comprehensive coverage — 56 chapters, 7 appendices, and a glossary — means that it can be used in both business law and legal environment of business courses. The text and cases throughout the book have been written and edited by business law instructors who are recognized experts in their respective fields.

Clear Presentation

Throughout the book, the text, the cases, and the problems have been written and edited to make the law clear to students. All technical words are explained in the text and are included in the glossary. Legal concepts are developed logically, and the use of four levels of headings will help students to understand the concepts as they are developed. Examples are used frequently to explain legal concepts. Actual court decisions have been very carefully edited so that they too are comprehensible to students and clarify the text rather than cause confusion. Most of the court decisions begin with an edited summary of the facts and procedure of the case.

Total Integration

Perhaps the characteristic that contributes the most to the high quality of this book is the total integration of its materials. In each chapter, the text that explains legal concepts flows naturally into the cases that illustrate those concepts. The lead-in to each case explains the relationship between the case and the preceding text material. Furthermore, each case is followed by case review questions that require the student to relate the text material to the case, thereby highlighting the important points that the student should learn from reading and analyzing the case. Finally, each chapter concludes with review questions and case problems. A student who can answer all of the review questions for a chapter will have gained a basic understanding of the most important points of the chapter. The case problems, which have been carefully developed so that they can be fully answered on the basis of the material presented in the chapter, require the students to apply the law that they have learned rather than just to memorize it.

The 7 appendices consist of the Constitution of the United States, the Uniform Commercial Code, the Uniform Partnership Act, the Uniform Limited Partnership Act, the Revised Uniform Limited Partnership Act, the Model Business Corporation Act, and selected antitrust statutes. The appendices have been placed in a separate volume in order to facilitate their use. When studying topics that require reference to material in an appendix, the student can look at the text and the appendix at the same time. We have found this to be much more convenient than having to refer to appendices that are located in the back of the book.

THE ORGANIZATION OF THE BOOK

The organization of this book has been developed to present information in an order that will help the reader to learn about and to understand law. The book is divided into 10 parts.

Part I: The Legal Environment of Business

Part I consists of 7 chapters that introduce the student to the study of law and to the legal environment in which business functions. Chapter 1 presents an approach to the study of law that will help the student not only to memorize legal rules but also to understand how those rules operate in the business world. The analytical framework that is presented to the student explains in simple terms the sources of laws, the effects of laws, and the possible goals of law.

Chapter 1 also carefully explains how court decisions are used in the study of law, instructs the student on how to brief a case, and presents a practice court decision for the student to read and analyze in the manner recommended in the chapter. Although all of the introductory topics usually found in the first chapter of business law books are included in Chapter 1, the chapter has been organized in a way that permits the students to understand the significance of each of the topics as well as their relationships to one another and to topics presented later in the book.

In Chapters 2 through 4, students learn about the structure and process of the legal system — including the process of legal reasoning that contributes to the environment in which business operates. In Chapters 5 and 7, two areas of the law — tort law and criminal law — that are not related exclusively to business, but which are such pervasive legal topics that they are important aspects of the legal environment of business, are explained and discussed.

Also included in Part I is coverage of product liability in Chapter 6. This chapter has been placed after the chapter on tort law in order to illustrate how the courts have applied tort law to the issue of product liability. Chapter 6 is also included in Part I to show students one of the areas in which business has an impact on society and how society has responded to that impact.

Parts II through IX

The next 8 parts of the book — Parts II through IX — provide accurate and comprehensive coverage of those areas of law that directly affect business:

Part   II: Contract Law (11 chapters)
Part   III: Sales Law (6 chapters)
Part   IV: Negotiable Instruments Law (4 chapters)
Part   V: Debtor – Creditor Law (2 chapters)
Part   VI: Agency Law (4 chapters)
Part VII: Partnership Law (3 chapters)
Part VIII: Corporation Law (4 chapters)
Part   IX: Property Law (3 chapters)

Part X: The Regulatory Environment of Business

Part X contains 12 chapters. It begins with 2 chapters that carefully explain the structure and process of government regulations of business. The remaining 10 chapters deal with various areas of business activity that are regulated by the government through antitrust law, consumer protection regulation, insurance law, securities regulation, labor law, employment discrimination law, environmental law, and land-use regulation.

SUPPLEMENTS TO THIS BOOK

Four supplements are available to users of this book. The purpose of each of the supplements is to enhance the effectiveness of the book as a tool for teaching and learning about business law and the legal environment of business.

Study Guide

A study guide that helps the students to derive the most benefit from using this book has been prepared by Professor Janine Hiller of Virginia Polytechnic Institute and State University. In the study guide, each chapter of the book has been outlined. Included in the outline are references to the cases in the chapter, the case review questions, the review questions, and the case problems. A list of key words and objective study questions are also included for each chapter.

Instructor's Manual

A comprehensive instructor's manual prepared by the authors is available to instructors who adopt this book. The manual contains the same chapter outline with references that is found in the Study Guide. In addition, the instructor's manual includes case summaries and answers to the case review questions, the review questions, and the case problems.

Test Bank

An extensive test bank of effective true–false, multiple-choice, and essay questions prepared by William Burke of the University of Lowell is available to instructors who adopt this book. This test book is available on software disks for Apple, TRS-80, and IBM-PC compatible computers.

Transparencies

A set of acetate teaching transparencies is also available free to adopters.

In summary, we hope our book provides both instructors and students with an effective tool for the study of business law. We are anxious to receive feedback from you letting us know in what ways we have succeeded and in what ways we might improve our efforts. Please feel free to write us to give us your views. In the meantime, we hope you enjoy and benefit from using this book.

John W. Collins
Patrick J. Cihon
Mary Ann Donnelly
Richard Hartzler
James P. Karp
Frederick J. Naffziger
Arthur D. Wolfe

ACKNOWLEDGMENTS

The authors wish to acknowledge the many people who have made significant contributions to the completion of this book.

Professor Sandra N. Hurd of Syracuse University wrote Chapter 5, *Tort Law,* and Chapter 7, *Criminal Law.* Professor Edward Graves of the American College wrote the original draft of Chapter 50, *Insurance Law.* Chapter 53, *Employment Discrimination,* is adapted from *A Basic Guide to Federal Labor Law: The Private Sector,* second edition, pp. 155–173, © 1975, 1981, by Fred J. Naffzinger and Keith Knauss.

We have benefitted from the thoughtful manuscript reviews of Jenny Bennett, Sandra Hurd (Syracuse University), Jack Karns (University of North Dakota), Charles Patten (University of Wisconsin-Oshkosh), Eric Richards (Indiana University), Michael Schuster (Syracuse University), George Spiro (University of Massachusetts, Amherst), and Frances Zollers (Syracuse University).

For help in the production of the manuscript we thank Gloria Burhyte, Roberta Chamberlin, Sheila Forsyth, Jill Cooper, Colleen Woodward, Mary Ann De Michele, Joseph Callahan, Jon Canis, Matthew McCabe, William Kiessling, Patti Vassalo Hoversten, and Denise Androvette.

The following permissions to reprint materials are acknowledged: Drawing by Robt. Day, © 1950, 1978 The New Yorker Magazine; partnership agreement by Matthew Bender and Company, Inc.; excerpts from the Restatement (Second) of Agency, © 1958, the Restatement (Second) of Contracts, © 1981, and the Restatement (Second) of Torts, © 1965, all copyrighted by the American Law Institute; Uniform Commercial Code, © 1978, The American Law Institute and the National Conference of Commissioners on Uniform State Laws; adaptations of CPA examination questions, all copyrighted by the American Institute of Certified Public Accountants; stock certificate provided by Maura Rodgers; specimens of bank documents provided by Key Bank of Central New York through Mr. Richard Liddle.

We are greatly indebted to the talented, understanding, and patient people at

John Wiley & Sons who have contributed so much to our efforts: Barbara Heaney, Rafael Hernandez, Jan Lavin, Elizabeth Meder, Kevin Murphy, Chris Ross, Alida Setford, Susan Winick, and especially our editor, Lucille Sutton. Thanks also to Steve Perine, whose tough blue pencil has become so familiar to us.

Finally, we wish to thank our families, friends, and students, whose support and patience have been indispensable.

J.W.C.
P.J.C.
M.A.D.
R.H.
J.P.K.
F.J.N.
A.D.W.

TABLE OF CONTENTS

PART I

THE LEGAL ENVIRONMENT OF BUSINESS

PART II
CONTRACT LAW

PART III

SALES LAW

PART IV

NEGOTIABLE INSTRUMENTS LAW

PART V

DEBTOR–CREDITOR LAW

PART VI

AGENCY LAW

PART VII

PARTNERSHIP LAW

PART VIII
CORPORATION LAW

PART IX
PROPERTY LAW

PART X
THE REGULATORY ENVIRONMENT OF BUSINESS

PART I

THE LEGAL ENVIRONMENT OF BUSINESS

"*What burns me up is that the answer is right here somewhere, staring us in the face.*"

INTRODUCTION TO LAW AND THE LEGAL SYSTEM

Studying a subject involves not only learning specific information but also *understanding* and *evaluating* the information that is learned. When a person begins the study of a new subject, it is thus helpful to have an analytical framework. An analytical framework provides a way of looking at a subject so that the relationships among and significance of the various pieces of information learned about the subject can be understood and evaluated.

In this chapter, we will present an analytical framework for understanding and evaluating laws and the legal system. We will begin by considering where the rules, principles, and standards that are the law are found. Then we will discuss the effects of the existence of the law and its application by the legal system and the goal of law. Finally, we will consider the relationships among these topics and how they can be used as an analytical framework for understanding and evaluating laws and the legal system. Additionally, at the end of the chapter you will apply this analytical framework to a court decision.

WHERE THE LAW IS FOUND

Look at the cartoon we've reproduced here. Notice all the books and the frustration of the lawyers. You might also find it interesting to note that most people assume that the three people in the cartoon are lawyers even though the fact that they are lawyers is not expressly stated.

Why do we assume that these people are lawyers? The way they are dressed may be a clue. But most likely, it's because they are looking for an answer to a question, and the answer is hidden away somewhere in the hundreds of books in their library. In the following sections, you will read about the kinds of things that lawyers find inside those books. (Today, of course, lawyers may find the law at a computer terminal rather than in a book.)

Constitutions

A **constitution** is a document that sets forth the basic principles of a government, such as the authority of the government, the division of authority within the government, and the rights of the people. You are probably somewhat familiar with the United States Constitution, but you may not be aware that your state, as well as all of the other states, also has a constitution. Because the U.S. Constitution is the "supreme law of the land," however, the provisions of a state's constitution may not violate any of the provisions of the U.S. Constitution.

Sometimes the answers to legal questions are found in a constitution, and the U.S. Constitution will be referred to many times in this book. In the next chapter, for instance, you will learn that the Constitution dictates the kinds of lawsuits that can be heard in federal courts. The U.S. Constitution is reprinted in its entirety in Appendix A. If you have never actually read the Constitution, you may want to do so now.

Statutes

The U.S. Constitution, as well as the constitution of each state, establishes a legislature, sometimes referred to as the legislative branch of government. The primary function of a legislature is to enact laws in the form of **statutes.** Frequently, the answers to legal questions are found in a statute.[1] For instance, if a corporation wants to know whether it is legal for it to purchase another corporation, the answer may be found in Section 7 of the Clayton Act, an antitrust statute adopted by the U.S. Congress. If you want to see what a statute looks like, the Clayton Act is reprinted in Appendix G. Many statutes will be referred to throughout the book.

The provisions of a statute adopted by a legislature may not violate the provisions of any applicable constitution. Thus, the U.S. Congress may not adopt a statute that violates any provision of the U.S. Constitution, and a state legislature may not adopt a statute that violates the provisions of either that state's constitution or the U.S. Constitution. A statute that violates the provisions of an applicable constitution is said to be *unconstitutional.*

Precedents

The U.S. Constitution and the state constitutions also create court systems, sometimes called the judiciary or the judicial branch of government. The pri-

---

[1] We also use the term statute to refer to ordinances enacted by the elected law-making bodies of local governments such as villages, towns, cities, and counties.

mary function of courts is to resolve conflicts, which take the form of lawsuits, by applying the law. When a court decides a lawsuit, it must apply any constitutional provision or statute that is applicable to the lawsuit. For instance, a court that has to decide a lawsuit in which the issue is whether a corporation did something illegal when it purchased another corporation would have to apply Section 7 of the Clayton Act.

Sometimes, however, there is no constitutional or statutory provision that will answer a legal question raised in a lawsuit. When this happens, a court will look to previous court decisions, called **precedents,** to find the law that will answer the legal questions. For instance, in Chapter 5 you will read about cases in which one person has sued another on the grounds of negligence. For the most part, the law of negligence is not found in constitutions or statutes. Instead, the early law of negligence was developed by judges who decided on their own, without the guidance of a constitution or statutes, how lawsuits based on negligence should be decided. In subsequent lawsuits based on negligence, the judges looked to these precedents for legal principles to apply. In other words, the precedents themselves created the law of negligence. If you want to see an instance in which a court created law to be applied in future cases, read the case of *Gastonia Personnel Corp. v. Rogers* on page 61.

Even in lawsuits in which a court applies a constitution or a statute to answer a legal question, the court may refer to precedents to see how the constitutional or statutory provisions were applied in similar situations. For instance, in the case of *Lewis v. Curry College* in Chapter 2 (see page 22), the Supreme Court of Washington State referred to two earlier cases, *International Shoe Co. v. Washington* and *Hanson v. Denckla,* to interpret a Washington statute and the due process clause of the U.S. Constitution.

Executive Orders

The federal and state constitutions also create the executive branches of the federal and state governments. The president is the chief executive officer of the federal government, and the chief executive officer of a state government is the governor. The primary function of the executive branch of government is to execute, which means to carry out, the law.

In carrying out the law, the president or a governor may issue an *executive order.* For instance, Presidential Executive Order 11245, which requires all businesses that have contracts in excess of $10,000 with the federal government for construction or the supply of goods and services to agree not to discriminate in employment on the basis of race, color, creed, religion, sex, or national origin, is the subject of the *Liberty Mutual Insurance Co. v. Friedman* case on page 1002. An executive order has the force of law unless the chief executive officer does not have the constitutional or statutory authority to issue it. Executive orders must therefore be considered in answering legal questions.

Administrative Regulations

Federal and state constitutions do not create administrative agencies. Instead, these agencies are created by statutes adopted by federal, state, and local legislatures for the purpose of implementing government regulatory policies. For instance, the Securities and Exchange Commission implements policies intended to protect investors, the Environmental Protection Agency implements environmental policies, and the National Labor Relations Board implements policies concerning labor-management relations.

Administrative agencies frequently combine legislative (law making), executive (law execution), and judicial (law application) functions (see Chapter 45). In carrying out its legislative function, an administrative agency may adopt *regulations.* For example, a regulation adopted by the Consumer Product Safety Commission requiring that all new baby cribs have a maximum spacing of 2.375 inches between slats is discussed on page 975.

An administrative regulation has the effect of law as long as it falls within the authority delegated to the agency by the legislature, the agency followed proper procedures in adopting the regulation, and the regulation is reasonable and is supported by substantial evidence. A person answering a legal question must therefore consider administrative regulations. The regulatory environment of business is the subject of Chapters 45 through 56 of this book.

Treaties

A treaty is an agreement between nations. Article II, Section 2 of the U.S. Constitution provides that the president has the power to make treaties for the United States, subject to the approval of two-thirds of the members of the Senate. In Article VI, the Constitution provides that these treaties are the supreme law of the land. Treaties, too, must therefore be considered when answering legal questions.

Secondary Sources

Each of the sources of law discussed thus far is called a *primary source* of the law, which means that it is a source where actual law can be found. There are also other sources that lawyers, judges, and others frequently turn to that contain descriptions of the law rather than actual law. These sources are called *secondary sources* of the law.

For example, there are many legal encyclopedias, books, and periodicals that contain descriptions of the law. A series of books called Restatements has been particularly influential in the development of the law, and they are often cited (referred to) by the courts. Each Restatement is an attempt by the American Law Institute, a private group of law experts, to state sound principles of law in a particular legal field. For instance, you will find numerous references to the Restatement of Contracts and the Restatement of Agency when you read about contracts and agency in this book.

THE EFFECTS OF THE LAW

Although finding the law is sometimes a difficult task, as it apparently is for the lawyers in the cartoon that appears earlier in this chapter, it is usually the easiest part of legal analysis. Finding and knowing the law are of little value to a person who does not know how to apply it. To understand how the law is applied, it is essential to understand the effects that result from the existence of the law and its application by the legal system. Sometimes, these effects are referred to as the functions or purposes of the law. In this section, you will read about the various effects of the law and its application.

Conflict Resolution

An important effect of the law and the legal system is the resolution of conflicts that arise when different needs and desires—that is, different interests—are felt by the people and organizations that make up society. The law resolves conflicts by recognizing and protecting certain interests and by not recognizing or protecting others. However, the interests that are protected can change over time; there is always pressure on the legal system to recognize new interests and to reevaluate the recognition of old interests. For instance, the law that determines the liability of a manufacturer to a consumer who is injured by a defective product has changed dramatically during the last 150 years. You will learn about the interests that have been recognized and protected at different times and why the law of product liability has changed over the years when you read Chapter 6.

When conflicts arise between individuals, the interests involved may appear to be only those of the individuals themselves. Usually, however, the individuals in conflict are expressing not only their own interests but also the interests of others who are in similar situations.

For example, in a conflict between an individual landlord and an individual tenant concerning the amount of maintenance the landlord must provide for the tenant's apartment, the landlord and the tenant are indeed representing their own interests. But, at the same time, they are also representing the interests of other landlords and other tenants. The way in which the particular conflict is resolved will affect not only the two parties in conflict but also other landlords and tenants because the decision will serve as a precedent for the resolution of future landlord-tenant conflicts.

That society resolve conflicts is important. Otherwise, society will suffer the disruptive effects that result from the continuation of conflict and the possible use of violent methods to resolve the conflict by the people involved. That society resolve conflicts effectively is also important. The slow and unfair resolution of conflicts can be as disruptive to society as no resolution at all. Conversely, the quick, fair, and wise resolution of conflicts can have a beneficial effect on the well-being of society.

Conflict Prevention

Although much attention is paid to the conflict resolution effect of law and the legal system, the prevention of conflict may be an even more important effect of law. Because the law indicates how legal conflicts will be resolved if they occur, many people regulate their behavior so as to avoid conflicts they would lose. In other words, the law can be used by people and businesses for planning purposes.

Deterring Unwanted Behavior One way in which the law guides behavior is by deterring (discouraging) behavior that is believed to be detrimental to society. A clear example of this function of the law is found in the designation of certain behaviors as criminal and the imposition of penalties on those who engage in these behaviors. Similarly, some behavior is deterred by laws providing that a person who injures another while engaged in that behavior will be made to compensate the injured party for the losses he or she incurs. In some instances, extra penalties, called *punitive damages,* are imposed in addition to the actual losses incurred as a further effort to deter certain behavior.

Channeling Desired Behavior Not only does the law seek to deter certain socially detrimental behavior, it also seeks to encourage certain socially beneficial behavior. Encouraging desired behavior is called the channeling function of law. An example of the way in which the law channels behavior is found in contract law, which provides that the courts will generally enforce the promises of people who enter into contracts. People are thus encouraged to enter into contracts because they know that a court will provide a remedy if the other party fails to keep his or her contract promises. This has the socially beneficial effect of stimulating economic activity and creating economic growth.

Allocation of Authority

The law also has the effect of allocating (distributing) decision-making authority within society. For instance, the U.S. Constitution allocates the authority of the federal government among the executive, the legislative, and the judicial branches. In Chapter 2, you will read about the decision-making authority that is allocated to the federal courts.

Some statutes, such as those that create administrative agencies, also allocate authority. In turn, an administrative agency will adopt regulations to allocate its authority among the various people who work for the agency. The U.S. Constitution also allocates some authority to the states, which in turn allocate their authority among the branches and agencies of their state governments. The net sum of all of these actions is the present allocation of governmental authority in the United States.

Process Requirements

In addition to determining *who* has the authority to make decisions, the law may also have the effect of determining *how* decisions are made. In other words, the law may require the use of *particular processes* when decisions are made. In Chapter 2 and 3, you will read about the decision-making processes that the courts follow in resolving legal conflicts, and in Chapter 46, you will read about the processes used by administrative agencies.

THE GOAL OF LAW

The final step in legal analysis is often an evaluation of whether the effects of a particular law are good or bad. This question can only be answered, however, if we know what the goal of law is so that the effects of a particular law can be evaluated in terms of that goal. Unfortunately, there is no agreement as to what the goal of law should be. Instead, there are various theories about the goal of law. In this section, we will discuss these theories. As you read about them, you should consider your personal view of what the goal of law is.

The Goal of Promoting Morality

One view of law emphasizes the relationship between law and morality. Those who have thought of law in this way, including St. Thomas Aquinas, have believed that what is moral can be determined by the use of reason. The reasoning process begins with a determination of the essence of human nature, which is believed to be a reflection of God's will. Law should therefore promote and protect the essence of human nature.

For instance, since the will to survive is an essential part of human nature, law should promote survival. Any law that has the effect of promoting survival, such as a statute that provides that a person who kills another person will be punished, is thus a good law. This view of law is usually called the *natural law* theory.

The Goal of Serving Power

Another view of law emphasizes the relationship between law and political power. Those who have thought of law in this way, Thomas Hobbes among them, have believed that law serves to promote the interests of those people who have political power. Law is thus seen as a political issue, not a moral issue. This view of law is usually called *legal positivism.*

The Goal of Reflecting Custom

A third view of law emphasizes the relationship between law and social custom. Those who have thought of law in this way, including Sir Henry Maine, have believed that law should reflect the customs of the people who make up society rather than the will of a supreme being or the interests of those who have political power. Law is thus seen as a reflection of society, not a command to it. This view of law is usually called *historical jurisprudence.*

The Goal of Social Welfare

A final view of law emphasizes the relationship between law and social welfare. Those who have thought of law in this way, such as Roscoe Pound, have believed that law should serve society by recognizing and balancing the interests of all the members of society. Law is thus seen as a tool to improve human existence rather than as either a command to or a mere reflection of society. This view of law is usually called *sociological jurisprudence.*

AN ANALYTICAL FRAMEWORK

The topics discussed thus far in this chapter and the relationships among them comprise our analytical framework. They can be summarized as shown in

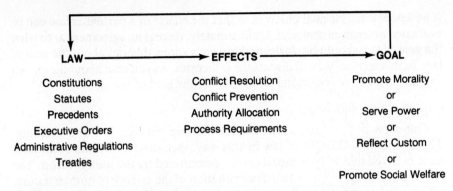

FIGURE 1-1
An Analytical Framework for Studying Law

Figure 1-1. As you read this book, you may want to use this analytical framework as a basis for learning, understanding, and evaluating the law. Most people, when they study law, focus on simply *learning* the law itself; that is, they merely learn the rules, principles, and standards that are found in constitutions, statutes, precedents, executive orders, administrative regulations, and treaties.

To understand the law, however, you must also focus on the effects of the law you learn about. What conflict of interests make a particular law necessary? What interests are or are not recognized and protected by the way the law resolves the conflict? What behavior is discouraged or encouraged by the law? Does the law allocate decision-making authority or require certain decision-making processes? Only if you can answer questions such as these can you be said to *understand* the law and how the legal system will apply it in particular situations.

In addition, as a student of law, you should learn to evaluate the law. To accomplish this, you must first make a personal determination of the goal of law and then decide whether the effects of a particular law are compatible with that goal. Only if these steps are taken can you *evaluate* the law and thus participate as a citizen in making the law work to improve society.

In Figure 1-1, you should note the arrow that goes from the goal of law back to the law itself. This arrow signifies that the goal of law serves not only as a basis for evaluating the existing laws but also as a basis for changing old laws and adopting new ones. As was mentioned earlier, you will read about evaluation and change in the law of product liability when you read Chapter 6.

A PRACTICE CASE

In this book, you will read many court case decisions, something you may never have done before. You may have some difficulty reading these cases at first, but after you have read a few, your ability to read and understand them should improve. By all means, don't be intimidated by this new experience. Literally millions of students have mastered the necessary skills for reading and analyzing cases, and you will too.

When you read a case, you may want to prepare what is called a "brief" of the case. Briefing a case means that you analyze it by writing down the following information concerning the case:

1. The *parties* involved in the case.
2. The relevant *facts* of the case.
3. The *procedure* followed in the case prior to the court's decision.
4. The *issue* of the case, meaning the legal point that will determine the outcome of the case and about which the parties disagree.
5. The *decision* of the court.
6. The *reasoning* of the court in reaching its decision, as well as the *reasoning* of any judges who do not join in the court's opinion but instead write separate opinions of their own.

The following case and the case review questions that follow it will give you some practice in reading cases. You will also apply some of the information that you have read about in this chapter. We have attempted to make this case and the others in this book as understandable as possible for you. For instance, the bracketed paragraphs at the beginning of most cases provide a summary of the facts and the procedure followed in the case. Furthermore, the decisions themselves have been edited to delete extraneous discussion and, except where necessary for understanding, citations to sources of the law. In the following case, however, some citations have been left in so that you can see where the court found the law that it applies.

Although there were two people against whom the legal action was brought in this case, by tradition only the name of one appears in the title of the case. The information just below the title of the case tells where the decision was published—in this case, Volume 562 of the South Western Reporter, 2nd Series, page 62—and in what court system or court and year the decision was made.

After you read the court's decision, which was written for the court by Justice Holt, you will find that Justice Fogleman disagreed with the majority of the justices of the court and decided to write what is called a *dissenting opinion*. Although a dissenting opinion has no immediate legal effect, Justice Fogleman no doubt hoped that it would contribute to changing the law in the future. You will learn more about dissenting opinions in Chapter 3.

EVANS LABORATORIES, INC. v. MELDER
562 S.W.2d 62 (Arkansas 1978)

[Evans Laboratories, Inc. (Evans) is in the termite and pest control business. Evans employed D.O. Melder as the manager of one of its branch offices in McGhee, Arkansas, and Louis Cingolani as a route-man servicing customers in the McGhee area. The employment contracts of Melder and Cingolani were for an unspecified length of time and could be terminated by either party upon ten days' notice. The contracts included a clause, called a restrictive covenant, that provided that, for two years following the termination of their employment, Melder and Cingolani would not accept or solicit business from any of Evans' customers that they had serviced.

Melder and Cingolani quit working for Evans and went into business as Delta Pest Control. Evans brought a legal action against its two former employees asking the court to enforce the restrictive covenant in the employment contract by enjoining (stopping) them from engaging in certain activities.

The trial court in which the case began refused to enjoin the activities of Melder and Cingolani. Evans then appealed the trial court's decision to the Supreme Court of Arkansas. (You will read about beginning a lawsuit in Chapter 2 and about trials and appeals in Chapter 3.) Because Evans brought the appeal, it is referred to in the decision as the appellant. Melder and Cingolani are called the appellees.]

HOLT, Justice

Appellant correctly states the central issue to be resolved on appeal is the validity of the restrictive covenants. Appellant concedes that the restriction covenant is inapplicable to appellee Melder, because, as a branch manager, he serviced no former customers.

The validity of a restrictive covenant not to compete in an employment contract depends upon the facts and circumstances of the particular case. *United Ins. Agency, Inc. v. Martin; McLeod v. Meyer.* Further, it is well established that we are reluctant to uphold employment contracts which have negative provisions, as here, with reference to future employment elsewhere by the employee. *McLeod v. Meyer.*

Appellees argue that the restrictive covenant in question here is invalid because it constitutes a restraint of trade which is void against public policy. Appellant argues that this restrictive covenant is necessary because the relationship between the routeman and the customer is the most important element in developing and maintaining business in this industry.

In determining whether or not a restraint of trade imposed by a contract is reasonable, we consider "whether it is such only as to afford a fair protection to the interests of the party in whose favor it is given, and not so large as to interfere with the interests of the

public." *Orkin Exterminating Co. v. Murrell.* Here the record indicates that when appellant's prior customers defected from it to Delta, the newly organized firm, it was not due to any solicitation on appellee Cingolani's part but due to their satisfaction with his prior servicing.

In the circumstances we are of the view that the provision which prohibits Cingolani from accepting the requests of appellant's former customers, whom he formerly serviced, is undue interference with the interests of the public's right to the availability of a serviceman it prefers to use. In other words, it results in an unreasonable restraint of trade.

Affirmed. [Meaning that the appellate court upholds the trial court's decision.]

FOGLEMAN, Judge (dissenting)

The court's reluctance to uphold a contract having restrictive covenants with reference to future employment has led it up a one-way blind alley from which it cannot see the basic purpose for these covenants and the legitimate right of an employer to protect himself against unfair competition. By so doing, employers are deprived of their right to contract to protect themselves from business piracy. I feel so strongly that it is high time this court reexamine the posture it has taken in these cases, that I am compelled to voice those feelings, even though time will not permit elaboration to the extent I would like.

It appears to me that the view of employment contract covenants not to compete taken by this court over the last thirty years clearly indicates that the basic reasons for permitting these contracts in restraint of trade at all have become obscured. Originally, no such contract was enforceable. Later development produced the rule that a general restraint was invalid, but a partial restraint was valid, recognizing that a purchaser of a business or an employer was entitled to protection, not from competition, but from unfair competition, or business piracy. Ultimately, the rule of partial restraint gave way to the rule of reasonableness, i.e., reasonable restraints are to be enforced. *Orkin Exterminating Co. v. Murrell.* The test of reasonableness turns on the facts and circumstances of the particular case, and that rule has been recognized ceremonially by this court. *United Insurance Agency v. Martin; McLeod v. Meyer.* Perhaps no better test could be provided, because in every case there is a clash of two important freedoms, freedom to contract and freedom to work.

It is widely recognized that the most important of the legitimate interests of the employer which are entitled to protection is the stock of customers he has been able to develop. It is the personal relationship existing between the employee and the customers of the employer which has to be taken into account as indicating the likelihood that the employee when leaving might be able to take his employer's customers with him. This depends upon the extent to which the customer identifies him with business in hand and replaces the contact he would otherwise have with the employer, which is likely when the employee is the main, if not the sole, contact of the employer with the customer. Customer lists are generally taken in other states to be confidential information sufficiently important to warrant protection. . . .

Furthermore, it is generally recognized that the right of an employer to keep his trade or business secrets for himself and to retain the advantage of such special knowledge as he may possess of names and special needs of potential customers is subject to protection by a restrictive covenant.

The concept of reasonableness is broken down into three separate and distinct elements, i.e., reasonableness as to the employer, reasonableness as to the employee and reasonableness as to the public. The first and most important of the three is reasonableness as to the employer, the party in whose favor the covenant is given. *Orkin Exterminating Co. v. Murrell.*

The rules governing such contracts are flexible, and, if the public is not involved, and the restriction of the employee is no greater than protection to the other party requires, the contract may be sustained. There is no hard and fast rule as to what contracts are void, and each case must be judged according to its own facts and circumstances. Such a covenant is reasonable, where there is no public injury, "[if] it is such only as to afford fair protection to the interests of the party in whose favor it is given," and the employee is not deprived of his means of making a living. *Edgar Lumber Co. v. Cornie Stove Co.*

A review of the facts in this case will demonstrate the reasons I feel so strongly that the legitimate interests of the employer are not outweighed by the interests of the public, insofar as appellee Cingolani is concerned. I agree that the contract with Melder is unenforceable.

I would reverse the [trial court's decision] and direct the entry of an appropriate injunction [an order to stop certain activity] against Cingolani.

CASE REVIEW QUESTIONS

1. In the court's decision (written by Justice Holt), where did the court find the law to apply to resolve the conflict between Evans and Melder and Cingolani? Where did Justice Fogleman find the law that he applied in his dissenting opinion?
2. What are the interests of Evans and Cingolani that are in conflict? Which interests does the court recognize and protect?
3. Will anyone other than Evans, Melder, and Cingolani be affected by the outcome of this case? Explain.
4. What behaviors are discouraged or encouraged by the decision in this case?
5. Does the decision in this case allocate any decision-making authority or require that particular decision-making processes be used?
6. Which of the possible goals of law do you think are reflected in the majority and dissenting opinions? Explain.
7. What is the basis of the disagreement between Justice Holt and Justice Fogleman concerning the proper resolution of the conflict between Evans and Cingolani?
8. Do you agree with the decision written by Justice Holt or with the decision written by Justice Fogleman? Explain.

REVIEW QUESTIONS

1. Where is the law found?
2. What are the effects of the law? Give an example not given in the text of each of the effects of the law.
3. What are the various theories concerning the goal of the law? With which theory do you most agree?

4. What are the relationships among the law, its effects, and the goal of law?
5. What things should be included in a brief of a case?

CASE PROBLEM

[This case problem concerns the same legal issue that you read about in *Evans Laboratories, Inc. v. Melder*. It is much longer than the case problems for the rest of the chapters in this book. We believe, however, that presenting a case problem in this chapter that provides substantial background information will better help you to understand how legal conflicts develop and how the law affects them. When you consider how the conflict in this case problem should be resolved, you may want to use the case of *Evans Laboratories, Inc. v. Melder* as a precedent.]

Dr. Joseph Karpinski is an oral surgeon in the city of Auburn in Cayuga County, New York. Nearly all of an oral surgeon's business is the result of referrals from dentists, so when Dr. Karpinski decided to expand his business, he set out to develop connections with dentists in the four nearby counties of Tompkins, Seneca, Cortland, and Ontario.

Dr. Karpinski's plan was successful, and after several years 20 percent of his practice consisted of treating patients referred to him by dentists located in those counties. Several of those dentists informed him, however, that some of their patients found it difficult to travel from their homes to Auburn. As a result, Dr. Karpinski decided to open a second office in the more centrally located city of Ithaca.

He began looking for an assistant and, in the course of his search, met Dr. Paul Ingrasci, who was just completing his training in oral surgery at Buffalo General

Hospital and wanted to enter private practice. Dr. Ingrasci was interested in becoming associated with Dr. Karpinski and, after a number of discussions, they reached an understanding. They agreed that Dr. Ingrasci would live in Ithaca, an area with which he had no prior familiarity, and would work there as an employee of Dr. Karpinski, who would rent and fully equip an office at his own expense.

Dr. Karpinski was concerned, however, that Dr. Ingrasci might take advantage of their arrangement. He knew that the dentists who sent their patients to Dr. Ingrasci in Ithaca would get used to dealing with him. Thus, if Dr. Ingrasci later went into practice on his own, he might be able to take a substantial amount of Dr. Karpinski's business with him. Dr. Karpinski believed that he needed protection against this possibility, so he insisted that a promise by Dr. Ingrasci not to compete be a part of their agreement. Dr. Ingrasci agreed to this requirement. The doctors entered into a written agreement under which Dr. Karpinski promised to maintain an office in Ithaca and employ Dr. Ingrasci there for five years and Dr. Ingrasci promised to work for Dr. Karpinski for five years. Dr. Ingrasci further promised never to practice oral surgery in the counties of Cayuga, Cortland, Seneca, Tompkins, or Ontario unless in association with Dr. Karpinski or unless Dr. Karpinski fired him and employed another oral surgeon.

When the five year period was over, the two men

had extended discussions concerning whether they should continue in business as employer and employee or as partners. Dr. Karpinski was willing to continue to employ Dr. Ingrasci, but Dr. Ingrasci wanted to be a partner. Because they were unable to agree, Dr. Ingrasci left Dr. Karpinski's employ. A week later, he opened his own office in Ithaca for the practice of oral surgery, thus breaking his promise not to compete. The dentists in the area began referring their patients to Dr. Ingrasci rather than to Dr. Karpinski. Within two months, Dr. Karpinski's practice from the Ithaca area dwindled to almost nothing, and he closed his office in that city.

The courts in New York have decided in prior cases that a promise by an employee not to compete is valid and enforceable by the courts if the promise is reasonable under the circumstances of the particular case.

What is the conflict between Dr. Karpinski and Dr. Ingrasci? In whose favor do you think a court should resolve the conflict?

2

BEGINNING
A LAWSUIT

The American judicial system encompasses both criminal law, through which society punishes people who break its laws, and civil law, through which injured persons seek compensation for their injuries. Because most legal issues involving business fall under civil law, this area of the law is the focus of Chapters 2 through 4. In these chapters, you will read about the structure and processes of the judicial system and about the things that judges consider when they make decisions.

The topics of judicial structure, process, and decision making are presented here so that when the various substantive areas of law—such as contracts, negotiable instruments, and corporations—are discussed later in the book you will be better able to understand how that law has been developed. Without a basic understanding of these matters, the legal system might well appear to be nothing but a bewildering bureaucratic machine that cranks out irrational decisions.

Like any other institution that makes decisions affecting others, the legal system must be concerned with its legitimacy. This means that those who are affected by court decisions must generally find them acceptable, even though they may not like the outcome of a particular case. Establishing legitimacy is especially difficult for the courts as approximately half of the people subject to judicial decisions *don't* like the outcome because it goes against them. It is therefore very important for the structure and process of the legal system to be such that court decisions are viewed as having been reached fairly, especially by the losing parties. As you read the following chapters, you should evaluate the judicial system in terms of whether you believe it to be legitimate. Could our judicial system be improved? In what ways?

In this chapter, we will discuss matters that affect the beginning of a lawsuit. More particularly, we will be concerned with the questions of *where* and *how* a person may begin a lawsuit.

JURISDICTION

Conflicts arise among people when different individuals have different needs or desires. Although submitting conflicts to the judicial system is one method of resolving them, not all conflicts are resolved by the courts. Conflicts can be ignored, they can be settled by the parties themselves, or they can be resolved by nonjudicial processes, such as arbitration.

Still, many important conflicts are resolved by the courts. If a person decides to resort to the courts, that person must first find a court that has the power to resolve the conflict in which he or she is involved. The power of a court to resolve a particular conflict or controversy is called **jurisdiction.** In the United States, finding a court with jurisdiction is complicated by the fact that there are fifty-one judicial systems—fifty state systems and the federal system—from which to choose. In the following section, you will learn about the bases of federal court and state court jurisdiction.

Federal Courts

The jurisdiction of the federal courts is authorized by Article III of the United States Constitution. Under Article III, the most important jurisdictional powers given to federal courts are the power to decide (1) cases concerning federal questions and (2) cases involving diversity of citizenship.

A case concerns a **federal question** when at least one of the legal issues of the case will require the court to apply the Constitution, laws, or treaties of the United States. The federal courts have limited the extent of this type of jurisdiction by requiring that the federal question or questions in a case be *substantial* in order for a federal court to take jurisdiction. This means that cases that are primarily concerned with state-law issues and that involve only minor or peripheral federal questions will be rejected by the federal courts.

Diversity of citizenship means that the opposing parties in a case are citizens of different states. When this situation arises, Congress has provided that federal jurisdiction is limited to cases in which the amount of money actually in controversy is more than $10,000. For diversity of citizenship to exist, the opposing parties must be citizens of different states at the time the lawsuit is begun. An individual is a citizen of the state in which he or she **is domiciled,** meaning the state of his or her permanent residence to which, if absent, he or she intends to return. For diversity of citizenship purposes, a corporation is considered to be a citizen of both the state in which it is incorporated and the state in which it has its principal place of business. If the opposing party is a citizen of either of these states, diversity of citizenship does not exist.

The powers of the federal courts are merely authorized by the constitutional provisions. It is therefore necessary for Congress to adopt legislation that actually provides for federal jurisdiction. Congress has given the federal courts *exclusive jurisdiction* over certain controversies arising under particular federal statutes, thus denying state courts jurisdiction over these controversies. Examples of this include actions to recover federal income taxes, cases involving the infringement of federal patents, and federal bankruptcy proceedings.

In a case in which federal jurisdiction exists but that jurisdiction is not exclusive, the prospective **plaintiff** — the person bringing the legal action — may choose to bring suit in either a federal court or a state court. This situation is called *concurrent jurisdiction.* If the plaintiff chooses a state court, the **defendant** — the party against whom the legal action is brought — may choose to remove the action to a federal court if the case involves a substantial federal question or if the defendant is not a citizen of the state in which the suit is brought.

State Courts

Conflicts over which the federal courts do not have jurisdiction or over which they do not have exclusive jurisdiction may be resolved in state courts. Indeed, it is in the state courts that most litigation takes place. Not all states have jurisdiction over all cases, however.

Bases of State Court Jurisdiction When considering the jurisdiction of the state courts, it is important to recognize that it is the plaintiff who must seek a state that has jurisdiction over the defendant. The plaintiff himself or herself consents to a state's jurisdiction simply by bringing suit in that state. The circumstances in which a state has jurisdiction over a defendant are explained in the following sections.

Jurisdiction Based on Presence of the Defendant The most fundamental basis of state court jurisdiction is when the defendant is present in the state at the time he or she receives formal notification through the personal service of a summons of the beginning of a legal action. Exemption from jurisdiction is provided in certain circumstances, such as when the prospective defendant enters the state solely to be a witness in a judicial proceeding or when he or she has been brought into the state by force. To take jurisdiction over a defendant who has been brought into a state by force would be a denial of the right to due process of law, which is guaranteed by the Constitution.

Jurisdiction Based on Domicile of the Defendant A state court has jurisdiction over all persons who are domiciled within its boundaries, whether or not they are present within the state at the time a suit is brought. Remember, a person is domiciled in his or her state of permanent residence to which, if absent, he or she intends to return. A corporation is domiciled in the state in which it is incorporated.

Because everyone has one state of domicile, there will always be at least one state in which a plaintiff may bring a legal action against a defendant. If the prospective defendant cannot be found or is outside of the state in which the legal action is begun, formal notification of the beginning of the legal action may be accomplished by means other than the personal service of a summons. For instance, the summons may be delivered to someone else at the defendant's usual dwelling place or the summons may be mailed to the defendant's last known address.

Jurisdiction Based on Consent of the Defendant Consent is a basis of jurisdiction because the defendant can waive (give up) the defense of lack of jurisdiction over him or her. By consenting to jurisdiction, the defendant subjects himself or herself to the decision-making power of the court.

In some cases, a defendant may *expressly* consent to jurisdiction in a state because he or she has no objection to the case being heard there. Express consent to the jurisdiction of a particular state can also be given before a conflict arises. For instance, when forming a contract, the parties may expressly agree in the contract that a particular state will have jurisdiction over any conflicts that may arise in the future with respect to the contract.

The mobility of the population in the twentieth century has led to the need for states to assert jurisdiction over nonresidents. Often, for instance, a nonresident automobile driver will injure a state resident and then leave the state before he or she can be personally served with a summons giving notice of a lawsuit. The prospective defendant is not present or domiciled in the state and has not expressly consented to that state's jurisdiction. Thus, if presence, domicile, and express consent were the only bases of state court jurisdiction over individuals, the injured state resident would probably be forced to travel to another state to bring a suit. Similarly, if domicile and consent were the only bases of jurisdiction over corporations, a nonresident corporation could carry on business within a state through people who were not employees of the corporation and thereby protect itself from the jurisdiction of that state's courts because the corporation would not be domiciled in the state and would not have consented to jurisdiction.

Beginning in the 1920s, the states began to deal with this problem by adopting statutes providing that nonresident drivers and nonresident corporations are deemed to have given their consent, meaning that their consent is *implied,* to the jurisdiction of the state's courts in legal actions arising out of driving an automobile or doing business in the state. "Doing business" in this context means conducting continuous and systematic, as opposed to casual and isolated, business activity.

These statutes are called "long-arm" statutes because they extend a state's jurisdiction beyond its boundaries. The courts have upheld the theory of implied consent on the basis that states have the power to regulate the use of their highways and the doing of business within their boundaries by corporations and can therefore condition these activities on consent to jurisdiction.

Jurisdiction Based on Activities Within the State During the 1960s, the states extended their "long arm" jurisdiction even further by adopting statutes that provide for jurisdiction in cases in which the connection between the nonresident defendant and the state is very slight. These statutes may provide that the transaction of *any* business within the state, even if the nonresident business never enters the state, or the commission of *any* act that causes injury within the state is enough to give the state jurisdiction over a nonresident defendant. For example, these statutes have been applied to obtain jurisdiction over a nonresident manufacturer that sent defective goods into a state where they caused injury, even though the manufacturer itself never did business within the state.

Jurisdiction Based on the Presence of Property Owned by the Defendant Jurisdiction based on the presence, domicile, consent, or activities of the defendant rests on a state's power over the defendant's *person* and is called jurisdiction *in personam* or personal jurisdiction. If a state does not have personal jurisdiction over a defendant, it may still have jurisdiction over *property* owned by the defendant within the state, which is called *in rem* jurisdiction. A court with *in rem* jurisdiction cannot bind the defendant personally. It can only determine rights in the defendant's property.

Often, cases based on *in rem* jurisdiction involve disputes over the ownership of the property. However, they may also involve disputes that are not related to the property located in the state. In such cases, the property owned by the defendant is used as the basis of jurisdiction, but it is the unrelated dispute that is litigated. If the plaintiff wins the case, the judgment may be satisfied only out of the property located in the state.

In rem jurisdiction can put the defendant in a difficult position. If he or she goes to the state asserting *in rem* jurisdiction in order to protect his or her property by defending against the unrelated claim, does this constitute consent to personal jurisdiction? In some states, limited appearance without consent to personal jurisdiction is allowed; in others it is not. Note the defendant's dilemma when limited appearance is not allowed.

Choice of Law Because there are several bases of state court jurisdiction, a plaintiff may be able to find more than one state with jurisdiction over the defendant. In such situations, the plaintiff chooses where to bring the suit. If the law is different in two states that have jurisdiction over the defendant and each state applies its own law to determine who will win a case, the plaintiff would naturally choose that state in which the law was most favorable to him or her.

Having the outcome of a case be determined by where the suit is brought would call the legitimacy of the legal system into question. Therefore, no matter which state the plaintiff chooses, the court there will apply *choice of law* principles that have been developed to determine which state's law will be applied to resolve a particular conflict. Generally, this means that the same law will be applied in a case no matter where the plaintiff chooses to bring the action. For instance, in a case in which a plaintiff is suing for damages incurred in an automobile accident, the courts of two or more states may have jurisdiction. However, in whichever state the plaintiff chooses to bring the lawsuit, the court will apply the law of the state in which the accident occurred to determine whether the defendant is liable for the plaintiff's injuries.

Forum Non Conveniens Even when a state has jurisdiction over a defendant, the courts of that state may sometimes decline to exercise jurisdiction on the basis that it would make more sense to have the case brought elsewhere. For example, if most of the evidence and witnesses are located in another state and it would be expensive to bring them to the state where the suit has been begun, a court might refuse jurisdiction because it would be more convenient to bring the suit elsewhere. This principle, called *forum non conveniens,* is applied only in extreme circumstances and only when the more convenient state also has jurisdiction over the defendant.

Subject Matter Jurisdiction There are some situations in which a state will lack jurisdiction, even though the defendant is present or consents, because of the subject matter of the dispute. For instance, states may not enforce the criminal laws or tax laws of another state, dissolve the marriage of an out-of-stater, or resolve disputes over title to land located outside the state.

Minimum Contacts with State Although jurisdiction over the person of the defendant has generally been found in the situations discussed earlier, jurisdiction cannot be found if it would violate the defendant's right to due process of law that is guaranteed by the United States Constitution. Due process, as it affects jurisdiction, requires that it be reasonable for the defendant to have to defend in the particular state.

Whether or not requiring the defendant to defend in a particular state is reasonable depends on whether the defendant has had sufficient *minimum contacts* with the state so that resolving the suit in that state does not offend traditional notions of fair play and substantial justice. For instance, if a nonresident who does not enter a state causes an injury within the state, the courts of that state may not exercise jurisdiction if the prospective defendant does not have the requisite minimum contacts. In the two cases that follow, the courts were confronted with the problem of whether the respective defendants had the necessary minimum contacts with a state to allow a court in that state to take jurisdiction.

LEWIS v. CURRY COLLEGE
573 P.2d 1312 (Washington 1978)

[Lewis brought a legal action in the state of Washington against Curry College, which is located in the state of Massachusetts, for reasons discussed by the court in its decision. The trial court dismissed the case on the grounds that the Washington courts did not have jurisdiction over Curry College. Lewis appealed.]

ROSELLINI, Associate Justice

The facts are not in dispute. The appellant [Lewis] is a Washington resident who has a learning disability, known as dyslexia. He was a student at Curry College for a portion of the academic year 1974–1975. The college has never registered to do business in this state and has no agents or operations here. The college has a small student body of about 800 students, most of whom are from eastern states. In its entire 100-year history, the college has had only one student from the state of Washington, that student being the appellant.

In 1970, a part-time faculty member at Curry College visited the state of Washington and made a speech to a group interested in learning disabilities. She was not authorized to speak as an agent of the college, and, so far as the record shows, did not purport to do so. In the course of the speech she told the group that Curry College had a program for students with dyslexia. Jerry Winger, an employee of the Seattle Public School District, heard the teacher's speech. He had already had some knowledge of the program, which he had gleaned from reading articles in education publications about it. He requested the college to send him more information about the program and later recommended to the appellant that he contact the college.

The appellant wrote to the college requesting information. The information which he received in response to this request included a catalogue and copies of articles which had been written about the dyslexia program. The record does not disclose the author or authors of these articles. They reported the fact that the college had such a program, that the program was innovative, and that it was helping students with learning disabilities. The articles did not solicit enrollment in the program.

In November 1972, the appellant formally applied for admission to the college. He was accepted and was enrolled in August 1974. His expenses were to be paid through a national defense loan, a grant arranged by the college, and a grant from the Washington State Department of Social and Health Services, made with the cooperation of the college.

Before many months had passed, the appellant expressed dissatisfaction with the learning disability program. He was dismissed before the end of the school year. In this action he alleged, in substance, that he was induced to enroll in the school by false representations and that the school was guilty of a breach of contract in failing to provide a satisfactory program of assistance for persons with his learning disability. He asked for damages in the amount of $25,000 for mental suffering, frustration, and loss of time, and for the return of $256.36, that amount which he owed on the national defense loan.

To support his theory that the courts of this state have jurisdiction over the college, the appellant relies upon the following provisions of [the Washington statutes]:

(1) Any person, whether or not a citizen or resident of this state, who in person or through an agent does any of the acts in this section enumerated, thereby submits said person . . . to the jurisdiction of the courts of this state as to any cause of action arising from the doing of any of said acts:
(a) The transaction of any business within this state;
(b) . . . .

In *International Shoe Co. v. Washington,* the United States Supreme Court held that, in order to subject a nonresident to jurisdiction over his person, if he is not present within the territory of the forum, it must appear that he has had certain minimum contacts with it, such that the maintenance of the suit does not offend traditional notions of fair play and substantial justice. The court went on to say that due process requires that, before a binding *in personam* judgment can be entered, the defendant must have had some contacts, ties, or relations with the state. This requirement was further clarified in the case of *Hanson v. Denckla* wherein the court said that "minimal contacts" are required, that it is essential in each case that there be some act by which the defendant purposefully avails himself of the privilege of conducting activities within the forum state, thus invoking the benefits and protection of its laws.

In implementing this requirement of the federal and state constitutions, we have laid down the following rules:

(1) The nonresident defendant must purposefully do some act or consummate some transaction in the forum state; (2) the cause of action must arise from, or be connected with, such act or transaction; and (3) the assumption of jurisdiction by the forum state must not offend traditional notions of fair play and substantial justice, consideration being given to the quality, nature and extent of the activity in the forum state, the relative convenience of the parties, the benefits and protection

of the laws of the forum state afforded the respective parties, and the basic equities of the situation.

Applying these criteria to the facts before us in this case, we find no showing that the college purposefully did any act or consummated any transaction in this state. While it supplied information to residents and institutions of this state, it did so only upon request. There is no showing that it engaged in advertising or solicitation of students here. The complaint [the statement of the plaintiff's claim] shows that the appellant was indeed advised to attend the college, but the advice came from a Washington resident not connected in any way with the college. The contract of enrollment was entered into in Massachusetts and the institution's services were performed there. . . .

No case cited has suggested that by publishing its catalogue and material describing its courses and programs, and furnishing these publications to persons or institutions requesting them, a nonprofit institution of learning, located exclusively in one state, subjects itself to the reach of the long-arm statute. Here, the [college] did nothing to invoke the protection of the laws of this state; and, as we have noted, it did not advertise for students or send its agents into the state to solicit enrollment. It carried on no activities here. The requirement of minimal contacts was not met.

The judgment is affirmed.

DAVIS METALS, INC. v. ALLEN
198 S.E.2d 285 (Georgia 1973)

[Davis Metals, Inc. (Davis) entered into an employment contract with Allen on January 6, 1969. The contract included a promise by Allen that if he left Davis' employment, he would not compete with it. At that time, both Davis and Allen were residents of Georgia and the contract was entered into in Georgia. The contract provided that it was to be interpreted under the laws of Georgia, and Allen went to work in Davis' Georgia office.

Later, Allen quit his job with Davis and moved to Alabama. There he entered into business in competition with Davis. Davis then brought a legal action in a Georgia state court, asking the court to order Allen to stop competing with Davis.

Allen moved to dismiss the case on the basis that the Georgia courts did not have jurisdiction over him. The trial court agreed with Allen and dismissed the case. Davis appealed. The Georgia Court of Appeals affirmed the trial court's decision. Davis then appealed to the Georgia Supreme Court.]

GUNTHER, Justice

We consider the judgment of the Court of Appeals to be erroneous, and it must be reversed. We perceive

the defect in the decision of the Court of Appeals to be contained in one sentence: "Defendant's liability here, if any, did not arise from any business transaction in Georgia, but instead from the defendant's competing outside Georgia in the State of Alabama."

The competition by the appellee in Alabama in and of itself would not give rise to a cause of action in favor of the appellant. If there was no contract in existence between the parties, then appellee would be completely free to compete with the appellant in Alabama and anywhere else. The act that gives birth to a cause of action because of the competition carried on in Alabama is the contract entered into by the parties in the State of Georgia. The Georgia contract gives the appellant a cause of action if a breach occurs, and it is immaterial if the breach occurs within or without the State of Georgia.

Our Long Arm Statute provides that a court of this state may exercise personal jurisdiction over a nonresident, as to a cause of action arising from any act of the nonresident, if the nonresident "transacts any business within this State." The only requirement is that the act or acts of the nonresident, giving rise to the cause of action, must have some relationship to the

State of Georgia. There must be minimum contacts with this state.

In this case the appellee, at the time a resident of Georgia, executed a contract in the State of Georgia and the contract provided that it was to be construed and interpreted pursuant to the laws of Georgia. Both parties therefore invoked the protection of the law of Georgia with respect to their individual rights and liabilities under the contract.

These are sufficient contacts with the State of Georgia to comply with the requirement of transacting "any business within this state."

Under our Long Arm Statute jurisdiction over a nonresident exists on the basis of transacting business in this State if the nonresident has purposefully done some act or consummated some transaction in this state, if the cause of action arises from or is connected with such act or transaction, and if the exercise of jurisdiction by the courts of this state does not offend traditional fairness and substantial justice.

We hold that the trial court had personal jurisdiction over the appellee in this case.

Judgment reversed.

CASE REVIEW QUESTIONS

1. Which of the bases of state court jurisdiction discussed earlier are the respective plaintiffs asserting in each of the two cases?
2. Why did the court in the *Lewis* case decide that it lacked jurisdiction whereas the court in the *Davis Metals* case decided that it had jurisdiction?
3. In the courts of what state could Lewis find jurisdiction over Curry College? Explain.
4. In the courts of what state other than Georgia could Davis have found jurisdiction over Allen? Explain.
5. Would the federal courts have jurisdiction in either the *Lewis case or the Davis Metals* case? Explain.

ORIGINAL JURISDICTION AND VENUE

Once the plaintiff has selected a judicial system with jurisdiction over the defendant, he or she must next choose the correct court within that system. A lawsuit must begin in a court that has *original jurisdiction.* Most litigation will begin in a trial court that has *general original jurisdiction.* In the federal system, this court is called a federal district court. There are 94 district courts in the federal system.

The states refer to their courts of general original jurisdiction by various names, such as *court of common pleas, district court,* or *superior court.* In addition, the states have created various courts with *limited original jurisdiction.* For instance, the states have created courts that are restricted to cases involving small sums of money, for example, *small claims court, justice of the peace court,* and *county court.* The jurisdiction of other courts may be restricted in the subject matter that can be litigated, for example, *probate courts,* which are concerned with decedents' estates, *family courts,* and *juvenile courts.* In the federal system, there are courts whose original jurisdiction is restricted to cases involving custom duties, patents, and certain claims against the United States.

The plaintiff must also be concerned about the geographical location of the court that has original jurisdiction within the proper judicial system. Judicial systems are divided territorially, and statutes, called **venue** statutes, designate the particular territorial division within the judicial system in which an action may be brought. In the federal court system, for instance, an action in which jurisdiction is based on diversity of citizenship may be brought in the district court that is located where all of the plaintiffs or all of the defendants reside or where the claim arose. For venue purposes, a corporation is considered to reside where it is incorporated or anywhere it is licensed to do business or is doing business. State venue provisions vary a great deal, but they generally require that an action be brought in the territorial division of the state, usually a county, where the defendant resides or is doing business or where the claim arose.

PLEADINGS

The first stage of a lawsuit involves the **pleadings,** which are formal written statements made by the parties. In this section, we will discuss the various pleadings that are exchanged by the parties, amendments to pleadings, and motions that may be made by the parties during the pleadings stage of a law-suit.[1]

At one time, the pleadings contained more extensive factual statements than they do today, and the parties continued to exchange pleadings until the matters in dispute were determined. As you will read, pleadings now provide only general assertions of the parties' claims and defenses, without stating their factual bases in detail. In addition, the number of exchanges between the parties is very limited.

Summons and Complaint

After choosing a court that has jurisdiction, a plaintiff begins a lawsuit by filing with the court a **complaint** containing the statement of his or her claim (see Figure 2-1). The clerk of the court then issues a **summons,** which is a notice that a legal action has been begun (see Figure 2-2). The summons and the complaint are served on (delivered to) the defendant. All jurisdictions have enacted **statutes of limitations,** which provide that legal claims must be brought within specified periods of time or the right to bring them is lost. A legal claim is brought when the lawsuit based on the claim is begun.

In the complaint, the plaintiff must state the basis of the court's jurisdiction, make a short and plain statement of the legal claim that shows that he or she is entitled to a remedy from the court, and state the particular remedy that he or she wants the court to provide. The defendant is thereby put on notice of the general nature of the legal action and what the plaintiff wants the court to do.

---

[1] The civil procedure outlined in the remainder of this chapter and in the following chapter is based primarily on the procedure followed in federal courts under the Federal Rules of Civil Procedure. These or similar rules have also been adopted in many states. The outline provided in the text is a broad one, designed for fundamental understanding. It does not contain all of the qualifications necessary for total accuracy.

UNITED STATES DISTRICT COURT FOR THE NORTHERN
DISTRICT OF NEW YORK

Civil Action, File Number 7426

JOHN DOE, PLAINTIFF
v.   *COMPLAINT*
MARY ROE, DEFENDANT

Plaintiff, for his complaint, hereby states:

1. Plaintiff is a citizen of the State of New York and defendant is a citizen of the State of Pennsylvania. The matter in controversy exceeds, exclusive of interest and costs, the sum of ten thousand dollars.

2. On August 21, 1985, in a public highway called North Main Street in Sunnyvale, New York, defendant negligently drove a motor vehicle against plaintiff who was then crossing said highway.

3. As a result plaintiff was thrown down and had his leg broken and was otherwise injured, was prevented from transacting his business, suffered great pain of body and mind, and incurred expenses for medical attention and hospitalization in the sum of twelve thousand dollars.

WHEREFORE, plaintiff demands judgment against defendant in the sum of one hundred thousand dollars, interest, and costs.

John Smith
Attorney for the Plaintiff
312 South Main Street
Sunnyvale, New York

FIGURE 2-1
A Complaint

UNITED STATES DISTRICT COURT FOR THE NORTHERN
DISTRICT OF NEW YORK

Civil Action, File Number 7426

JOHN DOE, PLAINTIFF
v.   *SUMMONS*
MARY ROE, DEFENDANT

To the above-named Defendant:

You are hereby summoned and required to serve upon John Smith, plaintiff's attorney, whose address is 312 South Main Street, Sunnyvale, New York, an answer to the complaint that is herewith served upon you, within 20 days after service of this summons upon you, exclusive of the day of service. If you fail to do so, judgment by default will be taken against you for the relief demanded in the complaint.

John Simpson
_____
Clerk of Court.

[Seal of Court]

Dated: December 16, 1985

FIGURE 2-2
A Summons

Remedy The statement in a complaint concerning the remedy that the plaintiff wants the court to provide may affect the procedure followed in a case. At one time every state and the federal government had two coexisting systems of courts, one called *law courts* and the other called *equity courts,* and each court system had its own body of procedural rules. Whether a case would be heard in a law court or in an equity court depended on what remedy the plaintiff was seeking.

The use of two court systems was a method of resolving legal issues that was brought to the United States from England. Equity courts, sometimes called Chancery courts, were originally created in England because of dissatisfaction with the law courts, which generally refused to grant any remedy other than money damages. The courts of equity, however, granted such remedies as the **injunction** (a court order that someone stop doing a specified act), **specific performance** (a court order that someone perform a specified act), and **reformation** (a court order that a document be rewritten to conform with the actual agreement of the parties).

During the last half of the nineteenth century, the states and the federal government began to merge the two systems of courts. Today, in almost all states and at the federal level, there is only one system of courts, and the judges in that system may grant both legal and equitable remedies. Nonetheless, whether a legal or equitable remedy is sought by the plaintiff can still have some minor effects on the procedure followed in a case. The most important of these effects is that there will be no jury in cases that seek an equitable remedy. Generally, however, the distinction between law actions and equity actions is no longer of any importance.

Answer

When a defendant is served with a summons and a complaint, he or she has a certain amount of time, usually twenty days, to respond. Common responses include contentions that the court lacks jurisdiction, that venue requirements have not been satisfied, and that the claim stated by the plaintiff does not show that he or she is entitled to a remedy plus admissions or denials of the facts forming the basis of the plaintiff's claim and statements of additional facts, called *affirmative defenses,* which will free the defendant of liability if proven to be true.

In addition, the defendant may wish to assert a claim of his or her own against the plaintiff. If the defendant's claim is asserted in response to the complaint, it is called a **counterclaim.** In actions in federal courts and in some states, the defendant *must* assert a counterclaim in response to the plaintiff's complaint if the defendant's claim arises out of the same transaction or occurrence as the plaintiff's claim. If the defendant fails to do so, he or she will lose his or her claim. The reason for this *compulsory counterclaim* rule is to save the time and expense of having to conduct two trials that involve the same witnesses and testimony. On the other hand, the defendant is permitted, but is not compelled, to assert any unrelated claims he or she may have against the plaintiff. This is called a *permissive counterclaim.*

Generally, the defendant's responses are contained in a written statement called an **answer** (See Figure 2-3). If the defendant counterclaims, the plaintiff is required to respond to the counterclaim in a written statement called a **reply** in a manner similar to the way in which the defendant must answer a complaint. The complaint, answer, and reply, along with other written statements used in particular situations, are collectively called the pleadings.

UNITED STATES DISTRICT COURT FOR THE NORTHERN
DISTRICT OF NEW YORK

Civil Action, File Number 7426

JOHN DOE, PLAINTIFF
v.   *ANSWER*
MARY ROE, DEFENDANT

Defendant hereby makes the following Answer to the Complaint of plaintiff, John
Doe:

First Defense

Defendant admits the allegations contained in paragraph 1 of the complaint and
denies each and every other allegation contained in the complaint.

Second Defense

If defendant negligently caused injury to the plaintiff as alleged in the complaint,
the plaintiff was guilty of contributory negligence in that he was crossing the highway
at the time of the accident in defiance of traffic signals, and in that he failed to pay
heed to the signals given by the defendant, and that this negligence on the part of the
plaintiff contributed to the alleged injury suffered by the plaintiff.

Counterclaim

1. On August 21, 1985, in a public highway called North Main Street in Sunnyvale, New York, plaintiff negligently crossed said highway in front of defendant's
motor vehicle.

2. As a result defendant was thrown about her motor vehicle and had her neck
sprained and was otherwise injured, was prevented from transacting her business,
suffered great pain of body and mind, incurred expenses for medical attention and
hospitalization in the sum of four thousand dollars, and incurred damage to her
motor vehicle in the sum of two thousand dollars.

WHEREFORE, defendant demands judgment against plaintiff in the sum of fifty
thousand dollars, interest, and costs.

Lawrence Russo

Attorney for the Defendant
714 South Central Street
Anywhere, Pennsylvania

Dated: December 30, 1985

FIGURE 2-3
An Answer

Amending Pleadings

The pleadings contain the allegations of the parties. After making these allegations, a party may discover that he or she made a mistake, or a party may obtain more information concerning the case. It may then be necessary to amend the pleadings. Before trial, some amendments require permission of the court whereas others do not. When permission is required, it is generally given freely. Even after trial has begun, the court will normally give permission to amend the pleadings unless the amendment would prejudice the other party. Generally, prejudice arises when an amendment would result in the other party being caught by surprise and unprepared to respond to the new claims or defenses asserted in the amendment.

Motions Related to Pleadings

A small number of responses to claims, answers, or counterclaims may be made by motion rather than in the pleadings. A *motion* is an application to the court for an *order*. A motion to *dismiss the complaint* (in some states called a *demurrer*) is a request that the court order dismissal of a claim or counterclaim because it suffers from a fatal flaw, such as lack of jurisdiction by the court, failure to meet venue requirements, or failure to state a claim, that makes further proceedings in the case unnecessary.

A motion for *judgment on the pleadings* requests the court to declare the party making the motion the winner of the case on the grounds that, even if the allegations of the other party are true, the party making the motion will win the case. For instance, if the defendant's answer fails to allege facts that could make for a successful defense, the plaintiff is entitled to a judgment on the pleadings.

Because the pleadings contain only allegations and can be amended, a motion to dismiss the complaint or a motion for a judgment on the pleadings will seldom be successful. Instead, the party against whom the motion is sought will be given the opportunity to correct his or her pleadings. If a proper correction is made, the motion will be denied and the case will proceed. If not, the motion will be granted.

In most cases, the pleadings and motions are drafted for the parties by a lawyer. Sometimes, however, a party will try to proceed without a lawyer. In the case that follows, the plaintiff personally drew up a complaint and had it served on several defendants, including Joseph Califano, who was Secretary of Health, Education and Welfare at the time. The defendants, through their attorneys, moved to dismiss the complaint.

BROWN v. CALIFANO
75 F.R.D. 497 (Dist. of Columbia 1977)

SIRICA, District Justice

This suit is the latest foray in a virtual onslaught of litigation filed by plaintiff over recent years against countless public and private individuals and organizations. Plaintiff alleges widespread misconduct by defendants actionable variously under the Constitution, numerous federal statutes and nearly all theories of recovery known to the common law. In eight rambling counts, plaintiff claims "fraud, psychiatric, medical, educational repressions, harassments, and intimidations, nuisances, tortures, aggravations, malpractice, entrapments, counterproductivity; invasions and violations of personal privacy; commitments and imprisonments, brutality, detentions, false personation, and false pretenses, false arrest, political surveillances and monitoring; tormentations, duress, distress, tensions, persecutions, wrongful death and attempted homicide by euthanasia; for reverse discrimination; for damages, injuries and conversions" and so forth. The matter is presently here on the motions of all defendants to dismiss the complaint because it is vexatious, frivolous and wholly fails to state a cause of action. For the reasons that follow, the Court finds that dismissal is required on the ground that the complaint fails to comply with the dictates of Rule 8(a) of the Federal Rules of Civil Procedure.

Rule 8(a) sets out a minimum standard for the sufficiency of complaints, providing that a complaint: "shall contain . . . (2) a short and plain statement of the claim showing that the pleader is entitled to relief. . . ." The purpose of the rule is to give fair notice of the claim being asserted so as to permit the adverse party the opportunity to file a responsive answer and prepare an adequate defense. Beyond this, the rule serves to sharpen the issues to be litigated and to confine discovery and the presentation of evidence at trial within reasonable bounds.

The burden imposed by the rule is by no means exacting. Quite to the contrary, the provision generously accords the plaintiff wide latitude in framing his claims for relief. This is particularly the case where, as here, the plaintiff is proceeding *pro se* [on his own behalf]. Yet despite the liberality envisioned by the rule, even a *pro se* complaint is subject to dismissal if the pleading fails reasonably to inform the adverse party of the asserted cause of action.

The pleading filed by the plaintiff in this case is indeed a confused and rambling narrative of charges and conclusions concerning numerous persons, organizations and agencies. The complaint contains an untidy assortment of claims that are neither plainly nor concisely stated, not meaningfully distinguished from bold conclusions, sharp harangues and personal comments. Nor has plaintiff alleged with even modest particularity the dates and places of the transactions of which he complains. It belabors the obvious to conclude that the complaint filed in this action falls far short of the admittedly liberal standard set if Rule 8(a).

Ordinarily, the remedy for noncompliance with Rule 8(a) is dismissal with leave to amend. But where, as here, the plaintiff has shown that he is no stranger to the courts, having filed seven previous lawsuits akin to this one, dismissal with prejudice is not inappropriate. To permit plaintiff to institute this lawsuit another time will needlessly waste time and effort.

For these reasons, plaintiff's complaint must be, and the same hereby is, dismissed with prejudice.

CASE REVIEW QUESTIONS
1. Why, specifically, was the motion to dismiss the complaint granted?
2. The text preceding the case stated that the person against whom a motion to dismiss the complaint is made will generally be given the opportunity to correct the pleadings. Why didn't Judge Sirica give such an opportunity to Brown?

REVIEW QUESTIONS

1. What does it mean for a court to have jurisdiction?
2. What are the most important bases of federal court jurisdiction?
3. What are the bases of state court jurisdiction?
4. What is a venue statute and how does it relate to jurisdiction?

5. Explain the difference between a motion to dismiss the complaint and a motion for a judgment on the pleadings.

CASE PROBLEMS

1. Blue was injured when his car was struck by a truck belonging to National Ford Corporation (National) and driven by one of its employees. Blue brought a legal action asking for $50,000 in damages against National in a federal court in Pennsylvania. National asked the court to dismiss the action on the basis that it did not have jurisdiction because there was not diversity of citizenship between the parties. National was incorporated in Delaware and had its principal place of business in Pennsylvania. Blue was born in Pennsylvania and lived there until a year before bringing suit against National, when he moved to Glassboro, New Jersey. He moved there because he had been accepted as a graduate student at Glassboro State College. He was also given a job as a dormitory advisor, and he lived in a residence hall for students where he kept all of his personal belongings. He hoped to earn a degree and get a job at the college as an administrator. He paid New Jersey income taxes and had a New Jersey driver's license, but he was not registered to vote anywhere.

   Blue visits his grandfather, with whom he previously resided, in Pennsylvania every two weeks. He also visits other friends and relatives in Pennsylvania two or three times a year. What arguments could each of the parties make concerning whether the court has jurisdiction? Who will win the case? Explain.

2. Bouse, age 20, was expelled from a public high school because of a high incidence of tardiness and absenteeism, very poor grades, the use of drugs, and for having overly long hair. He brought a legal action in a federal court, asking the court to require the school to readmit him. Part of his case was based on the fact that federal courts had previously decided that the right to wear one's hair any length is protected by the United States Constitution. With regard to the other bases of dismissal, Bouse argued that there was insufficient evidence to expel him. The school asked the court to dismiss the case on the basis that it did not have jurisdiction. Should the court take jurisdiction over the case? Explain.

3. Ms. DeLeon was driving her car in Iowa when she ran into Mr. Peters, causing extensive injuries to him. DeLeon is a resident of Wisconsin and Peters is a resident of Minnesota. DeLeon, however, has been sent to Alaska by the company she works for for a two-year period, at the end of which she intends to return to Wisconsin. If Peters decides to bring a legal action against DeLeon, in what courts of what states may the action be brought? Explain. Is it possible that the case may be litigated in a federal court? Explain.

4. Ms. Brown is a resident of Georgia, where she purchased a power saw manufactured by Fastest Saw Corporation. While Brown was using the saw, the blade came loose and caused severe facial injuries to her. Her hospital and doctor bills alone totalled $11,000. Fastest Saw is incorporated in Arkansas and has its manufacturing plant and principal place of business in Arkansas. It sells all of its products to a wholesaler in Arkansas, who then distributes them to retail outlets throughout the southeast United States, including Georgia. Fastest Saw itself does no business in Georgia. Georgia has a statute that provides for jurisdiction over any nonresident who transacts any business or causes any injury within the state.

   If Brown decides to bring legal action against Fastest Saw, in what courts in what states may the action be brought? Explain. Is it possible that the case may be litigated in a federal court? Explain.

5. Peters sued Duggan. The complaint that was served on Duggan stated that Peters had been walking down a flight of stairs with Duggan when he fell and suffered substantial injuries. The complaint also stated a valid for basis the court's jurisdiction and asked the court to award Peters

$10,000 in damages. Duggan made a motion requesting the court to dismiss the complaint. On what basis might Duggan have made his request? Should the request be granted? Explain.

6. Purvis purchased a piano from the Smith Piano Company, agreeing to pay the purchase price in installments. When Purvis fell behind in his payments, Smith went to his house to collect the amount due. Purvis and Smith got into a heated argument over the value of the piano. One thing led to another, and Purvis and Smith became engaged in a fight, which Purvis lost. Smith then sued Purvis for the balance due on the piano. If Purvis wishes to sue Smith for assault, must he counterclaim in response to Smith's complaint? Explain.

7. Parsons sued Dillenger. The complaint stated that Dillenger had borrowed Parsons' car, had driven it negligently, and had damaged it. Dillenger's answer stated (1) that he had not borrowed the car, (2) that it was already damaged when he borrowed it, and (3) that it was not damaged when he returned it to Parsons. Parsons made a motion for a judgment on the pleadings, arguing that the motion should be granted because the statements in Dillenger's answer were contradictory and could not possibly all be true. Should the trial court judge grant Parsons a judgment on the pleadings? Explain.

3

TRIAL AND APPEAL

In Chapter 2, you learned about the initial stage of a lawsuit, which is called the pleadings. In this chapter, you will read about the stages of a lawsuit that follow the pleadings, which are called the *pre-trial proceedings,* the *trial,* and the *appeal.*

PRE-TRIAL PROCEEDINGS

As you read in the previous chapter, modern pleadings provide only general notice of the parties' claims and defenses, without stating their factual bases in detail, and the number of pleadings exchanged between the parties is very limited. Under modern pleadings, the parties are therefore often in the dark at the beginning of the proceedings about relevant facts. They also may not know how their adversary intends to prove the allegations that have been made in the pleadings. Although this information will come out at trial, it may be too late then to allow the effective rebuttal of the other party's factual claims. If a party tries to search out this information prior to trial, the adverse parties or persons friendly to the adverse parties, who may possess the information, may choose not to provide it voluntarily.

Modern pleadings also do not serve to narrow the issues to be litigated at trial. It is important to focus the trial on the issues actually in dispute so that the court's time will be used most efficiently. To narrow the issues for trial, it is necessary to eliminate uncontested matters and to pinpoint those matters that will involve the greatest conflict. Most jurisdictions today therefore provide for various pre-trial discovery procedures and a pre-trial conference to assist the parties in unearthing all the relevant evidence, to prevent surprise at trial, and to narrow the issues to be tried. These devices also serve to encourage settlement prior to trial by making the parties aware of the relative strengths of their cases.

Pre-Trial Discovery

There are several **pre-trial discovery** devices by which a party may uncover the facts of a case or learn how the other party intends to prove claims or defenses. Generally, these discovery devices are initiated by the parties themselves without the involvement of the court. Any information may be sought as long as it is *relevant,* meaning that it will help to prove the allegations made in the parties' pleadings, and is not *privileged,* meaning that the party with the information has no legal basis for withholding it. Responses to discovery requests are made under oath. The most common pre-trial discovery devices are explained in the following sections.

Requests for Admission A party may request another party to admit either the genuineness of documents or the truth of facts. Called a **request for admission,** this device can help to weed out matters of fact that are not really in controversy, thus saving time and expense for both the parties and the court. The person to whom a request for admission is made must admit or deny, in whole or in part, the genuineness of the documents or truth of the facts, must state why an admission or denial cannot be made, or must object that the request concerns matters that are irrelevant or privileged. Failure to respond is deemed to be an admission.

Oral Depositions A party may examine any person by taking an oral deposition. In an **oral deposition,** the *deponent* (the person being examined) is questioned by attorneys for both parties in a manner similar to the questioning of a witness at trial. The questions and answers are recorded stenographically. Objections to questions may be made on the basis of relevance or privilege. A court order preventing or limiting an oral deposition will be granted if it can be shown the examination would be conducted in bad faith or to annoy, embarrass, or oppress the deponent or a party to the lawsuit.

Written Interrogatories A party may also seek to examine any person by **written interrogatories** (questions). The attorney for the other party may then prepare *cross interrogatories.* When all of the written questions are prepared, they are delivered to an examining officer who asks them of the deponent and has the answers recorded stenographically. Objections to interrogatories may be made for the same reasons as objections to depositions.

Written interrogatories may be submitted directly to an adverse party in the lawsuit rather than through an examining officer. When this is done, the questions are usually answered by the adverse party with the aid of his or her lawyer. As a result, these interrogatories are of limited use, but they are a simple and inexpensive means of discovering an adversary's version of the facts.

Physical and Mental Examinations If the physical or mental condition of a party is in controversy, a court order requiring that party to submit to an examination by a physician may be sought. The findings and conclusions of the physician are then reported to the party who sought the order, and that party is also entitled to receive the report of any other medical examination of the party examined.

Production of Documents and Things for Inspection When appropriate, an order may be obtained allowing a party to enter into the property of another party to inspect or photograph the premises or any object or operation thereon. Similarly, a party may request the court to provide a relevant document or other tangible object for inspection, copying, or photographing. In the following case, the plaintiff made a Motion for Production of Documents and the defendant opposed the motion.

HESS v. PITTSBURGH STEEL FOUNDRY & MACHINE COMPANY
49 F.R.D. 271 (W.D. Pa. 1970)

[Richard A. Hess was employed by Pittsburgh Steel Foundry & Machine Company (Pittsburgh) for more than twenty years. In 1967, Pittsburgh installed a new grinding process, which included an Osborn ramron grinding wheel, in the plant in which Hess worked. Hess had a bronchial asthmatic condition, which had been inactive. His condition worsened dramatically after installation of the new process, and he died in January of 1968.

Hess' wife brought a legal action against Pittsburgh and Osborn Manufacturing Company (Osborn), the manufacturer of the Osborn ramron grinding wheel. The ramron grinding wheel contains a polyurethane bond. The polyurethane bond contains a chemical known as tolyene diisocyanate, which is dangerous to individuals with bronchial conditions.

During the pre-trial discovery process, Mrs. Hess made a Motion for Production of Documents. She requested the court to order Osborn to produce certain documents relating to the ramron grinding wheel and the chemical decomposition of the polyurethane bond. Osborn opposed the motion.]

COURLEY, Senior District Judge

The liability of the defendant manufacturer is substantially disputed. The immediate matter before the Court is a Motion for Production of Documents which relate to the ramron grinding wheel and the chemical decomposition of its bond, which issue is at the center of the controverted facts in this case.

The [argument of the plaintiff] for production of documents is that the defendant Osborn should make available all inter-company correspondence relative to the complaints which existed on the part of three companies [other than Pittsburgh] and the recommendations made by Osborn to correct conditions, that is, the experience of fumes, odors, smells and chemicals being released when the grinding wheels were used.

The Court has reviewed and considered all the pleadings, discovery processes previously developed, which included depositions and interrogatories, heard oral argument, thoroughly and completely reviewed the record at time of argument, considered the briefs of counsel, and concludes the Motion should be granted.

Under Rule 34 of the Federal Rules of Civil Procedure, a party is entitled as part of the discovery to documents for inspection and copying where the purpose is to assist in the trial or preparation of the case. This is designed to aid parties in prosecuting and defending actions without unnecessary expense, formality or delay. The framework within which the rules are to be interpreted is to secure the just, speedy, and inexpensive determination of every action, and to this end, the rules are to be liberally construed.

We must start out with the basic legal proposition in ruling on any request for discovery regardless of its nature, whether or not the evidence might be admissible or reasonably calculated to lead to any evidence that might be found material or relevant in the determination of the issues involved in the proceeding.

Since this was a new product that was never heretofore on the market, the reasonableness of the possibility of what might be found important or relevant is far beyond the mind or the legal training of a lawyer and judge. Letters and records can well be construed or understood in a manner that would be entirely different or at variance with what a mind would apply where the individual is trained in the field of chemistry, a physicist or an engineer who is specially qualified and competent to review and evaluate all the experiences, complaints and findings that have taken place from the manufacture and use of an instrumentality such as a grinding wheel of this nature that has been found to be an innovation or something that was not heretofore known to science for industrial use.

Under the circumstances, although the defendant herein involved has been most cooperative, through its distinguished counsel, this plaintiff is entitled to all the information involved in the instant Motion that has not been heretofore produced or made available.

Cases of this nature must rest basically on the records of the manufacturer and what information was known to him. After all data has been assembled, it has been my experience as a trial judge during the last twenty-five years, that opinions of experts are required before an adjudication factually or legally can be resolved. In view thereof, any and all information as to the experience with the instrumentality involved in this action, whether used under similar or dissimilar circumstances, becomes of the greatest importance.

It is also important to note that the information subject to the Motion cannot be derived from any other source and unquestionably the production thereof will greatly facilitate the pre-trial and adjudication of this involved and intricate litigation.

An appropriate Order is entered.

CASE REVIEW QUESTIONS
1. What do you think was the defendant's argument for not granting the plaintiff's motion?
2. Why specifically was the plaintiff's Motion for Production of Documents granted?

Pre-Trial Conference

Prior to trial, the judge may call a conference with the attorneys. The procedure for pre-trial conferences varies among jurisdictions, but the general purpose is to supplement the pre-trial discovery of facts and to narrow the issues in order to facilitate the trial.

At the conference, the judge may seek to have the parties admit to facts and documents over which there is no real dispute so as to avoid unnecessary proof at trial. The effect of these admissions is similar to that of those obtained by a request for admission, discussed earlier.

A primary function of the pre-trial conference is to limit the issues for trial to those not disposed of by admissions or by agreements of counsel. Following the conference, the judge will issue an order reciting the action taken at the conference, thus controlling the trial in terms of the issues that can be raised. The parties need not submit evidence at the trial to prove the facts that are stipulated in the order, and evidence contrary to these facts will not be admitted.

The pre-trial conference also offers the parties an opportunity to settle their case. Some judges may go so far as to urge the parties to enter into a settlement, but the possibility of settlement is apt to come up during the pre-trial conference of any case regardless of whether the judge urges it.

Motion for Summary Judgment

A case should, of course, go to trial only if there are issues that need to be tried. The pleadings represent merely the *allegations* of the parties. During the pre-trial proceedings, it may become evident that there is, in fact, no genuine dispute as to any material fact because one of the parties has no evidence to support the allegations made in his or her pleadings. In such a situation, the party who believes that the other party is destined to lose the trial may make a motion for **summary judgment.**

When the court reviews a motion for summary judgment, it will consider affidavits submitted by the parties as well as pre-trial depositions, interrogatories, and admissions. The role of the judge in deciding whether to grant or to deny a motion for summary judgment is to determine whether the submitted documents show evidence of a genuine dispute between the parties, not whether these documents are true or false. If it appears from the documents that a dispute exists, the motion will be denied.

THE TRIAL

Most legal actions that are actually begun by the exchange of pleadings between the parties are either voluntarily stopped or settled by the parties, or they are dismissed by the court. For those that are not, the next stage in the judicial process is the trial.

During the pleadings stage, discussed in the previous chapter, the parties make allegations concerning their conflict. At the trial, the parties are called upon to present evidence to prove their allegations, and the facts of the case are determined on the basis of the evidence presented. The law is then applied to the facts of the case and a verdict made. The verdict, in turn, becomes the basis for a judgment issued by the court.

The Jury

The jury is a group of randomly selected and impartial people — usually 12 in number, but sometimes fewer — who are asked to determine the facts of a case on the basis of evidence presented to them. The United States Constitution and the constitutions of the individual states provide that a person is entitled to a jury trial in any case for which there would have been the right to trial by jury under the law of England at the time of the adoption of the Constitution. Because the right to trial by jury was not available in equity court at that time, there is no right to trial by jury today in cases in which the plaintiff is seeking an equitable remedy (see page 29).

Many types of legal action that were unknown at the time the Constitution was adopted have since been created, so determining whether a right to a jury trial exists in a particular case is sometimes difficult. In some instances, when new legal actions are created by statute, the right to trial by jury is provided for or denied in the statute itself. In most common kinds of civil litigation, however, the right to a jury trial exists, so a jury will be used to determine the facts of the case unless all parties agree to waive the use of a jury. When a jury is not used, the case will be tried before the judge alone, and he or she will determine the facts of the case. The remaining discussion of the trial will assume the use of a jury.

Generally, prospective jurors are selected randomly from voter lists within the territorial jurisdiction of the court so that they will be fairly representative of the community in which the trial will take place. The initial selection process is accomplished by an officer of the court, often called a *commissioner of jurors.* The persons selected who are not disqualified or excused are called the *general jury panel.*

The jurors for a particular trial are chosen from the general jury panel. Each party, through his or her attorney or through the judge, is allowed to question prospective jurors concerning matters that might cause them to be biased in determining facts and reaching a verdict. If a party believe a juror would be biased, a **challenge for cause** can be made to the judge. If the judge agrees that such bias may be present, the challenge will be granted and the prospective juror will be dismissed. There is no limit to the number of challenges for cause that can be made.

The parties may also make a limited number of **peremptory challenges** to jurors. No reason need be given for a peremptory challenge, and it may be used, for instance, to reject someone from the jury about whom an attorney has nothing more than a "funny feeling."

When the proper number of jurors have been selected, the jurors are sworn in.

Presentation of Evidence

Opening Statement Following the selection and swearing in of the jurors, the attorney for each party makes an *opening statement,* in which he or she outlines for the jury the allegations he or she intends to prove. This is done so that the jury will be better able to understand the presentation of evidence.

Plaintiff's Case The attorneys then introduce their evidence. The plaintiff's attorney proceeds first, calling witnesses to present testimony that the attorney believes will establish the essential elements of the plaintiff's claim. Usually, witnesses will appear at a trial voluntarily. If a witness will not appear voluntarily, however, the court will issue a **subpoena** ordering that person to appear and to give testimony. If a witness is required to appear and to produce a document that is in his or her possession, a **subpoena duces tecum** will be issued.

The testimony is brought out through the *direct examination* of each witness, during which the plaintiff's attorney asks questions of the witness. When the plaintiff's attorney is finished, the defendant's attorney may cross-examine the witness. During *cross-examination,* the defendant's attorney may seek to bring out testimony favorable to the defendant's case or to raise questions about the credibility of the witness. Redirect examination and recross-examination may then alternate until each party's attorney is done with the witness.

The plaintiff's attorney continues to call witnesses until he or she is satisfied that the plaintiff's case has been completely presented, at which point the plaintiff's case is rested.

Defendant's Case Generally, the defendant's attorney then proceeds to present the defendant's case, following the same procedures used in the presentation of the plaintiff's case. However, the defendant may choose not to offer any proof and may instead simply argue to the jurors that they should not accept the plaintiff's evidence as true. This course is not usually followed, though.

When the defendant's case has been fully presented, the defendant's attorney rests his or her case.

Rebuttal and Rejoinder Still following the procedures for the presentation of testimony, the plaintiff may then present evidence in *rebuttal,* which is limited to responses to new evidence brought forth by the defendant. When the rebuttal, if there is one, is concluded, the defendant may offer evidence in *rejoinder.* This continues back and forth until both parties have fully presented their evidence and have rested their cases.

Rules of Evidence The presentation of evidence is guided by rules of evidence that limit the way in which proof of facts can be offered. These rules require that all of the evidence presented by the parties be both relevant and competent. **Relevant evidence** is evidence that tends to prove or disprove a fact over which the parties are in dispute. If the parties agree to a fact or if the determination of a fact would have no bearing on the outcome of the trial, evidence concerning that fact is irrelevant and is therefore inadmissible. **Competent evidence** is evidence that a qualified witness can provide as a result of his or her personal knowledge. This means that the evidence must concern something that the witness personally said or did or knows, rather than, for example, something that someone else told the witness.

If one attorney believes that an opposing attorney is attempting to present irrelevant or incompetent evidence, he or she may object. The judge must then determine the relevancy or competency of the evidence in question. If the judge errs in making this determination, the error may serve as a basis for appeal, as will be discussed later in this chapter.

Summation Following the presentation of evidence, the attorney for each side is allowed to present a *summation* to the jury. At this time, each attorney in turn will review the evidence and explain how it tends to support the case of his or her client in an effort to convince the jurors that his or her client should win.

Instructions, Verdict, and Judgment

The primary function of the jury is to evaluate the evidence that is presented to them and then to determine the facts of the case on the basis of that evaluation. In addition, the jury is usually directed by the judge to apply the law to the facts they have found and, after doing so, to declare who should win the case. The jury's declaration is called a **verdict.**

Following the presentation of evidence by the parties, the judge gives **instructions** to, or **charges,** the jury, explaining to the jury how it should carry out its tasks. In these instructions, the judge will usually review the issues in dispute, summarize the evidence that has been heard, and explain the applicable law. Frequently, the parties will request that particular instructions be given, but the final determination of what the instructions will include lies with the judge.

One of the matters about which the judge will instruct the jury is who has the **burden of proof,** meaning who it is that must prove what. Generally, the burden of proof is allocated between the parties on the basis of the allegations made in the pleadings. This means, for instance, that the plaintiff normally has the burden of proving the allegations in the complaint whereas the defendant normally has the burden of proving the defenses in the answer.

The jury in a civil case may only find facts for the party having the burden of proof if a *preponderance of evidence* concerning that fact favors that party. In other words, the jury must believe that the evidence of the party having the burden of proof outweighs — is more convincing than — the evidence of the other party. If the jury finds the evidence to be balanced evenly, the burden of proof has not been met.

After the judge has instructed the jury, it then goes to the jury room and deliberates until a verdict is reached. Usually, the verdict is simply a statement of which party the jury declares to have won the case on the basis of the evidence presented, which is called a *general verdict*. If a general verdict is for the plaintiff, it will also state the amount of money to which the plaintiff is entitled. Occasionally, a jury is asked to deliver a *special verdict* or to answer *special questions,* which means that it is asked to make a special finding on each relevant fact in dispute and to report those findings to the judge. The judge then applies the law to the facts as found by the jury to determine which party should win the case.

Traditionally, a jury has had to be unanimous in its findings in order to report a verdict to the judge. However, some states now require something less than unanimity, such as a three-quarters or five-sixths finding, for the jury to reach a verdict. The Federal Rules of Civil Procedure also allow the parties themselves to agree on a less than unanimous jury finding. Whatever degree of unanimity is necessary, if, after deliberation, the jury is unable to agree sufficiently, the judge will dismiss the jury. Unless the parties can now settle their case, a new trial will be required.

When the judge receives the verdict of the jury, he or she will enter a judgment for the party in whose favor the jury has found, unless either a motion for judgment n.o.v. or a motion for a new trial, both of which are discussed in the following section, is granted. The **judgment** is the official declaration of the court that states the winner of the case and the remedies, if any, to which the parties are entitled.

Motions During Trial

At various times during the trial, the parties may make certain motions. If granted, these motions will have a significant impact on the outcome of the case. In the discussions of the motions that follow, you should note when each motion can be made, the basis for granting it, and the effect it will have on the case.

Plaintiff's Motion for Nonsuit Anytime the plaintiff wishes to stop the trial, a motion for a *voluntary nonsuit* can be made. If the defendant agrees to the motion or if the judge finds that the need to stop the trial is not due to the laxity of the plaintiff's attorney and that stopping the trial will not cause undue harm to the defendant, the motion will be granted. The plaintiff is free to take up the case against the defendant at a later time.

Defendant's Motion for Nonsuit This motion may be made by the defendant's attorney following the presentation of the plaintiff's evidence. If the judge determines that the plaintiff's attorney has failed to present sufficient evidence to allow the jury reasonably to find the necessary facts to support plaintiff's case, the motion will be granted. This motion is called a *compulsory nonsuit*. It results in a judgment for the defendant, which prohibits the plaintiff from bringing the same case against the defendant again.

Mistrial Either party may make a motion for a **mistrial** at any time. If the judge determines that there has been a major procedural defect, a prejudicial error that cannot be corrected, or an extraordinary event that is disruptive—such as the death of one of the attorneys—or that the jury is deadlocked, the motion will be granted. The parties are then in the same position they were in prior to the start of the trial.

Directed Verdict A motion for a **directed verdict** may be made by either party following the presentation of all the evidence. If the judge determines that, on the basis of the evidence presented, the jury could reasonably return a verdict only for the party making the motion, the motion will be granted. Because of the determination that the jury could reasonably come to only one conclusion, the judge does not ask the jury for a verdict. Instead, the judge issues a judgment for the party whose motion for a directed verdict has been granted.

Judgment N.O.V. A motion for **judgment n.o.v.** (*non obstante vedicto*, meaning "notwithstanding the verdict") may be made after the jury announces its verdict by the party against whom the verdict has been found. If the judge determines that, on the basis of the evidence presented, the jury could only have reasonably returned a verdict for the party making the motion, the motion will be granted. In other words, the standard for granting this motion is the same as for a directed verdict, but this motion is made *after* the jury has returned its verdict rather than before.

New Trial A motion for a *new trial* may also be made after the jury announces its verdict by the party against whom the verdict has been found. It requests the judge to set aside the jury's verdict and to grant a new trial. If the judge determines that the jury grossly misinterpreted the weight of the evidence or that it failed to follow the instructions it was given to the prejudice of the losing party or if the judge finds that he or she, as judge, made an error that affected the outcome of the case, the motion will be granted. Judgment will not be issued for either party, and, unless the parties can now settle their case, a new trial will be held.

In the case that follows, a trial court judge considers a motion for a judgment n.o.v. and a motion for a new trial. As you read the decision, keep in mind the standards that are applied by the courts in considering such motions. How are those standards applied in this case?

MALANDRIS v. MERRILL LYNCH, PIERCE, FENNER & SMITH, INC.
447 S.Supp. 543 (D. Col. 1977)

MATSCH, District Judge

After a four day trial with sharply conflicting testimony and upon instructions by the judge that liability could be found for fraud and deceit and for the intentional infliction of emotional distress, a jury of six persons returned a verdict for the plaintiff for [$4,030,000, consisting of $30,000 for damages resulting from fraud and deceit, $1,000,000 for damages resulting from the intentional infliction of emotional distress, and $3,000,000 in punitive (penalty) damages, meaning damages that are imposed to punish a person who has harmed another maliciously or wantonly]. The defendant seeks a judgment notwithstanding the verdict or, alternatively, a new trial. A proper consideration of these motions requires some comment on the evidence.

The plaintiff, Jung Ja Malandris, is a naturalized citizen of the United States who was born and raised in the Republic of Korea. She has had no formal education of any kind and she is unable to read or write in any language. The plaintiff married Steven Malandris when he was on active duty as a truck driver in the United States Army in Korea.

After discharge, Mr. Malandris obtained employment as a baggage handler for United Airlines working first in New Jersey and later at Stapleton International Airport in Denver, Colorado. Recognizing that as an uneducated and unskilled worker his earning capacity is entirely dependent upon his physical strength, Steven Malandris has relentlessly worked double shifts and all of the overtime and holiday time which he could obtain from his employer.

Steven and Jung Ja Malandris have pursued an extraordinary life style, wholly dominated by a search for financial security. Although their income has been maximized, Mr. and Mrs. Malandris have avoided most of the expenditures ordinarily incurred by other couples in comparable circumstance. They have not gone to restaurants or movies; they have not subscribed to magazines or newspapers; they have not visited in the homes of others or had guests in their apartment; and they have lived at a subsistence level. In sum, Mr. and Mrs. Malandris have existed in an isolated environment wholly separate from the society surrounding them.

Steven's hard work and their unusual life style enabled Mr. and Mrs. Malandris to accumulate more than $60,000 and, as a result of a posting of the price and income record of United Airlines stock on an employees' bulletin board, they invested all of their savings in United's common stock.

Jung Ja Malandris was the dominant marriage partner and, although Steven earned it, she controlled the couple's money. In this way, she also controlled her husband.

When the plaintiff became disquieted and uncomfortable about the future of United Airlines stock, she directed her husband to sell it and to put the proceeds into bank deposits. Mr. Malandris went to Merrill Lynch [a stock brokerage firm] for that purpose and there he met Mr. John Barron, an account executive who was a retired army officer. While the testimony of Steven Malandris and John Barron sharply conflicts in most important respects, taken as a whole the evidence supports the version of Mr. Malandris. He said that John Barron induced him to leave the proceeds of the United Airlines sale with Merrill Lynch because the firm could make money for him just as banks made income from the investment of funds placed on deposit. Steven Malandris testified that John Barron said that there would be a "partnership" with Merrill Lynch with an assured gain and no possibility of any loss. The plaintiff's husband also said that he was induced to mislead his wife and to forge her signature on a power of attorney by the representations and later the threats of John Barron. What remains undisputed is that [an] account was opened in the name of Jung Ja Malandris and that a number of transactions were made on the Chicago Board of Options Exchange for this account. The account was closed with a loss of approximately $30,000.00.

The conflicting testimony of John Barron was that Steven Malandris came to him and directed him not only to sell the United Airlines Stock, but also instructed him to open [an] account in his wife's name and . . . gave specific directions for each of his options trades.

After viewing the demeanor and manner of these two witnesses while they testified during the trial and after consideration of the other evidence in the case, including the documents in evidence and the unexplained absence of some of the routine documentation, I join the jury in rejecting the testimony of John Barron as lacking credibility. The evidence fully supports the finding that John Barron knew he was dealing with a man and his wife who were wholly innocent of the risks involved in the securities market; that he knew of the extraordinary efforts to achieve the life savings brought to him; and he knew that the airlines stock was in the name of the plaintiff and that Mr. Malandris had delivered all of his earnings to his wife; that he deliberately manipulated Steven Malandris to deceive his wife and to conceal from her the investments which were made; that he knew Jung Ja Malandris was a Korean from a background of poverty and deprivation to whom financial security was of great importance; [and] that he knew of the extraordinary life style which this couple followed , and, finally, that he, Barron, had no previous experience with options trading.

The evidence also shows, beyond doubt, that Jung Ja Malandris has sustained permanent emotional injury which has destroyed her ability to function as a human being. She has rejected this world and lives only in the anticipation of life after death. This results in her total preoccupation with religion.

The defendant urges that the verdicts be set aside because they are "so grossly excessive as to shock the judicial conscience." What is most relevant in this case is not the judicial conscience, it is the conscience of the community as represented by the six people who served on the trial jury. They heard this evidence and they considered whether the conduct of John Barron went beyond the bounds of decency and was utterly intolerable in a civilized community. The defendant's counsel wish to make much of the fact that there was only a $30,000 economic loss. They, like their client, fail to understand that such economic losses can and do result in human suffering which cannot be evaluated arithmetically. This is not a case of lost investment, it is the tragedy of a lost life. Is $1,000,000 too great a value to place upon that life?

The defendant denies that there is any showing of proximate causation between its acts and plaintiff's emotional state. The jury was correctly instructed as follows:

> Proximate cause means that cause which in natural and probable sequence produced the claimed injury. It is the cause without which the claimed injury would not have been sustained.

The evidence showed that Jung Ja Malandris did have a predisposition to suffer severe emotional injury from any economic loss and the psychiatric testimony that she was greatly affected by the loss of control of her husband is an important aspect in this case. That loss of control was a consequence of the defendant's interference in this couple's relationship. It is apparent to me, as it must have been to the jury, that, knowing that which he did know about the plaintiff, John Barron should be held to know that a reasonably foreseeable consequence of the manipulation of Steven Malandris and the deceit of his wife would be the collapse of her ability to function. The defense has pointed out that there were other factors contributing to plaintiff's emotional condition. Yet, it failed to produce any evidence which would separate the effects of its wrongful conduct from the effects of other influences. The law in Colorado is clear that the aggravation of a preexisting condition can result in liability if the wrongdoer is unable to isolate the impact.

During the third day of trial on Thursday, September 15, 1977 at approximately 4:30 P.M. while plaintiff's counsel was questioning John Barron on cross examination, Jung Ja Malandris, seated in the public area of the courtroom, began to cry uncontrollably. As her counsel was helping her from the courtroom and while the jury was leaving under the Court's instructions, Steven Malandris also lost control of his emotions and began shouting. The record is not clear as to what the jury may have heard and seen at that time, but the jury was returned and given a cautionary instruction when the trial resumed at 4:45 P.M. Mr. and Mrs. Malandris were not then present. Trial continued on Friday, September 16, 1977, without either Mr. or Mrs. Malandris being present. The case was given to the jury on the following Monday, September 19, 1977. The intervening day of testimony and weekend between the Malandris' court conduct and closing arguments and submission to the jury must be considered in evaluating any effect of this unfortunate incident on the jury's deliberation. Additionally, the conduct of Mr. and Mrs. Malandris must be viewed in the context of the trial. There is nothing to indicate that either of these people engaged in any theatrics or that they deliberately attempted to use this as a means to communicate with the jury. Having observed the entire trial, including the incident in question, it is my finding and conclusion that these outbursts were genuine human reponses to testimony which was not credible and which went directly to the pivotal issues in the case. Mrs. Malandris' actions were entirely consistent with the testimony of both psychiatrists. Mr. Malandris' reaction to the testimony of Mr. Barron can best be characterized as instinctive, uncontrolled anger. It is not possible to try lawsuits in a sterile chamber, wholly free from the effects of human emotions, particularly in a case in which the injury complained of is severe emotional distress.

Considering the evidence as a whole, in my judgment, this jury verdict was produced not by any passion, prejudice or sympathy generated by the plaintiff's conduct or that of her husband; it was, rather, the product of a sense of outrage and indignation about the callous and cavalier conduct of the defendant's agent acting in complete disregard of the rights and sensitivities of the plaintiff whose emotional and economic security was in his hands.

The defendant also claims that it was error to exclude testimony of its witness, Jeavons, concerning the options trading. Such testimony was irrelevant and prejudicial. The facility with which one who is truly expert in a specialized aspect of securities trading might be able to explain and simplify it to a jury would, in my judgment, mislead and misdirect the jury as to the issues in the case. What was important was what Mr. Malandris and Mr. Barron knew and said to each other about such activity.

The constitutional right of trial by jury is nothing less than the right to have human conflict resolved by the considered judgment of representative members of the community. Any interference with such a community judgment must be justified by compelling circumstances showing unfairness in the manner in which the issue was presented or considered. In evaluating a motion to set aside a jury verdict, it must be remembered that the Seventh Amendment of the United States Constitution specifically preserved the right of trial by jury as it existed in the common law courts of England.

I have reflected carefully on this trial and the results achieved and in my view the trial was fair and the ver-

dict was within the discretion of the people who sat on this jury. Accordingly, it is

ordered, that the defendant's motion for judgment notwithstanding the verdict and for a new trial are denied.

CASE COMMENT

You will read about appeals in the next section of this chapter, but you may be curious now as to whether there was an appeal from the trial court's decision that you just read. Merrill Lynch did appeal the decision. An appellate court ruled that the punitive damages imposed by the jury were excessive and should be reduced from $3 million to $1 million. However, the appellate court approved of all other aspects of the trial court's decision, leaving Jung Ja Malandris with a judgment for $2,030,000. Later, the United States Supreme Court refused to hear arguments in the case, leaving the appellate court's decision and Malandris' $2,030,000 judgment intact.

CASE REVIEW QUESTIONS

1. The defendant made motions for a judgment n.o.v. (notwithstanding the verdict) and for a new trial. From reading the decision of the court, what arguments do you think the defendant made in support of these motions?
2. How did the judge respond to each of these arguments?

APPEAL

A party dissatisfied with the final outcome of a trial has the *right* to appeal to an appellate court, requesting that higher court to reverse or modify the trial court's judgment. Actually, only a relatively small number of trial court judgments are appealed. An appeal is expensive, and unless a party who has the right to appeal firmly believes that the appeal will be successful, there is usually no reason for bringing it.

Levels of Appeal

The federal court system and the larger states have two levels of appellate courts—intermediate appellate courts and a final or highest court. Intermediate appellate courts are generally aligned geographically, each reviewing the decisions of the trial courts located within a designated territory. In the federal system, there are 13 intermediate appellate courts, called *courts of appeals.* Smaller states, which have relatively few cases, usually have only a single appellate court—the state's highest court—to hear all the appeals from its trial courts.

In those legal systems that have two levels of appellate courts, there are only a very limited number of situations in which a party who is dissatisfied with the outcome of the first appeal has the *right* to a second appeal to the highest court. Generally, there is no such right, and a party who wants to bring an appeal to the system's highest court must *request* that court to hear the appeal. Such a request is called a **writ of certiorari.** A highest court uses its discretion in deciding whether to grant a writ of certiorari, usually granting it only in cases that raise important legal issues or that will allow the highest court to resolve contradictory decisions made by various lower courts.

Under certain narrow circumstances, there is a *right* to appeal a decision of the highest court of a state to the Supreme Court of the United States, which is the highest court in the federal court system. If a state's highest court has decided that a federal law or treaty violates the U.S. Constitution or that a state law does not violate the U.S. Constitution and if that decision has affected the outcome of the case, there is a right to appeal the state court's decision to the Supreme Court.

Bases of Appeal

You will recall that during the trial certain matters, such as the admissibility of evidence and what instructions to give to the jury, are ruled on by the judge, whereas other matters, particularly the determination of the facts of the case, are decided by the jury. Those matters decided by the judge are called *questions of law,* and those matters decided by the jury are called *questions of fact.*

A party who appeals is restricted to basing the appeal on questions of law. The appellant must convince the appellate court that the trial court judge decided a question of law erroneously and that the judge's error was prejudicial in that it may have led to an incorrect judgment. For example, a party bringing an appeal might argue that the trial judge erroneously excluded certain relevant evidence that would possibly have led the jury to return a different verdict.

Questions of fact decided by the jury are not subject to appeal. When the jury determines the facts, it can evaluate the witnesses' demeanor, meaning their behavior while giving testimony, to help determine which witnesses know and are telling the true facts of the case. Because the appellate court does not see or hear the witnesses, the final determination of the facts of a case is left to the trial court jury.

Appellate Court Procedure

Appellate court procedure is quite different from trial court procedure. An appeal does not involve a retrial of the case but, rather, is limited to a review of any claimed errors raised by the parties concerning questions of law. The party who brings the appeal is called the **appellant,** and the other party is called the **appellee.** The number of judges who will hear an appeal varies among jurisdictions from three to nine.

Both parties submit written briefs containing their arguments on the issues raised on appeal. In addition, the court receives copies of the pleadings and a written record of the trial, including a transcript of the testimony. The parties, through their attorneys, are usually allowed to present oral arguments to the appellate court, during which the judges may ask questions to help clarify unclear points.

After oral argument, the judges individually review the case and then meet together to review and decide the case. Frequently, one of the judges will prepare a written opinion explaining the reasons for the court's decision. If a majority of the judges agrees with this written decision, it is called the **majority opinion.** A judge who agrees with the court's decision but who does not agree with the explanation of the reasons for it given in the court's written opinion may choose to write a **concurring opinion** in which he or she separately states his or her view of the case. A judge who disagrees with the court's decision may choose to write a **dissenting opinion** explaining why he or she disagrees with the majority of the court.

The decision of the appellate court will either *affirm, modify,* or *reverse* the trial court's judgment. If the trial court's judgment is reversed, the appellate court will **remand** (send back) the case to the trial court either for further proceedings consistent with the appellate court's decision or for the trial court to give a final judgment to the appellant. Two situations in which the trial court will be directed to give a final judgment to the appellant are (1) when the appellate court decides that the trial court should have granted the appellant's motion for a directed verdict or a judgment n.o.v. during the trial and (2) when the appellate court reverses the trial court's grant of a motion for a judgment n.o.v. and reinstates the jury's verdict.

In the case that follows, you should note the question of law that forms the basis of the appellant's appeal and the action taken by the court as a result of its decision.

SEGELKE v. PET, INC.
528 P.2d 929 (Colo. App. 1974)

ENOCH, Judge

Plaintiff Richard Segelke initiated this action to recover damages for breach of contract. The jury returned a verdict for plaintiff in the amount of $41,212.96. Defendant's motion for judgment notwithstanding the verdict was granted, and the court also granted defendant's motion for a directed verdict which had been taken under advisement when made at the close of plaintiff's case and before the case was submitted to the jury. Plaintiff appeals from this judgment. We reverse.

The contract which the parties executed in February 1966 provided that plaintiff was to sell to defendant 30,000 hundred-weights (cwt.) of potatoes during the coming season. Plaintiff was to deliver the potatoes for storage at Julesburg or Sedgwick for ultimate processing into potato chips at defendant's plant in Houston, Texas. The contract required the potatoes to be U.S. Commercial Grade and of such quality as to chip satisfactorily "upon arrival." The parties presented conflicting testimony as to whether the conditions of both grade and chip potential were to apply upon the delivery of potatoes to storage or whether the latter condition was to be met when the potatoes reached the plant for processing.

After harvesting of his crop in the fall of 1966, plaintiff delivered in excess of 30,000 cwt. of potatoes to the stipulated storage facilities. Plaintiff testified that in the fall and winter of 1966 defendant took eleven 450 cwt. loads of the potatoes from storage for processing in defendant's plant in Denver. Defendant paid plaintiff for these potatoes that were processed. However, defendant refused to make any further payment under the contract, claiming that plaintiff had delivered nonconforming potatoes, that were neither U.S. Commercial Grade, nor chippable.

The court granted defendant's motions on the ground that plaintiff had failed as a matter of law to prove delivery of U.S. Commercial Grade potatoes to Julesburg and Sedgwick. Plaintiff contends that there was sufficient evidence that plaintiff delivered to defendant U.S. Commercial Grade potatoes and that the jury verdict should be reinstated.

The standards for evaluating motions for directed verdict and motions for judgment notwithstanding the verdict are essentially the same. The trial court must view the evidence in the light most favorable to the party moved against and apply every reasonable inference of fact that can legitimately be drawn therefrom in that party's favor. Then, such motions may be granted only where the evidence, so considered, is such that no reasonable man could decide the contested issues against the moving party.

Defendant contends that plaintiff and his other witnesses, who were also potato farmers, were not qualified to testify that the specified grade of potato had been delivered because the witnesses did not know the exact government definition of U.S. Commercial Grade potatoes. However, farmers are competent to offer expert testimony concerning matters within their experience in a particular locality. Plaintiff was the son of a potato farmer and had raised potatoes for eight years prior to 1966. Even though he misstated the technical definition of U.S. Commercial Grade, he did testify that in his opinion the potatoes delivered met the conditions of the contract. Plaintiff's neighbor, who had grown potatoes for twenty-eight years, testified that the plaintiff's crop was the best he had ever seen, and that when he took some of plaintiff's potatoes out of storage, they very easily met U.S. Commercial Grade. The neighbor described the applicable general grade specifications more stringently that it had been even in 1966, admitting that he could no longer recall certain percentage defect factors. It is noted that this trial took place six years after the harvest in question. Plaintiff's father-in-law, a potato grower for approximately twenty years, also testified that plaintiff's potatoes met the neighbor's over-stringent specification. Furthermore his testimony as to the specifications of the required grade of potatoes was reasonably accurate. Two experienced employees of plaintiff supplemented the above testimony by agreeing that the condition of the potatoes upon entry into storage was excellent. Defendant's agent admitted accepting and paying for certain of plaintiff's potatoes after removing them from storage, although asserting that none of these achieved requisite contract grade. Though defendant presented conflicting evidence, plaintiff's evidence was sufficient to require that the case be submitted to the jury, and thus it was error for the court to grant defendant's motions.

Judgment is reversed and the cause remanded with directions to reinstate the jury verdict and enter judgment thereon.

CASE REVIEW QUESTIONS
1. Trace the procedural steps in the case from beginning to end.
2. What was the basis of the plaintiff's successful appeal?
3. Why do you think the trial court judge waited until after the jury returned its verdict to grant defendant's motion for a directed verdict?

THE EFFECTS OF FINAL JUDGMENT

If there is no appeal from a trial court's judgment or if no further appeals can be made, the trial court makes a *final judgment*. At that time, the trial court will also issue a *final order* that directs the parties to do those things that are consistent with the judgment. For instance, if the final judgment is that the defendant is liable to the plaintiff in the amount of $50,000, the final order will direct the defendant to pay that amount to the plaintiff. Similarly, if the final judgment is that the plaintiff is entitled to an injunction, the court will issue a final order directing the defendant to stop doing a specific act.

Generally, a defendant will obey a court's order. However, if a defendant does not obey a court's order, there are processes that can be used by a plaintiff to enforce the order. For instance, an order to pay money can be enforced, subject to certain limitations, by having a law enforcement officer seize and sell the defendant's property or **garnish** the defendant's income, which means that a part of defendant's income is periodically paid by his or her employer directly to the plaintiff until the amount due is paid. An order directing the defendant to stop doing a specified act can be enforced by having the defendant held in **contempt** of court. A person in contempt of court can be fined or jailed.

A valid final judgment may be enforced in the state where it was granted or in another state. The *Full Faith and Credit Clause* of the U.S. Constitution provides that a state's courts must enforce a decision of the courts of another state and must give to that decision the same recognition that it would receive in the state in which it was made.

A final judgment is said to be ***res judicata,*** or "a matter settled by judgment." This means that the plaintiff may not bring another legal action against the defendant based on the same claim that has been resolved by the final judgment.

REVIEW QUESTIONS

1. What are the primary functions of pre-trial discovery and the pre-trial conference?
2. Compare and contrast requests for admission, oral depositions, and written interrogatories.
3. Compare and contrast the following motions: summary judgment, defendant's motion for nonsuit, directed verdict, and judgment n.o.v.
4. Give an example of circumstances in which a prospective juror could be successfully challenged for cause.
5. Give an example of circumstances in which an attorney might use a peremptory challenge to reject a prospective juror?

6. Give an example of testimony by a witness that would not be admitted as evidence because it was not relevant.
7. Give an example of testimony by a witness that would not be admitted as evidence because it was not competent.
8. Compare and contrast the roles of the judge and the jury.
9. Compare and contrast questions of law and questions of fact.
10. Compare and contrast a final judgment and a final order.

CASE PROBLEMS

1. Paladin sued Daniels. The complaint stated that Paladin was injured as a result of Daniels' negligence while driving a car. Daniels' answer denied that he was negligent. Daniels took oral deposi-

tions from all of the five witnesses to the accident, except Paladin, and their testimony indicates that Daniels was not negligent. Daniels submitted the depositions of the witnesses to the court and made a motion for a summary judgment. Paladin submitted an affidavit stating that he intends to testify that Daniels was negligent. Should the judge grant the motion for summary judgment? Explain.

2. Lambert brought an action against a doctor for medical malpractice. Brandt, a prospective juror, was questioned by Lambert's attorney. Brandt said that he had a speaking acquaintance with the doctor, that his mother had worked for the doctor six years prior to the trial, that the doctor had treated him for a broken leg more than ten years earlier, and that he believed him to be a good doctor. Brandt also said that he would not believe the doctor any more than any other witness, that the doctor could make mistakes like all human beings, and that he was confident that he could give Lambert a fair trial. Lambert's attorney challenged Brandt for cause. Should the trial judge grant the challenge? Explain.

3. Reid sued the railroad to collect damages because of the death of her cow, which had strayed on the railroad's track. There had been no negligence by the train crew. Under the law of the state where the accident occurred, the railroad would be liable if the cow got onto the track through a fence that the railroad had failed to repair, but it would not be liable if the cow got onto the track through an open gate at a private crossing.

At the trial, the plaintiff's witnesses testified that part of the fence between the cow's pasture and the track was down and out of repair and that a gate opening into the pasture had been left open prior to the accident. The cow was killed at a point equidistant from the break in the fence and the gate. After the presentation of the evidence by plaintiff as just summarized, the railroad made a motion for a nonsuit, arguing that Reid had not met her burden of proof. Should the motion be granted? Explain.

4. A plane owned by the United States government completed a test flight and landed at an airport. With permission from the control tower, the plane parked on a seldom used runway and the pilot requested that a tractor be sent to tow the plane to a parking area. Shortly thereafter, an experimental plane owned by Douglas Aircraft landed and, with the control tower's permission, used the same runway on which the government plane was parked. Because of the shape of the experimental plane, the pilot could not see directly ahead, so he zigzagged at 15 degree angles to improve his visibility. While taxiing in this manner, the experimental plane collided with the parked government plane.

The government brought legal action against Douglas on the basis of negligence to recover for the damages to its plane. After the presentation of the evidence, as just described, the government requested the court to grant it a directed verdict. Should the court grant the directed verdict for the government? Explain.

5. Stewart sued Randolph to collect a real estate agent's commission. Randolph's defense was that someone else, not Stewart, had actually made the sale. The jury was instructed that Stewart was entitled to $1,900 if she was entitled to recover at all. The jury returned a verdict for Stewart for $950. What motion might Randolph choose to make in light of the jury's verdict? Should the trial judge grant Randolph's motion? Explain.

4

LEGAL REASONING

In Chapters 2 and 3, you read about the *procedure* that is followed in law cases as they move through the legal system. The focus of this chapter is the *reasoning* that is used when legal decisions are made. This chapter considers the setting in which legal decisions are made, the reasoning process by which decisions are made, and judicial philosophies.

THE DECISION SETTING

A court generally requires that certain conditions be met before it will make a legal decision. If these conditions are met in a particular case, the case is said to be **justiciable,** meaning that it is a case that can properly be decided by a court. The necessary conditions are as follows:

1. A real conflict must exist.
2. The parties before the court must be directly affected by the court's decision.
3. The legal issues to be decided must be framed as narrowly as possible to resolve the conflict.
4. The issues in the case must be judicial, meaning that they must be the kinds of issues that courts may decide.

Each of these conditions is explained and discussed in the following sections.

Real Conflict

Ripeness Courts will generally not give **advisory opinions.** This means that courts will generally not make a legal decision unless there exists a *real conflict* between the parties to the legal action. Sometimes, however, people want to know in advance what a court will do if a conflict arises at some later time.

For instance, an employee who has agreed in an employment contract not to compete with his or her employer may believe that the contract is invalid and could not be enforced by the employer if he or she should quit and go into competition. The problem, however, is that the employee doesn't know whether a court will agree that the contract is invalid. If the employee brings a legal action asking a court to rule on the validity of the contract before he or she actually quits and goes into competition with the employer, the court may dismiss the action because a real conflict does not yet exist. Such a legal action is said to be not yet **ripe** because more events must occur before a real conflict will exist between the parties.

Some states have adopted legislation that allows their courts to give advisory opinions under very restricted circumstances even though the conflict involved is not yet ripe. Generally, these opinions may only be requested by the governor or the legislature, and they may only concern a proposed statute that is being considered by the legislature. Furthermore, an advisory opinion given by a court under these circumstances is usually not binding on the court with regard to future decisions pertaining to the statute in question.

The United States Supreme Court has declared that federal courts cannot give advisory opinions because Article III of the U.S. Constitution limits judicial power to the deciding of "cases and controversies." The Court has, however, upheld as constitutional Congress' Federal Declaratory Judgment Act, which allows the federal courts to declare the legal rights between parties to a suit even though the conflict involved may not yet be technically ripe. Whether a court will issue a **declaratory judgment** is up to the discretion of the court, and such judgments are normally limited to situations in which a real controversy between adverse parties exists and the risks and costs to the parties if the conflict is allowed to fully ripen are very great. Many states also allow declaratory judgments under these circumstances.

Mootness If a conflict has existed between parties but has been resolved in some manner other than by legal action, a court will dismiss a legal action concerning the prior conflict on the basis that it has become **moot.** For example, an employer may bring a legal action for an injunction against a former employee who has entered into competition with the employer in violation of an employment contract. If, after the legal action has begun, the employee withdraws from competition and no further competition by the employee is threatened, the court will dismiss the legal action seeking an injunction on the basis that it has become moot.

Reasons for the Real-Conflict Condition The courts do not decide unripe or moot cases and will generally not give advisory opinions because it is believed that the parties in such situations will not feel compelled to present their arguments in the strongest possible manner. When a real conflict exists, the parties are more apt to make their arguments in the most careful and complete manner possible. The better the parties argue their cases, the more likely it is that the court will make the best decision. Also, it is felt that the court's limited and valuable time can best be spent resolving real rather than hypothetical conflicts.

Affected Parties

Adversary Process Another way in which the courts attempt to stimulate the most effective presentation of arguments is to require that the arguments be presented by parties who care about the outcome of the case because they will be directly affected by the court's decision. It is believed that, when there is a disagreement about the facts or law of a case, the best way to determine the facts or the correct law is for the judge to remain passive and neutral while the most directly affected parties are given full opportunity to present their arguments in as forceful a manner as possible. This procedure, in which each side presents the most favorable version of its case to a passive and neutral court, is called the **adversary process**.

Because of the adversary requirement, the courts will not decide a case in which the parties concoct a conflict simply to obtain an advisory opinion that a court would otherwise refuse to provide. In such a case, which is called a **feigned controversy** or **collusive suit**, the parties appear to be in conflict but in reality are not.

Standing Another result of the adversary requirement is that the parties involved in a legal action must have **standing** in order to present their arguments. This means that the parties can assert only their own rights, not the rights of others. For example, if Smith injured Jones, Jones' friend Brown does not have standing to sue Smith to recover damages, unless he brings the suit as a legally recognized representative of Jones. Brown does not have standing because he is not as much of an adversary of Smith as is Jones, the person who was actually injured, who will probably pursue the legal action with more zeal than would Brown.

Class Actions Sometimes a large group of people have similar legal claims that could be brought by each of them individually, but even though the total of the claims is large, each individual claim is so small that it is unlikely to be pursued. If the group of people sharing such a claim is so large that it would be impractical to bring them all before a court, a member of the group may bring a **class action** on his or her own behalf and on the behalf of all of the members of the group. If the court finds that such a group exists and that the person bringing the action would adequately represent the rights of all of the members of the group, it will allow the class action to be brought.

Reasons for the Affected-Parties Condition Because of the view that the best arguments will be presented to a court by the parties who will be the most affected by the outcome of the case, it is believed that the requirement that only affected parties may come before the courts makes it more likely that correct decisions will be made. It is also believed that a court that remains passive, rather than seeking out legal conflicts and involving itself in the presentation of legal arguments, will be seen by the parties and by society as being unbiased in its decisions. Through these means, it is hoped that the decisions of the courts will be accepted by all those who are affected by them.

Narrow Issues

When a court resolves a conflict, it does so on as narrow a basis as possible. By narrowing the legal issues to include only those that must be decided in order to resolve the conflict, a court will be more likely to decide those issues properly. The narrower the questions asked are, the more likely it is a court's answers will be correct.

In their written decisions, judges will sometimes make general statements of law that go beyond what is necessary to decide the case. These general statements, called **dicta**, have no binding legal effect. Only the **holding** of the case, that part of the decision that is necessary to resolve the conflict before the court, is binding for future application. By narrowing the issues as much as possible, the courts insure that their decisions will be clearer and will therefore be more likely to be correctly applied in the future.

It is also believed that by narrowing the legal issues to be decided, the courts make their decisions more acceptable to the parties and to society. Furthermore, by limiting the scope of their decisions and by avoiding general statements of law, judges are less likely to be seen as being swayed by their personal viewpoints.

Judicial Issues

The federal and state courts were established by the federal and state constitutions. These constitutions also created two other branches of government, the executive branch and the legislative branch, and assigned certain powers to them. The courts have taken the position that these other governmental branches, or the people through their votes, have the final say on certain matters called **political questions**. Because of the separation of powers among the three branches of government that is constitutionally required, political questions are not judicial issues, so decisions concerning them cannot be reviewed by the courts. For example, the courts will not review decisions by the executive or legislative branches concerning foreign relations or foreign policy.

Administrative agencies are not constitutional creations but, instead, are created by legislation. These agencies are often given the power to resolve conflicts. Sometimes the creating legislation specifically prohibits the review of an agency's decisions by the courts, thus giving the agency, rather than the courts, the final say in resolving certain conflicts. Even when the decisions of administrative agencies may be reviewed by the courts, the review allowed is very limited and is usually restricted to questions of law decided by an agency, not questions of fact. As a result, many conflicts raise administrative questions rather than judicial issues. In all cases, however, the courts, not the agencies, have the final say on constitutional issues.

Case Example of Justiciability

In the following case, the court decided that not all of the conditions for justiciability had been met. As you read the case, try to identify the unmet conditions that made the case not justiciable.

BAIRD v. STATE
574 P.2d 713 (Utah 1978)

[Lamar Baird is a resident of Utah. When the Utah legislature adopted an Occupational Safety and Health Act (OSHA), Baird (the plaintiff) brought a legal action against the state of Utah and the Occupational Safety and Health Division (the defendants) seeking a declaratory judgment that OSHA is unconstitutional. In his complaint, Baird stated that he sought the declaratory judgment on his own behalf as an employer and as an employee and on behalf of all employers and employees subject to the act. In their answer, the defendants argued that OSHA was constitutional. The trial court ruled that the act was unconstitutional. The defendants appealed.]

MAUGHAN, Justice

Based on the record before us, the trial court should have dismissed this action for a declaratory judgment *ex mero motu* [on its own motion without request from either party]. It should have done so on the ground it lacked jurisdiction to render an advisory opinion.

The alleged adverse actions of defendant consisted of the creation, administration, and enforcement of a legislative act. The allegations concerning the unconstitutionality of the act were all pleaded in the abstract. There were no concrete facts pleaded indicating any specific injury sustained or threatened to plaintiff personally. There were no allegations that plaintiff had sustained a particularized injury that set him apart from the public generally and would give him standing to challenge the constitutionality of the act.

The courts are not a forum for hearing academic contentions or rendering advisory opinions. To maintain an action for declaratory relief, plaintiff must show that the justiciable elements requisite in ordinary actions are present, for a judgment can be rendered only in a real controversy between adverse parties.

The courts have no jurisdiction to render a declaratory judgment in the absence of a justiciable or actual controversy. A mere general contention between parties, which has not been formulated into a definite controversy, does not warrant declaratory relief. Judicial adherence to the doctrine of separation of powers preserves the courts for the decision of issues between litigants capable of effective determination.

A party seeking a declaration of the constitutionality of a statute must have a real interest therein as against his adversary, whose rights and contentions must be in opposition to those of the plaintiff. A party to whom a statute is inapplicable cannot question its constitutionality by seeking a declaration of rights.

The general rule is applicable that a party having only such interest as the public generally cannot maintain an action. In order to pass upon the validity of a statute, the proceeding must be initiated by one whose special interest is affected, and it must be a civil or property right that is so affected.

The necessity of alleging in the pleading a justiciable controversy is regarded as of such importance as to require the court to raise the question of its own motion, if the parties neglect or fail to do so. A plaintiff may seek and obtain a declaration as to whether a statute is constitutional by averring [stating] in his pleading the grounds upon which he will be directly damaged in his person or property by its enforcement; by alleging facts indicating how he will be damaged by its enforcement; that defendant is enforcing such statute or has a duty or ability to enforce it; and the enforcement will impinge upon plaintiff's legal or constitutional rights. A complaint is insufficient which merely challenges the constitutionality of a statute, without in some way indicating that plaintiff will be affected by its operation or is subject to its terms and provisions.

To grant standing to a litigant, who cannot distinguish himself from all citizens, would be a significant inroad on the representative form of government, and cast the courts in the role of supervising the coordinate branches of government. It would convert the judiciary into an open forum for the resolution of political and ideological disputes about the performance of government.

In his allegations, plaintiff neither asserted a legally protectable interest in the subject matter of the action nor did he plead any facts indicating he would be directly affected by enforcement of the act. The wrong of which he complained was public in character, and his complaint disclosed no special injury affecting him differently from other citizens. He, therefore, had no standing to urge the unlawfulness of the governmental action. It is not the duty of this Court to sit in judgment upon the action of the legislative branch of government, except when a litigant claims to be adversely affected on a particular ground by a legislative act.

Plaintiff may assert only his own legal rights. He may not base his claim upon the legal rights of third parties. The denial of equal rights can be urged only by those who can show they belong to the alleged discriminated class. An asserted violation of due process can be urged only by those who claim an impairment of their rights in the application of the statute to them. Plaintiff's claims are presented as abstract propositions, he does not allege he has been denied these rights by enforcement of the act. Challenges such as these may only be urged by those whose rights are impaired by the contested legislation.

Where an appeal from an action of an administrative body is provided by statute, a remedy by way of declaratory judgment will be denied. The proper procedure to challenge the statute and the administration thereof is by judicial review after final administrative action has been taken.

Reversed.

CASE REVIEW QUESTIONS
1. Carefully trace the procedural steps in this case from beginning to end.
2. According to Justice Maughan's decision, what conditions for justiciability had not been met? Explain.
3. If Baird had stated in his complaint that he was subject to and currently in violation of the act, would the court have decided that the case was justiciable? Explain.

DECISION MAKING

When a proper decision setting is present, a court with jurisdiction will resolve a conflict between the parties in a legal action. To resolve a conflict, the court must determine the facts of the case and the applicable law and then apply the law to the facts in order to reach a decision. In Chapter 3, we focused primarily on the procedures through which a court determines the facts of a particular case. Now we will focus on the process for determining the applicable law.

The primary sources from which a court selects the applicable law for a particular case are *constitutions, statutes,* and *previous court decisions.* Once the applicable law has been selected, it may then be necessary to interpret its meaning. The meaning of constitutional provisions, statutes, and previous court decisions is often unclear and must therefore be interpreted by a court.

Interpretation of Constitutional Provisions and Statutes

Each state, as well as the federal government, operates under a constitution, a document that sets forth the basic principles of government. These principles address matters that include the authority of the government, the division of that authority among the branches of government, and the rights of the people. If a court is asked to decide whether a government or a branch of government has exceeded its authority or whether an individual's rights have been violated, it becomes necessary for the court to determine the meaning of constitutional provisions.

The primary authority of the legislature, one of the three branches of government, is to enact laws in the form of statutes. Today, statutes affect all phases of business and social activity. When conflicts arise under them, it becomes necessary for a court to determine their meaning.

The relevant considerations for interpreting the meaning of constitutional provisions and statutes are discussed in the following sections.

What Does the Constitutional Provision or Statute Say? The language of a constitution or a statute is, of course, an important consideration. Presumably, the drafters understood the meanings of words and chose their words carefully. If a constitution or statute will be interpreted in a court according to the *plain meaning* of its words, the people who are affected by it will be able to read and understand that plain meaning and conduct their activities in accordance with it without fear that the words will be interpreted in some other way.

The interpretation of a constitutional provision or a statute may also be facilitated by the *textual context* of a word or phrase. In this method of interpretation, the meanings of the words may be determined by considering the constitution or the statute as a whole, not just the isolated word or phrase being interpreted. For instance, the use of the same or a different word or phrase elsewhere in the constitution or statute may shed light on the meaning of the word or phrase being interpreted.

Why Was the Constitutional Provision or Statute Adopted? Another possible consideration in constitutional or statutory interpretation is the purpose for which the constitutional provision or statute was adopted. If the court can determine how the drafters intended the law to function, they may want to make their interpretation consistent with that intention. The two primary sources for determining the purpose of a constitutional provision or a statute are the circumstantial context and the legislative history.

In considering the *circumstantial context,* a court will try to identify the problem that the drafters were attempting to solve and interpret the constitutional provision or statute in terms of how it contributes to the effective solution of that problem. *Legislative history* includes such documents as legislative committee reports and transcripts of legislative debates. If the purpose of a constitutional provision or statute can be determined from its legislative history, a court may choose an interpretation that contributes to the fulfillment of that purpose.

What Are Society's Needs and Expectations? In addition to the language and the purpose of a constitutional provision or statute, a court may want to consider society's needs and expectations in its interpretation. Although it is impossible to determine exactly what interpretation the members of society would give to a particular constitutional provision or statute, there are various clues that a court may use to determine society's needs and expectations.

For instance, there may be certain *public declarations,* such as other statutes, executive orders, or administrative rulings, that do not apply directly to the case before the court but may suggest how the law that does apply should be interpreted. In addition, custom and *public opinion* may be helpful in determining society's needs and expectations.

Interpretation of Previous Court Decisions

A nationwide system of courts was first established in England about 900 years ago when representatives of the king were given jurisdiction to resolve certain controversies. These early judges had no constitution or statutes to look to for guidance, so they determined how the conflicts that came before them should be resolved on their own.

As conflicts arose that raised issues similar to those decided in prior cases, the judges began to refer to their previous decisions, called **precedents,** for principles to apply. The body of legal principles that was developed in England in this manner came to be known as the **common law,** and it was adopted by early American courts for resolving conflicts here as well.

Today, the resolution of many conflicts is controlled by constitutions and statutes, but the courts still look to the common law for legal principles when necessary. The tendency of the courts to apply legal principles found in precedents to later cases is called *stare decisis* (let the decision stand). Part of this process, however, involves the interpretation of the previous cases. The relevant considerations in interpreting precedents are discussed in the following sections.

What Have the Courts Said in Previous Decisions? Just as it makes sense to look at the language of a statute when interpreting that statute, it is important to review what legal principles the court said it was applying in making its decision when interpreting a previous case. One of the purposes of written decisions is to provide an explanation to society of what the law is so that people will know how similar cases will be decided in the future. Moreover, similar decisions in similar cases give the law a certainty that allows people to conduct themselves in ways that avoid legal problems.

Why Were Previous Cases Decided As They Were? When looking at precedents, a court may also consider the reasons given by the earlier court for deciding the case the way it did. The court can then decide whether the same reasons apply to the case before it. The court may even question whether the reasons given for making the previous decision are still valid.

What Are Society's Needs and Expectations? A court may also choose to consider society's needs and expectations in interpreting precedents. Such things as statutes, executive orders, and administrative rulings may imply how previous cases should be interpreted even though they do not apply directly to the case before the court. In addition, society's customs and public opinion may contribute to interpretation. Taken together, formal public declarations, customs, and public opinion make up a society's **public policy.** Sometimes, current public policy may even lead a court to overrule the legal principles used in previous court decisions.

In the case that follows, a court was asked by the defendant to give a new interpretation to the word "necessaries" in cases involving contracts made by minors. As you read the case, note what the court takes into consideration in deciding how to interpret the word "necessaries."

GASTONIA PERSONNEL CORP. v. ROGERS
172 S.E.2d 19 (North Carolina 1970)

[Bobby L. Rogers graduated from high school in 1966 at the age of 17. Shortly thereafter, he married, moved into a rented apartment with his wife, and started taking courses toward an associates' degree in civil engineering at Gaston Tech. Rogers' wife was employed, and he received no financial aid from his parents. Because his wife was expecting a baby, Rogers decided to quit school and go to work.

Rogers went to Gastonia Personnel Corporation (Gastonia), an employment agency, for help in finding a job. He talked to a personnel counselor and signed a contract that, among other things, provided: "If I accept employment offered me by an employer as a result of a lead from you within twelve months of such lead, I will be obligated to pay you as per the terms of this contract." The contract included a fee scale based on starting salary.

Gastonia referred Rogers to Spratt-Seaver, Inc., where he was employed at a starting salary that entitled Gastonia to a fee of $295 according to the fee scale in the contract. When Rogers refused to pay the fee, Gastonia sued to recover the $295. In his answer, Rogers admitted that he had not paid the fee, but he argued that he was not indebted to the plaintiff in any amount because he was under 21 years old when he signed the contract with Gastonia and could therefore elect to avoid the contract.

At trial, Gastonia presented evidence to show that there was a contract between it and Rogers and that it

was entitled to payment under the terms of the contract. The parties stipulated (agreed) that Rogers was under 21 when the contract was created and performed.

Following the presentation of the plaintiff's evidence, Rogers moved for a nonsuit. The trial court granted the motion. Gastonia appealed to an intermediate appellate court, which affirmed the trial court's decision. Gastonia then appealed to the Supreme Court of North Carolina.]

BOBBITT, Chief Justice

Under the common law, persons, whether male or female, are classified and referred to as *infants* until they attain the age of twenty-one years.

An early commentary on the common law, after the general statement that contracts made by persons (infants) before attaining the age of twenty-one "may be avoided," sets forth "some exceptions out of this generality," to wit: "*An infant may bind himselfe to pay for his necessary meat, drinke, apparell, necessary physicke, and such other necessaries,* and likewise for his good teaching or instruction, whereby he may profit himselfe afterwards." . . . It appears also in later decisions of this Court: *Turner v. Gaither; Cole v. Wagner; Barger v. M. & J. Finance Corp.*

In accordance with this ancient rule of the common law, this Court has held an infant's contract, unless for "necessaries" or unless authorized by statute, is voidable by the infant, at his election and may be disaffirmed during infancy or upon attaining the age of twenty-one. . . .

[The court then reviewed several North Carolina cases concerning infants' contracts. In almost all of the cases, the courts had allowed the infant to disaffirm his or her contract despite claims by the adults involved that the contracts involved "necessaries." One case was quoted as saying, "the dominant purpose of the law . . . is to protect children and those of tender years from their own improvidence, or want of discretion, and from the wiles of designing men." The rationale for the exception made in cases involving necessaries was explained in another decision as being based on the premise that "infants had better be held liable to pay for necessary food, clothing, etc., than for the want of credit, to be left to starve."

The court also reviewed a number of North Carolina statutes in effect that allowed infants to enter into certain kinds of contracts, such as borrowing money for educational costs, obtaining automobile insurance, opening bank accounts, obtaining safe deposit boxes and life insurance, and, if married, buying and financing real and personal property. It was also noted that statutes provided that minors 18 years of age or older could marry and enter into certain hazardous occupations.

Finally, the court pointed out with approval the lowering of the age of majority by the legislature in England from 21 years of age to 18.]

Admittedly, the decisions of the District [trial] Court and of the [intermediate] Court of Appeals rest squarely on the ancient rule of the common law as applied in prior decisions of this Court. However, without awaiting additional statutory changes, whether general or piecemeal, it seems appropriate that this common-law rule, which is rooted in decisions made by judges centuries ago, should be modified at least to the extent set forth below.

In *State v. Culver*, Vanderbilt, C. J., in accord with cited quotations from impressive legal authorities, including Coke's Fourth Institute, Professor Williston, Dean Pound, Mr. Justice Holmes and Mr. Justice Cardozo, said:

One of the greatest virtues of the common law is its dynamic nature that makes it adaptable to the requirements of society at the time of its application in court. There is not a rule of the common law in force today that has not evolved from some earlier rule of common law, gradually in some instances, more suddenly in others, leaving the common law of today when compared with the common law of centuries ago as different as day is from night. The nature of the common law requires that each time a rule of law is applied it be carefully scrutinized to make sure that the conditions and needs of the times have not so changed as to make further application of it the instrument of injustice.

In general, our prior decisions are to the effect that the "necessaries" of an infant, his wife and child, include only such necessities of life as food, clothing, shelter, medical attention, etc. In our view, the concept of "necessaries" should be enlarged to include such articles of property and such services as are reasonably necessary to enable the infant to earn the money required to provide the necessities of life for himself and those who are legally dependent upon him.

The evidence before us tends to show that defendant, when he contracted with plaintiff, was nineteen years of age, emancipated [free from parental care and custody], married, a high school graduate, within "a quarter or 22 hours" of obtaining his degree in applied science, and capable of holding a job. To hold, as a matter of law, that such a person cannot obligate himself to pay for services rendered him in obtaining employment suitable to his ability, education and specialized training, enabling him to provide the necessities of life for himself, his wife and his expected child, would place him and others similarly situated under a serious economic handicap.

In the effort to protect "older minors" from improvident or unfair contracts, the law should not deny to them the opportunity and right to obligate themselves for articles of property or services which are reasonably necessary to enable them to provide for the proper support of themselves and their dependents. The minor should be held liable for the reasonable value of articles of property or services received pursuant to such contract.

Accordingly, the judgment of the Court of Appeals is reversed and the cause is remanded to the Court with direction to award a new trial to be conducted in accordance with legal principles stated herein.

CASE COMMENT

Reading this case is apt to make you want to know more about the contract liability of minors. This topic will be explained fully in Chapter 14. For now, however, focus your complete attention of the *reasoning process* used by the court in determining when a minor is liable for breach of contract because he or she has purchased "necessaries." Postpone until later learning about all of the aspects of a minor's contract liability.

CASE REVIEW QUESTIONS

1. Carefully trace the procedural steps in this case from beginning to end.
2. Was it a constitutional provision, a statute, or previous court decisions that the court interpreted?
3. Explain the reasoning on which the court based the decision that this case falls within the "necessaries" exception to the general rule that minors can avoid contracts. What things did the court consider in interpreting the meaning of "necessaries"?
4. Do you agree with the court's decision? Why?

JUDICIAL PHILOSOPHIES

In the preceding section of this chapter, three possible considerations for interpreting law were discussed. Frequently, all of these considerations yield the same result. In other words, when language, purpose, and society's needs and expectations are all considered, each may suggest the same interpretation of a constitutional provision, a statute, or a precedent.

Sometimes, however, different considerations suggest different interpretations. In a particular case, for instance, the plain meaning of a statute may suggest one interpretation, whereas the purpose of the statute may suggest another. The perceived needs and expectations of society may support one or the other of these interpretations, or they may raise a third possibility. In such a situation, which interpretation should a judge choose?

When different considerations suggest different interpretations, the decision as to which interpretation to choose often depends on the court's judicial philosophy. Some people believe that the interpretation of law should focus almost exclusively on language, whereas others emphasize the importance of purpose or society's needs and expectations.

Judicial Conservatism

Judicial conservatives argue that the function of the courts is to resolve conflicts by enforcing the law as it is written. According to this view, then, a court should restrict its interpretation of statutes and constitutional provisions to the plain meaning of the words used in those documents, and it should adopt the legal principles that earlier courts have said they were applying in their decisions of previous cases. Judges who follow this view are sometimes referred to as *strict constructionists.*

This judicial philosophy sees the formal institutions of the government — the three branches of government and the administrative agencies — as the sources of the law that should be applied in deciding cases. Emphasis is placed on interaction among the branches of government as the proper means of achieving society's goals. It is the function of the legislature and, to a lesser extent, the executive branch and the administrative agencies, but not of the courts, to determine what the law should be. The function of the courts is simply to interpret the law in a consistent manner according to its plain meaning.

The conservative view of the role of the courts has certain advantages. Because it greatly limits the matters a court can consider when interpreting law, it tends to make the law more certain than it would be if additional matters were considered. By making the law relatively certain, it is hoped that those who are affected by the law will be able to know and understand it and will then be able to behave in accordance with it.

Judicial Activism

Functional Analysis Judicial activists argue that the role of the courts should involve more than simply enforcing the law as it is written. They believe that a court should consider not only the plain meaning of the words used in constitutions, statutes, and prior cases but also the functions of those documents and precedents.

This approach, sometimes referred to as *functional analysis,* sees reason as playing an important role in the interpretation of law. Why should a court enforce a law in a way that will not further the purpose of that law, its advocates ask. They believe that consideration should be given to the spirit, not just the letter, of the law. Furthermore, if the spirit of the law, meaning its purpose or function, and the letter of the law conflict, they feel that emphasis should be placed on the spirit.

This functional view of the role of the courts also has certain advantages. Because it expands the number of matters considered by a court in interpreting the law, it tends to make the law more flexible than it would be if only the language of the law were considered. By making the law more flexible, it is hoped that the courts will be better able to resolve conflicts in those ways that are most beneficial to society. Limiting the interpretation of the law to only its language, it is argued, can lead to unjust and socially detrimental results in particular cases.

Those who would limit interpretation of law to its language respond that functional analysis is too imprecise. Who, they question, can say with certainty what the purpose of a constitutional provision, a statute, or a precedent is? They argue that, because the purpose of a law cannot be determined precisely, a judge who says he or she is considering the law's purpose in an interpretation is really imposing his or her own personal view of the law's purpose. The imposition of personal views, they conclude, is not a proper function of a judge.

Public Policy Analysis Some judicial activists go even further and argue that the function of the courts is to interpret the law in accordance with the needs and expectations of society. Although they acknowledge that society's needs and expectations cannot be determined precisely, they believe that public policy, as reflected in the law, society's customs, and public opinion, can be looked to for guidance and that legal conflicts can thereby be resolved as society desires and in its best interests.

This approach to legal interpretation, sometimes referred to as *public policy analysis,* sees the people, who comprise society, as the ultimate source of the law that should be applied in deciding cases. If the needs and expectations of society conflict with the letter or even the purpose of the law, emphasis should be placed on society's needs and expectations.

The primary advantage of the public policy approach is that, to the extent the courts' decisions actually reflect the needs and expectations of society, those decisions will be perceived by the members of society as beneficial. Limiting interpretation of the law to the language and function of constitutional provisions, statutes, and previous cases, it is argued, can lead to decisions that are out of step with society's current needs and expectations and that are therefore unacceptable to society. To the extent that the legal system's decisions are unacceptable, the system will be perceived as illegitimate.

Conversely, others argue that public policy analysis is too imprecise and is subject to abuse. Who can say with certainty what the needs and expectations of society are at any particular moment in time, they ask. They argue that the only proper way to determine the people's will is to look to the official governmental actions that apply to the particular case. To the extent that a judge goes beyond these official actions in interpreting the law, he or she is really imposing his or her personal view of society's needs and expectations. The imposition of personal views, they conclude, is not a proper function of a judge.

Case Example

In the previous section, you read the majority opinion of the North Carolina Supreme Court in the case of *Gastonia Personnel Corp. v. Rogers,* which held that the "necessaries" of an infant include not only such things as food, clothing, shelter, and medical attention but also those articles of property and those services that are reasonably necessary to enable an infant to earn the money required to provide the necessities of life for himself or herself and those who are legally dependent upon him or her.

Four of the seven judges of the North Carolina Supreme Court concurred in the majority opinion. Three judges dissented, and two of them wrote dissenting opinions. One of those dissenting opinions follows. As you read it, notice the ways the judicial philosophy of Judge Lake, who wrote it, appears to differ from that of Judge Bobbitt, who wrote the majority opinion.

GASTONIA PERSONNEL CORP. v. ROGERS
172 S.E.2d 19 (North Carolina 1970)

LAKE, Justice (dissenting)

As the majority opinion shows clearly, since a time prior to Columbus' discovery of America, it has been the well settled rule of the common law, repeatedly stated by this Court, that an infant's contract may be disaffirmed by him without liability, unless it is a contract for what the law calls "necessaries." If the contract is one for necessaries, the infant is liable for the reasonable value of what he received.

For five hundred years English and American societies and economies have thrived under this rule and infants have found employment. It may well be that a better rule can be devised. I find nothing in this record, or in current social and economic conditions, to support the conclusion that either our society or our economy would suffer substantially if we adhere to the rule for one more year. Then the General Assembly [the North Carolina legislature] will be in session and can make such changes as may be necessary.

After reciting several instances in which the Legislature of this State has modified the common law rule, the majority, "without awaiting additional statutory changes, whether general or piecemeal," now changes the law upon which the decisions of the lower courts "rest squarely." In justification, the majority opinion quotes former Chief Justice Vanderbilt of the Supreme Court of New Jersey as saying: "The nature of the common law requires that *each time* a rule of law is applied it be carefully scrutinized to make sure *that the conditions and needs of the times have not so changed as to make further application of it the instrument of injustice.*" (Emphasis added.)

This is not my conception of the nature of the common law, nor is it my understanding of the authority conferred upon this Court by the people of North Carolina. The authority of the people, through their representatives in the State Government, to change the common law when conditions and needs have so changed as to render the law unjust or unwise is clear. They have, however, seen fit [in the North Carolina Constitution] to vest this authority in the Legislature and not in us. This power to change established law to meet changes in conditions is the essence of the legislative power.

The tragic turmoil in our public schools had its beginning in the decision of another court to assume the power to change the law of the land to conform to its conception of justice in a new time. No such social upheaval will result from the decision of the majority in this case, of course, but it is the same kind of error. It weakens, however so slightly, the wall of separation which the people of this State built between the proper functions of the several divisions of their government. The majority opinion, itself, shows this step is unnecessary for it cites at least six instances in which the Legislature has acted in recent years to make changes in this small field of law. I am not persuaded that there is such an urgent necessity for the change now made by this decision that it cannot safely wait another year. The majority opinion shows that in England the change felt desirable there was made by Act of Parliament [the English legislature].

If some change is necessary, the majority opinion gives the trial courts no standard to guide them in other cases. The majority opinion expressly approves this statement from [the] Indiana Law Journal: "But this protection must not become a straightjacket stifling the economic and social advancement of infants who have the need and maturity to contract." How are the trial judges tomorrow to distinguish between the infant who does and the infant who does not have "maturity"? What is the test of an infant's "need" to contract? Again, the majority opinion says the previously accepted concept of "necessaries" should be enlarged to include "articles" and "services" which are "reasonably necessary" to enable the contracting infant to earn money to provide necessities of life for himself and his dependents. Are the services of an employment agency more necessary for this purpose than is an automobile for use in going from home to work? Is a nineteen year old, who has almost finished an engineering course, mcre in need of such an auto-mobile than a seventeen year old drop-out from high school?

I am unable to find in current events overwhelming evidence that today's nineteen year olds have more maturity of judgment than did those of a century ago and so have less need of protection. The present defendant, an exceptionally well educated one, has evaluated his economic credit and reputation for integrity in business transactions at something less than $295. In this I find little evidence of maturity of judgment.

CASE REVIEW QUESTIONS

1. What reasons are given in the dissenting opinion for maintaining the traditional interpretation of the "necessaries" exception to the general rule that minors can avoid contracts?
2. What type of judicial philosophy is represented by the majority opinion in this case, which you read earlier? What type of judical philosophy is represented by the dissenting opinion? Explain your answers.
3. Which of the two opinions in this case do you agree with? Why?

REVIEW QUESTIONS

1. What are the four conditions of justiciability? Give concrete examples of situations in which each of the conditions would not be met. What functions are served by these conditions?
2. What things might a judge consider when inter-preting a constitutional provision, a statute, or a previous case?
3. If you were a judge, would you most likely be a judicial conservative or a judicial activist? Explain the reasons for your choice.

CASE PROBLEMS

1. Cole was a candidate for Congress. He decorated his automobile and trailer with large campaign posters. On August 15, Verville, the chief of police, informed Cole that he intended to enforce against him a town ordinance that said, "No person shall operate a vehicle on any street or highway for the primary purpose of displaying advertising signs." Cole then brought suit against Verville on the grounds that the ordinance was unconstitutional because it violated Cole's right to free speech. He asked the court for an injunction stopping Verville from interfering with Cole's operation of his auto-mobile bearing the campaign posters. On November 10, when the time came to argue the case before the court, the defendant submitted an affidavit stating that Cole had been defeated in the primary election on September 15 and that the successful candidate in that primary had been de-

feated in the general election on November 3. Cole submitted an affidavit stating that he intended to use the same car and trailer, decorated with posters, in a future political campaign. What action should the court take? Explain.

2. Johnson, a landlord, was upset when a price-control act was adopted that established maximum rents that could be charged for rental property. He was anxious to test the constitutionality of the statute. He asked one of his tenants, a man named Roach, if he would act as the plaintiff in a lawsuit to test the validity of the statute. Roach agreed, as long as there would be no cost to him. Johnson said he would pay all expenses and told Roach that he would not even have to appear in court. A lawsuit against Johnson was then begun in Roach's name. The suit claimed that rent in excess of that allowed under the statute had been collected. Johnson moved to dismiss the suit on the basis that the statute was unconstitutional. The court then learned that Roach had not read the complaint filed in his name; had not employed, paid, or met with the attorney who appeared on his behalf; and did not know who had paid the court fees. What action should the court take? Explain.

3. The legislature of the state of Pennsylvania adopted a statute that required students in barber schools to serve lengthy apprenticeships before they would be eligible to apply for a barber license. Barbering without a license is subject to a substantial fine. The Pennsylvania Barber School Association brought an action on behalf of its members against the state and the Barber License Commission seeking a declaratory judgment that the statute was unconstitutional. The defendants moved to dismiss the action on the grounds that it was not justiciable. What arguments can the parties make concerning defendants' motion? Who will win the case? Explain.

4. The Laidley Field Athletic Board was created for the purpose of constructing certain athletic facilities. Some construction contracts were awarded by the board without competitive bidding. The Contractors Association, which has a membership of 131 building contractors, protested this action, but the board responded that it had no legal obligation to submit the particular contracts to competitive bidding. The Contractors Association then brought legal action against the board seeking a declaratory judgment that the contracts were in violation of state laws requiring competitive bidding and were therefore void. The board moved to dismiss the action on the basis that a justiciable controversy did not exist. What arguments should the parties make concerning this issue? Who will win the case? Explain.

5. The city of Petersburg maintains the Peoples Memorial Cemetery. The city wanted to widen a road that runs along one side of the cemetery. To accomplish this, the city purchased an acre of land adjacent to the cemetery with the intention of moving the bodies that were interred in that part of the cemetery that was to be used for widening the road to the newly purchased land. The Temples lived in a residence they owned that was located across the street from the land that the city had purchased. The brought a legal action seeking an injunction against the city. They based their case on a state statute that provides: "No cemetery shall be established within two hundred fifty yards of any residence without the consent of the owner of such residence." The Temples argued that they lived within 250 yards of the land the city intended to use as a cemetery and they had not consented to such use. The city admitted that these facts were true, but it argued that the statute was not applicable because the city was not "establishing" a cemetery but was only extending an already established cemetery. What arguments could the parties make concerning the meaning of the word "established" in the statute? Who will win the case? Explain.

6. In 1923, a state legislature enacted a statute that prohibited bringing into the state "horses, cattle, hogs, pigs, sheep, or livestock of any kind" without first having the animals inoculated against Hopkins disease. It placed authority for enforcement of the statute with the State Department of Agriculture. However, there has been no outbreak of Hopkins disease in the state since the 1920s, and outbreaks elsewhere in the world have become extremely rare. The disease is spread only by actual contact between animals. Last week, Fernando

brought an exhibit of Peruvian culture, including two live llamas that have not been inoculated against Hopkins disease, into the state. The Department of Agriculture ordered Fernando to remove the llamas from the state. An opinion poll conducted by the state's largest newspaper indicates that only four percent of those polled believe that Fernando should be prevented from showing his animals. If Fernando appeals the Department of Agriculture's order to a court, what arguments might each party present to the court? Who will win the case? Explain.

7. James Tallon was employed as a guard on a train operated by Rapid Transit, Inc. He was injured while on his way to work. He was in uniform and was riding on one of his employer's trains. Tallon did not have to pay to ride on his employer's train because he had been given a pass when he was hired. By statute, if Tallon was injured in an accident that occurred in the course of his employment, he was entitled to collect only workers' compensation. Otherwise, he could sue Rapid Transit for negligence and would probably be awarded a larger sum of money.

In a previous decision in the jurisdiction, an employee had been injured while traveling in a truck that was provided by his employer to take employees to and from a train station when they were going to an out-of-town work site. In the earlier case, the court had decided that the employee was injured in the course of his employment be-

cause, according to that court: "The vehicle was provided by the employer for the specific purpose of carrying employees to and from the place of employment and in order to secure their services." What arguments could Tallon and Rapid Transit make concerning the issue of whether Tallon's accident occurred in the course of his employment? Who will win the case? Explain.

8. In the early part of the twentieth century, the courts of New York decided several cases in which injured consumers had sued manufacturers for negligence. In these cases, the courts said that the manufacturer was liable to the consumer only if the product was "inherently dangerous." In the cases decided under this standard, poisons, a painter's scaffold, and a large coffee urn were found to be inherently dangerous, but a balance wheel on a circular saw and a steam boiler were found not to be inherently dangerous.

MacPherson, a consumer, brought a legal action against Buick Motor Company, a manufacturer, in a New York court in 1915. He alleged that the wheel of the car he had purchased had been negligently produced by Buick and that he had been injured as a result. He sought money damages. Buick argued that it was not liable even if it had been negligent because a car is not an inherently dangerous product. What arguments might each party have made concerning the issue of whether the car was an inherently dangerous product? Who should have won the case? Explain.

5

TORT LAW

Broadly defined, a **tort** is a civil (as opposed to a criminal) wrong, other than breach of contract, for which a court will provide a remedy. Tort law pertains to a large, miscellaneous group of wrongs that have evolved throughout legal history and continue to evolve today. As it becomes clear that a particular individual interest is entitled to protection, the courts respond by creating a new tort. In this way, tort law responds to the changing needs of society and insures protection against harm for society's members.

This chapter examines the purposes of tort law, the kinds of remedies that may be granted in tort cases, the various types of torts, the legal requirements for proving each tort, the defenses to tort actions, and the particular torts that may be described as business torts.

PURPOSES OF TORT LAW

When one individual harms another, loss results. For example, if A strikes B and B must go to a hospital emergency room for treatment, B suffers loss in the amount of money he will have to pay the hospital. One of the purposes of tort law is to allocate this loss, that is, to decide whether B must bear the loss or whether B is entitled to be compensated for his loss by A. In order to make this determination, the law must strike a balance between B's interest in protection against harm and A's interest in freedom of action. Thus, if A improperly interfered with B's interests—for example, if A's attack was deliberate—A must compensate B. But, if A acted properly—for example, if A acted in self-defense—she need not compensate B.

Another purpose of tort law is to prevent future harm by influencing behavior. The theory is that the imposition of liability will discourage repetition of the conduct that gave rise to the liability. A person who is held liable for damages will be more careful in the future, and the general threat of liability will be an incentive to everyone to conduct themselves in accordance with legally recognized standards of behavior.

CAUSATION

In order for liability to be imposed for the commission of a tort, there must be a causal relationship between the wrongful conduct of the defendant and the injury to the plaintiff. A plaintiff must prove causation to establish a defendant's liability for any tort. The law recognizes two kinds of causation: (1) cause in fact and (2) legal cause, which is often referred to as *proximate cause.* Both kinds of causation must be present for there to be liability.

Cause In Fact

The requirement of cause in fact is expressed in the negative: a defendant's conduct is not a cause in fact of a plaintiff's injury if the injury would have occurred in the absence of the defendant's conduct. For example, the failure of a railroad to install crossing signals would not be the cause in fact of injuries to someone who drove his or her automobile into the fifty-third boxcar of a passing train. The purpose of crossing signals is to warn motorists of approaching trains. In this example, it was not the railroad's failure to warn that caused the collision but rather the driver's failure to notice the passing train. The railroad's conduct, therefore, is not the cause in fact of the resulting injury.

Ordinarily, cause in fact questions are easy to answer. The only type of situation in which the cause in fact test does not work is when two causes bring about an event and either one of them by itself would have been sufficient to cause the event. For example, if A stabs C at the same time B shoots C and either wound in and of itself would have caused C's death, whose conduct is the cause in fact of C's death? Under the general rule, both A and B would escape liability because it could be said that the death would have occurred without the conduct of either. Consequently, a broader rule has emerged from such cases. A defendant's conduct is a cause in fact of a plaintiff's injury if that conduct was a material element and a substantial factor in bringing about the injury. Many states now follow this later rule.

Proximate Cause

Once cause in fact has been established, it must next be determined whether a defendant's conduct was the proximate cause of a plaintiff's injuries. Just as a stone thrown into a still pond causes many ripples, a single act may cause a multitude of reactions and results. The law does not hold an individual liable for each and every ripple. The concept of **proximate cause** is used to limit a person's responsibility for his or her conduct to those people and consequences that have a reasonable connection, in terms of justice and fairness, to that conduct.

For example, suppose A goes through a red light and strikes B's car. The force of the impact sends B's car over the curb and into a utility pole, knocking it down. As a result, four square blocks of the city are left without electricity. A's conduct is the cause in fact of any harm that results from the lack of electrical power. However, the rules of proximate cause may excuse A from liability for some, if not all, of the harm that results from the lack of electricity because justice and fairness dictate that those harms are simply too far removed from the conduct of a careless driver.

Many courts have resolved the question of where to draw the line in determining proximate cause by holding defendants liable only for those consequences of their wrongful conduct that are foreseeable and that result in harm to people within the area of foreseeable harm.

If a plaintiff proves that a defendant's wrongful conduct was both the cause in fact and the proximate cause of the plaintiff's injuries, then he or she has established the element of causation, without which there can be no tort liability.

DAMAGES

In addition to causation, another essential element of a plaintiff's proof in any tort action is damages. Three types of damages may be awarded in tort actions: nominal, compensatory, or punitive. As you will see as you read the following sections, the differences among these kinds of damages lie in the purpose for which each is awarded.

Compensatory Damages

Compensatory damages are designed to restore the plaintiff to the position he or she was in before the tort occurred, insofar as it can be done with money.

Compensation for Personal Injuries An injured plaintiff will be awarded money damages for all of the adverse physical and mental effects of the defendant's tortious conduct. The types of harm that are commonly compensated are economic loss, physical pain, mental distress, and physical impairment. Economic loss includes reasonable medical expenses; lost wages, earnings, or profits; the cost of substitute labor hired to do the work that the plaintiff cannot do; and the cost of custodial care if the plaintiff cannot care for himself or herself. Future losses and expenses are also included. Moreover, these losses need not be established with certainty. It is only necessary that it is probable that they will be incurred and that there is a reasonable basis for determining what they will be.

Both past and future physical pain, commonly called "pain and suffering," may be compensated. The dollar value of pain and suffering in a particular case is left largely to the discretion of the jury. In addition to physical pain, most courts recognize damage for mental harm due to fright and shock; anxiety about the future, both physical and economic; loss of peace of mind, happiness, or mental health; humiliation, embarrassment, or loss of dignity; mental distress from the loss of the ability to enjoy a normal life; and inconvenience caused by the injury. Finally, physical impairment, such as loss of eyesight or the use of a limb, whether temporary or permanent, partial or total, is valued and compensated.

If the plaintiff is especially vulnerable to some illness or injury, the defendant will still be liable for the harm caused even though a normal person would not have suffered the particular illness or injury under the same circumstances. This principle is known as the *eggshell skull rule.*

Normally, the plaintiff may be awarded compensatory damages even though he or she has already been or will be reimbursed by another source, such as workers' compensation, insurance, social security, or public assistance. It is felt that it would be more unjust for the defendant to escape liability because of these payments than it is for the plaintiff to recover twice. In some situations, however, the plaintiff will not be entitled to double recovery. For example, the workers' compensation law requires that the plaintiff repay the workers' compensation fund out of any damages collected from the defendant. This requirement insures that the plaintiff is compensated, the fund is maintained, and the defendant bears the loss.

For the protection of the defendant, the plaintiff has a duty to mitigate damages, that is, to make reasonable efforts to limit the losses resulting from the injury and to take steps to prevent further harm. The defendant will not be liable for losses that result from the plaintiff's failure to mitigate damages. In a few states, the duty to mitigate includes taking safety precautions such as wearing available seat belts. Under this rule, a defendant would not be liable for those injuries of a plaintiff that could be attributed to the plaintiff's failure to wear an available seat belt.

Compensation for Property Damage The damages awarded for harm to personal property depend on whether or not the injury to the property amounts to a taking of the property, which is referred to as *conversion.* The measure of damages for the conversion of personal property is the value of the property at the time of conversion. The plaintiff may also recover damages resulting from the loss of the property's use. For example, if A takes B's car and disposes of it, B is entitled to recover from A the value of the car at the time it was taken as well as the cost of renting a substitute until a replacement can be obtained.

For harm to personal property that does not amount to a conversion, the plaintiff may recover either the difference in the value of the property before and after the tort or the reasonable costs of repair and restoration.

Nominal Damages

Nominal (very small) damages are awarded if the plaintiff establishes the defendant's liability for a tort but fails to prove any actual damages. Failure of proof may arise in one of two situations. In the first, the plaintiff proves that he or she has sustained some actual damage but is unable to establish a dollar amount for the damage either because the injury cannot be valued or because the appropriate proof is not available. In the second situation, which usually involves intentional torts, there is no actual damage, but the plaintiff is entitled to recognition of the inference with his or her rights. For example, suppose A trespasses on B's land but does not cause any physical harm to the property. There is therefore no actual damage. Nevertheless, A has interfered with B's property rights and B, should he wish to pursue it, is entitled to an award for damages that recognizes the interference. In this situation, B will be given nominal damages, for example, a penny or a dollar.

Punitive Damages

As mentioned earlier, the primary purpose for awarding tort damages is to compensate a person for losses incurred because of the tort. The purpose of **punitive** (penalty) **damages** is not to compensate the person who has been harmed but to punish the defendant and to deter similar conduct by others. Such damages may be awarded in cases of intentional or strict liability torts, both of which will be discussed later in this chapter, if the defendant has acted with a wrongful or a hostile motive. Thus, if A trespasses on B's property with a malicious intent to destroy B's prize roses, B may be awarded punitive damages. You may recall that such damages were awarded in the *Malandris* case that you read in Chapter 3 (see page 44). Although punitive damages are generally not allowed in cases involving negligent conduct, some courts will permit punitive damages if the defendant's negligence amounts to wanton carelessness.

Damages from Multiple Defendants

When several defendants are liable for a plaintiff's injuries, the problem arises of how to allocate the damages among the defendants. If different defendants are responsible for identifiable parts of the plaintiff's harm, then each defendant will be liable for the harm he or she actually caused. If several defendants are responsible for the same harm, they are called *joint tortfeasors*. The term **tortfeasor** refers to a defendant who has been found liable for a tort. The ultimate liability of each joint tortfeasor will be based on the proportion of relative fault. The liability of joint tortfeasors is *joint and several*. This means that the plaintiff may obtain a judgment in the full amount against each defendant. He or she may then choose from which defendant to collect the judgment. Thus, for example, if A and B are found liable to the plaintiff, the plaintiff may choose to collect the entire amount from either A or B, or the plaintiff may choose to collect some portion of the judgment from each of them. This procedure helps to insure that the plaintiff will actually be paid. In most jurisdictions, a defendant who pays more than his or her share is entitled to reimbursement by the other defendants. Therefore, if it is determined that A is 60 percent liable and B is 40 percent liable, A may collect 40 percent from B if A has paid the entire judgment.

TYPES OF TORTS

There are three general categories of torts: intentional torts, negligence, and strict liability. The following sections explain these categories, give examples of each, and discuss defenses that can be used against them. As you read this material, you should pay particular attention to the elements of each tort, that is, what the plaintiff must prove to recover from the defendant, and on what grounds the defendant may seek to avoid liability.

Intentional Torts

An **intentional tort** is committed if an intentional invasion of a protected interest causes injury. To understand intentional torts, it is necessary to know what the law means by "intent." Intent is not necessarily a hostile state of mind or a desire to cause harm. Rather, it is a conscious objective to bring about a certain result, a result that in fact invades the interests of another person. Thus, a defendant may be liable even though he or she acted in fun or honestly believed that no harm would be caused. For example, if A drives a car in the direction of B for the purpose of surprising B, A will be liable if B is actually harmed as a result of A's horseplay.

Intentional torts may be divided into two subcategories: intentional interferences with a person and intentional interferences with a person's property. Conduct such as hitting a person or inflicting mental distress falls into the first subcategory; stealing a television or vandalizing a building falls into the second. These subcategories may be further subdivided into more specific types of wrongs.

Intentional Interferences with a Person There are a number of torts that involve intentional interference with a person. As you read the following material, you should notice that the wrongful conduct may be directed against either the physical or the emotional well-being of an individual.

Battery A **battery** consists of an unconsented touching of another person. This tort protects an individual's interest in his or her freedom from intentional and unpermitted physical contact with his or her person, including not only the body but also all those things in contact with or closely connected to the body, such as clothing or an object being held. The person being touched need not be conscious of it at the time. For instance, a person who is asleep, under anaesthesia, or otherwise unaware of being touched is still protected.

Assault An **assault** is an act by one person that results in a reasonable apprehension by another person of an imminent battery. Apprehension, as distinct from fear, is all that is required. Thus, if A raises her hand to strike B, there is apprehension even if B is certain he can ward off the blow and is therefore not afraid. A raised fist accompanied by the statement "I am going to hit you the next time I see you" would not be an assault because the words of futurity indicate that no imminent battery is threatened. Likewise, a threatening gesture made by a person who is under restraint would not be an assault because the restrained person could not in fact carry out a battery.

False Imprisonment The tort of **false imprisonment** consists of wrongfully confining or restraining another person. This tort protects an individual's interest in being free to move about at will. A person is imprisoned when he or she is involuntarily confined within boundaries — such as a room, a building, or a particular geographical area — set by another person. The confinement may be accomplished by means of physical barriers or by force or the threats of force. Moral or social pressure, however, is not sufficient. Also, the confinement must be total; that is, there can be no reasonable or safe means of escape.

Two common situations in which claims of false imprisonment arise are the detention of suspected shoplifters and arrest. At one time, the courts held that a store owner would be liable for false imprisonment if he or she detained a suspected shoplifter and the suspect was not guilty of shoplifting. Because of the magnitude of the economic loss caused by shoplifting, however, most states have enacted statutes that give shopkeepers the authority to detain customers for a reasonable time to investigate suspected shoplifting. Conversely, any arrest made without legal authority is a false arrest and the resulting confinement is false imprisonment.

Intentional Infliction of Mental Distress The tort of **intentional infliction of mental distress** is committed if a person conducts himself or herself in an outrageous and extreme manner that is calculated to cause and actually does cause very serious mental distress to another. For example, if A calls B and tells him falsely that his wife has been seriously injured in an automobile accident, A has intentionally inflicted mental distress. Certain business practices may constitute the intentional infliction of mental distress. For example, collection agencies or other creditors who use extreme high-pressure methods, such as around the clock telephone calls, to collect debts may be liable for the mental distress they cause.

Defamation The tort of **defamation** consists of harming an individual's good name or reputation. It includes two torts: written defamation, which is called **libel,** and spoken defamation, which is called **slander.** Because the interest protected is a person's good name or reputation, an essential element of defamation is that the defamatory statements be communicated to someone other than the person being defamed. If the communication is only to the individual involved, there can be no defamation, although there may be the intentional infliction of mental distress. Truth is an absolute defense to a tort action for defamation in most states. If the defamatory statements are true, it does not matter that the person who communicated them did so for bad reasons or even that the person did not himself or herself believe that they were true.

Invasion of Privacy There are four kinds of conduct that may constitute the tort of **invasion of privacy:** intrusion upon a person's solitude or seclusion; appropriation of a person's name or likeness; giving unreasonable publicity to private facts; and placing a person in a false light in the public eye. Invasion of an individual's home, eavesdropping on private conversations, making persistent and unwanted phone calls, and unauthorized prying into a bank account are all examples of intrusion. Appropriation often takes the form of using a person's name or picture without consent to advertise a product. The public disclosure of private facts that are offensive and objectionable to a reasonable person of ordinary sensibilities is an invasion of privacy even if the facts are true and would therefore not be defamatory. Erroneously attributing an inferior poem to a successful poet would place the poet in a false light in the public eye and would thus be an invasion of privacy.

Fraud The tort of **fraud** consists of using trickery or deceit to deprive another person of money or property. To prove the tort of fraud, a plaintiff must establish each of the following five elements:

1. There has been a false representation of fact.
2. The defendant knew or believed that the representation was false.
3. There was intent to induce another to act.
4. There was justifiable reliance on the misrepresentation.
5. Damage resulted from this reliance.

For example, suppose A approaches B about investing $10,000 in a proposed business venture of A's. In fact, A has no intention of starting a new business but intends instead to collect money from a number of investors and then leave the country. B checks with several banks and businesses in the area and learns that A has a good reputation for honesty and fair dealing and has launched several successful businesses in the past. B therefore invests the $10,000. Assuming that A indeed leaves with the money, B will be able to prove each of the five elements of the tort of fraud. (Fraud, as it applies in contract law, is discussed in Chapter 11.)

Prima Facie Tort In addition to the traditional categories of intentional torts, the law now recognizes a general principle of intentional tort liability called **prima facie tort.** A person who intentionally injures another without justification may be liable for committing a prima facie tort even though his or her conduct does not fall within the definition of an existing tort. This principle allows the law to be flexible and responsive to the changing needs and interests of society. For example, some courts now recognize a tort claim based on wrongful discharge from employment, as will be discussed in Chapter 19.

Intentional Interferences with Property This subcategory of torts pertains to conduct that infringes on a person's interest in being free from interference with his or her property rights.

Trespass to Land A **trespass to land** is any intentional entry onto land possessed by another. The interest protected is the individual's right to the exclusive possession of his or her real property. The land included is not only the surface of the land but also the air space and subsurface space to the height or depth that the individual can reasonably use such space.

The trespasser need not intend to trespass; he or she need only intend to commit the act that constitutes the trespass. For instance, if A walks on B's land with he honest belief that the land is her own, a trespass has nevertheless occurred. For entry to occur, there must be a physical invasion of B's land. It is not, however, necessary for the trespasser to come onto the land; flooding the land or throwing rocks on it, for example, would be sufficient.

Trespass to Chattels A **chattel** is an item of personal property. **Trepass to chattels** is an intentional act that interferes with another's possessory rights in the chattel. Interference may consist of damage, alteration, use, or movement of the chattel that deprives the owner of possession or control of the chattel for a period of time, even if only briefly. For example, if A takes B's coat and tears the lining, A has committed the tort of trespass to chattels and is liable to B for the cost of repairing the coat.

Conversion The tort of **conversion** is intentional conduct that deprives another of his or her personal property permanently or for an indefinite period of time. Conversion is essentially a trespass to chattel that is so serious or so aggravated that the defendant must pay full value for the chattel. For example, if A takes B's coat and burns it, A has *converted* the coat and is liable to B for its full value.

Defenses to Intentional Torts The defense most commonly asserted by a defendant to an alleged intentional tort is that the plaintiff has failed to prove the necessary elements of the alleged tort. But even if the plaintiff successfully proves all of the necessary elements of the alleged tort, the defendent can still raise certain defenses, called *affirmative defenses,* to avoid liability. The most important of these defenses are discussed in the following sections.

Privilege The defense of privilege can be asserted if the defendant has acted to further an interest of such social importance that public interest outweighs the plaintiff's interest in the protection of his or her rights from the defendant's conduct. For example, a defamatory statement made by a legislator in a legislative debate is privileged. In addition, the more social importance a defendant's privilege has, the greater it becomes. Thus, the acts of judges that are performed under authority of law are absolutely privileged, even if they are malicious or corrupt.

Consent A defendant can avoid liability for an intentional tort if the plaintiff consented to the defendant's conduct. When a person indicates his or her willingness for certain conduct to occur, consent has been given. Consent may be inferred from words, from conduct, or even from silence. The test is whether, under the circumstances, a reasonable person would have believed that the plaintiff was consenting to the defendant's conduct. For example, a person who plays football consents to ordinary tackles and whatever harm results, even a severe injury.

Discipline A parent, or someone standing in the place of a parent, will avoid liability for injuries that result from using force to control his or her child to the extent that the force is reasonably necessary to accomplish a permissible purpose. In some states, this right also extends to a schoolteacher to the extent that the use of force is necessary to maintain order in the school. The parent or the teacher will, however, be liable to the child if the force used is excessive.

Necessity The defense of necessity may be raised when a defendant intentionally commits an act that is reasonably necessary to prevent imminent harm, for which the plaintiff is not responsible, to his or her property or self or to others or the property of others and in so doing causes injury to the plaintiff's *property.* The law distinguishes between a *public necessity* and a *private necessity.* If the danger affects the entire community, for example, the defendant may be excused from liability entirely. If the defendant acts to protect a private interest, however, the defense of necessity is limited, and the defendant may have to compensate the plaintiff for his or her loss. Thus, a defendant who sets fire to a house to stop the spread of a fire that threatens the entire town may not be liable to the owner of the house. On the other hand, a defendant who sets fire to a house solely to protect his or her adjoining property may have to compensate the owner.

Defense of Self and Others A person has the right to take reasonable steps to protect himself or herself from harm. Self-defense is a valid defense to a tort claim even if the defendant was mistaken about the threat of harm, as long as he or she reasonably believed that self-defense was necessary.

In defending himself or herself, a person may only use as much force as is or reasonably appears to be immediately necessary under the circumstances. Force likely to cause serious physical injury or death may only be used if the defendant reasonably believes that he or she is in danger of similar harm. In some states, a person's right to self-defense is further limited by a duty to retreat or escape if it is safe to do so, unless the threat of harm occurs in the defendant's own dwelling.

An individual may also come to the defense of any third person. In such situations, the defendant stands in the position of the third person and acquires his or her right of self-defense.

Defense of Property A person's interest in the peaceful possession and enjoyment of his or her property gives rise to a limited right to defend that property against imminent intrusions. A person may therefore use reasonable force to expel or repel an intruder, but the force used must be the minimal amount required under the circumstances and in no instance may it rise to the level of deadly physical force. This limitation stems from society's belief that human life is always more important than property. The following case involves the limits to an individual's right to defend his or her property.

KATKO v. BRINEY
182 N.W.2d 657 (Iowa 1971)

[Katko (the plaintiff) sued Mr. and Mrs. Briney (the defendants) for injuries that resulted from being shot by a 20-gauge, spring-set shotgun rigged up by the Brineys in a bedroom of an old farm house that they owned that had been uninhabited for several years. Katko and his companion, McDonough, had broken into the house to steal old bottles and dated fruit jars that they considered to be antiques. The jury returned a verdict in favor of Katko for $20,000 in damages. The Brineys moved for a judgment notwithstanding the verdict and for a new trial. The trial judge denied both motions. The Brineys appealed.]

MOORE, Chief Justice

The primary issue presented here is whether an owner may protect personal property in an unoccupied boarded-up farm house against trespassers and thieves by a spring gun capable of inflicting death or serious injury.

For about 10 years, [from] 1957 to 1967, there occurred a series of trespassing and house-breaking events [at the farm house] with loss of some household items, the breaking of windows and "messing up of the property in general." The latest occurred June 8, 1967, prior to the event on July 16, 1967 herein involved.

Defendants through the years boarded up the windows and doors in an attempt to stop intrusions. They had posted "no trespass" signs on the land several years before 1967. The nearest one was 35 feet from the house. On June 11, 1967 defendants set a "shotgun trap" in the north bedroom. After Mr. Briney cleaned and oiled his 20-gauge shotgun, the power of which he was well aware, defendants took it to the old house where they secured it to an iron bed with a barrel pointed at the bedroom door. It was rigged with wire from the doorknob to the gun's trigger so it would fire when the door was opened. Briney first pointed the gun so an intruder would be hit in the stomach but at Mrs. Briney's suggestion it was lowered to hit the legs.

He admitted he did so "because I was mad and tired of being tormented" but he "did not intend to injure anyone." He gave no explanation of why he used a loaded shell and set it to hit a person already in the house. Tin was nailed over the bedroom window. No warning of its presence was posted.

Plaintiff lived seven miles from the old house. He had observed it for several years while hunting in the area and considered it as being abandoned. He knew it had long been uninhabited. In 1967 the area around the house was covered with high weeds. Prior to July 16, 1967 plaintiff and McDonough had been to the premises and found several old bottles and fruit jars which they took and added to their collection of antiques. On [that] date about 9:30 P.M. they made [another] trip to the Briney property. They entered the old house by removing a board from a porch window which was without glass. While McDonough was looking around the kitchen area plaintiff went to another part of the house. As he started to open the north bedroom door the shotgun went off striking him in the right leg above the ankle bone. Much of his leg was blown away.

The main thrust of defendants' defense in the trial court and on this appeal is that "the law permits use of a spring gun in a dwelling or warehouse for the purpose of preventing the unlawful entry of a burglar or thief." They repeated this contention in their exceptions to the trial court's instructions [2 and 5 to the jury].

[In its instructions] the trial court stated [that] plaintiff and his companion committed a crime when they broke and entered defendants' house. In instruction 2 the court referred to the early case history of the use of spring guns and stated under the law their use was prohibited except to prevent the commision of [serious crimes] of violence and where human life is in danger. The instruction included a statement [that] breaking and entering is not a [serious crime] of violence.

Instruction 5 stated:
You are hereby instructed that one may use reasonable force in the protection of his property, but such right is

subject to the qualification that one may not use such means of force as will take human life or inflict great bodily injury. Such is the rule even though the injured party is a trespasser and is in violation of the law himself.

The overwhelming weight of authority, both textbook and case law, supports the trial court's statement of the applicable principles of law.

Prosser on Torts states:

. . . the law has always placed a higher value upon human safety than upon mere rights in property, it is the accepted rule that there is no privilege to use any force calculated to cause death or serious bodily injury to repel the threat to land or chattels, unless there is also such a threat to the defendant's personal safety as to justify a self-defense. . . . Spring guns and other mankilling devices are not justifiable against a mere trespasser, or even a petty thief. They are privileged only against those upon whom the landowner, if he were present in person would be free to inflict injury of the same kind.

The facts in *Allison v. Fiscus* are very similar to the case at bar. There plaintiff's right to damages was recognized for injuries received when he feloniously broke a door latch and started to enter defendant's warehouse with intent to steal. As he entered a trap of two sticks of dynamite buried under the doorway by defendant owner was set off and plaintiff seriously injured. The court held the question whether a particular trap was justified as a use of reasonable and necessary force against a trespasser engaged in the commission of a felony should have been submitted to the jury.

The legal principles stated by the trial court in instructions 2 [and] 5 are well established and supported by the authorities cited and quoted. There is no merit in defendants' objections and exceptions thereto. Defendants' various motions based on the same reasons stated in exceptions to instructions were properly overruled.

Affirmed.

LARSON, Justice (dissenting)

I respectfully dissent because the majority wrongfully assumes that by installing a spring gun in the bedroom of their unoccupied house the defendants intended to shoot any intruder who attempted to enter the room. Under the record presented here, that was a fact question. Unless it is held that these property owners are liable for any injury to an intruder from such a device regardless of the intent with which it is installed, liability under these pleadings must rest upon two definite issues of fact, i.e., did the defendants intend to shoot the invader, and if so, did they employ unnecessary and unreasonable force against him?

Although the court told the jury the plaintiff had the burden to prove "That the force used by defendants was in excess of that force reasonably necessary and which persons are entitled to use in the protection of their property," it utterly failed to tell the jury it could find the installation was not made with the intent or purpose of striking or injuring the plaintiff. There was considerable evidence to that effect. As I shall point out, both defendants stated the installation was made for the purpose of scaring or frightening away any intruder, not to seriously injure him. It may be that the evidence would support a finding of an intent to injure the intruder, but obviously that important issue was never adequately or clearly submitted to the jury.

At the trial of this case Mr. Briney, one of the defendants, testified that the house where plaintiff was injured had been the home of Mrs. Briney's parents. He said the furniture and other possessions left there were of considerable value and they had tried to preserve them and enjoy them for frequent visits by Mrs. Briney. It appeared this unoccupied house had been broken into repeatedly during the past ten years and, as a result, Mr. Briney said "things were pretty well torn up, a lot of things taken." To prevent these intrusions the Brineys nailed the doors and some windows shut and boarded up others. Prior to this time Mr. Briney testified he had locked the doors, posted seven no trespassing signs on the premises, and complained to the sheriffs of two counties on numerous occasions. Mr. Briney further testified that when all these efforts were futile and the vandalism continued, he placed a 20-gauge shotgun in a bedroom and wired it so that it would shoot downward toward the door if anyone opened it. He said he first aimed it straight at the door but later, at his wife's suggestion, reconsidered the aim and pointed the gun down in a way he thought would only scare someone if it were discharged. On cross-examination he admitted that he did not want anyone to know it was there in order to preserve the element of surprise.

Although I am aware of the often-repeated statement that personal rights are more important than property rights, where the owner has stored his valuables representing his life's accumulations, his livelihood business, his tools and implements, and his treasured antiques as appears in the case at bar, and where the evidence is sufficient to sustain a finding that the installation was intended only as a warning to ward off thieves and criminals, I can see no compelling reason why the use of such a device alone would create liability as a matter of law.

I would reverse and remand the matter for a new trial.

CASE REVIEW QUESTIONS

1. What intentional tort did Katko claim the Brineys had committed?
2. What did Katko have to prove to have the court decide that the Brineys were liable to him for the commission of that tort?
3. On what grounds did the Brineys seek to avoid liability?
4. Why did the majority of the appellate court believe that the Brineys were liable to Katko?
5. The majority opinion quotes Mr. Briney as testifying that he did not intend to injure anyone. In light of this testimony, why did the court decide that Mr. Briney had committed an intentional tort?
6. Do you think that the result would have been different if the gun had been visible from outside the farm house or warnings about its presence had been posted? Explain.
7. Why did Judge Larson, who wrote the dissenting opinion, believe that the Brineys were entitled to a new trial?

Negligence

Negligence can be broadly defined as conduct that is careless; it is conduct that should be recognized by the person acting as creating an unreasonable risk of harm to others. Negligence is distinct from intentional torts in that it does not require that the tortfeasor have an intent to bring about a certain result.

For example, assume that while driving her car, A ran B down in the street. If it was A's desire to hit B, A's conduct was intentional and A has committed a battery. On the other hand, if A was simply not paying attention to the road, she has not committed an intentional tort. Instead, assuming A's failure to watch the road created an unreasonable risk of harm to other drivers and pedestrians, B among them, A has committed the tort of negligence.

A plaintiff who sues on the basis of negligence must prove the four elements of negligence:

1. The defendant owed a duty of care to the plaintiff.
2. The defendant breached that duty of care.

3. The plaintiff was injured.

4. The plaintiff's injury was caused by the defendant's breach of duty.

All four elements must be proven. If any one is missing, there can be no liability.

Duty of Care A duty of care is an obligation to conform to a particular standard of conduct toward another. Whether there is a duty of care in any given situation depends on whether the plaintiff's interests are entitled to legal protection against the defendant's conduct. Therefore, whether or not a person owes a duty of care can vary with circumstances.

For example, suppose that A, the owner of an apartment building, has neglected to keep the fire escape in a safe and usable condition. A fire breaks out. B, a tenant, and C, a burglar, climb down the fire escape to flee the burning building. Each falls because the fire escape is in an unsafe condition and each is injured. Both B and C sue A. In each case, A's careless failure to fix the fire escape caused the injury, but B will recover damages and C will not. The difference in liability is explained by the fact that A has a legal duty to B, a tenant who was rightfully in the building, to maintain the fire escape in a reasonably safe condition, whereas A does not owe this duty to C, a burglar who had no right to be on the premises. Because A owes no duty of care to C, she cannot be held liable to C for negligence.

The duty of care may also be established by statute. The principle of **negligence per se** allows a plaintiff to use a defendant's violation of a statute as proof that the defendant was negligent as long as the plaintiff is within the class of individuals that the statute is intended to protect and the harm caused is the kind the statute is intended to prevent.

For example, state statutes setting speed limits are enacted to protect persons using public roadways. Suppose that A, a pedestrian on a public street, is injured as a result of B's driving in excess of the posted speed limit. A is within the class to be protected because she was using a public roadway. Furthermore, the harm suffered by A — personal injury — is of the kind that the legislature wanted to prevent. A may therefore use B's violation of the speed limit as proof of negligence. Most states would treat B's violation of the speed limit as *conclusive proof* of negligence. However, some states would treat it only as *evidence* of negligence that a jury may accept or reject.

Breach of Duty of Care There must be a breach of the duty of care owed to the plaintiff by the defendant for there to be liability for negligence. The defendant will have breached the duty of care if his or her actions fall below the particular standard of conduct toward the plaintiff that the law requires. To understand what conduct the law requires of people — that is, what duties people owe — we must refer to that fictitious individual created by the law called the "reasonable person."

The reasonable person is based on society's judgment of how an individual should behave in each of the infinite number and variety of situations in which there is potential or actual risk of harm. A defendant's conduct is usually measured against what the reasonable person would do under the same or similar circumstances. If the defendant's conduct falls short of the reasonable person's conduct, the defendant has breached his or her duty; that is, the defendant has failed to live up to the required standard of care.

For example, suppose that the fire escape in the earlier example was unsafe because several steps had come loose. Suppose also that A had been repeatedly notified of the loose steps and had put off getting them fixed. A's conduct would fall below the standard of what a reasonable person would do under the circumstances and would thus be a breach of duty. On the other hand, suppose that A had just discovered the loose steps in the course of a daily inspection of the fire escape, had immediately called a reliable repairperson, and had begun to notify the tenants of the danger when the fire broke out and B was injured falling from the fire escape. In this situation, we could say that A had acted as a reasonable person under the circumstances and conclude that she had not breached her duty to B.

Although the reasonable person standard is objective and uniform, it does take into account certain individual attributes of the particular defendant, such as physical disabilities, superior skill and knowledge, or age. Thus, a person who has a hearing impairment will be judged by the standard of what a reasonable person with a hearing impairment would do under the circumstances. Similarly, a doctor who specializes in neurosurgery will be judged against the standard of a reasonable neurosurgeon rather than the standard of a reasonable doctor, and a child will be judged according to what can reasonably be expected of children of like age, intelligence, and experience.

In the following case, the plaintiff sued the defendant for negligence. The defendant argued that it did not owe a duty of care to the plaintiff and that, even if it did owe a duty of care, it had not breached its duty. Note how the court deals with each of these arguments.

KLINE V. 1500 MASSACHUSETTS AVENUE APARTMENT CORPORATION
439 F.2d 477 (D.C. Cir. 1970)

[Kline (the plaintiff) sued the 1500 Massachusetts Avenue Apartment Corporation (the defendant), the owner of the apartment building in Washington, D.C., in which Kline resided, to recover for injuries sustained when she was criminally assaulted in a common hallway of the building. The trial court found for the corporation and Kline appealed.]

WILKEY, Circuit Judge

The appellant, Sarah B. Kline, sustained serious injuries when she was criminally assaulted and robbed at approximately 10:15 in the evening by an intruder in the common hallway of an apartment house at 1500 Massachusetts Avenue. This facility, into which the appellant Kline moved in October 1959, is a large apartment building with approximately 585 individual apartment units. It has a main entrance on Massachusetts Avenue, with side entrances on both 15th and 16th Streets. At the time the appellant first signed a lease a doorman was on duty at the main entrance twenty-four hours a day, and at least one employee at all times manned a desk in the lobby from which all persons using the elevators could be observed. The 15th Street door adjoined the entrance to a parking garage used by both the tenants and the public. Two garage attendants were stationed at this dual entranceway; the duties of each being arranged so that one of them always was in position to observe those entering either the apartment building or the garage. The 16th Street entrance was unattended during the day but was locked after 9:00 P.M.

By mid-1966, however, the main entrance had no doorman, the desk in the lobby was left unattended much of the time, the 15th Street entrance was generally unguarded due to a decrease in garage personnel, and the 16th Street entrance was often left unlocked all night. The entrances were allowed to be thus unguarded in the face of an increasing number of assaults, larcenies, and robberies being perpetrated against the tenants in and from the common hallways of the apartment building. The landlord had notice of these crimes and had in fact been urged by appellant Kline herself prior to the events leading to the instant appeal to take steps to secure the building.

Shortly after 10:00 P.M. on November 17, 1966, Miss Kline was assaulted and robbed just outside her apartment on the first floor above the street level of this 585 unit apartment building. This occurred only two months after Leona Sullivan, another female tenant, had been similarly attacked in the same commonway.

At the onset we note that of the crimes of violence, robbery, and assault which had been occurring with mounting frequency on the premises at 1500 Massachusetts Avenue, the assaults on Miss Kline and Miss Sullivan took place in the hallways of the building, which were under the exclusive control of the appellee landlord. Even in those crimes of robbery or assault committed in individual apartments, the intruders of necessity had to gain entrance through the common entry and passageways. These premises fronted on three heavily traveled streets, and had multiple entrances. The risk to be guarded against therefore was the risk of unauthorized entrance into the apartment house by intruders bent upon some crime of violence or theft.

While the apartment lessees themselves could take some steps to guard against this risk by installing extra heavy locks and other security devices on the doors and windows of their respective apartments, yet this risk in the greater part could only be guarded against by the landlord. No individual tenant had it within his power to take measures to guard the garage entranceways, to provide scrutiny at the main entrance of the building, to patrol the common hallways and elevators, to set up any kind of a security alarm system in the building, to provide additional locking devices on the main doors, to provide a system of announcement for authorized visitors only, to close the garage doors at appropriate hours, and to see that the entrance was manned at all times.

As a general rule, a private person does not have a duty to protect another from a criminal attack by a third person. Among the reasons for the application of this rule to landlords are: judicial reluctance to tamper with the traditional common law concept of the landlord-tenant relationship; the notion that the act of a third person in committing an intentional tort or crime is a superseding cause of the harm to another resulting therefrom; the oftentimes difficult problem of determining foreseeability of criminal acts; the vagueness of the standard which the landlord must meet; the economic consequences of the imposition of the duty; and conflict with the public policy allocating the duty of protecting citizens from criminal acts to the government rather than the private sector.

But the rationale of this very broad general rule falters when it is applied to the conditions of modern day urban apartment living, particularly in the circumstances of this case. The rationale of the general rule exonerating a third party from any duty to protect another from a criminal attack has no applicability to the landlord-tenant relationship in multiple dwelling houses. The landlord is no insurer of his tenants' safety, but he certainly is no bystander. And where, as here, the landlord has notice of repeated criminal assaults and robberies, has notice that these crimes occurred in the portion of the premises exclusively within his control, has every reason to expect like crimes to happen again, and has the exclusive power to take preventative action, it does not seem unfair to place upon the landlord a duty to take those steps which are within his power to minimize the predictable risk to his tenants.

In the instant case, the landlord had notice, both actual and constructive, that the tenants were being subjected to crimes against their persons. For the period just prior to the time of the assault upon appellant Kline the record contains unrefuted evidence that the apartment building was undergoing a rising wave of crime. Under these conditions, we can only conclude that the landlord here "was aware of conditions which created a likelihood" (actually, almost a certainty) that further criminal attacks upon tenants would occur.

Upon consideration of all pertinent factors, we find that there is a duty of protection owed by the landlord to the tenant in an urban multiple unit apartment dwelling.

We now turn to the standard of care which should be applied in judging if the landlord has fulfilled his duty of protection to the tenant. Although in many cases the language speaks as if the standard of care itself varies, in the last analysis the standard of care is the same — reasonable care in all the circumstances.

The specific measures to achieve this standard vary with the individual circumstances. It may be impossible to describe in detail for all situations of landlord-tenant relationships, and evidence of custom amongst landlords of the same class of building may play a significant role in determining if the standard has been met.

In the case at bar, appellant's repeated efforts to introduce evidence as to the standard of protection commonly provided in apartment buildings of the same character and class as 1500 Massachusetts Avenue at the time of the assault upon Miss Kline were invariably frustrated by the objections of opposing counsel and the impatience of the trial judge.

The record as to custom is thus unsatisfactory, but its deficiencies are directly chargeable to defendant's counsel and the trial judge, not appellant.

We therefore hold in this case that the applicable standard of care in providing protection for the tenant is that standard which this landlord himself was employing in October 1959 when the appellant became a resident on the premises at 1500 Massachusetts Avenue. The tenant was led to expect that she could rely upon this degree of protection. While we do not say that the precise measures for security which were then in vogue should have been kept up (e.g., the number of people at the main entrance might have been reduced if a tenantcontrolled intercom-automatic latch system had been installed in the common entryways), we do hold that the same relative degree of security should have been maintained.

The risk of criminal assault and robbery on any tenant was clearly predictable, a risk of which the appellee landlord had specific notice, a risk which became reality with increasing frequency, and this risk materialized on the very premises peculiarly under the control, and therefore the protection of the landlord to the injury of the appellant tenant. The question then for the Trial Court becomes one of damages only.

Reversed and remanded.

CASE REVIEW QUESTIONS

1. What tort did Kline allege the landlord had committed? What did Kline have to prove to win her case?
2. On what basis did the trial court decide that the landlord was not liable to Kline?
3. Why did the appellate court disagree with the trial court?
4. Why do you think the appellate court sets out the facts of the case in such detail in its decision?

Res Ipsa Loquitur In some situations, a plaintiff will not be able to offer any clear or direct evidence of a defendant's breach of the duty of care. For example, a plaintiff would probably not be able to offer an eyewitness account of a food processor's act of negligence that resulted in the presence of a foreign substance in a sealed food container. Negligence, however, does not always require direct evidence; it may also be established by *circumstantial evidence,* which is evidence from which the fact to be determined may reasonably be inferred. A set of human footprints in newly fallen snow, for instance, is circumstantial evidence of the fact that someone has recently walked there.

One type of circumstantial evidence is termed *res ipsa loquitur,* which translated literally means "the thing speaks for itself." There are, however, four conditions that must be met before a plaintiff will be allowed to use *res ipsa loquitur* as evidence of a defendant's negligence:

1. The event that caused the plaintiff's injury must be one that does not usually occur unless someone is negligent.
2. The injury must have been caused by an agent or instrument under the defendant's exclusive control.
3. The injury must not have been due to any voluntary action on the part of the plaintiff.
4. The evidence as to whether the defendant was in fact negligent must be more readily accessible to the defendant than to the plaintiff.

Once these conditions have been met, the burden of proof shifts to the defendant, who must then show that he or she has not been negligent. If the defendant cannot show that reasonable care was exercised, the jury is entitled to find for the plaintiff.

For example, suppose that A sustains a shoulder injury while unconscious during an appendicitis operation. A sues the doctor and the hospital employees present during the surgery. If A is unable to offer direct evidence to explain her injury, the court may use the doctrine of *res ipsa loquitur* as evidence of the defendants' negligence and thereby shift the burden of explanation to the defendants. If the defendants fail to show that A's injury was not the result of their negligence, A will win her lawsuit.

Causation and Injury To be successful in a legal action based on negligence, a plaintiff must prove not only that the defendant had a duty of care and breached that duty but also that he or she was *injured* and that the injury was *caused* by the defendant's breach of duty. Earlier in the chapter you read that economic loss, physical pain, mental distress, and physical impairment are the common kinds of injuries for which tort law awards compensatory damages. You also read about causation. In all tort cases, the plaintiff must prove that the defendant's wrongful conduct was both the cause in fact and the proximate cause of his or her injury.

Generally, proving causation in a negligence case is not difficult. In the case that follows, however, the defendant argued that although his negligence was a cause in fact of the plaintiff's injuries, it was not the proximate cause because injury to the plaintiff was not a foreseeable consequence of the defendant's conduct.

GEORGE v. BREISING
477 P.2d 983 (1971)

[George (the plaintiff) sued Breising (the defendant) for personal injuries he sustained when he was struck by an automobile stolen from the grounds of Breising's automobile repair business. The trial court granted Breising's motion for summary judgment. George appealed.]

SCHROEDER, Justice

This is an appeal in a damage action arising from personal injuries sustained by the plaintiff, a pedestrian, in an automobile accident in Wichita, wherein the plaintiff was struck and injured by a stolen automobile driven by one Stephen Williams. The defendant was the owner and operator of a private automobile garage repair business and was charged with negligence by the plaintiff for leaving the keys in the automobile while it was parked on the private grounds of the defendant's place of business.

The underlying questions are: (1) Whether it is negligence to leave an automobile on private property, unattended and unlocked with the keys in the ignition, and if so; (2) whether that negligence is a proximate cause of the injury sustained by the plaintiff herein.

John E. Breising (defendant-appellee) operates his automobile garage repair business under the name of K.B.S. Motor Company at its present location of 2648 North Arkansas Avenue, Wichita, Kansas. The zoning classification for Breising's property is commercial. Located to the north of the premises in question is the Ramsey Dairy; to the east is a vacant lot; to the south is the residence of Loretta Seavey; and to the west across the street is the Ramsey-Kester used car lot.

While the appellant herein attempts to depict Mr. Breising's place of business as located in the middle of a slum area filled with criminals and juvenile delinquents, the area and neighborhood surrounding the business premises in question is shown by photographs in the record to represent a fairly normal location for business activity.

On the 9th day of November 1967, Harold Roberts brought his 1963 Oldsmobile to Breising for repair. The repairs were completed on the 13th day of November 1967, and pursuant to the request of Roberts, Breising parked the car on his premises just outside the building. On the afternoon of the day in question Roberts had called at Breising's shop and asked whether the repairs to his automobile had been completed. Breising told Roberts that if the repairs were completed during the afternoon of November 13, 1967, he would park the car in front of the shop so that Roberts could pick it up. Roberts informed Breising he would come by about 6:30 that evening, and if the car was not out on the lot he would assume Breising had not completed repairs. There was nothing said about leaving the keys in the ignition when the conversation took place. At approximately 6:00 P.M. Mr. and Mrs. Roberts drove by and saw their automobile in the garage with the hood up. Mr. Roberts assumed the repairs had not been completed inasmuch as there was an agreement to park it outside only if the repairs had been completed. At about 6:45 P.M. Breising parked Roberts' 1963 automobile in the parking lot outside of the building with the keys in the ignition. Breising then closed the shop and went home for dinner. When he returned to the shop at about 8:00 P.M. for some evening work, he noticed the automobile was gone and assumed Mr. Roberts had picked it up.

Sometime between 6:45 and 8:00 P.M. on the evening in question the Roberts car had been stolen from its location on Breising's premises by two boys, Roger Wyant (age 15) and Paul Allen (age 14). These boys drove the car around Wichita until approximately 7:30 that evening. They then parked it in front of KWBB radio station located at 28th and Salina Streets and started home. On the way home they met Stephen Williams in the Safeway parking lot at 25th and Arkansas Avenue and told him about the automobile.

The three boys went back to the automobile and

Stephen Williams drove it around for awhile. Later Stephen Williams was returning the automobile to Breising's place of business, but upon noticing him in the garage working, drove on to 25th and Shelton where all three boys left the automobile and went to their respective homes.

The next morning, November 14, 1967, Stephen Williams returned alone to the automobile and drove it again. He picked up a friend, Dennis Stout, and while driving the automobile around Wichita he struck the plaintiff near 13th and Santa Fe Streets.

The appellant stresses facts disclosing that teenage or younger children frequented the general area and Breising occasionally saw them walking down the alley behind his garage, walking down the sidewalk in front or cutting across his property. He stresses thefts reported of automobiles from the Ramsey-Kester used car lot on June 16, 1967, August 25, 1967, and September 30, 1967. He also stresses that police records reflect break-ins at the Ramsey Dairy on June 15, 1967, and December 14, 1967. He relies on the fact that Breising had knowledge of these car thefts and break-ins. He also relies on the fact that on Memorial Day, May 30, 1967, a 1961 Rambler sedan was stolen from Breising's lot. This automobile and its keys had been delivered by the owner, Sutherland, to a Mr. Ramsey who in turn delivered the automobile and keys to Breising. Apparently the vehicle was left on the K.S.B. lot with the keys in the ignition.

Loretta Seavey, who lived near the premises, testified by deposition the neighborhood was not too good and had deteriorated in recent years. . . . She had observed boys getting in and out of cars on the used car lots, and read of boys getting into trouble, many of them having addresses around the neighborhood.

Assuming it was negligent for Breising to leave the keys in Roberts' car on his property unlocked and unattended, the issue is not whether it was foreseeable that Roberts' vehicle would be stolen as the appellant urges in his brief; rather, the inquiry is whether the independent intervening act of negligence committed by Williams, the successor in possesssion to the thieves, in driving the stolen vehicle was reasonably foreseeable. Under the weight of authority such an independent intervening act of negligence is not foreseeable as a matter of law, thereby rendering Breising's act of negligence to be a remote cause and the intervening act of negligence of Williams to be the direct and proximate cause of the injury sustained by the appellant.

Whether the negligent conduct of the original wrongdoer is to be insulated as a matter of law by the intervening negligent act of another is determined by the test of foreseeability. If the original actor should have reasonably foreseen and anticipated the intervening act causing injury in the light of the attendant circumstances, his act of negligence would be a proximate cause of the injury. Foreseeability of some injury from an act or omission is a prerequisite to its being a proximate cause of the injury for which recovery is sought. When negligence appears merely to have brought about a condition of affairs or a situation in which another and entirely independent and efficient agency intervenes to cause the injury, the latter is to be deemed the direct and proximate cause and the former only the indirect or remote cause.

Affirmed.

CASE REVIEW QUESTIONS
1. What tort did George allege Breising had committed? What did George have to prove to win his case?
2. On what basis did Breising defend?
3. What standard does the court apply in determining whether Breising's negligence was the proximate cause of George's injury?
4. Do you think Breising would be liable to Roberts for any property damage to Roberts' car? Explain.

5. Do you think Breising would have been liable to the plaintiff if the plaintiff had been injured by Wyant and Allen on the evening they stole the car? Explain.
6. Whose negligence was the proximate cause of George's injury? Why do you think that George didn't sue that person instead of Breising? Explain.

Defenses to Negligence The defense most commonly raised by a defendant to a claim of negligence is that the plaintiff has failed to prove one of the necessary elements of negligence — duty, breach of duty, injury, or causation. Indeed, this was the defendant's contention in the two previous cases. There are, however, other defenses, called *affirmative defenses,* in which the defendant argues that even if he or she were negligent, liability should not be imposed because of some conduct of the plaintiff.

Contributory Negligence **Contributory negligence** is conduct on the part of the plaintiff that falls below the standard of care that the plaintiff must exercise for his or her own protection and that contributes as a legal cause to the injury suffered by the plaintiff. At one time, the law in all states held that when a plaintiff was contributorily negligent, no matter how slightly, he or she was denied any recovery from the defendant. For example, assume A carelessly failed to look both ways before driving out of a parking lot and was struck by B, who was driving negligently because he was driving too fast to stop. A suffered $10,000 in injuries. If A sued B for negligence, B could successfully defend on the grounds of A's contributory negligence because A did not act with due care and contributed to her own harm.

Comparative Negligence The doctrine of contributory negligence is very harsh on plaintiffs. It places the entire loss on the plaintiff when both the plaintiff and the defendant were in fact responsible for the plaintiff's injury. As a result, many states have now adopted a rule of comparative negligence in place of the rule of contributory negligence.

Under the rule of **comparative negligence,** a plaintiff's negligence is not a complete bar to recovery. Instead, the plaintiff's total damages are calculated and are then reduced by the proportion for which the plaintiff is at fault for his or her own injury. For instance, if A's own negligence in the preceding example caused 25 percent of her injury and B's negligence caused 75 percent of her injury, A would recover $7,500 of the $10,000 claim.

Assumption of the Risk **Assumption of the risk** occurs when someone voluntarily consents to encounter a known danger created by another person's negligence. If a plaintiff assumes a risk that results in injury to him or her, the defendant is relieved of any liability for that injury even if the defendant owed the plaintiff a duty of care and breached that duty. To establish assumption of the risk, the defendant must show that the plaintiff had actual knowledge of the risk, appreciated the degree of the danger, and freely and voluntarily consented to encounter it. Note that the test here is subjective — Did the particular plaintiff assume the risk? — rather than objective — Would a reasonable person have assumed the risk?

For example, suppose that A, the owner of a baseball stadium, has a duty to provide a screen in front of the seats behind home plate but fails to screen those seats. B, a frequent spectator at baseball games, chooses to sit in the unscreened area behind home plate and is injured by a foul ball. Under the circumstances, B has assumed the risk of his injury. On the other hand, C, who has never seen a baseball game and does not know the danger, cannot be said to have assumed the risk of the same injury.

In the following case, the court deals with the question of whether the defense of assumption of the risk is precluded in a state that has moved from the rule of contributory negligence to the rule of comparative negligence.

GONZALEZ v. GARCIA
142 Cal. Rptr. 503 (Cal. 1977)

[Gonzalez (the plaintiff) and Garcia (the defendant) were co-workers at a power plant and members of the same carpool. The two men went to several bars for their customary few drinks after finishing their 10 P.M.–6 A.M. shift. During the next three hours, Gonzalez had a number of beers while Garcia drank beer, tequila, and other alcoholic beverages. Several times during their travels between bars, Gonzalez tried to convince Garcia to let him drive, and he also attempted to find alternate transportation. He was unsuccessful in both efforts. Gonzalez finally fell asleep in the car. Garcia lost control of the car and it rolled over, landing on its side in the median strip of the freeway. Garcia was clearly intoxicated at the time of the accident and his blood alcohol level was 0.20. Gonzalez was injured in the accident. He brought a negligence action against Garcia to recover damages for his injuries.

Prior to the trial of this case, the California Supreme Court in *Li v. Yellow Cab Co.* had abolished the defense of contributory negligence and substituted the defense of comparative negligence in its place. In this case, the defendant wanted to use the defense of assumption of the risk, but the trial judge would not allow it to be used.

The jury returned a verdict in favor of the plaintiff and the defendant appealed. The sole issue presented by the defendant's appeal was whether the trial judge had erred in refusing to instruct the jury on assumption of the risk.]

STEVENS, Associate Justice

The defense of assumption of risk was a late development in the law of negligence. The elements most frequently cited as essential to find assumption of risk are that the plaintiff have actual knowledge of the specific risk, appreciate the magnitude of the danger and freely and voluntarily encounter it.

Most commentators recognize at least three kinds of assumption of risk: (1) express — where plaintiff, in advance, gives consent to relieve defendant of a legal duty and to take his chances of injury from a known risk; (2) implied — where plaintiff acts reasonably in voluntarily encountering a risk with the knowledge that defendant will not protect him; and (3) implied — where the plaintiff acts unreasonably in voluntarily exposing himself to a risk created by defendant's negligence.

So long as contributory negligence and assumption of risk were both complete bars to recovery, the distinction between the two was never completely clarified. Usually, if a distinction was made, it was based upon the fact that assumption of risk requires knowledge of the danger and intelligent and deliberate acquiescence, whereas contributory negligence is concerned with fault or departure from the reasonable man standard of conduct, frequently inadvertently. Also the standard for determining whether the defense is available is different—assumption of risk using a subjective standard of the particular individual and circumstances and contributory negligence using an objective, reasonably prudent man standard with which to compare plaintiff's conduct.

Assumption of risk has been rather unpopular due to the harshness of the "all or nothing" recovery, and there has been considerable effort to abolish it completely, particularly in view of the emergence of the comparative negligence doctrine.

Throughout the opinion in *Li v. Yellow Cab Co.,* the Supreme Court emphasized that the existent contributory negligence rule must give way to a system " which assesses liability in direct proportion to fault," eliminating the harshness of the "all-or-nothing" doctrine for reasons of logic, practical experience and fundamental fairness. The court discussed the "all-or-nothing" rule as "inequitable in its operation because it fails to distribute responsibility in proportion to fault," and as contrary to all notions of fairness which require the extent of fault to govern the extent of liability.

Each statement is equally applicable to the doctrine of assumption of risk. Slightly changing the theory behind the "all-or-nothing" recovery rule and calling it assumption of risk does not alter the fact that it is fundamentally unfair for one person to bear the total burden of damages for which two people are by hypothesis responsible.

In the instant case defendant's negligent driving was the direct cause of plaintiff's injuries, and plaintiff's only negligence was in riding in the same car. Thus, in this case plaintiff's conduct is of the type which is variant of contributing negligence which "exists when a plaintiff unreasonably undertakes to encounter a specific known risk created by defendant's negligence."

Regardless of the extent of assumption of risk which still exists as a separate defense and complete bar to recovery, in this case plaintiff's conduct clearly falls into the overlapping area, the area of choosing an unreasonable alternative when reasonable ones were available, thereby evidencing a lack of due care for his own safety. Plaintiff had actual knowledge that defendant was intoxicated, he had been advised by a police officer that he should drive, he demonstrated that he probably had knowledge of the risk by his attempts to contact his wife, he had the alternative of remaining [where he was] or calling a cab and yet he chose to ride with defendant. Where there is a reasonably safe alternative open, the plaintiff's free choice of the more dangerous way is unreasonable and amounts to both contributory negligence and assumption of the risk. To that extent the doctrines are merged under *Li. v. Yellow Cab Co.* into the doctrine of comparative negligence.

There was no error in the court's refusal to give the instruction on assumption of risk as requested.

The judgment is affirmed.

CASE REVIEW QUESTIONS

1. What tort did Gonzalez allege Garcia had committed? What did Gonzalez have to prove to win his case?
2. On what basis did Garcia defend?
3. How might the jury's verdict have been different if the trial court *had* instructed the jury on the defense of assumption of the risk? Explain.
4. Why didn't the court allow the defense of assumption of the risk to be used?

Strict Liability

Under certain circumstances, the law imposes tort liability without fault; that is, it imposes liability for conduct that is neither intentional nor negligent. There are a number of forms of this kind of tort liability, often called **strict liability,** that have been created both by common law and by statute. The common denominator in all situations in which strict liability is imposed is the determination that, even if due care were exercised, the individual benefitting from the activity that causes the harm rather than the party who suffers the harm ought to bear the losses that result. In the discussion of each situation that follows, you should note why this determination has been made.

Abnormally Dangerous Activities Strict liability is imposed for harm resulting from abnormally dangerous activities because certain activities, though socially useful or even necessary, are sufficiently dangerous or create sufficient risks that public policy considerations mandate that they be carried on only if those engaged in them are willing to insure others against the harm that may result. In determining whether a particular activity is abnormally dangerous, courts consider the following factors:

1. Whether the activity involves a high probability of causing some harm to the person or property of others.
2. Whether the harm that may result is likely to be great.
3. Whether the risk can or cannot be eliminated by the exercise of reasonable care.
4. Whether the activity is an uncommon one.
5. Whether the activity is inappropriate to the place where it is being carried on.
6. What the value of the activity is to the community.

For instance, storing large quantities of explosives or using explosives in the midst of a large city will result in strict liability whereas the same activity in a remote rural area will not. Likewise, the transportation of toxic or hazardous substances through a populated area is an abnormally dangerous activity whereas the storage of the same materials in an unpopulated area is not.

Vicarious Liability Vicarious liability is a form of strict liability in which A is held liable to C for the tort of B simply because A and B are in a particular relationship and B was acting within the scope of that relationship when he committed the tort. The most common situation in which there is vicarious liability is when the person who commits a tort is the employee of the person on whom the injured party seeks to impose liability. There are five primary justifications for the imposition of vicarious liability on employers:

1. The employer has a measure of control over the conduct of his or her employee.
2. The employer initiated the conduct out of which the tort arose.
3. The employer selected the employee.

4. Liability is the business cost of employing others.
5. The employer is more likely than the employee to have the means—the so-called "deep pocket"—to compensate a plaintiff.

The vicarious liability of an employer for the torts of an employee is discussed extensively in Chapter 33.

Strict Liability by Statute A number of regulatory statutes create strict liability. For example, **workers' compensation** statutes impose strict liability on employers for job-related injuries. If an employee covered by workers' compensation is injured in a work-related accident, the resulting injury or death is compensated according to a fixed schedule of benefits, irrespective of anyone's fault. One of the rationales for imposing strict liability on employers in such cases is that the employer, rather than the employee, should bear the expense of the employee's injury as a cost of doing business. Another rationale is that the imposition of liability will promote safety in the workplace.

Another example of statutorily created strict liability can be found in dram shop acts, which are laws that make individuals who sell alcoholic beverages strictly liable for the injuries of those harmed by the conduct of intoxicated customers. The justification for this type of legislation is that those who sell alcoholic beverages ought to bear the losses that may result as a cost of doing business. Generally, liability is imposed only in situations in which the sale itself is unlawful, as in selling alcoholic beverages to a minor or to an already intoxicated person, for instance.

Product Liability One of the most recent applications of strict liability has been in the area of the liability of manufacturers and sellers to consumers for injuries resulting from defective products. Because of the importance of this form of strict liability to business, it is discussed extensively in the next chapter.

BUSINESS TORTS

Although virtually all of the torts previously discussed in this chapter may be commited by a business organization, there are a number of torts that occur only in commercial settings. These torts fall into three categories: interference with business conduct; interference with business relations; and unfair trade practices.

Interference with Business Conduct

Although free competition is one of the fundamental principles of American society, an individual's freedom to engage in a business is circumscribed in two situations. First, a person may not engage in a business for the sole purpose of driving another person out of business. Second, a person may not interfere with another person's business by engaging in business in violation of restraints that have been imposed by law. Thus, if the Federal Communications Commission has granted a television station the exclusive right to broadcast on a certain frequency, another business may not interfere with that right. A person who interferes with another's business may be subject to an injunction (a court order to stop the interference) and, in addition, may be liable for damages. If the interference is a violation of a regulatory statute, the individual may also incur penalties under the statute.

In the following case, the court determined that there are limits to an individual's right to engage in the business of his or her own choice.

TUTTLE v. BUCK
119 N.W. 946 (Minn. 1909)

[Tuttle (the plaintiff) sued Buck (the defendant) for intentionally interfering with his business. Buck demurred (moved to dismiss the complaint). The trial court overruled Buck's demurrer and he appealed.]

ELLIOTT, [Judge]

This appeal was from an order overruling a demurrer to a complaint in which the plaintiff alleged:

That for more than ten years last past he has been and still is a barber by trade, and engaged in business as such in the village of Howard Lake, Minnesota, where he resides, owning and operating a shop for the purpose of his said trade. That until the injury hereinafter complained of his said business was prosperous, and plaintiff was enabled thereby to comfortably maintain himself and family out of the income and profits thereof, and also to save a considerable sum per annum, to wit, about $800. That the defendant, during the period of about twelve months last past, has wrongfully, unlawfully, and maliciously endeavored to destroy plaintiff's said business, and compel plaintiff to abandon the same. That to that end he has persistently and systematically sought, by false and malicious reports and accusations of and concerning the plaintiff, by personally soliciting and urging plaintiff's patrons no longer to employ plaintiff, by threats of his personal displeasure, and by various other unlawful means and devices, to induce, and has thereby induced, many of said patrons to withhold from plaintiff the employment by them formerly given. The defendant is possessed of large means, and is engaged in the business of a banker in said village of Howard Lake, at Dassel, Minnesota, and at other places, and is nowise interested in the occupation of a barber; yet in the pursuance of the wicked, malicious, and unlawful purpose aforesaid, and for the sole and only purpose of injuring the trade of the plaintiff, and of accomplishing his purpose and threats of ruining the plaintiff's said business and driving him out of said village, the defendant fitted up and furnished a barber shop in said village for conducting the trade of barbering. That failing to induce any barber to occupy said shop on his own account, though offered at nominal rental, said defendant, with the wrongful and malicious purpose aforesaid, and not otherwise, has during the time herein stated hired two barbers in succession for a stated salary, paid by him, to occupy said shop, and to serve so many of the plaintiff's patrons as said defendant has been or may be able by the means aforesaid to direct from plaintiff's shop. That at the present time a barber so employed and paid by the defendant is occupying and nominally conducting the shop thus fitted and furnished by the defendant, without paying any rent therefor, and under an agreement with defendant whereby the income of said shop is required to be paid to defendant, and is so paid in partial return for his wages. That all of said things were and are done by defendant with the sole design of injuring the plaintiff, and of destroying his said business, and not for the purpose of serving any legitimate interest of his own. That by reason of the great wealth and prominence of the defendant, and the personal and financial influence consequent thereon, he has by the means aforesaid, and through other unlawful means and devices by him employed, materially injured the business of the plaintiff, has largely reduced the income and profits thereof, and intends and threatens to destroy the same altogether, to plaintiff's damage in the sum of $10,000.

It has been said that the law deals only with externals, and that a lawful act cannot be made the foundation of an action because it was done with an evil motive. Such generalizations are of little value in determining concrete cases. They may state the truth, but not the whole truth. Each word and phrase used therein may require definition and limitation.

We do not intend to enter upon an elaborate discussion of the subject, or become entangled in the subtleties connected with the words "malice" and "malicious." We are not able to accept without limitations the doctrine above referred to, but at this time content ourselves with a brief reference to some general principles.

It must be remembered that the common law is the result of growth, and that its development has been determined by the social needs of the community which it governs. It is the resultant of conflicting social forces, and those forces which are for the time dominant leave their impress upon the law. It is of judicial origin, and seeks to establish doctrines and rules for the determination, protection, and enforcement of legal rights. Manifestly it must change as society changes and new rights are recognized. To be an efficient instrument, and not a mere abstraction, it must gradually adapt itself to changed conditions. Necessarily its form and substance have been greatly affected by prevalent economic theories.

For generations there has been a practical agreement upon the proposition that competition in trade and business is desirable, and this idea has found expression in the decisions of the courts as well as in statutes. But it has led to grievous and manifold wrongs to individuals, and many courts have manifested an earnest desire to protect the individual from the evils which result from unrestrained business competition. The problem has been to so adjust matters as to preserve the principle of competition and yet guard against its abuse to the unnecessary injury to the individual. So the principle that a man may use his own property according to his own needs and desires, while true in the abstract, is subject to many limitations in the concrete. Men cannot always, in civilized society, be allowed to use their own property as their interests or desires may dictate without reference to the fact that they have neighbors whose rights are as sacred as their own. The existence and well-being of society require that each and every person shall conduct himself consistently with the fact that he is a social and reasonable person. The purpose for which a man is using his own property may thus sometimes determine his rights. . . .

To divert to one's self the customers of a business rival by the offer of goods at lower prices is in general a legitimate mode of serving one's own interest, and justifiable as fair competition. But when a man starts an opposition place of business, not for the sake of profit to himself, but regardless of loss to himself, and for the sole purpose of driving his competitor out of business, and with the intention of himself retiring upon the accomplishment of his malevolent purpose, he is guilty of a wanton wrong and an actionable tort. In such a case he would not be exercising his legal right, or doing an act which can be judged separately from the motive which actuated him. To call such conduct competition is a perversion of terms. It is simply the application of force without legal justification, which in its moral quality may be no better than highway robbery.

Affirmed.

CASE REVIEW QUESTIONS

1. What tort did the plaintiff allege the defendant committed? What would the plaintiff have to prove to win his case?
2. What are the competing interests of the plaintiff and the defendant?
3. On what basis did the appellate court uphold the trial court's decision?

Interference with Business Relations

There are two types of business torts that fall into the general category of interference with business relations. They are interference with contracts and interference with employment.

Interference with Contracts Business is generally carried on through the making of contracts. The right to enter into a contract and to benefit from its performance is a property right protected by law. There are three types of activities that constitute tortious interference with these contract rights: interference with the making of a contract, refusal to deal, and interference with contract performance.

Interference with the Making of a Contract A person tortiously interferes with the making of a contract when, acting with malice, he or she induces another not to enter into a contract with a third party. (While "malice" is almost impossible to define precisely, it generally means "without legal justification" or "through illegal means.") For example, if A convinces B not to enter into a contract to buy C's car simply because A does not like C, A has committed a tort. Likewise, if A induces B not to buy C's car by making fraudulent statements about the condition of the car, A has again tortiously interfered with the making of a contract. In both of these instances, A would be liable to C for damages.

Refusal to Deal Although an individual is generally free to choose with whom he or she will or will not contract, there are situations in which refusing to deal is a tort. For instance, refusing to contract because of race or religion may violate the Civil Rights Act of 1964 and may thus give rise to a cause of action for a business tort. Refusing to sell a product to another in an attempt to create an illegal monopoly is also tortious.

Interference with Contract Performance Inducing someone to breach his or her contract with another is the most common form of interference with contract performance. However, any act that impairs contract performance or decreases the value of that performance to one of the contracting parties may subject the person committing the act to tort liability.

Thus, if A has contracted with B to deliver 1,000 widgets on January 1st, C may not induce A to breach the contract by, for example, threatening not to reorder goods from A if she makes delivery to B. For this tort to be committed, a valid contract must exist and the defendant must know of its existence.

Interference with Employment There are certain situations in which interfering with an employer-employee relationship is a tort. For example, an employer may be liable if he or she induces someone else's employee to leave his or her employment in violation of an employment contract.

Unfair Trade Practices

Businesses may create their own trade advantages — by marketing a unique product, for example — or good will — by having a superior customer service department, for example. They are entitled to protection from unfair competitive business practices that would impair the benefits they can expect to obtain from their efforts. The most common unfair business practices that give rise to tort liability are fraudulent marketing; trademark, patent, and copyright infringement; and unlawful appropriation of trade secrets.

Fraudulent Marketing The intentional misrepresentation of either the source or the maker of a product is *fraudulent marketing* and is a tort. For example, if a department store displays a sign saying "A Brand" to indicate that all of the sweaters on a sweater counter are "A Brand" when in fact only a few are, it is fraudulently marketing the sweaters. Likewise, a dress shop that has a sign in its window falsely claiming "Dresses by A" is engaging in fraudulent marketing.

Imitating or copying another's product may also be tortious. For example, if a company packages its products in a manner so similar to that used by another company that a consumer would have difficulty distinguishing between the products, a tort has been committed. This specific kind of fraudulent marketing is known as *palming off.*

Not all imitations create liability, however. Liability depends on the way in which the product is copied. For instance, if Company A sends a designer to Company B's store to examine nonpatented Paris originals and Company A then reproduces the designs in a ready-to-wear line, no tort has been committed; the designer has merely copied something that is on public display. However, if Company A bribes an employee of Company B to show A's designer a dress so that he or she can copy it, Company A has secured the design through improper means and may be sued for fraudulent marketing.

Trademark, Copyright, and Patent Infringement When a business chooses a name for a product, creates an original work, or develops a new product, it wants to protect itself from unfair competition. It may do this by securing a *trademark,* a *copyright,* or a *patent,* each of which creates a protected property right. Infringing on this right is a tort.

Trademark Infringement A **trademark** is any word, symbol, device, or design that is adopted and used to identify an article for sale and is placed on or atached to the article or its container. A business is entitled to the exclusive use of its trademark, which may be registered with the state or federal government. A company that intentionally or unintentionally uses, for example, a name for its product that is so similar to another company's trademark that a prospective purchaser is likely to be confused as to the source of the product has committed the tort of *trademark infringement.*

Sometimes, a product name is so widely and commonly used that it becomes a generic term for a type of goods. When this occurs, the term may then be used by anyone to describe that type of goods as long as there is no attempt to misrepresent the product as the original. For instance, the name "aspirin," which was formerly a trademark, has become a generic term and may now be used by anyone.

Copyright Infringement Any original literary, dramatic, musical, or similar work may be protected by **copyright.** Anyone who then publishes a copy of the work without the permission of the copyright holder has infringed on the originator's copyright and is liable for damages. There is, however, no protection against someone who independently creates a similar work. Thus, if A is unaware of B's previously copyrighted computer program and through her own efforts creates a program very similar or identical to it, there has been no *copyright infringement* and, consequently, no tort.

Patent Infringement An inventor who creates a process, a machine, a product, a composition of matter, or a plant may be able to **patent** his or her invention and thus acquire the exclusive right to market it. In order to be patented, an invention must be useful, novel, and nonobvious in light of the prior state of the art. Anyone who makes or sells a patented article without the permission of the patent holder has committed the tort of *patent infringement.* Unlike a copyright, however, a patent is an exclusive right. Thus, someone who independently invents a previously patented process may not use or sell it. Like trademarks, copyrights and patents may be registered with the government.

Unlawfully Appropriating Trade Secrets A **trade secret** is any manufacturing or engineering process, formula, compilation of information such as a customer list or marketing survey, or other device that is known only to the company that created it and that gives the company a competitive advantage. For example, suppose that a company is the first to develop an unpatented machine to make flexible hoses such as those used on coin operated telephones. The machine gives its developer a competitive advantage and is therefore a trade secret. If another company acquires that trade secret dishonestly — through industrial espionage, for instance — it has unlawfully appropriated the trade secret. No registration with the government is necessary for a trade secret.

The following case examines the question of whether aerial photography of a plant under construction is an unlawful appropriation of a trade secret.

E.I. DUPONT DE NEMOURS & COMPANY, INC. v. CHRISTOPHER
431 F.2d 1012 (5th Cir. 1970)

[E.I. DuPont de Nemours & Company, Inc. (DuPont) sued Rolfe and Gary Christopher for wrongfully obtaining trade secrets. The trial court found for DuPont and the Christophers appealed.]

GOLDBERG, Circuit Judge

This is a case of industrial espionage in which an airplane is the cloak and a camera the dagger. The Christophers were hired by an unknown third party to take aerial photographs of new construction at [DuPont's] Beaumont plant. Sixteen photographs of the DuPont facility were taken from the air on March 19, 1969 and these photographs were later developed and delivered to the third party.

Dupont employers apparently noticed the airplane on March 19 and immediately began an investigation to determine why the craft was circling over the plant. By that afternoon the investigation had disclosed that the craft was involved in a photographic expedition and that the Christophers were the photographers. DuPont contacted the Christophers that same afternoon and asked them to reveal the name of the person or corporation requesting the photographs. The Christophers refused to disclose this information, giving as their reason the client's desire to remain anonymous.

Having reached a dead end in the investigation, DuPont subsequently filed suit against the Christophers, alleging that the Christophers had wrongfully obtained photographs revealing DuPont's trade secrets, which they then sold to the undisclosed third party.

DuPont contended that it had developed a highly secret but unpatented process for producing methanol, a process which gave DuPont a competitive advantage over other producers. This process, DuPont alleged, was a trade secret developed after much expensive and time-consuming research and a secret which the company had taken special precautions to safeguard. The area photographed by the Christophers was the plant designed to produce methanol by this secret process, and because the plant was still under construction parts of the process were exposed to view from directly above the construction area. Photographs of that area, DuPont alleged, would enable a skilled person to deduce the secret process for making methanol.

The question is whether aerial photograhy of plant construction is an improper means of obtaining another's trade secret. We think that the Texas rule is clear. One may use his competitor's secret process if he discovers the process by reverse engineering applied to the finished product; one may use a competitor's process if he discovers it by his own independent research; but one may not avoid these labors by taking the process from the discoverer without his permission at a time when he is taking reasonable precautions to maintain its secrecy. To obtain knowledge of a process without spending the time and money to discover it independently is *improper* unless the holder voluntarily discloses it or fails to take reasonable precautions to ensure its secrecy.

[W]e realize that industrial espionage of the sort here perpetrated has become a popular sport in some segments of our industrial community. However, our devotion to freewheeling industrial competition must not force us into accepting the law of the jungle as the standard of morality expected in our commercial relations. Our tolerance of the espionage game must cease when the protections required to prevent another's spying cost so much that the spirit of inventiveness is dampened. Commercial privacy must be protected from espionage which could not have been reasonably anticipated or prevented.

We do not mean to imply, however, that everything not in plain view is within the protected vale, nor that all information obtained through every extra optical extension is forbidden. Indeed, for our industrial competition to remain healthy there must be breathing room for observing a competing industrialist. A competitor can and must shop his competition for pricing and examine his products for quality, components, and methods of manufacture. Perhaps ordinary fences and roofs must be built to shut out incursive eyes, but we need not require the discoverer of a trade secret to guard against the unanticipated, the undetectable, or the unpreventable methods of espionage now available.

In the instant case DuPont was in the midst of constructing a plant. Although after construction the finished plant would have protected much of the process from view, during the period of construction the trade secret was exposed to view from the air. To require DuPont to put a roof over the unfinished plant to guard its secret would impose an enormous expense to prevent nothing more than a school boy's trick. We introduce here no new or radical ethic since our ethos has never given moral sanction to piracy. The market place must not deviate far from our mores. We should not require a person or corporation to take unreasonable precautions to prevent another from doing that which he ought not do in the first place. Reasonable precautions against predatory eyes we may require, but an impenetrable fortress is an unreasonable requirement, and we are not disposed to burden industrial inventors with such a duty in order to protect the fruits of their efforts.

"Improper" will always be a word of many nuances, determined by time, place, and circumstances. We therefore need not proclaim a catalogue of commercial improprieties. Clearly, however, one of its commandments does say:

> Thou shall not appropriate a trade secret through deviousness under circumstances in which countervailing defenses are not reasonably available.

The decision of the trial court is affirmed.

CASE REVIEW QUESTIONS

1. What tort did DuPont allege the Christophers had committed? What did DuPont have to prove to win its case?
2. On what grounds do you think the Christophers defended?
3. Do you think the court's conclusion would have been different if the process for producing methanol would have been visible from the air after construction of the plant was completed? Explain.

REVIEW QUESTIONS

1. What are the purposes of tort law?
2. What is the difference between cause in fact and legal or proximate cause?
3. Define an intentional tort. What are the most common defenses to intentional torts?
4. Define negligence. What are the most common defenses to negligence?
5. Define strict liability. What are some of the reasons strict liability is imposed?
6. What are the three major categories of business torts? Give an example of each.

CASE PROBLEMS

1. Two conductors for the Long Island Railroad assisted a passenger onto a train that was pulling out of the station. A plain brown package that the passenger was carrying was dislodged and fell to the

platform. The package, which contained fireworks, exploded. The concussion from the explosion knocked over a weighing station several hundred feet down the platform. The scales fell on Mrs. Palsgraf, injuring her. She sued the railroad company and the two conductors. What tort can Mrs. Palsgraf allege the two conductors committed? On what basis can Mrs. Palsgraf argue that the railroad company is liable for the tort of its employees. What legal argument would the railroad make in its defense? Explain.

2. For several months, the neighborhood children had played softball in the empty lot next to Collins' home. Because of several broken windows and the noise, Collins told the children not to play in the lot anymore. Angered by this, one of the children painted "Collins is a mean person" on the front of Collins' garage. To what damages will Collins be entitled? Explain.

3. As Johnson was walking across a parking lot to his car, he saw Smith standing next to the driver's side of the car, bending over. Believing that Smith was trying to break into his car, Johnson grabbed him and wrestled him to the ground. A crowd gathered. Johnson yelled at Smith, accusing him of trying to steal his car. Smith struggled to free himself, protesting, but Johnson held him down and raised his fist as if to strike Smith. A passing police officer stopped to investigate. Johnson told the police officer that he caught Smith breaking into his car. The officer arrested Smith. Smith, finally given the opportunity to explain, said that the car's lights had been left on and he was merely checking to see if the car was unlocked so he could turn them off. The lights were in fact on and a witness confirmed that Smith looked at the car but did not touch it. What torts were committed by Johnson? Explain.

4. Farady surprised an intruder in his home late one evening. As Farady called out to the intruder, she turned toward him. Seeing a glint of metal and believing the intruder had a knife in her hand, Farady shot her in the arm. In fact, the intruder was unarmed and the reflection Farady saw was from her watchband. The intruder sues Farady for battery. What defense will Farady raise? Will he be successful?

5. Gregory chartered a yacht for a weekend cruise in the Caribbean. On the second day out, the yacht hit an underwater obstruction and sank. Gregory and the crew spent four days in a lifeboat before being rescued. Although the yacht had been equipped with sonar, the sonar had not detected the obstruction. In her suit for negligence against the yacht's owner, Gregory argued that a more sophisticated piece of sonar equipment that would have detected the obstruction in time for it to be avoided was on the market and that the yacht should have been equipped with it. The newer equipment, with which this and other boat owners were familiar, was not commonly used because of its expense. Will Gregory be successful in her negligence claim? Explain.

6. An employee of the Coca Cola Bottling Company delivered several cases of Coca Cola to the restaurant where Escola worked as a waitress. As Escola was putting one of the bottles of Coca Cola in the refrigerator, it exploded in her hand, inflicting a deep cut which severed the blood vessels, nerves, and muscles of the thumb and palm. Escola wants to sue the Coca Cola Bottling Company, but she can offer no direct proof of the company's negligence. How might Escola be able to prove that the company was negligent? Explain.

7. Stiffel Company patented and manufactured a pole lamp. The pole lamp was a commercial success. Soon thereafter, Sears, Roebuck & Company began marketing a basically identical lamp, which it sold for less than the Stiffel lamp. Stiffel sued Sears for patent infringement. The court held that Stiffel was not entitled to patent protection. Stiffel then sued Sears for engaging in an unfair trade practice, specifically, fraudulent marketing. Will Stiffel's suit be successful? Explain.

6

PRODUCT LIABILITY

A person who is injured by a product usually wants to be compensated for those injuries. Today, a person's ability to recover can be based on three legal theories of product liability—negligence, warranty, and strict liability in tort. In this chapter, you will learn about the historical development of these theories.

As you read this chapter, you should notice that each of the legal theories of product liability is related in some way to tort law, which was the subject of the previous chapter. You should also notice the kinds of things that judges have considered as they have interpreted and changed the law of product liability over the years. Considerations in the interpretation of law was one of the topics discussed in Chapter 4 (see pages 58–67).[1]

TORT LAW AND PRODUCTS

In the past, people made simple products and sold them directly to the purchasers who used them. If the maker was careless in making a product and

---

[1] The focus of this chapter is on the historical development of product liability and its current status based upon negligence and strict liability. Although warranties are discussed in this chapter in terms of how they have affected the historical development of product liability, the current law of sales warranties is not included here. A complete discussion of sales warranties appears in Chapter 22, "Liability of Sellers."

the purchaser was injured as a result of the maker's carelessness, the purchaser could bring a legal action against the maker based on the tort of negligence.

You may recall from the previous chapter, however, that traditionally an absolute defense to a legal action based on negligence was that the injured party's own negligence had contributed to his or her injuries (see page 91). This defense, known as *contributory negligence,* was almost always available to product makers in lawsuits brought by purchasers in earlier times. In a simple economy in which buyers purchased few products, the products that were purchased were uncomplicated, and the buyers dealt directly with manufacturers. It was therefore believed that an ordinary buyer had sufficient knowledge and skill to inspect products and to discover any defects in them. A buyer's failure to discover a defect in a product that later injured him or her was considered to be contributory negligence, which barred recovery for the maker's negligence. *Caveat emptor,* meaning buyer beware, was a fitting slogan for those times.

But over time, the variety of products available to consumers multiplied, and their complexity became sufficient to confound the mind of the ordinary person. The specialization and efficiency that accompanied modern capitalism raised the standard of living to dizzying heights. Specialization progressed to the point that new methods of marketing were required. Manufacturers gradually stopped selling directly to the consumer. Instead, they sold to dealers who in turn sold to the consumers. Thus, the consumer became hard-pressed to acquire the knowledge and skill to conduct reasonable inspections of his or her purchases. And, no longer dealing directly with the manufacturer, the consumer was unable to evaluate the manufacturer's character and skill.

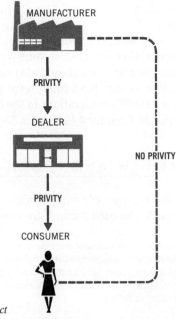

FIGURE 6-1
Privity of Contract

The Problem of Privity of Contract

As society and the economy changed, the old laws were stretched to fit increasingly complicated circumstances. Furthermore, the dealer in the new distribution scheme created a difficult problem for the courts. According to the law at the time, a plaintiff could not recover damages from a defendant unless he or she was in **privity of contract** with the defendant, meaning that there had to be a contractual relationship between the two parties.

The existence of one or more dealers between the manufacturer and the consumer meant that the consumer was *not* in privity of contract with the manufacturer (see Figure 6-1). The manufacturer was in privity with the dealer, who was unlikely to be harmed by the manufacturer's negligence; and the consumer was in privity with the dealer, who was unlikely to be responsible for the defect in the product that harmed the consumer. Thus, the dealer was not liable to the consumer because he or she was not negligent, and the manufacturer was not liable to the consumer because there was no privity of contract between them.

The case that follows was decided in England in 1842. The judges state the rule saying that there can be no liability for negligence without privity of contract and give the reasons for it. As you read the case, watch carefully for the reasons given by the judges and consider whether you agree with them.

WINTERBOTTOM v. WRIGHT
152 Eng. Rep. 402 (Ct. of Exchequer 1842)

[The defendant contracted with the Postmaster-General to supply mail coaches to carry the mail and to see to it that the coaches were "kept in a fit, proper, safe, and secure state and condition for said purpose." Atkinson, knowing of the contract, agreed to supply horses and drivers to the Postmaster-General for the coaches. The plaintiff was one of the drivers provided by Atkinson. While driving a coach provided and serviced by the defendant, the plaintiff was thrown to the ground and lamed for life when the coach broke down because it had been negligently constructed. Plaintiff brought a legal action seeking compensation damages for his injuries.]

LORD ABINGER, Chief Baron

I am clearly of the opinion that the defendant is entitled to our judgment. Here the action is brought simply because the defendant was a contractor with a third person; and it is contended that thereupon he became liable to everybody who might use the carriage. If there had been any ground for such an action, there certainly would have been some precedent of it, but with the exception of actions against innkeepers, and some few other persons, no case of a similar nature has occurred in practice. That is a strong circumstance, and is of itself a great authority against its maintenance. It is however contended, that this contract being made on behalf of the public by the Postmaster-General, no action could be maintained against him, and therefore the plaintiff must have a remedy against the defendant. But that is by no means a necessary consequence—he may be remediless altogether. There is no privity of contract between these parties; and if the plaintiff can sue, every passenger, or even any person passing along the road, who was injured by the upsetting of the coach, might bring a similar action. Unless we confine the operation of such contracts as this to the parties who entered into them, the most absurd and outrageous consequences, to which I can see no limit, would ensue. The plaintiff in this case could not have brought an action on the contract. By permitting this action, we should be working this injustice, that after the defendant had done everything to the satisfaction of his employer, and after all matters between them had been adjusted, and all accounts settled on the footing of their contract, we should subject them to be ripped open by this action of tort being brought against him.

ALDERSON, Baron

I am of the same opinion. If we were to hold that the plaintiff could sue in such a case, there is no point at which such actions would stop. The only safe rule is to confine the right to recover to those who enter into the contract; if we go one step beyond that, there is no reason why we should not go fifty. The only real argument in favour of the action is, that this is a case of hardship.

ROLFE, Baron

The breach of the defendant's duty is his omission to keep the carriage in a safe condition; and when we examine the mode in which that duty is alleged to have arisen, we find a statement that the defendant took upon himself, under and by virtue of the contract, the sole and exclusive duty, charge, care, and burden of the repairs, state, and condition of the said mail-coach, and, during all the time aforesaid, it had become and was the sole and exclusive duty of the defendant, under and by virtue of his contract, to keep and maintain the said mail-coach in a fit, proper, safe, and secure state and condition. The duty, therefore, is shown to have arisen solely from the contract; and the fallacy consists in the use of that word "duty." If a duty to the Postmaster-General be meant, that is true; but if a duty to the plaintiff be intended (and in that sense the word is evidently used), there was none. This is one of those unfortunate cases in which there certainly has been *damnum* [loss], but it is *damnum absque injuria* [loss without injury in the legal sense]; it is, no doubt, a hardship upon the plaintiff to be without a remedy, but by that consideration we ought not to be influenced. Hard cases, it has been frequently observed, are apt to introduce bad law.

Judgment for the defendant.

CASE REVIEW QUESTIONS

1. Why wasn't there privity of contract between the plaintiff and the defendant?
2. What reasons do the judges give for why the plaintiff should not recover because there was no privity of contract?
3. Why couldn't the plaintiff sue his employer, Atkinson?

Reasons for the Winterbottom Decision Why the court made the decision it did in *Winterbottom v. Wright* is a matter open to debate. But an examination of the historical context of the decision can lead to some plausible theories.

First of all, the court appears not to have recognized the changes in distribution techniques that were taking place. As discussed earlier, the distribution pattern had grown from a simple agreement between a product maker and a consumer into a more complex arrangement usually involving one or more intermediary dealers. While this case did not involve a dealer as such, it exemplified the increasing intricacy of distribution arrangements. Yet the court was still thinking in terms of a simple contract between a product maker and a consumer. The *Winterbottom* case also presented another twist: goods for hire passed to an employer and then to an employee.

Second, legal history reveals that at the time of the decision the tort duty of care was commonly regarded as having grown out of contracts; historical evidence now suggests that the reverse was actually the case. As the court saw it, there was no duty of care if there was no contract between the parties.

Third, the defendant was part of the transportation industry, a highly regarded English institution because the development of transportation was an important part of the Industrial Revolution. The court was unlikely to impose any constraint on this favored industry.

Finally, the court showed concern for manufacturers in general. A growing economy requires growing industry. It was commonly felt that industrialists should not be burdened with "absurd and outrageous" liabilities.

Chipping Away at Privity

The case of *Thomas and Wife v. Winchester* posed a dilemma concerning privity for the New York court that decided it in 1852. Mrs. Thomas had been injured when she swallowed a liquid extract from a bottle that had been mislabelled by Winchester, a druggist in New York City. Winchester's negligence was clear, but Mrs. Thomas was not in privity of contract with the druggist because the mislabelled bottle had passed through the hands of several intermediate dealers before it was sold to Mrs. Thomas by Alvin Ford, a druggist in Cazenovia, New York, who knew nothing of the mislabelling. On the theory of *Winterbottom v. Wright,* there could be no remedy for Mrs. Thomas and her husband, who had brought suit against Winchester.

Nonetheless, the court decided that the Thomases were entitled to recover from Winchester. As you read the case, note the reasoning that the court used to reach this conclusion.

THOMAS and WIFE v. WINCHESTER
6 N.Y. 397 (N.Y. 1852)

[The trial court denied the defendant Winchester's motion for a nonsuit. The jury returned a verdict for plaintiffs, Mr. and Mrs. Thomas. Winchester appealed.]

RUGGLES, Chief Judge

This is an action brought to recover damages from the defendant for negligently putting up, labelling and selling as and for the extract of dandelion, which is a simple and harmless medicine, a jar of the extract of belladonna, which is a deadly poison.

The case depends on the first point taken by the defendant on his motion for a nonsuit; and the question is, whether the defendant, being a remote vendor of the medicine, and there being no privity or connection between him and the plaintiffs, the action can be maintained.

If, in labelling a poisonous drug with the name of a

harmless medicine, for public market, no duty was violated by the defendant, except that which he owed to Aspinwall [the dealer to whom Winchester sold the product], in virtue of his contract of sale, this action cannot be maintained. If A builds a wagon and sells it to B, who sells it to C, and C hires it to D, who in consequence of the gross negligence of A in building the wagon is overturned and injured, D cannot recover damages against A, the builder. A's obligation to build the wagon faithfully, arises solely out of his contract with B. The public have nothing to do with it. Misfortune to the third persons, not parties to the contract, would not be a natural and necessary consequence of the builder's negligence; and such negligence is not an act immediately dangerous to human life. This is the rule in *Winterbottom v. Wright.*

But the case in hand stands on a different ground. The defendant was a dealer in poisonous drugs. The death or great bodily harm of some person was the natural and almost inevitable consequence of the sale of belladonna by means of a false label.

The defendant's negligence put human life in imminent danger. Can it be said that there was no duty on the part of the defendant to avoid the creation of that danger by the exercise of greater caution? Or that the exercise of that caution was a duty only to his immediate vendee [buyer], whose life was not endangered? The defendant's duty arose out of the nature of his business and the danger to others incident to its mismanagement. Nothing but mischief like that which actually happened could have been expected from sending the poison falsely labelled into the market; and the defendant is justly responsible for the probable consequences of the act.

Judgment affirmed.

CASE REVIEW QUESTIONS

1. If the rule in *Winterbottom v. Wright* had been applied in the *Thomas* case, who would have won the case? Explain.
2. Why do you think the court did not apply the rule in *Winterbottom v. Wright* to the *Thomas* case?
3. If you had owned a manufacturing company at the time of the decision in the *Thomas* case, under what circumstances would you have been held liable to a consumer for negligence after that decision?

After *Thomas and Wife v. Winchester,* the law was that a manufacturer owed a duty of care only to the immediate purchaser except when the product involved was imminently dangerous to human life, in which case the duty was also owed to the one who was most likely to be injured by the negligence, the ultimate consumer. The New York court had taken one step toward providing legal protection for the consumer.

If the courts had continued to devote their attention to the development of laws to protect consumers when they could not protect themselves, the problems created by *Winterbottom v. Wright* might have been eliminated. But the lawyers and jurists of the time were not interested in such problems. They were more interested in logically applying laws to facts. Rather than determining just results on the basis of the needs of society and shaping the laws accordingly, the legal profession was shaping justice according to the law.

For fifty years, the main legal question pertaining to product liability was not how to protect consumers or even whether to maintain a favorable legal environment for business but rather: "What kind of products are inherently dangerous to human life?" In one case during that period, it was decided that a negligently manufactured steam boiler that exploded and killed a person was not inherently dangerous, so the estate of the person killed could not recover from the manufacturer because there was no privity of contract between the person killed and the manufacturer. However, in another case, a court held that a scaffold 90 feet high was inherently dangerous, so the estate of a worker who was killed when the scaffold collapsed was able to collect from the person who negligently constructed the scaffold even though there was no privity between the worker and the scaffold builder.

Privity's Last Stand

The final challenge to the privity rule came with the development of a product of unprecedented complexity, the automobile. The average citizen puttering about in a horseless carriage had no intimate knowledge of the mechanics involved, and yet the contraption could go up to 50 miles an hour!

This technological wonder did not immediately bring about a change in the law, however. In a 1915 case, *Cadillac Motor Car Co. v. Johnson,* a man was injured when a wheel on his car collapsed and the car turned over. That the wheel was made of rotten wood was undisputed, yet the court found for the manufacturer. The judge reasoned that the automobile was not inherently dangerous; it was only dangerous if defectively made. Because the product was not inherently dangerous, the manufacturer had no liability to the purchaser of the automobile, with whom the manufacturer was not in privity of contract.

A dissenting judge argued that manufacturers of a machine as complicated and potentially dangerous as the automobile had a duty to construct a safe machine. This dissent signaled that it was time for a change in the law. In 1916, a landmark decision did change the law.

MacPHERSON v. BUICK MOTOR COMPANY
111 N.E. 1050 (N.Y. 1916)

[MacPherson (the plaintiff) purchased an automobile from a retail dealer. The car had been manufactured by the Buick Motor Company (the defendant). MacPherson was injured in an accident while driving the car caused by a defective wheel on the car. MacPherson brought a legal action based on negligence against the Buick Motor Company. The trial court found for MacPherson. The Buick Motor Company appealed.]

CARDOZO, Judge

The defendant is a manufacturer of automobiles. It sold an automobile to a retail dealer. The retail dealer resold to the plaintiff. While the plaintiff was in the car, it suddenly collapsed. He was thrown out and injured. One of the wheels was made of defective wood, and its spokes crumbled into fragments. The wheel was not made by the defendant; it was bought from another manufacturer. There is evidence, however, that its defects could have been discovered by reasonable inspection, and that inspection was omitted. The charge is one of negligence. The question to be determined is whether the defendant owed a duty of care and vigilance to any one but the immediate purchaser.

The foundations of this branch of the law, at least in this state, were laid in *Thomas v. Winchester*. A poison falsely labeled is likely to injure anyone who gets it. Because the danger is to be foreseen, there is a duty to avoid the injury.

Thomas v. Winchester became quickly a landmark of the law. In the application of its principle there may at times have been uncertainty or even error. There has never in this state been doubt or disapproval of the principle itself. The defendant argues that things imminently dangerous to life are poisons, explosives, deadly weapons — things whose normal function is to injure or destroy. But whatever the rule in *Thomas v. Winchester* may once have been, it has no longer that restricted meaning.

We hold, then, that the principle of *Thomas v. Winchester* is not limited to poisons, explosives, and things of like nature, to things which in their normal operation are implements of destruction. If the nature of a thing is such that it is reasonably certain to place life and limb in peril when negligently made, it is then a thing of danger. Its nature gives warning of the consequences to be expected. If to the element of danger there is added knowledge that the thing will be used by persons other than the purchaser, and used without new tests, then, irrespective of contract, the manufacturer of this thing of danger is under a duty to make it carefully. We have put aside the notion that the duty to safeguard life and limb, when the consequences of negligence may be foreseen, grows out of contract and nothing else. We have put the course of the obligation where it ought to be. We have put its source in law.

Beyond all question, the nature of an automobile gives warning of probable danger if its construction is defective. This automobile was designed to go fifty miles an hour. Unless its wheels were sound and strong, injury was almost certain. The defendant knew the danger. It knew also that the car would be used by persons other than the buyer. This was apparent from its size; there were seats for three persons.

There is nothing anomalous [abnormal] in a rule which imposes upon A, who has contracted with B, a duty to C and D and others according as he knows or does not know that the subject matter of the contract is intended for their use. The court left it to the jury to say whether the defendant ought to have foreseen that the car, if negligently constructed, would become "imminently dangerous." Subtle distinctions are drawn by the defendant between things inherently dangerous and things imminently dangerous, but the case does not turn upon these verbal niceties. If danger was to be expected as reasonably certain, there was a duty of vigilance, and this whether you call the danger inherent or imminent.

We think the defendant was not absolved from a duty of inspection because it bought the wheels from a reputable manufacturer. It was not merely a dealer in automobiles. It was a manufacturer of automobiles. It was responsible for the finished product. It was not at liberty to put the finished product on the market without subjecting the component parts to ordinary and simple tests. Under the charge of the trial judge nothing more was required of it. The obligation to inspect must vary with the nature of the thing to be inspected. The more probable the danger, the greater the need for caution.

Affirmed.

BARTLETT, Chief Judge (dissenting)

I do not see how we can uphold the judgment in the present case without overruling what has been so often said by this court and other courts of like authority in reference to the absence of any liability for negligence on the part of the original vendor [seller] of an ordinary carriage to any one except his immediate vendee [buyer]. The absence of such liability was the very point actually decided in the English case of *Winterbottom v. Wright*. [T]he opinion of Chief Judge Ruggles in *Thomas v. Winchester* assumes that the law on the subject was so plain that the statement would be accepted almost as a matter of course. In the case at bar the defective wheel on an automobile moving only eight miles an hour was not any more dangerous to the occupants of the car than a similarly defective wheel would be to the occupants of a carriage drawn by a horse at the same speed; and yet unless the courts have been all wrong on this question up to the present time there would be no liability to strangers to the original sale in the case of the horse-drawn carriage.

CASE REVIEW QUESTIONS

1. Did the court in the *MacPherson* case change the rule that had been set down in the case of *Thomas v. Winchester?* Explain.

2. In his dissent, Judge Bartlett said, "Unless the courts have been all wrong on this question up to the present time there would be no liability. . . ." How would you respond to this statement?

3. If you had owned a manufacturing company at the time of the decision in the *MacPherson* case, under what circumstances would you have been held liable to a consumer for negligence after that decision?

Res Ipsa Loquitur

The *MacPherson* case removed the privity of contract limitation on the liability of product manufacturers to consumers in lawsuits based on negligence. The wisdom of the decision was recognized by courts throughout the nation, and the court's conclusion was generally adopted. *Cadillac Motor Car Co. v. Johnson,* discussed in the text prior to the *MacPherson* case, is remembered today only as an interesting example of a court's inability to adjust the law to meet the needs of the times.

Despite the removal of the privity limitation, consumers still faced difficult problems when they sued product manufacturers. For instance, the consumer had to present evidence of the manufacturer's negligence in the production of the particular product that caused injury to the consumer. This could be done if the manufacturer's system of production or the design of the product were negligent. But how could the consumer prove that the particular defective product that had caused an injury had been produced negligently in other cases?

Suppose, for instance, that the consumer of a carbonated beverage was injured when the glass bottle containing the beverage exploded. The consumer then sues the manufacturer of the beverage for negligence. Prior to trial, the consumer discovers that the manufacturer's inspection process used to test for defects in its bottles is the most advanced in the industry. Also, the manufacturer uses high-grade glass in its bottles, and there is nothing wrong with the product's design.

In such a case, the plaintiff is apt to suspect that negligence by the manufacturer occurred during the inspection process. Even if the inspection *process* itself is the finest in the industry, there could be negligence on the part of an employee in *carrying out* the process. Perhaps the employee who was supposed to inspect the bottles on an assembly line left the line for an important phone call, allowing some bottles to go by without being inspected. Maybe the inspector simply fell asleep or was negligent in some other way.

The problem for the plaintiff is that, most likely, there will not be any evidence to prove that the inspector was negligent when the particular bottle that caused the injury was supposed to be inspected. Ordinarily, if the plaintiff cannot prove negligence, the manufacturer cannot be held liable.

In such situations, the courts have allowed plaintiffs to use a method of proof called *res ipsa loquitur,* which means "the thing speaks for itself." This method of proof of negligence was discussed in the previous chapter (see page 87). It is mentioned again here because one of its most common applications has been in product liability cases. Without this method of proof, consumers would have little chance of proving negligence in product liability cases.

In a negligence case, the burden is ordinarily on the plaintiff to prove that the defendant was negligent. When *res ipsa loquitur* is applied, however, the burden switches to the defendant, who must prove that he or she was not negligent. In other words, in a product liability case, the burden of proving that the product was not negligently manufactured is placed on the manufacturer. The plaintiff in the following case was successful because she was able to use the doctrine of *res ipsa loquitur.*

ESCOLA v. COCA COLA BOTTLING CO. OF FRESNO
150 P.2d 436 (Cal. 1944)

[Escola (the plaintiff) was a waitress. She was injured when a Coca Cola bottle exploded in her hand. She brought legal action against the Coca Cola Bottling Company of Fresno (the defendant) for negligence. She had no evidence that the particular bottle that had injured her had been negligently manufactured. Instead, she argued that her case was based on *res ipsa loquitur.* Coca Cola presented evidence that approved methods of inspection had been used. The jury returned a verdict for Escola. Coca Cola appealed.]

GIBSON, Judge

The question is whether plaintiff may rely upon the doctrine of *res ipsa loquitur* to supply an inference that defendant's negligence was responsible for the defective condition of the bottle at the time it was delivered to the restaurant.

An explosion such as took place might have been caused by an excessive internal pressure in a sound bottle, by a defect in the glass of a bottle containing safe pressure, or by a combination of these two possible causes. The question is whether under the evidence there was a probability that defendant was negligent in any of these respects. If so, the doctrine of *res ipsa loquitur* applies.

The bottle was admittedly charged with gas under pressure, and the charging of the bottle was within the exclusive control of the defendant. As it is a matter of common knowledge that an overcharge would not ordinarily result without negligence, it follows under the doctrine of *res ipsa loquitur* that if the bottle was in fact excessively charged an inference of defendant's negligence would rise. If the explosion resulted from a defective bottle containing safe pressure, the defendant would be liable if it negligently failed to discover such flaw.

It appears that there is available to the industry a commonly used method of testing bottles for defects not apparent to the eye, which is almost infallible. Since Coca Cola bottles are subjected to these tests by the manufacturer, it is not likely that they contain defects when delivered to the bottler which are not discoverable by visual inspection. The used bottles are not again subjected to the tests referred to above, and it may be inferred that defects not discoverable by visual inspection do not develop in bottles after they are manufactured. Obviously, if such defects do occur in used bottles there is a duty upon the bottler to make appropriate tests before they are refilled, and if such tests are not commercially practicable the bottles should not be re-used. It follows that a defect which would make the bottle unsound could be discovered by reasonable and practicable tests.

Although it is not clear in this case whether the explosion was caused by an excessive charge or a defect in the glass, there is sufficient showing that neither cause would ordinarily have been present if due care had been used. Further, defendant had exclusive control over both the charging and inspection of the bottles. Accordingly, all the requirements necessary to entitle plaintiff to rely on the doctrine of *res ipsa loquitur* to supply an inference of negligence are present.

The judgment is affirmed.

CASE REVIEW QUESTIONS
1. If the rule in *Winterbottom v. Wright* had been applied in the *Escola* case, who would have won the case? Explain.
2. If the rule in *Thomas and Wife v. Winchester* had been applied in the *Escola* case, who would have won the case? Explain.
3. If the plaintiff in the *Escola* case had not been allowed to use the doctrine of *res ipsa loquitur,* who would have won the case? Explain.
4. If your answer to any of the above questions was that the defendant manufacturer, the Coca Cola Bottling Company of Fresno, would have won the case, why do you think the actual outcome of the case was in favor of Escola?

WARRANTIES AND PRODUCTS

As you have seen, when consumers first began to bring legal actions against manufacturers to recover for injuries caused by defective products, they usually based their actions on the tort of negligence. Often, however, these suits would be unsuccessful because either the consumer was contributorily negligent or was unable to prove negligence by the manufacturer.

The Advantage of the Warranty Theory to Consumers

Two cases decided in 1918 dramatize the shortcomings of negligence actions brought by consumers. The defendant in both cases was the Childs Dining Hall Company, and the decision in each case was rendered in the same court, on the same day, by the same judge. In *Ash v. Childs Dining Hall Co.,* the plaintiff was injured by a tack in a piece of blueberry pie served to her at the dining hall. Evidence indicated that the tack had come from a wooden berry basket and was so small that it might have been imbedded in a blueberry. The plaintiff therefore could not demonstrate that the presence of the tack was due to the negligence of the dining hall. The judge reasoned that it might have already been stuck into a blueberry before it reached the hands of the cooks and that reasonable vigilance on the part of the dining hall employees would not necessarily have been sufficient to prevent the tack from getting into the pie. The court decided for the dining hall.

In *Friend v. Childs Dining Hall Company,* the plaintiff broke several teeth when she bit into some stones in a dish of baked beans. Rather than claiming that the dining hall had been negligent, Friend claimed that the dining hall had breached an implied warranty (an implied promise that the food was fit to be eaten). The court decided in favor of the plaintiff.

The outcomes of the two cases were different because two different theories of law were used. The seller's liability in tort is rooted in the duty to use due care, which is met by engaging in reasonable conduct. The seller's liability in warranty is rooted in the terms of the contract between the parties, and the seller is obligated to fulfill the terms of the contract.

A **warranty,** which is a promise about the quality or performance of goods, has for a long time been regarded as a contract right of a buyer.[2] A seller of food, for instance, has a contract duty to provide food that is fit for human consumption. If unfit food is served, the seller has breached his or her duty. The buyer does not have to prove that the seller's breach was due to negligence by the seller. The buyer need only show that the food was not fit for consumption in order to recieve damages. The reason for the unfitness of the food is irrelevant. The *Friend* case illustrates this thinking.

If Ash had based her case on the theory of breach of warranty rather than on the theory of negligence, she would have won her case, too. However, under the old common law method of pleading a case, a theory of law had to be selected as the basis for a recovery claim; if the wrong theory was chosen, the case was lost.

The Nature of Warranties

The law of warranties has a long history. It began as a legal action for deceit. If a merchant made an untrue statement about goods offered for sale, he or she could be held liable for deceit. In time, the action for deceit evolved into the tort of fraud (see page 78). Eventually, untrue statements made by sellers as part of a contract for sale were separated from other kinds of untrue statements and were treated, not as fraud, but as breaches of warranty. Since warranty actions were identified with contracts of sale, they became regarded as contract actions rather than tort actions.

The law not only provided a remedy to a buyer when the seller made an express statement (an express warranty) that was untrue; it also provided a remedy for breach of an implied warranty. An implied warranty is a promise by the seller that is not actually made by the seller but instead is imposed by law. For example, the law imposes a warranty on a seller that the goods being sold are fit for their ordinary purpose, regardless of whether the seller actually makes such a promise. This is called a *warranty of merchantability.*

At the time that implied warranty promises were first imposed on contracts of sale, manufacturers and growers sold directly to consumers. When marketing became more complex and dealers began coming between manufacturers and consumers, the courts made a decision much like the *Winterbottom* decision. Since implied warranties had until then been attached to sales by manufacturers, it was decided that implied warranties did not attach to sales by

---

[2] For a complete discussion of sales warranties, see Chapter 22.

dealers. Implied warranty protections were thus lost by consumers. England quickly changed this rule and imposed implied warranties on dealers, but change in the United States did not occur until most states adopted the Uniform Sales Act in 1906.

Warranties and Privity

Under the Uniform Sales Act (which has been superseded by the Uniform Commercial Code), a purchaser could recover from a dealer for injury caused by a defective product on the basis of a breach of implied warranty theory. Alternatively, as you have seen earlier in this chapter, the purchaser could recover from the manufacturer on a tort theory if negligence could be proven. If a product is defective, the manufacturer's negligence is much more likely to be the cause of the defect than is negligence by the dealer. But, because it may be difficult to prove the manufacturer's negligence, it may be easier to recover from the dealer for breach of warranty.

Consumers, however, encountered another problem in breach of warranty actions against dealers. If the consumer of the product was not the actual purchaser of the product, could the consumer recover for a breach of implied warranty from the dealer? Suppose, for instance, that a mother purchased an electric appliance from a dealer for her son. Suppose further that the appliance was defective and severely shocked the son while he was fixing a snack. The electrical charge paralyzed the son's arm so that he could not let go and the appliance then exploded, seriously injuring him. Under the Uniform Sales Act, could the son recover?

The courts' answer to this question was no. A consumer who was not a purchaser could not recover from a dealer on a theory of implied warranty because the consumer was not in privity with the dealer (see Figure 6-2). And because neither the consumer nor the purchaser was in privity with the manufacturer, there could also be no recovery from the manufacturer under the implied warranty theory. Yet, when implied warranties had been developed as a legal theory for the protection of consumers, consumers usually purchased directly from the manufacturer. As in negligence cases, dealers had again come between the manufacturer and the consumer to defeat the protections of the law the consumer had already gained. And again, the courts lost sight of the original reasons for the law. They applied the law mechanically to the facts and seemed unaware of any responsibility to protect those consumers who could not protect themselves.

The cases that led the way to overcoming the privity requirement for warranty theory involved food products. Traditionally, sellers of food products have been held to stricter standards than other merchants because of the obvious vulnerability of the consumer when food is the item consumed. Before the development of industry, few products could cause harm to a human being, whether or not they were defective, unless they were specifically designed to do so, as in the case of weapons and poisons. Food was virtually the only thing a person might purchase that could unexpectedly do harm.

Thus, the law that protects consumers against defective food has a very long

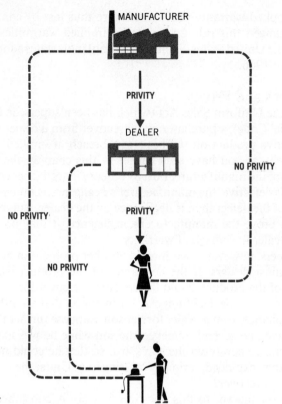

FIGURE 6-2
Privity of Contract and Third Parties

history, as the judge in the following case points out. In this case, all the members of the Capps family were injured and one child died as the result of consuming sausage prepared by the defendant manufacturer and sold in its containers to retail dealers, one of whom sold a package of the sausage to Mr. Capps. An action was brought against the manufacturer on a theory of implied warranty.

JACOB E. DECKER & SONS, INC. v. CAPPS
164 S.W.2d 828 (Texas 1942)

[Mrs. Capps brought a lawsuit for herself and two other lawsuits as the legal representative of two of her children against Jacob E. Decker & Sons, Inc. (Decker) for damages for injuries sustained as a result of eating contaminated sausage. The three suits were tried together. The jury found that the sausage was contaminated and poisonous and unfit for human consumption at the time it was processed and manufactured. The jury also found that the contamination of the sausage and the failure to discover it were not the result of negligence by Decker. The trial court awarded damages to plaintiff, and this decision was affirmed by an intermediate appellate court. Decker appealed to the Supreme Court of Texas.]

ALEXANDER, Chief Justice

[T]he question to be determined is whether a non-negligent manufacturer, who processes and sells contaminated food to a retailer for human consumption is liable to the consumer for the injuries sustained by him as a result of eating of such food. So far as we have been able to ascertain, this exact question has not heretofore been before this court.

After having considered the matter most carefully, we have reached the conclusion that the manufacturer is liable for the injuries sustained by the consumers of the products in question. We think the manufacturer is liable in such a case under an implied warranty imposed by operation of law as a matter of public policy. We recognize that the authorities are by no means uniform, but we believe the better reasoning supports the rule which holds the manufacturer liable. Liability in such a case is not based on negligence, nor a breach of the usual implied contractual warranty, but on the broad principle of the public policy to protect human health and life. It is a well-known fact that articles of food are manufactured and placed in the channels of commerce, with the intention that they shall pass from hand to hand until they are finally used by some remote consumer. It is usually impracticable, if not impossible, for the ultimate consumer to analyze the food and ascertain whether or not it is suitable for human consumption. Since it has been packed and placed on the market as a food for human consumption, and marked as such, the purchaser usually eats it or causes it to be served to his family without the precaution of having it analyzed by a technician to ascertain whether or not it is suitable for human consumption. In fact, in most instances the only satisfactory examination that could be made would be only at the time and place of the processing of the food. It seems to be the rule that where food products sold for human consumption are unfit for that purpose, there is such an utter failure of the purpose for which the food is sold, and the conse-

quences of eating unsound food are so disastrous to human health and life, that the law imposes a warranty of purity in favor of the ultimate consumer as a matter of public policy.

Since very early times, the common law has applied more stringent rules to sales of food than to sales of other merchandise. It has long been a well-established rule that in sales of food for domestic use there is an implied warranty that it is wholesome and fit for human consumption.

The rule which imposes a warranty, as a matter of public policy, of the soundness of food sold for human consumption is not of modern origin. As far back as the year 1266 A.D. the statute of Pillory and Tumbrel and the assize [court] of bread and ale provided in part: "It is ordained that none shall sell corrupt victuals. . . ." This implied warranty was not based on any reliance by the buyer upon the representations of the seller, or upon his skill and judgment, but was grounded squarely upon the public policy of protecting the public health.

It must be conceded that many courts have denied recovery against the manufacturer and have insisted strictly on the requirement of privity. There is a growing tendency, however, to discard the requirement of privity and to hold the manufacturer liable directly to the ultimate consumer.

Many of the courts which have allowed a recovery where there was no direct contractual relationship between plaintiff and defendant have done so by indulging in fictions, such as presumed negligence, fraud, . . . and agency of the buyer [dealer] for the consumer. Such fictions are indulged merely because it is thought necessary to do so in order to get away from the rule which requires privity of contract where recovery is sought on an implied warranty growing out of a contract. We believe the better and sounder rule places liability solidly on the ground of a warranty not in contract, but imposed by law as a matter of public policy.

A party who processes a product and gives it the appearance of being suitable for human consumption, and places it in the channels of commerce, expects someone to consume the foods in reliance on its appearance that it is suitable for human consumption. The invitation extended by him is not only to the housewife to buy and serve his product, but to the members of the family and guests to eat it. In fact, the manufacturer's interest in the product is not terminated when he has sold it to the wholesaler. He must get it off the wholesaler's shelves before the wholesaler will buy a new supply. It would be but to acknowledge a weakness in the law to say that he could thus create a demand for his products by inducing a belief that they are suitable for human consumption, when as a matter of fact, they are not, and reap the benefits of the public confidence thus created, and then avoid liability for the injuries caused thereby merely because there was no privity of contract between him and the one whom he induced to consume the food. The mere fact that the manufacturer or other vendor may thus induce the public to consume unwholesome food evidences the soundness of the rule, which imposes a warranty, as a matter of public policy on the sale of food or other products intended for human consumption. If a man buys food and his whole family and guests eat it and all become ill, it would be arbitrary and unreasonable to say that only the man who bought the food would have a remedy for his sufferings.

It will also be noted that in many cases liability is placed on negligence in the processing of the food, and this has led some courts to conclude that proof of negligence was essential to a recovery. Since the warranty of suitableness is imposed by law as a matter of public policy, there is no need for proof of negligence.

In fact, a rule which would require proof of negligence as a basis of recovery would in most instances, by reason of the difficulty of making such proof, be equivalent to a denial of recovery. It would be impracticable, if not impossible, for a consumer to prove the circumstances under which a particular can of beans or meat eaten by him had been processed.

We hold that the defendant, as the manufacturer and vendor of the sausage in question, was liable to the plaintiffs, as the consumer thereof, for the injuries caused to them by the contaminated and poisonous substances in the sausage at the time the defendant manufactured and sold the same, even though the defendant was not negligent in the processing thereof.

Affirmed.

CASE REVIEW QUESTIONS

1. Were any of the plaintiffs in privity of contract with the defendant? Were any of the plaintiffs in privity with the retailer who sold the contaminated sausage to Mr. Capps? Explain.
2. On what grounds do you think that the defendant argued that privity of contract was necessary in order for the plaintiffs to succeed in their legal actions?
3. What reason does the court give for deciding that privity of contract is not necessary in order for the plaintiffs to win their cases?
4. What reason does the court give for saying that proof of negligence by the defendant is not necessary for the plaintiffs to win their cases?
5. The court says that other courts have allowed recovery by consumers even though they were not in privity of contract with manufacturers "by indulging in fictions, such as presumed negligence, fraud, . . . and agency of the buyer [dealer] for the consumer." Can you explain in what sense the court speaks of "fictions," and how the examples cited by the court would be used in an actual case?

Disclaimers of Warranties

During the 1950s, the courts gradually eliminated the privity requirement for breach of warranty in consumer cases that did not involve food products.

Manufacturers therefore sought ways to protect themselves from this increased liability being imposed by the courts. Anticipating the complete removal of the privity of contract doctrine and its immunizing effect on manufacturers' product liability, the manufacturers of many products developed contracts of sale for use between retail dealers and consumers that contained clauses disclaiming virtually all liability for harm caused by product defect. These disclaimer clauses were often labeled "warranties" or "guarantees," which deceived the legally uneducated purchaser into believing that the manufacturer and the dealer were doing him or her a favor rather than disclaiming liability.

In a 1953 case, *Shafer v. Reo Motors,* a bus was destroyed by fire when its defectively manufactured gasoline tank broke loose from its supports, dragged along the street, and ignited from the friction. In a legal action for breach of warranty brought by the buyer of the bus against the manufacturer of the bus, the court considered the legal effect of the contract between the manufacturer and the buyer. The contract contained the following paragraph:

> We warrant each new Reo Truck and Reo Bus manufactured by us, to be free from defects in material and workmanship under normal use and service, our obligation under this Warranty being limited to making good at our factory any part or parts thereof, including all equipment or trade accessories (except tires) supplied by the Truck Manufacturer, which shall, within 90 days after making delivery of such vehicle to the original purchaser or before such vehicle has driven 4,000 miles, whichever event shall first occur, be returned to us with transportation charges prepaid, and our examinations shall disclose to our satisfaction to have been thus defective; this Warranty being expressly in lieu of all other Warranties expressed or implied and of all other obligations or liabilities on our part, and we neither assume or authorize any other person to assume for us any liability in connection with the sale of our vehicles.

It is interesting to note the organization of the paragraph. It begins by stating that the manufacturer warrants the bus to be "free from defects," which is certainly something the purchaser wants to hear. Then comes a promise to repair or replace defective parts, which may seem proper to the purchaser, although this promise is actually quite limited. Notice that the purchaser must pay the transportation charges for delivering the product to the factory. The disclaimer from liability does not come until the end of the paragraph, but it turns out to disclaim virtually all liability.

The court decided that the defendant, Reo Motors, was not liable to the buyer of the bus. In the view of the court, the matter was straightforward. The manufacturer had disclaimed almost all obligations and the plaintiff had accepted the contract; therefore, the plaintiff had to abide by the terms of the contract.

Manufacturers like Reo Motors have argued that a buyer who is dissatisfied with a contract is under no compulsion to accept it. What, though, are the buyer's alternatives? Bargaining is not a real choice when the contract terms have been dictated by the manufacturer to the retail dealer, although one might think that the terms of a warranty/disclaimer that differ from the protection provided by law should be the subject of bargaining. When bargaining is impossible, the manufacturers argued, the seller is free to go elsewhere. Yet, at the time of the decision in *Shafer v. Reo,* all of the auto manufacturers in the United States had agreed to sell their products with identical disclaimers. Thus, if a person wanted to buy a car, he or she had to accept the disclaimer. There were no alternatives available.

Privity's Last Stand (The Sequel)

The relative strengths of consumers and automobile manufacturers in the 1950s were so unequal that it was only a matter of time before the legal conscience was aroused. On the one side, the buyers were ignorant of the law and inexperienced with the complexities of the automobile, and they lacked bargaining power. On the other side, the sellers had banded together to close off any options for the buyer. The following case was a direct response to this situation in the auto industry.

HENNINGSEN v. BLOOMFIELD MOTORS
161 A.2d 69 (N.J. 1960)

FRANCIS, Judge

Plaintiff Claus H. Henningsen purchased a Plymouth automobile, manufactured by defendant Chrysler Corporation, from defendant Bloomfield Motors, Inc. His wife, plaintiff Helen Henningsen, was injured while driving it and instituted suit against both defendants to recover damages on account of her injuries. Her husband joined in the action seeking compensation for his losses. The complaint was predicated upon breach of express and implied warranties and upon negligence. At the trial the negligence counts were dismissed by the court and the cause was submitted to the jury for determination solely on the issues of implied warranty. Verdicts were returned against both defendants and in favor of the plaintiffs. Defendants appealed.

On May 7, 1955, Mr. and Mrs. Henningsen visited the place of business of Bloomfield Motors, Inc. They were shown a Plymouth which appealed to them and the purchase followed. Mr. Henningsen intended the car as a Mother's Day gift to his wife. His intention was communicated to the dealer. When the purchase order or contract was prepared and presented, the husband executed it alone. His wife did not join as a party.

The reverse side of the contract contains 8½ inches of fine print. In the seventh paragraph, about two-thirds of the way down the page, the warranty, which is the focal point of the case, is set forth. It is as follows:

7. It is expressly agreed that there are no warranties, express or implied, *made* by either the dealer or the manufacturer on the motor vehicle, chassis, or parts furnished hereunder except as follows.

The manufacturer warrants each new motor vehicle (including original equipment placed thereon by the manufacturer except tires), chassis or parts manufactured by it to be free from defects in material or workmanship under normal use and service. Its obligation under this warranty being limited to making good at its factory any part or parts thereof which shall, within ninety (90) days after delivery of such vehicle *to the original purchaser* or before such vehicle has been driven 4,000 miles, whichever event shall first occur, be returned to it with transportation charges prepaid and which its examination shall disclose to its satisfaction to have been thus defective; *this warranty being expressly in lieu of all other warranties expressed or implied and all other obligations or liabilities on its part,* and it neither assumes nor authorizes any other person to assume for it any other liability in connection with the sale of its vehicles. . . . (Emphasis is ours.)

The new Plymouth was turned over to the Henningsens on May 9, 1955. It had no servicing and no mishaps of any kind before May 19. That day, Mrs. Henningsen drove to Asbury Park. She was proceeding at 20–22 miles per hour. Suddenly she heard a loud noise "from the bottom, by the hood." It "felt as if something cracked." The steering wheel spun in her hands; the car veered sharply to the right and crashed into a highway sign and a brick wall. No other vehicle was in any way involved. As a result of the impact, the front of the car was so badly damaged that it was impossible to determine if any of the parts of the steering wheel mechanism or workmanship or assembly were defective or improper prior to the accident. The insurance carrier's inspector, with 11 years of experience, advanced his opinion based on the history and his examination, that something definitely went "wrong from the steering wheel down to the front wheels."

The terms of the warranty are a sad commentary upon the automobile manufacturers' marketing practices. Warranties developed in the law in the interest of and to protect the ordinary consumer who cannot be expected to have the knowledge or capacity or even the opportunity to make adequate inspection of mechanical instrumentalities, like automobiles, and to decide for himself whether they are reasonably fit for the designed purpose. But the ingenuity of the Automobile Manufacturers Association, by means of its standardized form, has metamorphosed [transformed] the warranty into a device to limit the makers's liability.

The manufacturer agrees to replace defective parts for 90 days after the sale or until the car has been driven 4,000 miles, whichever is first to occur, *if the part is sent to the factory, transportation charges prepaid, and if examination discloses to its satisfaction that the part is defective.* It is difficult to imagine a greater burden on the consumer, or a less satisfactory remedy. Aside from imposing on the buyer the trouble of removing and shipping the part, the maker has sought to retain the uncontrolled discretion to decide the issue of defectiveness. But in this instance, after reciting that defective parts will be replaced at the factory, the alleged agreement relied upon by Chrysler provides that the manufacturer's "obligation under this warranty" is limited to that undertaking; further, that such remedy is "in lieu of all other warranties, express or implied, and all other obligations or liabilities on its part." The contention has been raised that such

language bars any claim for personal injuries which may emanate from a breach of the warranty. [I]t has been successfully maintained [in other cases] that the exclusion "of all other obligations and liabilities" precludes a cause of action for injuries based on negligence. *Shafer v. Reo Motors.*

Putting aside for the time being the problem of the efficacy [effectiveness] of the disclaimer provisions contained in the express warranty, a question of first importance to be decided is whether an implied warranty of merchantability by Chrysler Corporation accompanied the sale of the automobile to Claus Henningsen.

Under modern conditions the ordinary layman, on responding to the importuning of colorful advertising, has neither the opportunity nor the capacity to inspect or to determine the fitness of an automobile for use; he must rely on the manufacturer who has control of its construction, and to some degree on the dealer who, to the limited extent called for by the manufacturer's instructions, inspects and services it before delivery. In such a marketing milieu [environment] his remedies and those of persons who properly claim through him should not depend "upon the intricacies of the law of sales. The obligation of the manufacturer should not be based alone on privity of contract. It should rest, as was once said, upon 'the demands of social justice.' "

Accordingly, we hold that under modern marketing conditions, when a manufacturer puts a new automobile in the stream of trade and promotes its purchase by the public, an implied warranty that it is reasonably suitable for use as such accompanies it into the hands of the ultimate purchaser.

[A]utomobile manufacturers, including Chrysler Corporation, undertake large scale advertising programs over television, radio, in newspapers, magazines, and all media of communication in order to persuade the public to buy their products. [M]anufacturers who enter into promotional activities to stimulate consumer buying may incur warranty obligations. [T]he form of express warranty made part of the Henningsen purchase contract was devised for general use in the automobile industry as a possible means of avoiding the consequences of the growing judicial acceptance of the thesis that warranties run directly to the consumer.

In the light of these matters, what effect should be

given to the express warranty in question which seeks to limit the manufacturer's liability to replacement of defective parts, and which disclaims all other warranties, express or implied? In assessing its significance we must keep in mind the general principle that, in the absence of fraud, one who does not choose to read a contract before signing it, cannot later relieve himself of its burdens. And in applying that principle, the basic tenet of freedom of competent parties to contract is a factor of importance. But in the framework of modern commercial life and business practices, such rules cannot be applied on a strict, doctrinal basis.

The traditional contract is the result of free bargaining of parties who are brought together by the play of the market, and who meet each other on a footing of approximate economic equality. In such a society there is no danger that freedom of contract will be a threat to the social order as a whole. But in present-day commercial life the standardized mass contract has appeared. It is used primarily by enterprises with strong bargaining power and position.

The warranty before us is a standardized form designed for mass use. It is imposed upon the automobile consumer. He takes it or leaves it, and he must take it to buy an automobile. No bargaining is engaged with respect to it. In fact, the dealer through whom it comes to the buyer is without authority to alter it; his function is ministerial — simply to deliver it. The form warranty is not only standard with Chrysler, it is the uniform warranty of the Automobile Manufacturers Association.

There is no competition among the car makers in the area of the express warranty. Where can the buyer go to negotiate for better protection? Such control and limitation of his remedies are inimical to the public welfare and, at the very least, call for great care by the courts to avoid injustice through application of strict common-law principles of freedom of contract.

It is undisputed that the president of the dealer with whom Henningsen dealt did not specifically call attention to the warranty on the back of the purchase order. The form and the arrangement of [certain fine print clauses on the front of the contract that referred to the back of the contract] certainly would cause the minds of reasonable men to differ as to whether notice of a yielding of basic rights stemming from the relationship with the manufacturer was adequately given.

But there is more than this. Assuming that a jury might find that the fine print referred to reasonably served the objective of directing a buyer's attention to the warranty on the reverse side, and, therefore, that he should be charged with awareness of its language, can it be said that an ordinary layman would realize what he was relinquishing in return for what he was being granted? Any ordinary layman of reasonable intelligence, looking at the phraseology, might well conclude that Chrysler was agreeing to replace defective parts and perhaps replace anything that went wrong because of defective workmanship during the first 90 days or 4,000 miles of operation, but that he would not be entitled to a new car. It is not unreasonable to believe that the entire scheme being conveyed was a proposed remedy for physical deficiencies in the car. *In the context* of this warranty, only the abandonment of all sense of justice would permit us to hold that, as a matter of law, the phrase "its obligation under this warranty being limited to making good at its factory any part or parts thereof" signifies to an ordinary reasonable person that he is relinquishing any personal injury claim that might flow from the use of a defective automobile. No one can doubt that if the will to do so were present, the ability to inform the buying public of the intention to disclaim liability for injury claims arising from breach of warranty would present no problem.

The task of the judiciary is to administer the spirit as well as the letter of the law. On issues such as the present one, part of that burden is to protect the ordinary man against the loss of important rights through what, in effect, is the unilateral act of the manufacturer. The status of the automobile industry is unique. Manufacturers are few in number and strong in bargaining position. In the matter of warranties on the sale of their products, the Automobile Manufacturers Association has enabled them to present a united front. From the standpoint of the purchaser, there can be no more arms length negotiating on the subject. Because his capacity for bargaining is so grossly unequal, the inexorable conclusion which follows is that he is not permitted to bargain at all. In the framework of this case, we are of the opinion that Chrysler's attempted disclaimer of an implied warranty of merchantability and of the obligations arising therefrom is so inimical to the public good as to compel an adjudication of its invalidity.

Both defendants contend that since there was no privity of contract between them and Mrs. Henningsen, she cannot recover for breach of any warranty made by either of them. On the facts, as they were developed, we agree that she was not a party to the purchase agreement.

The precise issue presented is whether Mrs. Henningsen, who is not a party to their respective warranties, may claim under them. We are convinced that the cause of justice in this area of the law can be served only by recognizing that she is a person who, in the reasonable contemplation of the parties to the warranty, might be expected to become a user of the automobile. Accordingly, her lack of privity does not stand in the way of prosecution of the injury suit against the defendant Chrysler.

It is important to express the right of Mrs. Henningsen to maintain her action in terms of a general principle. To what extent may lack of privity be disregarded in suits on such warranties? [I]t is our opinion that an implied warranty chargeable to either an automobile manufacturer or a dealer extends to the purchaser of the car, members of his family, and to other persons occupying or using it with his consent. It would be wholly opposed to reality to say that use by such persons is not within the anticipation of parties to such a warranty of reasonable suitability of an automobile for ordinary highway operation. Those persons must be considered within the distributive chain.

Affirmed.

CASE REVIEW QUESTIONS

1. What reasons does the court give for deciding that an implied warranty by Chrysler Corporation accompanied the sale of the car from Bloomfield Motors to Mr. Henningsen?
2. What reasons does the court give for not allowing the disclaimer of implied warranties contained in the contract between Mr. Henningsen and Bloomfield Motors?
3. Were either of the plaintiffs in privity of contract with the defendant Chrysler Corporation? Were either of the plaintiffs in privity with the defendant Bloomfield Motors? Explain.
4. What reasons does the court give for deciding that privity of contract is not necessary in order for the plaintiffs to succeed in their legal action against Chrysler?
5. Why do you think the plaintiffs' negligence action was dismissed by the trial court?

STRICT LIABILITY IN TORT

Strict liability in tort is a modern approach to the problem of product liability. Whereas negligence is based on fault and warranty is grounded in contract, strict liability in tort allows for recovery regardless of fault and apart from any contractual relationship between the parties. It developed from concepts of liability already present in the many areas of the law. Warranty itself is a form of strict liability because recovery is available regardless of fault on the part of a seller who warrants the goods. The concept of strict liability was explained in the previous chapter (see pages 94–95). Here we will consider its application in product liability cases.

Limitations of Negligence and Warranty

The complexity of modern technology often makes it difficult to establish that the manufacturer of a defective product was negligent. Even where the doctrine of *res ipsa loquitur* is used to assist in finding that a manufacturer was negligent, contributory negligence or comparative negligence can eliminate or reduce an injured person's recovery.

Recovery based on warranty can be limited or excluded by disclaimers of warranty or by the doctrine of privity, which limits recovery to purchasers or such closely related persons as family members or guests. Even when warranties are made by a retail seller of goods, an injured party may not be able to recover from the manufacturer because the manufacturer made no warranty. In addition, certain procedural requirements, such as the giving of notice of a breach of warranty, may prevent recovery even though a warranty was made.

Reasons for Strict Liability

The reasons for imposing strict liability on a manufacturer of a product were discussed by Justice Traynor in a concurring opinion to the case of *Escola v. Coca Cola Bottling Co. of Fresno,* which you read earlier in this chapter (see page 114). Although the majority decided the case in favor of the plaintiff on the basis of negligence, Justice Traynor offered strict liability as another theory of recovery and explained the advantages of this theory.

ESCOLA V. COCA COLA BOTTLING CO. OF FRESNO
150 P. 2d 436 (Cal. 1944)

TRAYNOR, Justice (concurring)

I concur in the judgment, but I believe the manufacturer's negligence should no longer be singled out as the basis of a plaintiff's right to recover in cases like the present one. In my opinion it should now be recognized that a manufacturer incurs an absolute liability when an article that he has placed on the market, knowing that it is to be used without inspection, proves to have a defect that causes injury to human beings. *MacPherson v. Buick Motor Co.* established the principle that irrespective of privity of contract, the manufacturer is responsible for an injury caused by an article to any person who comes in lawful contact with it. [T]he source of the manufacturer's liability was his negligence in the manufacturing process or in the inspection of component parts supplied by others. Even if there is no negligence, however, public policy demands that responsibility be fixed wherever it will most effectively reduce the hazards to life and health inherent in defective products that reach the market. It is evident that the manufacturer can anticipate some of the hazards and guard against the recurrence of others, as the public cannot. Those who suffer injury from defective products are unprepared to meet its consequences. The cost of an injury and the loss of time or health may be an overwhelming misfortune to the person injured and a needless one, for the risk of injury can be insured by the manufacturer and distributed among the public as a cost of doing business. It is to the public interest to discourage the marketing of products having defects that are a menace to the public. If such products nevertheless find their way into the market it is to the public interest to place the responsibility for whatever injury they may cause upon the manufacturer, who, even if he is not negligent in the manufacture of the product is responsible for its reaching the market.

The injury from a defective product does not become a matter of indifference because the defect arises from causes other than the negligence of the manufacturer, such as negligence of a submanufacturer of a component part whose defects could not be revealed by inspection . . . or unknown causes that even by the device of *res ipsa loquitur* cannot be classified as negligence of the manufacturer. The inference of negligence may be dispelled by an affirmative showing of proper care. . . . An injured person, however, is not ordinarily in a position to refute such evidence or identify the cause of the defect, for he can hardly be familiar with the manufacturing process as the manufacturer himself is. In leaving it to the jury to decide whether the inference has been dispelled, regardless of the evidence against it, the negligence rule approaches the rule of strict liability. It is needlessly circuitous to make negligence the basis of recovery and impose what is in reality liability without negligence. If public policy demands that a manufacturer of goods be responsible for their quality regardless of negligence there is no reason not to fix that responsibility openly.

The retailer, even though not equipped to test a product, is under an absolute liability to his customer, for the implied warranties. . . . The courts recognize, however, that the retailer cannot bear the burden of the warranty, and allow him to recoup any losses by means of the warranty of safety attending the wholesaler's or manufacturer's sale to him. . . . Such a procedure, however, is needlessly circuituous and engenders wasteful litigation.

As handicrafts have been replaced by mass production with its great markets and transportation facilities, the close relationship between the producer and consumer of a product has been altered. Manufacturing processes, frequently valuable secrets, are ordinarily either inaccessible to or beyond the ken of the general public. The consumer no longer has means or skill enough to investigate for himself the soundness of a product, even when it is not contained in a sealed package, and his erstwhile vigilance has been lulled by the steady efforts of manufacturers to build up confidence by advertising and marketing devices such as trade-marks. . . . Consumers no longer approach products warily but accept them on faith relying on the reputation of the manufacturer or the trade mark. . . . The manufacturer's obligation to the consumer must keep pace with the changing relationship between them; it cannot be escaped because the marketing of a product has become so complicated as to require one or more intermediaries. Certainly there is greater reason to impose liability on the manufacturer than on the retailer who is but a conduit of a product that he is not himself able to test.

The manufacturer's liability should, of course, be defined in terms of the safety of the product in normal and proper use, and should not extend to injuries that cannot be traced to the product as it reached the market.

CASE COMMENT

Although Justice Traynor's approach to liability was rejected by the majority in the case of *Escola v. Coca Cola Bottling Co. of Fresno* (see pages 114–115), the doctrine of strict liability was later adopted by the California court and a number of other jurisdictions. Subsequently, the *Restatement of Torts 2nd* defined strict liability in tort in §402A as follows:

(1) One who sells any product in a defective condition unreasonably dangerous

to user or consumer or to his property is subject to liability for physical harm thereby caused to the ultimate user or consumer, or to his property if

(a)   the seller is engaged in the business of selling such a product, and

(b)   it is expected to and does reach the user or consumer without substantial change in the condition in which it is sold.

(2)   The rule stated in subsection (1) applies although

(a)   the seller has exercised all possible care in the preparation and sale of his product, and

(b)   the user or consumer has not bought the product from or entered into any contractual relation with the seller.

CASE REVIEW QUESTIONS

1.   What public policy supports the imposition of strict liability on sellers of defective products?
2.   What problems does Justice Traynor identify as likely if negligence is used as a means of compensating a person injured by a defective product?
3.   What changes have occurred in society that call for the imposition of strict liability?
4.   Is the standard set by §402A of the Restatement of Torts 2nd broader or narrower than the standard suggested by Justice Traynor for the imposition of liability?

Defect

Although an injured party need not prove fault in order to recover for strict liability, he or she must prove the existence of a defect in the product that was present at the time the product was sold. A defect can occur in a variety of ways. It can result from some breakdown in the manufacturing process, a weakness in a component part, inadequate labeling that fails to warn a user of dangers, or a failure in the design of a product.

The exact nature of a defect is often difficult for an injured person to prove. Sometimes, for example, an accident will cause substantial destruction or mutilation of the product, making it difficult to establish the exact cause of the accident. For this reason, some courts accept circumstantial evidence as proof of a defect, arguing in effect that if there had been no defect there would have been no accident. In other cases, expert testimony is used to establish proof of a defect.

Strict Liability and Privity

Strict liability was developed in part to overcome the doctrine of privity. Section 402A states that strict liability is applicable even though "the user or consumer has not bought the product from or entered into any contractual relation with the seller." However, because §402A speaks of "the user or consumer," strict liability has not been applied by all courts to cases involving the so-called bystander — that is, a person who is injured by a product but who is not the person using the product.

In the following case, the court discusses the reasons for extending coverage to a bystander and the proof necessary to establish the defect.

ELMORE v. AMERICAN MOTORS CORPORATION
451 P.2d 84 (Cal. 1969)

[Sandra Elmore purchased a 1962 Rambler from Mission Rambler Company on March 16, 1962. Mission serviced the car after it had been driven 1,500 miles. Subsequently, Elmore noticed that the car shimmied when it was driven between 60 and 65 miles per hour. Her husband checked the car and could barely detect the shimmying, so he did not think it sufficiently serious for her to take time off from work to have it serviced.

On April 29, 1962, an accident occurred in which Elmore's vehicle crossed to the wrong side of the road and struck a car driven by Waters, who was killed. Elmore received head injuries and could remember nothing about the accident. Elmore and Waters' estate sued American Motors Corporation.

At the trial, a Mr. Hendley testified that he had followed Elmore for about a mile before the collision. He stated that she was traveling about 45 miles per hour when sparks began coming from under her car and the car itself began "fishtailing," which ultimately caused the collision. A highway patrol officer testified that he found gouge marks on the pavement near the accident that he had not observed when he patrolled the area about an hour earlier.

Mr. Snyder, a mechanical engineer and automobile expert, gave his opinion that a piece of metal of some kind from the vehicle came in contact with the highway and caused the gouge mark. Mr. Ausburn, a licensed engineer, testified that in his opinion there was a defect in the car prior to the accident, namely a disconnected drive shaft.

The lower court dismissed the suits following the trial. Both plaintiffs appealed.]

PETERS, Justice

A manufacturer is strictly liable in tort when an article he places on the market, knowing that it is to be used without inspection for defects, proves to have a defect that causes injury to a human being. [Citation omitted.]

It [has been] recognized that a plaintiff is entitled to establish the existence of the defect and the defendant's responsibility for it by circumstantial evidence.

When the evidence is viewed, as it must be, most strongly in favor of the plaintiffs, it furnishes an inference that their injuries were proximately caused by a defect in the Rambler which existed at the time of sale. Ausburn testified that in his opinion the car was defective prior to the accident in that the drive shaft was disconnected, and in light of the presence of the gouge mark, and Mr. Hendley's testimony as to the sparks, it could properly be inferred that the disconnected drive shaft gouged the roadway and caused the rear of the car to lift and to swerve or be thrown around which in turn caused the Rambler to go to the wrong side of the road. Thus, it could properly be found that the disconnected drive shaft was a proximate cause of the accident.

Ausburn also testified that the cause of a drive shaft falling would be either loose fastenings or metal failure and would not be "anything the driver did" or normal wear and tear. The car had been driven less than 2,800 miles. In these circumstances, it is not unreasonable to conclude that the defect in the metal or in the fastenings existed at the time of sale.

The authors of the [R]estatement have refrained from expressing a view as to whether the doctrine of strict liability of the manufacturer and retailer for defects is applicable to third parties who are bystanders and who are not purchasers or users of the defective chattel.

In *Greenman v. Yuba Power Products, Inc.*, we pointed out that the purpose of strict liability upon the manufacturer in tort is to insure that the "costs of injuries resulting from defective products are borne by the manufacturers that put such products on the market rather than by the injured persons who are powerless to protect themselves."

It has been pointed out that an injury to a bystander

is often a perfectly foreseeable risk of the maker's enterprise, and the consideration for imposing such risks on the maker without regard to his fault do not stop with those who undertake to use the chattel. [A restriction on the recovery by bystanders] is only the distorted shadow of a vanishing privity which is itself a reflection of the habit of viewing the problem as a commercial one between traders, rather than as part of the accident problem. [Citation omitted]

If anything, bystanders should be entitled to greater protection than the consumer or user where injury to bystanders from the defect is reasonably foreseeable. Consumers and users, at least, have the opportunity to inspect for defects and to limit their purchases to articles manufactured by reputable manufacturers and sold by reputable retailers, where as the bystander ordinarily has no such opportunities. In short, the bystander is in greater need of protection from defective products which are dangers.

An automobile with a defectively connected drive shaft constitutes a substantial hazard on the highway not only to the driver and passenger of the car but also to pedestrians and other drivers. The public policy which protects the driver and passenger of the car should also protect the bystander, and where a driver or passenger of another car is injured due to defects in the manufacture of an automobile and without any fault of their own, they may recover from the manufacturer of the defective automobile.

All of the foregoing considerations are as applicable to the bystander's action as that of the purchaser or user, and we are satisfied that the doctrine of strict liability in tort is available in an action for personal injuries by a bystander against the manufacturer and the retailer.

The judgments are reversed.

CASE REVIEW QUESTIONS
1. What evidence was offered that the Rambler was defective?
2. Was the court able to determine precisely what caused the defect? Did it matter with regard to the recovery awarded to the plaintiffs?
3. Did Waters have privity with the seller or the manufacturer of the Rambler?
4. What reasons does the court give for deciding that bystanders should be allowed to recover for injury caused by defective products?
5. Would Waters have recovered if the rule in *Winterbottom v. Wright* had been applied? Explain.

Product Liability Today

In many jurisdictions today, there are a variety of causes of action available for a person who is injured or who suffers economic loss because of a defective product. Depending upon the facts of the case and the position taken by the courts in a particular jurisdiction, an injured person may be able to bring a cause of action for negligence, breach of warranty, or strict liability in tort against the seller of the product, the manufacturer, or both. The law of each state must be examined to determine the availability of these remedies.

Even when strict liability has been adopted by a jurisdiction, a number of problems still exist. For example, recovery for economic loss or property damage may not be available. Although §402A of the Restatement of Torts 2nd speaks of a product that is unreasonably dangerous to a consumer's or user's property, a number of courts do not allow recovery for economic loss or property damage in an action based on strict liability in tort.

Another problem is referred to as the *second collision.* In these cases, the plaintiff alleges that his or her injuries are more severe than they should have been because the product, usually an automobile, was not designed to protect consumers against injury in the event of an accident. This is sometimes described as the problem of crashworthiness. Put another way, is a product defective if it does not protect the user from injury in a foreseeable accident even though the accident is not caused by a defect in the product? Or, in terms of negligence, is the manufacturer negligent for failing to design a product that protects the consumer against injury in a foreseeable accident? For example, is a manufacturer liable if a person is injured in a collision because he or she is hurled against some projection in the automobile? Some courts would find the manufacurer liable; others would not.

The development of comparative negligence (see page 91) presents problems for an injured party even when the doctrine of second collision is accepted. For example, what is the liability of a manufacturer if a person was injured when he or she was ejected from an automobile because of a faulty door latch that allowed the door to open upon impact even though the automobile was equipped with seat belts, which the injured party was not wearing? Under some comparative negligence statutes, it may be necessary for a court to determine what injuries would have occurred if the injured party had not been negligent and had been wearing the seat belt. Recovery would then be allowed for those injuries.

REVIEW QUESTIONS

1. What is privity?
2. What relationship does privity have to negligence, warranty, and strict liability?
3. How is *res ipsa loquitur* used in product liability cases?

4. What advantages does breach of warranty have over negligence in product liability cases?
5. What advantages does strict liability have over negligence and breach of warranty in product liability cases?

CASE PROBLEMS

1. James Phipps, an employee of Marbert Motors, Inc., was injured while test driving an automobile that had been delivered to Marbert for servicing. The accident occurred when the accelerator of the

car stuck, causing the car to accelerate to high speed, leave the highway, and strike a tree. The accident was caused by defects in the automobile's accelerator mechanism and in the carburetor. Phipps has sued the manufacturer for negligence in the design and manufacture of the automobile, for breach of warranties, and for strict liability in tort. Who will win the case? Explain.

2. Greenman wanted a combination power tool that could be used as a saw, a drill, and a wood lathe. After carefully reading the manufacturer's brochure that described the ruggedness of its product, he selected a Shopsmith. Greenman's wife bought the power tool for him as a Christmas present in 1955. Two years later, Greenman purchased the necessary attachments to use the Shopsmith as a lathe. While turning a piece of wood to construct a chalice, the piece of wood flew out of the machine and struck Greenman on the forehead, causing serious injuries. Greenman sued the retailer and the manufacturer. His expert witnesses testified that the screws used to hold the various parts of the machine together were inadequate, which allowed the machine to separate from the wood under even normal vibrations. The experts also testified that there were other methods of fastening the machine that could have prevented the accident. On what bases can Greenman sue the retailer and the manufacturer? Explain.

3. Mrs. Baker's doctor prescribed the drug Dicumarol for phlebitis, which Mrs. Baker suffered during a pregnancy. Subsequently, the child was born with severe and irreperable birth defects due to bleeding in the fetal brain. The package insert for the drug contained a warning that the drug passes through the placental barrier and can cause bleeding in the fetus. A similar warning had been printed at one time in the *Physician's Desk Refer-*

ence, but it had been eliminated several years before Mrs. Baker was hospitalized. The doctor testified that he was unaware of the warning. The drug company had not provided the the warning information to physicians when its salesmen made personal calls on them, nor had it used "Dear Doctor" letters or notices in medical journals to bring the problem to doctors' attention. When Mrs. Baker brought suit against the drug company, it argued that the package insert was a sufficient warning. What arguments can be made on behalf of Mrs. Baker?

4. On a clear day, Christino Paglia was driving his Chrysler automobile southbound on a highway, going 45 to 50 miles per hour, when he suddenly became unable to control the steering. His car crossed the solid line in the center of the highway into the northbound lane and crashed into a car in which Marcia Codling and her husband, Frank, were traveling. Paglia, who had recently purchased the automobile from the Jones dealership, had experienced no prior difficulty with the steering mechanism. As a result of the accident, the Codlings and Paglia suffered a number of serious injuries and both automobiles were destroyed. What causes of action do the Codlings and Paglia have and against whom? Explain.

5. Bolm was involved in a head-on crash while riding a Triumph motorcycle. The accident was not caused by Bolm's negligence or by any defect in the motorcycle. Bolm suffered pelvic injuries when his body was hurled forward during the crash, striking a luggage rack that rested on the gas tank in front of the saddle. The top of the rack was about three inches higher than the saddle. Bolm sued Triumph Motors Corporation. Who will win the case? Explain.

7

CRIMINAL LAW

A **crime** is a violation of a duty that an individual owes to the community. Legislation creates the duty to the community and makes the violation of the duty a criminal offense that may be punished. There must be a statute prohibiting particular conduct for that conduct to be a crime. The existence of a prohibiting statute is essential because of the due process clause of the Constitution, which requires that there be prior notice of what conduct may result in a fine, imprisonment, or execution.

A crime is classified as either a **felony** or a **misdemeanor.** Felonies, the classification for more serious crimes, are generally punishable by imprisonment for more than a year, whereas misdemeanors are generally punishable by imprisonment for a year or less. Legislation may also provide for various degrees of felonies and misdemeanors that reflect the seriousness of the particular crime. For example, assault in the third degree only requires that the defendant inflict physical injury, whereas assault in the second degree requires that the defendant inflict *serious* physical injury. In addition to crimes, there are statutes that create **violations,** which are generally less serious than felonies and misdemeanors. The violations with which you are probably most familiar are found in a state's vehicle and traffic laws. For example, speeding and failure to yield the right of way are violations. Other violations may be found in laws relating to agriculture, restaurants, and domestic animals.

In this chapter, we will examine the purpose and substance of criminal law, the constitutional protections that apply in the criminal law, and the criminal liability of corporations and their executives.

THE PURPOSE OF THE CRIMINAL LAW

The purpose of the criminal law is to prevent conduct that society has deemed undesirable in order to protect the public. Criminal law achieves this goal by punishing criminal conduct, often by imposing a prison sentence. There are six theories of punishment. As you will see, some are aimed at the criminal who commits a crime and some are aimed at the conduct of others. The theories are

1. Punishment prevents the criminal from committing future crimes.
2. Punishment isolates the criminal from society.
3. Punishment rehabilitates the criminal so that he or she will not want or need to commit future crimes.
4. Punishment deters others from engaging in criminal conduct.
5. Punishment, through the publicity that attends it, educates the public as to what conduct is prohibited.
6. Punishment helps maintain respect for the law and reduces the number of acts of personal vengeance.

Debates rage on the appropriateness and the effectiveness of each of these theories of punishment. What is clear, however, is that society desires to punish those who engage in undesirable conduct and it will continue to do so.

SUBSTANTIVE CRIMINAL LAW

Elements of a Crime

A crime generally consists of two elements: (1) an act or a failure to act when there is a duty to do so and (2) the state of mind that accompanies the act or failure to act. For example, a person may be guilty of the crime of assault if he or she intentionally (the state of mind) causes physical injury to another person (the act itself).

A criminal act may be a physical activity, such as pulling the trigger on a gun, or merely a verbal activity, such as lying under oath. The required criminal state of mind, which will be specified by the statute creating the crime, may be intent, knowledge, recklessness, or negligence. These states of mind are defined as follows:

1. A person acts intentionally with respect to a result or to conduct when his or her conscious objective is to cause such a result or to engage in such conduct.
2. A person acts knowingly with respect to conduct or to a circumstance when he or she is aware that his or her conduct is of such a nature or that such a circumstance exists.
3. A person acts recklessly with respect to a result or to a circumstance when he or she is aware of and consciously disregards a substantial and unjustifiable risk that such a result will occur or that such a circumstance exists.
4. A person acts negligently with respect to a result or to a circumstance when

he or she fails to perceive a substantial and unjustifiable risk that such a result will occur or that such a circumstance exists.

For both reckless and negligent criminal conduct, the risk involved must be of a nature and a degree that disregard of the risk constitutes a gross deviation from the standard of conduct that a reasonable person would observe in the situation. Crimes that require a particular state of mind are said to be *mala in se,* or wrong in themselves.

Some crimes, however, do not require any particular state of mind. A person will be guilty of this type of crime if he or she commits the prohibited act, regardless of his or her state of mind. This is known as **strict liability.** For example, a person who sells adulterated food may be criminally responsible for the sale, whatever his or her state of mind may be. Strict liability crimes are said to be *mala prohibita,* which means they are wrong simply because they are prohibited by legislation.

Defenses to Crimes

There are a number of defenses that may relieve a defendant from criminal responsibility, even though the necessary elements of the crime are present. These defenses fall into two general categories: (1) defenses that are based on the lack of responsibility of the defendant and (2) defenses that establish a justification or an excuse for the criminal act.

Defenses Relating to Lack of Responsibility There are three defenses that a defendant may assert to demonstrate lack of responsibility. They are insanity, intoxication, and infancy.

Insanity A defendant is not criminally responsible if he or she was insane at the time of acting. The legal definition of insanity used in a majority of jurisdictions provides that a person is insane if, as a result of mental disease or mental defect, he or she lacks substantial capacity to know or appreciate either the nature and consequence of his or her conduct or the fact that such conduct is wrong. Although the insanity defense has come under attack, the prevailing view is that it is not appropriate to punish a person whose conduct results from mental illness. In fact, very few defendants assert the insanity defense, and of those that do, only a small number are found not guilty as a result. Defendants who are found not guilty by reason of insanity are generally sent to a mental health facility for treatment.

Intoxication In some instances, voluntary drug or alcohol intoxication is a defense. This defense is based on the theory that extreme levels of intoxication may negate the state of mind that a particular crime requires. However, many courts are reluctant to allow voluntary intoxication to be used as a defense, both because the defendant chose to put himself or herself in an intoxicated state and because of the perceived likelihood of false claims of intoxication. As a result, these courts require that very extreme intoxication be shown before they will excuse the defendant from responsibility. This requirement is, of course, relaxed in the very rare situations in which the intoxication is involuntary.

Infancy Infancy may also operate as a defense to a criminal charge because children up to a certain age, generally 16, are considered to be incapable of committing a crime. The age at which a person becomes criminally responsible is determined by state statute and may vary from crime to crime. Thus, in some states, a 13-year-old may be charged with murder but not with burglary. Defendants who have not attained the statutory minimum age are tried in a juvenile or family court where the primary concern is for their welfare, not their punishment.

Defenses Relating to Justification or Excuse A defendant may raise any of a number of defenses to establish justification or excuse for his or her conduct. The most common of these defenses are discussed in the following material.

Consent Generally, consent by the victim is not a defense because a crime is a wrong against society and society does not allow that wrong to be condoned by the individual harmed. Thus, the fact that the fraternity or sorority pledges consented to it is not a defense to the crime of hazing. Certain crimes, however, are defined in terms of the victim's lack of consent. For example, rape is generally defined as sexual intercourse by forcible compulsion. A person's consent to sexual intercourse would therefore negate a necessary element of the crime of rape and would be a defense to that crime.

Duress A person who commits a crime under a threat of harm, either to himself or herself or to a third party, may be justified in committing the act under a theory of duress. The rationale of this defense is that the actor has lost the mental capacity to act criminally because of the threat of harm. Thus, if A is armed with an explosive and threatens B with death unless B assists A in robbing a bank, B is not guilty of the robbery because it is better for society as a whole that B help A than that B's life be lost.

Entrapment When a government official or someone acting on his or her behalf originates the idea for a crime and induces another person to commit the crime when that other person is not predisposed to do so, the defense of **entrapment** is available. The rationale for this defense is that the legislature does not really intend statutes to cover conduct that results from entrapment by a government agent.

Mistake It is often said that "ignorance of the law is no excuse." Although this statement is true in general, ignorance may provide a defense if it negates the state of mind necessary to commit a crime. For example, a creditor may honestly but mistakenly believe that he or she is legally entitled to take another person's property to satisfy a debt owed by the other person. In most states, if the creditor takes the other person's property, his or her "mistake of law" will prevent a conviction for larceny.

Another type of mistake that may be a defense is a "mistake of fact." Generally, an honest and reasonable mistake of fact will negate criminal liability. For example, a person who possesses oregano in the mistaken belief that it is marijuana cannot be convicted of illegal possession of drugs.

Self-defense A person who is unlawfully attacked by another is permitted to take certain steps to protect himself or herself from physical harm, and he or she may be excused if the steps taken constitute a crime against the aggressor. For example, a person who has injured or killed another may argue that he or she did so in **self-defense.** There are, however, limits to the actions that may be taken in self-defense. A person may only use such force as reasonably appears to be necessary to prevent the threatened harm. Deadly force, which is force that is likely to inflict serious injury or death, may not always be used to prevent harm. It may only be employed when it appears reasonably necessary to prevent immediate death or serious physical injury. What is reasonably necessary is judged by the standard of what a reasonable person in the defendant's position would have concluded was required under the circumstances. The following case illustrates that the reasonableness of the defendant's conduct should be evaluated in light of all of the facts and circumstances within his or her knowledge.

WASHINGTON v. ALLERY
682 P.2d 312 (Wash. 1984)

[Sherry Allery, the defendant, was convicted of second degree murder in the shooting death of her husband, Wayne Allery. She appealed her conviction, arguing that the court's instruction to the jury on self-defense, which directed the jury to consider self-defense in terms of the defendant's reasonable apprehension of danger in the circumstances as they appeared to her at the time of the shooting, was inadequate. She also argued that the court erred in excluding expert testimony on the battered woman syndrome, which was offered as evidence of her fear of imminent danger at the time of the shooting.]

DORE, Justice

The defendant married Wayne Allery in 1975. Shortly after the marriage, she began to experience what was to become a consistent pattern of physical abuse at the hands of her husband. She suffered periodic pistol whippings, assaults with knives, and numerous beatings from her husband's fists throughout the marriage. In 1978, Mrs. Allery was hospitalized after her husband struck her on the head with a tire iron. During the last year of their marriage, the beatings increased in frequency and severity. Finally on October 24, 1980, Mrs. Allery initiated divorce proceedings and

served her husband with restraining orders [orders by a court directing the husband not to interfere with her].

The shooting occurred early in the morning of November 1, 1980. The defendant testified that she entered her house late at night not expecting to find her husband there because of the restraining orders. She bolted the door locked when she entered. As she moved through the house and into the kitchen, a light came on by the couch. Mr. Allery was lying there and said to her, "I guess I'm just going to have to kill you sonofabitch. Did you hear me that time?"

The defendant went into the bedroom and tried unsuccessfully to open the window to escape. She heard a metallic noise from the kitchen and thought Mr. Allery was getting a knife. While in the bedroom, the defendant loaded one shell into a shotgun. She moved from the bedroom to the kitchen area and fired the shot that killed her husband while he remained lying on the couch.

The trial court gave only one instruction on self-defense:

Homicide is justifiable when committed in the lawful defense of the slayer when the slayer, even though mistaken, has reasonable ground to believe that the person slain intends to inflict death or great bodily harm and there appears to the slayer to be imminent danger of such harm being accomplished.

The slayer may employ such force and means as a reasonably prudent person would use under the same or similar conditions as they appeared to the slayer at that time.

It is a complete defense to a charge of homicide that it was justifiable.

If, after considering all of the evidence in the case, you have a reasonable doubt as to whether the killing was done in self-defense, you must return a verdict of not guilty.

Defendant contends this instruction did not adequately convey the . . . standard applied to self-defense. . . . We agree.

The justification of self-defense must be evaluated from the defendant's point of view as conditions appeared to her at the time of the act. The jurors must understand that, in considering the issue of self-defense, they must place themselves in the shoes of the defendant and judge the legitimacy of her act in light of all that she knew at the time.

In the instant case, the jury was instructed to consider the self-defense issue in terms of the defendant's reasonable apprehension of danger as circumstances appeared to her at the time of the incident. The instruction is inadequate because it does not instruct the jury to consider the conditions as they appeared to the slayer, taking into consideration all the facts and circumstances known to the slayer at the time and prior to the incident.

Defendant's theory of the case was that her intimate familiarity with her husband's history of violence convinced her that she was in serious danger at the time the shooting occurred. There was substantial evidence of the history of violence throughout the marriage between defendant and the victim. The jury should have been instructed to consider the self-defense issue from the defendant's perspective in light of all that she knew and had experienced with the victim.

At trial, defendant offered the expert testimony of Karil Klingbeil to explain the battered woman syndrome. After extensive voir dire [questioning of the potential witness] conducted out of the presence of the jury, the trial judge refused Klingbeil's testimony.

The record shows that Klingbeil would have described her professional analysis of the behavior and emotional patterns of women suffering from repeated physical abuse by their husbands and lovers. She would have testified that in her opinion defendant Allery displayed the behavioral and emotional characteristics of a battered woman. Defense counsel was very specific in explaining the purpose of Klingbeil's testimony. It was offered (1) to explain the mentality and behavior of battered women generally, (2) to provide a basis from which the jury could understand why defendant perceived herself in imminent danger at the time of the shooting, and (3) to explain why a battered woman remains in a relationship that is both psychologically and physically dangerous.

The admissibility of expert testimony . . . depends upon whether (1) the witness qualifies as an expert, (2) the opinion is based upon an explanatory theory generally accepted in the scientific community, and (3) the expert testimony would be helpful to the trier of fact.

The qualifications of Klingbeil were well established at trial and are not an issue here. The particular issue before us is whether the scientific understanding of the battered woman syndrome is sufficiently developed so that expert testimony on the syndrome is admissible.

Klingbeil testified that the battered woman syndrome is a recognized phenomenon in the psychiatric profession and is defined as a technical term of art in professional diagnostic textbooks. The syndrome is comprised of three distinct phases. In the first phase, tension mounts between the woman and her partner and minor abuse occurs. More serious violence follows and the woman experiences a sense of powerlessness to do anything to stop her husband. Psychologists describe a phenomenon known as "learned helplessness," a condition in which the woman is psychologically locked into her situation due to economic dependence on the man, an abiding attachment to him, and the failure of the legal system to adequately respond to the problem. Finally, there is a temporary lull in the physical abuse inflicted on the battered woman, and she forgives her assailant, hoping that the abuse will not reoccur.

We join those courts which hold expert testimony on the battered woman syndrome admissible. We find that expert testimony explaining why a person suffering from the battered woman syndrome would not leave her mate, would not inform police or friends, and would fear increased aggression against herself would be helpful to a jury in understanding a phenomenon not within the competence of an ordinary lay person.

Where the psychologist is qualified to testify about the battered woman syndrome, and the defendant establishes her identity as a battered woman, expert testimony on the battered woman syndrome is admissible. This evidence may have a substantial bearing on the woman's perceptions and behavior at the time of the killing and is central to her claim of self-defense.

[T]he jury must consider all the facts and circumstances known to the woman at the time of the killing in evaluating her claim of self-defense. To effectively present the situation as perceived by the defendant, and the reasonableness of her fear, the defense has the option to explain her feelings to enable the jury to overcome stereotyped impressions about women who remain in abusive relationships. It is appropriate that the jury be given a professional explanation of the battering syndrome and its effects on the woman through the use of expert testimony.

We reverse defendant's conviction and remand for a new trial.

CASE REVIEW QUESTIONS

1. State in your own words what was wrong with the instruction given to the jury by the trial court judge concerning self-defense.
2. What was the relevance of the expert testimony on the battered woman syndrome to the defendant's claim of self-defense?
3. Do you think the defendant established the elements of a claim of self-defense? Explain.

Common Crimes

Crimes Affecting Business This section outlines many of the crimes that may affect businesses. As you read this material, you should pay particular attention to the necessary elements for each crime discussed, that is, to the prohibited conduct and the required state of mind.

Arson A person is guilty of **arson** if he or she intentionally damages a building by fire or explosion. The degree of arson will depend on such considerations as the type of building involved and whether the defendant knew or should have known that there were people in the building.

Bribery Businesses must be concerned with three different kinds of **bribery:** bribery of foreign officials, bribery of public officials, and commercial bribery. The Foreign Corrupt Practices Act, passed by Congress in 1977, prohibits payments to any foreign official and any foreign political party or party official for the purpose of influencing decisions in order to obtain business. Payments to foreign administrative officers who are not involved in making policy decisions are not covered by the Act, however. Thus, a payment to a foreign official for the purpose of obtaining his or her government's contract for the purchase of tractors from your business is illegal, but a payment to a customs inspector to speed up the delivery of spare parts is not illegal.

Bribery of public officials occurs when one confers, or offers to confer, any benefit upon a public servant for the purpose of securing his or her vote, opinion, judgment, action, or exercise of discretion as a public servant.

A business person is guilty of commercial bribery if he or she confers, or offers to confer, any benefit upon an employee of another company without the consent of the other company, with the intent to influence the employee's conduct in relation to the employer's affairs. For example, if to minimize competition A pays B, C's employee, to convince C not to go into production with a new product line, A is guilty of commercial bribery.

Burglary and Trespass A person is guilty of **burglary** if he or she knowingly enters or unlawfully remains in a building with the intent to commit a crime while in the building. Notice that the law does not require that a person break into a building; it is sufficient that the person merely be in the building unlawfully. The degree of burglary depends on the type of building, whether the person is armed with a weapon, and whether physical injury results to someone not participating in the crime. A related crime, **trespass,** occurs when a person knowingly enters or unlawfully remains on another's property. For trespass, there is no requirement of intent to commit another crime.

Forgery Most people think of forgery as occurring when one person imitates the signature of another. Forgery, however, has a much broader definition. A person is guilty of **forgery** if he or she falsely makes, completes, or alters a written instrument with the intent to defraud, deceive, or injure another. The definition of "written instrument" is all-inclusive. New York, for example, defines a "written instrument" as any instrument or article containing written or printed matter or the equivalent thereof, used for the purposes of writing, embodying, conveying, or recording information, or constituting a symbol or evidence of value, right, privilege, or identification, that is capable of being used to the advantage or disadvantage of some person. This definition would include deeds, contracts, commercial instruments, prescriptions, money, stocks, and bonds. The degree of forgery depends on the particular kind of instrument forged. The most commonly forged instrument is a check.

Larceny A person steals property and commits **larceny** when he or she wrongfully takes, obtains, or withholds the property from its owner with the intent to deprive the owner of the property or to appropriate the property to himself or herself or a third person. Larceny includes thefts committed by trespass, trick, embezzlement, false pretense, acquiring lost property without taking reasonable steps to return it, issuing a bad check, extortion, and false promise.

Robbery **Robbery** is forcible stealing. A person forcibly steals property when he or she uses or threatens to use immediate physical force upon another person in the course of committing a larceny. Robbery is a crime that is committed intentionally. The degree of the crime depends upon the degree of risk to others. Thus, it is a more serious crime to commit a robbery when armed with a deadly weapon than when unarmed. Note that the difference between robbery and larceny is that robbery involves the use of force whereas larceny does not.

Theft of Services As technology advances and people become more ingenious, legislatures must frequently enact new laws to keep pace. For example, in early prosecutions of individuals who used magnets to slow down the meters measuring their use of electricity or used "blue boxes" to make long-distance calls without the phone company's knowledge, the defendants argued that the crime of larceny had not been committed because what was taken was not a "thing" that fell within the legal definition of property. Because criminal statutes must be strictly interpreted in order to meet the requirements of due process, many courts were forced to agree with the defendants and dismiss the charges. The response of legislatures was to make theft of services a crime. A person is guilty of **theft of services** if he or she obtains services with the intent to avoid payment. Services include such things as gas, water, electricity, meals, rooms, telecommunications, and transportation.

Usury A person is guilty of criminal **usury** when he or she knowingly charges, takes, or receives money or other property as interest on a loan in excess of the amount that is legally permitted by statute. In many states, criminal usury statutes traditionally did not apply to loans made to corporations. Lenders used this distinction to extract usurious interest rates from individuals by forcing them to incorporate and then borrow in the corporate name. Most states have now eliminated this loophole by disregarding the corporate form in consumer transactions.

White-Collar Crime Although the term *white-collar crime* is widely used, there is disagreement about its meaning. Three broad definitions are generally used. The first describes white-collar crime as any crime committed by a person of respectability and high social status in the course of his or her occupation. The second characterizes it as any illegal act committed by such nonphysical means as concealment or guile to obtain money, property, business, or personal advantage or to avoid the loss of money or property. The third definition is a combination of the first two. It defines white-collar crime as a nonviolent crime typically committed by a wealthy individual or organization. While there is disagreement about the exact definition of white-collar crime, there is no disagreement that its cost to society is tremendous, not only in terms of dollars (estimates range to over $400 billion annually), but also in terms of human suffering and loss of respect for the law.

White-collar crime often goes undetected or unprosecuted. For example, it may be impossible for a business to determine that its loss of inventory is a result of theft by employees. Also, a business may prefer to deal privately with an embezzling officer rather than risk the adverse publicity of prosecuting him or her. When white-collar criminals are successfully prosecuted, the courts tend to treat them more leniently than other offenders. Fines and alternative forms of sentencing are common, and jail terms, when imposed, are generally shorter than those given to other criminals.

Computer Crimes Computer crime falls into one of four general categories:

1. The introduction of fraudulent data into a computer system.
2. The alteration or deletion of data banks.
3. The unauthorized use of computer time or programs.
4. The electronic theft of money, property, services, or information.

The substantial increase in the use of computer technology has made government and industry extremely vulnerable to computer criminals. The growth of nationwide data networks, the widespread use of remote terminals that access large computer systems via telephone lines, and the number of sophisticated users of personal computers are all factors that have contributed to the rise in computer crime.

Computer crime is particularly attractive because it offers large potential profits with minimal risk of arrest. Efforts to combat computer crime have been aimed at increasing security and enacting state and federal legislation specifically authorizing the prosecution of computer crimes.

CONSTITUTIONAL PROTECTIONS

Any person who is or may be a criminal defendant is afforded certain protections by the United States Constitution and the constitution of the state in which the person is brought to trial. In many of the sections and amendments of the United States Constitution, the word "person" has been interpreted by the courts to include corporations. However, corporations are not entitled to all the constitutional safeguards that are afforded human beings. Thus, as we shall see, a corporation is treated as a person within the meaning of the Fourth Amendment's prohibition against unreasonable searches and seizures, but it is not treated as a person with respect to the Fifth Amendment privilege against self-incrimination.

The following protections found in the Constitution and its amendments are those that are most often invoked by criminal defendants.

Article I, Section 9

Neither Congress nor any of the states may pass ex post facto legislation. An **ex post facto** law is any law that operates in any way to the disadvantage of an individual accused of a crime committed prior to the enactment of the law. Thus, none of the following could be applied to a prior act of a defendant: a law creating a new crime, a law making an existing crime more serious, a law increasing the penalty for a crime, or a law permitting less or different evidence to be sufficient for conviction. This prohibition is directed at legislation only; it does not apply to court decisions.

The Fourth Amendment

The Fourth Amendment provides:

The right of the people to be secure in their persons, houses, papers, and effects, against unreasonable searches and seizures, shall not be violated, and no Warrants shall issue, but upon probable cause, supported by Oath or affirmation, and particularly describing the place to be searched, and the persons or things to be seized.

Arrest and Search Warrants The Fourth Amendment requires that probable cause be shown before an arrest warrant or a search warrant may be issued. The purpose of requiring that warrants be issued and that they be issued by judicial officers is to insure that a neutral and objective person determines that the likelihood of an individual's criminal involvement is sufficiently high to justify the intrusion of an arrest or a search. Probable cause exists when the facts and circumstances, as presented to the judge in a sworn statement, would lead a reasonably discreet and prudent person to believe that, for an arrest warrant, a person committed a crime, or, for a search warrant, identified evidence of a specific crime will be found in a particular place.

Warrantless Arrests and Searches The Fourth Amendment does not require a warrant in every situation. For example, a police officer who witnesses a crime may immediately make an arrest, and a police officer who sees illegal drugs may immediately seize them.

There are a number of other exceptions to the requirement for a warrant. Of most concern to businesses is the warrantless administrative search or inspection. Many regulatory statutes permit or require warrantless searches as part of the investigatory process. One justification for warrantless inspections is the need for surprise to preclude hazardous conditions from being covered up prior to an inspector's visit. Another is the administrative burden that would result if a warrant were required for each of the thousands of inspections made each year.

The courts' concern about these statutes is that they may give regulatory agencies too much discretion, they may lead to abuses, and they may undermine constitutional safeguards, especially when the information obtained is used as the basis for a criminal prosecution. The prevailing view is that such legislation is constitutional if it contains sufficient "assurances of regularity," that is, if it affords substantially the same protections as would a warrant. The following case examines warrantless inspection legislation in relation to constitutional protection.

MARSHALL v. BARLOW'S INC.
436 U.S. 307 (Sup. Ct. 1978)

[The Occupational Safety and Health Act (OSHA) empowers agents of the Secretary of Labor to search the work area of any employment facility within the act's jurisdiction to inspect for safety hazards and violations of OSHA regulations. No search warrant is expressly required under the act. In September of 1975, an OSHA inspector attempted to search the work areas of Barlow's, Inc., an electrical and plumbing installation business. The inspector did not have a search warrant. Mr. Barlow, the president of the corporation, refused the inspector admission to the employee work area based on his Fourth Amendment rights and sought an injunction against the search. A lower court issued the injunction, ruling that the Fourth Amendment required a search warrant for the inspection and that the statutory authorization in the OSHA for warrantless inspections was unconstitutional. The Secretary of Labor Marshall appealed to the Supreme Court.]

WHITE, Justice

This Court has already held that warrantless searches are generally unreasonable and that this rule applies to commercial premises as well as homes. . . .

It therefore appears that unless some recognized exception to the warrant requirement applies, [the decisions made in previous cases] would require a warrant to conduct the inspection sought in this case.

The Secretary urges that an exception from the search warrant requirements has been recognized for "pervasively regulated business[es]" . . . and for "closely regulated" industries "long subject to close supervision and inspection." . . . These are indeed exceptions, but they represent responses to relatively unique circumstances. . . .

[T]he Secretary attempts to support a conclusion that all businesses involved in interstate commerce have long been subjected to close supervision of employee safety and health conditions. But the degree of federal involvement in employee working circumstances has never been of the order of specificity and pervasiveness that OSHA mandates. It is quite unconvincing to argue that the imposition of minimum wages and maximum hours . . . prepared the entirety of American interstate commerce for regulation of working conditions to the minutest detail. . . .

The Secretary nevertheless stoutly argues that the enforcement scheme of the Act requires warrantless searches and that the restrictions on search discretion contained in the Act and its regulations already protect as much privacy as a warrant would. The Secretary thereby asserts the actual reasonableness of OSHA searches, whatever the general rule against warrantless searches might be. Because "reasonableness is

still the ultimate standard," the Secretary suggests that the Court decide whether a warrant is needed by arriving at a sensible balance between the administrative necessities of OSHA inspections and the incremental protection of privacy of business owners a warrant would afford. He suggests that only a decision exempting OSHA inspections from the Warrant Clause [of the Fourth Amendment] would give "full recognition to the competing public and private interests here at stake."

The Secretary submits that warrantless inspections are essential to the proper enforcement of OSHA because they afford the opportunity to inspect without prior notice and hence to preserve the advantages of surprise. While the dangerous conditions outlawed by the Act include structural defects that cannot be quickly hidden or remedied, the Act also regulates a myriad of safety details that may be amenable to speedy alteration or disguise. The risk is that during the interval between an inspector's initial request to search a plant and his procuring a warrant following the owner's refusal of permission, violations of this latter type could be corrected and thus escape the inspector's notice.

We are unconvinced, however, that requiring warrants to inspect will impose serious burdens on the inspection system or the courts, will prevent inspections necessary to enforce the statute, or will make them less effective. . . .

When the Secretary proceeds to secure a warrant . . . his entitlement to inspect will not depend on his demonstrating probable cause to believe that conditions in violation of OSHA exist on the premises. Probable cause in the criminal sense is not required. . . . A warrant showing that a specific business has been chosen for an OSHA search on the basis of a general administrative plan for the enforcement of the Act derived from neutral sources such as, for example, dispersion of employees in various types of industries across a given area, and the desired frequency of searches in any of the lesser divisions of the area, would protect an employer's Fourth Amendment rights. . . .

Finally, the Secretary urges that requiring a warrant for OSHA inspectors will mean that, as a practical matter, warrantless-search provisions in other regulatory statutes are also constitutionally infirm. The reasonableness of a warrantless search, however, will depend upon the specific enforcement needs and privacy guarantee of each statute. . . .

Nor do we agree that the incremental protections afforded the employer's privacy by a warrant are so marginal that they fail to justify the administrative burdens that may be entailed. The authority to make warrantless searches devolves almost unbridled discretion upon executive and administrative officers, particularly those in the field, as to when to search and whom to search. A warrant, by contrast, would provide assurances from a neutral officer that the inspection is reasonable under the Constitution, is authorized by statute, and is pursuant to an administrative plan containing specific neutral criteria. Also, a warrant would then and there advise the owner of the scope and objects of the search, beyond which limits the inspector is not expected to proceed. . . .

We conclude that the concerns expressed by the Secretary do not suffice to justify warrantless inspections under OSHA or vitiate the general constitutional requirement that for a search to be reasonable a warrant must be obtained. . . .

The judgment of the District Court is therefore affirmed.

STEVENS, Justice (dissenting)

Congress has determined that the regulation and supervision of safety in the workplace furthers an important public interest and that the power to conduct warrantless searches is necessary to acomplish the safety goals of the legislation.

[T]he Court has no authority to impose an additional burden on the Secretary unless that burden is required to protect the employer's Fourth Amendment interests. The essential function of the traditional warrant requirement is the interposition of a neutral magistrate between the citizen and the presumably zealous law enforcement officer so that there might be an objective determination of probable cause. But this purpose is not served by the new fangled inspection warrant.

[T]he inspection warrant adds little to the protections already afforded by the statute and pertinent regulations, and the slight additional benefit it might provide is insufficient to identify a constitutional violation or to justify overriding Congress' judgment that the power to conduct warrantless inspections is essential.

The case before us involves an attempt to conduct a warrantless search of the working area of an electrical and plumbing contractor. The statute authorizes such an inspection during reasonable hours. The inspection is limited to those areas over which Congress has exercised its proper legislative authority. The area is also one to which employees have regular access without any suggestion that the work performed or the equipment used has any special claim to confidentiality. Congress has determined that industrial safety is an urgent federal interest requiring regulation and supervision, and further, that warrantless inspections are necessary to accomplish the safety goals of the legislation. While one may question the wisdom of pervasive governmental oversight of industrial life, I decline to question Congress' judgment that the inspection power is a necessary enforcement device in achieving the goals of a valid exercise of regulatory power.

I respectfully dissent.

CASE REVIEW QUESTIONS

1. What arguments did OSHA make to try to convince the court that the OSHA provision allowing warrantless searches did not violate the Fourth Amendment?
2. State in your own words the reasons why the court decided that the OSHA provision allowing warrantless searches violated the Fourth Amendment.
3. After the decision in this case, what would OSHA be required to show in order to obtain a search warrant from a judge? Do you think that this requirement provides adequate protection to those employers who are subject to the act? Explain.
4. Do you agree with the majority opinion or the dissenting opinion in this case? Explain.

The Fifth Amendment

The Fifth Amendment provides:

> No person shall be held to answer for a capital, or otherwise infamous crime, unless on a presentment or indictment of a Grand Jury, except in cases arising in the land or naval forces, or in the Militia, when in actual service in time of War or public danger; nor shall any person be subject for the same offence to be twice put in jeopardy of life or limb; nor shall be compelled in any criminal case to be a witness against himself, nor be deprived of life, liberty or property, without due process of law; nor shall private property be taken for public use, without just compensation.

Indictment by a Grand Jury A **grand jury** is a group of citizens who reviews the evidence against a person suspected of committing a serious crime and determines whether there is reasonable cause to believe that he or she committed the crime. The purpose of the grand jury is to act as a buffer between citizens and the prosecutorial might of the state. If a majority of the members of the grand jury finds that the evidence establishes reasonable cause, the grand jury will vote an **indictment,** also called a *true bill,* against the person. The district attorney may then begin prosecution of the person on behalf of all of the citizens of the state. This procedure explains why criminal cases are referred to as, for example, "The People v. Defendant" or "State v. Defendant."

Double Jeopardy The Fifth Amendment prohibition against **double jeopardy** means that a person may not be tried more than once for the same criminal offense. Although this rule would appear to be simple, it is not always clear whether a defendant has been previously put in "jeopardy" and, if he or she has been previously put in jeopardy, whether it was for the "same" crime. In examining these issues, it is important to keep in mind that the purpose of the double-jeopardy prohibition is to prevent the government, with all of its resources and power, from making repeated attempts to convict an individual for the same offense, thereby subjecting him or her to continuing embarrassment, expense, anxiety, and insecurity as well as increasing the likelihood of convicting the person even if he or she is innocent.

A person has been placed in jeopardy if he or she has been tried by a court and either acquitted or convicted. The government may neither appeal nor begin a second prosecution for the same offense. If a defendant has been tried but the jury cannot reach a verdict, a second trial is permissible on the theory that it is not a second prosecution but merely a continuation of the first. A defendant waives his or her right to be protected from double jeopardy when he or she appeals a guilty verdict. If the conviction is set aside on appeal, the defendant may be tried again.

The test for determining whether multiple charges against a defendant are for the same offense is whether the same evidence is required to prove each charge. For example, if A enters B's house unlawfully to steal money, is discovered by B, and hits B in order to escape, A has committed a burglary and an assault. Because different evidence is required to prove each of these crimes, they are not the same offense and separate trials would not be prohibited by the rules of double jeopardy. Many states, however, protect a defendant from the burden of consecutive trials in this kind of situation by requiring that all charges arising out of a single incident be brought at the same time. On the other hand, one act may in fact constitute two different offenses. For example, if A steals money from a federally insured state bank, A has violated a state law prohibiting larceny and a federal law prohibiting stealing from a federally insured financial institution. A may therefore be prosecuted by both governments without being subjected to double jeopardy.

Self-incrimination The guarantee against self-incrimination in the Fifth Amendment has several applications. The first is that a defendant in a criminal trial cannot be required to take the witness stand. As part of this protection, no inference against the defendant can be made because of the failure to testify, and it may not be commented on by the prosecution. If the defendant chooses to take the stand, he or she waives the Fifth Amendment protection against self-incrimination and may not then refuse to answer any questions.

Issues concerning self-incrimination may also arise before a grand jury, a congressional committee, or an administrative tribunal. Because no criminal charges have been brought, a person cannot refuse to be a witness before these bodies. Once under oath, however, the witness may decline to answer questions on the grounds of self-incrimination. A witness may not only refuse to give answers that are admissions of guilt but may also refuse to give answers that will furnish evidence of guilt or that may lead to such evidence.

Testimony that would otherwise be protected can be compelled by granting the witness immunity from prosecution. Thus, by promising you that your testimony will not be used as the basis for a prosecution against you, the government can require you to provide answers that will incriminate you.

Evidence that is nontestimonial is not covered by the Fifth Amendment. Thus, an individual may not refuse to be in a line-up, to provide a handwriting example, or to give a hair or blood sample. Personal books and papers may be protected. Thus, the Fifth Amendment will protect an individual from being forced to turn over personal records in his or her own possession, but it will not protect him or her from a legal search for and seizure of those records. Similarly, requiring that materials in the hands of an accountant or an attorney be produced does not violate Fifth Amendment rights because the individual who is compelled to produce them is not the person who might be incriminated by them. The attorney–client privilege, however, will protect documents in the hands of an attorney if they were given to the attorney by the client for the purpose of obtaining legal advice and the client could have withheld them.

A corporation is not protected by the Fifth Amendment right against self-incrimination and may not, therefore, refuse to produce corporate records. Similarly, a corporate official may not refuse to testify or to produce documents on the grounds that the corporation would be incriminated, nor may the custodian of corporate books and records withhold them on the grounds that he or she might be personally incriminated by the information contained in them.

Due Process The concept of due process reflects society's belief that the legal system must be a fair one. The due process rights found in the Fourth, Sixth, Seventh, and Eighth Amendments as well as in the Fifth Amendment deal primarily with protections against abuses in the criminal process. For instance, using physical coercion to extract a confession is fundamentally unfair and is therefore a violation of an individual's rights of due process in general as well as a violation of his or her specific right against self-incrimination.

Because society's values change and evolve, due process rights change and evolve also. For example, it was not until 1966 that the concept of due process required law enforcement officers to advise criminal suspects of their constitutional rights. However, after several decades of expanding the protections for criminal suspects, the trend today is to reexamine the fairness and necessity of those protections.

The Sixth Amendment

The Sixth Amendment provides:

> In all criminal prosecutions the accused shall enjoy the right to a speedy and public trial, by an impartial jury of the State and district wherein a crime shall have been committed, which district shall have been previously ascertained by law, and to be informed of the nature and cause of the accusation; to be confronted with the witnesses against him; to have compulsory process for obtaining witnesses in his favor, and to have the Assistance of Counsel for his defence.

Right to Counsel Because of the technical complexities of the law, the right to counsel is one of the most important constitutional safeguards. An individual has the right to the assistance of an attorney at every "critical stage" of criminal proceedings. A critical stage may occur long before charges are filed. Thus, an individual has the right to be represented at a line-up or during police questioning if he or she is in custody and is the target of the investigation. Because of the importance of competent legal help, a person who cannot afford a lawyer will be provided one free of charge by the government. As with other constitutional rights, the right to counsel may be waived, but the waiver must be made knowingly and intelligently and must be agreed to by the court, which will carefully examine all of the facts and circumstances to determine whether the defendant is capable of representing himself or herself.

The Exclusionary Rule

Although the exclusionary rule is not specifically mentioned in the Constitution, it is an important safeguard that has been developed by the courts to give full effect to the protections of the Fourth, Fifth, and Sixth Amendments.

Under the **exclusionary rule,** evidence that has been obtained in violation of a person's constitutional rights may not be used as evidence against that person at trial. The purpose of the exclusionary rule is twofold: (1) to deter police misconduct and (2) to preserve the integrity of the criminal justice system. The rule applies to such identification evidence as line-ups, confessions, and physical evidence. For instance, marijuana found in an illegal search of A's home may not be admitted at trial as evidence against A. Likewise, a coerced confession is inadmissible against the person from whom it was taken.

Also not allowed under the exclusionary rule is "fruit of the poisonous tree," which refers to evidence that is obtained as a result of an initial illegality. For example, suppose A, without having been advised of his constitutional rights, confesses to a homicide and tells the police where the murder weapon is hidden. Not only will the confession be excluded, but the weapon will also be excluded because it was found as a result of the illegally obtained confession.

There is an important exception to the exclusionary rule — the *inevitable discovery rule.* If evidence that first comes to light through an illegality would have been found anyway — that is, if it would have been found during normal, routine police investigation — the evidence will not be excluded. Thus, in the previous example, if the police would have found the murder weapon in the course of their routine criminal investigation, it may be used as evidence.

CORPORATE AND EXECUTIVE CRIMINAL RESPONSIBILITY

Corporate Criminal Responsibility

At one time, the courts held that a corporation could not be guilty of a crime because it had no mind with which to form the necessary intent and no body that could be put in prison. The English courts that initially found corporations to be criminally responsible dealt only with crimes that did not require a state of mind. Corporations were first found guilty of crimes of nonfeasance — that is, the failure to perform a duty required by law — and then, somewhat later, they were found guilty of crimes of misfeasance — that is, the improper performance of a lawful act. The courts were very clear, however, in their stand that a corporation could not be indicted for acts of personal violence or immorality. With the growth and development of the corporate form of business in the modern world, these restrictive views have undergone substantial change. Today, corporations can be successfully prosecuted for almost any type of criminal activity.

State of Mind Crimes Because a corporation has no mind and can act only through its members, its criminal responsibility must be based on imputing the acts and states of mind of the members to the corporation itself. The scope of corporate liability will depend, to a substantial extent, on the determination of whose individual acts and states of mind will be ascribed to the corporation. For the purpose of making this determination, the members of a corporation can be divided into three groups: first, the board of directors and high-level corporate officers who formulate policy and run the corporation; second, middle-level managers in supervisory and managerial capacities who are involved to a lesser extent in corporate decision making; and, third, subordinate employees who are generally responsible for carrying out corporate business and executing policy decisions.

"Intent" Crimes For crimes that require the state of mind of intent, the courts in different states have disagreed as to when a corporation can be said to have criminal intent. In some states, the courts have ruled that criminal intent must be a matter of corporate policy for the corporation to be criminally responsible. Under this rule, only the acts and intent of the directors, high-level officers, or, in some instances, middle-level managers can subject the corporation to liability. In other states, the courts have ruled that the acts and intent of any employee, including the most subordinate employee of the corporation, are sufficient. Which of these rules of liability is applied depends on whether, as a matter of public policy, the court believes corporate responsibility should be restricted or expanded. Some courts believe that it is unfair to impose criminal liability on a corporation for the conduct of lower-level employees over whom the corporation actually has relatively little control. These courts apply the first rule. Other courts, however, believe that corporations should be responsible to society for the harmful consequences of their business activities, regardless of who acted unlawfully. These courts apply the second rule.

Whichever rule is applied, the criminal act or omission involved must fall within the scope of authority or employment of the person who performed it, and it must have been done with the intent to benefit the corporation. Note that it does not matter whether the corporation *actually* benefited from the act or omission, so long as the *intent* of the person who performed it was to benefit the corporation.

"Knowing" or "Willful" Crimes Many statutes define crimes that can only be committed "knowingly" or "willfully." For example, possession of stolen property is a crime that must be committed "knowingly." Thus, a corporation would only be guilty of possession of stolen property if it could be shown that the corporation knew — that is, was aware — that, say, several truckloads of stolen computers were being held in one of its warehouses. Courts have had no difficulty imputing knowledge or willfulness when the actor is a member of the board of directors, a high-level manager, or a middle-level manager who actually makes policy decisions. The difficulty here arises in those situations in which the actors are subordinate employees. Some courts have resolved this dilemma by holding the corporation liable for the collective knowledge of its employees. In effect, this means that any information that is commonly known to the employees will be ascribed to the corporation.

In some jurisdictions, corporations may assert a "due diligence" defense to knowing or willful crimes. If the corporation can demonstrate that the high-level managers who had responsibility for the conduct out of which the crime arose acted with due diligence to prevent the commission of the crime, corporate liability can be avoided under this defense.

The following case illustrates corporate responsibility for the violation of a statute that defines a willful crime.

UNITED STATES v. CARTER
311 F.2d 934 (Sixth Cir. 1963)

[Pilsener Brewing Company (Pilsener) and George S. Carter, president, chief executive officer, and a member of the board of directors of Pilsener, were indicted and convicted of violating the provisions of the Taft-Hartley Act, which makes it a crime for an employer to pay any money to an official of a union that represents its employees. Pilsener and Carter appealed. The following discussion by the court concerns the criminal liability of Pilsener.]

O'SULLIVAN, Circuit Judge

For some years . . . Carter, as president of Pilsener and [John J.] Felice, as head of the Teamster's Local, participated in the labor negotiations between Pilsener and the Teamsters Union. . . . While Carter and Felice described their relationship as that of intimate and social friends, their association and acquaintance had beginnings in labor negotiations in which they had both participated. Sometime prior to April 17, 1956, Felice arranged to purchase two homes. . . . Felice told Carter of his contemplated acquisition of the new homes and said that he would likely need some cash to close the purchase. . . . Later Felice told Carter that he needed $4,500.00. Carter, according to Felice, replied, "Give me a few days. See me at the office."

Following the above talks, Carter . . . called one William Zeidler at the Chicago office of City Products [Pilsener's parent company] and told Zeidler that Felice wanted to borrow some money and asked whether "we should loan him the money." Zeidler called him back and said, "Go ahead, make the loan."

Carter advised the Controller of Pilsener, one Nero, that Pilsener was making a loan to Felice of $4,000.00 He advised Nero that a company check should not be used to transfer the funds, but that payment was to be made with an official bank check or in cash. . . . Later that day, Felice arrived at the Pilsener office and was given [a] $4,000.00 check and $500.00 in

cash. He signed a promissory note [made payable to Carter] which had been prepared by Carter.

In directing and completing the transaction, Carter told Pilsener's controller, Nero, that the transaction was to be kept "confidential" and that no attempt should be made to collect the note; that he, Carter, "would handle it." The note to Carter was not endorsed by him to Pilsener, but was delivered to its controller, retained by it and entered on the company's books under notes receivable. . . . [N]o effort was made to collect it and in 1959 it was charged off.

[A] corporation, through the conduct of its agents and employees, may be convicted of a crime, including a crime involving knowledge and wilfulness. . . . It is essential, however, to corporate guilt, that its officer's or agent's illegal conduct be related to and done within the course of his employment and have some connection with the furtherance of the business of such corporation.

[W]e believe that the authority of George S. Carter and the activity in which he was engaged at the time of the offense involved, brought criminal responsibility to the corporation of which he was president. As president, he was Pilsener's chief executive officer with the general supervisory authority that attends such office. Aside from his implied authority as president, he was the one who actually ran the company. . . . We think that it can fairly be inferred that in acceding to Felice's request for money and providing such money out of the corporation's funds Carter, however illegal and misguided his actions were, did so in the course of his employment with, and in furtherance of the business interests of, his company. . . . Proof of an actual benefit to the corporation in such circumstances is not essential.

We are of the opinion, too, that Carter's knowledge and wilfulness must be charged to Pilsener. The corporate person can only act and know through its officers, and the guilty knowledge and willful conduct of its chief executive officer will be charged to the corporate person.

[The Court then went on to consider whether there had in fact been a wilful violation of the statute.]

Under [the statute] wilfulness is a necessary ingredient of the crime charged. . . . Carter disclaimed any knowledge of the relevant provisions of the Act in question. We do not think it necessary to a finding of wilfulness that it be shown that the one so charged had read the statute which makes his conduct illegal. . . .

The word 'wilful,' even in criminal statutes, means no more than that the person charged with the duty knows what he's doing. It does not mean that, in addition, he must suppose that he is breaking the law.

[T]he wilfulness of Carter is properly imputed to the Pilsener Corporation and . . . there was sufficient evidence from which wilfulness of the corporation could be found.

Affirmed.

CASE REVIEW QUESTIONS
1. From what facts does the court conclude that Carter's conduct was wilful?
2. If Carter in fact did not know that he was breaking the law, why would that not relieve the corporation from liability?

Strict Liability Crimes Many federal and state regulatory statutes create **strict liability crimes.** No particular state of mind is required to commit a strict liability crime; the fact that the prohibited conduct or result occurred is sufficient for criminal liability. A corporation will be found guilty of one of these crimes if its agents or employees, acting within the scope of their employment, have violated the applicable statute. The fact that the activities of the agents or employees were contrary to company policy or to express instructions given to them is not a defense to prosecution for a strict liability crime. In the following case, which illustrates this rule, you should pay particular attention to the policy reasons the court gives for its finding of responsibility.

UNITED STATES v. HILTON HOTELS CORPORATION
467 F.2d 1000 (Ninth Cir. 1972)

[Operators of hotels, restaurants, and other businesses in Portland, Oregon, formed an association to attract conventions to the city. Hilton Hotels Corporation (Hilton) was a participating member of the association. To help finance the association, companies selling supplies to hotels were assessed an amount equal to one percent of their sales to hotel members. To aid collections, hotel members agreed to give preferential treatment to suppliers who paid their assessments and to boycott those who did not. Hilton was convicted of violating Section 1 of the Sherman Act, which prohibits conspiracies in restraint of trade or commerce. Hilton appealed, arguing that a corporation could not be liable for the unauthorized acts of its employees.]

BROWNING, Circuit Judge

The manager of appellant's Portland hotel and his assistant testified that it was the hotel's policy to purchase supplies on the basis of price, quality, and service. They also testified that on two occasions they told the hotel's purchasing agent that he was to take no part in the boycott. The purchasing agent confirmed receipt of these instructions, but admitted that, despite them, he had threatened a supplier with loss of the hotel's business unless the supplier paid the association's assessment. He testified that he violated his instructions because of anger and personal pique toward the individual representing the supplier. . . .

Congress may constitutionally impose criminal liability upon a business entity for acts or omissions of its agents within the scope of their employment. . . . The intention to impose such liability is sometimes express, but it may also be implied. The text of the Sherman Act does not expressly resolve this issue. For the reasons that follow, however, we think the construction of the Act that best achieves its purpose is that a corporation is liable for acts of its agents within the scope of their authority even when done against company orders.

It is obvious from the Sherman Act's language and subject matter that the Act is primarily concerned with the activities of business entities. . . .

The statute

was designed to be a comprehensive charter of economic liberty aimed at preserving free and unfettered competition as the rule of trade. It rests on the premise that the unrestrained interaction of competitive forces will yield the best allocation of our economic resources, the lowest prices, the highest quality and the greatest natural progress, while at the same time providing an environment conducive to the preservation of our democratic political and social institutions.

With such important public interests at stake, it is reasonable to assume that Congress intended to impose liability upon business entities for the acts of those to whom they choose to delegate the conduct of their affairs, thus stimulating a maximum effort by owners and managers to assure adherence by such agents to the requirements of the Act.

Legal commentators have argued forcefully that it is inappropriate and ineffective to impose criminal liability upon a corporation, as distinguished from the human agents who actually perform the unlawful acts . . . , particularly if the acts of the agents are unauthorized. . . . But it is the legislative judgment that controls, and "the great mass of legislation calling for corporate criminal liability suggests a widespread belief on the part of legislators that such liability is necessary to effectuate regulatory policy." Moreover, the strenuous efforts of corporate defendants to avoid conviction, particularly under the Sherman Act, strongly suggests that Congress is justified in its judgment that exposure of the corporate entity to potential conviction may provide a substantial spur to corporate actions to prevent violations by employees. . . .

Sherman Act violations are commercial offenses. They are usually motivated by a desire to enhance profits. They commonly involve large, complex, and highly decentralized corporate business enterprises, and intricate business processes, practices, and arrangements. More often than not they also involve basic policy decisions, and must be implemented over an extended period of time.

Complex business structures, characterized by decentralization, and delegations of authority, commonly adopted by corporations for business purposes, make it difficult to identify the particular corporate agents responsible for Sherman Act violations. At the same time, it is generally true that high managerial officials, for whose conduct the corporate directors and stockholders are the most clearly responsible, are likely to have participated in the policy decisions underlying Sherman Act violations, or at least to have become aware of them.

Violations of the Sherman Act are a likely consequence of the pressure to maximize profits that is commonly imposed by corporate owners upon managing agents and in turn, upon lesser employees. In the face of that pressure, generalized directions to obey the Sherman Act, with the probable effect of foregoing profits, are the least likely to be taken seriously. And if a violation of the Sherman Act occurs, the corporation, and not the individual agents, will have realized the profits from the illegal activity.

In sum, identification of the particular agents responsible for a Sherman Act violation is especially difficult, and their conviction and punishment is peculiarly ineffective as a deterrent. At the same time, conviction and punishment of the business entity itself is likely to be both appropriate and effective.

For these reasons we conclude that as a general rule a corporation is liable under the Sherman Act for the acts of its agents in the scope of their employment, even though contrary to general corporate policy and express instructions to the agent.

Affirmed.

CASE REVIEW QUESTIONS
1. What acts of Hilton's employee resulted in its liability?
2. What policy reasons does the court give for deciding that a corporation can violate the Sherman Act as a result of acts of its employee even when those acts violate specific instructions given to that employee?
3. Do you think that these policy reasons justify imposing liability on a corporation when an employee acts contrary to express instructions *and* with purely personal motives? Explain.
4. Why is the corporation liable even though the employee acted out of personal motives and did not intend to benefit the corporation? Explain.

Executive Liability

Officers and other employees of a corporation may be personally liable for criminal acts they commit while acting on behalf of the corporation. However, as a general rule, there is no vicarious liability in the criminal law. This means that one person will generally not be held criminally responsible for the acts and omissions of another person and one person's state of mind will not be imputed to another person. To be criminally liable, a person must actually engage in criminal conduct. An employee, therefore, will not be held responsible for a crime unless he or she actually committed the wrong or authorized, approved, ratified, or in some other way personally participated in its commission.

In the case of strict liability crimes, however, it is possible for an employee, usually the president or chief executive officer, to be held criminally liable for the acts of his or her subordinates. In the following case, the president of a corporation was found liable, not because he had personally violated the law or had been negligent in managing the corporation, but because he was in a position of responsibility for the situation out of which the criminal charges arose.

UNITED STATES v. PARK
421 U.S. 658 (Sup. Ct. 1975)

[Acme Markets, Inc., is a national retail food chain with approximately 36,000 employees, 874 retail outlets, 12 general warehouses, and 4 special warehouses. Its headquarters, including the office of the president, John R. Park, who is also chief executive officer, are located in Philadelphia. Acme and Park were charged with violating the Food, Drug, and Cosmetic Act. The government alleged that the defendant's Baltimore warehouse was accessible to rodents and that, as a result, the food stored in it became contaminated. Acme pleaded guilty. Park pleaded not guilty, was convicted at trial, and appealed. The Court of Appeals reversed the conviction and ordered a new trial. The government appealed to the Supreme Court. Note that the government is the petitioner and Park is the respondent.]

BURGER, Chief Justice

[At trial, an] FDA consumer safety officer testified concerning evidence of rodent infestation and other insanitary conditions discovered during a 12-day inspection of the Baltimore warehouse in November and December of 1971. He also related that a second inspection of the warehouse had been conducted in March 1972. On that occasion the inspectors found that there had been an improvement in the sanitary conditions, but that "there was still evidence of rodent activity in the building and in the warehouse and we found some rodent-contaminated lots of food items."

The government also presented testimony by the Chief of Compliance of FDA's Baltimore office, who informed respondent by letter of the conditions at the Baltimore warehouse after the first inspection. There was testimony by Acme's Baltimore division vice president, who had responded to the letter on behalf of Acme and respondent, and who described the steps taken to remedy the insanitary conditions discovered by both inspections. The government's final witness, Acme's vice pesident for legal affairs and assistant secretary, identified respondent as the president and chief executive officer of the company and read a bylaw prescribing the duties of the chief executive officer. He testified that respondent functioned by delegating "normal operating duties," including sanitation, but that he retained "certain things, which are the big, broad, principles of the operation of the company," and had "the responsibility of seeing that they all work together."

Respondent was the only defense witness. He testified that, although all of Acme's employees were in a sense under his direction, the company had an "organizational structure for responsibilities for certain functions" according to which different phases of its operation were "assigned to individuals who, in turn, have staff and departments under them." He identified those individuals responsible for sanitation and related that upon receipt of the January 1972 FDA letter, he had conferred with the vice president for legal affairs, who informed him that the Baltimore division vice pesident "was investigating the situation immediately and would be taking corrective action and would be peparing a summary of the corrective action to reply to the letter." Respondent stated that he did not "believe there was anything [he] could have done more constructively than what [he] found was being done."

On cross-examination, respondent conceded that providing sanitary conditions for food offered for sale to the public was something that he was "responsible for in the entire operation of the company," and he stated that it was one of the many phases of the company that he assigned to "dependable subordinates." . . . [R]espondent admitted that the Baltimore problem indicated the system for handling sanitation "wasn't working perfectly" and that as Acme's chief executive officer he was responsible for "any result which occurs in our company." . . .

[In a previous case, *United States v. Dotterweich,* the Supreme Court had upheld the conviction, under the Food, Drug, and Cosmetic Act, of the president and general manager of a corporation that had purchased drugs from manufacturers and shipped them in interstate commerce under its own label. The Court had held that in the interest of a larger good, the lives and health of people who cannot protect themselves, it was appropriate to put "[t]he burden of acting at hazard upon a person otherwise innocent but standing in a responsible relation to a public danger."]

Dotterweich and the cases which have followed reveal that in providing sanctions which reach and touch the individuals who execute the corporate mission — and this is by no means necessarily confined to a single corporate agent or employee — the Act imposes not only a positive duty to seek out and remedy violations when they occur but also and primarily, a duty to implement measures that will insure that violations will not occur. The requirements of foresight and vigilance imposed on responsible corporate agents are beyond question demanding, and perhaps onerous, but they are no more stringent than the public has a right to expect of those who voluntarily assume positions of authority in business enterprises whose services and products affect the health and well-being of the public that supports them. . . .

The Act does not, as we observed in *Dotterweich,* make criminal liability turn on "awareness of some wrongdoing" or "conscious fraud." The duty imposed by Congress on responsible corporate agents is, we emphasize, one that requires the highest standard of foresight and vigilance, but the Act, in its criminal aspect, does not require that which is objectively impossible. The theory upon which responsible corporate agents are held criminally accountable for "causing" violations of the Act permits a claim that a defendant was "powerless" to prevent or correct the violation to "be raised defensively at a trial on merits."

[The decision of the Court of Appeals is reversed.]

CASE REVIEW QUESTIONS

1. What were Park's corporate duties and how did they relate to the violation with which he was charged?
2. What reasons did the court give to support the criminal liability of executives in cases such as this?
3. What defense may be available to an executive charged with a strict liability crime?
4. Do you agree with the outcome of the case? Explain.
5. Why didn't the government's appeal to the Supreme Court constitute double jeopardy?

REVIEW QUESTIONS

1. What is the difference between a state of mind crime and a strict liability crime? Give an example of each not given in the text.
2. In what situations does the protection against double jeopardy apply? When does this protection not apply?
3. Under what circumstances will a corporation be held responsible for criminal acts committed by its employees?
4. What is the standard used to determine whether a corporate executive will be criminally liable for the corporation's violation of a strict liability statute?

CASE PROBLEMS

1. What crimes have been committed in the following situations?
   a. John encounters Pat, the paper boy, one evening while Pat is making his collections. John pushes Pat to the ground and takes the money he has collected.
   b. John breaks into Fran's house looking for money. He doesn't find any and leaves without taking anything.
   c. John sees Betsy leave her purse unattended in a shopping cart at the grocery store. He takes it.
   d. John cuts through Carol's backyard on the way to school after having been told not to.
   e. John alters the amount of money on a check written to him.
2. The Gun Control Act of 1968 authorizes officials to enter into the premises of firearms dealers during business hours for the purpose of inspecting

records and documents and firearms stored on the premises. The statute does not require a warrant. Biswell, a pawnshop operator, was visited one afternoon by Treasury agents who inspected Biswell's books and requested entry into a locked gun room. Biswell asked whether the agents had a search warrant. He was told that they did not and that the statute authorized them to inspect without one. Biswell unlocked the storeroom, and the agents found and seized two sawed-off rifles that Biswell was not licensed to possess. When Biswell was tried for illegal possession of weapons, he moved to exclude the seized guns, arguing that the search of his business premises violated the Fourth Amendment. Is Biswell correct? Explain.

3. Internal Revenue agents visited Fisher and interviewed him in connection with an investigation of possible civil or criminal liability under the federal income tax laws. Shortly after the interview, Fisher obtained from his accountant certain documents relating to the preparation of his tax return by the accountant. The documents were analyses by the accountant of Fisher's income and expenses, which had been constructed by the accountant from Fisher's cancelled checks and deposit receipts. After obtaining the documents, Fisher retained an attorney to represent him in connection with the investigation and transferred the documents to the lawyer. Is the Internal Revenue Service entitled to get Fisher's documents from his attorney? Explain.

4. Police officers obtained a warrant to search Johnson's home for stolen television sets. While searching the bedroom, an officer opened a bureau drawer and found heroin. Johnson was arrested for the illegal possession of a dangerous drug. Is the heroin admissible against Johnson at his trial? Explain.

5. Canadian Fur Trappers, Inc., operated a business selling fur coats on the installment plan. The general manager and the salespeople of the store devised a scheme in which they took multiple cash deposits for the same fur coat, kept the coat in storage, and delivered it to whoever paid off the balance first. A fur of inferior quality was then delivered to each of the other persons who had made deposits and who subsequently completed their payments. This plan resulted in substantial extra profit to the corporation. Canadian Fur Trappers, Inc., was indicted for larceny. In a trial, who will win the case? Explain. Would your answer be different if the general manager and the salespeople had kept the extra profit instead of turning it over to the corporation? Explain.

6. Annbest Apartments, Inc., employed Walter Raphael as superintendent for the apartment building it owned on West 21st Street in New York City. Raphael received a number of complaints from tenants that unsafe space heaters were being used in the building. Raphael failed to investigate these complaints. Several days later, one of the heaters shorted out and caused a fire in which three tenants were killed. The corporation was charged with reckless homicide. Reckless homicide is committed when a person is aware of and consciously disregards a substantial and unjustifiable risk of death. Is the corporation criminally responsible? Explain.

7. Dean Starr, the secretary-treasurer of Cheney Brothers Food Corporation, was charged with violating the Food, Drug, and Cosmetic Act by allowing the contamination of food stored in a company warehouse. The warehouse had been infested with mice after an adjoining field was plowed for farming. Starr, the officer in charge of sanitation problems, was told of the problem and ordered Marks, the warehouse janitor, to take certain corrective measures. Marks did not do anything. During an FDA inspection one month later, Marks told the inspector that there were mice in the warehouse and that he had not taken the corrective steps as ordered. Marks also falsely suggested to the inspector the existence of additional violations. If the government prosecutes Starr for violating the Food, Drug, and Cosmetic Act, who will win the case? Explain.

8. In May and June of 1972, the FDA inspected a multifood storage warehouse owned by Y. Hata & Co., Ltd., a corporation on the island of Maui, Hawaii. The inspectors discovered that birds were flying in and out of the warehouse, perching on overhead sprinkler pipes and bags of rice, and eat-

ing from the bags of rice. Bird droppings were found on some of the rice bags. Hata, the president of the corporation, was aware of the bird infestation problem as early as August 1971. He tried numerous devices to prevent birds from entering the warehouse, but none were completely successful. At the time of the FDA inspections in 1972, the corporation was planning to enclose the food storage area of the warehouse in a huge wire cage that it believed would successfully keep the birds out. If Hata is prosecuted for violating the Food, Drug, and Cosmetic Act by storing adulterated food, on what basis might he defend? Who will win the case? Explain.

PART II

CONTRACT LAW

8

INTRODUCTION TO CONTRACT LAW

When people speak of a contract, they are often referring to a written document. In the law of contracts, however, a document is only evidence of a contract. The actual contract is the legal relationship between the parties and the rights and duties that they owe to each other. In other words, a contract has no physical existence; instead, it is a concept recognized by the courts. This chapter will introduce you to the law of contracts by considering its underlying rationale, providing an overview of contract law, outlining the sources of contract law, and recommending a helpful approach for analyzing contract cases and problems.

PROMISES, PROMISES

Contract law focuses on promises. A classic definition states that a contract is "a promise or set of promises for the breach of which the law gives a remedy, or the performance of which the law in some way recognizes as a duty."[1] A briefer definition is that a contract is an *enforceable promise*.

The Economic Basis of Contract Law

There is nothing inherent in the nature of promises that requires the courts to enforce them. If these promises were not enforced, the world would not come to

---

[1] Restatement (Second) of Contracts §1 (1979).

an end. What would happen, though, is that the pace of economic activity within society would be dramatically slower than it is under a system in which promises are enforced. A reason that society chooses to enforce promises, then, is to encourage reliance on them and thus facilitate economic activity. This, in turn, contributes to economic growth, which is one of society's goals.

When a promise is made, it creates an expectation concerning the future in the mind of the person who receives it. For example, if I say to you, "I promise to deliver to you 1,000 widgets on December 1, if you promise to pay me $1,000 for them" and you promise to pay the money, you now have the expectation that I will deliver 1,000 widgets to you on December 1. You have this expectation even though my promise is **executory,** meaning that it has not yet been performed.

If you are confident that your expectation will be fulfilled because I will execute my promise, you are apt to act in reliance on my promise. For instance, you may rent a store in which to sell the widgets at retail, you may purchase advertising space to announce the sale of the widgets, or you may buy a new television set, which you plan to pay for from the profits you anticipate from reselling the widgets. Your confidence that I will perform my promise may stem in part from my reputation as an honest person who keeps promises. Nevertheless, the fact that the courts will enforce my promise if I fail to keep it will certainly increase your confidence.

Of course, if you are not confident that your expectation will be fulfilled, you will hesitate to act in reliance on my promise, and you may not enter into the other transactions until I actually deliver the widgets. And if I don't deliver the widgets to you and your expectation is not protected, you will not enter into the other transactions at all. In either case, your economic activity will be slowed greatly. A function of contract law, then, is to protect certain expectations by enforcing promises so that people may rely on them and, as a result, feel free to engage in economic activity. Therefore, not only the person having the expectation, but society as well, desires that promises be enforced because it stimulates the economy.

The Moral Basis of Contract Law

Although protecting expectations to stimulate economic growth is the dominant function of contract law today, the notion that promises voluntarily made are sacred and should be enforced on a moral basis is always lurking in the background. Under this theory, the emphasis is on the individual freedom and responsibility of the promise maker, the **promisor,** rather than on the reliance of the receiver of the promise, the **promisee.**

Because many promises are broken and are not enforced by the courts, we know that the moral basis for the enforcement of promises is a subsidiary, not a primary, basis of contract law. Nonetheless, when studying contract law, you should consider the extent to which the courts appear to consider the morality of keeping promises as a basis for enforcement in place of or in addition to the economic basis of protecting expectations.

AN OVERVIEW OF CONTRACT LAW

Because contract law includes so many topics, a brief overview of the material you will read in Chapters 9 through 18 will help you to see how the various topics relate to one another and to contract law in general. In contract law cases, the legal issues that may arise are (1) whether a contract was created between the parties, (2) whether it is the kind of contract the courts will enforce, (3) whether the promises contained in the contract were performed or otherwise discharged, and (4) by what means a contract promise that has not been performed should be enforced.

Was A Contract Created?

Generally, there are four essential prerequisites (requirements) that must exist before a contract is created in order for the promises of the parties to the contract to be enforceable. These prerequisites are as follows:

1. There must be an *agreement* between the parties. The formation of an agreement through the bargaining process of offer and acceptance is the subject of Chapters 9 and 10.
2. *Consideration* must support the promises of the parties. Whether a promise is supported by consideration is the subject of Chapter 12.
3. The parties must have the legal *capacity* (legal ability) to create a contract. The subject of capacity is discussed in Chapter 14.
4. The agreement must have a *legal purpose.* What constitutes an illegal agreement is the subject of Chapter 15.

Is the Contract Enforceable?

Even if the essential prerequisites exist and a contract has been created, a party to the contract may in some cases argue successfully that his or her promise is not enforceable. For instance, if one of the parties has bargained in a manner that the courts believe to be unfair, the other party's promise will not be enforced. Fairness in the bargaining process is the subject of Chapter 11.

Another situation in which the courts will sometimes refuse to enforce a contract is when it is not in a form that the law requires. Some contracts, *but not all contracts,* must be in writing to be enforceable. When a writing is required and what kind of writing is required to make a contract enforceable are considered in Chapter 13.

A party to a contract may also be able to argue that his or her promise is not enforceable by the particular person who is trying to enforce it. This argument is made when the person who wants to enforce the promise is someone who is not a party to the contract. You will learn when a person who is not a party to a contract may nonetheless enforce it in Chapter 16.

Were the Promises Performed or Discharged?

To win a lawsuit for breach of contract, a person must show not only that an enforceable contract promise was made but also that the promise was not discharged. The usual way in which contract duties are discharged is by per-formance of the contract promises. You will read about performance and the other ways in which contract duties are discharged in Chapter 17.

How Should a Contract Promise Be Enforced?

If a court decides that an enforceable promise has been made and has not been discharged, the court will enforce the promise. Your first thought about the enforcement of promises may be that the court will make a party actually perform a promise that has not been kept. As you will read in Chapter 18, however, requiring the actual performance of an unkept promise is not the usual remedy in contract cases. Instead, the courts generally require the party who has breached the contract — that is, the party who has not kept his or her promise — to pay money damages to the party who has been injured by the breach.

SOURCES OF CONTRACT LAW

To answer the questions about contracts just discussed, it is necessary to learn contract law. Unfortunately, all the law that applies to contracts is not found in one place. The courts find contract law in court decisions, the Restate-ment of Contracts, legislation, administrative regulations, and the Uniform Commercial Code.

Court Decisions

Contract law is primarily common law, which means that it has been created for the most part through court decisions. The traditional emphasis of these decisions has been on the policy of freedom of contract. This policy leaves it to the contracting parties to determine the terms of economic transactions — that is, the rights and duties of each of the parties — through private agreements. The courts have often said that they will only enforce terms that have been agreed to by the parties; they will not make a contract for the parties.

Restatement of Contracts

Because there are many judicial systems in the United States, the decisions of the courts in the various states concerning the law of contracts sometimes conflict. In 1932, the American Law Institute, an organization composed of legal practitioners, judges, and scholars, published the Restatement of Con-tracts in an attempt to sort out the conflicts and to state the contract principles that it believed to be the soundest in a form similar to a series of statutes. Although the Restatement was written by a private organization and therefore does not have the force of the law, it is an important authority that is often looked to by the courts as a source of contract law. An updated version of the

Restatement, referred to as the Restatement (Second) of Contracts, was completed in 1979.

Legislation and Administrative Regulations

Although contract law is still primarily common law and while freedom of contract remains a basic principle of that law, the rights and duties of contracting parties are being increasingly determined by statutes and regulations adopted by legislatures and administrative agencies. This is occurring because the classic contract model of two equal parties bargaining to reach an agreement is not applicable in many cases today. It is often replaced by situations in which one party has substantially greater economic power than the other and may therefore be able to force contract terms on the weaker party. Whether the weaker party actually has freedom of contract is thus called into question. Legislatures and administrative agencies, and in some instances the courts, have taken steps to prevent the stronger party from taking advantage of his or her economic power in such situations. Examples of this kind of legislative and administrative action include the adoption of standardized insurance terms (see Chapter 50), limitations on employment contracts (see Chapter 53), and consumer protection provisions (see Chapter 49).

Uniform Commercial Code

The Uniform Commercial Code (UCC) is another legislative influence on contract law. It has been adopted by all the states except Louisiana, which has adopted it only in part, as well as the District of Columbia and the Virgin Islands. Article 2 of the UCC states the law that is to be applied to contracts for the sale of goods, one category of contracts in general. Article 2 changed the traditional law of contracts — the law that had been created by court decisions — in a number of important ways. As a result, there are some situations in which there is one contract rule for contracts for the sale of goods and another rule for all other contracts.

Increasingly, however, the courts are applying Article 2 contract principles and rules to all contracts, not just sales contracts. When the areas in which this has occurred are discussed in the chapters on contract law, both the modern contract rule, found in the UCC, and the traditional contract rule will be explained. You should learn both the modern rule and the traditional rule so as to fully understand the operation of contract law. In Part III of this book (Chapters 19 through 24) you will learn more about the Uniform Commercial Code and the law of sales and sales contracts. The UCC is reprinted in full in Appendix B.

Because of the various sources of contract law and the fact that there are fifty-one different judicial systems, contract law is not uniform throughout the United States. The Restatement of Contracts and the Uniform Commercial Code have added considerably to the degree of uniformity among the states, but much diversity remains. In the contract law chapters that follow, the mainstream of American contract law will be set forth. Variations among the states will be noted only when important differences exist or when they facilitate understanding the predominant rules.

ANALYZING CONTRACT CASES AND PROBLEMS

In Chapter 1, a method of analyzing law cases called "briefing" a case was explained. However, before briefing a contract case and when doing the case problems in the contract law chapters, we suggest that you answer the following questions concerning the case or problem:

1. Who is trying to enforce a promise? You might refer to this party as the *enforcer.*
2. Who does the enforcer say made the promise that he or she is trying to enforce? You might refer to this party as the *maker.*
3. What *promise* does the enforcer say the maker made?
4. On what grounds does the maker argue that the promise should not be enforced? In other words, what is the maker's *defense?*

Answering these questions as the first step in your analysis of contract cases and case problems will help you to understand better contract law and its application.

You can practice answering these questions with the following case. As you read the majority opinion and the dissenting opinion in this case, you should keep in mind that the primary reason for enforcing promises, as explained earlier, is to encourage people to rely on expectations that are created by promises and thus to promote economic activity.

WILLIAMS v. WALKER-THOMAS FURNITURE COMPANY
350 F.2d 445 (D.C. Cir. 1965)

[Williams first purchased furniture from Walker-Thomas Furniture Company (Walker-Thomas), a retail store, in 1957. In subsequent years, she made other purchases amounting to $1,800, including a stereo set for $514 on April 17, 1962. All of the purchases were on credit. Each time Williams made a purchase, she signed a contract in which she promised that if she failed to pay any of the monthly installment payments as they became due, Walker-Thomas could repossess *all* of the furniture purchased by Williams since her first purchase.

When Williams purchased the stereo, she owed Walker-Thomas $164. Shortly after purchasing the stereo, she failed to pay one of the monthly installment payments. She had, however, made payments totaling $1,400 since her first purchase.

Walker-Thomas brought a legal action to enforce Williams' promise and to repossess all the furniture. Williams defended on the grounds that the court should not enforce her promise because the contract with Walker-Thomas was unconscionable. (You will read about unconscionable contracts in Chapter 11.

For now, however, you only need to know that unconscionable means very unfair.) In other words, Williams argued that the court should not enforce her promise to let Walker-Thomas repossess all of the furniture she had ever purchased from them if she failed to make a monthly installment payment because that promise was very unfair to her. The trial court rejected Williams' defense and found for Walker-Thomas. An intermediate appellate court affirmed. Williams appealed to the highest court for the District of Columbia. In the decision, Williams is referred to as the appellant and Walker-Thomas is referred to as the appellee.]

WRIGHT, Circuit Judge

Appellant's principal contention, rejected by both the trial and the appellate courts below, it that [the contract is] unconscionable and, hence, not enforceable. In its opinion in *Williams v. Walker-Thomas Furniture Company,* the District of Columbia Court of Appeals explained its rejection of this contention as follows:

> Appellant's second argument presents a more serious question. The record reveals that prior to the last purchase appellant had reduced the balance in her account to $164. The last purchase, a stereo set, raised the balance due to $678. Significantly, at the time of this and the preceding purchases, appellee was aware of appellant's financial position. The reverse side of the stereo contract listed the name of appellant's social worker and her $218 monthly stipend from the government. Nevertheless, with full knowledge that appellant had to feed, clothe and support both herself and seven children on this amount, appellee sold her a $514 stereo set.
>
> We cannot condemn too strongly appellee's conduct. It raises serious questions of sharp practice and irresponsible business dealings. A review of the legislation in the District of Columbia affecting retail sales and the pertinent decisions of the highest court in this jurisdiction disclose, however, no ground upon which this court can declare the contracts in question contrary to public policy. We note that were the Maryland Retail Installment Sales Act, or its equivalent, in force in the District of Columbia, we could grant appellant appropriate relief. We think Congress should consider corrective legislation to protect the public from such exploitive contracts as were utilized in the case at bar.

We do not agree that the court lacked the power to refuse enforcement to contracts found to be unconscionable. In other jurisdictions, it has been held as a matter of common law that unconscionable contracts are not enforceable. Since we have never adopted or rejected such a rule, the question here presented is actually one of first impression [i.e., this is the first time this court has had to answer this question].

Congress has recently enacted the Uniform Commercial Code, which specifically provides that the court may refuse to enforce a contract which it finds to be unconscionable at the time it was made. The enactment of this section, which occurred subsequent to the contracts here in suit, does not mean that the common law of the District of Columbia was otherwise at the time of enactment, nor does it preclude the court from adopting a similar rule in the exercise of its powers to develop the common law for the District of Columbia. In fact, in view of the absence of prior authority [i.e., previous cases] on the point, we consider the congressional adoption of the UCC persuasive authority for following the rationale of the cases from which the section is explicitly derived. Accordingly, we hold that where the element of unconscionability is present at the time a contract is made, the contract should not be enforced.

Because the trial court and the appellate court did not feel that enforcement could be refused, no findings were made on the possible unconscionability of the contract. Since the record is not sufficient for our deciding the issue as a matter of law, the case must be remanded to the trial court for further proceedings.

Remanded.

DANAHAR, Circuit Judge (dissenting)

The District of Columbia Court of Appeals obviously was as unhappy about the situation here presented as any of us can possibly be. Its opinion in the *Williams* case concludes: ''We think Congress should consider corrective legislation to protect the public from such exploitive contracts as were utilized in the case at bar.''

There are many aspects of public policy here involved. What is a luxury to some may seem an outright necessity to others. Is public oversight to be required of the expenditures of relief funds? A washing machine, e.g., in the hands of a relief client might become a fruitful source of income. Many relief clients may well need credit, and certain business establishments will take long chances on the sale of items, expecting their pricing policies will afford a degree of protection commensurate with the risk.

   I mention such matters only to emphasize the desirability of a cautious approach to any such problem, particularly since the law for so long has allowed parties such great latitude in making their own contracts. I dare say there must annually be thousands upon thousands of installment credit transactions in this jurisdiction, and one can only speculate as to the effect the decision in these cases will have.

CASE REVIEW QUESTIONS

1. Who is trying to enforce a promise in this case?
2. Who made the promise that the enforcer is trying to enforce?
3. What promise does the enforcer say the maker made?
4. On what grounds does the maker argue that the promise is unenforceable?
5. The primary reason for enforcing promises is to encourage people to rely on the expectations that are created by promises. Does the decision in this case encourage such reliance? Explain.
6. If the decision in this case does not encourage reliance on promises, which of the reasons for not enforcing a promise discussed earlier in the chapter did the court apply? Explain.
7. What reasons did Judge Danahar give for agreeing with the decisions of the two lower courts?
8. What was the source of the law that Judge Wright applied?

REVIEW QUESTIONS

1. What is a contract?
2. Why does the law enforce promises?
3. What are the legal issues that may arise in a contract law case?
4. What are the sources of contract law?
5. What questions should you ask when beginning an analysis of a contract law case or problem?

9

THE BARGAINING PROCESS: OFFER

Before entering into a contract, people generally engage in negotiation. As negotiation progresses, one party may make an **offer.** An offer is a promise that is conditional upon receiving something that is demanded in return. A person making an offer is called an **offeror.** The person receiving an offer is called an **offeree.**

For example, if Buyer and Seller are negotiating the sale of widgets, Seller may at some point say, "I promise to deliver 10,000 widgets to you on February 1, if you promise to pay me $10,000." Seller's statement is an offer, and Seller is an offeror because she is making a promise ("I promise to deliver 10,000 widgets to you on February 1 . . .") that is conditional upon receiving something in return (". . . if you promise to pay me $10,000.").

Buyer, the offeree, may then transform Seller's promise into a contract, thus making it legally enforceable, by accepting the offer. **Acceptance** occurs when the offeree meets the condition demanded by the offeror. In our hypothetical case, if Buyer responds, "I promise to pay you $10,000 for the widgets," he has accepted the offer. Acceptance is fully explained and discussed in the next chapter.

Through the process of offer and acceptance, the parties have reached a mutual agreement, an essential prerequisite to the creation of a contract. If, in addition to the mutual agreement, the other essential contract prerequisites are met, a contract is created between the parties and their promises are legally enforceable. The other essential prerequisites, which are consideration, capacity to contract, and legality of purpose, will be discussed in later chapters.

At this point, our focus is on the promise aspect of the offer rather than the condition. Before a court will determine that an offer was made, three things must be true:

1. A promise or promises must have been made.
2. The promise(s) must have been made with the intent that it (they) be legally binding if accepted.
3. The promise(s) must be reasonably certain and definite.

WAS A PROMISE MADE?

In determining whether a promise was made, the courts do not ask whether the offeror intended to make a promise. Instead, they apply an "objective" standard and ask: "Could a reasonable person, familiar with the business being transacted, justifiably believe that a promise was made?" If the answer to the question is yes, then in the eyes of the law a promise has been made. This can lead to some unexpected results from a layman's point of view because no matter what the alleged promisor says—or *doesn't* say—application of the objective standard may result in the finding that a promise was made. If the promise is made in words, it is called an express promise. Promises manifested by conduct are said to be implied in fact.

You may wonder why the courts apply an objective standard in determining whether or not a promise was made. The reason is that it allows a person who reasonably believes that another person has made a promise to rely on that promise without worrying about whether the person who appeared to make the promise really intended to do so. In other words, the law will protect reasonable expectations in order to stimulate economic activity.

Promises are distinguishable from such things as predictions, opinions, statements of future intent, and preliminary negotiations, but whether or not a particular statement is a promise can only be determined by application of the objective standard. In certain recurring situations, however, such as those discussed below, the courts have developed more certain rules for determining whether a promise was made.

Advertisements

The courts have generally ruled that an advertisement is not an offer. In other words, those who read an advertisement may not justifiably believe that the person placing it is making a promise. This rule serves to protect sellers because, if advertisements were treated as offers, a seller would be bound to a contract with everyone who accepted the offer, regardless of whether the seller had enough of the goods to fulfill all the contracts. On the other hand, if an advertisement contains clear words that indicate a promise by the advertiser, a court will determine that the advertisement is an offer.

Auctions

Generally, an auctioneer requesting bids is not making an offer or a promise to sell. Instead, the bidder makes an offer to buy when he or she makes a bid. Acceptance is generally manifested by the fall of the hammer, but the auctioneer is also free to reject all bids and withdraw the goods any time before acceptance. On the other hand, if goods are put up for auction "without reserve," the goods cannot be withdrawn after bids are called for unless no bid is made.

In the following two cases, the plaintiffs are suing for breach of contract, and the defendants are defending on the basis that they did not make a promise. You should note the standard that the courts apply in determining whether a promise has been made and how that standard is applied in each case.

HORNE v. PATTON
287 So.2d 824 (Ala. 1973)

[Horne brought a legal action against Dr. Patton. Dr. Patton moved to dismiss the complaint and the court granted the motion. Horne appealed.]

BLOODWORTE, Justice

This case is alleged to have arisen out of the disclosure by Dr. Patton, defendant herein, to plaintiff's employer of certain information acquired in the course of a doctor–patient relationship between plaintiff Horne and defendant doctor, contrary to the expressed instructions of patient Horne.

The [basis of plaintiff's claim] is that the alleged disclosure breached an implied contract to keep confidential all personal information given to the defendant by his patient. [It] alleges that defendant doctor entered into a physician–patient contractual relationship wherein the plaintiff agreed to disclose to defendant all facts which would help him in his diagnosis and treatment of the plaintiff, that defendant agreed to treat the plaintiff to the best of his medical ability, and to keep confidential all personal information given to him by the plaintiff. It is alleged that this agreement is implied from the facts through common custom and practice.

This court has often stated that an implied contract arises where there are circumstances which, according to the ordinary course of dealing and the common understanding of men, show a mutual intent to contract. Defendant admits in his brief that the facts and circumstances alleged are such as to show a mutual intent to contract according to the ordinary course of dealing between a physician and his patient. The point of difference between the parties appears to be whether or not there is an implied term in the ordinary course of dealing between a doctor and a patient that information disclosed to the doctor will be held in confidence.

This question is one of first impression in this state. Few courts have considered this question. One of the fullest discussions on this point appears in *Hammonds v. Aetna Casualty & Surety Co.*:

> Any time a doctor undertakes the treatment of a patient, and the consensual relationship of physician and patient is established, two [legal] obligations (of significance here) are simultaneously assumed by the doctor. Doctor and patient enter into a simple contract, the patient hoping that he will be cured and the doctor optimistically assuming that he will be compensated. As an implied condition of that contract, this Court is of the opinion that the doctor warrants that any confidential information gained through the relationship will not be released without the patient's permission. Almost every member of the public is aware of the promise of discretion contained in the Hippocratic Oath, and every patient has a right to rely upon this [promise] of silence. . . . Consequently, when a doctor breaches his duty of secrecy, he is in violation of part of his obligations under the contract.

We have not been cited to, nor have we found in our

research, any case in which a cause of action for the breach of an implied contract of confidentiality on the part of the doctor has been rejected. Moreover, public knowledge of the ethical standards of the medical profession or widespread acquaintance with the Hippocratic Oath's secrecy provisions or the AMA's Principles of Ethics or Alabama's medical licensing requirements of secrecy (which is a common provision in many states) singly or together may well be sufficient justification for reasonable expectation on a patient's

part that the physician has promised to keep confidential all information given by the patient.

Again, of course, any confidentiality between patient and physician is subject to exceptions. . . where the supervening interests of society or the private interests of the patient intervene. These are matters of defense.

The judgment of the trial court is therefore due to be reversed and remanded.

O'KEEFE v. LEE CALAN IMPORTS, INC.
262 N.E.2d 750 (Ct. App. Ill. 1970)

MCNAMARA, Justice

Christopher D. O'Brien brought suit against defendant for an alleged breach of contract. O'Brien died subsequent to the filing of the lawsuit, and [O'Keefe, the legal representative of O'Brien's estate] was substituted in his stead. Plaintiff and defendant filed cross-motions for summary judgment. The court denied plaintiff's motion for summary judgment and granted defendant's motion. This appeal follows. The facts . . . are not in dispute.

On July 31, 1966, defendant advertised a 1964 Volvo Station Wagon for sale in the *Chicago Sun-Times.* Defendant had instructed the newspaper to advertise the price of $1,095 for said automobile in the advertisement. O'Brien visited defendant's place of business, examined the automobile and stated that he wished to purchase it for $1,095. One of the defendant's salesmen at first agreed, but then refused to sell the car for the erroneous price listed in the advertisement.

Plaintiff appeals, contending that the advertisement constituted an offer on the part of the defendant, which O'Brien duly accepted and thus the parties formed a binding contract.

It is elementary that in order to form a contract there must be an offer and an acceptance. A contract requires the mutual assent of the parties.

The precise issue of whether a newspaper advertisement constitutes an offer which can be accepted to form a contract or whether such an advertisement is merely an invitation to make an offer has not been determined by the Illinois courts. Most jurisdictions which have dealt with the issue have considered such an advertisement as a mere invitation to make an offer, unless the circumstances indicate otherwise. As was stated in Corbin on Contracts:

> It is quite possible to make a definite and operative offer to buy or to sell goods by advertisement, in a newspaper, by a handbill, or on a placard in a store window. It is not customary to do this, however, and the presumption is the other way. Neither the advertiser nor the reader of his notice understands that the latter is empowered to close the deal without further expression by the former. Such advertisements are understood to be mere requests to consider and examine and negotiate, and no one can reasonably regard them as otherwise unless the circumstances are exceptional and the words used are very plain and clear.

In *Craft v. Elder & Johnston Co.* defendant advertised in a local newspaper that a sewing machine was for sale at a stated price. Plaintiff visited the store, attempted to purchase the sewing machine at that price, but defendant refused. In holding that the newspaper advertisement did not constitute a binding offer, the court held that an ordinary newspaper advertisement was merely an offer to negotiate. In *Ehrlich v. Willis Music Co.* defendant advertised in a newspaper that a television set was for sale at a mistaken price. The actual price was ten times the advertised price. The court found that no offer had been made, but rather an invitation to patronize defendant's store. The court also held that [plaintiff] should have known that the price was a mistake. In *Lovett v. Frederick Loeser & Co.* a newspaper advertisement offering radios for sale at 25% to 50% reductions was held to be an invitation to make an offer.

We find that in the absence of special circumstances a newspaper advertisement which contains an erroneous purchase price through no fault of the defendant advertiser and which contains no other terms is not an offer which can be accepted so as to form a contract. We hold that such an advertisement amounts only to an invitation to make an offer. It seems apparent to us in the instant case that there was no meeting of the minds nor the required mutual assent by the two parties to a precise proposition.

The judgment of the Circuit Court is affirmed.

CASE REVIEW QUESTIONS
1. What promise did Horne argue that Dr. Patton had made?
2. Did the court agree with Horne that Dr. Patton had made the alleged promise? Explain.
3. What promise did O'Keefe argue that Lee Calan Imports had made?
4. Did the court agree with O'Keefe that Lee Calan Imports had made the alleged promise? Explain.

INTENT TO BE LEGALLY BOUND

The courts also apply an objective standard to determine whether the person who makes an offer intends to be legally bound by the promise it contains. On this issue, the question asked is, "Could a reasonable person, familiar with the business being transacted, justifiably believe that the person making the promise intended to be legally bound by it?"

It doesn't matter, therefore, what the person making the promise *actually* intended, that is, the promisor's "subjective" intent. Regardless of the offeror's actual or subjective intent, if the person receiving the promise could reasonably believe that the person making the promise intended to be legally bound by it, the offeror is bound to a contract upon acceptance of the offer. Promises made with the intent to be legally bound are distinguishable from such things as jokes, statements made in anger, and social promises, but whether such intent exists can only be determined by application of the objective standard.

A common situation in which the intent to be legally bound is called into question occurs when the parties, while negotiating, indicate an intent to put their final agreement in writing. If the parties reach an otherwise legally binding agreement, does a contract exist, or is the creation of the contract delayed until it is put in writing and signed by the parties?* This question must be answered in any case in which one of the parties attempts to withdraw from an agreement prior to its being put in writing and signed by the parties. Whether such a withdrawal is possible depends on whether the parties intended that there be no contract until the agreement was put in writing or whether the writing was simply intended to be a "convenient memorial" of their already legally binding agreement.

Unless their intent one way or the other is very clear, this matter will be a question of fact that must be determined by the jury using the objective standard discussed above. Some of the important factors to be considered in applying the objective standard include whether the contract is a type that is usually put in writing, whether the agreement is simple or detailed, and the amount of money involved. The more complex and important the agreement, the more likely it is that the parties don't intend it to have legal consequences until the agreement is reduced to writing and signed by them.

In the two cases that follow, the plaintiffs are suing for breach of contract and the defendants are defending on the basis that they did not intend to be legally bound. You should carefully note the standard that the courts apply in determining whether the defendant intended to be legally bound and how that standard is applied in the particular case.

* Not all contracts need be in writing to be enforceable (see Chapter 15).

MacDONALD v. FEDERAL LIFE AND CASUALTY COMPANY
410 F. Supp. 1126 (E.D.N.Y. 1976)

[MacDonald was an employee of Federal Life and Casualty Company (Federal), who was hired during April 1970. He was to be paid a weekly salary plus an annual bonus based on performance. A bonus agreement was arrived at during the year 1972. The bonus formula was signed by MacDonald and returned to Federal. In March 1973, the 1972 bonus checks were mailed along with a letter stating that an "arbitrary after the fact" reduction in the bonus had been made by Federal. MacDonald's bonus under the formula would have been $25,000, but the bonus check he received was for only $10,649.

MacDonald informed Federal that he considered the check to be only a partial payment of the bonus due to him. After being discharged by Federal in November 1973, MacDonald brought a legal action for breach of contract against Federal to collect the full amount of his 1972 bonus. Federal moved for a summary judgment for reasons discussed by the court. Federal is referred to in the court's opinion as "the movant."]

BRUCHHAUSEN, District Judge

In support of the motion for summary judgment, the movant states that the document in question is not contractual in nature, and that paragraph 6 provides:

> This arrangement may be modified or terminated at any time by the company and in no way constitutes a contractual obligation by Federal Life and Casualty Company.

This document was signed by the plaintiff and returned to the defendant. The movant urges that it is perfectly clear no contractual intent was intended between the parties, and that the movant retained full unilateral authority to modify the bonus arrangement. This was necessary because of financial reversals that might occur during any year. During the years 1972–1973, the movant lost money, therefore, the downward bonus modification. The contention of the movant is simply this proviso, above stated, creates no contract. The employer is free to or not to pay a bonus in its sole discretion.

It is well settled that on a motion for summary judgment, the court cannot try issues of fact, it can only determine whether there are issues to be tried.

In the case at bar, the court is obliged to grant the relief sought.

There is no contention that the plaintiff did not know or understand the contents of the bonus arrangement document. The affidavits, exhibits and deposition of the plaintiff clearly indicate his complete knowledge of the bonus arrangement. He is simply disappointed in not receiving his expected bonus.

The reservation, contained in the bonus arrangement for 1972, clearly negates any intent of the promisor to be contractually bound with an employee. If this were not true, there would be no plausible explanation for it being inserted in the document. It is merely an indefinite promise to pay a bonus which determination is wholly optional on behalf of the promisor, and, therefore, unenforceable.

The court after due deliberation of the arguments and applicable law grants the motion of the defendant, dismissing the complaint.

SCHECK v. FRANCIS
260 N.E.2d 493 (N.Y. 1970)

[George Scheck brought a legal action against Connie Francis for breach of an employment contract. Francis moved to dismiss the complaint, for reasons discussed below in the court's opinion, and the motion was granted. Scheck appealed.]

FULD, Chief Judge

For many years, the plaintiff, George Scheck, had been the personal manager of defendant Connie Francis, a popular singer. He brings this suit against her, alleging a breach of employment agreements covering a five-year period.

In February, 1968, about a year after an earlier employment agreement had expired, the parties entered into negotiations for a new contract. The defendants' attorney, Marvin Levin, Esq., had submitted a number of proposed agreements for the plaintiff's approval which he found unsatisfactory. After a final negotiation session Mr. Levin mailed to the plaintiff the four agreements here involved in quadruplicate, with a covering letter, dated April 15, 1968, requesting the plaintiff to "sign all copies" and "have Connie sign" them. . . . According to the plaintiff, he signed the agreements promptly; they were, however, never signed by Miss Francis as called for by the letter. He continued to work for the defendants until August 12, 1968, when their attorney notified him that he was not to "enter into new negotiations for (Connie Francis') services, unless and until she notifies you in writing to the contrary." In March, 1969 . . . the plaintiff was advised by the defendants' new attorneys that there were "no contracts in existence between (him) and our client." The present suit for damages followed.

It is well settled that, if the parties to an agreement do not intend it to be binding upon them until it is reduced to writing and signed by both of them, they are not bound and may not be held liable until it has been written out and signed. In the *Schwartz* case, for instance, involving the purchase and sale of stock, the parties met for the purpose of signing a written contract dealing with the transaction. Each signed his own copy but, because the check offered by the buyer was not certified, each picked up his contract and left, arranging to meet the next day. The defendant then refused to go through with the agreement, and this court upheld a determination in his favor on the ground that "(i)t is entirely plain, . . . that the parties did not intend to be bound until a written agreement had been signed and delivered."

The writings before us likewise evidence the intention of the parties not to be bound until the agreements were signed. The plaintiff urges that there was, at least, a triable issue whether Mr. Levin's letter constituted proof that the parties had agreed upon the terms of the contracts. . . . We do not agree. It appears quite clear, from Mr. Levin's letter alone, that the agreements were to take effect only after both parties had signed them. Thus, he had instructed the plaintiff

that he was to sign them and "have Connie sign" them, expressly advising him to call if there were "any questions or comments." Although the agreements themselves were not required to be delivered to the plaintiff's attorney (Mr. Granett) before the parties had signed, a copy of the covering letter was sent to him. This combination of circumstances unquestionably gave the plaintiff an opportunity to decline to go through with the deal before he signed. Certainly, the defendant Francis enjoyed the same privilege, and she never did sign. In short, both parties must plainly have understood that the agreements were to take effect only after they had signed them, and until that time, the matter was still in the stage of negotiations.

Order affirmed.

CASE REVIEW QUESTIONS

1. What promise did MacDonald argue had been made by Federal?
2. Did the court agree with Federal that its promise had not been made with the intent to be legally bound? Explain.
3. What promise did Scheck argue had been made by Francis?
4. Did the court agree with Francis that her promise had not been made with the intent to be legally bound? Explain.

DEFINITENESS AND CERTAINTY

Before a court will enforce a contract, the material terms of the agreement must be definite enough to make the promises of the parties certain. This requirement is based on the fact that the courts will not make a contract for the parties; it will only enforce the terms agreed to by them. If these terms cannot be determined by the court because they are indefinite, the court will not know what promises to enforce. This problem can arise either because terms are omitted entirely or because the language is too vague.

Omitted Terms

When material terms of a contract have been omitted, a court must decide whether it can enforce the contract despite the omissions. Although a court will not make a contract for the parties, it may conclude that the parties intended the omitted terms to be supplied by implication.

For example, if parties enter into an agreement for the sale of goods but fail to state the price at which the goods are to be sold, should the court enforce the contract anyway and, if so, at what price? In this situation, the courts have held that the parties intend that the goods be sold at a reasonable price and that this price must be determined on a case-by-case basis. Similarly, if no time for delivery is set, delivery within a reasonable time is implied.

On the other hand, when there is no standard by which an omitted material term can be reasonably determined, the courts have refused to enforce the contract. Examples of such omissions include the kind and quantity of goods to be sold. In such cases, there is rarely any basis on which a court can determine the missing term by implication.

Vague Terms

In cases in which terms are included in a contract but are left vague by the parties, the courts have traditionally not felt as free to determine the terms by implication as they have in cases in which terms are omitted. This has also been true when the parties have only agreed to agree to material terms at a future time. The reason for this is that a court may feel as though it is making a contract for the parties if it gives meaning to the vague term, whereas it may not feel this in a case in which it must determine a term that has been omitted.

The Modern View

As a result of the application of the traditional rule requiring a high degree of definiteness in the drafting of agreements, it has frequently turned out that parties who believed that they had an enforceable contract actually did not. If no contract is found to exist, the reasonable expectation of one of the parties is not protected. Often, however, omitted or indefinite terms or agreements to agree are used in commercial situations with good reason.

For example, parties may wish to enter into a long-term supply contract, but they may not be able to agree on a single price for the entire term of the agreement because of possible fluctuations in the market. They may therefore agree on the sales term of their contract but leave the price term to be agreed on at a later time.

Similarly, people in business may wish to enter into requirements or output contracts. In a **requirements contract,** one party promises to purchase all the requirements for a certain product from the other party. In an **output contract,** one party agrees to sell his or her entire output of a product to the other. In both cases, a question of definiteness arises because the *specific* quantity of goods to be sold is not actually agreed upon.

Should such agreements be enforced even though there are indefinite terms? The modern view, as reflected in Section 2-204(3) of the Uniform Commerical Code, is that they should be enforced even though they do not meet the traditional standards of definiteness. This view is more in keeping with the expectations of the parties, and it places less emphasis on technical formalities required by law.

There is, of course, a limit to how far a court will go in enforcing indefinite contract terms. The UCC states that if the parties intend to contract, a contract should not fail because of indefiniteness even though terms are left open provided that "there is a reasonably certain basis for giving an appropriate remedy." If a contract is too indefinite, however, the court may be unable to find such a basis.

In the case that follows, the plaintiff has brought a legal action for breach of contract. The defendant argues that no contract exists because the terms of the parties' agreement are not certain and definite enough for the court to enforce. Notice the reasoning used by the courts to determine if the defendant's argument is valid.

MAG CONSTRUCTION CO. v. McLEAN COUNTY
181 N.W.2d 718 (North Dakota 1970)

STRUTZ, Judge

In April 1966, McLean County advertised for bids for [the] loading and hauling of gravel, to be delivered on highways or in stockpiles.

Pursuant to this call for bids, the plaintiff submitted the following bid:

Gravel Loading & Hauling Bids to McLean Co.
Loading—14½ per cubic yard
Hauling—0.25 per yard for first 3 miles
    0.07 per yard mile thereafter
Mag Construction Company
By (signed) David Gregory, Pres.

This bid was "accepted" by the Board of County Commissioners and the plaintiff was notified of its acceptance. However, the plaintiff never was called upon to do any loading and hauling of gravel for the defendant. Such loading and hauling as was done for the defendant County was done by parties other than the plaintiff.

The plaintiff brings this action against the County, demanding that it be paid for loading and hauling done for the County by others, and that such payment be on the basis of the plaintiff's bid which had been accepted by the defendant. The trial court dismissed the plaintiff's complaint and the plaintiff has appealed to this court.

The only issue to be determined on this appeal is whether the parties had entered into a contract which would support an action by the plaintiff for its breach. The call for bids requested that bids be submitted for loading and hauling gravel to be delivered on highways or in stockpiles. Such call for bids did not mention any amount of gravel to be loaded, hauled, and delivered, and did not bind the County to have a single yard delivered. The bid submitted by the plaintiff to haul and stockpile for the figures set forth therein did not require the plaintiff to haul any amount of gravel. The call for bids furthermore did not fix a period of time within which the loading and hauling was to be done.

The courts do not favor the destruction of contracts because of uncertainty, but will, if feasible, construe agreements so as to carry into effect the reasonable intention of the parties, if that can be determined.

To be valid and enforceable, however, a contract must be resonably definite and certain in its terms so that a court may require it to be performed. It must spell out the obligations of each of the parties with reasonable definiteness. Indefiniteness as to any essential element of the agreement may prevent the creation of an enforceable contract. Thus contracts must be definite enough to enable a court to ascertain just what is required of the respective parties in the performance thereof. Courts will not uphold agreements which are indefinite and uncertain as to the obligations imposed upon the parties thereto.

Where an agreement is so uncertain and incomplete as to any of its essential terms that it cannot be carried into effect without new and additional stipulations between the parties, it will be held to be invalid.

An agreement which contains no definite provisions as to its duration may be unenforceable as being too indefinite. Thus it has been held that a contract to mine ore at a certain pit, "as long as we can make it pay," is too indefinite to allow prospective profits in case the work is stopped by the other party to the contract. Therefore, where one party to a contract retains the right to determine the extent of his performance, his promise has been held to be too indefinite for reasonable enforcement.

Let us now examine the alleged contract in this case to determine whether it is enforceable. The defendant's call for bids did not mention what amount of gravel, if any, was to be hauled for it, so the defendant was not obligated to have any amount of gravel hauled and delivered. On examination of the plaintiff's bid submitted in response to such call for bids, we find that the plaintiff did not bind itself to haul a specific amount of gravel. All that can be said is that the plaintiff offered to load and haul any gravel which the defendant might request it to haul for the consideration set forth in the bid. The defendant, however, did not request the plain-tiff to haul any gravel, and the plaintiff did not haul a single yard of gravel. Therefore there has been no performance under the contract.

Where the County advertised for bids to haul gravel for county roads without agreeing that it would have any gravel hauled, and where the plaintiff submitted its bid to haul gravel for county road purposes without agreeing that it would haul all or any definite amount of the gravel which defendant needed hauled during any stated period of time, and the plaintiff was advised that its bid had been "accepted," but the County did not agree to have any gravel hauled, and where the defendant thereafter did not request the plaintiff to haul any gravel, and the plaintiff fails to show that it has done anything in performance of its bid, no contract was entered into by the parties which the courts will attempt to enforce. A contract is a promise or set of promises, for the breach of which the law gives a remedy, or the performance of which the law recognizes as a duty. In this case, neither party made any promise, for the breach of which the law will give a remedy.

For reasons stated in this opinion, the judgment of the trial court dismissing the plaintiff's complaint is affirmed.

CASE REVIEW QUESTIONS

1. What promise did Mag Construction argue had been made by McLean County? Do you think the parties believed they had a contract?
2. Did the court agree with McLean County that the terms of their agreement with Mag Construction were not certain and definite enough to enforce? Why?
3. If Mag Construction had failed to haul and load as it had promised and McLean County had brought a legal action for breach of contract, who would have won the case? Explain.

REVIEW QUESTIONS

1. Does a person actually have to make a promise in order to be held liable for breach of contract? Explain.

2. Give an example of an agreement that people would ordinarily expect not to be legally binding until put in writing. Give an example of an agree-

ment that people would ordinarily expect to be legally binding even though not yet put in writing.

3. How does the modern view concerning omitted and vague terms in contracts differ from the traditional view? Why has the modern view been adopted?

CASE PROBLEMS

1. Richards wrote Flowers on January 15, "We would be interested in buying your lot on Gravatt Drive, Oakland, California, if we can deal with you directly and not through a realtor. If you are interested, please advise us by return mail of the cash price you would expect to receive." On January 19, Flowers responded, "Thank you for your inquiry regarding my lot on Gravatt Drive. As long as your offer would be in cash, I see no reason why we could not deal directly on this matter. Considering what I paid for the lot and the taxes that I have paid, I expect to receive $4500 for this property. Please let me know what you decide." On January 25, Richards telegrammed Flowers, "Have agreed to buy your lot on your terms." When Flowers later refused to convey the property to Richards, Richards sued Flowers for breach of contract. Did the parties have a contract? Explain.

2. Embry worked for McKittrick under a written contract which expired on December 15. Prior to the expiration of the contract, Embry tried to reach an understanding with McKittrick concerning his employment for another year but was put off. On December 23, Embry visited McKittrick's office and said that he had received an offer from another company and that if McKittrick wished to retain his services any longer he would immediately have to have a contract for another year. Otherwise, he would quit right then. McKittrick said to Embry, "Go ahead, you're all right. Get our orders out and don't let things worry you." Embry continued on the job until February 15. On that day, he was notified that he was fired. If Embry sues McKittrick for breach of contract, how might McKittrick defend himself? Who will win? Explain.

3. Grissim was in the livestock business. When he was first starting his business, he received a great deal of aid and advice from Murray, and the two became lifelong friends. When Murray became ill, Grissim ran his farm for him and never asked for payment. When Murray died, his son inherited the farm. The son requested that Grissim continue to manage the farm, and Grissim said he would. This arrangement continued for ten years. When the son sold the farm, Grissim requested payment for his services. The son refused to pay. If Grissim sues the son, on what basis might the son defend? Who will win the case? Explain.

4. On April 6, the Great Minneapolis Surplus Store advertised in the newspaper:

> Saturday 9 A.M. Sharp
> 3 Brand New Fur Coats
> Worth up to $100.00
> $1.00 Each
> First Come, First Served

Lefkowitz was the first person in the store on the designated morning, ready and able to buy one of the advertised coats. The store, however, refused to sell a fur coat to Lefkowitz for a dollar. If Lefkowitz sues the store for breach of contract, how might the store defend? Who will win the case? Explain.

5. Armstrong became disgusted with his valuable horse after a long ride because it seemed jaded and lame. He offered to sell the horse to a number of people around the stable for $5.00. McGhee agreed, and Armstrong said he would deliver the horse to McGhee the next day. The next day, however, Armstrong visited McGhee and said

that he had been joking and would not deliver the horse. If McGhee sues Armstrong for breach of contract, who will win? Explain.

6. Susan Woods lived at the Hotel Alms. John Woods, her adult son, lived about a mile away. John visited his mother regularly and helped her in managing her securities portfolio. John did not ask for payment and was never paid, but Mrs. Woods told John on a number of occasions that he would be paid. She also told several of her friends that her son was taking care of her business and that he would be paid for his services. After his mother's death, John filed a claim with her estate for services rendered on her behalf, arguing that he had a contract with his mother. The estate defended against the claim on the basis that Susan Woods had not intended to be legally bound by her promise to John. Who will win? Explain.

7. Rivers sued the Beadles for breach of contract. She put into evidence their agreement, which read as follows:

> In consideration of Vera Rivers Realty handling our purchase of 3 lots located at Center Avenue, San Rafael, without brokerage, we hereby agree as follows:
> 1. To build on each lot a house, which is to be placed on the market for sale immediately upon completion.
> 2. To give Vera Rivers Realty the exclusive right to sell the houses and pay 8 percent commission on selling price, this right to continue for one year from date of completion on each house.

The Beadles sold the lots without having built any houses on them. Rivers presented evidence indicating that homes near the three lots generally sold for $50,000. The Beadles argued that the agreement was too indefinite for the court to enforce. Who will win the case? Explain.

8. Atlas Moving & Storage Warehouse, Inc., entered into a contract with Truly Nolen, Inc. The agreement, entitled "Lease for Rental of Building Space for Advertising Purposes," applied to the top half of the front of the Atlas Moving & Storage Warehouse Building. It provided that,

> The lessor [Atlas] shall pay for the cost of painting an appropriate sign and shall illuminate the wall area from 7 P.M. to midnight every evening.
> The lessor agrees to maintain the sign in first class condition at all times.

Other terms of the contract included the rent to be paid by Nolen and the start and end dates of the lease. The day after the agreement was signed, Atlas informed Nolen that it would not honor the agreement. If Nolen sues Atlas for breach of contract, how might Atlas defend? Who will win? Explain.

9. Peterson was general manager of Pilgrim Village, Inc. He was in charge of the construction and sale of houses in Pilgrim Village Plot, a tract developed by the company. On several occasions over a ten-year period, Gifford, an officer of the corporation, told Peterson that he would receive a share of the corporation's profits from the sale of the houses in addition to his monthly salary. Pilgrim Village recently fired Peterson and refused his demand for a share of the profits made by the company during the perod of his employment. If Peterson sues Pilgrim Village, on what basis might the company defend? Who will win? Explain.

10. The proprietors and vendors of a medical preparation called the Carbolic Smoke Ball inserted the following advertisement in the Pall Mall Gazette of November 13, 1891, and in other newspapers:

> £100 reward will be paid by the Carbolic Smoke Ball Company to any person who contracts the increasingly epidemic influenza, colds, or any disease caused by taking cold, after having used the ball three times daily for two weeks according to the printed directions supplied with each ball. £100 is deposited with the Alliance Bank, Regent Street, showing our sincerity in the matter.
> One Carbolic Smoke Ball will last a family several months, making it the cheapest

remedy in the world at the price—10s., post free. The ball can be refilled at a cost of 5s. Address—Carbolic Smoke Ball Company, 27 Princess Street, Hanover Square, London.

Carlill, on the faith of the advertisement, bought one of the balls and used it as directed three times a day from November 20, 1891, to January 17, 1892, when she came down with influenza. When the company refused to pay the £100, she brought suit for breach of contract. What arguments do you think the company made in its defense? Who do you think won the case? Explain.

10

THE BARGAINING PROCESS: ACCEPTANCE

If a contract offer is made, an **acceptance** of the offer will result in the creation of a contract between the parties. Before a court will determine that an offeree has accepted an offer, four things must be true:

1. The offeror's demand must be met.
2. The offeree must have intended to accept the offer.
3. The offeree must have accepted by a proper means.
4. The offer must still be in existence when accepted.

The material in this chapter considers these four requirements.

WAS THE OFFEROR'S DEMAND MET?

An offer, as explained in the previous chapter, is a promise that is conditional upon receiving that which is demanded in return. An acceptance occurs when the offeror's demand is met. Contract law has traditionally maintained that the offeror is the master of the offer and that a response to the offer by the offeree is an acceptance only if it precisely fulfills the terms of the offer. Under this rule, if the offeree's response to the offer varies in any material (important) way from the demand contained in the offer, no contract results.

Unilateral and Bilateral Contracts

An offer that demands a promise in return is called an offer to enter into a **bilateral contract**. An offer that demands something other than a promise (usually an act) in return is called an offer to enter into a **unilateral contract**.

Often, however, it is difficult to tell whether an offer demands a promise or an act. People don't usually say, "I promise to deliver 10,000 widgets to you if you promise to pay me $10,000." Instead, they are apt to say something like, "I'll sell you 10,000 widgets for $10,000." In the latter statement, is it an act or a promise that is being demanded in return for the offeror's promise to sell?

You are likely to be tempted to say that it is an act that is being demanded in return—the act of paying $10,000. The law, however, says that it is a promise that is being demanded in return—a promise to pay $10,000. This is so because the law presumes that unless an offeror makes it very clear that he or she is demanding an act, the offeror is demanding a promise in return for his or her promise in the offer.

The reason the law makes this presumption makes very good sense. If an offeror demands an act in return for his or her promise, no contract will be formed between the parties until the act is actually performed. For instance, using the earlier widget example, no contract would be formed until the offeree actually paid the $10,000. In the meantime, neither party would be legally bound to perform the contract, meaning that either party could back out at any time prior to the payment of the $10,000.

It is clear that in most cases this is not what contracting parties want. Instead, they want to exchange promises and thus legally bind each other. Then each party can rely on the fact that the other party will either perform his or her promise or will have to pay damages for failing to perform his or her promise. The law therefore presumes that the offeror in the widget example is demanding a promise to pay $10,000 for the widgets in return for the promise to sell them. As soon as the buyer makes such a promise, a contract is formed between the buyer and seller.

Demand for Immediate Shipment

Suppose a buyer makes an offer to buy goods from a seller and asks that the goods be shipped immediately. How should the seller accept such an offer—by promising to ship the goods or by shipping the goods? In the previous section it was stated that the law presumes that an offer demands a promise in return. Wouldn't it be natural, however, for the seller not to bother with the promise and to ship the goods immediately instead? But if the presumption is applied and the offer demands a promise to ship rather than the act of shipping, immediate shipment would not constitute an acceptance. The buyer thus could change his or her mind and reject the goods when they are delivered because no contract has been formed between the parties.

Such a result is not in harmony with usual commercial needs and understandings. Both the Uniform Commercial Code and the courts have attempted to bring commercial law more into line with the intentions of people engaged in such a transaction. Today, therefore, an order asking for prompt shipment of goods can be accepted by either a prompt promise to ship the goods or by actual prompt shipment of the goods.

Additional or Different Terms

One application of the traditional rule that an offeree's response to an offer is an acceptance only if it precisely fulfills the terms of the offer in all material matters has been in cases in which the offeree's response contains terms additional to or different from those offered. In such cases, the courts have traditionally held that no contract is created. This result, however, has often proved detrimental to the consummation of commerical transactions under contemporary conditions. Today, business is frequently transacted by companies through the mails on printed forms. Under the traditional rule, if the form used by the offeree varies in any material way from that used by the offeror, as would be expected, the offeree has not accepted the offer and no contract is formed.

In order to bring the law into greater conformity with commercial understandings, Uniform Commercial Code §2-207 now provides that, unless the offeree expressly makes the acceptance conditional on assent by the offeror to additional or different terms, a definite expression of acceptance of an offer constitutes an acceptance even though it contains such terms. Between merchants, the new terms become a part of the contract, unless (a) the offer expressly limited acceptance to the terms of the offer, (b) the new terms materially alter the offer, or (c) the offeror objects to the new terms within a reasonable time. If a nonmerchant is a party to the transaction, the new terms are merely proposals for additions to the contract and are without effect unless assented to by the offeror.

The practical impact of the UCC provision is that if an offeree expressly states that he or she wishes to accept an offer, there is an acceptance even though it also states additional or different terms, and the additional or different terms generally *do not* become a part of the contract. The only situation in which the new or different terms do become a part of the contract is when the contract is one between *merchants* (i.e., dealers or experts in the subject matter of the contract) and the offeror does not object to the additional or different terms prior to or after receiving them and they do not materially change the offer. In this very narrow situation, it is presumed that the offeror has no objection to the additional or different terms.

In the following case, the court had to decide whether there had been an acceptance by the defendants and, if so, whether the additional terms proposed by the defendants became a part of the contract. Note also that the court had to deal with the fact that the defendants' acceptance was not precisely in accordance with the method of acceptance suggested by the offeror.

McAFEE v. BREWER
203 S.E.2d 129 (Va. 1974)

PANDON, Justice

Don D. McAfee, plaintiff, instituted this action against the defendants, Jack R. Brewer and his wife, Virginia Brewer, to recover the balance due on an alleged contract between the parties for the sale of certain furniture. The case was tried without a jury, and the trial judge held for the defendants on the ground that they had not accepted plaintiff's offer to sell since there was no "meeting of the minds" of the parties on the exact furniture items to be purchased. [Plaintiff appealed.]

Plaintiff contends that the trial court erred in not holding that his offer to sell was accepted by the defendants, and in denying him recovery on the contract.

The evidence shows that plaintiff and another were co-owners of the Dower House in McLean, Virginia, which the defendants had contracted to buy. Several weeks prior to the May 7, 1971, settlement date for purchase of the property, the defendants began negotiations with the plaintiff for the purchase of certain items of furniture in the house.

On April 30, 1971, plaintiff sent the defendants a letter containing the following: a list of furnishings to be purchased by defendants at specified prices, a payment schedule of $3,000 due upon acceptance, $3,000 due 60 days after the acceptance date, and $2,635 due 120 days after the acceptance date, a blank space for the defendants' signatures and the date the signatures were affixed, and a clause reading, "if the above is satisfactory please sign and return one copy with the first payment."

The delivery of the furniture was to be accomplished by leaving the items in the house; in fact, the items remained in the house after the settlement date.

On June 3, 1971, the defendants sent the following letter to plaintiff:

Exams were horrible but Florida was great! Enclosing a $3,000 ck. — I've misplaced the contracts. Can the secretary send another set? We're moving into Dower House on June 12 — please include the red secretary on the contract for the entrance foyer. I'll have to stop by some time during the month & order a coffee table.

Hope all is well —

Sincerely —
/s/Va. & Jack

Plaintiff, in turn, sent the defendants a letter dated June 8, 1971, in which he enumerated the various items of furniture purchased by them. Except for several additionally approved items, the list on the June 8th letter corresponded precisely with the list in the April 30th letter. Believing he had a contract with the Brewers to sell them the listed items of furniture, the plaintiff purchased new furniture to furnish his new home.

The defendants moved into Dower House around the middle of June 1971. Shortly thereafter the defendants made a number of telephone calls to plaintiff's office in an attempt to advise him that there had been a misunderstanding relating to their purchase of the listed items. Their calls were not returned. After unsuccessful efforts to settle the matter, the defendants refused to send plaintiff any more money, and this action was instituted.

Defendants testified that no argreement ever existed on what furniture was to be purchased. Defendant Jack R. Brewer further testified that he sent the $3,000 check only to buy several of the listed items, which totalled approximately $2,600, not to accept plaintiff's offer comprising all of the items listed. Brewer said he was not concerned about the overpayment because plaintiff was a friend, and he desired to buy some additional items from him.

It is elementary that an agreement based on mutual assent is essential to a valid contract.

The Uniform Commercial Code is applicable here since the alleged contract is for the sale of "goods."

Code §2-207 of the UCC provides, in pertinent part:

A definite and seasonable expression of acceptance or a written confirmation which is sent within a reasonable time operates as an acceptance even though it states terms additional to or different from those offered or agreed upon, unless acceptance is expressly made conditional on assent to the additional or different terms.

Here the defendants' letter of June 3rd constituted a definite and seasonable acceptance or written confirmation sent within a reasonable time after receipt of plaintiff's offer to sell. The enclosure of the $3,000 check, the amount due upon acceptance of the contract, and the request to "include the red secretary on the contract" manifested defendants' assent of confirmation of the specific items enumerated in the April 30th letter. The reference to the red secretary was not expressed in language making acceptance conditional upon inclusion of the secretary. This item was merely a proposal for an addition to the contract.

While it is true that defendants did not sign and return one copy of the contract in the manner requested by plaintiff, their acceptance of the offer by letter was reasonable under the circumstances because they had misplaced the contract and the copy thereof. Moreover, there was no indication by the plaintiff that if the offer was not accepted in the suggested manner it would not be acceptable to him. Section 2-206 of the UCC rejects the technical rules of acceptance in providing that "an offer . . . shall be construed as inviting acceptance in any manner and by any medium reasonable in the circumstances."

For the reasons stated, the judgment of the court below is reversed and final judgment in the amount of $5,635 is hereby entered for plaintiff.

CASE REVIEW QUESTIONS

1. Why specifically did the court decide that Brewer had accepted McAfee's offer?
2. Why do you think the trial court decided that Brewer had not accepted McAfee's offer?
3. Did the additional term in Brewer's acceptance become a part of the contract? Explain.

DID THE OFFEREE INTEND TO ACCEPT?

For an acceptance to be legally effective it must be made with the intent to be legally bound. As we previously saw was true of the offer, an objective standard is used in determining intent to be bound. This means that if the offeree communicates to the offeror an appearance that a reasonable person could justifiably believe to be an acceptance, the courts will treat the appearance as an acceptance regardless of the actual (subjective) intent of the offeree. Such an appearance can be created by words, conduct, or, under some circumstances, silence. Acceptances made in words are called express acceptances. If an acceptance is made by conduct or silence, it is said to be implied in fact.

Acceptance by Silence

Suppose a seller sends an unsolicited offer to a buyer that includes the statement, "Unless I hear from you by May 1, I will assume that you have accepted my offer." In this situation, the courts have held that it is unfair for the seller to impose a duty to reply on the buyer; therefore, if the buyer does not intend to accept, the silence does not constitute an acceptance. Under these circumstances, in other words, the seller cannot justifiably believe that the buyer's silence is an acceptance. On the other hand, if the buyer intends for the silence to indicate acceptance, it will operate as an acceptance and a contract will be formed.

Under what circumstances may silence create the justifiable belief in a reasonable person that an acceptance is intended? One situation is when the offeree expressly states that silence will constitute acceptance. A statement by the offeree such as, "Unless you hear from me by May 1, you may assume that I have accepted your offer," would create such a situation, and silence by the offeree until after May 1 would be treated as an acceptance.

Similarly, a custom of doing business between parties may create a situation in which silence constitutes acceptance. If, for example, the buyer has often in the past accepted and paid for unrequested goods sent by the seller, the retention of goods may be determined to be an acceptance under the objective standard.

Still another possible case of acceptance by silence occurs when a person receives services that one would reasonably believe are provided by the offeror with the expectation of compensation. If there is a reasonable opportunity to reject the services, but they are silently accepted instead, the acceptance of the services will be treated as an acceptance of the offer, and the person receiving the services will be legally bound to pay for them.

What if a person receives unsolicited goods, rather than services, under circumstances that imply payment is desired, and the person remains silent? Traditionally, the courts have decided that acceptance occurs only if the receiver "exercises dominion" over the goods. This means that if the goods are put aside and simply held for the sender, no acceptance occurs; however, if the goods are used in a way that indicates that the receiver is exercising ownership rights over them, an acceptance does occur.

More recently, certain states and the federal government have adopted statutes intended to discourage the sending of unsolicited goods. These statutes provide that unsolicited goods may be kept and used without such actions constituting an acceptance. In other words, the receiver may treat the unsolicited goods as a gift.

DID THE OFFEREE ACCEPT BY A PROPER MEANS?

As part of an offer, an offeror can state that a particular means of acceptance is to be used by the offeree. If the offer stipulates that only one means of acceptance may be used, that exclusive means must be used in order for the acceptance to be effective. For instance, if the offer explicitly requires that the acceptance be made by mail, no other means of communication will serve as an acceptance no matter how clear the intent of the offeree to accept may be.

If the offer merely suggests, but does not require, a particular means of acceptance, the offeree may use the suggested means or any other means that is reasonable under the circumstances. If no means of acceptance is referred to in the offer, any means that is reasonable under the circumstances will suffice.

In the two cases that follow, the defendants, who are being sued for breach of contract, argue that no contract exists because the respective plaintiffs failed to accept the defendants' offers by proper means. In the first case, the court agrees with the defendant because the plaintiff failed to meet the terms of the offer. In the second case, the court applies the objective standard and decides that the plaintiff did accept the defendant's offer.

GOLDEN DIPT COMPANY v. SYSTEMS ENGINEERING AND MANUFACTURING COMPANY
465 F.2d 215 (7th Cir. 1972)

SWYGERT, Chief Judge

[Systems Engineering and Manufacturing Company (SEMCO) submitted a proposal to Golden Dipt Company to construct a pneumatic bulk flour handling system. The proposal included a statement of terms which required a twenty-five percent first payment to be submitted with the order. It also provided that, "This Proposal, when approved by the Purchaser and submitted to and accepted by the Company, expresses the entire agreement of the parties."]

On August 22, 1968, Viviano [president of Golden Dipt] conversed by telephone with Dennis W. Warneke, Marketing Manager of SEMCO. At that time, Viviano said that his New York headquarters had approved SEMCO's proposal, that SEMCO should "start on it immediately" and that the paperwork would follow. Warneke "expressed his appreciation" and said that "they would start on it immediately."

Warneke then submitted a copy of the proposal to SEMCO's accounting department. On September 3, 1968, the accounting department notified him that there was a mathematical error in the computations and that the total price should be increased approximately $30,000. Warneke telephoned Viviano on the same day and told him that the price would have to be adjusted upward. Viviano told Warneke that he regarded the proposal at the previous price as having been made a firm contract, and Warneke stated that SEMCO would not perform without the additional charge. Viviano stated that on September 3, 1968, he caused a check in the amount of $45,000 to be drawn to the order of SEMCO and executed and dated the proposal on behalf of Golden Dipt. However, he never transmitted the check or the signed proposal to SEMCO. Warneke confirmed the price change upward in the amount of $31,795 by letter dated September 4, 1968.

Upon SEMCO's refusal to perform at the original price of $198,654, Golden Dipt let the contract on September 6 to a theretofore unsuccessful bidder at a cost of $215,534.43, and this lawsuit followed. The sole question raised by this appeal is whether a contract ever came into existence between the parties. We hold that no contract was created.

Unquestionably, the proposal submitted by the defendant was an offer to contract. We thus turn to the crucial question of whether the offer was validly accepted by the plaintiff. It is clear that an offeror may, by the terms of his offer, restrict the mode of acceptance. As Professor Corbin stated the principle:

> The offeror creates the power of acceptance, and he has full control over the character and extent of the power that he creates. He can prescribe a single and exclusive mode of acceptance. It makes no difference how unreasonable or difficult the prescribed mode may be, if the offeror clearly expresses, in the terms of the communicated offer itself, his intention to exclude all other modes of acceptance.

Illinois case law [applicable in this case] adheres fully to the foregoing principles.

We believe that the language of the proposal clearly establishes the requirement by defendant of an exclusive mode by which plaintiff could accept the offer. That mode was expressly stated in the requirement that a twenty-five percent down payment accompany the placement of an order and the statements under the title "Acceptance" which provided: *"This Proposal, when approved by the Purchaser and submitted and accepted by the Company,* expresses the entire agreement between the parties." Those provisions undoubtedly require that acceptance be in the form of the delivery of a copy of the proposal signed by the plaintiff's authorized agent together with a down payment of twenty-five percent of the purchase price.

It is also clear from the facts described above that plaintiff never accepted the offer, for neither the signed copy of the proposal nor the twenty-five percent down payment was ever delivered to the defendant. Plaintiff argues that the exclusive mode of acceptance, should we determine there was one, was met because Viviano signed the proposal and drew a check for $45,000 prior to notification of the change by Warneke. Even if the drawing of a check in the amount of twenty-five percent down payment and the signing of the proposal by Viviano would constitute acceptance without delivery of the documents to defendant, it is clear that plaintiff did not comply with the prescribed mode of acceptance in any event. That is so because the proposal's requirement of a down payment of twenty-five percent of the proposal price was not met—twenty-five per-

cent of the original price of $198,564 would have been $49,641, not $45,000 which is the amount for which Viviano had the purported down payment drawn.

We conclude, therefore, as did the district court, that the offer stated an exlcusive mode by which it could be accepted, that the plaintiff did not accept the offer in the exclusive manner it authorized, and that, consequently, no contract was ever formed between the parties.

The judgment of the district court is affirmed.

FUJIMOTO v. RIO GRANDE PICKLE COMPANY
414 F.2d 648 (5th Cir. 1969)

BOLDBERG, Circuit Judge

This appeal involves claims by George Fujimoto and Jose Bravo against the Rio Grande Pickle Company upon written contracts of employment. The questions before us are of contract formation and construction.

Rio Grande Pickle Company, a Colorado corporation engaged in the business of raising and selling cucumbers for the pickling industry, hired Fujimoto in the Spring of 1965 and Bravo in the following Fall. Both of these employees were given important jobs. Fujimoto was employed as the supervisor of planting and growing operations, while Bravo functioned as the labor recruiter.

In order to encourage them to work with zeal and not to leave the company's employ, Rio Grande offered contracts with profit sharing bonus provisions to both Fujimoto and Bravo. Prior to the offer of the written contracts, the company had responded to the offerees' demands for more compensation by orally agreeing to pay them a salary plus a bonus of ten percent of the company's annual profits. Bravo told the president of Rio Grande that he wanted the agreement in writing, and the president replied, "I will prepare one and send you a contract in writing." The contractual documents sent to Fujimoto and Bravo did not specify how the acceptances should be communicated to the

company. Under these circumstances Fujimoto and Bravo signed their respective contracts but did not return them to the company. Believing that they had accepted the company's offers and that they were working under the proffered bonus contracts, the two employees remained in the employ of Rio Grande until November 30, 1966.

The written contracts called for the employees to devote their best efforts to Rio Grande and promised in return that the company would pay each offeree a bonus amounting to ten percent of the company's net profits for each fiscal year. Each employee was to agree to return half of his bonus to the company as an investment in company stock.

Partly as a consequence of projected changes in the nature of the corporation's business, Fujimoto and Bravo quit their jobs with Rio Grande on November 30, 1966. Shortly thereafter the company ceased doing business in Texas. Fujimoto and Bravo then brought this suit, claiming that they had accepted the offered contracts and that they had not received the ten percent of the company's net profits for the fiscal year ending September 30, 1966, and ten percent of the profits of the subsequent two months, October and November, 1966.

[T]he jury found that Fujimoto and Bravo each had entered into a written contract in October, 1965. It was then determined that Fujimoto and Bravo should each recover the sum of $8,964.25 as damages for the company's breach of contract.

On appeal Rio Grande argues that there is insufficient evidence in the record to support the jury's finding that Fujimoto and Bravo had accepted the offered bonus contract. . . .

Rio Grande argues that there were no contracts because Fujimoto and Bravo did not accept the written bonus offers by signing and returning the written instruments to the company. Each contract was signed by the respective employee, but neither was returned. Thus the first issue is whether the offers, which by their terms did not specify the means by which they could be accepted, could be accepted by a mode other than the return of the signed instruments.

Neither written offer specified a particular mode of acceptance, and there is no evidence that Rio Grande ever manifested any intent that the offers could be accepted only by the return of the signed instruments. Moreover, there is substantial and convincing evidence to the contrary. The record is replete with evidence that the company conditioned the bonus offers primarily upon the offerees remaining in the company's employment and that the employees understood that they did not have to return the signed contracts in order to have contracts under which they would each get a ten percent bonus.

Since we have found that the return of the signed documents was not the exclusive means by which the offerees could convey their acceptances, we must now determine whether Fujimoto and Bravo in fact adequately communicated such acceptances to the company. Where, as here, the offer and surrounding circumstances are silent as to permissible modes of acceptance, the law requires only that there be some clear and unmistakable expression of the offeree's intention to accept.

In the case at bar there is substantial evidence to support the jury's finding that the company knew that the offerees had agreed to the terms of the proffered bonus contracts. Of particular importance is the fact that Fujimoto and Bravo, who had threatened to quit unless their remuneration was substantially increased, continued to work for the company for fourteen months after receiving the offers. Moreover, during this fourteen-month period they did not again express dissatisfaction with their compensation. There is also evidence that Fujimoto and Bravo discussed the bonus contracts with the company president in such circumstances and in such a manner that their assent and acceptance should have been unmistakable to him. In view of these circumstances, Rio Grande could not have been besieged with any Hamlet-like doubts regarding the existence of a contract. Since Rio Grande knew that Fujimoto and Bravo had accepted its offer, there was a valid and binding contract.

Affirmed.

CASE REVIEW QUESTIONS
1. Why specifically did the court decide that SEMCO's offer had not been accepted by Golden?
2. Suppose Golden had argued that its telephone call was an offer that had been accepted by SEMCO. How should SEMCO respond to such an argument?
3. Why specifically did the court decide that Rio Grande's offer had been accepted by Fujimoto and Bravo?
4. Which of the circumstances discussed in the section of the text "Acceptance by Silence" is present in the *Fujimoto* case?

WAS THE OFFER STILL IN EXISTENCE WHEN ACCEPTED?

To be effective, acceptance must be made before the offer is terminated. Termination of an offer can occur in a number of ways, each of which is discussed below. Notice that sometimes termination occurs because of the will of or action taken by the parties while in other situations it occurs by operation of law, regardless of the will of the parties.

Termination by Lapse of Time

If an offer provides that it must be accepted within a certain period of time, failure to accept within the designated period results in termination of the offer. Even if a time for termination is not stated in the offer, the law provides that acceptance must occur within a reasonable length of time.

What constitutes a reasonable length of time is a judgment that must be made in light of all the circumstances of a particular case. The means used to communicate the offer may suggest what period of time for acceptance is reasonable. For example, telegraphic offers are generally interpreted as requiring the offeree to accept during the business day on which the telegram is received.

The stability of the market for the type of goods being traded may also be an important consideration. The more frequently prices change, the less time the offeree has to accept. This prevents the offeree from delaying acceptance until after market trends can be determined.

Termination by Rejection or Counter-offer

Generally, a **rejection** of an offer or the making of a counter-offer by an offeree terminates the original offer. A **counter-offer** is an offer made by an offeree to the offeror that deals with the same subject matter as the original offer, but demands new terms.

A counter-offer is not made if the offeree simply *suggests* different terms, but doesn't indicate rejection of the original offer. Similarly, any *comment* on the terms of the original offer that does not imply rejection is not a counter-offer.

For example, if the seller offers to sell goods to the buyer for $100, the buyer's statement, "I'll take them for $90," would be a counter-offer. The statements, "Would you sell them for $90?" or "I accept, but they're only worth $90," by the buyer would not constitute counter-offers. The former statement is merely a request for a modification of the original offer with no rejection implied, whereas the latter is sometimes referred to as a "grumbling acceptance."

Termination by Revocation

Revocation of an offer occurs through action taken by the offeror. Any action that would indicate to a reasonable person in the position of the offeree that the offeror no longer intends to be legally bound by the promise(s) contained in the offer is a revocation. For example, revocation would occur if the offeror expressly told the offeree that the offer was withdrawn or if the offeree learned that the subject matter of the offer had been sold to someone else.

Are All Offers Revocable? Not all offers can be revoked by the offeror. For instance, if the offeree pays to have the offer kept open, it becomes irrevocable. Such an arrangement is called an **option.**

The Uniform Commercial Code and statutes in some states provide that a *written* promise to hold an offer open will make it irrevocable even if no payment is made. The Code provision will be discussed in more detail in Chapter 20.

The courts of several states have held that an offer is also irrevocable if the offeror can reasonably expect that the offeree will rely on the offer and the offeree does in fact so rely. This technique of making an offer irrevocable is called promissory estoppel and will be discussed further in Chapter 12.

When May a Revocable Offer Be Revoked? A revocable offer to enter a *bilateral* contract may be revoked at any time before acceptance. It is necessary, therefore, to know when a revocation and an acceptance take effect.

A revocation is generally not effective until it is received by the offeree. An acceptance, however, generally takes effect when it is dispatched by the offeree, if it is communicated in a manner that is authorized by the offeror.

What constitutes an authorized means of communication of an acceptance is determined in a variety of ways. If the offeror does not expressly authorize a certain means of communication, it is implied that the means used to communicate the offer as well as any other means customary where and when the offer is received are authorized. The Uniform Commercial Code considers authorized means of communication to include any means that are reasonable under the circumstances.

If the offeree uses an unauthorized means of communicating the acceptance, it generally will not be effective until receipt by the offeror. If the offeror expressly *requires* a certain means of communication, however, the use of any other means will be totally ineffective and no contract will result.

How should attempted revocations of offers to enter into *unilateral* contracts be handled? If the rule discussed above is applied — revocation may occur any time before acceptance — the offeror could revoke the offer any time before performance is completed by the offeree since acceptance does not occur until then. This would be unfair, however, to an offeree who had almost completed the performance demanded by the offeror and at the last moment had the offer withdrawn. Therefore, the courts have held that once performance is begun by the offeree, the offer becomes irrevocable. If the offeree then completes performance within the time allowed by the offer, a contract is formed between the parties.

Termination by Death or Lack of Capacity of the Parties

After an offer is made, but prior to its acceptance, the death or legally certified incapacity of either the offeror or the offeree will serve to terminate the offer. This occurs whether or not the death or incapacity is known to the other party.

Termination by Death or Destruction of the Subject Matter

The death of a person or the destruction of a thing that is essential to the performance of the contract prior to acceptance terminates the offer. For example, if goods that are the subject of a contract are destroyed in a warehouse fire, there is no contract when a subsequent acceptance occurs.

Termination by Intervening Illegality

If performance of the contract becomes illegal prior to acceptance, the offer is terminated, whether or not the parties are aware of the intervening illegality.

Case Example of Termination

There are two issues in the following case. The first concerns whether the original offer made by the plaintiff was still in existence at the time the defendant tried to accept it or whether it had terminated by lapse of time. The second issue illustrates that if an offer terminates prior to acceptance, an attempted acceptance of the terminated offer will itself be an offer that can be accepted by the original offeror.

TEXTRON, INC. v. FROELICH
302 A.2d 426 (Pa. 1973)

[Textron, Inc., brought a lawsuit against Froelich. Froelich counterclaimed against Textron for breach of contract. After the presentation of evidence, Textron moved for a directed verdict on Froelich's counterclaim. The trial court granted the motion, deciding there was no contract. Froelich appealed.]

HOFFMAN, Judge

The existence of a contract in this case depends on (1) whether the oral offer here necessarily terminated at the end of a telephone conversation, or, (2) if it did, whether there was a counter-offer made and accepted.

The facts as set forth in the appellant's case are as follows. The appellee, a fabricator of steel and wire products, orally offered the appellant, a steel broker, a specified quantity of two different sizes of steel rods at specified prices. The appellant responded that he thought he wanted the rods but he wanted to check with his customers. Some five weeks later the appellant called the appellee and agreed to buy one size of rods and then two days later agreed to purchase the other size at the prices originally discussed. The appellee replied, ''Fine. Thank you.'' to both phone calls.

The trial judge based his decision on the rule set forth in *Boyd v. Merchants and Farmers Peanut Co.*, that an oral offer ordinarily terminates with the end of the conversation. The dictum in *Boyd,* however, does not preclude the possibility that in some cases an oral offer does continue past the conversation. The general rule is that:

1. The power to create a contract by acceptance of an offer terminates at the time specified in the offer, or, if no time is specified, at the end of a reasonable time.
2. What is a reasonable time is a question of fact, depending on *the nature of the contracts proposed, the usages of business and other circumstances of the case which the offeree at the time of his acceptance either knows or has reason to know.* [Emphasis added]

There may be times when a judge could find as a matter of law that an oral offer made in the course of a conversation terminates with the end of the conversation. If there is any doubt as to what is a reasonable interpretation, the decision should be left to the jury. In this case, the appellant has informed the appellee that he wanted time to contact some customers before accepting the offer, which was only natural for a steel broker. Under the circumstances, it is possible that a jury could have found that the oral offer continued beyond the end of the conversation.

We need not, however, decide this appeal on that issue. Even if the original offer by appellee had lapsed, a jury could find that the required elements to offer and acceptance were present in appellant's two subsequent telephone conversations with appellee and that a contract therefore existed. If appellee's original offer lapsed, appellant's telephone calls agreeing to purchase the specific size and quantity of rods they had previously discussed at a price also previously agreed upon, constituted new offers. Appellee's response, in-

cluding the statement, "Fine. Thank you.", indicated an acceptance of these offers. "Unless otherwise unambiguously indicated by the language or circumstances . . . an offer to make a contract shall be construed as inviting acceptance in any manner and by any medium reasonable in the circumstances. . . ." Here, appellee accepted in the same manner and medium and during the same conversation in which appellant's offers were made.

Viewing appellant's case in the light most favorable to him, there was sufficient evidence supporting his contractual counterclaim to go to the jury.

The order of the court below is reversed and the case remanded for a new trial.

CASE REVIEW QUESTIONS

1. What are the two reasons given by the court for their conclusion that the jury could find that a contract existed between Textron and Froelich?
2. Why specifically did the court believe that a jury could find that Textron's offer was still in existence when it was accepted by Froelich?

REVIEW QUESTIONS

1. What four things must be true for an acceptance to occur?
2. Under what circumstances may an offeree's silence result in an acceptance?
3. Describe the ways in which an offer can terminate.
4. What problem is created if an offeree says that he or she accepts an offer, but changes the terms of the offer by stating additional or different terms? How have the courts handled this problem?

CASE PROBLEMS

1. Hills, Inc., ordered 34 men's suits from a salesman of Kessler, Inc., using a printed form supplied by the salesman. The printed form provided that the order would not become a binding contract until it had been accepted by Kessler at its home office. A week later Kessler's home office advised Hills by a form letter that "you may be assured of our very best attention to this order." A month later, however, Kessler wrote Hills:

"This is to inform you that we find it will be impossible to ship the order that you placed. We dislike very much having to inform you of this, but we trust that you will understand when we say that because of previous commitments it is necessary to cancel your order." It was then too late for Hills to buy other suits for the fall season. Hills brought a legal action against Kessler for breach of contract. Kessler defended on the grounds that they had not accepted Hills' offer and, therefore, no contract existed. Who will win the case? Explain.

2. Roto-Lith, a merchant, offered to buy a drum of emulsion from F.P. Bartlett & Co., also a merchant. The offer said the emulsion must be warranted as not harmful to Roto-Lith's equipment. Bartlett sent a response to Roto-Lith stating that the offer was accepted and further providing that "All goods sold without warranties, express or implied." Roto-Lith did not object to the terms, accepted delivery of the goods and paid for them. When the emulsion proved defective and caused extensive damage to Roto-Lith's equipment, Roto-Lith brought an action for breach of warranty. Bartlett defended on the grounds that the exclusion of warranties contained in the acceptance became a term of their contract. Who will win the case? Explain.

3. The Commodity Credit Corporation invited bids for the purchase of off-condition raisins. Pearl Distilling Company telegraphed a bid on August 3: "Offer ten cents per pound for 9599 boxes of raisins located Cleveland, Ohio." Pearl's bid was the highest received by Commodity Credit and on August 9 they telegraphed Pearl: "CCC accepts your August 3 offer to purchase 9599 boxes raisins at 10 cents per box. Forward certified check in the amount of $2,138.92." When Pearl received the telegram it did nothing, and no check was sent to Commodity Credit Corporation. Ten days later, when the time for receipt of the check had expired, the Commodity Credit Corporation looked into the matter and discovered that their August 9 telegram had been in error. They then telegraphed Pearl: "August 9 contract covering sale of raisins should read ten cents per pound instead of 10 cents per box. Also, certified check should be in the amount of $25,176.52 instead of $2,138.92." Again Pearl did nothing and refused to take delivery of the raisins. Commodity Credit sold the raisins at a loss and brought a legal action against Pearl for breach of contract. Pearl defended on the grounds that their offer had not been accepted. Who will win the case? Explain.

4. Killebrew, a cotton grower, offered to sell his cotton crop to Hohenberg, a cotton buyer, pursuant to the terms of a one-page contract form that Killebrew had signed. Hohenberg then sent an acceptance to Killebrew on a three-page purchase contract form that Hohenberg had signed. The three-page form was longer than, but not materially different from , the one-page form. Later Killebrew refused to deliver the cotton to Hohenberg. If Hohenberg brings a legal action against Killebrew for breach of contract, on what grounds might Killebrew defend? Who will win the case? Explain.

5. Jones, an independent insurance agent, insured Prescott's building through the Manchester Fire Insurance Company. On December 4, Jones notified Prescott that he would renew the policy for a further term of one year from January 1, under the same terms and conditions as the previous year, unless notified to the contrary by Prescott. Prescott did not insure his building with anyone else because he assumed Jones would take care of the matter as he said he would. On January 5, Prescott's building was destroyed by fire. Jones, however, had failed to insure the building and the insurance company refused to pay for the damage. Prescott brought legal action against Jones for breach of contract. On what grounds may Jones defend? Who will win the case? Explain.

6. Martin entered into a contract to purchase real estate from Basham. When Basham refused to convey the property, Martin threatened to bring suit seeking specific performance of the contract. When the parties negotiated a possible settlement of the case on October 1, Martin offered to settle for $5,000, but Basham did not accept the offer. Trial was then held before a judge, who announced on October 16, following the presentation of evidence, that he was of the opinion that Martin was entitled to specific performance of the contract. Immediately following the judge's decision, Martin said he would still take $5,000 to settle the case. On October 29, Basham told Martin she would agree to pay the $5,000. When she mailed a check for that amount on November 16, Martin returned the check and said that he had

decided he wanted the house instead. Basham brought a legal action against Martin to enforce the settlement agreement. Martin defended on the grounds that Basham had not accepted the settlement offer before it terminated. Who will win the case? Explain.

7. Ina Ward applied to the Gallia County Board of Education for a teaching position. On June 4, the Board voted to offer her a teaching contract, and June 15 a contract was mailed to her for her signature. She received the contract on June 18. Miss Ward did not return the contract immediately and on July 2, unknown to Miss Ward, another teacher was hired to fill the position that had been offered to her. On July 5, Miss Ward signed and returned the contract to the Board of Education, but they refused to employ her. She brought legal action against the Board for breach of contract. The Board defended on the grounds that she had not accepted their offer before it terminated and, therefore, no contract existed. Who will win the case? Explain.

8. Langellier wrote to Shaefer: "I own lot 4, block 5, West St. Paul proper, and I understand you own lot 3, same block. I would ask what is your price for lot 3, and on what terms you will sell it. If you don't want to sell it, what will you give me for lot 4?" Shaefer replied by letter: "I am in need of money and will sell lot 3 for $800, cash. I don't want lot 4." Langellier then responded: "Your offer to sell me lot 3, block 5 is accepted, although I am afraid I am paying $100 to $200 too much for it. I should prefer to pay in installments if you would sell it that way; but if you prefer not, I will pay cash." When Shaefer refused to complete the transaction Langellier brought a legal action against Shaefer for breach of contract. Shaefer defended on the grounds that his offer had not been accepted. Who will win the case? Explain.

9. Thoelke owned property located in Orange County, Florida. On November 20, Morrison, who was in Florida, signed a contract to purchase the property and mailed it to Thoelke, who was in Texas. On November 27, Thoelke received the contract, immediately signed it and placed it in the mail addressed to Morrison. After Thoelke mailed the contract, but prior to its receipt by Morrison, Morrison telephoned Thoelke and said that he wished to cancel the contract. Thoelke refused, and when Morrison would not pay for the property, Thoelke sued for breach of contract. Who will win the case? Explain.

10. One evening Smith discovered a leak in the roof of his house. He called Firstrate Roofing Company, but because it was night he reached Firstrate's telephone answering service. The message he left said, "Bad leak in my roof at 419 Main Street, I hope you can do something about it." The next day Firstrate sent an employee over to fix the roof. No one was home, but the employee began to fix the roof anyway. When Smith came home and discovered the roofer, he told him to stop immediately because he had decided to fix the roof himself. Because the roofer was almost done with the job, however, he refused to stop and finished the work. Smith has received a bill from Firstrate for $350.00, which he refuses to pay. If Firstrate brings legal action against Smith for breach of contract, on what grounds might Smith defend? Who will win the case? Explain.

11

FAIRNESS IN THE BARGAINING PROCESS

Contract law is based on the premise that economically efficient exchange will take place if individuals and businesses are left free to make independent decisions in the marketplace. This assumes that contract promises will not be coerced and will be made on the basis of correct information. Exchanges in which one party is coerced or acts out of ignorance will not be efficient, and the economy will suffer as a result. On the other hand, it is important to encourage people to resist coercion and to seek out the truth actively. The legal topics of misrepresentation, fraud, duress, undue influence, unconscionability, and mistake, which are discussed in this chapter, indicate how the courts have handled such issues.

MISREPRESENTATION

If one person misrepresents an important fact to another and the second person relies on the misrepresentation in deciding to enter into a contract, an inefficient exchange will take place. The law, therefore, provides that in such cases the party who relies on the misrepresentation may elect to avoid (get out of) the contract.

Note that the contract is **voidable**. This means that it actually comes into existence, but one party may avoid it. To do so he or she must prove that:

1. There was a misrepresentation of fact.
2. The fact was material.
3. There was justifiable reliance on the misrepresentation.

Only if all three of these elements are proved will a court grant **rescission**, the remedy that allows a party to avoid a contract on the grounds of **misrepresentation**.

Misrepresentation of Fact

A misrepresentation is any false assertion by one party to another, regardless of whether there was any intent to deceive. Questions arise in this area of the law because the courts have not treated all false assertions as misrepresentations of fact. For instance, a distinction has been made between facts and opinions. Calling a product the best or finest of its kind is generally treated as just a seller's opinion, sometimes called **puffing**, rather than a misrepresentation, even if the product is not the best.

A prediction, not in the form of a promise, such as an assertion that the value of a product will double in a year, is also usually treated as an opinion, not a fact. Similarly, statements of value or representations of law are generally considered opinions rather than facts. In all these instances, however, opinions will be treated as facts if they are made by a person who is or claims to be an expert, or who has significantly better access to the true facts, or who is in a relationship with the deceived party that calls for special trust and confidence.

On the other hand, a statement that may sound like a mere opinion may actually constitute a misrepresentation of fact. Although statements, such as "I believe the machine is perfectly safe" or "I know the machine is perfectly safe," may appear only to express opinions about the safety of a machine, they are also assertions of fact concerning the state of mind or knowledge of the speaker. If the state of mind or knowledge is in fact different from what is asserted, that is, if the speaker in the above examples does not in fact believe or know that the machine is safe, then he or she has misrepresented the fact of his or her state of mind or knowledge.

Silence as Misrepresentation Another problem in this area arises when there has not been an actual misrepresentation, but instead a party to a transaction has been silent concerning an important fact. Suppose, for example, that a person is selling a house. What facts must the seller disclose to the buyer? Must he or she reveal that the house lies in a landing pattern to an airport, that the neighbors are noisy, or that the foundation is eroding, if the buyer doesn't ask about such matters?

As a general rule there is no duty to disclose any information to the other party to a transaction. The assumption is that each party will be diligent in asking questions and otherwise obtaining information concerning the important facts of the transaction. Under certain circumstances, however, a duty to speak will arise. For instance, if the undisclosed information is very important, if only one party has it, and if the other party does not have access to it and is not likely to inquire about it, a duty to provide the information is imposed.

Similarly, if a party takes affirmative action to conceal certain facts or to prevent the other party from discovering them, misrepresentation will be found. Also, failure to disclose information will be treated as a misrepresentation if a statute, such as the Federal Truth-in-Lending Act, requires its disclosure or when a relationship exists between the parties such that an expectation of full disclosure is justified.

Materiality of the Fact

A misrepresented fact is only material if it would be likely to affect the conduct of a reasonable person. In other words, would a reasonable person who knew the truth have entered into the contract under the same terms? If the misrepresented fact is significant enough that the answer is no, there is good reason not to enforce the contract because the misrepresentation was a contributing factor in entering the contract and the resulting exchange is economically inefficient.

Justifiable Reliance

A party to whom a material misrepresentation of fact has been made may only use the misrepresentation to avoid the contract if he or she has justifiably relied on it in deciding to enter the contract. If someone agrees to contract based on his or her own investigation and knowledge of the facts rather than on a misrepresentation of the facts by the other party, there has been no reliance, and the contract cannot be avoided.

How cautious must a person be in accepting the representations of people with whom they contract? To what extent must a contracting party make an independent investigation rather than rely on representations? Until early in this century, courts usually decided that justifiable reliance was not present if a person either knew or *should have known* that statements were false. Today, however, the courts generally protect those who rely on misrepresentations and don't know that statements are false even if they could have discovered the truth had they sought it out on their own.

FRAUD

To prove **fraud,** a person must show the existence of the three elements (discussed above) that make up misrepresentation, and, in addition, he or she must show that the misrepresentation of fact was intentional. Intent in these circumstances means that the person making the misrepresentation knew that his or her assertion was false and made it with the intention of deceiving the other party.

Intentional misrepresentation of the facts includes situations in which a person recklessly disregards the truth. For instance, if a used car seller says, "This car has had only one prior owner," when he or she doesn't know how many prior owners there have been and there have, in fact, been two or more prior owners, the seller's misrepresentation is intentional.

Remedies

If a party to a contract can prove the elements of misrepresentation, he or she may avoid the contract through an action for rescission. In such a situation, the court will attempt to return the parties to the position they would have been in had no contract been made. This means that both parties must return what they have received from the other. The transactions, made inefficient by the misrepresentation, is thus erased.

If a party to a contract can prove the elements of fraud, a more stringent remedy is available against the intentional misrepresenter. In this situation, the party who has been deceived is given the option to affirm the contract, rather than rescind it, and to collect damages in a tort action for any injury caused by the fraud. For instance, if a seller of land makes an intentional misrepresentation, the buyer may choose to keep the land and recover from the seller the difference between the amount paid and the actual value of the land. On the other hand, the buyer could choose to rescind the contract by simply proving the elements necessary to show misrepresentation.

Whether a party to a contract seeks to rescind the contract because of misrepresentation or to affirm it and seek damages because of fraud, the legal action must be begun within a reasonable length of time after the false assertion is discovered. This prevents the deceived party from gaining the advantage of waiting to see whether he or she has made a good deal before deciding to bring legal action. Unreasonable delay in bringing a claim is called **laches.**

Case Examples of Misrepresentation and Fraud

The two cases that follow raise several of the issues discussed in this section. In the first case, the court is concerned with whether silence by the defendant constituted a misrepresentation and, if it did, whether the misrepresentation was intentional. The second case deals with whether the plaintiff's reliance on a misrepresentation was justified and, if it were, whether the plaintiff's legal action was begun within a reasonable time after discovery of the misrepresentation.

ELIZAGA v. KAISER FOUNDATION HOSPITALS, INC.
487 P.2d 870 (Oregon 1971)

[In January 1969 Kaiser Foundation Hospitals, Inc. (Kaiser) hired Elizaga, a citizen of the Philippines, for a hospital position called a preceptorship starting July 1, 1969. At the time of the hiring, Kaiser's officials had good reason to believe that the program under which they hired Elizaga would be canceled by the Board of Medical Examiners of the State of Oregon as of June 30, 1969. They did not inform Elizaga of this, however. After Elizaga moved his family to the United States, Kaiser was officially notified that the program was canceled. Kaiser then notified Elizaga that he would not be hired. He eventually found a position as an intern at about half the salary he would have received from Kaiser.

Elizaga brought a legal action against Kaiser seeking damages for fraud. After the trial Kaiser moved for a directed verdict, but the court denied the motion. The trial court then awarded judgment to Elizaga. Kaiser appealed.]

DENECKE, Justice

Plaintiff brought this action alleging that defendant's offer of a preceptorship for July 1, 1969, constituted [fraud]. Defendant's principal assignment of error is that the trial court erred in denying its motion for a directed verdict. The first contention is that there was no evidence of a misrepresentation. It is recognized that nondisclosure of material facts can be a form of misrepresentation where the defendant has made representations which would be misleading without full disclosure.

Plaintiff made it clear in his correspondence that he was concerned about whether he would qualify for the preceptorship. Defendant assured him that he would and then offered him a position. When taken as a whole, a jury could find that the negotiations amounted to a representation that the preceptorship would continue after June 30, 1969. In order to avoid misleading plaintiff, defendant was under a duty to disclose the fact that the Board of Examiners might well terminate the program.

Defendant's next argument is that even if there was a misrepresentation, there was no evidence of defendant's intent to mislead. The requisite intent to mislead consists of a defendant misrepresenting a material fact for the purpose of misleading the other party or with the knowledge he is misleading the other party or in reckless disregard of the fact he is misleading the other party. As discussed, the record in this case contains evidence of the following. The Board of Medical Exam-

iners had questioned the continuation of the preceptorship for a number of years. In 1965 the Board stated its intention to terminate the program as of June 30, 1966. Defendant obtained an extension for a year, partly because of its expressed intention to obtain an approved residency program. The residency, however, was not forthcoming. In the summer of 1968, after an additional extension, defendant was told that its program had terminated in fact. Defendant obtained one final extension, but at this time the indications were the program would end June 30, 1969. In spite of these facts, defendant offered plaintiff a job without disclosing that the program would probably terminate June 30, 1969. Moreover, defendant persisted in its nondisclosure after learning that plaintiff intended to come to Portland well before the job was to begin. We hold that in light of all this evidence a jury could conclude that defendant knew the preceptorship probably would not be renewed; that defendant nevertheless offered plaintiff a job beginning July 1, 1969; and that plaintiff accepted the offer with the firm belief there would be a job for him. Under these facts a jury could also decide that the misrepresentation produced by the failure to disclose was done in reckless disregard of the fact plaintiff was being misled.

Affirmed.

WOODTEK, INC. v. MUSULIN
503 P.2d 677 (Oregon 1972)

BRYSON, Justice

Plaintiff, an Oregon corporation, brought this suit seeking rescission of a contract to purchase a lumber mill business from defendants Matt and Mike Musulin, who are father and son. Plaintiff alleged that defendants had materially misrepresented the financial condition of the business. From a decree dismissing the suit, plaintiff appeals.

In April, 1969, defendant Matt Musulin began construction of a mill in Prineville, Oregon, under the name of Musulin, Inc. The mill began production in late October, 1969. Soon thereafter Matt Musulin, Charles E. Bernert, vice president and general manager of plain-

tiff, and Coral Alan Nyman, plaintiff's comptroller and certified public accountant, began negotiations for a sale of the defendants' mill to plaintiff. Bernert and Nyman requested a financial statement of Musulin, Inc., as of November 30, 1969. Mervin Hanscam, accountant for Musulin, Inc., prepared a "Statement of Financial Condition," each page of which carried the following: "Prepared from the Records Without Audit Verification."

After reviewing Hanscam's figures and data, plaintiff's Board of Directors approved the purchase. On January 9, 1970, Bernert, acting on behalf of plaintiff, and defendants signed a "Contract for Stock Purchase" whereby plaintiff acquired from defendants all of the outstanding shares of Musulin, Inc., for shares of Woodtek, Inc. The contract stated, in part:

4. REPRESENTATIONS AND WARRANTIES.

Each of the Sellers represents and warrants to the Purchaser, with total liability of the Seller limited to the amount of stock sold by him, that: . . . .

(e) The balance sheet of the Company as of the 30 day of November, 1969, and related statements of income and expenses for the period ended on that date, a copy of which has heretofore been delivered to the Purchaser, are a true and accurate statement as to the financial condition of the Company on the 30 day of November, 1969, and the results of its prior operation, prepared in conformity with generally accepted accounting principles consistently applied.

Plaintiff assumed control of the mill some five days after the contract was executed. On August 20, 1970, plaintiff notified defendants that it was rescinding the stock purchase agreement because of defendants' material misrepresentations of the financial condition of Musulin, Inc. Defendants deny any misrepresentation. . . .

Plaintiff first contends that "the trial court erred in concluding that plaintiff knew or should have known of the true extent of Musulin's liability to Trans-Pacific Leasing, Inc., long before rescission was attempted and that, therefore, plaintiff was not entitled to the remedy of rescission."

The trial court found:

. . . I believe that the only material misrepresentation was that concerning the liability under the Trans-Pacific lease. I believe the misrepresentation was innocent. I believe in all the circumstances plaintiff's reliance upon the representation concerning the liability to Trans-Pacific was not really justified. Further, I believe that the plaintiff knew, or in the exercise of reasonable care should have known, of the true extent of the liability to Trans-Pacific long before rescission was attempted and that plaintiff, therefore, is not entitled to a decree . . . for rescission by failure to promptly elect to pursue that remedy.

Plaintiff was justified in relying on the financial statement produced by the accountant for Musulin, Inc. Bernert and Nyman requested the statement so that plaintiff's Board of Directors could make their decision. Nyman testified that the financial statement was represented to him as being reasonably accurate. The Hanscam statement and a report prepared by Nyman, using Hanscam's figures, were considered by plaintiff's Board of Directors in reaching their decision.

The warning accompanying the statement that it was compiled "without audit verification" was sufficient to apprise its reader that the statement was not accurate in every particular but did not abrogate the oral representations by Hanscam that the figures were reasonably accurate. Under these circumstances, Nyman and plaintiff's Board of Directors justifiably relied on the Hanscam statement for what it represented.

We believe, however, as did the trial court, that plaintiff knew or should have known of the true extent of liability of Musulin, Inc., to Trans-Pacific Leasing, Inc., long before it attempted to rescind the stock purchase agreement. The record discloses that prior to January 9, 1970, the contract date, Bernert and Nyman thoroughly discussed the Trans-Pacific lease with the Musulins, including the terms of the lease, the amount of the monthly payments, and the machinery covered by the lease. Approximately two weeks after the purchase agreement was executed, Bernert and Nyman held additional discussions with defendants concerning the equipment lease in an attempt to extend the term of the lease and decrease monthly payments. In February and March, 1970, Nyman made certain adjusting entries in the Musulin, Inc., books in order to change the accounting presentation of the Trans-Pacific lease. He did not discuss these changes with the other members of plaintiff's staff:

The general rule is that the corporation is affected or charged with knowledge of all material facts of which its officer or agent received notice or acquires knowledge while acting in the course of his employment and within the scope of his authority, even though the officer or agent does not in fact communicate his knowledge to the corporation through its other officers or agents, or its board of directors. . . .

The evidence indicates that Bernert and Nyman, while acting within the scope of their duties for plaintiff, learned the true extent of Musulin, Inc.'s liability under the Trans-Pacific lease and chose either to ignore the facts or to keep them a secret.

Affirmed.

CASE REVIEW QUESTIONS

1. Why do you think Elizaga sued Kaiser on the basis of fraud rather than misrepresentation?
2. Why did Kaiser's silence concerning the possible cancelation of the position for which Elizaga had applied constitute a misrepresentation?
3. Why was Kaiser's misrepresentation determined to be intentional?
4. Why do you think Woodtek, Inc., sued the Musulins on the basis of misrepresentation rather than fraud?
5. On what grounds did the trial court in the *Woodtek* case find for the defendants?
6. Did the appellate court agree or disagree with the findings of the trial court in the *Woodtek* case? Explain.

DURESS AND UNDUE INFLUENCE

Duress

Another situation in which the courts will provide relief to a person who has entered into a contract occurs when that person's promise has been induced by fear of a wrongful threat or act by the other party. The use of such wrongful threats or acts is called **duress.**

The most extreme example of duress is the use or threat of violence to coerce a party into entering a contract. If the promisor's arm is twisted or a gun is held to the promisor's head and, as a result, the promise is made, the exchange that takes place is based on fear, not on the promisor's expectation of an efficient allocation of resources. To protect individual freedom and to promote efficient exchange, the courts will not enforce a coerced promise.

The difficult question, however, is what threats or acts should be considered wrongful. Any act that is either criminal or tortious qualifies as wrongful. Such wrongful acts would include assault, battery, false imprisonment, and blackmail.

Noncriminal, nontortious acts or threats may also be labeled wrongful in limited circumstances. If a legal right is exercised oppressively or abusively, it may be treated as wrongful. If a person asserts a legal right for the purpose of coercing someone into a contract that is unfair and that is not related to the right being asserted, the legal right is being abused, and the party who is coerced may escape the contract on the basis of duress. For instance, an employer who has a legal right to fire an employee without cause may not use the threat of firing to force the employee into a contract not related to the employment.

In the case that follows, the plaintiff argued that an agreement to settle the plaintiff's claim against the defendant had been obtained because of economic duress by the defendant and, therefore, should not be enforced. The court had to determine whether the plaintiff had made out a case of duress.

INTERNATIONAL UNDERWATER CONTRACTORS, INC. v. NEW ENGLAND TELEPHONE AND TELEGRAPH COMPANY
393 N.E.2d 968 (Mass. 1979)

BROWN, Justice

The plaintiff, International Underwater Contractors, Inc. (IUC), appeals from the entry of summary judgment for the defendant, New England Telephone and Telegraph Company (NET).

The plaintiff, which had entered into a written contract with the defendant to assemble and install conduits under the Mystic River for a lump sum price of $149,680, . . . seeks additional compensation in a total amount of $811,816.73 for a major change in the system from that specified in the contract. The plaintiff asserts that the change, which was necessitated by delays caused by the defendant, forced the work to be performed in the winter months instead of during the summer, as originally bid, making the equipment originally specified unusable. This major change was made, the plaintiff alleges, at the direction of the defendant, and upon the defendant's assurances that it would pay the resulting additional costs.

The defendant moved for summary judgment with a supporting affidavit, wherein it argued in defense a release signed by the plaintiff settling the additional claim for a total sum of $575,000. The plaintiff [which also submitted affidavits] argues that the release is not binding because it was signed under economic duress.

[T]he affidavits show a dispute as to whether NET gave assurances to IUC that if IUC made the change in installation of equipment and continued to perform that work to completion, NET would pay the additional costs and would not permit IUC to lose money. The affidavits also raise a question whether IUC's financial difficulties were attributable to such acts of the defendant and whether plaintiff was forced because of such difficulties to accept a disproportionately small settlement which it would not otherwise have accepted.

Such allegations are material and, if true, would make out a case for duress. Here, if the plaintiff's allegations are true, the defendant's acts in (1) insisting on a deviation from the contract and repeatedly assuring the plaintiff that it would pay the additional cost, which was substantially greater than the original, if the plaintiff would complete the work and (2) then refusing to make payments for almost a year caused the plaintiff's financial difficulties . . . could be considered "wrongful" acts. . . .

The unequal bargaining power of the two parties (both in terms of their comparative size and resources as well as the financial difficulties into which the plaintiff had fallen, allegedly because of the defendant's acts) is a factor to be considered in determining whether the transaction involved duress. In addition, the disparity between not only the plaintiff's alleged costs ($811,816) but also the amount NET's engineers had recommended in November, 1974, to the board for settlement ($775,000) and the amount offered on a "take-or-leave-it" basis in December and accepted in settlement ($575,000) raises the possibility there may have been a disproportionate exchange of values and should be considered in determining whether the release was signed under duress.

The defendant argues that it did not have to settle the case but could have "exercised its lawful right to litigate the rights of the parties under the agreement" and that "[d]oing or threatening to do what a party has a legal right to do cannot form the basis of a claim of economic duress." However, if the assertions of the plaintiff are true, the defendant did more than assert a legal right, as its acts created the financial difficulties of the plaintiff, of which it then took advantage. The defendant also argued that the plaintiff cannot be found to have acted under duress because it had an adequate remedy at law. However, "if recourse to courts of law is not quick enough to save the victim's business or property interests, there is no adequate legal remedy." Here, if the allegations of the plaintiff are true, the plaintiff, as a result of the defendant's wrongful acts, was not "free either to rely on [its] legal rights or . . . voluntarily to accept the terms proposed.''

In summary, we find that the affidavits raise issues of material fact, and we are therefore unable to say as a matter of law that the signing of the release was voluntary. Accordingly, it was error to enter summary judgment.

Judgment reversed.

CASE REVIEW QUESTIONS

1. Why do you think that the trial court granted the defendant's motion for summary judgment?
2. Why specifically did the appellate court decide that the motion for summary judgment should have been denied?

Undue Influence

Undue influence differs from duress in that, rather than being concerned with wrongful acts of coercion, it deals with unfair persuasion. Unfair persuasion is present when a person in a dominant position or a position of trust and confidence uses the power of that position unfairly to persuade a dependent person to enter a contract to which the dependent person would not have otherwise agreed. Threats or deception need not be present, only unfair persuasion. This occurs when the person in the dominant position uses high pressure techniques, such as dealing at a time or in a place that makes the dependent person especially vulnerable and/or insisting on an immediate decision, without giving the dependent person the opportunity to consult advisors.

If duress or undue influence are present, the resulting contract can be avoided by the party who has been wrongfully coerced or unfairly persuaded to enter the contract. If, however, after the duress or undue influence are no longer present, the coerced or unfairly influenced party acts or accepts benefits under the contract or fails to act to avoid it with reasonable promptness, the contract is ratified (approved of) and the defense or action for duress or undue influence is lost.

UNCONSCIONABILITY

Another situation in which a promisor may be given relief despite having made a promise occurs when a court finds that the contract or a portion of the contract agreed to is **unconscionable.** Although this concept is now generally applied to all contracts rather than just to sales contracts, the most precise statement concerning unconscionability is found in Section 2-301 of the Uniform Commercial Code, which provides:

(1) If the court as a matter of law finds the contract or any clause of the contract to have been unconscionable at the time it was made, the court may refuse to enforce the contract, or it may enforce the remainder of the contract without the unconscionable clause, or it may so limit the application of any unconscionable clause as to avoid any unconscionable result.

(2) When it is claimed or appears to the court that the contract or any clause thereof may be unconscionable the parties shall be afforded a reasonable opportunity to present evidence as to its commercial setting, purpose and effect to aid the court in making the determination.

What Does Unconscionable Mean?

You may have noticed that, although the UCC provision quoted above allows the court to do certain things if it finds unconscionability, it does not define the term itself. The word *unconscionable* is not, in fact, expressly defined anywhere in the Code. What, then, does unconscionable mean? A clue to its meaning is found in the Official Comment to Section 2-302, which reads in part:

> The basic test is whether, in the light of the general commercial background and the commercial needs of the particular trade or case, the clauses involved are so one-sided as to be unconscionable under the circumstances existing at the time of the making of the contract. Subsection (2) makes it clear that it is proper for the court to hear evidence upon these questions. The principle is one of the prevention of oppression and unfair surprise . . . and not of disturbance of allocation of risks because of superior bargaining power.

Another definition sometimes used by the courts comes from an eighteenth-century English case in which a judge said that an unconscionable contract was one "such as no man in his senses and not under delusion would make on the one hand, and as no honest and fair man would accept on the other." Yet another definition suggests that an unconscionable contract is one that "affronts the sense of decency."

A Question of Law

Another interesting point about Section 2-302 is that it makes the issue of unconscionability a question of law to be determined by a judge rather than a question of fact to be determined by a jury. In determining the question of unconscionability, the trial court judge must give the parties the chance to present evidence concerning the commercial setting and the purpose and effect of the contract or clause.

Making the issue of unconscionability a question of law is significant in that it makes the trial court judge's determination on the issue reviewable on appeal, as is true of all questions of law. As a result, although the word unconscionable is undefined, precedents can accumulate and provide guidelines for people in business and for the courts.

Remedies Available

The UCC states that if a contract or contract clause is found to be unconscionable, the court may refuse to enforce the contract, may refuse to enforce the unconscionable part of the contract, or may limit the application of the unconscionable part of the contract. The courts have fully applied this flexibility in the determination of remedies that are appropriate to a particular case.

In fact, the courts may have gone beyond the remedies designated in the UCC. Although traditionally the courts have said that they would not make a contract for the parties involved in a contract dispute, some courts have virtually remade contracts in cases where unconscionability has been found. For example, there have been cases in which courts have reduced an unconscionable contract price and then enforced the contract.

Precedents

As mentioned earlier, although the courts will provide a remedy for the victim of an unconscionable contract or contract clause, the term itself is undefined. As a consequence, to gain an understanding of the concept of unconscionability it is necessary to be familiar with the kinds of situations in which the courts have applied it and the factors that the courts have considered important in those situations.

Consumers have been the primary beneficiaries of the doctrine of unconscionability. In consumer cases, excessive price has often been a very important factor considered by the courts. For instance, there have been several cases where consumers have paid more than twice the value for goods sold to them and the courts have declared the price term of the contract to be unconscionable. It is probably significant in these cases that the consumer was not aware that he or she was paying an excessive price.

Another factor present in a number of consumer cases in which the courts have found unconscionability is that the consumer has been handicapped by a language difficulty or the lack of education or experience. For example, in several cases, oppressive contracts that were negotiated in Spanish but were written in English, and were not translated or explained, have been found to be unconscionable.

Contracts and clauses found to be unconscionable usually involve gross one-sidedness, and often the existence of the one-sidedness is hidden in small print and complicated language. For example, contract provisions calling for full payment by a consumer even if the full services to be received under the contract are not used have been found to be unconscionable in some cases.

The Official Comment to Section 2-302 states that its purpose is not to disturb the "allocation of risks because of superior bargaining power." Nonetheless, in many of the cases in which unconscionability has been found, inequality in bargaining power has been present. Although such bargaining inequality alone is not grounds for a finding of unconscionability, it is an important factor when linked to other factors, such as those discussed above.

The case that follows is an example of a consumer case in which a trial court applied the doctrine of unconscionability. You should note carefully the factors considered by the court in making its determination as to whether the contract was unconscionable.

BROOKLYN UNION GAS COMPANY v. JIMENIZ
371 N.Y.S.2d 289 (1975)

SHILLING, Judge

Plaintiff, Brooklyn Union Gas Company, is suing defendant Rafael Jimeniz for breach of contract. The plaintiff alleges entering into a contract with defendant on or about June 15, 1971, for the delivery and installation of 1 400 Economite Gas Conversion Burner, 1 L400G-A Aquastat, 1 P404A Pressuretrol, 1 Backdraft Diverter. Plaintiff further claims that pursuant to the contract entered into herein the payments to be made by the defendant were deferred for twelve months and that the above items upon delivery and installation had a one year unconditional satisfaction guarantee.

The purported written agreement was presented to the defendant in English only. Defendant, a non-English speaking and writing individual who only spoke and wrote Spanish fluently, admits to signing the papers introduced into evidence by plaintiff, the contract, but also testified that no one ever explained the contract to him. Defendant also testified that when he asked for an interpretation of the contract and an explanation of what the plaintiff's agent, one David H. Mann, said regarding the alleged contract, a woman named Carmen told him to sign it. Plaintiff never sold or negotiated with defendant but induced defendant's tenants to pressure defendant into signing the contract. Plaintiff's agent, Mann, had defendant sign this purported contract at 673 Snediker Avenue, Brooklyn, N.Y., and not at plaintiff's main office at Montague Street, Brooklyn, N.Y., where a Spanish interpreter would have been available.

Defendant could neither write nor speak English and testified to the fact that when one month later he attempted to make a payment at the Montague Street branch, he was told by an employee that he need not pay for another year. After one year passed defendant started to make payment. On or about May 22, 1973, during second year, defendant complained to plaintiff that the unit involved herein was not functioning. Plaintiff's field repairmen found that a transformer burned out. An order for the part was placed with plaintiff's office. However, after discovering that defendant had made no payments past 1972, no further action was taken by plaintiff to supply the necessary part. Defendant, not receiving satisfaction, made no attempt to make further payments and plaintiff made no attempt to repair.

Under UCC §2-302,

> If the court as a matter of law finds the contract or any clause of the contract to have been unconscionable at the time it was made, the court may refuse to enforce the contract.

That is the situation here—this court finds, as a matter of law, that the contract introduced by plaintiff is unconscionable and, thereby, under the UCC, unenforceable. . . . The Court of Appeals has made it plain in *Wilson Trading Corp. v. David Ferguson* that whether a contract or any clause of the contract is unconscionable is a matter for the court to decide against the background of the contract's commercial setting, purpose and effect. This court has the power and the discretion to determine whether a contract is unconscionable. It is up to the court as a matter of law to determine if the contract is or is not unconscionable and the court can strike the clause, clauses or the entire contract as a result if it finds the contract to be unconscionable.

An unconscionable sales contract contains procedural elements involving the contract formation process,which the use of high-pressure sales tactics, failure to disclose the terms of the contract, misrepresentation and fraud on the part of the seller, a refusal to bargain on certain critical terms, clauses hidden in fine print, and unequal bargaining power aggravated by the fact that the consumer in many cases cannot speak English. . . . The term *caveat emptor* has been eroded by the Code. No longer can a seller hide behind it when acting in an unconscionable manner.

In making an agreement, the contracting parties create obligations as between themselves—the law of contracts generally contemplates that the parties will meet each other on a footing of social and approximate economic equality. The basic test of unconscionability of a contract is whether under the circumstances existing at the time of the creation of the contract the parties were in equality to each other on all levels. The court can look into the contract to make its determination and ascertain how the contract was printed, whether both parties to the contract spoke English, how the contract was made and if the contract was one-sided.

The defendant, in this case, was not looking for any arrangement but was induced to enter into this agreement by the plaintiff. The plaintiff, through its agent, made no attempt to explain to the defendant directly or indirectly what was involved. High-pressure sales tactics were used and a Spanish-speaking interpreter was not provided by the plaintiff before the contract was signed. "Apparent throughout the trial of this matter [was] that the defendant had a reasonable though limited comprehension of day to day English language usage. On technical or legal issues, however, he demonstrated an uncertainty with various terms and difficulty in expressing himself often found in people in this city for whom English remains a second language" (as in this case, in the present case, an interpreter was used throughout the trial). [Citation omitted.]

> The doctrine of unconscionability is used by the courts to protect those who are unable to protect themselves and to prevent injustice, both in consumer and non-consumer areas. . . . [U]nequal bargaining powers and the absence of a meaningful choice on the part of one of the parties, together with contract terms which unreasonably favor the other party, may spell out unconscionability.

In this case, the defendant had a limited knowledge of the English language and no knowledge of the technical or legal tools of English. The plaintiff never provided an interpreter to explain the contract. The bargaining positions, therefore, were unequal. The defendant was and is, under these facts, unable to protect himself. Since he cannot protect himself, the court must protect him and thus this court declares the contract unconscionable and a nullity.

[Judgment for defendant.]

CASE REVIEW QUESTIONS

1. What factors did the court consider in making its determination that the contract was unconscionable?
2. What remedy did the court give to Jimeniz as a result of its decision that the contract was unconscionable?

Unconscionability in Contracts between Merchants People in business have not had much success in using the doctrine of unconscionability. This is so because it is generally felt that such people, more than consumers, should be able to look out for their own interests. For example, in one case a clause that allowed a brewing company to terminate an exclusive distributorship without cause was not found to be unconscionable. Similarly, in a lawsuit against a telephone company seeking damages for omitting the plaintiff's listing from yellow pages, a contract clause limiting the telephone company's liability to the amount it charged to place the listing was held not to be unconscionable.

On the other hand, in a few cases businesses, especially small businesses, have received protection under the doctrine of unconscionability. For example, in a case involving a contract for the sale of yarn, the contract provided that the buyer could not make any claims against the seller for defects in the yarn "after weaving, knitting, or processing, or more than 10 days after shipment." The court held that such a clause in the contract would be unconscionable if defects in the yarn could not reasonably be discovered within the time provided in the clause.

MISTAKE

Mistakes in contract transactions occur in various ways. A mistake by one or both of the parties may be significant because it may make the contract void (i.e., prevent its formation) or voidable (i.e., allow it to be avoided by one or both of the parties) or it may be grounds for reformation (correction).

Set out below are a number of common mistake situations that occur in contract transactions. In each situation, you should note under what circumstances a mistake is legally significant and what that significance is.

Mutual Mistake of Fact

A mistake of fact is present when a party believes something to be true, but his or her belief is not in accord with the real facts. If both parties are mistaken in their beliefs, there is a **mutual mistake.** If the fact about which they are mistaken was a significant factor in their decision to contract, the party whose performance is thereby made significantly more difficult is given the legal right to avoid the contract on the basis of a mutual mistake of fact.

For example, a buyer and seller may both believe that certain goods exist when, in fact, they have been destroyed in a fire about which neither has yet heard. If they contract to buy and sell the destroyed goods, the seller is in a difficult situation because he or she no longer has the goods. The seller may therefore avoid the contract.

In such cases, it is important to note whether there has been a mistake of fact on the one hand or a conscious uncertainty on the other. For instance, if two parties believe they are contracting to sell a topaz, but the stone turns out to be a much more valuable uncut diamond, the transaction can be avoided by the seller. If the parties aren't sure about the kind of stone they are contracting to sell, however, and it turns out to be a diamond, there is no mistake because the parties did not believe something to be true that was not in accord with the facts. The contract, therefore, cannot be avoided by the seller under such circumstances.

Also, there are certain defenses available to the party who opposes avoidance of the contract. First, if that party has acted in reliance on the contract and would therefore be substantially harmed if the court allowed rescission, the remedy of rescission will not be granted. Second, the party opposed to avoidance may be able to show that the party seeking rescission in some way affirmed the contract. This may happen, for instance, if after discovering the mistake, the party delays unduly before seeking avoidance. Undue delay is prohibited so that the party with the right to avoid cannot take advantage of that right to wait and see whether avoidance or affirmance would be more beneficial.

In the case that follows, a party to a contract is seeking to rescind the contract because of a mutual mistake of fact.

BEACHCOMBER COINS, INC. v. BOCKETT
400 A.2d 78 (N.J. 1979)

[Beachcomber Coins, Inc., a retail dealer in coins, brought a legal action against Ron Bockett, a part-time coin dealer, seeking rescission of a contract to buy and sell for $500 a dime purportedly minted in 1916 in Denver. The trial court found for Bockett. Beachcomber appealed.]

CONCORD, Judge

Plaintiff asserts a mutual mistake of fact as to the genuineness of the coin as Denver-minted, such a coin being a rarity and therefore having a market value greatly in excess of its normal monetary worth. Plaintiff's evidence at trial that the "D" on the coin signifying Denver mintage was counterfeited is not disputed by defendant.

The proofs were that the seller had himself acquired this coin and two others of minor value for a total of $450 and that his representative had told the purchaser that he would not sell the dime for less than $500. The principal [owner] of plaintiff firm spent from 15 to 45 minutes in close examination of the coin before purchasing it. Soon thereafter he received an offer of $700 for the coin subject to certification of its genuineness by the American Numismatic Society. That organization labeled it a counterfeit, and as a result plaintiff instituted the present action.

The evidence and the trial judge's findings establish this as a classic case of rescission for mutual mistake of fact. As a general rule:

    . . . where parties on entering into a transaction that affects their contractual relations are both under a

mistake regarding a fact assumed by them as the basis on which they entered into the transaction, it is voidable by either party if enforcement of it would be materially more onerous to him than it would have been had the fact been as the parties believed it to be.

Moreover, "negligent failure of a party to know or to discover the facts as to which both parties are under a mistake does not preclude rescission or reformation on account thereof." It is undisputed that both parties believed that the coin was a genuine Denver-minted one. The mistake was mutual in that both parties were laboring under the same misapprehension as to this particular, essential fact. The price asked and paid was directly based on that assumption. That plaintiff may have been negligent in his inspection of the coin (a point not expressly found but implied by the trial judge) does not, as noted above, bar its claim for rescission.

Defendant's contention that plaintiff assumed the risk that the coin might be of greater or lesser value than that paid is not supported by the evidence. It is well established that a party to a contract can assume the risk of being mistaken as to the value of the thing sold. The *Restatement* states the rule this way:

    Where the parties know that there is doubt in regard to a certain matter and contract on that assumption, the contract is not rendered voidable because one is disappointed in the hope that the facts accord with his wishes. The risk of the existence of the doubtful fact is then assumed as one of the elements of the bargain.

However, for the stated rule to apply, the parties must be conscious that the pertinent fact may not be true and make their agreement at the risk of that possibility. In this case both parties were certain that the coin was genuine. They so testified. Plaintiff's principal thought so after his inspection, and defendant would not have paid nearly $450 for it otherwise. A different case would be presented if the seller were uncertain either of the genuineness of the coin or of its value if genuine, and had accepted buyer's judgment on these matters.

Reversed.

CASE REVIEW QUESTIONS
1. Why do you think that the trial court gave judgment to the defendant?
2. What evidence would the defendant have to present in order to successfully employ the defenses available to a party who opposes avoidance of a contract on the grounds of mutual mistake?

Unilateral Mistake of Fact

It has traditionally been the rule that if only one of the parties to a contract has a belief that is not in accord with the facts, that is, if there is a **unilateral mistake,** that party's mistake has no effect on the contract. The only exception to this general rule has been in those cases where one party makes a mistake of fact and the other party realizes it. In such a case, there is no contract.

For example, under this rule, if two parties are engaged in a contract to purchase and sell a stone, and the seller believes the stone to be a topaz (mistake) and the buyer believes it to be a diamond (no mistake), the seller cannot avoid the contract unless the buyer knows of the seller's mistake at the time of contracting.

Modern Trend There has been a recent trend, however, of allowing a party to avoid a contract under certain circumstances when he or she has made a mistake but the other party hasn't. First, the mistake must be one that makes the performance of the contract substantially more difficult for the mistaken party. Second, the party not making the mistake must not be substantially harmed as a result of rescission of the contract. Applying these conditions to the previous example, if the difference in value between a topaz and a diamond is substantial, and the stone had either not been delivered yet or, if delivered, the buyer had not done anything, such as, reselling the stone, to change his or her position, the seller can rescind the contract. In such cases, the choice is made by the court to deny the legitimate expectations of the party not making a mistake in favor of protecting the mistaken party.

Note that in these cases the mistake must be a mistake of fact, not simply an error in judgment. For instance, if both parties believe that the stone is a diamond, the fact that the buyer pays too much for it will not allow him or her to avoid the contract since there has been a mistake of judgment, not of fact.

Common contemporary situations in which the new attitude of the courts toward unilateral mistakes can be seen are cases in which a contractor misinterprets the specifications in an invitation for bids or makes a computational error in calculating a bid. In such cases, if the contractor's error is substantial and the other party will not be substantially harmed by rescission of the contract, the contractor can avoid the agreement. Again, however, such relief is not available in cases in which the contractor has only made an error in judgment rather than a computational error or a misinterpretation of specifications. In the case that follows, the court had to determine whether the mistake involved was the kind that would allow rescission of the contract or was an error in judgment.

Finally, the same defenses that apply to cases of mutual mistake—that is, action in substantial reliance on the contract or affirmance of the contract—are also applicable to cases of unilateral mistake.

BALABAN-GORDON COMPANY, INC. v. BRIGHTON SEWER DISTRICT
342 N.Y.S.2d 435 (1973)

[Brighton Sewer District advertised for bids to construct two sewer treatment plants. Bids were received for the general construction, plumbing, wiring, and electrical work for each facility. Bidders could bid on the contracts separately or in combination. Balaban-Gordon Company, Inc., was the lowest bidder for the construction of both plants. Its total bid for the work was $2,249,700—$530,000 below the next lowest bidder. Balaban-Gordon also bid on the plumbing contract, for which it was the high bidder. Its bid was $376,230 higher than the low bid.

Upon learning of the difference in the bids, Balaban-Gordon's representatives checked with Brighton's engineers and then reexamined their worksheets. They determined that they had incorrectly interpreted the specifications and had included in the bid for the plumbing contract the cost of several pieces of mechanical equipment that should have been included in the bid for general construction.

Balaban-Gordon explained its error in detail at a conference with Brighton's representatives and asked that its bid be withdrawn. Brighton would not allow withdrawal of the bid and demanded that Balaban-Gordon sign the contracts for general construction. Balaban-Gordon refused to do so, and Brighton readvertised for bids.

Balaban-Gordon brought a legal action to rescind their bid. The trial court granted rescission. Brighton appealed. In the decision that follows, the appellate court refers to Brighton as appellant and Balaban-Gordon as respondent.]

SIMONS, Justice

The parties are in agreement that relief is available where the mistake is clerical or arithmetical. In such a case, the mistaken bid does not express the true intention of the bidder. If he were to recompute the bid or if another person were to do so, the obvious error would be discovered and corrected. Its existence may be objectively determined. In those circumstances, there is said to be no meeting of the minds because the bid was one which the bidder never intended to make.

On the other hand, it is commonly recognized that a bidder will not be relieved from an error in a value judgment in estimating the requirements or costs necessary to fulfill a contract. Mistakes of this type are inherent business risks assumed by contractors in all bidding situations. If the specifics of the job were recalculated by the bidder, his bid would be the same, for these estimates do not involve oversights. They represent subjective judgments deliberately made with respect to the requirements of the job. Another person calculating the bid might or might not make the same "mistake," depending upon his mental evaluation of the work to be performed, but in any event, the minds of the bidder and the offeree meet because the bid is precisely what the bidder intends even though his judgment later proves faulty.

The appellant claims that the error must be considered one of these two types, either clerical and arithmetical, or an error of judgment, relief by rescission being available in the former case but not in the latter. Since the incorrect interpretation of the specifications was not clerical or arithmetical appellant claims that respondent should be held to the bid. . . . Unfortunately, not all mistakes by contractors are categorized so easily. Applying the reasoning of the two types of mistakes to the facts of this case illustrates the difficulty. If respondent's representatives were to recompute its bid, they doubtless would interpret the specifications the same way. It that sense, the bid accurately reflected the contract respondent was willing to make and there was a meeting of the minds. Nevertheless, the error was objectively discoverable. Another contractor computing the bid would not, and in fact no other did, make the same mistake in interpretation and in that sense the bid did not represent the bid intended because respondent was working under a misapprehension with respect to the particulars called for by the specifications. Reasonable care probably dictated that respondent should have asked the engineers to clarify the meaning of the ambiguous specifications (at least one other bidder did so), but respondent's failure to investigate should not prevent it from obtaining relief.

The decisive factual question is whether the mistake is one the courts will excuse. Then, if the mistake concerns a material matter in an executory [unperformed] contract under circumstances where relief to the bidder results in no damage to the municipality but enforcement results in serious harm to the bidder, rescission will be granted. Manifestly, rescission may be allowed more readily for a mistake made by a bidder which is objectively established and which does not evolve from an inherent risk of business. Even though the mistake is the product of negligence on the part of the bidder, relief should be granted because the assurance exists from the objective proof that the transaction is free from mischief. This satisfies a fundamental purpose of the public bidding statutes.

The error in this case did not pertain to an evaluation of risks or estimation of requirements or costs by the bidder and the effect of the mistake was verifiable in much the same way as a clerical error, the impossibility of performance or an arithmetical error. That being the case, it should be excused and rescission granted. In these days of multi-million dollar construction contracts, the public interest requires stability in bidding of public contracts under rules that protect against chicane [trickery] and overreaching. Nevertheless, little is to be gained if a contractor is forced to perform a contract at an extravagant loss or the risk of possible bankruptcy. If a mistake has been made under circumstances justifying relief, the municipality should not be allowed to enforce the bargain. Its remedy to avoid loss is to award the contract to the next bidder or assume the responsibility of rebidding.

The judgment granting respondent rescission of its bid . . . should therefore be affirmed.

CASE COMMENT

Because a bid is only an offer, you may wonder why Balaban-Gordon couldn't simply withdraw its bid, that is, revoke its offer, before the contract with Brighton was signed. The answer is that, under the statutes that provide for bidding on government contracts, such bids are irrevocable for a specified period after they are opened. A bid on a government contract is therefore a binding offer to make a contract. This rule prevents bidders from withdrawing their bids after they find out what other bidders have bid on the same contract.

CASE REVIEW QUESTIONS
1. Why specifically did the court allow Balaban-Gordon to rescind its binding offer to make a contract?
2. Why did the court decide that Balaban-Gordon's mistake was a misinterpretation of Brighton's specifications rather than a mistake in judgment?

Mistake in Performance

If one party to a contract pays money to the other or otherwise performs because of a mistaken belief that such payment or performance is required by the contract, the payment or value of the performance may be recovered. Such recovery, called **restitution,** is based on the unjust enrichment of the party receiving the payment or performance. It can be obtained even if the mistake was unilateral or even negligent. For example, if an insurance company makes payment on a life insurance policy as the result of the mistaken identification of a deceased person, and the mistake comes to light when the insured later turns up alive, the company can recover the money that it paid to the beneficiary of the policy.

A defense to an action for restitution is that the party that has received the payment or performance has acted detrimentally in innocent reliance on it so that requiring him or her to pay restitution would be unfair.

Ambiguity of Language

Words often have more than one meaning. If a material term of a contract has more than one reasonable meaning, each party may have a mistaken belief as to the meaning of the term intended by the other party. If both or neither of the parties realizes that the material language of the contract is ambiguous (i.e., has more than one reasonable meaning), there is no contract between the parties unless they both intended the term to have the same meaning. If there is no contract, it is void and neither party is able to enforce the contract against the other.

On the other hand, if only one party realizes that an ambiguity exists in a material term of the contract, a contract exists and the court will interpret the term according to the meaning intended by the party who did not realize the ambiguity existed. This rule places a duty on contracting parties to clear up any ambiguities in language that they realize exist.

For example, in a recent case the seller agreed to sell her "Swiss coins" to the buyer. The seller meant by the term "Swiss coins" those coins contained in her "Swiss Coin Collection," whereas the buyer meant all the Swiss coins owned by the seller. Under the particular circumstances of this case, the court would not enforce the seller's promise because it found the meaning intended by each party to be reasonable but different. The court said, therefore, that no contract had come into existence.

Mistake in Drafting Writing

If the parties to a contract reach an agreement and then elect to put their agreement into a written document, which they then sign, there may turn out to be a variance between their oral agreement and the terms stated in the written document. For example, an oral agreement to sell Lot 52 may show up in a written document as an agreement to sell Lot 25. Is there then a contract to sell Lot 52, Lot 25, both, or neither?

In such a situation, either party may bring a legal action for reformation of the written document to change it to match the original oral agreement of the parties. In the previous example, for instance, either party could have the document changed to read Lot 52 instead of Lot 25.

Of course, legal action to reform a written document is necessary only if one of the parties resists changing the written terms. The party who resists generally takes the position that the written terms do in fact correctly reflect the original oral agreement. If legal action is necessary, the party seeking reformation must prove by "clear and convincing evidence" that the writing does not correctly reflect the parties' original oral agreement. This degree of proof is higher than the burden of "a preponderance of the evidence" that is most commonly required in civil cases.

REVIEW QUESTIONS

1. What things must a party to a contract show to prove misrepresentation or fraud? Why might a person choose to prove misrepresentation rather than fraud?
2. How do duress and undue influence differ from one another?
3. What does unconscionable mean?
4. Today, under what circumstances may a party to a contract seek relief for a unilateral mistake of fact?

CASE PROBLEMS

1. Bell bought a business from Phillips. One of the assets of the business was $22,000 in accounts receivable. In negotiating the sale, Phillips told Bell that all of the accounts receivable were "collectible," meaning that they were current and there was no reason to believe they would not be collected. At the time Phillips made the statement, all the accounts receivable were current. It did, in fact, appear that all of the receivables would be collected, and Phillips so believed. In time, however, although Bell tried hard to collect all of the accounts, $7,000 worth had to be written off as bad debts. If Bell brings legal action against Phillips, what will he have to prove to win

his case? How might Phillips defend? Who will win? Explain.

2. Kallgren purchased a resort from Steele. The resort is located on United States government land in a National Forest and is adjacent to a state highway. The resort was maintained on government land under a special permit from the Federal Forest Service. The permit provided that the Forest Service could terminate the permit at any time for any reason. At the time of the sale, the Forest Service made no objection to the transfer of the permit to Kallgren. Shortly thereafter, the Forest Service notified Kallgren that the permit would be revoked. The reason given was that the

resort was too close to the state highway. This was the first time that Kallgren learned that the resort was within or too close to the state highway right of way. Steele had known this fact, but he had said nothing to Kallgren. The buildings are located on the side of a canyon, so it is impossible to move them further away from the highway. On what basis might Kallgren bring legal action against Steele? What will he have to prove to win his case? On what basis might Steele defend? Who will win? Explain.

3. Warr sold land that he owned to Creech for $43 per acre. Prior to the sale, Creech told Warr that he intended to use the land to develop a tree farm. In reality, Creech was buying up property on behalf of a power company for the purpose of constructing a lake, and he had paid other land owners up to $200 per acre. If Warr brings legal action against Creech, what will he have to prove to win his case? On what basis might Creech defend? Who will win? Explain.

4. Groening was interested in purchasing a residence that Opsata had advertised for sale. The residence was located on a bluff overlooking a lake, and Groening was concerned that the bluff might erode away, causing damage to the residence. Before contracting to purchase the residence, Groening asked about the danger of the bluff collapsing, and Opsata replied, "I don't think anything will go wrong." After the contract for sale was agreed to by the parties, Groening once again expressed his concern, and Opsata said, "I have built many houses on these bluffs and I know that they are perfectly safe." In fact, Opsata knew that erosion along the shoreline of the lake had damaged several other residences on bluffs similar to his. Indeed, a few years earlier, he had joined with some of his neighbors to seek assistance from the government in dealing with the problem. A few months after Groening purchased the residence, the bluff collapsed and the residence was destroyed. On what basis might Groening bring legal action against Opsata? What will he have to prove to win the case? On what basis might Opsata defend? Who will win? Explain.

5. In January, Brown purchased a movie theater from Hassenstab. Prior to the sale, Hassenstab told Brown that he had been making about $30,000 a year profit from the theater. He also showed his books to Brown, but they provided no information because many entries had not been made and totals were missing. In April, Brown began to suspect that his profit would be a great deal less than $30,000. He asked Hassenstab for all of the past records and gave them to an accountant. The accountant reconstructed the income and expenses for the two years prior to purchase and determined that the profits for those two years had been $5,500 and $200, respectively. This information was reported to Brown in May. In July, Brown brought an action against Hassenstab to rescind the contract. What will Brown have to prove to win his case? On what basis might Hassenstab defend? Who will win? Explain.

6. Laemmar was an employee of J. Walter Thompson Company (Thompson) for many years. During that time, he purchased a number of shares of Thompson stock from the company under an agreement that gave Thompson the right to repurchase the stock if Laemmar's employment were terminated for any reason. Laemmar was asked by the company to sell his stock to Thompson and was told that if he refused he would be fired. Because of the threat of losing his job, Laemmar contracted to sell his stock to the company. On what basis might Laemmar seek to rescind his contract with Thompson? How might Thompson defend against Laemmar? Who will win? Explain.

7. Odorizzi, a public schoolteacher, was arrested for shoplifting. After his arrest, he was questioned, booked, arraigned in court, and released on bail. During this time, he went without sleep for about 40 hours. Before he was able to get any sleep, he was visited in his apartment by the principal of his school. The principal said he had Odorizzi's best interests in mind and advised him to resign immediately. He also warned Odorizzi that if he didn't resign, the school district would hold a public dismissal hearing, as required by law. If he resigned, however, there would be no hearing and he could secure employment elsewhere. Odorizzi

resigned immediately. After the charges against Odorizzi were dismissed, he sought reinstatement by the school district. The district refused to reinstate him, saying that his resignation was binding. On what basis might Odorizzi try to avoid his promise to resign? What will he have to prove to win his case? How might the school district defend against Odorizzi? Who will win? Explain.

8. A Spanish-speaking salesman for Frostifresh Corporation negotiated orally in Spanish with Reynoso for the sale of a refrigerator-freezer. Reynoso, who had a family, explained to the salesman that he could not afford to buy the appliance because he only had a week left on his job. The salesman distracted and deluded Reynoso by advising him that the appliance would cost him nothing because he would be paid a bonus of $25 for each refrigerator bought by a friend or neighbor. The salesman then submitted to Reynoso a contract entirely in English, without translation or explanation. The contract, which Reynoso signed, provided for a price of $900 for the refrigerator and a credit charge of $245. The cost of the appliance to Frostifresh was $348. When Reynoso failed to pay the contract price, Frostifresh brought a legal action for breach of contract. Reynoso defended on the grounds that the contract was unconscionable. Who will win? Explain.

9. Walker promised to sell Sherwood a particular cow for $80. Both parties believed the cow was sterile. The price was much less than the $750 the cow would have sold for if she were fertile. Before the time for delivery of the cow, the seller discov-

ered that the cow was pregnant. He then refused to deliver the cow. If Sherwood brings legal action against Walker for breach of contract, on what grounds might Walker defend? Who will win? Explain.

10. The city of Syracuse requested bids for the construction of a new school. Martens submitted a bid for $1,799,690. The bid was calculated by totaling 99 different items that were assembled in a short time. The preparation for the bidding was immense and required almost constant work by an estimator day and night for a week. The bid was completed only a few minutes before the deadline for submission, and there was no opportunity to double-check the figures. Martens' bid was the lowest, but he became suspicious that it might contain an error. When he recalculated the bid, Martens discovered that a $387,990 item had been omitted. Because he only expected to make $100,000 profit, he told the city that he was withdrawing his bid. If the city sues Martens for breach of contract, on what basis might Martens defend? Who will win? Explain.

11. Raffles agreed to sell Wickelhouse 125 bales of cotton due to arrive on the ship *Peerless* from Bombay. The buyer knew only of a ship named *Peerless* that was due to arrive in October. The seller knew only of a ship named *Peerless* that was due to arrive in December. When the cotton arrived in December, the buyer refused to take delivery. If Raffles brings legal action against Wickelhouse for breach of contract, on what grounds might Wickelhouse defend? Who will win? Explain.

12

CONSIDERATION

If Jones says to Smith, "I promise to give you $1,000 on May 1," and Smith replies, "I gratefully accept your promise," should Smith be able to enforce Jones' promise in a court if Jones refuses to pay the $1,000 on May 1? From a moral standpoint, you may believe that a court should enforce Jones' promise simply because she made it and should therefore be bound to perform it.

Are there any reasons for *not* enforcing Jones' promise? There are two possibilities you may want to consider. First, should Jones be protected in case she failed to give sufficient deliberation to her promise? It is possible that she made the promise without considering its impact upon herself and her family and that enforcement of her promise will cause serious problems for them. Would these circumstances make you hesitant to call for enforcement of Jones' promise on a "moral" basis?

Second, should the power of the government be used to enforce promises in cases where no economic exchange takes place? The fundamental rationale for the legal enforcement of promises is to encourage trade in order to stimulate economic growth. The transaction between Jones and Smith does not involve an exchange; Jones' promise is simply gratuitous (a gift). Should the absence of an exchange cause a court to refuse to enforce Jones' promise?

Indeed, the courts have traditionally sought to protect people from their impulsive promises, and they normally refuse to enforce promises that are not part of an economic exchange. In other words, gratuitous promises such as Jones' are not enforced. A promise is enforced by the courts only if it is "supported by consideration."

WHAT IS CONSIDERATION?

There are three elements that must be present in order for a promise to be supported by **consideration:**

1. The person making the promise (the promisor) must request (bargain for) something in return for the promise.
2. That which is requested must have legal value.
3. The promisor must receive that which was requested.

If Jones says to Smith, "I promise to pay you $1,000 on May 1, if you promise to deliver 1000 widgets to me on that day," and Smith replies, "It's a deal," will Smith be able to enforce Jones' promise in a court if Jones refuses to accept delivery of the widgets and pay the $1,000 on May 1? Yes, if Jones' promise is supported by consideration. Is it?

Did Jones request something in return for her promise? Yes, she requested Smith's promise to deliver 1000 widgets. Did Smith's promise have legal value? Yes, because he promised to do something that he was not legally obligated to do. Did Jones receive what she requested? Yes, Smith's response is a promise to deliver the widgets pursuant to Jones' request. Because all three elements are present, we can conclude that Jones' promise is supported by consideration and will therefore be enforced by a court.

Because Jones' promise is supported by consideration, we may conclude that she deliberated about the transaction (i.e., she gave thought to what she offered and what she wanted in return) and that it is part of an economic exchange. But will the presence or absence of consideration always be proof of the existence or nonexistence of deliberation and exchange? You should keep this question in mind as you read this chapter.

APPLICATION OF THE DOCTRINE OF CONSIDERATION

In seeking out the three elements of consideration, the courts have been confronted with a number of common and recurring situations. In this section, we will describe some of these situations and explain how the courts have reacted to them.

Past Consideration

Because consideration is based on something that is requested by a promisor, something that has already been received by the promisor cannot serve as consideration for a promise. The courts have taken this position on the grounds that a person will not bargain for something that he or she already has. In other words, a person will not bargain for past consideration.

For example, a promise to pay $500 "in consideration of the fact that you have named your child after me" is not supported by consideration because the naming of the child has already taken place and can no longer be requested or bargained for. On the other hand, consideration would exist if the child had not yet been named, the promisor requested a certain name, and the parents were induced by the promise to give the child the name requested.

Adequacy of Consideration

One of the elements of consideration is that whatever is requested must have legal value. Generally, this means that the person receiving the promise must suffer a legal detriment; that is, the person must do or promise to do something that he or she is not already legally obligated to do or must refrain or promise to refrain from doing something that he or she is privileged to do. It is also permissible for the detriment to be suffered by someone other than the promisee.

Note that it is not necessary for the promisor to receive any benefit as long as the promisee or someone else suffers a detriment. In the case that follows, a bank loaned money to a corporation and the corporation gave a promissory note to the bank promising to repay the loan. The note was guaranteed by the defendant, meaning that the defendant promised the bank that he would repay the loan if the corporation failed to do so. When the bank sued the defendant, he argued that he was not liable because he had received no benefit from the loan.

COLLINS v. GWINNETT BANK & TRUST COMPANY
255 S.E.2d 122 (Georgia 1979)

McMURRAY, Presiding Judge

This is a suit on a note brought by Gwinnett Bank & Trust Company against Ed V. Collins Contracting, Inc., and Ed V. Collins, an individual. Ed V. Collins, as president of the corporation, executed the note in the corporate name and also signed the instrument as guarantor in his individual capacity. Summary judgment was granted in favor of Gwinnett Bank & Trust Company and against Ed V. Collins Contracting, Inc., so that the only issues remaining upon the trial of the case were those relating to the action against Ed V. Collins, individually.

At trial the verdict was directed in favor of Gwinnett Bank & Trust Company and against Ed V. Collins. Ed V. Collins appeals the direction of the verdict against him contending that he was denied his defense of failure of consideration.

There is no contention that the corporate defendant did not receive the proceeds of the loan. The failure of consideration defense upon which Ed V. Collins, the individual, relies is that he personally received no consideration for the loan.

The evidence presented at trial failed to provide any support for the failure or want of consideration defense upon which the individual defendant relies. Ed V. Collins, the individual defendant, contends and the evidence shows that he personally received none of the money for which the note was given. This, however, is not determinative of the question of whether consideration was given. It is not necessary that the promisor receive anything, as loss, trouble or disadvantage undergone by the promisee is a sufficient consideration. The trial court did not err in directing the jury to return a verdict in favor of the plaintiff. Indeed, the evidence disclosed that defendant, Ed V. Collins, felt an obligation as president of the corporation making the note to borrow the money to pay debts and keep the good name of the corporation. He, therefore, received value for executing the guaranty of payment.

Judgment affirmed.

CASE REVIEW QUESTIONS
1. What did Collins ask for in return for his promise to guaranty the loan?
2. Did the bank give Collins what he asked for? Explain.
3. Did what the bank gave to Collins in return for his promise to guaranty the loan have legal value? Explain.

How Much Consideration Is Adequate? As long as the consideration that is requested in exchange for a promise has *some* value, a court will not examine whether it is approximately equal in value to the promise. For example, if I offer to sell my new Chevrolet Corvette to you for $50, and you accept my offer, my promise is supported by consideration even though my promise is much more valuable that the $50 I am to receive in return.

The rationale for the courts' refusal to consider adequacy of consideration is based on the concept of freedom of contract. It is up to the contracting parties to determine the terms of their agreement, and the courts will not protect competent parties from entering into bad bargains. Inadequacy of consideration may serve, however, as evidence of the existence of fraud, duress, undue influence, unconscionability, or mistake in the transaction (see Chapter 11). A court may also consider the adequacy of consideration when deciding whether to grant certain remedies (see Chapter 18).

Preexisting Duties

Although a court will not examine the adequacy of consideration, it will look to see whether the alleged consideration for a promise has any legal value at all. One situation in which no value exists occurs when a person does or promises to do something that he or she is already legally obligated to do or refrains from or promises to refrain from doing something that he or she is not privileged to do.

Contract Modification A common situation in which there is a preexisting duty occurs when parties seek to modify a contract on one side but not the other. For example, a land owner may enter a contract with a building contractor to build a building for $500,000. Before the building is completed, the contractor may refuse to continue to work unless the land owner promises to pay any extra $100,000. If the land owner promises to pay the additional sum, is the promise enforceable?

Most courts would conclude that the land owner's promise was not supported by consideration because he or she did not receive anything of value in return for the promise. The building contractor simply promised to do something that he or she was already legally obligated to do under the original contract between the parties. This conclusion might be justified on the basis that it protects the land owner from economic coercion by the contractor. The coercion might take the form of a threat by the contractor to delay completion of the building, to the economic detriment of the land owner.

On the other hand, where coercion does not appear to be present, there would not seem to be any justifiable reason for not allowing competent parties to modify their contracts. The requirement of consideration to uphold a contract modification presumes that the absence of consideration is conclusive evidence of coercion in the obtaining of the new promise. To avoid application of the rule in cases where no coercion appears to be present, the courts have created a number of devices for circumventing it. A few jurisdictions reason that a modification constitutes an implied termination of the original contract by the parties. This erases the preexisting obligation and creates a new contract that calls for both parties to undertake new duties. Other courts have taken the position either that no consideration is necessary to modify a contract or that the consideration in the original contract is imported into the new contract.

Unforeseen Difficulties A more common exception to the general requirement for consideration in upholding a contract modification occurs in cases where substantial unforeseen difficulties have arisen that affect the performance of one of the parties under the original contract. Where performance becomes more burdensome because of substantial unforeseen problems, and the party confronted with the additional burden requests or is offered additional payment, a court may reason that it was the unforeseen burden, not economic coercion, that led the other party to promise to pay the additional sum.

In the following case, the court had to determine whether the difficulties that resulted in a modification of a contract without consideration were substantial and unanticipated, as is required for the application of the unforeseen difficulties exception to the requirement for consideration in contract modification cases.

MOBILE TURNKEY HOUSING, INC. v. CEAFCO, INC.
321 So.2d 186 (Alabama 1975)

[Mobile Turnkey Housing, Inc. (Turnkey) contracted with Commercial Contractors, Inc. (Commercial) to act as general manager on a construction project. Commercial subcontracted with Ceafco, Inc. (Ceafco) to do the grading and site work on the project. The subcontract included a clause that provided, "Subcontractor acknowledges that he has visited the site and appraised himself of all conditions, including latent subsurface conditions, and agrees that the lump sum price set forth herein will be compensation in full on work performed by him regardless of any conditions encountered in the execution of the contract." Another clause provided, "Subcontractor will be paid sixty-five cents per cubic yard if any undercutting is required as a result of unsatisfactory material below the surface."

Ceafco encountered soil that could not be compacted to the required density. The situation could only be corrected by bringing in large amounts of fill. Ceafco ceased work and demanded more money to pay for the fill to be brought in. Commercial agreed, but when the work was done, they would only pay the originally agreed to amount.

Ceafco brought legal action against Commercial for breach of contract. The trial court found for Ceafco for the reasons set forth in the opinion that follows. Commercial appealed.]

ALMON, Justice

In their answer, Commercial set out the following defense to the complaint:

> . . . that, because Ceafco was already legally bound to provide borrow fill under the original contract of February 20, 1969, there was no consideration for any oral promise that might have been made between Ceafco and Commercial at the meeting of May 19.

The trial judge told the jury in his charge that the doing of an act which you are already legally obligated to do is not sufficient consideration to support a contract. But an exception to this rule exists when due to unforeseen and extraordinary difficulties in performance the law must sustain the promise based upon standards of honesty and fair dealing.

Following these instructions the jury returned [a verdict] to the effect that the new promise to pay by Commercial to Ceafco was supported by adequate consideration.

In its final decree the court found as follows:

> That while the Court considered and finds said written contract of February 20, 1969, to be unambiguous and required Ceafco to perform the work for which the new promise to pay additional money was made, it further finds that Commercial Contractors, Inc., made a new promise to Ceafco, Inc., to pay it additional money for the additional backfill material or borrow, that such new promise was supported by a valid consideration; that the instant fact situation constitutes an exception to the general rule that a promise to pay additional compensation for the doing of that which the promisee is already legally bound to do or perform is insufficient consideration for a valid and enforceable contract, that the instant fact situation properly comes within the "unforeseeable difficulties exception"; that the Court recognizes the promise of Commercial Contractors, Inc., to Ceafco, Inc., for additional compensation based upon what the Court finds to have been extraordinary and unforeseeable difficulties in the performance by Ceafco,

Inc., of the said written contract of February 20, 1969; and that in the circumstances of this case the Court sustains the consideration for said new promise, based upon standards of honesty and fair dealing and affording adequate protection against unjust or coercive exactions.

Upon these findings, the court ordered that a judgment in the amount of $112,929.75 be entered against Commercial in favor of Ceafco.

We view the dispositive issue [the issue that determines the outcome of the case] to be whether the trial judge was in error in finding consideration for the new promise to pay additional money simultaneously with a finding that the original subcontract covered the additional work encountered.

It is manifestly clear from the court's findings and the provisions of the contract that Ceafco contracted to do the work regardless of any soil conditions that might be encountered. Further, the evidence tends to show that the provision of the contract which provided for the payment of an additional sixty-five cents per cubic yard for undercutting required as a result of unsatisfactory material below the surface was negotiated by the parties to provide for the very contingency which is the subject of this litigation.

The alleged "unforeseeable consequences" can hardly be termed as such when the contract in unambiguous terms provided for just such a contingency.

The principle of law which we follow seems on occasion to be rather harsh. Yet to hold otherwise would permit one party to a valid and unambiguous contract to use his failure of performance as a coercive force to extract a higher price than was originally contracted for.

The decree is due to be reversed and the cause remanded.

CASE REVIEW QUESTIONS

1. Why did the appellate court believe that the unforeseen difficulties exception was not applicable to Commercial's promise to pay more than originally agreed to for the fill to be brought in?

2. Which decision — that of the trial court or that of the appellate court — do you find to be more consistent with the policy behind the unforeseen difficulties exception?

Contract Modification under the UCC Uniform Commercial Code §2-209 provides that a modification of a contract for the sale of goods "needs no consideration to be binding." Note that this provision of the UCC is in direct contradiction to the traditional rule that one-sided contract modifications are not enforceable because they are not supported by consideration. The traditional requirement of consideration is premised on the concern that one party to a contract may coerce the other into a modification that benefits only the first party.

Although the Code does allow for contract modification without consideration, it recognizes the potential threat of coercion in modification situations. Instead of presuming coercion when consideration is not present, however, the UCC requires that the modification be made in **good faith,** which is defined as "the observance of reasonable commercial standards of fair dealing in the trade." This means that if the party who agrees to a modification can persuade the court that the demand for such modification was unreasonable, the court will not enforce it. This will occur not because the promise to modify was not supported by consideration, but because it was not obtained in good faith.

Satisfaction of Debts

A situation closely related to the one discussed in the previous section arises when a creditor promises to discharge a debtor upon the partial payment of the debt that is owed. Suppose, for example, that a debtor who owes $100 agrees to pay $50 if the creditor will promise to discharge him or her from paying the other $50. Is the creditor's promise supported by consideration? If not, it is unenforceable and the creditor may seek full payment of the original amount owed.

Whether the promise to discharge the balance of the amount due is enforceable will generally depend on whether the debt is liquidated or unliquidated. A **liquidated** debt is one in which the existence of the debt and the amount due are not in dispute. The majority of courts rule that a promise to discharge a debtor upon partial payment of a liquidated debt is not supported by consideration because the creditor has not received anything of value from the debtor that the creditor was not already entitled to.

On the other hand, if either the existence of the debt or the amount of the debt are in dispute, the debt is **unliquidated.** In this situation, it is usually held that the promise to discharge the balance of the debt upon partial payment is supported by consideration because, in addition to making the partial payment, the debtor gives up the right to assert his or her arguments concerning the disputed claim.

For example, if the creditor argues that the debtor owes $100 while the debtor argues that only $50 is owed, a promise by the creditor to discharge the debt in return for payment of $75 is supported by consideration. In addition to the $75, the creditor is bargaining for the surrender by the debtor of the claim that he or she owes only $50.

In the following case, the defendant argued that he did not owe the original amount of the debt because the plaintiff had promised to accept a lesser amount. Assuming that the plaintiff had in fact made such a promise, what will the court have to determine to decide whether the plaintiff's promise was supported by consideration?

RHOADES v. RHOADES
321 N.E.2d 474 (Ohio 1974)

[When Mr. and Mrs. Rhoades were divorced, Mr. Rhoades was ordered by the court to pay $80 per week for the support of his two children. He paid that amount for a time, but then began to pay $50 per week instead of $80. When he later requested the court to change its order from $80 to $50, Mrs. Rhoades asked the court to require Mr. Rhoades to pay her a sum equal to the total amount that he had failed to pay previously since each payment had been $30 less than it should have been.

The trial court granted Mrs. Rhoades' request and ordered Mr. Rhoades to pay the arrearages (the amount due but unpaid) in a lump sum. Mr. Rhoades appealed the court's decision on the grounds that Mrs. Rhoades had agreed to reduce the amount of the support payments.]

PER CURIAM [by the Court]

Although defendant characterizes the testimony relative to the purported extrajudicial "agreement" [i.e., an agreement made by the parties outside of court] between the parties, reducing support payments, as "undisputed," our perusal of the record indicates that such is not the case.

It appears that defendant had resigned his employment in this state to accept another position in Illinois at a sharply reduced salary. He testified that because of his reduced income he could not pay the support ordered by the court and telephoned plaintiff to so advise her. He claims that in that telephone conversation, secretly audited by a woman now the defendant's wife, he offered to pay the total sum of $50 per week (instead of $80 as ordered) and that plaintiff accepted the offer. Plaintiff, however, testified that while she recalled a telephone conversation in which defendant told her of his inability to pay as ordered and his inten-

tion to remit a lesser amount, she did not make any agreement with him.

Defendant has cited to us a number of decisions treating with the law governing extrajudicial agreements between parents altering support orders made by courts, urging that the case of *Tressler v. Tressler* "serves as a review of all the case law dealing with extrajudicial agreements."

We believe that *Tressler* pronounces accurately the law in Ohio bearing upon the subject with which we are concerned here. Consequently, we have searched the record to determine whether there is evidence sufficient to have required the court below to find that an agreement had been made between the parties. Especially, we have searched for evidence to establish that there was consideration for any such agreement.

If, in the case at bar, the defendant gave up nothing, there could be no agreement.

It is elementary that neither the promise to do a thing, nor the actual doing of it will constitute a sufficient consideration to support a contract if it is merely a thing which the party is already bound to do, either by law or a subsisting contract with the other party.

All that we can perceive defendant here promised to do, and for all material purposes did, was to pay a sum less than that which he was already obligated to pay to plaintiff. Hence, there was no consideration sufficient to support the purported agreement even if plaintiff's testimony that she did not recall agreeing to defendant's proposal is brushed aside.

Upon this state of the record, viewed in light of the law as we comprehend it to be, we can find no error committed below in rendering the lump sum judgment.

Judgment affirmed.

CASE REVIEW QUESTIONS
1. Was the original debt owed by Mr. Rhoades to Mrs. Rhoades liquidated or unliquidated? Explain.
2. Of what importance was the court's determination concerning whether the debt was liquidated or unliquidated?

Statutes Concerning Satisfaction of Debts Some states have adopted statutes that make a promise in writing to release a claim enforceable even if it is not supported by consideration. Such a release would be enforceable, therefore, regardless of whether the debt was liquidated or unliquidated. In this situation, as was noted in the earlier discussion of contract modifications that are enforceable under the Uniform Commercial Code even if they are not supported by consideration, the promise to release the claim will not be enforced if the promisor can show that it was obtained by coercion, duress, fraud, or the like.

EXCEPTIONS TO THE DOCTRINE OF CONSIDERATION

Thus far, we have seen that the courts will usually require that a promise be supported by consideration for it to be enforceable, although under certain specific circumstances, devices may be used to circumvent the consideration requirement when its application seems to create a result inconsistent with the doctrine's underlying rationale. In this section, more generalized exceptions to the doctrine of consideration are set forth.

Promissory Estoppel

Courts have at times been confronted by cases involving gratuitous promises (nothing was requested in return for the promise or that which was requested did not have legal value) and unaccepted offers (that which was requested has not been received) that the promisees argue should be enforced. The promisors, of course, contend that neither gratuitous promises nor unaccepted offers are supported by consideration and that they are therefore unenforceable.

Common examples of situations in which such cases arise involve promises to pay a gratuitous retirement benefit to an employee at will (i.e., an employee not working under a contract who may be discharged without liability at any time) and bids by subcontractors that are used by general contractors in bidding on an overall contract. Should such promises be enforceable?

Under certain circumstances, the courts will enforce gratuitous promises and unaccepted offers. If the promisor should reasonably expect the promisee to act in reliance on the promise and the promisee does take such action, a court will enforce the promise in order to avoid injustice. The basis of such enforcement is called **promissory estoppel.**

For example, the employee may be induced to retire in reliance on the promise to pay a pension or the general contractor may be induced to submit a particular bid on the overall project in reliance on the subcontractor's bid. Neither of these actions was requested or bargained for and, therefore, will not serve as consideration for the promise. However, since the action in each case could be expected by the promisor, the court will enforce the promise under the doctrine of promissory estoppel if doing so is necessary to avoid injustice.

In the two cases that follow, the plaintiffs attempted to use the doctrine of promissory estoppel to win their cases. As you read the cases, consider why it was necessary to use the doctrine and why only one plaintiff was successful in doing so.

HUNTER v. HAYES
533 P.2d 952 (Colo. App. 1975)

KELLY, Judge

Defendants, Gordon Hayes and Winslow Construction Co., appeal from a $700 judgment for plaintiff, Kathleen Hunter, in an action based on defendant's unfulfilled promise to employ Hunter as a flag girl on a construction job. Trial was to the court, which found that defendants had offered Hunter a job to begin on June 14, 1971, and that Hunter, relying on this offer, terminated her position at the telephone company and was unemployed for two months, despite her efforts to find other employment.

On appeal the defendants urge as grounds for reversal . . . that there was no evidence of a meeting of the minds, and thus, no contract existed which could have been breached. . . .

The defendant's contention that there was no evidence of a meeting of the minds on all the terms of a contract is accurate, but irrelevant in this case. The plaintiff both pleaded and proved her detrimental reliance on defendant Hayes' promise of employment. The trial court's findings and judgment were clearly based on the doctrine of promissory estoppel, which was approved and applied by this court in *Mooney v. Craddock,* quoting the *Restatement of Contracts* §90, as follows:

A promise which the promisor would reasonably expect to induce action or forbearance of a definite and substantial character on the part of the promisee and which does induce such action or forbearance is binding if injustice can be avoided only by enforcement of the promise.

Here, the record shows that Hayes not only offered Hunter a job which was to begin on June 14, 1971, but also told her to terminate her position at the telephone company. Having done as she was bidden — as Hayes should have foreseen she would — Hunter was out of work for two months.

These circumstances permit the application of the doctrine of promissory estoppel and allow the enforcement of the promise without evidence of a meeting of the minds or consideration. Thus, the absence of evidence of a meeting of the minds was immaterial.

The defendant's argument that Hunter failed to prove that she was damaged is also without foundation. The damages awarded by the trial court were based on Hunter's monthly wages at the telephone company, namely, $350 per month, and on the period of her unemployment. When a plaintiff's recovery is predicated on findings of a promise and detrimental reliance thereon, there is no fixed measure of damages to be applied in every case. Rather, the amount of damages should be tailored to fit the facts of each case and should be only that amount which justice requires. Here, the damages awarded compensated Hunter only for the direct loss she suffered as a result of her reliance on the promised employment. This amount was not unreasonable.

Judgment affirmed.

REAMER v. UNITED STATES
532 F.2d 349 (Fourth Cir. 1976)

HAYNSWORTH, Chief Judge

In this action for breach of an enlistment contract, the plaintiff claims that the military agreed to delay his period of active duty in the reserves until after he had finished a semester of school. The district court found that the contract contained no agreement for a delay. We affirm.

In the summer of 1968, Richard Reamer was ready to enter his second year of law school, but the Selective Service had classified him as 1-A. After contacting various reserve units, he was given an opportunity to join the army reserves in Salisbury, North Carolina. On August 24, 1968, he signed an enlistment contract, which Captain Dominick and Warrant Officer Wall had negotiated on behalf of the military.

Reamer's enlistment contract is in the usual form. Its first fifty-three paragraphs contain information about him and about the obligations that he was undertaking. Paragraph 54 provides:

> I have had this contract fully explained to me, I understand it, and certify that no promise of any kind has been made to me concerning assignment to duty, geographical area, schooling, special programs, assignment of government quarters, or transportation of dependents except as indicated in attached acknowledgement of understanding of service requirements.

In paragraph 55 Reamer signed to attest his understanding of and truth of the information in the preceding clauses. The 56th paragraph, entitled "Remarks," contains the typed statement: "Delayed from entry on ACDUTRA or active duty until 1 Feb 1969." After that the oath of enlistment, signed by Reamer, and the confirmation of the enlistment, signed by Dominick.

The "acknowledgement of understanding of service requirements," referred to in the body of the enlistment contract, is a separate document, which Reamer signed at the same time that he executed the contract. That form supplies the enlistee with a variety of information about military obligations, including the statement: "I will enter on active duty for training for a period of _____ weeks within 120 days of this date,

unless a delay for a longer period is authorized or directed by the Department of the Army."

At a hearing, Captain Dominick testified that the statement in paragraph 56 was only a recommendation and that the officers tried to explain that to enlistees. He did not remember discussing it with Reamer. Mr. Wall, however, testified that he told the plaintiff twice that he could not bind the military to a delay and that special permission must come from the Third Army. Reamer testified that he thought that the statement in the contract did operate to delay his active duty. Under that impression, he began the fall semester at the University of North Carolina School of Law and incurred a number of expenses necessary for his studies. When the Army ordered him to active duty on December 3, 1968, he was obliged to leave school without finishing the semester.

Reamer filed this suit against the United States, Wall and Dominick to recover his expenditures for the unfinished semester. The district court dismissed the complaint, finding that the "Remarks" section of the form was not a part of the contract because the plaintiff had signed in the preceding paragraph. It found, as a fact, that Wall had told plaintiff that he could not bind the army to a delay and that he did not misrepresent facts concerning the plaintiff's reporting date. Accordingly, it held that the defendants had made no express or implied representation that Reamer would not be called to active duty before February 1, 1969.

The plaintiff says that his claim of promissory estoppel should have been considered even after the contract claim failed. He relies on the Restatement's provision that "[a] promise which the promisor should reasonably expect to induce action or forbearance on the part of the promisee or a third person and which does induce such action or forbearance is binding if injustice can be avoided only by enforcement of the promise." The essence of the denial of the contract claim is that no promise of a delay was made. Furthermore, even if the contract were technically construed to contain a promise, the defendants could not reasonably have expected the plaintiff to rely, and the plaintiff could not reasonably have relied, on the statement in paragraph 56 after he had twice been told that permission for the delay must come from higher authorities.

Since we find no merit in the other claims of error concerning the admission of evidence in the trial to the court, we affirm the judgment of the district court.

Affirmed.

CRAVEN, Circuit Judge (Dissenting)

Nothing could be clearer than the words "delayed from entry on ACDUTRA or active duty until February 1969" appearing in the enlistment contract. But it is an empty promise, so the majority holds, because the delay was not "authorized or directed by the Department of the Army." My brothers hold that the officers of the Army with whom Reamer dealt and who obtained his signature to the enlistment contract represented the Department of the Army for the purpose of getting him to sign the contract, but not for the purpose of putting the words of delay in it. It is a distinction too fine for me, and one to which I cannot assent.

In the new era of the volunteer Army, I am surprised that the government would want what it now has obtained: a decision which, if publicized, must be read by prospective enlistees to mean: Warning! You may not safely rely upon the terms of your enlistment contract.

CASE REVIEW QUESTIONS

1. In the *Hunter* case, was the promise of Hayes and Winslow Construction Company an example of a gratuitous promise or of an unaccepted offer? Explain.
2. In the *Reamer* case, why did Reamer's argument that the doctrine of promissory estoppel should apply against the Army fail?

Charitable Subscriptions

A pledge to a charitable institution is generally a gratuitous promise not supported by consideration. In order to protect such institutions in their important role in society, the courts have historically used legal fictions to find consideration for promises to charities where, in fact, none exist.

With the growth of the concept of promissory estoppel, some courts have enforced charitable promises without consideration on the basis that they induce action by the charity in reliance on the promise. The difficulty with this approach is that action in reliance on a particular pledge is often difficult to prove. The trend today is toward enforcing charitable subscriptions without either consideration or reliance.

Promise to Pay a Debt Discharged by Law

A new promise to pay a contractual debt that has been discharged by law is enforceable even though it is not supported by consideration. The most common examples of this exception are situations in which a new promise is made by a debtor whose debt has been discharged either by the running of a statute of limitations or through bankruptcy proceedings.

The new promise to pay such a debt must be clear and explicit and, in most states, in writing to be enforceable. In cases involving the statute of limitations, voluntary partial payment of the debt is treated as an implied new promise to pay the former debt and is enforced against the debtor unless the creditor is advised that no such new promise is being made.

This exception, it should be noted, applies only to contractual debts that have been discharged by law. Therefore, a debt that has been *voluntarily* discharged by a creditor is not revived by a new promise to pay.

Statutory Exception

Pennsylvania is the only state that has adopted a statute called the Model Written Obligations Act. One of the provisions of this act states:

> A written release or promise, hereafter made and signed by the person releasing or promising, shall not be invalid or unenforceable for lack of consideration, if the writing also contains an additional express statement, in any form of language, that the signor intends to be legally bound.

This statute substitutes a written document that includes a statement of intent to be legally bound for the traditional requirement of consideration. There is no indication, however, that other states intend to follow Pennsylvania's lead.

Contracts under Seal

Before the courts in England developed the doctrine of consideration, they would only enforce promises under seal. A **seal** consisted of wax affixed to a document and imprinted with a distinctive mark, usually made by a ring. At a later date, the courts would enforce promises that were either under seal or supported by consideration.

Today, only a few states will enforce promises under seal that are not supported by consideration. In these few states, the seal is usually not an impression in wax. Instead, it is designated simply by the word "seal" or the letters "L.S." (*locus sigilli,* the place of the seal) at or near the place where the signature appears. In other states, the seal is inoperative; that is, its use has no effect.

REVIEW QUESTIONS

1. What are the three elements that must be present in order for a promise to be supported by consideration?

2. In what way is the doctrine of consideration an issue when parties to a contract modify their agreement by having one of the parties promise to do something more than that party originally agreed to?

3. In what way is the doctrine of consideration an issue when a creditor promises to discharge a debt if the debtor makes a partial payment of the debt?

4. Under what circumstances will a court apply the doctrine of promissory estoppel?

CASE PROBLEMS

1. William E. Story, Sr., was the uncle of William E. Story, II. When the nephew was 15 years old, his uncle promised him that if he (the nephew) would refrain from drinking, using tobacco, swearing,

and playing cards for money until he was 21, he (the uncle) would pay him $5,000. The nephew assented and fully performed the conditions. When the nephew became 21, the uncle refused to pay the $5,000. The nephew brought suit to enforce the promise, and the uncle defended the suit on the grounds that his promise was not supported by consideration. Who will win the case? Explain.

2. Manwill and Oyler were close friends. When Oyler fell on hard times, Manwill gave him several thousand dollars over a period of years to see him through. Oyler did not promise to repay the money, and Manwill did not expect to be repaid when he gave the money to Oyler. When Oyler's fortune improved, he was so grateful to Manwill that he promised to repay all of the money that Manwill had given to him. Later, however, when Manwill asked for the money, Oyler replied that he had changed his mind and refused to pay back the money. Manwill brought a legal action to enforce the promise to repay all of the money. Oyler defended on the grounds that his promise was not supported by consideration. Who will win the case? Explain.

3. Suttle was a mine promoter and owner. Friedman, at various times, had looked up and written up mining properties for Suttle. Suttle asked Friedman to look for good prospects for him, telling him that he would examine any property that Friedman brought to his notice and, if the property were satisfactory, purchase it. Friedman brought the property known as "Three Black Buttes" to Suttle's notice. He showed Suttle written reports concerning the property and samples of ore from it and told him its location and the name of the owner. Friedman advised Suttle that the purchase price was $36,000 and that he desired a commission of $4,000 for his services. Suttle was interested in the property and told Friedman that he would pay the commission if he bought the property.

Suttle subsequently bought the property, but he refused to pay the commission. Friedman brought legal action to collect the commission. Suttle defended on the grounds that his promise to pay the commission was not supported by con-

sideration since Friedman had given him all the information about the mine before he made the promise. Who will win the case? Explain.

4. The county of Allegheny in Pennsylvania wished to widen a highway, so they took a portion of Quarture's land. Quarture hired an attorney, Sniderman, to represent him in a legal action to recover money from the county for taking the land. Sniderman and Quarture signed an agreement that called for Sniderman to "institute, conduct, superintend or prosecute to final determination, including any appeals, an action against the County of Allegheny on account of taking property in the widening of State Highway 545." Quarture was to pay Sniderman "10 percent of all that is recovered" as a fee.

The Board of Viewers of Allegheny County awarded $1,650 for the land after listening to Sniderman's presentation on behalf of Quarture. Quarture told Sniderman that he wanted to appeal the Board's decision. Sniderman said he would bring the appeal to the Court of Common Pleas only if Quarture would enter into a new agreement providing for a fee of 33⅓ percent of the amount awarded on appeal. The new agreement was entered into and Sniderman brought the appeal. The Court of Common Pleas awarded $2,961 for the land taken by the county. Sniderman demanded $987 (one-third of the award on appeal) from Quarture. When Quarture would only pay $296.10 (10 percent of the amount awarded) Sniderman brought legal action to recover $690.90. Quarture defended on the grounds that his promise to pay 33⅓ percent of the amount awarded on appeal was not supported by consideration. Who will win the case? Explain.

5. Pittsburgh Testing Laboratory entered into a written subcontract with Farnsworth in which Pittsburgh agreed to do all of the testing and inspection of materials required under a master contract between Farnsworth and Douglas Aircraft for the construction of concrete ramps and runways. Farnsworth was to pay Pittsburgh a fee of $24,450 for its services. During preliminary negotiations, Farnsworth had estimated that the job would be completed in seven months. This

estimate provided the basis for Pittsburgh's fee, but there was no guarantee in the contract of a completion date.

Before the end of the seven-month period, it became clear that the contract would not be completed within the estimated time, due mainly to the necessity of moving 1,200,000 tons of dirt instead of an estimated 600,000 tons. A controversy then arose between the parties. Pittsburgh told Farnsworth that it would not proceed unless a new contract was entered into that provided payment for the remaining work at the rate of $3,492 per month until the completion of the work. Farnsworth agreed to these new terms, and Pittsburgh continued to provide the same services as before. When the work was completed, Farnsworth refused to pay anything more than the $24,450 originally agreed to. Pittsburgh brought legal action to recover the additional amounts due under the second agreement. Farnsworth defended on the grounds that its promise to pay the additional amounts under the new contract was not supported by consideration. Who will win the case? Explain.

6. Dr. Foakes owed Julia Beer $2,000 plus interest. He promised to pay $500 at once and the balance in installments if Mrs. Beer would forget about the interest. Mrs. Beer agreed. After Foakes had finished making the payments as agreed, Mrs. Beer demanded that he also pay the interest. He refused. When Mrs. Beer brought a legal action to collect the interest, Dr. Foakes defended on the grounds that she had promised not to collect the interest. Mrs. Beer countered by arguing that her promise was not binding because it was not supported by consideration. Who will win the case? Explain.

7. Jaffray sold goods to Davis on which $7,714.37 was owed. Jaffray promised to accept $3,462.24 in full payment of the purchase price if Davis would sign a promissory note for that amount and give Jaffray a mortgage on the inventory, fixtures, and other property used in Davis' business. Davis gave Jaffray the note and the mortgage and, in the course of the following year, paid the $3,462.24. At that time, Jaffray demanded payment of the full original purchase price. Davis refused. When Jaffray brought a legal action to collect the balance of the debt, Davis defended on the grounds that Jaffray had promised not to collect the balance of the original debt. Jaffray countered by arguing that his promise was not binding because it was not supported by consideration. Who will win the case? Explain.

8. Amino Brothers Construction Co. contracted with Elk County to build an earthen dam. During the course of construction, it was determined that extra work would be required to complete the dam. The parties entered into a contract modification providing that extra compensation would be paid for the extra work. The amount of extra compensation was left for later determination after a study of the costs involved.

When work was completed, Amino was paid the initially agreed upon contract price. Amino then submitted its cost records to the county, along with a bill for $22,342.96 for the extra work. The county, however, believed that only $2,944.72 should be paid for the extra work. The county sent a check for that amount to Amino. On the face of the check was the statement: "Endorsement constitutes a receipt in full when check is paid." Amino endorsed and cashed the check. It then brought legal action against Elk County seeking the balance of its claim for extra work. Elk County defended on the grounds that endorsement of the check constituted a promise to discharge the balance claimed by Amino. Amino countered by arguing that its promise was not supported by consideration. Who will win the case? Explain.

9. Mrs. Bredermann was an employee at will of Vaughan Manufacturing Company for many years. When her son became ill she considered leaving her job but did not feel that she could live on the pension she would receive if she retired at that time. The president of the company, after hearing of Mrs. Bredermann's problem, told her, "I have tried to work something out for you. I know you have been worried and you have been nervous. I want you to take your retirement now, and we will—the company will—pay you full salary for the rest of your life." Mrs. Bredermann then decided to retire.

The company sent her a check for her full salary for three years but then reduced the payments by half. Four years later, the company discontinued the checks altogether. Mrs. Bredermann brought a legal action seeking damages for the company's failure to pay her full salary as had been promised. The company defended on the grounds that the promise was not supported by consideration. Who will win the case? Explain.

10. Universal Credit Company delivered five cars to Lusk to be reconditioned and resold. It was agreed that possession of the cars was at the "sole risk of Lusk as to all loss and injury." Afterwards, Universal notified Lusk that it would carry fire and theft insurance on the cars. As a result, Lusk did not insure the cars. Later, through no fault of Lusk, the cars were destroyed by fire. Universal demanded payment in full from Lusk. Lusk insisted that if the cars had been insured and payment for the loss were made by the insurance company, Universal's claims would be satisfied. Universal had not insured the cars, however, even though they had said they would. Universal brought a legal action against Lusk to collect the value of the cars. Lusk defended on the grounds that Universal had promised to insure the cars. Universal countered by arguing that their promise was not binding because it was not supported by consideration. Who will win the case? Explain.

13

CONTRACTS IN WRITING

The fact the courts enforce promises creates the danger that people may lie and say that someone made a promise to them when in fact no such promise was made. Or, if a promise was made, the parties may disagree over exactly what it was that was promised. For example, a buyer may believe that the agreed upon purchase price in a sales contract was $500, whereas the seller may believe that the price agreed to was $600.

One way to deal with both lying and honest disagreement is to require that the parties put their agreement in writing and then to limit enforcement to the promises contained in the written document. In this chapter, you will see that this is the approach that the law has used to provide certainty in contracts and to prevent perjury. You will also see, however, that this approach has caused some serious problems of its own with which the law has had to deal.

In this chapter, you will also be introduced to the problem of imprecision in contract language. How should the language of a contract be interpreted by a court when the parties disagree over its meaning? Also, what should be done about technical legal language that is used to make contract terms more precise but may not be comprehensible to one not trained in law?

STATUTE OF FRAUDS

The procedures used by the English courts in the seventeenth century to determine the facts of a case were grossly inadequate for getting at the truth, and people frequently used the procedures for fraudulent purposes. For instance, a person who wanted the property of another might simply go to court, allege that the owner had promised to sell the property, and ask the court to enforce the promise. Because of the inadequacy of the procedures for proving facts used at the time, the party bringing such an action might be able to convince the court that the promise had been made even though there was no real evidence to prove the allegation.

The abuse of the courts' procedures to enforce promises that had not in fact been made became a serious problem. When it appeared that the courts were unable to do anything about the problem, the English Parliament enacted the **Statute of Frauds** in 1677. This act required that, to be enforceable, certain promises had to be in a writing that was signed by the party against whom the promise was to be enforced. By requiring a signed writing, Parliament hoped to stop the enforcement of promises that had not been made. For the same reason, the legislatures of all the states in the United States have enacted statutes that are virtually identical to the one adopted by Parliament in 1677.

When Is a Writing Necessary?

The Statute of Frauds does not require that all promises be in a signed writing to be enforceable. Unless a promise falls within one of the following categories, it is enforceable regardless of whether it is in writing or not:

1. Contracts for the sale of land or an interest in land.
2. Contracts for the sale of goods for a price of $500 or more.
3. Contracts in consideration of marriage.
4. Contracts not to be performed within one year.
5. Contracts containing a promise to pay the debt of another.
6. Contracts containing a promise by an **executor** or **administrator** (i.e., persons appointed by a court to represent the estate of a deceased person) to pay the debts of the decedent from the executor's or administrator's own funds.

Why have these particular contracts been singled out as the only ones that must be in writing to be enforceable? The reasons vary. Some of them—contracts for the sale of land, for the sale of goods for a price of $500 or more, and in consideration of marriage, for example—are especially important both to the individuals involved and to society. Requiring that they be in writing promotes deliberation by the parties and makes society more certain that they have been made.

Contracts not to be performed within one year are required to be in writing because of the concern that the parties and witnesses to a contract will not be able to recall the terms of an oral agreement correctly after an extended period. Requiring a writing in such cases promotes certainty in commercial transactions since the parties can be sure that only the exact promises they have actually made will be enforced. A **collateral contract,** which is a contract whereby one person promises to pay the debt of another, is required to be in writing because of an inherent suspicion as to whether such a promise has in fact been made. A writing also promotes deliberation in the making of such promises and limits enforcement to the exact promise that has been made.

Preventing perjury, promoting certainty, and encouraging deliberation are all worthy functions of the Statute of Frauds. If applied mechanically, however, the Statute can also promote dishonesty. Suppose, for instance, that two parties enter into an oral agreement. That agreement, even though oral, creates expectations in the parties. Contract law, in order to stimulate economic activity, will generally encourage reliance by the parties on their expectations by enforcing such promises. If the oral contract falls within one of the categories of the Statute of Frauds, however, it may not be enforced even though the promisor admits to having made the promise and to having made it after deliberation. In other words, there may be times when the enforcement of the Statute will defeat the very policies that contract law seek to promote.

Some courts have taken the position that in such cases they have no choice but to enforce the Statute as written. More typically, however, the courts have found various ways of avoiding application of the Statute in order to avoid injustice. In some cases, this has been accomplished by the courts by creating exceptions for certain contracts even though they fall within the categories of the Statute that require a writing. For example, courts have held that an oral contract to pay the debt of another is enforceable if the other person's original debt is thereby discharged or if the promise is made to the original debtor rather than to the creditor. Partial performance of a contract may also lead a court to make an exception, especially if the kind of partial performance unequivocally indicates that a contract has been made and what its terms are.

In other cases, the courts have given a narrow construction to the Statute, leading to the conclusion that certain contracts that appear to fall within one of the categories requiring a writing actually do not. A promise to pay the debt of another, for example, may be enforced even though it is not in writing if the promisor's main purpose for making the promise was to benefit himself or herself. Similarly, a contract that is not to be performed within a year will be enforced if it could *possibly* be fully performed within a year, even though performance within a year is unlikely or did not in fact occur. Application of these two exceptions can be seen in the two cases that follow.

STUART STUDIO, INC. v. NATIONAL SCHOOL OF HEAVY EQUIPMENT, INC.
214 S.E.2d 192 (N.C. App. 1975)

[Stuart Studio, Inc. (Stuart) is an art studio. Stuart negotiated with Gilbert S. Shaw, chairman of the Board of Directors of the National School of Heavy Equipment, Inc. (National) concerning the preparation and printing of 25,000 catalogues for National. The parties discussed payment, and Shaw told Stuart that payment would be within ten days after billing. Shaw further stated that if National could not pay the amount due, he, Shaw, would stand good for the entire bill. Shaw's promise was not in writing.

After performing under the contract, Stuart could not obtain payment from either National or Shaw. He brought a legal action against both of them. At the completion of the presentation of Stuart's evidence at the trial, Shaw moved for a directed verdict on the grounds that his promise was not enforceable because it was not in writing as required by the Statute of Frauds. The trial court granted the motion. Stuart appealed.]

CLARK, Judge

The North Carolina Statute of Frauds, a substantial prototype of the historic English statute, contains the provision that

> no action shall be brought . . . upon a special promise to answer the debt . . . of another person, unless the agreement upon which such action shall be brought, or some memorandum or note thereof, shall be in writing, and signed by the party charged therewith. . . .

The promise of Gilbert S. Shaw to stand good for the debt of National School of Heavy Equipment, Inc., to be incurred for the printing of catalogues was not in writing and was within the Statute of Frauds unless plaintiff has offered evidence to invoke the application of the "main purpose rule," which is a well-known exception to the rule requiring that such promises be evidenced by a written memorandum.

The "main purpose rule" is stated in *Burlington Industries v. Foil* as follows:

> . . . [W]henever the main purpose and object of the promisor is not to answer for another, but to subserve some pecuniary or business purpose of his own, involving either a benefit to himself, or damage to the other contracting party, his promise is not within the statute, although it may be in form a promise to pay the debt of another, and although the performance of it may incidentally have the effect of extinguishing that liability.

Shaw's personal and pecuniary interest in the transaction was evident; he was the founder of the School, owned 100% of the Class A voting stock and 49% of the Class B stock, was Chairman of the Board of Directors, and as an officer drew a monthly salary of $2,000. At this time, 6 March 1972, it is reasonable to assume that the School was facing financial difficulty; Shaw personally advanced $12,000 to the School during this period of financial distress. The school went into receivership in December 1972, and bankruptcy in March 1973. Apparently, Shaw sought, in a final effort to avoid the School's financial ruin, to attract new students through an advertising campaign, which included the production and circulation of new catalogues.

In this case, the evidence offered by the plaintiff tends to show that Gilbert S. Shaw had a personal and direct interest in the School; and the evidence is clearly sufficient to raise an issue for jury determination. We find that the trial court improvidently granted defendant's motion for directed verdict and the judgment is modified and the cause remanded for trial on the issue of the liability of Gilbert S. Shaw on the printing contract of 6 March 1972.

Modified and remanded.

KEYSTONE INTERNATIONAL, INC. v. INGHAM
593 S.W.2d 354 (Texas 1979)

[Ingham, a manufacturer's representative, agreed to represent Keystone International, Inc. (referred to in the case as SEMCO, the name under which it did business) in selling equipment to the Nestle Company at their plant in Freehold, New Jersey. SEMCO orally agreed to pay a 5 percent commission on all such sales made by Ingham. Ingham made a sale to Nestle and sought payment of the commission. Because of a dispute between Ingham and SEMCO over how much the sale to Nestle was worth, SEMCO refused to pay the full amount demanded by Ingham.

Ingham brought suit against SEMCO for breach of contract to collect the amount he believed due to him. One of Keystone's defenses was that their contract with Ingham was unenforceable because it was not in writing as required by the Statute of Frauds. The trial court ruled that the contract did not fall within the requirements of the Statute of Frauds and gave judgment to Ingham. SEMCO appealed.]

RAY, Justice

SEMCO insists that the agreement confirmed by the letter is unenforceable as a contract because it was not to be performed within one year from the date of its making. . . . The argument of SEMCO is that the Texas Statute of Frauds applies because Ingham testified that the Nestle project would "probably take more than a year to build." The authorities do not support appellant's position. As a general rule, to fall within the statute of frauds and be unenforceable ". . . the agreement must be one of which it can truly be said at the very moment it is made, 'This agreement is not to be performed within one year'; in general the cases indicate that there must not be the slightest possibility that it can be fully performed within one year. . . ." It makes no difference how long the parties expect performance to take or how reasonable and accurate those expectations are, if the agreed performance can possibly be completed within a year. The Texas cases are consistent with this reasoning. In *Hall v. Hall* our Supreme Court held that,

> . . . in order to fall within the statute, it must appear from the terms of the contract that performance cannot be completed within one year. . . . A corollary to the foregoing is that where the term of performance is uncertain in the sense that the contract merely provides for the performance of a particular act or acts, such as building of a house, which can conceivably be performed within one year, the statute does not apply, however improbable performance within one year may be.

We do not believe that the testimony of Ingham that the project would "probably take more than a year" is conclusive evidence that the contract could not be performed within one year.

Judgment affirmed.

CASE REVIEW QUESTIONS

1. In *Stuart,* which provision of the Statute of Frauds appears to require that the contract be in writing? What is the purpose or function of requiring a writing in such a case?
2. In *Stuart,* why doesn't the court require a writing? Does the exception applied by the court defeat the purpose or function of the Statute of Frauds' requirement?
3. In *Ingham,* which provision of the Statute of Frauds appears to require that the contract be in writing? What is the purpose or function of requiring a writing in such a case?
4. In *Ingham,* why doesn't the court require a writing? Does the court's interpretation of the Statute of Frauds defeat the purpose or function of the Statute's requirement?

What Kind of Writing Is Required?

The Statute of Frauds requires that, in order to be enforceable, contracts falling within its provisions must be in a written memorandum that is signed by the party against whom a promise is to be enforced. The writing, however, need not be in any particular form. Although it will generally take the form of a formal written agreement between the parties, letters, telegrams, business records, or any other form of writing will suffice. Furthermore, the writing need not have been made with the Statute in mind, nor need the writing be made at the time the contract is made. Indeed, the writing need not even be in existence at the time the suit is begun as long as it did exist at one time.

Usually, all of the necessary contents of the written memorandum will be contained in one document, but two or more documents may be used to show the necessary contents in some instances. If all of the documents have been signed and clearly relate to the same transaction, if the documents are attached to one another, or if the signed document expressly refers to the unsigned documents, the requirement of the Statute is met. Some courts will also allow the promisee to present evidence to show that documents are connected if they refer to the same transaction, even though they do not expressly refer to one another.

To meet the requirements of the Statute, the memorandum must state with reasonable certainty the parties to the contract, the subject matter of the contract, and the essential terms of the contract. In addition, as noted above, it must be signed by the party against whom the promise contained in the contract is to be enforced. The signing may take any form as long as it was made with the intent to authenticate the writing. In the following case, the court had to determine if the terms contained in a written agreement were sufficient to meet these requirements.

McDANIEL v. SILVERNAIL
346 N.E.2d 382 (Ill. App. 1976)

[Alfreda Silvernail owned some land. She entered into an agreement with McDaniel, who had been renting a house located on the land, to sell part of the land. The agreement read:

I agree to sell to George McDaniel the house on R.D. 2, in which he now lives, plus two acres, for $600 to be agreed.

/s/Alfreda Silvernail

When Silvernail refused to perform her promise, McDaniel brought a legal action against her for breach of contract. Silvernail defended on the grounds that the written agreement was not sufficient to meet the requirements of the Statute of Frauds, and, therefore, her promise was not enforceable. The trial court found for Silvernail. McDaniel appealed.]

SIMKINS, Justice

Manifestly, this writing is insufficient to satisfy the Statute of Frauds. A contract for the sale of land can-

not be specifically enforced by a court unless the writing contains: (1) the names of the vendor and vendee; (2) a description of the property which is sufficiently certain so that it can be identified; (3) the price, the terms and conditions of sale; and (4) the signature of the party to be charged.

From this document, a court would be unable to locate the boundaries of the property to be conveyed. Plaintiffs rely on the *Callaghan* case and upon *Draper v. Hoops.* Both are readily distinguishable. In *Callaghan,* the property was described as:

[T]he Altha Martin property located on Route 25, north of the city of Batavia, Illinois. This area comprises five acres more or less. The space now occupied by 20 trailers is properly licensed and zoned by the State of Illinois and Kane County Zoning Dept. . . .

There was no evidence in *Callaghan* that the seller owned more than 5 acres at that location. The description therefore is referrable to the entire property held by the seller. In the case at bar [plaintiff alleges] defendant is the owner of a quarter-quarter Section but the contract refers to only two acres of that land.

In *Draper* the property was described as "158 acres in Lee County, Illinois." That was sufficient when supplemented by a definite written description given to the buyer simultaneously with the agreement. However, two parcels of property described as a frame residence in Walnut, Ill., and a two-story house in Franklin Park, Week Resubdivision, east of W.C.R.R. were both so indefinite that specific performance could not be ordered.

The case at bar is similar to *Wetmore v. Watson.* In *Wetmore,* the seller agreed to convey 100 acres of real estate situated in Fayette County, Illinois, on condition that he inherit the land from his aunt. This description was too indefinite because the aunt owned 600 acres at the time the contract was entered into. It was impossible to determine which 100 acres he meant to be conveyed. Similarly, it is impossible to determine which two acres are meant to be conveyed by this contract.

Judgment affirmed.

CASE REVIEW QUESTIONS

1. Which provision of the Statute of Frauds required the contract in the above case to be in writing? What is the purpose or function of requiring a writing in such a case?
2. Why specifically have the requirements of the Statute of Frauds not been met in this case?
3. Has the purpose or function of requiring a writing in cases such as this been carried out in this case?

The Effect of Failure to Comply

The Statute of Frauds provides that, if a contract that falls within one of the categories requiring a writing has not been put in writing, the contract is unenforceable. This is why McDaniel was not able to enforce his contract with Silvernail in the case that you just read.

Notice that, when the *McDaniel* case went to court, neither McDaniel nor Silvernail had performed the promises they had made. Suppose, however, that Silvernail had given McDaniel a deed to the two acres of land on which the house stood and McDaniel had paid the $600 to her. Would performance by both parties of their promises have changed the outcome of the case? The answer is yes. When the statute applies, it makes contracts unenforceable, not void or voidable. Therefore, once both parties have fully performed their contract promises, neither party has the legal right to rescind the contract, even though it is not in writing.

What if one party to an oral contract that falls within one of the categories of the statute has performed his or her promise, but the other has not? Suppose, for instance, that a salesperson whose employment contract must be in writing to be enforceable makes sales for a company. Can the company refuse to compensate the salesperson on the ground that its promise to compensate is not enforceable because of the Statute of Frauds?

The company is correct in its argument that its promise is unenforceable. However, the law gives a party who has performed under a contract that is not enforceable because of the Statute of Frauds the right to recover the value of any benefit that he or she has provided to the other party. This recovery, called a **quasi-contract** remedy, provides **restitution** for someone who has acted in reliance on the existence of a contract that is later determined to be unenforceable because of the Statute of Frauds. Therefore, the salesperson in our example would be entitled to compensation for the fair value of his or her services. The remedies of restitution and quasi-contract are fully explained in Chapter 18.

Modern Trends

The Statute of Frauds, except as it applied to contracts for the sale of land and to pay the debt of another, was repealed by the English Parliament in 1954. Although it has been severely criticized in the United States because it often promotes rather than prevents frauds, repeal of the Statute has not been seriously considered and seems unlikely. Nevertheless, there have been efforts in the United States to maintain the desirable functions of the Statute while minimizing the harm it can cause.

One change in the law is found in §2-201 of the Uniform Commercial Code, which applies to the Statute of Frauds requirement concerning the sale of goods for a price of $500 or more. Under the Code, if a person "admits in his pleading, testimony or otherwise in court that a contract for sale was made," the contract is enforceable even though it is not in writing, but only to the extent of the quantity of goods admitted to. Prior to the enactment of this provision, oral contracts that were required by the Statute to be in writing to be enforceable were not enforced even if the promisor admitted that a contract existed. The Code also provides for other changes in the Statute's requirements with regard to the sale of goods. These will be discussed in Chapter 19, which concerns the law of sales.

Another modern trend is the increasing use by the courts of the concept of promissory estoppel, discussed earlier in Chapter 12. In cases in which a promise has been made that the promisor could reasonably expect the promisee to rely on and the promisee does in fact detrimentally rely on the promise, courts are enforcing such promises with increasing frequency, even though they fall within one of the categories of the Statute of Frauds and are not in writing. The concept of promissory estoppel is applied by the court in the following case.

LUCAS v. WHITTAKER CORPORATION
470 F.2d 326 (Tenth Cir. 1972)

[Lucas entered into a verbal employment agreement with Whittaker Corporation. To accept the employment, Lucas had to resign from the job he already had in Missouri and move his family to Denver, Colorado, where he assumed his duties. The terms of the verbal employment contract included a $27,000 annual salary for a fixed period of two years. After thirteen months Lucas was fired.

Lucas sued Whittaker for breach of contract. Whittaker defended on the grounds that its promise to employ Lucas was not enforceable because it was not in writing as required by the Statute of Frauds. The trial court held that under the circumstances the doctrine of promissory estoppel prevented Whittaker from asserting the Statute of Frauds as a defense. Whittaker appealed.]

PICKETT, Circuit Judge

The contract having been consummated in California, Colorado law requires the application of California law in determining its validity.

In California the doctrine of estoppel to assert the statute of frauds is applied to prevent fraud that would result from a refusal to enforce an oral contract. It is said that "[s]uch fraud may inhere in the unconscionable injury that would result from denying enforcement of the contract after one party has been induced by the other seriously to change his position in reliance on the contract. . . ."

The nub of Whittaker's argument is that Lucas gave up no more than any person who leaves his present employment for what he thinks is a better job. The trial court held that Lucas' detrimental reliance on the two-year contract in moving to Colorado was more than that suffered in the ordinary change of jobs.

Lucas, in accepting the offered employment by Whittaker, resigned from what appeared to be a secure job with a company for whom he had worked for nine years, including incidents of that employment—medical and life insurance benefits, stock options, accrued vacation time and a college tuition supplement for eligible dependents. He sold a custom-built house in which he and his family lived for only eight months. He gave up business and social contacts. All of this obviously was lost because of Lucas' reliance on the oral agreement. The trial court's fact finding of unconscionable injury is not clearly erroneous. That Lucas earned more during his thirteen months with Whittaker than he would have earned in two years at his old job is irrelevant in determining unconscionable injury.

Affirmed.

CASE REVIEW QUESTIONS
1. Which provision of the Statute of Frauds requires that the contract between Lucas and Whittaker be in writing?
2. If Whittaker had been allowed to assert the Statute of Frauds as a defense, in what manner discussed earlier in the chapter might the court have interpreted the Statute so as to avoid its application in this case?
3. Why specifically was Whittaker not allowed to assert the Statute of Frauds as a defense?

PAROL EVIDENCE RULE

The Statute of Frauds, as you have read, encourages people to put their agreements in writing and seeks thereby to prevent lying. The **parol evidence rule** seeks to achieve a similar purpose, but in a different manner. Like the Statute of Frauds, though, the parol evidence rule has at times caused problems of its own.

The parol evidence rule states that a written document that is intended by the parties to be a complete and final expression of their agreement (a complete and final expression is called an **integration**) cannot be contradicted or supplemented by evidence of an oral agreement made between the parties either prior to or at the same time as the written contract or by other **extrinsic evidence.** You should note that the parol evidence rule applies to all written contracts, not just those that must be in writing because of the Statute of Frauds.

Intent of the Parties

Problems concerning the parol evidence rule have arisen because of different interpretations of the part of the rule that requires that the parties "intend" their written contract to be a complete expression of their agreement, that is, an integration. How is such an intent to be determined?

Traditionally, the courts have said that the intent of the parties concerning this issue should be determined by looking only at the writing itself. If the writing contains a **merger clause**—that is, an express statement that it contains the parties' complete agreement—or otherwise appears to be an integration, it will be treated as such.

Even when the courts determine the parties' intent in this way, the parol evidence rule may in some cases promote dishonesty rather than discourage it. Suppose, for instance, that a person wishes to store furniture in a warehouse. The written form of agreement, provided by the company, states that the risk of destruction to the furniture by fire is retained by the furniture owner. The warehouse company's representative, however, says "Don't let that worry you, we'll be happy to pay for any fire loss." If the furniture is destroyed by fire, and a court determines that the written contract appears to be the parties' complete agreement, the furniture owner will not be allowed to present evidence of the oral statement made by the warehouse company's representative because it contradicts the integration. In such a case, the parol evidence rule would protect the very dishonesty it was intended to prevent. Under such a rule, then, it is essential that the parties make certain that the writing contains all of the terms of their agreement.

Today, there is a trend away from the traditional approach to determining whether the parties intend that their written contract be a complete and final expression of their agreement. The modern view does not limit the search for the parties' intent to the written document. Instead, the court will consider all relevant evidence of the parties' intent even when the writing contains a merger clause.

Under this approach, the furniture owner would be allowed to testify about the representative's statement concerning the risk of destruction of the furniture by fire to show that the written contract was not intended to be an integration. If the court agrees that the writing was not intended to be a complete expression of the agreement, the parol evidence rule would not be applicable, and the furniture owner would be allowed to contradict the writing with evidence of the oral statement by the representative.

In the case that follows, the court was confronted with evidence of an oral agreement between the parties that was different from their written agreement. The court therefore had to decide whether or not the parol evidence rule was applicable.

NATIONAL CASH REGISTER COMPANY v. I.M.C., INC.
491 P.2d 211 (Or. 1971)

[A salesman for National Cash Register Company (NCR) approached the bookkeeper for I.M.C., Inc. (IMC) about leasing an accounting machine. IMC's bookkeeper agreed on behalf of her company to lease the machine. She signed a printed form contract provided by the salesman. One provision of the form read that IMC would rent the equipment "for a term of ____ year(s)." When the bookkeeper signed the form, the blank space in this provision had not been filled in. The form contract also included a provision on the back in small print to the effect that the contract could only be terminated after payment of not less than 12 months' rent.

When the salesman returned to his office, he filled in the blank space to read "for a term of 1 year(s)." The contract was thereafter signed by another employee of NCR who did not know that the blank had not been filled in when the contract was signed by the bookkeeper. No copy of the contract, as thus filled in and signed by NCR, was sent to IMC.

After leasing the machine for only a few months, IMC notified NCR that it was terminating the agreement. NCR then brought a legal action against IMC for breach of contract claiming that the minimal rental period was for one year.

IMC defended on the grounds that NCR's salesman had told IMC's bookkeeper that the equipment rental was on a month-to-month basis, that this was the reason why the blank was not filled in, and that the small print on the back of the form would not apply. The bookkeeper testified at the trial that when she signed the contract she recognized that it was "incomplete," and that she only signed it so that the salesman could "get an order through."

NCR's salesman testified that he had explained to IMC's bookkeeper that the equipment could only be leased for a minimum period of one year. NCR also argued that the trial court judge should not consider the bookkeeper's testimony that she believed the rental to be on a month-to-month basis because to do so would violate the parol evidence rule.

The trial court found for IMC because "the term of the lease agreement was on a monthly basis and not for a period of one year." NCR appealed.]

TONGUE, [Judge]

In this case the question is presented whether or not there was ever an integration of the oral agreement into the written contract as a "memorial" of the terms of the previous oral agreement. It is well established [in Oregon] that parol evidence is admissible to show that the parties never intended to integrate their oral agreement into a written contract.

[D]efendant's bookkeeper testified that although she understood that the equipment was to be rented on a month-to-month basis, when she signed the written form contract she recognized that it was "incomplete," but signed it so that plaintiff's salesman could "get an order through" for the equipment and so that he would have "some record" to show that the equipment had been delivered. From this evidence it follows that although the parties orally agreed to lease the equipment on a month-to-month basis, as found by the trial court, they did not agree to an integration of that oral agreement into a written lease agreement.

It necessarily follows that since no valid written contract was agreed upon by the parties, plaintiff is not entitled to recover judgment for rental payments for the remainder of the alleged one year term, as held by the trial court. It also follows that we must affirm the judgment of the trial court in denying plaintiff such a remedy.

Affirmed.

CASE REVIEW QUESTIONS

1. State specifically why the court believed that the parol evidence rule was not applicable in this case.

2. Which of the two views concerning the determination of the intent of the parties that their written contract is to be a complete expression of their agreement does the court follow?
3. How would the case have been decided if the court had believed that the parol evidence rule was applicable?

Narrow Interpretation of the Parol Evidence Rule

Because of the possible problems caused by application of the parol evidence rule, the courts have generally interpreted it narrowly. Thus, the rule is not applicable in the following situations:

1. When a party wishes to present evidence to prove that a contract is void or voidable. For example, a party to a contract can show that the writing was signed under duress even if the writing contains a provision stating that it was not signed under duress. In such a situation, the party is not seeking to contradict or supplement the agreement, but to show that no contract exists.
2. When a party wishes to present evidence to prove an agreement entered into subsequent to the written contract. For example, a party to a written contract can show that it was modified by a subsequent oral agreement because the rule only applies to prior or simultaneous oral agreements.
3. When a party wishes to present evidence to prove additional, noncontradictory terms that would naturally be made but that were not included in the writing. In such a situation, the courts have said that the writing was not intended to be a complete expression of the parties' agreement and that consistent additional terms may be added.

In the case that follows, the court had to determine whether the parol evidence rule was applicable. Follow the procedure in the case carefully so that you understand how the issue of the applicability of the parol evidence rule arose.

CUNNINGHAM v. BROWN
276 S.E.2d 718 (N.C. App. 1981)

[Lance Cunningham was driving a motorcycle on which his wife, Pamela Cunningham (hereinafter referred to as plaintiff–wife) was a passenger. Louise Brown (hereinafter referred to as defendant) was traveling on the same highway and in the same direction as the Cunninghams, separated from them by a tractor-trailer. As Lance Cunningham passed the tractor-trailer, defendant turned from her right lane of travel into her left lane of travel and into the path of the motorcycle, resulting in a collision.

Allstate Insurance Company, insurer for Lance Cunningham, paid plaintiff–wife $4,975.00. In return for the payment, plaintiff–wife signed a document called a release. The document stated that plaintiff–

wife "released and forever discharged Lance Cunningham *and any other person, firm or corporation charged or chargeable with responsibility or liability* from any and all claims, particularly on account of personal injury sustained in consequence of" the accident described above. [Emphasis added.]

Plaintiff – wife later brought a legal action against defendant. Defendant moved for summary judgment, seeking dismissal of plaintiff – wife's claim on the basis of the release that plaintiff – wife had signed. Plaintiff – wife submitted an affidavit in opposition to defendant's motion, arguing that although she had signed the release, she had not read it, had not been given a copy of it, had thought it was merely a receipt for the insurance company's check, and had been told by the Allstate representative that signing it would not affect her claim against defendant.

The trial court excluded plaintiff – wife's affidavit on grounds of the parol evidence rule, granted defendant's motion for a summary judgment, and dismissed plaintiff – wife's claim. Plaintiff – wife appealed.]

WHICHARD, Judge

A release, like any other contract, is subject to avoidance by a showing that its execution resulted from fraud or mutual mistake of fact. This rule of contract law is founded on the proposition that there can be no contract without a meeting of the minds; and that when a contract is executed under circumstances amounting to fraud or mutual mistake, the requisite meeting of the minds does not occur. Thus, plaintiff – wife here could avoid the effect of the release pleaded by defendant . . . by showing that the release was procured under circumstances amounting to fraud or mutual mistake.

This she sought to do by the introduction of the affidavit which the trial court excluded. The trial court specifically stated in its order allowing defendant's motion for summary judgment that the objection to introduction of the affidavit was made "on the grounds of the parol evidence rule." This rule . . . provides that a written contract cannot be contradicted by evidence of prior or contemporaneous negotiations or conversations. It in effect establishes a presumption that the writing accurately reflects the matters on which the minds of the parties ultimately met.

The parol evidence rule does not, however, preclude admission of extrinsic evidence when one of the parties seeks to prove that a written agreement was executed under circumstances amounting to fraud or mutual mistake. In these circumstances the offering party does not seek to contradict a written agreement, but seeks to show the existence of facts which prevented a meeting of the minds and the consequent formation of a contract. The question presented, then, by plaintiff – wife's assignment of error to the exclusion of her affidavit on grounds of parol evidence rule, is whether the facts contained in the affidavit sufficiently raised issues of fraud or mutual mistake in the execution of the release. If so, pursuant to the rule permitting extrinsic evidence to demonstrate the existence of fraud or mistake, the affidavit should have been admitted for the purpose of showing matter in avoidance of defendant's plea of the release as a bar to plaintiff – wife's claim.

[The court then reviewed the factual allegations contained in the affidavit to determine whether they sufficiently alleged fraud or mistake.]

We conclude that the affidavit offered by plaintiff – wife in avoidance of defendant's motion for summary judgment was admissible pursuant to the above cited authorities which permit the introduction of parol evidence tending to show that execution of a written agreement was procured under circumstances amounting to fraud or mutual mistake. The trial court therefore erred in sustaining defendant's objection lodged on the basis of the parol evidence rule.

Because exclusion of the affidavit was error, it follows that the granting of defendant's motion for summary judgment was also in error. It is elementary that summary judgment is proper only when the pleadings and affidavits demonstrate that no genuine issue as to any material fact exists and that the moving party is entitled to judgment as a matter of law. Plaintiff – wife's affidavit, which we hold here should have been allowed into evidence, raised genuine issues of fact as to whether the release in question was executed under circumstances amounting to fraud or mutual mistake. Because these genuine issues of fact were raised, entry of summary judgment dismissing plaintiff – wife's claim was error.

Reversed and remanded.

CASE REVIEW QUESTIONS

1. State specifically how the issue of the applicability of the parol evidence rule arose in the Cunningham case.
2. Which of the situations discussed in the text immediately before the case did the court believe was applicable?

INTERPRETATION OF CONTRACTS

Although putting a contract in writing will usually make clear what it is that the parties have agreed to, parties will sometimes disagree over what their contract requires of them. This is to be expected since many words have more than one meaning and the parties may interpret the words of their contract in different ways.

If such a disagreement leads to a legal conflict between the parties, a court will have to choose between the alternative interpretations of the parties. In making this choice, the courts are guided by principles called rules of construction. The principal rule of construction in contract interpretation is that a court should give the words of a contract the meaning intended by the parties.

To determine the intent of the parties, the courts have followed certain additional rules of construction. These rules include the following:

1. Words should generally be given their ordinary meanings.
2. Technical terms should generally be given their technical meanings.
3. A writing should be interpreted as a whole.
4. The purpose of the parties in entering the contract should be given great weight.
5. When general and specific provisions conflict, the specific provisions usually qualify the general provisions.
6. When handwritten and printed provisions conflict, the handwritten provisions are to be preferred.
7. Words are to be interpreted most strongly against the party who wrote them.
8. Conduct of the parties subsequent to the formation of the contract, called a **course of performance,** that indicates a particular interpretation of the contract by them should be considered.
9. Conduct of the parties in previous transactions, called a **course of dealing,** that indicates a particular interpretation of the contract by them should be considered.
10. Any regular practice or method of dealing in a particular trade, called **trade usage,** that indicates a particular interpretation of the contract by the parties should be considered.
11. A reasonable, lawful, and effective interpretation is preferred.

When you read the case that follows, keep these rules of construction in mind. Which of the rules does the court apply?

STENDER v. TWIN CITY FOODS, INC.
510 P.2d 221 (Wash. 1973)

[Stender, a pea grower, entered into a written contract with Twin City Foods, Inc. (TCF), a food processor. The contract was a mimeographed form prepared by TCF and signed by both parties.

Under the contract, Stender was required to plant, fertilize, and cultivate 120 acres of peas. In turn, TCF was obligated to harvest the peas at their proper maturity and to pay a stipulated price for them, depending on the quality of the peas. TCF had executed similar contracts with other pea growers for several years. Under these contracts, TCF made an assignment of planting dates that were staggered so that various crops would mature at different times, thus allowing TCF to harvest the crops of all its contract growers in a systematic manner. Stender, an experienced grower, knew of these similar contracts.

When Stender's peas reached proper maturity for harvesting, TCF did not harvest them. The reason for TCF's failure was that severe fluctuations in temperature during the growing season had resulted in a totally unexpected number of crops becoming ready for harvesting at the same time. Despite substantial efforts by TCF, some crops, including Stender's, went unharvested.

Stender brought a legal action for breach of contract against TCF. TCF's defense was based on a provision of the contract which read:

> In the event of circumstances resulting from *adverse weather conditions* that may delay harvest of the pea crop, TCF has the option to divert that portion of Grower's acreage for seed or feed purposes as the quality of the salvage may dictate. [Emphasis added.]

The trial court held that TCF had been excused from harvesting the peas at maturity by operation of the "adverse weather conditions" clause. Stender appealed on the grounds that the trial court had improperly interpreted that clause.]

WRIGHT, Associate Justice

Determination of the intent of the contracting parties is to be accomplished by viewing the contract as a whole, the subject matter and objective of the contract, all the circumstances surrounding the making of the contract, the subsequent acts and conduct of the parties to the contract, and the reasonableness of respective interpretations advocated by the parties.

Both the plaintiff and the defendant were heavily involved in the Washington pea industry, plaintiff as a grower with 8 years of experience and the defendant as a large processor. This fact would indicate that the contract should be construed in light of the usages of the pea industry existing at the time the contract was executed.

The record supports the trial court's conclusion that the reason that the defendant bypassed the plaintiff's crop is that the weather conditions increased the size of the crops ready for processing beyond any reasonable expectations.

The definition of adverse weather conditions must be determined in light of reasonable industry custom and usage. Once a contract is established, usage and custom are admissible into evidence to explain the terms of the contract. And, parol evidence is admissible to establish a trade usage even though words in their ordinary or legal meaning are unambiguous. In view of custom and usage of the pea industry, it can be most reasonably stated that the term "adverse weather conditions" includes unusual temperature fluctuations resulting in an unexpected maturation of an entire pea crop which have been systematically planted with the objective of partial maturation over a period of time to allow for orderly harvesting. This construction of the term in question is especially valid when both parties to the contract were well aware that the purpose of scheduling crops was to avoid maturity of all the contract crops at once and to provide for systematic harvesting.

The contract provides for payment for pea crops which are harvested beyond the optimum maturity for freezing as a processed food by the defendant. The trial court properly awarded plaintiff damages computed on the basis of a permissible bypass of the plaintiff's crops, as provided by the parties' contract.

Affirmed.

CASE REVIEW QUESTIONS
1. What do you think the alternative interpretations of the "adverse weather conditions" clause suggested by Stender and Twin City Foods were?
2. Which of the rules of construction set out in the text immediately preceding the case does the court apply?
3. Does the court fail to apply any of the rules of construction that might be helpful to Stender's case?
4. How could the parties have made their contract clearer so that the court would not have had to interpret the "adverse weather conditions" clause?

Interpretation and the Parol Evidence Rule

An issue over which the courts of different states disagree is the effect of the parol evidence rule on the interpretation of contracts. In determining the meaning of words in an integrated writing, should oral agreements made between the parties either prior to or at the same time as the written contract be considered? Suppose, for example, that two people agree to buy and sell cotton arriving on a ship named *Peerless* and there are two ships by that name, one arriving in October and the other in December. Will one of the parties be allowed to present evidence of an oral conversation between the parties that indicates that they both agreed to the ship named *Peerless* that was to arrive in October?

Some courts say no, on the grounds that consideration of such oral agreements would violate the parol evidence rule. Other courts, however, will consider oral agreements in interpreting contracts. These courts take the position the oral agreements are being used only to determine the meaning of the contract, not to contradict or supplement the contract, which is what is prohibited by the parol evidence rule. In other words, the words of the written contract cannot be varied or contradicted until after their meaning is known.

PLAIN LANGUAGE

As American industry has grown, business contracts have become longer, more detailed, and more complex. Similarly, the expansion of consumer goods production and sales has been accompanied by growth in the length, detail, and complexity of consumer contracts. In some cases, consumer contracts have been made complex purposely in order to discourage purchasers from reading or questioning them. More frequently, though, the complexity has resulted from the attempts of business lawyers to respond to court decisions and to new statutory and regulatory requirements.

An unfortunate result of the growth in the complexity of consumer contracts is that they frequently cannot be understood by the consumers. To deal with this problem, New York enacted a statute in 1977 that requires the use of plain language in consumer agreements. It requires that consumer contracts in New York be written in a clear and coherent manner, using words with common and everyday meanings. Also, the sections of these contracts must be appropriately divided and captioned. In short, consumer contracts must be written so that they can be understood by the average user.

Some states have followed New York's example and have adopted similar plain language statutes of their own. Other states can be expected to enact such statutes in the near future. Federal plain language legislation has been proposed in Congress, but it has not yet been adopted.

At present, all plain language legislation applies only to consumer contracts. In time, however, the requirement could be extended to business contracts. In particular, small businesses may seek adoption of a plain language requirement in their contracts with large businesses. Also, as business firms become more familiar and more experienced with the use of plain language, they may voluntarily choose to use it in their contracts even though not required to do so by law.

REVIEW QUESTIONS

1. What kinds of contracts must be in writing in order to be enforceable?
2. In what kinds of situations may application of the Statute of Frauds lead to an unjust result? How have the courts dealt with such situations?
3. What are the two different approaches that courts have used in determining if parties to a written contract have intended their writing to be a final and complete expression of their agreement?
4. Under what circumstances may parties to a written contract present parol evidence without violating the parol evidence rule?
5. What is the primary rule of construction used by courts when interpreting the language of a contract?
6. Why have consumer contracts become more complex? How does plain language legislation attempt to deal with the complexity of consumer contracts?

CASE PROBLEMS

1. Mrs. Kerner was admitted to Eastern Hospital. Because of her illness, she was very confused and was not able to carry on a coherent conversation. A representative of the hospital called Mr. Kerner, who was legally separated from his wife, and explained the situation to him. Mr. Kerner said, "I will pay the bills." When Mr. Kerner refused to pay the bills, Eastern brought a legal action against him for breach of contract. Mr. Kerner defended on the grounds that his promise was not enforceable because it was not in writing as required by the Statute of Frauds. Who will win the case? Why?

2. Sahlin, an elderly man, orally promised the Strandbergs that, if they would live with and care for him and keep his house in good repair, they would receive the house when he died. The Strandbergs lived with Sahlin for about ten years before he died. During that time, they raised portions of the house and garage, put in new footings and sills, installed a drainage basin and piping, constructed new entrance doors, built patios and walks, replaced most of the plumbing, and insulated and paneled several rooms. They received no compensation for their services and paid for their share of the food. They also paid for all the building materials for the various projects they undertook. Sahlin died without leaving a will. The Strandbergs brought legal action against his estate, asking the court to have the property conveyed to them. The estate defended on the basis that Sahlin's promise was not enforceable because it was not in writing as required by the Statute of Frauds. Who will win the case? Why?

3. Gore and Middleton entered a contract under which Middleton would drill an oil well on

Gore's land and Gore would pay for the work. Because he had good reason to believe that Gore would not be able to pay for the work, Middleton refused to drill the well. Abraham owned land next to Gore's land and would benefit substantially if Gore's oil well produced oil. Abraham told Middleton that, if he would go ahead and drill the well, he (Abraham) would pay for the work if Gore did not. Gore did not pay for the work, and Abraham refused to pay Middleton. Middleton brought suit against Abraham for breach of contract. Abraham defended on the basis that his promise was not enforceable because it was not in writing as required by the Statute of Frauds. Who will win the case? Why?

4. Gilliam hired Kouchovcos to operate a business for him. Under their agreement, which was oral, Kouchovcos was to share in the profits of the business. The term of employment was for a period of ten years or until the death of Kouchovcos. Shortly after the business opened, Gilliam fired Kouchovcos. When Kouchovcos brought legal action for breach of contract, Gilliam argued that his promise was not enforceable because it was not in writing as required by the Statute of Frauds. Who will win the case? Why?

5. Schmoll in Chicago agreed by phone to sell horse hides to Wheeler in Boston. Schmoll shipped the hides and mailed to Wheeler an invoice itemizing the goods sold, the prices, and terms of shipment. The total price for the hides was $6,000. After Wheeler received the invoice, but before he received the hides, he sent a letter to Schmoll acknowledging receipt of the invoice but stating that he would refuse to accept the hides. When the hides arrived in Boston, Wheeler refused to accept them, and they were returned to Schmoll. Schmoll brought legal action against Wheeler for breach of contract. Wheeler defended on the basis that his promise was not enforceable because it was not in writing as required by the Statute of Frauds. Who will win the case? Why?

6. Brickhouse took Spitz, an architect, to visit a vacant lot. Brickhouse told Spitz that he only had $75,000 to spend on a new house. He asked Spitz if a six-room, ranch-style house could be built on the lot for that amount. Spitz said it could, but that before beginning work on plans for the house, Brickhouse would have to sign a standard form of contract. The contract provided that the architect's fee would be 10 percent of the cost of building the house and that a down payment of 10 percent of the architect's fee was to be paid at the time the contract was signed. The contract said nothing, however, about how much the house would cost to build. Brickhouse signed the contract and gave Spitz a check for $750, as he was instructed to do by Spitz.

When the plans were completed by Spitz, Brickhouse asked several building contractors for their estimates of the amount it would cost to build the house. All of the contractors agreed that it would cost at least $100,000. Brickhouse refused to pay any additional money to Spitz under their contract and demanded the return of the $750 he had already paid. If Spitz brings a legal action against Brickhouse for breach of contract, will Brickhouse be allowed to argue that he does not have to pay the fee because the parties had an oral agreement that the maximum cost of the house would not exceed $75,000? Who will win the case? Explain.

7. Butler made fraudulent oral representations to induce Ganley to enter into a road construction contract. A clause in their contract provided:

Ganley has examined the specifications and plans of the work to be done, is familiar with the location of said work and the conditions under which it must be performed, knows all the requirements, and is not relying upon any statement not included in this contract made by Butler.

When Ganley discovered that Butler had committed fraud, he brought a legal action to rescind the contract. Will Ganley be allowed to present evidence of the fraudulent oral representations made by Butler? Who will win the case? Explain.

8. Lath owned a farm he wished to sell. Across the road, on land belonging to Lunn, Lath had an icehouse that he had the right to remove at any time. Mitchell was considering buying Lath's farm for use as a summer residence. However, she found the icehouse objectionable. Lath entered into a written contract with Mitchell to sell her the farm at a specified price. At the same time,

Lath made an oral promise to Mitchell to remove the icehouse. After the sale of the farm was completed, Mitchell took possession of the farm and spent a substantial amount of money improving the property. Lath, however, refused to remove the icehouse. If Mitchell brings a legal action against Lath for breach of contract for failure to remove the icehouse, on what basis can Lath defend? Who will win the case? Explain.

9. Congress adopted the Mineral Leasing Act to allow the United States government to lease public lands to private citizens for the purpose of searching for oil and gas. The Act provides that "such leases shall require payment of rental of not less than 25 cents per acre per year." Essley entered into such a lease, which was in writing. It provided that Essley would pay "a rental of 50 cents for each acre for the first year and a rental of 25 cents for each subsequent year." In the first year of the lease, Essley paid the government 50 cents per acre. In the second year of the lease, however, Essley told the government that under the terms of her lease she only owed a total rent of 25 cents. The government brought a legal action against Essley to collect 25 cents *per acre*. How much should the court determine is owed by Essley? Explain.

10. Gross enrolled in the Stormville Parachute Training School (School), located in New York State. He signed a form, entitled "Responsibility Release," which provided: "I hereby waive any and all claims I may have against the Stormville Parachute Training School for any personal injuries that I may sustain or that may arise out of my learning, practicing, or actually jumping from an aircraft." Gross suffered injuries when he landed after his first jump from a plane.

Gross brought a legal action against the School for negligence. The School defended on the basis that Gross had waived any claims for negligence against it by signing the Responsibility Release. Gross argued that the Responsibility Release did not explain in a clear and coherent manner that he was waiving claims based on negligence and was therefore in violation of New York's plain language legislation. Who will win the case? Why?

14

CAPACITY TO CONTRACT

As we have seen, the core of a contract is a mutual agreement of exchange. When such an agreement exists, it is generally considered to be in society's interest to enforce it. There may, however, be reasons for not enforcing the agreement.

One reason the courts may refuse to enforce an agreement is that they do not recognize the ability of certain people to contract. In some situations, the ability to contract is limited to protect the public. For instance, convicts, corporations, and public agencies all have limits placed on their power to contract.

In other situations, a person's ability to contract is limited to protect that person. An obvious example of such a limitation would involve a person with severe mental infirmities. Also, the courts have traditionally felt that minors, sometimes referred to as infants, need protection when contracting.

When a court refuses to enforce a contract because it does not recognize the ability of a party to enter into the contract, that party is said to lack the **capacity** to contract. In this chapter, we will consider primarily the contractual capacity of minors and, to a lesser extent, the capacity of the mentally infirm.

CAPACITY OF MINORS

When a minor enters into a contract, the contract is **voidable** by the minor. This means that if the minor wants to get out of the contract, he or she may do so. This right is given to minors to protect them from entering into disadvantageous contracts.

The minor's decision to get out of a contract is called a **disaffirmance**, which is sometimes referred to as a **renunciation**. This decision can be made at any point until a reasonable time after the minor becomes an adult has passed. Historically, a person was considered to be a minor until the age of 21. Today, however, the age of majority in most states is 18.

Disaffirmance occurs when the minor demonstrates an unwillingness to be bound by the contract. This unwillingness can be demonstrated in any way; no special form is required. Note, though, that a minor's contract is voidable, not void, and that the decision to disaffirm or affirm the contract is up to the minor.

A decision to affirm a contract is called a **ratification**. Although the minor may disaffirm at any point until a reasonable time after becoming an adult, the choice to ratify can only be made after adulthood has been reached. The choice to ratify can be demonstrated either expressly or by implication.

One way ratification is implied is by the minor's failure to make a timely disaffirmance. If the minor does not act within a reasonable time after becoming an adult, the contract is ratified. What constitutes a reasonable time depends on the circumstances of the particular case, considering such things as whether either party has performed their promise and the amount of prejudice caused the other party by the minor's delay in disaffirming. Whether a disaffirmance or a ratification has taken place will often be a question of fact for a jury to decide.

In the first of the two cases that follow, the court had to decide whether or not the actions of the minor constituted a disaffirmance, that is, whether or not the minor demonstrated an unwillingness to be bound by his contract. In the second case, the court had to decide whether the minor acted to disaffirm within a reasonable time after becoming an adult.

LOGAN COUNTY BANK v. TAYLOR
295 N.E.2d 743 (Ill. App. 1973)

SMITH, Justice

While a minor, defendant [Taylor] executed a [promissory] note. While still a minor, he claims he renounced or disaffirmed it. He used the proceeds of the note for the purchase of an automobile. He made two payments, was then drafted, and left the car with a friend "when I went into the service and it set there until I contacted the bank to pick it up." He was twenty [and a minor in Illinois] when all this occurred. The bank did pick it up and sold it for salvage — $30. The note when executed in December, 1964, was for $377.40. Subsequently, in 1969, the bank called defendant in and demanded payment. Defendant advised them that he was a minor at the time the loan was executed, but was told in return that such fact was of no consequence, and he thereupon agreed to make payments of $10 or $15 a month — which he never did. In February, 1972, the bank [obtained a] judgment against him [using a procedure that did not require Taylor's presence in court]. Defendant sought to have such [judgment] set aside arguing that he had timely disaffirmed the note. The court, however, confirmed the judgment and he appealed.

We are not presented with the question more often present than not, as to whether the disaffirmance, if such was the case, was timely, that is, made within a reasonable time after reaching majority. Here, the disaffirmance, if there was one, was prior to majority and therefore about as timely as it could be. A minor can in most instances disaffirm a contract during his minority. But the question remains, was the act of calling the bank, and telling them to "pick it up" a renunciation or disaffirmance. For defendant here to avoid the note, the renunciation must be unequivocal.

The bank argues that defendant's direction to pick the car up was not an act of disaffirmance and points to the fact that defendant did not demand the return of two payments previously made. It argues further, that disaffirmance can only come after majority—thus whatever the implications of picking up the car might be, it has no bearing in our context.

We think otherwise. . . . [A] minor can disaffirm his contract during minority, and the question here is whether he did so in having the car picked up by the bank. Disaffirmance or renunciation is a question of intent and it seems to us that when he told the bank to pick up the car it was his intent to disaffirm the note. There are no circumstances present that militate against such conclusion by implication, such as making another payment, or expressly, by advising the bank at the time that he still intended to pay off the note. In our opinion, his contacting the bank and telling them to pick up the car was an unequivocal renunciation and disaffirmance. True, he could have sent them a letter, registered mail, telling them just that, and maybe such could be characterized as "more unequivocal," but there is no requirement for the nth degree of unequivocalness. As defendant points out, to impose specificity and formality on the act of disaffirmance is to disregard the basis for the policy of the law that protects minors from the improvident actions and which accords to them the right to disaffirm.

The bank points to the subsequent conversations with it in 1969 and characterizes such a "reaffirmance." But you can't reaffirm that which has been disaffirmed. In our opinion, there was *nothing* to reaffirm — defendant's disaffirmance in legal effect obliterated the note. Reaffirmance cannot be premised on an effort to reverse that which has been legally avoided. . . . Accordingly, we hold that defendant disaffirmed the contract during his minority.

The judgment appealed from is reversed and the cause is remanded with directions to vacate the judgment and enter judgment for defendant.

EASTERN AIRLINES, INC. v. STAHL
318 N.Y.S.2d 996 (1970)

[Herman A. Stahl used airline tickets he had purchased from Eastern Airlines. He paid for the tickets with checks drawn on a bank account in the name of "Herman A. Stahl Management Services." The checks bounced, and some time later Eastern brought suit against Stahl. Stahl defended on the grounds that he was a minor when he entered into the contract with Eastern and that he had disaffirmed the contract after becoming an adult. At the end of the trial Stahl moved for a directed verdict.]

KASSAL, Judge
[T]he plaintiff presented evidence consisting of two Dun & Bradstreet business information reports showing the defendant in business as early as 1960, which the defendant conceded, and which date is three and four years prior to the date of the checks herein. The two checks, identified by the bank witness as bearing the defendant's signature, were drawn on a business account, namely, "Herman A. Stahl Management Services."

Therefore, addressing the defense of disaffirmance, the court concludes that the same is not a valid defense herein since it had not been exercised within a reasonable time after the defendant attained his majority. The defendant attained his majority on April 21, 1964, but he did not disaffirm these checks until September 26, 1964, a period more than five months after.

Some of the considerations which lead to the conclusion that this was not a reasonable period are these: The five months hiatus, the said disaffirmance did not occur until asserted as a defense in legal action, the fact that the defendant is not truly an "infant" in the moral or business concept of this principle since he had admittedly been actively involved in various and numerous business enterprises for at least three years prior thereto or from his 17th birthday on.

Obviously, these all add up to a person who had more than sufficient mental capacity and his disaffirmance, five months after attaining his majority [21 in New York at the time], with regard to the issuance of checks in his twentieth year, should not under these circumstances be considered a disaffirmance within a reasonable period. In the court's opinion, some of the elements that should be considered in determining a reasonable period for a disaffirmance are the business experience, awareness and general acumen of the said infant. We have, in this instance, an example of a very world-wise man attempting, by the device of invoking a disaffirmance, to avail himself of a "free ride" both literally and figuratively.

For the reasons set forth, the court denies all the motions made by the defendant during and at the end of the trial. . . .

CASE REVIEW QUESTIONS

1. Why was there any question in the *Taylor* case as to whether or not Taylor had disaffirmed his contract with the bank?
2. What specifically did Taylor do to demonstrate his unwillingness to be bound to his contract with the bank?
3. What circumstances were present in the *Stahl* case that led the court to conclude that Stahl did not disaffirm within a reasonable time after becoming an adult?
4. Why was Stahl's failure to disaffirm within a reasonable time after becoming an adult treated as a ratification?

Rights of Adults When Minors Disaffirm

Frequently, when a minor chooses to disaffirm a contract, he or she has already received the benefit of the other party's performance. For example, after a minor purchases a car from an automobile dealer, the minor may choose to avoid the transaction. This means that if the minor disaffirms, he or she may not only discontinue making payments, but may also recover all amounts already paid.

At this point, the question arises of whether a party with whom a minor contracts may also need some protection. Should the minor be allowed to keep the benefit of the other party's performance without having to pay for it? When the minor disaffirms a contract, any tangible goods received from the other party that the minor still possesses must be returned. The minor in the example just given, for instance, must return the car to the automobile dealer. But what if the minor has purchased something intangible or no longer has the goods, or the goods have depreciated or have been damaged?

The traditional view, still followed in many states, is that the minor need only return the goods received from the other party and still in his or her possession, regardless of their condition, in order to disaffirm. In the automobile example, the minor need only return the car, even if it has been abused or wrecked. If the car is no longer in the minor's possession, for whatever reason, the minor can disaffirm the contract without returning anything. An exception to this occurs if the minor sells or exchanges goods purchased from the other party and still possesses the money or property received in the sale or exchange. In such cases, the original goods are **traced** and the minor must turn over the money or property received in the sale or exchange, if it is still in his or her possession, in order to disaffirm.

The emphasis of the traditional view is on the protection of minors from improvident contracts. Some courts, however, have felt that although minors need such protection and should be able to disaffirm, they should also be required to restore the adult to the position he or she was in at the time the contract was formed. Such courts require the minor to pay for any depreciation that has occurred while the goods were in the minor's possession or for any value received if the purchase is of an intangible or if for any other reason the minor no longer possesses whatever he or she purchased. This view, which seems to be growing, provides minors with some protection, but it also makes them pay for benefits received, which provides protection for the other party as well. In the following case, the court applies this view to an unusual situation.

BOYCE v. DOYLE
273 A.2d 408 (N.J. 1971)

[Boyce was injured while riding a motorcycle driven by March that collided with a car driven by Doyle. Shortly after the accident Boyce, who was then 19 (and a minor under New Jersey law), was paid $450 by March, and he signed a document releasing March from any further liability. After spending the money and while still a minor, Boyce brought suit against both March and Doyle based on the accident. March counterclaimed for the return of the $450 he had paid to Boyce for the release.

Before the case went to trial, Boyce became an adult. March moved for a summary judgment on his counterclaim. The judge reserved decision on March's motion and the case went to trial. The jury returned a verdict in favor of Boyce against Doyle but against Boyce in favor of March. The judge then made a decision on March's motion for summary judgment on his counterclaim.]

OSBORNE, [Judge]

There can be no doubt but that contracts not of necessity may be voided by an infant either before or a reasonable time after he obtains his majority. Thus the institution of suit while plaintiff was still a minor and the continuous prosecution of the case, culminating in a trial more than three years later, operated as a rescission of the release executed while plaintiff was an infant.

Now, however, after plaintiff has rescinded his release, proceeded to trial and lost on the merits as to defendant March, he asserts that he is not obligated to restore to the other party the consideration he received.

The court recognizes that the majority rule followed in most jurisdictions is that an infant is not obligated to return the consideration received by him where, during his minority and before disaffirmance, he has wasted, squandered, destroyed, used or otherwise disposed of such consideration. Nor is the infant liable, in such a case, to return the equivalent of the consideration or otherwise to account for its value. However, the soundness of this rule has come under increasing attack.

It appears that New Jersey follows the minority rule that an infant must restore the other party to the *status quo* to the extent of the benefits the infant has received, if the other party is free from fraud or bad faith. Cf., *Pemberton B. & L. Ass'n v. Adams.*

The court in *Pemberton* would not permit the infant defendant to rescind a mortgage commitment without returning the money he had received.

> [The infant], after coming of age, retained the possession of this property, and claimed and enjoyed all benefits of a conveyance thereof, and now raises this defense of infancy without offering to return the consideration money. Under these circumstances, his liability continues, even though there has been no fraud.

The infant in *Pemberton* had purchased property with the money borrowed from a bank, and to that extent the case is distinguishable in that he had not completely squandered the proceeds prior to obtaining his majority. The consideration for the release in the present instance is not easily traceable.

Subsequent New Jersey decisions have embraced the philosophy enunciated in *Pemberton.* In *Carter v. Jays Motors, Inc.,* defendant urged reversal of a judgment entered against him on the grounds that the infant involved had not made restitution of an automobile. While the court found against defendant because of his failure to counterclaim for the automobile, it quoted approvingly from *Levine v. Mallno Oldsmobile Co., Inc.:*

> The law is of course clear that where a contract to purchase is by the infant alone, he may avoid it and recover back money paid on account, subject perhaps to a counterclaim for damages for partial destruction of the property.

Finally, in *Sacco v. Schallus,* the court extended the proposition to its logical conclusion. In reaching a determination that an adult dealing with an infant was entitled to dissolve a partnership . . . the court broadly stated that:

> . . . [R]ecovery by an infant cannot be had without a restoration to the other party of the consideration received, or an allowance from such recovery as compensation for the benefit conferred upon the infant seeking to avoid the contract.

This language is apposite to the present circumstances. Though there has been no evidence of fraud or misrepresentation on the part of the plaintiff, and while the proceeds cannot directly be traced, he received a benefit of immediate consequence upon signing the release. The court has permitted the infant to utilize the shield and rescind his release, but will not permit him offensively to assert his right to retain the consideration for that release now that he has elected to rescind and has recovered a judgment against the codefendant. This I consider to be the thrust of the decisions in this State as well as the better rule.

Defendant March's motion for summary judgment on the counterclaim is granted.

CASE REVIEW QUESTIONS

1. What contract did Boyce and March enter into while Boyce was a minor? What benefit had Boyce received under that contract? Did Boyce still possess that benefit?
2. What legal standard did the court apply in this case?
3. What result would the court have reached in this case if it had applied the traditional view concerning the duty of a minor to return what has been purchased when he or she disaffirms a contract?
4. What did the court mean when it said, "The consideration for the release in the present instance is not so easily traceable"? What is the legal significance of the court's statement?

Misrepresentation of Age

Another situation in which a person contracting with a minor might need protection arises when the minor lies about his or her age. If the correct age is known, one can avoid the problem of the disaffirmance of contracts by minors simply by refusing to contract with them. But what if a minor looks like and claims to be an adult?

Here again, the traditional view protects the minor and gives him or her the choice of disaffirming the contract by returning to the other party those goods received and still in his or her possession. There is, however, a trend away from this position and toward providing protection to the party to whom the minor has lied.

Protection for persons contracting with minors who have lied about their age has been accomplished in a variety of ways. Some states have provided such protection by statute. In other states, the courts have used such techniques as estopping (prohibiting) the minor who misrepresents his or her age from using lack of capacity as a defense or holding the minor liable for the tort of fraud because of the intentional misrepresentation of age. With increasing frequency, the need for such protection is being recognized, as is indicated in the case that follows.

HAYDOCY PONTIAC, INC. v. LEE
250 N.E.2d 808 (Ohio 1969)

[Jennifer L. Lee purchased a car from Haydocy Pontiac, Inc. (Haydocy). At the time of the purchase Lee was a minor of the age of 20 years, but she told Haydocy that she was an adult, and Haydocy believed her. Shortly after the purchase, Lee delivered the car to an auto repair company for service. The auto repair company went bankrupt, and Lee was unable to get the car back.

Lee made no payments on the purchase price to Haydocy. Haydocy brought legal action against Lee, seeking either to recover the car or to obtain payment of the purchase price. Lee defended on the basis that she was a minor at the time of purchase and had not ratified the purchase after becoming an adult. The trial court found for Lee. Haydocy appealed.]

STRAUSBAUGH, Judge

The cases we have examined in this regard all relate to the question [of] whether the infant can recover

from the vendor the purchase price paid and the right of the vendor to counterclaim rather than the facts of this case where the vendor seeks to recover the property, or in lieu thereof, the balance due on the purchase price. Many of the cases use language to the effect that when the property received by the infant is in his possession, or under his control, to permit him to rescind the contract without requiring him to return or offer to return it would be to permit him to use his privilege as a "sword rather than a shield."

At a time when we see young persons between 18 and 21 years of age demanding and assuming more responsibilities in their daily lives; when we see such persons emancipated, married, and raising families; when we see such persons charged with the responsibility for committing crimes; when we see such persons being sued in tort claims for acts of negligence; when we see such persons subject to military service; when we see such persons engaged in business and acting in almost all other respects as an adult, it seems timely to reexamine the case law pertaining to contractual rights and responsibilities of infants to see if the law as pronounced and applied by the courts should be redefined.

To allow infants to avoid a transaction without being required to restore the consideration received where the infant has used or otherwise disposed of it causes hardship on the other party. We hold that where the consideration received by the infant cannot be returned upon disaffirmance of the contract because it has been disposed of, the infant must account for the value of it, not in excess of the purchase price, where the other party is free from any fraud or bad faith and where the contract has been induced by a false representation of the age of the infant. Under this factual situation the infant is estopped from pleading infancy as a defense where the contract has been induced by a false representation that the infant was of age.

The common law has bestowed upon the infant the privilege of disaffirming his contracts in conservation of his rights and interests. Where the infant, 20 years of age, through falsehood and deceit enters into a contract with another who enters therein in honesty and good faith and, thereafter, the infant seeks to disaffirm the contract without tendering back the consideration, no right or interest of the infant exists which needs protection. The privilege given the infant thereupon becomes a weapon of injustice.

The judgment is reversed and the cause is remanded in accordance with this opinion.

CASE REVIEW QUESTIONS
1. What legal standard did the court apply in this case? Explain in your own words why the court adopted this standard.
2. What result would the court have reached in this case if it had applied the traditional view concerning the protection of a minor who lies about his or her age?
3. Which method of protecting a person who contracts with a minor discussed in the paragraph immediately preceding the case did the court adopt?

Necessaries

The fact that minors may disaffirm their contracts makes people hesitant to contract with them. Although this will protect a minor from improvident bargains, it may also make it impossible for a minor to buy important goods and services, even those that are necessary for survival. To encourage the sale of such goods and services to minors, an exception to the general policy of allowing minors to escape liability is made in cases of minors' contracts for **necessaries** when the party furnishing the necessaries has already provided them.

The precise meaning of the term "necessary" is elusive. It is a relative term, and its meaning in a particular case is influenced by the life style of the particular minor. Even in situations involving food, clothing, and shelter, whether what has been provided to the minor is a necessary will depend on such things as whether the minor is **emancipated** (free from parental care and custody) or married. The minor's status in life will also determine whether such things as education, working tools, automobiles, or furniture are necessaries. Often this issue will be a question of fact for a jury to determine.

Similarly, the minor's liability to someone who has provided necessaries is dependent on whether the minor has another source for them. For instance, a minor will not be held liable to someone who provides goods that he or she already possesses or that parents or guardians are willing and able to provide.

Liability for necessaries, when it occurs, it not considered to be contractual because the minor lacks the capacity to contract. Instead, recovery from the minor must be based on what is called a quasi-contract remedy. (The remedy of quasi-contract is explained in Chapter 18.) Because of this, the person providing the necessaries is not entitled to the contract price agreed to by the minor. The minor is liable only for the fair value of the necessaries provided. The determination of the fair value is also often a jury question.

Many states have adopted statutes concerning such things as insurance, banking, and military enlistments that specifically provide minors with the capacity to enter into certain kinds of contracts.

In the following case the court had to decide whether the item purchased by a minor was a necessary and, if so, the amount that the seller was entitled to recover.

CIDIS v. WHITE
336 N.Y.S.2d 362 (1972)

GITELMAN, Judge

In this action, plaintiff, a duly licensed optometrist, was requested by defendant, Carol Ann White, an infant, 19 years of age, to furnish her with contact lenses. She advised plaintiff that she urgently desired them as soon as possible. She agreed to pay $225.00 for the lenses and gave the doctor her personal check for $100.00. Plaintiff, accordingly, after examining infant defendant's eyes, immediately ordered the lenses from his laboratory and incurred an indebtedness of $110.00. The examination was held on Thursday evening, the lenses were ordered on Friday and received by the doctor on Saturday. On Monday morning the infant called and disaffirmed her contract on advice and insistence of her father, and stopped payment on her check. The infant was 19 years of age, working, and although living at home with her parents, paid for her room and board.

The plaintiff established that the contact lenses could be used by no one but the infant and have no market value at all, thus resulting in an absolute loss to the plaintiff of $110.00.

The question presents itself as to whether or not the contact lenses were "necessaries." The term "necessaries" as used in the law relating to the liability of infants therefor is a relative term somewhat flexible, except when applied to such things as are obviously requisite for the maintenance of existence, and also depends on the social position and situation in life of the infant.

An analogy may be drawn between the instant case and the situation that existed in the case of *Vichnes v. Transcontinental & Western Air, Inc.,* and *Bach v. Long Island Jewish Hospital.* In the *Vichnes* case an infant purchased a round trip ticket to California and after using it tried to disaffirm and recover the money he paid. The Appellate Term reversed the Municipal Court and dismissed his claim. In the *Bach* case, an emancipated infant attempted to disaffirm her consent to a cosmetic operation performed on her. The Supreme Court, Nassau County, refused to permit her to do so. In both of these cases, the infant had received full benefit and could not place the defendant in status quo. So also in this case, since the contact lenses are of no value to anyone except the infant defendant, the plaintiff has suffered a loss and cannot be put back in status quo except by payment of a reasonable sum.

The Court has in mind the case of *International Text Book Co. v. Connelly,* which holds that an infant is not liable for a sum in excess of the fair value of the necessaries furnished even though he has contracted to pay more.

Accordingly, and for the purpose of doing substan-

tial justice between the parties, judgment is granted in favor of the plaintiff and against the defendant, Carol Ann White, in the sum of $150.00. . . . During the trial the father urged that his daughter should not be penalized for obeying her father. The Court suggests that there is nothing to prevent the father from paying the judgment for his daughter, if he is so minded.

[Judgment for plaintiff.]

CASE REVIEW QUESTIONS

1. What considerations in the *Cidis* case led the court to conclude that White's purchase was a necessary?
2. Why did the court award Cidis a judgment of $150.00 rather than the $225.00 purchase price that White had agreed to pay?
3. Is White entitled to receive the contact lenses?
4. Do the facts in the *Vichnes* and *Bach* cases, cited by the court in its decision, appear analogous to the facts in this case? How would you explain the decisions in those cases?

CAPACITY OF THE MENTALLY INFIRM

Much of what has already been discussed concerning the capacity of minors and their right to disaffirm contracts is also applicable to contracts entered into by the mentally infirm. The traditional standard for determining whether a person lacks the capacity to contract because of mental infirmity has been whether the person was able to understand the nature and consequences of his or her act at the time of entering into the contract. If such understanding was not present, the person did not have contractual capacity.

Another standard, in addition to the traditional one, adopted by the Second Restatement of Contracts, defines lack of contractual capacity as when a person "by reason of mental illness or defect . . . is unable to act in a reasonable manner in relation to the transaction and the other party has reason to know of this condition." Note that under this standard, the mental infirmity need not be as great, but the other party must be on notice of it. Under these two standards, lack of capacity to contract is not limited to persons who have been declared incompetent by a court. It can also include mentally retarded, senile, drugged, and intoxicated people.

Historically, there has been a greater concern for persons who contract with the mentally infirm than for those who contract with minors. Generally, when the person has performed under the contract, had no reason to know of the lack of capacity, and did not take advantage of the incompetent, the mentally infirm person may only disaffirm the contract if he or she fully reimburses the other party. As discussed earlier in this chapter, there is a trend toward treating minor's contracts in this manner as well.

A mentally infirm person may disaffirm at any time until a reasonable time after gaining competency. After regaining competency, the person may also choose to ratify the contract. If a **guardian** is appointed for the incompetent, the guardian has the power to disaffirm or ratify. Liability for necessaries is treated as it is with minors.

In the following case, the court is confronted with the issue of determining whether one of the parties to a contract lacked the capacity to contract because of a mental infirmity.

KRASNER v. BERK
319 N.E.2d 897 (Mass. 1974)

BRAUCHER, Justice

The plaintiff and defendant, both doctors, occupied a suite of medical offices from 1964 to 1969, and shared the rent equally. In April, 1969, they renewed the lease for three years beginning June 1, 1969, and on May 22, 1969, they agreed in writing that each would pay half the rent and taxes due under the lease, even if one of them moved out or was "unable to occupy his suite as a result of disability or for any other reason." The written agreement was drawn up by the plaintiff's attorney. The defendant, aged fifty-three, was diagnosed in November, 1969, as suffering from presenile dementia, and in July, 1970, he closed his office and moved out. It was stipulated that his share of the rent and taxes for the period from August 1, 1970 to the expiration of the lease, May 31, 1972, was $7,754.18, and that the only issues to be tried were whether the defendant was of unsound mind and mentally incapable of entering into the lease and the agreement. . . .

The defendant's wife and brother testified to his behavior. In September, 1967, he began to be absent-minded and confused, he missed appointments with patients and records piled up in his office. He was unable to answer direct questions with direct answers, and was forgetful and oversolicitous of everyone. While skiing in New Hampshire, he would get lost and be unable to find the lifts. On a trip in August, 1968, he

kept getting lost and sometimes could not find his hotel room or his tickets. He failed to keep an appointment with his brother in 1968. In the fall of 1968 he began to consult doctors about his health. As of 1968 his brother could no longer permit him to write prescriptions for patient–employees at the brother's company in Maine, although he continued to examine them. In the winter or spring of 1969 he went to the movies and climbed over the seats while his brother walked down the aisle. Early in 1969 he could not use his dictaphone; he ran over his medical bag in the parking lot several times; if his watch stopped, he would not know how to fix it. He would forget there were patients waiting for him. Sometimes he would leave his car at his ski lodge in New Hampshire and hitchhike home to Newton; at least once every two weeks he would forget his car at the office and hitchhike home. The defendant's wife talked to the plaintiff about these matters and the plaintiff said that he knew her husband and he seemed to be the same as he always was.

A neurologist called as a witness by the defendant testified that the defendant was referred to him on June 5, 1969, and was found to be a friendly, cooperative man with a disorder of immediate recall; beyond this the neurological examination was entirely unrevealing. At this time there was discussion about the defendant's giving up his practice. In November, 1969, the witness saw the defendant again. This time the hospital record showed a diagnosis of disturbance of brain function manifested by memory impairment and episodic confusion. The patient refused a definitive study because of the fear that it might demonstrate a pathology of which he was fearful. A neuropsychological test showed a verbal IQ of 116 (above average) and a performance IQ of 76 (very dangerously low, at the moronic level), indicating that the defendant was unable to reason, unable to form proper judgment, and unable to learn new material. . . . Very probably the defendant could be expected to function at an adequate level in situations with which he was thoroughly familiar and where success depended simply on the use or reinstatement of earlier learned material. In situations which might demand new learning or independent judgment or any genuine degree of adaptation, he would probably do very poorly.

Based on the findings, the diagnosis was presenile dementia. The patient had a disease in which there was premature senility of the brain; at the age of fifty-three, he had a loss of higher mental abilities resembling that of very old age dementia. The condition had been developing slowly for a matter of years and was permanent. The witness advised the defendant to give up his practice.

The plaintiff requested the judge to rule that as a matter of law the evidence was insufficient to warrant a finding that at the time the lease and agreement were entered into by the defendant he was of unsound mind and mentally incapable of making these agreements. The judge denied the request with the following comment: "The evidence of Dr. John F. Sullivan, a qualified neurologist (exceptional qualifications) that the defendant was unable to reason, unable to form proper judgment or learn new material, combined with same testimony from lay witnesses established sufficient evidence." The Appellate Division held that it was prejudicial error to deny the plaintiff's request and ordered judgment for the plaintiff for $7,754.18.

We have said that in an inquiry into capacity to contract, "the true test is, was the party whose contract it is sought to avoid, in such a state of insanity at the time, as to render him incapable of transacting the business." If he "could not understand the nature and quality of the transaction or grasp its significance, then it was not the act of a person of sound mind. There may

be intellectual weakness not amounting to lack of power of comprehend. But an inability to realize the true purport of the matter in hand is equivalent to mental incapacity." We have required proof that the person in question "was too weak in mind to execute the deed with understanding of its meaning, effect and consequences." These expressions do not differ in substance from the statement of the rule in Restatement 2d: Contracts: "A person incurs only voidable contractual duties by entering into a transaction if by reason of mental illness or defect . . . he is unable to understand in a reasonable manner the nature and consequences of the transaction."

Even where there is sufficient understanding, a contract may in some circumstances be voidable by reason of failure of will or judgment, where the person contracting, by reason of mental illness or defect, is unable to act in a reasonable manner in relation to the transaction and the other party has reason to know of his condition. There was evidence in the present case to support a finding that the defendant had a terrible fear of presenile dementia and could not bring himself to face that prospect. There was evidence also that the defendant's wife discussed the defendant's condition with the plaintiff, and that the plaintiff's attorney drew up a written agreement referring explicitly to inability to occupy the suite "as a result of disability." Perhaps it might be inferred that the plaintiff, contrary to his testimony, had reason to know of the defendant's condition. But the case had not been argued in these terms, and there is no indication that the trial judge or the Appellate Division drew any such inference. We therefore do not put our decision on this ground.

On the sufficiency of understanding, the case is a close one. . . . If the judge had found that the defendant was competent to contract, we would have had no difficulty in upholding the finding. There was evidence that the plaintiff and the defendant discussed the possibility of moving to other offices before deciding to renew the lease but could not find suitable office space, that the defendant read the agreement before he signed it and then said that it was fair, and that four months later he was able to dictate a letter of complaint to the landlord showing some understanding of the terms of the lease.

We think, however, that we would invade the province of the trial judge if we drew inferences as to capacity to understand from actions of the defendant which in the setting may have been equivocal. "Where a person has some understanding of a particular transaction which is affected by mental illness or defect, the controlling consideration is whether the transaction in its result is one which a reasonably competent person might have made." Restatement 2d: Contracts. When the defendant made the lease and the agreement, his medical practice had already been curtailed, and the judge could infer that this was the result of his mental condition. Within two weeks after signing the agreement he consulted a doctor specializing in brain disease, and discussed giving up his practice, and within six months that doctor advised him to give up the practice of medicine. The agreement made was an improvident one for a doctor who was about to consider whether he should give up his practice. We think the judge could find that he was not competent to make it.

The order of the Appellate Division must be reversed.

CASE REVIEW QUESTIONS
1. State the two legal standards that the court considered in this case.
2. On which of the two legal standards considered by the court did it base its conclusion that Berk was not mentally competent to enter into the contract with Krasner?
3. What are the most relevant facts in the case for deciding that Berk was not mentally competent? What makes those facts relevant?

REVIEW QUESTIONS

1. Fully state the general principles concerning the rights of a minor who enters into a contract and the policy that supports such a rule.
2. Why do you think that there has been a trend in the direction of requiring a minor who disaffirms a contract to fully compensate the other party for any benefits received?
3. State two possible exceptions to the general rule that, when a minor disaffirms a contract, the minor need only return goods received still in his or her possession, regardless of their condition.
4. Why do you think the courts have shown greater concern for persons who contract with the mentally infirm than for those who contract with minors?

CASE PROBLEMS

1. Marilyn Weiand, a minor, was injured as a result of negligence by an employee of the city of Akron. The insurance carrier for the city, Nationwide Insurance, agreed to pay her medical bills and to make other compensation in return for her agreement not to sue the city. Shortly after she became an adult, Weiand sent Nationwide some bills amounting to $40. A check was sent to her for this amount, but she returned it and notified the city and the insurance company that she disaffirmed her contract not to bring suit against the city. When she brought suit against the city based on its employee's negligence, the city defended on the basis of the previous agreement not to sue. May Weiand disaffirm her promise? Explain.
2. Icovino, a minor, entered into a contract with Haymes for a course of instruction in voice consisting of 36 lessons to be completed in 12 weeks. At the time of the signing of the contract, Icovino paid Haymes $500. After receiving 14 of the lessons, Icovino disaffirmed the contract. When Haymes refused to return the $500, she brought an

action against Haymes to recover the money on the grounds that she was a minor and elected to disaffirm. Haymes defended on the basis that Icovino had not returned the benefits received under the contract. Who should win? Explain.

3. Wilson, a minor, was an orphan. His aunt brought a legal action to be appointed his guardian. Wilson objected to her appointment and wished to have someone else appointed his guardian. Porter, a lawyer, represented Wilson in the action for appointment of a guardian. After the action was concluded (the aunt winning and being appointed guardian) Wilson refused to pay Porter his fee. Porter brought legal action to recover the fee. Who will win the case? Explain.

4. Wilkerson, a minor, bought two mated pairs of chinchillas from Hogue for $1,850. Four babies were born of the two pair after the sale, but later one of the adult chinchillas and one of the babies died because of Wilkerson's carelessness. He then sought to disaffirm the contract and offered to return the six remaining animals. When Hogue refused to accept the chinchillas and to return the money, Wilkerson brought an action against Hogue to recover the money on the grounds that he was a minor and elected to disaffirm. On what basis might Hogue defend? Who should win? Explain.

5. Chagnon bought a used car from Keser for $1,025. Chagnon was one month and ten days short of becoming an adult, but he falsely told Keser that he was already an adult, which Keser believed. Three months later, Chagnon advised Keser of his desire to disaffirm the contract and return the car. When Keser refused to refund the purchase price, Chagnon brought an action against Keser to recover the money on the grounds that he was a minor at the time of contracting and now elected to disaffirm. On what grounds might Keser defend? Who should win? Explain.

6. Robertson, a minor, purchased a pickup truck from Julian Pontiac. Robertson had quit school three years earlier and had earned his own living since that time, working for a construction company and traveling around to different jobs with his father in his father's truck. He lived at home with his parents. Robertson had mechanical difficulties with the truck and returned it to the dealer for repair, but the defective condition was not remedied. Two months later, after Robertson had become an adult, the truck caught fire and was destroyed. If he now seeks to disaffirm the contract because he was a minor at the time of purchase, on what basis might Julian Pontiac defend? Who would win? Explain.

7. Mr. and Mrs. Craig, both minors, were both employed and lived with Mr. Craig's parents. They purchased a house trailer from Ballinger on credit, but shortly thereafter decided they could not afford it and returned it to Ballinger. Ballinger refused to accept the trailer and brought legal action against the Craigs to collect the purchase price. On what basis might Ballinger argue that he is entitled to payment from the Craigs? Who will win? Explain.

8. Alice Sosik borrowed $3,600 from Conlon and gave him a mortgage on property she owned to secure the loan. At that time, some of her mannerisms were peculiar and there were some oddities in her speech and dress. There was, however, nothing unusual about the loan agreement. When Sosik defaulted on her payments six months later, Conlon foreclosed on the mortgage and became owner of the property. A year after the foreclosure, a doctor examined Sosik and found her to be suffering from chronic mental illness and incapable of managing her affairs. She then brought a legal action to disaffirm her original agreement with Conlon because of lack of capacity and to have her property returned to her, submitting as evidence the above facts. On what grounds might Conlon defend? Who should win? Explain.

9. Martinson, while obviously drunk, borrowed money from Matz and signed a promissory note. Although pressured by Matz to pay the note, Martinson made only two payments, both two years after signing the note. Five years after signing the note, Martinson sought to disaffirm his contract with Matz on the basis that he lacked mental capacity at the time of contracting. Matz then brought suit against Martinson to collect the note. Who will win? Explain.

15

ILLEGALITY

In the previous chapter, we saw that some agreements of exchange are not enforced because of a characteristic of one of the parties. Another reason for not enforcing some exchange agreements may be found in the nature of the agreement itself. If a court determines that an agreement is "illegal," it must decide what effect to give to it. In this chapter, we will consider what constitutes an illegal agreement and the effect of such illegality.

WHEN IS AN AGREEMENT ILLEGAL?

There are two reasons why a court may determine that an agreement is illegal. First, an agreement may violate a statute that has been adopted by the legislature. Second, an agreement may be in violation of accepted public policy as viewed by the court.

Violations of Statute

Legislatures adopt criminal and civil statutes in order to help society to achieve its goals. Criminal statutes are enacted for the purpose of deterring activities that are believed to be detrimental to society. Fines and imprisonment are imposed on those who violate these statutes by engaging in the specified prohibited activities. An agreement to engage in criminal activity is illegal.

For example, there are criminal laws that prohibit gambling. A **wagering agreement** is therefore illegal. It is necessary, however, to distinguish illegal wagering agreements from risk-shifting and **speculative bargaining agreements,** which are legal. A wager occurs when the parties agree that a payment will take place between them depending on the outcome of an uncertain event in which they have no interest other than their agreement. A bet on a sporting event, for instance, would be a wager, which is illegal.

If, however, a person is subject to an existing risk, it is not illegal for another person to agree to accept that risk. For example, an owner of a building is always subject to the risk that the building will be damaged or destroyed. Most building owners protect themselves from such risks by entering into contracts with insurance companies under which the insurance company agrees to accept the risk of damage to or destruction of the building in return for a payment called a premium. On the other hand, if a person without any financial interest in the building—that is, a person not subject to any risk because of damage or destruction of the building—enters into an insurance contract covering the building, the agreement would be an illegal wager.

A speculative bargaining agreement, such as an agreement to buy and sell stock or commodities in the future, is not an illegal wager as long as the parties are legally bound by their agreement to actually deliver and receive the subject matter of the transaction. This is so regardless of whether the parties actually complete the delivery and receipt of the goods. On the other hand, a bet as to the future price of a corporation's stock or a commodity, unaccompanied by a legal obligation for delivery and receipt, would constitute an illegal wager.

Some civil statutes are also adopted to deter activities believed to be detrimental to society. Unlike criminal statutes, however, civil statutes provide for remedies other than fines and imprisonment. An agreement to violate a civil statute will generally be considered illegal. Also, under some statutes, such as **usury** legislation (which limits interest rates) and **Sunday laws** (which prohibit contracts from being formed on Sunday), certain agreements are expressly declared void or voidable.

Civil statutes frequently require the members of a specified trade or profession be licensed. For example, doctors, lawyers, real estate agents, insurance agents, stockbrokers, barbers, plumbers, electricians, pawnbrokers, and liquor distributors and sellers are all commonly required to be licensed. If a person without a license engages in one of the trades or professions for which a license is required, and while so engaged enters into an agreement, the agreement will generally be held to be illegal. A person who practices law without a license, for instance, would generally not be able to enforce an agreement with a client to collect a fee. As you will read later in this chapter, however, some agreements that are illegal because one of the parties does not have a required license are, nonetheless, enforceable.

In the following case, the court had to decide whether a company that was not registered as a broker–dealer, as was required by law, could collect fees in payment for services it had rendered.

REGIONAL PROPERTIES, INC. v. FINANCIAL AND REAL ESTATE CONSULTING COMPANY
678 F.2d 552 (Fifth Cir. 1982)

[Regional Properties, Inc. (Regional) contracted with Financial and Real Estate Consulting Company (Financial). Under the contract, Financial promised to sell to investors limited partnership interests in certain of Regional's projects, and Regional promised to pay a fee for such service. Financial sold some interests and some, but not all, of the fees were paid. Regional later discovered that Financial was not registered as a broker–dealer with the Securities and Exchange Commission as required by the Securities Exchange Act and had thus violated the Act by selling the partnership interests.

Regional brought a legal action to rescind its contract with Financial. Financial counterclaimed for the fees as yet unpaid by Regional. The trial court held that Financial could not recover any unpaid fees. The Appellate Court affirmed this part of the trial court's decision for the reasons stated below.]

RODIN, Circuit Judge

An unregistered broker could not enforce an executory contract engaging him to sell securities using interstate facilities. The fact that the unregistered broker has performed his part of the contract should not alter that result. Were this not the result there would be no civil remedy for the failure to register. Because fees are usually contingent, as they were here, the broker who has not performed is entitled to no fee. If the broker who has performed can recover his commission despite nonregistration, then the prohibition is a toothless tiger.

The illegality of the transaction precludes the recovery of damages for breach and any other judgment aimed at enforcement of the tainted contract. Thus, persons who perform services without obtaining a required occupational license have been denied recovery. . . . This precept has been applied to bar compensation to unlicensed lawyers, physicians, real estate brokers, architects and engineers, building contractors, and plumbers. We, therefore, agree with the district judge that the contract employing Financial was voidable, at the option of Regional, and that Financial is not entitled to any fees as yet unpaid.

[Affirmed in part.]

CASE REVIEW QUESTIONS
1. Financial performed a valuable service for Regional. Is it fair that Regional does not have to pay for this service? If not, how can the outcome of the case be explained?
2. Do you think Financial should be allowed to keep the fees it has already received from Regional? You will learn how the law answers this question later in the chapter.

Violations of Public Policy
Courts have found in some cases that certain agreements are illegal, even though they do not violate any criminal or civil statutes, because they violate public policy that the courts believe exists. The difficulty in these cases is that it may not always be clear what public policy is.

A court tries to determine what public policy is by considering the Constitution, statutes, executive orders, court decisions, and the customs and opinions of society. If the court can determine from these sources that society has a particular goal, it may find illegal an agreement that, if performed, would detrimentally affect the ability of society to attain that goal.

There follow two examples—agreements in restraint of trade and exculpatory clauses—of the kinds of agreements that, under certain conditions, courts have found to be in violation of public policy. It should be kept in mind, however, that the concept of public policy is continuously evolving. Thus, the kinds of agreements that are declared by the courts to be in violation of public policy and therefore illegal are continuously changing also. In addition, it must be remembered that legislatures are free to step in and declare particular types of agreements either legal or illegal by statute.

Restraint of Trade An agreement in restraint of trade is one that has the effect of reducing competition. Two common situations in which such agreements are used occur when a person buys a business and desires protection from competition by the seller and when an employer hires an employee and desires protection from the employee leaving the job and disclosing trade secrets or taking customers away. In these situations, the sale or employment agreement may include a provision in which the seller or employee promises not to compete with the buyer or employer. Such a provision is called a covenant not to compete.

When first confronted with such agreements, the courts said that all promises to restrain trade were illegal and unenforceable because they violated public policy. The public policy that the courts were referring to is found in the economic theory of capitalism, which maintains that, generally, maximum competition will best benefit society by encouraging low prices, high quality, and maximum choice for the consumer.

In time, however, the courts began to realize that, in some cases, covenants not to compete would promote trade rather than restrain it. For instance, the owner of a business may not be able to sell the business if an enforceable covenant not to compete cannot be included in the contract of sale. Potential buyers may fear that the owner's customers will continue to do business with the owner if he or she sets up a new place of business after selling the existing one. Similarly, an employer considering the expansion of a business by hiring new employees may fear that those employees will later be in a position to take trade secrets or customers away from the employer unless an enforceable covenant not to compete can be included in the employment contract.

In order to encourage the sale and expansion of businesses—that is, to promote trade—the courts now enforce covenants not to compete if they are a part of such a contract and are reasonable. In determining whether a covenant not to compete is reasonable, a court will take into consideration the effect it has on the parties to the contract and on society. If the buyer of a business or an employer has a legitimate need for protection from competition, a covenant not to compete will generally be enforceable as long as the buyer or employer receives no more protection than is necessary and the effect of the restraint on the seller or employee and the public is not overwhelming. In determining whether the buyer or employer has received more protection than is necessary under the circumstances, a court will consider the extent of the restraint of trade in terms of how long and in what geographic area the seller or employee is prohibited from competing.

For example, a promise by the seller of a small bakery not to compete with the buyer for three years within the county in which the bakery is located would probably be found reasonable and enforceable. On the other hand, a promise by the same seller not to compete anywhere in the entire state for ten years would probably be found unreasonable because it provides more protection from competition from the seller than the buyer needs to keep the bakery's customers.

Courts of different states do not treat unreasonable covenants not to compete in the same way. Most courts have held that if such a covenant is unreasonable, it is void and unenforceable. Some courts, however, have held that an unreasonable covenant not to compete can be reformed by the court to make it reasonable and enforceable.

Another approach used by some courts is to enforce the reasonable provisions of a covenant not to compete while not enforcing the unreasonable provisions. This is called the "blue-pencil" theory of severability since the unreasonable provisions are severed by scratching them out with a theoretical blue pencil. The court then enforces the reasonable provisions that remain. In the following case, a court explains why it has chosen to reject the blue-pencil theory.

MOORE v. CURTIS 1000, INC.
640 F.2d. 910 (Eighth Cir. 1981)

[Moore was employed as a sales representative by Curtis 1000, Inc. (Curtis) from 1975 to 1979, selling business paper products in a territory that included parts of Kansas City and surrounding areas. The parties had agreed to an employment contract under which Moore had agreed that for two years following termination of his employment he would not (i) solicit orders for products sold by Curtis in any territory in which he had solicited business for Curtis or from anyone from whom he had solicited such business, (ii) call upon any customers of Curtis in any territory in which he had solicited business for the company, and (iii) solicit orders for products sold by Curtis in any town or city in which he had acted as a sales representative for the company.

Moore left his employment with Curtis in 1979 and in December formed a business for the purpose of distributing business paper products in the Kansas City area. In March 1980, he brought a legal action seeking a declaratory judgment regarding the validity of the employment contract. Curtis counterclaimed against Moore, seeking damages for breach of contract and a preliminary injunction.

The trial court granted the preliminary injunction and Moore appealed. The appellate court said that the trial court's decision to grant the preliminary injunction for Curtis was only correct if Curtis was likely to win the case. It then held that Curtis was unlikely to win the case for the reasons stated within the decision.]

ROSS, Circuit Judge

In *Coffee System of Atlanta v. Fox,* the Supreme

Court of Georgia stated that they have "customarily considered three separate elements" in determining the reasonableness of restrictive covenants in employment contracts. The three elements are: "(1) the restraint in the activity of the employee, or former employee, imposed by the contract; (2) the territorial or geographic restraint; and (3) the length of time during which the covenant seeks to impose the restraint."

When considering the territorial restrictions placed on an employee, the Georgia courts have indicated that territorial restrictions will generally be enforced when they relate to the area in which the employee worked but restrictions which relate to the entire area in which the employer does business are generally unenforceable.

Our research of Georgia law also shows that the Georgia courts have continually "rejected the blue-pencil theory of severability as applied to restrictive covenants in employment contracts. Therefore, if any of the subparagraphs of the restrictive covenant are invalid, the entire covenant must fall."

Due to Georgia's rejection of the "blue-pencil theory of severability," it seems clear that any evaluation of the likelihood of success in enforcing this employment contract must be done through evaluation of all the clauses of the restrictive covenant.

In this case Curtis 1000's motion for a preliminary injunction sought enforcement of only subparagraphs (i) and (ii) contained in the restrictive covenant. Subparagraphs (i) and (ii) directly related to the former territory in which Mr. Moore worked and are, therefore, *prima facie* valid. However, Curtis 1000's motion ignored subparagraph (iii) of the restrictive covenant which provides [that Moore could not]:

> Solicit orders for printing, envelopes, or other products marketed by the Company or perform any other duties for which employed by the Company, whether as Sales Representative, Sales Supervisor, or District Sales Manager, *in any town or city* in which such duties were

performed during the two years preceding the termination of this Agreement. [Emphasis added.]

This subparagraph is, under the facts of this case, extremely broad and not linked to Mr. Moore's former territory. Mr. Moore's former territory included, for example, small portions of downtown Kansas City, Missouri, and North Kansas City and part of Kansas City, Kansas. If subparagraph (iii) was enforced as written, Mr. Moore would be barred from soliciting in all of Kansas City, Missouri, North Kansas City and Kansas City, Kansas.

Our review of Georgia law leads to the conclusion that the district court applied an erroneous legal premise. First, Georgia requires that every subparagraph of the covenant be enforceable before the covenant as a whole is found enforceable. Second, subparagraph (iii) extends the territorial restriction of this contract to an area considerably larger than Mr. Moore's former territory and such restrictions are generally unenforceable under Georgia law. For these reasons, we do not believe Curtis 1000 has shown a probability of success on the merits.

The reluctance of Georgia courts to "blue-pencil" employment contracts is also based on policy considerations. As noted in *Howard Schultz & Assoc. v. Broniec*:

> It is these very requests [to "blue-pencil" employment contracts] which are the reason for rejecting severability of employee covenants not to compete. Employers covenant for more than is necessary, hope their employees will thereby be deterred from competing, and rely on the courts to rewrite the agreements so as to make them enforceable if their employees do compete. When courts adopt severability of covenants not to compete, employee competition will be deterred even more than it is at present by their overly broad covenants against competition.

Therefore, after considering each of the relevant factors, we hold that the district court's issuance of the preliminary injunction . . . must be reversed.

CASE REVIEW QUESTIONS

1. Explain why subparagraphs (i) and (ii) of Moore's covenant not to compete were enforceable.
2. Explain why subparagraph (iii) was unenforceable.
3. Explain the policy reason the court gives for rejecting the blue-pencil theory.

Exculpatory Clauses An **exculpatory clause** is a provision in a contract by which one party promises not to hold the other party liable for damages caused by the other party's negligence. Such clauses are frequently found in sale's contracts—the buyer promising not to hold the seller liable for negligence in the design or manufacture of the product being sold—and in employment contracts—the employee promising not to hold the employer liable for injuries caused by the employer's negligence.

Exculpatory clauses are also frequently found in **bailment** contracts in which one party, called a **bailor,** gives possession and control of personal property to another party, called a **bailee.** Examples of bailment contracts include leaving a coat in a checkroom, parking a car in a parking lot, and storing furniture in a warehouse. Checkrooms, parking lots, warehouses, and other bailees may try to free themselves from liability by posting signs or including exculpatory clauses on identification tickets.

Courts have questioned the legality of exculpatory clauses because public policy, as reflected in tort law, generally provides that one whose negligence causes injury to another should be required to compensate the injured person. On the other hand, public policy, as reflected in contract law, generally provides that parties are free to agree to whatever contract terms they desire, so long as their agreement does not do harm to society.

The view of the courts is that exculpatory clauses do not necessarily violate public policy. If certain conditions are present, however, an exculpatory clause will be held to violate public policy and to be unenforceable. For instance, if a company that provides public service, such as a common carrier or public utility, requires a customer to agree to an exculpatory clause, the clause will not be enforced. Similarly, if substantial inequality of bargaining position exists between the parties and the stronger party requires the acceptance of the exculpatory clause, the clause will not be enforced. Also, as reflected in the following case, an exculpatory clause will not be enforced if it tries to free a party from liability for gross negligence or recklessness.

FIDELITY LEASING CORPORATION v. DUN & BRADSTREET, INC.
449 Fed. Supp. 786 (E.D. Pa. 1980)

[Fidelity Leasing Corporation (Fidelity) was considering extending credit to Intercontinental Consulting Corporation (Intercontinental). Intercontinental furnished Fidelity with a financial report. Fidelity also contacted Dun & Bradstreet, a large credit reporting agency that contracts to sell credit information to subscribers, and requested a credit report on Intercontinental. The Dun & Bradstreet credit report gave substantially the same figures as the financial report supplied directly by Intercontinental.

Fidelity then extended credit to Intercontinental in the amount of $18,939.84. Intercontinental made monthly payments on the amount due for about 20 months, at which time all payments ceased. Intercontinental still owed $11,442.82. Fidelity then discovered that Intercontinental was a sham organization with no active business activities. It had been set up to obtain credit by another company with a poor credit rating.

Fidelity brought a legal action claiming that negligence, gross negligence, and recklessness by Dun &

Bradstreet had caused Fidelity's loss. Before trial, Dun & Bradstreet moved for a summary judgment on the grounds that it was protected from liability by an exculpatory clause in its contract with Fidelity.]

LORD, Chief Judge

Fidelity has alleged that Dun & Bradstreet's negligence, gross negligence and recklessness have caused it to suffer a business loss. The contract between the plaintiff and the defendant includes the following exculpatory provision:

> Because of the large number of informational sources upon which Dun & Bradstreet, Inc. must rely and over which Dun & Bradstreet has no control, the subscriber acknowledges that Dun & Bradstreet, Inc., does not and cannot guarantee the correctness or completeness of information furnished. Such information is to be considered a complete and current response according to Dun & Bradstreet, Inc.'s procedures. Such responses usually are not the product of independent investigation prompted by each subscriber inquiry. . . . Dun & Bradstreet, Inc., therefore, shall not be liable for any loss or injury caused in whole or in part, either by its negligent acts of omission or commission or that of its officers, agents or employees or by contingencies beyond its control, in procuring, compiling, collecting, interpreting, reporting, communicating or delivering information. . . .

Pennsylvania courts have uniformly honored contract clauses where entered into freely, so long as they do not contravene public policy. The contract between Fidelity and Dun & Bradstreet was entered into freely by parties concerning their private affairs. . . . Moreover, Lawrence Perlmutter, president and co-shareholder of Fidelity, responsible for the transactions with Dun & Bradstreet, is not an inexperienced business person. I find the clause to be valid and enforceable, and the plaintiff therefore cannot assert a claim for damages based on defendant's negligence.

It is also a long-standing principle of Pennsylvania law that contracts that eliminate a party's liability for negligence are not favored, and therefore are strictly construed. The Pennsylvania Supreme Court has instructed that contracts that limit liability for violation of otherwise legally protected rights "must spell out with the utmost particularity the intention of the parties."

The exculpatory clause at issue in this case speaks to the negligent acts of the defendant or its officers, agents or employees. The question is whether this clause exculpates the defendant from acts of gross negligence or recklessness.

As noted above, exculpatory clauses are strictly construed against the party asserting the immunity. In addition, the burden to establish immunity is on the party asserting it and the defendant here has offered no reason or precedent for construing the clause to cover gross negligence. I find therefore that the exculpatory clause in the contract does not insulate the defendant from liability for gross negligence or recklessness.

[Motion for summary judgment denied.]

CASE REVIEW QUESTIONS

1. Assuming Dun & Bradstreet was negligent, is it fair that they do not have to pay for the financial damage they caused Fidelity?
2. Explain by reference to the specific facts of the case the public policies in conflict in determining the validity of the exculpatory clause.

EFFECT OF ILLEGALITY

If one of the parties to an illegal agreement asks the court to enforce the agreement, what should the court do? The reaction of the courts to such a request depends on whether or not either party has performed any of the terms of the agreement.

Where There Has Been No Performance

If neither party has performed under an illegal agreement—that is, the agreement is **executory**—the general rule is that the agreement is void. For instance, if A promises to pay B $1,000 for injuring C and B promises to injure C in exchange for A's promise, but A has not yet paid the money and B has not yet injured C, the contract is void. This is true no matter which party tries to enforce the contract. In other words, even though A's promise to pay money is not illegal, B cannot enforce it because B's illegal promise to injure C will not serve as consideration for A's promise.

There are, however, some exceptions to the general rule that an executory illegal bargain is void. These exceptions are:

1. If one party is justifiably ignorant of the fact that the agreement is illegal and the other is aware of its illegality, the party not aware of the illegality may enforce the contract upon showing that he or she would have performed the contract but for the illegality. For example, a person who contracts with an unlicensed company that is operating a business that by law requires a license, but who is unaware of the fact that the company lacks a license, can recover from the company in an action for breach of contract.

2. Sometimes a legal act is made illegal because of the purpose of the party performing the act. For example, if a person buys goods for the purpose of smuggling them illegally into another country, the act of purchasing the goods is illegal. As was stated in the previous paragraph, if the seller is ignorant of the buyer's purpose, the seller would be able to enforce the contract. In addition, where the bargain is made illegal solely because of the purpose of one of the parties, the other party may enforce the contract even if he or she knew of that purpose if the intended purpose does not involve serious **moral turpitude** and the innocent party does nothing to facilitate the illegal purpose.

3. When an agreement is illegal because of a statute that was enacted for the purpose of protecting one of the parties, that party may enforce the contract. For example, generally someone who contracts to purchase stock can enforce the contract even though the seller has violated a statute concerning the legal sale of stock that was adopted by a legislature to protect stock purchasers.

In the following case, however, a purchaser of stock was not allowed to enforce his purchase contract that was in violation of such a statute. The court explains why in its opinion.

McCAULEY v. MICHAEL
256 N.W.2d 491 (Minn. 1977)

[McCauley was a broker–dealer in securities. Michael had organized a corporation. They entered into a contract under which McCauley was to invest $500 in Michael's corporation and receive 1000 shares of stock in return. Because of certain actions by Michael, this agreement was illegal under Minnesota's "Blue Sky Laws," laws which were adopted to protect investors from fraud.

McCauley paid the $500, but Michael refused to deliver the stock. McCauley then brought legal action to enforce the contract. The trial court held that, because the contract was illegal, McCauley could not enforce it. Instead, he was only entitled to recover his $500. McCauley appealed.]

SCOTT, Judge

Generally speaking, innocent purchasers of stock issued or sold in violation of "Blue Sky Laws" may recover by rescission or damages. The revised Minnesota Blue Sky Law specifically provides for such recovery. . . . On the other hand, if a purchaser is *in pari delicto* [equally guilty] with the seller, he is barred from recovery. There is some ground between "innocent" and "in pari delicto"; in cases where the purchaser is less than innocent but not *in pari delicto* the law will generally favor the purchaser, since the Blue Sky Laws are intended for his protection.

The purchaser will be permitted, in most cases if he has less than full knowledge of the illegality, to rescind the contract and receive back upon tender what he paid for the stock, or if he no longer owns the stock, to recover damages from the seller. The law thus seeks to return the parties to their positions prior to the illegal contract.

Enforcement of illegal stock contracts, however, is another matter. Earlier cases held that stock subscriptions made without complying with the Blue Sky Laws cannot be enforced against the subscriber [purchaser]. This follows logically from the above rules because Blue Sky Laws are intended to protect the purchaser. The present case, however, is one in which the purchaser seeks to enforce an assumedly illegal stock contract. Innocent members of the class protected by Blue Sky Laws, including purchasers, may enforce bargains made in contravention of those laws.

It would again follow that while innocent purchasers may enforce, as well as rescind, contracts violating the Blue Sky Law, purchasers *in pari delicto* could not.

This appears to be somewhat stricter on the purchaser than when only rescission or damages are sought, but this distinction has a logical basis. In seeking to rescind an illegal contract, the purchaser asks only for his original consideration, thus returning him to his status prior to the bargain. Enforcement of the contract, by specific performance or damages, however, is a much stronger contractual remedy, and may cause considerable loss to the seller. Even though the Blue Sky Laws do not intend to protect sellers who have acted unlawfully, neither do they intend to offer remedies to less-than-innocent purchasers. Further, the right to enforce an illegal stock contract offers an opportunity to the unscrupulous purchaser to elect his remedy; if the stock rises, enforcement; if the stock falls or becomes valueless, rescission. This right of election should be offered only to purchasers [who are] either "wholly innocent" or "guillible participants."

The facts of this case show that McCauley does not satisfy the standard applicable for enforcement. McCauley is a registered broker–dealer, and has been employed in the securities field since 1961. He cannot, therefore, be characterized as "guillible" in regard to purchasing stock of "insiders." Nor can he be regarded as an innocent purchaser. McCauley's knowledge and experience generally as a licensed broker–dealer, and his specific knowledge of this particular transaction, will not allow him to enforce the stock contract with Michael if that contract contravenes the Blue Sky Laws.

The rule might be thus stated: Where a contract for the sale of stock contravenes the securities laws, it may be enforced only by the innocent or guillible purchaser, who has purchased in good faith and without knowledge of any facts leading him to believe that the contract for sale may be illegal. In all other instances, enforcement will be denied. The evidence in this case shows, as stated above, that McCauley does not come under this narrow category, and hence he cannot enforce his contract with Michael if that contract is found to be illegal.

Affirmed.

CASE COMMENT

You may have noticed that the contract between McCauley and Michael was not executory because one of the parties, McCauley, had performed his part of the contract. As explained in the next section of the text, in such a situation the contract would be called "partially executed."

Why, then, did the court consider applying one of the three exceptions to the general rule concerning illegal contracts that are applied to executory contracts? As you will read in the next section, the court did this because the three exceptions are applied to partially and fully executed contracts as well as to executory contracts.

CASE REVIEW QUESTIONS

1. Why is a purchaser of stock generally allowed to sue for breach of contract even if the contract by which the stock is sold is illegal under the Blue Sky Laws?
2. Explain why the court did not allow McCauley to sue for breach of contract.

Where There Has Been Partial or Full Performance

If there has been partial or full performance under an illegal agreement, that is, if the agreement has been partially or fully executed, the general rule remains that the courts will leave the parties to the contract where it finds them. In other words, despite the fact that there has been performance, neither party is entitled to any remedy from the court. For example, a person who enters an illegal agreement by bribing a public official in return for a promise to award a government contract can neither sue for breach of contract nor recover the bribe money if the public official fails to keep the promise.

There are, however, some exceptions to the general rule. Three exceptions that a court will apply were discussed in the previous section of the text. They are, briefly, cases in which the party enforcing the contract (1) was unaware of the illegality, (2) did not facilitate the purpose of the other party that made the contract illegal, and (3) is the party intended to be protected by the statute that makes the contract illegal.

Additional exceptions, applied only when an illegal contract has been partially or fully performed, are as follows:

1. A court will enforce an agreement that violates a criminal statute if it believes that the legislature intended the penalty provided in the statute to be the only penalty to be imposed on a party violating the statute. For example, if a person fails to obtain a license to do a kind of business for which a license is required, a court will allow the person to enforce an agreement entered into as part of that business if the licensing statute was

passed simply to raise revenue for the state rather than to protect the public from fraud or incompetence.

2. A court will enforce an agreement if it believes that the illegality involved in the transaction is too remotely connected to the contract. For example, if two parties enter into a legal agreement but illegally fail to report it to the tax authorities, the contract will be enforced. The contract is said to be collateral to the illegal act and is therefore enforceable. Similarly, if a party to an illegal agreement enters into a second contract with an innocent third party to deposit money derived from the illegal agreement, the third party cannot avoid enforcement of the second contract by asserting the illegality of the first agreement. Again, the second contract is collateral to the illegality.

3. If a party performs a lawful promise contained in a contract, a court will enforce any lawful promise made by the other party even though the other party may have also made an illegal promise. For example, if Jones sells and delivers goods to Smith in return for Smith's promise to illegally influence a public official and to pay $5,000, Jones can enforce the promise to pay the $5,000. This exception holds unless the illegal promise is highly criminal or immoral. If, for instance, Smith promised to pay $5,000 and to have the public official beaten up, Jones would not be able to enforce the promise to pay the money. Note that this exception is made only for the party who has not made an illegal promise. If Smith performed first, he would not be able to enforce Jones' promise to sell the goods, unless the illegal act was very slight in degree.

4. A person who is not guilty of serious moral turpitude and who is not as implicated in the illegality as the other party can recover any consideration given to the other party or the fair value of that consideration, but he or she cannot enforce the other party's promises. For instance, if White uses fraud, duress, or undue influence to get Brown to enter into an illegal agreement, Brown would be said not to be *in pari delicto* (equally guilty) with White and would be entitled to recovery from White. Similarly, if the transaction is illegal because of a statute that was enacted to protect a class of persons of which Brown is a member, Brown is not *in pari delicto* with White and can recover any consideration paid. Some courts have decided, for example, that a bettor is not *in pari delicto* with a professional bookie because gambling laws are primarily aimed at organized gambling, not at bettors.

5. Even a person who is *in pari delicto* with the other party to an illegal agreement can recover any consideration given to the other party or the fair value of that consideration if he or she withdraws from the agreement in time to prevent the illegal aspect of the contract from happening. The purpose of this exception, called *locus poenitentiae* (place of repentance) is to encourage parties to illegal contracts to refuse to perform them. Therefore, withdrawal from the contract must occur before the illegal purpose has been substantially performed.

In the following case, a court chose to enforce a contract that had been performed despite the presence of illegality. It referred to two of the exceptions just discussed in reaching its conclusion.

GOLD BOND STAMP COMPANY v. BRADFUTE CORPORATION
463 F.2d 1158 (Second Cir. 1972)

[Bradfute designs and operates sales-building contests for retail stores. It contracted with Colonial Stores, Inc. (Colonial), a grocery store chain, to operate a bingo-type game. Cards were to be distributed in Colonial's stores and numbers would be published in Colonial's newspaper advertisements. Another party to the contract was Gold Bond Stamp Company (Gold Bond), who promised to provide the prizes for the contest.

Bradfute assured Gold Bond that the number of prizes was limited by a mathematical formula, thus limiting Gold Bond's risk. Bradfute also assured Gold Bond that the promotion was legal, stating: "Full Legal Protection is guaranteed by contract. Thoroughly checked for legality in your area before we start."

Due to errors in the game that were not discovered by Bradfute's employees, the number of contest winners and prizes distributed greatly exceeded the number Gold Bond had anticipated. Gold Bond brought a legal action against Bradfute to collect its excess costs. One of Bradfute's defenses was that the contract with Gold Bond was unenforceable because the promotion was an illegal lottery under the law of Georgia, where the promotion took place.]

MOORE, Chief Justice

Georgia law unfortunately offers no precise answer to the issue before us. [I]f the party seeking to enforce the collateral agreement merely had knowledge of the other's illegal purpose, the agreement is enforceable. The issue of enforceability becomes clouded, however, when the party seeking to enforce the agreement not only knew of the other's illegal purpose but also participated in it. Early Georgia cases indicated that any degree of participation would make the agreement unenforceable. More recent cases, however, indicate that a party's peripheral participation in the illegal scheme of the other, in addition to knowledge that the scheme is illegal, does not necessarily prevent that party from having a collateral agreement enforced. In *Bernstein,* a party which not only delivered liquor it knew was to be involved in an illegal tax avoidance scheme but also explained how the scheme might be implemented was permitted to bring an action for the purchase price of the liquor. The court reasoned that if the delivery was lawful and if no further aid was rendered after the delivery, the collateral agreement would be enforceable. Counsel have not cited and research has failed to disclose any further case delimiting the degree of participation which will make a collateral agreement unenforceable.

Here, not only was Gold Bond unaware it was participating in an illegal sales promotion, its participation in the operation of the promotion was minimal. It merely supplied the prizes at Bradfute's direction. It is therefore concluded that the collateral prize agreement is enforceable.

We need not, however, rest our determination on this conclusion alone. Even if the collateral agreement were tainted by the illegality, Georgia law would still require finding the agreement enforceable.

While illegal contracts are, as a general rule, unenforceable, Georgia courts have noted:

> there are instances in which contracts may be immoral or illegal but the parties to which are not equally culpable, and where, because of such inequality of guilt, the agreement may be enforced at the instance of the one less at fault.

Herein, Bradfute not only convinced Gold Bond to participate in the promotion after representing that it was legal, though, in fact it did not know whether its representation was true, but also created, designed and supervised the entire promotion. In addition, its negligence was the cause of errors which appeared in the game. Under these circumstances, we find that the parties are not *in pari delicto.*

Affirmed.

CASE REVIEW QUESTIONS

1. Which of the exceptions to the general principle that the courts will leave parties to an illegal contract where it finds them does the court apply in the *Gold Bond* case?
2. Explain in terms of the facts of the *Gold Bond* case why these exceptions to the general rule are made.

REVIEW QUESTIONS

1. Give three examples not specifically presented in the text of contracts involving illegality that would be unenforceable.
2. Why are courts hesitant to enforce covenants not to compete and exculpatory clauses in contracts? Why are they nonetheless sometimes enforced?
3. Give three examples not specifically presented in the text of contracts involving illegality that would be enforceable.

CASE PROBLEMS

1. Freeman, a clothing salesman, contracted with Stone to have Stone arrange a sale to the French Supply Council (FSC). Under the contract, Freeman was to pay Stone a commission for arranging the sale, and Stone was to use a part of the commission to bribe the purchasing agent of FSC. Such a bribe is illegal under state law. Stone arranged the sale but did so without having to pay the bribe. When Freeman learned that no bribe had been paid, he sued Stone to recover that part of the commission that was supposed to be used to pay the illegal bribe. Who will win the case? Explain.

2. Sawyer and Wilson engaged in a dice game in which Wilson won $1,400. Sawyer made out two I.O.U.'s for $700 each. When Wilson sought payment, Sawyer refused to pay. Wilson then brought a legal action to collect the I.O.U.'s. Sawyer argued that the court should not allow Wilson to collect because the I.O.U.'s were a payment of a gambling debt. He pointed out that the state constitution provided that "gambling is a vice and the legislature shall pass laws to suppress it." He also cited a state statute that read, "The law grants no action for the payment of what has been

won at gaming or by a bet." Who will win the case? Explain.

3. Kahn authorized Harris, a stock broker, to buy cotton contracts for him. A cotton contract is for 100 bales of cotton. In October, Harris purchased seven contracts on the New Orleans Cotton exchange for December delivery. When Kahn refused to pay Harris the amount due on the contracts, Harris resold them in October at a loss. He then brought legal action against Kahn for commissions and the loss sustained. Kahn argued in his defense that his contract with Harris was an illegal gambling contract because he had never intended to take delivery of the cotton. Instead he had been speculating that the price of cotton would rise before December and he would be able to resell the contracts at a profit. Who will win the case? Explain.

4. Lifetone Corporation sold a fire alarm system to Leach. As part of the agreement, Leach provided Lifetone with a referral list of prospective purchasers. For each sale made by Lifetone to one of the people on the referral list, Leach was to receive a commission of $100. Lifetone assured Leach that his commissions would be adequate to

cover the price he paid for the fire alarm system. Leach received no commissions and refused to pay for the alarm system. Lifetone brought a legal action for breach of contract. Leach defended on the grounds that the sales contract was illegal because the commission provision was an illegal lottery under state law. The state law defines an illegal lottery as "a scheme for the distribution of money by chance among persons who have paid for the chance." Who will win the case? Explain.

5. Securities Acceptance Corporation (Securities), a consumer loan company with 89 offices in 15 states, hired Brown to work in its office in North Platte, Nebraska. Brown signed an employment contract that provided, "For a period of 18 months after the termination of his employment for any reason, the employee will not engage in any business competitive with the employer's business in any city in which employee shall have been employed by the employer." Brown worked in the North Platte office for seven years, when he was transferred to the Omaha office. Shortly thereafter Brown quit his job and went to work for a competitor of Securities in North Platte. Securities brought a legal action for breach of contract. On what basis might Brown defend? Who will win the case? Explain.

6. Lally sold his business, Lally's Barber Shop, located in Rockville, to Mattis. The contract of sale provided that, "The Seller agrees that he will not engage in the barbering business for a period of five years in the City of Rockville or within a radius of one mile from the barber shop." Lally was 58 years old and not in good health. He had been a barber for 40 years and was unfamiliar with other work. He opened a restaurant, but it was unsuccessful. He then went to work for Mattis. After working for Mattis for nine months, Lally left and opened a barber shop in his own home 300 yards from the shop he had sold to Mattis. At the time of the opening of the new shop three years still remained under the covenant not to compete. Mattis brought a legal action to enforce Lally's covenant not to compete. Who will win the case? Explain.

7. Jenkins wished to obtain a place to park her car close to her place of work. Parker operates a parking lot in connection with his gas station. When Jenkins spoke to Parker about using his lot, she was told the monthly fee, that she would have to leave her keys each day so that the car could be moved if necessary, and that Parker would not be responsible for loss by fire or theft. There was also a large sign on prominent display which said, "Not responsible for loss by fire or theft." Jenkins agreed to park her car in the lot and paid for one month's parking in advance. Jenkin's car was stolen from the lot. She brought a legal action for negligence against Parker to recover the value of the car. Parker defended on the basis of Jenkins' agreement with Parker that he was not responsible for loss by theft. How might Jenkins respond to this defense? Who will win the case? Explain.

8. Dias, a landlord, and Houston, a contractor, entered into a contract providing that Houston would remodel Dias' building for $4,000. Houston, however, refused to do the work because of a dispute with Dias. Dias hired another contractor to do the job, and then brought suit against Houston for breach of contract. Houston argued in his defense that the contract was illegal because he did not have a contractor's license as required by state law. When the parties had contracted, Dias had not been aware that Houston did not have the required license. Who will win the case? Explain.

9. Zakzaska owed Chapman $1,695 in payment for a used car. He later discovered that, before selling the car, Chapman had changed the odometer on the car from 60,000 miles to 21,000 miles. A state statute provides, "No used motor vehicle shall be offered for sale unless the odometer shall be turned back to zero." Violation of the statute is a misdemeanor, punishable by a fine and/or imprisonment. When Zakzaska refused to pay the amount due, Chapman brought a legal action for breach of contract. Zakzaska argued that the court should not enforce the contract because of the illegality. Who will win the case? Explain.

10. Calhoun Corporation planned to have a building

constructed from plans drawn by an architect. It contracted with Hillstrom to do the electrical work. The architectural drawing did not contain plans and specifications for electrical installation, so Hillstrom made such plans as best he could. Hillstrom then applied for a permit as required by law to install the electrical work. He did not, however, file the plans and specifications of the electrical installation with the Department of Buildings, which was also required by law. After Hillstrom completed the work, Calhoun refused to pay him. When Hillstrom brought a legal action for breach of contract, Calhoun defended on the basis of illegality. Who will win the case? Explain.

16

RIGHTS OF THIRD PARTIES

Thus far, our consideration of contract law has focused on the actual parties to the contract. We know that if a promisor fails to keep a promise, the promisee may sue for breach of contract. Generally, it is only the actual parties to the contract who will be concerned about its performance.

Sometimes, however, other people become interested in a contract. In this chapter we consider three situations in which this may happen:

1. A promisee may wish to transfer his or her rights under a contract to another person. Such a transfer is called an **assignment.**
2. A promisor may wish to transfer his or her duties under a contract to another person. Such a transfer is called a **delegation.**
3. The performance of the contract between the promisor and promisee may benefit someone who is not a party to it. Such a contract is called a **third-party beneficiary contract.**

ASSIGNMENT OF RIGHTS

Smith, a manufacturer and seller of widgets, has entered into a contract with Brown. Under their agreement, Smith has delivered 10,000 widgets, but Brown has not yet made payment of the contract price of $10,000. Suppose Smith discovers that he needs money right away in order to pay for some raw materials. He may consider either selling his contract right to collect $10,000 from Brown or using the right as security for a loan. Can he do this? If so, how? What rights and duties would someone who bought Smith's right to payment have? What rights and duties would Smith and Brown have after Smith sells his right to payment from Brown?

The law provides that Smith may sell his right to collect money from Brown or use it as security for a loan. In either case, Smith's transfer of his right is called an **assignment,** Smith himself is called the **assignor,** and the person to whom the right is sold is called the **assignee.** Brown is referred to as the **obligor** or promisor.

Although assignments generally occur when rights are sold or used as security for a loan, the law does not require that an assignment be supported by consideration. This means that a person can also make an assignment as a gift. If no consideration is received, however, the assignor may be able to revoke the assignment.

Traditionally, the courts have not required that an assignment be in writing, but today there are statutes that require many assignments to be in writing.

Limitations on Assignments

In the previous example, there doesn't appear to be any reason not to allow the assignment by Smith of the right to collect money from Brown. It would not seem to make any difference to Brown whether he pays the money to Smith or to the assignee, as long as his debt is discharged when he makes payment.

But what if the contract with Brown entitles Smith to other kinds of rights? Suppose, for example, that Brown is an employee under a contract in which Brown has promised to work for Smith for two years. Should Smith be able to assign his contract right to have Brown work for him for two years to an employer in another city? If Smith is allowed to make such an assignment, and the law requires Brown to perform his duties under the contract for the assignee, people like Brown will be discouraged from entering into contracts. To avoid this undesirable result, the law provides that rights are not assignable over the objection of the obligor in the following situations:

1. If the assignment would materially alter the duties of the obligor. This limitation prevents an employer from assigning the right to services by an employee in many, but not all, cases.
2. If the assignment would materially increase the risk or burden of the obligor. This limitation would prevent a person from assigning a fire insurance policy because an insurance company issues a policy, in part, on the basis of the character of the insured.

In addition, the courts will not enforce an assignee's claim against an obligor if the assignment is prohibited by a statute or by public policy. Many states, for example, have statutes that prohibit or restrict a person's power to assign his or her right to future wages.

Traditionally, if the parties expressly provide in their contract that an assignment of rights under the contract shall be void, the courts have enforced such provisions and not recognized an assignee's claim. The trend today, however, is to restrict the ability of contracting parties to prohibit assignment of rights to receive money. This has been done in the interest of business convenience. On the other hand, a provision expressly providing that rights under the contract are assignable will be enforced even though the rights would otherwise not be assignable, unless the assignment would violate a statute or public policy.

In the following case, a professional basketball player is trying to escape a contract with a basketball club on the grounds that the club has made an invalid assignment of its contract rights. The court must decide whether the rights are assignable over the player's objection.

MUNCHAK CORPORATION v. CUNNINGHAM
457 F.2d 721 (Fourth Cir. 1972)

[Southern Sports Corporation, whose primary stockholder and manager was James C. Gardner, owned and operated the Carolina Cougars basketball club. Cunningham entered into a contract with Southern Sports Corporation to play basketball with the Carolina Cougars at a specified salary. The contract provided that, if during the term of the contract Cunningham played basketball for another team, the Cougars could obtain a court order stopping him from playing for the other team. It also provided that his contract with Southern Sports could not be assigned to another "club" without his consent.

Southern Sports Corporation assigned Cunningham's contract to Munchak Corporation as part of a transaction in which Munchak became the owner and operator of the Carolina Cougars basketball club. Cunningham was not asked to consent, nor did he consent to the assignment.

When Cunningham sought to play basketball for the Philadelphia 76ers basketball club during the term of his contract with Southern Sports, which had been assigned to Munchak, Munchak sought a court order stopping him. One of Cunningham's defenses was that his contract was not assignable and that the attempted assignment from Southern Sports to Munchak excused him from performance of the contract. The trial court refused to give the order which Munchak asked for, and Munchak appealed.]

WINTER, Circuit Judge

We recognize that . . . the right to performance of a personal service contract requiring special skills and based upon the personal relationship between the parties cannot be assigned without the consent of the party rendering those services. But . . . some of such contracts may be assigned when the character of the performance and the obligation will not be changed. To us it is inconceivable that the rendition of services by a professional basketball player to a professional basketball club could be affected by the personalities of successive corporate owners. Indeed, Cunningham had met only Gardner of Southern Sports Club, and had not met, nor did he know, the other stockholders.

The policy against assignability of certain personal service contracts is to prohibit an assignment of a contract in which the obligor undertakes to serve only the original obligee. This contract is not of that type, since Cunningham was not obligated to perform differently for plaintiffs than he was obligated to perform for Southern Sports Club. We, therefore, see no reason to hold that the contract was not assignable under the facts here.

Reversed and remanded.

CASE REVIEW QUESTIONS

1. Which of the limitations on assignments discussed in the text did Cunningham want the court to apply to his case?
2. State specifically why the court did not apply the limitation that Cunningham argued was applicable.

Status of Assignee

Suppose the assigned right is a right to receive payment of money and the obligor pays the debt to the assignor after the right to collect the money has been assigned to the assignee. Can the obligor assert the defense of payment in an action by the assignee to collect the debt? The answer depends on whether the obligor had notice of the assignment. After the obligor receives notice of the assignment, the rights of the assignee will not be affected either by an agreement between the original parties to the contract or by payment to the assignor.

For example, assume that O'Riley owes money to Rogers. Rogers assigns her right to receive the payment of the money to Edwards. If O'Riley has not received notice of the assignment and pays Rogers, he is discharged from the debt. Edwards would then have to seek payment from Rogers. On the other hand, if O'Riley has received notice of the assignment and he still pays Rogers, he is not discharged from the debt and must pay Edwards. O'Riley, however, would be entitled to be paid by Rogers.

Another reason why the assignee should notify the obligor of the assignment is to obtain protection in case the assignor wrongfully assigns the same rights to a second assignee. In such a situation, the courts in some states have decided that only the first assignee to notify the obligor is entitled to performance by the obligor. The other assignee is left only with a claim against the assignor. In other states, the courts have decided that the first assignee is entitled to performance by the obligor regardless of whether notice was given to the obligor.

For example, assume again that O'Riley owes money to Rogers. Rogers assigns her right to receive the payment of the money to Edwards. Then Rogers improperly assigns to Emerson the same right to receive the payment from O'Riley. Does Edwards or Emerson have the legal right to payment from O'Riley? As the previous paragraph indicates, in some states it would be the first assignee—either Edwards or Emerson—to notify O'Riley. In other states, it would be Edwards, the first assignee, regardless of who notified O'Riley first.

When an assignment of a right is made, the assignee stands in the same position as the assignor. This means that if the obligor has a legal defense to the assignor's right, that defense may be used by the obligor against the assignee. For example, if the assignor used misrepresentation to obtain the obligor's promise, the obligor may use the defense of misrepresentation in a legal action brought by the assignee for breach of contract.

In the following case, the assignees (the Litwins) of certain rights were unsuccessful in their suit against the obligor (Timbercrest Estates, Inc.) because they were viewed as being in the same position as their assignors (the Murphys).

LITWIN v. TIMBERCREST ESTATES, INC.
347 N.E.2d 398 (Ill. App. 1976)

[Mr. and Mrs. Murphy contracted with Timbercrest Estates, Inc. (Timbercrest) for the construction of a house. Under the contract, Timbercrest promised that "Construction will conform to and meet the requirements and building codes of Schaumburg, Illinois." Upon completion, the Murphys took possession of the house. Shortly thereafter, the Murphys complained of a few minor defects in the house, which Timbercrest repaired.

Three years later, the Murphys sold the house to Mr. and Mrs. Litwin. At the time of the purchase the Litwins were not aware of any defects in the house. Two years later, however, the Litwins became aware of some defects. They then asked the Murphys to assign to them any rights which the Murphys had against Timbercrest.

The Murphys made such an assignment and the Litwins brought legal action against Timbercrest. The complaint alleged breach of the contract with the Murphys, assignment of the Murphys' claim to Litwin, and the damages incurred from correcting the defects in the house. A motion for summary judgment by Timbercrest was denied and, after trial judgment was entered for the Litwins, Timbercrest appealed on the grounds that the summary judgment should have been granted.]

SULLIVAN, Judge

Plaintiffs' action is predicated on alleged breaches of conditions in the construction contract — principally the failure of defendants to build in accordance with the requirements of the Schaumburg building code. However, inasmuch as plaintiffs were not parties to the original contract, their cause of action necessarily depends upon whether they acquired any rights against defendants by the Murphy assignment. . . .

As a general rule, an assignment is a transfer of some identifiable property, claim or right from the assignor to the assignee. The assignment operates to transfer to the assignee all the right, title or interest of the assignor in the thing assigned. It is an elementary principle of law applicable to all assignments, that they are void unless the assignor has either actually or potentially the thing which he attempts to assign. In any event, the assignee can obtain no greater right or interest than that possessed by the assignor, inasmuch as one cannot convey that which he does not have.

Our examination of the record herein leads us to conclude that at the date of the assignment some two years after the sale of the house, the Murphys possessed no [claim against Timbercrest]. The record discloses that at the time of the sale to plaintiffs, the Murphys were unaware of any building code violations or other defects in defendants' performance under the contract. The parties agree that the alleged defects were unknown to both buyer and seller at the time of the 1968 sale to plaintiffs. It is true that shortly after they took possession in December of 1965, the Murphys had complained of a leak causing damage to plaster and of the width of the drive. It appears, however, that the leak was repaired and the driveway widened, and Murphy testified that at the time of the sale to plaintiffs he had no claim or difficulty with the premises and had no intention of making any claim against defendants.

In view thereof, we can only conclude that on the day of the assignment, the Murphys had no actual or potential claim because of the alleged contract violations and that they had no [claim against Timbercrest] which might be the subject of an assignment.

Reversed.

CASE REVIEW QUESTIONS
1. State specifically why the court concluded that the Litwins did not have a right against Timbercrest because of defects in the house.

2. Would the outcome of the case have been different if the Murphys had assigned their rights against Timbercrest at the time they sold the house to the Litwins?
3. Would the outcome of the case have been different if the Murphys had known of the defects at the time that they sold the house to the Litwins?

Status of an Assignor

When an assignor receives value for the right assigned, he or she is held by the law to make certain promises to the assignee, called **implied warranties,** concerning the assignment to the assignee, unless the parties expressly agree otherwise. These promises are:

1. That the assigned right is valid and is not subject to any defenses, except as stated or apparent.
2. That any document representing the assigned right given to the assignee is genuine.
3. That the assignor will not do anything to impair the value of the assignment.

Notice that the assignor does not promise that the obligor is solvent or will perform. This means that, unless otherwise agreed, the assignee takes the risk of performance under the contract by the obligor.

DELEGATION OF DUTIES

Besides transferring rights, a party to a contract may also wish to transfer his or her duties under a contract. For example, a construction company may wish to hire a subcontractor to perform some of the tasks it has promised to carry out under a construction contract. Should it be allowed to do so if the other party to the construction contract objects?

The transfer of a contract duty is called a **delegation,** the transferor is called the **delegator,** and the transferee is called the **delegate.** Generally, duties can be delegated, except in those cases where the other party to the contract would be expected to have a particular interest in having the delegator, the original promisor, perform the duties.

Under this standard, most construction contracts and promises to deliver goods can be delegated because the performance of the duties can be objectively measured and could be performed equally well by many people. On the other hand, the performance of promises to paint a portrait, to perform surgery, or to represent a client in court could not be delegated without the consent of the original promisee because the promisee in such cases is relying on the personal skill, judgment, and character of the promisor. Duties also may not be delegated if the original contract so provides or if prohibited by a statute or by public policy.

If performance of a duty may be delegated, the delegation does not free the delegator from liability for nonperformance of the duty. This means that if the delegate fails to perform the delegated duties, the promisee can still bring suit for breach of contract against the delegator. Only if the promisee agrees to release the delegator in exchange for the delegate's agreement to assume the duties, can the delegator escape such liability. Such an agreement by the promisee is called a **novation.**

The liability of the delegate for nonperformance of duties he or she has agreed to carry out runs to the delegator (i.e., the original promisor) to whom the delegate made a promise to perform the duties. The delegate may also be liable for nonperformance to the original promisee on the basis that the original promisee is a third party beneficiary of the delegated contract. This type of liability is discussed in the next section of the text.

In the following case, one party to a contract is trying to escape the contract on the ground that there has been an invalid delegation of the other party's duties under the contract. The court must decide if the duties are delegable.

MACKE COMPANY v. PIZZA OF GAITHERSBURG, INC.
270 A.2d 645 (Md. 1970)

[Pizza of Gaithersburg, Inc. (Pizza) was owned by Ansell. Pizza operated pizza shops at six locations. It contracted to have cold drink vending machines owned by Virginia Coffee Service, Inc. (Virginia) installed in each of its pizza shops. The contract was for a period of one year.

During the term of the contract, the assets of Virginia were purchased by the Macke Company (Macke) and the contract with Pizza was assigned by Virginia to Macke. Pizza then attempted to terminate the contract.

Macke brought suit against Pizza for breach of contract. Pizza defended on the grounds that Virginia's duties under the contract were not delegable to Macke. The trial court found in favor of Pizza, and Macke appealed.]

SINGLEY, Judge

In the absence of a contrary provision—and there was none here—rights and duties under contract may be assigned and delegated, subject to the exception that duties under a contract to provide personal services may never be delegated. . . .

We cannot regard the agreements as contracts for personal services. They were . . . assignable by Virginia unless they imposed on Virginia duties of a personal or unique character which could not be delegated.

The appellees earnestly argue that they had dealt with Macke before and had chosen Virginia because they preferred the way it conducted its business. Specifically, they say that service was more personalized, since the president of Virginia kept the machines in working order, that commissions were paid in cash, and that Virginia permitted them to keep keys to the machines so that minor adjustments could be made when needed. Even if we assume all this to be true, the agreements with Virginia were silent as to the details of the working arrangements and contained only a provision requiring Virginia to "install . . . the above listed equipment and . . . maintain the equipment in good operating order and stocked with merchandise."

Moreover, the difference between the service the Pizza Shops happened to be getting from Virginia and what they expected to get from Macke did not mount up to such a material change in the performance of obligations under the agreements as would justify the appellees' refusal to recognize the assignment.

As we see it, the delegation of duty by Virginia to Macke was entirely permissible under the terms of the agreements.

Reversed.

CASE REVIEW QUESTIONS

1. State specifically why the court decided that Virginia's duties in the case were delegable.
2. Why does the court reject Pizza's argument that the duties were not delegable on the grounds that it chose to do business with Virginia because its service was more personalized, the president of Virginia kept the machines in working order, commissions were paid in cash, and Virginia permitted Pizza to keep keys to the machines?
3. If Macke failed to perform the duties that were delegated to it, against whom could Pizza bring a legal action for breach of contract?
4. If Macke failed to perform the duties that were delegated to it, to whom would it be liable for its failure?

THIRD-PARTY BENEFICIARIES

Who can bring a legal action for breach of contract? In most cases, the party asserting that a contract promise has been broken is the person to whom the promise was made and who exchanged something (consideration) for the promise. For example, suppose Anderson loans Baker money and Baker promises that he will repay it. There is no question that Anderson, the person to whom the promise was made and who loaned Baker money in exchange for the promise, can sue for breach of contract if Baker fails to repay the money.

Suppose alternatively that Baker fails to keep his promise to repay the money, but Anderson, for whatever reason, doesn't bring legal action against Baker. Should Carlson, a friend of Anderson, be allowed to bring the action against Baker for breach of contract? The courts have said no on the grounds that Carlson is not a party to the contract. In legal language Baker and Carlson are said to be not in **privity** of contract.

Now suppose we complicate the situation a bit. If Anderson owes Carlson $500 and in exchange for loaning Baker $500 he has Baker promise to repay Carlson $500 — thus wiping out Anderson's debt to Carlson — should Carlson be allowed to sue Baker for breach of contract if Baker doesn't keep his promise? Notice that Baker and Carlson are not in privity of contract, as in the previous example. On the other hand, Carlson has a much closer "connection" to Baker's promise than he did in the previous example. Should a person who has a close connection to the promise be allowed to sue for breach of contract even though privity is lacking? If so, what kind of connection should be necessary before such a suit will be allowed?

Types of Beneficiaries

United States courts have generally decided that a contract made with the intent to benefit a third person—that is, someone who is not a party to the contract—may be enforced by that third person, who is called a third-party beneficiary. Traditionally, the courts have found that a contract is made with the intent to benefit a third person when the promisee enters into the contract with the objective intent to confer a gift (the promisor's promise) on the third party or to discharge an obligation that the promisee owes to the third party. If the intended benefit is a gift, the third party is called a **donee beneficiary**. If the benefit discharges an obligation of the promisee, the third party is called a **creditor beneficiary**. In all other cases, the third party is called an **incidental beneficiary** and may not sue to enforce the promisor's promise.

Note that the standard that is used is the objective intent of the promisee to benefit a third party. For example, if Mrs. Johnson enters a loan contract with a bank for the specified purpose of obtaining college tuition money for one of her children, and the bank promises to pay the money directly to the child, Mrs. Johnson's intent to benefit her child is clear and the child is a donee beneficiary who can enforce the bank's promise to loan the money even though he or she is not a party to the contract. Similarly, if Mrs. Johnson enters a loan contract with a bank for the express purpose of obtaining money to pay off her creditors, and the bank agrees to pay the money directly to the creditors, the creditors to whom payment was promised are creditor beneficiaries who can enforce the bank's promise even though they are not parties to the contract.

On the other hand, if Mrs. Johnson obtains the loan without mentioning how the borrowed funds are to be used, and the funds are to be paid directly to her, there is no evidence of her intent to make a gift or to discharge an obligation. Therefore, her creditors, children, and all other people are mere incidental beneficiaries of her contract with the bank and may not sue to enforce the bank's promise if the bank later refuses to keep its promise to loan her the money.

Rights and Duties

If a third-party beneficiary brings suit against a promisor, the promisor may usually assert any defenses that could be asserted against the promisee if the promisee were suing on the contract. In other words, the third-party beneficiary generally stands in the same position as the promisee and is subject to such defenses as misrepresentation or mistake, unless the promisor and promisee have agreed otherwise.

What about modifications in the contract made by the promisor and promisee after the third-party beneficiary contract is formed? For instance, can the promisee discharge the promisor from the contract without the consent of the third-party beneficiary? The answer is yes, unless the third party justifiably relies on the promise, has already brought suit on it, or assents to it in a manner provided by the promisor or promisee before being notified that the contract has been discharged or modified.

Of course, the promisor and promisee can provide in their original agreement that the consent of the third party either is or is not required to amend or discharge their contract, and the third party would be bound by such a provision. For example, virtually all life insurance policies provide that the beneficiary's consent is not required to terminate the policy or change the beneficiary.

If the third party is a creditor beneficiary, he or she does not lose any rights against the original debtor when the debtor enters into a contract with someone else to pay the debt. This is true unless the creditor agrees to a novation, an agreement discharging the original debtor and promising to look only to the new party for payment in return for the new promise to pay the debt.

In the case that follows, the court had to determine whether the plaintiff, who was suing the defendant for breach of contract but was not in privity of contract with the defendant, could nonetheless sue as a third-party beneficiary.

BUCHMAN PLUMBING COMPANY, INC. v. UNIVERSITY OF MINNESOTA
215 N.W.2d 479 (Minn. 1974)

[The University of Minnesota (University) entered into a contract with James Steele Construction Company (Steele) for the construction of two additional floors to a building. It also entered into a substantially identical contract with Buchman Plumbing Company, Inc. (Buchman) for the mechanical installations that were a part of the construction project. Both contracts provided that the work was to be completed within 200 days.

Buchman complained numerous times about delays in the project, claiming that Steele was responsible for the delays. After the project was completed, Buchman brought a legal action against the University and Steele. The claim against Steele was based on breach of contract by Steele of its contract with the University. Steele defended on the basis that Buchman was not in privity of contract with Steele. Buchman argued that it was a third-party beneficiary of the University–Steele contract. The trial court found for Steele, and Buchman appealed.]

MULALLY, Justice

Buchman asserts that even though it and Steele signed separate contracts with the University, it was a creditor beneficiary of the Steele–University contract. For Buchman to maintain an action against Steele on a creditor–beneficiary claim, Buchman must establish a duty owed to it by the University, which duty was to be performed by Steele. Buchman claims that the University owed it the duty to create conditions which would allow it to complete its work within 200 days. Furthermore, Buchman claims that it was necessary for all contractors to cooperate to attain the end result of a completed addition. . . .

The primary test used in Minnesota in determining whether a party may sue as a third-party beneficiary is the "intent to benefit" test. This intent must be found in the contract as read in light of all the surrounding circumstances. If the intent to benefit is shown, the beneficiary is an intended beneficiary. If no intent to benefit is shown, a beneficiary is no more than an incidental beneficiary and cannot enforce the contract.

In determining whether the necessary intent to benefit is present, many courts have inquired: To whom is performance to be rendered? If, by the terms of the contract, performance is directly rendered to a third party, he is intended by the promisee to be benefited. Otherwise, if the performance is directly rendered to the promisee, the third party who also may be benefited is an incidental beneficiary with no right of action.

[W]e hold that there was no "intent to benefit" Buchman. Steele's performance was to be rendered directly to the University. The 200-day [provision was] intended to benefit the University. Buchman was at most an incidental beneficiary.
Affirmed.

CASE REVIEW QUESTIONS

1. On what basis did Buchman argue that it was a creditor beneficiary of the University–Steele contract?
2. State specifically why the court decided that Buchman could not sue as a third-party beneficiary of the University–Steele contract.

REVIEW QUESTIONS

1. Under what circumstances may a person not assign a contract right that he or she has if the obligor objects? Give an example of each of these circumstances.
2. What promises (implied warranties) does an assignor make to an assignee when an assignment is made? Give an example of how the assignor might breach each of these promises.
3. Under what circumstances may a person not delegate a contract duty to another if the original promisee objects? Give an example not mentioned in the text of a duty that could not be delegated.
4. Name and define three kinds of third-party beneficiaries. What are the legal rights of each kind?

CASE PROBLEMS

1. Anderson entered into a contract with Farragut Academy, a private school, under which Anderson would conduct a fund-raising campaign for one year and the school would pay Anderson $225 a week for one year. Shortly thereafter, Anderson borrowed money from Newton Bank and assigned his contract right to the weekly payments to the bank as security for the loan. As part of the loan transaction, Farragut Academy signed a document stating that it knew of the assignment, that the unpaid balance was $7,500, and that it agreed to make all future payments to Newton Bank. It made three such payments to the bank but then refused to make any more because Anderson failed to conduct any further fund-raising activities. Newton Bank brought legal action against Farragut Academy to collect the remaining payments due under the contract. Who will win the case? Explain.

2. Mary Paalzow owned a large office building called the James Building. She entered into negotiations with Seymour Berger concerning leasing the building to him. During the negotiations, she had the background and financial status of Berger investigated. She discovered that he was an experienced and efficient manager of office buildings and was a millionaire. Paalzow then entered into a contract with Berger to lease the building to him. Berger assigned the contract to his niece. When a lease naming the niece as lessee was sent to Paalzow to sign, she refused to sign it. Berger then brought a legal action asking the court to require Paalzow to sign the lease. Paalzow defended on the basis that Berger's rights in the contract were not assignable over her objection. Who will win the case? Explain.

3. Vickers contracted with Industrial Construction Company (ICC) for the building and equipping of a canning factory according to detailed specifications attached to the contract. ICC was experienced in such construction. Before beginning construction, ICC assigned its rights and delegated its duties under the contract to Johnson, who was wholly inexperienced in constructing such factories. Vickers was not notified of the assignment. Johnson satisfactorily completed construction of the factory, but Vickers refused to accept it and pay for the work on the grounds that the contract was unassignable. If Johnson brings a legal action against Vickers for breach of contract, who will win the case? Explain.

4. Wichita State University (WSU) entered into a contract with Golden Eagle under which Golden Eagle was to supply a qualified flight crew to fly the WSU football team to away games. As part of the contract, WSU promised to provide passenger liability insurance. During the term of the contract a plane carrying the WSU football team to an away game, and being flown by a Golden Eagle flight crew, crashed. WSU had failed to purchase passenger liability insurance. Brown, an injured survivor of the crash, brought suit against WSU, arguing that WSU had promised to obtain passenger liability insurance in its contract with Golden Eagle and its failure to do so was a breach of contract. WSU defended on the grounds that Brown was not in privity of contract with WSU and, therefore, could not bring the suit. What argument can Brown make that may allow him to bring the suit? Who will win? Explain.

5. The Masters, Mates, and Pilots Union (Union) had a contract with the Washington Toll Bridge Authority (Authority). A provision of the contract prohibited the employees covered by the contract from going on strike. As a result of the inability of the Union and the Authority to agree on terms of a new contract, the workers went on strike in violation of their contract. A law suit was brought against the union for breach of their contract with the Authority by hotel owners, shop owners, and others who were inconvenienced or economically harmed as a result of the strike. The Union defended on the grounds that the plaintiffs were not in privity of contract with the Union and, therefore, could not bring the suit. What argument can the plaintiffs make that may allow them to bring the suit? Who will win? Explain.

6. Emmick entered into a contract with Hamm, an attorney, under which Hamm promised to draft a will in return for the payment of a fee. After Emmick died, it was discovered that because of an error by Hamm in the drafting of the will Lucas would receive $75,000 less than he would have received if the will had been drafted correctly. Lucas brought legal action against Hamm arguing that Hamm's failure to draft the will correctly constituted a breach of contract. Hamm defended on the grounds that Lucas was not in privity of contract with Hamm. What argument can Lucas make that may allow him to bring the suit? Who will win? Explain.

7. Nancy Pruitt entered into a contract with her son, Alexander Pruitt, to convey to him a piece of real estate. In return, Alexander promised to pay a specified sum of money to Nancy's other son, Joseph, when Joseph became 21 years old. At the time the contract was made, Joseph was five years old. Before Joseph had any knowledge of the contract, Nancy and Alexander agreed that Alexander would return the real estate to Nancy and she would discharge him from his promise to pay the sum of money to Joseph. Alexander then returned the real estate to Nancy.

   After becoming 21 years old, Joseph brought legal action against Alexander, arguing that Alexander's failure to pay the sum of money to Joseph constituted a breach of contract. On what grounds might Alexander defend? Who will win the case? Explain.

17

DISCHARGE OF CONTRACT DUTIES

The making of a contract usually creates duties for the parties to it. Those duties exist until they are discharged. In this chapter, you will learn about the ways in which a contract duty may be discharged.

DISCHARGE BY PERFORMANCE

The most common way in which a party discharges a contractual duty is by performing it. When a party completes performance as promised, the other party's expectation resulting from the promise is fulfilled. Sometimes, however, it can be difficult to determine whether performance has occurred. In this section, we will consider some of these difficulties and how they are handled by the courts.

What Constitutes Performance?

If a party performs a contractual duty exactly as promised, he or she is, of course, discharged. If performance is not exact, the deviation from exact performance, if it is trivial, will be ignored under the doctrine of *de minimis non curat lex* (the law does not concern itself about trifles) and the performance will be treated as exact. But what if the deviations are not merely trivial but are slight? Should the performing party be discharged?

In some cases, the answer is no, because the exact performance of the promisor's promise can be accomplished and measured precisely. For example, a contractual promise to pay money in exchange for goods can only be discharged by payment of the exact amount of money agreed to and nothing less.

On the other hand, exact performance of the promisor's promise is not easily accomplished or measured in some situations. For example, a promise by a construction company to erect a building pursuant to a complex and detailed set of blueprints and specifications will seldom, if ever, be performed exactly, no matter how hard the company tries to do so. In such a situation, if the promisor's performance deviates only slightly, though more than trivially, from what was promised so that the promisee's expectation is substantially fulfilled, and the promisor has made a good faith attempt to perform fully, the promisor is said to have given **substantial performance.** This will allow the construction company to collect the contract price agreed to by the other party, less any damages to the other party that occurred as a result of the company's failure to perform exactly. This is done because the promisee's expectation has been substantially fulfilled by the substantial performance.

Material Breach

Failure to perform contract duties either exactly or substantially generally results in a material breach of the contract unless the party who fails to perform has an excuse, which is discussed in the next section of the text. A party who materially breaches a contract has no contract rights against the other party, that is, the other party is discharged from performance of his or her contractual duties. The party who materially breaches is also liable for damages that result to the other party from the breach. The calculation of such damages will be discussed in the next chapter.

In some cases, material breach of contract can occur even before a party's performance under a contract becomes a duty. If a party expressly states that he or she intends to breach the contract, or if such intent can be implied from the party's actions, an **anticipatory breach** occurs, which has the same legal effect as a material breach. For example, an anticipatory breach occurs if a person who has contractually promised to sell a house tells the buyer that he or she is going to refuse to give the buyer a deed when the time agreed to for doing so arrives or if the seller sells the house to someone other than the buyer.

In the case that follows, the court had to determine whether a construction company has substantially performed or materially breached its contract to build a road.

ALASKA STATE HOUSING AUTHORITY v. WALSH & COMPANY, INC.
625 P.2d 831 (Alaska 1980)

[Walsh & Company, Inc. (Walsh) entered into a contract with the Alaska State Housing Authority (ASHA) whereby Walsh agreed to construct a gravel surface road. According to the plans, which were incorporated into the contract, a 12-inch layer of compacted wood chips was to be placed below the gravel surface, in order to insulate the surface from the tundra material below.

When Walsh completed the road final inspection by ASHA revealed that the average thickness of the wood chip layer underlying the surface was only nine inches. ASHA then refused to pay Walsh the entire price agreed to in the contract.

Walsh brought a legal action to recover the entire contract price. ASHA denied liability, arguing that Walsh had materially breached the contract. Walsh argued that it had substantially performed. The trial court found that there had been substantial performance and awarded Walsh the contract price less damages resulting from Walsh's performance. ASHA appealed, arguing that the trial court had erred in finding substantial performance.]

CONNER, Justice

[T]he doctrine of substantial performance permits recovery by a contractor who has substantially, though imperfectly, performed his contractual undertaking. In such circumstances the contractor is entitled to recover the contract price, less the reasonable costs of remedying the defects in the work or materials. The initial burden of proving substantial performance is on the contractor. If his evidence shows substantial performance, the burden is then upon the owner to prove that certain deficiencies in the work require set-off [reduction in the contract price]. Substantial performance is determined by considering such factors as the character of the performance that was promised, the purpose that the contract was meant to serve, and the extent to which any nonperformance by the contractor has defeated the purposes or ends which were meant to be achieved. This means that in many cases substantial performance becomes a matter of degree, to be determined by weighing a number of factors together.

In the case at bar the trial court stated:

In reaching the conclusion that Walsh did substantially perform its obligations I especially considered the extent of Walsh's performance, the lack of any willful noncompliance with the technical specifications, and the fact that the roadway as constructed has not required any inordinate or special maintenance by ASHA.

We now address ASHA's contention that the trial court erred in finding that there was substantial performance by Walsh. ASHA's argument is that the departures from the contract specifications were so grave that the owner was deprived of what it bargained for in that the road it received in its entirety averaged only 75% of the specified insulation depth, with a 2,000 foot section averaging only 40% of the design insulation depth.

However, the court had before it evidence that the road was substantially serving its intended purpose and did not require rebuilding. The evidence on this point consisted of both oral testimony and documentary evidence, from which inferences could be drawn both for and against a finding that Walsh had substantially performed. We conclude that the trial court did not err in deciding that substantial performance had been rendered.

Affirmed.

CASE REVIEW QUESTIONS

1. What factors did the court consider in determining that Walsh had substantially performed his contract duties? How were those factors applied in this particular case?

2. How do you think the damages to ASHA, and thus the reduction in the contract price, should be calculated? Should it be the cost of reconstructing the road in order to bring it in line with the original plans? What if the cost of bringing the road in line with the original plans would now cost more than the original contract price? (This issue will be dealt with in Chapter 18.)

Personal Satisfaction

A recurring situation in which there is frequently a problem in determining whether performance or breach of contract has occurred is when a promisor promises to perform to the personal satisfaction of the promisee. If the promisee says he or she is not satisfied, will a court ever decide that performance has occurred anyway? The answer is yes, if the performance can be objectively evaluated and the promisee's dissatisfaction with the performance is found to be unreasonable. The sale of most goods and services would fall into this category.

On the other hand, if the performance can only be evaluated subjectively because it concerns matters of individual taste, preference, or convenience, a court will accept the adverse judgment of the promisee unless it is given in bad faith. Such things as works of art and services of a personal nature would be included in this category.

Third-Party Satisfaction

A similar situation occurs when a promisor promises to perform to the satisfaction of a third person who is not a party to the contract. Such promises are frequently made by construction companies when they promise to perform to the satisfaction of a particular architect or engineer. The satisfaction is shown by the issuance of a certificate indicating approval of the construction work done. In such cases, a court will accept the judgment of the architect or engineer unless it is shown that it was made in bad faith, constitutes a gross mistake, or that issuance of the certificate was prevented by the other party to the contract.

Late Performance

Another situation in which it may be difficult to determine whether material breach of contract has occurred is when the promisor fails to perform on time. Generally, the courts have decided that a promisor does not breach the contract even though performance is later than provided by the contract as long as it is within a reasonable time after the time provided.

On the other hand, a court will hold that late performance constitutes a breach if the parties intend that timely performance is very important. Such intent is generally shown by the inclusion of a clause in the contract stating that "time is of the essence." But, as the following case indicates, a court will sometimes determine that the parties intended time to be of the essence even though such a clause was not included in the contract.

CREASY v. TINCHER
173 S.E.2d 332 (W. Va. 1970)

[Creasy offered to buy certain real estate from Tincher for $30,000. The offer was in a writing which also provided: "This sale shall be completed and all necessary papers executed and delivered within 90 days from the date of acceptance hereof by Seller." Tincher accepted the offer the next day.

Because of various delays, the 90-day period expired without the sale of the land being completed. About one week before the expiration of the 90-day period, Creasy asked the real estate agent who represented Tincher to obtain an extension of the 90-day period. The real estate agent, however, did not talk to Tincher until after the expiration of the 90-day period. When the extension was requested, Tincher said he considered the agreement terminated and no extension would be granted.

Creasy brought a legal action, requesting that the court order Tincher to sell the land to Creasy. The trial court refused to grant the order on the grounds that the 90-day time period was of the essence of the contract. Tincher appealed, arguing that the trial court was incorrect in deciding that time was of the essence.]

CAPLAN, Judge

Whether or not time is of the essence of a contract is determined from the language used in the instrument and the circumstances surrounding it. The principle object is to determine the intent of the parties. Time is often made the essence of a contract and if the parties clearly so intend, by word or action, it will be so regarded.

> It is clear therefore that the parties may make time of the essence of their contract by stipulating therein that 'time is of the essence', although those exact words are not essential. Any words which show that the intention of the parties is that time shall be of the essence of the contract . . . will have that effect.

Applying the above principles to the instant case we are of the opinion that the time expressed in the agreement in which the contract shall be consummated is of the essence of the agreement. The language used is clear and unequivocal. It provides that the sale shall be completed within ninety days from the date of acceptance by the seller. As herein noted the contract need not include the words "time is of the essence." Here, we believe, the language clearly shows the intention of the parties.

In addition to the clear language of the contract, the circumstances surrounding the transaction show that the parties intended time to be of the essence of the agreement. Mrs. Tincher testified that she and her husband wanted to get this sale consummated promptly and that they thought ninety days in which to do it was too long; that they finally but reluctantly agreed to that time period; and that she attempted to get Mrs. Creasy to close within the specified time. The plaintiff, by requesting an extension of the ninety-day period, very obviously revealed her belief that such time was of the essence of the agreement. Otherwise, why would she bother to seek such extension of time?

Affirmed.

CASE REVIEW QUESTIONS

1. Do you agree with the court that the language of the contract "is clear and unambiguous" that the 90-day period is of the essence of the contract? Explain.
2. What are the circumstances surrounding the transaction that the court believes shows an intent that the 90-day period be of the essence of the contract? Do you agree that these circumstances show such an intent?
3. How would you answer the court's question in the last sentence of the decision?

EXCUSES FOR NONPERFORMANCE

If a party fails to perform contract duties, a breach of contract will result unless that party can provide a legal excuse for the nonperformance that has discharged the duty to perform. In previous chapters, you have read of some circumstances in which parties have been allowed to rescind their contract. For example, a party who can prove the existence of the elements of misrepresentation can avoid the contract through an action for rescission. A party who rescinds is, of course, excused from performance of his or her duties under the contract.

Operation of Conditions

One excuse for nonperformance is that the duty created by the contract is not owed by the promisor because of the operation of a condition in the contract. A contract condition is an act or event that affects the duty to perform as promised.

If a contract provides that a certain event must occur before the duty to perform arises, the event is called a **condition precedent.** If the condition does not occur, the conditional duty is discharged. For example, if an insurance company issues a policy promising to pay a certain sum of money in case of the accidental death of the policy holder, the company's duty of payment does not arise unless the policy holder dies as the result of an accident during the period of the policy.

If the terms of a contract say that the parties are to exchange performances at the same time, the performances are **concurrent conditions.** For example, if two students agree to buy and sell a textbook, payment and delivery are concurrent conditions, unless the students expressly agree otherwise. In order for the duty of either party to perform to arise under such a contract, the other party must **tender** (offer) performance of his or her duty under the contract. Therefore, if neither party shows up at the time and place agreed to for the sale, both parties are discharged because the concurrent condition of each performance has not occurred.

A contract provision that states that a contractual duty that has already arisen will be discharged upon the occurrence of a certain event is called a **condition subsequent.** An insurance policy, for instance, may provide that the company's duty to pay for a loss cannot be enforced after 12 months from the time the loss occurs. The duty to pay under such a contract arises when the loss occurs; that is, the occurrence of the loss is a condition precedent to the company's duty to pay. Failure to submit a claim within 12 months of the occurrence of the loss will discharge the company's duty to pay; that is, the failure to submit the claim within the designated time is a condition subsequent.

Some contract conditions are expressly created by the terms of the contract. Words in a contract like "if," "provided that," and "when" may introduce conditions, but it is the intent of the parties, not just the language of the contract, that determines the existence of an express condition. Other contract conditions are imposed by law rather than by the intent of the parties. These conditions are called **constructive conditions.** An example of a constructive condition is discussed in the next section of the text.

In the following case, the court had to decide if the failure of the operation of a condition in a contract excused the performance of the contract duties of one of the parties.

UNITED STEEL WORKERS v. U.S. STEEL CORPORATION
292 F.Supp 1 (N.D. Ohio 1980)

[In 1977, United States Steel Corporation (U.S. Steel) considered closing its plants in the Mahoning Valley (Youngstown), Ohio. At that time, however, it elected to keep those plants open, telling the employees, "With your help, this effort will continue and if and when there will be a phase-out depends on the plants' profitability, but no timetable has been set."

In 1979, U.S. Steel decided to close the Mahoning Valley plants, causing the layoff of about 3,500 workers. The union that represented the workers brought a legal action to keep the plants open on the grounds that the company had promised to keep them open so long as they remained profitable. The union asked the court to enforce U.S. Steel's promise.

The court refused to enforce the alleged promise for several reasons. One reason was that the plaintiffs had failed to prove the condition precedent to the defendant's liability, the profitability of the steel mills.]

LAMBROS, District Judge

Plaintiffs attempted to demonstrate profitability by defining minimum profitability as the "gross profit margin," which William R. Roesch, President and Chief Operating Officer of United States Steel, described as "the revenues minus the variable costs of performing the operation to produce the product." He admitted that "technically, if you are losing money at the gross margin operation, there is no way to make that operation profitable." Plaintiffs then turned to their exhibits 32 through 37, which were summary sheets of operating profitability for the Youngstown facilities for 1977, 1978, 1979, and 1980. These exhibits revealed that the gross profit margin for 1977 was $24,899,000.00, that for 1978 was $41,770,000.00, that for 1979 was $32,571,000.00 and that the projected gross profit margin for 1980, as of November 20, 1979, was $32,396,000.00.

These figures do indicate that at the variable-cost margin, the plant was, in a sense, profitable. It should be remembered, however, that even with the projected $32,396,000.00 gross profit margin projected for

1980, the over-all projection for the year was a loss of $9,387,000.00. This suggests that with a different definition of profit, especially one that would include fixed costs, the outcome of an accounting analysis could be made to be nonprofitability. Mr. Roesch testified that the gross profit margin "does not represent the profit of the operation" nor does it represent that the operation is necessarily profitable, considered as a whole. He explained that "[t]here are other factors involved because, once you have the gross margin, you have to subtract the depreciation for the equipment which was involved and depreciate it over a period of time; you have to subtract the selling expenses which are necessary; and you have to subtract the administrative charges, the taxes, and so forth." He also explained that, because of the integrated system of the national corporation, many of the unseen costs of the Youngstown Works were absorbed by other plants and operations in the steel company. Mr. Roesch testified that it was primarily the obsolescence of the plant facilities that made the plant unprofitable.

The testimony of David Roderick, Chairman of the Board of Directors and Chief Executive Officer of United States Steel, confirmed Mr. Roesch's opinion. In answer to the question "And through the end of October, 1979, . . . the performance of that year was in the area of about the break even, was it not?" Mr. Roderick replied ". . . the actual number was about a $300 thousand loss, as of the end of October, cumulative for the year. And further, as I recall, they had lost money three out of the four months preceding it." Further, Mr. Roderick explained the opinion of the Board of Directors on the trend of the loss in this way:

> Well, what I really mean by an irreversible loss is based on our best judgment, or my best judgment, the loss would be incurred and there was nothing the plant could do to avoid that loss, that the market was working negatively and that it was our projection that the plant would lose money in five out of six months of the second half, that the loss for the year would be quite substantial in 1979, and with all the facts that we could see on the horizon for 1980, plus the actual perform-

ance for the second half of 1979, we felt there was no way that the loss trend could be reversed for the calendar year of 1980.

This Court is loathe to exchange its own view of the parameters of profitability for that of the corporation. It is clear that there is little argument as to the production figures for the Youngstown mills — the controversy surrounds the interpretation of those figures. Plaintiffs read the figures in light of a gross profit margin analysis of minimum profitability. Defendant sees capital expenditure, fixed costs and technical obsolescence as essential ingredients of the notion of profitability. Perhaps if this Court were being asked to interpret the word "profit" in a written contract between plaintiffs and defendant, some choice would have to be made.

Given the oral nature of the alleged promises in the case at bar and the obvious ambiguity of the statements made, this Court finds that there is a very reasonable basis on which it can be said the Youngstown facilities were not profitable. Further, plaintiffs have made no showing of bad faith on the part of the Board of Directors in the Board's determination of profitability, nor have they given any grounds to suggest that defendant's definition of profitability is an unrealistic or unreasonable one. The condition precedent of the alleged contract and promise — profitability of the Youngstown facilities — was never fulfilled, and the contract [action] . . . cannot be found for plaintiffs.

[Judgment for defendant.]

CASE REVIEW QUESTIONS
1. The court in the *U.S. Steel* case treats profitability of the plants as a condition precedent. Could profitability be treated as a condition subsequent? Would it effect the outcome of the case? Explain.
2. How did the steelworkers interpret the word "profitable" in their alleged contract with U.S. Steel? How did U.S. Steel interpret the word "profitable"? Which interpretation did the court use? Explain.
3. Can you see any other contract law reasons why the court might refuse to enforce U.S. Steel's promise to keep the plants open?

Impossibility

Another excuse for nonperformance that the courts accept is that the promised performance has become impossible because of an unexpected event. This excuse is allowed when the court determines that the parties to the contract believed that certain facts would continue to exist, although they did not expressly state so in their contract, making those facts a constructive condition precedent to the promisor's duty. Because the condition is not met, the performance is excused.

A common instance of impossibility occurs when something that is necessary to the promisor's performance is destroyed and cannot be replaced. For example, if a farmer promises to deliver tomatoes that are to be grown on a particular farm, destruction of the crop through no fault of the farmer would excuse performance. Another common situation in which performance becomes impossible occurs when, after a contract is formed, a law or regulation is adopted that makes performance illegal. Similarly, performance is excused by the serious illness or death of the promisor if personal performance is required under the contract. On the other hand, contracts that do not call for personal performance will not be excused by illness or death.

At one time, the courts would accept nothing short of absolute impossibility before excusing performance. Events that made performance extremely more difficult, but not impossible, were rejected as excuses for nonperformance. More recently, however, some courts have relaxed this requirement somewhat. They now excuse performance, even though it is possible to perform, in cases where the cost of performance is much greater than expected because of the occurrence of an unforeseen contingency that changes the manner of performance that was contemplated by the parties. This is called **commercial impracticability** or **commercial frustration.**

For example, in one case a large city entered into a long-term contract to dispose of the sewage of a nearby suburb, charging the suburb a specified price. The state government subsequently passed a law requiring sewage treatment techniques that substantially increased the cost to the city of performance under the contract. The new law had not even been proposed at the time the contract was first entered into, and neither party had considered the possibility of the adoption of such a law when negotiating the contract. Although performance by the city was not impossible, a court discharged the city from its duties under the contract on the basis of commercial impracticability.

To use impossibility or impracticability as an excuse, the promisor must prove that the difficulty in performance is objective, not subjective. This means that the promisor must show that performance would be impossible or more difficult for anyone, not just for the particular promisor. For example, if a buyer of goods develops serious financial problems so that he or she cannot make payment, the excuse of impossibility or impracticability is not available because it is only that particular buyer who cannot perform.

In the case that follows, a court is being asked to adopt the doctrine of commercial frustration in a case where the promisor would not be excused on the basis of impossibility.

HOWARD v. NICHOLSON
556 S.W.2d 477 (Missouri App. 1977)

[Nicholson signed a lease with Honey's International, Ltd. (Honey's) to rent a bridal salon to Honey's for 20 years in a building that Nicholson was to have built pursuant to Honey's plans and specifications. Nicholson then entered into a contract with Howard under which Howard would construct the building in accordance with Honey's plans and specifications for a price of $199,740.

Prior to the completion of the building, Honey's went bankrupt, discharging them from their lease with Nicholson. Nicholson then notified Howard that he would not accept or pay for the building.

Howard sued Nicholson for breach of contract. The trial court found that Nicholson was excused from performance of his contract duty to pay for the building on the grounds of commercial frustration. Howard appealed.]

MCMILLAN, Presiding Judge
The applicability of the doctrine of commercial frus-

tration presents a question of first impression in Missouri. Under the doctrine, if the happening of an event not foreseen by the parties and not caused by or under the control of either party has destroyed or nearly destroyed either the value of the performance or the object or purpose of the contract, then the parties are excused from further performance. The doctrine of commercial frustration is close to but distinct from the doctrine of impossibility of performance. Both concern the effect of supervening circumstances upon the rights and duties of the parties but in cases of commercial frustration "[p]erformance remains possible but the expected value of performance to the party seeking to be excused has been destroyed by a fortuitous event. . . ."

[C]ases and commentators have approached the doctrine of commercial frustration as a problem of "allocating, in the most generally satisfactory way, the risks of harm and disappointment that result from supervening events." The problem in commercial frustration cases (is) "whether an unanticipated circumstance, the risk of which should not be fairly thrown on the promisor, has made performance vitally different from what was reasonably to be expected." If the event was reasonably foreseeable, then the parties should have provided for its occurrence in the contract and its absence indicates an assumption of risk by the promisor.

Courts consider the relation of the parties, the terms of the contract and the circumstances surrounding its formation in determining whether the supervening event was reasonably foreseeable.

It is also necessary to establish that there was a total or practically total destruction of the purpose or object of the transaction.

The doctrine of commercial frustration, like that of impossibility of performance, grew out of the demands of the commercial world to excuse performance in cases of extreme hardship. Sound public policy, while requiring that the doctrine be limited in its application so as to preserve the certainty of contract, requires the law to be flexible and equitable in situations where unexpected contingencies operate to make performance valueless and the allocation of contractual risks capricious or fortuitous.

In this case the proposed building could have been built. But in view of the findings by the trial court that the building had been specifically designed for use as a bridal salon by Honey's and for the sale of bridal fashions and accessories and that it was not suited for other uses, the value of the building as such was destroyed by the supervening circumstance of the bankruptcy of Honey's, the proposed tenant. In addition, appellant was at all times aware of respondents' ultimate purpose in purchasing the property and in construction of the building, its use as a Honey's Bridal Salon. Both parties to the construction contract contemplated construction of a building to be used as a Honey's Bridal Salon.

The other factor to consider in the application of commercial frustration as an excuse of performance is the foreseeability of the supervening event — was the bankruptcy of Honey's a reasonably foreseeable event that should have been provided for in the construction contract? While the possibility of bankruptcy of businesses in general is a foreseeable and all-too-frequent occurrence, the future bankruptcy of a particular company, the continuing existence of which was essential to complete the entire transaction, was not reasonably within the contemplation of the parties at the time of contracting such that the parties would have made provision for such an event. The bankruptcy of Honey's was a fortuitous and unexpected supervening event over which neither party had any control. The doctrine of commercial frustration "reads into" a contract an implied condition that Honey's would be able to rent the proposed building and use it as a bridal salon. The bankruptcy of Honey's effectively destroyed the value of the building which was suitable only for such use and excused performance by the respondents.

In this case it is not inequitable to maintain that appellant had assumed part of the risk in the contract in light of appellant's active participation and knowledge of the entire transaction. Appellant was aware that the construction of the proposed building was for one purpose only, the long-term lease by Honey's and operation as a bridal salon. Inasmuch as the bankruptcy of Honey's made this objective unattainable and destroyed the value of performance of the contract, the doctrine of commercial frustration will operate to excuse further performance under the contract.

Affirmed.

1. Why did the court decide to adopt the doctrine of commercial frustration?
2. State specifically why the court finds the doctrine of commercial frustration applicable in this case.

Agreement of the Parties

A party to a contract is also excused from performance of his or her contractual duties if the other party agrees to discharge such performance. For instance, the parties may mutually agree to terminate a contract they entered into. Such an agreement, called a **mutual rescission,** discharges both parties from their duties under their contract. A mutual rescission also occurs if the parties substitute a new contract for one they already have.

If only one party discharges the other from contractual duties, such action is called a **release.** In any situation involving a release, it is important to make sure that the promise to discharge is supported by consideration or there is a substitute for consideration (see Chapter 12) or a valid gift has been made (see Chapter 42).

Operation of Law

Finally, contract duties may be discharged by the operation of laws other than contract law. For instance, the statute of limitations may run on a contract claim (see Chapter 2), or contract duties may be discharged by bankruptcy (see Chapter 30). The law also provides that a party to a written contract who alters the contract with fraudulent intent discharges the other party from his or her contract duties.

REVIEW QUESTIONS

1. Explain the difference between substantial performance of a contract and material breach of a contract.
2. Under what circumstances can a court decide that a promisor has performed his or her contract duties even though the promisee or a third party is not satisfied with the performance and the contract provides that such satisfaction is necessary for performance to occur?
3. State three kinds of conditions that a contract may contain and give an example of each kind.
4. What is the difference between the concept of "impossibility" and the concept of "commercial impracticability"? Give an example of each.

CASE PROBLEMS

1. Loeffler contracted to sell Roe a motel for a specified price. Before the contract was performed, a survey of the property revealed that three corners of the roof of the building extend beyond the lines of the property on which the motel is located. In each instance, the roof extends over public property (a sidewalk and an alley) for a distance of less than two feet. A large proportion of business build-

ings in the city in which the motel is located have roofs with similar minor overhangs of public property, and the city government has never objected to any of them. Roe notified Loeffler that he refused to buy the motel as he had promised because the overhangs constituted a breach of contract by Loeffler, discharging Roe. Loeffler then brought legal action against Roe on the basis of breach of contract. Who will win the case? Explain.

2. Jones hired Haverty to install plumbing, heating, and ventilation equipment in a building being built on Jones' property. Total cost of the building was to be $186,000, and Haverty was to be paid $27,332. When Haverty finished his work, Jones refused to pay on the grounds that the work done was defective in 12 ways. Nine of these defects can be corrected at a total cost of $99.21. The other three defects can only be corrected at a cost that is greater than is justified by their importance. Because of these three defects, the building was worth $2,180 less than it would be if the work had been done correctly. If Haverty sues Jones for breach of contract, who will win the case? If Haverty will win, how much will he be entitled to collect? Explain.

3. Old World Arts, Inc. (OWA) entered into a contract to have printing done for a specified price by Design and Lithography Center, Inc. (D&L). The contract provided that the printing was to be done to OWA's satisfaction. When the printing was completed, OWA rejected it. D&L brought a legal action against OWA for the price agreed to under the contract. It presented testimony by several printers and advertisers that the printing was satisfactory for its intended commercial purpose. OWA defended on the basis that the printing was not satisfactory to it. Who will win the case? Explain.

4. Hangen entered into a contract with Raupach to build a house at a specified price according to an architect's plans. Final payment by Raupach was conditioned on production by Hangen of a certificate from the architect certifying that the house had been completed pursuant to the architect's plans. When Hangen completed construction of the house, the architect told him that there had been substantial performance of the contract.

Raupach, however, insisted that the architect raise certain insignificant objections, and no architect's certificate of completion was issued to Hangen. When Hangen sued Raupach for the specified price of construction of the house, Raupach defended on the grounds that production of an architect's completion certificate was a condition precedent of his liability. How should Hangen respond to this defense? Who will win the case? Explain.

5. Logan entered into a contract to sell Bogojavlensky a vacant lot and then to build a house on the lot for a specified price. The contract stated that the work was to be completed by Logan and the house was to be ready for occupancy by Bogojavlensky on October 1. Bogojavlensky made a down payment of $2,000 and Logan began work. Although Logan worked diligently, the house was not ready by October 1. When Logan told Bogojavlensky that the house would not be finished until October 10, Bogojavlensky said he was rescinding the contract and demanded repayment of the deposit he had made. If Bogojavlensky brings a legal action to recover the $2,000 deposit, on what basis can Logan defend? Who will win the case? Explain.

6. Lach entered into a contract to buy Cahill's house for a specified price. He gave Cahill a $1,000 deposit at that time. A provision of the contract stated: "This agreement is contingent upon buyer being able to obtain a mortgage." Lach applied for a mortgage at six different banks, but all of his applications were denied. Lach then notified Cahill that he was unable to obtain a mortgage and wanted his $1,000 back. Cahill refused to return the $1,000. If Lach brings a legal action to recover the deposit, on what basis can he argue that he was discharged from his promise to buy the house? Who will win the case? Explain.

7. The Santa Barbara Hotel (Hotel) entered into a contract with La Combre Golf Club (Club) under which Club would allow the Hotel's guests to use its golf course and the Hotel would pay the Club $300 per month. The Hotel was destroyed by fire. There were still two years remaining in the term of the contract. The Hotel was not rebuilt, and it stopped making payments on the contract because it had no guests. If Club sues Hotel to recover $7,200, the amount due for the final 24 months of

the contract, on what basis can Hotel defend? Who will win the case? Explain.

8. On June 1, 1939, Wood leased property to Bartolino "for use solely as a gas station" for $100 a month. The term of the contract was for five years. In January, 1942, the federal government enacted a number of rules that restricted sales of cars, tires, and gasoline. As a result, tourist travel in the United States declined substantially. Most of Bartolino's business until then had come from tourists. As a result, Bartolino began to suffer large financial losses from the operation of the business. In July, 1942, Bartolino closed his gas station and refused to pay any more rent. Wood brought a legal action for breach of contract. How might Bartolino have defended himself in the case? Who do you think won the case? Explain.

9. Bailey entered into a contract to build a house for Martin at a specified price according to certain plans. The contract stated that Bailey could not deviate from the plans "without prior written approval of Martin." During construction, Martin orally instructed Bailey to make a number of additions and changes. The cost to Bailey in following these instructions was $751.77, and he added this cost to the price of the house when he billed Martin. Martin refused to pay the additional amount. If Bailey brings legal action to recover the additional amount, on what basis can Martin defend? Who will win the case? Explain.

18

REMEDIES

When a contract is formed, it creates expectations in the parties to the contract. Generally, these expectations are met because the parties fully or substantially perform the promises they made in the contract. If one of the parties fails to perform his or her contract promises, however, a court will try to protect the expectations of the other party by providing an appropriate remedy. As you should recall, protection of expectations is the primary purpose of contract law.

The rights and duties created by a contract are *primary* rights and duties. When the contract is breached, the law substitutes *secondary* rights and duties for the primary ones. The law concerning remedies defines these secondary rights and duties.

As a general proposition, the purpose of contract remedies is to put a party who is harmed as the result of a breach of contract in as good an economic position as that party would have been in if the contract had been performed. In this way, the law fulfills the expectations of the party who has been harmed. You should keep this purpose in mind as you read about the various contract remedies that the law provides.

MONEY DAMAGES

The most common remedy for breach of contract is the payment of money damages by the party who breaches the contract to the party who is injured by the breach. The purpose of the payment of money damages is to put the party who is harmed by the breach of the contract in the same economic position as he or she would have been in if the contract had been performed. Damages assessed by a court for this purpose are called **compensatory damages.**

A number of the rules concerning compensatory damages that have been developed are applicable to the breach of particular kinds of contracts, such as, contracts for the sale of goods (see Chapter 24), employment contracts, real estate sales contracts, and construction contracts. The general principle applied in measuring damages under all contracts, however, is that the party who has been harmed by the breach of the contract is entitled to collect for losses caused or gains prevented by the breach.

General Damages

General damages are damages that arise naturally from the breach of the contract. They result directly from the fact that the transaction that is the subject of the contract does not occur because of the breach. For instance, if the subject of the contract is the sale of a car and the contract is breached by the buyer, the seller is obviously damaged by not collecting the purchase price. If the seller breaches, the buyer is damaged by not getting the car. In either case, the general damages are calculated by determining the difference between the contract price and the market price.

Examples of General Damages Suppose a used car dealer contractually promises to sell a particular car to a customer for $10,000. The dealer later breaches the contract by refusing to deliver the car. If the market price for such cars (i.e., the price at which such cars are generally sold at present) is $11,000, the customer has suffered damages of $1,000 and is entitled to recover that amount of money damages from the dealer. The customer can then purchase the same kind of car elsewhere, and the actual cost to the customer will be $10,000; that is, the $11,000 paid less $1,000 damages collected.

Using the same example, suppose it is the buyer rather than the dealer who breaches the contract by refusing to accept delivery of the car. If the dealer can prove that the market price for the car is only $9,000, the dealer's general damages are $1,000. This is calculated by determining the difference between the contract price ($10,000) and the market price ($9,000). If the dealer collects the $1,000, he or she can now sell the car for $9,000, and still have a total of $10,000. This is the amount the dealer expected to have under the contract that the original buyer breached.

If the seller is selling services rather than something tangible and the buyer breaches the contract, the calculation of the general damages is somewhat different. For example, suppose a landowner contracts with a construction company to have a house built for $100,000. Before the construction company begins work, however, the landowner has a change of heart and tells the company not to build the house, thereby breaching the contract. (You will read later in this chapter why the company should follow the landowner's instructions and not begin work on the house.) How should the construction company's general damages be measured?

The answer is that the company is entitled to the difference between the contract price, $100,000, and the estimated cost of building the house, say $90,000. In other words, the company is entitled to $10,000, which represents the anticipated profit on the contract. Similarly, if the company has already begun work when the landowner breaches, the company is entitled to the anticipated profit plus the expenses incurred in starting the work. In either case, the payment of the damages will put the construction company in the same position it would have been in if the landowner had not breached; that is, all expenses will be paid and a $10,000 profit realized.

You may have noticed in reading these examples of general damages that a party to a contract will not always be harmed by the other party's breach of the contract. For instance, if the contract price of goods being sold is the same as the market price, neither party will be harmed by a breach. Similarly, if the cost of building a house is $100,000 and the contract price is $100,000, the construction company would not be harmed if the landowner breached their contract. In such cases the courts award only nominal damages, as will be explained later.

Special or Consequential Damages

The courts have been confronted with a difficult problem in determining how far to extend liability for compensatory damages. The primary function of contract law is to stimulate economic activity by encouraging people to enter into contracts. If liability for breaching promises is too great, though, people will be hesitant to enter into contracts.

This problem has been dealt with by the development of two categories of compensatory damages. The first category, general damages, discussed in the preceding section of the text, includes all those damages that arise naturally from the breach of contract. The second category, called **special damages** or **consequential damages,** includes additional damages that did not arise naturally from the breach but were foreseeable by the party committing the breach. Any damages that do not fall into one of these two categories cannot be awarded by a court to a party who has been harmed by breach of contract.

The Case of Hadley v. Baxendale An example of the application of these concepts is found in the historically important case of *Hadley v. Baxendale,* decided in England in 1854. In that case, a mill owner had to stop the operation of his mill because of a broken shaft. He requested a shipping company to deliver the broken shaft to an engineering company, which would manufacture a new shaft using the broken one as a model. The shipping company neglected to send the shaft for several days. The mill was therefore shut down for a longer period than it otherwise would have been, resulting in a greater loss of profits than would have occurred had the shaft been sent without delay.

The mill owner sued the shipper for the lost profits of the mill that resulted from the delay in the delivery of the shaft. The shipper argued that such damages were too remote, and that he should therefore not be held liable for them. The court agreed with the shipper, and stated the following standard for determining the extent of liability for damages resulting from breach of contract:

> Where two parties have made a contract which one of them has broken, the damages which the other party ought to receive in respect of such breach of con-

tract should be such as may fairly and reasonably be considered either arising naturally, i.e., according to the usual course of things, from such breach of contract itself, or such as may reasonably be supposed to have been in the contemplation of both parties, at the time they made the contract, as the probable result of the breach of it.

In applying this standard the court believed that the loss of profits resulting from the breach of contract by the shipper did not "arise in the usual course of things"—that is, they were not general damages—because it was possible that the mill had a substitute shaft on hand and did not have to shut down production while a new shaft was manufactured. The court also believed that the possibility of lost profits was not "in the contemplation of both parties at the time they made the contract"—that is, they were not consequential damages—because the possibility of such losses had not been communicated by the miller or otherwise made known to the shipper. Because they did not arise naturally from the breach of contract and were not otherwise foreseeable, the court decided that the shipper was not liable to the mill owner for the lost profits.

In the case that follows, the court was confronted with a contemporary business situation that required application of the standard for determining contract damages first stated in *Hadley v. Baxendale* more than 130 years ago.

TRAYLOR v. HENKELS & McCOY
585 P.2d 970 (Idaho 1978)

[Traylor entered into a contract with Henkels & McCoy, Inc., under which Traylor was to dig a trench in which a gas main would be installed for a specified price. While the work was being done, the parties modified the agreement a number of times to allow for the removal of hard rock and other "extras." Before the work was completed, Henkels & McCoy removed Traylor from the job and had someone else finish the work.

Traylor brought a legal action for breach of contract, seeking $24,831.41 for the removal of the hard rock, $14,593.61 for other "extras," and $538.20 for the balance due on the original specified price, for a total of $39,963.22. Traylor also sought damages for the loss of goodwill, the loss of value on his equipment, and the loss of future profits as a consequence of the forced closing of his business. He asserted that these additional damages were caused by Henkels & McCoy's failure to pay the $39,963.22. Henkels &

McCoy counterclaimed, seeking damages against Traylor for the cost of having someone else perform the work.

The trial court gave judgment to Traylor in the amount of $103,171.14. It found against Henkels & McCoy on the counterclaim. Henkels & McCoy appealed on the grounds that the judgment was excessive to the extent it exceeded $39,963.22.]

SHEPARD, Chief Justice

Idaho is in accord with the orthodox rule that contract damages are recoverable only for the direct consequence of a breach in absence of a special agreement to the contrary. The rule was stated in *Hadley v. Baxendale.*

It is clear in the instant case that the damages sought by Traylor in excess of $39,963.22 are not such as may be expected to ordinarily result from the breach of a contract to excavate a trench. Henkels & McCoy might, however, be liable if, according to the second principle set forth in *Hadley v. Baxendale,* those damages were "in the contemplation of both parties, at the time they made the contract, as the probable result of the breach of it." Traylor does not seriously contend that those damages were in contemplation of the parties at the time they made the basic contract and we deem it to be a somewhat remote possibility that Henkels & McCoy would enter a contract conditioned upon its acceptance of liability for the liquidation of Traylor's business in the event of a breach by Henkels & McCoy.

Traylor rests his claim for consequential damages on the assertion that Henkels & McCoy had agreed to take responsibility for the financial stability of the business at the time of the modification of the basic contract. The parties are, of course, free to modify a contract. If the parties contemplated liability for special damages (for allegedly forcing the liquidation of Tray-

lor's business) at the time the contract was modified, then the defaulting party must accept the consequences of that agreement. Traylor contends that there was a series of contract modifications regarding extras and that at some point Henkels & McCoy agreed with him for the performance of the extras, knowing full well that Traylor was depending upon the payment therefor in order to remain in business. The record does not sustain that contention.

It appears clear that the jury could have awarded damages due for the rock work, the extras and on the basic contract for $39,963.22, but that amount is exceeded in the jury's verdict by some $63,207.92. That amount could only have been awarded to compensate Traylor for the injury to and loss of his business and loss of future profits.

Reversed.

CASE REVIEW QUESTIONS

1. How much did Traylor claim for general damages? How much did he claim for consequential damages?
2. State specifically why the court believed that Traylor was not entitled to damages for the loss of good will and the loss of future profits as a consequence of the forced closing of his business.
3. Why don't courts hold those who fail to keep their contract promises liable for all the damages caused by such failures rather than holding them liable only for those damages that are foreseeable?
4. On what basis do you think Henkels & McCoy counterclaimed for the cost of having someone else perform the work after Traylor was removed from the job?

The Requirement of Certainty

In addition to the requirement of foreseeability, liability for contract damages will only be imposed if they can be proved with reasonable certainty. For example, contract law suits seeking damages for lost profits resulting from the breach of a contract to produce an entertainment show have generally been unsuccessful because of the plaintiff's inability to prove with sufficient certainty the amount of profit that would have been made had the show gone on. On the other hand, in a legal action by an established business firm seeking lost profits on a type of transaction in which the firm has frequently engaged in the past, lost profits are apt to be provable with sufficient certainty.

In the following case, the court had to decide whether certain evidence that was offered would contribute to the proof of lost profits with reasonable certainty.

BATTISTA v. LEBANON TROTTING ASSOCIATION
538 F.2d 111 (6th Cir. 1976)

[Lebanon Trotting Association (Lebanon) was a partnership that conducted harness horse racing meets. Lebanon entered into a contract for the years 1967–1969 with Peter Battista under which Battista was to produce and sell programs for the racing events. He intended to charge 35 cents each for the programs and was to pay Lebanon 10 cents for each program sold.

After one year John Carlo, one of the partners of Lebanon, notified Battista on behalf of Lebanon that he would no longer be allowed to produce and sell the programs. Shortly thereafter Battista brought a legal action for breach of contract against both Lebanon and Carlo. In the trial court, Battista presented evidence concerning profits for 1968 and 1969 that he lost because of the breach of contract. He testified that his profits for 1967 were $8,700, but that he planned to raise the price of the programs from thirty-five cents to fifty cents during the final two years of the contract. At the end of the trial, Battista received a judgment against Carlo for $38,000 for compensatory damages.

Carlo appealed on several bases. One was that Battista's testimony about raising the price of the programs was inadmissible because it was speculative, and that a jury should not be allowed to award damages for lost profits based on speculation.]

WEICK, Circuit Judge

The rule of law on lost profits is that the anticipated profits may be recovered only where such profits could reasonably have been contemplated by the parties as a probable result of the breach; such profits cannot be speculative or conjectural but must be shown with reasonable certainty.

The evidence showed that in 1967 Battista's net profit from the contract was $8,700. Battista testified

that since he had decided in January 1968 to raise the price to fifty cents per program, he computed his lost profits, using the fifty cent figure, to be $50,000 for the years 1968 and 1969. Battista, however, never told anyone of his plan to increase the program price.

While it was proper, in proving lost profits to a reasonable certainty, for the parties to show the past profit performance of the enterprise or the amount of profit called for in the contract, we believe it was wholly speculative for Battista to testify here that he would have realized an increase of annual profits of more than 300% of the 1967 contract if the contract had not been repudiated. Whatever might have been the result had that subjective intent been communicated to Lebanon, or otherwise corroborated, it does not by itself rise to the level of proof to a reasonable certainty.

Had Battista told Lebanon that he intended to increase the selling price to fifty cents per program, Lebanon might very well have insisted on increasing its price for the concession. On the other hand, it might also have taken action to prevent the price increase in order to protect the volume sales it depended on for its own profits from the transaction. We need not decide here what Lebanon might have done had Battista carried through with his unilateral decision to increase the price; the two possibilities suggested merely illustrate the complete uncertainty of any profits based on any uncommunicated price increase.

Because Battista did not inform Lebanon of his proposed price increase, the jury when computing compensatory damages should not have been permitted to consider his testimony that he intended to increase the price. It was error to admit such testimony.

Reversed.

CASE REVIEW QUESTIONS
1. State specifically why the appellate court found that the testimony of Battista concerning the raising of the price of programs was inadmissible for the purpose of proving lost profits.

2. Aside from the evidence concerning the raising of the price of programs, does it appear that Battista would be able to prove his lost profits with reasonable certainty? Explain.

Failure to show lost profits with sufficient certainty does not necessarily mean that the party seeking damages will have no recovery at all. A party may also collect expenses that could foreseeably be expected to be spent in reliance on the contract. An entertainment promoter, for instance, who is unable to collect for lost profits, as discussed previously, could nonetheless collect for such expenses as advertising costs incurred in preparation for the staging of the event.

Another alternative to the recovery of lost profits arises in cases in which a breach of contract by one party prevents the use and operation of property from which profits would be made. In such a case, even if lost profits cannot be proved with sufficient certainty, the party who has been damaged may collect the fair rental value of the property for the period during which he or she did not have the property because of the breach. For example, failure to deliver a machine may result in lost profits to a manufacturer. If the manufacturer cannot prove the amount of the lost profits with sufficient certainty, it can still recover the rental value of the machine for the period during which it did not have the machine because of the breach.

Mitigation of Damages

Another way in which liability for contract damages is limited is by the courts imposing a duty on the party who has been harmed by a breach of contract to mitigate (keep to a minimum) the damages resulting from the breach. In other words, the party who has been harmed may not sit idly by and watch the damages accumulate.

For example, if an employer breaches an employment contract by firing an employee, the employee is entitled to money damages equal to the entire salary that would have been earned during the remaining term of the contract. The employee, however, must try to mitigate these damages by seeking other comparable employment. If the employee reasonably tries to obtain new comparable employment but fails, the entire amount of lost salary can be collected from the original employer. On the other hand, if the employee is successful in finding new work, the damages that must be paid by the original employer will be reduced by the amount earned from the new employer. Similarly, if the employee does not make a reasonable attempt to find comparable employment, the original employer's damages will be reduced by the amount it is estimated the employee would have earned had an attempt to find new work been made.

Liquidated Damages

Sometimes, the parties to a contract will include as a term of their agreement the amount of damages to be imposed if the contract is breached. Such a provision is called a **liquidated** (expressly agreed to) **damages** clause. If reasonable, it will generally be enforced by the courts. On the other hand, the courts will not enforce a liquidated damages clause if it determines that the purpose of the parties in including the clause in their contract was not to compensate the party who would be harmed by breach of contract but, instead, was intended to impose a penalty on the party who breached the contract.

The purpose of providing a penalty in a contract is to discourage a party from breaching it and to provide a special punishment if the contract is breached anyway. The courts have refused to enforce such penalties on the ground that only the government, not private individuals, can determine appropriate remedies for breach of contract.

The purpose of a nonpenalty liquidated damages clause is only to help determine the correct amount of damages, not to provide an additional remedy. The courts have said that a liquidated damages clause will be enforced if (1) accurate determination of the actual damages would be difficult or impossible, (2) the parties intend to provide for damages and not a penalty, and (3) the amount agreed to is a reasonable estimate of the probable damages.

In the following case, the court had to determine whether a teachers' contract contained a valid liquidated damages clause or if, instead, the clause provided for a penalty. The problem was complicated by the fact that the contract provision in question specifically used the term "penalty."

UNIFIED SCHOOL DISTRICT NO. 315 v. DeWERFF
626 P.2d 1206 (Kan. 1981)

[DeWerff was employed by Unified School District 315 as a teacher and basketball coach. On June 28, 1978, DeWerff gave notice of his resignation. He was informed that his resignation would be accepted upon payment of $400 as required by the teachers' employment contract.

The contract provision in question provided:

Penalty for breaking contracts:

1. It is the intent of the Board to negotiate an agreement that will tend to make teachers as responsible for the compliance of their contracts as they will expect the Board of Education to be.
2. . . .
3. In all cases where a teacher under contract fails to honor the full term of his or her contract, a lump sum of $400 is to be collected if the contract is broken before August 1, and after August 1 a penalty of $75 will be charged for each month remaining on his or her contract.

4. The Board reserves the right to waive the provisions of this penalty policy.

DeWerff refused to make the payment and the school district sued. The trial court found the provision to be a valid liquidated damages clause, the agreed amount of $400 to be reasonable, and that the board had applied the provision impartially and fairly in the past. Accordingly, judgment was rendered for the plaintiff for $400. The defendant appealed, arguing that the damages clause in the contract provided for a penalty rather than liquidated damages.]

PRAGEL, Justice Presiding

It is well settled that parties to a contract may stipulate to the amount of damages for breach of the contract, if the stipulation is determined to be a liquidated damages clause rather than a penalty. A stipulation for damages upon a future breach of contract is valid as a liquidated damages clause if the set amount is determined to be reasonable and the amount of damages is difficult to ascertain. The distinction between a provision for liquidated damages and one for a penalty is that a penalty is to secure performance, while a liquidated damages provision is for payment of a sum in lieu of performance. Liquidated damages provisions, if otherwise valid, are generally enforceable in employment contracts for the employee's wrongful termination of employment.

The use of term "penalty" throughout the provision does not, as a matter of law, defeat the trial court's finding that the provision was, in fact, a liquidated damages clause.

As noted, the characteristic of a penalty is that it is designed to secure performance rather than to estimate reasonable damages in case of breach. The present case is complicated by the fact that the provision in question states that its purpose is to "make teachers . . . responsible for the compliance to their contracts." However, the stated purpose of the provision is not necessarily controlling where the stipulated sum is reasonable and the amount of actual damage for breach would be difficult to determine. Here the evidence established that the provision in question was drafted by nonlawyer negotiators who were not trained in the intricacies of the law. It was further undisputed that such provisions are frequently included in employment contracts negotiated between school boards and teachers organizations. The damages provided in those contracts are comparable in amount to that provided for in the contract presently before us for consideration.

Generally, a contract provision will be considered a penalty where there is no attempt to calculate the amount of actual damages that might be sustained in case of breach. An indication of this lack of calculation is deemed present when the amount of stipulated damages is the same for a total or partial breach, or for breach of minor or major contract provisions. In the present case, the contract provision required payment of a greater sum as the school year commenced and progressed. There was trial testimony that it became increasingly difficult, after the April 15 contract deadline, to procure qualified teachers. The terms of the contract, when coupled with the evidence, suggest that there was indeed an attempt to calculate the amount of damages that might result from the teacher's breach. The stated purpose of the provision to secure contract performance is not, in itself, sufficient to render it an unenforceable penalty.

A valid liquidated damages clause must be a reasonable calculation of damages difficult to establish with certainty. Where actual damages are readily ascertainable, a provision purporting to be a liquidated damages clause will be construed as a penalty, with the injured party recovering only those damages established by proof. At trial, the district's school superintendent, Dr. Douglas Christensen, testified to the actual expenses incurred in advertising for defendant's vacancy. He testified that substantial man-hours were spent recruiting, interviewing, and hiring. Teachers were shuffled as a result of defendant's resignation when the district was unable to find an exact replacement. He testified that the time spent interviewing and hiring took time away from other activities, and that budget and curriculum preparation suffered as a result. He also testified that it was extremely difficult to find replacements at such a late date, particularly for a teacher–coach position such as that vacated by defendant.

The requirements of a valid liquidation damages clause—that the sum be reasonable and the actual damages be difficult to ascertain—have been met by the provision in question. The district court's judgment that the provision constituted an enforceable liquidated damages clause is affirmed.

Affirmed.

CASE REVIEW QUESTIONS

1. State specifically why the court determined that the damages clause in the contract was a valid liquidated damages clause rather than a penalty.
2. What arguments can you make for DeWerff that the damages clause is in fact a penalty clause?

Attorney's Fees

Generally, the award of contract damages does not include the attorney's fees of the successful party. Often, however, a contract will provide that if attorney's fees are incurred as a result of a breach of contract, the party harmed by the breach is entitled to collect such fees in addition to any other damages. Most states enforce such provisions.

Nominal Damages

Sometimes, a person brings a legal action for breach of contract and proves that a breach actually occurred but fails to prove that any actual damages have been suffered. This may happen, for example, because of the rules discussed previously for measuring damages and requiring that damages be foreseeable and proved with certainty. In such a situation the plaintiff will be awarded **nominal** (very small) **damages,** usually six cents or a dollar.

Punitive Damages

As mentioned previously, the primary purpose of awarding damages for a breach of contract is to compensate a person for losses incurred as a result of the breach. The purpose of **punitive** (penalty) **damages** is not to compensate the party who has been harmed, but to punish a person who harmed another maliciously or wantonly. Punitive damages are seldom awarded in contract cases.

SPECIFIC PERFORMANCE

When a court orders a party to perform the promises made in a contract, it is granting a remedy called **specific performance.** Failure to obey the court's order is treated as contempt of court and can result in the court fining or imprisoning the party who disobeys its order.

As noted earlier, the preferred remedy for breach of contract is the payment of money damages. Upon receiving damages, the injured party can buy substitute performance for the promise the other party failed to keep. Specific performance is therefore ordered by the court only if the remedy of money damages is inadequate.

The most common situation in which a court will grant the remedy of specific performance is when a person who promises to sell real property (land) fails to keep the promise. Granting specific performance in such cases began in medieval England because status and power were closely related to land ownership at that time. It was felt, therefore, that the payment of damages alone would not put the buyer in as good a position as he or she would have been in had the promise been performed because each parcel of land was unique and substitute performance was not obtainable. Although parcels of land may not be considered unique today, the courts continue to grant the remedy of specific performance to injured purchasers of real estate.

In cases involving the sale of personal property (goods), it is quite rare for a court to grant specific performance. However, such things as valuable works of art, patents, and copyrights that are in fact unique are subject to the remedy of specific performance. Under the Uniform Commercial Code (Section 2-716), specific performance will also be granted even if goods are not unique or in other proper circumstances. These circumstances are present if the goods can't be purchased from another seller because of a market shortage or because the seller who has breached the contract has a monopoly. But, again, the granting of specific performance in cases involving personal property is not common because the buyer can usually purchase substitute goods on the open market.

In the following case, a purchaser of cotton is seeking specific performance of a contract to buy cotton. Before reading the case, consider under what circumstances a purchaser of cotton might be entitled to such a remedy.

WEATHERSBY v. GORE
556 F.2d 1247 (Fifth Cir. 1977)

[Weathersby, a cotton buyer, entered into a contract with Gore, a cotton farmer, that obligated Gore to sell to Weathersby the cotton produced by him on 500 acres of land during the 1973 crop year. Two months after making the contract and many months before the cotton was to be picked, Gore gave Weathersby notice that he was canceling the contract.

Weathersby brought a legal action against Gore for breach of contract, asking the court to enforce specific performance of the contract. The trial court found for the plaintiff and ordered specific performance by Gore.

Gore appealed, arguing that the trial court had erred in finding a breach of contract and that the remedy of specific performance should not have been granted. The appellate court held that the defendant was entitled to a new trial on the issue of whether the contract had been breached. Its decision concerning whether the remedy of specific performance was proper in this case follows.]

CLARK, Circuit Judge

The parties are in considerable disagreement over the meaning of UCC §2-716: "Specific performance may be decreed where the goods are unique or in other proper circumstances." Various authorities have been cited to the court indicating that crop contracts historically have been treated as susceptible to specific performance treatment more readily than other types of contracts. However, cotton contracts have not been

given such treatment in Mississippi when other cotton was readily available on the open market. In *Austin v. Montgomery,* the Mississippi Supreme Court permitted without discussion the specific performance of a cotton output contract that had been entered in March 1973 and breached by the farmer–seller in July. The plaintiff buyer contended that it was impossible to obtain cotton elsewhere when notice was given in July that the farmer would refuse to deliver at harvest. The farmer did not attempt to refute this contention. Consequently the seller would have had to default on his contract to deliver the cotton to a textile mill. Since the parties here are in agreement that other cotton was available when the notice cancellation was sent in May by Gore, the *Austin* decision is not in point.

Far predating Mississippi's adoption of the Uniform Commercial Code, but indicating the reasons why specific performance is not suitable here, is *Scott v. Billgerry.* Billgerry was the purchaser of seventy-five bales of cotton from Scott. The purchase price of $3,900 was paid at the time the contract was entered. Upon Scott's subsequent refusal to deliver, Billgerry sought specific performance. Though the court was not referring to an output contract but rather to the simple purchase of cotton bales, the language is equally applicable here:

It is altogether immaterial whether there was a sale of certain specific bales of cotton, or an agreement to sell and deliver a certain number of bales out of a particular lot, or a general agreement to sell and deliver a certain number of bales, without any designation of the specific bales, or of the particular lot out of which they are to come. All such cases depend upon the same general principle. The rule is, not to [grant] specific performance of agreements respecting goods . . . unless, under the particular circumstances of the case, there can be no adequate compensation in damages. . . .

The adoption of the Uniform Commercial Code by Mississippi does not suggest the considerations expressed in *Scott v. Billgerry* are now to be rejected. Other than to indicate the Code intended to "further a more liberal attitude than some courts have shown in connection with the specific performance of contracts of sale," the comments accompanying UCC §2-716 are of little guidance. The comments also state that "[o]utput and requirements contracts involving a particularly or peculiarly available source of market present today the typical commercial specific performance situation," but the interpretation of this language appears to range from suggesting all output contracts should be specifically enforceable to a mere observa-

tion that output contracts form a suitable factual background in most cases in which specific performance may be sought.

The general rule applicable when specific performance is requested has been stated in *Roberts v. Spence:* "specific performance of a contract will not be awarded where damages may be recovered and the remedy in a court of law is adequate to compensate the injured party." Considering the reluctance expressed in Roberts to authorization of the specific performance remedy, we hold that the Mississippi Supreme Court would apply a restrictive reading of §2-716. Weathersby was adequately protected from any damages occasioned by Gore's breach of the contract, if any occurred. He could have acquired additional cotton on the open market when Gore informed him he would no longer perform under the contract. He did not do so and thus, if entitled to damages at all, must settle for the difference between the contract and the market price at the time Gore canceled.

Reversed and remanded.

CASE REVIEW QUESTIONS

1. Why did the court believe that the remedy of specific performance was improper?
2. Under what different circumstances might a court grant specific performance of a contract to buy cotton?

Specific Performance of Employment Contracts It is even more rare for a court to order specific performance for a breach of a promise to perform personal services. To do so would probably violate the United States Constitution's prohibition of involuntary servitude.

It is also very rare for a court to order the specific performance of an employer's promise to employ someone. Such a remedy would not involve involuntary servitude, but it could be difficult for the court to make sure the employer treated the employee fairly, rather than just giving him or her a job, and it might require the continuance of a bad employment relationship. Recently, however, some courts have ordered the reinstatement of certain government employees as a remedy for violations of civil service laws by the government. It may be, therefore, that the courts will begin to look more favorably on granting specific performance against employers for breach of employment contracts in the private sector.

Restrictions on the Use of Specific Performance Because granting specific performance rather than money damages is an exceptional remedy, the courts have placed some restrictions on its use under certain circumstances. One such limitation is that a court may choose not to grant specific performance to a party who has driven a very hard bargain. For example, if the party seeking specific performance has only paid a nominal price or if the contract is otherwise so grossly one-sided that it is oppressive to the other party, a court may deny the remedy sought.

Specific performance may also be denied to a party who has delayed in bringing the legal action if the delay has prejudiced the other party. Such prejudicial delay is called **laches**. Delay can be prejudicial, for instance, because of the loss of evidence or the death of a witness that would have been important to the other party's case or because of a significant change in the value of the subject matter of the contract.

Finally, a court may choose not to grant specific performance in a case in which the party seeking the remedy has **unclean hands.** This does not mean that the party's hands are literally dirty. It is, instead, a figure of speech indicating that the party seeking specific performance has engaged in improper conduct, such as lying or cheating, in the transaction. For example, one court refused to grant specific performance of a contract for a professional sports team that had contracted with a college athlete in violation of collegiate rules and had then kept the contract secret so that the athlete could continue to play as an amateur in college.

If a court refuses to grant specific performance because money damages would be an adequate remedy or because of actions of the party seeking the remedy, the party suing for breach of contract may still seek money damages, as discussed previously, or the party may pursue the remedy of restitution, which is discussed in the next section of the text.

RESTITUTION

At the beginning of this chapter, we stated that the usual purpose of contract remedies is to put a party who is harmed as the result of a breach of contract in as good an economic position as that party would have been in if the contract had been performed. Usually, this is accomplished by an award of money damages, although, occasionally, specific performance is granted.

Another remedy that is sometimes used in contract cases is called **restitution.** This remedy has a different purpose than the remedies of money damages and specific performance. Rather than putting an injured party in as good a position as he or she would have been if the contract had been performed, when restitution is awarded the purpose is to prevent the unjust enrichment of one of the parties.

Restitution is given in three different kinds of contract situations: (1) cases in which a contract is rescinded; (2) cases in which a contract has been breached; and (3) cases in which no contract ever existed.

Contract Rescission Cases

Throughout the chapters on contract law, you have learned of several instances in which a party is entitled to rescind a contract and recover any value that has already been given to the other party to the contract, less any value received under the contract. For instance, recovery may be available when a party performs under an agreement that turns out to be unenforceable because of duress, undue influence, misrepresentation or mistake (see Chapter 11), lack of capacity (see Chapter 14), or impossibility (see Chapter 17).

Such recovery is a form of restitution. It returns the parties to the same economic position they were in prior to the formation of the contract that is rescinded. Note that this remedy is not awarded because of a breach of the contract, but because the contract has been rescinded. To allow the parties to retain the benefits already received in such a situation would unjustly enrich them.

Breach of Contract Cases

Suit by Party Who Has Not Breached Earlier in this chapter, you learned that in order to collect money damages for a breach of contract the injuries incurred must have been reasonably foreseeable and must be proved with reasonable certainty. If these standards cannot be met, or if for any other reason an injured party chooses to do so, a party injured by a material breach of contract may seek restitution rather than money damages.

For example, suppose Sam Student enters State College and pays a year's tuition in advance. If Sam is wrongfully expelled from the college, he would probably not be able to prove his future economic injuries with reasonable certainty and would not, therefore, be entitled to collect money damages. He would, however, be entitled to the remedy of restitution, which would allow him to collect the amount of tuition previously paid by him, less the value of the services he received prior to being expelled. This remedy would prevent the unjust enrichment of the college.

Suit by Party Who Has Breached In the previous chapter, we said that a party who materially breaches a contract has no contract rights against the other party; that is, the other party is discharged from performance of his or her contractual duties. The application of this principle by the courts has the effect of encouraging people to perform their contract promises rather than breaching them.

Sometimes, however, the application of this principle can cause a great deal of hardship to a person who breaches a contract. For example, the New Hampshire Supreme Court was once confronted with a case in which an employee, Britton, had promised to work for an employer, Turner, for one year for a specified amount of money. Before the year was up, Britton left his job without good cause or Turner's consent. Turner refused to pay Britton anything for the work he performed before quitting on the ground that Britton's quitting was a breach of contract and, therefore, Turner was discharged from his contract duty to pay the specified amount of money.

The court agreed that Turner was discharged from the contract because of Britton's breach and that Britton could receive nothing under the contract for the work already performed. The court, however, also held that Turner was liable to Britton for the reasonable value of the work performed by Britton. Turner's liability was not based on the contract because Britton's breach had discharged Turner's duties. Instead, it was based on **quasi-contract,** meaning "as if it were a contract." Quasi-contracts are also sometimes called implied-in-law contracts or constructive contracts.

In most states today, such a case would be covered by a statute that requires periodic payments to workers, rather than a lump-sum payment at the end of the employment contract, and the payment of all accrued wages when the employment is terminated. Quasi-contractual recovery may be obtained, however, in other situations by a party who breaches a contract and therefore has no contract rights. For example, in some states a person who breaches a short-term service contract may nonetheless recover in quasi-contract for the reasonable value of his or her services even though performance is less than substantial. Of course, the person who breached the contract would be liable for the breach of contract, as discussed earlier in this chapter.

The essence of a legal action based on quasi-contract and the remedy of restitution is to prevent the enrichment of one party by another under circumstances in which it would be unjust to allow the party who has been enriched to retain the benefit without paying compensation for the value of the benefit.

No Contract Cases

Another situation in which someone may seek restitution would be a case in which no contract ever existed. This could occur, for instance, because the other party had not made a promise or the promise was not definite enough for the court to enforce (see Chapter 9). For example, if a doctor provides emergency medical attention to someone who is unconscious, the doctor would not be able to bring a contract action to recover a fee. This is so because the unconscious patient could not have promised to pay at the time the medical services were provided. The doctor would, however, be able to recover in quasi-contract for the reasonable value of the services. This remedy has been provided by the courts in order to prevent unjust enrichment by someone who refuses to pay under such circumstances.

In the case that follows, the plaintiff and the defendant clearly had no contract. Nonetheless, the plaintiff sued to collect damages from the defendant on the ground of quasi-contract, arguing that the defendant had been unjustly enriched.

ARTUKOVICH, INC. v. RELIANCE TRUCK COMPANY
614 P.2d 327 (Arizona 1980)

[Artukovich, Inc., leased a crane to the Ashton Company for use by Ashton in a construction project. Ashton hired the Reliance Truck Company to transport the crane to the construction site. Before transporting the crane, Reliance, without the permission of Artukovich or Ashton, used the crane to put into place a 246,000-pound transformer for a utility company, which paid Reliance for the work. Reliance then transported the crane pursuant to its agreement with Ashton.

When Artukovich learned of the unauthorized use of the crane by Reliance, it brought a legal action to recover damages. The trial court found for plaintiff, but the intermediate appellate court reversed. Plaintiff appealed to the Arizona Supreme Court. In the decision that follows, the court discusses Artukovich's right to recover damages from Reliance under the circumstances of this case.]

HOLOHAN, Vice Chief Justice

Contracts implied-in-law or quasi-contracts, also called constructive contracts, are inferred by the law as a matter of reason and justice from the acts and conduct of the parties and circumstances surrounding the transactions and are imposed for the purpose of bringing about justice without reference to the intentions of the parties.

Restatement of Restitution, §1 provides, "A person who has been unjustly enriched at the expense of another is required to make restitution to the other." Comment (a) to that section notes that a person is enriched if he received a benefit and is unjustly enriched if retention of that benefit would be unjust. Comment (b) defines a benefit as being any form of advantage. The facts in this case show that the defendant did receive a benefit or advantage through the use of plaintiff's crane. Defendant received $6,000.00 for putting the transformer in place pursuant to a contract with Arizona Public Service. The defendant has acknowledged throughout the litigation that it recognized and intended to pay someone a reasonable rental value for the crane's use.

Unjust enrichment does not depend upon the existence of a valid contract, nor is it necessary that plaintiff suffer a loss corresponding to the defendant's gain for there to be a valid claim for an unjust enrichment. . . . Thus, even though plaintiff had no right to use the crane at the time of defendant's unauthorized use, the defendant is liable to plaintiff because the defendant received a benefit by using plaintiff's crane to perform the contract with Arizona Public Service. To allow the defendant to use plaintiff's crane without compensating plaintiff for its use would unjustly enrich the defendant and would be inequitable.

[Judgment for plaintiff.]

CASE REVIEW QUESTIONS
1. Why did the court base its decision on quasi-contract rather than breach of contract in this case?
2. How should the amount of damages to be paid by Reliance to Artukovich be measured?

REVIEW QUESTIONS

1. How does the remedy of money damages fulfill the primary purpose for awarding contract damages?
2. What are general damages and consequential damages and what role do they play in the field of contract damages?
3. How is a liquidated damages clause distinguished from a penalty clause?
4. Under what circumstances is a party to a contract entitled to the remedy of specific performance?
5. Under what circumstances is a party to a contract entitled to the remedy of restitution?

CASE PROBLEMS

1. Christensen entered into a contract to have a house built by Hoskins for a specified price. Because of defective waterproofing by Hoskins, water seeped through a wall, causing extensive dry rotting in the floor and supporting beams of the living room. The damage to the house caused by these problems reduced the market value of the house by $8,000. The defects and damage to the house could be corrected for $500. If Christensen brings a legal action against Hoskins for breach of contract, how much will he be entitled to for compensatory damages? Explain.

2. Peevyhouse owned a farm containing coal deposits. He leased his land to Garland Coal & Mining Company (Garland) for coal mining purposes. The land was to be strip-mined; that is, the coal was to be taken from pits on the surface of the land rather than from underground mine shafts. In the lease, Garland expressly promised to restore the land by filling in the pits and smoothing out soil banks. When Garland had completed its strip-mining, however, it refused to restore the land as it had promised. Peevyhouse brought a legal action against Garland for breach of contract. Peevyhouse presented evidence that it would cost $29,000 to have the restoration work done. Garland presented evidence that the market value of the farm would only be increased by $300 if the restoration work were done. How much is Peevyhouse entitled to collect in damages from Garland? Explain.

3. Macondray, residing in Manila, Philippine Islands, is an employee of Kerr Steamship Company (Kerr). Macondray cabled his employer in New York requesting instructions regarding the loading of freight on one of the company's ships. In response to Macondray's request, Kerr delivered to RCA Telegraph Company (RCA) a telegram instructing him to load the freight. The telegram was in a code that could not be understood by any of the employees of RCA. RCA charged Kerr $26.97 to deliver the telegram. RCA inadvertently failed to deliver the telegram to Macondray. As a result,

the freight was not loaded, and Kerr lost $6,675.29, the amount it would have earned had it carried the freight. Kerr brought a legal action against RCA for breach of contract, asking the court to order RCA to pay money damages of $6,675.29. On what basis could RCA argue that it was not liable for damages in that amount? What should the court decide as to the amount of damages for which RCA is liable? Explain.

4. Morristown Lincoln-Mercury, Inc. (Morristown), an automobile dealer, wanted to have a sale. It entered into a contract with Lotspeich Publishing Company (Lotspeich) to have advertisements announcing the sale carried for three days in a newspaper published by Lotspeich. Lotspeich failed to run the advertisements as it had promised. Morristown brought a legal action against Lotspeich seeking $6,000 in compensatory damages. It argued that, because of Lotspeich's failure to run the advertisements, it had to reduce its order of 30 new cars from the manufacturer to 10, and that it would have made a profit of $300 on each of the cars it had cancelled. On what basis can Lotspeich defend itself on the issue of damages? If Morristown is not entitled to $6,000, how much is it entitled to? Explain.

5. Clark entered into a contract to have a painting cleaned and repaired by Marsiglia for a specified price. After Marsiglia began the work of cleaning and repairing, Clark notified him to stop the work. Nevertheless, Marsiglia completed the job. Clark refused to pay for the work. If Marsiglia brings a legal action to collect the price specified in the contract, on what basis can Clark defend? If Marsiglia is not entitled to the specified price, how should his damages be calculated? Explain.

6. Kuznicki entered into a contract for the installation of a fire detection system in his home by Security Safety Corporation (Security) for $498.00. Security anticipated making a profit of $100 on the transaction with Kuznicki. The contract provided that, "In the event of cancelation of this agreement the owner agrees to pay 33⅓ percent of the con-

tract price as liquidated damages." One day after the contract was formed, Kuznicki told Security not to install the system. At that time Security had not begun to install the system and had done nothing in reliance on Kuznicki's promise. If Security brings a legal action against Kuznicki, seeking $166.00 in liquidated damages, on what basis can Kuznicki defend himself on the issue of damages? If Security is not entitled to $166.00, how much is it entitled to? Explain.

7. Campbell Soup Company (Campbell) entered into a contract with Wentz, a farmer, under which Campbell would buy and Wentz would sell all of the Chantenay red cored carrots to be grown on Wentz's farm at the price of $30 a ton. Wentz harvested approximately 100 tons of carrots. Because of adverse weather conditions during the growing season, at the time of harvesting Chantenay red cored carrots were virtually unobtainable on the open market, and their price had risen to $90 a ton.

Wentz refused to deliver his carrots to Campbell at the contract price. If Campbell brings a legal action against Wentz for breach of contract seeking the remedy of specific performance, on what basis might Wentz argue that Campbell is not entitled to that remedy? How should the court rule on this issue? Explain.

8. McKee entered into a contract with Burke. McKee was to knock down with a bulldozer and remove from Burke's land a large number of trees and then level the land. Burke was to pay a specified sum per hour for the work. McKee knocked down all of the trees and removed some of them, but did not level any of the land. Burke refused to pay for any of the work. If McKee brings a legal action to recover for the time spent knocking down and removing the trees, on what basis could Burke defend? Who should win the case? If McKee wins, how should his damages be calculated? Explain.

PART III

SALES LAW

19

INTRODUCTION TO SALES LAW

A sale is a common transaction in the commercial world. The purchase of a 50-cent candy bar from a vending machine is a sale; trading in your old car for a new one is a sale; ordering computer-controlled assembly line equipment is a sale. Each of these transactions involves a sales contract.

Contract law is concerned with enforcing promises. Many contracts contain a promise to sell something such as goods, services, or real estate. Goods present some special problems. Unlike services, goods because they are tangible (meaning that they can be touched) may be damaged or lost. Unlike real estate (land and buildings), goods are moveable and may be transported from place to place. Contracts for the sale of goods therefore raise special legal issues. To deal with these issues, law that is unique to the sale of goods, known as the law of sales, or sales law, has been developed. This chapter and the five that follow will explain and discuss sales law.

UNIFORM LAW FOR SALES

Goods subject to sales contracts are often transported across state lines. Problems arise if a legal conflict develops, for example, between a seller in Illinois and a buyer in California. Which state's law will be used to resolve the conflict? The choice of one state's law over another can have serious consequences. For example, if the law applicable to the problem is different in each state, the seller might win under California law but lose under Illinois law.

Lack of uniformity in the law governing commercial transactions, including the law of sales, raises significant problems. Large companies do business in several states, and some do business in every state. To the extent that commercial law is not the same or similar among the states, businesses may need to use different forms or different provisions in their sales contracts for each state in which they do business. Not only is this a nuisance to the business firms, but it also creates expenses that are ultimately paid for by consumers.

It is desirable, therefore, for all states to have uniform laws governing commercial transactions. To this end, the National Conference of Commissioners on Uniform State Laws was formed to draft and promote uniform laws throughout the United States. One of the earliest laws proposed by this commission was the Uniform Sales Act. It was distributed for adoption in 1906 and was subsequently adopted by a number of states. Other uniform laws governing commercial transactions were also proposed and were widely adopted.

In the 1930s, it became clear that these uniform commercial laws needed to be updated to reflect more accurately the needs of contemporary commerce. A project was therefore begun to develop the **Uniform Commercial Code (UCC),** often referred to simply as the **Code,**to modernize and unify the Uniform Sales Act and the other uniform acts that dealt with commercial transactions.

The Code was first adopted by Pennsylvania in 1954, and many other states adopted it during the 1960s. The Code has now been adopted by all the states except Louisiana, which has only adopted it in part.* It has also been adopted by the District of Columbia and the Virgin Islands. The UCC is reproduced for your use in Appendix B.

The Uniform Commercial Code

The Code is divided into articles, each of which deals with a specific subject.

Article 1 — General Provisions Contains material that applies to all the types of commercial transactions governed by the Code. Article 1 has, for example, definitions of terms used throughout the Code.

Article 2 — Sales Governs sales contracts.

Article 3 — Commercial Paper Governs paper used as a substitute for money such as checks.

Article 4 — Bank Deposits and Collections Contains provisions governing banks in their handling of checks and other items for their depositors' accounts.

Article 5 — Letters of Credit Governs the issuing by a bank of a letter promising that the bank will make payments on behalf of the customer who arranged to have the letter issued. For example, a buyer of goods may have his or her bank issue a letter of credit that assures the seller of the goods that payment for the goods will be made when it is demanded.

Article 6 — Bulk Transfers Sets specific requirements that must be met when all or substantially all of the materials, supplies, merchandise, or other inventory of a business are transferred to a new owner. In many of

* Louisiana has adopted Articles 1, 3, 4, and 5.

these transfers, notice of the sale must be given to the creditors of the transferor. These provisions are made to insure that the creditors will be repaid.

Article 7—Warehouse Receipts, Bills of Lading and Other Documents of Title Governs documents that are used when goods are stored in warehouses or transported by carriers such as railroads, airlines, or trucking companies.

Article 8—Investment Securities Governs the issuing, transferring, and registering of securities such as stocks or bonds.

Article 9—Secured Transactions, Sales of Accounts and Chattel Paper Specifies the rights and obligations of a creditor who takes collateral (property) to insure that a debtor will repay a loan.

Article 10—Effective Date and Repealer Specifies when the Code becomes effective—that is, becomes the law—in a state adopting it. Article 10 also provides for repeal (cancellation) of the earlier laws that the Code replaces.

Article 11—Effective Date and Transition Provisions This article became part of the Code in 1972 when a number of amendments, especially to Articles 8 and 9, were proposed by the Commission on Uniform State Laws. Article 11 provides for the date these amendments will become effective in states that adopt them.

The articles of the Code are subdivided into parts, and each part is subdivided into sections. In a reference to the Code—Section (§)2-102, for example—the number before the hyphen refers to the article, the number after the hyphen refers to the part, and the remaining two numbers refer to the section. Thus "§2-102" is a reference to Article 2, Part 1, Section 2.

Throughout the chapters dealing with sales (Chapters 19–24), negotiable instruments (Chapters 25–28), and secured transactions (Chapter 29), all references to sections are references to the Uniform Commercial Code unless you are told otherwise.

An important feature of the Code is the Official Comments. In them, the drafters of the Code set out the policies the various provisions are intended to reflect. The purpose of the comments is to increase the likelihood that the courts in the different states will give uniform interpretation to the sections of the Code. The Official Comments are not reproduced in this book because of their length, but they are mentioned occasionally in the text and in some of the cases.

Understanding the Code One of the drafters of the Code, especially of Article 2, was Karl Llewellyn. As a commercial lawyer and a legal philosopher concerned with how things really happen, Llewellyn observed the commercial community in operation and drafted sections of the Code to deal with business needs in a realistic way. Thus, a section often describes a type of situation in giving the rule to govern that situation. When reading the Code, you should try to understand the situation being described, what the rule is, and why the rule should apply.

A simple example will demonstrate this point. The situation: A has agreed to sell B 100 widgets. All of the details of the agreement are worked out except for the price. The written contract signed by both parties specifies that the price is to be fixed by an agreement between them at the time for delivery of the widgets. On delivery, however, A and B are unable to agree on a price. The problem, then, is how much should the widgets cost when A and B have not agreed. The rule: the price for widgets will be a reasonable price [§2-305(1)(b)]. The reason: if A and B have in fact agreed to buy and sell the widgets, the contract should be enforceable despite the absence of a price. The Code therefore provides a standard for determining the price that can be used by the parties or by a court. What is a reasonable price will, of course, depend upon the facts involved such as market conditions at the time of delivery.

SALES (ARTICLE 2)

Article 2 applies to contracts for the sale of goods. Because the Code specifies that "this Article applies to transactions in goods" [§2-102], a number of courts have applied Article 2 to other commercial transactions involving goods, such as the leasing of goods and service contracts that involve the use of goods, as when a plumber supplies a new faucet to replace a broken one. The following material discusses the concepts of *sale* and *goods*.

Sale

A **sale** is the passing of title (ownership) from a seller to a buyer for a price [§2-106(1)]. Note that a sale occurs *only* if title to the goods passes from the buyer to the seller *and* a price is paid. The price can be paid in money or in anything else of value such as services, real estate, or other goods [§2-304].

A sale is different from a **gift** because, when a gift is made, title is passed but no price is paid. To make a gift, the *donor* (the giver) must deliver the gift to the *donee* (the recipient) with the intent to make a gift (see Chapter 42).

A sale is also different from a **bailment,** which is a transaction that occurs when there is a transfer of possession but no transfer of title. Depending on the circumstances, a price may or may not be involved in a bailment. For example, there is a bailment when a business ships goods via railroad or some other carrier. The carrier has possession of the goods and charges a price to carry them, but it does not have title to the goods. Lending a sweater to a friend, however, is a *gratuitous bailment* because no money or other payment was exchanged for the loan. It is a bailment because the friend does not own the sweater even though he or she has possession of it. In all bailments, the person in possession of the goods is called the **bailee.** The person who transfers possession is the **bailor** (see Chapter 42).

Contract for Sale: Present Sale and Contract to Sell Goods at a Future Time
All sales involve the making of a contract. When the making of the contract accomplishes the transfer of title, as in the purchase of a candy bar from a vending machine, the transaction is called a **present sale** [§2-106(1)]. If the

goods do not yet exist or will be selected and delivered at some future time, as is often the case in the purchase of assembly line equipment, for example, there is a contract to sell goods at a future time [§2-106(1)]. Both the present sale and the contract to sell goods at a future time are contracts for sale and are governed by Article 2.

It is not always clear whether a contract is a contract for the sale of goods governed by Article 2 or a contract for services governed by general contract law. In the following case, for example, a patient received a transfusion of impure blood. The court had to determine whether the transfusion was a sale. If it was a sale, then warranties (promises about the quality of goods) imposed by Article 2, called *implied warranties,* would apply and the hospital would be liable for the injury.

FOSTER et al. v. MEMORIAL HOSPITAL ASSOCIATION OF CHARLESTON
219 S.E.2d 916 (W.Va. 1975)

[Ethel Foster and her husband, the plaintiffs, sued Memorial Hospital Association of Charleston, the defendant, for damages caused by a transfusion of blood containing hepatitis. Foster argued that the hospital had warranted (promised) under the UCC that the blood was fit for transfusion. The trial court ruled in favor of the hospital on the grounds that the transfusion was the performance of a service and not a sale governed by Article 2. Foster appealed.]

NEELY, Justice

The facts of this case do not disclose whether the transfer of blood was characterized as a "sale" by the parties at the time of the transfusion. . . .

The simplest method for disposition would be for this Court to characterize the transaction as either a "sale" or a "service" as a matter of law and to permit that linguistic characterization to be dispositive of the issue; however, such a course provides merely a result without reason. The issue in this case is not simply whether ownership of personal property passed from one person to another, but rather whether the transfer of personal property in this case is of the type contemplated under the law of [sales].

The great weight of authority in the United States under the common law, the Uniform Commercial Code, and the old Sales Act, is that a transaction involving blood is not a "sale" creating an implied warranty. . . . The landmark case on the subject is *Perlmutter v. Beth David Hospital,* in which the court held that the essence of the contractual relationship between hospital and patient is one in which the patient bargains for, and hospital agrees to make available, the human skill and physical material of medical science to the end that the patient's health is restored. The Court said:

Such a contract is clearly one for services, and, just as clearly, it is not divisible. Concepts of purchase and sale cannot separately be attached to the healing materials —such as medicines, drugs or, indeed, blood—supplied by the hospital for a price as part of the medical services it offers. That the property or title to certain items of medical material may be transferred so to speak, from the hospital to the patient during the course of medical treatment does not serve to make each such transaction a sale. "'Sale' and 'transfer' are not synonymous," and not every transfer of personal property constitutes a sale. It has long been recognized that, when service predominates, and transfer of personal property is but an incidental feature of the transaction, the transaction is not deemed a sale. . . .

This Court agrees with the reasoning of *Perlmutter,* . . . and holds that a court must look to the underlying contract in a close case such as [this] one. . . . The provisions of [§2-314] create a warranty "if the seller is a merchant with respect to goods of that kind." A hospital or a doctor does not exactly fit into the model of a "merchant" in the transaction of furnishing blood to a patient in the course of medical treatment. Obviously the ownership of personal property passed for a consideration; however, is it the type of transfer to which the law of warranty applies? There is a reasonable difference between a merchant on the one hand who is engaged in the active promotion and sale of his product such as Coca Cola bottles, automobile axles, or standardized drugs and a doctor, dentist or lawyer on the other hand who supplies medicine, blood, tooth fillings, or legal briefs in the course of his professional relationship with a patient or client.

In the practice of medicine there is inevitably a balancing of risks and benefits to any patient involving a highly sophisticated set of probabilities which must be analyzed by medical practitioners in order to do the maximum possible good for the patient with the minimum possible risk. Accordingly, we hold that where an individual contracts for professional services involving an incidental transfer of personal property as a necessary part of such service, and where the appropriate use of such personal property depends primarily upon the skill and judgment of the person rendering the service, such a transfer of personal property by the professional is not within the contemplation of [Article 2] and any injury or damage resulting from such transferred personal property must be recovered by an action grounded in negligence and not by an action grounded in warranty. Therefore, the judgment of the [trial] Court is affirmed.

Affirmed.

CASE REVIEW QUESTIONS
1. Did ownership of the blood pass from the hospital to Foster?
2. Was there a sale of the blood? Why?
3. Why wasn't the court content to settle the question by merely characterizing the transfusion as a "sale" or a "service"?
4. Would a druggist who recommends and sells a brand-name cold remedy be exempt from implied warranties under this decision? Explain.

Goods

Goods are all things that are moveable except for money that is used to pay for goods, investment securities such as stocks, and **things in action,** which are legal rights to obtain money, personal property, or services [§2-105(1)]. Examples of things in action are the right to be repaid a loan or the right to receive services that are to be performed under a contract. Although money that is used to pay for goods is not goods, money that is the subject matter of a transaction, such as a coin collection, is goods. Things that cannot be moved, such as real estate, and things that are intangible (that is, cannot be touched), such as copyrights, bank accounts, and services, are not goods.

The determination of whether the subject matter of a contract is moveable is not made when the contract is formed but, rather, when the goods are *identified to the contract*. **Identification** generally occurs when particular goods are designated as the goods that are the subject matter of the contract [§2-501(1)]. For example, when a buyer orders assembly line equipment, the machines are identified to the contract when the manufacturing process is completed and the goods are marked or otherwise designated by the seller as the goods referred to in the seller's contract with the buyer.

Future Goods and Unborn Animals Goods that exist but are not identified to the contract and goods that do not exist, and thus cannot be identified to the contract, are called **future goods** [§2-105(2)]. Specially manufactured goods, which are goods produced according to specifications agreed upon by the seller and the buyer, do not, by their very nature, exist when the contract is made, so they are future goods until they are identified to the contract. The ownership of something that hasn't been identified or doesn't exist cannot be transferred, so any sale of future goods cannot be a present sale but must be a contract to sell goods at a future time.

Are unborn animals future goods? The Code says that an unborn animal can be identified to a contract when it is conceived [§2-501(1)(c)] and is therefore goods [§2-105(1)]. Until the animal is conceived, however, it would be future goods.

Goods or Real Estate? Some things that are sold, such as buildings, crops, or timber, are closely associated with **real estate** (land). Are these things goods or are they part of the real estate? The Code provides the following rules in such situations:

1. The sale of minerals (including oil and gas) or a building or other structure that is be to removed from real estate by a seller for a buyer is a contract for the sale of goods and is governed by Article 2 [§2-107(1)]. However, if the buyer is going to remove the minerals or the structure from the real estate, the contract is for the sale of land and is governed by general contract law and real property law (see Chapter 43).
2. The sale of growing crops or timber is a contract for the sale of goods regardless of who removes the goods [§2-107(2)].
3. The sale of other things attached to real estate is a contract for the sale of goods if they can be removed without damaging the real estate, regardless of who removes them. If they cannot be removed without causing material damage to the real estate, they are considered to be part of the real estate. For example, a refrigerator that can be removed without causing harm to a house would be goods, but an in-ground swimming pool would be real property.

Goods or Services? In many situations, a seller is selling both services and goods. A plumber, for example, may repair a leak and, in so doing, replace the faucet. Is the plumber's contract to repair the leak a contract for the sale of services (repairing the leak) or a contract for the sale of goods (selling the faucet)? The courts have generally answered this question by determining whether the sale of goods is the predominant part of the transaction or is only incidental to it. If the sale of goods predominates, it is a transaction in goods governed by Article 2.

In the following case, there was a contract for the sale and installation of used bowling alley equipment. The court had to determine whether or not Article 2 applied to the contract.

BONEBRAKE v. COX
499 F.2d 951 (Eighth Cir. 1974)

[The Cox brothers, the defendants, had run a bowling alley called the Tamarack Bowl for 20 years. On February 5, 1968, the bowling alley was gutted by fire. The Cox brothers decided to rebuild. On April 17, 1968, they entered into a written contract with Woodrow B. Simek, a dealer in new and used bowling equipment, for the purchase and installation of used bowling equipment for a total price of $20,000.

Simek died before installation was completed, and Frances Bonebrake, the plaintiff, was appointed as administratrix (representative) of his estate. The Cox brothers obtained the balance of the equipment they needed from another source, and Bonebrake brought a legal action against the Cox brothers for breach of contract.

A number of issues in the case involved the possible application of Article 2. One of the issues was whether the contract between Simek and the Coxes was a contract for the sale of goods or a contract for services. The trial court determined that the Code was not applicable to the contract. The Coxes appealed.]

SMITH, Senior District Judge

We now consider whether the contract of April 17, 1968, comes under the Code. The fire suffered by defendant's bowling alley on February 5, 1968, had destroyed its equipment. This contract with Simek was to replace those goods. The "following used equipment" was purchased: lane beds, bail returns, chairs, bubble ball cleaning machine, lockers, house balls, storage racks, shoes and foundation materials. The equipment was to be delivered and installed by Simek. He warranted that the lanes would be "free from defects in workmanship and materials," and that they would "meet all ABC [American Bowling Congress] specifications."

The language thus employed is that peculiar to goods, not services. It speaks of "equipment," and of lanes free from "defect in workmanship and materials." The rendition of services does not comport with such terminology.

The [trial court], however, ruled that the above-described contract

is not the type of contract which falls within the statutory scheme of the U.C.C. It involved substantial amounts of labor, as well as goods, with a lump sum price. The Code was meant to cover contracts for the commercial sale of goods, not non-divisible mixed contracts of this type.

In such holding there is error. Article 2 of the Code, here involved, applies to "transactions in goods" [§2-102]. The definition of "goods" is found in §2-105(1):

"Goods" means all things (including specially manufactured goods) which are movable at the time of identification to the contract for sale other than the money in which the price is to be paid, investment securities . . . and things in action.

As [has been pointed] out, [§2-102] is divided into two parts, the first affirmative, defining the scope and reach of Article 2, the second negative, excluding certain transactions. To come within the affirmative section, the articles [the "things"] must be movable, and the movability must occur at the time of identification to the contract. The applicability of the Code to the April contract is clear from and within its four corners. The "things" sold are all items of tangible property, normally in the flow of commerce, portable at the time of the contract. They are not the less "goods" within the definition of the act because service may play a role in their ultimate use. The Code contains no such exception.

Services always play an important role in the use of goods, whether it is the service of transforming the raw materials into some usable product or the service of distributing the usable product to a point where it can easily be obtained by the consumer. The §2-105(1) definition should not be used to deny Code application simply because an added service is required to inject or apply the product.

In short, the fact that the contract "involved substantial amounts of labor" does not remove it from inclusion under the Code on the ground [as found by the trial court] that "the Code was [not] meant to cover non-divisible mixed contracts of this type."

In contrast to the language of the April contract before us, in which "the following used equipment" was purchased, we note the contractual terminology employed in *Computer Servicenters, Inc. v. Beacon Mfg. Co.,* wherein the court, in holding that the contract there before it was one for service, rather than for the sale of goods, held as follows:

> Article 2 of the Commercial Code deals with "transactions in goods" [§2-102]. "Goods" [are defined in §2-105(1)]. That definition is indeed broad, however, it must be noted that the article deals with, and the definition of goods is cast in terms of, the contract for sale. "Sale" consists in the passing of title from the seller to the buyer for a price [§2-106(1)]. The fact of the matter here is that the alleged contract was simply not for the sale of goods as contended by the plaintiff. Rather it was that certain services be provided the

defendant by the plaintiff. The written proposal states that it is an agreement "for performance of data processing services." The proposal indicated that there would be a separate charge for supplies unless the defendant provided them. The payment contemplated was for the analysis, collection, storage, and reporting of certain data supplied the plaintiff by the defendant. It was not for the sale of goods, and to claim to the contrary strains the imagination.

Finally, on this phase of the case, we find a dearth of authority going to a point relied upon by the [trial court], namely, that the Code was not meant to cover "non-divisible mixed [goods and services] contracts of this type." Rather, the cases presenting mixed contracts of this type are legion. The test for inclusion or exclusion [under the Code] is not whether they are mixed, but, granting that they are mixed, whether their predominant factor, their thrust, their purpose, reasonably stated, is the rendition of service, with goods incidentally involved (e.g., contract with artist for painting) or is a transaction of sale, with labor incidentally involved (e.g., installation of a water heater in a bathroom). The contract before us, construed in accordance with the applicable standards of the Code, is not excluded therefrom because it is "mixed," and, moreover, is clearly for the replacement of the equipment destroyed by fire, i.e., "goods" as defined by the Code.

The judgment of the district court is reversed.

CASE REVIEW QUESTIONS
1. Is used bowling alley equipment goods? Why?
2. Is a contract to install bowling alley equipment a sale? Why?
3. Is a contract to provide computer services a sale? Explain. Would your answer be different if the computer service company installed terminals in its customer's office to relay data to the main office? Explain.

Merchants

The Code designates certain buyers or sellers who are professionals in business as merchants. According to the Code, a **merchant** is a person who deals in a particular kind of goods, who holds himself or herself out as having special knowledge or skill related to a particular kind of goods, or who employs someone who has such knowledge or skill [§2-104(1)]. A merchant, then, is distinguished from a casual or inexperienced seller or buyer.

A person can be a merchant in some situations and not in others. For example, the owner of a hardware store is a merchant when he or she sells tools to a customer because a hardware store owner deals in tools. The same person is not a merchant, however, when he or she sells a rare book from a small collection kept as a hobby because a hobbyist does not deal in books.

A sale of goods may occur between two parties who are merchants, between one party who is a merchant and another who is not, or between two inexperienced parties. For example, an automobile manufacturer may sell a car to an auto dealer (two merchants), the dealer may then sell the car to an individual customer (a merchant and an inexperienced party), and the customer may later sell the car to a friend (two inexperienced parties).

Traditional contract law would apply the same rules to all three transactions. The drafters of the Code, however, set out a number of special rules in Article 2 that apply to merchants in certain situations. Some of these rules apply to transactions "between merchants," that is, when both the seller and the buyer are merchants [§2-104(3)], whereas others apply when only one of the parties is a merchant. Figure 19-1 provides a summary of the sections of Article 2 that contain special rules for merchants. At this point in your study of sales law, you may not understand all of the provisions in Figure 19-1. You may wish to refer to it again after you have read the six sales law chapters.

Good Faith

The Code imposes an obligation of performance in good faith on all parties to all contracts governed by it [§1-203]. **Good faith** is defined as "honesty in fact in the conduct or transaction concerned" [§1-201(19)]. Merchants, however, are held to a higher standard of good faith. Article 2 defines good faith for a merchant as honesty in fact and "the observance of reasonable commercial standards of fair dealing in the trade" [§2-103(1)(b)]. Whenever a merchant appears in a court case, therefore, it is relevant to inquire not only into his or her honesty but also into the applicable standards of fair dealing.

Statute of Frauds

Statute of Frauds is legislation that requires certain promises to be in a writing signed by the party who is to be held responsible for the promises or the promises will not be enforced. As discussed in Chapter 13, the Statute of Frauds has been criticized for causing injustice in many cases. Nonetheless, repeal of the statute appears unlikely. The drafters of the Code attempted, however, to design the writing requirement for sales contracts so as to avoid injustice.

The original Statute of Frauds enacted in England in 1677 specified that

> no contract for the sale of any goods, wares, and merchandises, for the price of
> ten pounds sterling or upwards, shall be allowed to be good, except the buyer shall
> accept part of the goods . . . and actually receive the same, or give some thing in
> earnest . . . or in part of payment or that some note or memorandum in

Sections of the Uniform Commercial Code Applicable to Merchants

Section	Subject	Provision
2-103(1)(b)	Good faith	Good faith for merchants requires honesty in fact *and* observance of commercial standards
2-201(1)(b)	Statute of Frauds	Between merchants, a memo signed by either seller or buyer may satisfy the statute for both parties
2-205	Firm offer	Merchants can create irrevocable offers without consideration
2-207(2)	Acceptance	Between merchants terms added to an acceptance can become part of the contract without specific agreement
2-209(2)	Contract modification	A merchant's form that prohibits modification of the contract except by a signed writing must have a separate signature line for such prohibition to be effective against a nonmerchant
2-312(3)	Warranty against infringement	A merchant seller warrants that there will be no trade infringement claims against the buyer
2-314	Warranty of merchantability	A merchant seller guarantees that the goods sold are fit for their ordinary use
2-326(3)	Consignment sales	Delivery of goods to a merchant buyer with the seller retaining title may not protect the seller from the buyer's creditors
2-327(1)(c)	Sale on approval	Merchant buyers must follow reasonable instructions in returning goods received on approval
2-402(2)	Rights of sellers' creditors	Retention of goods sold by a merchant for a reasonable time is not a fraud on creditors
2-403(2)	Entrusting	A merchant seller has the power to transfer the ownership rights of any person who entrusts goods to the merchant to a buyer in the ordinary course of business
2-509(3)	Risk of loss	Merchant sellers who themselves deliver goods to a buyer have the risk that the goods will be lost or damaged until the goods are actually received by the buyer
2-603	Rejection of goods	A merchant buyer must follow the seller's reasonable instructions about returning or caring for rejected goods and must attempt to sell rejected perishable goods
2-605(1)(b)	Reasons for rejection	Merchant buyers must state all objections concerning goods or their delivery when asked for objections by a merchant seller in a writing
2-609(2)	Adequate assurance of performance	Between merchants, commercial standards will be used to test the reason why a merchant demands assurance

FIGURE 19-1
Sections of the Uniform Commercial Code Applicable to Merchants

writing . . . be made and signed by the parties to be charged . . . or their agents thereunto lawfully authorized.

Article 2 retains the principle of the original statute and the same general language. Under the Code, contracts for the sale of goods for $500 or more must be evidenced by a signed writing. The Code, however, modifies the requirements concerning the kind of writing and provides some exceptions. It is important to remember that meeting the requirements of the Statute of Frauds, either by a writing or through an exception, does not prove the existence of a contract. In other words, compliance with the requirements only gets a party into the courtroom; he or she must still prove that an enforceable promise was made.

What Kind of Writing Is Required by the Code? A writing can be very informal. A note on a piece of scrap paper written in pencil can satisfy the statute if it contains the required material. Moreover, a writing is not necessarily insufficient for meeting the writing requirement simply because it omits or incorrectly states certain terms agreed to by the parties. There are, however, three definite and invariable requirements for what must be in the writing. If these requirements are met, the statute is satisfied and the contract can be enforced [§2-201(1)].

First, the writing must indicate that a contract for the sale of goods has been made between the parties. The writing must provide a basis for believing that a contractual relationship that can be proven by oral testimony actually exists. A writing that merely states an offer does not indicate the existence of a contract because there is no evidence of acceptance.

Second, the writing must be signed by the party against whom the enforcement of a contractual promise is sought. The signing requirement can be met by the use of "any symbol executed or adopted by a party with a present intention to authenticate a writing" [§1-201(39)]. This means that the use of initials or even a letterhead could meet the signing requirement as long as the intent is to authenticate (make valid) the writing.

Third, the writing must specify a quantity of goods to be sold. The Code provides that a contract that must be in writing to be enforceable is not enforceable beyond the quantity of goods shown in the writing. For example, suppose a memo signed by a seller states that "John Doe ordered 500 widgets." Even if the number 500 is an error and the parties actually agreed to the sale of 5,000 widgets, the agreement can not be enforced beyond the 500 widgets specified in the writing.

Exceptions to the UCC Writing Requirement The Code provides for four exceptions to the writing requirement. If one of those exceptions applies to a particular situation, an oral contract for the sale of goods for $500 or more can be enforced even though there is no writing or there is a writing that does not satisfy the three requirements.

Confirmation between Merchants Some business deals are made over the phone or under other circumstances that do not allow the contract between the parties to be put in writing when the agreement is reached. To deal with this situation, the Code provides that the contract will be enforceable if written confirmation is sent and the following conditions are met:

1. The agreement is between merchants.
2. One of the merchants sends to the other merchant a written confirmation of the agreement that satisfies the writing requirement against the merchant sending the confirmation.
3. The confirmation is sent within a reasonable time.
4. The merchant receiving the confirmation has reason to know of its contents.
5. The merchant receiving the confirmation does not object to the contents within ten days of receipt.

Once these conditions are met, the contract will be enforceable against the merchant who receives the confirmation even though he or she has not signed a writing [§2-201(2)].

For example, suppose a retail bookstore owner telephones a wholesaler and orders 500 books. The next day the wholesaler sends a signed letter to the retailer saying, "This is to confirm your purchase of 500 books." If the retailer receives the letter and does not object within ten days, his or her promise to buy the books is enforceable even though he or she has not signed a writing. The contract is, of course, enforceable against the merchant who sent the written confirmation because the confirmation must meet all the writing requirements of §2-201(1).

As we have noted, the written confirmation exception is available only when both the seller and the buyer are merchants. In the following two cases involving oral contracts, the courts first had to determine whether both parties were merchants.

CAMPBELL v. YOKEL
313 N.E.2d 628 (Ill. App. 1974)

[Frank and Robert Yokel, the defendants, are farmers. They orally agreed to sell 6,800 to 7,200 bushels of soybeans at a price of $5.30 per bushel to Campbell Grain and Seed Company, the plaintiffs. Following the oral agreement, Campbell sent the Yokels a signed written confirmation of the oral agreement. The Yokels received the confirmation, never signed it, and never objected to its contents. The Yokels refused to deliver the soybeans, arguing that they had never signed a contract. Campbell sued to enforce the con-

tract. The Yokels raised the Statute of Frauds as a defense. The trial court ruled in favor of the Yokels. Campbell appealed.]

CREBS, Justice

The [trial] court (held) . . . that the defendants were not "merchants" within the meaning of [§2-201(2) that provides:]

Between merchants if within a reasonable time a writing in confirmation of the contract and sufficient against the sender is received and the party receiving it has reason to know its contents, it satisfies the requirements of subsection (1) against such party unless written notice of objection to its contents is given within ten days after it is received.

Plaintiffs contend that the court erred in finding that the defendant farmers were not "merchants" and that [§2-201(2)] was not applicable. We agree.

Growing crops are "goods" within the meaning of Article 2 of the Commercial Code [§2-105(1)]. The . . . definition of "merchant" leads us to the conclusion that a farmer may be considered a merchant in some instances and that one of those instances exists when the farmer is a person "who deals in goods of the kind . . . involved in the transaction."

The defendants in the instant case have admitted that they have grown and sold soybeans and other grains for several years. They have sold to the plaintiffs and to other grain companies in the past. We believe that a farmer who regularly sells his crops is a person "who deals in goods of that kind."

The authors of the comments to the Uniform Commercial Code state that the term "merchant" applies to a "professional in business" rather than to a "casual or inexperienced seller or buyer" [§2-104, Uniform Commercial Code Comments 1 and 2]. The defendants admittedly were not "casual or inexperienced" sellers. We believe that farmers who regularly market their crops are "professionals" in that business and are "merchants" when they are selling those crops.

Our decision does not place a great burden on farmers. As the comments to [§2-103] point out, the provisions in Article 2 of the Commercial Code dealing with "merchants" involve "normal business practices which are or ought to be typical of and familiar to any person in business." . . . Placing this small burden upon farmers in certain instances lessens the possibility that the statute of frauds would be used as an instrument of fraud. For example, assuming that an oral agreement had been reached in the instant case, that the farmers had received the written confirmation signed by the plaintiffs and that the farmers were not "merchants," the farmers would be in a position to speculate on a contract to which the grain company was bound. If the market price fell after the agreement had been reached, the farmers could produce the written confirmation and enforce the contract. If the market price rose, the farmers could claim the protection of the statute of frauds and sell [the] crop on the open market. Our holding reduces the possibility of this type of practice in cases in which the farmer is a person who regularly sells crops of the kind involved in the transaction at hand.

For the foregoing reasons, we hold that the court erred when it determined that the defendants were not merchants. Our decision is not tantamount to a finding that a contract did exist between the plaintiffs and the defendants. We hold merely that, since the defendants were merchants, [§2-201(2)] operates to bar the defendants from asserting the defense of the statute of frauds. The burden of persuading the trier of fact that an oral contract was in fact made prior to the written confirmation is unaffected.

Reversed and remanded.

CASE REVIEW QUESTIONS

1. Why did the court find that Yokel was a merchant?
2. Why was the Statute of Frauds applicable to the contract?
3. Why could the contract be enforced against Yokel if he never signed anything? Explain.
4. Could Yokel enforce the contract against Campbell? Why? Would your answer be different if Yokel were not a merchant? Explain.
5. On a retrial, what will Campbell have to prove in order to enforce the contract?

TERMINAL GRAIN CORP. v. FREEMAN
270 N.W.2d 806 (S.D. 1978)

[Following several telephone conversations in which Freeman, the defendant, allegedly agreed to sell 4,000 bushels of wheat at $1.655 a bushel before January 1, 1973, and 4,000 bushels of wheat at $1.71 per bushel after January 1, 1973, Terminal Grain Corporation, the plaintiff, prepared two written confirmations of the oral agreements and mailed them to Freeman on August 31, 1972. Kenneth Wheeler, an independent trucker, negotiated deals between various farmers and Terminal Grain and was involved in the Freeman deal. In September of 1972, Wheeler delivered 4,000 bushels of Freeman's grain to Terminal. Freeman was paid for the grain. In January of 1973, Freeman informed Wheeler that he would not deliver the remaining 4,000 bushels. The price of wheat at the time varied between $2.25 and $2.30 per bushel.

Freeman alleged that he never agreed to sell to Terminal, that he thought the sales were with Wheeler, and that he did not know of the confirming memoranda until late in the fall. His attorney advised him that the confirmations did not constitute valid binding contracts, so he refused to deliver any wheat under them. Terminal sued Freeman for breach of contract. The trial court refused to instruct the jury on the Statute of Frauds provision relating to merchants in §2-201(2). Terminal appealed.]

RANSON, Justice

As a farmer, Freeman contends he is not a "merchant" within the contemplation of [§2-201(2)] and it therefore has no application to him.

The official comment to [§2-104] of Uniform Commercial Code definition of "merchant" . . . states in part:

1. This Article assumes that transactions between professionals in a given field require special and clear rules which may not apply to a casual or inexperienced seller or buyer. . . .
2. The term "merchant" as defined here roots in the "law merchant" concept of a professional in business.

The professional status under the definition may be based upon specialized knowledge as to the goods, specialized knowledge as to business practices, or specialized knowledge as to both and which kind of specialized knowledge may be sufficient to establish the merchant status is indicated by the nature of the provisions.

In similar factual cases the courts which have considered whether or not a "farmer" is or may be considered a "merchant" under the above Uniform Commercial Code provisions are almost equally divided in their opinions. The courts in Illinois, Texas, Missouri, Ohio, and North Carolina have held farmers to be merchants under various facts and circumstances. . . .

On the other hand the courts in Iowa, New Mexico, Utah, Kansas, Arkansas, and Alabama have held that a farmer is not a merchant. . . .

In arriving at its conclusion that the defendant farmer/seller was not a "merchant" within the meaning of the Uniform Commercial Code, the Kansas Court, said

[T]he appellee neither "deals in wheat" as that term is used in [§2-104] nor does he by his occupation hold himself out as having knowledge or skill peculiar to the practices or goods involved in the transaction. The concept of professionalism is heavy in determining who is a merchant under the statute. The writers of the official UCC comment virtually equate professionals with merchants — the casual or inexperienced buyer or seller is not to be held to the standard set for the professional in business. The defined term "between merchants" used in the exception proviso to the statute of frauds . . . contemplates the knowledge and skill of professionals on each side of the transaction. The transaction in question here was the sale of wheat. Appellee as a farmer undoubtedly had special knowledge or skill in raising wheat but we do not think this factor, coupled with annual sales of a wheat crop and purchases of seed wheat, qualified him as a merchant in that field.

We agree with the reasoning of the Kansas Court and with the other courts which hold the average farmer, like Freeman, with no particular knowledge or experience in selling, buying or dealing in future commodity transactions, and who sells only the crops he raises to local elevators for cash . . . is not a "merchant" within the purview of the exception provision to the Uniform Commercial Code statute of frauds. Through training and years of experience a farmer may well possess or acquire special knowledge, skills, and expertise in the production of grain crops but this does not make him a "professional," equal in the marketplace with a grain buying and selling company, whose officers, agents, and employees are constantly conversant with the daily fluctuations in the commodity market, the many factors affecting the market, and with its intricate practices and procedures. Accordingly, the trial court did not err in refusing to instruct the jury on this issue.

On a retrial of the issues involved . . . the trial court would be obligated to instruct the jury that the Uniform Commercial Code statute of frauds contained in [§2-201(1)] applied to the transaction. . . . As Freeman is not a "merchant" within the contemplation of [§2-201(2)], the defense of the general statute of frauds would bar any recovery of damages by Terminal Grain. . . .

[Affirmed.]

CASE REVIEW QUESTIONS
1. Why did the court find that Freeman was not a merchant?
2. Which decision do you prefer — *Campbell v. Yokel* or *Terminal Grain Corporation v. Freeman?* Why?
3. Is either Freeman or Yokel a casual or inexperienced seller?
4. Could Freeman enforce the contract against Terminal Grain? Explain. Why didn't he?

Specially Manufactured Goods Sometimes parties agree that goods are to be manufactured especially for the buyer. In this situation, a seller could be damaged if a buyer could escape his or her promise to buy the goods on the basis of the fact that the promise was not in a signed writing because the specially manufactured goods might not be readily sold to anyone else. The Code therefore provides that a contract for specially manufactured goods will be enforceable against the buyer even though he or she has not signed a writing if the following conditions are met [§2-201(3)(a)]:

1. The goods are to be specially manufactured for the buyer.
2. The goods are not suitable for sale to others in the ordinary course of the seller's business.
3. The seller either makes a substantial beginning on the manufacture of the goods or makes a commitment for the procurement of goods needed for their manufacture before receiving notice that the buyer no longer wants to purchase the goods.
4. The circumstances reasonably indicate that the goods are for the buyer.

For example, suppose a drapery maker enters into an oral agreement to supply custom-made drapes for a newly remodeled hotel ballroom. The size and color scheme of the drapes are such that the seller would have no other readily available buyer for them. If the buyer refuses to take the drapes, the drapery maker will be able to sue for damages even though the contract was oral. The seller will still have to prove the existence of the contract. Merely showing up with specially manufactured goods does not prove that there is a contract, but it is enough evidence to open the door to the court room.

Performance Performance can provide strong evidence that the parties entered into a contract even though they did not put their agreement in a signed writing. For instance, if a buyer pays for goods or a seller delivers goods that the buyer accepts and does not return, there is every reason to believe that the parties had a contract. In general, people do not accept either money or goods without having made some type of agreement. Therefore, when payment has been made by a buyer and accepted by the seller *or* when goods have been received and accepted by a buyer, the Code provides that the contract will be enforceable against either party even though there is no signed writing [§2-201(3)(c)].

For example, suppose that a buyer orally agrees to purchase a car. If the buyer pays the seller the purchase price, the seller's promise to sell the car is enforceable even though it is not in a signed writing because payment was made by the buyer and accepted by the seller.

An interesting problem is presented by this exception. The original statute enacted in England made reference to partial payment as a means of satisfying the Statute of Frauds. The Code does not mention partial payment. It speaks only of "goods for which payment has been made and accepted" [§2-201(2)(c)]. In addition, the Code makes it very clear that contracts are not enforceable beyond the quantity shown. Suppose, for instance, that A and B have an oral contract for the sale of two television sets, each priced at $550. B makes a $200 down payment. If A refuses to deliver the second television set, claiming that there is only a contract for one, should B be able to enforce the agreement and get the second set? The best solution is that B should not be able to enforce the agreement. The $200 is evidence of a contract, but it does not indicate a quantity greater than the one set A is willing to deliver. This solution allows the payment exception to operate in conjunction with the Code's stated policy of not enforcing a contract beyond a stated or indicated quantity.

Admissions in Court The UCC provides that, if a person admits in his or her pleadings or in testimony or in some other way in court that a contract for sale was made, the contract is enforceable even though it is not in a signed writing, but only to the extent of the quantity of goods stated in the admission [§2-201(3)(b)]. Prior to the enactment of this provision, oral contracts that had to be in writing to be enforceable were not enforced even if the promisor admitted in a legal proceeding that the contract existed.

In the following case, the court discusses this exception. The court had to determine whether the admission must be explicit or whether the statute is satisfied when the party testifies to facts that prove the existence of a contract.

LEWIS v. HUGHES
346 A.2d 231 (Md. 1975)

[Mrs. Lewis, the plaintiff, negotiated with Dr. Hughes, the defendant, for the sale of her mobile home in a trailer park owned by Dr. Hughes. Dr. Hughes refused to pay for the trailer, and Mrs. Lewis sued to enforce the contract. The only writing evidencing the contract was signed by Mr. Baer, an attorney for Dr. Hughes, whom the trial court held was not authorized to sign contracts for Dr. Hughes. Mr. Baer had conducted some of the negotiations with Mrs. Lewis for the sale of the trailer. The trial court ruled in favor of Dr. Hughes because there was no writing signed by him. Mrs. Lewis appealed.]

DIGGES, Judge

Whether the writing requirement of the Statute of Frauds contained in [§2-201] prevents the enforcement of an oral contract for the sale of a mobile home is the question we must settle in this case. [W]e conclude that it can be enforced under [§2-201(3)(b)] since Dr. Hughes admitted in his testimony at trial that the contract was made. Consequently we will reverse and remand the case for an assessment of damages.

According to §2-201(3),

> A contract which doesn't satisfy the requirements of [§2-201(1)] but which is valid in other respects is enforceable. . . .
> (b) If the party against whom enforcement is sought admits in his pleading, testimony or otherwise in court that a contract for sale was made, but the contract is not enforceable under this provision beyond the quantity of goods admitted. . . .

The appellant asserts that Dr. Hughes repeatedly acknowledged the existence of the contract in his testimony and that therefore, regardless of its enforceability under §2-201(1), the agreement is enforceable under §2-201(3)(b).

The next step is to determine just what, if anything, Dr. Hughes did admit concerning the agreement during the course of his testimony at trial. An examination of the record discloses that the doctor testified as follows:

Q. This . . . conversation (with Mr. Baer), did you regard that as a meeting of the minds that you were to buy a trailer from Mrs. Lewis for $5,000 then or in the immediate future?

A. No sir, I did not.

Q. What was your understanding of your relationship with Mrs. Lewis at that time?

A. My understanding was we were in a negotiation state really of reaching an agreement as to the purchase of the trailer, and I did not really agree to the terms how to purchase the trailer. But the price I had agreed with Mr. Baer on.

Q. Did you tell (Mr. Baer), as he says, "O.K. I will buy it at that price," or not?

A. Yes.

Q. . . . But am I correct when you said, "O.K. I will buy it at that price," that in your mind, at that time, you meant that you would buy it for $2,500 down, whatever it is, plus the rest over a period of time, although you did not say so?

A. That is right.

In sum, it is apparent from this, as well as from other portions of the appellee's testimony not here quoted, that at the trial the doctor admitted he told Mr. Baer, without mention of any terms of payment, that he would purchase the mobile home for $5,000. Of course, it is legally irrelevant, in the fact of Dr. Hughes' objective manifestation of unconditional assent to the offer, that the doctor thought the contract was still being negotiated and had a subjective desire to impose certain conditions on the manner of payment. . . . Consequently, when on May 9 the lawyer, in accordance with his authority, informed appellant of Dr. Hughes' assent, there was an acceptance of the offer and a contract, as a matter of law, came into existence. . . .

We come then to the basic issue in this case, which is whether the Statute of Frauds is satisfied pursuant to [§2-201(3)(b)] when the party denying the existence of the contract and relying on the statute takes the stand and, without admitting explicitly that a contract was made, testifies to facts which as a matter of law establish that a contract was formed. While we have no case specifically deciding this question, numerous cases dealing with [§2-201(3)(b)] seem to say that in such a situation the requirements of the statute have been fulfilled. . . . We hold that the Statute of Frauds does not bar enforcement of the contract involved in this case.

Since it is implicit in the trial judge's findings of fact that he concluded that there was a breach of contract by the appellee, we will remand the proceedings to the [trial] court for entry of judgment in favor of the appellant and for assessment of such damages as that court finds appellant suffered as a result of the breach of contract.

[Reversed.]

CASE REVIEW QUESTIONS

1. Could the contract have been enforced against Dr. Hughes if he had told the managers of the trailer park that he had a contract? Why?
2. Could Mrs. Lewis have enforced the contract if she had sent Dr. Hughes a letter signed by her and stating the terms of the contract? Explain.
3. On what basis does the court find that a contract existed?

Contract Modifications

It is often desirable to modify a contract after the parties have initially agreed, as for example, when prices change or delivery dates need to be revised. Prior to the enactment of the Code, modifying a contract was often difficult and, at the very least, required some consideration for the altered promises to be enforceable.

The problem created by the doctrine of consideration in the modification of contracts was discussed in Chapter 12. In order for a promise to be supported by consideration, the person who makes the promise must receive something of value in return for making it. If a party to a contract promises to do something extra under that contract, the new promise will not be supported by consideration unless the other party promises to do something extra as well (see page 224). In some instances, this rule protects people from economic coercion. When coercion does not appear to be present, however, the courts have developed a number of devices for circumventing it. These traditional contract law devices were explained in Chapter 12. The Code makes these devices unnecessary with regard to sales contracts. It allows a sales contract to be modified without consideration [§2-209(1)].

Sometimes a modification of a sales contract must be in writing in order to be enforceable. For instance, if the contract, as modified, falls within the terms of the Statute of Frauds — that is, if it is for the sale of goods for a price of $500 or more — the modification must be in writing to be enforceable [§2-209(3)].

Contract modifications must also be in writing, regardless of the price of the goods, when the parties have agreed in their original contract that any modifications must be in writing. The Code, however, provides some protection for nonmerchants. It provides a requirement that modifications be in writing contained in a form supplied by a merchant to a nonmerchant, must be signed separately by the nonmerchant [§2-209(2)]. This provision should at least bring the existence of the requirement to the attention of the nonmerchant.

Even though a modification may be required to be in writing, it may still have some effect even if it is not in writing because a court can treat an agreement to modify a contract as a waiver [§2-209(4)]. A waiver occurs when someone knowingly and voluntarily gives up a right that he or she has. For example, suppose a buyer orally agrees to a different delivery date for a new automobile. The buyer's oral promise is not enforceable because the contract falls within the Statute of Frauds and the modification is not in writing. A court, however, can treat the promise as a waiver of the delivery date called for in the original contract. Because of the waiver, there is, in effect, no delivery date specified in the original contract. A court could then fix a delivery date that is reasonable considering all the circumstances.

In all contract modifications, the new promises must be asked for and made in good faith and both parties must agree to them. In the following case, the court discusses modifications of contracts. It also has to determine whether or not a modification was made in good faith.

PALMER v. SAFE AUTO SALES, INC.
452 N.Y.S.2d 995 (Civ. Ct. City of N.Y. 1982)

[Leonard Palmer, the plaintiff, entered into a contract with Safe Auto Sales, Inc., the defendant, for the purchase of a 1980 Toyota Tercel, deluxe model, at a price of $5,822.04. When the automobile arrived, the seller informed Palmer that he would have to pay an additional $250, which reflected an increase in the cost of the car to the dealer between the time it was ordered and the date of delivery. Palmer needed the car, so he paid the additional amount in order to obtain possession of it. Palmer then sued to recover the additional charge.]

SAXE, Judge

The issue that I must resolve . . . is: Whether a modification of a contract between a merchant and a consumer for the sale of a new automobile under which the consumer is obligated to pay an increased price over that specified in the original contract of sale to be entitled to obtain delivery and possession of the vehicle, is a bad faith modification of the original con-

tract under the provisions of the Uniform Commercial Code which may accordingly entitle the buyer to recover damages. . . .

It is undisputed by either party that the defendant did not perform according to the terms of the original contract. The primary issue to be resolved, therefore, is whether that original contract was effectively modified by a subsequent agreement between the parties. . . . At common law, the rule was that where a party did or promised to do what he was already legally obligated to do, there existed no sufficient consideration to support the new promise. This rule was known as the pre-existing duty rule. Applied to the facts of this case, it would appear to bar Dr. Palmer's promise to pay an additional amount for delivery of the same vehicle that he had ordered or one differing in an immaterial respect only.

The Code has eliminated the ''pre-existing duty'' rule in sales contracts [§2-209(1)]. It has been generally recognized that:

Contract modification is a common business practice. Experience has proven to us time and again that instability in economic conditions, legislative enactment, administrative fiat, and a change of heart can cause the parties to a contract for the sale of goods to have second thoughts about their original contract.

Modification of sales contracts are consequently expressly authorized and no consideration is necessary to support the modification. The modifications must however be in writing [§2-209(2)] and additionally must be made "in good faith" [§2-209, Comment 2].

[§1-201(19)] provides that: "'Good faith' means honesty in fact in the conduct or transaction concerned." A more stringent standard appears in [§2-103(1)(b)], as follows: "'Good faith' in the case of a merchant means honesty in fact and the observance of reasonable commercial standards of fair dealing in the trade." [T]he party against whom violation of the good faith standard has been asserted is a "merchant" [§2-104(1)].

The issue then is whether the modification of the original sales contract has met the good faith standard of [§2-103(1)(b)], . . . Official Comment 2 to [§2-209] states that: "The test of 'good faith' between merchants or as against merchants includes 'observance of reasonable commercial standards of fair dealing in the trade' [§2-103], and may in some situations require an objectively demonstrable reason for seeking a modification." The Comment further provides, however, that "such matters as a market shift which makes performance come to involve a loss may provide such a reason. . . ."

Although the Comment does not specifically state, it would appear that a modification of a sales price term arising out of a market shift will generally be held enforceable only in a context involving "merchants." [I]n a case involving merchants [a court has observed] that:

In the context of a lengthy, on-going business relationship, seeking modification of a sales price is not uncommon and, given increased costs, is a fair method of doing business in order to preserve the desirability of the relationship for both parties. . . .

However, while such modification might be expected in a sales transaction between merchants, a different rule is appropriate where one of the parties is a consumer. I hold that where, as here, a sophisticated merchant attempts to coerce a consumer into assenting and paying a price increase for the vehicle that had previously been contracted for, such a modification does not meet the good faith requirement of Article 2 of the UCC. The consumer who purchases goods, such as an automobile, makes, it is presumed, a reasoned decision based among other things upon the price factors and the necessity of receiving delivery of the vehicle within certain time parameters. The purchase of an automobile entails a large expenditure for the average consumer. It is not a transaction undertaken frequently. Therefore, having signed a contract and furnished a deposit, the consumer reasonably believes that he has contracted for a vehicle at a price certain. The attempt by the dealer to exact a further charge to deflect a price increase to it, is an unfair and manifestly unreasonable requirement. In short, it is a modification lacking in good faith [§2-103(1)(b)].

While the modification to reflect the price increase might be deemed a modification "honest in fact," I hold that the modification does not conform to the additional standard relevant to this transaction, i.e., "the observance of reasonable commercial standards of fair dealing in the trade" [§2-103(1)(b)]. The transaction must be viewed in the totality of the circumstances: a price increase modification in the context of a single consumer transaction as opposed to one in "a lengthy, on-going business relationship" between merchants. If both parties were merchants, I would hold otherwise.

Accordingly, the claimant is entitled to recover damages from defendant.

CASE REVIEW QUESTIONS

1. Why did the contract modifications have to be in writing?
2. Why was there no consideration for the modifications? Was any needed under the Code? Explain.

3. Why could Palmer demand a repayment of the additional price since he agreed to pay it? Explain.
4. What standard of good faith is applicable to this case? Why?

Parol Evidence Rule

Under traditional contract law, the **parol evidence rule** states that a written contract that is intended by the parties to be a complete and final expression of their agreement cannot be contradicted or supplemented by evidence of an oral agreement made between the parties either prior to or at the same time as the written contract (see Chapter 13). The Code modifies this traditional rule. It still prohibits the contradiction of a writing that is intended to be a final expression of the parties' agreement by evidence of a prior or contemporaneous oral agreement [§2-202]. However, it does allow the terms of the final written expression of the parties' agreement to be explained or supplemented by *course of dealing* (the conduct of the parties in previous transactions [§1-205]), *course of performance* (the conduct of the parties after the contract has been formed [§2-208]), and *usage of trade* (regular practices or methods of dealing in the kind of business in which the parties are engaged [§1-205]) [§2-202(a)]. (For a full explanation of these terms see pages 364–366.)

The Code also allows the terms of a writing to be supplemented by additional, noncontradictory terms, unless a court finds the writing to have been intended not only as final but also as a complete and exclusive expression of the parties' agreement [§2-202(b)]. For example, suppose that a contract for the sale of a car says nothing about the tires or about the writing being a complete and exclusive expression of the parties' agreement. The buyer would be allowed to try to supplement the terms of the writing with evidence that, before delivery, the seller agreed to put radial tires on the car.

Parol evidence can also be introduced to prove that a contract is either void or voidable under general contract law or to prove that an agreement was entered into *subsequent* to the written contract [§1-103]. These situations are discussed fully on page 248.

In the following case, the court had to determine whether parol evidence was admissible to explain the quantity terms of a contract.

HEGGBLADE-MARGULEAS-TENNECO, INC. v. SUNSHINE BISCUIT, INC.
131 Cal. Rptr. 183 (Cal. App. 1976)

[Heggblade-Marguleas-Tenneco, Inc. (HMT), the plaintiff, contracted to sell potatoes to Sunshine Biscuit, Inc., and Bell Brand Foods, Inc. (hereinafter referred to together as Bell Brand). HMT resulted from two mergers: the Kern County Land Company (KCL) merged with Tenneco in 1967 and Heggblade-Marguleas merged with Tennecc in 1970. Before the merger, Heggblade-Marguleas marketed agricultural products for different companies, including KCL. Heggblade-Marguleas never marketed processing potatoes. KCL had grown but never marketed processing potatoes. After the 1970 merger, HMT took over the agricultural operations of KCL.

In May of 1970, HMT decided to grow and market potatoes to processors. Later that summer, John Thomas, executive vice-president of HMT, met with Lon Doty, president of Bell Brand, which produced potato snack foods such as chips and french fries. A tentative agreement was reached for the sale of 100,000 sacks of potatoes to be delivered between May and July of 1971. Later, for reasons discussed in the court's decision, HMT brought a legal action against Bell Brand for breach of contract. The trial court granted a judgment for Bell Brand. HMT moved for a new trial, but the motion was denied. HMT appealed.]

FRANSON, Acting Presiding Judge

Mr. Thomas understood that the figure mentioned by Mr. Doty at the meeting was variable because of Bell Brand's commitments to its other customers. Thomas told Doty that HMT would overplant "a little bit" since this would be their first contract and they wanted to be sure they could produce the quantity needed.

Mr. Thomas received a letter from Mr. Doty on August 10, 1970, which read in part:

> After analyzing our needs and obligations to those people who have performed well for us in the past, we would like to start with you on the basis of obtaining 100,000 sacks of Kennebec potatoes from your operation between May 17 and July 17, 1971. The price would be $2.35 in one ton bins. . . .

Thomas replied by letter on August 31, 1970:

> Just a note to let you know that we are going ahead with our contract to furnish you 100,000 sacks of Kennebec potatoes. . . .

Doty was aware that HMT had had no prior marketing experience with processing potatoes. Thomas testified that while he understood that the quantity agreed upon would not be exact to the last sack of potatoes he believed that the amount taken by Bell Brand would be fairly close to the contract terms. Doty did not mention to Thomas that the quantity term was merely an estimate.

Jean Smith, potato buyer for Bell Brand, became concerned after reading Doty's letter to Thomas stating that the quantity was too high. . . . Smith talked to Thomas at least twice concerning a reduction of the quantity and was advised in early October that HMT had already procured the seed necessary to produce the specified amount. On October 17, 1970, Smith went to Thomas' office for the purpose of executing Bell Brand's form contract at a reduced figure. At that meeting Thomas told Smith that he considered the two letters between him and Doty as a contract, so Smith executed the formal contracts in conformity with the letters.

Smith and Gary Riopelle, president and general manager of Bell Brand, testified that because the contracts are executed eight or nine months before the harvest season, the custom in the processing potato industry is to treat the quantity solely as a reasonable estimate of the buyers' needs based on the customers' demands and the growers' ability to supply based on the anticipated yield for the delivery period.

Because of a decline in demand for Bell Brand products in May through July 1971, Bell Brand's sales for the late spring and summer of 1971 were down substantially. As a result Bell Brand's need for potatoes from its suppliers was severely reduced. . . . By the end of the harvest season, Bell Brand was able to take only 60,105 sacks from HMT on the two contracts.

Appellant contends that the quantity terms in the contracts are definite and unambiguous, hence it was error to admit into evidence the custom of the processing potato industry that the amounts specified are reasonable estimates. Appellant's contention is without merit.

[§2-202] states the parol evidence rule applicable to the sale of [goods]:

> Terms with respect to which the confirmatory memoranda of the parties agree or which are otherwise set forth in a writing intended by the prties as a final expression of their agreement with respect to such terms as are included therein may not be contradicted by evidence of any prior agreement or of a contemporaneous oral agreement but may be explained or supplemented "(a) By course of dealing or usage of trade. . . ."

[§2-202(a)], permits a trade usage to be put in evidence "as an instrument of interpretation." The Uniform Commercial Code comment to [§2-202(a)] states that evidence of trade usage is admissible

> . . . in order that the true understanding of the parties as to the agreement may be reached. Such writings are to be read on the assumption that . . . the usages of trade were taken for granted when the document was phrased. Unless carefully negated they have become an element of the meaning of the words used. . . .

Under [§2-202(a)] established trade usage and custom are a part of the contract unless the parties agree otherwise. Since the contracts in question are silent about the applicability of the usage and custom, evidence of such usage and custom was admissible to explain the meaning of the quantity figures.

Appellant contends that because Mr. Thomas did not understand that the quantity figure was an estimate, the trade custom must be excluded from the contract. . . .

[P]ersons carrying on a particular trade are deemed to be aware of prominent trade customs applicable to their industry. The knowledge may be actual or constructive, and it is constructive if the custom is of such general and universal application that the party must be presumed to know of it.

KCL had been involved in farming for many years and had grown potatoes for processing. Heggblade-Marguleas had been involved in the marketing of agricultural products on a large scale although it had never marketed processing potatoes. Because potatoes are a perishable commodity and their demand is dependent upon a fluctuating market, and because the marketing contracts are signed eight or nine months in advance of the harvest season, common sense dictates that the quantity would be estimated by both the grower and the processor. Thus, it cannot be said as a matter of law that HMT was ignorant of the trade custom.

We conclude that the trial court properly admitted the evidence of usage and custom to explain the meaning of the quantity figures in the contracts.

The judgment is affirmed.

CASE REVIEW QUESTIONS
1. Was the usage of trade used to contradict the parties' agreement or was it used to explain the agreement? Explain.
2. Why didn't the court also refer to the parties' course of dealing or course of performance to help interpret their agreement?
3. Why did the court consider usage of trade in the interpretation of the parties' agreement even though Doty did not know of it?
4. Is there anything that Doty could have done to prevent the consideration of usage of trade in the interpretation of the contract?

REVIEW QUESTIONS

1. Define sale, gift, and bailment.
2. What type of contracts are governed by Article 2 of the Uniform Commercial Code?
3. What are goods, future goods, and specially manufactured goods?
4. Are oil in the ground, crops, and unborn animals goods? Explain.
5. What is a merchant?
6. What is good faith? What is good faith for a merchant?
7. Explain the three requirements for a writing that will satisfy the Statute of Frauds.
8. Explain the four exceptions to the writing requirement of the Statute of Frauds.
9. When does the parol evidence rule apply?

CASE PROBLEMS

1. De Filippo and Fleishman were Ford dealers in West Philadelphia. When their dealership was destroyed by fire, they negotiated with Ford for the purpose of purchasing a new dealership. Eventually, De Filippo and Fleishman signed a contract to buy all of the assets except for the real property of another Ford dealership, Presidential Motors. Ford never signed the contracts. According to the contract, Ford was to lease the real estate to the two dealers. The contract also specified that the assets to be transferred included equipment, new and used vehicles, improvements to the building, accounts receivable, and contracts covering services. The value of the movable assets was three times the value of the other assets. When Ford refused to honor the contract, the two dealers sued to enforce the contract. Ford argued that the contract was not enforceable because of the Statute of Frauds. The plaintiffs argued that the Uniform Commercial Code Statute of Frauds was not applicable because the sale was the sale of a business, not of goods. Who will win the case? Explain.

2. Warners Motors, Inc., entered into a dealership contract with Chrysler Motors Corporation. The contract specified that its purpose was to establish a relationship "to provide a means for the sale and service of DeSoto and Plymouth passenger cars, parts, and accessories." The agreement required Chrysler to supply various services to Warners, and it contained provisions governing the rights and obligations of the parties to the franchise with regard to such matters as the payments required for the use of the DeSoto and Plymouth names. In a dispute over an alleged breach of the contract, it was argued that Article 2 was applicable to the contract. How should the court rule on this issue? Explain.

3. Berry raised cattle that he regularly sold to meat packers. On one occasion, however, Berry sold some cattle to Perschbacker, who regularly purchased cattle for resale to other ranchers. Berry's cattle, which were resold by Perschbacker to a rancher, turned out to be diseased. The rancher sued Perschbacker to recover damages for breach of the warranty of merchantability, a warranty that is only made by merchants in the sale of goods. Perschbacker, in turn, sued Berry on the grounds that Berry had breached his warranty of merchantability. Will the rancher recover for breach of warranty from Perschbacker? Will Perschbacker recover from Berry? Would your answer be different if Perschbacker were a meat packer? Explain.

4. Robett Manufacturing Company sent the following letter to John Alice following an oral discussion in which Alice informed Robett that the General Services Administration (GSA) had solicited Alice's bid for the supply of certain clothing.

> Confirming our telephone conversation, we are pleased to offer the 3,500 shirts at $4.00 each and the trousers at $3.00 each with delivery approximately ninety days after receipt of order.
> Thanking you for the opportunity to offer these garments, we are
> > Very truly yours,
> > ROBETT MANUFACTURING
> > COMPANY, INC.

The signature was typed; there was no handwritten signature. Alice submitted a bid to GSA based on Robett's figures. Later, Robett received a solicitation from GSA to bid for the same job, and Robett submitted a bid. GSA awarded the contract to Robett. Alice sued Robett for breach of contract, arguing that Robett had breached the contract it had with Alice by bidding on the same job. Robett moved to dismiss the cause of action. Alice argued that Robett's letter was a confirming memorandum that satisfied the Statute of Frauds. Who will win the case? Explain.

5. Thomaier ordered a Corvette from Hoffman Chevrolet, Inc. Thomaier signed a purchase offer and gave Hoffman $1,000. Hoffman never signed the contract, but it did send an order for a Corvette to General Motors. The order listed Thomaier as the buyer and referred to the car as

sold rather than as inventory. Hoffman refused to deliver the Corvette to Thomaier, who then sued for delivery. Hoffman raised the Statute of Frauds as a defense. Who will win the case? Explain.

6. Jim Patents, Inc. (Patents) and Jack Frost are both merchants. Following a telephone conversation in which Jack Frost ordered a quantity of merchandise, Patents' president shipped the merchandise accompanied by invoices specifying the quantity, price and terms. Frost retained the goods for three weeks and then tried to return them. Patents was unwilling to take the goods back and sued for the price. Frost argued that his promise was not enforceable because the requirements of the Statute of Frauds had not been met. Who will win the case? Explain.

7. Southern Crate and Veneer (Southern) manufactures and distributes wooden crates. A necessary component of the crates is wooden cleats. Maderas Tropicals (Maderas) was created to produce wooden cleats following an oral agreement between Southern and Haynes Willingham. The agreement called for Southern to purchase the entire output of Maderas if Willingham was able to set up the business. Southern's president wrote and signed the following letter:

> We stand willing and able to purchase all the cleats that he can manufacture. Hopefully, he will find an adequate supply of lumber at prices economical to the production of cleats and can have his operation in full swing in a matter of several months.

Maderas was set up and began producing cleats. Southern purchased all of the cleats for a while, but it later notified Maderas that due to reduced demand for crates Maderas should cut its production level. Maderas sued Southern for breach of contract because Southern refused to purchase Maderas' output. Southern argued that its promise is not enforceable because the requirements of the Statute of Frauds had not been met. Maderas argued that the statute was satisfied on the grounds that the goods were specially manufactured goods because Maderas was un-

able to sell many cleats following Southern's breach. Who will win the case? Explain.

8. On April 1st, Gary Self, an agent for CIM, entered into an option agreement with McCollum Aviation. Self sent the following telegram to McCollum: "This confirms your option to purchase Bill Wilco's helicopter. . . . This offer shall expire at midnight April 11th. /s/ Gary Self." On April 11th, McCollum and Self orally agreed to extend the option for two additional weeks. One week later, McCollum sent a check as payment for the helicopter. The check was returned because CIM had already sold the helicopter to a third party. McCollum sued CIM. CIM argued that the option had expired and was not modified by the oral agreement. Who will win the case? Explain.

9. Gold Kist, Inc. (Kist) entered into a contract with Will Pillow for the purchase of soybeans. The contract called for Pillow to deliver 5,000 bushels of soybeans in September at a price of $5.59 per bushel and 5,000 bushels in January at a price of $7.22 per bushel. When Pillow made the September delivery, he orally asked Kist to pay him the higher price for that delivery instead of the January delivery because he needed the money. Kist orally agreed and paid Pillow $7.22 per bushel. Pillow never made the January delivery, and Kist had to buy the remaining 5,000 bushels of soybeans at the January market price of $6.50 per bushel. Kist sued Pillow for breach of contract and asked for the difference between the $6.50 market price and the $5.59 contract price Kist would have paid Pillow as damages. Pillow defended on the grounds that the oral modification of the contract was not effective. He also argued that the contract price of $7.22 for the January delivery was higher than the price Kist had to pay for the soybeans, so Kist had not suffered any loss. Who will win the case? Explain.

10. Columbia Nitrogen Corporation entered into a contract with Royster Company to sell it a specified quantity of phosphate at a specified price. Royster refused to purchase the full amount, arguing that the prices and quantities had to be adjusted to reflect a declining market. When Columbia sued for breach, Royster offered evidence

that the usage of trade and the prior course of dealing of the parties indicated that a buyer of phosphate had no duty to accept the quantity stated in the contract at the prices stated if there were changes in demand in the market place. Is this evidence admissible? Explain.

11. George and Davoli entered into a written contract for the sale of Indian jewelry. According to the contract, the jewelry could be returned to the seller if the buyer decided not to purchase it. Nothing was stated in the contract about when the jewelry must be returned if the buyer was not going to purchase it. The seller offered evidence that the parties had orally agreed that the jewelry would be returned by the Monday evening following the making of the contract. Should the court admit the evidence? Explain.

20

SALES CONTRACTS

Sales contracts are simply one category of contracts in general. As such, they are subject to the usual rules of contract law discussed in Chapters 8 through 18, except where those rules have been displaced by specific provisions of Article 2 of the Uniform Commercial Code. For any contract problem, therefore, the first step is to determine the type of contract involved. If the contract is for the sale of goods, the next step is to determine whether the problem presented by the contract is covered by any of the provisions of Article 2. If it is, Article 2 governs; if it is not, the governing principle must be sought in traditional contract law.

The drafters of the Code were not concerned with rewriting the entire body of contract law that applies to sales contracts. Instead, they addressed certain problems that they believed were created when traditional contract law was applied to sales contracts. These problems and the solutions to them found in the Code are discussed in this chapter.

OFFER AND ACCEPTANCE

The Code contains a number of sections that change the traditional contract principles concerning offer and acceptance, which were discussed in Chapters 9 and 10. These changes are explained and discussed in the following sections of the chapter.

Definiteness and Certainty

Traditionally, contract law has required that the parties to a sales contract must reach a clear and complete mutual agreement on all important terms, such as the description and quantity of the goods to be sold, the price to be paid, and the time for delivery. If the parties omitted any important terms or if a court felt that their agreement on these terms was too vague, the court would decide that no contract had come into existence due to lack of a mutual agreement (see Chapter 9). As a result, the courts often determined that there was no contract even though the parties believed that one existed.

The Code encourages courts to find that contracts for the sale of goods exist despite the absence of precise agreements. In certain situations, it even allows courts to supply vague or missing terms.

When terms are vague or are left open, the basic policy of the Code is to enforce the contract if it appears that the parties intended to enter into a contract and there is a reasonably certain basis for giving an appropriate remedy [§2-204(3)]. In looking for a reasonably certain basis for giving a remedy, a court can consider such things as the parties' course of dealing, usage of trade, or the parties' course of performance. In addition, the Code itself has provisions that supply open (missing) terms. Each of these points will be discussed in more detail in the following materials.

Finding a Contract The Code allows a contract to be made in any manner as long as there is evidence that the parties have entered into an agreement. The existence of a contract can be established, for example, if the parties are behaving as though there is an agreement [§2-204(1)]. For instance, if A is delivering widgets and B is paying for them, the natural implication is that A and B have a contract for the sale of widgets.

A contract can be enforced even though the exact moment that the contract came into existence is undetermined [§2-204(2)]. For example, if C and D have sent a number of letters back and forth, the determination of which letter was the offer and which was the acceptance is unimportant if C and D are behaving as though there is a contract. The terms of the contract can be determined from the various letters.

In the following case, one of the parties argued that there was no contract because there was no single document that set forth the parties' agreement. The court had to determine whether or not there was a contract.

**SALT RIVER PROJECT AGRICULTURAL IMPROVEMENT & POWER DISTRICT
v. WESTINGHOUSE ELECTRIC CORP.**
37 U.C.C. Rptg. Serv. 75 (Ariz. 1983)

[In 1973, the plaintiff, Salt River Project Agricultural Improvement & Power District (SRP), purchased a local maintenance controller (LMC), a device to be used on a gas turbine unit previously purchased from Westinghouse. SRP was the second largest electric utility in Arizona. In 1976, an explosion and fire caused by a malfunction in the LCM damaged the turbine. SRP sued Westinghouse for the damage to the turbine, alleging a breach of warranty covering the LMC. Westinghouse defended on the grounds that its contract had disclaimed liability for such damage. The trial court ruled in favor of Westinghouse. On appeal, SRP argued that the parties had never entered into an agreement about who should bear the risk if the LMC malfunctioned. The court had to determine the existence and the nature of the contract between the two parties.]

CORCORAN, [Judge]

This is an appeal from a . . . judgment entered in favor of appellee Westinghouse Electric Corporation. . . . We affirm.

The sale of the LMC was documented in part by SRP's "Purchase Order" and Westinghouse's "Acknowledgment." Paragraph 1 of the "Terms and Conditions of [SRP's] Purchase Order" states:

> This Purchase Order becomes a binding contract, subject to the terms and conditions hereof, upon receipt by Buyer at its Purchasing Department of the acknowledgment copy hereof, signed by Seller, or upon commencement of the performance by Seller, whichever occurs first. *Acceptance of this Purchase Order must be made on its exact terms and if additional or different terms are proposed by Seller such response will constitute a counter-offer,* and no contract shall come into existence without Buyer's written assent to the counter-offer. Buyer's acceptance of or payment for material shipped shall constitute acceptance of such material subject to the provisions herein, only, and shall not constitute acceptance of any counter-offer by Seller not assented to in writing. [Emphasis added.]

Westinghouse's "Acknowledgment" states:

> YOUR ORDER HAS BEEN ENTERED AS OUR GENERAL ORDER (GO) NUMBER AS SHOWN ABOVE. . . . SEE REVERSE SIDE FOR TERMS AND CONDITIONS
>
> [Reverse Side]
> TERMS AND CONDITIONS
> The conditions stated below shall take precedence over any conditions which may appear on your standard form, and no provisions or condition of such form except as expressly stated herein, shall be binding on Westinghouse. . . .

Anticipating this court's findings that the provisions of the Westinghouse Acknowledgment control as the contract, SRP argues that . . . [t]he parties never executed a single document setting forth all the terms of

their agreement, never resolved the inconsistencies between SRP's Purchase Order and Westinghouse's Acknowledgment, and never agreed to a risk allocation with respect to . . . defect. . . .

We have reviewed the commercial setting in which the transaction in this case took place. . . .

[§2-204] provides:

> (1) A contract for sale of goods may be made in any manner sufficient to show agreement, including conduct by both parties which recognizes the existence of such a contract.
> (2) An agreement sufficient to shown a contract for sale may be found even though the moment of its making is undetermined.
> (3) Even though one or more terms are left open the contract for sale does not fail for indefiniteness if the parties have intended to make a contract and there is a reasonably certain basis for giving an appropriate remedy.

Thus, we find no support in the Uniform Commercial Code for SRP's argument that a contract under the UCC cannot arise upon the exchange of documents and conduct of the parties until and unless the parties have engaged in all negotiations necessary, and until and unless that parties sign a single integrated document containing all of the agreed terms and provisions inside its four corners. Furthermore, we find that SRP and Westinghouse *did in fact* "negotiate the risks to be allocated to each [party]." The sequence of events leading up to the sale of the LMC was as follows:

1. SRP sent a Purchase Order to Westinghouse in which SRP said, in effect, that it must have full warranties on the LMC product, that Westinghouse may not limit either warranties or its liability, and that if Westinghouse proposed additional or different terms than those contained in SRP's Purchase Order, Westinghouse's proposal would constitute a counter-offer.

2. Westinghouse replied to the SRP offer by sending to SRP its Acknowledgment. In bold face type the Westinghouse Acknowledgment states, in essence, that Westinghouse would sell the LMC only on its terms and conditions, and thus, gave notice of objection to SRP's terms.

3. SRP received the Westinghouse Acknowledgment and did not object to its terms. Instead, SRP received delivery of the LMC; permitted it to

be installed at the . . . power plant; paid for the LMC and used it for more than two years.

While SRP may be operating under the subjective belief that the exchange of documents in this case did not constitute negotiation, this court must look to the objective conduct of the parties—SRP made an offer to purchase the LMC, Westinghouse made a counter-offer concerning the purchase, and SRP, without protest, accepted the terms of that counter-offer by accepting the delivery of the LMC unit and by paying for it.

The judgment of the trial court is affirmed.

CASE REVIEW QUESTIONS

1. Why is Westinghouse's "Acknowledgment" an offer?
2. What effect does Westinghouse's "Acknowledgment" have on SRP's "Purchase Order"?
3. What actions by SRP and Westinghouse indicate the existence of a contract?
4. At what precise point was the contract made? Does it matter?
5. What could SRP have done to have prevented Westinghouse's terms from controlling?

Course of Dealing, Usage of Trade, and Course of Performance If an agreement between parties is vague or if certain terms are not even discussed, a court can look to the actions of the parties or of the industry to supply the missing terms.

Course of dealing refers to the conduct of the same parties in previous transactions between them, which indicates that they have a common understanding concerning the terms of their agreement [§1-205(1)]. For example, suppose that a restaurant owner has telephoned a frozen food dealer every Monday for a year and said, "Send over some french fries." Each week the dealer has delivered five cases of french fries, and each time the restaurant has accepted and paid for them. Then one day, after ordering the french fries in the usual way, the restaurant owner refuses to accept delivery of them, claiming that there was no contract because "send over some french fries" is too vague an agreement for a court to enforce. Under the Code, a court could look to the parties' course of dealing (their actions over the past year) and find a reasonably certain basis for deciding that the parties had a contract for the purchase and sale of five cases of french fries.

Usage of trade refers to a practice or method of dealing so common in a particular business that it can be expected to be part of the parties' agreement even though they have not expressly included it [§1-205(2)]. For example, suppose the frozen food dealer and the restaurant owner said nothing about the price to be paid for the french fries when the first order was made. If it is customary when buying and selling frozen foods for the price to be the retail market price on the day that the goods are delivered, usage of trade will determine that the price for the french fries will be the retail market price on the day they are delivered.

Course of performance refers to conduct by the parties under a single contract that involves repeated acts by either party when the other party has knowledge of those acts and an opportunity to object to them. Any conduct during the course of performance that is accepted without objection is treated as being part of the parties' agreement even though it is not expressly included in the contract [§2-208]. For example, suppose the frozen food dealer and the restaurant owner enter into a year-long agreement that calls for the dealer to deliver french fries each week but says nothing about the day delivery is to be made. Each week for six months, the dealer delivers on Tuesday. If the restaurant owner suddenly demands delivery on Monday, the dealer can say that the delivery day is Tuesday even though the parties never expressly agreed to a day for delivery. The results would be the same even if the contract called for a Monday delivery but the restaurant owner had always accepted the Tuesday deliveries without objection.

In the case that follows, the parties disputed whether a particular charge made by the seller had been agreed to by the parties in their contract. The seller argued that the charge had been expressly agreed to by the buyer and that, even if it had not been expressly agreed to, it was a part of their agreement because of course of dealing, usage of trade, and course of performance.

LOIZEAUX BUILDERS SUPPLY CO. v. DONALD B. LUDWIG CO.
366 A.2d 721 (N.J. 1976)

[Loizeaux Builders Supply Company (plaintiff), a concrete supplier, brought a legal action against Donald B. Ludwig Company (defendant), a general contractor, to collect an amount allegedly due for concrete deliveries. One of the items making up the total amount claimed to be due was a $79.18 "less than truckload" charge that was imposed when less than a full truckload was delivered.]

DREIER, [Judge]

On or about February 13, 1973, plaintiff, a concrete supplier, contracted with defendant for the sale and delivery of concrete for use by defendant, a general contractor, at the "Smith Transport job" in Woodbridge, N.J. The initial contract terms were agreed to over the telephone. Mr. Krause, plaintiff's vice-president in charge of production, testified that he notified defendant's president, Donald B. Ludwig, of the price

defendant would be charged per cubic yard of concrete, and further alerted defendant to the additional "usual" charges that would be imposed if [necessary].

The testimony of the parties also indicates that the deliveries ran through March 1974. The routine procedure was for defendant to call plaintiff and order a specified number of cubic yards of concrete . . . such orders would then be delivered to defendant's job site in plaintiff's trucks. Defendant was billed on the tenth, twentieth and thirtieth of each month by invoices. . . .

Donald Ludwig testified that he did not consider himself bound in any way to order his supplies from plaintiff. He felt no obligation to deal exclusively with plaintiff but rather stated that if a supplier at a lower price had come to his attention, he could have dealt with it instead of plaintiff. Krause agreed that defendant could have bought its supply of concrete elsewhere. Accordingly, the relationship between the parties is best characterized as a series of separate contracts, with the added element that several of the contract terms related back to the parties' original agreement.

With respect to the . . . disputed [less than truckload charge], defendant, while acknowledging these charges to be customary, maintains that they were not specifically agreed to at the outset, and therefore were not a part of the contract. This was strenuously denied by plaintiff.

Defendant's position is untenable for two reasons. First, it assumes the existence of a single . . . contract which, as noted above, did not exist. . . . But even if defendant's version of the original conversation were [accepted] by this court, defendant was alerted to these additional charges at the time he received his first invoice from plaintiff, which contained an itemization of these additional charges. If defendant disagreed with these charges, it was free to cease ordering its supplies from plaintiff [§2-208(1)].

In addition, the disputed charges were established by plaintiff to be subject of an industry-wide pricing policy, which may be recognized by the court as relevant in determining the meaning of the agreements between the parties. These charges being customary in the trade strongly corroborates plaintiff's version of the initial negotiation between the parties. The court is mindful that it should not undertake to write a contract for the parties. Where, however, it is evidence that the parties intended to contract, it is within the province of the court to construe the terms of their contract consistent with a result that is fair and just [§2-204]. The construction including recognized additional charges accomplishes that end. The "less than truckload" charge falls within the category of usual charges for which defendant is responsible.

Accordingly, judgment will be entered for plaintiff. . . .

CASE REVIEW QUESTIONS

1. In what ways, if at all, did the court use the concepts of course of dealing, usage of trade, and course of performance in concluding that the "less than truckload" charge was included in the parties' agreement?
2. On what basis could the court have found the existence of one or more contracts?
3. On what basis did the court find that there was a series of contracts?
4. Does the existence of several contracts have an impact upon whether the court is actually applying the concept of course of dealing or course of performance?

Open Terms If it is determined that the parties have entered into a contract but have failed to include certain terms in the agreement that cannot be supplied by application of course of dealing, usage of trade, or course of performance, the Code provides several terms that can be used to fill in terms that have been left open. The following materials discuss these terms, which are sometimes referred to as gap-fillers.

Price Sometimes a buyer and a seller may not agree upon a price. They may simply neglect to determine a price from the start, or they may be unable to agree on a price even though they earnestly desire to do business. If they are unable to agree on a price, they may agree that the price is to be fixed by the market or by a third party, or they may decide to agree to a price at a later date. Whenever no price is agreed to or the agreed upon method (market or third party) fails to fix the price due to unforeseen circumstances, the Code provides that the price is a reasonable price at the time of delivery [§2-305(1)].

If one of the parties wrongfully interferes with the method agreed upon for determining the price, say, by refusing to cooperate in naming the third party to fix the price, the other party has the choice of canceling the contract or fixing a reasonable price himself or herself [§2-305(3)]. On the other hand, if the parties' intent is that there is no contract unless a price is agreed to or fixed by an agreed upon method, there is no contract unless the price is actually agreed to or fixed by that agreed upon method [§2-305(4)].

Place for Delivery If the buyer and the seller do not specify the place for delivery, the place is the seller's place of business if he or she has one; otherwise, it is the seller's home [§2-308(a)]. Accordingly, if A agrees to buy five bushels of ripe tomatoes from farmer B but the parties do not say anything about where the tomatoes are to be delivered, A must go to B's farm to pick them up unless the custom in the area is that farmers deliver to their customers. If there is no such custom and B refuses to deliver the tomatoes to A's home, B has not breached the contract because B has no obligation to deliver to A's home. The place for delivery is B's farm.

If the parties contract for the sale of specified, existing goods and they know where the goods are located, the place for delivery is the location of the goods when the contract is made [§2-308(b)]. For example, if C agrees at a meeting in New York City to buy D's yacht, which C and D know is located at Martha's Vineyard, the place for delivery is Martha's Vineyard.

Time of Performance If the parties neglect to agree upon a time for delivery of goods or for performing any other action required in the contract, the Code declares that the delivery or the performance of the other action shall be done within a reasonable time [§2-309(1)]. What constitutes a reasonable time is a judgment that must be made in light of all of the circumstances of the particular case. The underlying principle is that the parties must perform within a time that is commercially acceptable given the nature, purpose, and circumstances of the action to be taken. For example, if A and farmer B have not agreed on the time for delivery for the tomatoes, A must pick up the tomatoes when they are ripe. It would be unreasonable for A to pick them up six weeks later and then complain that they are rotten.

Duration of Agreement If a contract calls for a series of actions, such as a series of deliveries by the seller, but the parties have not agreed as to how long the actions are to continue, the parties are bound to continue the actions for a reasonable time. Either party may terminate the agreement at any time [§2-309(2)]. However, notice of termination must be given sufficiently in advance of the actual termination to allow the other party a reasonable amount of time to make other arrangements [§2-309(3)].

Shipping Arrangements If a contract calls for the shipping of goods and the parties have not agreed on shipping arrangements, the seller may make the necessary arrangements. In doing so, he or she must act in good faith and in a commercially reasonably manner [§2-311(1) and (2) and §2-504].

Assortment of Goods If the parties have not agreed on the assortment of goods, the buyer may determine the assortment [§2-311(2)]. For example, if the parties have agreed to buy and sell 100 widgets but have not agreed on color and the widgets come in several different colors, the buyer may choose how many widgets of each color are to be sent. He or she could pick 50 blue, 25 red, and 25 green, for instance. The selection must be made in good faith and within the limits set by commercial reasonableness. For example, if the widgets only come in sealed packages of 50, it may be unreasonable for the buyer to demand that two packages be broken apart in order to get 25 red widgets and 25 green ones.

Time of Payment If the parties do not agree on when the seller is to make payment, payment is due at the time and the place where the buyer is to receive the goods [§2-310]. In the following case, the parties had not agreed on the time for payment. One of the parties argued that this failure to agree resulted in no contract being formed.

SOUTHWEST ENGINEERING COMPANY v. MARTIN TRACTOR COMPANY
473 P.2d 18 (Kansas 1970)

[Cloepfil, a representative of Southwest Engineering Company (Southwest), the plaintiff, and Hurt, a representative of Martin Tractor Company (Martin), the defendant, met in Springfield to discuss the purchase by Southwest of a generator from Martin. Hurt gave Cloepfil a written memorandum quoting a price of $21,500 for the generator. Southwest accepted the offer to sell at $21,500, but Martin refused to deliver a generator. Southwest bought a generator from another company for $27,541 and brought an action to collect $6,041 from Martin for breach of contract. The trial court entered judgment for plaintiff. Defendant appealed.]

FOXTRON, Justice

The basic disagreement centers on whether the meeting between Hurt and Cloepfil at Springfield resulted in an agreement which was enforceable under the provisions of the Uniform Commercial Code.

It is quite true, as the trial court found, that terms of payment were not agreed upon at the Springfield meeting. Hurt testified that as the memorandum was being made out, he said they wanted 10 percent with the order, 50 percent on delivery and the balance on acceptance, but he did not recall Cloepfil's response. Cloepfil's version was somewhat different. He stated that after the two had shaken hands in the lobby preparing to leave, Hurt had said their terms were 20 percent down and the balance on delivery, while he (Cloepfil) said the way they generally paid was 90 percent on the tenth of the month following delivery and balance on final acceptance. It is obvious the parties reached no agreement on this point.

However, a failure on the part of Messrs. Hurt and Cloepfil to agree on terms of payment would not, of itself, defeat an otherwise valid agreement reached by them. [§2-204(3)] reads:

> Even though one or more terms are left open a contract for sale does not fail for indefiniteness if the parties have intended to make a contract and there is a reasonably certain basis for giving an appropriate remedy.

The Official U.C.C. Comment is enlightening:

> Subsection (3) states the principle as to "open terms." . . . If the parties intend to enter into a binding agreement, this subsection recognizes that agreement as valid in law, despite missing terms, if there is any reasonably certain basis for granting a remedy. The test is not certainty as to what the parties were to do nor as to the exact amount of damages due the plaintiff. Nor is the fact that one or more terms are left to be agreed upon enough of itself to defeat an otherwise adequate agreement. Rather, commercial standards on the point of "indefiniteness" are intended to be applied, this Act making provision elsewhere for missing terms needed for performance, open price, remedies and the like.
>
> The more terms the parties leave open, the less likely it is that they have intended to conclude a binding agreement, but their actions may be frequently conclusive on the matter despite the omissions.

The above Code provision and accompanying Comment were quoted in *Pennsylvania Company v. Wilmington Trust Co.,* where the court made this observation:

> In an article entitled "The Law of Sales in the Proposed Uniform Commercial Code," [the author] wanted to limit omissions to "minor" terms. He wanted "business honor" to be the only compulsion where "important terms" are left open. Nevertheless, his recommendation was rejected. This shows that those drafting the statute intended that the omission of even an important term does not prevent the finding under the statute that the parties intended to make a contract.

So far as the present case is concerned, [§2-310] supplies the omitted term. This statute provides in pertinent part:

> Unless otherwise agreed
>
> (a) payment is due at the time and place at which the buyer is to receive the goods even though the place of shipment is the place of delivery. . . .

In our view the language of the two Code provisions is clear and positive. Considered together, we take the two sections to mean that where parties have reached an enforceable agreement for the sale of goods, but omit therefrom the terms of payment, the law will imply, as part of the agreement, that payment is to be made at the time of delivery.

We do not mean to infer that terms of payment are not important under many circumstances, or that parties may not condition an agreement on their being included. However, the facts before us hardly indicate that Hurt and Cloepfil considered the terms of payment to be significant, or of more than passing interest. Hurt testified that while he stated his terms he did not recall Cloepfil's response, while Cloepfil stated that as the two were on the point of leaving, each stated their usual terms and that was as far as it went. The trial court found that only a brief and casual conversation ensued as to payment, and we think that is a valid summation of what took place.

Moreover, it is worthy of note that Martin first mentioned the omission of the terms of payment, as justifying its breach, in a letter written by [a lawyer] . . . more than four months after memorandum was prepared by Hurt. On prior occasions Martin attributed its cancellation of the Springfield understanding to other causes. . . . In explaining the meaning of the letter to Cloepfil, Hurt said that Martin was doing work for the Corps of Engineers in the Kansas City and Tulsa districts and did not want to take on additional work with them at this time.

The entire circumstances may well give rise to a suspicion that Martin's present insistence that future negotiations were contemplated concerning the terms of payment is primarily an afterthought, for use as an escape hatch. Doubtless the trial court so considered the excuse in arriving at its findings.

The judgment of the trial court is affirmed.

CASE REVIEW QUESTIONS

1. Is there a basis for believing that Southwest Engineering and Martin Tractor had a contract? Explain.
2. Did the court agree with Martin that the terms of their agreement with Southwest Engineering were not certain and definite enough to enforce? Why?
3. The court says that Martin did not raise the issue of the omitted terms of payment until sometime after it had canceled its arrangement with Southwest. What is the relevance of this point?
4. On what basis did the court arrive at a remedy of $6,041?

Unless Otherwise Agreed Provisions In addition to providing specific terms, such as price or payment terms, to fill the gaps left open in order to create a contract, the Code also has a number of provisions that apply to a sales contract if the parties do not agree to different terms. Some of these provisions specify when certain things will happen, such as when goods will be identified as the goods belonging to a contract [§2-501(1)], when risk of loss passes from the seller to the buyer [§2-509], or when title to the goods passes [§2-401]. Other sections provide for the availability of certain remedies [§2-719] or specify certain rights, such as the right to inspect goods [§2-513]. Still others define and discuss the implications of using certain terms, such as the delivery terms (free on board) [§2-319] or COD (cash on delivery) [§2-513(3)(a)].

These "unless otherwise agreed" provisions serve two functions. First, they flesh out the contract between the parties when the parties do not specify how these matters are to be handled. Second, they flag those areas where the parties are free to vary the Code requirements through their own agreements.

Firm Offer

Under traditional contract law, an offer can generally be revoked (withdrawn) any time before it has been accepted unless the offeree (the party to whom the offer was made) gives something of value (consideration) to the offeror (the party making the offer) to keep the offer open. The Code, however, provides for an irrevocable offer, called a *firm offer,* that needs no consideration to be binding. In order for an offer to be a firm offer, all of the following conditions must be met [§2-205]:

1. There must be an offer.
2. The offer must be made by a merchant.
3. The offer must be to buy or sell goods.
4. The offer must be in writing.
5. The writing must be signed by the merchant.
6. The writing must give assurance that the offer will remain open.

If a firm offer states the period of time that it will be held open, it may not be revoked during that period. If no time is stated, a firm offer must be held open for a reasonable time. In any event, however, a firm offer may not be held open for more than three months [§2-205].

Note that only merchants can make firm offers and that they can be made only through the use of a signed writing. The Code, however, provides that a symbol, rather than the traditional handwritten signature, may be used to authenticate a writing [§1-201(39)]. Accordingly, an offer that has simply been typed on a merchant's letterhead may be considered a signed writing. The test is whether the letterhead was intended to authenticate the offer.

Firm Offers in Form Contracts Sometimes a seller of goods will supply its sales people with forms to be used by a buyer for making an offer to purchase the seller's goods. This may be done for a variety of reasons. For instance, the seller may want to achieve some uniformity and to insure that certain terms will appear in all its sales contracts. Also, the seller may not want to be the offeror. If the buyer makes the offer, the seller will then have the opportunity to determine that sufficient goods are on hand to fill the offer. Similarly, if the sale is to be on credit, the seller will have time to check the credit rating of the buyer before accepting the offer and forming a contract.

Because a buyer in this type of situation would be unlikely to be familiar with the seller's form, the Code specifies that a buyer cannot make a firm offer unless the buyer separately signs the provision that assures that the offer will remain open [§2-205]. Thus, for a buyer (offeror) to make a firm offer to a seller (offeree) on the seller's form, there must be a separate signature line near the firm-offer provision that the buyer must sign. This requirement prevents the seller turning the buyer's offer into a firm offer without the buyer's knowledge. While the buyer–offeror model just discussed is the most common, the rule also applies to a buyer prepared contract form on which the seller makes the offer. Of course, in either situation, the offeror must be a merchant in order for a firm offer to be created.

Acceptance by Proper Means

When an offer is accepted, it is sometimes important to know whether it was accepted by an authorized means. If an offer expressly stipulates that there is only one means of acceptance, such as a response by registered mail, that exclusive means must be used in order for the acceptance to be effective (see page 188). The Code does nothing to change this rule.

Even if an offer does not require an exclusive means of acceptance, the use of an authorized means of acceptance is still significant. If an authorized means of acceptance is used, the acceptance is effective when it is dispatched. On the other hand, if the means used to accept is not authorized, the acceptance is not effective until it is received by the offeror (see page 193).

Whether an acceptance becomes effective when it is dispatched or when it is received will usually not be important. It becomes important, for instance, when the offeror revokes the offer between the time the acceptance is dispatched and the time it is received.

For example, suppose that A makes an offer to B. B accepts by mail and deposits the acceptance in a mailbox. Before the acceptance is received, A tells B that the offer is revoked. If the acceptance was effective when it was dispatched — that is, when it was placed in the mailbox — it is too late for A to revoke the offer and the parties have a contract. However, if the acceptance will not be effective until it is received by A, the revocation of the offer occurred before acceptance and the parties do not have a contract.

Under traditional contract law, the courts have said that the authorized means of communicating an acceptance are (1) any means expressly authorized by the offeror, (2) the means used by the offeror to communicate the offer, and (3) any other means customary where and when the offer was received. For sales contracts, the Code has added to this list any means that is reasonable under the circumstances [§2-206(1)(a)].

Unilateral and Bilateral Acceptances

How should a seller accept an offer to buy goods then the offer asks for prompt or immediate shipment? Should the seller accept the offer by promising to ship the goods and thereby create a bilateral contract, or should the seller accept simply by shipping the goods and thereby create a unilateral contract? (See page 184.)

The Code states that an offer can be accepted in any manner that is reasonable under the circumstances unless the offeror expresses an unambiguous intent to enter into either a unilateral or a bilateral contract [§2-201(1)(b)]. Therefore, an order asking for the prompt shipment of goods can be accepted either by a prompt promise to ship the goods or by actual prompt shipment of the goods.

Even a shipment of goods that do not conform to the terms of the offer constitutes an acceptance, which makes the shipper-seller liable for breach of the contract that has just been created. A seller who ships nonconforming goods can avoid making a contract, however, by notifying the buyer that shipment is made only to accommodate the buyer [§2-206(1)(b)].

For example, suppose that A orders 500 blue widgets, Model No. 2873, from B. B is out of Model No. 2873 but has a supply of Model No. 2874, which is a darker shade of blue. If B ships 500 Model No. 2874 widgets without notifying the buyer that the shipment is being made only to accommodate the buyer, B will have accepted the offer and A can recover damages, if there are any, caused by B's failure to deliver the proper goods. As we will see in Chapter 23, B may have an opportunity *to cure,* that is, to send the correct Model No. 2873 widgets, if A rejects Model No. 2874. If, however, B notifies A that the shipment is only an accommodation, then B is, in effect, only making an offer to sell A 500 Model No. 2874 widgets.

Acceptance Varying the Terms of an Offer

Under traditional contract law, the parties must be in complete agreement concerning all the important terms of the contract. Unless and until complete agreement is reached, no contract is formed and the promises of the parties are therefore not enforceable (see page 183).

For example, suppose that Alpha Company sends a purchase order form to

Beta Company ordering 50 television sets. Alpha's form contains numerous detailed provisions concerning the sale. Beta accepts Alpha's order by sending an acceptance on Beta's own form, which also contains numerous detailed provisions concerning the sale. Do Alpha and Beta *believe* that they have a contract at this point? In all probability, they do. But, under traditional contract law, there is no contract if any of the material terms on Beta's form do not match those on Alpha's form, which is likely to be the case, because Alpha and Beta have not agreed on all of the important terms of the contract. Instead, traditional law would hold that Beta has made a counter-offer. Thus, not only would there be no acceptance and therefore no contract, but Beta's counter-offer would also operate as a rejection that would terminate Alpha's offer.

This problem, sometimes called "the battle of the forms," is dealt with by the Code. It provides that any communication that contains a definite expression of acceptance *is an acceptance* even though it contains terms in addition to or different from the terms of the offer, unless the communication expressly states that it is an acceptance only if the offeror agrees to the additional or different terms [§2-207(1)]. Under the Code, therefore, Alpha and Beta would have a contract, just as they believe.

There is still the question, though, of what the terms of the contract are. The additional terms — that is, those terms in Beta's acceptance that were not in Alpha's offer — become proposals or offers for additions to the contract [§2-207(2)]. The law is not clear, however, as to what happens to the terms in Alpha's and Beta's forms that conflict. For example, suppose Alpha's form says that payment is due ten days after delivery whereas Beta's form says that payment is to be made upon delivery. There are two ways to deal with the situation. First, the conflicting terms might be dropped from the contract and replaced in accordance with the Code's provisions for missing terms. Second, the terms of the offer can control. You should be aware, though, that even the leading legal scholars do not agree on which solution is preferable.*

If Alpha and Beta are both merchants, the additional terms in Beta's form — that is, the proposals for additions to the contract — become a part of the contract unless (1) the offer (Alpha's form) expressly limits acceptance to the terms of the offer, or (2) the additions materially alter the offer, or (3) the offeror (Alpha) objects to the additional terms within a reasonable time [§2-207(2)]. If either Alpha or Beta is not a merchant, the additional terms can only be proposals for additions to the contract. They do not become terms of the contract unless they are actually agreed to by the offeror.

In a battle of the forms situation between merchants, an important question is often whether or not an additional term is material. If it is material, the offeror need not object in order for the term to be excluded from the contract. If the term is not material, however, failure to object to it will result in the term becoming a part of the contract. In the following case, the parties to the contract are both merchants who have engaged in a battle of the forms. The court must decide whether or not an additional term in the acceptance became a part of the contract. The offeror had not objected to the additional term.

* White and Summers, *Uniform Commercial Code,* 2nd ed., West Publishing Co., 1980, pp. 27–31.

MARLENE INDUSTRIES CORP. v. CARNAC TEXTILES, INC.
380 N.E.2d 239 (N.Y. 1978)

[Marlene Industries Corporation (Marlene) entered into a contract with Carnac Textiles, Inc. (Carnac), under which Marlene was to purchase certain fabrics from Carnac. In negotiating the contract, the parties did not expressly discuss the method by which disputes about the contract would be resolved.

When a dispute about the contract arose between the parties, Carnac sought to take the dispute to arbitration, a method of resolving conflict through the use of a private, unofficial person rather than a court. Marlene went to court and requested that the court issue a stay (an order) forbidding Carnac from taking the case to arbitration.

The trial court denied the stay, and an intermediate appellate court affirmed. Marlene then appealed to the Court of Appeals, the highest New York State court.]

GABRIELLI, [Judge]

This appeal involves yet another of the many conflicts which arise as a result of the all too common business practice of blithely drafting, sending, receiving, and filing unread numerous purchase orders, acknowledgments, and other diverse forms containing a myriad of discrepant terms. Both parties agree that they have entered into a contract for the sale of goods; indeed, it would appear that there is no disagreement as to most of the essential terms of their contract. They do disagree, however, as to whether their agreement includes a provision for the arbitration of disputes arising from the contract.

The dispute between the parties, insofar as it is relevant on this appeal, is founded upon an alleged breach by Marlene of a contract to purchase certain fabrics from . . . Carnac. The transaction was instituted when Marlene orally placed an order for the fabrics with Carnac. Neither party contends that any method of dispute resolution was discussed at that time. Almost immediately thereafter, Marlene sent Carnac a "purchase order" and Carnac sent Marlene an "acknowledgment of order." Marlene's form did not provide for arbitration, . . . Carnac's form, on the

other hand, contained an arbitration clause placed in the midst of some 13 lines of small type "boilerplate" [standard, printed contract provisions]. When a dispute subsequently arose, Carnac sought arbitration, and Marlene moved for a stay.

This case presents a classic example of the "battle of the forms," and its solution is to be derived by reference to [§2-207] of the Uniform Commercial Code, which is specifically designed to resolve such disputes.

Subdivision (2) of [§2-207] is applicable to cases such as this, in which there is a consensus that a contract exists, but disagreement as to what terms have been included in that contract. Subdivision (1) of [§2-207] was intended to abrogate the harsh "mirror-image" rule of common law, pursuant to which any deviation in the language of a purported acceptance from the exact terms of the offer transformed that "acceptance" into a counter-offer and thus precluded contract formation on the basis of those two documents alone. Under subdivision (1) of [§2-207], however, an acceptance containing additional terms will operate as an acceptance unless it is "expressly made conditional on assent to the additional or different terms." Having thus departed from the common law doctrine, it became necessary for the Code to make some provision as to the effect upon the contract of such additional terms in an acceptance. Subdivision (2) was designed to deal with that problem.

Before continuing, we would note that the section speaks of both acceptance and written confirmations. It is thus intended to include at least two distinct situations: one in which the parties have reached a prior oral contract, and any writing serves only as confirmation of that contract; and one in which the prior dealings of the parties did not comprise actual formation of a contract, and the writings themselves serve as offer and/or acceptance. In either case, the writing or writings may contain additional terms, and in either case the effect of such additional terms under the Code is the same. Thus, on this appeal, since the prior discussions of the parties did not reach the question of dispute resolution, it is necessary to determine whether those discussions rose to the level of contract formation, or whether no contract was created until the exchange of forms. Therefore, whether Marlene's form is an offer and Carnac's an acceptance, or whether both are mere confirmations of an existing oral contract, the result in this case is the same, and that result is dependent upon the operation of [§2-207(2)].

The parties to this dispute are certainly merchants, and the arbitration clause is clearly a proposed additional term. . . . As such, it became a part of the contract unless one of the three listed exceptions in [§2-207(2)(b)] is applicable. We hold that the inclusion of an arbitration agreement materially alters a contract for the sale of goods, and thus, pursuant to [§2-207(2)(b)], it will not become a part of such a contract unless both parties explicitly agree to it.

It has long been the rule in this State that the parties to commercial transaction "will not be held to have chosen arbitration as the forum for the resolution of their disputes in the absence of an express, unequivo-cal agreement to that effect; absent such an explicit commitment neither party may be compelled to arbitrate. . . ." The reason for this requirement, quite simply, is that by agreeing to arbitrate a party waives in large part many of his normal rights under the procedural and substantive law of the State, and it would be unfair to infer such a significant waiver on the basis of anything less than a clear indication of intent. . . .

Since an arbitration agreement in the context of a commercial transaction "must be clear and direct, and must not depend upon implication . . . [its] existence . . . should not depend solely upon the conflicting fine print of commercial forms which cross one another but never meet. . . ." Applying these principles to this case, we conclude that the contract between Marlene and Carnac does not contain an arbitration clause; hence, the motion to permanently stay arbitration should have been granted.

Accordingly, the order appealed from should be reversed.

CASE REVIEW QUESTIONS

1. How could Marlene have avoided the costly and lengthy litigation to prevent arbitration of the dispute with Carnac?
2. Is it relevant in the case that both Marlene and Carnac are merchants? Why?
3. Why did the court decide that the inclusion of an arbitration clause was a material alteration of the contract?
4. Suppose that the use of arbitration were the accepted and nearly universal practice in the textile industry. Would the outcome of the case have been different?

FAIRNESS IN THE BARGAINING PROCESS

The Uniform Commercial Code was instrumental in bringing the concept of *unconscionability* into the prominent position it now holds in contract law. The Code provides in §2-301:

(1) If the court as a matter of law finds the contract or any clause of the contract to have been unconscionable at the time it was made, the court may refuse to enforce the contract, or it may enforce the remainder of the contract without the unconscionable clause, or it may so limit the application of any unconscionable clause as to avoid any unconscionable result.

(2) When it is claimed or appears to the court that the contract or any clause thereof may be unconscionable the parties shall be afforded a reasonable opportunity to present evidence as to its commercial setting, purpose and effect to aid the court in making the determination.

Because the concept of unconscionability is now applied by the courts to all contracts, it is explained and discussed fully in Chapter 10 (see pages 207–212).

EXCLUSIVE DEALING ARRANGEMENTS

Sometimes a buyer and a seller enter into a contract that provides for **exclusive dealing,** which means that the buyer promises to buy from no one but the seller or the seller promises to sell to no one but the buyer. In such situations, the question arises of whether the person who receives such a promise has received anything of value. Neither party is actually obligated to do anything. The buyer may decide not to buy anything from the seller or anyone else, and the seller may never have anything to sell. Because neither party is obligated, there is no consideration to support the promise.

Suppose, for example, that a manufacturer (seller) awards an exclusive distribution franchise to a wholesaler (buyer). In return, the wholesaler promises to buy stereo systems from the manufacturer, but no quantity is mentioned. Is the buyer's promise supported by consideration? The wholesaler might argue that the manufacturer's promise has no value because it is only a promise for an exclusive distribution franchise. It is not a promise to make and sell any stereos. If the manufacturer stops manufacturing and selling stereos, of what value is the exclusive dealership?

The Code provides that if a buyer and a seller promise to deal exclusively with one another, the seller has a duty to use his or her best efforts to supply the goods and the buyer has a duty to use his or her best efforts to promote the sale of the goods [§2-306(2)]. In other words, the manufacturer in our example cannot arbitrarily shut down operations. Instead, the manufacturer must use his or her best efforts to supply the stereos. This makes the manufacturer's promise valuable, which provides consideration for the wholesaler's promise and binds the parties to a contract.

Output and Requirements Contracts

Output contracts and **requirements contracts** also provide for a type of exclusive dealing. These contracts serve a useful purpose in the commercial community. A manufacturer may seek an output contract to insure that there is a buyer for all the goods produced by his or her factory. Similarly, a buyer, who wishes to insure that he or she has a steady supply of materials may seek a requirements contract. For example, a candy producer may enter into a contract with a sugar seller whereby the sugar seller will provide all the sugar the candy producer will need for a year. This type of contract assures the candy producer of a supply of sugar at fixed prices, though it does allow some leeway in the event that candy sales increase or decrease during the year.

Under traditional contract law, output and requirements contracts were considered to be unenforceable for several reasons. For one thing, the promises were said to be illusory (an illusion) or lacking in mutuality. Because no one promised to produce (output) or to need (require) anything, there was no promise that could be enforced. In addition, these contracts, by their very nature, do not specify a quantity.

Under the Code, an output or requirements contract is enforceable even though, by definition, the parties have not agreed on an exact quantity of goods to be sold. The Code provides that the quantity to be sold is the amount of actual output or actual requirements that may occur, as long as the party manufacturing the output or needing the requirements acts in good faith. In no case, however, is there an agreement to sell an amount unreasonably different from an express estimate in the contract or, if there is no estimate, unreasonably different from any normal or comparable output or requirements [§2-306(1)]. Under the Code, the promise is no longer illusory or lacking in mutuality because the parties must produce the goods in good faith or must exercise good faith in creating needs.

In the following case, the producer of goods who had an output contract stopped producing. The court had to determine whether or not the producer acted in good faith.

FELD v. HENRY S. LEVY & SONS, INC.
335 N.E.2d 320 (N.Y. 1975)

[Feld, the plaintiff, operated a business known as the Crushed Toast Company, and Henry S. Levy & Sons, Inc. (Levy), the defendant, is engaged in the wholesale bread baking business. The parties entered into a written contract dated June 19, 1968, in which Levy agreed to sell and Feld agreed to purchase "all bread crumbs produced by the Seller in its factory at 115 Thames Street, Brooklyn, New York, during the period commencing June 19, 1968, and terminating June 18, 1969." The agreement was to "be deemed automatically renewed thereafter for successive renewal periods of one year," with either party having the right to cancel by giving not less than six month's notice to the other by certified mail. No notice of cancellation was served, but Levy stopped producing bread crumbs. Feld sued for damages. The trial court ruled in favor of Feld but required a trial on the amount of damages. Both parties appealed.]

COOKE, Judge

Interestingly, the term "bread crumbs" does not refer to crumbs that may flake off bread; rather, they are a manufactured item, starting with stale or imperfectly appearing loaves and following by removal of labels, processing through the grinders, the second of which effects a finer granulation, insertion into a drum in an oven for toasting and, finally, bagging of the finished product.

Subsequent to the making of the agreement, a substantial quantity of bread crumbs, said to be over 250 tons, were sold by defendant to plaintiff but defendant stopped crumb production on about May 15, 1969.

There was proof by defendant's comptroller that the oven was too large to accomodate the drum, that it was stated that the operation was "very uneconomical," but after said date of cessation no steps were taken to obtain more economical equipment. The toasting oven was . . . completely dismantled in the summer of 1969. . . . It appears, without dispute, that defendant indicated to plaintiff at different times that the former would resume bread crumb production if the contract price of 6 cents per pound be changed to 7 cents, and also that, after the crumb making machine was dismantled, defendant sold the raw materials used in making crumbs to animal food manufacturers.

Defendant contends that the contract did not require defendant to manufacture bread crumbs, but merely to sell those it did, and, since none were produced after the demise of the oven, there was no duty to then deliver and, consequently from then on, no liability on its part. Agreements to sell all the goods or services a party may produce or perform to another party are commonly referred to as "output" contracts and they usually serve a useful commercial purpose in minimizing the burdens of product marketing. The Uniform Commercial Code rejects the ideas that an output contract is lacking in mutuality or that it is unenforceable because of indefiniteness in that a quantity for the term is not specified. Official Comment 2 to [§2-306] states in part:

> Under this Article, a contract for output . . . is not too indefinite since it is held to mean the actual good faith output . . . of the particular party. Nor does such a contract lack mutuality of obligation since, under this section, the party who will determine quantity is required to operate his plant or conduct his business in good faith and according to commercial standards of fair dealing in the trade so that his output . . . will proximate a reasonably foreseeable figure.

The real issue in this case is whether the agreement carries with it an implication that defendant was obligated to continue to manufacture bread crumbs for the full term. [§2-306] of the Uniform Commercial Code, entitled "Output, Requirements and Exclusive Dealing" provides:

> (1) A term which measures the quantity by the output of the seller or the requirements of the buyer means such actual output or requirements as may occur in good faith, except that no quantity unreason-

ably disproportionate to any stated estimate or in the absence of a stated estimate to any normal or otherwise comparable prior output or requirements may be tendered or demanded.

> (2) *A lawful agreement* by either the seller or the buyer *for exclusive dealing* in the kind of goods concerned *imposes* unless otherwise agreed an obligation *by the seller to use best efforts to supply the goods* and by the buyer to use best efforts to promote their sale. [Emphasis supplied.]

The Official Comment thereunder reads in part:

> Subsection (2), on exclusive dealing, makes explicit the commercial rule embodied in this Act under which the parties to such contracts are held to have impliedly, even when not expressly, bound themselves to use reasonable diligence as well as good faith in their performance of the contract. . . . An exclusive dealing agreement brings into play all of the good faith aspects of the output and requirement problems of subsection (1).

Under the Uniform Commercial Code, the commercial background and intent must be read into the language of any agreement and good faith is demanded in the performance of that agreement and, under the decisions relating to output contracts, it is clearly the general rule that good faith cessation of production terminates any further obligations thereunder and excuses further performance by the party discontinuing production.

This is not a situation where defendant ceased its main operation of bread baking. Rather, defendant contends in a conclusory fashion that it was "uneconomical" or "economically not feasible" for it to continue to make bread crumbs. . . . The seller's duty to remain in crumb production is a matter calling for a close scrutiny of its motives. . . . It is undisputed that defendant leveled its crumb making machinery only after plaintiff refused to agree to a price higher than that specified in the agreement and that it then sold the raw materials to manufacturers of animal food.

The parties by their contract gave the right of cancellation to either by providing for a six month notice to the other. The apparent purpose of such a stipulation was to provide an opportunity to either the seller or buyer to conclude their dealings in the event that the transactions were not as profitable or advantageous as desired or expected, or for any other reason. Correspondingly, such a notice would also furnish the receiver of it a chance to secure another outlet or source of supply, as the case might be. Short of such a cancellation, defendant was expected to continue to perform in good faith and could cease production of the bread crumbs, a single facet of its operation, only in good faith. Obviously, a bankruptcy or genuine imperiling of the very existence of its entire business caused by the production of the crumbs would warrant cessation of production of that item; the yield of less profit from its sale than expected would not. Since bread crumbs were but a part of defendant's enterprise and since there was a contractual right of cancellation, good faith required continued production until cancellation even if there be no profit.

The order should be affirmed.

CASE REVIEW QUESTIONS

1. What quantity of bread crumbs was Levy obligated to produce? Explain.
2. Why does the court discuss exclusive dealing in conjunction with an output contract?
3. Why can't Levy stop producing bread crumbs?
4. Under what circumstances could Levy stop producing bread crumbs? Explain.

REVIEW QUESTIONS

1. Can a court enforce a contract that is vague or is even missing such terms as the price or delivery date? Explain.
2. Explain when course of dealing, usage of trade, or course of performance would be applicable to a contract?
3. How is price determined if the parties do not agree upon or specify a price in their conract?
4. What is the place for delivery if no place is specified?
5. What is the time for payment if the contract does not specify a time?
6. What elements are necessary to create a firm offer?
7. How can a seller acept an offer that states, "Ship 500 widgets promptly"?
8. What is the effect of a new term being included in a party's acceptance if both parties are merchants? What is the effect if one party is not a merchant?
9. What are the buyer's and seller's obligations in an exclusive dealing contract?

CASE PROBLEMS

1. On April 30, 1971, Don McAfee, who was selling his house and furniture, sent two copies of a letter to Jack Brewer that listed a number of pieces of furniture at specified prices. The letter included a payment schedule calling for $3,000 to be paid on acceptance of the offer, with additional amounts due periodically over the following four months. The letter also contained the following sentence: "If the above is satisfactory please sign and return one copy of the letter with the first payment." The letter contained a blank line for Brewer's signature. Brewer did not sign and return McAfee's letter, but he did send a check for $3,000 along with a letter that read in part: "Enclosing a $3,000 ck. — I've misplaced the contracts. Can secretary send another set? . . . [P]lease include the red secretary [a type of desk] for the entrance foyer." Do McAfee and Brewer have a contract for the sale of the furniture? Does the contract include the red secretary? Explain.

2. Southwestern Stationery wished to purchase a used printing press from Harris Corporation. Harris sent Southwestern a purchase order form with instructions as to how Southwestern should submit its offer. On April 29, 1976, Southwestern filled out the form, signed it, included a check for the down payment, and sent it to Harris. The order form contained the following:

> This order is subject to acceptance by Seller at its home office written herein. Thereupon, Seller shall mail to Purchaser a signed duplicate copy hereof, and the same shall constitute the entire contract between the parties, which shall be changed only by written agreement of the parties.
>
> The banking by Seller or other disposition of funds paid by purchaser to Seller or the disposition by Seller of any trade-in equipment offered by Purchaser to Seller hereunder shall not constitute an acceptance of this order by Seller.

The form also contained a signature block:

> This order is hereby accepted and dated at Seller's Cleveland, Ohio, Office on _____
> HARRIS CORPORATION, a Delaware Corporation, Sheet Fed Press Division,
> By _____

Harris received the purchase order form from Southwestern but never signed it. On June 10, 1976, Harris notified Southwestern that it would be unable to make the sale and returned Southwestern's check. Southwestern purchased a printing press elsewhere and sued Harris for the difference in the price. Who will win the case? Explain.

3. Spartan Grain and Mill Company (Spartan) offered a deal to a number of chicken farmers whereby Spartan promised to buy all the eggs produced by a farmer provided the farmer promised to buy only Spartan feed. A farmer named Ayers accepted Spartan's offer but later backed out. When Spartan brought suit for breach of contract, Ayers argued the contract was not enforceable because it did not specify a price. Ayers believed that the price Spartan charged for its feed was too high. He said, "The product is chicken feed, but the price is not." Spartan argued that, even though its price for feed was greater than that of other feed suppliers, the price was justified because it was part of a marketing package. Spartan pointed out that no other feed supplier agreed to buy the eggs. Who will win the case? Explain.

4. Stop and Shop advertised certain records for sale. When supplies ran out, Stop and Shop issued "rain checks" that read, "This rain check will entitle you to purchase the item listed at today's advertised sale price." The rain checks name the particular recordings, the price, and the date. They were signed by an employee of Stop and Shop. Two weeks later, when the records were again in stock, Stop and Shop refused to honor a customer's rain check. The customer purchased the record elsewhere at a higher price and sued Stop and Shop to recover the difference between the price on the rain check and the price paid elsewhere. Who will win the case? Explain.

5. On April 22, E.A. Coronis, a steel fabricator, wrote the following letter to the Gordon Construction Company, which had solicited bids for a construction project:

> We are please to offer:
>
> All structural steel including steel girts and prulins, both buildings delivered and erected .... $155,413.
> NOTE: This price is predicated on an erected price of 0.1175/lb of steel and we would expect to adjust the price on this basis to conform to actual tonnage of steel used in the project.
>
> Thank you very much for the opportunity to quote.
>
> Very truly yours
>
> C.A. Coronis
> /s/ Arthur C. Pease

Gordon Construction Company was the low bidder and was awarded the construction contract. Gordon did not at that time expressly accept Coronis' offer. In June, Coronis sent Gordon a telegram that read, "Withdrawing our proposal of

April 22nd." Gordon replied by telegram, "We are holding you to your bid of April 22nd." Coronis refused to perform, and Gordon was forced to purchase steel elsewhere. Gordon sued Coronis for breach of contract, arguing that the letter of April 22nd was a firm offer and was not revocable. Who will win the case? Explain.

6. Fox, a retail jeweler doing business in Ohio, sent a purchase order to Baumgold Brothers, Inc., a New York wholesale jeweler, requesting the immediate delivery of a specified small selection of diamonds. An employee of Baumgold filled the order, wrapped the diamonds securely, addressed the package to Fox, and delivered it to the U.S. Postal Service, specifying registered mail and insuring the package. Fox never received the diamonds and refused to pay for them. Baumgold sued for breach of contract. Fox defended on the grounds that there was no contract for sale as Baumgold had never accepted Fox's offer. Who will win the case? Explain.

7. In the previous problem, when Baumgold's employee sent the diamonds, he enclosed a copy of "Baumgold's All Risk Memorandum," which read in part:

> The merchandise is delivered to you at your risk from all hazards, regardless of the cause of the loss of damages. . . . Receipt of the merchandise constitutes your agreement to the foregoing terms. . . .

These terms were in addition to those contained in Fox's purchase order form. However, Baumgold and Fox had done business on the basis of these terms before. When Baumgold sued, Fox argued that Baumgold's acceptance, if there had been one, was conditional on Fox's assent to the additional terms, and he had never assented to them. He also argued that, if there were a contract, Baumgold's additional terms did not become a part of it because they materially altered the terms of the offer. Who will win the case? Explain.

8. Lady Duff-Gordon, a well-known fashion designer and clothing manufacturer, hired Otis F. Wood to market her products for a period of one year. Under their contract, Wood had the exclusive right to sell her designer clothing. Lady Duff-Gordon was to receive 50 percent of all the profits Wood made selling her clothes. During the year, Lady Duff-Gordon entered into another contract with Designer Sales, Ltd., to sell her clothes. Lady Duff-Gordon refused to give Wood 50 percent of the profits from the contract with Designer Sales. Wood sued her for breach of contract. Who will win the case? Explain.

9. Kinsey Cotton Company and Ferguson signed an agreement that read in part:

> The Producer and Seller agrees to sell all the cotton produced by the Producer and Seller during the crop year 1973 on approximately 230 acres situated in Bartow County, Georgia, and Polk County, Georgia.

Ferguson refused to deliver the cotton, arguing that there was no contract. Kinsey sued for breach of contract. Who will win the case? Explain.

10. McCasland and Prather entered into an agreement for the sale of McCasland's business. As part of the contract, Prather agreed to purchase all the brine and fresh water he needed for the operation of the business from McCasland. McCasland sued for breach of contract when Prather failed to purchase any brine or fresh water despite McCasland's repeated requests that he do so. Prather argued that there was no contract because (1) his promise was not supported by consideration and (2) the agreement was not definite and certain since no price was stated for the brine and fresh water and no term was set during which they had to be supplied. Who will win the case? Explain.

21

LOSS AND OWNERSHIP

Once a contract for the sale of goods has been made, the question arises as to what rights the seller and the buyer have in the goods. Prior to the enactment of the Uniform Commercial Code, the rights of the parties were usually determined on the basis of who had title to (ownership of) the goods. The Code, however, determines the rights of the parties on the basis of the rules it has set up for the particular situation rather than on the basis of title. The Code describes the various types of situations that can arise and then specifies what rights the parties have in each situation. For example, the Code deals with such matters as when a buyer has sufficient ownership interest in the goods to be able to obtain insurance and who loses if the goods are destroyed while they are being shipped to the buyer via railroad. The various situations in which questions about rights arise, along with the rules that apply to those situations, will be discussed in this chapter.

IDENTIFICATION OF GOODS TO THE CONTRACT

In order for a buyer to have any rights in goods, the goods must be both existing and identified. Goods that are not both existing and identified are called future goods [§2-105(2)]. When **identification** of the goods occurs is determined by the application of §2-501. The parties to the contract can agree on the time and the manner in which the goods will be identified [§2-501(1)]. Often, however, the parties will not even discuss, much less agree on, the identification of the goods.

For those instances when the parties do not have an agreement concerning identification, the Code describes three situations and tells how and when identification occurs in each situation. First, if the goods already exist and the contract between the parties refers to specific goods, these goods are identified to the contract when the contract is made [§2-501(1)(a)]. For example, if an electronics dealer sells Buyer A a television set Model No. XYZ (Serial No. 357), which has been used as a demonstration model, the buyer is purchasing a specific television set and that set is identified to the contract when the contract is made.

Second, if the goods are future goods—that is, if they do not exist or are not specifically referred to in the contract—the goods will be identified to the contract when they are "shipped, marked or otherwise designated by the seller as the goods to which the contract refers" [§2-501(1)(b)]. For example, if the electronics dealer sells Buyer B a television set Model No. XYZ for delivery in one week and the dealer has 20 Model No. XYZ televisions in the storeroom, a particular television set is identified to the contract when the dealer takes that set off the storage shelf and tags it for Buyer B.

Third, the Code has some very specific rules for crops and unborn young. Crops are generally identified to a contract when they are planted. Unborn young are identified to a contract when they are conceived [§2-501(1)(c)].

Insurable Interest

Once goods are identified to a contract, the buyer has an **insurable interest** in the goods. Upon identification, then, the buyer has a sufficient ownership interest in the goods to obtain insurance to cover any loss he or she may suffer if the goods are damaged. Of course, having an insurable interest is not the same thing as having insurance, but a person cannot obtain insurance unless he or she has an interest that can be insured.

As long as the seller retains title to (ownership of) the goods or a security interest (e.g., a mortgage) in the goods, the seller also has an insurable interest in the goods [§2-501(2)]. Thus, both the buyer and the seller may insure the goods at the same time.

Special Property

The identification of goods to a contract also gives the buyer a right called special property. **Special property** enables a buyer who has paid all or part of the purchase price to obtain the goods from the seller if the seller becomes insolvent (has debts in excess of assets) within ten days after the buyer has made the first payment. However, if the seller becomes insolvent more than ten days after the buyer has made the first payment, the buyer is treated like any other creditor.

The buyer must, of course, pay any unpaid portion of the price in order to obtain the goods [§2-502]. For example, suppose Buyer C makes a downpayment on a television set on Monday. On Tuesday the dealer tags a set for Buyer C, thereby identifying it to the contract. The dealer then becomes insolvent and files for bankruptcy on Friday. Buyer C may obtain the tagged television set if he or she pays the rest of the purchase price.

Buyer C will be able to get the particular television set tagged by the seller even if it is not the model that he or she ordered. Once goods are identified, the buyer acquires both an insurable interest and a special property right in the goods even if they do not conform to the contract [§2-501]. Goods do not conform to a contract when they do not meet the obligations or specifications included in the contract [§2-106(2)].

If the seller has not identified any goods to the contract, a buyer who has paid all or part of the price may identify the goods in the event the seller becomes insolvent. However, the buyer can only identify and obtain goods that conform to the contract [§2-502(2)]. Otherwise, the buyer might be unjustly enriched if he or she could identify and obtain goods that were of better quality than the goods ordered.

RISK OF LOSS

Frequently, a buyer does not take possession of the goods when the contract for sale is made. For instance, the goods may have to be shipped to the buyer or they may remain in a warehouse for some time until the buyer is ready to take possession of them or the goods may remain with the seller until the buyer picks them up at the seller's place of business. If the goods suffer casualty — that is, if they are damaged, lost, or destroyed — before the contract is fully performed, it must be determined whether the seller or the buyer will bear the loss. Traditionally, this question was settled by determining who had title. The logic was based on the idea that the party who owned the goods should suffer the loss.

The Code takes a different approach. The drafters of the Code analyzed the various types of situations in which goods may suffer casualty and established rules for distributing the risk of loss for each situation based upon the interests of the parties in the goods and their ability to control the goods and insure against lost.

Effect of Risk of Loss

When goods suffer casualty and are damaged, lost, or destroyed, the rules concerning the allocation of **risk of loss** determine who loses — the seller or the buyer. Suppose, for example, that a seller and a buyer contract for the sale of 50 television sets for $15,000, but the sets are destroyed in a fire before the buyer takes possession of them. What difference does it make whether the buyer or seller has the risk of loss?

Risk on Buyer If the buyer has the risk of loss when the goods suffer casualty, the buyer must pay the seller the contract price for the goods [§2-709(1)(a)]. The buyer owes the seller $15,000 even though he or she doesn't get the television sets. Thus, the buyer loses because he or she must pay for goods that have little or no value. Of course, if the buyer has insured against this type of loss, he or she can collect from the insurance company.

Risk on Seller If the seller has the risk of loss when the goods suffer casualty, the results depend on whether or not the goods were identified to the contract when the contract was made. If the goods were identified when the contract was made, the contract is void if the goods are totally lost or destroyed. This means that neither the buyer nor the seller have any rights against the other, provided that the casualty to the goods is not the fault of either party [§2-613(a)]. If the identified goods are not totally lost or destroyed, the buyer can inspect the goods and choose either to avoid the contract or to accept the goods with an appropriate reduction in their price [§2-613(b)].

If the goods are not identified to the contract when the contract is made and the seller has the risk of loss when the goods suffer casualty, the seller still has the duty to deliver the goods and will breach the contract if he or she fails to deliver them as promised.

Returning to our example, if the risk of loss of the 50 destroyed television sets is still with the seller, the rights of the buyer will depend on whether or not the television sets were identified to the contract when the contract was formed. If the television sets were not identified to the contract when the contract was formed, the seller still has the duty to deliver 50 television sets to the buyer. The seller, therefore, will have to either obtain other sets to honor the contract or pay damages for breach of contract.

If the television sets were identified to the contract when the contract was made—say, for example, that they were the last 50 sets of a discontinued model—the contract is void and the buyer and seller have no rights against one another. The seller loses because he or she no longer has the 50 television sets, although he or she may be able to recover from an insurance company if the goods were insured.

There is a logical reason for the two different rules when the risk of loss is on the seller. When goods are identified to the contract when the contract is made, the parties understand that the performance of the contract depends on continued existence of the specific goods. If the identified goods are lost or destroyed or damaged, delivery by the seller becomes impossible. Alternatively, when the parties have not contracted for the sale of specific goods, the seller has simply promised to deliver unspecified goods and can still do so even through the goods he or she expected to use to fulfill the promise have been destroyed or damaged.

Who Has the Risk of Loss?

Under the Code, the allocation of risk of loss varies depending on the situation. The simplest situation occurs when the parties actually agree as to when risk of loss will pass from one to the other. If the parties have such an agreement, risk of loss will pass from the seller to the buyer at the time specified in the agreement [§2-509(4)]. The agreement may be made expressly or, as discussed in the previous chapter, it may be implied from trade usage, course of dealing, or course of performance.

For those instances when the parties have not agreed as to when the risk of loss will pass, the Code describes four basic types of situations [§2-509].

1. The seller is a merchant, and the goods are not to be shipped by a carrier nor are they in the hands of a bailee.

2. The seller is a nonmerchant, and the goods are not to be shipped by a carrier nor are they in the hands of a bailee.
3. The goods are to be shipped to the buyer by carrier, and the seller is either a merchant or a nonmerchant.
4. The goods are to be delivered without being moved and are held by a bailee — that is, by a third party who has possession of the goods but does not own them — and the seller is either a merchant or a nonmerchant.

The rules for determining when risk of loss passes from the seller to the buyer in each of these situations are explained and discussed in the following sections of the chapter.

Merchant Seller If a merchant seller is not going to ship the goods to the buyer by a carrier and the goods are not going to remain in the hands of a bailee, the risk of loss passes to the buyer when the buyer actually receives the goods [§2-509(3)]. Goods are received by a buyer when he or she takes physical possession of them [§2-103(1)(c)].

For example, suppose a store delivers a new mattress to a customer's home. The store's delivery person arrives when no one is at home and leaves the mattress on the front porch. At that point, the buyer has not received the goods, and the seller continues to bear the risk of loss for any theft or damage that may occur until someone arrives home and takes physical possession of the mattress.

The following case concerns risk of loss when the seller is a merchant and the buyer is to pick up the goods at the seller's place of business.

CAUDLE v. SHERRARD MOTOR CO.
525 S.W.2d 238 (Texas 1975)

[Sherrard Motor Company (Sherrard), the plaintiff, contracted to sell John Caudle, the defendant, a house trailer. Caudle made a down payment of $2,685 by check. While Sherrard was getting the trailer ready, Caudle was sent out of town to Dallas on business. Because the trailer was not ready, Caudle told Sherrard that he would return and pick it up later. Before Caudle returned, the trailer was stolen from Sherrard's place of business. Upon learning of the theft, Caudle stopped payment on the check he had given Sherrard for the down payment and refused to pay for the trailer.

Sherrard brought a legal action against Caudle for breach of contract. The issue in the case was whether or not the risk of loss had passed to Caudle before the theft of the trailer occurred. If it had, Caudle owed Sherrard the purchase price of the trailer; if it had not,

the contract was void and Caudle consequently owed nothing. The trial court gave judgment to Sherrard. Caudle appealed.]

AKIN, Justice

Plaintiff contends . . . that . . . the risk of loss passed to the defendant pursuant to [§2-509(4)]. This section provides that a buyer and seller may specifically enter into a contract contrary to the other provisions of §2-509. Plaintiff argues that such a contrary agreement was made because the terms of the contract for the sale of the trailer provided that the risk of loss passed to the defendant when the contract was signed by the parties.

The pertinent clause of the sales contract states: No transfer, renewal, extension or assignment of this agreement or any interest hereunder, and no loss, damage or destruction of said motor vehicle shall release buyer from his obligation hereunder.

We hold that this language is insufficient to constitute a "contrary agreement" between the parties pursuant to [§2-509(4)]. A contract which shifts the risk of loss to the buyer before he receives the merchandise is so unusual that a seller who desires to achieve this result must clearly communicate his intent to the buyer. . . . This clause was apparently intended to fix responsibility for loss after the defendant had taken possession of the trailer. This interpretation is consistent with other provisions of the contract. For example, the contract provides that the "buyer shall keep said motor vehicle in good order and repair. . . ." [I]t would indeed be difficult for the buyer to honor this responsibility without having acquired actual possession of the trailer. Furthermore, since risk of loss is not specifically mentioned in the contract, we cannot say that agreement to the contrary may be inferred from reading the document as a whole. We, therefore, conclude that it was not the intention of the parties to transfer risk of loss of the trailer prior to delivery of possession to the buyer. To hold otherwise would be to set a trap for the unwary. If parties intend to shift the burden of the risk of loss from the seller to the buyer before delivery of the goods, then such must be done in clear and unequivocal languages.

It is the defendant's contention that pursuant to [§2-509(3)] the risk of loss remained with the plaintiff because [the buyer] had not taken actual physical possession of the trailer. We agree. To determine if this section applies, the following questions must be resolved: (1) was the plaintiff a merchant? and (2) did the defendant receive the trailer? The plaintiff is a merchant under Article 2 of the Code as it "deals in goods of the kind . . . involved in the transaction. . ."

[§2-104(1)]. The language "receipt of the goods" is defined in the Code as "taking physical possession of them" [§2-103(1)(c)]. It is undisputed that the defendant never took physical possession of the trailer; therefore, he had not received the goods. Accordingly, we hold that the risk of loss did not pass to the buyer before the trailer was stolen. It follows, therefore, that no breach of contract occurred.

Our holding is in accordance with the underlying principles of [§2-509] dealing with the risk of loss. Under the Uniform Commercial Code, the risk of loss is no longer determined arbitrarily by which party had title to the goods at the time of the loss. Instead, as the drafters of the Code state: "The underlying theory of these sections on risk of loss is the adoption of the contractual approach. . ." [§2-509, Official Comment 1]. In addition, [§2-509(4)] provides that the buyer and seller are free to adjust by contract their rights and risks contrary to the other provisions of [§2-509]. Subject to the placement of a contractual approach at the analytic center of risk of loss problems is the policy that a party who had control over the handling of goods should bear their loss. Strong policy reasons support this approach. The party in control is in the best position to handle properly the goods . . . and to insure the goods. This theory is particularly applicable when the buyer is not a merchant and is unfamiliar with the problems of handling the goods. . . .

[A] merchant who is to make delivery at his own place of business continues to maintain control over the goods and can be expected to carry insurance to protect his interest in them. On the other hand, the buyer has no control over the goods and may not have had the foresight to obtain insurance on the undelivered merchandise. . . .

Accordingly, this cause is reversed.

CASE REVIEW QUESTIONS

1. On what basis do you think the trial court held that risk of loss had passed to Caudle?
2. Why did the appeals court hold that Sherrard had risk of loss?
3. Why must a merchant seller clearly and unequivocally notify a buyer that risk of loss will pass to the buyer prior to the buyer's taking possession of the goods?

4. Why wasn't the clause in Sherrard's contract sufficient to shift the risk of loss to the buyer?

Nonmerchant Seller If the seller is not a merchant and is not going to ship the goods to the buyer via a carrier and the goods are not going to remain in the hands of a bailee, risk of loss passes to the buyer on tender of delivery [§2-509(3)]. **Tender of delivery** means that the seller (1) makes and holds available for the buyer goods that conform to the contract and (2) gives the buyer any notification reasonably necessary to enable the buyer to take delivery [§2-503(1)]. Unless otherwise agreed, tender of delivery must be at a reasonable hour, and the goods must be kept available long enough for the buyer to take possession of them. Suppose, for instance, that a nonmerchant sells a used car to a friend and agrees that the friend will pick up the car at 8 A.M. the next morning. The seller has the risk of loss until 8 A.M. At that time, which is the agreed upon time for tender of delivery, the risk of loss passes to the buyer. Therefore, even if the buyer does not come to pick up the car at 8 A.M., if it is damaged after that time, the buyer will have to pay for the car.

The result, of course, would be different if the seller of the automobile were a merchant who had agreed to an 8 A.M. delivery time. The merchant seller would continue to bear the risk of loss if the buyer did not pick up the car at the scheduled time because risk of loss would not pass to the buyer until the car was actually received by the buyer [§2-509(3)].

This distinction between merchant and nonmerchant sellers is made because it is customary for merchants to insure the goods they have for sale, whereas a buyer may not think to insure purchased goods until he or she takes possession of them. Thus, the merchant is better prepared to take the loss. The situation is apt to be different, however, when a person who is not a merchant sells something. In this case, the seller is not any more likely to have insurance than the buyer.

Shipment by Carrier When a contract calls for the seller to ship goods to the buyer using a carrier, such as a trucking company, a railway company or some other business that is engaged in shipping goods, the question of who must bear risk of loss hinges upon whether the contract for sale is a **shipment contract** or a **destination contract**. The categorization of a contract as a shipment contract or a destination contract is generally determined by the agreement of the parties concerning the delivery terms. Common delivery terms are *FOB place of shipment, FOB place of destination, FAS, ex-ship,* and *CIF* or *C & F*. The significance of each of these terms, as determined by the Code, is discussed in the following sections.

FOB Place of Shipment The abbreviation **FOB** stands for *free on board*. FOB place of shipment means that the seller must bear the expense of delivering the goods to an appropriate carrier at the place of shipment, but it is the buyer's responsibility to pay the carrier. The buyer may pay the carrier by forwarding the necessary amount to the seller, or the cost of the carriage may be included as a separate item in the sales contract [§2-319(1)(a)].

A sales contract that contains this kind of arrangement is a shipment contract. Under the Code, sales contracts that call for the carriage of goods are presumed to be shipment contracts unless the parties clearly specify otherwise [§2-503 Official Comment, Paragraph 5]. In a shipment contract, the risk of loss passes to the buyer when conforming goods are duly (properly) delivered to the carrier in the manner agreed to in the contract or required by the Code [§2-509(1)(a)]. For example, suppose the seller is located in Chicago and the buyer is in Denver. If the contract states that the sale is "FOB Chicago," the risk of loss will pass to the buyer when the seller properly delivers the goods to the carrier in Chicago. Thus, any loss that occurs while the goods are in transit to Denver will be the responsibility of the buyer.

When shipment contracts are used, a seller must select an appropriate carrier and make appropriate arrangements for the carriage of the goods in keeping with the nature of the goods, the time for delivery, and any other pertinent aspects of the contract. Appropriate arrangements include such things as insurance, refrigeration, care of livestock, or any special packaging. In addition, it is the seller's duty to obtain and deliver to the buyer the necessary shipping documents and to give the buyer prompt notice that the goods have been shipped [§2-504].

FOB Place of Destination FOB place of destination means that the seller is obligated to deliver the goods to the destination [§2-319(1)(b)]. The seller pays for the cost of carriage and must tender delivery of the goods at their destination, though the actual tender may be made by the carrier according to the rules for tender previously discussed.

A sales contract with this kind of arrangement is called a **destination contract.** In a destination contract, risk of loss passes to the buyer when conforming goods are duly tendered by the carrier to the buyer at the destination point [§2-509(1)(b)]. For example, if the seller is in Chicago and the buyer is in Denver and the contract states that the sale is "FOB Denver," risk of loss will pass to the buyer when the carrier properly tenders the goods in Denver. Thus, any loss that occurs while the goods are in transit to Denver will be the responsibility of the seller.

Under a destination contract, the seller must give the buyer reasonable notification of when the goods will be available, and the buyer must provide reasonable facilities to receive the goods [§2-503(1)]. For example, in a destination contract if a buyer does not have space in his or her warehouse when a shipment arrives at a reasonable time and the buyer refuses delivery, he or she will assume the risk of loss even though the goods remain in the carrier's possession because the carrier has duly tendered delivery.

Delivery FAS *FAS,* which stands for free alongside, is a delivery term that may be used when the carrier is a ship. It means that the price of the goods includes delivery by the seller alongside — that is, next to — the ship that transports them at the place specified in the agreement [§2-319(2)]. Thus "FAS New Orleans" would mean that the price of the goods includes delivery of the goods alongside a ship in New Orleans. This type of contract is a shipment contract; therefore, when the seller meets this delivery requirement, the risk of loss passes to the buyer [§2-509(1)(a)].

Delivery Ex-Ship A contract term calling for the delivery of goods ex-ship requires that the seller be responsible for the goods until they have been unloaded from the named ship at the destination port [§2-322]. The Code specifies that this type of contract is a destination contract, and that the seller has the risk of loss until the goods are unloaded [§2-502(1)(b)].

Delivery CIF and C&F The delivery term CIF means that the price of the goods includes the cost (C) of the goods, insurance (I) on the goods, and the freight (F) charged to deliver the goods to the destination specified in the contract. The term C&F means that the price of the goods includes the cost of the goods and freight charges. Even though the cost of carriage is included in the cost of the goods, the Code classifies any contract that uses either of these terms as a shipment contract [§2-320]. Risk of loss therefore passes to the buyer when conforming goods are properly delivered to an appropriate carrier [§2-509(1)(a)].

The following case concerns a contract that lacked a delivery term. The judge had to decide whether the contract was a shipment contract or a destination contract in order to determine who had the risk of loss.

EBERHARD MANUFACTURING CO. v. BROWN
232 N.W.2d 378 (Mich. 1975)

[Eberhard Manufacturing Company (Eberhard), the plaintiff, brought a legal action against Brown, the defendant, for the price of goods sold pursuant to a distributorship agreement. Brown counterclaimed for damages for breach of the distributorship agreement. The trial court gave judgment against Eberhard on the action for the purchase of the goods and for Brown on the counterclaim.

Eberhard appealed. One part of the appeal was based on a claim by Eberhard that the trial court had erred in giving Brown a credit of $559.03 for goods that had been lost while being delivered to him by carrier. Eberhard argued that the risk of loss for those goods had passed to the buyer before they were lost. Brown argued that the risk of loss had not passed before the goods were lost.]

GILLIS, Presiding Judge

On appeal both parties point to [§2-509(1)] as controlling. Plaintiff, however, cites subsection (a) and defendant subsection (b). Subsection (a) states the rule where the contract is a "shipment" contract, in which case risk of loss passes to the buyer when the goods are duly delivered to the carrier; subsection (b) states the rule where a contract is a "destination" contract, in which case risk of loss passes to the buyer when the goods are duly tendered at the destination.

An agreement of the parties would control as to who has the risk of loss. . . [§2-509(4)].

The parties here did not expressly agree on who was to bear the risk of loss. The contract contained no F.O.B. [or other delivery] term. . . . There was testimony by plaintiff that its goods are sold F.O.B. place of shipment, plaintiff's factory. That testimony might be evidence of a usage of trade. . . . It was not proof that the parties had agreed, expressly or in fact, as to who had the risk of loss.

Under Article 2 of the Uniform Commercial Code, the "shipment" contract is regarded as the normal one and the "destination" contract as the variant type. The seller is not obligated to deliver at a named destination and bear the concurrent risk of loss until arrival, unless he has specifically agreed so to deliver or the commercial understanding of the terms used by the parties contemplates such delivery [§2-503, Official Comment 5]. Thus a contract which contains neither an F.O.B. term nor any other term explicitly allocating loss is a shipment contract.

Defendant argues that since the goods were to be shipped to defendant's place of business in Birmingham, the contract required plaintiff to deliver the goods "at a particular destination" . . . Defendant's position is that "ship to" substitutes for and is equivalent to an F.O.B. term, namely F.O.B. place of destination. But that argument is persuasively refuted by the response that a "ship to" address must be supplied in any case in which carriage is contemplated. Thus a "ship to" term has no significance in determining whether a contract is a shipment or destination contract for risk of loss purposes.

Other buyers have occasionally argued that the "ship to" term made the contract into a destination contract. Courts have properly rejected this argument. . . .

Since the presumption of a shipment contract controls in this case, the trial court should not have given defendant the $559.03 credit for the lost shipment. . . .

Therefore, judgment for defendant is affirmed in part and reversed in part. Defendant's recovery is reduced by $559.03 from $6,315.82 to $5,756.79.

CASE COMMENT

In a carriage contract, the allocation of risk of loss is really a determination of who sues the carrier for the loss suffered. If the carrier is a common carrier (one whose business it is to carry the goods of the general public), the carrier is strictly liable — that is, it is responsible regardless of fault — for the goods during carriage with only five exceptions. A carrier is not liable for damage caused by (1) an "act of God," such as an earthquake or a flood; (2) an act of the public enemy, that is, damage caused by the armed forces of an enemy nation; (3) acts of the public authority, such as an order by a state that all trains must stop; (4) acts of the shipper (seller), such as the seller's failure to package the goods properly; (5) the nature of the goods, such as mold in cantaloupe due to claudisporium rot that cannot be detected prior to shipment and occurs even though the goods have been properly refrigerated.

In all other situations, the carrier will be strictly liable for any damage even though it has been as careful as possible. For example, the carrier will be liable if the goods are damaged when a train robber blows up a section of track in order to stop a train or if the delay caused by the derailment causes some of the goods to spoil.

CASE REVIEW QUESTIONS

1. Why did the buyer have to pay for goods that were never received?
2. What reasons can you give for the shipment contract being the normal type of sales contract?

3. Why would a ''ship to'' term be needed in a shipment contract if the seller is not required to deliver the goods to a destination?

Delivery without Movement Sometimes the goods subject to a contract for sale are not in the possession of the seller but are instead in the possession of a **bailee,** such as a warehouseman. The seller and buyer may agree that the goods are not to be delivered to the buyer but are to remain in the warehouse. In other words, they are to be "delivered" without being moved.

Suppose, though, that these goods are destroyed in a fire. Does the buyer or the seller have the risk of loss? The Code describes three ways in which risk of loss passes from the seller to the buyer when goods are held by a bailee and are to be delivered without being moved. The underlying principle of each is that the risk of loss will pass to the buyer when the buyer either is assured or has had the opportunity to be assured that he or she can obtain the goods from the bailee without problems.

Risk of loss passes from the seller to the buyer when one of the following three conditions is met:

1. *The buyer receives a negotiable document of title covering the goods.* A document of title is written evidence that a person has the right to possession of goods that are being held by a bailee. (Documents of title will be explained more fully later in the chapter.) The transfer of a **negotiable document of title** normally results in the buyer becoming the owner of the goods and gaining the right to receive the goods from the bailee free from any excuses by the bailee as to why the goods can't be delivered and free from any claims of ownership of the goods by others [§7-502]. Since the buyer effectively has ownership of the goods upon transfer of the document of title, the buyer also assumes the risk of loss at that point.

2. *The buyer receives a nonnegotiable document of title, and the buyer has had reasonable time to present the document to the bailee* [§2-509(2)(c)]. A **nonnegotiable document of title** does not give the buyer the same unqualified ownership of the goods that a negotiable document of title gives. For example, the seller can still stop delivery of the goods after giving the buyer a nonnegotiable document of title [§7-504 and §2-705]. Moreover, although a seller makes a proper tender of the goods by tendering a nonnegotiable document of title to the buyer, tendering the document does not in itself transfer risk of loss to the buyer. Risk of loss does not pass to the buyer until the bailee acknowledges (admits) the buyer's rights to the goods or the buyer has had a reasonable period of time in which to seek the bailee's acknowledgment and the buyer has failed to do so [§2-503(4)(b)]. If the bailee refuses to honor the document, the tender of the goods is not proper and risk of loss remains with the seller.

3. *The bailee acknowledges the buyer's right to possess the goods.* If no document of title has been issued, the seller can instruct the bailee to acknowledge the buyer's right to possess the goods. When acknowledgment is made by the bailee, risk of loss passes to the buyer.

Sale on Approval and Sale or Return Contracts There are two situations in which the buyer has possession of the goods but also has a right to return the goods to the seller even though there is nothing wrong with them. One of these situations is the **sale on approval** contract, which occurs when goods that can be returned are delivered to the buyer primarily for his or her personal use [§2-326(1)(a)]. This is the typical "ten days free home trial" situation, in which the buyer may return the goods if he or she decides not to buy them. The other situation occurs when goods are delivered to the buyer primarily for resale to others. If the buyer does not succeed in reselling the goods, they may be returned to the original seller. This type of arrangement, which is sometimes called a **consignment,** is called a **sale or return** contract by the Code [§2-326(1)(b)].

When a contract calls for a sale on approval, risk of loss does not pass to the buyer until the goods are accepted by the buyer [§2-327(1)]. Acceptance may occur in one of three ways [§2-606].

1. The buyer elects to keep the goods.
2. The buyer fails to return the goods within the allotted time.
3. The buyer treats the goods as his or her own by using them in ways not contemplated by the contract.

For example, if a buyer has taken a stereo system home for a ten-day trial, the loan of that system to a friend would constitute an acceptance. During the trial period in a sale on approval contract, the return delivery of the goods to the seller is at the seller's risk and expense, although a merchant buyer must follow any reasonable instructions given by the seller [§2-327(1)(c)].

In a sale or return contract, risk of loss passes to the buyer when it would in a normal sales contract and remains with the buyer until the goods are returned to the seller. The return delivery of the goods, therefore, is at the buyer's risk [§2-327(2)(b)].

Effect of Breach on Loss

The rules for the risk of loss that have just been discussed apply to situations in which the contract has not been breached by either the seller or the buyer. When one of the parties has breached the contract, however, that party may have to bear the risk of loss.

Seller's Breach There are many ways in which a seller may breach a sales contract (see Chapter 23, pages 434–436). For example, the seller may deliver goods that do not conform to the contract — that is, the goods may be defective or they may be different from the goods specified. Also, the manner of delivery may not conform to the terms of the agreement. In most cases in which the seller breaches the contract, the buyer has the right to reject the goods. Until the seller cures (remedies) the defect or until the buyer accepts the goods in spite of the problem, risk of loss remains with the seller [§2-510(1)].

Sometimes, though, the buyer may not discover the defect until after he or she has already accepted the goods. When the buyer has the right to revoke his or her acceptance because of a previously undiscovered defect, risk of loss is treated as having stayed with the seller [§2-510(2)]. The risk born by the seller is limited in this situation, however. The seller must pay for the loss only to the extent that the buyer's insurance fails to cover the loss. For example, suppose the buyer can revoke acceptance and return some goods worth $3,000. Before the buyer returns the goods, they are destroyed in an accident. If the buyer's insurance only covers $1,000 of the loss, the seller must pay the remaining $2,000. If the buyer's insurance covers the entire loss, the seller suffers no loss.

Buyer's Breach The buyer may also be the one to breach the contract. The buyer breaches a contract, for example, when he or she enters into a contract with a seller to purchase certain goods but then changes his or her mind and refuses to honor the contract. Similarly, if a buyer fails to make a payment for the goods that is due before they are delivered, he or she breaches the contract. As soon as a breach occurs, the seller can treat the risk of loss as being with the buyer, but only to the extent that the seller's insurance coverage is inadequate. The Code stipulates, however, that the risk of loss is with the buyer only "for a commercially reasonable time" [§2-510(3)]. During this time, the seller can purchase insurance if it is needed to cover the risk.

TRANSFER OF TITLE

As discussed earlier, the drafters of the Code provided rules for such issues as risk of loss regardless of who actually owns the goods. It was also necessary, however, to include provisions for determining when **title** (ownership) passes from seller to buyer. These provisions are needed in situations where a question of ownership arises in areas not covered by the UCC. For example, state law may impose a sales tax on the transfer of title from the seller to a buyer. Similarly, the rights of creditors to goods held by the seller may depend on who has title.

When Title Passes

Title to goods cannot pass from the seller to the buyer prior to the time the goods are identified to the contract [§2-401(1)]. Therefore, when a contract is made for future goods (goods not existing or not identified to the contract), the buyer gets no title at that point. Subject to this precondition, buyers and sellers can make any agreements they wish concerning passage of title.

If the parties make no specific agreement, the general rule under the Code is that title passes when the seller completes his or her required performance concerning the physical delivery of the goods [§2-401(2)]. For example, under a shipment contract, title passes to the buyer when the goods are delivered to the carrier [§2-401(2)(a)]. Under a destination contract, title passes when the goods are duly tendered to the buyer at their destination [§2-401(2)(b)].

If goods are identified to the contract when it is made, title passes at that time if no documents of title are to be delivered and delivery is to take place without the goods being moved [§2-401(3)(b)]. This provision would apply, for example, when a buyer purchases some furniture from a store. If the furniture is marked with the buyer's name at the time of the sale, it is identified to the contract when the contract is made. If the buyer is going to move the furniture himself or herself, he or she becomes the owner of the furniture as soon as the contract is made.

When delivery is to be made without moving the goods and the seller is to give a document of title to the buyer, title passes when the document of title is delivered [§2-401(3)(a)]. This provision would apply, for example, when the goods are in a warehouse. The buyer becomes the owner of the goods when he or she is given the document of title that will allow him or her to obtain the goods from the warehouse.

Passage of Title in Sale on Approval and Sale or Return Contracts Under a sale on approval contract, in which goods are delivered to the buyer primarily for his or her personal use, title passes to the buyer when the goods are accepted [§2-236(1)(a) and §2-327(1)]. Under a sale or return contract, in which goods are delivered primarily for resale and the buyer has the right to return the goods if they are not resold, title passes to the buyer according to the usual rules for passage of title found in §2-401.

A buyer who has received delivery of goods under either a sale on approval or a sale or return contract appears to own the goods. Are they, as a result, subject to the claims of the buyer's creditors? The Code provides that goods held by the buyer under a sale on approval contract are not subject to the claims of the buyer's creditors until they have been accepted. Conversely, goods held by the buyer under a sale or return contract can be treated by the buyer's creditors as being owned by the buyer even if the seller and the buyer have agreed that the seller is to retain title to the goods [§§2-326(2), (3)].

There are, however, three ways in which the seller in a sale or return contract can protect his or her interest in the goods from the buyer's creditors. The seller can (1) file notice of his or her interest in the goods as provided in Article 9 of the Code (see Chapter 29), (2) comply with a state law that provides protection for sellers if they erect a sign near the goods that states their interest in the goods, or (3) establish that the buyer is generally known by his or her creditors to be selling goods that belong to others.

In the case that follows, there was a dispute between the seller in a sale or return contract and the buyer's creditors.

BUFKOR, INC. v. STAR JEWELRY CO., INC.
552 S.W.2d 522 (Texas 1977)

[Bufkor, Inc., the defendant, was a creditor of Tavernier Jewelers (Tavernier). Bufkor had brought suit against Tavernier to collect a debt. Bufkor had received a judgment in this suit and was entitled to have some of Tavernier's goods seized by a sheriff. Star Jewelry Company (Star), the plaintiff, had an agreement with Tavernier whereby Star delivered certain items of jewelry to Tavernier for the purpose of sale by Tavernier under a consignment arrangement. Ownership of the jewelry was to remain with Star unless Tavernier was able to sell it.

On April 2, 1975, Bufkor, pursuant to legal procedure, had a sheriff seize the assets of Tavernier, including the jewelry that had been delivered by Star. The goods were to be sold and the proceeds were to be used to pay off the judgment Bufkor had against Tavernier.

Star then brought a legal action against Bufkor, claiming that the jewelry it had sent to Tavernier could not be seized and sold by the sheriff because it belonged to Star, not to Tavernier. The trial court gave judgment, and the jewelry, to Star. Bufkor appealed.]

DIES, Chief Justice

It is true that the term "consignment" was used in the dealings of the parties but it is also true that Tavernier maintained a place of business for the purpose of selling jewelry merchandise and had authority to sell this merchandise. . . .

Transactions which once might have been regarded as consignments are now regarded as sales by the Uniform Commercial Code. The purpose of this change was to permit people to deal with a debtor upon the assumption that all property in his possession is unencumbered, unless the contrary is indicated by their own knowledge or by public records. . . .

[Article 9] provides a method by which Star could have given notice of its lien [interest], i.e., by filing a financing statement with the Secretary of State. Tav-

ernier's president Dolleshanger gave Star the form and suggested that such a statement be filed. This was not done by Star. [§2-326] provides:

(2) Except as provided in Subsection (3), goods held on approval are not subject to the claims of the buyer's creditors until acceptance; goods held on sale or return are subject to such claims while in the buyer's possession. (3) Where goods are delivered to a person for sale and such person maintains a place of business at which he deals in goods of the kind involved, under a name other than the name of the person making delivery, then with respect to claims of creditors of the person conducting the business the goods are deemed to be on sale or return. The provisions of this subsection are applicable even though an agreement purports to reserve title to the person making delivery until payment or resale or uses such words as "on consignment" or "on memorandum."

The intention of the parties is no longer determinative of the question of whether a transaction is a sale or consignment. . . .

Consequently, we hold that these goods should be held to have been delivered for "sale or return," and thus, that neither the title nor the right to possession of these goods was retained by plaintiff Star Jewelry Company.

Star, having neither title nor right to possession, may not prevail. . . .

We, therefore, proceed to render the judgment that the trial court should have rendered; that plaintiff take nothing by reason of its suit and that . . . the goods [be] returned to defendant Bufkor, Inc.

Reversed.

CASE REVIEW QUESTIONS
1. Why was the sale by Star to Tavernier a sale or return?
2. What could Star Jewelry have done to protect its interest?
3. Why do you think the Code treats a delivery of goods in the situation described in §2-326(3) to be a sale or return as far as creditors are concerned?

Who Can Transfer Title?

Logically, it makes sense that a buyer must purchase goods from someone who has title to them or is authorized to transfer title to them in order to become the owner of the goods. In other words, a person cannot get title to goods by purchasing them from a finder or a thief who has no title to them. Nevertheless, a person who purchases goods acquires all the title that the seller has or has authority to transfer [§2-403(1)].

There are, however, situations in which a buyer can acquire title to goods even though the seller does not have good title to them. These situations arise when a seller does not have good title but does have the *power* to transfer good title.

Voidable Title One situation in which a seller without good title has the power to transfer ownership to a buyer occurs when the seller has voidable title. A person has **voidable title** when the person who sold him or her the goods has a legal right to get the goods back. This right to recover the goods may be due to duress, undue influence, misrepresentation, or impossibility in the original sale (see Chapter 17).

In addition, the Code identifies some specific situations in which a buyer will have voidable title. For example, if a person purchased goods with a check that was later not paid, he or she merely has voidable title [§2-402(1)(b)]. Payment by check is a conditional payment and becomes ineffective as payment if the check is not paid [§2-511(3)].

A person with voidable title has the power to transfer good title to a good-faith purchaser for value [§2-403(1)]. In the case of a nonmerchant, a good-faith purchaser for value is basically a person who has no knowledge of the fact that the seller's title is voidable and who either pays or promises to pay the seller for the goods [§§1-201(19), (44)]. For a merchant to qualify as a good-faith purchaser for value, he or she must also conform to reasonable commercial standards of fair dealing in the trade [§2-103(1)(b)].

Entrusting A second situation in which a seller without good title has the power to transfer ownership to a buyer occurs when a person entrusts possession of goods to a merchant who deals in goods of that kind. **Entrusting** refers to any section that involves leaving goods with a merchant for any reason [§2-403(3)]. The merchant has possession of the goods but no title.

If the merchant to whom the goods are entrusted sells the goods to someone who qualifies as a buyer in the ordinary course of business [§1-201(9)], the buyer will acquire whatever rights the person who entrusted the goods to the merchant had in the goods [§2-403(2)]. The concept of a buyer in the ordinary course of business is narrower than the concept of a good-faith purchaser for value. The concepts are similar in that a buyer in the ordinary course of business must act in good faith and must give value. In addition, though, a buyer in the ordinary course of business can only buy from a merchant, and the sale must be made in the way in which the merchant usually sells his or her goods.

Suppose for instance, that the owner of a watch leaves it to be repaired with a merchant who repairs and also sells used watches. If the store sells the watch to another customer who is a buyer in the ordinary course of business, the purchaser will acquire good title to the watch. The original owner will, of course, have the legal right to collect damages from the store, but he or she will not be able to recover the watch. However, if the person who left the watch was not the owner and was not acting on behalf of the owner in bringing the watch to be repaired, the customer would not acquire good title, and the original owner would have the legal right to recover the watch. Thus a thief cannot deprive the true owner of his or her property by selling goods to a merchant who then sells them to a customer.

The law concerning entrusting reflects an effort to balance ownership interests against the need for goods to flow freely in the marketplace. Imagine the length of the checkout line in the supermarket if each buyer had to satisfy himself or herself that the grocer did indeed have title to or the right to sell the goods the buyer wishes to purchase. Note that entrusting does not give the seller the *right* to sell goods entrusted to him or her, but it does give a merchant seller the *power* to transfer ownership interests in those goods to a buyer in the ordinary course of business. The merchant seller will be liable to the original owner of the goods, but the new buyer will be entitled to keep them.

Estoppel A third situation in which a seller without good title has the power to transfer ownership to a buyer occurs when the real owner of the goods does something that makes it appear to a third party that the goods are owned by the person selling them. If the buyer justifiably relies on the appearance of ownership and pays for the goods, the real owner is estopped (prohibited) from presenting evidence in court that the goods did not belong to the seller.

For example, suppose Anderson loans Bentley a television set. Sometime later, Bentley offers to sell the set to Coleman during a conversation overheard by Anderson. Anderson says nothing to Coleman about the fact that she (Anderson), not Bentley, actually owns the set. Coleman pays Bentley for the set. If Anderson brings a legal action against Coleman to recover the set, Anderson will lose because she will be estopped from denying that Bentley was the owner of the television set.

Rights of Seller's Creditors

Sometimes disputes arise between the creditors of a seller and a buyer who has paid for goods but has not yet received possession. If title has not passed to the buyer, his or her only right is the special property right, discussed earlier in this chapter, that enables a buyer who has paid all or part of the purchase price to obtain the goods from the seller if the seller becomes insolvent within ten days after the buyer made the first payment [§2-502(1)] (see page 384).

When title to the goods has passed to the buyer, the seller's creditors must have rights superior to the buyer's ownership rights if they are to prevail. The creditors may gain superior rights if the buyer has allowed the seller to retain possession of the goods. By leaving the goods in the seller's possession, the buyer is contributing to the impression that the seller owns more assets than actually belong to him or her.

The Code specifies that the seller's creditors have no rights superior to the buyer's rights when the retention of the goods by the seller was in good faith, was in the course of trade, and was only for a commercially reasonable time after the sale [§2-402(2)]. The retention of goods beyond a commercially reasonable time may be considered fraudulent, and the creditors may be given rights superior to the buyer's title.

In some states, the protracted retention of possession by the seller is always treated as fraudulent — that is, it is fraud per se — and the creditors are given rights superior to the buyer in the goods involved. Other states treat the extended retention of possession only as evidence of fraud, and the buyer is allowed to refute the evidence if he or she can. If the buyer is successful in showing that there was no intent to defraud creditors, he or she may keep the goods. Otherwise, the creditors are given superior rights to the goods involved.

DOCUMENTS OF TITLE

A **document of title** is any written document that is treated in the regular course of business as adequate evidence that the person in possession of the document is the person entitled to receive, hold, and dispose of the document and the goods it covers [§1-201(15)]. There are two basic types of documents of title: **bills of lading,** which are issued by carriers, and **warehouse receipts,** which are issued by warehousemen.

Documents of title serve a number of purposes. First, a document of title serves as a receipt that specifies the type and quantity of goods received by a warehouseman for storage or by a carrier for delivery. Second, the document of title is the contract between the issuer and the person to whom it is issued. It sets the terms for the care and delivery of the goods.

Third, a document of title can be used to collect the price for the goods when the seller and the buyer are in different cities. For example, a seller in Chicago cannot collect from a buyer in New York in the same way that a grocery store owner can get money at a checkout counter — that is, here are the groceries, give me the money or you don't get them. The seller in Chicago can, however, collect from the buyer in New York by sending a document of title and a paper called a draft, which is a demand for money (see page 487) to an agent in New York. The agent notifies the buyer, and the buyer must pay the draft in order to get possession of the document of title, which will, in turn, allow him or her to get possession of the goods. A carrier or warehouseman will not deliver the goods to anyone who does not have the document of title. In this way, the seller is able to retain control over the goods until he or she receives payment.

Fourth, a document of title can be used to help finance the seller's business. For example, rather than waiting until the goods have arrived in New York and the seller's agent has collected from the buyer, the seller can take the document of title to a Chicage bank and borrow against it; that is, the seller can use the document as collateral for a loan. In effect the seller gets the proceeds of the sale without having to wait for the goods to reach New York. The Chicago bank forwards the document of title and a draft to its agent in New York, who collects from the buyer and transmits the money to the Chicago bank. When the bank receives the money, it treats it as payment of the loan made to the seller.

Finally, a document of title can be used as a trading device. By selling a document of title, the seller can transfer ownership of the goods. For example, wheat stored in a grain elevator may be traded or sold to a succession of buyers simply by selling the document of title. Often a buyer may be acting as a broker or grain speculator and may not actually want the grain.

Collection at a distance, financing, and trading work only with a magic type of document called a **negotiable document of title.** A document of title is negotiable if it specifies that the goods are to be delivered "to the bearer" or "to the order of" a person named in the document [§7-104(1)(a)]. The words "bearer" or "order" are the magic. If these words are in the document, the document is negotiable; if they are not, the document is a **nonnegotiable document of title.**

Negotiable documents of title have many similarities to the checks with which you are undoubtedly familiar. If a document of title specifies delivery "to bearer," the bearer of the document can transfer it (negotiate it) to another person simply by delivery. If the document specifies delivery "to the order of" a person named in the document, that person must indorse (sign) the document and deliver it in order to negotiate it that is, to transfer ownership of the document to another person [§7-501]. A document of title is "duly negotiated" when it has been negotiated (delivered if a bearer document or delivered and properly indorsed if an order document) to a new owner (holder) who purchases the document for value, in good faith, and without any notice that someone else has a claim to it or that anyone has a defense to it, that is, a reason not to allow the delivery of the goods to the holder [§7-501(4)].

When a document of title has been duly negotiated, the holder of the document has title to the document and title to the goods. In addition, the holder takes the document free from any claims or defenses of the issuer of the document except for those that come about because of terms in the document or rules in the Code [§7-502]. For example, if a bearer document of title was duly negotiated by delivery to a holder who paid value and acted in good faith, the issuer of the document (the warehouseman or the carrier) must deliver the goods to the holder even though the document was stolen from the person to whom it was originally issued. A person to whom a document of title has been duly negotiated is the owner of the goods.

A nonnegotiable document of title is usually referred to as a **"straight" bill of lading** or **"straight" warehouse receipt.** It will serve as a receipt and as a contract, but it cannot be used effectively for other purposes because a nonnegotiable document is subject to all claims and defenses. A nonnegotiable document of title does not, therefore, give the buyer the same ownership rights as does a negotiable document of title.

Certificate of Title

A certificate of title is different from a document of title. A **certificate of title** is issued not by carriers or warehousemen but by a state pursuant to a law requiring a certificate for the purpose of establishing ownership of movable goods, typically an automobile. Indeed, a number of states have adopted the

Uniform Motor Vehicle Certificate of Title and Anti-Theft Act. As its title suggests, one of the purposes of this act is to make it more difficult for a thief to sell an automobile.

Whether the delivery of a certificate of title is necessary to transfer title is subject to dispute. Some jurisdictions have decided that title does not pass unless the certificate of title has been delivered. The better view seems to be that title passes according to the rules set forth in the Code as discussed in this chapter.

REVIEW QUESTIONS

1. How are goods identified to a contract? Explain.
2. What is the effect on a buyer if goods are destroyed after risk of loss has passed to him or her?
3. Why does it matter whether goods were identified to a contract when the contract was made if the goods are damaged while the seller has the risk of loss?
4. When does risk of loss pass if the seller is a merchant? What if the seller is a nonmerchant?
5. What is a shipment contract? What is a destination contract? How do you know which kind of contract an agreement is?
6. When does risk of loss pass to a buyer if the goods being sold are held by a bailee?
7. When does risk of loss pass to the buyer in a sale on approval contract?
8. When does title pass to a buyer if the goods are going to be shipped?
9. What is entrusting?
10. What is a document of title? How is it used?

CASE PROBLEMS

1. Crump entered into a contract for the purchase of a TV antenna from Lair Distribution Company. The contract called for Crump to make installment payments for a ten-year period and specified that title would remain with Lair until all payments were made. The antenna was installed at the Crump home. Several months after installation, the antenna was struck by lightning and damaged. Lair repaired the antenna at Crump's request, but Crump refused to pay for the repairs. Lair sued Crump for the cost of the repairs. Crump defended on the grounds that he was not responsible for the damage because he did not have title to the antenna. Who will win the case? Explain.

2. Mitchell agreed to purchase a used tractor from the Highway Equipment Company (Highway), which was selling some of its outdated equipment. Mitchell agreed to pick up the tractor on the morning of June 29th. At 2 A.M. on the morning of June 29th, a fire of undetermined origin seriously damaged the tractor. Mitchell refused to pay for the tractor even though Highway was willing to discount the price because of the damage. Highway sued Mitchell for the price. Will Highway recover the price? Explain.

3. Johnny Appleseed, an apple grower in Oregon, wrote to the Old Pioneer Store located nearby in the state of Washington. Appleseed offered to sell his entire crop, which consisted of 500 bushels of apples, to Old Pioneer. No delivery terms were mentioned. On the day Appleseed received a letter from Old Pioneer accepting the offer, lightning struck the barn where the apples were stored. The barn and the apples were a total loss. Johnny Appleseed sued Old Pioneer for the price of the apples. Old Pioneer counterclaimed for breach of contract. Who will win the case? Explain. If Old

Pioneer loses, will it be able to collect on its insurance policy that covers any goods for which Old Pioneer has title? Explain.

4. John Bellamy purchased a registered quarter horse, Holiday Dandy, from Meadowland Quarter Horse Ranch, which breeds horses and sells them at public auction. The catalogue distributed prior to the auction indicated that Holiday Dandy was in foal by Silver Right. Two days after Bellamy purchased, paid for, and took possession of Holiday Dandy, he learned that she was not in foal. Holiday Dandy was returned to Meadowland to be rebred according to the custom of the industry. While at Meadowland, Holiday Dandy died. Bellamy sued to recover the purchase price. Meadowland argued that risk of loss had passed to the buyer. Who will win the case? Explain.

5. Mark La Casse, a Massachusetts college student, helped finance his education by selling pocket calculators to other students. La Casse called Stan Blaustein, a New York dealer in calculators, and ordered 23 calculators. Blaustein normally used United Parcel Service (UPS) to deliver orders. Because UPS was on strike, Blaustein was reluctant to agree to the sale. Finally, Blaustein agreed to make the sale, demanding payment in advance. La Casse left it to Blaustein to determine the manner of shipment if the strike was not settled before the calculators were to be shipped. Several days later, Blaustein received a letter from La Casse enclosing payment for the calculators, a blank check, and the following statement: "Please find a blank check to cover postage. Please ship to my resident address if you will, as this is easier for me." Blaustein packed the calculators and delivered them to the U.S. Post Office. Although the price of the calculators was $2,744, Blaustein only insured them for $400. The cost of postage and insurance was only $9.98, well below the $50 that La Casse had indicated in his letter was the amount in his bank account. Full insurance would have cost $16.26. La Casse never received the calculators and sued to recover his payment. Blaustein argued that risk of loss had

passed to buyer when the calculators were delivered to the post office. Who will win the case? Explain.

6. Boutell Driveaway, Inc., operated an automobile delivery service. Boutell's employee, Samuel Frisch, delivered a Cadillac from a seller, XYZ Motors, to a buyer, H & B Chevrolet-Cadillac, Inc. Frisch delivered the car by parking it in H & B's lot at 9:30 P.M., after business hours, and slipping the key under the dealership's front door. Frisch did not notify anyone that the car had been left in the lot, nor was there any prior agreement as to the procedures to be followed upon delivery. The Cadillac was not in the lot at 8:30 the next morning when the showroom was opened, nor was the key found on the floor. H & B sued Boutell for failure to deliver the car. Boutell argued that risk of loss had passed to H & B. Who will win the case? Explain.

7. James purchased an automobile from Hudiburg Chevrolet. He made the down payment on the car with a check that was later returned unpaid. When Hudiburg tried to recover the car, the dealer discovered that James had taken it to Georgia and had obtained a certificate of title under the assumed name of Denison. Denison (James) then took the car to Wisconsin, where he obtained another certificate of title and sold the car to a Milwaukee dealer who purchased it in good faith. The Milwaukee dealer then sold it to Ponce. Hudiburg sued Ponce for return of the automobile. Who will win the case? Explain.

8. Liberty Bank entered into a contract with Brady Auto Sales, Inc. (Brady) whereby Liberty Bank loaned money to Brady and was given a mortgage on the auto dealer's inventory. The inventory was defined as "goods or merchandise now owned or hereinafter acquired by the dealer which are held for sale or lease." Mr. Cosgriff bought a new auto from Brady. When he was later unable to sell his old car, a 1980 Dodge station wagon, Mr. Cosgriff asked Brady to sell it for him. Before the station wagon was sold, Brady defaulted on its loan. Liberty Bank seized and sold all of Brady's inventory, including the station wagon. Cosgriff sued

Liberty Bank to recover the station wagon. The Bank argued that the station wagon was inventory covered by the bank's security interest, that it had title to the car as a buyer in the ordinary course of business, and that Cosgriff's only rights were against Brady. Who will win the case? Explain.

9. Smith ordered a new truck from Palmer's Granite Garage, Inc. (Palmer). Smith took possession of the truck on October 3rd. However, he did not pay for the truck nor initiate the registration process nor apply for a certificate of title because Palmer had not received the invoice and other paperwork from the manufacturer. Smith put his own dealer's plates on the truck and drove it away. Palmer later received the invoice and set the payment date for October 6th. On October 5th, Smith was killed in an accident while driving the truck. Fulater, who was injured in the same accident, sued Palmer as the owner of the vehicle. Palmer argued that title had passed to the buyer. Who will win the case? Explain.

10. Mr. and Mrs. Alan Gerber purchased a new home in Salt Lake City and hired Jensen Interiors as decorators. Between February 13th and March 20th, Jensen delivered and installed a variety of home furnishings valued at $12,000. The agreement between Mr. and Mrs. Gerber and Jensen was that the furnishings were delivered "on approval" until the entire decorating plan was completed. At that time, a contract for sale would be executed for those items the Gerbers were going to keep. Some goods were tagged "Not Returnable after Three Days." The Gerbers were told that this return policy was not strictly enforced and did not apply to them. After the decorating was completed and the furnishings had been in the Gerber home for two months, the Gerbers used the furniture as security for an $11,000 loan from the South Davis Security Bank. Subsequently, the Gerbers went into bankruptcy. South Davis Security Bank claimed the right to the furnishings. Jensen objected on the grounds that, at the time the Gerbers used the furniture as collateral, the Gerbers had no ownership interest in the goods because they were in the home "on approval" only. Whose rights to the goods are superior, Jensen Interiors' or South Davis Security Bank's? Explain.

22

LIABILITY OF SELLERS

Throughout the history of commercial law, two opposing forces have been at work. On one side, sellers of goods want to be free of burdensome legal obligations to buyers. On the other, buyers want protection against injuries and losses caused by defective products. Out of this conflict, several legal theories have been developed concerning the responsibilities of sellers to buyers.

There are three main legal grounds on which a seller's liability for a defective product can be based. Two of these — negligence, and strict liability in tort — were discussed in Chapter 6. This chapter will discuss a seller's liability based on warranty as set forth in the Uniform Commercial Code (UCC).

SALES WARRANTIES

Many areas of the law have warranties. There are warranties in real property transactions (see Chapter 43) and when checks are transferred (see Chapter 27) as well as in the sale of goods. A **warranty** is a promise that something is true. Sales warranties are promises about the nature and quality of goods. For example, a seller may warrant that a toaster is free from any manufacturing defect.

A sales warranty can be made by an explicit promise, or in certain situations, it may be imposed by law. For example, the Code imposes a warranty that goods will meet certain standards if the seller is a merchant. The various types of sales warranties will be discussed in this chapter.

Transactions in Goods

Sales warranties also apply to other transactions in goods. The leasing of goods, for example, is sometimes considered to be analogous to the sale of goods. The lessor makes a profit, and the lessee pays for the use of the goods. Some courts have therefore held that the leasing of goods, such as construction equipment or automobiles, is a transaction in goods and have applied the Code's sales warranties to these leased goods [§2-102].

Contracts that provide primarily for services are not subject to sales warranties. For example, the transfusion of blood is a service that is not subject to sales warranties (see Chapter 19, pages 337–338). Sales warranties have, however, been applied to service-type contracts when the goods involved are more than incidental to the service being performed. For example, the use of a hair-coloring preparation by a beautician could be covered by a sales warranty.

BREACH OF WARRANTY

To appreciate why warranties are important, you should understand what happens if a warranty is breached. A breach of warranty occurs if the goods are not as warranted; that is, if they do not conform to the promise that was actually made about them or that was imposed by law in the situation. For example, a warranty is breached if a toaster warranted to be free of defects won't toast bread.

To obtain a remedy for a breach of warranty, a buyer must prove three things:

1. A warranty pertaining to the goods was made.
2. The goods are not as warranted; that is, the goods do not conform to the promise made.
3. Loss was suffered and the lack of conformity was the proximate (immediate) cause of the loss.

For example, in order to obtain a remedy, the buyer of the toaster that won't toast will have to prove (1) that the seller warranted the toaster to be free of defects; (2) that the toaster was defective, that is, it won't toast; and (3) that because the toaster won't toast, the buyer has suffered a loss because he or she does not have the toaster for which he or she paid. Fault is not an element in a recovery for breach of warranty. Therefore, a seller who makes a warranty is strictly liable. Even though the seller may have been as careful as he or she could be, a buyer can still recover if the goods are not as warranted.

Remedies for Breach of Warranty

There are two basic types of remedies available for breach of warranty.

1. The buyer can return the defective goods in some situations. For example,

the buyer of the toaster that won't toast could immediately return it to the seller. This remedy will be discussed in more detail in the next chapter.

2. The buyer can recover monetary damages for the loss caused by the breach of warranty. Monetary damages can compensate the buyer for the loss of the bargain and for consequential damages.

Consequential damages are losses caused to property (economic loss) or persons (personal injury) by defective goods [§2-715(2)]. Suppose, for example, that a buyer plugs in a new toaster and, instead of toasting the bread, it shoots sparks that damage the buyer's kitchen cabinet and burn the buyer's hands. The buyer has lost the benefit of the bargain; that is, he or she has lost the price of the toaster. The buyer has also suffered economic loss in the damage to the kitchen and personal injury in the burning of his or her hands.

Will the buyer be able to recover these losses from the seller? In general, the answer is yes. The Code provides that a buyer may recover for loss caused by any goods that do not conform to their warranties. The measure of damages is the difference between the value of the goods when the buyer received them and the value they would have had if they had been as warranted [§2-714(2)]. Put another way, the amount of damages received by the buyer should put the buyer in as good a position as he or she would have been in if the goods had been as warranted.

The Code requires that a buyer notify a seller of a defect within a reasonable time after the buyer discovers the breach [§2-607(3)(a)]. What is a reasonable time depends upon all the circumstances, including whether the buyer is a business person, who should be aware of the notification rules, or a consumer, who may not be aware of the rules. Failure to notify the seller in a timely fashion bars a buyer from obtaining any remedy [§2-607(3)(a)]. The purpose of the notice is to inform the seller that there is a problem with the goods so that the seller can attempt to remedy the problem and avoid litigation.

In the following case, the court had to decide how the amount of damages due to the buyer was to be determined when a warranty (a promise) that the seller had title to (ownership of) a used car was breached.

ITOH v. KIMI SALES, LTD.
345 N.Y.S.2d 416 (Civ. Ct. City of N.Y. 1973)

[Itoh, the plaintiff, purchased a used automobile from Kimi Sales, Ltd., the defendant. Kimi warranted that it had title to the car. Kimi had checked the identification number of the car with the police and had been told that the car was not stolen. Apparently, though, the number had simply been changed. After purchasing the car, Itoh was stopped by the police and the automobile was seized as stolen property.

Itoh sued Kimi for breach of warranty of title and moved for summary judgment. The court granted judgment but required a trial on the amount of damages due. The court discussed the types of damages available and the basis on which they were to be determined.]

COHEN, Judge

Plaintiff sues Kimi for damages of $2,692.79 consisting of $2,173.00, the purchase price of the automobile paid in May of 1970, $493.63, paid by plaintiff for additions and improvements to the automobile; and $26.16, paid by plaintiff for the hiring of an automobile to enable him and his family to return home when the police picked up the stolen automobile while they were driving away from home. . . .

As far as damages are concerned, there are triable issues of the fact concerning all items claimed except with respect to the purchase price paid which, if a proper item of damage, could be awarded on this motion for summary judgment. There is a question, however, as to whether this latter item is a proper item of damage. [T]he value of a stolen item may have depreciated in value — as may be the case with automobiles generally (although not necessarily as in the case of, for example, antiques). . . . The object [of awarding damages] is to reflect what the buyer has "actually lost" and . . . award ". . . to him only the loss which has directly and naturally resulted, in the ordinary course of events, from the seller's breach of warranty." [§2-714] states:

> (1) Where the buyer had accepted the goods and given notification he may recover as damages for any non-conformity of tender the loss resulting in the ordinary course of events from the seller's breach as determined in any manner which is reasonable.
> (2) The measure of damages for breach of warranty is the difference at the time and place of acceptance between the value of the goods accepted and the value they would have had if they had been as warranted, unless special circumstances show proximate damages of a different amount.

> (3) In a proper case any . . . consequential damages under the next section may also be recovered.

As stated in the Official Comment [§2-714], "Subsection (2) describes the usual, standard and reasonable method of ascertaining damages in the case of breach of warranty, but it is not intended as an exclusive measure." It recognizes the possibility of a different measure where "special circumstances show proximate damages of a different amount" and subsection (3) allows "In a proper case any . . . consequential damages. . . ." A case involving breach of warranty of title, where stolen tangible property is taken away from the buyer at some time after the purchase, is one where there are special circumstances so that the measure of damages should be the value of such property when it is taken away. In this way, the buyer will recover what he has "actually lost." He will get the benefit of any appreciation in value, including items of value he may have added to the stolen property — as claimed by plaintiff; and, on the other hand, he will not be unduly enriched by depreciation in the value of the property, from the use of which he benefitted until it was taken from him. . . . In addition, plaintiff may seek to recover for . . . consequential damages [§§2-714(3) and 2-715] which may include expenses for hiring an automobile. . . .

Since all of the items of damage to which plaintiff may be entitled involve triable issues of fact, the Court while granting plaintiff's motion for summary judgment against Kimi, directs that there be an assessment of damages after which judgment shall be entered in favor of plaintiff against defendant for the amount of damages determined upon such assessment.

[Trial on the amount of damages ordered.]

CASE REVIEW QUESTIONS

1. What warranty (promise) did Kimi make?
2. How was the warranty breached?
3. What has Itoh actually lost?
4. Should Itoh recover the purchase price of the car? Explain.
5. Why should Itoh recover the cost of renting an automobile to return home?

When Does Breach Occur?

A breach of warranty occurs when tender of delivery of the goods is made even if the buyer does not discover the breach until a later time. For example, in the case of the stolen car, the warranty that the seller had title was breached when the car was delivered to the buyer even though the buyer did not learn of the breach until the police seized the car.

If a warranty explicitly extends to the performance of the goods at a future time, a breach occurs when the buyer discovers or should have discovered the breach.

In the following case, the goods were as warranted at the time of delivery, but they no longer conformed to the warranty a few months later. The court had to determine whether the goods were still covered by the warranty.

GLEN PECK, LTD. v. FRITSCHE
651 P.2d 414 (Colo. App. 1982)

[Glen Peck, Ltd. (Peck), the plaintiff, purchased a bull from Jerome Fritsche and Alan Main, the defendants, for breeding purposes. The sales brochure contained the following warranty:

BREEDING GUARANTEE: BULLS—Should any bull fourteen (14) months of age or over fail to prove a breeder after being used on cows known to be breeders, the matter shall be reported in writing to the seller within six (6) months following date of purchase or six (6) months after the bull has reached 14 months of age. The seller will then have the right and privilege of 6 months to prove the bull a breeder. . . .

The bull was bought on January 12, 1979, and was kept under good conditions by Peck on its farm until June. On June 12, 1979, the bull's semen was tested and the bull was found to be sterile. Peck sued for breach of warranty. The trial court found for the defendants, and Peck appealed.]

PIERCE, Judge

Buyer argues . . . that the trial court erred in concluding as a matter of law that there was no breach of warranty because the . . . warranty did not "explicitly extend to a future performance" so that any breach would have to occur at the time of purchase and that no breach did occur since there was evidence that tended to establish that [the] bull [was a] breeder on the date of the sale. We agree with the buyer.

[§2-725(2)] states in pertinent part:

A breach of warranty occurs when tender of delivery is made; except that where a warranty explicitly extends to future performance of the goods and discovery of the breach must await the time of such performance, the cause of action accrues when the breach is or should have been discovered.

[T]he trial court here concluded as a matter of law that [§2-725(2)] did not apply. This conclusion was erroneous, and we hold that the . . . warranty here extended explicitly to future performance.

Normally, a cause of action for breach of . . . warranty accrues at the time of purchase of the goods. The . . . warranty here, however, was prospective. The warranty promised the performance of the bulls as breeders, not only at the moment of purchase but at some future date as well, namely, "after being used on cows known to be breeders." The warranty was also "explicit." It was adequately stated so that there was no doubt as to its meaning.

The parties do not dispute that the bulls were found sterile within the six month provision. Therefore, the breach was discovered within the time of performance as provided under [§2-725(2)].

The judgment is reversed and the cause is remanded for determination of damages and entry of judgment for plaintiff.

CASE REVIEW QUESTIONS
1. Why was the warranty breached?
2. When did the breach occur?
3. Why does the court say that the warranty explicitly extends to future performance?

CODE WARRANTIES

Article 2 of the Uniform Commercial Code specifies four types of warranties that can be made about goods being sold.

1. Warranty of title [§2-312].
2. Express warranty [§2-313].
3. Implied warranty of merchantability [§2-314].
4. Implied warranty of fitness for a particular purpose [§2-315].

Warranty of Title

In every contract for sale, there is a warranty of title. A seller does not have to say or do anything to create this warranty. A **warranty of title** is a promise that [§2-312]:

1. The buyer will have good title.
2. The seller has the right to transfer title.
3. The goods are transferred free of liens (claims by other persons).
4. The buyer will not be subject to claims for patent or other trade infringements if the seller is a merchant.

Good Title In all sales, the seller warrants that the buyer will have good title to the goods; that is, the seller promises that the goods will belong to the buyer free from the claims of anyone else [§2-312(1)(a)]. For example, in the case of *Itoh v. Kimi Sales, Ltd.* presented earlier in this chapter (page 407), the car dealer warranted that Itoh would have good title to the car.

Rightful Transfer A seller not only warrants that the buyer will have good title to the goods but also that the seller has the right to convey title [§2-312(1)(a)]. In Chapter 21, you learned that a merchant has the power but not the right to transfer title of goods entrusted to the merchant by their owner. A buyer in the ordinary course of business would get good title to these goods. Therefore, if the buyer were to be sued by the original owner to recover the goods, the buyer would win. The merchant seller, however, would be liable to the buyer for any losses the buyer incurred defending his or her ownership of the goods. The merchant's warranty of title would have been breached because warranty of title not only protects the buyer from the loss of the goods but also from any losses caused by a need to defend the right of ownership of the goods.

Freedom from Liens A seller also warrants that the goods transferred are free from any **liens** or **encumbrances;** that is, the seller promises that the goods are not subject to any third party's interest in or rights to the goods. A lien would exist, for example, if a creditor of the seller has taken an interest in the goods as collateral for a loan. However, if the buyer knows of any third person's claims when the contract for sale is made, there is no warranty that the transfer is free of those claims.

Infringements A merchant seller warrants that, in a transfer of goods of the type in which the merchant deals, the goods will be delivered free from any claims of any third persons that their patents, trademarks, or copyrights have been infringed [§2-312(3)]. For example, a merchant who sells designer items that are trademarked warrants in the sale of these items that they are the real items and that the designer's trademark rights have not been violated. If the buyer furnishes a merchant seller with the specifications for making goods, the seller does not warrant that the goods are free from infringement claims. In this situation, it is the buyer who, in effect, warrants to the seller that there are no infringements in the specifications [§2-312(3)].

Disclaimer of the Warranty of Title A seller can **disclaim a warranty;** that is, he or she can exclude or negate a promise made or a promise imposed by the Code. A seller can also **modify a warranty,** for example, by limiting its coverage. In order to be effective, any disclaimer or modification of a warranty must be made in the manner specified by the Code.

A warranty of title can be disclaimed or modified only by explicit language or by circumstances that indicate that the seller either does not have title or is selling only such rights as the seller or a third party may have. For example, a sheriff who is selling goods that have been seized to pay a judgment makes no warranty of title. An example of an explicit modification would be a statement by the seller that he or she does not warrant title but warrants only that he or she knows of no liens against the goods being sold.

Express Warranties

Express warranties are specific promises that are explicitly or implicitly bargained for by the parties and become part of the basis of the bargain in the agreement between them. In other words, express warranties are promises about what it is that the seller is agreeing to sell and the buyer is agreeing to buy.

The Code recognizes three ways in which express warranties can be created.

1. By any affirmation of fact or promise made by the seller that relates to the goods and becomes part of the basis of the bargain [§2-313(1)(a)].
2. By any description of the goods that is made part of the basis of the bargain [§2-313(1)(b)].
3. By any sample or model of the goods that is made part of the basis of the bargain [§2-313(1)(c)].

Express Warranty by Affirmation of Fact No particular words are needed to make an express warranty, so any statement of fact about the goods is an express warranty if it relates to what the seller intends to sell. The statement must, however, be a statement of fact. Puffing or sales talk — such as "This is the greatest" or "It will last forever" or "I've used it and loved it" — are statements of opinion, not fact, and do not create warranties.

There is overlap between the various types of express warranties; for example, a description is also an affirmation of fact. In the following case, the court did not determine which type of express warranty was involved, but it did find that a statement on the cardboard box that contained a ladder was an express warranty. The manufacturer had therefore made certain promises about the quality and performance of the goods.

CANTRELL v. AMARILLO HARDWARE CO.
602 P.2d 1326 (Kan. 1979)

[In February of 1974, Cantrell, the plaintiff, purchased a Mark V ladder from a retail seller who had purchased it from Amarillo Hardware Company, a wholesaler. The ladder had been manufactured by R.D. Werner Company, Inc., in January of 1974. Cantrell was injured when the ladder collapsed, and he brought suit against Amarillo and Werner, the defendants. Judgment was granted to Cantrell, and the defendants appealed.]

HOLMES, Justice

On June 26, 1974, plaintiff was using the ladder at his place of business, in a proper manner and upon a clear, level concrete floor. As plaintiff proceeded up the ladder, the front rails or legs below the first step suddenly collapsed throwing plaintiff to the floor. He was knocked unconscious, suffered a . . . fracture of the right wrist, bruises and abrasions to the head and face and soft tissue injuries to the back and hips. Expert testimony revealed permanent disability to plaintiff's right arm, back and hips.

Cantrell brought this action for actual . . . damages based upon a breach of express . . . warranty in the design, material, and workmanship of the Mark V ladder.

The evidence revealed that the Mark V ladder was an aluminum six-foot stepladder warranted to be satisfactory under loads of up to 200 pounds. Plaintiff weighed 165 pounds. The ladder, at the time in ques-

tion, was in the same condition as when it left defendant's factory. The cardboard box covering the top of the ladder bore the following message:

GOOD QUALITY: LIGHT-STRONG-SAFE; RATED LOAD 200 LBS.; FOR SAFETY'S SAKE BUY ME. I'M LIGHT AND STRONG! FIVE YEAR GUARANTEE. . . . The manufacturer guarantees the ladder, under normal use and service to be free from defects in material and workmanship, for five years from date of purchase.

Werner argues there is no evidence in the record indicating that any component, design feature or material used in the ladder was defective. . . . Werner contends that the proof of a defect is the basic element necessary for recovery in an action founded upon breach of contract. We have no quarrel with the broad general statement . . . that "[r]egardless of the theory upon which recovery is sought for injury . . . , proof that a defect in the product caused the injury is a prerequisite to recovery."

The cause of action at bar is based on a breach of express warranty. [§2-313] reads as follows:

(1) Express warranties by the seller are created as follows:

(a) Any affirmation of fact or promise made by the seller to the buyer which relates to the goods and becomes part of the basis of the bargain creates an express warranty that the goods shall conform to the affirmation or promise.

(b) Any description of the goods which is made part of the basis of the bargain creates an express warranty that the goods shall conform to the description.

(c) Any sample or model which is made part of the basis of the bargain creates an express warranty that the whole of the goods shall conform to the sample or model.

[T]his court discussed the scope of express warranties by manufacturers as follows:

> A manufacturer may by express warranty assume responsibility in connection with its products which extends beyond liability for defects. All express warranties must be reasonably construed taking into consideration the nature of the product, the situation of the parties, and surrounding circumstances. However, defects in the product may be immaterial if a manufacturer warrants that a product will perform in a certain manner and the product fails to perform in that manner. Defects may be material in proving breach of an express warranty, but the approach to liability is the failure of the product to operate or perform in the manner warranted by the manufacturer.

[T]his court quoted favorably, as follows:

> In an action of the present character, the burden of proof resting upon the plaintiff entails merely demonstration that the goods did not have the properties warranted. In the absence of controverting evidence adduced by the defendant, which convinces the jury that the goods were as warranted, plaintiff should prevail. The plaintiff is not required to show the technical causation of the goods' failure to match their warranty. . . .

[W]e have no hesitancy in finding there was sufficient competent evidence to support the jury's award of actual damages and that there was a violation of the express warranty of the appellant which was the cause of plaintiff's injuries.

The judgment is affirmed.

CASE REVIEW QUESTIONS

1. Did the manufacturer make any affirmations of fact or promises about the ladder? Describe them.
2. Were these statements part of the basis of the bargain?
3. How did the ladder fail to conform to the warranties made?
4. What did the buyer, Cantrell, have to prove to establish a breach of warranty?

Express Warranty by Description Express warranties can arise from a description of the goods. The description need not be in words. It can be found in blueprints or other technical specifications. In addition, prior deliveries can establish a description of quality or quantity based upon the course of dealing between the parties. As with all express warranties, the test is whether the description is part of the basis of the bargain; that is, whether it describes what the seller intends to sell and the buyer, to buy.

In the following case, the court had to decide whether a picture in a catalogue was a description.

RINKMASTERS v. CITY OF UTICA
348 N.Y.S.2d 940 (1973)

[Rinkmasters, the plaintiff, brought a cause of action against the city of Utica, the defendant, for refusing to accept and pay for certain goods that were delivered by Rinkmasters. The city of Utica defended on the grounds that the goods were not as warranted and sought to have the suit against it dismissed.]

HYMES, Judge

The plaintiff is a manufacturer of equipment for ice skating rinks. It publishes a "Purchasing Guide" in which items for sale are described and illustrated.

The defendant, the City of Utica, maintains an outdoor skating rink. At its request, the plaintiff forwarded a copy of the "Purchasing Guide" to the defendant. Through its Purchasing Agent, the defendant submitted an order for a resurfacing tank. . . . Upon [its] arrival at the city skating rink, the package [was] opened, examined and [was] found by the manager of the skating rink not to be in accordance with what he ordered. The plaintiff was so notified and the item [was] returned by the defendant. . . .

The resurfacing tank was a steel triangular tank placed on a carriage with rubber wheels. There was a pushing handle at one end and a water-release handle on top of the tank. As the tank was pushed over the ice, water was released from the tank onto a blade of cloth or rubber extending horizontally across the front of the tank at ice level so that a thin film of water was deposited upon the ice, creating a smooth surface. The description in the plaintiff's brochure gave the dimensions of the tank and stated that special sizes were made to order. There was no other word description. However, there was an illustration which showed a resurfacing tank with a water-release handle near the pushing bar and a blade in front of the tank which extended considerably beyond the width of the tank.

When the item was ordered by the Department of Purchase, it described the unit in the exact terms as set forth in the description in the "Purchasing Guide." However, the item that was delivered did not match the illustration in two important respects. The water-release handle at the top of the tank, by which the operator of the machine could control the flow of water onto the ice, was located beyond the reach of the person pushing the tank. This would necessitate stopping the movement of the tank in order to operate the release handle. Also, the blade near the surface of the ice was only as long as the width of the water tank. The illustra-

tion showed a blade that extended considerably beyond the width of the tank. . . .

The plaintiff has asserted that the items delivered were the items ordered. At the same time, the general manager for the plaintiff admitted on the stand that they varied from the illustrations. He claimed that the items delivered were new and improved models.

However, it is apparent from the testimony, that the items delivered were not in accordance with the descriptions contained in the catalogue. Under these circumstances, the plaintiff cannot recover a judgment against the defendant.

The Uniform Commercial Code, Section 2-313(1)(b) states,

> Any description of the goods which is made part of the basis of the bargain creates an express warranty that the goods shall conform to the description.

Most of the cases had involved the word description of merchandise. However, there has been an increased use of illustrated catalogues and brochures by businesses in search of trade. The traveling salesman has been replaced by the catalogue. Multi-colored catalogues are thrust upon the public as invitations to purchase. Description by words is limited, but drawings, photographs and blueprints are profusely used to guide and entice the purchaser. It is axiomatic that "a picture is worth a thousand words." The description of goods set forth in the Uniform Commercial Code certainly covers illustrations as well as words.

The plaintiff could have relieved itself of the responsibility of delivering items in conformity with the illustrations in its "Purchasing Guide" by merely indicating that the items were "Not As Illustrated." It failed to give the buyer any such warning. It is therefore bound by the warranty to deliver the goods according to the descriptions and illustrations.

Judgment is granted to the defendant dismissing the complaint.

CASE REVIEW QUESTIONS
1. In what way did the court find that the seller had made an express warranty?
2. Must an express warranty be made in words? Why?

3. In what ways did the resurfacing tank not conform to the warranties made?
4. What could the seller have done to avoid making those warranties?

Express Warranty by Sample or Model An express warranty can be made by showing the buyer a sample or a model of the goods. The term *sample* implies goods actually taken from the bulk of goods from which delivery will be made. The term *model* implies goods of the type that will be delivered. In either case, if the sample or model becomes part of the basis of the bargain, there is an express warranty that the goods delivered will be like those shown to the buyer.

For example, if a seller solicits orders for clothing by sending a small piece of fabric to prospective purchasers, the seller can fairly be said to be seeking to induce people to buy on the basis of the fabric sample. The sample thus becomes part of the basis of the bargain, and the fabric in the clothing delivered must be of the same quality as the small piece.

Implied Warranties

An **implied warranty** is a warranty that is imposed by law in particular situations. The Code recognizes two implied warranties: (1) the warranty of merchantability and (2) the warranty of fitness for a particular purpose.

Warranty of Merchantability A **warranty of merchantability** is made if the seller of the goods is a merchant with respect to that kind of goods [§2-314(1)]. The essence of this warranty is that the goods should be merchantable; that is, they should be capable of being sold (merchandised) by the buyer. Just as a buyer of goods should not have to defend his or her title to them in a law suit, a buyer who purchases goods covered by a warranty of merchantability should be able to resell the goods without any fears about their quality. The warranty of merchantability is also made to consumers who will use rather than resell the goods.

The Code sets forth a list of requirements that goods must meet to conform to the warranty of merchantability. The list covers only minimum requirements, so what is merchantable is not limited to what is specifically stated in the statute. Other attributes of merchantability may be developed by case law or through usage of trade.

Goods are merchantable under the Code requirements if they are of average quality; are of a quality that they would usually be accepted without objection by buyers; are fit for the ordinary purposes for which they are to be used; are adequately contained, packaged, and labeled as required by contract or the nature of the goods; and conform to any promises or affirmations that appear on the packaging or labeling [§2-314(2)].

In the past, there was a question about whether a sale had occurred when a person was served food in a restaurant. It was argued that, until the meal was paid for, there was no sale and that, until there was a sale, there were no warranties. The Code settles this question by stating that where the seller of food is a merchant, as a person operating a restaurant would be, "the serving for value of food or drink" is "a sale" [§2-314(1)]. Under the Code, if a patron of a restaurant who has not yet paid is rushed to the hospital deathly ill from having consumed some of the restaurant's food, there is no longer any question about whether or not the sales warranties apply. They do.

In the following case, a woman choked on a fish bone. The court had to determine whether the warranty of merchantability was breached.

WEBSTER v. BLUE SHIP TEA ROOM, INC.
198 N.E.2d 309 (Mass. 1964)

[Webster, the plaintiff, choked on a fish bone in a dish of fish chowder served by the Blue Ship Tea Room, the defendant. Webster sued to recover damages, alleging a breach of warranty. The jury found for the plaintiff, and the defendant appealed.]

REARDON, Justice

This is a case which by its nature evokes earnest study not only of the law but also of the culinary traditions of [Massachusetts] which bear so heavily upon its outcome.

The plaintiff, who had been born and brought up in New England (a fact of some consequence), ordered clam chowder and crabmeat salad. Within a few minutes she received tidings to the effect that "there was no more clam chowder," whereupon she ordered a cup of fish chowder. Presently, there was set before her "a small bowl of fish chowder." . . . "The fish chowder contained haddock, potatoes, milk, water and seasoning. The chowder was milky in color and not clear. The haddock and potatoes were in chunks" (also a fact of consequence). "She agitated it a little with the spoon and observed that it was a fairly full bowl. . . . It was hot when she got it, . . . [and she] stirred it in an up and under motion. She denied that she did this because she was looking for something, but it was rather because she wanted an even distribution of fish and potatoes." "She started to eat it, alternating between the chowder and crackers which were on the table. . . . She ate about 3 or 4 spoonfuls then stopped. She looked at the spoonfuls as she was eating. She saw equal parts of liquid, potato and fish as

she spooned it into her mouth. She did not see anything unusual about it. After 3 or 4 spoonfuls she was aware that something had lodged in her throat because she couldn't swallow and couldn't clear her throat by gulping and she could feel it." At the Massachusetts General Hospital . . . a fish bone was found and removed. The sequence of events produced injury to the plaintiff which was not insubstantial.

We must decide whether a fish bone lurking in a fish chowder, about the ingredients of which there is no other complaint, constitutes a breach of implied warranty under applicable provisions of the Uniform Commercial Code. As the judge put it in his charge,

> Was the fish chowder fit to be eaten and wholesome? . . . [N]obody is claiming that the fish itself wasn't wholesome. . . . But the bone of contention here—I don't mean that for a pun—was this fish bone a foreign substance that made the fish chowder unwholesome or not fit to be eaten?

The defendant asserts that here was a native New Englander eating fish chowder in a "quaint" Boston dining place where she had been before; that "[f]ish chowder, as it is served and enjoyed by New Englanders, is a hearty dish, originally designed to satisfy the appetites of our seamen and fishermen"; that "[t]his court knows well that we are not talking of some insipid broth as is customarily served to convalescents." We are asked to rule in such fashion that no chef is forced "to reduce the pieces of fish in the chowder to minuscule size in an effort to ascertain if they contained any pieces of bone." "In so ruling," we are told (in the defendant's brief), "the court will not only uphold its reputation for legal knowledge and acumen, but will, as loyal sons of Massachusetts, save our world-renowned fish chowder from degenerating into an insipid broth containing the mere essence of its former stature as a culinary masterpiece." Notwithstanding these passionate entreaties we are bound to examine with detachment the nature of fish chowder. . . .

Chowder is an ancient dish pre-existing even "the appetites of our seamen and fishermen. . . ." The word "chowder" comes from the French "chaudiere," meaning a "caldron" or "pot." In the fishing villages of Britany . . . "faire la Chaudiere" means to supply a caldron in which is cooked a mass of fish and biscuit with some savoury condiments. . . . Our literature over the years abounds in references not only to the delights of chowder but also to its manufacture. A namesake of the plaintiff, Daniel Webster, had a recipe for fish chowder which has survived into a number of modern cookbooks and in which the removal of fish bones is not mentioned at all. [The court quoted the entire recipe.] The recitation of these ancient formulae suffices to indicate that in the construction of chowders in these parts in other years, worries about fish bones played no role whatsoever. This broad outlook on chowders has persisted in more modern cookbooks. The all embracing Fannie Farmer states in a portion of her recipe, fish chowder is made with a "fish skinned, but head and tail left on. Cut off head and tail and remove fish from backbone. Cut fish in 2-inch pieces and set aside. Put head, tail, and backbone broken in pieces, in stewpan; add 2 cups cold water and bring slowly to boiling point. . . ." The liquor thus produced from the bones is added to the balance of the chowder.

Thus, we consider a dish which for many long years, if well made, has been made generally as outlined above. It is not too much to say that a person sitting down in New England to consume a good New England fish chowder embarks on a gustatory adventure which may entail the removal of some fish bones from his bowl as he proceeds. We are not inclined to tamper with age old recipes by any amendment reflecting the plaintiff's view of the effect of the Uniform Commercial Code upon them. In any event, we consider that the joys of life in New England include the ready availability of fresh fish chowder. We should be prepared to cope with the hazards of fish bones, the occasional presence of which in chowders is, it seems to us, to be anticipated, and which, in the light of a hallowed tradition, do not impair their fitness or merchantability.

We are most impressed, however, by . . . a case where the plaintiff was injured by a piece of oyster shell in an order of fried oysters, [in which the Court] held that "the possible presence of a piece of oyster shell in or attached to an oyster is so well known to anyone who eats oysters that we can say as a matter of law that one who eats oysters can reasonably anticipate and guard against eating such a piece of shell. . . ."

Thus, while we sympathize with the plaintiff who has suffered a peculiarly New England injury, the order must be

Judgment for the defendant.

CASE REVIEW QUESTIONS
1. What warranty had the Blue Ship Tea Room made?
2. What aspect of the warranty do you think Webster was claiming was breached?
3. Why didn't Webster recover against the Blue Ship Tea Room since she proved she was injured?
4. On what basis did the court find that there was no breach of warranty?

Warranty of Fitness for a Particular Purpose The warranty of merchantability requires that goods be fit for the ordinary purpose for which such goods are used [§2-314(2)(c)]. The **warranty of fitness** applies to particular purposes; that is, it requires that goods be fit for specific purposes. For example, a sleeping bag is ordinarily used for sleeping in the outdoors in moderate weather. A sleeping bag for use in winter weather would be a sleeping bag for a particular purpose.

A **warranty of fitness** for a particular purpose is implied in a sale of goods contract if, at the time the contract is made, the seller knows or has reason to know the following [§2-315]:

1. The buyer needs the goods for a particular purpose.
2. The buyer is relying on the seller to select or furnish suitable goods.

Both elements must be met for the warranty of fitness to apply.

If a buyer has a particular purpose in mind for a product and fails to tell the seller about it or if the buyer orders a particular model, the seller makes no implied warranty of fitness and has no duty to deliver goods that are suitable for other than ordinary purposes. If the buyer is later disappointed because the product is not suitable for the particular purpose he or she had in mind, the buyer must suffer the consequences. For example, if a buyer purchases a sleeping bag for four-season use but does not inform the seller of this purpose, there is no breach of warranty when the bag is not warm enough for winter camping.

In order for a warranty of fitness to be implied, the seller must know of the buyer's particular needs either explicitly because of what the buyer says or implicitly because the circumstances are such that the seller must know the buyer's purpose. For example, a restaurant owner has reason to know that his or her customers are relying on his or her skill and judgment to furnish food that is fit to eat. In this instance, both the ordinary and particular purpose for the goods overlap.

In the following case, the court had to determine whether or not a warranty of fitness was made and breached.

SAM'S ETC. v. ADMAR BAR & KITCHEN, ETC.*
425 N.Y.S.2d 743 (Civ. Ct. Kings County 1980)

MILLER, Judge

When realization does not live up to a buyer's expectations should the seller be charged with breaching a warranty of fitness for use and merchantability.

This is the tale of a pushcart that wouldn't push. Or so plaintiff claims in this action for $10,000 damages.

Plaintiff-buyer is the purveyor of franks, ice cream and soda in Brooklyn's sylvestral Marine Park. These exotic epicurean edibles are separately sold from small picturesque pushcarts pursuant to a permit plaintiff purchases every three years from the New York City Department of Parks.

As plaintiff's business prospered and parched palates of peripatetic pedestrians and ball players clamored for an augmented array of gastronomic

* The official case name uses "ETC." probably because the actual names are very long. The actual names are "Sam's Marine Park Enterprises, Inc. v. Admar Bar & Kitchen Equipment Corporation."

goodies, plaintiff decided to expand its enterprise. Plaintiff . . . met with defendant-seller, a manufacturer of vending equipment, and ordered two "special carts," at a cost of $6,480.00, specifying the inclusion of both insulated and refrigerated compartments for cooking franks, heating knishes, onions, sauerkraut, cooling ice cream and soda, brewing coffee and hot chocolate, pretzels, cake, and sandwich showcases, condiment dispensers, etc. A cabinet to house two cylinders of bottled gas was also necessarily incorporated. To accommodate another of buyer's design requests, one of the two large classic wheels was reduced in size and hidden from view under the cart by a metal apron shield.

Buyer approved the blueprint prepared by the seller and gave him $3,300 on account, subsequently inspected [the] dream wagons on two occasions, and upon completion, paid the full balance and accepted delivery. On the first sunny day thereafter, one of the plaintiff's employees proudly sallied forth to Marine Park with his sleek, six-foot long, stainless steel "Stutz Bearcart." (Only the anachronistic gaily striped umbrella could provide a clue to a pedestrian that this floating kitchen was the progeny of the pushcart of sainted memory!) Buyer claims to have made a distressing discovery — the pushcart allegedly no longer pushed! One cart was used, nevertheless, during the summer season. Buyer brought this action for return of his payment plus consequential damages after unsuccessful discussions with the seller concerning possible remedial measures.

The implied warranty sections of the Uniform Commercial Code [§2-314 Merchantability and §2-315 Fitness for a Particular Purpose] were intended to hold a seller responsible when inferior goods are passed along to an unsuspecting buyer and said goods, upon delivery, are not of a merchantable quality or are unfit for their particular purpose. Normally, a buyer with a specific use peculiar to the nature of his business would be protected both under Common Law and the Uniform Commercial Code, particularly where the skill or judgment of the seller is reasonably relied upon by the buyer to furnish goods suitable to meet their particular use. However, no implied warranty of fitness for a particular purpose arises when seller manufactures goods following the specification given by the buyer and acts upon his advice as to design.

Seller herein attempted to fulfill buyer's own design mandates and produced "very good wagons," according to the testimony of buyer's president. The only item of dissatisfaction stems from the claimed lack of mobility.

If buyer cannot use these carts in the particular manner it had intended, that is not a sufficient basis on which to charge defendant with a breach of warranty. Since this Court was able to move the wagon in front of the courthouse without physical difficulty or discomfort, the buyer should perhaps look towards more hearty and different personnel, motorization or installation in the conventional location of the larger traditional wheel that has successfully served such vehicles for generations.

For all of the foregoing reasons, the complaint herein is dismissed with judgment for the defendant.

CASE REVIEW QUESTIONS

1. What warranties did the buyer say were breached?
2. Why did the court hold that there was no warranty of fitness for a particular purpose?
3. Why wasn't the warranty of merchantability breached?

EXCLUSION OR MODIFICATION OF WARRANTIES

The Code allows sellers to exclude (disclaim) or modify (limit) each of the warranties. The way in which each type of warranty may be excluded or modified is specified by the Code. You have already read how the warranty of title may be excluded or modified (see page 411).

Exclusion or Modification of Express Warranties

Once an express warranty has been made, it is difficult to exclude that warranty. It can be modified, however. The policy of the Code is to protect buyers from such exclusionary language as, "The seller makes no express warranties."

Any language used to exclude or limit an express warranty must be consistent with the express warranty made [§2-316(1)]. Thus, the seller cannot say, "I am selling a television set but I do not warrant that it is a television set." The two statements are inconsistent. The seller can, however, say, "I am selling a television but I do not warrant that it will operate for more than ninety days."

The Code specifies that warranties can be cumulative; that is, there can be more than one and they can overlap. In general, any warranties should be construed as being consistent with one another. When this is impossible or unreasonable, the intention of the parties shall determine which warranty has priority. The Code sets some guidelines for determining priority:

1. Exact or technical specifications, such as a blueprint, have priority over an inconsistent model or sample or general language describing the goods.
2. A sample taken from the bulk of the same goods that are to be delivered takes priority over general language describing the goods.
3. Express warranties have priority over inconsistent implied warranties of merchantability. For example, a statement by a merchant seller that a used appliance may not operate properly is inconsistent with the implied warranty of merchantability that the goods being sold are fit for the ordinary purposes for which such goods are used [§2-314(2)(c)]. In this situation, the express warranty that the appliance may not operate properly will have priority.

Exclusion or Modification of Implied Warranties

The implied warranty of merchantability can be excluded either orally or in writing. The disclaimer must use the word "merchantability." If the disclaimer is made in writing, it must be done in a way that is conspicuous [§2-316(2)]. In other words, the seller must make some effort to draw the buyer's attention to the exclusion or limitation of the warranty of merchantability.

A warranty of fitness for a particular purpose can only be disclaimed or modified by a statement in writing; an oral disclaimer is not effective. The written statement must be conspicuous. The Code specifies that the statement, "There are no warranties which extend beyond the description on the face hereof," is sufficient to exclude the warranty of fitness provided that it is conspicuous.

The implied warranties of merchantability and fitness can also be excluded by employing certain phrases commonly used in business that communicate to a buyer that warranties are being excluded; for example, goods sold "as is" or "with all faults." When these phrases are used, according to the Code, the implied warranties are excluded if the words are sufficiently conspicuous even if the word "merchantability" is not used [§2-316(3)(a)].

If the seller demands that the buyer inspect the goods as fully as he or she desires before purchasing them, there are no implied warranties with respect to defects that an examination ought to reveal or would have revealed if the buyer who declined to inspect the goods had done so [§2-316(3)(b)]. If an inspection is demanded, the buyer's skill and the normal method of examining the goods in question will determine what defects are excluded from the implied warranties. For example, things that can only be discovered by testing, such as the chemical composition of the goods, would not be excluded by an examination unless chemical testing were a normal part of an examination of the particular goods.

The implied warranties can also be limited or excluded by course of dealing, course of performance, or usage of trade [§2-316(3)(c)]. For example, if a seller has always limited a warranty in past contracts to a period of three months, the same warranty limitation may apply to a new contract for the same type of goods even if it were omitted by accident because the buyer has reason to know that the seller only warrants goods for three months.

Limitation of Damages

The Code allows sellers to limit the amount of damages that may be recovered for a breach of warranty. The limitation may be a **liquidated damages** provision, which is a provision that specifies the amount of money due in the event of breach [§2-718].

A seller may also limit the type of remedy available. For example, a warranty that provides for the repair or replacement of defective goods would be a limited remedy [§2-719(1)(a)]. Warranties that limit recovery to repair or replacement are effective as limitations only if the repair or replacement actually occurs.

Whenever a limited remedy is not effective — if, for example, repairs are not made or a replacement is not given — the Code states that the warranty providing for a limited remedy has "failed of its essential purpose" [§2-719(2)]. At that point, all warranties and remedies provided by the Code become available to the buyer. For example, suppose that a merchant seller has excluded the warranty of merchantability and has substituted a warranty promising to repair any defect, but the seller does not repair the defect. The buyer can sue for breach of the warranty of merchantability and recover monetary damages instead of merely having the defect repaired.

Although the Code allows sellers to limit remedies for breach of warranty and even to exclude consequential damages, a seller may not exclude consequential damages if to do so would be unconscionable [§2-719(3)]. The Code specifically says that to exclude consequential damages due to physical injury to a person caused by defective consumer goods is, on the face of it, unconscionable. Whether an exclusion of consequential damages is unconscionable when the loss is economic, such as damage to a person's property, depends upon the circumstances. Knowledgeable buyers and sellers can agree between themselves on the allocation of certain risks. For example, a seller of farm equipment may exclude consequential damages for the loss of crops if the equipment fails to operate as warranted. If the seller is not acting unconscionably — that is, in a one-sided, unfair, oppressive way — in excluding the consequential damages, the farmer buyer will have to bear the loss.

The following case deals with a used car sale. The court was concerned with the types of warranties the buyer received, the attempted exclusion and limitation of warranties by the seller, and the availability of a remedy for the buyer.

STREAM v. SPORTSCAR SALON, LTD.
397 N.Y.S.2d 677 (Civ. Ct. City of N.Y. 1977)

[Stream, the plaintiff, purchased a used car from Sportscar Salon, Ltd., the defendant. The car was delivered on March 10, 1976. It broke down in early April after having been driven for about 300 miles. The defendant put a new engine in the car. Nevertheless, the engine continued to leak oil and the car broke down again. Stream had the car towed to the Sportscar Salon and sued to recover the purchase price, alleging breach of warranty.]

COHEN, Judge

This action is one for breach of warranty presenting the question of whether a product — the engine of a car — was defective. The breakdown of the car a few weeks after its sale to plaintiff, particularly when the engine had been losing large amounts of oil, supports a finding that the engine was defective when sold. The second breakdown, again with the loss of large amounts of oil, this time only a few days after defendant installed a replacement engine, even more readily supports a finding of a defective engine.

The contract of sale on defendant's form dated February 28, 1976 states in paragraph 7:

It is expressly agreed that there are no warranties, express or implied, made by either the dealer or the manufacturer on the motor vehicle, chassis or parts furnished hereunder. . . .

The bill of sale on defendant's form dated March 5, 1977 has stamped on it the statement "Limited Used Car Warranty" without further explanation. In another one of defendant's forms entitled "One Year Mechanical Guarantee" dated March 9, 1976 (referred to as a warranty in testimony given by defendant's service manager) and signed by both parties, defendant

agrees that it will protect the purchaser from any cost of repairs other than normal maintenance and wear on the vehicle . . . during the term of this guarantee for one repair or replacement on each of the specified parts, subject to the terms and conditions set forth: A. Engine. . . . This guarantee is only valid for a mechanical failure. This does not cover normal wear.

Defendant does not rely on the express denial of warranties as set forth on the contract of sale. It could hardly do so since the subsequent bill of sale it issued declares that there is a "Limited Used Car Warranty" and the "Guarantee" makes what defendant itself regards as certain warranties. The court finds, after consideration of the language used in the papers in question, which were prepared by defendant, that defendant warranted that the engine was not defective [§2-313].

Although the car was not purchased for any particular purpose [§2-315] so that the implied warranty of fitness for a particular purpose does not come into play, consideration must be given to the more general implied warranty of merchantability found in [§2-314]. . . . "Goods" includes a car and defendant, a car dealer, is a merchant with respect to the car. This implied warranty of merchantability, then, is applicable . . . unless excluded or modified in accordance with [§2-316(2), (3)] which contains the following language:

(2) Subject to subsection (3), to exclude or modify the implied warranty of merchantability or any part of it the language must mention merchantability and in case of a writing must be conspicuous. . . .

(3) Notwithstanding subsection (2)

(a) unless the circumstances indicate otherwise, all implied warranties are excluded by expressions like "as is," "with all faults" or other language which in common understanding calls the buyer's attention to the exclusion of warranties and make plain that there is no implied warranty.

There is no mention of the word "merchantability" in any of the papers involved in this case. Therefore, the implied warranty of merchantability remained in effect by virtue of [§2-316(2)] unless [§2-316(3)] came into effect. The phrases quoted in subsection (3) were not used in the various papers involved. . . . Accordingly, the implied warranty of merchantability is applicable to the sale of this car.

The court finds that by virtue of the defective engine in the car, defendant breached the express warranty relating to the engine as set forth in the "Guarantee" and also breached the implied warranty of merchantability in that the car, with that defective engine, was not fit for driving — the ordinary purpose for which it was to be used.

Defendant contends that under no circumstances can plaintiff recover the purchase price. It contends that its obligation was limited to the repair and replacement of defective parts and that it satisfied this obligation by replacing the car's engine. However, in determining whether plaintiff [can recover the purchase price] consideration must be given to any attempt to limit or modify remedies in accordance with [§2-316(4)] which states:

Remedies for breach of warranty can be limited in accordance with the provisions of this Article on liquidation or limitation of damages and on contractual modification of remedy [§2-718 and §2-719].

§2-719 entitled "Contractual Modification or Limitation of Remedy," states in subsection (1) and (2) as follows:

(1) Subject to the provisions of subsections (2) and (3) of this section . . .

(a) the agreement may provide for remedies in addition to or in substitution for those provided in this Article and may limit or alter the measure of damages recoverable under this Article, as by limiting the buyer's remedies to return of the goods and repayment of the price or to repair and replacement of non-conforming goods or parts; and
(b) resort to a remedy as provided is optional unless

the remedy is expressly agreed to be exclusive, in which case it is the sole remedy.

(2) Where circumstances cause an exclusive or limited remedy to fail of its essential purpose, remedy may be had as provided in this Act.

An examination of the language used in the express warranty reveals that while reference is made to "repairs" and "replacement," it is not expressly agreed that plaintiff's remedy was limited to repair and replacement. Indeed, the language used is in terms of limitation of "liability" rather than in terms of "remedies." As pointed out in [Official Comment 2 to §2-719]:

Subsection (1)(b) creates a presumption that clauses prescribing remedies are cumulative rather than exclusive. If the parties intend the term to describe the sole remedy under the contract, this must be clearly expressed. . . .

Accordingly, the court concludes that the remedy of "repair and replacement" is not exclusive and that the remedy permitting the recovery of the purchase price is available to plaintiff.

Moreover, the court notes that in the beginning of the "Guarantee" there is a provision for "one repair or replacement" of the engine. In this case, there was a repair and replacement which still left the car with a defective engine. Even if the "Guarantee" were effective in limiting plaintiff's remedy to repair and replacement, under these circumstances such an exclusive or limited remedy failed "of its essential purpose," and under [§2-719(2)] any "remedy may be had as provided in this Act." Indeed, under the circumstances of this case, if plaintiff's remedy were to be limited to "one repair or replacement" of the engine, such a limitation might very well be unconscionable. . . .

Also, there is, in addition to the express warranty, the implied warranty of merchantability. Since there has been no mention of merchantability in the papers prepared by defendant, there may be no limit on the remedy available to the plaintiff — who seeks to recover the purchase price — by reason of the breach of the implied warranty of merchantability.

Judgment is directed in favor of plaintiff against defendant for the sum of $2,688 with interest from May 6, 1976.

CASE REVIEW QUESTIONS
1. Why couldn't the seller rely on the express denial of warranties in the contract for sale?
2. Why wasn't the warranty of merchantability disclaimed by the denial of warranties in the contract?
3. Was the "One Year Mechanical Guarantee" an express warranty or a limitation of warranty? Or was it both?
4. Why would the remedy of one repair be unconscionable?

WARRANTY COVERAGE

Up to this point, we have discussed warranties as extending from sellers to buyers. Under traditional law, the doctrine of **privity of contract** provided that only a buyer of goods could recover from the seller for breach of warranty. As discussed in Chapter 6, recent legal developments have extended the seller's liability to persons other than the buyer. The drafters of the Code recognized these developments and provided the states with the option of selecting who can recover for breach of warranty [§2-318, Alternatives A, B, and C]. A seller may not exclude the coverage provided by any of these alternatives if the person covered suffers physical injury due to a breach of warranty.

Under Alternative A, any seller's warranty extends to any "natural person" (a term that excludes corporations) who is a member of the family or the household of the buyer or who is a guest in the buyer's home if it is reasonable to assume that the person may use or be affected by the goods warranted. The person injured can recover from the seller of the goods only for physical injury suffered.

Alternative B provides coverage for any natural person who suffers physical injury regardless of his or her relationship to the buyer. Alternative C provides coverage for any person, meaning both natural persons and corporations, regardless of that person's relationship to the buyer and for any type of loss — economic loss or property damage as well as physical injury.

Because each state can select one of these alternatives, you should determine which alternative has been adopted by your state.

MAGNUSON–MOSS WARRANTY ACT

Warranties are excluded or modified in many consumer sales situations. Frequently, recovery for breach is limited to repair, refund, or replacement. Responding to nationwide consumer complaints that such remedies were ineffective, Congress enacted the Magnuson–Moss Warranty Act in 1975. The act's purpose was to improve the quality of the information about warranties available to consumers, to prevent deception, to improve competition in the marketing of consumer goods, and to encourage warrantors to establish procedures whereby consumer disputes are fairly and expeditiously settled through informal mechanisms.

The act applies to consumer products, which are defined as "any tangible personal property . . . which is normally used for personal, family, or household purposes . . . [MMWA §101(1)]. [Note: References in this part of the text are to the Magnuson–Moss Warranty Federal Trade Commission Improvement Act found in Title 15 of the United States Code Annotated.]

The act requires certain sellers to disclose the type of warranty being given by labeling it as either "full" or "limited." The act also sets forth standards that must be met in order for a warranty to be labeled as "full." For example, to label a warranty "full," a seller must provide a remedy without cost and within a reasonable time for any breach of a written warranty [MMWA §104(a)(1)].

A written warranty is any written affirmation of fact or written promise made in connection with a sale that relates to the nature of the consumer goods and promises that they are free of defects or will meet a certain level of performance over a period of time [MMWA §101(6)(A)]. A written warranty is also made if the seller promises in writing to refund, repair, replace, or take any other remedial action if the consumer goods fail to meet certain specifications [MMWA §1-1(6)(B)].

If a warranty meets the requirements set forth in the act, the warranty must be conspicuously labeled a "full warranty." If it does not meet the requirements, it must be conspicuously labeled a "limited warranty." The purpose of the act is to put buyers on notice that a warranty may not meet certain standards. The buyer can then protect himself or herself by selecting products with appropriate warranties.

Recognizing that sellers often attempt to disclaim implied warranties, the act states that any seller who makes a written warranty or enters into certain service contracts with the buyer may not disclaim or modify any implied warranties, such as those provided by the UCC. Any attempted disclaimer is ineffective [MMWA §108]. Thus, in all states that have adopted the UCC, the warranties of merchantability and fitness cannot be disclaimed if a written warranty is made.

In the following case, the court had to determine whether a written warranty had been made in order to determine whether the goods were covered by implied warranties.

MARINE MIDLAND BANK v. CARROLL
471 N.Y.S.2d 409 (A.D. 2d Dept. 1984)

[Newcomb, an automobile dealer, sold a Titan mobile home to the Carrolls, the defendants. The Carrolls were going to pay for the trailer in installments over a period of years. Newcomb assigned the right to re- ceive these payments to Marine Midland, the plaintiff. The Carrolls refused to make the payments because problems arose with the mobile home. Marine Midland sued to recover the payments. The Carrolls defended on the grounds of breach of warranty. Marine Midland argued that the warranties had been disclaimed. The Carrolls argued that under Magnuson–Moss, the seller had made a written warranty and could not disclaim the implied warranties. The trial court dismissed the Carrolls' defense. The Carrolls appealed.]

CASEY, Judge

The determinative question is whether the "Dealer's PreDelivery Inspection Requirements" form, completed and signed by Newcomb's service manager, constituted a "written warranty" within the meaning of the Federal act, although the form made no representation as to the future condition or performance of the items inspected and despite a disclaimer in the sales contract that the "seller makes no warranties, express or implied, and hereby disclaims all warranties. . . ." The inspection form was filled out, checked and signed on the day before the sale, and thus became "part of the basis of the bargain" [MMWA §101(6)]. Under the act, a "written warranty" is defined as "any written affirmation of fact . . . made in connection with the sale of a consumer product by a supplier to a buyer which relates to the nature of the material or workmanship and affirms or promises that such material or workmanship is defect free" [MMWA §101(6)(A)].

We find that the inspection form herein constituted a "written warranty" under the act, since it represented that the motor home had been inspected and tested and was found to "perform, function, operate and/or serve exactly as intended." As to the disclaimer relied on by plaintiff, [MMWA §108(a)] of the act provides, in pertinent part, that "[n]o supplier may disclaim or modify . . . any implied warranty to a consumer with respect to such consumer product if (1) such supplier makes any written warranty to the consumer with respect to such consumer product. . . ." This provision effectively invalidates plaintiff's disclaimer. We, therefore, reverse that part of the order of Special Term based upon the conclusion that the Magnuson–Moss Warranty Act had no applicability to the transaction and reinstate the third affirmative defense. . . .

Order modified, on the law, by reversing so much thereof as dismissed defendants' third affirmative defense as so modified, affirmed.

CASE REVIEW QUESTIONS

1. Why was Magnuson–Moss applicable to the Carroll's contract?
2. In what way had the seller made a written warranty?
3. Why was the seller's disclaimer invalid?
4. What warranties are applicable to the transaction?

REVIEW QUESTIONS

1. What is a warranty?
2. What must a buyer prove to recover for a breach of warranty?
3. How are damages measured for a breach of warranty?
4. When does a breach of warranty occur?
5. Name and describe four types of warranties specified by the Code.
6. How can each of these warranties be disclaimed or modified?
7. How is a warranty of merchantability different from a warranty of fitness?
8. What limitations can a seller place upon a recovery for a breach of warranty?
9. Who can recover for a breach of warranty and for what type of loss?
10. Under the Magnuson–Moss Warranty Act, what impact does making a written warranty have on the implied warranties available under the UCC?

CASE PROBLEMS

1. In October 1958, Mrs. Mittasch purchased a casket and a burial vault for her deceased husband. Seal Lock Burial Vault, Inc., the seller, provided a certificate of assurance that: "We hereby certify that this Vault is free from material defects or faulty workmanship and will give satisfactory service at all times." In June 1970, Mrs. Mittasch wished to move her husband's body to a different cemetery. When the body was exhumed, it was discovered that water had leaked into the vault. Mrs Mittasch sued Seal Lock for breach of warranty. Who will win the case? Explain.

2. In 1932, Mrs. Erna Menzel purchased a painting in Europe for the equivalent of $150. The painting was by Marc Chagall. During the Second World War, Mrs. Menzel fled Europe and the painting was apparently seized by the Germans. Sometime later, the painting was purchased by a New York art dealer named Klaus Perl. Perl sold the painting to a gentleman named List in 1955 for $4,000. In 1962, Mrs. Menzel was reading an art book and saw a reproduction of the painting. The book noted that List was the owner. Menzel recovered the painting from List. At the time List turned the painting over to Menzel, it had a market value of $22,500. List brought an action against Perl for breach of warranty of title. Who will win the case? Explain. What will be the measure of damages?

3. Clinton Construction Company ordered 300 gallons of antifreeze from Bryant and Reaves, Inc., a dealer in automobile supplies. Clinton informed Bryant that it needed the antifreeze to protect its heavy-duty construction equipment over the winter when it would not be in use. No brand name was stated, but the order did specify that the product be "of a good, first-class, permanent quality." Bryant did not have any antifreeze and contacted Luther Kelly, a manufacturer of antifreeze. Kelly shipped some antifreeze directly to Holly Springs where Clinton was located. Clinton paid Bryant $1,100 for the antifreeze. In the spring, Clinton was unable to start and use much of its equipment due to broken water lines. A chemical analysis of the antifreeze showed a 0.5 percent chloride content, which can cause damage to en-

gines. Clinton paid $30,000 for repairs to the construction equipment and lost $10,000 in earnings due to the down time of the machinery during repairs. Clinton sued Bryant for $40,000. Bryant defended upon the grounds that it was not responsible for the antifreeze since it had been shipped to Clinton by Kelly. Who will win the case? Explain. What damages will be awarded? Why?

4. Hensley went to Colonial Dodge, Inc., to purchase a used car. In the show room was a large sign that read, "Colonial Dodge USED CARS—ONE YEAR WARRANTY." Hensley selected a car and signed a purchase agreement. On the back side of the agreement was printed:

   No warranties, express or implied, are made by the dealer with respect to used motor vehicles except as may be expressed in writing by the dealer.

   Hensley drove the car home, which was about three miles away. Half way there, the engine failed to operate properly and the car slowed to 25 miles an hour. Hensley took the car to a mechanic, who discovered busted and bent push rods. Hensley asked the dealer to replace the engine. After various unsuccessful negotiations with the dealer, Hensley finally had a new engine installed by another mechanic. Hensley sued Colonial Dodge for the cost of the repairs to the engine. Who will win the case? Explain.

5. AFA Corporation maufactures bottle caps that are sold to distillers. AFA incorporates cardboard liners covered with a thin plastic film in the caps. The liners serve to seal off the contents of the bottles. Phoenix Closures manufactures liners. In 1975, Phoenix supplied AFA with samples of liners including Lasan and Vinylite liners, which Phoenix recommended for use on liquor bottles. AFA purchased a quantity of liners from Phoenix. Subsequently, AFA received numerous complaints from the distillers that the liners were leaking. Phoenix examined the liners in AFA's possession and took them back, admitting that the liners supplied were not the same as the samples. AFA sued Phoenix to recover damages, alleging breach

of warranty. What, if any, warranties were breached? Explain.

6. El Fredo Pizza negotiated with Roto-Flex Oven Company for the purchase of a pizza oven for a new restaurant it planned to open. El Fredo Pizza went to Roto-Flex because it already had a Roto-Flex oven in one of its restaurants. Roto-Flex manufactured and installed a new oven for the new El Fredo restaurant. The new oven heated unevenly. As a result, El Fredo had to hire extra employees to monitor the baking of pizzas. Roto-Flex attempted to correct the problem but was unsuccessful, and El Fredo replaced the oven.

   El Fredo sued Roto-Flex for breach of the implied warranty of fitness and alleged as damages the costs of the additional employees and profits lost due to loss of customers. El Fredo argued that the delay in getting pizzas baked resulted in the loss of clientele. Who will win the case? Explain. What damages will be awarded? Why?

7. Robert Matzkin Company (Matzkin) needed an adhesive to laminate aluminum sheets to plywood. A sales representative of Basic Adhesives, Inc. (Basic) visited the work site and told Matzkin that Basic's scientists had formulated a special adhesive for laminated aluminum and plywood. Matzkin ordered 60 gallons. A five-gallon container was delivered first. Later, Matzkin received a 55-gallon container. Each container bore the following label:

   NONWARRANTY: Since we have no control over the conditions under which these goods are transported or stored, handled or used, we make no warranty, either express or implied, with respect to these goods or their fitness for any purpose or the results to be obtained from their use. No representative of ours has the authority to waive or change this provision, which applies to all sales. IF THE PURCHASER DOES NOT ACCEPT THE GOODS ON THESE TERMS, THEY ARE TO BE RETURNED AT ONCE, UNOPENED.

   Matzkin used the adhesive, but the laminated plywood delaminated, so Matzkin refused to pay for the adhesive. Basic Adhesive sued to recover the price. Who will win the case? Explain.

8. Alexis McLaughlin purchased a Ford truck and a camper unit that was affixed to the back of the truck. While traveling with her daugher Mary Ann and her niece Jocelyn Wolfe, Alexis had an accident that was found to be the result of a breach of warranty made by Ford. All three women sued Ford for physical injuries suffered in the accident and for damages to property. Who will win the case? Explain.

9. Ventura purchased a new Ford automobile from Marino Auto Sales (Marino). The front page of the sales contract conspicuously contained the following language:

   The seller, MARINO SALES, Inc., hereby expressly disclaims all warranties, either express or implied, including any implied warranty of merchantability or fitness for a particular purpose.

   On the back of the contract paragraph 7 repeated the disclaimer language. It read in part:

   It is expressly agreed that there are no warranties . . . except, in the case of a new motor vehicle, the warranty expressly given to the purchaser upon the delivery of such motor vehicle. The selling dealer also agrees to promptly perform and fulfill all terms and conditions of the owner service policy.

   The warranty provided by Ford read in part:

   LIMITED WARRANTY (12 MONTHS OR 12,000 MILES). . . . Ford warrants for its 1978 model cars . . . that the Selling Dealer will repair or replace free any parts except tires, found under normal use . . . to be defective in factory materials or workmanship within the earlier of 12 months or 12,000 miles. . . . THERE IS NO OTHER EXPRESS WARRANTY ON THIS VEHICLE.

   Ventura's new automobile was seriously defective and the dealer was unable to repair it. Ventura sought to return the automobile, alleging breach of warranty. Marino refused to refund the purchase price. Ventura sued to recover the price. Who will win the case? Explain.

23

PERFORMANCE

When a seller and a buyer have entered into a sales contract, each party must perform the promises made. If one of the parties does not perform one or more of his or her promises, that party breaches the contract and the other party is entitled to a remedy. This chapter will discuss the parties' obligations in the performance of sales contract. The next chapter will discuss the remedies available for a failure to perform.

A buyer's basic obligation is to accept the goods and pay the seller for them. A seller's basic obligation is to deliver goods that conform to the specifications in the contract. The manner in which a seller or a buyer is to perform his or her obligations is determined by the agreement of the parties. If the contract does not specify the manner of performance, it is determined by specific provisions in the Code or by any relevant course of dealing, usage of trade, or course of performance. The material that follows discusses the performance obligations imposed by the Code in the absence of any explicit or implied agreement.

PAYMENT BY THE BUYER

If the parties have not agreed on the manner of payment, payment by the buyer is due at the time and place the buyer is to receive the goods [§2-310(a)]. For example, payment for groceries is due at the check out counter.

If the seller is transferring the goods by delivering a document of title (a piece of paper that represents the goods, see Chapter 21), the buyer must pay for the goods at the time and place he or she is to receive the document [§2-310(c)]. For example, if a seller in Chicago is shipping goods to a buyer in New York City and the bill of lading (a document of title issued by a carrier) is to be delivered to the buyer by seller's agent in New York, the buyer must pay for the goods when the seller's agent notifies the buyer that the document has arrived in New York.

When goods that are shipped by carrier are sold to the buyer on credit — for example, in accordance with an agreement that payment is due in 30 days — the period for payment begins to run from the date of the shipment or the date of the invoice, whichever is later [§2-310(d)]. For example, if goods that are to be paid for in 30 days are shipped on November 1st, payment would be due November 30th. If the invoice is dated November 5th, however, payment would not be due until December 5th even if the goods were shipped on November 1st.

A buyer may make a required payment by any means or in any manner customary in the ordinary course of business [§2-511(2)]. A buyer will therefore generally be able to pay by check. Payment by credit card will also be appropriate in a number of situations. Payment by check, however, is conditional between a buyer and a seller [§2-511(3)]. If a check is dishonored (not paid), there has been, in effect, no payment by the buyer.

A seller can demand that payment be made in **legal tender,** which is coin or money that a creditor must by law accept as payment. In the United States, Federal Reserve bills (paper money) are printed with a statement that they are legal tender. If a seller demands payment in legal tender, the buyer must be given reasonable time to obtain the cash. A seller cannot, therefore, wait until the last minute to demand payment in cash. If a seller could do this, he or she could force a buyer who did not have cash in hand to breach the contract.

Breach by the Buyer

If a buyer fails to make a payment at the time and in the manner in which it is due, he or she is in breach of the contract. The seller may suspend his or her performance under the contract and is entitled to a remedy. For example, if the buyer does not pay at the time and place the seller is to deliver the goods, the seller is not obligated to leave the goods with the buyer.

Repudiation by the Buyer A buyer also breaches a sales contract when he or she **repudiates** the contract by telling the seller in advance of the time for performance that he or she will not honor the contract or pay for the goods when payment is due. A **repudiation** is an **anticipatory breach,** which means that the breach comes before the time for performance.

When there is an anticipatory breach, the seller may elect to do one or more of the following:

1. *The seller may wait a reasonable time for the buyer to change his or her mind* [§2-610(a)]. What is a reasonable time depends upon all the circumstances. For example, a seller of nonperishable goods with a stable market price can wait for a longer period than can a seller of perishable goods with a price that is dropping rapidly.

2. *The seller may seek any of the remedies for a breach provided by the Code* [§2-610(b)]. The Code remedies will be discussed in Chapter 24. The seller is not required to notify the buyer before seeking Code remedies because the buyer's repudiation serves as notice to the buyer that the contract has been breached. The buyer must, however, be given notice by the seller if the seller plans to take some action that requires notification for the seller to be acting in good faith. For example, suppose that the seller has reassured the buyer that he or she will continue to hold the goods for the buyer for two weeks despite the buyer's repudiation. Under the requirements of good faith, the seller would be obligated to notify the buyer if he or she changes his or her mind and decides to seek a remedy under the Code before the two-week period has expired.

3. *The seller may suspend his or her own performance* [§2-610(c)]. For example, if a buyer repudiates a contract for specially manufactured goods, the seller is not required to continue manufacturing the goods. If the buyer later changes his or her mind and reinstates (reestablishes) the contract, the seller will not be in breach if the goods are not completed at the time called for in the contract [§2-611(3)].

Retraction of a Repudiation A buyer can retract (withdraw) his or her refusal to honor a sales contract at any time up to the time for performance called for by the contract [§2-611(1)]. For example, if the buyer tells the seller on November 1st that he or she will not make a payment due on November 15th, the buyer can retract the repudiation at any time up to November 15th. The buyer, however, will not be able to retract if the seller has notified the buyer that the contract is cancelled or that the seller considers the buyer's action of repudiation as final or if the seller has changed his or her position in a material way because of the buyer's repudiation. The seller would have changed his or her position if, for example, he or she arranged to sell the goods to someone else because of the repudiation.

A buyer can retract a repudiation by any method that clearly indicates to the seller that the buyer intends to honor the contract. For example, a buyer could reinstate a contract by sending the seller the payment due for the goods.

Adequate Assurance When a buyer wishes to reinstate a contract, the seller can demand adequate assurance that the buyer will actually honor the terms of the contract. **Adequate assurance** is anything that gives the seller confidence that the buyer will perform, such as payment in advance or payment in **escrow** (payment to a third party to be held until the time for performance).

Adequate assurance can be demanded by either sellers or buyers at any time they have reason to believe that the other party will not perform in accordance with the contract. The demand for adequate assurance must be made in writing [§2-609(1)]. Between merchants, commercial standards will be used to test the reasonableness of a party's concern that the other party will not perform and the adequacy of any form of assurance offered [§2-609(2)]. When a demand for adequate assurance had been made, the party making the demand can suspend performance if the suspension is reasonable.

Excused Performance and Setoff

When a seller repudiates a contract, the buyer's rights are similar to the rights of a seller when a buyer repudiates. The buyer can wait a reasonable time for the seller to perform, the buyer can seek Code remedies, and the buyer is excused from making payments [§2-610].

If the seller has breached a contract, a buyer may not only withhold payment for future deliveries, but he or she may also setoff (withhold) payments due for goods already delivered to the extent that he or she is entitled to damages for the breach. The buyer must notify the seller that he or she intends to withhold the damages from the payment due [§2-717].

In the following case, the court had to determine whether the seller had repudiated the contract after partial performance and whether the buyer was entitled to a setoff. Notice that the seller, by failing to take appropriate action, became the party who breached the contract.

NATIONAL FARMERS ORG'N v. BARTLETT & CO., GRAIN
560 F.2d 1350 (8th Cir. 1977)

[National Farmers Organization, the seller and plaintiff, sued to recover $18,441.62 due on the price of grain sold and delivered to Bartlett & Company, Grain, the buyer and defendant. The buyer argued that it was not obligated to pay the amount due because the seller had repudiated and the buyer was entitled to a setoff for damages. The buyer and seller had 45 contracts between them, and the seller had made deliveries on 31 of the contracts. The buyer, however, had not completed all the payments due. On January 26, 1973, the seller notified the buyer that the seller "was not going to deliver any grain to [the buyer] on any of the 14 outstanding contracts between the parties unless and until [the buyer] paid [the seller] a substantial amount of money due on deliveries already made as of that date on contracts Nos. 22868, 1371, 1389 and 1824." The seller did in fact suspend performance on all 14 contracts as of January 27.

The buyer treated the notice as an anticipatory repudiation. The parties engaged in negotiations to settle the amounts due. A dispute remained about eight contracts. The trial court determined that the seller had anticipatorily repudiated the contracts and found for the buyer. The seller appealed.]

VAN OOSTERHOUT, Senior Circuit Judge

Accordingly, at issue herein is the propriety of claimed setoffs, totalling $18,441.62, on those contracts having delivery dates subsequent to January 31. . . . The resolution of this issue turns on the question whether the Seller's January 26 communication constituted an anticipatory repudiation of these contracts. The question tendered to us for decision . . . is a difficult and close one. Ultimately, its resolution is governed by [§2-610].

Before examining the . . . question directly, we find it useful for the purpose of comparison to consider what the Seller clearly could have done on January 26. [§2-609(1)] provides in part:

> When reasonable grounds for insecurity arise with respect to the performance of either party the other may in writing demand adequate assurance of due performance and until he receives such assurance may if commercially reasonable suspend any performance for which he has not already received the agreed return.

Comment 3 to this section states in part:

> Under commercial standards and in accord with commercial practice, a ground for insecurity need not arise from or be directly related to the contract in

question. . . . Thus a buyer who falls behind in "his account" with the seller, even though the items involved have to do with separate and legally distinct contracts, impairs the seller's expectation of due performance.

The example just cited conforms precisely to the facts before us. Plainly, the Seller could have availed itself of a [§2-609] remedy on January 26. Equally plainly, however, it did not do so.

Although the Buyer was on January 26 substantially behind on payment on some of the contracts . . . there is no indication that the Buyer's ability to pay was impaired.

With the above comments in mind, we turn to the controlling issue under [§2-610]. The district court, acknowledging that the issue was a close one, concluded that the Seller anticipatorily repudiated the contracts with delivery dates subsequent to January 31 when on January 26 it notified the Buyer that no grain would be delivered under any of the contracts unless and until the Buyer made a substantial payment for deliveries already made under contracts Nos. 22868, 1371, 1389, and 1824. The court reasoned:

> Plaintiff's imposition on January 26 of a condition . . . that defendant perform under various independent contracts clearly amounted to a statement of intention not to perform except on conditions which went beyond each of [the contracts not yet due]. . . . A party to a contract may not refuse performance simply because the other party has breached a separate contract between them.

The Code does not articulate what constitutes an anticipatory repudiation. Comment 2 to [§2-610], however, offers the following guidance:

> It is not necessary for repudiation that performance be made literally and utterly impossible. Repudiation can result from action which reasonably indicates a rejection of the continuing obligation. . . . Under the language of this section, a demand by one or both parties for more than the contract calls for in the way of counter-

performance is not in itself a repudiation nor does it invalidate a plain expression of desire for future performance. However, when under a fair reading it amounts to a statement of intention not to perform except on conditions which go beyond the contract, it becomes a repudiation.

It is the last sentence of this Comment which is of foremost concern to us. The communication of January 26, fairly read, amounts to a statement of intention not to perform future contracts except on conditions which go beyond those contracts. Under the language of the Comment, therefore, the communication was indeed an anticipatory repudiation of the future contracts.

The general rule is not subject to variance when the stated condition derives from a separate contract or contracts—regardless of the validity of the repudiator's claim under the separate contract or contracts. It is well established that the breach of one contract does not justify the aggrieved party in refusing to perform another separate and distinct contract.

[A]s noted peviously, . . . there is no indication that the Buyer's ability to pay was impaired. Measures short of suspending delivery on all contracts could have preserved the Seller's contractual right to payment. Moreover, as we have concluded above, a [§2-609] remedy was specifically available but not used. Despite the Buyer's wrongful withholding of payment on contracts not in default, the separate identities of the various contracts were unquestionably preserved, as all deliveries and payments were separately accounted for throughout the pertinent time period.

Taking all of the above-mentioned facts into account, we agree [there was] an anticipatory repudiation here.

The judgment appealed from is affirmed.

CASE REVIEW QUESTIONS

1. What was the seller's obligation under the contracts? What was the buyer's obligation?
2. In what way did the buyer breach the contract? In what way did the seller breach the contract?
3. Why was the buyer excused from making the full amount of payments due?

4. Of what relevance is the fact that there was more than one contract?
5. What should the seller have done that it did not do?

DELIVERY BY THE SELLER

A seller's basic obligation is to transfer and deliver goods that conform to the specifications in the contract to the buyer [§2-301]. If a seller who is not legally excused from delivering the goods fails to deliver the goods called for by the contract, the seller has breached the contract. Upon breach, the buyer can seek the remedies available under the Code, which are discussed in Chapter 24.

On first thought, it might seem that there would be no breach if the seller delivers the goods. In fact, though, the question of whether there has been a breach or not is quite complex. For instance, the goods, even though delivered, may not be the goods that were ordered; that is, the goods may not conform to the contract.

The buyer has various options as to how he or she may treat a delivery of goods that does not conform to the contract. For example, the buyer may keep (accept) or reject (return) the delivered goods. Figure 23-1 charts all the possible actions that may be taken when goods are delivered by a seller and indicates who will be in breach depending upon what actions are taken. Each of the actions in the figure will be described in the following materials.

The Seller Delivers the Goods

If the parties have agreed upon a manner for delivery, the seller must deliver the goods in that manner or be in breach of the contract. If the buyer and seller have not agreed upon the manner for delivery, the Code determines where, when, and how delivery must be made and the quantity of goods that must be delivered.

Where Must Delivery Be Made? In the absence of an express or implied agreement, the Code specifies the place for delivery. These specifications were discussed in detail in Chapter 20 (see page 367), so they will be summarized here.

The place for delivery is basically the seller's place of business or, if the seller has no place of business, his or her home [§2-308(a)]. If the goods are identified to the contract when it is made and are known by the parties to be located in some other place, that place is the place for delivery [§2-308(b)].

If the contract explicitly or impliedly requires the seller to deliver the goods to the buyer at the buyer's home or place of business, the delivery can be made by the seller using his or her own trucks or by a carrier. The obligations of the seller concerning delivery using his or her own trucks or a carrier are discussed in Chapter 20.

If the goods are to be delivered through the use of a document of title, such as

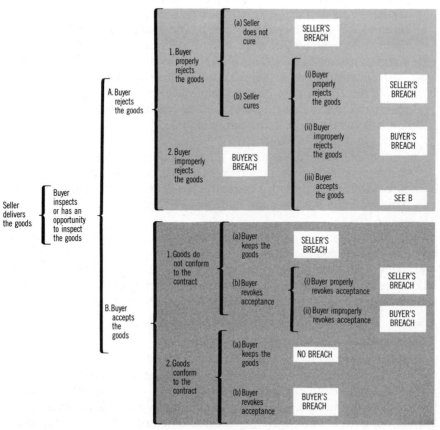

FIGURE 23-1
Buyer's and Seller's Options When Goods Are Delivered

a bill of lading issued by a carrier, the document may be delivered through the banking system; that is, the seller can send the document to a bank in the buyer's city. The bank is then obligated to notify the buyer that the document can be picked up. The place for delivery of the document in this situation is the bank [§2-308(c)].

When Must Delivery Be Made? In the absence of an agreement, delivery must be made at a reasonable time [§2-309]. For example, if a seller is authorized to ship a load of Christmas trees, the shipment must be made early enough before Christmas for the buyer to have an opportunity to sell the trees.

How Are the Goods to Be Delivered? A seller can satisfy his or her obligation to deliver goods in one of two ways, depending upon the circumstances. The seller must either tender (offer) delivery of the goods or make appropriate arrangements to ship the goods.

1. *The seller must tender the goods.* The seller or the seller's agent must tender the goods if the goods are to be delivered (1) at the seller's place of business, (2) at the buyer's place of business, or (3) by a carrier under a destination contract (see page 390). Tendering delivery of the goods is sufficient to satisfy the seller's obligation to deliver the goods [§2-507].

   If the parties have not agreed upon the manner of tender, the seller or the carrier (in the case of a destination contract) must give the buyer reasonable notice that the goods are available and must make the goods available to the buyer at a reasonable hour [§2-503(1)]. Tender is discussed in detail in Chapter 21.

2. *The seller must arrange to ship the goods.* If the authorized method of delivery is a shipment contract (see page 390), the seller must make appropriate arrangements with a carrier for the delivery of the goods [§2-504]. This provision was discussed in detail in Chapter 21.

How Many Goods Must Be Delivered? The quantity of goods to be delivered is specified in the contract. If the parties have not agreed otherwise, the seller must deliver all of the goods in a single delivery [§2-307]. In other words, the seller does not satisfy his or her obligation to deliver by tendering or shipping less than the full quantity of goods called for by the contract.

Excused Delivery

If the agreed upon method of delivering the goods becomes unavailable or commercially impracticable, the seller must use a reasonable substitute if one is available. In this situation, the buyer may not object to the substitute [§2-614(1)]. For example, if the contract calls for shipment to be made by rail but the railroads are not operating because of a strike, the seller may use a different type of carrier. Whether the seller should ship by truck or by plane depends upon the nature of the goods and other circumstances. If rapid delivery is important, the seller would probably choose the airlines. The buyer cannot allege that the seller is in breach of the contract even if delivery of the goods to an airport rather than a railyard requires the buyer to travel farther to pick them up.

If delivery of the goods or the means of delivery has become impracticable and no reasonable substitute is available, the seller may be excused from performance. In this situation, there are three conditions that must be met if the seller is to be excused [§2-615(1)]:

1. Something unexpected must have occurred.
2. The parties must have assumed that the unexpected event would not occur.
3. The occurrence of the event must make the seller's performance commercially impracticable; that is, there is no reasonable commercial substitute.

If the occurrence of an unexpected event affects only a part of a seller's performance, as might happen if part of the goods are destroyed, the seller can allocate the remaining goods among all of his or her customers in a fair and reasonable manner [§2-615(2)]. The seller must notify the buyer of a delay in delivery, a suspension of delivery, or a reduction in the quantity of goods to be delivered [§2-615(c)].

In the following case, the court had to decide whether the seller was excused from delivering some fertilizer.

NEAL-COOPER GRAIN CO. v. TEXAS GULF SULPHUR CO.
508 F.2d 283 (7th Cir. 1974)

[Neal-Cooper Grain Company (Neal-Cooper), the plaintiff, sued Texas Gulf Sulphur (TGS), the defendant, for failure to deliver a quantity of fertilizer (potash) ordered by the buyer. The parties had a written contract that allowed TGS to increase prices fifteen days after providing the buyer with a revised price list.

The contract also contained an exculpatory (excuse) clause that read:

> The Seller shall not be liable for failure or delay in shipments or completion of a shipment . . . when such failure or delay is caused by . . . the operation of statutes or law, interference of civil or military authority or other causes of like or different kind beyond the control of the seller. . . .

On December 2, 1969, Neal-Cooper sent TGS an order for ten thousand tons of potash. TGS did not respond to the order, but it did send a new price list about January 17th 1970. TGS refused to ship the December order at the December prices.

In early January 1970, TGS shut down its Moab mine as its principal source of supply. Thereafter, only small quantities of potash were produced from that mine. TGS's principal source of supply became the Allan mine in Canada. Canadian governmental regulations did not permit TGS to sell potash for less than 33.75 cents a unit, a price greater than TGS's contract price with Neal-Cooper. TGS argued that it was therefore excused from delivering potash to Neal-Cooper. The trial court ruled in favor of TGS. Neal-Cooper appealed.]

PELL, Circuit Judge

Under the Uniform Commercial Code three conditions must be met before a party is excused from per-

formance. TGS correctly states them in its brief: "(1) a contingency must occur (2) performance must thereby be made 'impracticable' and (3) the non-occurrence of the contingency must have been a basic assumption on which the contract was made." See [§2-615]. TGS cites the Draftsmen's Comments in support of its position, but the support is not there. The relevant comments provide:

> Neither is a rise or a collapse in the market itself a justification, for that is exactly the type of business risk which business contracts made at fixed prices are intended to cover. But a severe shortage of raw materials or of supplies due to a contingency such as . . . unforeseen shutdown of major sources of supply . . . which either causes a marked increase in cost or altogether prevents the seller from securing supplies necessary to his performance, is within the contemplation of this section. . . .
>
> There is no excuse under this section, however, unless the seller has employed all due measures to assure himself that his source will not fail [§2-615, Comments 4–5].

As TGS correctly states, the Code abandons the old rule of impossibility of performance or act of God and substitutes for it the rule of commercial impracticability. . . . Nevertheless, impracticability will not be deemed an excuse unless the intervening circumstances are ones which the parties assumed would not occur. The fact that performance has become economically burdensome or unattractive is not sufficient for performance to be excused.

In our opinion, the present case is one in which performance may have become burdensome but was not excused. Performance by TGS was not shown to have been impossible. There was no showing that the

Moab mine could not have produced sufficient potash to fill the contract. Indeed, in its new price list which by its terms was to be effective on January 1, 1970, this significant statement appears: "Shipments to be at Seller's option from either Allan, Saskatchewan; *Moab, Utah or Seller's warehouses.*" [Emphasis added by the court.]

Finally, we note that at the time [TGS] signed the contract . . . that company had been aware for many months that as of the following January it would turn to the Allan mine for its principal source of supply. It was TGS's decision to switch to the Canadian mine, not the governmental regulation of prices which caused the claimed price increase. . . . We will not allow a party to a contract to escape a bad bargain merely because it is burdensome. After one party has entered a contract for supply, he ceases to look for other sources and does not enter other contracts. To make duplicate arrangements for supply under such circumstances might assure the delivery of the material desired but also might well be productive of double liability and inability to dispose of the double deliveries. Barring circumstances not existent here, the buyer has a right to rely on the party to the contract to supply him with goods regardless of what happens to the market price. That is the purpose for which such contracts are made.

[We hold] . . . that performance by TGS was not excused, and that the contract was breached. . . .

[Reversed.]

CASE REVIEW QUESTIONS

1. What three elements does the court say must be met to excuse a seller from performance?
2. Why aren't those elements met in this case?
3. What could TGS have done to comply with the terms of the contract?

The Buyer Inspects the Goods

When goods have been tendered, delivered, or identified to a contract, a buyer has a right to inspect the goods [§2-513(1)] (see Figure 23-1). Unless the contract indicates otherwise, the buyer can inspect the goods before paying for them. A buyer will not be allowed to inspect the goods before payment, however, if the contract calls for delivery COD (cash on delivery) [§2-513(3)(a)] or if payment is made against documents of title [§2-513(3)(b)]. Payment against documents of title means that the buyer is obligated to pay for the document when it is presented and that the buyer cannot inspect the goods before payment even if the goods have arrived in the buyer's city. Delivery COD or payment against documents insures that the seller will get his or her money when the buyer gets the goods so that the seller already has his or her money if a dispute arises over the goods when the buyer inspects them. The buyer then has to decide whether any problem with the goods is serious enough to justify trying to get his or her money back from the seller.

When inspection is allowed before payment, the inspection must take place at a reasonable place and time and in a reasonable manner [§2-513(1)]. In other words, a buyer cannot normally demand to inspect the goods at 3 A.M.

If a buyer incurs expenses in inspecting the goods, either before or after payment, such as the cost of a chemical analysis, those costs must be paid by the buyer. If, however, the goods are not as ordered — that is, if they do not conform to the contract — the buyer can recover the costs of inspection in an action for breach of contract.

Inspection is a necessary prelude to the choice a buyer must make when the seller has delivered or tendered the goods. The buyer can choose to accept (keep) the goods or to reject (return) the goods. The opportunity to inspect the goods allows the buyer to determine whether the goods are as warranted (specified) in the contract. (For a discussion of warranties , see Chapter 22.)

The Buyer Rejects the Goods

A buyer who has inspected the goods and has discovered that they do not conform to the contract may be able to **reject** (return) the goods. (See Figure 23-1.) A buyer's rights with regard to rejecting nonconforming goods are determined by the type of contract involved. The Code distinguishes between single shipment contracts and installment contracts. An **installment contract** is a contract whereby the seller is required or authorized to make a series of shipments to the same buyer pursuant to the same agreement. For example, if a seller has a contract to deliver 1,000 pounds of sugar each month for six months, the contract is an installment contract. This is true even if the contract reads that "each shipment is a separate contract." Conversely, a contract to deliver 6,000 pounds of sugar in one shipment is a single shipment contract.

Single Shipment Contracts: The Perfect Tender Rule The Code provides a **perfect tender rule** for single shipment contracts, which allows a buyer to reject the shipment of goods if there is *any* breach in the performance of the contract. A buyer can reject or accept all the goods or reject some of the goods and accept the rest [§2-601].

A buyer can reject the goods if they do not conform to the specifications in the contract. For example, if the contract calls for 6,000 pounds of sugar and the seller delivers or tenders 5,950 pounds, the buyer can reject all the goods because 5,950 pounds does not conform to the 6,000 pounds specified in the contract. The buyer can also reject the goods if the manner of delivery is not in accord with the terms of the contract. For instance, if the contract calls for delivery on Tuesday morning, the buyer can reject the goods if they are delivered on Tuesday afternoon even if there is nothing wrong with the goods themselves.

In deciding whether to reject or accept some or all of the nonconforming goods, a buyer will have to consider such things as the seriousness of the breach, whether he or she has already paid for the goods, and his or her business needs. For example, suppose that the buyer ordered 6,000 pounds of sugar but received 5,950 pounds. If the buyer can easily obtain the additional 50 pounds of sugar, the breach is not too serious. If the buyer has already paid the seller, negotiating with the seller for a return of the sugar in exchange for the buyer's money may not be worth the trouble. If the buyer needs the sugar to meet his or her production requirements, a rejection would seem inappropriate.

If the nonconformity is serious, a buyer may have no choice except to reject the goods. Suppose that 6,000 pounds of sugar are delivered according to the contract but all of the sugar is contaminated with a pesticide. The buyer can reject the sugar because it is not fit to use under the warranty of merchantability (see page 415). Even if the buyer has paid for the sugar and needs it, he or she is likely to reject the entire shipment in this situation.

The perfect tender rule has limited applications. First, a buyer who is technically able to reject may not have suffered any damages because of the nonconformity. Suppose, for example, that the goods are to arrive on Tuesday morning but come instead on Tuesday afternoon. If the buyer had no immediate need for the goods on Tuesday morning, he or she has suffered no loss due to the breach. Second, the perfect tender rule is balanced by the seller's right to cure (correct) any defect. Cure will be discussed later in this chapter. Finally, the perfect tender rule is not applicable to installment contracts.

Installment Contracts When parties have a long-term contractual relationship created by an installment contract, the Code encourages the relationship by allowing the buyer to reject goods only for a substantial (serious) nonconformity. The buyer can reject an installment that is nonconforming only if the nonconformity substantially impairs the value of the delivery to the buyer [§2-612(2)].

For example, suppose that the contract calls for the delivery of 1,000 pounds of sugar each month for six months and a shipment arrives with only 550 pounds. If receiving only 550 pounds substantially reduces the value of the shipment to the buyer, he or she can reject the shipment. However, if the seller gives adequate assurance (see page 431) that he or she can correct the nonconformity—by promptly shipping an additional 450 pounds, for example—the buyer cannot reject the 550 pound shipment and must accept it [§2-612(2)]. Only if cure (correction) on the nonconformity is not possible can a buyer reject an installment.

Proper or Improper Rejection If a buyer has a right to reject goods under either the perfect tender rule that applies to a single shipment contract or because of substantial impairment in the case of an installment contract, the rejection must be made in the proper manner. If a buyer has no right to reject the goods or a buyer does not reject in the proper manner, he or she will be deemed to have accepted the goods (see Figure 23-1). The buyer's and seller's rights when the buyer has accepted goods are discussed later in this chapter.

Proper Rejection A buyer must reject goods within a reasonable time after the goods have been delivered or tendered for delivery, and he or she must give the seller notice of the rejection [§2-602(1)]. When a buyer has rejected goods, he or she cannot use them [§2-602(2)]. For example, suppose that the contract calls for a single delivery of 5,000 blue widgets, and a shipment of 2,000 red widgets arrives. The buyer must promptly notify the seller if he or she chooses to reject the shipment. If the buyer thereafter opens five packages of the red widgets and sells some of them to his or her customers, the buyer has exercised ownership over those five packages. The buyer's rejection of those five packages would therefore be ineffective.

The buyer must tell the seller the reason for a rejection, that is, what is wrong with the goods. If the buyer fails to do this and the seller could have cured (corrected) the defect, the buyer will not be able to use that defect to prove that his or her rejection was proper. Suppose, for instance, that a buyer rejected a shipment because it was short two items out of the 50 ordered, but the buyer notified the seller that the model number was incorrect. If the seller has only a few of the proper model number left, he or she may not attempt a cure. If the buyer sues the seller for breach of contract and the seller proves that the proper model number was delivered, the buyer will not be able to claim that the seller breached by only shipping 48 items because that is not what the buyer told the seller. The net effect of all this is that the buyer will be the one in breach for refusing to accept the goods.

If both parties are merchants and the seller demands in writing that the buyer provide a complete and final statement of all defects on which the buyer intends to rely to prove that his or her rejection was proper, the merchant buyer must provide the merchant seller with the requested list. Even though the seller may no longer be able to cure the defects, the buyer's list will help the seller to negotiate a settlement or to prepare for a trial. More importantly, the merchant buyer will not be able to claim at a trial any defect that is not on that list.

The Buyer's Duties on Rejection A buyer who has rejected goods has certain duties with regard to the goods. If the buyer has not paid all or even part of the price for the goods nor incurred any costs, such as expenses for inspection, he or she must hold the goods for a reasonable time and must take reasonable care of them so that the seller can take them back [§2-602(2)(b)]. A merchant buyer must also follow any reasonable instructions given by the seller concerning the care and reshipment of the goods [§2-603(1)].

If the seller gives no instructions to the buyer within a reasonable time after being notified that the goods are nonconforming, the buyer can make a judgment in good faith as to how to dispose of the goods [§2-604]. The buyer can store the goods, return them to the seller, or even resell them. A merchant buyer, however, is required to make reasonable efforts to sell rejected goods for the seller if they are perishable or if they are likely to decline in value [§2-603(1)]. For example, suppose that the buyer ordered pine Christmas trees but received a load of spruce Christmas trees one week before Christmas. If the seller does not give instructions, the buyer must try to sell the trees. Not only are the trees perishable, but they will also have seriously declined in value on the day after Christmas.

If the buyer resells the rejected goods, he or she is entitled to reimbursement for expenses incurred in making the sale, such as costs of storage, advertising, and commissions on the sale. A sale of rejected goods by the buyer is not an exercise of ownership over the goods; rather, it is done to mitigate, or reduce (see page 319), the damages that the seller will have to pay [§2-604].

The Seller's Cure

If a buyer has rejected goods because of a defect in the goods or in the manner of delivery, the seller has the option to **cure** — that is, to correct the defect — if the time for performance has not expired [§2-508(1)]. (See Figure 23-1.) For example, suppose that a contract calls for the delivery of 5,000 widgets before October 15th. If the seller delivers 4,000 widgets on October 12th but the buyer rejects them, the seller can cure by delivering a total of 5,000 widgets before October 15th.

The seller must give the buyer notice that he or she intends to cure. Furthermore, the seller can give the buyer notice of an intent to cure even if the seller has already taken the rejected goods back and has refunded the purchase price, provided that the time for performance has not expired.

If the seller shipped nonconforming goods with the belief that they would be acceptable to the buyer, perhaps with some adjustment in the price, the seller can have a reasonable period of time beyond the time for performance in which to make a cure. For example, suppose that a contract calls for 5,000 blue widgets to be delivered on October 15th. If the seller delivers 4,500 blue widgets (all he or she has) on October 15th and reduces the price but the buyer still rejects them, the seller will have a few more days to obtain and deliver the remaining 500 blue widgets.

In the following case, an inspection disclosed a nonconformity in the goods. The buyer rejected the goods and refused to accept a cure. You should pay special attention to the interplay between the seller and the buyer, which resulted in the buyer being the one in breach.

T.W. OIL, INC. v. CONSOLIDATED EDISON
57 N.Y.2d 574 (N.Y. 1982)

FUCHSBERG, Judge

In the first case to wend its way through our appellate courts on this question, we are asked . . . to decide whether a seller, who, acting in good faith and without knowledge of any defect, tenders non-conforming goods to a buyer who properly rejects them, may avail itself of the cure provision [§2-508(2)]. We hold that, if seasonable notice be given, such a seller may offer to cure the defect within a reasonable period beyond the time when the contract was to be performed so long as it has acted in good faith and with a reasonable expectation that the original goods would be acceptable to the buyer. . . .

In January, 1974, . . . the plaintiff [T.W. Oil, Inc.] purchased a cargo of fuel oil. . . . While the oil was still at sea en route to the United States in the tanker *M T Khamsin,* plaintiff received a certificate from the foreign refinery at which it had been processed informing it that the sulfur content . . . was .52%. Thereafter, on January 24, the plaintiff entered into a written contract with the defendant [Consolidated Edison (Con Ed)] for the sale of this oil. The agreement was for delivery to take place between January 24 and January 30, payment being subject to a named independent testing agency's confirmation of quality and quantity. The contract, following a trade custom to round off specifications of sulfur content at, for instance, 1%, .5%, or .3%, described that of the *Khamsin* oil as .5%. In the course of the negotiations, the plaintiff learned that Con Ed was then authorized to buy and burn oil with a sulfur content of up to 1% and would mix oils containing more and less to maintain that figure.

When the vessel arrived, on January 25, its cargo was discharged into Con Ed storage tanks. . . . In due course, the independent testing people reported a sulfur content of .92%. On this basis, acting within a time frame whose reasonableness is not in question, on February 14 Con Ed rejected the shipment. Prompt negotiations to adjust the price failed; by February 20, plaintiff had offered a price reduction roughly responsive to the difference in sulfur reading, but Con Ed, though it could use the oil, rejected this proposition. . . .

The very next day, February 21, plaintiff offered to cure the defect with a substitute shipment of conforming oil scheduled to arrive on the *S. S. Appollonian Victory* on February 28. Nevertheless, on February 22, the very day after the cure was proffered, Con Ed, adamant in its intention to avail itself of the intervening drop in prices, summarily rejected this proposal too. . . .

There ensued this action for breach of contract, which resulted in a nonjury decision for the plaintiff in the sum of $1,285,512.83. . . . To arrive at this result, the Trial Judge . . . decided as a matter of law that [§2-508(2)] was available to the plaintiff even if it had no prior knowledge of the non-conformity. Finding that in fact plaintiff had no such belief at the time of the delivery, . . . the court went on to hold that plaintiff's "reasonable and timely offer to cure" was improperly rejected. . . .

In support of its quest for reversal, the defendant now asserts that the trial court erred . . . in failing to interpret [§2-508(2)] to limit the availability of the right to cure after date of performance to cases in which the seller knowingly made a non-conforming tender. . . .

We turn then to the central issue on this appeal: Fairly interpreted, did [§2-508(2)] of the Uniform Commercial Code require Con Ed to accept the substitute shipment plaintiff tendered? In approaching this question, we, of course, must remember that a seller's right to cure a defective tender, as allowed by both subdivisions of [§2-508], was intended to act as a meaningful limitation on the absolutism of the old perfect tender rule, under which, no leeway being allowed for any imperfections, there was, as one court put it, just "no

room . . . for the doctrine of substantial performance" of commercial obligations. . . .

In contrast, to meet the realities of the more impersonal business world of our day, the Code to avoid sharp dealing, expressly provides for the liberal construction of its remedial provisions [§1-102] so that "good faith" and the "observance of reasonable commercial standards of fair dealing" be the rule rather than the exception in trade [§2-103(1)(b)]. . . . As to [§2-508] in particular, the Code's Official Comment advises that its mission is to safeguard the seller "against surprise as a result of sudden technicality on the buyer's part" [§2-106, Comment 2]. . . .

[§2-508] may be conveniently divided between provisions for cure offered when "the time for performance has not yet expired" [§2-508(1)] . . . and ones which by newly introducing the possibility of a seller obtaining "a further reasonable time to substitute a conforming tender" [§2-508(2)], also permit cure beyond the date set for performance. . . .

Since we here confront circumstances in which the conforming tender came after the time of performance, we focus on subdivision (2). On its face, taking its conditions in the order in which they appear, for the statute to apply (1) a buyer must have rejected a non-conforming tender, (2) the seller must have had reasonable grounds to believe this tender would be acceptable (with or without money allowance), and (3) the seller must have "seasonably" notified the buyer of the intention to substitute a conforming tender within a reasonable time.

In the present case, none of these presented a problem. The first one was easily met for it is unquestioned that the .92%, the sulfur content of the *Khamsin* oil did not conform to the .5% specified in the contract and that it was rejected by Con Ed. The second, the reasonableness of the seller's belief that the original tender would be acceptable, was supported not only by unimpeached proof that the contract's .5% and the refinery certificate's .52% were trade equivalents, but by testimony that, by the time the contract was made, the plaintiff knew Con Ed burned fuel with a content of up to 1%, so that, with appropriate price adjustment, the *Khamsin* oil would have suited its needs even if at delivery, it was to the plaintiff's surprise, to test out at .92%.

As to the third, the conforming state of the *Appol-*

Ionian oil is undisputed, the offer to tender it took place on February 21, only a day after Con Ed finally had rejected the *Khamsin* delivery and the *Appollonian* substitute then already was en route to the United States . . . it is almost impossible, given the flexibility of the Uniform Commercial Code definitions of "seasonable" and "reasonable," . . . to quarrel with the finding that the remaining requirements of the statute also had been met.

[We hold] that a seller should have recourse to the relief afforded by [§2-508(2)] as long as it can establish that it had reasonable grounds, tested objectively, for its belief that the goods would be accepted. *[Affirmed.]*

CASE REVIEW QUESTIONS
1. Why is it clear that Con Ed could reject the *Khamsin* oil?
2. Could Con Ed have rejected the oil if it were the fifth shipment in a ten-shipment contract?
3. Why did the oil company have reason to believe that the *Khamsin* shipment would be acceptable to Con Ed?
4. Con Ed argued that only a seller who knows that a nonconforming shipment is being sent can use §2-508(2) and have additional time to cure. Why should that argument be rejected?

The Buyer's Options on the Seller's Cure If the seller tenders a cure, the buyer's options are similar to those he or she had when the seller first delivered. The buyer first has an opportunity to inspect the goods to determine if they conform to the contract. After the inspection, three things may happen (see Figure 23-1):

1. The buyer might properly reject the goods (see page 440). If there is still time, the seller may attempt another cure. If the seller cannot or does not cure, the seller is in breach of the contract.
2. The buyer might improperly reject the goods. An improper rejection can operate as an acceptance. By improperly rejecting, the buyer has breached the contract.
3. The buyer might accept the goods. The buyer's options on acceptance will be discussed in the following material.

The Buyer Accepts the Goods

When the seller delivers or tenders delivery of the goods, either initially or as a cure, the buyer has the option of accepting the goods (see Figure 23-1). Acceptance of goods is a technical term in sales law. It means more than merely taking possession of the goods. A buyer's acceptance of goods establishes certain rights between the parties. For example, if the buyer accepts the goods, the seller can collect the contract price for them [§2-709(1)(a)]. If the buyer does not accept the goods, the seller cannot recover the price but will be able to use other remedies provided by the Code.

A buyer can accept the goods only after he or she has had a reasonable opportunity to inspect them. Because a buyer must sometimes take possession of or pay for goods before he or she is able to inspect them, neither payment nor taking possession constitutes acceptance. For example, the buyer who pays for goods delivered COD has not accepted the goods.

Acceptance occurs in one of three ways, but only after the buyer has had an opportunity to inspect the goods.

1. *The buyer signifies to the seller that the buyer will take or retain the goods* [§2-606(1)(a)]. No formal notification of acceptance is required. All that is necessary is that the buyer signify in some fashion that he or she is keeping the goods. For example, in a case where payment is due after the goods have been delivered, the buyer may be signifying acceptance by sending payment for the goods. The payment, of itself, is not proof that the buyer has accepted the goods, but it is some indication that such is the case. If the buyer can prove that the payment was made automatically upon receipt of the goods, the payment does not establish acceptance. However, if payment was made after a careful inspection of the goods, the payment does signify acceptance.

2. *The buyer fails to make an effective rejection* [§2-606(1)(b)]. After having an opportunity to inspect the goods, the buyer must tell the seller whether or not he or she will take or retain the goods. If the buyer fails to inspect the goods within a reasonable time or fails to reject them in the proper manner (see page 440), the buyer is considered to have accepted the goods.

3. *The buyer treats the property in a way that is inconsistent with the seller's ownership* [§2-606(1)(c)]. A buyer who treats received goods as though he or she owns them is acting inconsistently with the seller's rights of ownership. For example, suppose that a buyer has received a machine that, upon inspection, is found not to operate in accord with the contract specifications. The buyer intends to reject the machine, but in the meantime, he or she uses it. The buyer's use of the machine is inconsistent with the seller's ownership of the machine. By using the machine as though it were his or her own, the buyer has accepted the machine.

Reasonable Time for Inspection In establishing whether a buyer has accepted goods, the determination of what is a reasonable time for inspection is often relevant. What is a reasonable time depends upon all the circumstances, including any agreements between the parties. For example, if the contract calls for inspection to be made six weeks after delivery, the buyer cannot accept the goods until the six weeks have passed and the inspection has been made.

Even if the contract does not specify a time for inspection, the circumstances may indicate what constitutes a reasonable time. For example, suppose that a buyer is building an apartment house and purchases 10,000 square feet of carpeting, which is to be installed in the apartments just before the building is opened to tenants. If the seller knows that the building is under construction, the reasonable time for the inspection of the carpeting will be when it is unrolled and installed. It is unreasonable to expect the buyer to examine the carpeting for defects prior to that time. Accordingly, the buyer will not have accepted the goods before the carpeting has been unrolled and installed.

Revocation of Acceptance A buyer who has accepted goods cannot then reject them [§2-607(1)]. The buyer may, however, be able to **revoke acceptance,** but only if a nonconformity in the goods substantially impairs their value to the buyer [§2-608(1)]. (See Figure 23-1.) The buyer can revoke acceptance if he or she was unaware of a serious defect at the time of acceptance because the defect was difficult to discover [§2-608(1)(b)]. Because the buyer has the right to inspect the goods before acceptance, it is the buyer's responsibility to discover any defects at the time for inspection. Thus, if there is some obvious problem with the goods that could have been discovered easily upon inspection but was not due to the buyer's carelessness, the buyer forfeits the right to revocation.

A buyer can also revoke acceptance if he or she knew about the defect at the time of acceptance and reasonably assumed that the defect would be cured, but the seller has not cured the defect within a reasonable time [§2-608(1)(a)]. For example, suppose that a buyer purchases a copying machine. When the buyer inspects the machine, he or she discovers that about half the time the machine reproduces only a portion of the page being copied. When the buyer notifies the seller of the problem, the seller assures him or her that it can be easily fixed by replacing a part that the seller will have to order. Based on these assurances of cure, the buyer accepts the machine.

After the seller has installed the replacement part and has attempted to adjust the machine on several occasions, the machine still reproduces only a portion of the page being copied about 40 percent of the time. The buyer can revoke acceptance because the value of the machine is substantially impaired, and the seller has been unable to cure the defect. If the seller were able to fix the machine so that it operates properly 95 percent of the time, the buyer would not be able to revoke acceptance unless a 5 percent failure rate also constitutes substantial impairment.

A revocation of acceptance is not effective until the buyer notifies the seller of it [§2-608(2)]. The buyer must revoke acceptance within a reasonable time after he or she has discovered or should have discovered the defect. What is a reasonable time depends upon all the circumstances.

The buyer cannot revoke acceptance if the goods are substantially changed and the change was not caused by a defect in the goods. For example, a buyer can revoke acceptance of a machine that is damaged in a fire caused by a defect in the machine. However, the buyer cannot revoke acceptance if the goods have been substantially changed by external causes — water damage from a leak in the roof, for example — or through the deterioration that comes with use, even if the goods have a serious defect. For instance, if a buyer has had an automobile for seven years when a previously undiscovered defect causes a major accident, the buyer cannot revoke acceptance and return the automobile. The buyer can, however, recover damages for breach of warranty (see Chapter 22).

In the following case, the buyer took possession of an automobile that did not operate properly. In its decision, the court discusses the options of the buyer and the seller.

ZABRISKE CHEVROLET, INC. v. SMITH
240 A.2d 195 (N.J. Super. 1968)

DOAN, [Judge]

On February 2, 1967 defendant [Smith] signed a form purchase order for a new 1966 Chevrolet Biscayne Sedan which was represented to him to be a brand-new car that would operate perfectly. . . . On February 9, 1967 defendant tendered plaintiff [Zabriske Chevrolet, Inc.] his check for $2,069.50 representing the balance of the purchase price ($2,064) and $5.50 for license and transfer fees. Delivery was made to defendant's wife during the early evening hours of Friday, February 10, 1967. . . .

While en route to her home, about 2½ miles away, and after having gone about 7/10 of a mile from the showroom, the car stalled at a traffic light, stalled again within another 15 feet and again thereafter each time the vehicle was required to stop. When about half-way home the car could not be driven in "drive" gear at all, and defendant's wife was obliged to then propel the vehicle in "low-low" gear at a rate of about five to ten miles per hour, its then maximum speed. Defendant, considerably upset by this turn of events, thereupon . . . called plaintiff to notify them that they had sold him a "lemon," that he had stopped payment on the check and that the sale was cancelled. The next day plaintiff sent a wrecker to defendant's home, brought the vehicle to its repair shop and after inspection determined that the transmission was defective. . . . Plaintiff replaced the transmission with another one removed from a vehicle then on plaintiff's showroom floor, notifying defendant thereafter of what had been done. Defendant refused to take delivery of the vehicle as repaired and reasserted his cancellation of the sale.

Plaintiff urges that defendant accepted the vehicle and therefore under the Code [§2-606(1)] is bound to complete payment for it. Defendant asserts that he never accepted the vehicle and therefore under the Code properly rejected it; further, that even if there had been acceptance he was justified under the Code in revoking the same. Defendant supports this claim by urging that what was delivered to him was not what he bargained for, i.e., a new car with factory new parts, which would operate perfectly as represented. . . . The essential ingredient which determines which of these two remedies is brought into play is a determination . . . whether there had been an "acceptance" of the goods by the buyer. Thus, the primary inquiry is whether the defendant had "accepted" the automobile prior to the return thereof to the plaintiff. [§2-606] states in pertinent part:

> (1) Acceptance of goods occurs when the buyer
> (a) after a reasonable opportunity to inspect the goods signifies to the seller that the goods are conforming or that he will take or retain them in spite of their non-conformity; or
> (b) fails to make an effective rejection [§2-602(1)], but such acceptance does not occur until the buyer has had a reasonable opportunity to inspect them. . . .

Plaintiff contends that defendant had "reasonable opportunity to inspect" by the privilege to take the car for a typical "spin around the block" before signing the purchase order. If by this contention plaintiff equates a spin around the block with "reasonable opportunity to inspect," the contention is illusory and unrealistic. To the layman, the complicated mechanisms of today's automobiles are a complete mystery. To have the automobile inspected by someone with sufficient expertise to disassemble the vehicle in order to discover latent defects before the contract is signed, is assuredly impossible and highly impractical. Consequently, the first few miles of driving become even more significant to the excited new car buyer. This is the buyer's first reasonable opportunity to enjoy his new vehicle to see if it conforms to what it was represented to be and whether he is getting what he bargained for. How long the buyer may drive the new car under the guise of inspection of new goods is not an issue in the present case. It is clear that defendant discovered the nonconformity within 7/10 of a mile and minutes after leaving plaintiff's showroom. Certainly this was well within the ambit of "reasonable opportunity to inspect." That the vehicle was grievously defective when it left plaintiff's possession is a compelling conclusion, as is the conclusion that in a legal sense the defendant never accepted the vehicle.

Even if defendant had accepted the automobile tendered, he had a right to revoke under [§2-608]:

> (1) the buyer may revoke his acceptance of a lot or commercial unit whose non-conformity *substantially impairs its value* to him if he has accepted it:
> (a) on the reasonable assumption that its non-conformity would be cured and it has not been seasonably cured; or
> (b) without discovery of such non-conformity if his acceptance was reasonably induced either by the difficulty of discovery before acceptance of by the seller's assurances. . . . [Emphasis added by the court.]

There having been no acceptance, the next issue presented is whether defendant properly rejected under the Code. That he cancelled the sale and rejected the vehicle almost concomitantly with the discovery of the failure of his bargain is clear from the evidence. [§2-601] delineates the buyer's rights following non-conforming delivery and reads as follows:

> Subject to the provisions of this Chapter on breach in installment contracts . . . , if the goods or the tender of delivery *fail in any respect to conform* to the contract, the buyer may
> (a) reject the whole. . . .
> [Emphasis added by the court.]

[§2-602] indicates that one can reject after taking possession. Possession, therefore, does not mean acceptance and the corresponding loss of the right of rejection. . . .

In the present case we are not dealing with a situation such as was present in *Adams v. Tramontin Motor Sales.* In that case, brought for breach of implied warranty of merchantability, the court held that minor defects, such as adjustment of the motor, tightening of loose elements, fixing of locks and dome light, and a correction of rumbling noise, were not remarkable defects, and therefore there was no breach. Here the breach was substantial. The new car was practically inoperable and endowed with a defective transmission. This was a "remarkable defect" and justified rejection by the buyer.

Lastly, plaintiff urges that under the [§2-508] it had a right to cure the nonconforming delivery. The inquiry is as to what is intended by "cure," as used in the Code. This statute makes no attempt to define or specify what a "cure" shall consist of. It would appear, then, that each case must be controlled by its own facts. The "cure" intended under the cited section of the Code does not, in the court's opinion, contemplate the tender of a new vehicle with a substituted transmission, not from the factory and of unknown lineage from another vehicle in plaintiff's possession. It was not the intention of the Legislature that the right to "cure" is a limitless one to be controlled only by the will of the seller. A "cure" which endeavors by substitution to tender a chattel not within the agreement or contemplation of the parties is invalid.

For a majority of people the purchase of a new car is a major investment, rationalized by the peace of mind that flows from its dependability and safety. Once their faith is shaken, the vehicle loses not only its real value in their eyes, but becomes an instrument whose integrity is substantially impaired and whose operation is fraught with apprehension. The attempted cure in the present case was ineffective.

[Judgment is rendered in favor of defendant.]

CASE REVIEW QUESTIONS

1. Why hadn't the buyer accepted the goods?
2. What constituted a reasonable time for inspection of the automobile?
3. If the buyer had accepted, the court ruled that the buyer could have revoked acceptance. Why?
4. Why was the buyer's rejection proper?
5. Why was the seller's offer to substitute a different transmission an ineffective cure?

The Buyer Retains the Goods A buyer can accept and keep goods that either conform or do not conform to the contract. If the goods conform to the contract, there is no breach by either party unless the buyer fails to pay for the goods. A buyer who has accepted goods must pay the price specified in the contract [§§2-607(1) and 2-709]. If a buyer accepts only part of the goods, the buyer must only pay for those goods he or she accepts.

A buyer who has accepted goods cannot then reject them [§2-607(2)]. A buyer who attempts to revoke acceptance of conforming goods is wrongfully revoking and thereby breaches the contract. If the goods or the manner of delivery do not conform to the contract, the remedies available to the buyer are revocation of acceptance, as previously discussed, or a recovery for breach of warranty.

Notification A buyer who has accepted goods must give the seller notice when he or she discovers any nonconformity [§2-607(3)(a)]. The notice must be given within a reasonable time after the buyer discovers the defect. Failure to give the seller notice will prevent the buyer from seeking any remedy.

The purpose of the notice is to alert the seller that the buyer is not satisfied with the delivery and that the seller may be facing a law suit. Prompt notification by the buyer enables the seller to begin negotiations to settle any dispute and avoid possible legal action by the buyer. Moreover, it allows the seller to prepare for any legal action by collecting the evidence while it is still available.

In the following case, the court discusses the purpose of the notification requirement. The question raised is whether the buyer is still under an obligation to notify the seller formally when both the seller and the buyer are aware of the breach. The answer hinges on whether the notification is meant only to inform the seller of a previously undetected breach or whether it is also intended to let the seller know that litigation might be forthcoming.

EASTERN AIR LINES, INC. v. McDONNELL DOUGLAS CORP.
532 F.2d 957 (Cir. 1976)

[Eastern Air Lines, the plaintiff, entered into a series of contracts with Douglas Air Craft, Inc., for the purchase of 99 airplanes. Douglas Air Craft subsequently merged with McDonnell Aircraft Corporation, which together became McDonnell Douglas Corporation (McDonnell), the defendant. There were repeated delays in the delivery of the airplanes. On the average, each of 90 of the planes was delivered 80 days after the month specified in the contract for delivery. Several months after all the planes had been delivered, Eastern wrote to McDonnell and presented a claim for damages caused by the late deliveries. Although the contracts contained a clause exempting McDonnell from excusable delay for causes beyond its control and not its fault, Eastern alleged that the delays were not excusable. McDonnell refused to pay Eastern's claim, and Eastern filed suit. A jury awarded Eastern the sum of $24,552,659.11. McDonnell appealed on several grounds.]

AINSWORTH, Circuit Judge

During the trial and in final instructions to the jury, the District Court held that Eastern need not prove, as a predicate for recovery in this suit, that it had given

McDonnell Douglas reasonable and timely notice of the delivery delays. McDonnell strongly contests the trial judge's rulings for Eastern on this issue and argues either that the airlines should, as a matter of law, be barred from any recovery or, alternatively, that the issue of timely notice should have been submitted to the jury.

The statute governing this question is §2-607(3)(a) of the Uniform Commercial Code. . . . McDonnell contends that the trial judge denied it the benefits of this provision, both by ruling that §2-607 does not apply to late deliveries and by holding in the alternative that Eastern gave adequate notice. Because we are unable to agree with the District Court's ruling on either ground, we hold that the question of timely notice under §2-607 should have been submitted to the jury.

Even though §2-607, by its very terms, governs "any breach," the trial court found the notice requirement to be inapplicable to delivery delays because a seller necessarily has knowledge of this sort of contract violation. [T]he District Judge concluded that notice is useless where a breach is apparent to both parties. The trial court apparently was of the view that the sole function of §2-607 is to inform the seller of hidden defects in his performance. Under this approach, the only purpose of notice is to provide the seller with an opportunity to remedy an otherwise unknown nonconforming tender. . . .

Section 2-607's origins, however, reveal that it has a much broader function. The Code's notice requirement was derived from decisional law in California and several other states which sought to ameliorate the harsh common law rule that acceptance of goods by the buyer waived any and all of his remedies. . . . The buyer, though was permitted to accept the [goods] without waiving any claims if he gave the seller prompt notice to this effect. . . . This approach reconciled the desire to give finality to transactions in which goods were accepted with the need to accommodate a buyer who, for business reasons, had to accept the tendered goods despite unsatisfactory performance by the seller. . . . Decisions in California and elsewhere, therefore, recognized that the primary purpose of notice is to inform the seller that, even though his tender has been accepted by the buyer, his performance is nonetheless a breach of contract. . . .

[T]he notice requirement developed in pre-UCC cases is entirely consistent with the Article 2 goals of encouraging compromise and promoting good faith in commercial relations. As Comment 4 to §2-607 indicates, the purpose of notice is not merely to inform the seller that his tender is nonconforming, but to open the way for settlement through negotiations between the parties. "[T]he sound commercial rule" codified in §2-607 also requires that a seller be reasonably protected against stale claims arising out of transactions which a buyer has led him to believe were closed. . . . Early warning permits the seller to investigate the claim while the facts are fresh, avoid the defect in the future, minimize his damages, or perhaps assert a timely claim of his own against third parties. . . .

Given these undeniable purposes, it is not enough under §2-607 that a seller has knowledge of the facts constituting a nonconforming tender; he must also be informed that the buyer considers him to be in breach of the contract. . . . Accordingly, . . . we find that the trial court erred in not applying §2-607 to the delivery delays at issue in this case. . . .

[W]e must determine whether the notice given by Eastern was both sufficient and timely as a matter of law. As will be demonstrated below, the adequacy and timeliness of notice under §2-607 typically depends upon the reasonableness of the buyer's efforts to communicate his dissatisfaction. . . .

Eastern contends that [the] facts are more than sufficient to constitute adequate notice as a matter of law. The Code, in Eastern's view, does not require the buyer to inform the seller that he is presenting a claim under the contract. This contention is based on Comment No. 4 to §2-607 which states, in part, that "[t]he content of the notification need merely be sufficient to let the seller know that the transaction is still troublesome and must be watched."

It appears that Comment No. 4 was aimed at remedying a rule adopted under . . . the Uniform Sales Act by some courts that a mere complaint of a breach was not adequate notice. In California and a number of other states, for example, a buyer was required to indicate that he intended to look to the seller for damages.

These technical requirements were dispensed with

because they frequently served to deny an uninformed consumer of what was otherwise a valid claim. As is noted in the draftsmen's comments, "the rule of requiring notification is designed to defeat commercial bad faith, not to deprive a good faith consumer of his remedy." Eastern is therefore correct in asserting that notice under §2-607 need not be a specific claim for damages or an assertion of legal rights. . . .

However, the fact that the Code has eliminated the technical rigors of the notice requirement under the Uniform Sales Act does not require the conclusion that any expression of discontent by a buyer always satisfied §2-607. [A] buyer's conduct under §2-607 must satisfy the Code's standard of commercial good faith. Thus, while the buyer must inform the seller that the transaction is "still troublesome," Comment 4 also requires that the notification "be such as informs the seller that the transaction is claimed to involve a breach, and thus opens the way for normal settlement through negotiation."

In arguing that these requirements have been complied with, Eastern cannot rely on the same minimal standards of notice developed for ordinary consumers. The measure of good faith required under the Code varies with a buyer's commercial status. Unlike an ordinary purchaser, a merchant's good faith is measured by "reasonable commercial standards of fair dealing in the trade." Therefore, as the Comments to §2-607 indicate, what constitutes adequate notice from an inexperienced consumer may not be sufficient in a transaction between professionals. While an ordinary purchaser is generally ignorant of his obligation to give timely notice, a merchant buyer should be well aware that some form of notice is a requirement of his trade.

Reviewing Eastern's entire course of conduct during the years 1965–1969, and recognizing that Eastern must be held to a higher standard of good faith than an ordinary consumer, we conclude that a jury could reasonably find, as one of its options, that adequate notice was not given. . . .

. . . Eastern's commercial good faith is subject to further challenges because it continued to negotiate new contracts and amend old ones throughout the period in which the delays occurred. Two of the agreements, in fact, were executed in October of 1967 after 44 of the planes were already late. At no time during the negotiation and execution of any of these contracts did Eastern seek a settlement of its claims or even dispute McDonnell's . . . excuse. This may very well have led McDonnell to believe that, even though Eastern was unhappy about the delays, it did not consider them to be a breach of the contract. . . .

. . . In conclusion, therefore, the issue of notice under UCC §2-607 should have been submitted to the jury with instructions that it determine whether Eastern's conduct throughout the life of the contracts constituted adequate and timely notice to McDonnell that it was considered to be in breach of the contracts.

Case remanded.

CASE REVIEW QUESTIONS

1. What purpose is served by the notice requirement of §2-607?
2. Why wasn't McDonnell sufficiently on notice of a breach if it knew that the deliveries were late?
3. What type of notice was required of Eastern? How did it differ from what would be expected of a consumer buyer?
4. How has the Code changed prior law?
5. What will be the results if a jury finds that Eastern's notice was not reasonably timely?
6. What would have been reasonable and timely notice?

REVIEW QUESTIONS

1. Where and when must a buyer pay for goods?
2. What is a repudiation?
3. When may a party demand adequate assurance of performance?
4. Under what circumstances is a buyer or a seller excused from performance?
5. When does a buyer have a right to inspect the goods?
6. Under what circumstances may a buyer reject goods? What if the contract is a single shipment contract? What if it is an installment contract?
7. What are a buyer's obligations when rejecting goods?
8. When may a seller cure?
9. Describe three ways in which a buyer can accept goods?
10. When may a buyer revoke acceptance?
11. What obligation does a buyer have to give the seller notice of a breach?

CASE PROBLEMS

1. Kenneth Dobson, doing business as Gate City Seed Company (Seed Co.), entered into a contract dated September 4th with Donald Whewell for the purchase of 400 Christmas trees. Whewell thereafter contracted with a Michigan firm for the purchase of 400 Christmas trees. In late September, Whewell received Seed Co.'s copy of the contract with the word "Canceled" written on it. Whewell attempted to cancel his contract with the Michigan firm but was unable to do so. On October 30th, Whewell's attorneys wrote to Seed Co. and demanded adequate assurance of Seed Co.'s intent to perform the contract. Seed Co. was given until November 6th to respond. Whewell received notice on November 6th that Seed Co. would not perform. Whewell then made numerous attempts to sell the trees, but only 124 trees were sold by late December. Whewell sued Seed Co. to recover damages. Seed Co. defended on the grounds that Whewell had waited too long before attempting to sell the trees. Who will win the case? Explain.

2. Charles Toppert entered into a series of contracts calling for the delivery of a number of bushels of corn to the Bunge Corporation. Bunge's normal policy is to pay when a farmer completes the deliveries called for by a contract. On November 9, 1973, Toppert completed delivery on contract 0355. After a demand by Toppert's attorney,

Bunge finally made payment on November 20, 1973. On December 3, 1973, Toppert completed delivery under contract 0364 and began delivery under contract 0366. Bunge refused to pay on contract 0364. Toppert delivered no more corn. Toppert met several times with representatives from Bunge to work out the problem, but the conversations were mostly about some contracts that Toppert's father and brother had not yet signed for Bunge. The last conversation took place on January 2, 1974. On January 4th, Bunge notified Toppert that it was cancelling the two remaining contracts (0366 and 6079). Toppert sued to recover payment on contract 0364. Bunge counterclaimed for damages under contracts 0366 and 6079. Who will win the case? Explain.

3. The United States contracted with Transatlantic Financing Corporation for the transportation of a full cargo of wheat from the United States to a port in Iran. On October 27th, 1956, the *S.S. Christos* sailed with the cargo of wheat on a course that would have taken the ship through the Mediterranean Sea and the Suez Canal. On November 2, 1956, the Egyptian government obstructed the Suez canal with sunken ships and closed it to traffic because of a dispute between Egypt, Israel, France, and Great Britain. The *S.S. Christos,* after notifying the United States, changed course and pro-

ceeded around Africa and the Cape of Good Hope. It delivered the grain to Iran on December 30, 1956. Transatlantic Financing Corporation sued to recover additional compensation for losses suffered because of the extended route. The United States argued that Transatlantic had breached the contract. Who will win the case? Explain.

4. Bose Corporation manufactures high-quality stereo speaker systems. The speakers are competitively priced through the use of vinyl-covered particle board in place of wood. Bevel-Fold Corporation entered into a contract with Bose that called for Bevel-Fold to specially manufacture 10,000 cabinets. Bose reserved the right to reject "at any time any cabinets defective in material and workmanship." The contract specifically called for two inspections: an immediate inspection of 10 percent of each shipment upon delivery and an inspection for Bose's quality standards after the units had been processed through the production line. Bevel-Fold shipped an average of 200 units per week from April 17th to October 14th. The first two shipments failed inspection and were returned. There were additional defects from time to time, which were frequently handled by Bevel-Fold's repairing the units and redelivering them. Bevel-Fold went out of business at the end of October. Bose inspected all the cabinets in Bevel-Fold's possession, took 788 of the cabinets, and refused 852. Bevel-Fold sued for breach, arguing that Bose's rejection was improper. Who will win the case? Explain.

5. Bead Chain Manufacturing Company negotiated with Saxton Products, Inc., for the manufacture and delivery of electrical components. In January 1973, Saxton ordered 5 million parts that were to conform to "Sketch S–1318." Bead prepared the necessary manufacturing equipment and began manufacturing the components as specified by the contract. Bead sent the first 100 samples in August, but they were lost. Upon inquiry by Bead, it learned of the loss and shipped more samples in October 1973 and February 1974. Small shipments were delivered in April and May of 1974. In July of 1974, when presented with the bill for the costs of tooling (obtaining and setting up the necessary manufacturing equipment), Saxton for the first time complained that the components were defective. Saxton claimed that the components did not meet some of its needs even though they conformed to the sketch. Bead sued for breach of contract. Saxton defended on the grounds that it had rejected the goods. Who will win the case? Explain.

6. Mrs. Kolley purchased a new color television set from Willie Wilson TV Appliances. When the set arrived at Mrs. Kolley's, it did not function properly in that the screen had a red cast when the set was turned on. Wilson examined the set and offered to remove the chassis in his shop to determine the problem and to adjust or repair the set. Wilson offered to replace the set if he could not repair it. Mrs. Kolley refused to authorize Wilson to remove the chassis and examine the set, and she demanded a new set. Wilson refused, and Mrs. Kolley sued to recover her money. Who will win the case? Explain.

7. Peter Werner purchased a wooden Friendship Sloop known as the "White Eagle" from Robert Montana, who had owned the boat for a number of years. Werner was concerned about the boat's seaworthiness. Montana assured Werner that the boat would "make up" so that the hull would be water tight when it had been in the water for several weeks. The bill of sale was signed in January. The purchase price was $13,250. In June, Werner put the boat in the water and allowed the time ordinarily sufficient for the wooden planking to swell or "make up." After six weeks in the water, the boat still leaked badly and could not be sailed. Werner subsequently discovered that the cost of repairs would be substantial. In September, Werner returned the boat and sued to recover the purchase price. Who will win the case? Explain.

8. Mr. Belmont owned a stable of horses that were used for racing and breeding purposes. Over a period of time, Belmont purchased three horses— Meadow Paige, Red Carpet, and King. Meadow Paige was purchased for breeding purposes. The contract called for Belmont to pay for Meadow Paige in June and to take possession of the horse at that time. The parties agreed that Meadow Paige's sperm would not be tested until after the racing

season. The tests, which were performed in November, showed that Meadow Paige was a "stud who was a dud."

Red Carpet was purchased at a race in Yonkers. Belmont did not have his trainer or veterinarian with him that day. Nevertheless, he took possession of Red Carpet and had the horse transported to his barns. On the following morning, Belmont's veterinarian inspected Red Carpet and discovered that the horse had a broken leg.

King was purchased at a claiming race. The "Daily Racing Form," the "Official Racing Program," and the "Affidavit of Ownership" all described King as a colt. In a claiming race, the buyer's "claim" or offer is placed in the claiming box at least fifteen minutes before the race. Belmont was the successful bidder. He paid for the horse and had the horse trucked to his barns fol-

lowing the race. The next day, Belmont saw a notice posted at the track that King was not a colt but a gelding. Belmont sought to reject the three horses. Each seller argued that Belmont had accepted the horses. Belmont sued each of them. Who will win the cases? Explain.

9. Margrove, Inc., accepted several deliveries of milk cartons from International Paper Products, Inc. (Paper) between November 1972 and February 1973. Margrove had difficulty filling the milk cartons, but no claim that the cartons were defective was made at that time. In fact, Margrove's vice-president sent Paper a letter on April 25, 1973, stating that the problem was with Margrove's machinery. On July 3, 1973, Paper sued to recover the purchase price of the cartons. In its answer, Margrove alleged for the first time that the cartons were defective. Who will win the case? Explain.

24

SALES REMEDIES

When a seller or a buyer does not receive the performance called for by a sales contract, the contract is breached, and the **aggrieved party** (the wronged party) is entitled to a remedy. An aggrieved seller or buyer can select one or more of the remedies available under the Uniform Commercial Code. Should a party select a remedy that is inappropriate in the circumstances, he or she is not prevented from obtaining another remedy. A court can award damages on the basis of any of the remedies available, regardless of which remedy is initially sought. This chapter will discuss the remedies available under the UCC.

BUYER'S BREACH: SELLER'S REMEDIES

When the buyer breaches a sales contract, the seller is entitled to a remedy. The Code lists the ways in which a buyer can breach as well as the remedies that are available to the seller [§2-703].

Buyer's Breach

The following material will briefly review the ways in which a buyer can breach a sales contract. This material was covered in detail in Chapter 23. A buyer breaches when [§2-703]:

1. *The buyer fails to make a payment when it is due.* For example, suppose that the buyer is to pay for goods on delivery. If the buyer refuses to pay when the goods are delivered, the contract is breached. (For a discussion of a buyer's duty to pay, see pages 429–430.)

2. *The buyer repudiates (refuses to perform in advance) a contract in whole or in part* [§2-610]. For example, the buyer repudiates a sales contract in part when the buyer tells the seller that he or she will not pay for more than 3,000 widgets even though the contract calls for the delivery of 6,000 widgets. (For a discussion of repudiation, see pages 430–433.)

3. *The buyer wrongfully rejects the goods* [§2-602]. For example, the buyer wrongfully rejects the goods if he or she waits too long to tell the seller that the goods are nonconforming. (For a discussion of rejection, see pages 430–441.)

4. *The buyer wrongfully revokes (cancels) acceptance of the goods* [§2-608]. For example, the buyer wrongfully revokes acceptance if the goods are returned for a minor nonconformity after they have been accepted. (For a discussion of revocation, see pages 446–448.)

Seller's Remedies

When a buyer breaches a sales contract, a number of remedies are available to the seller. Depending upon the situation, the seller may do one or more of the following [§2-703]:

1. Withhold delivery of the goods [§2-703(a)].
2. Stop delivery of goods in the hands of a bailee [§2-705].
3. Recover the goods from an insolvent buyer [§2-702].
4. Sell the goods to another buyer [§2-706].
5. Recover damages from the buyer [§2-706, §2-708(1), and §2-710].
6. Recover lost profit [§2-708(2)].
7. Recover the contract price for the goods [§2-709].
8. Cancel the contract [§2-703(f)].

Withhold Delivery If a buyer fails to make a payment or repudiates a sales contract before the seller has delivered the goods, the seller can withhold delivery of the goods. The seller is not required to deliver the goods in these circumstances because he or she will not receive payment for the goods. In addition to retaining possession of the goods, the seller can seek damages under one of the other remedies discussed in this chapter.

Stop Delivery Sometimes when a buyer does not pay for goods or repudiates a contract, the seller does not have possession of the goods because they have been delivered to a carrier for shipment or are in the hands of some other bailee, such as a warehouseman. In these circumstances, the seller can withhold delivery of the goods from a buyer who has breached by stopping the bailee from delivering the goods.

A seller cannot stop a delivery, however, if any of the following have occurred [§2-705(2)]:

1. The buyer has already received the goods.
2. The bailee has told the buyer that he or she is holding the goods for the buyer.

3. A negotiable document of title has been negotiated (transferred) to the buyer. (For a discussion of documents of title, see Chapter 21.)

In each of these situations, control of the goods has passed to the buyer and the seller can no longer claim possession of the goods.

If the goods are in the hands of a carrier, the seller can stop delivery of a shipment only if it is a whole carload, truckload, or planeload. However, if the buyer is **insolvent**—that is, if the buyer is not paying or cannot pay his or her debts [§1-201(23)]—the seller can stop delivery of any size, even if it is smaller than a carload, truckload, or planeload [§2-705(1)]. The Code distinguishes between solvent and insolvent buyers in this situation because recovering the goods may be the seller's only remedy when the buyer is insolvent. On the other hand, when the buyer is solvent, the seller will have an effective remedy even if the buyer gets possession of the goods because the seller can sue for breach of contract if the buyer does not pay.

Withhold Delivery or Recover Goods from an Insolvent Buyer If the seller has not delivered the goods, the seller can withhold delivery from an insolvent buyer unless the buyer pays cash for the delivery and for all previous deliveries made under the same contract [§2-702(1)]. In effect, then, the seller can demand payment in advance when a buyer is insolvent. The seller can do this even if the contract specifies that payment is due at a later date.

If a seller has already delivered goods to an insolvent buyer, he or she can recover any goods that have not been paid for, provided that he or she reclaims them within ten days after they have been delivered [§2-702(2)]. The seller can, however, reclaim goods more than ten days after delivery if the buyer has given the seller a written statement, such as a financial statement of the buyer's assets and liabilities, stating that the buyer is solvent within three months prior to the delivery of the goods [§2-701(2)].

The reclaiming of goods from an insolvent buyer excludes all other remedies. The seller who recovers his or her goods has an advantage over other creditors, so it would not be fair for this seller to seek additional damages from the assets of the buyer in competition with other creditors who cannot reclaim goods as a means of reducing their loss.

Resale If a buyer has breached a sales contract, the seller can **resell** the goods in his or her possession [§2-706]. The seller will have possession of the goods if he or she withheld delivery of the goods, if the buyer returned the goods, or if the seller reclaimed the goods.

The seller who resells goods must do so in good faith and in a commercially reasonable manner. The sale may be either public or private [§2-706(2)]. A public sale is a sale by auction; all other sales are considered to be private. The seller must give the buyer notice of any resale. If the resale is private, the seller is only required to give the buyer notice that he or she *intends* to resell [§2-706(3)]. If the sale is public, however, the seller must notify the buyer of the actual time and place for the resale, unless the goods are perishable or are rapidly declining in value [§2-706(4)].

In selecting the manner of resale, the seller must consider both the nature of the goods and the relevant practices in the trade. All aspects of the sale — the place, the time, the manner, and the terms — are subject to the test of commercial reasonableness [§2-706(3)]. For example, if the price received by the seller is disproportionately low given the quality of the goods, the sale would not be commercially reasonable.

If a seller conducts a resale in a commercially reasonable manner, he or she can recover the difference between the the resale price and the contract price as damages from the buyer. To this difference, the seller can add any incidental damages, but any expenses of the original sale that were not incurred, such as shipping charges, must be subtracted from it [§2-706(1)] (see Figure 24-1). **Incidental damages** include reasonable expenses incurred in stopping delivery; from the transportation, care, and custody of the goods after the buyer's breach; and from conducting the resale of the goods [§2-710].

If the resale price is greater than the contract price plus incidental expenses, the seller is not required to give the buyer any of the surplus. In addition, though a seller may appear to have suffered no loss and may even have made a profit in a resale, the seller may still be entitled to a remedy for loss of profits. This remedy will be discussed later in this chapter.

Seller's Right to Identify Goods to a Breached Contract If a buyer breaches a contract before the seller has identified goods as the goods belonging to the contract [§2-501], the seller can identify conforming goods and then use these goods as the goods to be resold under the resale remedy [§2-704(1)(a)]. (For a discussion of the identification of goods see pages 383–385.) The ability of a seller to identify conforming goods to the contract after breach by a buyer is important because a seller can resell goods at public auction only if the goods are identified.

Sometimes a seller has not completed manufacturing the goods when a buyer breaches. A buyer's breach that leaves unfinished goods in the possession of a manufacturer seller may be handled in one of two ways. The seller may, in the exercise of reasonable commercial judgment to avoid loss and to preserve his or her profit, either finish manufacturing the goods and identify them to the contract for resale purposes or stop manufacturing and sell the unfinished

Resale Remedy	
Contract price for 10,000 widgets	$10,000
Resale price of 10,000 widgets	− 8,000
	2,000
Costs of resale and storage	500
	2,500
Expenses saved — costs of delivery	− 200
Damages due the seller	$ 2,300

FIGURE 24-1
Resale Remedy

goods for their scrap or salvage value [§2-704(2)]. A seller who finishes manufacturing the goods and has identified them to the contract has the same remedies as if the goods had been finished when the buyer breached [§2-704(1)(b)]. In either situation, the seller may then sue for damages.

Nonacceptance A seller has a choice of two basic money damages remedies: (1) the resale remedy or (2) the nonacceptance remedy. If a seller has not properly conducted a resale, however, he or she will be limited to the nonacceptance remedy. Under the **nonacceptance remedy,** a seller is entitled to damages from the buyer in the amount of the difference between the market price for the goods at the time and the place where the goods were to be tendered and the unpaid contract price plus any incidental damages and minus any expenses saved [§2-708(1)].

In many situations, there will be little or no difference in the amount of money due under the resale or nonacceptance remedies. For example, suppose that the price of goods remains steady and is not subject to fluctuations. In this situation, the market price at the time and place for tender would be the same as the resale price. Therefore, the damages would be about the same regardless of the remedy selected (see Figure 24-2 and compare it to Figure 24-1).

Choice of Remedy: Resale or Nonacceptance When the market price for the goods is subject to fluctuation, the availability of a choice between the resale remedy and the nonacceptance remedy is very important. Figure 24-3 shows the impact of these remedies on the seller if (A) the market price is falling from the contract price and if (B) the market price is rising toward the contract price.

Suppose that the price of the goods is falling below the contract price, as shown in Figure 24-3A. If the only remedy available were nonacceptance damages, the seller would suffer a loss if the buyer breached the contract and purchased the widgets more cheaply from another seller. In terms of Figure 24-3A, the seller, Seller A, would suffer a $3,000 loss because he or she would receive only $7,000 for $10,000 worth of goods—$6,000 on the resale of the goods to another buyer, Buyer B, plus $1,000 from Buyer A under the nonacceptance remedy.

By breaching the contract with Seller A, Buyer A could buy 10,000 widgets

Nonacceptance Remedy	
Contract price for 10,000 widgets	$10,000
Market price at the time and place for tender	− 8,000
	2,000
Storage of goods	300
	2,300
Expenses saved—costs of delivery	− 200
Damages due the seller	$ 2,100

FIGURE 24-2
Nonacceptance Remedy

Contract for 10,000 widgets—Contract price $10,000

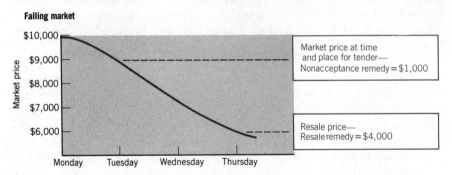

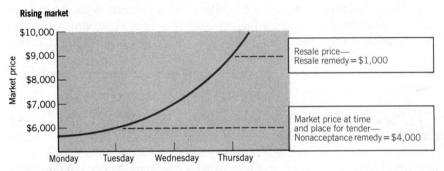

FIGURE 24-3
Seller's Remedies in a Fluctuating Market

for less than the $10,000 contract price even with the payment of damages to Seller A. For example, suppose that Buyer A breaches, waits until the price for 10,000 widgets drops to $6,000, and buys the widgets from Seller B. Buyer A will effectively pay $7,000 for 10,000 widgets—$6,000 to Seller B and $1,000 to Seller A as damages under the nonacceptance remedy.

The Code, however, also gives the seller the option of recovering damages under the resale remedy. In these circumstances, Buyer A is encouraged by the economic consequences to honor his or her contract with Seller A. In terms of Figure 24-3A, if Buyer A breaches, he or she will have to pay $4,000 (the resale remedy) plus any incidental damages incurred to Seller A as damages. Therefore, unless Buyer A can purchase 10,000 widgets from Seller B for less than $6,000, Buyer A will gain no economic advantage by breaching.

If the only remedy available in a rising market situation were resale damages, the seller might not suffer a loss but there would be no economic incentive for the buyer to honor the contract. In terms of Figure 24-3B, Buyer A could breach the contract at the time for tender and buy the widgets from Seller B for $6,000. Buyer A would only pay $7,000 for $10,000 worth of goods—$6,000 to Seller B and $1,000 to Seller A under the resale remedy.

Because the Code allows the seller the option of recovering under the nonacceptance remedy, however, the buyer has little economic incentive to breach. If

Buyer A breaches and buys from Seller B when the market price is $6,000, Buyer A still pays $10,000 for $10,000 worth of goods — $6,000 to Seller B, and $4,000 to Seller A under the nonacceptance remedy. In fact, Buyer A will pay more because Seller A can also claim incidental damages.

A seller does not have a completely free choice in the selection of a remedy. Under traditional contract law, a seller must mitigate (reduce) a buyer's damages. (For a general discussion of mitigation, see page 319.) In a falling market situation, for example, a seller cannot wait too long before reselling the goods.

Loss of Profit The purpose of remedies when a contract has been breached is to put a seller in as good a position as he or she would have been in if the buyer had performed. When the contract price and the market price or resale price are equal, a breach by the buyer leaves the seller with no significant recovery under either the resale or the nonacceptance remedy. In this situation, the seller has not been put in as good a position as he or she possibly would have been in had there been no breach.

A seller who resells goods really had two buyers — the breaching buyer and the buyer who actually bought the goods. If the first buyer had not breached the contract, the seller would probably have sold two items. Traditional contract law ignored the fact that the seller could have had the profit from two sales instead of one if the breach had not occurred.

The Code recognized this inadequacy in the traditional measurement of damages. Under the Code, therefore, when a seller has the capacity to sell more than one of the same item, the seller can recover the profits he or she would have realized if the additional sale had been made plus incidental damages [§2-708(2)]. This remedy is available, however, only in the situation where the seller sells goods at a standard price and can readily replace items sold. It is not available if the seller has only one item, such as a used car for sale.

Recovery of the Price A seller can recover the contract price of the goods only in three situations.

1. *The buyer has accepted the goods.* (For a discussion of acceptance, see pages 444–446.) Once a buyer has accepted the goods, he or she becomes obligated to pay for them [§2-709(1)(a)]. However, if the buyer wrongfully rejects the goods (see pages 440–441) or wrongfully revokes acceptance of the goods (see pages 446–449), the seller is not entitled to the contract price of the goods, though he or she can seek one of the other damage remedies such as nonacceptance [§2-709(3)].
2. *The goods are damaged or destroyed after risk of loss has passed to the buyer.* (For a discussion of risk of loss, see pages 385–395.) Even though the buyer may not receive any benefit from the goods, the buyer will have to pay for them if the buyer had risk of loss when the goods were damaged [§2-709(1)(a)].
3. *The seller is unable to sell goods that are identified to the contract.* For example, if the seller manufactures goods specifically for the buyer and the

goods cannot be resold by the seller at a reasonable price given a reasonable effort, the seller can recover the price of the goods from the buyer [§2-709(2)].

In addition to recovering the contract price for the goods, a seller can also recover incidental damages for such costs as storing and attempting to resell the goods. A seller must retain the buyer's goods. Nevertheless, if it becomes possible to sell the goods, the seller can sell them. If a profit is made on the sale, any amount in excess of the price and expenses belongs to the buyer. If the buyer pays for the goods, the buyer is entitled to any goods remaining with the seller.

In the following case, a buyer accepted five shipments of steel, but did not pay for all of them, and refused to take delivery of two shipments called for by the contract. In reading the case, you should notice how the seller uses the remedies available under the Code.

NEDERLANDSE, ETC. v. GRAND PRE-STRESSED CORP.
466 F.Supp. 846 (E.D. N.Y. 1979)

BARTELS, District Judge

Nederlandse Draadindustrie NDI B.V. ("NDI"), is a Dutch manufacturer of steel strand ("strand"), and defendant Grand Pre-Stressed Corporation ("Grand"), is a domestic manufacturer of prestressed concrete, of which strand is a component. In this . . . action, plaintiff seeks damages in the amount of $263,069.51 together with interest and costs for breach of a contract for the sale of approximately 1180 metric tons of steel strand to defendant. The sum claimed represents deficiencies allegedly due both for strand (a) delivered by plaintiff and accepted by defendant and (b) contracted for but rejected by defendant and either sold to third parties or not produced at all.

On May 2, 1975, the parties executed a written agreement for . . . steel strand amounting to approximately 1180 metric tons. . . . As stated in the . . . agreement, defendant was intending to use the strand as a component of pre-stressed concrete piles required for the construction of a sewage treatment plant. . . . Paragraph 3(f) of the agreement specified that payment was to be made by defendant on the 15th day of the month preceding the month of each delivery. . . .

During October and November 1975, plaintiff's di-

rector had several conversations with defendant's general manager both by telephone and in person during the course of which it became evident . . . that defendant had been purchasing strand from another supplier. . . . [In April the defendants told the plaintiff they would not take the last two shipments.]

[A]t the time of this first communication to plaintiff by defendant of its firm intention not to honor the terms of the May 1975 agreement, plaintiff had made five shipments, totalling 96 coils, and had submitted six invoices totalling $193,947.86. . . . Defendant, on the other hand, had made only two payments. . . .

[Plaintiff] determined to sell to third parties—and beginning in December 1975 did sell—portions of the strand originally intended for delivery to defendant. These sales were made at prices below that specified in the contract with the defendant, but at commercially reasonable amounts in accord with market levels generally at the time of sales. . . . Accordingly, . . . plaintiff sold to various third-party purchasers 317,891 metric tons of strand previously produced for defendant but for which defendant neither submitted payment nor requested delivery. . . .

Plaintiff first contends that it is entitled to recover

from defendant amounts due for strand accepted by defendant but for which no payment has been made. . . . Defendant has made no showing that any of the strand tendered by plaintiff and accepted by defendant was in any way defective or that defendant notified plaintiff of a nonconformity in the tender at any time, much less within a reasonable time as [§2-607(3)] requires. In the absence of such a showing, defendant is obligated to pay "at the contract rate" for all strand accepted [§2-709].

Plaintiff next seeks lost profit damages for the . . . strand covered by the contract but refused by defendant. . . . We conclude that defendant's refusal to accept further shipments was a breach of its obligations under the contract. Accordingly, plaintiff is entitled to recover lost profit damages on all strand provided for by the contract but not accepted by defendant.

Plaintiff cites [§2-708(2)] as the proper measure [of damages] in view of its capacity to produce strand not only under the contract but for third parties as well. Plaintiff reasons that any sales to third parties

would have been made regardless of defendant's breach. . . .

Here the evidence is clear that plaintiff had sufficient production capacity to supply not only the approximately 1180 metric tons of strand required by its contract with defendant but also the metric tons which were sold to third parties. [P]laintiff had a total estimated capacity of 12,500 metric tons, and actual sales of 8,788 metric tons in 1974 and 6,923 metric tons in 1975. These statistics leave little question as to plaintiff's capacity to supply both defendant and the third parties. . . .

Accordingly, . . . we find that the usual contract-market damages rule set forth in [§2-708(1)] is inadequate to put the plaintiff in as good a position as performance would have done and that plaintiff is entitled to the profit (including reasonable overhead) which it would have made from full performance by defendant.

Accordingly, judgment in accordance with the above is hereby ordered to be entered in favor of plaintiff against defendant. . . .

CASE REVIEW QUESTIONS

1. What remedies did NDI use? Why?
2. What other remedies could NDI have used? Explain.
3. What is the relevance of the seller's proof that it had an estimated production capacity of 12,500 metric tons?
4. The court notes that the sales to third parties were commercially reasonable. Why, then, didn't NDI sue for the resale remedy?

Cancel the Contract If a buyer breaches a sales contract, the seller can cancel the contract [§2-703(f)]. For example, if a buyer tells the seller that he or she will no longer honor a contract, the seller is not required to wait until the time for performance to see if the buyer will change his or her mind. The seller can cancel the contract immediately and make arrangements to sell the goods to another buyer. A seller who cancels a contract can also seek damage remedies under the Code, such as damages for loss of profits.

The seller's right to cancel a contract is particularly important if the contract is an installment contract; that is, if it is one in which there are a number of deliveries [§2-612(1)]. If the buyer's breach affects the whole contract, the seller can cancel the whole contract [§2-612(3)]. The seller need not wait for each installment to become due before making arrangements to resell the goods. The refusal by a buyer to pay for a single installment is not a breach of the whole contract, but it does give the seller the right to demand adequate assurance that all future payments will be made on time. (For a discussion of adequate assurance see page 431.)

A seller who wishes to cancel an installment contract must make his or her intention to do so clear to the buyer. A seller reaffirms the contract if he or she sues only to collect for overdue installments [§2-612(3)].

Liquidated Damages The parties to a sales contract can agree in advance on the amount of damages that are payable by either the buyer or the seller in the event of a breach. An amount of damages agreed upon at the time the contract is made is called **liquidated damages.** (For a discussion of liquidated damages see page 319.) Liquidated damages are available for breach of a sales contract only when proving the actual amount of damages is anticipated to be difficult or inconvenient [§2-718(1)]. A contract provision that fixes unreasonably large liquidated damages will not be enforced because a court will find the unreasonably large sum to be a penalty. Conversely, an unreasonably small amount may not be enforced because it is unconscionable.

Return of Down Payments Sometimes, a seller requires that a buyer make a down payment on goods. Suppose, though, that a buyer makes a down payment and then decides not to buy the goods and repudiates the contract. What right does the seller have to retain the down payment as liquidated damages for the buyer's breach? If the contract states that the down payment is to be kept in place of damages, the seller can keep the down payment as liquidated damages unless the amount is unreasonable or unconscionable.

If the contract does not provide for liquidated damages, the seller can keep $500 or 20 percent of the purchase price, whichever is less [§2-718(2)]. The seller can retain more than the minimum amount if he or she can establish damages, such as loss of profits or incidental damages [§2-718(3)]. The balance, if any, of the down payment must be returned to the buyer. Suppose a $5,000 down payment is made on a $10,000 computer but the buyer later changes his or her mind and demands the return of the down payment. The seller could retain a minimum of $500.

The following case was brought by a buyer who sought the return of the down payment claimed by the seller as liquidated damages. You should observe how the court computes the damages.

LEE OLDSMOBILE, INC. v. KAIDEN
363A.2d 270 (Md. App. 1976)

[Ada Kaiden, the plaintiff, sent Lee Oldsmobile, Inc., the defendant, $5,000 as a deposit for the purchase of a Rolls-Royce priced at $29,500. Lee Oldsmobile sent Kaiden a regular order form, which she signed and

Liquidated Damages

Difference between the Kaiden contract price of $29,500.00 and the resale price of $26,495.00	$3,005.00
Commission to salesman on second sale	601.00
Commission to broker on second sale	1,000.00
Interest due to bank	334.72
Transportation expenses	139.35
Total	$5,080.07

FIGURE 24-4
Lee Oldsmobile's Liquidated Damages

returned. Delivery was to be made in November. On November 21, 1973, Kaiden told Lee Oldsmobile that she had purchased another Rolls-Royce elsewhere. On November 29th, Kaiden refused to accept delivery of Lee Oldsmobile's Rolls-Royce and demanded the return of her deposit. The dealer refused. On January 17, 1974, Lee Oldsmobile sold the Rolls-Royce to another buyer for $26,495.00. Ada Kaiden sued to recover the $5,000 deposit plus interest. Lee Oldsmobile argued the $5,000 was liquidated damages. In support of its claim, it listed the amounts shown in Figure 24-4.

The trial court refused to allow liquidated damages and refunded the sum of $2,924.93 to Kaiden. Lee Oldsmobile appealed. Kaiden also appealed.]

POWERS, Judge

It may be seen . . . that Lee Oldsmobile holds $5,000.00 of Mrs. Kaiden's money, that Mrs. Kaiden breached her contract to buy a Rolls-Royce automobile; and that whatever damages flowed from the breach should reduce . . . Mrs. Kaiden's right to get her money back. The question of law presented is how to determine the damages. The question of fact is their amount.

The order form signed by Mrs. Kaiden contained a clause providing that the dealer shall have the right, upon failure or refusal of the purchaser to accept delivery of the motor vehicle, to retain as liquidated damages any cash deposit made by the purchaser. The Uniform Commercial Code . . . §2-718(1) provides:

> Damages for breach by either party may be liquidated in the agreement but only at an amount which is reasonable in the light of the anticipated or actual harm caused by the breach, the difficulties of proof of loss, and the inconvenience or nonfeasibility of otherwise obtaining an adequate remedy.

Running through many of the cases is the rule that not only must the amount be a reasonable forecast of just compensation, but that actual damages from a breach must be incapable or very difficult of accurate estimation. . . .

We reject the application of the liquidated damage clause in the present case . . . because it is clear that the actual damages are capable of accurate estimation. We do not say this from hindsight made possible because the actual figures claimed were in evidence. We say it because at the time the contract was made, it was clear that the nature of any damages . . . from a possible future breach was such that they would be easily ascertainable. . . .

The itemized claims totaled $5,080.07. The trial judge did not allow the item of $3,005.00, the difference between the contract price of $29,500.00 and the resale price of $26,495.00. That is why Lee Oldsmobile complains. The court did allow the other items, which come to a total of $2,075.07, and set that amount off against the $5,000 deposit, resulting in the judgment for the Kaidens in the amount of $2,924.93. That is why the Kaidens complain.

Several sections of the Uniform Commercial Code govern our resolution of the remaining issues. Under §2-703, where the buyer repudiates, the aggrieved seller may

> (d) Resell and recover damages as hereafter provided (§2-706);
> (e) Recover damages for nonacceptance (§2-708). . . .

For Lee Oldsmobile to be entitled to claim as damages the difference between the resale price and the contract price, the sum of $3,005.00 in this case, the resale must meet the requirements of §2-706. . . .

The trial court rejected as an item of damage the

difference between the resale price and the contract price because it held that the resale made by Lee Oldsmobile was not made in a commercially reasonable manner, and that no notification was given of its intention to resell at private sale. We need not decide whether the resale was made in a commercially reasonable manner. It is enough that Lee Oldsmobile did not give the Kaidens reasonable notification of its intention to resell. . . .

It will be seen that §2-708(1) authorizes two kinds of damage to an aggrieved seller. The first, the difference between the market price at the time and place for tender and the contract price was not claimed in this case, perhaps because Lee Oldsmobile's salesman testified in his deposition that the market price of a

Rolls-Royce was the sticker price. For the incidental damages authorized in §2-708 one turns to §2-710. . . .

Every item of damage claimed by Lee Oldsmobile which was allowable under §§2-708 and 2-710 was in fact allowed by the trial court. . . . The contentions of the Kaidens in the cross appeal that the incidental damages should not have been allowed, because the resale of the automobile was not made in a commercially reasonable manner, cannot prevail. Those incidental damages are allowable to an aggrieved seller under §2-710, whether he gets there through §2-706 or through §2-708.

Judgment affirmed.

CASE REVIEW QUESTIONS
1. Why was Lee Oldsmobile not entitled to the resale remedy?
2. Why couldn't Lee Oldsmobile keep the entire down payment as liquidated damages?
3. Why did Lee Oldsmobile keep more than the $500 minimum allowed by the Code?
4. What were the elements of incidental damages recovered by the seller?
5. Could Lee Oldsmobile have put in a claim for lost profits? Explain.

SELLER'S BREACH: BUYER'S REMEDIES

When a seller breaches a contract, the buyer may be affected in a number of ways. If the seller repudiates the contract or otherwise fails to deliver the goods, the buyer is left empty-handed. Often, substitute goods must be found as quickly as possible. If the goods are in some way unique, finding substitute goods may be particularly difficult or impossible. If the goods have been delivered but are nonconforming, the buyer may reject them or accept them. If the buyer rejects the goods, the buyer is left empty-handed. If the buyer accepts the goods, a different set of problems arises. The buyer may discover the nonconformity immediately or he or she may not discover it until later. A buyer's choice of remedies will depend upon the circumstances.

Seller's Breach
Before listing buyer's remedies, the Code catalogues seller's breaches. A seller breaches when:

1. *The seller fails to deliver the goods at the time or in the manner called for by the contract.* For example, when a contract calls for the seller to deliver goods on a Wednesday but he or she delivers them on the following Friday, the seller has breached the contract. (For a discussion of delivery obligations, see pages 434–436.)
2. *The seller repudiates a contract* [§2-610]. For example, a seller repudiates by telling the buyer in advance that he or she will not deliver the goods. (For a discussion of repudiation, see pages 430–431.)
3. *The seller delivers nonconforming goods and the buyer rightfully rejects the goods or properly revokes acceptance.* For example, suppose a seller ships blue widgets instead of the red widgets called for by the contract. If the buyer rejects the widgets and the seller cannot cure (provide the blue widgets), the seller breaches the contract. (For discussion of rejection and acceptance, see pages 439–441 and 444–446, respectively.)

Buyer's Remedies

When a seller breaches a sales contract, the buyer has a number of remedies. In appropriate circumstances, a buyer may do one or more of the following [§2-711]:

1. Purchase substitute goods (cover) [§2-712].
2. Recover damages from the seller [§2-712, §2-713, and §2-715].
3. Recover the goods from the seller [§2-502 and §2-716].
4. Recover any amounts already paid [§2-711(1), §2-707, and §2-717].
5. Recover for breach of warranty [§2-714].
6. Cancel the contract [§2-711(1)].

Cover When a seller has breached a sales contract by refusing to deliver goods or by delivering nonconforming goods, the buyer may **cover;** that is, he or she may purchase or make contracts to purchase goods that will substitute for the goods the seller has not properly delivered [§2-712(2)]. The buyer must cover within a reasonable time and must act in good faith. For example, under the doctrine of mitigation of damages (see page 319), the buyer cannot wait until the price of the goods has increased substantially unless there is a good reason for the delay, such as difficulty in finding substitute goods.

A buyer who has purchased substitute goods can recover from the seller the difference between the cost of the substituted goods and the contract price of the original goods [§2-712(1)]. However, the buyer must deduct any expenses saved from the difference. For example, if the seller does not ship the goods, the buyer will save any shipping costs that he or she might have been obligated to pay for the original goods.

The buyer can add incidental and consequential damages to the difference. **Incidental damages** include expenses reasonably incurred in the inspection, receipt, transportation, care, and custody of the original goods plus any other reasonable expenses caused by the seller's breach, such as expenses incurred in purchasing substitute goods [§2-715(1)]. **Consequential damages** include any

Cover Remedy

Cost of 10,000 red widgets purchased from Clyde	$12,000
Contract price for 10,000 red widgets from Sophia	−10,000
	2,000
Cost of returning blue widgets to Sophia and obtaining new contract with Clyde	+ 500
	2,500
Profits lost on contract with Helga	+ 500
	3,000
Expenses saved because only 8,000 widgets were shipped by Sophia	− 100
Damages due to buyer (Boyd)	$ 2,900

FIGURE 24-5
Cover Remedy

losses resulting from the buyer's unmet needs that the seller had reason to know at the time the contract was made, such as lost profits [§2-715(2)].

Suppose, for instance, that Sophia, the seller, has a contract with Boyd for 10,000 red widgets, but she ships 8,000 blue widgets. Suppose also that Sophia knows the widgets are to be incorporated into machines for Helga and that Boyd will have to reduce the price to Helga if the machines are delivered late. Figure 24-5 shows Boyd's damages if Boyd properly rejects the blue widgets, reships them to Sophia, promptly purchases red widgets from Clyde, but still suffers some loss on the contract with Helga due to the delays caused by Sophia's breach.

Nondelivery When a seller has breached a sales contract, the buyer is not limited to a remedy for cover. He or she may choose to recover for nondelivery of the goods. The measure of damages for nondelivery is the difference between the contract price and the market price at the time the buyer learns of the breach, plus any incidental and consequential damages, and minus any expenses saved [§2-713(1)]. For example, suppose that, as in the previous example, Sophia and Boyd have a contract for the purchase and sale of 10,000 red widgets. Sophia breaches by shipping 8,000 blue widgets. Suppose also that Boyd is unable to purchase the red widgets he needs to complete the machines for Helga. Figure 24-6 shows Boyd's damages for nondelivery. Note that the nondelivery remedy is available even though Sophia delivered some goods. The proper goods were not delivered, so effectively, there was no delivery.

Choice of Remedy: Cover or Nondelivery A buyer's remedies for cover and nondelivery parallel a seller's remedies for resale and nonacceptance. The Code allows a buyer to select either cover or nondelivery, depending on which will provide the buyer with the best remedy and which will create an economic incentive for the seller not to breach the contract when the market price has risen above the contract price. The buyer's choice is limited, however, by the doctrine of mitigation of damages (see page 319). In other words, a buyer must

Nondelivery Remedy

Market price of 10,000 red widgets when Boyd learns of the breach	$12,000
Contract price for 10,000 red widgets from Sophia	−10,000
	2,000
Cost of returning the blue widgets	+ 300
	2,300
Profits lost on contract with Helga	+ 1,000
	3,300
Expenses saved because only 8,000 widgets were shipped by Sophia	100
Damages due to buyer (Boyd)	$ 3,400

FIGURE 24-6
Nondelivery Remedy

purchase substitute goods if possible if the purchase can reduce the seller's consequential damages.

The choice of remedies is particularly important in a fluctuating market situation. Suppose that the price of widgets has risen above the contract price agreed upon between a buyer and a seller. The seller might be inclined to breach the contract so that he or she could sell the widgets at the higher price. Figure 24-7A shows how the buyer's choice of remedies could apply in a market situation where the market price of widgets is rising above the contract price. Figure 24-7B shows how the buyer's choice of remedies might apply when the market price is falling toward the contract price.

Recover the Price When the seller has breached the contract, the buyer can recover any amount already paid for the goods along with the other remedies already discussed. In addition to demanding that the seller return any amount already paid, the buyer has two other means of recovering amounts paid. The buyer can sell goods in his or her possession or he or she can withhold future payments.

Buyer's Right to Sell A buyer who has rightfully rejected goods or has justifiably revoked acceptance of goods may sell the goods in his or her possession as a means of recovering any amount already paid for the goods or any expenses incurred for inspection, receipt, transportation, care, and custody of the goods [§2-711(3)]. The buyer must conduct the sale in the same manner as an aggrieved seller would resell goods when a buyer breaches a contract [§2-706]. (For a discussion of the resale remedy, see pages 457–461.)

For example, the buyer must tell the seller that he or she is intending to sell the goods if the sale will be private. If the sale will be public, the buyer must give the seller reasonable notice of the time and place of the sale unless the goods are perishable or are rapidly declining in value.

If the buyer receives more than he or she has already paid for the goods and more than any expenses incurred, including the expenses of the resale, the

Contract for 10,000 widgets—Contract price $10,000

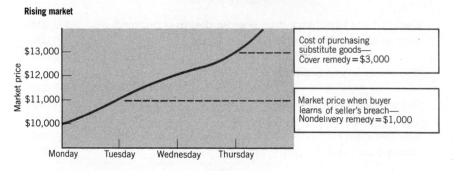

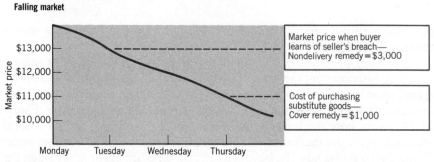

FIGURE 24-7
Buyer's Remedies in a Fluctuating Market

buyer must turn the excess over to the seller. The buyer, having rejected the goods, is really selling the goods for the seller.

Buyer's Right to Withhold Future Payments A buyer who is entitled to damages for a seller's breach of a sales contract can withhold the amount of the damages from any future payments that are due to be made under the contract, provided that the buyer notifies the seller that he or she intends to withhold the damages [§2-717].

For example, suppose that a buyer has a contract with a seller for the delivery of 10,000 widgets for $10,000. If the buyer has paid $5,000 and the seller only delivers 8,000 widgets, the buyer can deduct from the $5,000 still to be paid the amount due for the 2,000 undelivered widgets and any damages, such as, the costs of purchasing 2,000 widgets from another seller.

In the following case, the buyer sought remedies from the seller after revoking acceptance of a new automobile. The court had to determine whether the expenses of renting an automobile are included under a cover remedy. In its discussion, the court notes that the contract has a provision that limits the buyer's recovery for consequential damages. Limitation of damages is discussed later in this chapter.

McGINNIS v. WENTWORTH CHEVROLET CO.
668 P.2d 365 (Ore. 1983)

[McGinnis, the plaintiff, purchased a new El Camino automobile from Wentworth Chevrolet Company, the defendant, on July 25, 1978. The purchase price was $5,923. McGinnis had a number of problems with the automobile, ranging from cosmetic defects such as chipping paint to major mechanical problems such as the tendency for the engine to stall at intersections. Wentworth made several attempts to repair the automobile. After three months of problems, McGinnis' attorney wrote Wentworth revoking acceptance and requesting a return of the price or a new 1978 El Camino. Wentworth refused and again attempted to repair the automobile. On January 26, 1979, McGinnis, through her attorney, repeated her revocation, stored the automobile, and rented a substitute. Wentworth still refused to recognize the revocation. McGinnis sued to recover the purchase price plus incidental and consequential damages, including the car rental fees.

Upon trial, Wentworth raised the defense that recovery for these damages might be precluded by a limitation-of-liability clause set forth in the purchase contract. That clause provides that defendant, as seller, "shall not be liable in contract, tort or otherwise for injuries to persons or property or *for consequential damages* or commercial losses." [Emphasis added.]

The trial court ruled that McGinnis was entitled to a refund of the purchase price, less the value of her use of the automobile (which the court set at $1,000), but the trial court judge denied the request for additional damages, evidently concluding that in a revocation-of-acceptance case a plaintiff's remedy is limited to a refund of the purchase price.

The intermediate appellate court reversed the trial court and remanded for a determination of damages. The defendant appealed the granting of damages to the buyer for the rental of an automobile.]

CARSON, [Judge]

[T]he issue before us is whether, given plaintiff's justifiable revocation of her acceptance of the automobile, she is entitled to recompense for her automobile rental fees. . . .

Plaintiff's entitlement to damages, accordingly, is to be determined by reference to the UCC provisions governing a buyer's remedies upon rightful revocation of acceptance or rejection of nonconforming goods. The appropriate statute is [§2-711]:

> (1) Where . . . the buyer rightfully rejects or justifiably revokes acceptance then with respect to any goods involved . . . the buyer may cancel and whether or not he has done so may in addition to recovering so much of the price as has been paid:
>   (a) "Cover" and have damages under [§2-712] as to all the goods affected whether or not they have been identified to the contract; or
>   (b) Recover damages for nondelivery as provided in [§2-713]. . . .

Thus, a buyer in plaintiff's position is not relegated merely to cancellation of the contract and recovery of the price paid thereunder (as apparently held by the trial court); rather, she also potentially is entitled to a catalog of other remedies, one of which is "cover." [§2-712] provides:

> (1) After a breach within [§2-711] the buyer may "cover" by making in good faith and without unreasonable delay *any reasonable purchase of* or contract to purchase *goods in substitution* for those due from the seller.
> (2) The buyer may recover from the seller as damages the difference between the cost of cover and the contract price together with any *incidental or consequential damages* as defined in [§2-715] but less expenses saved in consequence of the seller's breach.
> (3) Failure of the buyer to effect cover within this section does not bar him from any other remedy. [Emphasis added by the court.]

In an appropriate case, where a buyer does not "cover," she or he may recover damages for non-delivery:

> (1) . . . [T]he measure of damages for nondelivery or repudiation by the seller is the difference between the market price at the time when the buyer learned of the breach and the contract price together with any incidental or consequential damages provided in [§2-715] but less expenses saved in consequence of the seller's breach.

In summary, a buyer who justifiably revokes acceptance of nonconforming goods purchased from a seller is entitled under the UCC to the following remedies:

1. The right to "cancel" this contract; and
2. Recovery of so much of the price as has been paid (including . . . certain expenses incurred incident thereto); and
3. "Cover" damages; or
4. "Nondelivery" damages; and
5. "Incidental" and "consequential" damages. . . .

The question presented is whether plaintiff's claim for rental recompense falls within one of the classes outlined above. The [intermediate appellate court] concluded that the renting of a replacement automobile was a reasonable way for plaintiff to cover and thus the rental costs, as a cost in effective cover, were recoverable as "incidental" damages under [§2-715(1)]. . . .

The Court of Appeals' opinion evinces a misconception as to the purpose and function of the UCC's "cover" remedy. Where a seller breaches a contract for the sale of goods by failing to deliver the agreed-upon goods, the buyer's traditional pre-code contract remedy was to seek "loss-of-bargain" damages. The measure of damages was calculated as the difference between the contract price and the fair market value of the goods. . . . This traditional remedy is reflected in the UCC's "market price" formula found in [§2-713].

The UCC's "cover" alternative was intended to enable the buyer to "obtain the goods he needs" by allowing the disappointed buyer to reenter the market place and make a reasonable purchase of substitute goods. This remedy also can obviate the often difficult calculation of the market price of the goods. . . . When a buyer makes a reasonable "cover," the measure of damages is the difference between the actual "cover" purchased and the contract price [§2-712(2)]. This formula results in a substantial departure from pre-code law where there was no assurance at what time or place the court would measure the market were the buyer to purchase substitute goods. Although [§2-712(3)] makes it clear that the buyer is not obligated to "cover" (except insofar as she needs to mitigate her consequential damages, see [§2-712, Comment 3], if the buyer does not "cover," her loss-of-bargain damages, if any, will be computed under [§2-713] the market price provision.

Incidental and consequential damages are defined in [§2-715]. . . . Whether a particular item of alleged damage is recoverable as incidental or consequential generally is not important provided that it is recoverable as either. In this case, however, the distinction may be significant because of the contract's exclusion clause which precludes "consequential damages."

The list of "incidental damages" in [§2-715(1)] is "not intended to be exhaustive but [is] merely illustrative of the typical kinds of incidental damage" [UCC §2-715, Comment 1]. The list and the employment of the term "incidental," however, connote a narrow ambit restricted to those costs and expenses incurred by the buyer which directly result from the fact of the breach. The dichotomy with the word "consequential" admittedly is vague.

Nonetheless, we conclude that plaintiff's rental expenses are not incidental damages. They relate to the particular circumstances of plaintiff relative to the goods, rather than being necessarily incident to a breach of this contract. Whether these expenses are recoverable as consequential damages under [§2-715(2)], and the effect, if any, of the contract's limitation-of-liability clause however, must be determined on remand.

In conclusion, that part of the opinion of the Court of Appeals granting plaintiff recompense for her automobile rental costs as an expense incidental to "cover" is reversed. This case is remanded to the trial court for further proceedings in accordance with this opinion. . . .

Reversed and remanded.

CASE REVIEW QUESTIONS

1. What remedies does the court say a buyer is entitled to in the event of a seller's breach?
2. Can McGinnis recover the cost of the rental car? Explain.

3. If McGinnis had purchased a new El Camino automobile to replace the one returned to Wentworth, would she have been able to recover the cost of the new automobile? Explain.

Specific Performance Suppose a buyer arranges to purchase a certain valuable painting, and the seller repudiates the contract. In this situation, money damages is an inadequate remedy because there is no substitute for the painting desired. The UCC states that in these circumstances the seller may be compelled by the court to relinquish the item called for by the contract [§2-716(1)]. This remedy is called **specific performance**. (For a general discussion of specific performance, see page 322.) Specific performance is available when the goods are in some way unique.

In addition to ordering the seller to deliver unique goods, a court can award appropriate damages. For example, if the seller knows that the buyer has made a contract with a third party to display the painting, a court could award damages for the profits lost when the buyer was unable to honor his or her contract with the third party.

What if the goods are not unique, but the buyer is unable to effect cover? The goods may be in short supply, for example. When the goods have been identified, the Code gives the buyer the right of **replevin**. This term refers to a person's right to obtain possession of goods. For example, suppose that a buyer has a contract for the purchase of 10,000 widgets, which the seller refuses to deliver. Suppose also that there are no other widgets available because all other widget manufacturers have contracts with other buyers. In this situation, a court can order the seller to deliver the widgets.

Insolvent Seller If a seller is insolvent, a buyer has a limited right to obtain possession of the goods belonging to the contract even if the goods are not unique or are not in short supply [§2-502]. The buyer can recover the goods if the following conditions are met:

1. The seller is insolvent.
2. The buyer has already paid all or part of the purchase price.
3. The buyer pays any unpaid portion of the purchase price.
4. The buyer claims the goods within ten days after the first payment was made for the goods.
5. The goods are identified to the contract. (For a discussion of the identification of goods, see pages 383–385.)

Either the seller or the buyer may identify goods as the goods belonging to the contract. If the buyer is the one who identifies the goods, however, he or she can only recover conforming goods [§2-502(2)]. Otherwise, the buyer could be unjustly enriched by selecting goods of a better quality.

The buyer can recover the goods under these limited conditions because he or she may be unable to recover the money paid for the goods. The insolvent seller may have already used the money by the time the buyer learns of the seller's insolvency.

Cancel the Contract When a seller has breached a sales contract, the buyer can cancel the contract [§2-711(1)]. For example, if a seller repudiates a contract and refuses to manufacture goods ordered by the buyer, the buyer is not obligated to wait for the seller to change his or her mind and comply with the contract. The buyer can cancel the contract and make a new contract with a seller who will manufacture the goods.

A buyer's right to cancel a contract is particularly important for an installment contract situation in which there are supposed to be a number of separate deliveries. When a seller has breached an installment contract, the buyer need not wait for each installment to become due. He or she can cancel the contract and then enter into new contracts for future deliveries.

Buyer's Damages for Accepted Goods A buyer may accept goods knowing that either the goods or their manner of delivery do not conform to the contract. For example, the goods may have been delivered two days late, which has caused the buyer to lose profits, but the buyer may choose to keep the goods rather than lose still more profits. Or the buyer may accept the goods and have no knowledge of a nonconformity that may only be disclosed at a later date. Or the buyer may be unable to revoke acceptance because the nonconformity is not substantial (see page 446).

Suppose, for example, that a seller ships only 9,950 widgets when the contract calls for 10,000. If the buyer accepts the shipment on the basis of the seller's promises to deliver the other 50 widgets, the buyer cannot revoke acceptance even if the seller does not deliver the remaining 50 widgets. The buyer is, of course, entitled to recover for the loss suffered from not receiving the other 50 widgets. The remedy may be as simple as an allowance against the price for those 50 widgets.

The buyer's remedy in these situations is determined by what is reasonable in the circumstances [§2-714(1)] and includes appropriate incidental and consequential damages [§2-714(3)]. In order to obtain a remedy, the buyer must notify the seller of the defect. (For a discussion of the buyer's obligation to give notice, see pages 449–451.)

Breach of Warranty The buyer who has accepted goods can also recover for breach of warranty. The measure of damages is essentially the difference between the value of the goods accepted and the value the goods would have if they had been as warranted [§2-714(2)] along with incidental and consequential damages [§2-714(3)]. The goal of the remedy is to put the buyer in as good a position as he or she would have been in if the goods had been as warranted. (For a discussion of warranty and the remedies available, see Chapter 22.)

LIMITATION OF REMEDIES

The remedies provided by the Code for breaches of sales contracts may not be available in every instance because the parties to a sales contract can agree to limit or exclude certain remedies. In addition, the Code provides a statute of limitations that sets limits on the time in which a suit can be brought for the breach of a sales contract.

Limited Remedy

A seller and a buyer can agree on the remedies that will be available in the event of a breach by either party. They can modify Code remedies, exclude certain remedies, or even create new remedies. For example, a contract can specify that in the event of a breach by the seller the buyer is entitled to return nonconforming goods and receive replacement goods.

If a limited remedy is not effective, an aggrieved party can claim any of the remedies available under the Code. For example, if the replacement of nonconforming goods is the exclusive remedy included in the contract and the seller will not replace nonconforming goods, the buyer can obtain damages through the Code remedies of cover or nondelivery along with incidental and consequential damages. (For more discussion of limited remedies, see Chapter 22.)

Limitation of Consequential Damages The Code allows parties to exclude consequential damages and, therefore, to agree on who will bear losses should they occur, provided that the agreement is not unconscionable [§2-719(3)]. The Code specifies, however, that excluding damages for physical (personal) injury caused by consumer goods in unconscionable. The exclusion of consequential damages in other situations may or may not be unconscionable, depending upon the circumstance.

Consequential damages are available to buyers for damages, including loss of profits, that result from needs of the buyer that the seller knows about and that cannot be prevented by cover [§2-715(2)(a)]. Consequential damages also include damages for physical injury to a person or injury to property that result from a breach of warranty [§2-715(2)(b)]. (For a discussion of consequential damages for breaches of warranty see Chapter 22.)

In the following case, the seller successfully disclaimed consequential damages and limited the buyer's recovery for damages.

KLEVEN v. GEIGY AGRICULTURAL CHEMICALS
227 N.W.2d 566 (Minn. 1975)

PETERSON, Judge

Plaintiffs, George and James Kleven, purchased herbicide from defendant, Ciba-Geigy Corporation, for use on the farmland. . . . Plaintiffs sued defendant for breach because the herbicide did not effectively provide weed control. The jury . . . found that defendant had breached an express warranty and found that, as a direct result of this breach, plaintiffs sustained damages of $2,146.20 for the reasonable cost of the herbicide and for the expenses incurred in applying the product. The trial court ordered judgment for plaintiffs in that sum.

Plaintiffs offered evidence to establish that the difference between the reasonable value of the corn actually in the field and the fair and reasonable value the corn would have had if the herbicide had been effective was $14,515 . . . [and] the cost of additional tilling, at $7,257.50. . . . The trial court ruled that any crop losses and tilling costs sustained by plaintiff constituted consequential damages and therefore declined to order judgment for such losses. Plaintiffs for that reason appeal from the judgment. . . .

The product in issue is a chemical herbicide, manufactured by defendant, known as Aatrex 80W. The bags in which the herbicide is contained are imprinted with this written warranty:

> The Directions For Use of this product reflect the opinion of experts based on field use and tests. The directions are believed to be reliable and should be followed carefully. However, it is impossible to eliminate all risks inherently associated with use of this product. . . . In no case shall Geigy or the Seller be liable for consequential, special or indirect damages resulting from the use or handling of this product. . . .

The trial court properly denied recovery to plaintiffs for their claimed crop damages and tilling expense on the ground that they were consequential damages excluded by the express terms of defendant's warranty. . . .

We address ourselves, in conclusion, to plaintiff's contention that the exclusion is in this case so unconscionable that it should not be enforced. [§2-302(1)] provides that unconscionable contract provisions may be either voided or limited by the court so as to avoid any unconscionable result. [§2-719(1), U.C.C. Comment 1], states that every sales contract should contain at least a fair quantum of remedy for breach of duties outlined in the contract. . . . We think the nature of the product and the risks related to its use affect the reasonableness of the exclusion in issue. . . .

Aatrex 80W is a highly technical specialized chemical developed and used for selective control of certain weeds or plants growing in common with other plants. . . . It is general knowledge, as the trial court in that rural area noted, that the eventual yield of a farm crop, such as corn, is affected by numerous and varied factors such as soil, weather, seed, weeds, and other conditions. Considering the nature of the product itself and the multitude of conditions and factors that affect its effectiveness or its degree of effectiveness, limited favorable results could be anticipated. Finally, it is clear that the risks of failure were fairly disclosed to plaintiffs at the time of purchase in these words:

> . . . Crop injury, ineffectiveness or other unintended consequences may result because of such factors such as weather conditions, presence of other materials, or the manner of use or application all of which are beyond the control of Geigy or the seller. All such risks shall be assumed by the Buyer.

We accordingly agree with the trial court's conclusion.

Affirmed.

CASE REVIEW QUESTIONS
1. Was the seller's disclaimer of consequential damages effective? Why?
2. Why wasn't the exclusion of consequential damages unconscionable?
3. Based on this case, what arguments would you expect to be made in the rehearing of *McGinnis v. Wentworth Chevrolet Co.* (See page 471)?

Statute of Limitations

If a buyer and a seller cannot resolve their problems, they may avail themselves of a court's help, but they must do this before the time permitted to bring a suit runs out. The Code provides for a **statute of limitations** — that is, a set time within which a suit for a breach of a sales contract must be brought. An aggrieved party must begin a suit within four years after a breach occurs, even if he or she does not discover the breach for some time [§2-715]. The four-year period during which a suit can be brought can be reduced by agreement of the parties, provided that they do not reduce the period to less than one year. The period cannot be extended, however.

[handwritten: WRONG PARTIES CAN CONTRACT TO EXTEND.]

The period in which suits can be brought is measured from the time the cause of action accrues. In general, a cause of action accrues when a breach occurs. For example, if a seller repudiates a contract, the cause of action accrues when the seller announces that he or she will not honor the contract. Similarly, if a buyer fails to make a payment when it is due, the breach occurs and the cause of action accrues on the date payment was due. If the period is not shortened by the parties' agreement, any suit for breach must be begun within four years from the date of the breach. If a suit is not begun within the four-year period, no suit is possible. The suit is said to be barred by the statute of limitations.

Breach of Warranty A cause of action for breach of warranty accrues when the goods are tendered for delivery unless there is a warranty that explicitly extends to the future performance of the goods. (For a discussion of when a breach of warranty occurs, see Chapter 22.)

REVIEW QUESTIONS

1. List eight remedies that are available to a seller when a buyer breaches a sales contract.
2. Under what circumstances can a seller withhold delivery of goods? Explain.
3. Explain the difference between the resale remedy and the nonacceptance remedy.
4. In what three circumstances can a seller recover the contract price for goods?
5. When are liquidated damages available?
6. List six remedies that are available to a buyer when a seller breaches a sales contract.
7. In what ways can a buyer recover the price paid for goods?
8. What are a seller's rights if the buyer is insolvent? What are a buyer's rights if the seller is insolvent?
9. Under what circumstances can a seller or buyer recover lost profits?
10. Under what circumstances can a seller exclude recovery for consequential damages?
11. How much time does an aggrieved party have to bring a suit for a breach of a sales contract?

CASE PROBLEMS

1. Alfred M. Lewis, Inc. (Lewis) was a wholesale grocer who sold frozen foods and other grocery items to retail outlets. Lewis entered into a contract to sell grocery items to Telemart Enterprises, Inc. (Telemart), a retail seller of groceries. During September, Lewis shipped $61,500 of groceries to Telemart using the services of Van Lines, Inc. Several hours after Lewis' shipment was loaded on Van Lines' truck, Lewis learned that Telemart had filed for bankruptcy. The Van Lines truck carrying the Lewis–Telemart ship- ment also had shipments for other buyers from sellers in the industrial complex where Lewis was located. What remedies are available to Lewis? Explain.

2. Norcross ordered 1,000 customized racks for greeting cards from Cesco Manufacturing Corporation (Cesco). Norcross promised to pay $100 per rack 30 days after the racks were delivered. No dates were specified for delivery, but Cesco was to ship the racks upon receipt of the shipping orders sent by Norcross. Cesco purchased the

necessary materials and began production. Over the period of a year, Cesco shipped 440 racks to Norcross. Finally, Norcross decided that the racks were too heavy even though they had been manufactured according to specifications. Norcross submitted no more shipping orders. At that point, 560 racks were undelivered. Of them, 480 were already manufactured and there was sufficient raw material on hand to manufacture the remaining 80. Cesco ceased manufacturing the racks and stored them in a warehouse. For several years, Norcross and Cesco tried to resolve the dispute. Although there was a market for card racks, Cesco did not have access to that market because the cost involved in finding buyers was prohibitive. Unable to resolve the dispute with Norcross, Cesco sold the remaining 560 racks at auction for $2,000 and the raw materials for $200. What remedies are available to Cesco? Explain.

3. Neri entered into a sales contract with Retail Marine Corporation (Marine) for the purchase of a boat having a sale price of $12,500. Neri made a down payment of $4,250. Within five days, Marine received the boat from the wholesaler. At the same time, Marine received a letter from Neri's attorney canceling the contract because Neri would be unable to make the payments due to medical problems. After storing the boat for four months at a cost of $675, Marine sold the boat to another purchaser for the price of $12,500. Marine's profit margin on the sale of the boat was $2,580. What remedies are available to Marine? Explain. How much, if any, of the down payment can Neri recover? Explain.

4. Varner, a fruit grower, agreed to sell to B.L. Lanier Fruit Company (Fruit Co.) all of the fruit grown on Varner's land. Fruit Co. was to pick the fruit before February 9th. The parties contemplated that there would be 22,000 boxes of fruit and set a price of $1.25 a box. The contract contained the following clause:

> Buyer has advanced to grower the sum of $11,000 which sum is an advance and part payment for the fruit at the price stated. . . . Should Buyer fail to comply with the terms,

this contract shall become null and void and the advance made shall be retained by Grower in full payment of liquidated damages.

Fruit Co. picked 12,000 boxes of fruit worth $15,000 but refused to pick any more. Some 9,500 boxes were left on the trees, and Varner was unable to sell them. Varner sued for breach of the contract. What remedies are available to Varner? Explain.

5. Dean Markel grew potatoes. He entered into an installment contract with David E. Dangerfield to sell 25,000 cwt. (hundredweight) of chipping potatoes during a six-month period. The contract price varied from month to month to reflect storage charges and possible price fluctuation. The low price per cwt. was $1.25 for field delivery in September. The price rose to a high of $2.30 in the sixth month of the contract. Markel delivered 10,000 cwt. of potatoes and then refused to deliver the balance. At the time Markel refused to deliver any more potatoes, the market price was $3.75 per cwt. Dangerfield made good-faith efforts to purchase the remaining 15,000 cwt. of potatoes but was unable to complete the purchase for 38 days. Because the market price of the potatoes was rising rapidly, the potatoes purchased by Dangerfield cost $4.41 per cwt. for 10,000 cwt. and $6.00 per cwt. for the remaining 5,000 cwt. Dangerfield incurred costs of $500 in arranging the contracts for the 15,000 cwt. of potatoes. What remedies are available to Dangerfield? Explain.

6. Huntington Beach High School District (School District) invited bids (offers) from companies to supply the school with an IBM or similar computer. The invitation noted that the School District had arranged to rent some peripheral equipment beginning on July 12th, the date the computer should be delivered. School District received two offers which were to remain open until July 12th. School District accepted Continental Information Systems Corporation's (Continental) bid which was $12,000 less than the other bid. On July 12th, Continental was still negotiating with a third party for the purchase of a system for School District. Believing in good faith that Con-

tinental would be able to complete the negotiations by July 31st, School District did not declare Continental in breach and did not, therefore, accept the other bid on the last day it was open. Continental did not deliver the computer, and School District ultimately purchases a system for $59,000 more than Continental's price. The computer was not installed until mid-October. During that three month period, School District had to pay $3,000 per month rental on the peripherals even though they were unusable. What remedies are available to School District? Explain.

7. Aeroglide manufactures a machine called Mini Dump, which turns small pickup trucks into small dumptrucks. Deaton entered into a distributorship agreement with Aeroglide. In February of 1978, Deaton ordered 24 Mini Dumps. When the units arrived, some were new, some were damaged, and others appeared used. Aeroglide admitted that two had been used for demonstration purposes. In May, Deaton wrote Aeroglide and stated that the Mini Dumps did not operate properly. Deaton demanded a return of its cash outlay and miscellaneous costs for storage and materials. Various negotiations followed. In September of 1978, Aeroglide offered to repurchase the units for $21,976.39. Deaton rejected the settlement offer. On June 30, 1980, Deaton sold the units at a private sale for $9,200. No notice of the sale was given to Aeroglide. Deaton sued Aeroglide to recover $15,047.22, the difference between the $9,200 and the purchase price. Deaton also claimed lost profits of $8,837.78 based on the difference between the purchase price and Aeroglide's suggested retail price and storage costs of $7,467.76. How much, if anything, should Deaton recover? Why?

8. Copylease Corporation had a contract with Memorex Corporation for the purchase of toner and developer used in copying machines. Memorex granted Copylease an exclusive territory. Memorex breached the contract and failed to deliver the toner and developer to Copylease. Copylease was unable to obtain an alternative source of toner because other brands were inferior to Memorex. Copylease sued for breach of contract. What remedies are available? Explain.

9. David Ferguson, Ltd., purchased a quantity of yarn from Wilson Trading Corporation. After the yarn was knitted into sweaters and the finished product washed, it was discovered that the yarn had shaded; that is, the color varied from sweater to sweater and even within the same sweater. The sweaters were unmarketable. Ferguson refused to pay for the yarn. Wilson sued to recover the purchase price pointing to language in the contract that read:

> No claims relating to . . . shade shall be allowed, if made after . . . knitting . . . , or more than 10 days after receipt of shipment. . . . The buyer shall within 10 days of the receipt . . . examine the merchandise for any and all defects. . . . It is expressly agreed that . . . no warranties, express or implied, have been . . . made by the seller except as stated herein, and the seller makes no warranty . . . as to the fitness for buyer's purposes of yarn purchased hereunder . . . except as expressly stated herein, being limited to the delivery of good merchantable yarn of the description stated herein.

Ferguson had notified Wilson of the defect as soon as it was discovered, but the discovery was not made until more than 10 days after the delivery. Who will win the case? Explain.

10. Daniel O'Brien sold 14 cows to Raymond Cube in July 1974. The cows were expressly and impliedly warranted to be merchantable in quality and fit for use as dairy cattle. In April 1975, the cattle were found to be afflicted with Brucellosis, a serious disease affecting cattle. In October 1978, Daniel O'Brien sued to recover compensatory damages for loss of the cattle and loss of milk production. Who will win the case? Explain.

PART IV

NEGOTIABLE INSTRUMENTS LAW

25

NEGOTIABLE INSTRUMENTS

Money is the medium of exchange in any advanced society. When we think of money, we usually picture gold, silver, currency, and coin. But suppose that all of our monetary transactions were made in these forms. Imagine the inconvenience, not to mention the risk, of paying your monthly bills in cash, either by sending the money through the mail or by carrying it in person to each of your respective creditors.

Negotiable instruments — checks, drafts, promissory notes, and certificates of deposit — were developed to make the exchange of money more convenient and safe. Historical evidence tells us that these types of instruments have existed in some form for thousands of years. It was not until the eighteenth century, however, that the law of negotiable instruments was developed and incorporated into English common law.

Consider the following scenario: In the early 1700s, an English textile company purchases cotton from an Egyptian supplier. The cotton is shipped from Alexandria to London by way of the Mediterranean. The method of payment involves shipping gold, silver, or English currency back along the same route to the Egyptian seller. From time to time pirates operating out of Tripoli in the Mediterranean make off with the money.

The English textile company has two main options for avoiding the pirates. It could switch to a West African supplier of cotton so that the product and payment could be shipped along a safer route. The textile company, though, prefers the type of cotton it obtains from the Egyptian supplier. The company's second option would be to revert to a form of barter that involved sending goods of some kind to Alexandria instead of gold. This method of payment would be cumbersome and impractical, however, especially if it were used throughout the business world.

The need for some safe, effective substitute for money spurred the development of the law of negotiable instruments. Suppose the English textile merchant, a man by the name of George Tilley, were to sign, date, and send to the Egyptian cotton supplier a piece of paper stating: "I, George Tilley, promise to pay to the order of Yasser Jabbar £1,000,* 90 days after this date." At the end of the 90 days, Yasser Jabbar would be entitled to the £1,000. Jabbar might collect the money in London or Tilley might pay it in Cairo, but either way the money might still have to be transported past the pirates in Tripoli.

If, however, the piece of paper signed by George Tilley were as good as money, Jabbar could use it like money to pay someone for something in Cairo. That person could, in turn, use it to pay someone else. Thus, through a network of bankers and merchants who trade by the land routes through the Near East and Europe, the piece of paper could avoid the pirates and make its way back to England. Each person who took the paper would pay the person who transferred it. Finally, George Tilley would pay the person who brought the paper to him.

NEGOTIABILITY

Negotiability is the legal theory that makes a piece of paper an acceptable means of payment and an effective substitute for money. The law provides a set of criteria for determining when a piece of paper is a negotiable instrument. The law also sets forth the rules governing **negotiation,** which is the effective transfer of a negotiable instrument.

Negotiation and Assignment Compared

The way a negotiable instrument is special can best be described by comparing it with a simple contract. Suppose George Tilley gave Yasser Jabbar a piece of paper that was not a negotiable instrument but was an enforceable promise to pay £1,000. Because the promise is stated in a contract, Jabbar could transfer his right to the £1,000 to Emir Abdul. Such a transfer is called an *assignment,* Jabbar being the *assignor* and Abdul being the *assignee.*

When an assignment of a contract right is made, however, the assignee stands in the same position as the assignor. If Tilley had a legal defense against Jabbar that would allow him to refuse to pay Jabbar, he could assert that defense against Abdul. As a result, Abdul might not be able to collect the £1,000. Tilley would have such a defense if, for example, Jabbar had lied about the quality of the goods. Tilley could use the defense of misrepresentation against Abdul because Abdul, as an assignee, has no greater rights than the assignor, Jabbar. (The subject of assignments is fully discussed in Chapter 16.)

Suppose, instead, that Tilley gave Jabbar a piece of paper that met all the criteria for being a negotiable instrument. When Jabbar transferred—or

---

* "£" is the symbol used to designate "pound," a denomination of English currency.

negotiated—the instrument to Abdul, Tilley would not be able to assert the defense of misrepresentation against Abdul because Abdul's rights would be greater than those of Jabbar. This occurs because the law governing negotiable instruments creates a status called a **holder in due course.** In addition, the law says that the negotiation of a negotiable instrument to a holder in due course cuts off certain defenses. Thus, if Abdul is a holder in due course, he takes the negotiable instrument free from the defense of misrepresentation.

There are three important questions that must be answered affirmatively if a person is to enjoy the status of holder in due course.

1. Is a piece of paper (an instrument) *negotiable* in form; that is, is it a negotiable instrument? This chapter will deal with the legal criteria for determining when a piece of paper is a negotiable instrument.
2. Has an instrument been duly *negotiated;* that is, has it been effectively transferred? The rules governing the transfer of a negotiable instrument will be covered in Chapter 26.
3. Is the person to whom an instrument has been negotiated a *holder in due course?* Chapter 26 will also discuss the criteria for becoming a holder in due course and will explain more fully the rights of a holder in due course.

All persons who deal with negotiable instruments, whether they are holders in due course or not, have certain rights and obligations that will be discussed in Chapter 27.

Statutory Law—UCC Article 3

The statutory law governing negotiable instruments is found in Article 3 of the Uniform Commercial Code. Throughout the chapters dealing with negotiable instruments, you will find numerous references to the UCC. We have therefore simplified these references as much as possible. For example, "§3-102(2)" is a reference to UCC Article 3, Section 102, Subsection 2. (Article 3 of the UCC is reproduced in Appendix B.) Reference is also made on occasion to the Official Comments to the Uniform Commercial Code. For information about the Uniform Commercial Code itself, see Chapter 19.

TYPES OF NEGOTIABLE INSTRUMENTS

There are two basic types of negotiable instruments: **notes,** which are promises to pay, and **drafts,** which are orders to a third party to pay.

Notes and Certificates of Deposit

Notes and certificates of deposit are two party instruments. The person who makes the promise to pay—that is, the person who signs the instrument—is the **maker.** The person to whom the promise is made is called the **payee.** (See Figure 25-1.) A note, usually referred to as a **promissory note** (see Figure 25-2), is a promise to pay [§3-104(2)(d)], and a **certificate of deposit** (see Figure 25-3) is an acknowledgment by a bank that it has received some money and a promise by the bank to repay the money [§3-104(2)(c)].

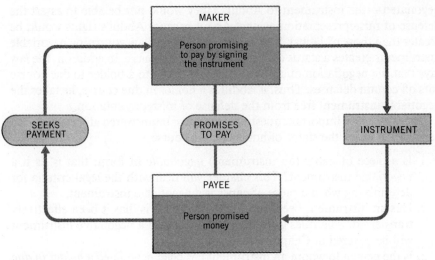

FIGURE 25-1
A Two Party Instrument

$ ___1,000.00___   ___January 1___ 19_85_

_____ I promise to pay to

the order of ___James J. Jones___

___One-Thousand and °°/₁₀₀_____ Dollars

Value received with interest at ___10___ per cent per annum

___Sandra S. Smith___

No._____ Due ___on demand___

FIGURE 25-2
A Promissory Note

CENTRAL BANK   No: 10519156

Negotiable Certificate of Deposit

Somewhere, New York ___Sept. 1___, 19_85_

THIS CERTIFIES to the deposit

in this BANK of the sum of $ _5,000.00_ .

___Five-thousand and °°/₁₀₀_____ Dollars

which is payable to bearer on the _1st_ day of _March_, 19_86_ upon presentation and surrender of this certificate, at the office of issue. This certificate bears interest at the rate of _8.89_ % per annum, to be computed for the actual number of days on the basis of a 360 day year, from date hereof until maturity. No interest will be allowed after maturity. Not payable before maturity.

CANCELLED

AUTHORIZED SIGNATURE

FIGURE 25-3
A Certificate of Deposit

The example of the English textile merchant involved the use of a promissory note, which was the earliest form of a negotiable instrument. Recall that Tilley signed, dated, and sent to Jabbar a piece of paper stating: "I, George Tilley, promise to pay to the order of Yasser Jabbar £1,000, 90 days after this date." Tilley is the maker and Jabbar is the payee. The words "to the order of" in this promise of payment are words of negotiability. They communicate the fact that George Tilley has not merely promised to pay a debt to Jabbar, but he has also promised to pay the debt as Jabbar orders. Jabbar himself may request payment from Tilley, or he may transfer the note to someone else. If Jabbar transfers the note to another person, he is ordering that payment be made to that person. Tilley has promised in advance to obey this order by his use of words of negotiability.

The payee's ability to order Tilley to pay a person other than the payee allows the payee to collect on the note immediately even when the note is not immediately payable. For example, Jabbar can take the note to some other person, say, Abdul, who is willing to pay Jabbar now and then wait to collect from Tilley when the note is due to be paid. Abdul may take the note in order to make a profit by discounting the note, that is, by paying Jabbar some percentage of the face value of the note and making a profit later when he collects the full amount of the note from Tilley. Jabbar can also use the note to pay for goods received from Abdul. Either way, Jabbar receives payment for the sale of his cotton to Tilley without having to wait for the due date of the note or having to go to England to collect.

Drafts

A **draft** is a three-party instrument. It is sometimes referred to as a **bill of exchange** [§3-104(2)(a)]. The draft was developed some time in the past when it occurred to merchants and bankers that the idea of the promissory note could be expanded. If the payee of a note could order the maker to pay a third party, why couldn't a third party be ordered to pay to the payee a sum of money that was held by the third party but belonged to or was due to the person who wrote the instrument. The draft was therefore created to allow a person to order a third party to pay the payee (see Figure 25-4).

The person who creates an instrument and orders the third party to pay is called a **drawer**. The word *draw* is used in two senses in connection with drawers. First, a drawer is said to draw—that is to sign—the instrument. Second, a drawer by signing an instrument is drawing upon—that is, is making a demand for money upon—a third person who has the drawer's money or owes the drawer money. The third party who has the money and who is ordered to make the payment is called a **drawee.** The person to whom payment is to be made is called a payee.

We can take a look at drafts in the context of our cotton merchant. If Tilley has previously sold his finished cotton products in the Middle East and Northern Africa, there must be purchasers of goods or debtors who owe Tilley money. If such a person is in the same general area as someone Tilley owes money to, why shouldn't Tilley draw on the person who owes him to pay the person he owes? Tilley could send to Jabbar the following document addressed to the

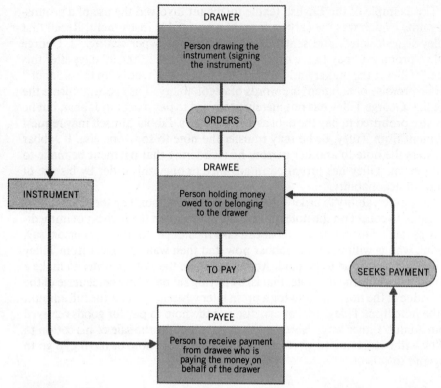

FIGURE 25-4
A Three Party Instrument

debtor: "Ali Nassar, pay to the order of Yasser Jabbar £1,000, 90 days after date." Again, the instrument would be dated and signed by Tilley. Yasser Jabbar is still the payee. Tilley, however, is not a promisor because he has made no promise to pay. Since he is drawing on Nassar, someone who owes him money, Tilley is now called the drawer. Ali Nassar, the person being drawn upon — that is, the person being ordered to make the payment — is the drawee.

Jabbar has two choices. He may keep the document for the 90 days and then present it to Nassar, or he may receive payment immediately by transferring the draft to some other person who is willing to collect from Nassar.

Checks The type of draft with which you are probably most familiar is the check. A check is a draft ordering a bank to make payment to a payee [§3-104(2)(b)]. In other words, if you give a store a check to pay for a purchase, you are the drawer, your bank is the drawee, and the store is the payee. (See Figure 25-5.)

Drafts in Sales Situations While most people are familiar with checks, other types of drafts are generally less well known. They are very well known in the commercial community, however, and are often used in contracts for the sale of goods. In a sales situation, a draft that is payable on demand, which means that

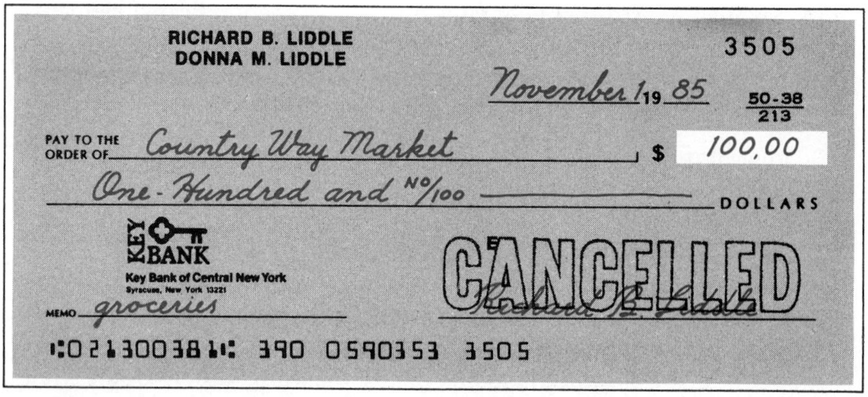

FIGURE 25-5
A Check

the draft must simply be presented to the drawee in order to obtain payment, is called a **sight draft.** A draft that is payable at a point sometime in the future is called a **time draft.** The example in Figure 25-6 names a buyer as the drawee because the buyer must pay for the goods. The buyer has the seller's money, because the buyer owes the seller the money for the goods. A bank is named as payee because the bank will receive the money for the seller's account. A seller is the drawer because the seller is ordering the buyer to pay the seller's bank.

THE FORM OF A NEGOTIABLE INSTRUMENT

The idea behind the development of the negotiable instrument was to create a contract that could serve as a substitute for money. An elaborate contract would involve too many complexities to be convenient, so the law creating the negotiable instrument that has evolved calls for a contract that is simple in

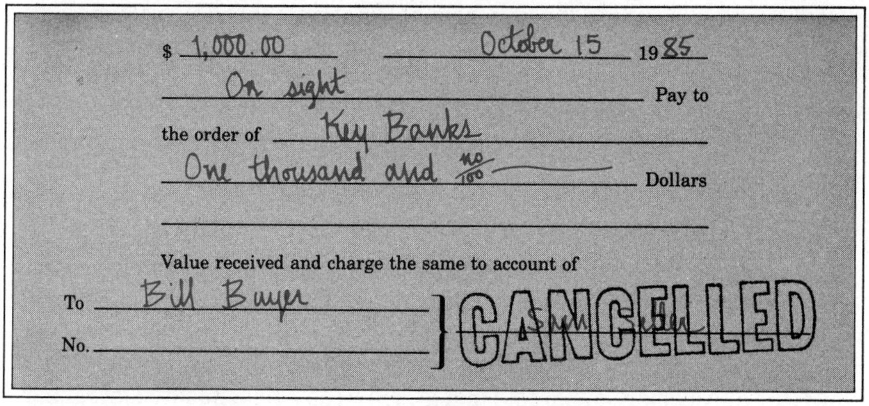

FIGURE 25-6
A Draft

form. A negotiable instrument contains only a few uncomplicated elements that have become traditional over the centuries.

The elements necessary to create a negotiable instrument today are set forth in §3-104. To be negotiable in form an instrument must

1. Be in writing.
2. Be signed.
3. Be unconditional.
4. Contain a promise (notes) or an order (drafts).
5. Be payable in money.
6. Be a sum certain (an identifiable amount of money).
7. Be payable on demand or at a definite time.
8. Contain the words of negotiability; that is, the word "order" or the word "bearer."

Each element will be explained in following sections of the text.

Negotiable and Nonnegotiable Instruments Compared

It is important to distinguish between negotiable and nonnegotiable instruments. An instrument that fulfills all eight requirements is negotiable. An instrument that does not is nonnegotiable.

The rights and liabilities of a party to a negotiable instrument are determined by the laws governing negotiability. The rights and liabilities of a party to a nonnegotiable instrument are determined by contract law. For example, a transferee of a negotiable instrument can become a holder in due course who takes the instrument free of certain defenses. The transferee of a nonnegotiable instrument can only be an assignee and is subject to all of the defenses that are good against the assignor.

The determination that an instrument is negotiable is only relevant for determining which set of laws apply. It is not a guarantee that the instrument will be paid. For example, a minor who signs a negotiable instrument may be able to avoid payment because of his or her minority status. On the other hand, if the signer of a nonnegotiable note has no defense that can be raised, the signer must honor the promise to pay. Nonnegotiable notes are therefore valuable and can be assigned and enforced like any other contract right. The importance of negotiable instruments is seen when there are defenses that can be raised. The holder of a negotiable instrument can be a holder in due course who is therefore free from most of defenses and will be paid; the person who has a nonnegotiable note will not be paid.

Writing

Because of the way it is used, a negotiable instrument must be in writing. Oral promises are not tangible, so they cannot be used as a substitute for money. How, for instance, can Tilley know that Abdul, who comes to England saying that Jabbar told him Tilley would pay, really was told that by Jabbar or that Abdul is the only person Jabbar told that to? How can Abdul be sure that Jabbar is telling the truth or that Jabbar hasn't also told others to seek payment from Tilley? The requirement that a negotiable instrument be in writing protects all the parties to the instrument and serves as evidence that the promise or order was actually made. The Code does not prescribe the manner in which the instrument must be written. It can be on scrap paper, a printed form, or even, as one occasionally sees in the newspaper, on some unusual item such as a watermelon or large plank of wood. The writing can be handwritten, typed, or printed.

The Code does, however, recognize certain priorities in the types of writing. If the terms of the instruments are in conflict, handwritten terms take precedence over typed or printed terms and typed terms take precedence over printed terms [§3-118(b)]. The underlying assumption is that changes or additions to a printed form will be typed or handwritten. Similarly, when a typed form is changed, the change will usually be handwritten. The Code also states that numbers written in words take precedence over numbers written in numerals unless the words are ambiguous, in which case the numerals control [§3-118(c)]. For instance, if the numerals on a check say "$20.25" but the words say "Two hundred and 25/100 dollars," it is reasonable to assume that the error was made in writing the numerals since a person is usually more careful when writing the words.

Signature

The written instrument is authenticated by the signature of the maker if the instrument is a note or the signature of the drawer if it is a draft. Another person can be authorized to sign an instrument on behalf of a maker or a drawer. According to the Code, a signature is "any symbol executed or adopted by a party with a present intention to authenticate a writing" [§1-201(39)]. The definition is broad enough to allow for stamped or machine written signatures, for the use of initials, or for any other method so long as the party intends the method used to be a signature authenticating the instrument.

Unconditional Promise or Order

A promise to pay money in a note and the order to pay money in a draft must be unconditional. This means that there can be no other promise, order, obligation, or power written into the instrument except as allowed by the Code. The chief exceptions are found in §3-105.

Why would a conditional promise be unsuitable? Remember that we are dealing with payments in the form of pieces of paper. We are not dealing with dollar bills, coins, gold, or silver, which are free of conditions. If one receives dollar bills or coins, one is paid. To make pieces of paper acceptable as a substitute for money, certainty of their payment is required. Suppose, for example, that Tilley had limited his promise to Jabbar by making payment subject to some other agreement by writing: "I, George Tilley, promise to pay to the order of Yasser Jabbar £1,000, 90 days after this date, provided that the cotton conforms to our purchase agreement." This promise hardly could serve as a substitute for money. Certainty of payment has been diminished by whatever uncertainties accompany the performance of the purchase agreement [§3-105(2)(a)]. The person taking the piece of paper would probably not even have the opportunity to look at the purchase agreement.

A mere notation or indication that the instrument results from a contract is allowed, though [§3-105(1)(b)]. For example, if Tilley stated in the note that "the note is in payment for cotton received" or "as per our purchase agreement," the note would still be negotiable.

Certain types of conditions and qualifications are allowed that enhance rather than detract from the certainty that the taker of the instrument will be paid. For example, a statement that there is security for payment in the form of a mortgage or other collateral can be included in a negotiable instrument [§3-105(1)(e) and §3-112(1)(b)]. Acceleration clauses, which allow for a demand that the entire amount due be paid immediately when, for example, there has been a failure to pay an installment that is due, are also permitted as conditions or qualifications [§3-105(1)(c)].

In the case that follows, the court had to determine whether a reference in a promissory note to a mortgage made the note nonnegotiable.

HOLLY HILL ACRES, LTD. v. CHARTER BANK OF GAINESVILLE
314 So.2d 209 (Fla. 1975)

[Holly Hills Acres, Ltd. (Holly), the defendant, purchased property from Rogers. In return, Holly gave Rogers a promissory note. Holly also gave Rogers a mortgage on the property as security for the payment of the note. The note contained the following provision:

> This note with interest is secured by a mortgage on real estate . . . made by the maker hereof in favor of the payee, and enforced according to the laws of the State of Florida. The terms of said mortgage are by this reference made a part hereof.

Rogers transferred the promissory note to Charter Bank of Gainesville (Bank) the plaintiff. When Holly refused to pay the promissory note, Bank brought a legal action to collect on the note. Holly defended on the basis of misrepresentation by Rogers in the sale of the property. Bank argued that the defense of misrepresentation could not be used against it because it was the holder in due course of a negotiable instrument. The trial court judge agreed and gave a summary judgment to Bank. Holly appealed, arguing that the promissory note was not a negotiable instrument.]

SCHEB, Judge

The note, incorporating by reference the terms of the mortgage, did not contain the unconditional promise to pay required by the U.C.C. Although negotiability is now governed by the Uniform Commercial Code, this was the Florida view even before the U.C.C. was adopted. E.g., the Supreme Court in *Brown v. Marion Mortgage Co.* held that certain bonds which were "to be received and held subject to" a certain mortgage were non-negotiable.

Appellee Bank relies upon *Scott v. Taylor* as authority for the proposition that its note is negotiable. *Scott,* however, involved a note which stated: "this note secured by mortgage." Mere reference to a note being secured by mortgage is a common commercial practice and such reference in itself does not impede the negotiability of the note. There is, however, a significant difference in a note stating that it is "secured by mortgage" from one which provides, "the terms of said mortgage are by this reference made a part hereof." In the former instance the note merely refers to a separate agreement which does not impede its negotiability, while in the latter instance the note is rendered non-negotiable.

As a general rule the assignee of . . . non-negotiable note . . . takes subject to all defenses available as against the [payee]. Appellant raised the issue of [misrepresentation] as between himself and [Bank, the assignee of the note]. . . .

Accordingly, the entry of a summary judgment is reversed and the cause remanded for further proceedings.

CASE REVIEW QUESTIONS

1. Who was the maker of the promissory note? Who was the payee?
2. Why was Holly's promissory note nonnegotiable?
3. Bank brought a law suit against Holly. As a result of the court's decision, has Holly won the law suit? Explain.

Payment from a Particular Source or Fund An instrument that requires that payment be made from a particular fund or source is nonnegotiable because it is conditional [§3-105(2)(b)]. Payment is uncertain because the fund or source may not have enough or even any money in it. For example, if Tilley made the following document, it would be nonnegotiable. "Ali Abdul, pay to the order of Yasser Jabbar £1,000, 90 days after date from the cotton textile fund." This order to pay is conditioned upon the existence of a cotton textile fund and upon its containing £1,000. If instead, Tilley wrote, "Pay the £1,000 first from the cotton textile fund," the instrument would be negotiable [§3-105(1)(f)]. Payment is not limited to a particular fund because payment is to be made by first exhausting the cotton textile fund and then by paying from any other funds belonging to Tilley. A modern check directs that payment be made first from a particular account because the check has an account number encoded on it in numerals that can be read by a computer to withdraw money from that account. But, if there are insufficient funds in that bank account, the check is still a negotiable instrument and the drawer is obligated to pay from some other fund.

Partnership and Trust Accounts Certain organizations, such as partnerships or trusts, can provide that payment of an instrument be made only from a particular source—that is, from partnership or trust assets. In effect, the Code allows partnerships or trusts to limit the personal liability of the partners or trustees by providing for payment from partnership or trust assets only. The individual partners or trustees have no personal liability to pay such an instrument if there are no partnership or trust assets [§3-105(1)(h)]. This is consistent with corporate law whereby a corporate creditor can look only to corporate assets for payment of a debt because shareholders of a corporation have no personal liability for the debts of the corporation.

A Sum Certain in Money

Why would a promise or order to pay other than a sum certain in money (an identifiable amount of money) be unsuitable? First, all economies of any importance employ a pricing system based on money, and it is money for which the negotiable instrument serves as a substitute. It can call for payment in dollars or pounds or drachmas, but it cannot call for payment in fish or coats or boats, which are things more suitable to a barter economy. The Code defines money as a medium of exchange adopted by a government, domestic or foreign, as a part of its currency. The amount to be paid must be expressed in money, but it need not be in U.S. dollars [§1-201(24) and §3-107].

Second, most forms of money—currency or coin—have identifiable face values. It is logical to require that a major substitute for money be no less certainly identified in value. Unlike cash, however, a negotiable instrument may often be a credit instrument that delays payment to a later date. Credit transactions often include installment payments, rates of interest that may differ before and after the due date, discounts for early payment and penalties for late payment, or agreements about the cost of collection and attorneys fees. Such terms may be included in a negotiable instrument even though they may affect the total amount of money to be received [§3-106].

Even if an instrument calls for the payment of interest, the sum is still certain because the value of the instrument can readily be determined from the information on the instrument if the interest rate is fixed, either by the instrument or by law. A note that reads "Pay to the order of Jabbar £1,000, with interest at 6 percent, 90 days from date" or "Pay to the order of Jabbar £1,000, with interest at 5 percent, 90 days from date, but interest at 7 percent from date if payment is not made at maturity" is negotiable because the interest rate is fixed by the instrument [§3-106(1)(a)].

A note that reads "Pay to the order of Jabbar £1,000, with interest 90 days from date" is negotiable even though it does not specify a rate of interest. The sum is certain because the law assumes that the judgment interest rate fixed by statute is intended [§3-118(d)]. The judgment interest rate is the percentage required by statute to be paid on damages recovered in a law suit. Suppose Tilley does not pay the note when due, and Jabbar sues Tilley, demanding judgment for £1,000 plus the interest. Suppose that, at the place for payment, the judgment interest rate is 8 percent annually. The amount of the judgment will be £1,000 plus the interest from the date of the note until the note is paid. If the note remains unpaid for one year, Jabbar would be entitled to £1,080.

Payable on Demand or at a Definite Time

A negotiable instrument must be payable on demand or at a definite time [§3-104(1)(c)].

Payable on Demand An instrument is **payable on demand** if no time for payment is stated or if the instrument states that it is payable on sight, that is, whenever it is presented for payment [§3-108]. A check states no time for payment because, by definition, it must be payable on demand [§3-104(2)(b)]. A postdated check (i.e., a check bearing a date later then the date on which it was issued) is treated not as a check but as a draft that is not payable until the date specified.

Payable at a Definite Time If a negotiable instrument is used for credit purposes, payment by the maker or drawer is often postponed to a later date.

When payment is postponed, the time for payment must be definite. With a demand instrument, a person in possession is able to say "I can be paid now" even though the holder of the instrument may choose to wait a while before collecting. If payment of the instrument is postponed, the holder must be able to say "I shall be paid then" and must know for sure at what definite point in time "then" is. If a person can ascertain the maturity date at any given time by simply looking at the instrument, the instrument is **payable at a definite time.** Instruments drawn like the following examples are payable at a definite time.

> Pay to the order of Jabbar on or before January 1, 1986. [§3-109(1)(a)]

Payment is due no later than January 1, 1986, although payment can be made earlier.

> A note dated January 1, 1986, which reads "Pay to the order of Jabbar 90 days after date." [§3-109(1)(a)]

This instrument is due to be paid on April 1, 1986. Notice that if the note were not dated, it would not be payable at a definite time. A person would have to ask "ninety days from when?" An undated note of this type would not be payable on demand because it specifies that it is not payable immediately but at some future time—90 days from the date. Since this type of undated note is not payable on demand or at a definite time, it would be nonnegotiable [§3-104(1)(c)]. When an undated note of this type is dated, however, it becomes negotiable [§3-115].

Although the negotiability of an instrument is not necessarily affected "by the fact that it is undated, antedated, or postdated" [§3-114(1)], an instrument that reads like the example—"90 days after date"—must have a date. Otherwise, the time certain for payment required for negotiability would not be present. On the other hand, a note that reads "Payable 90 days after June 1, 1986" and made on January 1, 1986, need not be dated "January 1, 1986" because the time certain for payment is not dependent upon the date the note was made.

> Pay to the order of Jabbar 90 days after sight. [§3-109(1)(b)]

This instrument will be payable 90 days after it is presented to Tilley for payment. While the time for payment cannot be expressed as a date, the date on which it must be paid can be controlled by the holder of the instrument. The holder knows that the money is payable 90 days after he or she shows Tilley the note and asks for payment.

> Pay to the order of Jabbar in monthly installments of $100 beginning on July 1, 1986, or on demand if buyer fails to make a payment on the first day of every month. [§3-109(1)(c)]

This instrument is due to be paid no later than July 1, 1986, and it may be payable sooner if the buyer defaults or fails to make a payment when it is due. The Code allows for **acceleration** which means making an instrument payable sooner than the date specified.

> Pay to the order of Jabbar on July 1, 1986, or at such time thereafter as the holder may select. [§3-109(1)(d)]

This instrument is payable on July 1, 1986, unless the person holding it elects to postpone the time for payment. Since the ability to extend the time for payment belongs to the holder of the instrument, he or she can select the definite time when payment will be due. If a maker rather than a holder could extend the time for payment indefinitely, the instrument would not be payable at a definite time since a holder would have no way of knowing when the instrument is payable. The instrument would be nonnegotiable. On the other hand, a maker can have an option to extend the time for payment to a later but specified date—for example, "Pay to the order of Jabbar on July 1, 1986, unless the maker elects to postpone payment until December 1, 1986." Because the ultimate date upon which the instrument is payable—that is, December 1, 1986—is specified, such an instrument is payable at a definite time.

> Pay to the order of Jabbar on July 1, 1986, unless the maker, Tilley, is unable to sell the shipment of cotton in which case payment will be made on July 1, 1987. [§3-109(1)(d)]

This instrument is payable by July 1, 1987, and it may be payable on July 1, 1986, if Tilley sells the cotton shipment. In other words, it is definitely payable on July 1, 1987, regardless of whether or not the cotton is sold.

The time for payment is not certain if payment is dependent upon the happening of an uncertain event—for example, "I promise to pay to the order of Jabbar upon the sale of my textile mill." Even when the sale of the mill has occurred, the defect is not remedied and the instrument remains nonnegotiable.

Payable to Order of Bearer

The word "order" and the word "bearer" are words of negotiability. The use of at least one of these words is essential to the creation of a negotiable instrument [§3–104(1)(d)]. An instrument that reads "pay to the order of John Smith" and an instrument that reads "Pay to John Smith or bearer" are both negotiable because both contain the words of negotiability. However, an instrument that reads "Pay to John Smith" is not negotiable because it lacks any word of negotiability. There are several exceptions to the requirement that the words of negotiability must be used. For example, an instrument reading "Pay to cash" is negotiable [§3-111].

Order or Bearer Instruments Negotiable instruments are classified as either order instruments or bearer instruments depending upon the word of negotiability used to make the instrument negotiable. As a general rule, instruments that use the word "order," such as "Pay to the order of John Smith" or "Pay to John Smith or order," are order instruments [§3-110].

Instruments that use the word "bearer," such as "Pay to bearer" or "Pay to John Smith or bearer," are bearer instruments [§3-111]. An instrument that uses both of the words, such as "Pay to the order of John Smith or bearer," will be a bearer instrument only if the word *bearer* is handwritten or typewritten [§3-110(3)].

Certain types of instruments are classified as bearer instruments even though the word "bearer" is not used. "Pay to Cash," for instance, is a bearer instrument. Similarly, "Pay to the order of cash" and "Pay to the order of Uncle Sam [a fictitious person]" are bearer instruments [§3-111].

As you will learn in the next chapter, these classifications are important in determining the proper method of transferring—or negotiating—an instrument.

In the case that follows, the court has to determine whether a promissory note that read "Pay to the order of _____" was a negotiable instrument.

HOSS v. FABACHER
578 S.W.2d 454 (Texas 1979)

[Hoss (plaintiff) brought a legal action against Fabacher (defendant). He claimed that Fabacher was liable to him on a document that read:

Freeport, Texas   15 April 1971   *$6002.19*
For value received, I, we, or either of us, the undersigned, promise to pay to the order of _____
In _____ monthly installments of $_____
each and one installment of $_____, the first installment to become due and payable on or before the *16* day of *July, 1971,* and one installment to be due and payable on the _____ day of each succeeding month until the whole of said indebtedness is paid with interest from *date* at the rate of *10* per cent per annum.

The document was signed by Fabacher.

Fabacher defended on the grounds that the document did not contain a promise to pay money to anyone. Hoss argues that the document was a bearer instrument and was, therefore, payable to the bearer, who was Hoss. The trial court gave judgment to Fabacher. Hoss appealed.]

PEDEN, Justice

Under the Texas Business and Commerce Code, "'instrument' means a negotiable instrument" [§3-102(1)(e)]. To be a negotiable instrument, the writing must (1) be signed by the maker or drawer, (2) contain an unconditional promise or order to pay a sum certain in money and no other promise, order, obligation or power given by the maker or drawer except as authorized by the Code, (3) be payable on demand or

at a definite time, and (4) be payable to order or to bearer [§3-104]. An instrument is payable to bearer when by its terms it is payable to (1) bearer or to the order of bearer; (2) a specified person or bearer; or (3) "cash" or the order of "cash," or any other indication which does not purport to designate a specific payee [§3-111]. The official comment to this section clearly states

> Paragraph (c) is reworded to remove any possible implication that "Pay to the order of _____" makes the instrument payable to bearer. It is an incomplete order instrument and falls under Section 3-115.

Section [3-115(a)] of the Code, titled "Incomplete Instruments," provides that when a paper whose contents at the time of signing show that it is intended to become an instrument is signed while incomplete in any necessary respect, it is unenforceable until completed. Comment 2 following that section defines "necessary" as "necessary to complete the instrument. It will always include the promise or order, the designation of the payee, and the amount payable." In our case the paper in question, stating: "pay to the order of _____" is not a bearer instrument, and it does not contain a promise to pay any amount. The trial judge was correct: it is unenforceable on its face and incomplete.

Affirmed.

CASE REVIEW QUESTIONS

1. Why do you think the Code provides that an instrument that states "Pay to the order of _____" is not a negotiable instrument?
2. What other requirement of negotiability does the court say have not been met? Do you agree?
3. What would have to be added to make the document in this case a negotiable instrument?

INCOMPLETE INSTRUMENTS

Sometimes, as in the preceding case, an instrument is issued with certain spaces left blank. If the information required by the blanks is necessary for the instrument — for example, the designation of the payee, the amount payable, or the promise or order to pay — the instrument is said to be incomplete and is nonnegotiable. As an incomplete instrument, it cannot be enforced, that is, the maker or drawer will not be required to pay [§3-115].

The question that arises is what happens if the blanks are filled in by someone other than the drawer or maker of the instrument. If the blanks are completed in an authorized manner, the instrument becomes negotiable and is enforceable as completed. This occurs, for example, when an employer gives an employee a check to pay for office supplies but is uncertain as to the exact amount required and leaves the amount payable blank. At that point the instrument is not negotiable. When the employee buys the supplies and fills in the correct amount due, the check has been completed as authorized. The check is then negotiable and the employer is obligated to pay.

On the other hand, if the instrument is completed in an unauthorized way, the answer as to whether the instrument is enforceable is not quite so simple. An unauthorized completion is called an alteration. Alterations are discussed in Chapter 27. In some situations, the maker or drawer will have to pay and in others the maker or drawer will not be obligated to pay. At this point it is sufficient to say that an unauthorized completion of an incomplete instrument may create a negotiable instrument. Whether the instrument is valid and can be enforced will be answered in Chapter 27.

REVIEW QUESTIONS

1. What is the legal significance of the determination of whether or not an instrument is negotiable?
2. What are the two basic types of negotiable instruments? How do they differ from one another? Of which type is your personal check an example?
3. List the elements required to create a negotiable instrument. Give an example, not presented in the text, for each element that demonstrates how the requirement might not be met.

CASE PROBLEMS

1. There follows a series of instruments. You should decide whether each is negotiable or nonnegotiable. If only a part of or a phrase from an instrument is given, you should assume that all other required elements of a negotiable instrument are present. (Note: Those portions of the following instruments that are italicized are normally written in by hand.)

    a. Money Order
        Nation Wide Check Corporation

        Pay the sum of *Ten Dollars and 00/100*

        $10.00

        Payable to *Bill Banks*

        From: _____
        Payable through Maryland National Bank
        Not valid over $100.00

    b. A note that promises to pay to the order of a named person "in the next 60 days the sum of five thousand dollars ($5,000) from jobs now under construction. . . ."

    c. For value received, the undersigned promises to pay to the Order of Bank of Viola, the principal sum of *$15,884.54* payable in installments or as follows: *Or payable $80.00 per week from Jack and Jill contract* with interest at the rate of *8.00* percent per annum from date until paid. */s/J. Nestrick 9-15-84*.

    d. A note handwritten by J. Andrea, which reads in its entirety: "I, J. Andrea, promise to pay to the order of J. Feinberg on demand, the sum of $15,000.00 as per contract."

    e. FOR VALUE RECEIVED, I, KOYT WOODWORTH EVERHART, JR., do promise to pay to JANE CARTER EVERHART or her order, ONE HUNDRED FIFTY THOUSAND DOLLARS ($150,000.00) in lieu of a property settlement supplementing certain Deed of Separation and Property Settlement, dated May 1, 1972, the terms of which are incorporated herein by reference.

        /s/Koyt Woodworth Everhart, Jr.

    f. A note that specifies that "in the event that the Chrysler Stock given as security for this note shall fall below $20 per share, the borrower shall provide additional security. . . ."

    g. A note that specifies that it is "to be paid solely from the assets of ABC & Daughters, a partnership."

    h. A note that states, "with interest at bank rates."

    i. A check on which the signature of the drawer has been forged.

    j. An installment note that specifies that "this note is secured by a mortgage of the same date which provides that the entire amount is due and payable upon certain defaults specified in the mortgage."

    k. A note payable to the order of Conrad Abend, payable in German marks.

    l. *Payable on demand $9,747.00*
        "No. _____ Pittsburgh, Pa. 8/4/64"
        For value received, I promise to pay to the order of MASTER HOMECRAFT COMPANY, the sum of *nine-thousand, seven hundred, forty-seven dollars and no cents* in _____ monthly installments of $_____ each, beginning on the _____ day of _____, 19____.

        /s/Edward T. Zimmerman

    m. A promissory note payable "30 days after demand."

    n. A promissory note payable "upon evidence of an acceptable permanent loan and upon acceptance of the loan commitment."

    o. A dated note that contains a promise to pay "within ten years after date."

    p. A note payable on April 15, 1985, that states: "In the event that the borrower becomes unemployed, the borrower may elect to extend the time for payment to December 31, 1985."

    q. A note that reads:

        _____, 19____

        For value received, I promise to pay to *John T. Doyle* the sum of *Five thousand and 00/100 dollars ($5,000), six months after date*.

        Ellen Larkins

r. A completely handwritten note that reads:

> Buyer promises to pay Seller (John Locke) the sum of $10,000 on June 1, 1984.
>
> David Hume

2. Are the following checks payable to the order of a specific person or to the bearer of the instrument?
   a. Pay to the order of _William P. Adams_ or bearer.
   b. Pay to the order of _bearer_.
   c. Pay to the order of _John Doe_.
   d. Pay to the order of _cash_.
   e. Pay to the order of _Helen M. Chapman or bearer_.
   f. Pay to bearer.

3. Fulkerson made an offer to sell his trailer park to How. The offer specified that if How wished to accept the offer he must "sign the contract and return it with a down payment of $10,000 by August 29th." On August 29th, How delivered the signed contract and a check for $10,000 dated September 1st. Fulkerson refused to transfer ownership of the trailer park to How, arguing that there was no contract because How had not complied with the terms of the offer because How had given him a postdated check. Was the postdated check a downpayment? Explain.

4. Anderson signed a note payable to the order of Holliday. The date for payment was left blank, and Anderson believed that he was to pay the note whenever he could. Later, Holliday, the payee, wrote "on demand" in the blank left to specify the date for payment. When Holliday sued Anderson on the note, Anderson argued that Holliday's writing in "on demand" had discharged Anderson from liability on the note. Who will win the case? Explain.

5. Terry Grothe purchased a horse at an auction and wrote a check to pay for the horse. Grothe did not fill in the name of the payee or the amount in words. He did sign the check, date it, and wrote in the figures "$125.00." An agent for Montgomery County Livestock Auction Company correctly filled in the name of the payee and the amount in words. Grothe did not have sufficient funds in his account to cover the check, and a criminal action was taken against him for issuing a bad check. Grothe argued that the instrument he gave to the auction company agent was not a check because it did not meet the requirements of a negotiable instrument. Is Grothe's argument correct? Explain.

26

NEGOTIATION AND THE HOLDER IN DUE COURSE

The last chapter discussed the criteria for answering the question: Is an instrument negotiable in form? This chapter will discuss the criteria necessary to answer two additional questions: (1) Has an instrument been duly negotiated? and (2) Is the person to whom an instrument has been negotiated a holder in due course? The answers to these questions are important. A negotiable instrument must be properly negotiated in order for the transferee to become a holder. Furthermore, a holder must satisfy certain legal requirements in order to qualify as a holder in due course.

Negotiable instruments were developed to be easy and effective substitutes for money. Money transfers easily from person to person. It is readily accepted as payment because a transferee of money will not be subject to the defenses that can be raised against an assignee of a contract interest. (See Chapter 16 on Assignments.) To encourage the acceptability of negotiable instruments, the law developed the concept of a holder in due course. This is a person who enjoys most of the rights of a transferee of money because he or she takes a negotiable instrument free from most of the defenses that could be raised by a maker or drawer to avoid payment of an instrument. A holder in due course has rights superior to a simple holder or to an owner of a nonnegotiable instrument.

NEGOTIATION

Negotiation is the transfer of an instrument in accordance with the legal requirements governing negotiation. It results in the transferee becoming a holder. A **holder** is a person who has possession of a negotiable instrument and is, by the terms of the instrument, entitled to possess it [§1-201(20)]. For example, if an instrument reads, "Pay to the order of John Smith," John Smith is the holder when he has possession of the instrument. When Jane Doe has possession of this instrument, she is not the holder because she is not the person named in the instrument. An instrument made payable to "Bearer" names the bearer—that is, the person who has possession of the instrument—as the person who is entitled to possess the instrument.

A holder has the legal power to transfer an instrument to another person, to enforce the payment of the instrument, or to **discharge** the instrument, which means to release the maker or drawer from the obligation of paying the instrument [§3-301]. A holder has these powers even though he or she may not be the owner of the instrument. For example, assume that Bob Roe is the owner of a check made payable to the order of "Bearer." If he gives the check to Betty Jones to deposit in the bank, she, as bearer and holder, would have the legal power or ability, although not the legal right, to tear up the check and thereby release the drawer of the check from the obligation to pay.

Requirements for Negotiation

How an instrument must be negotiated depends on whether it is classified as a bearer instrument or as an order instrument. As discussed in the last chapter, the classification of an instrument generally depends upon the word of negotiability used in it — *bearer* for a **bearer instrument** and *order* for an **order instrument.**

Negotiation of Bearer Instruments A bearer instrument is negotiated simply by the delivery of the instrument [§3-202(1)]. **Delivery** means a voluntary transfer of a possession [§1-201(14)]. Anyone who receives a bearer instrument by means of a voluntary transfer is a holder. In the example above, Betty Jones became a holder because Bob Roe voluntarily gave her the check made payable to the order of "Bearer."

Is someone who steals or finds a bearer instrument a holder? The answer is no because the thief or finder did not receive the instrument by delivery.

Is someone who is given an instrument by a thief or finder a holder? The answer is yes. For instance, suppose that Alice Smith stole the check made payable to the order of "Bearer" from Bob Roe. Alice Smith would not be a holder, but if she transfers the check to Ichabod Jones, Jones would become a holder because he has received the check by delivery.

Negotiation of Order Instruments Negotiation of an order instrument requires delivery and the signature, called an **indorsement,** of the person to whose order the instrument is made (notes) or drawn (drafts) [§3-202(1)].

Order instruments provide greater security to a holder than do bearer instruments. An order instrument can be negotiated only with the signature of the named payee or the person to whom the instrument is indorsed, that is, the person named in the indorsement as the next holder. For example, a check payable to June Rose that is indorsed to John Smith ("Pay to order of John Smith /s/ June Rose") can only be negotiated if John Smith's signature is on the check. Thus, the use of an order instrument minimizes the risk of the instrument falling into the hands of a thief or finder who could then negotiate it by delivery alone.

The thief or finder of an order instrument is not a holder. There has been no voluntary transfer, and the instrument does not name the thief or finder as the person entitled to possess the instrument. If the thief or finder forges the indorsement—that is, signs the name of the person to whose order the instrument is made, drawn, or indorsed—and then delivers the instrument to a third party, the third party has taken the instrument by delivery. The third party is not a holder, however, because the indorsement necessary for negotiation is missing. Only the real or authorized signature of the person to whose order the instrument is made, drawn, or indorsed is effective as an indorsement.

Suppose the name of a payee or indorsee—the new holder named in an indorsement—is misspelled. For example, what if an instrument says "Jon Smithe" when John Smith is the intended payee or indorsee? How should John Smith indorse the instrument? Either "Jon Smithe" or "John Smith" is acceptable as an indorsement if the signature is intended by Smith to be an indorsement because, according to the UCC, a signature is any sign or symbol adopted to authenticate a writing [§1-201(3)(b)]. Any questions that might be raised by bank tellers or the like can usually be avoided by indorsing "Jon Smithe (John Smith)" or vice versa [§3-203].

Right to an Indorsement Suppose John Smith gave Jane Doe an instrument that reads "Pay to the order of John Smith," but he neglected to indorse it. Is Jane Doe a holder? The answer is clearly no because delivery of an order instrument without indorsement does not constitute negotiation. Does Doe have any right to Smith's indorsement? The Code says that she does if she has paid for the instrument [§3-201(3)]. Even though she may have a right to an indorsement, however, there is no negotiation until the indorsement is placed on the instrument. Jane Doe does not become a "holder" until the instrument has been negotiated.

Indorsement

An indorsement is required for the negotiation of an order instrument, but an indorsement can be used on a bearer instrument as well. To be effective, an indorsement must be on the instrument itself or on an allonge, which is another piece of paper so firmly attached to the instrument that it effectively becomes a part of the instrument [§3-202(2)]. An indorsement is usually placed on the reverse side of an instrument, but it can be placed on the face of an instrument or on an allonge.

Indorsements When Checks Are Deposited A bank may require a person to indorse a check even though it is a bearer instrument, such as a check that reads, "Pay to the order of cash." Although an indorsement is not necessary to negotiate a bearer instrument, a bank will often require an indorsement because the indorser will thereby become liable to the bank if the check is not paid. This liability of an indorser will be discussed in more detail in Chapter 27.

Although an order instrument normally cannot be negotiated without the payee's or indorsee's signature, there is an exception when an order instrument is deposited in a bank. A bank may supply a customer's indorsement if the customer fails to do so [§4-205(1)]. Banks are allowed to do this to avoid the unnecessary delays in the bank collection process that would result if an unindorsed check had to be returned to the depositor. A bank is not allowed to supply a missing indorsement, however, if a check expressly requires that it be signed by the payee [§4-205(1)]. This requirement is commonly found on government and insurance company checks.

Forms of Indorsement Indorsements can be classified according to three pairs of forms designed to accomplish certain goals. Every indorsement is some combination of these three pairs. Indorsements are either (1) special or blank, (2) restrictive or nonrestrictive, and (3) qualified or unqualified.

Special Indorsements A **special indorsement** specifies the person to whose order the instrument is payable, just as the maker or drawer specifies the payee when creating an order instrument. A special indorsement makes the instrument an order instrument that can be further negotiated only by indorsement and delivery [§3-204(1)]. To make a special indorsement, the indorser writes, "Pay to the order of (indorsee's name)," on the instrument and then signs his or her own name (see Figure 26-1).

It must be noted that while the words of negotiability are essential to the creation of a negotiable instrument, these words need not be used in indorsements. An instrument is still negotiable and is still an order instrument even though the special indorsement might, for example, read "Pay Jane Doe, /s/ John Smith" or "Pay to Jane Doe, /s/ John Smith."

Blank Indorsements A **blank indorsement** does not specify any particular person who can further negotiate an instrument. A blank indorsement is made when the indorser simply signs his or her name. For example, when John Smith, as the payee of an instrument, simply signs, "John Smith," the indorsement is a blank indorsement (see Figure 26-2). A blank indorsement causes an instrument to become a bearer instrument, which means that it can be negotiated by delivery alone [§3-204(2)].

Order instruments are safer than bearer instruments because an order instrument requires the indorsement of the holder in order to be negotiated. Therefore, a holder of a bearer instrument has the right to convert a blank indorsement into a special indorsement [§3-204(3)]. Typically, this is done by inserting the necessary words above the blank indorsement. For example, a holder might write, "Pay to the order of (holder's name)," above the blank indorsement to make it into a special indorsement. For instance, Jane Doe could convert the indorsement in Figure 26-2 into a special indorsement by

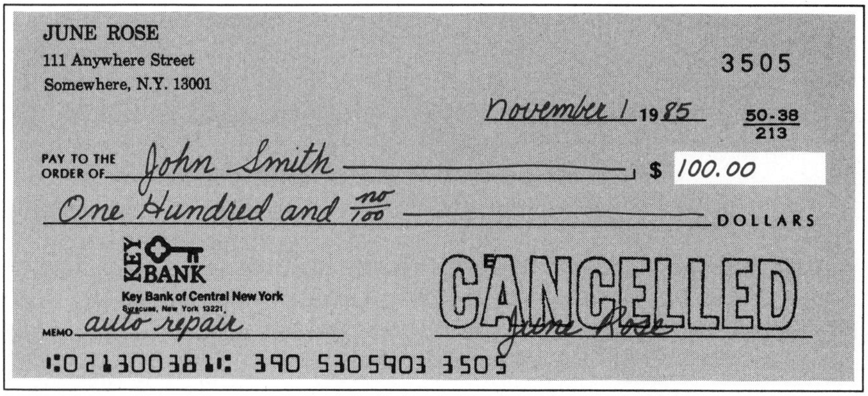

JUNE ROSE
111 Anywhere Street
Somewhere, N.Y. 13001

3505

November 1 19 85

50-38
213

PAY TO THE
ORDER OF *John Smith*

$ *100.00*

One Hundred and *no/100* DOLLARS

KEY BANK
Key Bank of Central New York
Syracuse, New York 13221.

MEMO *auto repair*

CANCELLED
June Rose

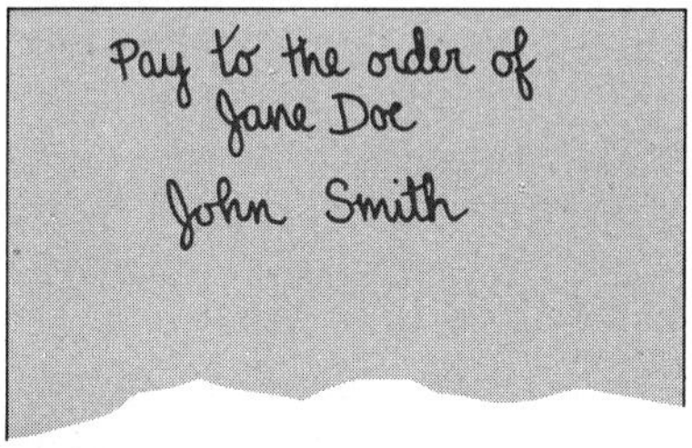

⑆0213003811⑆ 390 5305903 3505

FIGURE 26-1
A Special Indorsement

FIGURE 26-2
A Blank Indorsement

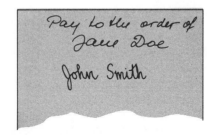

FIGURE 26-3
*A Blank Indorsement Turned into a
Special Indorsement*

writing, "Pay to the order of Jane Doe," above John Smith's signature (see Figure 26-3).

A bearer instrument can also be converted into an order instrument by the use of a special indorsement when it is negotiated. Even though no indorsement is required to negotiate a bearer instrument, a holder can affix an indorsement, either special or blank, when an instrument is negotiated to a new holder. When the indorsement is a special indorsement, a bearer instrument becomes an order instrument. For example, if Jane Doe, who is the holder of a bearer

FIGURE 26-4
A Blank Indorsement Followed by a Special Indorsement

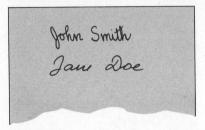

FIGURE 26-5
A Blank Indorsement Followed by a Blank Indorsement

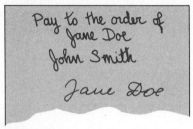

FIGURE 26-6
A Special Indorsement Followed by a Blank Indorsement

instrument, transfers it to Bob Jones by indorsing, "Pay to the order of Bob Jones, /s/ Jane Doe," the instrument becomes an order instrument that can be negotiated only by Bob Jones (see Figure 26-4). On the other hand, if Jane Doe made no indorsement or used a blank indorsement when making the transfer to Jones, the instrument would remain a bearer instrument (see Figure 26-5). It should be noted that an instrument that is specially indorsed will become a bearer instrument if it is subsequently indorsed in blank (see Figure 26-6).

In the case that follows, it was necessary for the court to trace a series of transfers of a promissory note in order to determine whether the party bringing the lawsuit, a hospital, was the holder of the note. The hospital had possession of the note, but the defendant argued that the hospital was not a holder entitled to enforce payment of the note.

WESTERLY HOSPITAL v. HIGGINS
256 A.2d 506 (R.I. 1969)

[Westerly Hospital, the plaintiff, brought a legal action to collect on a promissory note made by Mr. Higgins, the defendant. The trial court gave summary judgment to plaintiff. Defendant appealed.]

ROBERTS, Chief Justice

The record discloses that on July 13, 1967 [d]efendant—in consideration for services performed by plaintiff hospital in connection with the birth of a child to defendant's wife—executed and delivered a promissory note in the amount of $527.58 payable in 18 monthly installments of $29.31 to the order of plaintiff Westerly Hospital. It further appears that thereafter a duly authorized agent of the Westerly Hospital indorsed defendant's note in blank and by delivery negotiated it to the Industrial National Bank, hereinafter referred to as Industrial. . . . The indorsement contained an express clause guaranteeing payment [by the hospital] of the principal, interest, and the late charges on the note in question upon default by the maker.

Thereafter, defendant made three installment payments to Industrial, reducing the balance due on the note to $439.65. No further payments were made by defendant on the note, and according to the pertinent provisions thereof, the entire balance of the note, principal and interest, became due and payable immediately together with all costs of collection, including a reasonable attorney's fee. After default by defendant, Industrial, as holder of the note, made a demand upon plaintiff hospital for payment of the balance due in accordance with the terms of the contract of indorsement guaranteeing payment in full to the holder in case of default by the maker. After receiving the balance due on the note, Industrial negotiated the note by delivery to plaintiff hospital.

The defendant argues that this delivery of the note back to plaintiff was not sufficient to constitute a valid negotiation. He argues that the attempted [negotiation] by Industrial to Westerly Hospital was invalid for the lack of the signature of a duly authorized repre-sentative of Industrial and thereby Westerly Hospital was precluded from becoming a holder of the instrument. Thus, according to defendant, Industrial was the proper party to bring the action on this note. It seems rather obvious that had the transfer of the note from Westerly Hospital to Industrial been other than in blank, this argument would have merit, it being true that an authorized signature of an agent of Industrial would be necessary to negotiate the instrument.

However, §3-204(2) of the Uniform Commercial Code states, in pertinent part, that "An instrument payable to order and indorsed in blank becomes payable to bearer and may be negotiated by delivery alone until specially indorsed." Here Westerly Hospital as payee of the note caused its indorsement to appear thereon without specifying to whom or to whose order the instrument was payable. Instead, a blank indorsement, one specifying no particular indorsee, was made. The legal effect of such an indorsement and delivery was to authorize Industrial as the transferee and holder of the note to further negotiate the note without indorsement but by mere delivery alone.

In our opinion, then, the redelivery of the note in question by Industrial to Westerly Hospital accomplished a negotiation of the instrument. . . . It is our conclusion that in these circumstances defendant's contention that there was a genuine issue as to the identity of the proper party to bring the action on the note in question is without merit.

Affirmed.

CASE REVIEW QUESTIONS

1. Who was the maker of the note? Who was the payee?
2. Who was the first holder of the note? Explain. At this point was it a bearer instrument or an order instrument? Explain.
3. Who was the second holder of the note? Explain. At this point was it a bearer instrument or an order instrument? Explain.
4. Who was the third holder of the note? Explain. At this point was it a bearer instrument or an order instrument? Explain.
5. What would have been necessary for negotiation by the third holder of the note? Explain.

Restrictive and Nonrestrictive Indorsements In the past, further negotiation of an instrument could be prevented by writing "Pay to the order of (indorsee's name) only" above the indorser's signature. Under the UCC, however, no restriction stated in an indorsement can completely prevent further transfer or negotiation [§3-206]. The Code does, however, recognize certain types of restrictions called **restrictive indorsements**. One type of restrictive indorsement is the **conditional indorsement**, such as "Pay to the order of Jane Smith upon her delivery to me of the title to her motorboat. /s/ John Doe" [§3-205(a)]. The indorsee or any subsequent holder must await fulfillment of the condition before the instrument can be enforced against the indorser who set the restriction. The Code allows conditions in an indorsement that would make an instrument nonnegotiable if those conditions were found in the original promise or order (see Chapter 25).

More common restrictive indorsements are those that say, "For deposit only," "For collection," or "Pay any bank" [§3-205(c)]. "For deposit only" instructs the bank in which a check is deposited to credit the restrictive indorser's account. Thus, if someone presents such an instrument to a bank, the bank should not give that person cash for the instrument but should credit the indorser's account. Under a conditional indorsement or a "For deposit only" indorsement, a transferee will be a taker for value only if the transferee complies with the terms of the indorsement [§3-206(3)]. A bank that gives cash to a customer for a check indorsed "For deposit only" will not be a taker for value. To be a taker for value is one of the criteria for being a holder in due course, which will be discussed in more detail later in this chapter.

An indorsement that reads "Pay to Jane Doe for collection only, /s/ John Smith" is a restrictive indorsement [§3-205(d)]. Jane Doe is the holder of the instrument but only for the purpose of collecting payment for John Smith. The first taker of this instrument must pay or apply the value given in accordance with the indorsement in order to become a holder for value. For instance, if Jane Doe wants to negotiate the instrument to Bill Jones, she will have to indorse the instrument and deliver it to Bill Jones because the indorsement is both special and restrictive. Bill Jones should not pay Jane Doe. Rather, he should make sure that John Smith receives the payment in order to comply with the terms of the indorsement.

A nonrestrictive indorsement is one that is not restrictive; that is, it is not conditional, does not purport to restrict further transfer, does not say "For deposit only" or something similar, or does not state that the instrument is for the benefit or use of a person other than the holder.

In the following case, the bank stamped an indorsement on a check that had not been indorsed by the named payee. The court finds that the bank indorsement is sufficient to make it a holder. The Code allows banks to supply missing indorsements in certain situations in order to avoid the delays in the bank collection process that would result if a check had to be returned to a depositor for an indorsement [§4-205]. Unfortunately for the bank, its employee chose a stamp with a restrictive indorsement.

MARINE MIDLAND BANK v. PRICE, MILLER, EVANS & FLOWERS
455 N.Y.S. 2d 565 (1982)

[Marine Midland Bank, plaintiff, brought a legal action against the defendant, Price, Miller, Evans & Flowers, a law firm, to collect on a check that had been drawn by the defendant. The trial court gave judgment to the plaintiff bank. The defendant appealed, and the intermediate appellate court affirmed. The defendant appealed again, this time to the Court of Appeals, the highest court in New York.]

WACHTLER, Judge

The question on this appeal is whether the plaintiff, Marine Midland Bank can claim the status of a holder in due course of a check which it cashed without indorsement and stamped "credited to the account of the payee herein named," although the payee, who had presented the check, had no account at the bank. By a divided court the [intermediate appellate court] held that the bank had properly supplied the missing indorsement pursuant to subdivision (1) of section 4–205 of the Uniform Commercial Code and was otherwise a holder in due course. The defendant appeals on the basis of the dissent claiming primarily that the bank could not supply the missing indorsement because the payee was not a customer of the bank within the meaning of the statute; . . . and if the indorsement was effective the bank did not give value because it did not pay consistent with the indorsement.

The facts are not disputed. The defendant is a Jamestown law firm which in 1978 and 1979 represented clients in connection with construction contracts to be performed by Leo Proctor Construction Company, Inc., a Texas corporation. . . .

On January 3, 1979 the defendant made a progress payment on behalf of its clients by drawing and delivering two checks totaling $36,906.54. The checks were made payable to Proctor as the named payee and had been drawn by the defendant on a[n] . . . account it maintained for disbursement of client's funds at the First National Bank of Jamestown.

On January 4, 1979 a Proctor employee brought these two checks to one of the plaintiff's branch offices at Jamestown and presented them to the manager with a request that the funds represented by the checks be telegraphed to an account maintained by Proctor at the First National Bank of Bethany in Oklahoma. The checks were not indorsed by Proctor. However, an employee of the plaintiff bank stamped the reverse side of the checks "credited to the account of the payee herein named/Marine Midland Chautauqua National Bank" and then . . . transferred the funds to Proctor's account at the Oklahoma bank. Proctor has never maintained an account with the plaintiff bank.

After the defendant law firm delivered the checks to Proctor it was informed by one of its clients that Proctor was in default on the construction contracts and, at the client's request, stopped payment on the checks. . . .

The plaintiff made a . . . demand for payment of the checks by Proctor but was informed that Proctor had filed a petition in bankruptcy. The plaintiff then made a . . . demand for payment by the defendant, but the defendant refused to honor the checks. It is conceded that the plaintiff had no knowledge of Proctor's default on the construction contracts at the time it took the checks. . . .

The parties agree that the defendant has a valid defense against Proctor for lack of consideration and thus against the plaintiff, as Proctor's transferee, unless the plaintiff can qualify as a holder in due course.

Under the Uniform Commercial Code five requirements must be met before a party can obtain the special protections of a holder in due course. The party must be (1) a holder . . . (3) who took it for value. . . .

With respect to the first requirement the code provides that a holder is "a person who is in possession . . . an instrument . . . issued or indorsed to him or to his order or to bearer or in blank" [§1-201(20)]. In this case it is conceded that the bank is in possession of the check but [it is] also conceded that the bank accepted the check without indorsement. This would generally preclude a person from being a holder, and thus a holder in due course.

However, the bank contends . . . that [§4-405] excuses its failure to obtain Proctor's indorsement. The statute provides:

> A depository bank which has taken an item for collection may supply any indorsement of the customer which is necessary to title unless the item contains the words 'payee's indorsement required' or the like.

It appears that this section was designed to facilitate the collection process in the relatively common situation where a person having an account at the bank deposits a check without indorsement. . . . By its terms, however, the statute is not limited to that situation. The bank's statutory authority to supply a missing indorsement applies to any item submitted for collection by "a customer," which includes not only persons "having an account with a bank" but also anyone "for whom a bank has agreed to collect items." Thus the fact that Proctor had no account at the bank did not necessarily preclude the bank from supplying the missing indorsement.

If Proctor was the plaintiff's customer then the plaintiff was entitled to supply the missing indorsement and in our view satisfied that requirement in this case. Although Proctor did not in fact have an account at the bank capable of being credited that does not impair the effectiveness of the indorsement under the terms of the statute. The section is quite explicit that the statement the bank placed on the check in this case effectively serves as the customer's indorsement. And as noted earlier, being in possession of an indorsed item would qualify the bank as a holder [§1-201(20)].

However, in order to qualify as a holder in due course the bank must satisfy additional conditions, including a requirement that it give value within the meaning of the code. . . . With respect to this requirement the inconsistency between the indorsement and the manner in which the checks actually were paid is significant. On this point the code is equally explicit: [The court quoted §3-206(3).] Thus, a bank which has made a payment inconsistent with the indorsement cannot be said to have given value for the purpose of claiming the special protections afforded a holder in due course. . . . Furthermore, the statute does not limit the bank's obligation to pay consistent with a restrictive indorsement, to those cases where the restriction was imposed by the payee. Accordingly, inasmuch as the bank did not comply with the conditions of the indorsement which it supplied, it cannot be said to have given value within the contemplation of the code and therefore was not a holder in due course based on the indorsement. . . .

Accordingly, the order of the Appellate Division should be reversed . . . and judgment granted to the defendant.

CASE REVIEW QUESTIONS

1. Who is the payee, the drawee, and the drawer?
2. Is the bank a holder? Explain.
3. Was the bank's indorsement special or blank? Restrictive or nonrestrictive?
4. What could the bank have done to comply with the restrictive indorsement?
5. What rules should the bank make for its employees when the bank is supplying a missing indorsement?

Qualified and Unqualified Indorsements A **qualified indorsement** is an indorsement that limits the liability of an indorser in the event that a maker or drawee does not pay an instrument. Chapter 27 will discuss this and other liabilities of indorsers in some detail. For the moment, it is sufficient to know that if an indorser qualifies an indorsement by the use of words that disclaim liability, such as "Without recourse," the indorser is not making the usual promise made by an indorser that he or she will pay upon being notified that the maker or drawee did not pay [§3-414(1)]. An **unqualified indorsement** is one that does not contain the words "Without recourse" or similar words.

Relevance of Indorsements Indorsements are relevant from three perspectives. First, an indorsement is essential in order to negotiate an instrument if the instrument is made payable to the order of a named payee or indorsee. Second, the form of the indorsement determines whether the instrument is an order instrument or a bearer instrument and, therefore, what form the next negotiation of the instrument must take—that is, indorsement and delivery for order instruments or delivery alone for bearer instruments. Finally, indorsements determine the rights and obligations of the indorsers and the indorsees.

The following examples review the various types of indorsements.

Pay Mary Jones for collection only, /s/ Jim Black, Without Recourse

This indorsement is special, restrictive, and qualified. It is special because it names Jones as the person who can negotiate the instrument and who is the holder. The instrument is therefore an order instrument. The indorsement is restrictive because the instrument is indorsed for the benefit of Black, that is, it is to be collected for him. The indorsement is qualified because it specifies "Without recourse," thereby limiting Black's obligation to pay in the event that the maker or drawer **defaults,** that is, does not pay.

For deposit only, /s/ Bill Bones

This indorsement is blank, restrictive, and unqualified. It is blank because it does not specify the new holder. The instrument is therefore a bearer instrument. The indorsement is restrictive because any funds must be deposited to the account of Bill Bones. It is unqualified because there are no words such as "Without recourse."

THE HOLDER IN DUE COURSE

This section addresses the question of whether a person who has become a holder by negotiation is a **holder in due course.** The laws governing negotiable instruments provide that the negotiation of a negotiable instrument to a holder in due course gives that holder certain advantages over a mere or ordinary holder. The concept of a holder in due course was developed to allow negotiable instruments to be readily acceptable substitutes for money. This is accomplished by providing that a holder in due course takes an instrument free from most defenses and all claims that could be raised by a maker, a drawer, or any other party to the instrument.

Defenses and claims can be understood by considering the following: A **defense** basically means that someone is saying, "I won't pay because . . . ," giving a reason something like "you misrepresented the goods." A claim means, "Give me that instrument. It's mine; I have a right to it."

Requirements for Being a Holder in Due Course

In order to be a holder in due course, a person must have a negotiable instrument (see Chapter 25) that has been duly negotiated so that the person is a holder (discussed previously in this chapter). The person must also fulfill certain requirements, which will be discussed in the following material.

The UCC defines a holder in due course as a holder who takes an instrument [§3-302]

1. For value.
2. In good faith.
3. Without notice that it is overdue or has been dishonored or of any defense against it or claim to it on the part of any person.

The remainder of this chapter will discuss each of these requirements and the types of defenses and claims that cannot be asserted against a holder in due course.

Taking for Value Because being a holder in due course cuts off the ability of a maker or drawer to raise certain defenses, the Code defines taking for value in such a way as to insure that the holder has a sufficient monetary interest in the instrument so that it is fair to deprive the maker or drawer of a defense that might otherwise be available [§3-303]. A person who takes an instrument without giving value for it, which occurs when an instrument is given as a gift, cannot be a holder in due course and will not be able to collect on the instrument from a maker or drawer who has a defense because such a person has no monetary interest at stake. The Code describes four circumstances in which a holder has sufficient monetary interest to be a holder in due course.

Performance of Consideration A holder who has given or performed the consideration agreed to for the transfer of an instrument is a holder who has given value [§3-303(a)]. If the agreed consideration has not been given, the holder is not a holder for value. Suppose, for example, that Painter promises to paint Owner's house for $1,000. Owner pays Painter before the work is begun by giving her a check for $1,000 drawn by Company and naming Owner as the payee. Painter becomes the holder of the check when Owner indorses it and delivers it to her.

Before starting work, however, Painter learns from Company that it issued the check for goods sold to it by Owner, but that Owner had misrepresented the goods. Thus, Company has a defense against Owner, and Painter has learned of the defense before she has given value. The promise to paint the house does not constitute value because a holder gives value only to the extent that a promise is actually performed [§3-303(a)].

What should Painter do upon learning of Company's defense if three-fourths of the painting job is already completed? In this situation, Painter is a holder in

1000

due course to the extent of the value given—75 percent of $750, but not the remaining $250. A holder in such a situation can refuse to perform the rest of the promise that was made in return for the instrument. Painter, in other words, can stop painting. She will be able to collect the $750 from Company if she meets all the other criteria for being a holder in due course.

Payment for a Debt The taking of an instrument as payment for a debt constitutes value because the holder, by accepting payment, discharges the debt [§3-303(b)]. For example, if Painter owes Store $500 and she pays Store by indorsing and delivering to it a check drawn by Owner payable to the order of Painter, she no longer owes Store any money because Store, by accepting Owner's check as payment of Painter's debt, has canceled her debt. If Store cannot collect from Owner on the check, Store will suffer a loss because it no longer has a right to obtain payment of the debt from Painter. Assuming that Store meets the other criteria for being a holder in due course, it can collect from Owner even if Painter doesn't do the work for which Owner gave her the check.

Exchanges of Negotiable Instruments If a holder takes a negotiable instrument and gives a negotiable instrument in return, the holder takes for value. Consider the following example: Owner gives Painter a $750 check to buy paint, but Painter uses the check to make a loan to Jones instead. Jones gives Painter a negotiable promissory note promising to pay her $750 plus interest in return for the check from Owner. In giving Painter the note for the check, Jones has given value because Painter could at anytime negotiate the promissory note to a person who could qualify as a holder in due course. Jones would then have to pay that person on the note. However, since Jones has given value, he can collect on the check from Owner if he meets the other criteria for being a holder in due course. If Jones cannot recover from Owner on the check, though, he will suffer a loss.

Irrevocable Commitment An irrevocable commitment to do something for a third party constitutes giving value [§3-303(c)]. For example, if Bank issues an irrevocable letter of credit to Painter in return for a check that Owner had given to Painter naming her as payee, Bank has given value. The **letter of credit** is Bank's commitment to anyone who extends credit to Painter that she has a line of credit at Bank. Bank must, of course, honor the letter if Painter uses it to purchase supplies. Bank should therefore be allowed to collect from Owner on the check even if Painter never completes the job, provided that Bank meets the other criteria for being a holder in due course.

Good Faith A holder must not only take for value but must also take in good faith in order to become a holder in due course [§3-302(1)(b)]. The Code defines **good faith** as honesty in fact [§1-201(19)]. A person may be honest in fact and still not notice or be suspicious about things that a smarter or more reasonable person would question. The test is subjective and is sometimes referred to as the pure heart but empty-head test. For example, a gullible person who foolishly takes an instrument from a stranger or pays much less for an instrument than its face value is not necessarily acting in bad faith if that person was acting honestly.

What if a person has some suspicions about an instrument but has no actual knowledge of any irregularity? Must he or she pursue the suspicions to determine whether there is indeed a claim or defense? Generally, the answer is no, unless the suspicions are so compelling that a failure to inquire further could be characterized as a deliberate attempt to avoid learning of a claim or a defense.

Without Notice In addition to taking for value and in good faith, a holder to be a holder in due course must take an instrument without notice of any claim to it or any defense against its payment. In other words, if a transferee knows that another person claims an instrument as his or her own or that the maker or drawer has some defense or legal reason not to pay, the transferee cannot become a holder in due course. Notice of a claim or defense must be received by a transferee before the transferee becomes a holder in order for the notice to deprive the holder of holder in due course status. Similarly, a person who takes an instrument with notice that it is overdue cannot be a holder in due course. If a transferee has notice that the maker, drawer, or drawee has dishonored the instrument — that is, has refused for any reason to pay the instrument — the holder cannot be a holder in due course [§3-304 and §1-201(25)].

Incomplete and Irregular Instruments The Code is specific about the usual situations in which a purchaser of a negotiable instrument is deemed to have notice of a claim or defense [§3-304]. An instrument that is so incomplete as to raise questions of its validity, its term, its ownership, or who is to be paid gives notice of a claim or a defense [§3-304(1)(a)]. Similarly, if an instrument bears such visible evidence of forgery or alteration or is otherwise so clearly irregular that obvious questions should arise in the mind of a purchaser about its validity or ownership, the purchaser has notice of a claim or defense [§3-301(1)(b)].

Not every blank space or alteration need arouse suspicion. For example, when a teenager brings a check with the amount left blank to school to pay for a yearbook, there is no cause for suspicion unless the taker knows that the completion is improper [§3-304(4)(d)]. Even such obvious alterations as a change in the date from January 3, 1985, to January 3, 1986, if seen early in 1986, should not ordinarily raise any suspicion of irregularity.

In the words of the Code, the instrument must be "so incomplete" or "so irregular" that suspicion should be aroused. If the incompleteness or irregularity is blatant — as in a crude alteration of the words "Two and 00/100 dollars" by squeezing in "hundred" after the "two" and on top of the "and" — a court can find that any taker must have been suspicious. While the drawer may have a perfectly good explanation for why the alteration was made, a subsequent taker would be on notice that there might be a defense of material alteration that could be raised by the drawer, so the taker would not be a holder in due course.

Negotiation by a Fiduciary A **fiduciary** is a person who stands in a special relation to another person or institution because he or she manages money or property belonging to the other. The law imposes a strict duty of faithfulness upon a fiduciary. Some examples of fiduciaries are trustees, corporate officers, and agents. A fiduciary must, of necessity, handle checks and other negotiable instruments. Suppose a corporation treasurer negotiates an instrument that belongs to the corporation to pay a personal debt. The potential purchaser of the instrument may be on notice of the corporation's interest in the instrument. Is the purchaser barred from becoming a holder in due course simply because he or she recognizes the corporation's interest? It depends. A holder is not barred from being a holder in due course merely because the person who negotiated an instrument is or was a fiduciary [§3-304(4)(e)]. The statute requires that the holder actually know that a fiduciary is breaching a duty—that is, has no right to the personal use of instrument—in order to be on notice of the corporation's claim to the instrument [§3-304(2)]. If a holder knows that a fiduciary has no right to use an instrument, the holder cannot be a holder in due course.

Overdue Instruments A person who takes an instrument with notice that it is overdue cannot be a holder in due course. It is usually possible to determine whether a note or a draft is **overdue.** After all, a negotiable instrument must be payable on demand or at a definite time. An instrument payable at a definite time is overdue when the time specified for payment has passed. A demand instrument is overdue after demand for payment has been made and the purchaser has reason to know that fact. More commonly, a demand instrument is overdue when it gets old or stale. A demand instrument becomes stale after a reasonable interval from the time it was issued has elapsed. For example, a check more than 30 days old is presumed to be stale and thus overdue [§3-304(3)(c)].

A purchaser has notice that an instrument is overdue if he or she has reason to know that any amount of the instrument is overdue—if, for example, installments 2 and 3 of a ten-installment note have not been paid—or that the instrument has been accelerated—that is, a demand for early payment has been made [§3-304(3)]. Sometimes debtors and creditors create a series of notes rather than a single note to effectuate repayment in installments. If there has been an uncorrected default in one payment in a series of notes, a puchaser with knowledge of the default has notice that any other note in the series is overdue. On the other hand, if a debtor defaults on one note among many naming the same payee but the note is not part of a series, notice of the default does not bar a holder of any of the other notes from being a holder in due course because a default on one transaction does not mean that there is a defense to another note arising out of another transaction [§3-304(4)(f)]. Also, a holder is not barred from being a holder in due course by receiving notice that there has been a default in the payment of interest unless there is an accompanying notice of a default in the payment of principal [§3-304(4)(b)].

Effectiveness of Notice There is no notice of a claim or defense unless it is received at such a time and in such a manner as to give the transferee of an instrument a reasonable opportunity to act on the notice [§3-304(6)]. For example, if a corporation notifies a bank president at 9:15 A.M. that the corporate treasurer does not have the authority to cash checks, the notice is not effective—that is, it does not prevent the bank from being a holder in due course—if the corporate treasurer is at that moment approaching a teller's window to cash a corporate check. Even though the bank technically receives notice before it takes the check, there is not sufficient opportunity for the message to reach the teller before the check is cashed.

Some kinds of knowledge are not ordinarily considered notice. For instance, many people antedate (use a date earlier than the actual date) or postdate (use a date later than the actual date) checks. Of itself, knowing that a check is antedated or postdated does not give a holder notice of a defense because it is done by many people for reasons that have nothing to do with contract defenses [§3-304(4)(a)]. For example, antedating or postdating a check may be done as a matter of convenience to either the drawer or the payee.

Notice and Good Faith There is a close relationship between taking in good faith and taking without notice. Indeed, the question of what a holder of an instrument knows at the time of taking an instrument is often bound up with the element of good faith. In the following case, a cashier's check is postdated. The court must determine whether the plaintiffs took the check in good faith and without notice of any defense that the Habib Bank might have.

INDYK v. HABIB BANK LTD.
694 F.2d 54 (Second Cir. 1982)

CARDAMONE, Circuit Judge

On February 4, 1980 plaintiffs Evelyn and Leo Indyk contracted to sell to Dome Investment Company (Dome) 100 percent of the shares of Monroe Contract Corporation (Monroe), a Pennsylvania coal mining firm, for one million dollars. The closing [the time for performance of the contract] occurred on February 6, 1980 in the offices of Equibank in White Oak, Pennsylvania. . . . At the closing plaintiffs received, as payment on the balance of the purchase price, a cashier's check in the amount of $842,243.83 drawn on defendant Habib Bank Limited (Habib or Bank). The cashier's check was postdated June 4, 1980 and signed by Habib Assistant Vice President S. Hassan Ahmed. When plaintiffs presented the cashier's check on June 4, 1980 at Habib's New York City office, the Bank refused to pay claiming that the check was issued without either authority or consideration. . . .

Dome defaulted [failed to make payment] and Monroe went bankrupt. The Indyks subsequently brought a [legal] action . . . against Habib on the dishonored cashier's check. . . .

[T]he court below held that Ahmed's signature on the check was authorized . . . and that the Indyks were "holders in due course" of the Habib check and took it free of Habib's asserted defense of lack of consideration. Judgment was entered in favor of the Indyks against Habib. . . .

The effect of achieving holder in due course status is of course that the holder takes the instrument free from certain defenses, including the defense asserted here—lack of consideration.

Conceding that the Indyks took the cashier's check for value and in good faith, Habib asserts that the Indyks were not holders in due course because they took the postdated cashier's check with notice that defenses against the check existed. Specifically, Habib claims that the Indyks had notice because: they were aware that the cashier's check was postdated; their representative at Equibank, Mrs. Zell, expressed concern over the postdating and telephoned Mr. Ahmed at Habib to verify that the check was proper; banks normally do not use postdated cashier's checks; and the Indyks knew that Dome could not raise the necessary cash for the purchase of [Monroe's] stock until June 4, 1980 and, therefore, at least impliedly knew that Dome did not give any consideration for the cashier's check. We find Habib's contention that the Indyks took the check with notice unpersuasive.

Under New York law notice of defenses means actual, subjective knowledge of defenses. . . . Notice is not shown merely by the existence of suspicious circumstances. . . . There is no evidence in the record before us that the Indyks had actual, subjective knowledge that the Habib check was issued without consideration or subject to any defenses. The Indyks testified that they had never dealt with or even heard of Habib prior to the closing on February 6, 1980. The check, on its face, was conceded to be a regular Habib Bank cashier's check properly made out and signed by the Assistant Vice President in charge of the bank department that issued cashier's checks. The postdating of the check did cause the Indyks' banker some concern, which prompted her to telephone Mr. Ahmed at the Habib bank. Mrs. Zell was advised that the check had been properly issued and authorized. She reported this information to the plaintiffs. Moreover, the postdating of the check alone was not legally sufficient to give the Indyks notice of a defense [§3-304(4)(a)]. While postdated cashier's checks are not normally used by banks, the Indyks did not know and had no reason to know of this specific banking practice. The fact that the Indyks might have been aware of Dome's lack of funds does not necessarily demonstrate that they subjectively knew that Dome had not given consideration to Habib for the cashier's check. Dome might well have paid for Habib's check with a note or some other non-cash consideration. . . .

Absent any evidence that the Indyks had actual notice, the district court's conclusion that they were holders in due course entitled to judgment for the face amount of the check should be upheld.

CASE REVIEW QUESTIONS
1. Why is a postdated cashier's check suspicious?
2. Is suspicion enough to deprive a holder of holder in due course status?
3. Why do you think the cashier's check was postdated?
4. Why did the Indyks meet the good faith requirement to be a holder in due course?
5. Why did the Indyks not have notice of Habib Bank's defense?

The Payee as Holder in Due Course The Code specifically states that a "payee may be a holder in due course" [§3-302(2)]. Generally speaking, a payee is so closely associated with the underlying contract that the payee has notice of any contract claims or defenses. However, the Official Comment to §3-302(2) provides a number of examples of situations in which a payee can become a holder in due course. In all of the examples, a third party plays some role so that the payee does not deal directly with the marker or drawer and, hence, can meet the requirements for being a holder in due course—namely, taking for value, taking in good faith, and taking without notice.

For example, the preceding case does not indicate who was named as payee on the cashier's check. Suppose, however, that Dome had the Indyks named as payees when it obtained the check at the Habib Bank. Dome would be a *remitter,* a party who is issued an instrument payable to a different party. When Dome remitted, or delivered, the check to the Indyks at the closing, the Indyks themselves would not have done business directly with the Habib Bank. Since they would have no knowledge of the Habib Bank's defense of lack of consideration based on Dome's failure to pay the Habib Bank, the Indyks would be holders in due course even though named as payees.

Advantages of Being a Holder in Due Course

A holder in due course takes a negotiable instrument free from all claims and most defenses [§3-305]. Remember that a claim means someone saying "That's mine" and defense means someone saying "I won't pay because. . . ."

Defenses Available against the Ordinary Holder The Code provides that a person who is not a holder in due course takes a negotiable instrument subject to all valid claims as well as all defenses available in an action involving a contract [§3-306(a) and (b)]. The Code also lists other defenses, such as the failure to meet certain conditions, nondelivery of the instrument, acquisition by theft, and payment that would be inconsistent with restrictive indorsement, that are good against a holder who is not a holder in due course.

It is important to note that a holder's status is irrelevant if there are no claims to or defenses against the payment of an instrument. Holder in due course status is a shield that protects a holder against all claims and most defenses, but a maker, a drawer, or any other party cannot refuse to pay simply because a holder is not a holder in due course. The party must have some defense or claim in order to avoid payment.

The Shelter Rule If a holder takes an instrument from a holder in due course, in most cases the new holder will have the rights of the holder in due course. Thus, a holder may have the advantage of the shield — that is, the rights of a holder in due course — even though the holder does not meet the requirements to be a holder in due course. This rule, called the **shelter rule,** is important because commercial paper is supposed to flow freely and to be an acceptable substitute for money. If a holder in due course could not pass on the rights and advantages of being a holder in due course, the holder might not be able to transfer the instrument in the event that claims or defenses against the instrument became widely known.

For example, who would be willing to take a note made by Jane Doe after she takes out a full page ad in the financial section of the newspaper announcing that Bill Jones has sold her a car that is a lemon and stating that she will not pay the note she gave for the car? Without the shelter rule, innocent Betty Smith, who purchased the note from Bill Jones and thereby became a holder in due course, would be unable to use that note freely. Given the shelter rule, Smith can transfer the note to Jack Green, who can further negotiate the note or can collect from Doe. Even if Green had read Doe's advertisement before taking the note from Smith and therefore had notice of Doe's defense, he would have the status or rights of a holder in due course under the shelter rule [§3-201(1)].

A person who was a party to any fraud or illegality affecting the instrument cannot take advantage of the shelter rule to improve his or her status as a holder by simply waiting and taking the instrument from a holder in due course. Similarly, a prior holder who had notice of a claim or defense when he or she first acquired an instrument is not protected by the shelter rule if he or she reacquires the instrument from a holder in due course. In the example above, if Bill Jones purchases Jane Doe's note from Jack Green, Jones cannot claim holder in due course status.

Holder in Due Course Takes Free from All Claims A holder in due course or one who has the rights of a holder in due course takes free from all claims, such as ownership rights or other legal rights to an instrument. Consider the following scenario. Betty Smith draws a check for $50 that reads "Pay to the order of Cash." On the way to the bank, Smith loses her wallet with the check in it. Jane Doe finds the wallet and the check. She transfers the check to Bill Jones who pays her $50.

Can Smith get the check back from Jones? If Jones is a holder in due course of the check, Smith will not be able to say "That's mine" and recover the check. Smith's claim will be cut off [§3-305(1)].

Is Jones a holder in due course? The answer is probably yes. A check, by definition, is a negotiable instrument, so the law of negotiability applies. The check was negotiated to Jones because a check made payable to the order of cash is a bearer instrument that is negotiable by delivery alone. Although Doe was not a holder because she did not receive the check by a voluntary transfer, her transfer to Jones did constitute a delivery, so Jones is a holder. Note that Doe is not a holder because there was no delivery, so Smith could have recovered the check from Doe.

Jones gave value for the check — the $50. We must assume that he was acting in good faith, that he was honest in fact and had no notice of Smith's claim other than her signature. Because there are many reasons why Doe might have a check drawn by Smith, Smith's signature is not sufficient to give Jones actual knowledge that Smith lost the instrument and has a claim to it. Only if Jones were acting in bad faith in taking the check or had actual knowledge at the time of taking that the check belonged to Smith would Smith be able to recover the check.

One final note — even if Smith had the foresight and the opportunity to tell the bank on which the check was drawn to stop — that is, refuse — payment of the check when it was presented for payment, Smith would still have to pay Jones the $50. As we will see in more detail in Chapter 27, by drawing a check, a drawer promises to pay the check if the bank does not.

Defenses Available against a Holder in Due Course While a holder in due course takes free from all claims and most defenses, there are some defenses that can be effectively raised against a holder in due course [§3-305(2)]. All defenses that apply to negotiable instruments are divided into two types — real and personal. **Personal defenses** comprise most of the common defenses available for breach of contract, such as failure of consideration, conditional delivery (the payee was to use the check only in certain circumstances), breach of warranty, and misrepresentation of goods (the payee lied about the goods, which is sometimes called *fraud in the inducement*). Personal defenses are not good against a holder in due course.

Real defenses are not as common as personal defenses. They have been developed, in part, to protect those who cannot adequately protect their own interests in the business world. As a matter of public policy, real defenses are available against any holder of a negotiable instrument, including a holder in due course. Each of the real defenses is discussed in following sections.

Infancy Infancy or minority is a real defense, just as it is in a simple contract case. The purpose of the statute is to protect a minor against those who might take advantage of his or her age and lack of experience. If a negotiable instrument is issued by a minor, the minor's lack of capacity allows him or her to disaffirm the instrument to the same extent as he or she would be able to disaffirm any other contract [§3-305(2)(a)]. This means that a minor may usually disaffirm a negotiable instrument at any time until a reasonable time after becoming an adult, which occurs at 18 in most states. (See Chapter 14 for a complete discussion of a minor's right to disaffirm a contract.)

Incapacity, Duress, or Illegality Making Promise Void Some defenses make a contract promise null or **void,** which means that the promise never comes into existence under contract law. Other defenses make promises **voidable,** which means that the promise comes into existence, but it can be avoided by the party having the defense. A defense of lack of capacity to make the promise or order in an instrument by someone other than a minor—a mental incompetent, for example—can only be asserted against a holder in due course if the lack of capacity in the particular case makes the promise void, not just voidable, under contract law (see Chapter 14). Similarly, any defense based on duress (see Chapter 11) or illegality (see Chapter 15) that would make the promise or order in an instrument void under contract law may be asserted against a holder in due course [§3-305(2)(b)].

In the following case, the court had to determine whether the illegality of the contract involved made the promise of the maker of a note void or voidable.

NEW JERSEY MORTGAGE & INVESTMENT CORPORATION v. BERENYI
356 A.2d 421 (N.J. 1976)

[The Attorney General of the State of New Jersey brought a legal proceeding against Kroyden Industries, Inc. (Kroyden). At the conclusion of the proceeding, on May 25, 1964, the court issued an order directing Kroyden to stop committing certain acts or making certain representations to its customers in connection with the sale of carpeting.

Subsequent to the court order, in August 1964, an

employee of Kroyden offered, in violation of the court order, to give to Anna Berenyi carpeting worth $1,100 for free if she referred prospective customers to Kroyden. Berenyi agreed. Relying on the offer and the representations, she signed a promissory note for $1,521.

Kroyden then negotiated the note to New Jersey Mortgage and Invesment Corporation (N.J. M.I.C.), who met all of the requirements to be a holder in due course. Berenyi refused to pay the note. The plaintiff, N.J. M.I.C., then brought a legal action against the defendant, Berenyi. Berenyi defended on the grounds that her contract with Kroyden was illegal because Kroyden's actions were in violation of the court order and, therefore, she had a defense against the obligation to pay the note. The trial court gave judgment to the plaintiff. The defendant appealed.]

PER CURIAM [By the Court]

The controlling issue presented is whether the defense here asserted is a "real" defense or a "personal" defense. Real defenses are available against even a holder in due course of a negotiable instrument; personal defenses are not available against such a holder. We affirm since we are satisfied that the defense presented is not a "real" defense.

Defendant argues that since the transaction which resulted in the execution and delivery of defendant's note was engaged in by Kroyden in violation of the [court's order in the case of the Attorney General against Kroyden], the transaction was "illegal and thus a nullity [i.e., void] under [§3-305]," which provides in pertinent part as follows:

To the extent that a holder is a holder in due course he takes the instrument free from . . . (2) all defenses of any party to the instrument with whom the holder has not dealt except . . . (b) such other incapacity, or duress, or illegality of the transaction, as renders the obligation of the party a nullity; . . . .

However, the fact that it was illegal for Kroyden to enter into the transaction did not by reason of that fact render defendant's obligation under the note she executed a nullity.

On the contrary, as noted in the New Jersey Study Comment on [§3-305(2)(b)]:

In New Jersey, a holder in due course takes free and clear of the defense of illegality, unless the statute which declares the act illegal also indicates that payment thereunder is void. . . . [See e.g., N.J.S.A. 2A:40-3 which specifically provides that notes given in payment of a gambling debt "shall be utterly void and of no effect."] . . . [W]here no such statute is involved, it has been held that a negotiable instrument which is rooted in an illegal transaction or stems from a transaction prohibited by statute or public policy is not reason for refusing to enforce the instrument in the hands of a holder in due course.

There being no statute ordaining that a note obtained in violation of [a court order] is void and unenforceable, the illegality involved is not a real defense; the note is enforceable in the hands of a holder in due course who had no knowledge or notice of the injunction.

The judgment is affirmed.

CASE REVIEW QUESTIONS
1. Why did the court decide that Berenyi's defense was a personal defense and not a real defense?
2. What would Berenyi have had to prove in order to have had a real defense?
3. What would N.J. M.I.C. have to establish in order to be a holder in due course?

Fraud Fraud is intentional misrepresentation by one party about an important matter in a transaction that is justifiably relied on by the other party to the transaction (see Chapter 11). Whether fraud may be used as a defense against a holder in due course depends upon the type of fraud. There are two types of fraud—fraud in the inducement, which is a personal defense, and fraud in the execution, which is a real defense.

Suppose, for example, that a used car dealer deliberately misrepresents a material fact about a car in order to induce a buyer to purchase the car. The buyer signs a negotiable promissory note, which is then negotiated by the payee dealer to a holder in due course. Subsequently, the buyer discovers the fraud. Can the buyer refuse to pay the holder in due course? The answer is no. This type of fraud, known as fraud in the inducement, is a personal defense that can be asserted against an ordinary holder but not against a holder in due course.

The other type of fraud, known as fraud in the execution (also called fraud in the factum), is a real defense that is available against all holders, even a holder in due course [§3-305(2)(c)]. The defense of fraud in the execution is available when a maker or drawer of a negotiable instrument, through no fault of his or her own, is deceived about the nature of the document being signed, that is, if the maker or drawer does not know that the paper being signed is a negotiable instrument. For example, if the car dealer tricks the buyer into signing a negotiable note by switching forms, the buyer may be able to use the defense of fraud in the execution against a holder in due course.

This type of defense is most commonly used by people who are illiterate, close to illiterate, or extremely inexperienced in the business world. For example, if a person cannot read English and translators are unavailable, assurances that a document is a receipt when in fact it is a promissory note may constitute fraud in the execution.

In order to establish the real defense of fraud in the execution, excusable ignorance of the nature of the instrument being signed and the absence of reasonable opportunity to obtain the required knowledge must be proven. There are a number of factors that must be considered: age, intelligence, education, business experience, ability to read and to understand English, the types of representations made, the reasonableness of relying on the representations or the person making them, the presence or absence of third parties who might explain the document, and the apparent necessity or absence of necessity for acting without delay and so allowing no time to get the requisite knowledge. If fraud is found after all of these factors are considered, the maker or drawer can claim fraud in the execution as a real defense that will be good against a holder in due course.

Courts are hesitant to deprive a holder in due course of payment, so the defense of fraud in the execution is not readily available. In one case, a husband and wife in their forties who had some high school education were visited by a salesman promoting aluminum siding. The salesman told the family that their home would be a "show home" and that they would receive $100 for every contract made to install aluminum siding within 25 miles of their home. The family believed that in this way they would get their siding for nothing. The salesman gave them a printed contract form to read while he filled in the blanks on some other forms. The husband and wife read the printed form, but they signed the forms with the blanks filled in without reading them.

Later, the family discovered that they had signed notes and had mortgaged their home. The notes were negotiated by the salesman to a holder in due course. The family raised the defense of fraud in the execution. The court rejected the defense after looking at all the factors to be considered. The husband and wife had some education, both knew about mortgages because they had one on their home, both could speak and read English, and neither knew or had any reason to rely on the salesman nor did they check up on the grand scheme of getting something for nothing. The defense of fraud in the execution was therefore not available to them.

Discharge An important defense that is good against a holder in due course is that the debt created by an instrument was discharged in an insolvency proceeding such as a bankruptcy [§3-305(1)(d)]. When an insolvent debtor and his or her debts have been discharged through bankruptcy, the purpose of the Bankruptcy Act to allow a debtor a new beginning would be jeopardized if a holder in due course could still demand payment.

The Code also states that any other discharge of which a holder in due course has notice at the time of taking an instrument is a defense good against that holder [§3-305(1)(e)]. There are several types of discharges of which a holder in due course might have notice. For example, if a note has been partially paid and the amount paid is noted on the instrument, a holder in due course of that note knows that the amount due is discharged in part, that is, it has been reduced by the amount already paid. A maker of a note is discharged to the exent that a note has been paid. However, if a maker fails to have a payment noted on the instrument, the mere possession of a receipt that the payment has been made will not be effective against a holder in due course who subsequently takes the instrument and is unaware of the prior payment. The maker would, in effect, have to pay twice — once on the first payment and a second time to the holder in due course.

Forgery Although forgery is not specified by the Code as a defense in §3-305, the defense that a person's signature was forged or was otherwise unauthorized is available against a holder in due course. A person cannot be held liable on a negotiable instrument — that is, cannot be made to pay — unless his or her actual or authorized signature is on the instrument [§3-401]. Accordingly, not even a holder in due course can collect from a person who has not signed an instrument. A complete discussion of forgeries and unauthorized signatures can be found in Chapter 27.

ABUSE OF HOLDER IN DUE COURSE STATUS

The holder in due course concept has created a serious problem for consumers. Unscrupulous people have used it as a device to deprive consumers of defenses against the sellers of goods or services.

Consider, for instance, what happened in a small town in northern Indiana.

Some older women living on meager pensions, social security, or savings responded individually to an advertisement in the local newspaper stating that women with sewing skills were needed to do work in their homes. The advertisement said that the women could devote as little or as much time to work as they wished, depending on how much money they wanted to earn. The advertisement was actually placed to locate prospective purchasers of sewing machines. There was, in fact, no work.

A crew of sewing machine salesmen descended upon the town and appeared at the doors of the women who had responded to the advertisement. They proceeded to explain how much money the women could make doing simple sewing jobs right in their own homes. The women, seeing an opportunity to supplement their meager incomes, were easy customers. All the salesmen had to do was switch the conversation from work and pay to sewing machines and payments. This switch was accomplished by each salesman requesting to inspect the sewing machine of the victim to determine whether it was suitable for the work to be done. Of course, it was not. The immediate consternation of the victim, who saw all the money and security she was hoping for slipping through her fingers, was put to rest by the salesman. He could provide her with a proper sewing mchine, which she could pay for out of her earnings.

The victims were persuaded to make substantial down payments and to sign promissory notes for the balance due. In each case, the machine's price was several hundred dollars more than the market price in the town for the same or similar models, but the women were persuaded to believe that they were paying a wholesale price. The salesmen negotiated the promissory notes to a local bank for a discounted amount. Then, taking the down payments and the proceeds from the note, they left town never to be seen again. The bank tried to collect as a holder in due course after the women discovered the fraud.

Until recently, the bank would have succeeded because, as a holder in due course, it was free from the personal defense of fraud in the inducement. For many years, the courts have been aware of such frauds, and they have attempted to avoid enforcing such notes against their makers by interpreting the facts so as to preclude a holder from qualifying as a holder in due course. This interpretation was usually possible where payees negotiated notes to the same third party many times or where there was some other close business connection between the payee and the holder. In the first situation, the courts held that past practices gave notice of defenses about the newly offered instruments. In the second situation, they held that the close relationship made it impossible for the holder to have taken the instruments in good faith.

How to prevent these negotiable instrument frauds without doing harm to the function of negotiable instruments as freely transferable substitutes for money was the underlying social and economic problem. Some rebalancing of interests seemed necessary. The question to be resolved was whether the negotiable instrument was sufficiently a part of the ordinary business activity that its use would not be discouraged if a direct attack were made on the holder in due course concept itself in place of the indirect attacks being pursued by those courts that were deciding that some holders were not holders in due course.

A number of states have made direct attacks. They have declared either that no negotiable instrument can be created in a consumer transaction or that a holder of consumer paper cannot be immune to personal defenses. The second approach takes two forms. Either there can be no holder in due course for negotiable instruments that arise out of consumer transactions or the holder in due course has no immunity to consumer defenses. For transactions between businesses and nonconsumers, the UCC rules with respect to the holder in due course still apply.

The Federal Trade Commission's Holder in Due Course Rule

The Federal Trade Commission considered the problem to be a national problem, and in 1976 it adopted a rule that requires consumer credit contacts to contain the following notice in large bold face type.

NOTICE

ANY HOLDER OF THIS CONSUMER CREDIT CONTRACT IS SUBJECT TO ALL CLAIMS AND DEFENSES WHICH THE DEBTOR COULD ASSERT AGAINST THE SELLER OF GOODS OR SERVICES OBTAINED PURSUANT HERETO OR WITH THE PROCEEDS HEREOF. RECOVERY HEREUNDER BY THE DEBTOR SHALL NOT EXCEED AMOUNTS PAID BY THE DEBTOR HEREUNDER.

The Federal regulation requiring this notice is known as the Trade Regulation Rule Preserving Consumer Claims and Defenses. It strikes at three devices that are commonly used to separate a consumer's duty to pay from a seller's duty to peform. The first device is the holder in due course doctrine. The second is the **waiver-of-defense clause,** which is sometimes found in installment sales contracts. This clause declares that any defenses or claims that could be raised against a seller will not be used against any person to whom the seller may transfer, or assign, the contract. The third device is the **purchase money loan,** which involves the arranging by a seller of a direct loan of purchase money to a buyer from a bank or other financial institution. The buyer takes the loan money and makes a cash purchase from the seller who helped arrange the loan. The loan contract is with the lending institution not the seller, so the borrower must repay the loan even if problems develop with the goods. Whether a promissory note is negotiated or an installment sales contract is assigned to a bank or other financing company, the required notice must be part of the transaction. The result is that the consumer may assert the same defenses against the bank or other lending institution that could be asserted against the seller.

The Federal Trade Commission can only enforce its rule that the notice must be included in consumer credit contracts by ordering a seller or a lending institution to cease and desist from the unfair or deceptive practice of not including the notice. The failure of a seller to include the notice does not give the consumer any additional rights. A contract or negotiable instrument that does not have the notice is not illegal and, therefore, is not void. Nevertheless, most sellers and lending institutions know that the notice must be present in consumer credit contracts. Thus, it may be possible to charge a taker of a consumer credit contract with taking in bad faith if the notice is missing in circumstances where the taker should know that the instrument being transferred is a consumer credit contract.

REVIEW QUESTIONS

1. What is required in order to negotiate a negotiable instrument?
2. Why is it important for someone who is about to buy a negotiable instrument to note carefully the form of the previous indorsement?
3. Are there any circumstances in which mere suspicion, rather than actual knowledge, that there is something wrong wth an instrument will prevent a holder from being a holder in due course? Explain.

4. How would you distinguish between a personal defense to a negotiable instrument and a real defense?
5. Explain what the Federal Trade Commission has done to deal with the problem of abuses of the holder in due course concept.

CASE PROBLEMS

1. W.J. DeJarnatt executed a note as evidence of a loan made to him by David Haefele. The note was executed on a printed form showing the First National Bank of Paris, Texas, as payee instead of David Haefele. The bank came into possession of the note, indorsed it without recourse, and delivered it to David Haefele's former wife, who gave no value for it. The former wife indorsed the note without recourse and delivered it to David Haefele's daughter Davye Carter, who also gave no value for it. Davye Carter sued W.J. DeJarnatt to enforce the note. DeJarnatt defended on the grounds that Carter was not a holder of the note and, therefore, could not enforce it. Who will win the case? Explain.

2. A check was issued by Sumiton Bank payable to the order of John Smith. The check was stolen by an unknown person who indorsed the instrument "John Smith" and delivered it to Betty Jones who took it for value and in good faith. Betty Jones indorsed the instrument "Betty Jones" and delivered it to Peter White who also took it for value and in good faith. When Peter White attempted to collect the money from Sumiton Bank, they refused to pay it, arguing that Peter White was not a holder

of the check. Is White a holder of the check? Explain.

3. An agent for Elias Saka, a film producer, entered into an agreement with Mann Theaters (Mann). Mann agreed to show a film for two weeks. The price was $5,000 per week. The agent gave Mann two checks drawn by Saka, each payable to Mann for $5,000. Mann deposited the checks and began showing the film. Toward the end of the first week, one of the two checks was returned unpaid. Mann continued to show the film for the full two weeks. Mann sued Saka to recover the $5,000. Saka defended on the grounds that the agent had not followed his instructions in delivering the checks to Mann. Will Saka's defense be good against Mann?

4. Vernon Baszler was the manager and one of three equal co-owners of Mott Grain Company. Baszler deposited a number of checks payable to Mott Grain Company in his own account in the First National Bank and Trust Company. Some checks were indorsed with restrictive indorsements—for example, "Mott Grain Company/Vernon Baszler/ For deposit only"—and others were indorsed "Mott Grain Company/Vernon Baszler, owner" or "mgr." Mott Grain Company had supplied the

bank with a corporate resolution authorizing the bank to deal with Baszler when he was handling corporate funds. Baszler disappeared with the funds deposited to his account. If Mott Grain Company sues the bank to recover the amount of the checks deposited in Baszler's account, how may the bank defend? Who will win the case? Explain.

5. Perry purchased an overdue note from the Federal Deposit Insurance Corporation, which was acting as the liquidating agent for the payee of the note, the Surety Bank and Trust Company. The note was indorsed in blank by the payee. Perry sued to recover the amount of the note from the maker, Schlaikjer, who argued that he did not have to pay the note because he was induced to make the note by the payee's misrepresentations. Under what circumstances will Perry be able to recover from the defendant?

6. Agristor Credit Corporation sued Lewellen, the maker of a negotiable promissory note. Agristor established that it was a holder in due course. Lewellen raised the defense of usury and argued that the note was illegal and void under the state's usury law. The usury law provided that interest above a specified rate is illegal and must be refunded if collected. May Lewellen raise the defense of usury? Explain.

7. At the request of her husband, Jacqueline Quazzo executed a negotiable $1,000 note payable to her sister-in-law, Ada Quazzo. The husband, Ugo Quazzo, delivered the note to his sister, Ada, who gave her brother a check for $900 payable to him. Subsequently, Jacqueline refused to pay the note. Ada sued. Jacqueline defended on the grounds that (1) she never received any payment for the note since the money went to Ugo, (2) that Ada was not a holder in due course because she was the payee on the note, and (3) that Jacqueline had only signed the note because Ugo threatened to drop her out the window, smash her face, and terminate the marriage. Are any of Jacqueline's defenses good? Explain.

27

LIABILITY AND DISCHARGE

When a holder presents a negotiable instrument for payment, the holder should receive payment, and the story of that particular instrument, which may have passed through the hands of a number of persons, comes to an end. But when the maker or drawee does not pay, the instrument is dishonored. This chapter explores the liability—that is, the obligation to pay—of the various persons, such as makers of notes, drawers of drafts, indorsers, and sometimes drawees, who by signing become parties to a negotiable instrument. All persons who transfer negotiable instruments or who obtain payment or acceptance, whether they become parties or not, have liability based on warranties that will be explained in this chapter.

SIGNATURES

The primary rule of liability for a negotiable instrument is that no person is liable as a party to an instrument unless his or her signature appears on the instrument [§3-401]. A signature, as determined by the Code, is any symbol executed or adapted to authenticate a writing [§1-201(39)]. Any signature on an instrument is deemed to be that of an indorser unless the signature clearly indicates that it was made by someone in some other capacity, such as maker or drawer [§3-402].

Signature by an Agent

An agent is an authorized representative of a person or an organization called a principal (see Chapter 31). When a signature is made by an agent authorized by a principal to sign a negotiable instrument on behalf of the principal, the principal is liable on the instrument because the agent's signature is effectively the same as the principal's signature. An agent is liable on an instrument unless the instrument names the principal or indicates that the agent is signing in a representative capacity [§3-403(2)]. An agent is not liable to a payee if the payee understands that the agent is signing only in a representative capacity. An agent is liable to all other third parties who do not know of the principal or that the person is signing only as an agent.

Types of Signatures of Agents The following are examples of types of signatures that might be used by an agent.

Paula, the principal, has an agent, Albert, who is authorized to sign negotiable instruments. Any type of signature Albert uses will be Paula's signature. The liability of the agent for each type of signature is discussed.

Paula, principal, by Albert, agent

This is the best format. Albert is not liable because the signature discloses the principal and clearly identifies the agent. Paula is liable on the instrument; Albert is not.

Paula

Paula is liable; Albert is not. "Paula," as written by Albert, is effectively Paula's signature. Albert's signature is not required.

Paula/Albert

Paula is liable; Albert is liable except to a payee who knows and agrees that Albert is signing only as an agent. Albert is liable to any other person who takes the instrument because that person has no way of knowing from the instrument that Albert is an agent.

Albert, agent

Paula is liable; Albert is liable except to a payee who knows Albert is an agent, as in the previous example. Even though Albert's agency is disclosed, the principal is not disclosed, so any other party taking the instrument is relying on Albert.

Albert

Paula is liable; Albert is liable. Albert is liable because his signature is on the instrument without disclosing his principal or his agency status. Once again, though, Albert would not be liable to a payee who know that Albert was an agent for Paula.

In the first two examples, only Paula is liable. In the last three examples, Paula is liable and Albert can also be held personally liable. If a holder recovers from Albert, he then has a right to reimbursement from Paula. The right may be worthless, however, if Paula is insolvent or if she cannot be found. From an agent's point of view, the types of the signatures in the first two examples are preferable because they relieve an agent of any personal liability on an instrument.

In the following case, an officer of a corporation signed some corporate checks without indicating his position in the corporation. The court had to decide if the corporate officer was personally liable on the instrument.

FINANCIAL ASSOCIATES v. IMPACT MARKETING, INC.
394 N.Y.S.2d 814 (N.Y. County 1977)

SHERMAN, Judge

Plaintiff [Financial Associates] an alleged holder in due course moves for summary judgment in an action on two checks. Judgment is sought against [defendants] a corporation [Impact Marketing] and the individual drawer [Marc Eliot]. The question to be determined is whether the drawer who signed the checks without indicating his representative capacity can be held personally liable.

The checks were the last two of a series of six post-dated checks. All of the checks were purchased . . . by the plaintiff from the payee. Four were paid and payment [was] stopped on the last two.

The checks sued upon were drawn on the Chemical Bank payable to the order of "Barry E. Bell." [Bell negotiated the checks to Financial Associates.] "Impact Marketing, Inc." is printed on the checks and [they are] signed "Marc Eliot." [sic] The checks do not indicate that the individual defendant Marc Eliot, the drawer, signed in any representative capacity. However, he states that he drew the check as an officer of the defendant corporation for legal services to be performed for the corporation. . . . UCC Section 3-403 states:

> (2) An authorized representative who signs his own name to an instrument . . . (b) except as otherwise established between the immediate parties is personally

obligated if the instrument names the person represented but does not show that the representative signed in the representative capacity. . . .

The section is clear. It prevents a drawer or maker, who fails to indicate his representative capacity on an instrument, to contest the question of his individual liability against a holder in due course. . . . Accordingly, parol evidence [evidence from outside the instrument itself] in these circumstances is inadmissible to show agency or a representative capacity. . . . Nor does the fact that the checks contain printed corporate name change the result. For UCC Section 3-403 states that even where the instrument indicates the person represented, liability is imposed on the drawer or maker if he fails to show that he signed in a representative capacity. This the individual defendant failed to do and he is therefore personally liable. While this result may seem harsh, the rule is in keeping with the general intent and purpose of the negotiable instrument law to protect holders in due course. Commercial paper must be permitted to be freely negotiable without undue risk. . . .

Accordingly, the motion for summary judgment is granted against the individual defendant. . . .

CASE REVIEW QUESTIONS
1. Supposing that Marc Eliot is the treasurer of Impact Marketing, Inc., what form of signature should he have used?
2. If Barry E. Bell, the payee, had sued Marc Eliot, what would Eliot have had to prove to establish that he had no liability to Bell?
3. Why is a holder in due course protected in the situation found in this case?
4. Financial Associates is a holder in due course. Could Eliot have raised the defense of representative capacity against someone who was not a holder in due course?

Unauthorized and Forged Signatures

A **forged signature** is not the signature of the person whose name was forged. An **unauthorized signature** by an agent is not the signature of the principal because the principal did not authorize the agent to sign. Both types of signatures are unauthorized. Generally speaking, a person whose signature is unauthorized is not liable on a negotiable instrument because his or her signature is not on the instrument.

Although the policy of the Code is that a person whose signature is not authorized should not be held liable, the Code also states that if a person's negligence has contributed to the making of an unauthorized signature, that person may not use forgery or lack of authorization as a defense against a holder in due course or a person who pays the instrument in accord with reasonable commercial standards of behavior in the circumstances [§3-406].

For example, if an employer allows the same employee to write checks and to examine the returned checks for forgeries, the employer may be negligent by failing to discover the forgeries if this employee is forging checks. Similarly, a principal is precluded from asserting an agent's lack of authority when some action taken by the principal expressly or tacitly represented to a third party that the agent was authorized to sign an instrument.

An unauthorized signature can be ratified — that is, accepted as authorized — by a person whose signature was forged or by a principal whose agent was not authorized to sign. If a signature is ratified, it becomes the signature of the person ratifying it. The person ratifying the signature is then liable on the instrument.

Any signature operates as the signer's signature with regard to the protection of anyone who takes the instrument in good faith and for value. An unauthorized signer is, therefore, liable on an instrument because his or her signature is on the instrument even though it might not read like the unauthorized signer's usual signature. For example, if Alice, an agent for Peter, who is not authorized to sign an instrument, signs it "Peter", the signature really means "Alice." Alice is liable on the instrument; "Peter" is her signature as far as a person who took the instrument for value or paid it in good faith is concerned. But how do you find Alice? The signature offers no clue. Nevertheless, if you can find Alice, her signature "Peter" is on the instrument and she is liable.

FICTITIOUS PAYEES, IMPOSTERS, AND MATERIAL ALTERATIONS

In addition to forging signatures, there are other schemes that unscrupulous people use to victimize others. In the following sections, we will examine the liability of various persons in schemes involving fictitious payees, imposters, and material alterations.

Fictitious Payees

Employees sometimes embezzle funds by supplying the name or names of fictitious payees to the person who issues a company's checks. A **fictitious payee** is a person whose name is made up or taken from some list, such as a phone book, with no intent that the person named will actually receive any money. The employee takes the check and indorses it in the name of the fictitious payee, collects the money from a bank or other purchaser of the instrument, and then often disappears. The issue, then, is whether the bank or the purchaser may collect the amount of the check from the employee's company or whether the bank or purchaser must suffer the loss.

Based on what you have read up to this point, you would probably think that the bank or purchaser would suffer the loss because the check was not indorsed by the named payee. For example, if a check was made payable to the order of William Shaw, a fictitious payee, a bank did not pay the check to the order of William Shaw because William Shaw did not indorse the check.

The Code, however, has adopted a rule that imposes the loss on the employer rather than on a bank or purchaser when a faithless employee obtains a check naming a fictitious payee. An indorsement by any person in the name of the fictitious payee is deemed to be an effective indorsement [§3-405(1)(b) and (c)]. This makes a faithless employee's indorsement effective against his or her employer. The employer cannot claim that the indorsement was forged.

A check with a fictitious payee will be paid from the employer's account because the policy of the statute is that the loss ought to fall on an employer who hired and should control the faithless employee rather than on an innocent third party. This policy is based on the belief that an employer is in the best position to prevent such losses by exercising care in the selection and supervision of employees and can protect itself by purchasing insurance. An employer, of course, has rights against a faithless employee if he or she can be found and has enough money to reimburse the employer.

An employee's indorsement of a fictitious payee's name is effective as an indorsement, but it is also an unauthorized signature. Thus, the employee becomes a party to the instrument as far as anyone who in good faith pays the instrument or takes it for value is concerned [§3-404(1)]. Because the employee's signature is on the instrument, the employee is liable on the instrument [§3-404(1)].

In the following case, a company was tricked by its employee into drawing checks to a fictitious payee. The company argued that the usual policy of imposing liability on the employer in such cases should not be applied if the purchaser, a bank at which the checks were cashed, was negligent.

HICKS-COSTARINO COMPANY, INC. v. PINTO
233 UCC REP. Serv. 680 (N.Y.S. Ct. 1978)

[Hicks-Costarino Company, Inc., plaintiff, brought a legal action to recover payments that had been made on the company's checks. Plaintiff brought the action against several defendants: Amelia Pinto, who is a former employee of the plaintiff, Fanny De Marco, who conspired with Pinto to carry out a fictitious payee scheme, Citizens Savings and Loan Association (Citizens), which is the former employer of De Marco and the bank at which the checks were cashed, and Manufacturers Hanover Trust Company, which is the drawee bank. The decision concerns a motion by Citizens to dismiss the complaint.]

KUNZEMAN, Judge

Plaintiff alleges . . . that while defendant Amelia Pinto was in its employ she entered into a fraudulent scheme with defendant Fanny De Marco, who was an employee of Citizens Bank. Plaintiff alleges that defendant Pinto fraudulently procured its funds by drawing checks on plaintiff's account at Manufacturers Hanover Trust Company (hereinafter "Manufacturers") to the order of a fictitiously named payee, one J.C. Brancato, and thereafter forging the signatures of plaintiff's officers and cashing them at defendant Citizens bank through the alleged auspices and collusion of the defendant De Marco. It is alleged that these activities took place over a continuous period of two years and that approximately 90 checks were involved in the scheme. Plaintiff further alleges that on Dec. 19, 1975, it discovered fraud had been perpetrated upon it and promptly gave verbal notice to defendant Manufacturers. Plaintiff states that the dollar amount of the checks which were cashed as a part of the scheme amounted to $108,306 and that only $350 of that sum has been returned. Plaintiff contends that Citizens is liable by reason of its negligence in failing to properly supervise Miss De Marco and seeks to recover on this theory.

. . .

The fundamental legal question presented on this motion [to dismiss the complaint] is whether plaintiff is correct in its contention that a collecting bank [i.e., a bank which is not a drawee bank] such as Citizens may be held liable for its alleged negligence in paying a check drawn to a fictitious payee. An examination of the leading authorities indicates that this is not the law. Subdivision 4 of Official Comment [to §3-405(1)] provides:

> Paragraph (c) is new. It extends the rule . . . to include the padded payroll cases, where the drawer's agent or employee prepares the check for signature or otherwise furnishes the signing officer with the name of the payee. The principle followed is that the loss should fall upon the employer as a risk of his business enterprise rather than upon the subsequent holder or drawee. The reasons are that the employer is normally in a better

> position to prevent such forgeries by reasonable care in the selection or supervision of his employee, or, if he is not, is at least in a better position to cover the loss by fidelity insurance; and that the cost of such insurance is properly an expense of his business rather than of the business of the holder or drawee.

> The provision applies only to the agent or employee of the drawer, and only to the agent or employee who supplies him with the name of the payee. The following situations illustrate its application.

> a. An employee of a corporation prepares a padded payroll for its treasurer, which includes the name of P. P does not exist, and the employee knows it, but the treasurer does not. The treasurer draws the corporation's check payable to P. . . .

Accordingly, the rule that is accepted is that a collecting bank may not be held liable for the payment of an instrument drawn on a fictitious payee unless it has exercised "bad faith" in cashing the instrument. In the case at bar, on the admitted facts and after review of the extensive examinations before trial, this court is of the opinion that defendant Citizens did not exercise such "bad faith" sufficient to bar the application of §3-405 of the Code. While it is true that its employee was a participant in this scheme in that she arranged for the cashing of the checks, there had been no proof that plaintiff or plaintiff's [sic; defendant or defendant's] officers exercised "bad faith" or were guilty of gross carelessness. After Citizens was informed of the scheme, it discharged the employee and an examination of the banking practices which were reviewed in the examination before trial does not indicate that Citizens should have made a further inquiry or acted in "bad faith." Finally, it is relevant to point out that not only did plaintiff's employee initiate the scheme, but also on a regular basis plaintiff was receiving statements from Manufacturers Hanover Trust Company, which should have put it on notice of the mammoth fraud which was being perpetrated on it. Under the circumstances, this court is of the opinion, on the facts presented, that the responsibility for this fraud should fall upon the plaintiff. . . .

Accordingly, for the reasons stated above, this motion to dismiss is treated as a motion for summary judgment and, as such, is in all respects granted.

CASE REVIEW QUESTIONS

1. Can a collecting bank ever be held liable for payment of an instrument drawn on a fictitious payee? Explain.
2. What could the plaintiff, Hicks-Costarino Company, Inc., have done to protect itself?
3. Why doesn't the plaintiff just seek recovery against Amelia Pinto?
4. What liability does Amelia Pinto have on the instruments?

Imposters

An **imposter** is a person masquerading as another person. The imposter deceives the person issuing an instrument, who believes that the imposter is the other person.

In this situation, it is not a faithless employee who plays a trick but an outsider who induces a maker or drawer to issue an instrument naming the person the imposter is impersonating. The imposter then indorses the name of the payee and transfers the instrument to a bank or purchaser.

You would expect that an indorsement of a payee's signature by an imposter would be ineffective. Nevertheless, as in the case of a fictitious payee, the Code provides that an indorsement by any person in the name of the payee is effective where an instrument is issued to an imposter [§3-405(1)(a)]. A maker or drawer is therefore liable for payment to a bank or purchaser that takes the instrument.

The policy that imposes liability on a party who has been deceived by an imposter is the same as in the fictitious payee situation. The deceived party is in the best position to prevent the deception from occurring by exercising care in issuing instruments or by insuring against loss.

The imposter rule is only applicable if an instrument was intended to be issued to the person the imposter is impersonating. If an imposter represents that he or she is an agent of the named payee, the rule does not apply and an indorsement by anyone other than the named payee will be ineffective.

As in the fictitious payee situation, an imposter's signature is treated as the signature of the imposter, so that the imposter will be liable on the instrument. Of course, a defrauded maker or drawer will also have other legal rights against an imposter if he or she can be located and has money enough to reimburse the maker or drawer for the fraud.

Material Alteration

An alteration — that is, a change in an instrument — is material if it changes the duty of any party in any respect [§3-407]. For example, if after an instrument is issued, a second payee is added, or if an incomplete instrument is completed in an unauthorized manner or if the amount payable is raised, the change is a **material alteration.**

With several exceptions, if an alteration is both material and fraudulent — that is, made for a dishonest purpose — a party to an instrument whose duty has been affected will be **discharged** — that is, released — from the obligation to pay. However, if a party agrees to the changes made, the party is not discharged [§3-407(2)(a)]. A party may also be precluded from asserting the defense of discharge due to material alteration because of estoppel or negligence [§3-406].

If a material alteration is not fraudulent or a party is precluded from asserting the alteration, the party is not discharged. A party who is not discharged must pay any holder (even a holder who is not a holder in due course) of the altered instrument according to the instrument's original tenor, that is, as the instrument was before it was altered [§3-407(2)(b)]. A party's original obligation cannot be expanded by an alteration, but it also cannot be avoided unless the alteration is both material and fraudulent.

Even if a party is discharged, the defense of discharge due to a material alteration has limited effect upon a holder in due course. A holder in due course like any holder can enforce an altered instrument according to its original tenor. In addition, a holder in due course can enforce an instrument that was incomplete when issued according to the way it was completed even though the completion was unauthorized [§3-407(3)].

Completion of Incomplete Instruments An unauthorized completion of an incomplete instrument is a material alteration. The person who claims that the completion was unauthorized must prove the absence of authorization [§3-115]. If lack of authority cannot be proven, the instrument was, in effect, completed in an authorized manner and can be enforced as completed by any holder.

Even if lack of authority is proven, a holder in due course can enforce an instrument as completed [§3-407(3)]. The policy of the Code is to place the loss on the person who left an instrument incomplete rather than on an innocent holder in due course who has no knowledge that a completion is unauthorized. A holder who is not a holder in due course can enforce an instrument completed in an unauthorized way according to the way it should have been completed if it had been completed as authorized [§3-407(2)(b)].

A person can be a holder in due course even if the holder is aware that an incomplete instrument was completed. The test is whether the holder knew that the completion was unauthorized.

Suppose, for instance, that Alice made the following note on January 1, 1986:

I promise to pay to the order of Bert $100.00, ninety days from today. /s/Alice

The note is incomplete because it is not dated. A date is necessary to establish when payment is to be made. The note is not negotiable because without the date the note is not payable at a definite time (see Chapter 23). Assuming that Alice and Bert have no agreement as to the date to be put on the note, the implied authorized date is January 1, 1986. If any other date is put on the note, there will be a material alteration.

Suppose Bert wants to transfer the note to Carol. Suppose, further, that Carol notices the note is undated and mentions it to Bert, who immediately dates the note December 1, 1985. The note is now negotiable because it is now payable at a definite time. Carol knows that the note was completed but Carol is not on notice that the completion was unauthorized and that Alice may have a defense. Carol has no obligation to inquire into Bert's authority to date the note. Assuming that Carol is acting in good faith and gives value, Carol, as transferee of a negotiable note, is a holder in due course and can enforce the instrument as completed. Carol must be paid 90 days from December 1, 1985.

Suppose, though, that Bert had transferred the note by indorsement and delivery to Dole without dating it. Dole would not be a holder but merely an assignee because the note is not negotiable in that it is not payable at a definite time. Because Dole is not a holder in due course, Alice could refuse to pay Dole at any time other than 90 days from January 1, 1986 [§3-407(2)(b)].

Negligence Contributing to Alterations Whenever the carelessness or negligence of a person substantially contributes to the ability of another to alter an instrument, the defense of alteration is not available against a holder in due course or a holder who has paid the instrument in good faith following the reasonable standards of business governing care in paying instruments [§3-406]. This is the same rule that applies to forged or unauthorized signatures as discussed previously in this chapter.

What constitutes negligence is a question to be decided by looking at the facts of each case. Negligence is usually found where an instrument is issued while incomplete in any necessary respect or where spaces are left that allow for the insertion of numbers or names. For example, if Bert can easily raise the amount of a note drawn by Alice from $100.00 to $1000.00 because Alice left a space after the "$100" and before the ".00," Alice is negligent.

LIABILITY OF THE PARTIES

No person can be liable to pay a negotiable instrument unless his or her signature is on the instrument [§3-401]. The nature of a person's liability will depend upon the capacity in which the person signed the instrument. The Code speaks in terms of the "contract" of each of four types of parties: maker, acceptor, drawer, and indorser. You are already familiar with three of these parties—the maker, the drawer, and the indorser. An acceptor is a drawee who becomes liable on a draft by accepting the draft. The Code defines acceptance as "the drawee's signed engagement to honor the draft as presented" [§3-410(1)]. An acceptor is a drawee who, in effect, is promising to pay (honor) a draft at some point in the future when the draft is again presented to the drawee.

The maker and the acceptor are called primary parties because each has promised to pay simply on being asked [§3-413(1)]. The drawer and the indorser are called secondary parties because, although they have promised to pay, their agreement requires that a holder take certain steps in order to preserve their agreement to pay [§3-413(2) and §3-414(1)]. The nature of each party's contract and the steps necessary to enforce that contract are discussed in the following sections.

Primary Parties

Makers of notes and acceptors of drafts are primary parties to the instruments they sign. A maker or an acceptor promises to pay an instrument according to its tenor (terms) at the time he or she signs the instrument [§3-413(1)]. If an instrument is not complete at the time a maker or an acceptor signs it, the party promises to pay in accordance with the rules governing incomplete instruments discussed previously in this chapter. A primary party's obligation to pay is not affected by a holder's failure to present the instrument for payment at any required time. A primary party is obligated to pay even an overdue instrument.

A maker becomes a primary party by making the note. An acceptor becomes a primary party on a draft only when the draft is presented to a drawee who accepts it. Acceptance occurs when a drawee's signature is placed on a draft and the draft is delivered to the holder or the holder is notified of the acceptance [§3-410(1)].

Certified Checks A certified check is a check that has been accepted by a drawee bank [§3-411(1)]. Unless it has certified a check, a bank has no obligation on a check because its signature is not on the check. Moreover, a bank has no obligation to certify a check [§3-411(2)].

Most checks are not certified and pass through the bank collection process without any party becoming primarily liable. A drawee bank's payment of a check is not acceptance but merely the honoring of the bank's contract with its depositor to pay on demand a check that is properly payable [§4-401(1)]. If a drawee bank refuses to pay an uncertified check, the holder's recourse is to look to the drawer for payment.

If a payee or other holder of a check asks the drawer to get a check certified, the drawer continues to be liable on the instrument. If a payee or other holder gets the check certified, the drawer and any indorsers on the instrument at that time are discharged. The drawer and indorsers are no longer liable because the holder has elected to rely solely on the bank's credit with the bank primarily liable as the acceptor on the instrument [§3-411].

Certified checks are not used as frequently as in the past due to the computerization of the bank collection process. When a bank certifies a check, the bank withdraws the amount of the check from the depositor's account. A certified check with computer encoded account numbers on the bottom would automatically withdraw the amount of the check from the depositor's account a second time if the check passed through the system and was processed by the computers when the check was presented for payment. The encoded numbers must therefore be mutilated when a check is certified. This means that the check has to be processed by hand—a time and labor consuming activity. Since a bank has no obligation to certify a check [§3-411(2)], it will generally issue a cashier's check rather than certify a check that would have to be processed by hand. A cashier's check is an instrument drawn by a bank on itself. As such, it is really a note on which the bank, as maker, is primarily liable. The effect is the same as if the bank has become an acceptor of a drawer's check. A cashier's check can go through a computer system because the bank's, not the depositor's, account numbers are encoded on the check.

Secondary Parties

Drawers of drafts and checks and indorsers of all instruments are the secondary parties. Drawers and indorsers, by signing, promise to pay an instrument, but only if all of the following occur:

1. A holder has made a presentment of the instrument to the maker of the note or the drawee of a draft.
2. The maker or drawee has dishonored—that is, refused to pay—the instrument.
3. The drawer or indorser is given notice of the dishonor.
   [§3-413(2) and §3-414]

Each of these items will be discussed in some detail in the following sections.

An indorser or drawer who writes "without recourse" or similar words after his or her signature is a **qualified drawer or indorser** and is therefore an exception to the rule of secondary liability. A qualified drawer or indorser makes no promise to pay. Nevertheless, a qualified drawer or indorser may be liable for breach of the warranties imposed by the Code, and which are discussed later in this chapter.

Presentment **Presentment** occurs when a demand for acceptance or payment is made upon a maker, acceptor, drawee, or other payor by a holder or by someone on behalf of a holder [§3-504(1)]. It may be made by mail, through the bank collection process, or in person at the place of acceptance or payment if a place is specified in the instrument [§3-504].

Failure to make a timely presentment can result in the discharge of the secondary parties. The time for presentment depends upon the terms of an instrument and whether the instrument is presented for payment or for acceptance. While both notes and drafts can be presented for payment, only drafts can be presented for acceptance. If an instrument shows a specific date for payment, presentment can only be made on that date. The maker or drawee is not obligated to pay before that date, and a refusal to pay before the date specified is not a dishonor. On the other hand, a presentment for acceptance can be made at any time on or before the date specified for payment.

If no date is shown on an instrument or if payment of an instrument has been accelerated, presentment for payment must be made within a reasonable time. What constitutes a reasonable time depends upon the nature of the instrument, banking and trade practices, and the particular facts of the case. In order to preserve the drawer's liability, the Code specifies that a reasonable time to present most checks for payment or to begin the bank collection process is thirty days after the date on a check or the date the check was issued, whichever is later [§3-503(2)(a)]. To preserve an indorser's liability, the presumptive reasonable time period is seven days [§3-503(2)(b)].

The time period for indorsers is shorter because an indorser does not expect to have to pay on the instrument once the instrument has been transferred. Should there be a dishonor, an indorser wants prompt notice so that he or she can seek payment from other parties to the instrument. On the other hand, the drawer who issued a check expects to pay the amount stated from funds held by the drawee bank or from other funds owned by the drawer because of his or her liability due to the contractual agreement that caused the drawer to issue the check in the first place.

A person to whom presentment is made may require certain things. For example, the person may ask to see the instrument and the identification of the person making the presentment. If presentment is made on behalf of a third person, the person to whom presentment is made can ask for evidence of the authority of the presentor to receive the payment. The person presenting an instrument can be required to surrender the instrument if it is paid in full or to make a signed notation of receipt on the instrument of any payment, whether full or partial [§3-505(1)]. If a presenting party does not comply with these requirements within a reasonable time, the presentment is ineffective.

Presentment Excused Presentment may be excused in a variety of circumstances. For example, presentment is not required to preserve the liability of a secondary party if that party has waived the requirement of presentment expressly or by implication. A holder is not required to make presentment if a party has dishonored an instrument or has directed that payment not be made, because the party in question already knows that the instrument will not be honored [§3-511(2)(a)]. The presentment of a check to a drawee bank that has become insolvent would serve no purpose because it would be known in advance that the check would not be paid. In such cases, presentment is entirely excused [§3-511(3)(a)]. Presentment is also excused when it can not be made despite reasonable diligence by the holder [§3-511(2)(c)].

Delay in presentment is excused in situations where a holder does not know that presentment is due or where presentment is delayed due to circumstances beyond the holder's control, provided that the holder acts with reasonable diligence when the cause for the delay is removed. For example, if payment of a promissory note is accelerated by the terms of a note, a holder may not know that the conditions causing the acceleration have occurred and, therefore, may not make timely presentment. Similarly, a holder who is seriously ill may be delayed in making timely presentment [§3-511(1)].

Dishonor An instrument is **dishonored** when payment or acceptance is refused or is not made within the prescribed time period following the proper presentment of the instrument [§3-507(1)(a)]. If presentment is excused, an instrument is dishonored if it is not paid or accepted [§3-507(1)(b)].

The time prescribed for payment and the time prescribed for acceptance are different. Payment must be made before the close of business on the day a proper presentment is made. Acceptance must be made by the close of business on the day following presentment [§3-506(1)]. Dishonor does not occur, however, if the refusal to pay or accept is based on a demand that the holder meet one of the requirements of presentment such as the showing of identification.

Notice of Dishonor If proper presentment has been made or excused and an instrument has been dishonored, **notice of dishonor** must be given to preserve the liability of the secondary parties—the drawers and indorsers.

Notice may be given in any reasonable manner [§3-508(3)]. No special words need be used. A notice is sufficient if it identifies the instrument and declares that it has been dishonored [§3-508(3)]. Because notice of dishonor may have to be proved in court, however, it is best that notice be given in writing or, if given orally, confirmed in writing.

Notice can be given by any party who has received notice of the dishonor to any other party who may be liable on an instrument. A holder can give notice to his or her immediate transferor or to any or all indorsers and to the drawer as well if the instrument is a draft. Notice need not be given to the parties in any special order. Because it is not possible to foresee who will have sufficient resources to pay the instrument, notice of dishonor should be given to everyone who may be liable on an instrument.

Notice is sufficient if a secondary party receives it from any other party. The notice need not be given by the person seeking to enforce a secondary party's liability. For example, suppose Alex draws a check payable to Barbara, who indorses it to Carl, who indorses it to Donna. Suppose that when Donna presents the check for payment, it is dishonored. Donna may choose to give notice only to Carl, hoping that Carl will notify Barbara and Alex. Or Donna can give notice to Carl, Barbara, and Alex, which would be preferable. By giving notice to all the parties, Donna insures the secondary liability of all the parties. Donna's notice to Alex and Barbara also insures Carl's ability to hold these parties secondarily liable even if he fails to give notice himself.

Time for Notice of Dishonor Notice of dishonor is effective only if it is given in a timely manner. Notice must be given by a bank before its **midnight deadline,** that is, before midnight of the banking day following the banking day on which the bank dishonors the instrument or itself receives a notice of a dishonor from another bank or party [§4-104(1)(h)]. All other persons must give notice before midnight of the third business day after dishonor or after receipt of a notice of dishonor [§3-508(2)].

Notice of Dishonor Excused In some situations the giving of notice of dishonor would be a waste of time because it would provide no benefit to the party supposed to benefit from the requirement. For example, if a drawer has told the drawee bank to stop payment on a check, no purpose will be served by a holder giving the drawer notice of dishonor when the bank refuses to pay the check because it was the drawer who caused the dishonor to occur [§3-511(2)(b)].

Protest Sometimes notice of dishonor is given in a **protest,** which is a document that certifies the dishonor and is notarized or certified by certain specified persons [§3-509(1)]. Protest is optional for all negotiable instruments other than those drawn or payable outside the United States. A protest may be desirable, however, because it has certain advantages in a court as evidence that a notice of dishonor was given.

In the following case, the court discussed the process of presentment, dishonor, and notice of dishonor.

LAUREL BANK AND TRUST COMPANY v. SAHADI
345 A.2d 53 (Conn. 1975)

JACOBS, Judge

The major issue at controversy here is whether the defendant [Sahadi] is liable to the plaintiff [Laurel Bank and Trust Co.] for the proceeds of a check which was deposited by the defendant and was later dishonored. . . . [T]he court must hold that the plaintiff is entitled to recover the amount of $3950 plus interest. . . .

The court finds the following facts: On January 9, 1973, the defendant, as payee, endorsed a check from Corrine Harper. The amount of the check was $3,950, and it was drawn on the Valley Bank and Trust Company of Springfield, Massachusetts. The defendant presented this check to the plaintiff to be credited to his business checking account. The defendant deposited $3,050 of this amount and received $900 in cash. The check was dishonored by the Valley Bank and Trust Company, and the plaintiff was apprised of that situation. . . . The defendant's account was nevertheless credited with the deposited amount of $3,050, and the defendant withdrew those funds, among others in a series of transactions which culminated in his closing the account in March 1973. The defendant has never reimbursed the plaintiff for the $900 in cash taken on January 9, 1973, or for the $3,050 credited to his account on Janaury 9, 1973, and withdrawn at a later date. The plaintiff bank did not deduct any amount from the defendant's account at any time to reimburse itself for its losses.

The defendant . . . alleges that the plaintiff neglected to prove that proper notice of dishonor was given in a timely fashion, as required by the "midnight deadline" rule of [§3-508(2)] and as defined in [§4-104(1)(h)]. . . .

[W]as the defendant given proper notice that the check had been dishonored? . . . For our purposes, the "presentment" occurred when the plaintiff presented the check in question to the Valley Bank and Trust Company for acceptance and payment [§3-505(4)]. The Valley Bank and Trust Company refused to honor the check. In offering the check for presentment, the plaintiff was simply acting in the course of business. . . . But simply offering the check for presentment was not the full extent of the plaintiff's duty. After learning of the dishonor of the instrument, the plaintiff had the positive duty of notifying the defendant by midnight of the next full business day [§3-508]. . . .

The trial contains the following examination of Connell [bank manager] by the plaintiff's attorney.

Q. Mr. Connell, when you received notice of this check being returned uncollectible, did you make any attempts to reach Mr. Sahadi?

A. Yes, I did.

Q. And do you recall when you tried to reach him?

A. Yes, I [did]. It was the day that the check came back or the following day. I don't remember exactly what the date was.

Q. Okay, and how did you try to reach him; in what manner?

A. I called him on the phone.

Q. Did you speak with him?

A. Yes, I did.

Q. Could you relate to the court what you said to Mr. Sahadi?

A. I told him that the check he had negotiated at the bank had been returned to us from the Springfield Bank because the account had been closed.

The defendant did not offer any testimony concerning the notice or lack thereof, so on the basis of the testimony the court must hold that the notice of dishonor was given and that it was timely. Further, the oral method of notification adheres to the requirements of [§3-508(3)]. . . .

Let us now briefly analyze the legal basis for the plaintiff's claim, to see if the plaintiff has met its burden of proof.

It is well settled that "[n]o person is liable on an instrument unless his signature appears thereon" [§3-401(1)]. "Unless the instrument clearly indicates that a signature is made in some other capacity it is an indorsement" [§3-402]. The defendant signed the check in question, and this appears to satisfy the requirements of indorsement [§3-414(1)]. [Section 3-122(3)] provides: "A cause of action against a drawer of a draft or an indorser of any instrument accrues upon demand following dishonor of the instrument. Notice of dishonor is a demand."

Although the web of code provisions is woven loosely, the plaintiff in this case has assumed and proved its burden. First, the plaintiff alleged that it was the holder of the note. . . . The substance of this transaction is clear. The defendant attempted and is attempting to enrich himself at the expense of the plaintiff bank. The plaintiff satisfied the requirements of presentment, notice and demand following the dishonor [§§3-501(1)–(3)]. The defendant did nothing, although it is clear from the statutes that it was never intended that the bank should suffer loss in such a case. To hold otherwise cannot be supported.

The plaintiff has been deprived of $3,950 by the actions of the defendant. At the time of the dishonor, the plaintiff had the right of "charge-back" [i.e., the right to withdraw from Sahadi's account the amount previously credited]. The bank had the option of the charge back, but it was evident from the fluctuations of the account that there was not enough to cover the dishonored check. The bank instead chose to proceed on the obligation of the defendant to reimburse it. . . .

Judgment may enter accordingly.

CASE REVIEW QUESTIONS

1. Is Sahadi primarily or secondarily liable?
2. What steps must the bank take in order to preserve Sahadi's liability on his indorsement contract?
3. What is Sahadi obligated to do by virtue of his indorsement contract?
4. How did Laurel Bank give notice of dishonor? What better way of giving notice might the bank have used? Explain.

Effect of Omitted or Late Presentment or Notice of Dishonor The liability of secondary parties is conditional on timely and effective presentment, dishonor, and notice of dishonor. If presentment is not made or notice is not given, or if either are delayed without being excused, the secondary liability of an indorser is discharged [§3-502(1)(a)].

A drawer, however, is treated differently, more like a primary party, if the requirements for presentment and notice are not met. If presentment or notice of dishonor is excused, the drawer is not discharged. If presentment or notice is not excused, a drawer's liability can be discharged by a failure or delay in meeting these requirements only when a draft is payable at a bank and that bank becomes insolvent after the time for presentment is due. The drawer is discharged because the bank's insolvency deprives him or her of the funds in his or her account that he or she relied upon to pay the instrument [§3-502(1)(b)]. However, the drawer is discharged only if he or she assigns any right of recovery he or she may have against the insolvent bank for the amount due on the instrument to the holder of the instrument.

The reason for the distinction between indorsers and drawers is that they are related to an instrument in different ways. Generally, an indorser pays for an instrument upon receiving it. The indorser then receives payment in return when the instrument is negotiated to another person. Discharge due to late presentment or notice of dishonor does not result in any unexpected benefit to the indorser because the indorser has both given and received payment. If the drawer is discharged because of late presentment or notice of dishonor, the drawer will not pay for the instrument, even though he or she usually received payment when issuing it.

The difference between a drawer and an indorser can be seen in the following example. Suppose Allen draws a $100 check on Zenith Bank payable to Brown. Brown gives Allen goods worth $100. Brown indorses and delivers the check to Collins, who pays Brown $100. Collins makes a late presentment of the check for payment to Zenith, and the check is dishonored. Brown, an indorser, is discharged by the late presentment. Note that Brown gave $100 to Allen and received $100 from Collins. On the other hand, if Allen is discharged, he will come out $100 ahead because he received $100 from Brown but never had to honor the check on which he expected to pay $100 either out of his bank account or out of his pocket. Therefore, Allen, as the drawer, will be discharged only if the funds he had on deposit in the Zenith Bank have been lost because of the bank's becoming insolvent during the delay in presentment. If the bank is insolvent, Allen must assign his rights against Zenith to Collins in order to obtain a discharge [§3-502(1)(b)].

Order of Liability

If it is unclear in what capacity a person signed an instrument, a signature is presumed to be an indorsement [§3-402]. If more than one indorsement appears on an instrument, the indorsers are liable to each other in the order in which their signatures appear on the instrument [§3-414(2)].

Suppose, for example, that Alex makes a note payable to the order of Barbara. Barbara signs it and delivers it to Carl. Carl signs it below Barbara's name

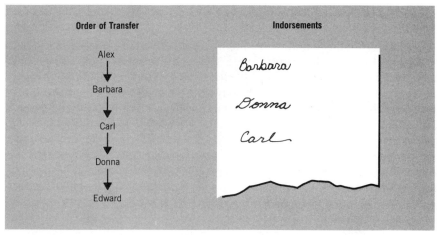

FIGURE 27-1
Order of Liability

and delivers it to Donna. Donna signs it above Carl's name and delivers it to Edward. (See Figure 27-1.) Alex does not pay the note. Barbara, Carl, and Donna are all indorsers. Barbara is liable to Carl, Donna, and Edward. Donna is liable to Carl and Edward unless she can prove that she signed at a later time than Carl, in which case she would be liable only to Edward.

Accommodation Party

An **accommodation party** is a person who signs in any capacity for the purpose of lending his or her name and credit to another party on an instrument. An accommodation party has no direct interest in the transaction. Nevertheless, an accommodation party is liable in the capacity in which he or she signed an instrument. For example, if Alex is visiting a friend away from his home town and finds himself short of cash, his friend Barbara can do him a favor by indorsing a check naming Alex as the payee after Alex has indorsed it and by cashing the check at a bank where she has an account. Even though the indorsement is made only as a favor, Barbara as well as Alex is liable as an indorser to subsequent holders.

An accommodation party may also sign an instrument as a maker, a drawer, or an acceptor. Suppose Carl wants to borrow some money. If the creditor is unsure of Carl's ability to repay, Carl may ask Doris, who has a better credit rating, to be a cosigner, that is, a comaker of the note. As between an accommodation party and a person accommodated, an accommodation can be established even by oral proof. The accommodation party can recover any sums that he or she has to pay on the instrument from the person accommodated. For example, if the comaker, Denise, pays the note upon Carl's default, Denise can prove the accommodation and recover from Carl.

DISCHARGE

A party's liability on an instrument, whether primary or secondary, continues until that liability is discharged, that is, until that party is released from any further obligation to pay. It is the liability of the party, not the instrument, that is discharged. Different parties may be discharged at different times, and a party may be discharged from liability to one or more persons but still remain liable to others.

Discharge is a defense against the obligation to pay an instrument — "I won't pay because I was discharged." The defense has limited effect against a holder in due course, however, because it is a personal defense. The defense is available against a holder in due course in the case of a discharge in an insolvency proceeding or in the case of a discharge of which the holder has notice when he or she takes the instrument, as may occur when the instrument has been partially paid [§3-305 and §3-602]. (See Chapter 26.)

You are already familiar with some of the situations that result in the discharge of a party. If a holder of a check has it certified, the drawer and any indorsers on the check at that time are discharged [§3-601(1)(g)]. Unexcused failure or delay in presentment or in giving notice of dishonor will discharge indorsers and may, in the case of bank insolvency, also discharge drawers, makers, and acceptors [§3-601(1)(i) and §3-502]. An alteration of an instrument that is both material and fraudulent will discharge any party whose contract is affected by the alteration, unless the party is prevented from claiming the discharge because of agreement, estoppel, or negligence [§3-601(1)(f) and §3-407]. The following sections will explain and discuss other ways in which discharge may occur under the provisions of the Code.

Payment and Tender of Payment

The simplest and most common form of discharge is payment [§3-601(1)(a) and §3-603]. If a maker or a drawee honors an instrument by paying the full amount due, all parties are discharged. If partial payment is made on an instrument, all parties are discharged to the extent of the payment [§3-603]. Whenever full payment is made, the person paying should demand the instrument and destroy it. Whenever partial payment is made, the person paying should require that the amount of the payment be written on the instrument. If an instrument is not canceled or a payment is not noted, a subsequent holder in due course will take the instrument free from the defense of discharge because he or she has had no notice of the payment.

If a party makes a **tender** (offer) of full payment on or after the date the instrument is due and the holder refuses to accept the payment, the party tendering payment continues to be liable, but he or she has no liability for any interest that accrues after the tender [§3-601(1)(b) and §3-604]. If a holder refuses payment, all parties except the party tendering payment are discharged.

Reacquisition of an Instrument

When a person who was a party to an instrument reacquires the instrument, any intervening parties are discharged and have no liability to the reacquiring party or to any subsequent holder who is not a holder in due course [§3-601(1)(e) and §3-208]. For example, a note made by Alex is negotiated to Barbara, Carl, and Donna, each of whom indorses it. If Donna negotiates the note back to Barbara, Carl and Donna are discharged with respect to Barbara and to any subsequent holders who are not holders in due course. Thus, if Barbara negotiates the note to Edward, who does not give value and therefore is not a holder in due course, Edward can look to Barbara but not to Carl or Donna for payment. If Edward negotiates the note to Frances, who is a holder in due course, Carl and Donna are liable to Frances.

Cancellation or Renunciation

The Code allows a holder to strike out any indorsements [§3-601(1)(c) and §3-605] (see also §3-208). The cancellation of a person's signature discharges that person because that person's signature is, in effect, no longer on the instrument [§3-605 and §3-401]. A canceled signature is notice to all subsequent holders that the party has been discharged. If, in the previous example, Barbara crosses out Carl's and Donna's signatures on reacquiring the note, Carl and Donna are discharged with regard to all subsequent holders. Neither Edward nor Frances could recover from them.

A holder may cancel an entire instrument by destroying it. This discharges all the parties to the instrument. A holder may also give up his or her right to enforce an instrument against a particular party or parties by delivering a **renunciation,** which is a signed writing that gives up the holder's interest, or by delivering the instrument itself to the party or parties to be discharged [§3-605(1)(b)]. A cancellation or renunciation is enforceable even if the party canceling or renouncing does not receive any consideration for the cancellation or renunciation [§3-605(1)].

Impairment of Recourse or Collateral

If a holder, by discharging one party, impairs another party's right of **recourse**—that is, the right to seek recovery—from the discharged party, the party whose right is impaired is also discharged [§3-601(1)(d) and §3-606]. In the previous example, if Edward cancels Carl's signature, Donna will also be discharged because Edward has impaired Donna's right to collect from Carl by removing Carl's signature from the instrument. Donna will not be discharged with respect to a subsequent holder in due course because that holder would have no notice that Donna is discharged since it could have been Donna who struck out Carl's signature.

A similar rule applies if a holder surrenders or returns **collateral,** which is property given by a party as security to guarantee payment. Any party who could have benefited from the collateral will be discharged, unless that party consented to the surrender of the collateral [§3-606(1)(b)].

In the following case, the holder of a note allowed the maker to sell the collateral—a motorcycle. The holder never received the money from the sale and demanded payment from the accommodation comaker of the note. The comaker defended on the ground that he was discharged because he had not consented to the sale of the collateral and could no longer pursue any rights he had in the motorcycle.

BENEFICIAL FINANCE COMPANY OF NORMAN v. MARSHALL
47 Okla. Bar Assn. J. 451 (Okla. Ct. of Appeals 1976)

BOX, [Judge]

An appeal by Beneficial Finance Company, plaintiff in the trial court, from judgment entered in favor of the defendant below, Alva D. Garren [an accommodation maker of a note signed by the Marshalls who are also defendants in this case], in an action to recover on a note.

The payee on a note brought an action against an accommodation maker [Garren] to recover the unpaid balance. The trial court held that the accommodation maker had been discharged under [§3-606] . . . and the payee appealed. The question is whether a non-consenting accommodation party is discharged under [§3-606(1)(b)] when the collateral is sold by the principal debtor with the express authority of the secured creditor.

Some time in the latter part of May 1974, Mr. and Mrs. Marshall contacted appellant Beneficial Finance Company of Norman (Beneficial) for the purpose of borrowing some money and were directed to Mr. Puckett, the office manager. After conferring with them for a few moments, Puckett reached the conclusion that the Marshalls were a bad credit risk. . . .

Shortly thereafter the Marshalls met with Garren, discussed their financial plight with him and asked him to co-sign. Garren agreed to do so and arranged a meeting with Puckett on May 29, 1974. At this meeting, Puckett told Garren that the Marshalls were a bad credit risk and advised Garren not to co-sign. Puckett's admonition did not dissuade Garren from signing a note but it did cause him to become concerned about having security for the obligation. Consequently he requested that Beneficial take a security interest in Mr. Marshall's custom built Harley Davidson motorcycle, then worth over a thousand dollars. Puckett acceded to this request and prepared a security agreement and accompanying papers for the Marshall's signature. Puckett then approved a loan in the total amount of $480.00, and a note was executed by all parties. Beneficial subsequently perfected a security interest in the motorcycle. . . .

The controversy leading to this action began shortly after execution of the note. A week before the first monthly installment was due Garren began to suspect that default was imminent. . . . It is clear . . . that Garren demanded that Beneficial do something to protect the collateral and that Beneficial refused because the Marshalls were not then in default.

Beneficial took no action until the Marshalls had defaulted on the first payment. Afterwards, on or about July 24, 1974, it notified Garren of the default and advised him that it was looking to him for complete payment. The crucial events of this case began unfolding in rapid succession thereafer. Upon learning of the default Garren sought out Mr. Marshall and demanded that he go to the Beneficial office and straighten the matter out. . . . Shortly thereafter Garren received a telephone call from a Beneficial employee and was told that Mr. Marshall was going to sell the motorcycle so that he could pay off the loan. . . .

The total purchase price was about $700. Marshall was to receive $345 from [the buyer] immediately and promised to apply this amount to the balance due and pay the remainder from his own pocket. The motorcycle sold that day. . . .

Puckett never received the proceeds [from the sale] and the record does not indicate what happened to it. Mr. Marshall left town and has not been seen since then.

Because it was unable to obtain the proceeds of the sale, Beneficial brought suit against Garren. . . . Garren's principal defense was that he signed the note as an accommodation party and was therefore entitled to invoke the suretyship defense of discharge under [§3-606(1)(b)] because the collateral for the loan had been impaired. The trial court agreed and granted judgment in favor of Garren.

Beneficial concedes Garren's status as an accommodation maker. Its sole contention is that notwithstanding his surety status, Garren is "absolutely liable" to Beneficial since he is a co-maker.

An accommodation party is liable "in the capacity in which he has signed" [§3-415]. Since Garren executed the note as a maker he was, as Beneficial urges, jointly and severally liable on the note as a co-maker [§3-118(e) and (f)]. This is settled law, . . . but it does not resolve the instant controversy. An accommodation party possesses certain defenses not ordinarily available to the maker or indorser, which can be asserted against all but holders in due course without notice of his accommodation status. The most important of these defenses are found in §3-606. Under §3-606(1)(b) the accommodation party is discharged when, without his consent, the holder "unjustifiably impairs any collateral for the instrument." The major question in this appeal is whether Garren was discharged under this section when the collateral for the loan was sold by the principal debtor with the express authority of the creditor. In order to resolve this question it is first necessary to consider the meaning of "impairment of collateral" as used in §3-606.

Section 3-606 does little to aid this inquiry because it does not define "impairment of collateral." . . .

[The Court quoted and discussed Official Code Comment 5, which discusses when an action is unjustifiable.]

We think that Comment 5 can most properly be considered as an effort by the draftsman to explain that the term "unjustifiable" as used in §3-606(1)(b) means that the holder's conduct in regard to the collateral is measured by a standard of reasonable care— whether he is or is not in possession of the collateral. In our opinion such an interpretation comports with the reality of modern commercial practice; a secured party can obviously act in many ways which impair collateral not in his possession, and which result in an increase in the surety's risk. Moreover, there is no reason to assume, without express language to that effect, that either the legislature or the Code draftsman intended that §3-606 impairment defense be unavailable to the surety in such instances. We conclude therefore that the impairment of collateral defense of §3-606 reaches conduct by a secured party which unjustifiably impairs collateral not in his possession or control.

We turn to the question of whether Beneficial impaired the collateral by authorizing its sale by the principal debtor. In order to determine this question it is necessary to consider legal consequences of the sale with respect to the surety Garren.

As we noted earlier, Beneficial had a security interest in the collateral security (the motorcycle) which had been perfected by filing. Beneficial subsequently gave Marshall, the principal debtor, the express authority to sell the collateral so that it could recover the unpaid balance due on the note. By so doing Beneficial completely relinquished the security interest in the collateral. This is necessarily so because under §9-306(2) when the debtor sells collateral pursuant to the authority of the creditor, the security interest is immediately cut off. . . . Obviously when the creditor has lost his security interest in the collateral the surety has also lost his right of recovery against the collateral—a right which more often than not prompted him to enter into the agreement in the first place.

The net result of the loss of security in this manner is that the surety's risk is greatly increased, and the law has traditionally held that conduct by the creditor which increases the surety's risk results in a discharge of the surety.

But would the creditor's consent to the sale of collateral not in his possession discharge the surety under the Uniform Commercial Code? . . .

The one unifying conclusion that can be drawn from [several cases discussed by the court], in our opinion, is that §3-606(1)(b) will be interpreted broadly to include, in addition to conduct by the creditor which diminishes the value of the collateral, unreasonable acts which make the collateral unavailable to the surety and thus increase his risks. This view seems to be in accord with both the common law of suretyship and the expectations of the parties to a suretyship agreement.

In the instant case the secured creditor (Beneficial) could hardly have made the collateral more unavailable to Garren, the surety. Accordingly, we hold that the sale of the collateral without Garren's express consent constituted an unjustifiable impairment of collateral within the meaning of §3-606, and that because the value of the collateral exceeded the value of the debt, Garren was totally discharged.

Affirmed.

CASE REVIEW QUESTIONS
1. Why is Garren an accommodation maker?
2. What are Garren's rights in the collateral and how were these rights impaired?
3. Why was Garren discharged by the sale of the motorcycle? Explain.
4. What liability do the Marshalls have on the instrument? Were they discharged by the sale of the collateral?

WARRANTIES

The Code imposes warranties in addition to the liabilities imposed by the contract made by each of the parties who sign an instrument. A **warranty** is a promise that certain facts, as stated or as imposed by the law, are true. Persons who transfer an instrument and receive consideration and persons who obtain payment or acceptance make warranties even if they do not sign the instrument [§3-417]. The warranties imposed when an instrument is transferred are different from those imposed when an instrument is presented for payment or acceptance.

Transfer Warranties

A transferor of an instrument who receives consideration warrants to his or her immediate transferee and, if the transferor indorses the instrument, to any subsequent holder who takes the instrument in good faith that:

1. The transferor has good title to the instrument or is authorized to act by one who has good title.
2. All signatures are genuine or authorized.
3. The instrument has not been materially altered.
4. No party on the instrument has a defense that can be successfully asserted against the transferor.
5. The transferor does not know of any insolvency proceedings against the maker, the acceptor, or the drawer of an unaccepted instrument.
   [§3-417(2)]

The warranty of good title in point 1 would be breached, for example, if the transferor of a bearer instrument had merely found the instrument. The warranties in both point 1 and point 2 would be breached if a necessary indorsement had been forged. If the transferor is not a holder in due course, all defenses could be asserted against the transferor and the warranty in point 4 would be breached if any defense exists. Even a transferor who is a holder in due course does not escape all warranty liability under point 4 because there may be a real defense that can be asserted against a holder in due course. The warranty in point 5 is breached only if the transferor knows of an insolvency proceeding. There may be an insolvency proceeding, but there is no breach if the transferor does not know about it.

If a party obligated to pay an instrument is discharged due to a material alteration, the warranty in point 3 has been breached. A holder can then recover from his or her transferor or from a prior indorser. You will recall that even a holder in due course can only enforce an altered instrument according to its original tenor. For example, if a note has been raised from $100 to $1,000, the maker would only be obligated to pay $100. The holder of the instrument could, however, recover the other $900 from his or her transferor based upon a claim for breach of warranty because there was a material alteration.

Importance of Transfer Warranties The warranty liability imposed on transferors is an important part of the law governing negotiable instruments. First, warranty liability expands the contract liability of persons who are parties to an instrument. Second, warranties also impose liability on a transferor who does not become a party to an instrument, as in the case of a person who transfers an instrument without making an indorsement or the case of a qualified indorser who disclaims liability as an indorser by indorsing "without recourse." Third, a person can take advantage of the transfer warranties even if a presentment or a notice of dishonor has been omitted or delayed. Finally, a person need not be a holder in due course in order to claim the benefit of the transfer warranties.

Although a qualified indorser has made no promise to honor an instrument, a qualified indorser who receives consideration upon transferring the instrument is not free of the warranties. All of the transfer warranties are made by a qualified indorser except that, under point 4, the qualified indorser merely warrants that he or she has no knowledge of any defense good against him or her. If there is a defense good against the qualified indorser, the warranty is breached only if he or she actually knew about the defense [§3-417(3)]. A person who receives consideration for the transfer of an instrument but makes no indorsement (qaulified or otherwise) makes all of the transfer warranties without any qualifications but only to the immediate transferee.

Presentment Warranties

A somewhat different set of warranties is made to a person who pays or accepts an instrument in good faith. A person who presents an instrument for payment or acceptance and all prior transferors warrants that:

1. The person presenting the instrument or the person for whom he or she is authorized to obtain payment has good title to the instrument.
2. The person presenting the instrument has no knowledge that the signature of the maker or drawer is unauthorized.
3. The instrument has not been materially altered.
   [§3-417(1)]

A holder in due course acting in good faith does not make the second and third warranties when payment is obtained from the maker or drawer of an instrument because it is expected that the maker or drawer can determine whether his or her signature is authorized or whether the instrument has been altered.

For similar reasons, the second warranty is not made by a holder in due course to an acceptor of a draft when the draft is presented for payment if the holder in due course took the draft after the acceptor became obligated on the instrument. No warranty that a drawer's signature is authorized is made by a holder in due course when he or she obtains acceptance of an instrument unless the holder knows that the signature is unauthorized [§3-417(1)(b)(iii)]. A drawee is supposed to know the drawer's signature.

A holder in due course makes no warranty that an instrument has not been materially altered to an acceptor of a draft if the alteration was made before acceptance and the holder in due course became a holder after the acceptance or if the alteration was made after acceptance [§3-417(1)(c)]. An acceptor is expected to know the nature and terms of the instrument that was accepted.

Finality of Payment Unless there has been a breach of one of the presentment warranties, any payment or acceptance of an instrument is final when it was made to a holder in due course or to any person who received payment and in good faith took steps that would cause loss if the payment had to be returned [§3-418]. For example, if after paying a check a drawee bank discovers that there were insufficient funds in the drawer's account to pay the check, the bank cannot recover the payment if the payment was made to a holder in due course or to a person who acted in good faith in reliance on the payment. Similarly, if the bank later discovers that the drawer's signature is forged, payment cannot be recovered unless the person who obtained the payment knew it was forged. Knowledge of the forgery would be a breach of the second presentment warranty. The policy behind this rule is that it is generally better to end a transaction when payment occurs than to reopen a whole series of transactions related to an instrument.

Liabilities Exemplified

Up to this point, we have discussed warranty liability separately from the other liabilities of the parties to an instrument. The interplay among the various liabilities of the parties and the warranty liabilities can sometimes be difficult to sort out. To help you understand these concepts, we will provide several examples involving a cast of characters who, for ease of identification, have been drawn from the rainbow.

Read the examples slowly and carefully. Charts have been provided to assist you in tracing the transactions involved. These examples are limited; other examples could be constructed using different indorsements or focusing on other warranties.

Yellow Butler owns and operates The Green Cotton Company. Green employs a number of farm hands. Yellow has a habit of gambling with his employees, which is illegal in his state. When the employees lose, they pay Yellow with promissory notes. Yellow also sells tools to his employees. Frequently, though, Yellow does not deliver the tools even though the employees have paid for them by signing negotiable notes. Red Smith, White Socks, and Blue Jones worked one summer for Yellow.

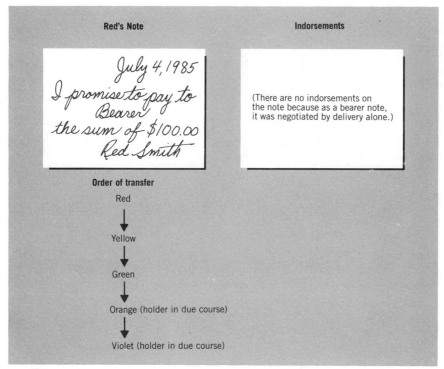

FIGURE 27-2
Red's Note

Red's Note Red Smith signed a bearer note to pay for gambling debts (see Figure 27-2). Yellow transferred the note to Green. Green negotiated the note to Orange Blossom, Inc., which paid full value. Orange, in turn, negotiated the note to the Violet National Bank, which paid full value. When Violet sought payment from Red, he refused to pay.

The bearer note was negotiated by delivery alone to Green, Orange, and Violet. Orange and Violet are both holders in due course. Green is not a holder in due course because it is too closely connected with Yellow to have taken the note in good faith and without notice of any defenses. Red's defense is a real defense and is good against the Violet Bank even though the bank is a holder in due course.

Red is the only person whose signature is on the instrument, but Red is not liable on his contract as maker because of the real defense that the note was given for a gambling debt. Red will not have to pay Violet.

From whom can Violet obtain payment? Orange is not liable as a party to the instrument because Orange did not indorse the note. But Violet can recover from Orange for breach of warranty. The warranty that there are no defenses that are good against the transferor has been breached by Orange because, even though Orange is a holder in due course, Red's defense is real.

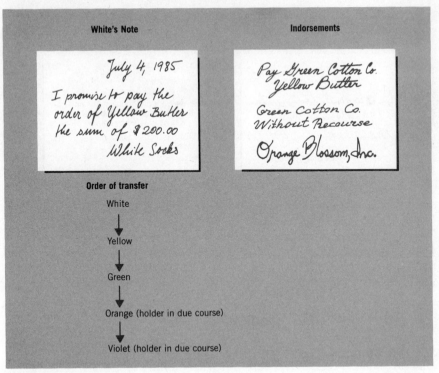

FIGURE 27-3
White's Note

Violet cannot recover from Green or Yellow because neither indorsed the note. Their signatures are not on the note, so they have no liability as parties to the instrument. Because they did not indorse, their warranties do not extend to Violet but only to their immediate transferees. Orange, however, can recover from Green because Green warranted to Orange simply by making the transfer and receiving value. Green, in turn, can recover from Yellow as its immediate transferor if Green gave Yellow consideration for the transfer.

White's Note Compare what happened with Red's bearer note to what happens with a note made by White Socks payable to the order of Yellow as payment of a gambling debt. White's note is negotiated to the same parties as Red's note (see Figure 27-3). In order to negotiate this note to Green, Yellow must indorse and deliver it. Yellow indorsed the note "Pay Green Cotton Company, Yellow Butler." Green transferred the note to Orange by indorsing, "Green Cotton Company/Without Recourse." Because Green's indorsement was a blank indorsement, no indorsement was required for Orange to negotiate the note. Nevertheless, Orange indorsed the note, "Orange Blossom, Inc.," when it negotiated the note to Violet. Green, Orange, and Violet each gave value for the note. White refuses to pay Violet.

From whom can Violet obtain payment? White, like Red, has a real defense

—the note is an illegal gambling contract—and is therefore not liable as a maker.

There are indorsements on this note, however. When the note is dishonored, Violet must give notice to any indorser it wishes to hold to an indorsement contract. If Violet gives proper notice to all indorsers, Violet can recover on an indorsement contract from Orange and Yellow but not from Green. Green, by its qualified indorsement, did not incur liability as an indorser.

Violet can, however, recover from Green for breach of warranty. Green warranted to Violet because Green indorsed the instrument and received value for the transfer to Orange. The warranty was breached because Green warranted that it did not know of any defense good against it, but it did know that Yellow took the note as payment of a gambling debt.

Violet could also recover from Orange for breach of warranty. By transferring the note and receiving consideration, Orange warranted to Violet that no defense was good against it. However, White's defense is good against Orange even though Orange is a holder in due course.

Violet can recover from Yellow if Yellow warranted to Violet. Yellow indorsed, but Yellow would only warrant if he received consideration from Green. If Yellow warranted, he breached a warranty because White has a defense good against him.

Blue's Note Compare what happened to Red's and White's notes, for which there were real defenses, with what happens to Blue's note. Blue signed a note payable to the order of Yellow to pay for tools. Blue never received the tools even though Yellow had Green deduct the amount due from Blue's salary. Blue's defenses are personal—failure of consideration and discharge by payment.

Blue's note was negotiated to the same parties as Red's and White's notes (see Figure 27-4). Yellow indorsed the note, "Yellow Butler/Without Recourse," and delivered it to Green. Because the note was indorsed in blank, Green negotiated it to Orange by delivery alone. Orange delivered it to Violet and indorsed it, "Orange Blossom, Inc." Both Orange and Violet gave value for the note. Blue refuses to pay Violet.

From whom can Violet collect? Blue, whose defenses are only personal, must pay Violet, who is a holder in due course. If Violet is unable to collect from Blue for some reason, such as Blue has no money, there are other persons from whom Violet can collect.

Violet can collect from Orange on its indorsement contract if Violet gives Orange a proper notice of dishonor. Violet will not be able to recover from Orange for breach of warranty because there was no breach. Orange warranted that there was no defense good against it, and Orange as a holder in due course has not breached this warranty because Blue's defenses are personal.

Violet cannot recover from Green. Green has no indorsement contract because Green's signature is not on the instrument. Violet cannot recover from Green for breach of warranty because Green only warranted to Orange as its immediate transferee. Orange, however, could recover from Green, its immedi-

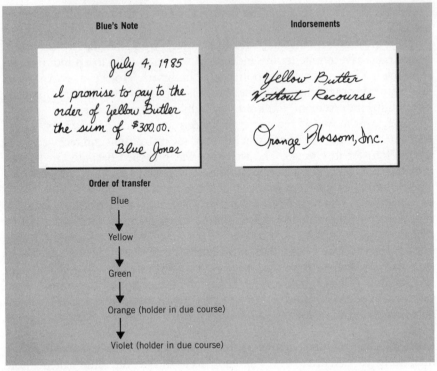

FIGURE 27-4
Blue's Note

ate transferor, for breach of warranty. Green is not a holder in due course because it knows of Blue's defenses, which are good against Green. Green has breached its warranty to Orange that no defense is good against it.

Violet can recover from Yellow but not on an indorsement contract because Yellow's indorsement is without recourse. Violet can recover from Yellow for breach of warranty because Yellow warranted that he know of no defense good against him when he knew that Blue has two defenses good against him—failure of consideration and discharge. Yellow warranted to Violet because he indorsed the note and received payment from Green.

REVIEW QUESTIONS

1. Describe two ways in which an agent who wants to avoid personal liability can sign a negotiable instrument on behalf of his or her principal? Explain.
2. Can a person whose signature is forged be liable on an instrument? Explain.
3. What is the policy reason for imposing liability on a maker or drawer who issues an instrument to an imposter?
4. What liability does a maker or a drawer have to the holder of an instrument that was issued while incomplete and was later completed in an unauthorized manner? Explain.
5. What is a certified check?
6. Describe the steps that a holder must take to enforce an instrument against an indorser?
7. Describe eight ways in which a party may be discharged on an instrument?

CASE PROBLEMS

1. Anita Willis indorsed a check as follows:

   /s/Anita Willis
   /s/Anita Willis, Inc.

   A subsequent holder of the check sued Anita Willis and Anita Willis, Inc. Anita Willis moved to dismiss the case against her personally because she had no personal liability on the instrument. Does she have personal liability? Explain.

2. The following note was issued to Rotuba Extruders, Inc. The underlined portions of the note were handwritten.

   $3,000.00   *February 11, 1976*
   May 25, 1976 after date *we* promise to pay to the order of *Rotuba Extruders, Inc. The Sum of $3,000 dols 00 cents*   Dollars at *Chemical Bank-Randall & Faile Sts., Bronx* Value Received No interest
                                        Kenbert Lighting, Inc.
   No. _____   Due *5/25/76*
                                        Kenneth Ceppos

   Rotuba Extruders, Inc., sued Kenneth Ceppos to enforce the note after Kenbert Lighting, Inc., a corporation of which Kenneth Ceppos was the chief executive officer, went into voluntary bankruptcy. Ceppos argued that he had no liability to Rotuba because he had not signed the note in a personal capacity, which Rotuba, the payee, as an immediate party should know. The only proof is Ceppos statement that he did not intend to sign in an individual capacity. Who will win the case? Explain.

3. An employee of Danje Fabrics submitted valid invoices from suppliers to Danje's bookkeeper, who prepared the checks. The employee then took the checks, forged the indorsements, and collected the funds for his own purposes. Danje's sought to recover the funds from the drawee bank, arguing that the indorsement signatures were not effective. Is Danje entitled to recover the funds? Explain.

4. Nora Ray, an elderly lady living alone, was visited by a gentleman, Robert Freeman, who said he was from the electric utility company. After examining her home, he told her she needed some electrical work done and that he would return after lunch to

do it. He also told her that there was a service fee of $1.50. Freeman offered to assist Ray in writing the check. He wrote the numbers "1.50" well to the right of the dollar sign. The amount in words was not written in. Ray testified that she signed the check because the amount was written in ink and couldn't be changed and she wanted Freeman out of the house. Freeman took the check, added "185" between the dollar sign and the "1.50" already written, and wrote in the words, "Eighteen hundred fifty one and 50/100." Freeman took the check to the drawee bank and cashed it. Ray sued the bank to recover $1,850. Must the bank repay Ray? Explain.

5. E.J. Drywall Company, Inc., as a maker executed a negotiable promissory note payable to the Community National Bank. The note contained an explicit waiver of the need for presentment and notice of dishonor. At the bank's request, Bernard K. Dawes, a vice-president of Drywall, signed the note below a heading "Assenting to Terms and Waivers on the Face of this Note." Drywall defaulted on the note and Community Bank sued Dawes for payment of the note. Dawes raised a number of defenses: (1) the language above the signature was ambiguous and did not indicate that Dawes was signing as a maker or as an indorser, (2) Dawes signed as an accommodation party and is not liable to the bank, and (3) because Dawes is, at best, an accommodation indorser who was not notified by the bank in a timely fashion of Drywall's default, he has no liability to the bank. Are any of Dawes' defenses good? Explain.

6. James Estepp applied to the United Bank for a loan. Estepp was required to obtain a cosigner who was a real property owner. Estepp asked Marvin Schaeffer, who had worked for eight years under Estepp at the local country club, to be a reference for him. Shaeffer owned real property, but he had only a third grade education and was not able to read. On the day the note was to be signed, Schaeffer indicated to the bank officer that he thought he was only signing as a character witness. The bank officer allowed Estepp to reexplain the situation to Schaeffer, but the bank officer left the

room during the explanation. When he returned, Estepp signed on the face of the note and Schaeffer signed on the back. The note read in part "It is agreed that any person . . . who writes his . . . signature on the face or back of this instrument . . . shall be regarded as a maker. . . ." Estepp defaulted on the note. The bank sued Schaeffer. Schaeffer defended on the grounds that (1) he was an indorser and not a maker, (2) he had not received proper notice of the dishonor, and (3) the note had been signed as a result of fraud in the factum. Are any of Schaeffer's defenses valid? Explain. If the bank recovers from Schaeffer, can Schaeffer recover from Estepp? Explain.

7. Robert T. Lee received a check from his insurance company to cover medical services rendered to Mr. Lee by Dr. John Schoonmaker. Lee indorsed the check and delivered it to Dr. Schoonmaker, who indorsed it, "Pay to Order of Metropolitan Bank of Syracuse, N.Y., John B. Schoonmaker, M.D." The doctor then returned the check to Lee who was to return it to the insurance company because the doctor believed that Lee was entitled to a larger amount from the insurance company. Lee never returned the check to the company. Instead, Lee crossed out the doctor's indorsement and cashed the check at the Merchants Bank. The check was dishonored when it was presented to the insurance company's bank because the insurance company stopped payment. The Metropolitan

Bank sought to recover from Schoonmaker. What arguments can be presented in Schoonmaker's defense? Explain.

8. Sid Blair executed a negotiable promissory note payable to Keith Everton. When Everton demanded that the note be paid, Blair defended on the grounds that Everton had orally renounced any claim to the note. Who will win the case? Explain.

9. On April 1st, Paul purchased some rare books and paid for them with a $2,000 note payable on demand to the order of Carmen, the seller. On April 2nd, Carmen indorsed the note "Carmen/Without Recourse" and gave it to Clare as a birthday present. On April 3rd, Clare indorsed the note "Pay Nancy for collection only — Clare," and gave it to Nancy. Nancy indorsed it "Nancy" and gave it to Michelle who gave Nancy $2,000 in cash. Nancy used the money to pay her doctor's bill. On April 6th, Michelle gave the note to Anne without indorsing it as payment for redecorating her apartment. On April 6th, Paul discovered that most of the rare books were fakes. On April 7th, Anne demanded payment from Paul, who refused to pay. Anne wants to know: (1) what rights she has against Paul; (2) what warranties each of the parties have made and to whom; (3) what liabilities each of the parties has to her; and (4) what steps she must take to secure her rights.

28

BANK DEPOSITS AND COLLECTIONS

Many negotiable instruments, most notably checks, are collected through banks. Article 4 of the Uniform Commercial Code, titled "Bank Deposits and Collections," governs the processes of payment and collection by banks. In order to provide for flexibility and to allow for development in the rules governing the bank collection process, the Code allows banks and their customers to vary the provisions of the Code through agreements [§4-103]. This chapter will discuss the rules governing bank collection as set forth in the Code. The student must bear in mind, though, that because banks can arrange for different rules by agreement, actual practices may vary from place to place even within the same jurisdiction. After a look at the bank collection process, the chapter will focus on the rights and duties of banks and bank customers.

THE BANK COLLECTION PROCESS

Banks process and collect more than checks. The Code uses the general term **item** to refer to any instrument, whether negotiable or not, that calls for the payment of money [§4-104(1)(g)]. Checks, promissory notes, and coupons from bonds are some of the items calling for the payment of money that are handled by the bank collection process.

Identifying the Banks
The Code identifies banks according to the roles they play in collecting items. Because a single bank may play more than one role in the collection process, it may have more than one identifying label.

A typical bank collection process can be seen by following a check drawn by John Jones on his account at the Northeast Bank, a New Jersey bank, to pay for goods purchased from National Catalogue, Inc., an Illinois-based company. Assume that National Catalogue deposits Jones' check in its bank in Chicago, the Midwest Trust Company. The route followed by Jones' check uses the Federal Reserve system, which was developed in part to provide an economical and efficient nation-wide bank collection system. Figure 28-1 shows the route taken by the check and identifies each of the banks through which it passes from the time it is deposited by the seller, National Catalogue, Inc., in its account at the Midwest Trust Company until it is paid by the Northeast Bank.

A **depositary bank** is the first bank to handle an item for collection, for example, the Midwest Trust Company [§4-105(a)]. A **collecting bank** is any bank that handles an item for collection, such as the Midwest Trust Company and the two Federal Reserve Banks [§4-105(d)]. An **intermediary bank** is any bank that handles an item but is neither the depositary bank nor the bank that must pay the item, such as the two Federal Reserve Banks [§4-105(c)]. If an item handled by the bank collection system, such as a bond coupon, is to be paid by some person or institution other than a bank, the last bank that handles the item is also called an intermediary bank. A **presenting bank** is the bank that presents an item for payment, such as the Federal Reserve Bank of New York [§4-105(e)]. Presentment is discussed in more detail in Chapter 27. A **payor bank** is a bank on which an item is drawn, such as the Northeast Bank. The payor bank has been previously referred to as the drawee bank. A payor bank is also a bank that has accepted an item [§4-105(b)]. Acceptance is also discussed in more detail in Chapter 27. A payor bank can be the depositary bank. This occurs when a check drawn upon a bank is deposited in that bank.

Bank Indorsements

It is interesting to look at the bank indorsements on a check that has gone through the bank collection process. The indorsements will disclose where the check has been. In the example in Figure 28-1, you could expect to find that each of the collecting banks have stamped an indorsement on the check that reads "Pay any bank" and includes the collecting bank's name — for example, "Pay any bank/Midwest Trust Company." This type of indorsement is a restrictive indorsement [§3-206]. (For more on restrictive indorsements see Chapter 26.) Only a bank may acquire the rights of a holder under this type of indorsement [§4-201]. The indorsement, in effect, prohibits transfer of the item outside of the bank collection system. A bank can, however, transfer an item outside the bank collection system by a special indorsement to a person who is not a bank or by returning the item to the customer who initiated collection [§4-201(2)]. For example, the depositary bank, Midwest Trust Company, would return Jones' check to National Catalogue if the check has been returned unpaid by the payor bank, Northeast Bank, because there were insufficient funds in Jones' account.

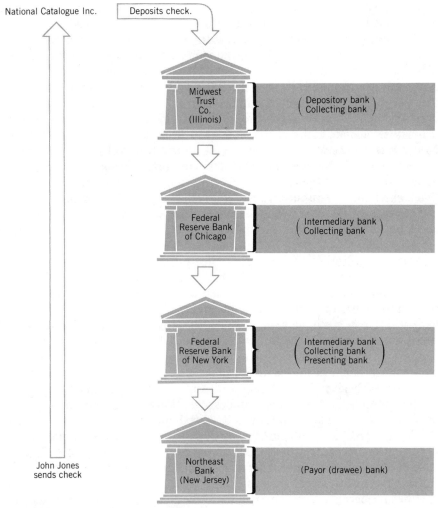

FIGURE 28-1
The Bank Collection Process

Midnight Deadline

A number of the provisions of the Code require a bank to take some action on an item in a timely fashion. The time for taking action is often phrased in terms of a "midnight deadline." The Code defines the midnight deadline as midnight on the next banking day following the banking day on which a bank receives an item or a notice or is in any other way obligated to take some sort of action [§4-104(1)(h)]. This definition is made slightly more complex by the fact that the Code allows a bank to declare a cut-off hour of 2 P.M. or later as the end of a banking day [§4-107]. All items received after the cut-off time become items of the next banking day. A **banking day** is a day on which the bank is open for carrying on substantially all of its business functions [§4-104(1)(c)].

The Code requires a collecting bank to transfer an item to the next collecting bank or to the payor bank before the collecting bank's midnight deadline [§4-202(2)]. An example of when collecting banks must transfer an item to the next bank is illustrated in Figure 28-2. When looking at the chart, bear in mind that the physical transfer of an item takes time. A collecting bank must, however, send items by a reasonably prompt method [§4-204]. Mail or transfer by a delivery service are common methods used to transfer items for collection. Notice that the check in the example took almost two weeks to be collected.

Because the time at which a bank acts is important, banks frequently date their indorsements. When looking at the indorsements on checks, you may find that banks handle items more expeditiously than Figure 28-2 indicates. Nevertheless, each of the banks in the example acted properly in transferring the check on the day of its midnight deadline.

Provisional Credits and Final Settlements

When a customer deposits a check, the depositary bank begins the collection process by forwarding the check in a timely fashion either directly to the payor bank or to the first of several intermediary banks. In many cases, the depositary bank will give its customer a **provisional credit;** that is, the bank will credit the depositor's account with the amount of the check, but it will reserve the right to reverse the entry and withdraw the amount in the event the check is dishonored by the payor bank. In the example in Figure 28-1, Midwest Trust Company would probably give National Catalogue, Inc., a provisional credit.

Each intermediary bank that handles a check usually gives its transferor a provisional credit. Thus, the Federal Reserve Bank of Chicago would make a **provisional settlement** with the Midwest Trust Company by provisionally crediting Midwest's account with the Federal Reserve Bank of Chicago. The Federal Reserve Bank of New York would make a similar settlement with the Federal Reserve Bank of Chicago.

When the check reaches the payor bank, the Northeast Bank, and is paid, all provisional settlements (credits) automatically become **final settlements** [§4-211(3) and §4-213(2)]. No notification of final payment need be given the depositary bank. However, a payor bank that dishonors an item must give notice of dishonor by its midnight deadline. This is clearly a case of no news being good news.

A payor bank that fails to give notice of dishonor by its midnight deadline is liable for the amount of the item in question [(§4-302)]. The purpose of this requirement is to force banks to act promptly even under adverse conditions. The Code does allow for two exceptions, though. First, collecting banks are allowed to extend the time limits imposed by the Code for a period of time not to exceed one banking day. The extention applies only to specific items and only for the purpose of making a good faith effort to secure payment. This might occur, for example, when a payor bank assures a collecting bank that an automatic payroll deposit will be made into the drawer's account the following day. The extention will allow a check presented by the collecting bank to be paid by

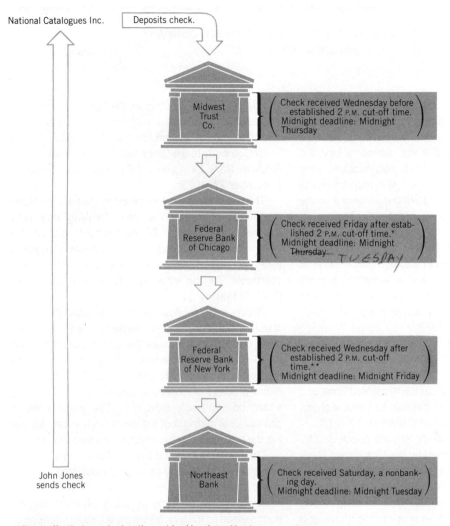

National Catalogues Inc.   Deposits check.

Midwest Trust Co.
Check received Wednesday before established 2 P.M. cut-off time. Midnight deadline: Midnight Thursday

Federal Reserve Bank of Chicago
Check received Friday after established 2 P.M. cut-off time.* Midnight deadline: Midnight ~~Thursday~~ *TUESDAY*

Federal Reserve Bank of New York
Check received Wednesday after established 2 P.M. cut-off time.** Midnight deadline: Midnight Friday

Northeast Bank
Check received Saturday, a nonbanking day. Midnight deadline: Midnight Tuesday

John Jones sends check

*Check effectively received on the next banking day— Monday.

**Check effectively received on the next banking day— ~~Monday.~~ *THURSDAY*

FIGURE 28-2
The Midnight Deadline

the payor bank. If the check could not be held until the following day, it would have to be dishonored [§4-108(1)].

Second, collecting banks and payor banks are excused for delays that are caused by the interruption of communication facilities, the suspension of payments by another bank, war, or emergencies beyond the control of the bank such as blizzards, acts of God, or floods. Even in these circumstances, however, a bank is required to exercise diligence [§4-108(2)].

In the following case, the payor bank did not return an item by its midnight deadline. The bank argued that it was excused.

BLAKE v. WOODFORD BANK AND TRUST COMPANY
555 S.W.2d 589 (Ky. 1977)

PARK, Judge

This case involves the liability . . . on two checks drawn on the Woodford Bank and Trust Company [defendant] and payable to the order of . . . Wayne Blake [plaintiff]. Following a trial without a jury, the [trial court] found that the bank was excused from meeting its "midnight deadline" with respect to the two checks. Blake appeals from the judgment of the [trial] court dismissing his complaint. . . .

The basic facts are not in dispute. On December 6, 1973, Blake deposited a check in the amount of $16,449.84 to his account at the Morristown Bank of Morristown, Ohio. This check was payable to Blake's order and was drawn on the K & K Farm Account at the Woodford Bank and Trust Company. The check was dated December 3, 1973.

On December 19, 1973, Blake deposited a second check in the amount of $11,200.00 to his account in Morristown Bank. The second check was also drawn on the K & K Farm Account at the Woodford Bank and Trust Company and made payable to Blake's order. The second check was dated December 17, 1973.

When Blake deposited the second check on December 19, he was informed by the Morristown Bank that the first check had been dishonored and returned because of insufficient funds. Blake instructed the Morristown Bank to re-present the first check along with the second check. Blake was a cattle trader, and the two checks represented the purchase price for cattle sold by Blake to James Knight who maintained the K & K Farm Account. Blake testified that he had been doing business with Knight for several years. On other occasions, checks had been returned for insufficient funds but had been paid when re-presented.

The two checks were forwarded for collection through the Cincinnati Branch of the Federal Reserve Bank of Cleveland. From the Federal Reserve Bank, the two checks were delivered to the Woodford Bank and Trust Company by means of the Purolator Courier Corp. The checks arrived at the Woodford Bank and Trust Company on Monday, December 24, 1973,

shortly before the opening of the bank for business. The next day, Christmas, was not a banking day. The two checks were returned by the Woodford Bank and Trust Company to the Cincinnati Branch of the Federal Reserve Bank by means of Purolator on Thursday, December 27, 1973.

The two checks were received by the bank on Monday, December 24. The next banking day was Wednesday, December 26. As the bank retained the two checks beyond its midnight deadline [§4-104(1)(h)], Blake asserts that the bank is "accountable" for the amount of the two checks under [§4-302(1)(a)]. . . .

Because of the payor bank's basic nonliability on a check, it was essential that some time limit be placed upon the right of the payor bank to dishonor a check when presented for payment. If a payor bank could hold a check indefinitely without incurring liability, the entire process of collection and payment of checks would be intolerably slow. . . . The payor bank is granted until midnight of the next business day following the business day on which it received the check.

The [trial] court found that the bank's failure to return the two checks by its midnight deadline was excused under the provisions of UCC §4-108.

The basic facts found by the [trial] court can be summarized as follows: (a) the bank had no intention of holding the checks beyond the midnight deadline in order to accommodate its customer; (b) there was an increased volume of checks to be handled by reason of the Christmas holiday; (c) two posting machines were broken down for a period of time on December 26; (d) one regular bookkeeper was absent because of illness. . . . The application of the exemption statute [§4-108(2)] necessarily will turn upon the findings relating to heavy volume, machine breakdown, and absence of a bookkeeper.

The bank's president testified that 4,200 to 4,600 checks were processed on a normal day. Because the bank was closed for Christmas on Tuesday, the bank was required to process 6,995 checks on December 26. . . .

Because of the cumulative effect of the heavy volume, machine breakdown, and absence of a regular bookkeeper, the bank claims it was unable to process the two checks in time to deliver them to the courier from Purolator for return to the Federal Reserve Bank on December 26. . . . The validity of this claim must be considered in light of the testimony of the bank's bookkeeper who processed the two checks.

Betty Stratton was the regular bookkeeper who posted all of the accounts from "D" through "K", and she processed the two checks in question on December 26. . . .

Ms. Stratton testified that she did not complete the posting of all the checks in the "H" through "K" accounts until after 4:00. Had it not been for the extra volume of checks to be handled and the breakdown in the posting machines, she should have completed the process of posting by 12:30 P.M. In accordance with her operating instructions, Ms. Stratton took the two checks to Susan Williams, the bank employee with the duty of handling any checks which were to be returned because of insufficient funds. Because of the lateness of the hour, Ms. Williams and all responsible officers of the bank had left for the day. Ms. Stratton left the two checks on Ms. Williams desk.

The increased volume of items to be processed the day after Christmas was clearly foreseeable. The breakdown of the posting machines was not an unusual occurrence, although it was unusual to have two machines broken down at the same time. In any event, it should have been foreseeable to the responsible officers of the bank that the bookkeepers would be delayed in completing posting of the checks on December 26. Nevertheless, the undisputed evidence established that no arrangements of any kind were made for return of "bad" items which might be discovered by the bookkeepers after the departure of the Purolator courier. . . .

Even though the bank missed returning the two checks by the Purolator courier, it was still possible for the bank to have returned the checks by midnight deadline. Under [§4-301(4)(b)] an item is returned when it is "sent" to the bank's transferor, in this case the Federal Reserve Bank. Under [§1-201(38)] an item

is "sent" when it is deposited in the mail. . . . Thus, the bank could have returned the two checks before the midnight deadline by the simple procedure of depositing the two checks in the mail, properly addressed to the Cincinnati branch of the Federal Reserve Bank.

This court concludes that circumstances beyond the control of the bank did not prevent it from returning the two checks in question before its midnight deadline on December 26. . . . The [trial] court erred in holding that the bank was excused under §4-108 from meeting its midnight deadline. The facts found by the trial court do not support its conclusion that the circumstances in the case were beyond the control of the bank.

. . . [T]he bank argues that the trial court erred in holding that there was no difference in the status of the two checks. The bank makes the argument that it is not liable on the first check, which had previously been dishonored by nonpayment. Blake received notice of dishonor when the first check was returned because of insufficient funds. The bank claims that it was under no further duty to meet the midnight deadline when the check was re-presented for payment. . . .

Even if it was unnecessary to give further notice of dishonor when the check was re-presented for payment in order to make Knight liable on the check and revive the underlying contract, it does not follow that the bank was relieved of its obligation to meet the midnight deadline. . . . Under §4-301(1), a payor bank may "revoke" a provisional settlement if, before its midnight deadline, the payor bank complies with [§4-301(1)(a), (b), i.e., returns the item or sends notice of dishonor]. . . .

Each collecting bank will have made a provisional settlement with its transferor, and, in turn, received a provisional settlement from the bank to which it forwarded the check. In this way, a series of provisional settlements are made as the check proceeds through the bank collection process.

Under [§4-213(2)], final payment of a check "firms up" all of the provisional settlements made under the collection process. Under [§4-213(1)(d)], a payor bank makes final payment of a check when it fails to revoke a provisional settlement "in the time and manner permitted by statute, clearing house rule or agreement." As to items not presented over the counter or by local clearing house this means that a payor bank is deemed to have made final payment of a check when it fails to revoke a provisional settlement by its midnight deadline. See [§4-213], Official Code Comment 6. In [an] article on check handling, [an author] has described §4-213 as the "zinger" section: "when provisional credit given by the payor bank becomes firm then — 'zing' — all prior provisional credits are instantaneously made firm." . . . [I]f a payor bank was not required to meet its midnight deadline with respect to previously dishonored items, then none of the other banks involved in the collection process could safely assume that the check had been paid. Consider the problems of the depositary bank. It must permit its customer to withdraw the amount of the credit given for the check when provisional settlements have become final by payment and the bank has had "a reasonable time" to learn that the settlement is final. See [§4-213(4)(a)]. The depositary bank will rarely receive notice that an item has been paid. In actual practice,

the depositary bank will utilize availability schedules to compute when it should receive the check if it is to be returned unpaid. . . . If a payor bank is not bound by its midnight deadline as to previously dishonored items, then there is no way for the depositary bank to know whether a previously dishonored item has been paid upon re-presentment except by direct communication with the payor bank. Such a procedure would impose an unnecessary burden upon the check collection process.

This court concludes that the [trial] court was correct in holding that there was no difference in the status of the two checks.

The judgment of the [trial] court on the appeal is reversed with directions to enter judgment in favor of Blake for the face amount of the two checks, less a credit for any amounts which Blake may have recovered from Knight. . . . All concur.

CASE REVIEW QUESTIONS

1. Why were the circumstances that delayed the processing of the checks not beyond the control of the bank?
2. What procedures should banks establish based on the decision in this case?
3. A final payment "zings" back through the chain of collecting banks. How long would it take a notice of dishonor to go from the payor bank to the depositary bank if there were two intermediary banks?
4. Why does the court say that a depositary bank rarely receives notice that a check has been paid?
5. When must a bank allow a depositor to withdraw funds deposited in the form of a check? Although the case does not discuss it, when can a depositor withdraw cash that was deposited in a bank? Consult §4-213(5).*

Final Payment

In the preceding case, the payor bank was deemed to have made a final payment when it failed to give notice of dishonor of the two checks by its midnight deadline. Notice of dishonor would have revoked the provisional settlement that the payor bank made with the presenting, collecting bank.

Failure to revoke a provisional settlement in a timely fashion is one of several

* Several states, most notably California and New York, have recently adopted statutes that limit the amount of time a bank can delay the availability of funds deposited to an individual depositor's account. For example, the New York statute requires that a consumer depositor should be able to withdraw the amount of a check six business days after the day of deposit if the check is drawn on a bank outside of New York State. Compare this to the amount of time it took the check in Figure 28-2 to be collected.

ways in which **final payment** occurs [§4-213(1)(d)]. Final payment also occurs
(1) if an item is paid in cash [§4-213(1)(a)], (2) if a settlement is made without
reserving any right to revoke [§4-213(1)(b)], or (3) if a payor bank has completed the process of posting an item to a depositor's account [§4-213(1)(c)].
The Code defines **posting** as "the usual procedure followed by a payor bank in
determining to pay an item and in recording the payment . . ." [§4-109]. The
procedure to be followed in posting is determined by each bank and may
include such things as verifying signatures, determining if there are sufficient
funds to pay an item, affixing a "paid" stamp to the item, making an entry to
the depositor's account, or correcting an entry or an erroneous action [§4-109].

A PAYOR BANK AND ITS CUSTOMER

When a check or some other item arrives at a bank where a person maintains
an account, a payor bank usually pays the check or item if there are sufficient
funds in the customer's account, which ends the story of that check or item.
Occasionally, however, an item is not paid by a bank when it should be or is paid
when it should not be. For example, a bank might dishonor a check even though
the customer's account has sufficient funds. This is called a **wrongful dishonor**.
Conversely, a bank might wrongfully pay a check even though there is a stop
payment order in effect or the customer has died or become incompetent. A
bank might also pay over a forged signature or a forged indorsement.

What are the rights and obligations of payor banks and customers in these
situations? The materials that follow discuss these and other situations.

Proper and Improper Payment

While a bank may charge a customer's account for any item that is properly
payable [§4-401], a bank incurs liability for paying improper items, such as a
check with a forged drawer's signature. The contract between a customer and
his or her bank requires the bank to pay only proper items. A bank must
therefore return to the depositor's account any amount that was improperly
paid on an item.

Overdrafts An **overdraft** occurs when a depositor has written a draft or a
check for an amount greater than the funds on deposit. If the item is otherwise
properly payable, a bank may choose to pay the overdraft but it is not obligated
to do so. The payment of an overdraft creates an implied promise by the
depositor to reimburse the bank.

Wrongful Dishonor

While a bank may choose not to pay an overdraft, it is liable if it mistakenly
or intentionally refuses to pay an item when a customer has sufficient funds on
deposit. The bank is also liable to its customer for damages that are directly
caused by the bank's wrongful dishonor [§4-402].

Consider the following situation: A buyer draws a check to make a payment to the seller of an automobile. The bank mistakenly refuses to pay the check even though the customer has sufficient funds to cover the amount of the check. As a result of the dishonor of the check, the seller repossesses the car and has the buyer arrested for writing a bad check. The bank is liable to its customer for the actual losses suffered by the customer that are proved to be caused directly (proximately) by the dishonor of the check. These damages would include not only the costs incurred by the customer in losing the automobile but also those damages caused by the arrest, such as the cost of defending against the criminal charge.

Death or Incompetence of a Customer

In the event of the death or incompetence of a customer, a bank still has the authority to accept, pay, or collect an item on behalf of the customer unless it knows that there has been an adjudication of incompetence or that the customer has died [§4-405(1)]. Even when a bank knows of a customer's death, it may for ten days after the date of death pay or certify checks drawn prior to death unless it is ordered to stop payment by a person claiming an interest in the account [§4-405(2)]. Most checks that clear after a person's death represent debts against his or her estate that would have to be paid in any event. Therefore, allowing the bank to pay them makes practical sense.

In the following case, a bank customer considered to be mentally incompetent had written checks for which he had insufficient funds in his account. At issue is the bank's authority to pay these checks. The question concerns not only whether the customer's incompetence revokes the bank's authority but also whether the checks were properly payable.

LINCOLN NATIONAL BANK v. PEOPLES TRUST BANK
379 N.E.2d 527 (Ill. 1978)

STATON, Judge

[William S.] Wyss had a checking account at Lincoln National Bank [defendant] and also owned a $50,000 certificate of deposit. . . .

This case raises the question of whether the Bank properly cashed checks. . . . Apparently, during the latter years of his life, Wyss' mind was somewhat unstable. Near the end of his life, he wrote three checks for which his account's funds were insufficient. The first, drawn on his Lincoln account and dated December 3, 1973 (#2223), was in the amount of $8,981.83. It was delivered by Wyss to Harold F. Allen [the apparent owner of Rudisill Motors] and was payable to Rudisill Motors. . . .

The main controversy involves the sequence of events culminating in the cashing of check #2223 for $8,981.83. On December 3, 1973, Harold F. Allen attempted to cash check #2223 at a Lincoln branch office. The Bank refused to cash the check. . . . Later the same day, after banking hours, Allen presented the check to a BankAmericard teller at Lincoln's main office. He indorsed the check with his name, followed by "Rudisill Motors." The teller accepted the check, credited part of the amount to Allen's BankAmericard account, and issued the remainder in the form of a cashier's check made out to Allen. The teller failed to abide by an internal bank rule, which required a manager's approval before a teller cashed or certified a check for over $500. Allen cashed the cashier's check at a savings and loan association the same day. . . .

Wyss died on January 29, 1974. Lincoln [charged] the amount of $9,581.83 (the sum of the three checks) against Wyss' certificate of deposit. [People's Trust Bank (plaintiff) on behalf of Wyss's estate hereafter referred to as Estate] sought to recover that amount.

Trial was brief. . . . [T]he trial court issued findings of fact and conclusions of law. The findings relevant to the appeal are as follows:

4. That prior to the presentment of check #2223 for payment at Lincoln an officer of said Bank was notified not to honor any checks of Wyss because Wyss was not mentally sound. . . .

7. That said teller, who was not an officer of the Bank, contrary to the internal rules of the Bank deducted the balance due BankAmericard and issued a Lincoln Cashier's Check for $8,354.08 to the individual, not the named payee of check #2223. . . .

9. That check #2223 was not properly payable from the account of Wyss nor did Lincoln make a good faith payment of said check.

The trial court concluded that the law was with the Estate and granted the Estate judgment against Lincoln in the amount of $9,581.83 plus interest in the amount of $1,725.00. . . . [Lincoln appealed.]

The only issue we must resolve then, is whether Lincoln properly cashed check #2223 and became entitled to set off $8,981.83 against Wyss' certificate of deposit.

Under the Uniform Commercial Code, Lincoln was authorized to cash check #2223, even though the account's funds were insufficient, so long as the check was properly payable [§4-401(1)]. Check #2223 was properly payable on its face. The check was completed and signed by the depositor and was not altered in any way. Thus, unless the check was not "properly payable" for some other reason, the trial court erred in finding (finding of fact #9) that the check was not properly payable.

The Estate argues that check #2223 was not properly payable for several reasons: it was cashed without sufficient funds to cover it; it was cashed without a

manager's approval; it had been dishonored previously; . . . .

The Estate's objections fail to establish that the check was not properly payable. [§4-401] clearly authorizes a bank to cash a check which creates an overdraft. The requirement of a manager's approval before cashing certain checks is an internal banking rule, the violation of which in this instance cannot be invoked for the benefit of the Estate. . . . Likewise, a previous dishonor of check #2223, whatever the reason, did not affect Lincoln's right to decide to pay the check upon a later presentment, again under [§4-401]. . . .

We hold that check #2223 was properly payable as a matter of law.

In its brief, the Estate claimed that the trial court's judgment for the Estate could be sustained on an alternative ground, that is, that Lincoln failed to exercise care in cashing check #2223. . . . [T]he Estate . . . argues that Lincoln, which was monitoring Wyss' account, was negligent in cashing a check when its officers knew of Wyss' mental instability.

The trial court's finding of fact #4, that the Bank had been notified not to honor Wyss' checks before check #2223 was presented on December 3, 1973, would appear to support such an argument. However, the finding is not supported by any evidence in the record. While Bank officers had been requested to "monitor" Wyss' account before the presentment of check #2223, the record shows that an actual "hold" was not placed on Wyss' account until December 5, 1973. A bank's duty to "monitor" an account cannot give rise to an action for negligence when a teller cashes a properly payable check.

Finally, it is not at all clear under what authority the bank would have stopped payment of checks drawn on Wyss' account. [§4-403] concerns the manner in which the "customer" may order a bank to stop payment on checks. In the case at hand, Wyss never requested that a "hold" be placed on his account. The "hold" was ordered by his attorney, who claimed that Wyss was mentally incompetent. . . . The record contains no evidence that Wyss was ever adjudicated to be incompetent [§4-405(1)]. Lincoln could not be held negligent in any way in cashing a properly payable check authorized by Wyss, simply because Wyss' attorney communicated to the Bank that Wyss was mentally unsound and in need of having his account monitored.

When Lincoln cashed check #2223, an overdraft on Wyss' account resulted. Wyss became indebted to Lincoln for the amount of the check. Lincoln had the right to charge the amount to Wyss' other deposits in the bank. . . . Therefore, Lincoln had the right to set

off the amount of $8,981.83 against the $50,000 certificate of deposit Wyss owned in the Bank.

With regard to check #2223, the trial court erred in concluding that the law was with the Estate and in granting the Estate judgment in the amount of $8,981.83. We reverse the award of $8,981.83 plus interest and remand to the trial court with instructions to enter judgment for Lincoln.

CASE REVIEW QUESTIONS

1. What arguments did the plaintiffs make that the check was not properly payable?
2. What reasons did the court use to establish that the check was properly payable?
3. Under what circumstances must a bank refuse to honor checks drawn on a customer's account when the customer is alleged to be incompetent?

Stop Payment Orders

A **stop payment order** is a direction by a customer to his or her bank to refuse payment of an item when it is presented. Only the bank customer—no one else—has the right to order his or her bank to stop payment of any item drawn by the customer [§4-403]. In order to be bound by a customer's stop payment order, the bank must receive the order and have time to act upon it before it pays or accepts an item. For example, a stop payment order on a check is too late if it is received by a bank vice-president five minutes before the holder of the check presents it to a teller for payment because the bank vice-president would not have a reasonable opportunity to notify the tellers to refuse payment.

Some states allow a stop order to be given orally, but an oral order is effective for only 14 days. A written order is effective for six months and may be renewed. An oral order must be followed by a written order to obtain protection for more than the 14 days covered by an oral notice. A bank is not acting properly if it pays a check that is the subject of a timely and effective stop payment order. Because payment is not proper, the bank cannot charge the customer's account for the amount of the check [§4-401].

Although banks are permitted to make agreements with their customers that allow for reasonable variations from the Code provisions, a bank cannot disclaim or limit its responsibility to act in good faith and to use ordinary care in handling stop payment orders or any other matters [§4-103(1)]. The following disclaimer would be invalid because it disclaims any liability, regardless of the care on the part of a bank, in the event payment is made after a stop payment order is received.

Should the check be paid through inadvertence, accident, or oversight, it is expressly agreed that the Bank will in no way be held responsible. The Bank receives this request upon the express condition that it shall not be in any way liable for its act should the check be paid by it in the course of its business. The undersigned agrees to be legally bound hereby.

Even if a customer signed such an agreement, a bank would be obligated to replace the money in the customer's account if the customer establishes that he or she has suffered a loss.

Stale Checks

A bank has no obligation to pay customers' checks that are **stale,** that is, more than six months old. Nevertheless, a bank that pays a check more than six months old is acting properly, provided that the payment is made in good faith. For example, a bank would be acting in good faith if it paid a stale dividend check because it knows or can assume that a company wants its shareholders to receive the dividends even if the check is deposited late.

Stop Payment Orders and Stale Checks Six months after receiving a written stop payment order, a bank is no longer obligated to stop payment unless the stop payment order has been renewed. Suppose that a stop payment order has expired and has not been renewed even though it remains on file. The check, now more than six months old, is presented for payment. What is the responsibility of the bank? One court has ruled that a bank could charge a depositor's account when a check more than 27 months old was paid by a bank clerk who did not check the stop payment order file before cashing the check. Because the stop payment order was more than six months old and was therefore no longer in effect, the bank did not act in bad faith and its payment was proper.

Bank's Right to Subrogation on Improper Payment

When a bank has made an improper payment by paying over a stop payment order or in some other circumstances to which a customer could object, the bank is **subrogated,** which means that it is substituted for or acquires the right of certain parties. Depending upon the circumstances, a bank that is subrogated may have (1) the rights of a holder in due course, (2) the rights of the payee, or (3) the rights of the maker or drawer of an item. The bank is entitled to exercise these rights only to the extent necessary to prevent loss to the bank and to prevent a person who should pay from being unjustly enriched [§4-407].

The following material illustrates the working of the statute. In each example, Jane Doe has purchased a television set from Bill Baker and has paid for it with a check. Jane Doe has then stopped payment on the check, but her bank has paid the check anyway. Jane Doe is demanding that the bank replace the funds in her account.

The Bank as Holder in Due Course Suppose that Bill Baker has negotiated the check to Carol Carter, who is a holder in due course. If the bank had not paid Carter, Jane Doe would have to pay her unless Doe had a real defense that could be asserted. If Doe would have to pay Carter, the bank should not lose because it paid Carter on Doe's behalf even though it had been directed not to pay. Accordingly, when Doe demands that the bank restore the funds to her account, the bank can claim Carol Carter's rights as a holder in due course and refuse to restore the money to Doe's account. If the bank had to replace the funds in Jane Doe's account, it would lose the amount of the check because it could not recover the money it paid Carol Carter. Jane Doe would therefore be unjustly enriched because her obligation to pay Carol Carter as a holder in due course would be satisfied not out of her funds but out of the bank's funds.

The Bank as Payee or as Drawer If Jane Doe's bank has paid the check to a nonholder in due course despite her stop payment order or has paid the check to a holder in due course when she has a real defense and can refuse to pay a holder in due course, the rights that the bank has depend upon what happened between Jane Doe and Bill Baker.

If Jane Doe actually got the television set, she should pay for it or she will be unjustly enriched. The bank need not replace the funds in her account because, otherwise, the bank would suffer loss by paying twice, once to Baker and once to Doe, and Jane Doe would get the television set for nothing. In this situation, the bank would be asserting the rights of the payee, Bill Baker, in order to avoid loss to the bank and unjust enrichment of Jane Doe.

If Jane Doe never got the television set, Bill Baker has been unjustly enriched because he has been paid for a set that was never delivered. In this instance, the bank must restore the funds to Doe's account and seek reimbursement from Baker. Jane Doe, as a party to the contract for the purchase of a television set, would have the right to the return of any payment made to the seller if the seller breached the contract by failing to deliver the television. The bank, in seeking payment from Baker, is asserting Jane Doe's rights in the underlying transaction; that is, the bank is asserting the drawer's rights to avoid loss to the bank and unjust enrichment of Baker.

Forged Drawer's Signatures and Alterations

A check that has been altered or a check on which the depositor's signature as drawer has been forged is not properly payable. A bank has a duty to a depositor to restore to the depositor's account any funds that were improperly paid. A depositor has a corresponding duty to give the bank prompt notice of any forgeries or alterations.

Customer's Duty to Report Forgeries and Alterations Upon receiving a monthly bank statement, a depositor must exercise reasonable care and promptness in checking the bank statement and looking over the returned checks. A depositor will be unable to recover from his or her bank any loss caused by a forgery or alteration if the depositor fails to discover any forgery of his or her signature or any alteration of the checks and if the bank also establishes that it suffered a loss due to the depositor's failure to use care and promptness in examining the bank statement and returned checks [§4-406(1)].

Suppose, for instance, that Clever forged Jane Doe's signature on a check that was paid by the Johnstown Bank. Doe did not examine the bank statement that contained the forged check for several months. When Doe finally examined the bank statement and notified the bank, the bank was unable to pursue and collect the money from Clever because Clever had left the country. If the bank establishes that it could have recovered the amount of the check if Doe had examined the bank statement earlier, the bank will not be required to replace the funds in Doe's account. On the other hand, if Doe promptly reports the forgery, the bank will have to replace the funds.

A discovery of a forged drawer's signature must be made within a reasonable time, which depends upon all of the circumstances. However, a depositor must discover and report any instances of forgery within one year from the date of the statement [§4-406]. A depositor must also report any other alterations within one year [§4-406].

If there are repeated forgeries or alterations by the same person, a depositor must report the first instance of forgery or alteration within 14 calendar days after receiving the bank statement that contains the evidence of the initial forgery or alteration. The failure to discover a forgery or alteration within the 14 days will preclude the customer from claiming against the bank for any subsequent forgeries or alterations by the same person [§4-406(2)].

Suppose Clever forged one check in June and several more during July and August. Jane Doe doesn't examine her June bank statement until sometime in August, however. Assuming that it is not unreasonable for Doe to be examining her June statement in August and that the forger is caught, Doe will nevertheless be unable to recover for any checks that were forged in July and August after she received the June bank statement plus a reasonable period of time not to exceed 14 days. If Doe received the June statement on July 1st, she and not the bank would suffer the loss due to any forgeries by Clever after July 14. The bank would be required to replace any funds paid on checks forged by Clever prior to that time.

If the forger is not caught and the bank cannot be repaid for the losses caused by the June and early July checks and the bank establishes that Jane Doe's failure to examine the June statement in July was unreasonable, she will suffer the loss for all of the forged checks. The lesson to be learned from this example is that bank statements should be examined within 14 days for forgeries and alterations.

Forged Indorsements

A check with a forged indorsement is not properly payable by a payor bank. A bank must restore to a customer's account any amount paid over a forged indorsement. However, a depositor will be unable to claim repayment if the bank does not receive proper notice of the forgery.

While a depositor must examine bank statements for forged indorsements, he or she will be less likely to discover a forged indorsement among the returned checks than a forged drawer's signature or an alteration. The depositor will probably discover the forged indorsement when the payee or an indorsee of the check eventually discloses that the check was never received or that it was stolen after it was received.

The statute gives a depositor a time limit of three years in which to notify a bank of a forged indorsement [§4-406]. If a depositor did not exercise reasonable care and promptness in examining a bank statement, the depositor cannot recover funds paid out over a forged indorsement, even if it is discovered before the three-year time limit is up.

A BANK'S WARRANTY RIGHTS

When a bank is required to replace funds in a customer's account, the bank does have the right, under some circumstances, to recover the funds from the party who presented the item for payment. The warranties of a customer or a collecting bank upon transfer or presentment are outlined in §4-207.

The warranties provided in §4-207 are similar to the warranties in §3-417 discussed in the previous chapter. These warranties are divided into (1) warranties made by customers and collecting banks to payor banks who pay or accept items and (2) warranties made by customers and collecting banks to their transferees and subsequent collecting banks who give settlements.

Transferor Warranties

Each customer and each collecting bank that transfers an item warrants to the transferee and to any subsequent collecting bank that takes the item in good faith that

1. The customer or the collecting bank has good title to the item or is authorized to obtain payment on behalf of one who has good title.
2. All signatures are genuine or authorized.
3. The item has not been materially altered.
4. There is no defense of any party good against the transferor.
5. The transferor has no knowledge of any insolvency proceedings with respect to the maker, acceptor, or drawer of an unaccepted item.
   [§4-207(2)]
   (For more explanation of these warranties, see Chapter 27.)

Presentment Warranties to a Payor Bank

All prior customers and all collecting banks warrant to a payor bank that they have good title or are authorized to obtain payment. In addition, they warrant that

1. They have no knowledge that the signature of the maker or drawer is unauthorized
2. The item has not been materially altered.

These two warranties are not made to makers, drawers, or acceptors who ought to recognize their own signature and remember the terms of any item they may have made, drawn, or accepted [§4-207(1)]. (For more explanation of these warranties, see Chapter 27.)

Warranties Exemplified Suppose a payor bank pays a check on which there is an indorsement that was necessary to negotiate the instrument but the indorsement was forged. The bank can recover from the prior customers and all collecting banks for breach of warranty because a person or bank who obtains payment from a payor bank warrants to the payor bank that the person or bank has good title to the instrument [§4-207(1)(a)]. The person or presenting bank does not have good title if a necessary indorsement is forged. (See Chapter 26.)

The situation is different in the case of a forged drawer's signature. A person or bank who obtains payment from a payor bank for an item guarantees only that the person or bank has no knowledge that the signature of the drawer is forged. The payor bank must prove that the person or bank who obtained payment of the instrument knew that the drawer's signature was forged. Otherwise, the payor bank must attempt to locate and collect from the actual forger.

In the following case, which concerns a forged indorsement, the payor (drawee) bank, Girard Bank, is suing the depository bank, Mount Holly State Bank, on the basis of warranty.

GIRARD BANK v. MOUNT HOLLY STATE BANK
474 F. Supp. 1225 (First Cit. 1979)

BROTMAN, District Judge

This case presents intriguing questions concerning commercial paper transactions and Articles 3 and 4 of the Uniform Commercial Code. . . . The drawee bank [Girard Bank, plaintiff] has sued the depository bank [Mount Holly State Bank, defendant] on its presentment warranty and now seeks summary judgment. . . .

Certain facts are not disputed by the litigants. On August 4, 1977 . . . Penn Mutual Life Insurance Company issued its check numbered 377406, dated August 4, for $28,269.54 to a Morris Lefkowitz of New York City, as a return of a policy premium. The check was drawn on Penn Mutual's account at plaintiff Girard Bank in Philadelphia. The check, prepared and signed in Philadelphia, was to be sent by mail to Penn Mutual's agency in New York for distribution to Mr. Lefkowitz.

On August 5 . . . [a person named] Darlene Payung deposited the check in her account at Mount Holly State Bank of Mount Holly, New Jersey. . . . The check bore a forgery of Mr. Lefkowitz's signature as an indorsement; the origin of the forgery is disputed. Ms. Payung also added her signature as an indorsement when she deposited the check. Mount Holly transferred the check through normal banking channels to Central Penn National Bank of Philadelphia,

which then presented it for payment to the drawee and payor, Girard. Mount Holly, the depositary and a collecting bank, recovered the full amount of the check from Penn [Mutual]. . . .

Girard has sued Mount Holly to recover on the latter's presentment warranty which it alleges was breached by the forged check.

Girard seeks recovery for Penn Mutual's breach of its presentment warranty under [§4-207(1)(a)]. . . .

The forged indorsement prevented Mount Holly, the depositary and collecting bank, from obtaining good title to the check, and Mount Holly therefore breached its warranty. . . . The overriding scheme of the Code is to place liability on the person who takes from the forger, which is often the depositary bank. The rationale is that this party is normally in the best position to detect the forgery and prevent the fraud. . . .

This policy is reflected throughout Articles 3 and 4 of the Code. Various sections indicate that a check bearing a forged indorsement is not "properly payable" within the terms of §4-401(1). . . . That section indicates that, absent . . . negligence on the part of the drawer, the drawee bank may not charge the drawer for a check that is not "properly payable."

However, the drawee which has paid the check may seek recovery against prior banks in the collection chain for breach of presentment warranty under §4-207. The depositary bank may also sue the prior transferring party under a similar warranty provided in §3-417. In the instant case, Mount Holly, if found liable to Girard, may be able to shift the loss back to the prior transferor, Ms. Payung. However, it is often the case that a depositary bank will be unable to recover from a prior party and will ultimately bear the loss.

The evidence in the record demonstrates that Mount Holly breached its §4-207(1)(a) presentment warranty to Girard. . . .

Summary judgment will be granted for plaintiff Girard in the amount of the Lefkowitz check, $28,269.54.

CASE REVIEW QUESTIONS

1. Did Mount Holly know that the indorsement of Morris Lefkowitz was forged?
2. Why is the depositary bank in the best position to detect a forged indorsement? Why didn't the bank detect the forgery?
3. Assume that the forged Lefkowitz indorsement is a blank indorsement. Why would the bank want Payung's indorsement?
4. What will Payung's liability be on the check if she is found?
5. Why are persons or banks suspicious of instruments with more than one indorsement?

REVIEW QUESTIONS

1. Identify and describe the role of each of the banks involved in the collection of a check drawn on a California bank and deposited in a bank in Virginia. Assume that the Federal Reserve Bank of San Francisco is involved in handling the check.
2. Chart the length of time it will take the check in the previous question to travel from the Virginia bank to the California bank if it was deposited in the Virginia bank on a Friday afternoon after 3 P.M.? Explain.
3. What is the effect of an indorsement by a bank that reads "Pay Any Bank?"
4. May a bank pay a check that is more than six months old? Explain.
5. May a bank pay checks drawn by a customer that are presented after the death of a customer? Explain.
6. What duty does a customer have to report a forged drawer's signature or a forged indorsement? Explain.

CASE PROBLEMS

1. David Graubart, Inc., received a check drawn by Prins Diamond Company on Bank Leumi. Graubart deposited the check in its account at National Bank, which forwarded the check through the bank collection process to Bank Leumi. The check was dishonored for insufficient funds and returned through the bank collection process to National Bank. Graubart redeposited the check at National

Bank, which re-presented the check to Bank Leumi through the bank collection process. Bank Leumi held the check for 12 days. Meanwhile Prins Diamond filed for bankruptcy. Graubart sued Bank Leumi for failure to return the check prior to its midnight deadline. Who will win the case? Explain.

2. The Paper Industry Pension Fund (Fund) drew a check for $100,000 payable to the order of Totowa Savings and Loan Association (Totowa Bank). The Fund delivered the check to an agent, Naiman, instructing him to open a certificate of deposit account in the Fund's name at the Totowa Bank. Instead, Naiman took the check drawn by the Fund to the drawee (payor) bank, the Chase Manhattan Bank (Chase). Even though the check was not indorsed by the Totowa Bank as the payee, Chase nevertheless took the check from Naiman, withdrew the $100,000 from the Fund's account, and issued a cashier's check naming Totowa Bank as the payee. The cashier's check did not name the Fund as the remitter. Naiman then took the check to the Totowa Bank and opened a CD account in the name of Playmate Enterprise Products, Inc. When the Fund was unable to recover the money from the Totowa Bank, the Fund sought to have Chase restore the $100,000 to its account. What arguments can be made on behalf of the Fund?

3. Sinwellan Corporation maintained a checking account at Farmers Bank. Farmers returned several checks drawn on the Sinwellan account and signed by P. A. Sinclair, Manager. The returned checks were stamped "Refused—Insufficient Funds" even though there was in fact a substantial balance in the account. Sinwellan and P. A. Sinclair sued for damages for alleged harmful publicity, loss of reputation, and embarrassment. In addition, damages were sought for the expenses caused by criminal proceedings that had been instituted against Sinclair. Who will win the case? Explain.

4. On Monday morning, C. E. Murphy gave a personal check for $15,000 drawn on the Smithtown Bank to David Brownsworth, a carpet dealer. Brownsworth immediately went to the Smithtown Bank and obtained a cashier's check to replace Murphy's personal check. On Monday afternoon Murphy became suspicious that Brownsworth was not going to deliver the carpet. Murphy called the Smithtown Bank and tried to stop payment on the check. The bank refused to stop payment. Murphy sued the bank to recover the $15,000. Who will win the case? Explain.

5. Ava Industries sold $19,500 worth of machinery to Woodhaven Knitting Mills, Inc. Woodhaven paid Ava with a check drawn on the Manufacturers Hanover Trust (Bank). Before Ava presented the check for payment, Woodhaven experienced some difficulty with the machinery and issued a stop payment order to the Bank. The Bank failed to honor the stop payment order and paid the check. Woodhaven demanded that the Bank return the $19,500 to its account because the check was not properly payable. The Bank restored the $19,500. Woodhaven brought an action against Ava for the defective machinery, which was settled by Ava giving Woodhaven certain new machinery and Woodhaven giving Ava $5000. The Bank sued Ava and Woodhaven to recover the $19,500 paid by Ava by the Bank. Who will win the case? Explain. If the bank wins, how much will be recovered from each defendant?

6. Titan Air Conditioning Company hired Stan Stone as a bookkeeper. Over several months, Stone prepared a number of checks on which he forged the indorsements and deposited the checks in the account of a dummy corporation. Because Stone also checked bank statements Titan did not discover the forgeries for almost a year. Titan sued its bank (Chase Manhattan Bank) to recover the funds arguing that checks with forged indorsements are not properly payable. What arguments can be made on behalf of the payor bank?

7. The Federal Reserve Bank of Richmond (Fed. Bank) as a collecting bank presented a check to North Carolina National Bank (N. C. Bank), which paid the check. Subsequently, it was established that the indorsement was forged. Upon being informed of the forgery, N. C. Bank restored the funds to its depositor's account and sued Fed. Bank for breach of warranty. N. C. Bank moved for summary judgment. Should the motion be granted? Explain.

PART V

DEBTOR-CREDITOR LAW

29

SECURED TRANSACTIONS

We have seen various ways in which commercial law facilitates economic exchange. The law of sales defines the rights and duties of buyers and sellers in sales transactions. The law governing commercial paper provides for convenient and safe means of payment in forms other than cash. The law of secured transactions, covered in Article 9 of the Uniform Commercial Code, facilitates economic exchange by reducing the risks taken by creditors in granting credit and thereby encourages the availability of credit services.

THE FUNCTION OF SECURITY

Credit is an indispensable part of our modern economy. Businesses and individuals often do not have the cash to pay for needed or desired goods or services. A direct loan of money by a lending institution or an extension of credit by a seller allows goods or services to be purchased now and paid for later. Creditors, however, often want security, which is something of value that assures them of repayment. When a debtor provides security, a creditor is assured of repayment in one of two ways. Either the debtor will repay in order to recover the property that was put up as security or, if the debtor does not repay, the creditor will be able to sell the property to recover the loan.

History of Security Interests
Prior to the enactment of the Uniform Commercial Code, the taking of security by a creditor was called by many names, and the rights of the creditor

and the debtor often depended upon the name used. Each type of security had its own set of rules. Furthermore, these rules varied from state to state.

Among the many types of security were conditional sales and chattel mortgages. In a conditional sale, goods were sold to and delivered to a buyer, but the seller retained title to the goods until the price was paid. If the buyer did not pay for the goods, the seller took them back. In a chattel mortgage situation, the debtor had title to the goods. The seller or lender, however, had the right to take the goods back provided that he or she had filed a chattel mortgage, which is akin to a real property mortgage, in the proper governmental office.

The enactment of the Code swept away the many forms of security in favor of a single basic type called a security interest. Under the Code, the giving of collateral by a debtor to a creditor creates a security interest that is subject to uniform rules and definitions regardless of the name used for the security.

A Secured Transaction Defined

A **secured transaction** occurs when a security interest is created. For example, when a bank lends a customer money to purchase a new car, the bank usually takes a security interest in the car. If the customer **defaults** — that is, does not repay the loan — the bank will be able to **repossess** the car — that is, take possession of the car — and sell it to repay the loan. In this situation, the creditor bank is the **secured party** [§9-105(1)(m)], the customer is the **debtor** [§9-105(1)(d)], and the car is the **collateral,** which is property that secures a loan and is subject to a security interest [§9-105(1)(c)]. The writings that evidence the security interest in the car and the promise to repay the loan are called **chattel paper** [§9-105(1)(b)].

The Scope of UCC Article 9

Article 9 governs security interests in *personal property* as distinguished from *real property.* Real property includes land, buildings, and other things attached to land. Thus, a real estate mortgage is not governed by the Code [§9-102]. In addition, certain other transactions in which a creditor has rights in a debtor's property are not covered by Article 9. For example, security interests that are subject to specific U.S. statutes, such as the Ship Mortgage Act, are excluded [§9-104(a)]. Some liens are also excluded. A **lien** refers to certain rights, created by law, that give a person a claim to the property of another. For example, a mechanic's lien gives a supplier of services or materials in the building or repair of an item rights to that item as a means of insuring that he or she will be paid [§9-104(c)].

If a transaction is not specifically excluded from coverage by Article 9, the test of whether a particular agreement is a secured transaction is to determine if it is intended to have effect as security. For example, the leasing of goods is a secured transaction if the lessee (i.e., the person to whom the goods are leased) can purchase the goods for little or no additional consideration over and above the rent or costs of the lease at the termination of the lease [§1-201(37)]. In this type of situation, the lease is really a thinly disguised sale in which the seller attempts to retain ownership rights as a lessor. A seller-lessor will therefore have to comply with the requirements of Article 9 in order to have rights in the leased goods.

Types of Property Governed by Article 9 A creditor can take a security interest in **goods,** which are basically things that are moveable but do not include things like money or minerals [§9-105(1)(h)]. A creditor can also take a security interest in **fixtures,** which are goods, such as shower stalls, furnaces, and window frames, that become so firmly attached to a piece of real estate that they are most often treated as real property [§9-313(1)(a)]. Security interests can also be created in things that are not goods. Such items are called **intangibles** and include accounts, chattel paper, money, and negotiable instruments such as promissory notes [§9-106].

An **account** is defined as a right to receive payment for the sale of goods or services that is not evidenced by chattel paper or some other type of instrument such as a promissory note [§9-106]. Accounts are often referred to as *accounts receivable.* An account receivable is created, for example, when a person uses a credit card issued by a seller to buy something. Before the buyer makes a payment on the charge account, the seller may need the money represented by the sale to purchase more inventory. The seller can obtain financing for new inventory by using the account receivable as security for a loan from a lending institution.

Article 9 distinguishes between four different types of goods: consumer goods, farm products, inventory, and equipment. **Consumer goods** are goods that are purchased or used primarily for personal, family, or household purposes [§9-109(1)]. **Farm products** are goods, such as crops, livestock, milk, eggs, or supplies, that are used in or produced by farming operations, provided that the goods are in the possession of a debtor who is engaged in farming [§9-109(3)]. **Inventory** includes goods that are held for sale or lease or that are raw materials used by a business to manufacture goods or provide services [§9-102(2)]. Goods are considered to be **equipment** if they are primarily bought for or used in business or farming and are not included in the definition of consumer goods, farm products, or inventory [§9-109(2)].

For Article 9 purposes, what type goods are considered to be is determined by the use to which they are put. For example, a refrigerator used by your family is a consumer good. In a store that sells refrigerators, the same type of refrigerator would be inventory. When used by a restaurant to keep food cold, the same type of refrigerator would be equipment.

CREATING A SECURITY INTEREST

There are two essential parts to the effective creation of a security interest. The first part, which involves the creation of rights between the secured party and the debtor, is called **attachment.** The second part, which involves the creation of rights between the secured party and other creditors of the debtor or persons who might purchase the collateral from the debtor, is called **perfection.**

Attachment

There are three conditions that must be met for a secured party to have an enforceable security interest in a debtor's property. When the three conditions are satisfied, the security interest is said to "attach" to the collateral. However, a debtor and a creditor can postpone the time for attachment by explicit agreement [§9-203(2)]. The three steps necessary for attachment are

1. There must be an agreement creating the security interest.
2. The creditor must give value.
3. The debtor must have rights—a legal interest—in the collateral.
   [§9-203(1)]

Agreement A debtor and a creditor must agree to create a security interest. If a secured party has possession of the collateral, the agreement creating the security interest need not be in writing. Possession by a secured party is sufficient evidence of the existence of an agreement and is a sufficient description of the collateral covered by the agreement. In all other cases, a written agreement called a *security agreement* [§9-105(1)(l)] must be signed by the debtor. The agreement must contain a description of the collateral [§9-203(1)(a)]. A written agreement reduces the possibility of future disputes over the terms of the agreement and what property of the debtor is collateral. No particular type of description is specified by the Code, but any description must reasonably identify the collateral [§9-110]. Figure 29-1 is an example of a written security agreement.

Value A creditor must give value to a debtor. The simplest way a creditor can satisfy this requirement is by giving money to a debtor. Other actions also constitute the giving of value, however. A creditor who makes an irrevocable commitment to extend credit to a debtor gives value even if the debtor does not immediately draw upon that credit [§1-201(44)(a)]. For example, a bank gives value when it approves a line of credit for a customer. In addition, a creditor gives value when the creditor acquires an interest in a debtor's property in order to insure the repayment of a loan granted by the creditor sometime prior to the taking of the security [§1-201(44)(b)]. Finally, a creditor who does anything that would be accepted as consideration for the making of a contract gives value [§1-201(44)(d)]. (See Chapter 12).

Debtor's Rights in the Collateral A debtor must have rights in the collateral. In the simplest form of meeting this requirement, a debtor has rights in anything that he or she owns. A debtor may also have rights in collateral that are sufficient to allow the attachment of a security interest even though the rights may fall short of full ownership. For example, under the law of sales, a buyer acquires what is called a *special property interest* when goods are identified as the actual goods being sold [§2-501]. (See Chapter 21, page 384.) Even though the buyer may not have title at that point, his or her special property interest is a sufficient ownership interest in the goods to satisfy the third requirement for attachment.

SECURITY AGREEMENT

DATE July 1, 1985

The Undersigned Wally B. Davidson

whose address is 101 Le Moyne Street

City Town or of Syracuse, New York 13200   County Onondaga
Village

(hereinafter called Debtor) is indebted to Key Bank of Central New York of Syracuse, New York, (hereinafter called Secured Party) in the sum of

Twenty-five thousand and no one-hundredths------------------ Dollars

($ 25,000.00) evidenced by a promissory note dated July 1, 1985

Now, as security for the payment of said note, and any and all renewals, modifications, extensions, and consolidations thereof, in whole or in part, and any and all other indebtedness, obligation and liability, of Debtor to the Secured Party, whether now existing or hereafter arising, including without limitation, any amounts advanced or incurred by Secured Party for taxes, assessments, insurance and all other charges and expenses as hereinafter provided (hereafter, all secured debt shall be collectively referred to as "Indebtedness"), Debtor hereby grants Secured Party a security interest in the following property, together with all accessories, attachments, parts, equipment, accessions and repairs now or hereafter affixed thereto or used in connection therewith and substitutions, replacements and proceeds thereof (hereinafter collectively referred to as "Collateral"). The Collateral will be used primarily for: personal, family or household purposes ☐   farm operations ☐   business purposes ☒

All equipment as now owned or hereafter acquired by the Debtor and used in the operation of the Debtor's business as now or hereafter conducted.

If the Debtor shall pay to the Secured Party the Indebtedness secured by this Agreement, which said Debtor hereby agrees to pay, then this Agreement and the security interest created hereby shall terminate. In the event of the assignment of the Secured Party's rights hereunder, the term "Secured Party" shall refer to the subsequent holder of this Agreement under such assignment. Debtor hereby authorizes the Secured Party (or successor to Secured Party's interest) to file a Financing Statement covering the Collateral without Debtor's signature in accordance with Uniform Commercial Code Section 9-402(2)(e).

This Agreement is subject to the provisions set forth on the reverse side hereof, the same being incorporated herein by reference.

Wally B. Davidson

BY _____

Witness: *Fredd Curman*

TITLE _____

Form No. 5228D 2/79

FIGURE 29-1
A Security Agreement

ADDITIONAL PROVISIONS TO SECURITY AGREEMENT

The Debtor hereby warrants and covenants that:

1. (a) Subject to the security interest granted hereby, Debtor is the true, lawful and sole owner of the Collateral and has the unrestricted right to enter into this Agreement.

(b) Except for the security interest granted hereby, the Collateral is free and clear of all liens and encumbrances and there are no financing statements, security agreements, or other similar documents on file in any public office wherever located covering any of the Collateral.

(c) Debtor will defend the Collateral against all claims of other persons except Secured Party.

2. The collateral is now located at the address stated on the face of this Agreement or, if not at that address, then at the following location:

_____

Debtor will notify the Secured Party in writing of any change in address from that shown in this Agreement.

3. Debtor will not sell or offer to sell or otherwise transfer the Collateral or any interest therein without the written consent of the Secured Party, except for the leasing thereof in the ordinary course of its business. The granting herein of a security interest in proceeds is not intended as implied or expressed authority for the sale or other transfer of the Collateral and should not be interpreted as a limitation on the restriction contained in this paragraph.

4. Debtor will keep the Collateral fully insured for all losses (with any loss payable to the Secured Party) and will furnish the Secured Party evidence of such insurance. Should Debtor fail to obtain such insurance coverage, Secured Party may, but is not obligated to, obtain such insurance coverage for its protection at Debtor's expense. Payment of said premiums shall be secured by this Agreement. Debtor hereby directs any insurance company to make payment directly to the holder of this Agreement for any return on unearned premiums and appoints said holder as attorney-in-fact to endorse any check, draft or order and sign any proof of loss. All such money received from such source will be applied toward the Indebtedness.

5. Debtor will keep the Collateral in good order and repair, will not use the same in violation of any policy of insurance thereon and will permit the Secured Party to inspect the Collateral at any reasonable time, wherever located.

6. In its discretion, Secured Party may, but is not obligated to, discharge taxes and other encumbrances at any time levied or placed on the Collateral, make repairs thereon and pay any necessary filing fees. Debtor agrees to reimburse Secured Party on demand for any and all expenditures so made and until paid the amount thereon shall be a debt secured by the Collateral.

7. Debtor may have possession of the Collateral until default. The occurrence of any one of the following shall constitute a default under this Agreement: (a) default by the Debtor in the performance of any of the conditions of this Agreement; (b) default by the Debtor in the payment, when due, of principal or interest or late charges upon the Indebtedness; (c) if the Debtor shall sell or in any manner dispose of, or attempt to sell, or dispose of the Collateral (except for the leasing thereof in the ordinary course of Debtor's business); (d) if said Collateral shall be misused or put to any illegal or unlawful use by Debtor or with Debtor's consent; (e) in case of the seizure of said Collateral by any process of law whatsoever; (f) in the event a petition under any provision of the Bankruptcy Act is filed by or against the Debtor; (g) if an application for receivership of any nature be filed by or against the Debtor; (h) if a receiver of the Collateral or assets of the Debtor be appointed; (i) if the Debtor shall die or terminate its existence. Upon default, the Secured Party may declare immediately due the entire amount then remaining unpaid upon the Indebtedness, and the Secured Party or its duly authorized agent may enter upon the premises of the Debtor or any other place where the Collateral may be and, without making any demand for possession, take possession thereof. Furthermore, upon default, Secured Party may require Debtor to assemble the Collateral and make it available to Secured Party at a place to be designated by Secured Party that is reasonably convenient to both parties. Upon obtaining possession of the Collateral, Secured Party shall have rights with respect to same as provided in the Uniform Commercial Code, including without limitation the right to sell the same at public or private sale. Secured Party will give Debtor at least five days prior written notice of the time and place of any public sale of the Collateral or of the time after which any private sale thereof is to be made. Debtor shall apply the net proceeds of the sale upon the Indebtedness in such order as Secured Party shall determine after first deducting therefrom the expenses of said sale, the expenses of taking possession and storing said Collateral, and reasonable attorney's fees and legal expenses. The Secured Party may become the purchaser at such sale, the same as any person not interested herein. If there be a deficiency after such sale, the Debtor agrees to pay the same.

8. Any securities or other property of Debtor in the possession of Secured Party may at all times be held as security for the payment of the Indebtedness. Regardless of the adequacy of Collateral, any deposits or other sums at any time credited by or due from Secured Party to Debtor may at any time after default be applied to or set off against the Indebtedness. Debtor hereby constitutes and appoints the Secured Party his/its true and lawful attorney-in-fact, irrevocably, in name, place and stead to endorse checks, drafts and orders received from the sale of the Collateral and apply the proceeds of any such checks, drafts or orders to the Indebtedness.

9. Secured Party is authorized to fill any blank spaces herein and to date this Agreement the date the loan is made. If there be more than one Debtor their obligations hereunder shall be joint and several. This Agreement shall bind and inure to the benefit of the heirs, legal representatives, successors and assigns of the parties, and shall take effect as a sealed instrument when signed by Debtor.

FIGURE 29-1 *(continued)*

After-Acquired Property When a creditor has given value, the creditor and the debtor can agree that a security interest will attach to property that the debtor does not have any rights to at the time a security agreement is signed. Such property is referred to as **after-acquired property** [§9-204]. The security interest attaches to this property at the time the debtor does acquire rights in it. The use of an after-acquired property clause in a security agreement provides a creditor with additional collateral either to replace collateral that has been sold, as occurs when inventory is sold and replenished, or to augment collateral that has depreciated in value. An after-acquired property clause is not effective with regard to consumer goods unless the consumer acquires the goods within ten days after the creditor has given value [§9-204(2)].

Perfection

Attachment is necessary to create rights between a secured party and a debtor. In order to protect the secured party against the claims of other creditors or persons who might purchase the collateral from the debtor, the secured party must "perfect" his or her security interest. There are two requirements that must be met to perfect:

1. The three conditions for attachment must be completed (see page 584).
2. All steps required for perfection must be taken.
   [§9-303]

The step necessary for perfection in most situations is the filing of a document called a **financing statement** with the appropriate government office [§9-302(1)]. (See Figure 29-2.) This creates a public record and gives notice to any interested party, whether a prospective buyer or a prospective creditor, that a security interest in the collateral in question already exists. An interested party can check with the governmental office to determine whether there are outstanding security interests in the collateral.

The three conditions for attachment and the steps required for perfection, such as filing, must all be completed for perfection to occur. No particular order of performance is necessary. For example, if a creditor completes the three conditions for attachment and then files a financing statement, perfection would occur upon the filing. However, if a creditor files a financing statement before giving value and having the debtor sign a security agreement, perfection would occur not upon the filing but upon the completion of the three conditions for attachment. Finally, suppose that an after-acquired property clause is used, and the creditor has given value, has had the debtor sign a security agreement, and has filed the financing statement. Has perfection occurred? The answer is no because a security interest cannot attach to any collateral until the debtor has rights in the collateral. When the debtor acquires rights in the collateral, the creditor's security interest attaches and is, at the same time, perfected because all the steps for attachment and perfection have been completed.

Filing The basic rule is that filing is necessary for security interests to be perfected unless there is a recognized exception [§9-302(1)]. Because filing is usually necessary for perfection, the mechanics of filing are important. Where a person must file depends on the law of the state in which the filing occurs and nature of the collateral [§9-401]. It is wise to exercise care in determining where filings are to be made. If a financing statement is not filed in the proper place or places, a security interest that can be perfected only by filing will not be perfected.

To allow each state to adapt the law to local custom and convenience, the drafters of the Code provided three alternative subsections that specify the place for filing [§9-401(1)]. State law must therefore be consulted to determine which subsection was selected by a particular state.

Under Third Alternative Subsection (1)—the most elaborate alternative—a financing statement for a security interest in farm equipment, farm products, accounts or intangibles arising from the sale of farm products by a farmer, or consumer goods must be filed in the designated office of the county where the debtor resides. If the collateral consists of crops growing or to be grown in a different county from where the debtor resides, a financing statement must also be filed in the county where the land is located [§9-401 Third Alternative Subsection (1)(a)]. A filing to perfect a security interest in fixtures, timber, or minerals must be made where a mortgage on the real property involved would be filed [§9-401 Third Alternative Subsection (1)(b)].

In situations not specifically covered by Third Alternative Subsection (1)(a) or (b), a filing must be made with the Secretary of State. If a debtor has a place of business in only one county, there must be two filings—one with the Secretary of State and the other in the designated office of the county where the business is located. If a debtor has no place of business, a filing must be made in the county where the debtor resides as well as with the Secretary of State.

The Financing Statement The form of a financing statement is described in §9-402(1) and is illustrated in §9-402(3). (See Figure 29-2.) Do not confuse a financing statement with a financial statement. A financ<u>ing</u> statement is the document required to be filed by Article 9 to perfect certain security interests. A finan<u>cial</u> statement is a statement of net worth showing assets and liabilities.

A financing statement must contain the names and addresses of the debtor and the secured party, a statement describing the collateral, and the signature of the debtor. A description is sufficient if it specifies the type of collateral being financed, such as "Equipment" or "All Cattle." A security agreement that meets the requirements of a financing statement can be filed [§9-402(1)]. However, a simpler financing statement is more commonly used.

Effective Filing Even though a financing statement has been physically filed, the filing will not be effective for purposes of perfection if there are errors in the financing statement that are seriously misleading [§9-402(8)]. The purpose of the filing requirement is to give notice to subsequent buyers and creditors. An error that frustrates this purpose is seriously misleading. For example, if a debtor's last name is misspelled, a searching creditor will probably not be able to find a filed financing statement.

This FINANCING STATEMENT is presented to a Filing Officer for filing pursuant to the Uniform Commercial Code.	No. of Additional Sheets Presented:	3. ☐ The Debtor is a transmitting utility.
1. Debtor(s) (Last Name First) and Address(es):	2. Secured Party(ies) Name(s) and Address(es)	4. For Filing Officer: Date, Time, No. Filing Office
Davidson, Wally B. 101 Le Moyne Street Syracuse, New York 13200	Key Bank of Central New York 201 South Warren Street Syracuse, New York	

5. This Financing Statement covers the following types (or items) of property:

    All equipment

6. Assignee(s) of Secured Party and Address(es)

7. ☐ The described crops are growing or to be grown on:*
☐ The described goods are or are to be affixed to:*
☐ The lumber to be cut or minerals or the like (including oil and gas) is on:*
*(Describe Real Estate Below)

☐ Products of the Collateral are also covered.

8. Describe Real Estate Here: ☐ This statement is to be indexed in the Real Estate Records:

9. Name of a Record Owner

No. & Street	Town or City	County	Section	Block	Lot

10. This statement is filed without the debtor's signature to perfect a security interest in collateral (check appropriate box)
☐ under a security agreement signed by debtor authorizing secured party to file this statement, or
☐ which is proceeds of the original collateral described above in which a security interest was perfected, or
☐ acquired after a change of name, identity or corporate structure of the debtor, or ☐ as to which the filing has lapsed, or already subject to a security interest in another jurisdiction:
☐ when the collateral was brought into the state, or ☐ when the debtor's location was changed to this state.

By _Wally B. Davidson_   By _____
    Signature(s) of Debtor(s)   Signature(s) of Secured Party(ies)

(1) Filing Officer Copy-Numerical
(5/82)   **STANDARD FORM - FORM UCC-1** — Approved by Secretary of State of New York

FIGURE 29-2
A Financing Statement

In order to perfect a security interest, an act legally sufficient to constitute a filing must be performed. In most cases, the simple act of tendering a financing statement and any required fee to a proper filing office constitutes a filing [§9-403(1)]. A filing is effective for five years. It then expires unless it is renewed by the filing of a continuation statement within the six-month period prior to expiration [§9-403(2) and (3)].

Exceptions to the Filing Requirement There are exceptions to the basic rule requiring filing to perfect [§9-302(1)]. In general, the exceptions provide alternative means of giving notice to buyers or prospective creditors of the already existing security interest.

Pledge If a creditor has possession of the collateral, the security interest is commonly known as a **pledge**. In this situation, no filing is necessary to perfect [§9-302(1)(a) and §9-305]. Because the debtor does not have possession of the collateral, he or she cannot sell the collateral or use it to obtain a loan from another creditor. Therefore, no notice need be given to third parties. A security interest in the form of a pledge is perfected when a creditor has possession of the collateral and the three steps for attachment have been completed.

Certificates of Title A number of states have enacted **certificate of title laws,** which require the use of a certificate of title in the transfer of various types of motor vehicles. If there is a certificate of title law, a filing "is not necessary or effective" [§9-302(3)]. Perfection is achieved by complying with the certificate of title law and completing the steps for attachment. Most certificate of title laws require that a secured creditor have the security interest noted on the certificate of title by the governmental office that issues the certificate. A subsequent buyer or creditor will have notice of any security interest since a vehicle cannot be transferred without the certificate of title.

Consumer Goods No filing is required to perfect a security interest in certain transactions involving consumer goods [§9-302(1)(d)]. If a creditor extends credit or makes a loan that enables a debtor to purchase goods in which the creditor takes a security interest, the security interest created is called a **purchase money security interest** [§9-107]. When a purchase money security interest is created in consumer goods, no filing is required. Once the necessary conditions for attachment have occurred, perfection is automatic and no other steps are required [§9-302(1)(d)].

There is an exception to this rule. A financing statement must be filed to perfect a security interest in a motor vehicle required to be registered that is a consumer good unless the state has a certificate of title law. Compliance with the certificate of title law is required in these states instead of a filing [§9-302(1)(d) and 9-302(3)].

Consumer Goods and Subsequent Creditors A creditor who takes a purchase money security interest in consumer goods has rights against the debtor and is protected against all subsequent creditors even though no notice is given to third parties by means of filing. The risk that a consumer buyer will mislead a subsequent creditor and use consumer goods subject to a purchase money security interest as collateral for a loan is considered to be minimal and acceptable.

Consumer Goods and Subsequent Consumer Buyers A consumer buyer is a person who buys goods for personal, family, or household purposes. A consumer buyer who buys consumer goods from a consumer debtor takes the goods free from the secured party's security interest unless the secured party has filed a financing statement or the consumer buyer knows of the secured party's security interest [§9-307(2)]. The secured party does not need to file in order to perfect if the transaction is a purchase money security interest in consumer goods, but the secured party may choose to file in order to protect against a subsequent consumer buyer.

In deciding whether or not to file, a secured party who is not required to file to perfect must weigh the risks that a debtor will sell the collateral to another consumer. If the resale value of the collateral is likely to remain high enough for repossession to be desirable, the creditor will probably want to file to protect against a subsequent consumer buyer. If the collateral is not particularly valuable, the creditor may decide not to incur the expense of filing. In the event that a debtor resells the collateral, a secured party who has not filed will lose the right to repossess the collateral but not the right to sue the debtor for default on the loan.

Floating Liens The term "floating lien" is used by courts and by the drafters of the Uniform Commercial Code as a means of graphically depicting part of the operation of Article 9. The term itself is not used in the Code. A floating lien, in effect, is one that floats above the collateral. When a debtor acquires rights in after-acquired property or has a turn over in inventory, the lien of the security interest drops down and attaches, but perfection dates from the initial agreement. A creditor who creates a floating lien arrangement through the use of an after-acquired property clause, insures that the security interest created will generally have priority over subsequent creditors, provided that the proper steps for perfection have been taken.

The following case discusses the steps necessary to create a perfected security interest.

EMPIRE MACHINERY CO. v. UNION ROCK & MATERIALS
579 P.2d 1115 (Ariz. 1978)

[Empire Machinery Company, the defendant, and Union Rock & Materials, the plaintiff, are both claiming a security interest in the same piece of equipment. A major issue presented to the court is whether Union had a perfected security interest in the equipment.]

OGG, Judge

The facts are not in dispute. On September 3, 1968, Empire, as lessor, and K & L Contracting Company, Inc., lessee, entered into a lease agreement and separate option to purchase equipment described as "1-New Caterpillar #12 Motor Grader, S/N 13K515." Empire perfected a security interest in the collateral by filing a financing statement on September 5, 1968.

On February 24, 1970, K & L exercised its option to purchase the motor grader it was leasing from Empire, pursuant to the agreement of September 3, 1968, and Empire and K & L entered into an installment sale security agreement covering this transaction [i.e., a contract calling for the payment of the price in a number of installments]. The [security] interest . . . was perfected effective September 5, 1968 because the collat-

eral was [a continuation of] the prior perfected security interest between Empire and K & L.

Four days earlier, on February 20, 1970, K & L entered into agreement with Union whereby Union was granted a security interest in all earthmovers and other equipment items which K & L owned or in which it had an interest and which were located on K & L property. Union perfected this security interest on February 24, 1970. . . . In early 1974 K & L defaulted . . . and Empire took possession of the grader for the purposes of selling it at a public sale. . . . The trial court determined that (1) Union had a perfected valid security interest in the collateral [in] February . . . 1970, but it was inferior to that perfected by Empire on September 5, 1968. . . .

We will first consider the issue of whether Union had a valid interest in the collateral. The prerequisite for creating a valid security interest is that it attach, or become enforceable, against the debtor. [§9-203 and the comments thereto] provide that attachment occurs when there has been an agreement, value given, and the debtor has rights in the collateral. [The statute] also provide[s] that the requirements of the agreement are that it (1) is written, unless the secured party takes possession of the collateral; (2) provides for a security interest; (3) is signed by the debtor; and (4) contains a description of the collateral. Empire's first contention is that the description of Union's collateral in the present case does not include the grader and thus the parties did not intend to create a security agreement in that equipment. The result, claims Empire, is that the required agreement that the grader be encumbered [i.e., subject to a security interest] was not made and the interest did not attach. The description of the collateral reads:

> All earthmovers, blades, rollers, laydown machines, trucks, automobiles and pickup trucks owned by or in which the Debtor has an interest, and now located at Debtor's place of business at 861 South Center Street, Mesa, Arizona, or located on any of the Debtor's business sites.

We find this description sufficient and [it] demonstrates a clear intent by Union and K & L to create a security interest in the grader. The Code requires only that the description reasonably identify the collateral [§9-110]. The Code also provides that the purpose of the description is merely to give notice of a security interest and that further inquiry is necessary to obtain the exact information [§9-402, Comment 2]. . . . The type of activity for which a Caterpillar motor grader is used is generally the same as that of an earthmover, blade, roller, laydown machine and truck. We find the description reasonably identifies the grader and evidences an intent to utilize all equipment of that type as collateral. Any ambiguity could have been eradicated by making reasonable inquiry based on the information contained in the financing statement. Courts have consistently held that the description of collateral is sufficient if it reasonably puts a third party on notice of an existing security interest so that inquiry can be made. We hold, therefore, that the description of the collateral was sufficient to satisfy the requirement of an agreement. . . .

Empire's next contention is that at the time K & L entered into the agreement with Union, [K & L] did not have any rights in the collateral as required by [§9-203(1)(c)], and, as a result, it was incapable of creating a security interest in it. . . . The Commercial Code does not require a party to have rights in the property *at the time the agreement is made.* The security interest merely remains unenforceable until all the events of the attachment occur (agreement, value given and debtor has rights in the property) [§9-203 and §9-204]. Similarly, the financing statement can be filed prior to the time of attachment but does not give a party priority rights until all the events of attachment have taken place [§9-303(1)]. If the events of attachment have occurred at some point in time, the Union had a valid security interest. Since there had been no contention that value was not given, the questions we must decide are whether there was an agreement that the interest attach and, if so, whether K & L, the debtor, at any time acquired rights in the property which was the subject of the agreement.

The facts indicate that Union and K & L made an agreement that the grader be subject to the security interest. As stated above, the written agreement contained an adequate description evidencing the parties' intent to encumber the type of equipment in which a motor grader is included. The agreement also stated it covered all such equipment which K & L owned or in which it had an interest, and was located on K & L property. By including a provision for equipment in which K & L had an interest, Union and K & L demonstrated an intent to include in the security agreement more than K & L owned outright. By limiting the description to equipment located on K & L property, the collateral was limited to a specific group. Since K & L had a definite interest, an option to purchase, and the collateral was in the specified group, we think it clear that Union and K & L agreed that the specific grader in question was to be covered by the agreement.

Although Union and K & L intended the security agreement to include the grader, K & L's contract interest at the time of the agreement did not satisfy the requirement of rights in the property. However, because it was agreed to include the grader as collateral, the steps necessary to create a security interest were completed when K & L exercised the option to purchase and obtained the rights to the property. . . .

Although Union perfected a security interest in the grader in February 1970, Empire had previously perfected an interest in the same collateral. Empire's interest had priority over Union's since it was perfected first. . . .

We affirm the opinion of the trial court.

CASE REVIEW QUESTIONS

1. Why was it necessary for Union and K & L to have a written security agreement?
2. Who had to sign the agreement?
3. Why didn't the description in the security agreement have to identify the grader by name and serial number? Explain.
4. At what point in time did Union's security interest attach? What were the steps necessary for attachment?
5. Why did Empire create a security interest in the grader when it was leased in 1968?

PRIORITIES

Problems of priorities arise in situations where there are two or more persons claiming an interest in the same collateral. For example, in the preceding case, both Union and Empire had perfected security interests in the grader. The rules governing priorities determine who has the first right to possession of collateral when there are several persons with competing interests. The types of persons who may have competing interests with a secured party are (1) other creditors with perfected or unperfected security interests, (2) lien creditors, and (3) subsequent buyers of the collateral.

Competing Creditors

When competing creditors have security interests in the same collateral, the rule that applies in most situations is that priority is determined according to the time of filing or the time of perfecting, whichever comes first. Remember that in most cases security interests are perfected by filing, so usually only the time of filing need be determined. The purpose of the statute is to provide notice to subsequent creditors of the existence or the possible existence of outstanding security interests. Hence, the Code gives priority to the creditor who files first even though the security interest may not be perfected until a later date, which may even be after another creditor has perfected. A second creditor would be on notice of the possible existence of the security interest as soon as the first creditor files.

For example, suppose that A enters into negotiation with B to obtain a loan using a printing machine as collateral. A signs a financing statement that B files. Before A and B complete their negotiations, A borrows from C using the same printing machine as collateral. C takes possession of the printing machine, thereby perfecting. Several days later, A and B complete their negotiations and B loans A some money. A then signs a security agreement covering the equipment. Because B has already filed, B's security interest perfects when the necessary steps for attachment are completed. In a subsequent dispute over who is entitled to the collateral, B or C, B will win because B was the first to file. C could have learned of B's outstanding security interest by checking the files.

First to Perfect If a creditor perfects a security interest in some collateral without filing prior to the time another creditor files or perfects a security interest in the same collateral, the creditor who perfects first has priority. For example, when a creditor takes a purchase money security interest in some consumer goods, the security interest perfects without filing. If the consumer subsequently pledges the goods to another creditor, the creditor with the purchase money security interest would have priority because that creditor was the first to perfect.

The time and manner of filing are critical in determining when and if a security interest has been perfected. The following case involves several questions concerning the effectiveness of filings.

MATTER OF TOPPO
474 F.Supp. 48 (W.D. Penn. 1979)

KNOX, District Judge

This matter is before the court on appeal from the orders of the Bankruptcy Judge . . . dealing with petitions . . . filed by First National Bank of Pennsylvania (hereinafter Pa.), and General Electric Credit Corporation (GE). . . .

The security agreement was duly filed by Pa. in the [filing] office of Mercer County and financing statements were also filed in the Office of the Secretary of the Commonwealth at Harrisburg, (Penna. Dept of State) on February 4, 1977. The time stamp shows that the financing statements were received at 9:37 A.M.

Meanwhile, GE had also entered into financing arrangements with the bankrupts and likewise filed financing statements covering their security agreement which financing statements were filed in the [filing] office of Mercer County and with the Penna. Dept. of State on February 4, 1977. The time stamp showed that the financing statement was received at 9:04 A.M.

The difficulty with the filings of the financing statements as required under [§9-401] was that the GE statement, while bearing a time stamp 33 minutes earlier than the time stamp on the Pa.'s financing statement, nevertheless was given a later number, 8650<u>243</u>, while Pa.'s statements had earlier numbers 8650<u>160</u>, 8650<u>162</u>, the Pa. statements being numbered 81 numerals ahead of GE's statements.

The Bankruptcy Judge has engaged in speculation in determining priority where the time stamp of GE is ahead of Pa.'s but Pa.'s numbers are ahead of GE's. It is sheer conjecture to imagine without evidence what might have occurred in the mail room of the Department of State which would explain this absurd situation, which so far as research by counsel and the court can determine is unique in the history of the Uniform Commercial Code.

There is nothing in the Uniform Commercial Code which says anything about the performance of quasi-judicial functions by the Department of State in determining whether to accept a financing statement for filing. Rather, under [§9-302(1)] reference is made to the filing of a financing statement and under [§9-312(5)(a)] the security agreement is perfected by "filing." We therefore hold that in the absence of evidence in this strange situation, the time stamps must control and therefore GE's security interest is superior to Pa.'s insofar as the rights of the parties are determined by the Uniform Commercial Code. This result gives GE a priority. . . .

[Affirmed.]

CASE REVIEW QUESTIONS

1. Whose financing statement was filed first, GE's or Pa.'s? Why?
2. Who has priority? Explain.

Competing Perfected and Unperfected Security Interests A creditor with a perfected security interest will have priority over a creditor with an unperfected security interest regardless of whose security interest attached first. For example, if A takes a security interest in X's property but fails to perfect and B subsequently takes a security interest in the same collateral and does perfect, B will have priority over A. If both creditors are unperfected, the first to attach has priority [§9-312(5)(b)].

Purchase Money Security Interests in Inventory or Equipment Filing is required to perfect a purchase money security interest in inventory or equipment. There is no exception for a purchase money security interest in these types of goods as there is for consumer goods [§9-302]. Nevertheless, a secured party who takes a purchase money security interest in inventory or equipment will have priority over other creditors provided certain conditions are met [§9-312(3) and (4)]. For instance, when the collateral is inventory, the purchase money security interest must be perfected when the debtor takes possession of the collateral. In addition, the secured party must give notice in writing to any other secured party who has filed a financing statement covering the same type of inventory [§9-312(3)]. A secured party who takes a purchase money security interest enjoys this priority in order to enable a debtor to purchase inventory on credit without it becoming subject to any after-acquired property clauses in already existing security agreements.

For example, suppose that A borrows from B, who takes a security interest in A's inventory, including all inventory presently owned or subsequently acquired. At a later date, A wishes to purchase some new inventory from C on credit. B already has filed a financing statement covering A's inventory, has entered into an agreement with A creating a security interest in A's subsequently acquired inventory, and has given value. The only step left to complete attachment, and therefore perfection for B, is for A to acquire rights in the subsequently purchased inventory. When C enters into a contract to sell A inventory, A will have rights in the collateral (§2-501) and B's security interest will perfect. C will have priority over B, however, provided that C's security interest is perfected at the time A receives possession of the collateral and C has given B written notice of the transaction [§9-312(3)]. Thus, C can sell inventory to A on credit and retain a security interest that, if properly and timely perfected, will have priority over other creditors, including prior creditors.

Lien Creditors **Lien creditors** acquire liens on property in several ways. A party to a judicial proceeding may have his or her property seized by court order so that a judgment rendered against the party may be satisfied out of the property. The party for whose benefit the property has been seized is a lien creditor. When a debtor makes an assignment of property for the benefit of creditors, the creditors are lien creditors from the time of the assignment. A **trustee in bankruptcy,** who is a person appointed by a bankruptcy court to manage the property of a bankrupt debtor, is a lien creditor of the assets of the debtor from the date of the filing of the bankruptcy petition [§9-301(3)].

A lien creditor has priority over an unperfected security interest provided that the lien creditor levies—that is, obtains his or her interest in the property—before the security interest is perfected [§9-301(1)(b)]. For example, a trustee in bankruptcy has priority over any secured party whose security interest in the debtor's property remains unperfected on the day the debtor files for bankruptcy.

In the following case, a creditor loses to a trustee in bankruptcy.

MATTER OF CRIPPS
31 B.R. 541 (W.D. Okla. 1983)*

ROBERT L. BERRY, Bankruptcy Judge

The trustee [in bankruptcy] for the debtor estate has received certain accounts receivable of the debtors' business. Petitioner [Cripps] seeks to obtain these sums, alleging that she is a bona fide purchaser of the same. Trustee counters, by alleging that he is a superior lien creditor pursuant to [the Bankruptcy Act], and therefore entitled to retain the funds.

The parties have stipulated to the following facts:

1. Jo Anne Brock ("petitioner") entered into discussions with Duane Cripps ("debtor") to purchase the accounts receivable of the debtors' business.
2. Petitioner agreed to purchase and debtor agreed to sell certain accounts receivable of the business.
3. Debtor sold certain accounts receivable to petitioner and executed a bill of sale.
4. The sale of accounts receivable was not a commercial financing transaction, nor a loan pledged as collateral.
5. Subsequent to purchase, petitioner took physical possession of the invoices, or copies thereof, of the accounts receivable and began to collect monies due on said accounts.

6. The debtors subsequently filed this Chapter 7 Bankruptcy.
7. No [financing statement] filing of the accounts receivable was made by petitioner.

A resolution of this case is provided for by Article 9. . . . [§9-102] provides in pertinent part: "(1) Except as otherwise provided in Section 9-104 on excluded transactions, this Article applies: . . . (b) to any sale of accounts or chattel paper."

The UCC Comment 2 to §9-102 states that:

[A] sale of such property (accounts, contract rights and chattel paper) is therefore covered by [§9-102(1)(b)] whether intended for security or not, unless excluded by §9-103 or §9-104. The buyer then is treated as a secured party, and his interest as a security interest.

None of the exclusions provided for in §9-103 or §9-104 cover the sale in the case as bar.

"Security interest" is defined at [§1-201(37)] as follows:

"Security interest" means an interest in personal property or fixtures which secures payment or performance of an obligation. . . . The term also includes any interest of a buyer of accounts or chattel paper which is subject to Article 9.

---

* B.R. is a reference to the Bankruptcy Reporter.

Clearly then, the sale of accounts creates a security interest, a security interest which is governed by the provisions of UCC Article 9. . . .

The import of this is that, should it be determined that petitioner had not properly perfected her interest in the accounts receivable, then, upon the filing of bankruptcy, the trustee as a lien creditor will have a security interest superior to that of petitioner, pursuant to [the Bankruptcy Act]. . . . The [Bankruptcy Act] interplays with [§9-301(1)(b)], which states:

> Except as otherwise provided in subsection (2), of this section, an unperfected security interest is subordinate to the rights of a person who becomes a lien creditor without knowledge of the security interest and before it is perfected. A "lien creditor" means a creditor who has acquired a lien on the property involved by attachment, levy or the like and includes . . . a trustee in bankruptcy from the date of the filing of the petition. . . .

By the terms of [the Bankruptcy Act], the trustee has the rights of a . . . lien creditor; under [§9-301(1)(b)] he accordingly prevails over Article 9 claimants whose interests are unperfected as of the filing of bankruptcy.

Perfection of a security interest under UCC Article 9 may occur by one of two methods; either by filing or by possession. The manner of perfection is contingent upon the nature of the items sought to be perfected.

Perfection of a security interest in accounts, contract rights and general intangibles may only be effectuated by filing. See UCC Comment 1 [§9-304 and §9-305].

> Even if the creditor collects ledger cards, journals, computer print-outs, sales slips and any other items believed to represent receivables he will not by those acts perfect a security interest in accounts.

In the instant case, perfection would only have been accomplished by filing. Failing to do so, petitioner, upon the filing of this bankruptcy, became subordinate to the rights of the trustee. . . .

Accordingly, the receivables which have been paid to the trustee are the property of the debtor estate.

CASE REVIEW QUESTIONS

1. What steps are necessary in order to perfect a security interest in accounts receivable?
2. Had Brock perfected her security interest in the accounts receivable?
3. Explain why a trustee in bankruptcy has priority over an unperfected security interest?

Rights of Buyers

If a secured creditor perfects his or her security interest, he or she has priority over most buyers who purchase secured property from a debtor.

In several situations, however, a buyer of collateral subject to a security interest takes free of the security interest even if it is perfected. For example, if a secured party authorizes the sale of collateral, a buyer takes free from the security interest [§9-306(2)]. Thus, if a creditor with a perfected security interest allows a debtor to sell the collateral as a means of securing the cash to pay the creditor, the creditor cannot repossess the goods if the debtor fails to repay him or her.

Buyers in the Ordinary Course of Business Even if a secured party has not authorized a sale, a buyer in the ordinary course of business [§1-201(9)] takes free of any security interest granted by the seller of the goods even though the buyer knows of the existence of the security interest. However, this rule does not apply to purchases of farm products from a person engaged in farming [§9-307(1)].

This section deals with the situation in which a debtor is a merchant [§2-104(1)] who is selling collateral as part of his or her business operations to a buyer who is purchasing goods in an ordinary way. Even if the buyer knows that the goods being sold are subject to a security interest, he or she takes free from the security interest. For example, if the credit manager of the bank who negotiated the inventory financing for a department store purchases some furniture from that store, the credit manager takes free from the bank's perfected security interest even though he or she knows of the bank's security interest in the furniture.

The rule that allows a buyer in the ordinary course of business to take free from a perfected security interest is based upon the balancing of the interests of the parties involved. The bank that financed the inventory and the debtor want the goods to be sold so that the debtor can repay the loan. Buyers want to avoid the confusion that would result if they had to obtain proof that the creditors who are financing the store's operation have indeed authorized the sale. By allowing buyers in the ordinary course of business to take free from any security interests created by the seller of the collateral, the law facilitates the sale of goods necessary for the debtor–seller to be able to pay the creditor. A creditor can protect his or her interest in the repayment of the loan or the credit extended to purchase the inventory by also taking a security interest in the proceeds from the sale of the inventory in the form of cash or accounts receivable.

The right of a buyer in the ordinary course of business to take free from a security interest is limited to situations in which the seller of the goods is the debtor in the secured transaction that created the security interest. For example, suppose A, as creditor, enters into a secured transaction with B, who is the debtor and is also a retail seller of the type of property that makes up the collateral. C, who buys some of the collateral from B, takes free from A's security interest. If C does not qualify as a buyer in the ordinary course of business, C would hold the property subject to A's security interest. Suppose that C is also a retail seller of the goods purchased from B. If C sells to D, who is a buyer in the ordinary course of business, D does not take free from A's security interest because C did not create the security interest with A. B did. D would take free of A's security interest only if C had created it.

Consumer Buyers If a debtor has granted a security interest in consumer goods he or she owns and then sells those goods, the rule is somewhat different. A buyer of the goods will take free of the secured party's perfected security interest only if he or she is buying the goods for personal, family, or household purposes and doesn't know of the secured party's interest and the secured party has not filed a financing statement [§9-307(2)].

Recall that a creditor who takes a purchase money security interest in consumer goods need not file to perfect. The creditor is protected against competing creditors and lien creditors, but he or she would lose the security interest if a consumer buyer who doesn't know about the security interest buys the goods. The creditor can, of course, pursue the debtor for repayment of the debt, but he or she cannot repossess the collateral. Thus, a creditor who takes a purchase money security interest in consumer goods has to balance the risk that another consumer will buy the goods against the expense and effort required to file.

The competing parties in the following case are the purchase money security interest holder and a pawn broker. The goods are consumer goods. The pawn broker presents several arguments.

KIMBRELL'S FURNITURE COMPANY, INC. v. FRIEDMAN
108 S.E.2d 803 (S.C. 1973)

LEWIS, Justice

This action . . . was brought by Kimbrell's Furniture Company, Inc., against the defendant Sig Friedman, d/b/a Bonded Loan, to determine the priority of conflicting liens held by them over a new television set and tape player. The facts are not in dispute.

The liens involve two separate purchases from Kimbrell—one of a new television set by Charlie O'Neal on July 11, 1972, and the other by his wife of a tape player on July 15, 1972. Each purchase was on credit and in each instance there was executed, as security, a conditional sale contract, designated a purchase money security agreement. Later, on the same day of each purchase, O'Neal carried the item to defendant Bonded Loan (a pawnbroker) and pledged it as security for a loan—the television for a loan of $30.00 and the tape player for a loan of $25.00.

Kimbrell did not record on the public records any financing statement or notice of either of the foregoing security agreements.

Bonded Loan (pawnbroker) holds possession of the television set and tape player as security for its loan and contends that its lien is prior to the unrecorded purchase security interest of Kimbrell. The lower court sustained this contention and Kimbrell has appealed.

The question to be decided is correctly stated by appellant as follows: Is a conditional seller of consumer goods required to file a financing statement in order to perfect his security interest against a pawnbroker who subsequently takes possession of such goods as security for a loan? . . .

Goods are classified or defined for purposes of secured transactions under [§9-109]. Subsection 1 defines "consumer goods" as those "used or bought for

use primarily for personal, family or household purposes." The property here involved was a television set and tape player. They are normally used for personal, family or household purposes and the purchasers warranted that such was the intended use. It is undisputed in this case that the collateral involved was consumer goods within the meaning of the foregoing statutory definition.

Kimbrell clearly held a *purchase money security interest* in the consumer goods sold to the O'Neals and, by them, subsequently pledged to Bonded Loan [§9-107(a)]. . . . [T]he UCC does not require filing in order to perfect a purchase money security interest in consumer goods. Pertinent here, [§9-302(l)(d)] provides:

> A financing statement must be filed to perfect all security interests except . . . (d) a purchase money security interest in consumer goods. . . .

Since filing was not necessary, the security interest of Kimbrell attached and was perfected when the debtors executed the purchase money security agreements and took possession of the property [§9-203 and §9-303(1)]. Therefore, Kimbrell's security interest has priority over the security interest of Bonded Loan by virtue of [§9-312(4)]. . . .

Bonded Loan, however, alleges that its interest takes priority over the security of Kimbrell by virtue of [§9-307(1)] which is as follows:

> A buyer in the ordinary course of business [§1-201(9)] other than a person buying farm products from a person engaged in farming operations takes free of a security interest created by his seller even though the

security interest is perfected and even though a buyer knows of its existence.

The above section affords Bonded Loan no relief. It was not a buyer in the ordinary course of business so as to take free of the security interest of Kimbrell. A buyer in the ordinary course of business is defined in [§1-201(9)]. . . .

[U]nder the foregoing definition, a buyer in ordinary course of business

must be "without knowledge that the sale to him is in violation of the ownership rights or security interests of a third party . . . " *and* the seller must be a "person in the business of selling goods of that kind. . . . " Thus [§9-307(1)] is limited to the *buyer out of inventory* who

may know of the inventory financer's security interest but does not know that the sale to him is unauthorized. [Emphasis added.]

Therefore, Bonded Loan could not have been a buyer in the ordinary course of business when O'Neal pledged the property to it, because O'Neal was not "a person in the business of selling goods of that kind."

The judgment of the lower court is accordingly reversed and the cause remanded for entry of judgment in favor of plaintiff, Kimbrell's Furniture Company, Inc., in accordance with the views herein.

CASE REVIEW QUESTIONS

1. Does Kimbrell have perfected security interests in the television set and the tape player? Why?
2. When does a purchase money security interest in consumer goods perfect?
3. Does Bonded Loan have a perfected security interest in the television set and the tape player? Why?
4. Whose security interest has priority—Kimbrell's or Bonded Loan's? Why?
5. Why isn't Bonded Loan a buyer in the ordinary course of business?
6. Why couldn't Bonded Loan argue that it was a consumer buyer?
7. If Sig Friedman had purchased the television from Charlie O'Neal for Sig Friedman's personal and family use, would Kimbrell's have been able to repossess the set?

PROCEEDS

In every secured transaction, there is always the possibility that the collateral will be sold or exchanged for different property. When inventory subject to a security interest is sold, the collateral becomes the cash or accounts receivable generated by the sale. When collateral that is insured is destroyed, the collateral becomes the insurance proceeds. The term proceeds is defined as whatever is received upon the sale, exchange, collection, or other disposition of collateral. Money, checks, deposit accounts, and the like are *cash proceeds.* All other types of proceeds are *noncash proceeds* [§9-306(1)].

A holder of a perfected security interest has a perfected security interest in proceeds for ten days after a debtor receives them. For example, a creditor with a security interest in inventory will have a security interest in the cash or accounts receivable from the sale of the inventory for ten days after the sale. This period of perfection can be extended by the proper filings or by obtaining possession of the proceeds before the end of the ten day period [§9-306(3)]. Tracing proceeds can sometimes be difficult, however. For example, it may be difficult to identify insurance proceeds from the loss of collateral if they are used to purchase new goods.

Proceeds are not the same as after-acquired property. Proceeds are the same collateral in a different form. After-acquired property is property in which a debtor acquires rights subsequent to the creation of the security interest. It is property in addition to rather than in substitution for the collateral specified in the security agreement.

Commingled Collateral

A similar tracing problem exists when goods subject to a security interest are mingled with other goods. The Code provides that when goods subject to a perfected security interest are mingled with other goods or become part of a manufactured product in such a manner that the goods lose their identity, the secured party has a security interest in a proportional share of the mass of the goods or the product [§9-315]. For example, a secured party's security interest in eggs is not lost when the eggs are used to make cakes.

If the collateral retains its identity but is incorporated into a product in such a way that it cannot be separated, the secured party retains a security interest only if the financing statement filed to perfect the security interest also covers the product into which the collateral has been incorporated. For example, a secured party who has a security interest in picture tubes will retain a security interest in television sets incorporating the picture tubes only if the financing statement lists picture tubes *and* television sets as collateral.

In the following case, a creditor traces its perfected security interest in vegetables right into the processing plant and, in effect, right into the canned product. The rule that a buyer of goods in the ordinary course of business takes free from a perfected security interest does not apply to farm products, so the processor who purchased the vegetables does not take free from the bank's security interest in the vegetables. Moreover, since some of the farm products had been sold by the processor, the secured party also traces its interest into the proceeds from the sales.

MATTER OF SAN JUAN PACKERS, INC.
626 F.2d 707 (9th Cir. 1983)

PER CURIAM [By the court]

This is a dispute between a secured creditor of a bankrupt food processor and a secured creditor of farmers from whom the food processor bought vegetables. The food processor, San Juan Packers, Inc., bought cans on credit from a can manufacturer, National Can Corporation, and granted the can manufacturer a floating lien on all of its inventory. In late summer, 1976, the food processor bought vegetables from many farmers, including the three involved in this litigation. These three farmers had obtained financing from

Peoples State Bank and had granted the bank a security interest in their crops and the "proceeds" thereof.

The food processor filed a petition in bankruptcy after it had received the farmers' vegetables and processed and sold a portion of them, but before it had finished paying all purchase price installments due the farmers. Not having been paid by the food processor, the farmers did not pay the bank. The bank brought this . . . proceeding in bankruptcy court against all of the food processor's secured creditors to establish the priority of the bank's security interest in the farmers' vegetables and in the cash proceeds thereof . . . .

The bankruptcy court found for the bank, and the can manufacturer appealed to the district court, which affirmed. The can manufacturer appeals to this court, advancing three contentions.

The can manufacturer first contends that money received by the food processor for the farmers' vegetables are not "proceeds" to which the bank's security interest attached under its security agreements with the farmers.

The Uniform Commercial Code (UCC) provides that "[p]roceeds includes whatever is received when collateral or proceeds is sold, exchanged, collected or otherwise disposed of" [Section 9-306(1)]. Under this definition, the money the food processor received for the farmers' vegetables is "proceeds" unless the vegetables ceased to be collateral when purchased by the food processor. . . .

The can manufacturer protests that under this view the bank could follow these vegetables into the hands of the ultimate consumer.* But this is precisely what the plain language of the UCC requires. . . .

The can manufacturer's second argument is that by the terms of §9-306(2) the bank's security interest continued only in "identifiable proceeds" and was lost because the food processor mixed together vegetables purchased from various farmers making it impossible to identify vegetables, or proceeds from the sale of vegetables remaining in the food processor's possession, as attributable to any particular farmer.

Section 9-315 of the UCC requires rejection of this argument. The bank had a perfected security interest in the farmers' vegetables, and those vegetables became part of a mass of vegetables in the hands of the food processor, so commingled that their identity became lost in the mass. By the express terms of §9-315(1), where collateral loses its identity by commingling or processing, the security interest continues in the mass or product — and it is not disputed that the proceeds in the fund established in this case can be traced to commingled vegetables in the hands of the food processor. . . .

Finally, the can manufacturer argues that if §9-315 is applied, the can manufacturer was entitled to share in the fund since the can manufacturer had a security interest in the vegetables in the food processor's possession grown by farmers other than the three in whose crops the bank had a security interest, and by the terms of §9-315 each party whose collateral is commingled in the mass in entitled to a ratable share of the proceeds of the sale of the mass. The bank resists application of §9-315 on the ground, relied upon by the district court, that §9-315(1) "requires the attachment of two security interests to the product or mass." The attachment of two security interests to the product or mass is an explicit condition only to the operation of §9-315(2), not §9-315(1). Moreover, this condition to the application of §9-315(2) was satisfied because both the bank's interest in the vegetables of the three farmers with whom the bank had its security arrangement and the can manufacturer's security interest in the other vegetables in the food processor's inventory attached to the mass of each variety of vegetables when the vegetables of the same variety purchased from various farmers were commingled. . . .

The judgment appealed from is therefore vacated, and the case is remanded for further proceedings:

1. to determine what proportion of each mass of the various vegetables was sold by the food processor prior to its bankruptcy;

---

* Section 9-307(1) provides that some buyers in the ordinary course of business take free of security interests, but specifically excludes "a person buying farm products from a person engaged in farming operations."

Although a person who does not purchase directly from farmers does not come within the farm products exception, he still does not take free of the original lender's security interest because that interest was not "created by his seller" [§9-307(1)]. [Footnotes combined.]

2. to apportion the available proceeds, if any, from such sales between the bank and the can manufacturer in accordance with §§9-315(2) and 9-306(4); and

3. to apportion the proceeds of sales made under

the bankruptcy court's supervision between the bank and the can manufacturer in accordance with §9-315(2).

[R]emanded.

CASE REVIEW QUESTIONS

1. Who are the competing creditors?
2. In what does the bank claim a security interest?
3. In what does the can company claim a security interest?
4. Why did the processor as a buyer not take free from the bank's security interest under §9-307(1)?
5. Would a purchaser of the canned vegetables from the processor take free from the bank's security interest? Why?
6. How far does the court state that a secured creditor can follow the collateral?

TERMINATION

If all goes well, a debtor pays a secured creditor for the amount of the loan or the credit extended. When all payments have been made and no additional credit is available under the terms of a security agreement, the secured transaction comes to an end. If the collateral is consumer goods, the debtor can demand in writing that the creditor file a termination statement in all offices where a financing statement was filed [§9-404(1)]. The termination statement gives notice that the collateral described in the financing statement is no longer subject to a security interest.

If the collateral is not consumer goods, the secured party need only provide the debtor with a termination statement for each office where a financing statement was filed [§9-404(1)]. Thus, the burden and expense of filing a termination statement is on a debtor when the collateral is not consumer goods.

A secured creditor is required to file in the case of consumer goods because a consumer debtor may not appreciate the necessity of filing a termination statement to clear the record. The rule does not place an undue burden on secured creditors since many security interests in consumer goods perfect without filing. For instance, purchase money security interests in consumer goods need not be filed to perfect. In addition, even though filing is required to perfect a purchase money security interest in a motor vehicle that is a consumer good, no filing need be made in those jurisdictions where perfection of the security interest depends upon compliance with a certificate of title law rather than upon filing. Moreover, a secured creditor who had to file to perfect has to file a termination statement only if the debtor demands it in writing.

A secured party must either file or send a termination statement within ten days after the demand is made by a debtor. A secured creditor who fails to do this is liable to the debtor for $100 plus any losses the debtor may suffer. For example, suppose a debtor demands a termination statement to clear the record of a security interest so that he or she can use the collateral for a new loan from a third party. Suppose further that the secured creditor fails to supply the termination statement as demanded and the loan is not made because the collateral is not cleared. Any loss that the debtor suffers because the new loan arrangement is not completed can be charged to the secured party who failed to supply the termination statement.

DEBTORS' AND CREDITORS' RIGHTS ON DEFAULT

Default by a debtor occurs when he or she fails to make a payment or in some other way breaches the terms of a security agreement.

Repossession

The basic right of a creditor upon default is to take possession of—that is, repossess—the collateral [§9-503]. A creditor may repossess without resorting to any judicial proceeding provided that the repossession occurs without a breach of the peace. This is called *self-help repossession.*

If self-help repossession is not feasible or if a creditor so chooses, the creditor can repossess collateral by means of a court action, which in most jurisdictions will be some form of an **action for replevin,** that is, an action to determine who has the right to possession of goods. In an action for replevin, a debtor must usually be given notice of the action and afforded the opportunity for a judicial hearing on the matter before the creditor can take possession of the collateral.

Right of Redemption A debtor has the right to redeem collateral that has been repossessed before it is sold by a creditor. If a debtor tenders the payment due on the debt plus reasonable expenses, a creditor must return the collateral to the debtor [§9-506]. The reasonable expenses that must be paid to redeem collateral include those costs incurred by a secured party in taking the goods, storing them, preparing them for resale, and arranging for the resale. In some situations, reasonable expenses also include attorney's fees. A debtor must pay all amounts that are due. If a security agreement accelerates payments—that is, makes future payments due immediately—a debtor must pay not only the overdue amounts but also the accelerated payments in order to redeem the collateral.* Frequently, a security agreement will accelerate all future payments in the event of a default. A debtor who has defaulted because of an inability to make one payment will probably not be able to pay all future payments plus expenses to redeem the goods.

---

* In some jurisdictions, this rule has been changed by consumer legislation to allow a debtor to redeem for overdue payments plus penalties only.

Disposition of Collateral

A secured party is required to proceed in a commercially reasonable manner when disposing of collateral, whether it is repossessed collateral or collateral that was already in the hands of the creditor, as in the case of a pledge [§9-504]. A sale of the collateral by a secured party may be private or public. Notice to the debtor of the resale is required in most situations. In the case of consumer goods, it is sufficient if a secured party notifies a debtor of the period of time after which there will be a disposition of the goods. A debtor can, however, waive the right to any notice [§9-504(3)].

In order to protect a consumer debtor, the Code provides some specific guidelines for the disposition of repossessed collateral. If a debtor has paid 60 percent of the cash price where the security interest is a purchase money security interest or 60 percent of a loan and has not waived his or her rights by a signed writing given to the creditor after the default, the creditor must dispose of the collateral in a commercially reasonable manner within ninety days [§9-505(1)]. A creditor who fails to comply with this rule will be subject to penalties provided by the Code [§9-507].

After a default, a debtor who has paid 60 percent or more may, in writing, waive his or her right to have the repossessed goods sold within ninety days. When this occurs, the secured party may simply keep the goods in lieu of any claim or deficiency judgment against the debtor. A **deficiency judgment** is a claim by the creditor for the difference between the amount received from the sale of the collateral and the unpaid amounts owed by the debtor plus the expenses incurred by the creditor upon default. In all other default situations —that is, for consumers who have paid less than 60 percent and for all other debtors regardless of the percentage paid—a creditor may after default propose to keep the collateral in lieu of any claims against the debtor or any surety for the debtor (i.e., a person who promises to pay if the debtor does not pay) [§9-505(2)].

If, after default, a debtor has not signed a waiver of his or her right to have a sale of the collateral within ninety days, a creditor must give the debtor written notice of any proposal to retain the collateral in satisfaction of the creditor's claims against the debtor. If the debtor wishes the creditor to dispose of the collateral, he or she must object in writing to the creditor's proposal to keep the collateral. The debtor's objection must be received by the creditor within twenty-one days of the date the notice was sent by the creditor.

Remedies for Failure of Creditor to Comply with Repossession or Resale Requirements

The Code provides various remedies for the failure of a secured party to comply with the rules [§9-507]. Disposition of collateral can be ordered or restrained, depending upon the circumstances. For example, if a creditor proposes to dispose of collateral in an unreasonable way, such as private sale to a friend without giving the debtor appropriate notice of the intent to sell, a court could enjoin the proposed sale and order a more appropriate sale.

If a creditor, by failing to repossess or resell in accordance with the law, causes a loss to a debtor, the loss can be recovered from the creditor. If a consumer debtor suffers loss, the law provides a formula that insures a minimum recovery as a penalty even though the actual loss may be less [§9-507(1)]. The consumer debtor can recover an amount not less than the service charge, which is the interest and other costs imposed by the creditor in the transaction, plus ten percent of the principal amount of the debt.

If a secured party disposes of collateral in an unreasonable manner or for an unreasonably low price, the creditor may be denied a deficiency judgment [§9-504(1) and §9-504(2)]. The fact that a better price could have been obtained does not, in and of itself, establish the fact that a sale was commercially unreasonable, but it is a factor to be considered [§9-507(2)]. Conversely, if a secured party realized a profit on a disposition, a debtor is entitled to any surplus over the amount of the loan less the expenses incurred by the creditor in the repossession and resale [§9-504(2)].

The following case explores the guidelines for the sale of collateral by a secured party. A substantial disparity between the sale price and the fair market value of the collateral was sufficient to raise an issue of fact as to the reasonableness of the sale.

SCHROCK v. CITIZENS VALLEY BANK
621 P.2d 96 (OT 1980)

CAMPBELL, Judge

Plaintiff [Schrock] executed two promissory notes to the defendant [Citizens Valley Bank] together with security agreements granting defendant a security interest in certain items of personal property, mostly farm equipment. Plaintiff defaulted on the notes. Defendant commenced an action for replevin, obtained immediate possession of the collateral, and proceeded to sell it by public auction. Plaintiff thereafter brought this action to recover damages sustained by defendant's alleged failure to conduct the public auction in a commercially reasonable manner. The jury returned a verdict in the amount of $30,000 in favor of the plaintiff. Defendant appeals. We affirm. . . .

A secured party taking possession of collateral on default may dispose of the collateral by sale or otherwise so long as every aspect of the disposition is commercially reasonable [§9-504(3)]. The debtor may recover from the secured party any loss caused by a failure to comply with this requirement [§9-507(1)]. By

returning a verdict in favor of plaintiff the jury necessarily found that the defendant did not conduct the public auction in a commercially reasonable manner.

> The normal measure of damages where there has been a failure to sell in a commercially reasonable manner is the difference between the price actually obtained and the price that could have been obtained by proceeding in a commercially reasonable manner. . . .

Defendant's sole argument is that plaintiff failed to introduce any evidence of the prices which could have been obtained had the auction in all respect been commercially reasonable. Defendant thus contends there was no proof of damages.

Proceeds from the auction totaled approximately $143,000. Four farm equipment dealers testified on behalf of plaintiff with respect to the fair market value of various items of equipment sold at the auction. Their testimony would have allowed the jury to find the aggregate fair market value of the equipment to have been more than $200,000. Several auctioneers testified that an auctioneer conducting a forced auction owed a duty to the debtor to obtain the highest price possible for the property. Two of them testified that, although a well run auction will bring a fair market price, receipt of 80 to 90 percent of the fair market value would be acceptable. The jury could reasonably have concluded that, had the auction been conducted in a commercially reasonable manner, it would have brought in $173,000 or more and that plaintiff suffered a loss in the amount of $30,000.

Affirmed.

CASE REVIEW QUESTIONS
1. What standard does the Code impose upon the sale of repossessed collateral?
2. What evidence is there that the standard was not met in this case?
3. What is the measure of damages where the standard has not been met?

REVIEW QUESTIONS

1. What are the three conditions for attachment?
2. What are the two steps for perfection?
3. Name three exceptions to the filing rule. Why are these exceptions allowed?
4. Explain the purpose of priorities.
5. Do buyers ever take free from security interests? Explain.
6. What are proceeds?
7. What are a creditor's rights and duties when a debtor defaults?

CASE PROBLEMS

1. Mid-American Dairy, Inc. (Dairy) loaned William H. Gallentine $3,081.91 to purchase a milk-holding tank. Gallentine signed a chattel mortgage and a financing statement. Dairy signed and filed the financing statement with the County Clerk of Hamilton County, the county where Gallentine resided. The financing statement gave the debtor's name and address as "William H. Gallentine, Aurora, Hamilton County" and the secured party's name and address as "Mid-American Daily, Inc., Omaha, Nebraska." The goods were described in the financing statement as "one farm bulk milk pickup tank, 1966, Kari-Kool plastic, 2100 gallons." After the financing statement was filed, Gallentine purchased a Kari-Kool milk tank as described. Subsequently, Gallentine sold the milk tank and some farm equipment to Newman Grove Cooperative Creamery Company, Inc. (Newman). When Dairy discovered the sale it sued Newman to recover the milk tank. Newman defended on the grounds that Dairy's security interest never attached inasmuch as Gallentine did not own the tank at the time the chattel mortgage was signed. Did Dairy's security interest attach? Explain.

2. The Friendly Loan Company made a loan to Harris taking a security interest in "All of the household consumer goods of every kind now owned or hereafter acquired by the Borrower in replacement of said consumer goods now or hereafter located in or about the residence of the Borrower. . . ." Over the next several years, Harris replaced all of the furniture in his home either by purchases or by way of gifts. Harris then filed for bankruptcy. The loan company claimed a security interest in all of Harris's furniture.

Does the loan company have a security interest in the furniture? Explain.

3. Dean Billings borrowed money from the Production Credit Association (PCA) to purchase livestock. Billings signed a security agreement describing certain livestock, inventory, equipment, and "all property similar to that described . . . which at any time may hereafter be acquired by Debtor. . . ." PCA filed a financing statement covering "All Machinery, All Cattle, All Feed, All Equipment, Auto and Truck." The financing statement was signed by Dean Billings. The following year, Billings purchased 66 head of cattle from Alfred Barth and signed a promissory note but no security agreement. Barth filed a financing statement. Billings went out of business, and PCA made arrangements to auction the cattle. After PCA's auctioneer had taken possession of the cattle, Barth attempted to repossess the 66 head of cattle from PCA's auctioneer.

   a. Does PCA have a perfected interest in all of Billing's cattle including the 66 head purchased from Barth? Explain.

   b. Does Barth have a perfected security interest in the 66 head of cattle? Explain.

   c. Who is entitled to the cattle? Explain.

4. Deere Company loaned money to John Ranalli who signed a security agreement and a financing statement covering certain equipment. Deere Company filed a handwritten financing statement that appeared to list the debtor's name as John Ranelli. The financing statement was indexed under John Ranelli. Is Deere Company's security interest perfected? Explain.

5. Frank J. and Hermelinda Montavon signed an agreement called "Security Agreement — Pledge." The Montavon's also endorsed two certificates of deposit (CDs) in blank and delivered them to the Alamo National Bank as collateral for a $25,000 loan that the Alamo Bank gave to Fipco, Inc., a company owned by the Montavons. Fipco defaulted. Although the bank attempted to obtain payment of the loan, it ultimately applied the CDs against the unpaid loan. The Montavons sued to recover the amount of the CDs, alleging that the bank had wrongfully converted their property since no financing statement had been filed. The bank defended on the grounds that it was merely executing its rights as a perfected security interest holder. Is the bank correct? Why? Explain.

6. Douglas Hill Staley purchased a stereo and a freezer from Goodyear Tire Company and signed a credit agreement that granted Goodyear a security interest in each item purchased until each item was paid for in full. Goodyear filed no financing statement. Staley subsequently defaulted in his payments and filed for bankruptcy. The bankruptcy court held that Goodyear had not perfected its security interest. Has Goodyear perfected its security interest? Explain.

7. White Star Distributors, Inc. (White Star) sold a used Winnebago motor home to William Scheuerle, who made a cash downpayment and signed a security agreement. Although the state where Scheuerle lives requires motor homes to be registered, it had not enacted a certificate of title statute. White Star never filed a financing statement. Scheuerle sold the Winnebago to Jan Jerge, who sold it to John Henchey, who sold it to Roy Kennedy. White Star attempted to recover the vehicle from Kennedy. White Star argued that no filing was needed to perfect a purchase money security interest in consumer goods. Should White Star be granted possession of the Winnebago? Explain.

8. DWG, Inc., sold Billy Peltier a lady's watch and two rings on credit. Peltier signed a security agreement and a financing statement. The security agreement described the watch as "1 – C/13 – M7325 – Gordon watch" and the rings as "ladies' bridal set — white gold." The financing statement described the watch as "Gordon watch M7325" and the rings as "a ladies' bracelet set — white gold." DWG immediately filed the financing statement. Subsequently, Peltier borrowed some money from the Grant Square Bank. The bank took possession of a watch and two rings. Peltier defaulted on his payments to both DWG and the bank. DWG sued the bank to recover possession of the watch and the rings. The bank argued that the descriptions in the financing statement were

inadequate and that the bank's interest should be superior to DWG. Who is entitled to the watch and the rings? Explain.

9. Doe planned on opening a new store. On June 1st, Doe entered into an agreement to borrow money from the Jones Bank (Jones). Doe was also negotiating with Smith for a loan. Smith obtained a signed financing statement from Doe on June 5th covering all of the inventory and equipment in Doe's new store. Smith immediately filed the financing statement but made no commitment to make a loan to Doe at that time. On June 27th, Jones filed a signed financing statement covering all of the inventory and equipment in Doe's new store. Negotiations for a loan continued between Doe and Smith. On March 5th, Smith loaned Doe money and Doe signed a security agreement giving Smith a security interest in all of the inventory and equipment in his new store. Doe failed to repay either Smith or Jones. Jones brought an action to obtain possession of Doe's inventory. Smith objected and claimed a priority over Jones. Do Jones and Smith both have perfected security interests? Who has priority? Explain.

10. Transport Oil Company, Inc., leased a filling station to Liddicoat, who did business under his own name, and entered into an agreement with Liddicoat to provide him with gasoline on a consignment basis. No financing statement was filed. Clark Oil and Refining Company, which had previously supplied gas and oil to Liddicoat, obtained a judgment against Liddicoat because he had failed to pay Clark for all the gas and oil it had delivered. Based on the judgment, Clark obtained a writ of attachment, a legal document that ordered the sheriff to seize any goods owned by Liddicoat. Among other goods, the sheriff seized some quantities of gas delivered to Liddicoat pursuant to his agreement with Transport. Transport sued to recover possession of the gas, claiming it had retained title to the goods under its consignment agreement and therefore had priority over Clark. Who gets possession of the gas seized by the sheriff? Explain.

11. Centennial Bank made a loan to Gochenaur Machine Company in return for a security agreement giving the bank a security interest in "all fixtures, machinery, and equipment of every kind and nature whatsoever." The filed financing statement covered "all equipment, furniture, and fixtures as now owned or hereafter acquired by the Debtor and used in the operation of the Debtor's business as now or hereafter conducted." Gochenaur defaulted and the bank took possession of all of the company's assets. Gochenaur then went into bankruptcy. The trustee in bankruptcy claimed the two vehicles, arguing that the bank had not perfected its security interest because Pennsylvania requires compliance with its certificate of title law to perfect a security interest in an automobile. The bank argued that it had perfected by filing the financing statement and by obtaining possession prior to the filing of the bankruptcy. Who is entitled to the automobiles? Explain.

12. Robert D. Weaver purchased a Dart from Wentworth Motor Company, Inc. (Wentworth) and signed a security agreement. The automobile was intended for personal and family use. Wentworth filed a financing statement. The state has no certificate of title law. Subsequently, Weaver traded the Dart for a new car from Hanson-Rock, Inc., of Hampton, an automobile dealer. Jones purchased the Dart from Hanson-Rock for personal and family use. Jones purchased in good faith and had no actual knowledge of Wentworth's security interest. Neither Hanson-Rock nor Jones had searched for any filing. Wentworth sued Jones to recover possession of the Dart, claiming a perfected security interest in it. Jones defended on the grounds that he was a buyer in the oridinary course of business and took free from Wentworth's security interest. Who is entitled to the automobile? Explain. Does Hanson-Rock have a right to the automobile? Explain.

13. Classic Construction Company (CCC) purchased a back hoe on a conditional sales contract and gave a security interest to General Electric Credit Corporation (Credit). When CCC defaulted by failing to make payments, Credit repossessed the back hoe. Credit sold the back hoe for the highest

offer it received, $10,500. Credits' own appraiser had valued the machine at $20,000 "as is" and at $25,000 if it were repaired. Credit sued CCC to recover the difference between the $10,500 received from the sale and the $21,000 balance owed under the conditional sales contract plus the costs of repossessing and selling the back hoe.

CCC defended on the grounds that the back hoe had not been sold in a commercially reasonable manner, as evidenced by the fact that the amount received was much lower than Credit's own appraiser's evaluation. Credit moved for summary judgment. How should the court rule?

30

BANKRUPTCY

Individuals and business organizations sometimes incur debts that they are unable to pay. Many reasons for this inability to pay can be given—poor management, the unwise use of credit, or unforeseen difficulties, for example. Some unpaid creditors will have security interests in the debtors' collateral. However, there are many instances when credit is not secured. For instance, employees are unsecured creditors of their employers, and public utilities deliver services without security. In addition, loans are often made and credit is often extended simply on the strength of a debtor's past credit history. Claims can also arise against an individual or a business as the result of contract or tort law. If a debtor is unable to pay all of his or her creditors and claim-holders, he or she may seek relief in federal bankruptcy or state debtor relief measures.

In biblical times, Mosaic Law provided for the periodic wiping out of all debts so that a person could begin again. Greco-Roman law, however, did not allow any relief to improvident or unfortunate debtors. English law accepted the biblical concept, though, and bankruptcy laws were enacted prior to the colonization of America. Our founding fathers provided for bankruptcy laws in Article I, Section Eight of the Constitution: "Congress shall have the power . . . to establish . . . uniform laws on the subject of Bankruptcies throughout the United States." Congress did not always exercise its power, so the various states developed their own forms of creditors' remedies and debtors' relief. This chapter will briefly discuss some of the state remedies available. Most of the chapter will then be devoted to bankruptcy law, referred to as the Bankruptcy Code.

STATE REMEDIES

State laws provide a variety of ways for insuring the creditors will be paid and for protecting debtors.

Security Interests

A creditor can protect himself or herself against the inability of a debtor to pay by creating a security interest in property belonging to the debtor (see Chapter 29). As long as the property in which a creditor holds a security interest is worth at least the amount of the unpaid loan, the creditor is protected since the property can be sold and the proceeds used to pay the loan. In many situations, however, it is impossible or impractical to create security interests. When a security interest has not been created or the value of the secured property falls below the amount due, creditors and claim-holders must seek other remedies.

Judgment Lien

Generally, state laws provide that a person who has obtained a judgment in a court proceeding can have a governmental official, typically a sheriff or some other law enforcement officer, seize some of a losing party's goods so that they can be sold to pay the judgment. The right of a person who has obtained a judgment to claim an interest in a debtor's property is called a **judgment lien** or **judicial lien.** The process whereby the goods are seized and sold is often referred to as levy and execution. State laws exempt certain types of property, such as clothes and furniture, from the claims of judgment-lien creditors when the debtor is an individual. These **exemptions** insure that the debtor will be able to maintain a reasonable life style and at least some measure of dignity. The debtor who must go about dressed in a barrel exists only in cartoons.

Garnishment

Most states provide that an employer of a debtor can be required to pay money owed to the debtor, such as wages, to an unpaid creditor as the money becomes due to the debtor. This process is usually called **garnishment.** Federal law limits the amount of a debtor's earnings that can be garnished under state laws.* This limitation insures that a debtor is not deprived of the income that provides for the minimal necessities of life.

Assignment for Benefit of Creditors, Receivership, and Composition

State laws provide several additional ways in which a debtor who cannot pay can seek relief. An **assignment for the benefit of creditors** occurs when all of a debtor's property is turned over to another person who then uses or sells the property to pay creditors in an equitable fashion. The person who holds the property and pays the creditors is called an assignee. A **receivership** occurs

---

* Restriction on Garnishment, 15 U.S.C.A. §1671 et seq.

when a court orders a debtor to turn over part or substantially all of his or her assets to a person, called a *receiver,* who then becomes responsible for paying the debtor's creditors. Finally, a debtor may be able to settle through a **composition** or **arrangement,** that is, by reaching agreements with his or her creditors to reduce the amount due or to extend the time for payment. Debtors seeking such agreements can often use the services of debt counseling agencies.

FEDERAL BANKRUPTCY LAW

Bankruptcy law in the United States is based upon the Constitution. Prior to 1898, there was no continual federal bankruptcy law. Debtors and creditors worked out their problems in accordance with state laws.

The three early federal bankruptcy acts, although of brief duration, laid down some important concepts that are reflected in the present law. The law in effect from 1800 to 1803 provided for bankruptcy relief only for debtors who were merchants, traders, or brokers and only if the relief were requested by creditors. A bankruptcy proceeding begun by creditors is called an **involuntary** bankruptcy. The 1841 act provided relief for all types of debtors and allowed for both involuntary and **voluntary** petitions, that is, this act allowed debtors themselves to seek bankruptcy relief. From 1867 to 1878, both voluntary and involuntary petitions could be filed, but creditors were prohibited from filing involuntary petitions when the debtor was a farmer.

Since 1898, federal bankruptcy relief has been continuously available. The Bankruptcy Reform Act of 1978 became effective on October 1, 1979. This act did not just amend the prior law, it took some substantially different approaches. It was found to be unconstitutional, however, because it created bankruptcy court judges with broad judicial powers even though they were not full federal court judges. The law was declared ineffective as of December 25, 1982. Bankruptcy courts nevertheless continued to operate under special rules. In 1984, Congress enacted the Bankruptcy Amendments and Federal Judgeship Act of 1984. This legislation restricts the jurisdiction of bankruptcy court judges and makes other changes in the 1978 Act. Where relevant, these changes will be discussed in this chapter.

The Bankruptcy Reform Act of 1978, as amended, will be referred to as the Bankruptcy Code unless otherwise noted. References to the sections of the Bankruptcy Code have been simplified in this chapter—for example, §303.

The Structure of the Bankruptcy Code

The Bankruptcy Code has eight odd-numbered chapters, 1 to 15. By eliminating even-numbered chapters, it retains the same numbering used in the prior law for key chapters. The Bankruptcy Code provides for three basic types of relief: Chapter 7 provides for liquidation; Chapter 11, for reorganization and arrangements; and Chapter 13, for adjustments of the debts of individuals with regular income, also called wage earner plans.

A Chapter 7 liquidation occurs when a debtor turns over all of his or her property except for exempt property to an official of the bankruptcy court—a trustee. The **trustee** then liquidates the property, that is, reduces it to cash for the purpose of paying creditors. A Chapter 11 reorganization or arrangement allows an individual or a business the opportunity of working out an agreement with creditors for the payment of debts or claims. The reorganization of a corporation's capital structure is also facilitated by a Chapter 11 proceeding. A corporation may, for example, create a new class of stock to provide new capital to pay off old debts. A Chapter 13 proceeding allows individuals with regular income the means of working out agreements with creditors to postpone or reduce the amounts to be paid. In a Chapter 13 proceeding, a debtor retains all of his or her property, but future income is subjected to the control of the court for several years.

Chapters 1, 3, and 5 provide general rules that apply to all three types of bankruptcy relief. Chapter 9 provides for the adjustment of the debts of a municipality. Chapter 15 provides for a pilot project to create a trustee system for the bankruptcy courts. This project is still underway.

The Purposes of Bankruptcy Law

Bankruptcy law has two fundamental purposes: (1) to rehabilitate debtors by giving them a fresh start and (2) to provide for the orderly collection and distribution of debtors' property for the benefit of their creditors.

Debtors who are unable to pay all of their debts or claims against them need the opportunity to become free from the burden of their debts in order to become productive and effective economic units in our society. Bankruptcy law deals with this need in two ways. First, it provides for a **discharge**—that is, the cancellation—of many of the debtor's debts. Second, the law protects certain types of property belonging to individual debtors from the claims of creditors through exemptions.

The orderly collection and distribution of a debtor's property is the second basic purpose of bankruptcy law. A sinking debtor is beset with the claims of many creditors. Some of these creditors may grab off part of the debtor's property and thus leave other creditors with little or no relief. Many provisions of the bankruptcy law are designed to prevent this type of grab law whereby one creditor receives a greater benefit from a debtor's estate than other creditors.

LIQUIDATION—CHAPTER SEVEN

Liquidation is a type of bankruptcy proceeding in which a debtor's property is liquidated, or turned into cash, and the cash is used to pay the debtor's creditors to the extent possible. In examining how liquidation works, it is necessary to refer to a number of sections that appear in Chapters 1, 3, and 5. These chapters contain general provisions that apply to all types of bankruptcy.

Commencement of a Case

A bankruptcy proceeding is begun by filing a petition with a bankruptcy court. The petition, which may be either voluntary or involuntary, is filed with the federal court in the district where the debtor has resided or has had his or her principal place of business for the preceding six months. It must be accompanied by a filing fee, although a debtor can petition for the right to pay the fee in installments. Failure to pay the filing fee can result in dismissal of a case. A debtor is also required to file schedules, which are prescribed lists that provide the court with information necessary to the case, such as the name and address of each creditor; a statement of the debtor's assets, liabilities, financial affairs, and executory contracts; and a list of the property the debtor claims as exempt property.

Voluntary Petitions A voluntary petition can be filed in a Chapter 7 liquidation by any type of debtor except railroads and most banks or insurance companies. The financial difficulties of banks and insurance agencies are handled by government bodies such as the Federal Deposit Insurance Corporation and state Superintendents of Banking. Railroads are not permitted to liquidate, but they can petition for relief under Chapter 11. Stockbrokers and commodities brokers are allowed to liquidate, but they are not allowed to use Chapter 11 because the complex special rules that apply to customers' accounts would seriously interfere with any attempted reorganization [§103 and §301]. A husband and wife can file a joint petition under any chapter [§302]. Figure 30-1 shows the official form promulgated by the United States Supreme Court for voluntary petitions.

A debtor need not be **insolvent** — that is, he or she need not have liabilities greater than assets — in order to file a voluntary petition. A debtor need not even allege that there are any debts. Indeed, there are few requirements that a debtor must meet in order to file a voluntary petition. Under the 1984 amendments, a consumer debtor must certify to the court that he or she knows about a Chapter 13 proceeding but has elected a Chapter 7 proceeding. If the debtor is represented by an attorney, the attorney must certify that he or she has explained the relief available under both Chapter 13 and Chapter 7. The purpose of this requirement is to encourage debtors to consider Chapter 13 proceedings.

No hearing or specific order of a bankruptcy judge is required for a voluntary petitioner to be declared a bankrupt. The mere filing of a voluntary petition constitutes an order by the bankruptcy court that the debtor is entitled to relief.

Abstentions A bankruptcy court may dismiss a debtor's petition if, after a hearing, the court determines that "the interests of creditors and the debtor would be better served by such dismissal or suspension" [§305(a)(1)]. This type of action is called an **abstention**. Neither the debtor nor the creditors can appeal to a higher court to have the case reinstated, but a party probably can seek a review of an abstention if the judge erred in applying the law or abused his or her discretion in dismissing the case. If conditions change, a new petition can be filed [§305(c)].

After a hearing, a court can also dismiss a petition for a Chapter 7 liquidation for such reasons as delays by a debtor that are prejudicial to the creditors. Even without receiving a request from a trustee or creditor, a court may dismiss a petition filed by an individual debtor whose debts are primarily consumer debts if the court finds that granting the debtor relief would cause a substantial abuse of the bankruptcy law. The Bankruptcy Code specifies, however, that there shall be a presumption in favor of granting a debtor's petition [§707]. This provision was enacted in the 1984 amendments as part of the reform of measures relating to consumer bankruptcy. It gives the court a means of dealing with potential abuses of the bankruptcy law.

Involuntary Petitions The Bankruptcy Code liberalized the rules governing involuntary petitions. Under the earlier law, a debtor had to commit one of seven listed acts of bankruptcy before creditors could petition for involuntary relief. Under the Bankruptcy Code, there are only two bases for seeking relief: (1) the debtor is generally not paying his or her debts as they become due [§303(h)(l)]; and (2) a custodian or receiver has been appointed by a court to

---

Official Form One — Voluntary Petition

UNITED STATES BANKRUPTCY COURT FOR THE
.... DISTRICT OF ....

In re	:	
.... ,	:	
Debtor [set forth here all names	:	Case No. ....
including trade names used by	:	
Debtor within last 6 years]	:	
Social Security No.	:	
and Debtor's Employer's Tax		
Identification No.	:	

Voluntary Petition

1. Petitioner's mailing address, including county, is ....
....

2. Petitioner has resided [*or* has had his domicile *or* has had his principal place of business *or* has had principal assets] within this district for the preceding 180 days [*or* for a longer portion of the preceding 180 days than in any other district].

3. Petitioner is qualified to file this petition and is entitled to the benefits of title 11, United States Code as a voluntary debtor.

4. [If appropriate] A copy of petitioner's proposed plan, dated .... , is attached [*or* petitioner intends to file a plan pursuant to chapter 11 *or* chapter 13] of title 11, United States Code.

FIGURE 30-1
A Voluntary Petition

take charge of the debtor's property. A creditor who wishes the debtor's affairs to be handled under federal bankruptcy law instead of state receivership law must petition for relief in bankruptcy within 120 days after the state receiver is appointed [§303(h)]. Because the Constitution gives Congress authority to govern bankruptcy, creditors always have the option of seeking relief under federal law if a state proceeding akin to a bankruptcy proceeding has been initiated.

Limitations on Involuntary Petitions Involuntary petitions can be filed only in Chapter 7 and Chapter 11 proceedings. No involuntary petitions can be filed against a debtor who is a farmer, a municipality, or an eleemosynary (charitable) corporation [§303(a)]. The law defines a farmer as a person who receives more than 80 percent of his or her income from a farming operation he or she owns or operates [§101(17)]. While a farmer can voluntarily seek relief through

---

5. [*If petitioner is a corporation*] Exhibit "A" is attached to and made part of this petition.

6. [If petitioner is an individual whose debts are primarily consumer debts.] Petitioner is aware that [he or she] may proceed under chapter 7 or 13 of title 11, United States Code, understands the relief available under each such chapter, and chooses to proceed under chapter 7 of such title.

7. [If petitioner is an individual whose debts are primarily consumer debts and such petitioner is represented by an attorney.] A declaration or an affidavit in the form of Exhibit "B" is attached to and made a part of this petition.

WHEREFORE, petitioner prays for relief in accordance with chapter 7 [*or* chapter 11 *or* chapter 13] of title 11, United States Code.

Signed: ....

Attorney for Petitioner

Address: ....

....

[*Petitioner signs if not represented by attorney.*]

....,

Petitioner.

I, ...,

the petitioner named in the foregoing petition, declare under penalty of perjury that the foregoing is true and correct.

Executed on ....

Signature: ....

Petitioner.

the bankruptcy law, creditors cannot force a farmer into bankruptcy because the farmer's inability to pay may be due to uncontrollable aspects of farming such as the weather. Municipalities are excluded because forcing them into bankruptcy would constitute federal invasion into sovereign state law. If a municipality elects to go bankrupt, it can file a petition under Chapter 9. Charitable organizations have traditionally been excluded, most likely to encourage their existence and to avoid the disruption of their operations.

Required Number of Creditors If a debtor has twelve or more creditors, a minimum of three of the creditors must join together to file an involuntary petition. The three creditors together must be owed at least $5,000 more than any security or liens they may have against the debtor's property [§303]. For example, if a creditor is owed $3,000 but has a security interest in collateral owned by the debtor that is valued at $2,000, that creditor can only count $1,000 toward the $5,000 minimum. There must be at least two other petitioning creditors who have unsecured claims of $4,000 or more to make a total of $5,000 in unsecured claims. If a debtor has twelve or more creditors and one creditor has an unsecured claim of $5,000, that creditor must be joined by two other creditors to meet the required minimum of three. This policy is designed to insure that a single creditor cannot force a debtor and all his or her other creditors into a bankruptcy proceeding when the debtor has twelve or more creditors.

A petitioning creditor must have an unsecured claim that is not subject to a dispute raised in good faith. For example, if a creditor has a suit pending against a debtor in which the debtor has raised a legitimate defense, the creditor involved cannot be one of the petitioning creditors.

If a debtor has fewer than twelve creditors, one creditor with an unsecured $5,000 claim that is not subject to a good faith dispute can file a petition. If there is no one creditor with an unsecured claim of at least $5,000, then any number of creditors with unsecured good faith claims can join together to reach the $5,000 requirement. This policy of the statute is to prevent the small debtor — one with fewer than twelve creditors — from being forced into bankruptcy unless he or she has a significant amount of debt.

Excluded Creditors Employees and insiders are excluded in determining the number of creditors needed to file an involuntary petition. The Bankruptcy Code has an extensive definition of **insider** (see Figure 30-2). Creditors who are employees or insiders are excluded *only* for the purpose of determining the total number of creditors, that is, in determining whether the debtor has twelve or more creditors. They are excluded because they may be friendly to the debtor and could block the relief sought by other creditors by refusing to join in a bankruptcy proceeding. For example, suppose that a debtor has two creditors, each of whom is owed $10,000, and twelve employees who are also creditors. The friendly employees could block the two big creditors from bringing an involuntary petition if all of them refused to join as the necessary third party. Once the employees are excluded in determining the number of creditors, however, the debtor would have fewer than twelve creditors, and either of the

Definition of an Insider

§101(25)

(25)   "[I]nsider" includes—

   (A) if the debtor is an individual—

      (i) relative of the debtor or of the general partner of the debtor;

      (ii) partnership in which the debtor is a general partner;

      (iii) general partner of the debtor; or

      (iv) corporation of which the debtor is a director, officer, or person in control;

   (B) if the debtor is a corporation—

      (i) director of the debtor;

      (ii) officer of the debtor;

      (iii) person in control of the debtor;

      (iv) partnership in which the debtor is a general partner;

      (v) general partner of the debtor; or

      (vi) relative of a general partner, director, officer, or person in control of the debtor;

   (C) if the debtor is a partnership—

      (i) general partner in the debtor;

      (ii) relative of a general partner in, general partner of, or person in control of the debtor;

      (iii) partnership in which the debtor is a general partner;

      (iv) general partner of the debtor; or

      (v) person in control of the debtor;

   (D) if the debtor is a municipality, elected official of the debtor or relative of an elected official of the debtor;

   (E) affiliate, or insider of an affiliate as if such affiliate were the debtor; and

   (F) managing agent of the debtor....

FIGURE 30-2
Definition of an Insider

---

creditors with the $10,000 claims could file a petition. Creditors that are excluded in determining the number of creditors are not prevented from being petitioning creditors if they so choose.

In the following case, employees were counted as petitioning creditors, but the involuntary petition was dismissed because the corporation is an eleemosynary (charitable) corporation and is therefore not subject to an involuntary petition.

IN RE UNITED KITCHEN ASSOCIATES, INC.
33 B.R. 214 (N.D. La. Bkrtcy. 1983)
Findings of Fact

SMALLENBERGER, Bankruptcy Judge

The issues at question are, first, may fifteen employees with claims in excess of $5,000.00 put an employer into involuntary bankruptcy, and second, is the entity in question an eleemosynary corporation, and therefore exempt from involuntary bankruptcy? . . .

Under [§303(b)(1)] a debtor may be put into involuntary bankruptcy through petition by three or more entities with . . . claims that aggregate to at least $5,000.00 more than the value of any lien on property of debtor if there are 12 or more creditors.

Under [§303(b)(2)] one or more creditors may file a petition for involuntary bankruptcy if such claim or claims aggregate to at least $5,000.00 and there are fewer than 12 such holders, excluding an employee or insider of such person. . . .

Under the plain meaning of [§303(b)(1) and (2)] employees of the debtor may be petitioning creditors for involuntary bankruptcy of the debtor. Employees are only excluded when determining if the debtor has twelve or more "nonfriendly" creditors. This exclusion does not apply when the employees desire to become petitioning creditors.

Therefore, fifteen employees with aggregate claims of $19,504.87 may file a petition to put a non-exempt debtor into involuntary bankruptcy.

Under [§303(a)] an involuntary case in bankruptcy may not be commenced against a "corporation" that is not a moneyed, business, or commercial corporation. Such eleemosynary institutions as churches, schools, and charitable organizations and foundations are, thus, exempt from involuntary bankruptcy. . . .

Under state law the debtor corporation was a nonprofit corporation, and based on the corporation's character and the nature of its activities the court finds that it is a non-profit corporation.

The facts indicate that the debtor corporation was incorporated under the laws of the State of Louisiana as a non-profit organization, for the stated purpose of providing meals to the elderly. The debtor corporation was organized on a nonstock basis. The corporation did issue memberships which were not ownership interests in the corporation, but instead were only rights to vote in the general membership meetings. The articles plainly state that none of the profits of the corporation, if any, shall ever be disbursed to a holder of membership certificate.

To summarize, though fifteen employees with claims in excess of $5,000.00 may file a petition of involuntary bankruptcy against an employer, United Kitchen Associates, Inc., is an eleemosynary corporation, and therefore is exempt from involuntary bankruptcy under [§303(a)].

[Petition dismissed.]

CASE REVIEW QUESTIONS

1. Could a single employee with a claim for $5,000 file an involuntary petition against United Kitchens if it were not an eleemosynary corporation?
2. Why should "friendly" creditors be excluded in determining the number of creditors a debtor has?
3. Why is United Kitchen Associates, Inc., an eleemosynary institution?
4. Could United Kitchens Associates, Inc., file a voluntary petition?

Contested Petitions A debtor can contest an involuntary petition and is entitled to a hearing on the issues. A bankruptcy court can dismiss or grant an involuntary petition following a hearing [§303(j)]. In order to prevent creditors from filing involuntary petitions as a means of pressuring or harassing debtors, bankruptcy courts can make awards to debtors who successfully defend against an involuntary petition. These awards can cover the debtor's attorney's fees and court costs and can even include punitive damage if the petition was filed by the creditors in bad faith [§303(i)]. If a debtor does not contest or is unsuccessful in contesting an involuntary petition, a bankruptcy court enters an order for the relief.

Automatic Stay The mere filing of a petition operates as an automatic stay. A debtor need not ask for one. The result of an automatic stay is to suspend most cases that are pending against a debtor and to prohibit the enforcement of any judgments against the debtor. A creditor cannot, at this point, seize any of a debtor's property to satisfy claims against the debtor. Both purposes of the Bankruptcy Code are achieved by a stay. A debtor gets respite from his or her creditors, and the creditors are prohibited from grabbing off pieces of the debtor's estate.

Conduct of a Case

After an order for relief has been entered, the court notifies the creditors concerning the filing of claims and any required meeting they must attend. A trustee is appointed or selected who is responsible for collecting the debtor's assets and making distributions to the creditors. The basic duties of a debtor and a trustee in the conduct of a case are set forth in the statute (see Figures 30-3 and 30-4).

A discharge is usually the goal sought by a debtor because it frees him or her from most types of creditors' claims. An individual debtor must attend the hearing at which a discharge is either granted or denied. The discharge hearing serves several purposes. First, the court will tell a debtor why a discharge was granted or denied. Second, the court will discuss with the debtor any agree-

A Debtor's Duties

Restated from §521

The debtor shall—

(1) file a list of creditors, and unless the court orders otherwise, a schedule of assets and liabilities, a schedule of current income and current expenditures, and a statement of the debtor's financial affairs;

(2) if an individual debtor's schedule of assets and liabilities includes consumer debts which are secured, the debtor must file with the court within a specified time a statement of the debtor's intention with regard to secured property, e.g., will the debtor retain or surrender the property, claim it as exempt, redeem the property or reaffirm the debt;

(3) if a trustee is serving in the case, cooperate with the trustee as necessary to enable the trustee to perform the trustee's duties under this title;

(4) if a trustee is serving in the case, surrender to the trustee all property of the estate and any recorded information, including books, documents, records, and papers, relating to property of the estate; and

(5) appear at the hearing required under section 524(d) of this title.

FIGURE 30-3
A Debtor's Duties

A Trustee's Duties

§704

The trustee shall—

(1) collect and reduce to money the property of the estate for which such trustee serves, and close up such estate as expeditiously as is compatible with the best interests of parties in interest;

(2) be accountable for all property received;

(3) ensure that the debtor shall perform his intention as specified in section 521(2)(b) of this title;

(4) investigate the financial affairs of the debtor;

(5) if a purpose would be served, examine proofs of claims and object to the allowance of any claim that is improper;

(6) if advisable, oppose the discharge of the debtor;

(7) unless the court orders otherwise, furnish such information concerning the estate and the estate's administration as is requested by a party in interest;

(8) if the business of the debtor is authorized to be operated, file with the court and with any governmental unit charged with responsibility for collection or determination of any tax arising out of such operation, periodic reports and summaries of the operation of such business, including a statement of receipts and disbursements, and such other information as the court requires; and

(9) make a final report and file a final account of the administration of the estate with the court.

FIGURE 30-4
A Trustee's Duties

ments he or she may wish to make concerning payments to creditors subsequent to the bankruptcy proceedings [§524(d)]. There are many reasons why a debtor might agree to pay a creditor whose claim would otherwise be discharged. For example, a debtor would probably want to continue to make car payments and mortgage payments on the family home. If a debtor is not represented by an attorney, the court must approve any agreements to repay loans not secured by property after determining that the agreements do not impose undue hardship on the debtor and are in his or her best interests [§524(c)].

Property of the Estate

One of the primary obligations of a trustee in bankruptcy is to collect the property of the estate (see Figure 30-4). In general, the property of the estate includes most of the property owned by the debtor on the date the petition is filed [§541]. In some situations, property can become a part of a bankrupt's estate subsequent to the filing. For example, if a debtor inherits property within 180 days of the commencement of a case, that property goes to the trustee in bankruptcy [§541(a)(5)]. In general, however, property received by a debtor subsequent to the filing belongs to the debtor unless that property is governed by a specific provision of the Bankruptcy Code. For example, if an individual debtor filed a petition in a Chapter 7 liquidation on Thursday and received a pay check on Friday, the pay check would not be included in the property of the estate that goes to the trustee. Any portion of the previous week's pay check in the debtor's bank account would, however, be part of the property of the estate.

A debtor is entitled to claim certain types of property as exempt from collection by the trustee. Exemptions are an important factor in the rehabilitation of an individual debtor. They will be discussed later in this chapter.

Trustee's Avoidance Powers The law gives a trustee in bankruptcy rights which can undo certain transfers of property that a debtor may have made prior to the bankruptcy. These rights that a trustee has are called avoidance powers because they allow the trustee to avoid certain transfers of property and to bring the property back into the debtor's estate. In many instances, the avoidable transfers occurred when a creditor grabbed a portion of a debtor's property. By avoiding a transfer, a trustee increases the property available in a debtor's estate to satisfy the claims of all the creditors. We will now examine the tools a trustee can use to avoid transfers of a debtor's property.

Preferences A preference is basically what it sounds like—one creditor is preferred over other creditors and receives more than other similar creditors. Basically, a trustee can avoid a transfer by a debtor to a creditor made on account of a previously owed debt—an antecedent debt—if the transfer was made while the debtor was insolvent and within ninety days of the date of the filing of the petition [§547]. The Bankruptcy Code defines *insolvent* as a financial condition in which the sum of a debtor's debts is greater than the worth of all of the debtor's property, excluding property that is exempt or property that has been conveyed in an attempt to hinder creditors. If a transfer is to a creditor who is also an insider (see Figure 30-2), a trustee can avoid a transfer made up to a year before the filing of the petition.

Certain types of transfers that meet the definition of a preference are protected from avoidance by the trustee. Most notable is the provision protecting the payment of debts incurred in the ordinary course of business, such as rent and utility bills [§547(c)]. In addition, a transfer that meets all the criteria of a preference is not considered to be a preference if the creditor receives no more than he or she would have received in a Chapter 7 liquidation.

A transfer creating a security interest under Article 9 of the Uniform Commercial Code will not be considered a preference even if a debtor is insolvent and on the verge of bankruptcy provided that certain requirements are met. In essence, if a secured creditor gives new value to a debtor by making a loan in return for the security interest, that creditor has not diminished the debtor's property. Indeed, a creditor who gives new value may infuse new life into a dying business. Contrast this with an unsecured creditor who is already owed money and who subsequently takes a security interest in some of an insolvent debtor's property in order to secure the unpaid debt. This creditor has essentially grabbed off a piece of the debtor's property and is now better off than other unsecured creditors. A trustee could avoid this security interest because it adds nothing of value to the debtor's estate and it diminishes the property available to pay other creditors. A trustee cannot, however, avoid a security interest that is created with the giving of new value if the terms of the statute are met [§547(c)].

In the following case, there are three liens against the debtor's property. The complainant seeks to avoid the liens as preferential transfers. A lien is considered to be a transfer of property because it gives a creditor an interest in or claim to the property against which the lien is placed. If a creditor's lien is perfected, the creditor has a claim to the property that takes precedence over other claims. The court rules that two of the liens constitute voidable preferences and one does not.

IN RE MARSTON
33 B.R. 597 (N.D. Ohio 1983)

SPEER, Bankruptcy Judge

The Debtor owned a parcel of property against which three (3) liens existed. The first lien was held by the Defendant, Ohio Citizens Trust Co. pursuant to a mortgage executed and recorded in December of 1977. The second lien belongs to the Defendant, Elliot Saferin, M.D., Inc., as the result of a judgment. . . . The judgment was rendered on October 14, 1980, and recorded on October 22, 1980. The third mortgage lien also belongs to Ohio Citizens Trust Co., and arose concurrently with the execution of a promissory note. The instrument was executed on November 6, 1979, but recorded on November 12, 1980. The Complaint seeks to avoid the lien of the Defendant, Elliot Saferin, M.D., Inc., and the second lien of Ohio Citizens Trust Co. The Bankruptcy Petition was filed on November 24, 1980.

A Trustee in bankruptcy is empowered to recover a debtor's property which has been transformed prior to the filing of the bankruptcy petition. This power is set forth in [§547], which states in pertinent part:

(b) . . . the trustee may avoid any transfer of property of the debtor—
  (1) to or for the benefit of a creditor;
  (2) for or on account of an antecedent debt owed by the debtor before such transfer was made;
  (3) made while the debtor was insolvent;
  (4) made—
    (A) on or within 90 days before the date of the filing of the petition; . . .

(5) that enables such creditor to receive more than such creditor would receive if—
  (A) the case were a case under chapter 7 of this title;
  (B) the transfer had not been made and
  (C) such creditor received payment of such debt to the extent provided by the provisions of this title.

. . .

(f) For the purposes of this section, the debtor is presumed to have been insolvent on and during the 90 days immediately preceding the date of the filing of the petition.

In Ohio perfection of a lien on real estate is accomplished by recording the lien with the proper Recorder's Office. Pursuant to [§547(e)(1)(A)], a transfer occurs when this recording is complete. A review of the record finds that the Defendants have each admitted that the transfers occurred within the preference period. It also reflects that the liens in question were, in fact, perfected or transferred within the ninety (90) days prior to the filing of the petition. Therefore, it must be concluded that the element of the statute requiring a transfer has been fulfilled.

The Defendants have also admitted the antecedent character of the debts. Defendant, Elliot Saferin, M.D., Inc., has admitted this character directly in his answer. Defendant, Ohio Citizens Trust Co., has admitted it by acknowledging that the perfection on the mortgage occurred more than one (1) year after the mortgage was executed. A debt is deemed to be of an antecedent character if the transfer made contemporaneously with the incurring of the debt is not perfected within the grace period provided by [§547(e)]. Therefore, the antecedent element has been fulfilled with regard to the second lien of Ohio Citizens Trust Co.

The Defendants have each denied that the Debtor was insolvent at the time of the transfer. However, they have offered no evidence to rebut the presumption of insolvency provided by [§547(f)]. . . . In view of the statutory presumption of insolvency and the absence of proof to the contrary, it must be held that the debtor was insolvent at the time of the transfer.

The remaining consideration that must be made is whether or not these Defendants received more by way of the transfer than they would have through a bankruptcy proceeding. A review of the Plaintiff's Affidavit finds that the Debtor's total indebtedness is ap-

proximately Five Hundred Thousand and no/100 Dollars ($500,000.00) while his total assets are less than Forty-five Thousand and no/100 Dollars ($45,000.00). The fixing of these liens would enable the creditors to follow the land until the judgments are paid, whereas avoidance of the liens would require them to participate as unsecured creditors. It is apparent that by requiring them to assume the latter status they will receive less than if their liens would be allowed to remain intact. Given the current asset to debt ratio they will receive only a small percentage of their claims. Therefore, they may not be allowed to obtain the greater advantage. . . .

It must be concluded that all the elements of [§547] have been satisfied and that the fixing of the liens constitute a voidable preference. It should be pointed out that this avoidance does not affect the first lien held by Ohio Citizens Trust Co.

CASE REVIEW QUESTIONS

1. How does the taking of the judgment and the recording of the judgment lien meet the requirements of a preference?
2. When did the voidable transfer occur in the mortgage recorded on November 12, 1980? Why?
3. What could the bank have done to have prevented the trustee from avoiding this mortgage?
4. Why is the first lien held by the Ohio Bank not avoidable by the trustee as a preferential transfer?
5. Why does the statute specify that a debtor is presumed insolvent during the ninety days prior to the filing of the petition?

Fraudulent Conveyances A fraudulent conveyance occurs when a debtor transfers property in a way that defrauds his or her creditors. The basic language of the statute is taken from a statute passed in England in 1570 during the reign of Queen Elizabeth I that prohibited transfers made with the intent to delay, hinder, or defraud creditors. Most states have similar legislation, which is often the Uniform Fraudulent Conveyances Act. Under the Bankruptcy Code, a trustee can avoid a transfer made with actual intent to hinder, delay, or defraud creditors. Even if there was no intent, a trustee can avoid a transfer if a debtor was insolvent when the transfer was made or became insolvent because he or she received less than reasonable value for the property transferred. A debtor who transfers property in a way that will hinder, delay, or defraud creditors usually conceals the transfer. Accordingly, the Bankruptcy Code provides that the trustee can avoid any fraudulent transfer that occurred as much as one year before the filing of the petition [§548].

A fraudulent conveyance is also grounds for denying a debtor a discharge of all debts owed. If a debtor is denied a discharge, he or she is still obligated to pay all debts owed to all creditors. In the following case, a debtor who put property in his wife's name is denied a discharge because the court found a fraudulent conveyance.

IN RE KAISER
32 B.R. 701 (S.D., N.Y.)

WERKER, District Judge

On February 11, 1981, Gerald Kaiser filed a voluntary petition in bankruptcy under chapter 7 of the Bankruptcy Code. The trustee commenced the first adversary proceeding in February 1982. That complaint . . . sought to prevent the discharge of the debtor . . . based upon the allegations that the debtor transferred certain of his property with the intent to hinder, delay or defraud his creditors within one year prior to the date of the filing of the petition. . . . This proceeding was brought against the debtor and Joan Kaiser, his wife, for the purpose of setting aside alleged fraudulent transfers made by the debtor traceable into a parcel of real property located at 6450 S.W. 102nd Street, Miami, Florida ("the Florida premises"), title to which was held in the name of Joan Kaiser.

[The Bankruptcy Judge found the transfers to be fraudulent, set aside the transfers, and denied the debtor's discharge. The debtor appealed.]

The record reveals that over the years Gerald and Joan Kaiser have resided on various properties title to which has been in the name of Joan Kaiser notwithstanding that Mr. Kaiser's funds were used for acquisition, maintenance, and improvement.

In October 1978, the real property located at 6450 S.W. 102nd Street, Miami, Florida, was purchased in the name of Joan Kaiser. The purchase price was $295,000. The down payment was $50,000 and was paid in cash solely with Gerald Kaiser's funds. The balance was covered by a . . . mortgage given by

"Gerald Kaiser and Joan Kaiser, his wife," securing a promissory note in the amount of $245,000, given by the Kaisers to the sellers. . . . From November, 1978, to February, 1981, monthly mortgage installments were paid with Gerald Kaiser's funds. The payments for maintenance and improvements on the premises were made with Mr. Kaiser's funds.

The payments made by Mr. Kaiser on the Florida property were made (1) directly from business entities under his control, (2) from accounts in the name of Joan Kaiser, Joan and Gerald Kaiser, the sole funding of these accounts was from Gerald Kaiser's business entities, (3) from cash received from Mr. Kaiser's businesses, by check payable to cash, Gerald Kaiser, or Joan Kaiser. [The] Judge . . . found that the practice of paying obligations from corporate or [other] accounts was designed to avoid the debtor's creditors. . . .

Appellants argue that since the trustee failed to establish actual fraudulent intent by direct evidence, the bankruptcy court could not have concluded that the subject transfers were made with actual intent to defraud creditors. By nature, fraudulent intent is not susceptible to direct proof. The text *Collier on Bankruptcy* states that

the finding of the requisite [fraudulent] intent may be predicated upon the occurrence of facts which, while not direct evidence of actual intent, lead to the irresistible conclusion that the transferor's conduct was motivated by such intent. Rarely will a fraudulent transferor disclose his fraudulent intent in a mode capable of direct proof.

. . .

With respect to proof of intent, it has been stated:

Circumstances from which courts have been willing to infer fraud include concealment of facts and false pretenses by the transferor, reservation by him of rights in the transferred property, his absconding with or secreting the proceeds of the transfer immediately after their receipt, the existence of unconscionable discrepancy between the value of property transferred and the consideration received therefor, . . . [and] the creation by an oppressed debtor of a closely-held corporation to receive the transfer of his property. While no finding of fraud can be predicated solely on the fact that a transaction resulting in a transfer of a debtor's property is between relatives or members of a family, such transactions are generally subjected to close scrutiny when challenged by the trustee. . . .

Gerald Kaiser has repeatedly exercised dominion and control over real property held in the name of his wife. . . . Courts will not sanction the use of wives as conduits through which funds of a debtor may be tapped while the same funds remain unreachable by creditors.

That Mr. Kaiser considered the Florida property his own militated in favor of such a finding. Mr. Kaiser included the Florida property among his assets on a January 30, 1980, personal financial statement delivered to a Florida bank, notwithstanding his wife's legal title. . . .

The mortgage on the Florida property was exe-cuted jointly by Gerald Kaiser and his wife as mortgagor and contained a statement by Gerald Kaiser that:

Mortgagor hereby covenants with Mortgagee that Mortgagor is indefeasibly seized with the absolute and fee simple title to said property; that Mortgagor has full power and lawful authority to sell, convey, assign, transfer and mortgage the same. . . .

In addition, as admitted by Mr. Kaiser, deductions for real estate taxes on the Florida property were taken by him in computing taxable income on his federal income tax returns for the years 1979 through 1981 . . . despite the fact that he was not entitled to these deductions since he was not the fee owner.

The facts show Gerald Kaiser's exercise of dominion and control over the Florida property and lead to the conclusion that Mr. Kaiser had his wife hold title to the Florida property and made payments for the purchase, maintenance and improvement of the property with the intent to shield the property and defraud his creditors.

The bankruptcy court properly denied the debtor's discharge. . . . While the value of the property transferred within the one year period may tend to negate fraudulent intent, where, as in this case, the record reveals a continuing concealment of property on the part of the debtor, courts look beyond the twelve month limitation in finding actual intent to defraud.

In accordance with the above, the judgement signed by [the] Bankruptcy Judge . . . is affirmed in all respects. . . .

So ordered.

CASE REVIEW QUESTIONS

1. What are the elements of a fraudulent conveyance?
2. How did the court establish intent?
3. What transfers occurred within one year before the petition was filed?
4. Why could the court look at actions that occurred more than one year prior to the filing of the petition?

Trustee's Lien The Bankruptcy Code gives a trustee a lien against a debtor's property. This lien, in effect, makes the trustee a creditor of the debtor as of the date the petition is filed. The trustee has the rights of an actual unsecured creditor to avoid transfers made by the debtor or the rights of a hypothetical *judicial lien creditor,* which is a creditor who has brought a successful suit against a debtor to recover the money owed him or her and has been awarded a judgment. A trustee is called a *hypothetical* judicial lien creditor because he or she has the rights of a judgment creditor even if there is actually no judgment creditor. In other words, the Bankruptcy Code gives a trustee rights as if he or she had brought a successful suit [§544].

The lien power of a trustee is sometimes referred to as "strong arm power." With this power, a trustee can avoid any security interests that are unperfected on the date the petition is filed. A creditor who has not perfected a security interest in the proper way under Article 9 of the Uniform Commercial Code will be treated as an unsecured creditor in a bankruptcy proceeding because of the trustee's lien. The UCC gives a lien creditor priority over a secured creditor if his or her lien is obtained before the security interest is perfected [§9 – 301(a)(b)]. A trustee's claim arises on the date of bankruptcy and is therefore prior to the claim of a security interest holder who has a security interest that is unperfected on the date of bankruptcy. (See Chapter 29.)

Trustee's Choice of Powers A trustee can choose which of the three avoidance powers he or she wishes to exercise. Suppose, for instance, that debtor D has entered into a security agreement in return for a loan from A. Subsequently, D files a petition in bankruptcy. The trustee may be able to avoid the security interest of A in one or more of the following situations:

1. If A failed to perfect the security interest, the trustee can avoid the security interest through the use of the strong arm provision of the trustee's lien [§544].
2. Even if A has perfected the security interest, the trustee would be able to avoid the security interest if the transfer was preferential [§547]. The transfer would be preferential if A failed to perfect the security interest during the grace period allowed by Article 9 but did perfect it within 90 days before the date the petition was filed and at a time when D was insolvent.
3. Even if D were solvent and the perfection were made in a timely manner, the trustee would be able to avoid the security interest if there had been a fraudulent conveyance. The conveyance would be fraudulent, for instance, if D created the security interest within one year before the date the petition was filed with the intent to hinder, delay, or defraud other creditors. More specifically, the conveyance would be fraudulent if A is D's in-law and the security interest has been given so that certain property cannot be claimed by other creditors.

Once a trustee in bankruptcy determines that a transfer can be avoided, he or she can take steps to recover the property for the estate. If necessary the trustee can institute a proceeding known as an *adversary proceeding* to recover the property.

Exemptions

Although virtually all the property belonging to a debtor on the date the petition is filed is property of the estate, an individual debtor is entitled to claim certain property as exempt. A debtor can select as exempt the types and amounts of property listed in §522(d) of the Bankruptcy Code or the types and amounts of property exempt under the law of the state where the debtor was domiciled for the greater portion of the 180 days immediately preceding the filing of the petition. The Bankruptcy Code, however, allows a state to **"opt-out"** of the list of exempt property in §522(d) and to require that a debtor exempt only property covered by state law. Figure 30-5 gives the list of exempt property under §522(d). Figure 30-6 is an example of a state opt-out statute. A majority of the states have enacted opt-out provisions. To determine what is exempt in any given state, the laws of that state should be consulted.

The following case involves an opt-out statute. The court traces some of the history and discusses the policies behind the exemption provisions.

IN RE NEIHEISEL
32 B.R. 146 (D. Utah Bkrtcy. 1983)

CLARK, Bankruptcy Judge

Objections to claimed exemptions have prompted the debtors in these . . . cases to challenge the validity of the Utah Exemptions Act under the Constitution of the United States. It is alleged that the Utah law violates the Supremacy Clause of Article VI [of the Constitution] by frustrating the federal fresh start policy of bankruptcy law.

Debtors claim exemptions for [a truck and a variety of furniture including a kitchen table and four chairs]. Under the Utah Exemptions Act as applied to these debtors, none of these items is exempt and, absent a finding that the Utah Exemptions Act is invalid, each must be surrendered to the trustee in each case for administration for the benefit of creditors.

In each of debtors' cases, the items claimed as exempt property would have been exempt under [§522(d)] if the Utah legislature had not enacted the Utah Exemptions Act, which prohibits debtors from electing the federal exemptions. Debtors persuasively argue that they need each item and that the loss of each item under the Utah law hinders their post-bankruptcy fresh start. . . .

In 1970, Congress created a Commission on Bank-

ruptcy Laws to "study, analyze, evaluate, and recommend changes" in bankruptcy law. In 1973, the Commission reported its findings to Congress and recommended a revised Bankruptcy Act. The Commission identified two equally important functions of bankruptcy law:

> The primary function of the bankruptcy system is to continue the law-based orderliness of the open credit economy in the event of a debtor's inability or unwillingness generally to pay his debts. Especially from creditors' perspectives, it is important to have rules that determine rights generally in the debtor's wealth, wherever situated, and thus guide conduct in the open credit economy. . . . Especially from debtors' perspectives it is important to have sanctuary from the jungle of creditors' pursuit of their individualistic collection efforts, both under law and outside of the law. Relief by way of stay of collection may be all that is needed. It is equally important to be able to obtain authoritative relief, through discharge, from the hardship of unpaid debts. The second function of the bankruptcy process, on a par with the first, is to rehabilitate debtors for continued and more value-productive participation, i.e., to provide a meaningful "fresh start." . . .

On September 8, 1977, after months of effort, the

House Committee on the Judiciary submitted its report on H.R. 8200 [the House bill].

H.R. 8200 set a federal floor for exemptions but permitted debtors to choose as an alternative the exemptions provided by state and federal nonbankruptcy law. . . . H.R. 8200 did not permit states to preempt the federal exemptions. . . . S. 2266 [the Senate bill] provided that exemptions would be governed solely by nonbankruptcy law, omitting the House's proposed Federal exemptions floor. [§522(b)] as enacted [allowing states to opt-out] is a compromise between the House and Senate proposals. . . .

Commentators agree that the exemptions compromise was a last-minute political expediency. Although courts have disagreed on the meaning of the exemptions compromise the prevailing view is now represented by the interpretation given the exemptions compromise by the Fifth Circuit:

[§522(b)] expressly grants the states broad discretion and an open-ended opportunity to determine what property may be exempt from the bankruptcy estate, as long as the state law does not conflict with property exempt under federal law other than the laundry list [in §522(d)]. Significantly, the section does not mandate that debtors be guaranteed a right to exempt particular types of property. The unambiguous language of [§522(b)] implicitly indicates a state may exempt the same property included in the federal laundry list, more property than that included in the federal laundry list, or less property than that included in the federal laundry list.

Fresh start is a flexible concept, encompassing multiple objectives and manifesting itself in many sections of the bankruptcy code. . . . The fresh start doctrine expresses both humanitarian and economic concerns. In theory, it espouses at least three fundamental tenets: that bankruptcy should not cause destitution by depriving debtors of property necessary for survival, if they have it, that bankruptcy should not create a burden on the state by transforming debtors into public charges, and that bankruptcy should aid in restoring debtors' capacity as productive participants in the economy. In practice, the fresh start is engendered by exemptions and discharge.

The exemptions compromise enacted by [§522(b)(1)] was not the resolution of a battle between forces favoring and opposing a fresh start. Both the

---

Federal Exemptions

Restated from §522(d)

(1) Homestead exemption—$7,500 in a debtor's residence or burial plot.

(2) One motor vehicle—$1,200.

(3) Household furnishings, household goods, wearing apparel, appliances, books, animals, crops or musical instruments held primarily for personal, family or household use, totalling no more than $4,000.

(4) Jewelry—$500.

(5) Any property—$400 plus any amount of the $3,750 not used in category (1).

(6) Implements, professional books or tools of the trade of the debtor—$750.

(7) & (8) Certain life insurance policies.

(9) Professionally prescribed health aids.

(10) Debtor's right to receive certain benefits such as social security benefits, veteran's benefits, disability benefits, alimony and certain pension type payments. (Pensions and alimony are exempt only to the extent reasonably needed for the support of the debtor and any dependent of the debtor.)

(11) The debtor's right to receive or property traceable to certain types of payments received in criminal or tort claims, or as life insurance or payments of future earnings to the extent reasonably necessary for support of the debtor and any dependent of the debtor.

FIGURE 30-5
Federal Exemptions

House and the Senate recognized a fresh start as a desirable goal of bankruptcy law. Their disagreement centered on whether Congress or the states should possess authority to fix exemptions. The House feared state stinginess. The Senate feared state munificence. By permitting states to forbid federal exemptions, the compromise left decision making authority on types and amounts of exemptions with the states.

In 1981, Utah banned the use, by Utah debtors in bankruptcy, of the federal exemptions by enacting the Utah Exemptions Act. The Utah Exemptions Act represents an effort not only to preempt federal exemptions in bankruptcy, but to modernize Utah exemption law. . . .

The Utah Exemptions Act is expressly authorized by [§522(b)(1)], under which states may preempt [§522(d)]. Although the Bankruptcy Reform Act expresses in many ways a federal policy favoring a fresh start for debtors, federal policy does not include minimum federal exemptions. That idea was proposed, but was rejected. Thus, debtors' argument that states must conform their exemption laws to [§522(d)] is without merit. If Congress has intended to require states to provide exemptions concomitant with those found in [§522(d)], it would have been easy to say so. Nothing was said.

The objections to the claimed exemptions in these cases are sustained.

Utah Exemption Act

Restated from Utah Code Annotated — Title 78 — Chapter 23

A. Homestead exemption — $8,000 for a head of a family, $2,000 for a spouse and $500 for each other dependent. (§78–23–3)

B. Other Exempt Property (§78–23–5)

   (1) Burial plot

   (2) Health Aids reasonably necessary for debtor or dependent

   (3) Benefits received or to be received for disability, illness or unemployment

   (4) Benefits paid for medical or hospital case to the extent used to pay for such care

   (5) Veterans benefits

   (6) Money or property for child support

   (7) One clothes washer, dryer, refrigerator, freezer, stove, sewing machine and all carpets in use along with provisions for three months, all wearing apparel except jewelry and furs and beds and bedding for the debtor and each dependent

   (8) Works of art depicting the debtor or the debtor and his resident family, or produced by the debtor or his family unless held as part of a trade or business

   (9) Proceeds of insurance or judgment due to bodily injury

C. Alimony, proceeds of life insurance policies and pension benefits to the extent reasonably necessary for support of individual or dependents. (§78–23–6)

D. Certain life insurance policies (§78–23–7)

E. (1) $500 worth of each type of property (not including property exempt in category B):

   (a) Household furnishings and appliances for one household

   (b) Animals, books and musical instruments reasonably needed for debtor and dependents

   (c) One heirloom or item of particular sentimental value

  (2) $1,500 of professional books or tools of the trade and one motor vehicle worth $1,500 as used in the debtor's business for other than transportation to and from the debtor's place of work.

FIGURE 30-6
Utah Exemption Act

CASE REVIEW QUESTIONS

1. What happens to property that is declared not exempt?
2. What purpose is served by allowing a debtor to exempt certain property from the claims of creditors?
3. What compromise did the House and Senate reach on the exemptions available to debtors in a bankruptcy proceeding?
4. Does the Utah Exemption Act frustrate the federal fresh start policy? Why?
5. In what way could the right of the debtor to exempt certain property affect a creditor's decision in the granting of credit?
6. Compare the federal list of exempt property (Figure 41-5) and the Utah list (Figure 41-6). Which list would you prefer? Why? Would it depend upon the type of property you owned? *Note:* In Utah you would not be allowed to choose between the federal or state list.

Avoiding Liens on Exempt Property The Bankruptcy Code ensures that a debtor's exempt property remains free from the claims of creditors not only by allowing the debtor to retain exempt property in a bankruptcy proceedings but also by allowing the debtor to avoid certain types of liens that creditors might place on his or her exempt property.

Judicial Liens A debtor can avoid any judicial lien on any exempt property [§522(f)] so that a creditor cannot grab off a piece of the debtor's property that is exempt in a bankruptcy proceeding. A judicial lien may sometimes be placed on exempt property because certain types of property may be exempt for bankruptcy purposes but may not be exempt from seizure by legal authorities to satisfy judgments.

The problem arises in several ways. All states have lists of property that cannot be seized by judgment creditors, but these lists may not be the same as the lists used in bankruptcy. If the state has not enacted an opt-out statute, a debtor could elect to exempt the property listed in the Bankruptcy Code which might differ from the property in the state's list. Thus, the debtor could avoid a judicial lien on property that has been seized by a creditor under applicable state law prior to the bankruptcy but is exempt in federal bankruptcy.

Even if the state has enacted an opt-out statute, some of the exempt property may be exempt only in a bankruptcy proceeding. For example, New York has enacted an opt-out statute that exempts automobiles valued up to $2,400 in a bankruptcy proceeding. An automobile, however, is not exempt from a judicial lien. Therefore, if a debtor whose automobile was seized by a judicial lien creditor files for bankruptcy, the creditor will have to return the automobile if the debtor claims it as exempt property.

Avoiding Security Interests in Exempt Property A debtor can avoid a security interest in exempt property and retain the property free from the claims of

Avoidance of Liens on Exempt Property

§522—Exemptions

(f) Notwithstanding any waiver of exemptions, the debtor may avoid the fixing of a lien on an interest of the debtor in property to the extent that such lien impairs an exemption to which the debtor would have been entitled under subsection (b) of this section, if such lien is

(1) a judicial lien; or

(2) a nonpossessory, nonpurchase-money security interest in any—

    (A) household furnishings, household goods, wearing apparel, appliances, books, animals, crops, musical instruments, or jewelry that are held primarily for the personal, family, or household use of the debtor or a dependent of the debtor.

    (B) implements, professional books, or tools of the trade of the debtor or the trade of a dependent of the debtor or

    (C) professionally prescribed health aids for the debtor or a dependent of the debtor.

FIGURE 30-7
Avoidance of Liens on Exempt Property

the secured creditor provided that three conditions are met:

1. The property subject to the security interest consists of household goods, tools or other essential work related articles used by a debtor in his or her occupation, or professionally prescribed health aids.
2. The property is in the debtor's, not the creditor's, possession; that is, the security interest is not a possessory interest such as a pledge.
3. The secured creditor did not lend the money or extend the credit that enabled the debtor to purchase the property; that is, the security interest is not a purchase money security interest. [§522(f), see Figure 30-7.]

If these conditions are met, the debtor can avoid a security interest in exempt property even if the security interest is perfected. The policy behind the provision is to protect these essential types of property from the claims of secured creditors.

If a creditor makes a loan to a debtor to enable the debtor to purchase these types of essential property, the creditor's interest cannot be avoided. Otherwise, creditors would not be willing to lend to debtors who must borrow in order to purchase essential property. The same need to protect a creditor is not present when a loan is made against already owned property and the creditor does not obtain possession.

If a debtor delivers possession of these types of essential property to a creditor, it can be argued that the debtor does not really need the property for daily living. When the property is in the creditor's possession, a debtor will not be able to avoid a security interest.

A debtor who is considering bankruptcy or creditors who are considering putting a debtor into bankruptcy should carefully examine the property owned by the debtor and the extent to which it may be exempt. From the debtor's perspective, bankrupcty not only provides an opportunity of being relieved of certain debts, but it also offers the possibility of freeing up certain property against which there may be liens, as could occur with a New York debtor whose automobile has been seized by a judgment creditor. From a creditor's perspective, there is probably no advantage in seeking bankruptcy if a debtor owns property that will be mostly exempt in a bankruptcy proceeding. The creditor will receive little or no payment in the bankruptcy, and he or she will be prevented from seeking payment in the future if the debtor receives a discharge.

Discharge

A discharge in a bankruptcy proceeding relieves an individual from having to pay most of his or her debts. Only an individual person is entitled to a discharge. A corporation does not need a discharge since it can be dissolved and, thus, be put out of existence. Either the trustee or a creditor can object to the granting of a discharge. If no objection is raised, the court must grant a discharge [§727].

A debtor can be denied a discharge on a number of grounds (Figure 30-8). For example, in the *Kaiser* case previously presented in this chapter, the debtor was denied a discharge because he had made a fraudulent conveyance. The effect of denying a debtor a discharge is that the debtor must continue to pay all of the debts and claims that he or she had prior to the bankruptcy.

A debtor who is not going to receive a discharge in bankruptcy should avoid a Chapter 7 liquidation and should seek some other method of dealing with creditors. In a Chapter 7 liquidation, all of a debtor's property except exempt property is sold (liquidated) and the proceeds are used to pay the creditors. If the debtor is denied a discharge and there is not enough money from the liquidation to pay all the claims of all creditors, the debtor will still owe the unpaid creditors. Thus, a debtor who does not obtain a discharge will lose all property but exempt property and will still owe his or her creditors. Contrast this with a debtor who does obtain a discharge. This debtor now has only exempt property, but he or she is free from all debts except for a few that are not dischargeable. Nondischargeable debts will be discussed later in this chapter.

In the following case, the court denies a discharge to a debtor at the request of a creditor.

MATTER OF WILSON
33 B.R. 689 (Bkrtcy. M.D. Ga. 1983)

HERSHNER, Bankruptcy Judge

On July 6, 1982, Defendant Henry David Wilson filed with this Court his voluntary petition under Chapter 7 of the Bankruptcy Code. On October 7, 1982, Plaintiff John A. Milam filed a ''Complaint . . . Objecting to Discharge under [§727].''

. . .

After reviewing the evidence and considering the arguments of counsel, the Court is of the opinion that Defendant should be denied a discharge in bankruptcy.

Defendant graduated . . . in 1963 with a Bachelor of Business Administration degree and is a certified public accountant. . . . Plaintiff was also an accountant. . . . Plaintiff decided to sell his [accounting] practice. After what best can be described as brief negotiations, Plaintiff and Defendant signed a sales agreement dated June 16, 1978. Defendant paid Plaintiff the initial down payment, but has made no other payments to Plaintiff.

Defendant admits that for the years 1980, 1981, and 1982, the only business record he maintained for the [accounting business] was a single checking account from which both business and personal expenses were paid. Defendant states that, in his view, this was all that was required for him to account for his business affairs. . . .

Because Defendant did not make the monthly payments as required by the June 16, 1978, sales agreement, Plaintiff brought suit against Defendant. . . . As a result of the suit, Plaintiff was awarded a judgment against Defendant in the amount of $57,569.00 on May 22, 1980. This is one of the debts that Defendant seeks to discharge in his bankruptcy case.

Plaintiff asserts five grounds in his complaint for the Court to deny Defendant a discharge in bankruptcy. . . . The five grounds are as follows:

. . .

3. That Defendant failed to maintain adequate books and records on the [accounting] practice from which the financial condition of the business could be ascertained.

. . .

When a party objects to the discharge of a debtor, that party bears the burden of proving that the case falls within one of the statutory exceptions to discharge. After carefully considering the evidence presented, the Court is of the opinion that the Plaintiff has

---

Grounds for Denial of Discharge

Restated from §727(a)

(1) The debtor is not an individual.

(2) The debtor has made a fraudulent conveyance within one year before filing the petition.

(3) The debtor has failed to keep or has destroyed records from which the debtor's financial condition and business transactions can be determined.

(4) The debtor has knowingly and fraudulently (a) made a false oath in connection with the bankruptcy case or (b) presented a false claim or (c) given, received or attempted to obtain money or property for acting or forbearing to act in the bankruptcy case or (d) withheld from the trustee or other officer of the bankruptcy case any information relating to the debtor's property or financial affairs.

(5) The debtor has failed to explain satisfactorily any loss or deficiency of assets.

(6) The debtor has refused to cooperate with the court by such acts as refusing to obey lawful orders of the court.

(7) The debtor has committed any act in category (2–6) within one year before the filing of the petition in connection with a case concerning an insider of the debtor.

(8) The debtor has been granted a discharge in a Chapter 7 or Chapter 11 proceeding in a case commenced within before the date of the filing of the petition.

(9) The debtor has been granted a discharge in a Chapter 13 in a case commenced within six years before the date of the filing of the petition unless in that case the debtor paid (a) 100% of the unsecured claims or (b) 70% of such claims in a plan proposed in good faith and completed by the debtor's best efforts.

(10) The court allows the debtor to waive a discharge.

FIGURE 30-8
Grounds for Denial of Discharge

sustained his burden on the third ground. Because the third ground is sufficient to bar Defendant's discharge, the Court need not address the other grounds. . . .

The objection is based on [§727(a)(3)] of the Bankruptcy Code. . . .

[§727(a)(3)] is intended "to enable creditors, with the assistance of proper books and records, to ascertain the true status of the debtor's affairs and to test the completeness of the disclosure requisite to a discharge." [§727(a)(3)] requires that a debtor produce some accurate written information that the creditors and trustee can rely on in tracing the debtor's financial history during the period preceding his bankruptcy. . . . Records are adequate when they are kept "so as to reflect, with a fair degree of accuracy, the debtor's financial condition and in a manner appropriate to his business."

. . .

From the above discussion, the Court concludes that the determination of whether a debtor is justified in failing to keep adequate books and records depends on the circumstances of each case. The issue of justification depends largely on what a normal, reasonable person would do under similar circumstances. The inquiry should include the education, experience, and sophistication of the debtor; the volume of the debtor's business; the complexity of the debtor's business; the amount of credit extended to debtor in his business; and any other circumstances that should be considered in the interest of justice.

In this . . . proceeding, the Court is convinced that Defendant did not keep adequate books and records. Defendant has not maintained accounts and ledgers in the [accounting] business since 1979. Nor has defendant filed a tax return since 1978. The only

record of receipts and disbursements made by Defendant since 1980 is in a checkbook. Defendant's checkbook records reflect only those receipts that were actually deposited in the checking account and in no way enable a creditor or the trustee to verify the total receipts of the [accounting business]. Any payment (e.g., a preferential payment) not made through the checking account would go undetected by creditors, if not disclosed by Debtor. Also, this checking account was used to pay both personal and business expenses. Clearly, it cannot be said that Defendant maintained sufficient records in his [accounting business].

The Court can perceive of no justification for Defendant's failure to keep adequate records. Defendant's . . . practice had gross revenues of approximately $40,000.00 to $45,000.00 per year. The Court is of the opinion that this volume of business warrants a more accurate method of accounting than a simple checkbook record.

Moreover, Defendant is a certified public accountant engaged in an accounting practice. . . . This is not the case of an unsophisticated wage earner who is unfamiliar with business practices. Rather, Defendant is specially trained in the ways of accounting, is certified by the state as having education and experience in accounting, and has practiced as an accountant for approximately eighteen years. Under these circumstances, the Court cannot condone Defendant's failure to keep adequate books and records. It cannot be said that a reasonable person in Defendant's position would have relied on a checkbook as his only business record.

[Discharge denied.]

CASE REVIEW QUESTIONS
1. Who has the burden of proving that a debtor should be denied a discharge?
2. Why must a debtor keep records of his or her financial condition?
3. What standard is applied to determine whether the debtor's financial records are adequate?
4. Why did the court hold that Wilson had failed to keep recorded information if he had recorded information in his checkbook?
5. Does Wilson still owe Milam $57,569.00?

Nondischargeable Debts

Restated from §523(a)

(1) Certain taxes or custom duties (a) which are given priority under §507 or (b) where the required return was not filed or (c) the debt made a fraudulent return or willfully attempted to evade the tax.

(2) Debts where the debtor obtained the money, property, services or an extension, renewal or refinancing of credit
   (a) by false pretenses or actual fraud or
   (b) by use of a written statement (i) that is materially false, (ii) concerning the debtor's financial condition, (iii) on which the creditor reasonably relied, and (iv) that the debtor made with intent to deceive or
   (c) by purchasing luxury goods or services with more than $500 from one creditor within 40 days of filing a petition or by taking cash advances aggregating more than $1,000 under an open ended credit plan from the same creditor within 20 days of filing a petition.

(3) Debts known to the debtor but not listed in the schedules (Unscheduled Debts).

(4) Debts created by fraud by a fiduciary, by embezzlement or by larceny (Breach of Fiduciary Duty).

(5) Certain types of alimony, maintenance or support for a spouse, former spouse or child.

(6) Debts arising because of willful or malicious injuries caused by the debtor.

(7) Certain fines or penalties due governmental units.

(8) Educational loans made or insured by a governmental unit or a non-profit institution unless the loan was first due more than five years before the filing of the petition or a denial of discharge would cause undue hardship to the debtor or the debtor's dependents.

(9) Debts incurred by a debtor as the result of a debtor's operation of a motor vehicle while legally intoxicated.

(10) The debt was listed or could have been listed in a prior bankruptcy proceedings where the debtor was denied a discharge under categories (2–7) of §727(a) or the debtor waived a discharge.

FIGURE 30-9
Nondischargeable Debts

Nondischargeable Debts Even if a debtor receives a discharge under §727, certain debts are not discharged [§523]. (See Figure 30-9.) A debtor must continue to pay these debts.

In the past, some creditors abused the exceptions to discharge. Often, a creditor would not seek a determination of the dischargeability of a debt during a bankruptcy proceeding. Instead, the creditor would bring a suit in a state court after the bankruptcy proceedings. The debtor might ignore the state court proceedings because he or she believed that the debt was discharged. The creditor would then obtain a default judgment — that is, a judgment rendered when a defendant doesn't show up and defend — and seize some of the debtor's property to satisfy the judgment. This abuse was so widespread that Congress enacted legislation to deal with the problem in the early 1970s, even before the enactment of the new Bankruptcy Code.

Under the new law, a creditor who claims that a debt is not dischargeable because it belongs in categories (2), (4), or (6) of §523(a) must seek a bankruptcy court determination of the nondischargeability of the debt. If a creditor does not seek a determination, the debt is discharged. Moreover, a creditor is enjoined (prohibited) by the order granting a discharge from pursuing the claim in any court subsequent to the bankruptcy.

If a creditor seeks a determination of the nondischargeability of a debt and fails to establish that the debt is not dischargeable, the debt will be discharged. In order to prevent creditors from harassing consumer debtors with suits to determine nondischargeability, the Bankruptcy Code requires that the judge must order an unsuccessful creditor to pay a consumer debtor's court costs and reasonable attorney's fees unless such payment would clearly be inequitable.

In the following case, the court carefully discusses each of the elements that the creditor must prove in order to establish that a debt is nondischargeable when the creditor claims that a debtor used a false financial statement.

IN RE ANDREWS
33 B.R. 970 (Bkrtcy. Mass 1983)

GABRIEL, Bankruptcy Judge

The Complaint of the Plaintiff, Martha's Vineyard Cooperative Bank ("the bank"), seeks a determination that two unsecured loans totalling $3,700 it granted the debtors, Bradford and Susan Andrews ("the debtors" or "the Andrews") are nondischargeable pursuant to [§523(a)(2)(B)]. A trial was held on November 16, 1982. Based upon the agreed facts, testimony and the documentary evidence the Court finds the following facts.

In May 1980 the debtor, Bradford Andrews, obtained a loan application from the bank to apply for a mortgage loan. The debtor, Susan Andrews, prepared the application dated August 29, 1980 which sought a mortgage loan of $45,000. . . . On page one of the application the debtors checked off the question "are you buying?", indicated a purchase price of $12,000, and that they were "building." The testimony of the only bank employee to testify, Mrs. Conroy, was that the bank knew the Andrews owned the Canterbury Land property and that the Andrews were building a home on this location. . . . The application stated that Mr. Andrews' monthly income as a mason contractor was $2,500 to $3,000. The application listed a checking account at the "M.V. National Bank." The applica-

tion did not request a statement of assets or secured debt. Rather, with respect to liabilities, the application only requested a list of "monthly obligations and open accounts." The Andrews listed total monthly obligations of $316.18, owed to four creditors. . . . The application was submitted to the bank. . . .

On October 8, 1980 the Andrews filed with the bank a personal loan application seeking $1,000. The purpose of this loan was: "to pay construction workers and contractors who are building our house—balance of this loan to be paid off with mortgage." Similar to the mortgage loan application the personal loan application contained no space for a list of assets or encumbrances on property but merely requested a statement of monthly obligations. The only mortgage obligation listed was $76.71 to Martha's Vineyard National Bank. The bank approved the $1,000 personal loan. . . . The bank's mortgage review board approved the Andrews' mortgage application on November 13, 1980, and forwarded the legal work. . . . On November 25, 1980 the bank received a letter from the law firm stating that their search revealed two mortgages on the Andrews' property and requesting pay-off figures.

At trial it was agreed that this search revealed that

the Andrews had executed a mortgage to Miles Homes for $51,275.40 on June 9, 1980. . . . The record further revealed that the Andrews had granted a . . . mortgage for $10,000 to the sellers which was recorded on May 23, 1980. Neither mortgage was listed on any of the loan applications submitted to the bank. Mrs. Andrews testified that although she did not list the $10,000 mortgage to the sellers on the loan applications, she did inform Mrs. Conroy that the purpose of the mortgage was to pay the balance of the purchase price. . . . Mrs. Andrews explained that she did not list the mortgage to Miles Homes because she and her husband were unaware that Miles had a mortgage on the property. They had selected a pre-fabricated home from Miles Homes. . . . They had executed a purchase contract with Miles, but the Andrews did not understand the document to be a mortgage. The Andrews did not learn of the Miles mortgage until they received a letter from the bank's attorney.

Mrs. Andrews was unable to explain the Miles transaction with clarity. It is clear that both she and her husband were and are unsophisticated in real estate transactions. Mrs. Andrews testimony was related in a sincere and credible manner, and I find that she did not understand that she and her husband had granted a mortgage to Miles Homes.

The bank seeks to except its debt from discharge pursuant to [§523(a)(2)(B)] which provides:

> a discharge does not discharge an individual debtor from any debt — for obtaining money, property, services or an extension, renewal or refinance of credit, by . . . (b) use of a statement in writing (i) that is materially false; (ii) respecting the debtor's financial condition; (iii) on which the creditor to whom the debtor is liable for obtaining money, property, services or credit reasonably relied; and (iv) that the debtor caused to be made or published with intent to deceive.

The lender has the burden of proving each element of its claim under this section by clear and convincing evidence.

There is no dispute that the loan applications submitted to the bank qualify as statements in writing concerning the debtors' financial condition.

The bank must demonstrate the financial statement was materially false, which means substantially untrue. The amount omitted from debtors' statements —

clearly transformed the application into an untruthful representation of the Andrews' financial condition, and the financial statements omitting the two mortgages were materially false.

The bank is also required to prove that it actually and reasonably relied on the false financial statements. The officer who approved the loan did not testify and there was no evidence presented concerning the basis for his decision. The plaintiff has failed to sustain its burden of demonstrating actual reliance.

Even if I were to find that the bank actually relied on the financial statements, this reliance cannot be considered reasonable. Where a financial statement fails to solicit sufficient information to accurately portray an applicant's financial condition, the creditor cannot claim its reliance on the application was reasonable. Here the application was so deficient it could not present an accurate picture of financial status. It fails to inquire into ownership of assets or encumbrances, such as mortgages. The bank's reliance on this inherently unreliable financial statement cannot be considered reasonable.

Finally the bank has also failed to demonstrate that the debtors intended to deceive it by submitting the false financial statement. Intent to deceive may be inferred where a person knowingly makes a false representation which the person knows or should know will induce another to make a loan. The debtor's credibility is an important factor in determining whether the requisite intent to deceive was present in a transaction. . . . A finding of intent to deceive is impermissible where a misrepresentation on a loan application was innocent and was caused by the deficiencies in the loan application itself.

Here the omission of the two mortgages by Mrs. Andrews, the preparer, cannot be considered intentionally deceptive. The application did not contain space for listing mortgage obligations.

. . .

The Plaintiff having failed to meet its burden of proof on the elements of [§523(a)(2)(B)] of the Bankruptcy Code, it is therefore ordered that the debt of the debtors to the Plaintiff as evidenced by loans . . . [is] discharged and judgment shall enter for the Defendants in this adversary proceeding.

CASE REVIEW QUESTIONS

1. What five elements must the bank prove in order to establish that the debts owed to it by the Andrews are nondischargeable?
2. Does the bank prove all the elements? Explain.
3. Of what relevance is the absence on the bank's form of any request for assets or secured debts?
4. Must the Andrews pay the debts owed to the bank?
5. If the court had found that the Andrews had intentionally given the bank a false financial statement, would the Andrews have been denied a discharge of all their debts?
6. Does the court ruling mean that the debtors are discharged from all their debts?

Payments to Creditors

One of the purposes of bankruptcy is the orderly collection of the debtor's property so that it can be used to satisfy the claims of creditors. In this section, we will discuss how and in what order creditors are paid.

Claims A creditor must file a claim in order to receive a payment, sometimes referred to as a dividend, in a bankruptcy proceeding. Creditors who are listed in a debtor's schedules are notified by the court that the debtor has been adjudicated a bankrupt. The creditors are given time limits within which claims must be filed. The debtor, another creditor, or the trustee can object to a claim. Certain claims can be disallowed completely or partially, as might occur when an insider's claim for services exceeds the reasonable value of the services rendered [§502].

Priorities Even if a creditor's claim is allowed, it does not mean that the creditor will be paid. Creditors are paid in order of priority [§507]. (See Figure 30-10.)

To fully understand the order in which creditors are paid, we must take a look at secured versus unsecured creditors. A secured creditor, for these purposes, is a creditor who has perfected a security interest pursuant to Article 9 of the Uniform Commercial Code (see Chapter 29) or some other statute that gives the creditor a right against specific property owned by the debtor, for example, the holder of a mortgage on real property. Because a secured creditor has an interest in specific property owned by a debtor, the secured creditor can take that property to satisfy his or her claim unless the security interest can be challenged or avoided by the trustee. The secured property does not become part of the property used to pay creditors.

To the extent that a secured creditor's claim is partially or totally satisfied by the secured property, that creditor has priority over other creditors. In other words, secured creditors could really be listed first in Figure 30-10. If the value of secured property is less than the value of a secured creditor's claim, that

Priorities

Restated from §507

(1) Administrative expenses — e.g., trustee's commissions; attorney's fees, appraiser's fees, etc. for professionals hired by the trustee; expenses of storing and selling debtor's property.

(2) Unsecured claims to the extent that the claim arose in an involuntary case in the ordinary course of the debtor's business and between the time the involuntary petition was filed and an order of relief is granted and a trustee appointed.

(3) Up to $2,000 of wages of employees of the debtor earned 90 days before the filing of the petition or the time the debtor ceased doing business, whichever occurs first.

(4) Contributions to employee benefit plans based on services rendered 180 days prior to the petition or end of the debtor's business, whichever occurs first, up to $2,000 times the number of employees and depending in part on any amount paid under category (3).

(5) Up to $900 for each deposit given to the debtor by an individual for the purchase, lease or rental of property or purchase of services for personal, family or household purposes.

(6) Governmental claims for certain types of taxes, e.g., income tax, excise tax, etc.

FIGURE 30-10
Priorities

creditor will be considered an unsecured creditor with respect to the surplus owed. Unsecured creditors who do not fall into categories (1) through (6) come after category (6) in what amounts to a seventh category.

The trustee pays claims by category. All claims in category (1) are paid in full first, then all claims in category (2) are paid in full, and so on. If there are not sufficient funds to pay all of the claims in any category in full, the creditors in that category receive a prorated share of the available funds in proportion to their claims. The next category receives nothing.

Because unsecured creditors without any priority status are paid last, they often receive little or nothing in a bankruptcy. In addition, a creditor with a dischargeable claim will receive nothing subsequent to the bankruptcy. Creditors with nondischargeable debts will receive their share of payment according to their level of priority. They can also pursue the debtor for the balance due subsequent to the bankruptcy. For example, alimony payments to a former spouse constitute a nondischargeable debt. Alimony has no priority, so the claim would be among the last to be paid. If creditors in the "seventh" category receive twenty-five cents per dollar of their claims, the ex-spouse would receive one-fourth of his or her claim. The ex-spouse could then demand payment of the remaining seventy-five percent from the debtor subsequent to the bankruptcy.

ADJUSTMENT OF DEBTS OF AN INDIVIDUAL WITH REGULAR INCOME — CHAPTER 13

A debtor who has regular income can use Chapter 13 provided that he or she has unsecured debts of less than $100,000 and secured debts of less than

$350,000. In a Chapter 13 proceeding, a debtor proposes a plan to pay off creditors, at least in part, over a specified period, usually three years. A debtor's property is not collected and sold by a trustee as in a Chapter 7 liquidation, so the debtor does not face the loss of nonexempt assets. Creditors are paid out of future earnings. In addition to preserving nonexempt property, Chapter 13 provides for the discharge of some debts that are not dischargeable in a liquidation.

The plan proposed by a debtor is the key aspect of a Chapter 13 proceedings. The plan must meet certain basic requirements. It must be proposed in good faith, and it must usually pay creditors at least as much as they would receive in a liquidation [§1325]. A Chapter 13 proceeding will allow a debtor to propose that a debt owed to a secured creditor be modified as to the amount owed or the duration of the payments [§1322].

A voluntary petition is required to commence a Chapter 13 proceeding. Furthermore, a debtor can convert a Chapter 13 proceeding into a Chapter 7 proceeding at any time. When a debtor proposes a plan, the court can reject the plan and dismiss the case or convert it to a Chapter 7 proceeding. If the debtor is a farmer, the court may not convert the case unless the farmer requests it.

In the following case, the court refused to confirm the debtor's plan.

IN RE CANADA
33 B.R. 75 (Bkrtcy. Ore. 1983)

HESS, Bankruptcy Judge

In this chapter 13 case Willamette University and Montana State University filed objections to confirmation of the debtor's plan.

From the fall of 1975 through the spring of 1977 the debtor attended Willamette University and accumulated $3,360.82 in direct student loans from Willamette. She took a year off and then entered Montana State University where she remained through the spring of 1980 accumulating direct student loans in the amount of $2,639.61 from Montana State. In the fall of 1980 the debtor attended Portland State University for one term. In March 1983 the debtor re-entered Portland State University and was classified as a junior.

During the next few years the debtor intends to complete her degree and work part time to cover her living expenses. . . . Her Chapter 13 Statement shows that after her expected monthly expenses she will have a surplus of $40 which, under her plan, she proposes to pay the trustee for distribution to credi-

tors. The Chapter 13 Statement lists unsecured debts totalling $7,569.33. No secured or priority debts are listed.

The debtor's plan proposes to pay unsecured creditors 14%. This would require 36 monthly payments. . . .

The universities assert three principal arguments against confirmation of the plan. They assert that 14% is not a substantial payment upon the student loans . . . and that the plan is not fundamentally fair and is contrary to the spirit of chapter 13.

The fact that utilizing the provisions of chapter 13 may permit a debtor to discharge debts which would not be dischargeable in a chapter 7 case, although an appropriate factor for the court to consider, is not a factor which by itself is controlling. . . . To hold that no chapter 13 plan can be confirmed unless it provides for payment in full of claims not dischargeable under §727 and §523, would be to abrogate §1328(a).

Congress has fixed no minimum percentage which must be paid to unsecured creditors except for §1325(a)(4) [which provides that the creditor not receive less than in a chapter 7 liquidation]. The plan in the present case meets this minimum requirement in that this would be a no asset case with no distribution to unsecured creditors were it converted to a case under chapter 7.

. . .

The Chapter 13 Statement shows that the debtor does not own any non-exempt property. Her earnings presently are such that no part of her wages would be subject to garnishment under Oregon law. The debtor is presently judgment proof. Should the debtor continue her schooling and her part time work none of her creditors could be successful in recovering any part of their debts through lawful collection procedures.

Under the circumstances it appears that at the present time there is no need for the debtor to obtain relief either under chapter 13 or chapter 7. . . .

Since it appears the debtor presently has no need for bankruptcy relief it would appear that the principal purpose is to obtain a discharge of the student loan obligations by paying only a small percentage of those debts.

The court therefore concludes that the debtor's plan is not proposed in good faith and is in violation of the spirit and purpose of chapter 13.

An order will be entered herein denying confirmation of the debtor's plan.

CASE REVIEW QUESTIONS

1. Would a student loan be a nondischargeable debt in a Chapter 7 proceeding? (See Figure 30-9.)
2. Can a plan be refused in a Chapter 13 proceeding because it seeks the discharge of a debt that would not be discharged in a Chapter 7 proceeding?
3. How much would the colleges have received if Canada had filed a Chapter 7 proceeding? Why?

REORGANIZATION—CHAPTER 11

A business or a debtor who does not qualify for Chapter 13 proceedings can use a Chapter 11 proceeding to work out an arrangement with creditors. Any debtor who can file a Chapter 7, except for a stockbroker or a commodities broker, can be a debtor in a Chapter 11 proceeding. A railroad, which cannot liquidate, can reorganize under Chapter 11. A Chapter 11 proceeding can be begun by either a voluntary petition or an involuntary petition, and it can be converted to a Chapter 7 proceeding in appropriate cases.

A Chapter 11 proceeding has several key features. First, Chapter 11 provides that a business can continue to operate during the reorganization. Indeed, the debtor, called the **debtor in possession,** may even continue to operate the business; it need not be turned over to a trustee. This is very important where management expertise may be important despite financial difficulties. Furthermore, a Chapter 11 proceeding may be desirable even when liquidation is the long range goal, since inventory sold by an ongoing business will bring greater value than inventory sold during a liquidation or forced distress sale. Finally, a

Chapter 11, like a Chapter 13, requires that a good faith plan be proposed for paying the debts. This plan can also propose a restructuring of equity ownership interests.

The 1984 amendments placed limitations on a business's ability to affect labor union contracts during a reorganization. The new legislation calls for consultation between the employees' representatives and the trustee or debtor in possession with regard to any modification of labor contracts. Court approval is required for the rejection or alteration of a labor contract [§1113].

The following case is offered to show the type of plan that can be proposed. Note the impact of the plan on the stockholders.

IN RE POLYTHERM INDUSTRIES, INC.
33 B.R. 823 (D.C. Wis. 1983)

CRABB, Chief Judge

This is an appeal by several creditors from an order of the United States Bankruptcy Court for the Western District of Wisconsin confirming the plan for reorganization of Polytherm Industries, Inc., under Chapter 11. . . .

Polytherm Industries, Inc., manufactures polystyrene foam insulation products. . . . On January 27, 1982, Polytherm filed a voluntary petition for reorganization. . . . On January 3, 1982, the debtor filed a proposed plan of reorganization. . . .

In August 1982, one of the . . . creditors . . . declined to accept preferred stock. Polytherm was unable to fill the ensuing $154,000 void in preferred stock subscription. As a result, Polytherm prepared and filed an amended plan for reorganization on November 12, 1982.

Polytherm proposed to fund the amended plan with cash proceeds from a new issue of common stock and from an improved operating position and earnings derived from internal restructuring and from the new product Thermomass™.

Polytherm's amended plan divides allowed claims and interests into six classes: (1) administrative expenses; (2) tax claims; (3) secured claims; (4) nonpriority unsecured claims of $100 or less; (5) other nonpriority unsecured claims; and (6) common stock. Under the amended plan, a holder of a nonpriority se-

cured claim could agree to reduce the claim to $100 in order to obtain Class 4 treatment of the claim.

In article III, the amended plan prescribes the treatment of each class of claims. All Class 1 administrative expense claims allowed by the court are to be paid in full on confirmation from the proceeds of the new common stock issue. Class 2 tax claims are to be paid with minimum monthly payments equal to one thirty-sixth of the claim amount beginning in January 1983. The amended plan provides for full payment of [overdue] interest . . . on Class 3 secured claims within a three year period according to [a] monthly payment schedule. . . . Under the amended plan, short-term notes are converted to loans at current commercial interest rates, with [overdue] interest paid as prescribed in the above schedule. . . . Class 4 claims, nonpriority unsecured claims of $100 or less, were to be paid in full in January 1983 from the proceeds of the new common stock issue. The amended plan proposes to pay 10% of all other nonpriority unsecured claims, Class 5 claims, within three years, with monthly payments of Class 5 claims at a minimum of one thirty-sixth of the claim amount scheduled to begin in January 1983. Finally, the amended plan cancels Class 6 claims; holders of old common shares lose their rights relating to those shares.

On December 22, 1982, the bankruptcy judge issued an order confirming the amended plan submitted to Polytherm.

On December 30, 1982, the Economic Development Administration filed a notice of appeal from the bankruptcy court's order of confirmation. The other appellants joined in this appeal.

In this bankruptcy action, Polytherm has elected to reorganize the corporation under Chapter 11 of the Bankruptcy Code rather than to liquidate under Chapter 7. Pursuant to that election, Polytherm had to submit a plan of reorganization. . . .

In a reorganization plan, creditors with valid, allowed claims are divided into classes according to the nature of their individual claims. . . . A reorganization plan must specify the treatment of each class of claims and accord all the claims of a particular class the same treatment unless the claimholder agrees to less favorable treatment.

The statutory provisions relating to reorganizations divide classes of claims into those that are impaired, i.e., materially and adversely altered under the reorganization plan and those that are not. . . . Only impaired classes have a right to vote to accept or reject a reorganization plan.

A bankruptcy court can confirm a plan that has the voluntary acceptance of all creditors, including "deemed" acceptances by unimpaired classes of creditors, provided the plan meets the eleven conditions precedent set forth in [§1129(a)].

If the reorganization plan meets all the requirements set forth in §1129(a) except for §1129(a)(8), the bankruptcy court may still confirm the plan under the cramdown provisions in §1129(b), that is, provisions which permit confirmation over objection. The cramdown provisions require a determination that adequate protection is afforded the dissenting impaired classes under the reorganization plan. In this case, I will first review the amended plan to determine if it meets the §1129(a) requirements. Only if the amended plan passes muster under these conditions precedent excluding §1129(a)(8) will I apply the §1129(b) cramdown provisions.

[The court reviewed the plan and found that it failed to meet certain requirements.]

The record does not contain the proposed compensation of insiders [officers of the bankrupt corporation] in the reorganized corporation. . . . Since section 1129(a)(5)(B) requires disclosure of proposed compensation, Polytherm is in noncompliance in this respect. . . .

Although the amended plan delineates the treatment accorded each class under the plan, it does not specify which classes are unimpaired under the plan. Therefore, it fails to comply with §1123(a)(2) and thus with §1129(a)(1).

Appellants . . . also assert that Polytherm proposed the reorganization plan in bad faith. . . . All the appellants contend that the services of the proposed officers would be contrary to the interests of creditors and public policy because of the alleged poor management of the present officers of the debtor corporation. Although continued service by prior management may be inconsistent with the interests of creditors, equity security holders, and public policy if it directly or indirectly perpetuates incompetence, lack of discretion, inexperience, or affiliations with groups inimical to the best interests of the debtor, the record is insufficient to permit an evaluation of the appellants' allegations of bad faith and inadequacy of current management. On remand, the bankruptcy court should evaluate the validity of the appellants' allegations in this regard, after the parties have developed a factual record sufficient for an informed evaluation. . . .

Also under §1129, the plan must accord dissenting holders of claims at least as much as would be received under liquidation. . . . To the extent they receive any payments or property under the amended plan, the Class 4 and 5 unsecured claimholders and the Class 6 holders of common stock would receive more than they would receive if Polytherm were liquidated under Chapter 7. The Class 3 secured creditors would retain the security to which their §111(b)(2) election applies. Therefore, the amended plan appears to comply with 11 U.S.C. §1129(a)(7). . . .

In its confirmation of the amended plan, the bankruptcy court explicitly found the plan to be feasible and fair and equitable, without specifying the grounds for the finding. A court may approve a Chapter 11 plan only if the plan is feasible. As defined in the Bankruptcy Code, feasibility requires that confirmation of the plan is not likely to be followed by liquidation or further financial reorganization of the debtor. Feasibility has been defined further in bankruptcy proceedings to require examination of the adequacy of the capital structure; the business's earning power; economic conditions; management's ability; the probability of the present management's continuation and any other factors related to the successful performance of the plan. As I have noted, the bankruptcy record does not permit a finding on this point. . . .

[The court then discussed what constitutes an impaired class and ruled that no unimpaired class accepted the plan since all but Class 3 were impaired.]

In this case, no impaired class has affirmatively accepted the debtor's reorganization plan. Therefore, this case fails to meet the requirement of §1129(a)(10) that at least one impaired class of creditors must affirmatively accept the plan. Accordingly, I conclude that the bankruptcy court was in error in confirming the reorganization plan.

It is ordered that the bankruptcy court's decision is reversed and the case is remanded for further proceedings.

CASE REVIEW QUESTIONS

1. How was the stock ownership of the corporation affected by the reorganization?
2. In what ways did the debtor's proposed plan fail to meet the required conditions for confirmation?
3. What steps must Polytherm take as a result of the decision?

REVIEW QUESTIONS

1. Define judgment lien, garnishment, assignment for benefit of creditors, and receivership.
2. What are the two purposes of bankruptcy law?
3. Who can file an involuntary petition? Against whom?
4. What are a trustee's three avoidance powers? Explain.
5. What is the role of exemptions?
6. What type of debts are nondischargeable?
7. In what order are creditors paid in a bankruptcy proceeding?

CASE PROBLEMS

1. The Green Briar Bank loaned $5,000 to Paul Johnson on a unsecured promissory note. Johnson has not made the last three payments despite repeated requests from the bank. The balance due on the loan is $4,000. The bank's credit manager has learned that Johnson owns an automobile worth $5,000 and has a weekly salary of $350.00. What steps could the bank take to recover the unpaid balance?
2. Smith owned 75 percent of the stock of the Green

Corporation. Jones owned 25 percent. Smith and Jones sold their stock to Averil, Inc., in return for a downpayment and a series of promissory notes. Smith and Jones owned an undivided interest in the notes in proportion to their stock ownership. Smith and Jones joined together with Doe, another creditor of Averil, and filed an involuntary petition against Averil. Averil defended upon the grounds that it had more than twelve creditors and that Smith and Jones were joint holders of an obligation that represented a single claim and should be treated as a single creditor. If the court rules that Smith and Jones are a single creditor, should the court dismiss the petition? Why?

3. Brian Bodey and Gary Bodey, two farmers who ran Bodey Farms, filed a voluntary petition for relief under Chapter 7 on February 4, 1983. During 1982, Bodey Farms had purchased feed and fuel oil supplies from Champaign Landmark, Inc. (Champaign) worth more than $60,000. In January 1983, the Bodeys still owed Champaign $17,000 in back bills even though all bills were supposed to be paid within thirty days. Champaign accepted a check for $5,000 in partial payment for the amount owed and insisted that all future payments be on time. During the rest of January, the Bodeys purchased an additional $4,000 in supplies. A payment of $4,000 was made at the end of January. It was established that the Bodeys had been insolvent for a number of months prior to the bankruptcy. The trustee brought an action against Champaign to recover the $9,000 arguing that the two payments were voidable preferences. Can the trustee recover the $9,000?

4. Between October 8, 1981, and November 10, 1981, Darryl R. Jones and William J. Trainor, the sole officers, stockholders, and directors of Tri-State Paving, Inc. (Tri-State) withdrew all the funds — $20,261 — in the Tri-State corporate bank account. The funds were used to finance a trip to Las Vegas for the purpose of winning enough money to pay the Tri-State corporate debt and the personal debts of Jones and Trainor. The plan failed and Tri-State filed a voluntary petition in bankruptcy on March 10, 1982. Jones and Trainor also filed petitions. The trustee for Tri-State sought (1) to recover the $20,261 from Jones and Trainor and (2) to have that amount owed to Tri-State declared a nondischargeable debt. Which avoidance power should the trustee use to recover the $20,261? Will Jones and Trainor's debt to the corporation be nondischargeable?

5. On April 8th, 1983, Agritrade delivered 510 bags of coffee to the General Coffee Corporation (General Coffee) pursuant to a sales contract entered into between Agritrade as seller and General Coffee as buyer. General Coffee failed to pay for the coffee and filed for bankruptcy on June 1, 1983. Agritrade argued that it had a vendor's lien (a security interest) on the goods for nonpayment of the price. Agritrade had not filed or perfected any security interest in the coffee. The trustee for General Coffee claimed the coffee for the debtor's estate. What avoidance power can the trustee use? What type of claim does Agritrade have against the debtor?

6. William Metzig was a remodeler of homes and commercial buildings. On December 30, 1982, Metzig filed a voluntary Chapter 7 petition. On the schedules, Metzig claimed a number of tools and some equipment as exempt under §522(d). The property consisted of $8,650.00 worth of saws, air compressors, staple guns, welding equipment, drills, mechanic's tool boxes, a half-ton pickup truck, salvage lumber, window units, filing cabinets, and office furniture. Metzig sought to avoid a nonpossessory, nonpurchase money security interest held by the Bank of the West on all of the $8,650 worth of property. The Bank of the West filed objections to Metzig's claimed exemptions. How much of the $8,650 can Metzig exempt?

7. G. Gilbride filed for bankruptcy. H. Jones, a creditor, objected to the granting of a discharge. The facts showed that Gilbride had served as a bank officer and an operator of a store and was at the time of the bankruptcy a bartender. In the year prior to the bankruptcy, Gilbride had received more than $100,000 in income. Gilbride's only explanation as to what had happened to the money was that he had spent it for living expenses. Gilbride submitted his current tax returns, bank statements, and cancelled checks but none for the year in which he had received substantial income. Gilbride's explanations about his assets were confusing and conflicting. Should Gilbride be denied a discharge?

8. Colleen Volpe borrowed $7,000 from the W.C.T.A. Federal Credit Union. The note was cosigned by her husband, Dale. Dale completed a

Ice Cream's Financial Statement

Liabilities

Creditor	Debt	Amount Due
Whipped Cream, former spouse	Alimony	4 mo. @ $300 = $1,200
Soda, employee	Salary	5 mo. @ $100 = 500
Sundae, employee	Salary	2 mo. @ $100 = 200
Internal Revenue Service	Back taxes	1,000
Cold Heart Bank	Vacation loan[1]	1,000
Strawberry computers	Home computer[2]	800
Blueberry computers	Business computer[2]	3,000
Chocolate Works	Inventory financing[3]	2,500
Double Scoop Loan Co.	Loan[4]	1,500
Walnut Bank	Home Mortgage[5]	75,000
Hot Fudge Utilities	Monthly bill[6]	350
Reindeer Gazette	Advertising[6]	400

[1] The loan application asked for all personal debts. Cream did not list any business debts. The bank loan officer knew Cream operated a business because Cream had taken business loans in the past.

[2] Each computer company took a security interest in the computer sold, but neither company filed a financing statement.

[3] Chocolate Works filed a financing statement to secure its loan.

[4] Double Scoop Loan Company took and perfected a security interest in Cream's household furnishings.

[5] Cream recently purchased the $80,000 home and paid $5,000 down. The bank properly filed the mortgage. Cream has made all payments to date on time.

[6] These are current bills. All previous bills have been paid.

Assets

Property	Value
1. Home	$80,000
2. Bank account	600
3. Inventory[7]	3,000
4. Household goods[7] (usual appliances and furnishings)	5,000
5. Ice cream making machines	2 @ $750 = 1,500
6. Office and store furnishings	1,000
7. Antique soda glasses[8]	2,500
8. Automobile	500
9. Delivery van	1,400

[7] Subject to security interests on mortgages.

[8] Two glasses each valued at $400 each were given to Cream by an aunt and uncle who formerly ran the business.

FIGURE 30-11
Ice Cream's Financial Statement

guarantor's statement that instructed the debtor to list "all debts such as doctor bills, real estate, automobile, repairs, furniture, installments, loans, etc." Dale did not list a Small Business Administration loan of $25,000, which was fully secured by business property, nor any of eighteen other business debts amounting to $10,000. Dale also did not list any of the business property, believing that he was not personally liable for the business debts. Dale and Colleen filed a joint bankruptcy petition. W.C.T.A. Federal Credit Union filed a complaint objecting to the discharge of the $7,000 debt. Should the debt be declared nondischargeable?

9. W. Frazier filed a petition for a Chapter 13 proceeding. The proposed plan called for paying $5,000 to the unsecured creditors who were owed $20,000. The trustee determined that the sale of the debtor's nonexempt property in a Chapter 7 proceeding would probably produce a dividend of $15,000 for the unsecured creditors. Should Frazier's plan be confirmed?

10. Ice Cream owns and operates an ice cream parlor and catering service in North Pole, U.S.A. At the present time, his liabilities and assets are as shown in Figure 30-11. Cream wants advice on the following questions:

a. How many creditors would be required to sign an involuntary petition? Can Cream be forced into bankruptcy? Why?

b. If Cream files for bankruptcy
   (1) What property will be exempt under the Bankruptcy Code? What property will be exempt under the Utah Exemption Act?
   (2) Will Cream receive a discharge?
   (3) Are any of the debts nondischargeable? Why?
   (4) In what order will the creditors be paid? How much will each creditor receive, assuming there is enough to pay all creditors in full except for unsecured creditors, who will receive fifty cents for each dollar in claims?
   (5) If Cream pays the utility and advertising bills immediately before the bankruptcy, will the trustee avoid the payments?

PART VI

AGENCY
LAW

31

THE AGENCY RELATIONSHIP

Commercial activity is generally conducted by agents. These agents are usually individuals who are acting on behalf of other individuals, partnerships, corporations, governments, or other legal entities. The legal relationship created by an **agent** on behalf of a **principal** with a third party is defined by that body of rules referred to as agency law. Agency law is a large part of the total legal framework that governs the employer–employee relationship. This law has been created primarily by state court decisions.

Because the law sometimes varies from state to state, studying agency law could be very confusing. We have attempted to simplify the presentation of agency rules by focusing on one widely recognized reference work, The Restatement of Agency, Second Edition, referred to hereafter as the Restatement. The Restatement was written by legal practitioners, jurists, and scholars who comprise the American Law Institute, an organization founded in 1923 to promote the clarification and simplification of the law.

The advantages in using agents to do one's work are numerous. Agents enable individuals, corporations, or other legal entities to extend their physical reach. One may safely negotiate a binding contract anywhere in the world by sending a properly authorized agent to conduct the negotiating and contracting. One's reach may be likewise extended by hiring experts or other specially trained individuals to act for and at the direction of the employer.

Most of the legal disputes that are resolved by the application of agency law involve at least three parties and, thus, three potential pairs of legal duties.

These three pairs of duties are:

$$\text{Principal} \longleftrightarrow \text{Agent}$$
$$\text{Agent} \longleftrightarrow \text{Third Party}$$
$$\text{Principal} \longleftrightarrow \text{Third Party}$$

Although many issues of agency law involve a third party, there is an important portion of agency law that involves only the principal and agent. For the sake of convenience, we will start by considering the creation of the agency relationship and then proceed to analyze the mutual legal duties of the principal and agent.

CREATION OF THE AGENCY RELATIONSHIP

Section 1 of the Restatement of Agency defines *agency, principal,* and *agent* as follows:

1. **Agency** is the fiduciary relation which results from the manifestation of consent by one person to another that the other shall act on his behalf and subject to his control, and consent by the other so to act.
2. The one for whom action is to be taken is the principal.
3. The one who is to act is the agent.

Most agency relationships are created by contract. As the definition indicates, however, it is the consent by the principal and the agent, not the existence of a contract, that is required. Therefore, a person who voluntarily consents to act at the direction of another is an agent, even though the agent receives nothing in return for such consent.

There are no formalities necessary to create an agency. It can be created orally or in writing or may even result from the conduct of a principal that implies the appointment of the agent. A common example of an agency created by a writing is a **power of attorney,** which is a document given by the principal to the agent that confers on the agent the authority to perform certain specified acts for the principal. Possession of such a document allows the agent to show third parties the exact extent of his or her authority.

Other common examples of agency relationships are the typical situations of employer (principal) and employee (agent) and lawyer (agent) and client (principal). In each of these situations there is mutual consent that the agent shall work on behalf of and subject to the control of the principal.

You may wonder about the principal's right to control the agent in the lawyer–client relationship. In this relationship the principal (client) has the right to tell the agent (lawyer) what to do and what not to do within the agency relationship. For instance, it is the client who decides whether to bring legal action. If the lawyer disagrees with the client's decision, he or she cannot legally overrule the client. The lawyer can, however, terminate the agency, in which event the client must then find a new lawyer.

There are some situations in which an agency does not exist but which are treated by a court as though an agency does exist in order to protect third parties. These situations will be discussed in the following chapters in which the rights of third parties are considered.

Capacity of Principal and Agent

Legal **capacity,** as we use the term here, refers to the legal qualification of one to contract (see Chapter 14). Most states have statutes defining this legal capacity. Generally, they state that minors, persons declared insane, and those deprived of their civil rights (e.g., convicts) lack this capacity. The law of some states may further provide that if a person is so under the influence of drugs or alcohol that he or she cannot understand or appreciate the legal effect of his or her acts, then that person lacks the legal capacity to accomplish the act.

In an agency relationship, it is most important that the principal have the legal capacity to act. If the principal has the capacity to give legally operative consent, then an agent may be appointed by the principal to conduct all of those transactions that the principal could conduct if he or she were present. This is so even if the agent lacks capacity to act, unless the agent is so drunk or similarly incapacitated that a third party would see that the agent did not know what he or she was doing.

For example, if a state declares that those under 18 years of age lack capacity to contract, a principal of legal age may appoint a 17-year-old agent to act, and the principal will be bound by contracts made for him or her by that agent. On the other hand, a principal who lacks legal capacity cannot appoint an agent, even when the agent is a person who has capacity to contract. In other words, when the capacity of the principal is removed, an agent who acts for the principal also loses capacity.

DUTIES OF THE AGENT TO THE PRINCIPAL

Because the agency relationship is usually created by contract, the agent has the duty under contract law to perform his or her promises in the contract. In addition, there are duties imposed on the agent because, as stated in the definition of agency, the agent is a fiduciary.

A **fiduciary** is a person who is vested with a special form of trust and who is required to display scrupulous good faith and candor. As a result, an agent has duties of loyalty and duties of service and obedience that are owed to the principal. These duties will be explained and discussed in the following sections of the text.

There are, however, limits to the application of these fiduciary duties. They apply only to acts conducted pursuant to the purpose of the agency. To determine if there is a breach of fiduciary duty by the agent, therefore, the first step is to determine the exact scope of the agency. This determination is made by defining the authority of the agent. The process for defining the scope of the agency and the authority of the agent is explained in the following chapters. It is sufficient for now for you to understand that an agent will only be held liable for a breach of fiduciary duty if the agent's acts are related to his or her authority, that is, if they are within the scope of the agent's employment.

Duty of Loyalty

The agent's fiduciary duty of loyalty requires that the agent act solely and completely for the principal's benefit in all matters associated with the agency. This duty is imposed not only on agents who are compensated for their work but on gratuitous agents as well. Following are several situations in which the duty of loyalty is applicable.

Accounting for Income An agent must give over to the principal all income received as a result of business transacted on behalf of the principal. This must be done even if the agent has not violated any duty to the principal in receiving the money. For example, if an agent takes out an insurance policy on the principal's behalf, using the agent's own money and taking out the policy in the agent's own name, he or she would have to pay over to the principal any rebates or dividends declared by the insurance company and paid to the agent. Money earned outside the scope of the agency, such as income from a second job, may, of course, be retained by the agent. The courts have also decided that an agent such as a waitress or doorman may keep money received as tips, even though it is received while acting on behalf of the principal.

Confidential Information The duty of loyalty requires that the agent not use or disclose to others any confidential information about the principal without the principal's informed consent. Confidential information includes any information that is not common knowledge outside of the principal's business, such as, customer lists, trade secrets, and financial information. This duty to keep secret the confidential information of the principal continues even after the agency relationship is terminated.

Commingling Property An agent must not commingle his or her own property with the property of the principal. Also, an agent must not hold or deal with the principal's property in such a way that it appears to be the agent's property. Unless the principal is fully informed about such activities by the agent and consents to them, they constitute a breach of the duty of loyalty. Therefore, if an agent deposits funds belonging to the principal in a bank account, they should not be deposited in the agent's own name. Instead, they should be deposited either in the principal's name or in the name of the agent expressly in trust for the principal.

Conflicts of Interest An agent may not deal with the principal, either on the agent's own behalf or on behalf of another, in any transaction connected to the agency without first informing the principal. The duty of loyalty is violated when an agent deals with the principal without the principal's knowledge even if the principal is not harmed by the transaction. In fact, the duty is breached even if the principal benefits from the transaction. For example, if P tells A to sell goods at a particular price and A secretly purchases the goods for his or her own benefit, A has breached the duty of loyalty to P even if the price A pays is equal to or greater than the price designated by P. Even if the agent deals with the principal with the principal's consent, the duty of loyalty requires the agent to disclose all information material to the transaction to the principal and to deal fairly with the principal.

Because conflicts of interest must be avoided, the agent must also not compete with the principal within the scope of the agency, either on his or her own behalf or on behalf of another, unless the principal is informed of the competition and consents to it. For instance, an agent employed to sell cars for a car dealer may not sell cars in competition with the principal, either for himself or for another car dealer, without the employer's knowledge and consent.

The duty not to compete applies not only in situations in which the agent is selling for the principal, but also, as in the case that follows, when the agent is buying something for the principal. The issue that the court had to deal with is whether the competition by the agent was within the scope of his employment. Note carefully the agent's arguments and the reason the court decided that there had been a breach of the fiduciary duty of loyalty by the agent.

NYE v. LOVELACE
228 F. 2d 599 (Fifth Cir. 1956)

[Nye, an Oklahoma oil investor, hired Lovelace as an agent to procure mineral interests under an area of land designated by Nye on a map. One parcel of land, the Johnson tract, was entirely within the designated area. Another parcel, the Crosby tract of 1,260 acres, had only 400 acres within the area designated on the map. One of the owners of the Crosby parcel, Hart, also owned the Gray tract, which was entirely outside of the designated area.

When Lovelace dealt with Hart concerning the purchase of the mineral interests in the Crosby parcel, he learned that Hart would only sell the rights within the area designated by Nye if the mineral interests in the 860 acres of the Crosby parcel outside of the designated area were also purchased. Lovelace agreed to this. At the same time Lovelace contracted with Hart to purchase for his (Lovelace's) own benefit the mineral interest in the Gray tract.

Nye brought a legal action against Lovelace on the grounds that Lovelace had breached his fiduciary duty of loyalty by purchasing the Gray tract for himself. The trial court found for Lovelace, holding that the Gray tract was properly purchased by Lovelace for his own benefit because it lay outside the designated area and its purchase was not necessary to the acquisition of interests within the area. Nye appealed.]

BROWN, Circuit Judge

The trial court placed great reliance on the fact that, since the Gray tract happened to be just outside of the lines on the plat, Nye had himself excluded it from the buying area. . . . The court recognized, however, that it could not automatically exclude from the agency all land outside of the designated buying area, since so much had been, and had to be, procured beyond it to acquire interests within it. In the trial court's view, the outside acreage was within the agency only when necessarily procured in a single transaction as a condition to acquiring acreage within the area. On this approach the court then held that these were two separate transactions, separately negotiated so that procurement of Gray was wholly unrelated to acquisition of the desired interest in Crosby. . . .

Disregarding Lovelace's subjective attitude whether this was one or two transactions . . . it is uncontradicted that so far as Hart was concerned, it was a common transaction, whether in one or two parts, or more, and under no circumstance would he have sold the Gray tract had not he been selling Crosby. While the trial court rejected, as Hart's conclusion, his insistence that it was one transaction, the court did not, could not, find that had Lovelace approached him solely to procure Gray, he would have made the trade. . . . Everything about the course of dealing between Lovelace and the owners of Crosby bespeaks the recognition by Lovelace that these people were not going to permit a purchaser to pick and choose the good and reject the bad. Requiring Lovelace to take [860] acres of Crosby outside the designated area to procure the interest in 400 within makes practically absolute Hart's assertion that Gray would not have been sold alone.

The trial court, we think, became so preoccupied with the notion that Hart did not require purchase of Gray as a condition precedent to delivery of Crosby, that the vital importance of Hart's unwillingness to sell Gray unless they bought Crosby completely escaped him. This meant that the opportunity to procure a valuable interest in Gray was due entirely to Lovelace's position as agent for Nye. It was not simply the case of an agent acquiring knowledge of an attractive opportunity through performance of the master's work. When the door was opened solely because of Lovelace's dealings for his principal—when the only way to exploit the collateral opportunity was to consummate concurrently the principal's transaction—he was under an obligation to tender the co-incidental benefits to his principal or at least advise him of his personal tentative interest in it. It is not for the agent to determine for the principal whether the fruits are, or are not, attractive or desired, nor is it open to the servant under his heavy obligation of high fidelity to analyze, in re-verse, what must have been in his principal's mind at the time the general outline of the area was made, or to determine that, because the particular tract was separately owned under a title unrelated to the larger purchase, the principal would adhere to the strict artificial lines of the area instead of acquiring, as was otherwise frequently done, interests in the seller's outside acreage.

Here, an unfaithful servant, whose activities from the inception were in breach of his heavy duties, undertook, with circumstances strongly suggesting a studied furtiveness, to capitalize upon the information which had come to him under an obligation of trust, and in doing so, he sought to make decisions and resolve questions for his principal in which he stood to gain or lose as self-interest prevailed or was submerged. That which he has obtained by these means, he must restore.

As we think the total record is an overpowering portrayal of an agent unfaithful to his trust, the denial by the trial court of relief to recapture the diverted fruits of his actions leaves us with the conviction that an injustice has been done and a mistake has been committed. . . . and the judgment, insofar as it concerns the Gray tract, must be reversed and rendered in favor of appellant, Clark C. Nye.

Reversed.

CASE REVIEW QUESTIONS

1. In what way did Lovelace violate his duty of loyalty to Nye?
2. Why did the court decide that the scope of Lovelace's agency was not limited to the property designated on the map?
3. Would Lovelace have been liable to Nye if he had purchased land that was a quarter mile away from the land designated on the map and was not related in any way to any parcel designated on the map?
4. The issue of legal remedies available to the principal when an agent breaches a duty to the principal will be discussed later in the chapter. For now, however, what remedy do you think the court should give to Nye?

Duty of Service

If an agency is created by contract, the agent has a contractual duty to perform the promises that he or she made in the contract. In addition, the agent has a duty of service imposed by agency law that must be honored, unless the principal otherwise agrees. Following are several situations in which the duty of service is applicable.

Care and Skill The duty of service requires that the agent act within the scope of the agency with the degree of care and skill normally expected of agents doing the kind of work the agent is employed to do. The agent must also exercise any special skill that he or she possesses. The agent can violate this requirement by doing such things as engaging in misconduct when negotiating with third persons or carelessly harming property of the principal. For example, a truck-driver for a company would breach the duty to exercise care and skill by negligently driving the company's truck.

Good Conduct Success in business is often related to a good reputation. An agent must not act in such a way as to bring disrepute on the principal or the principal's business. The kind of reputation to be maintained will vary among different businesses as well as with the particular job of the agent. For example, the personal reputation of a laborer will usually be relatively unimportant to the success of a business. On the other hand, if a bank officer gains a deserved reputation as a gambler, the duty of good conduct would likely be violated.

In addition, an agent has a duty to act in such a way as to maintain a good working relationship with the principal. An agent who is abusive to the principal breaches the requirement of good conduct.

Giving Information An agent must give to the principal any information that the agent has and that he or she should expect the principal would want to have or that is relevant to the transactions of the principal with which the agent is involved. For example, if a principal told an agent to sell certain property at a particular price, and the agent found a buyer who was willing to pay more than the fixed price, the agent would have the duty to give this information to the principal.

There is an exception to this duty in cases in which the agent has a superior duty to a third person not to disclose the information. For example, a lawyer who has obtained confidential information from a client would not have to disclose that information to a subsequent client, even if the information were relevant to the subsequent client's business. Because the lawyer cannot carry out the duty to give the information to the subsequent client, he or she should terminate the relationship with the subsequent client.

Keeping Records An agent is required to keep accurate financial records of all transactions within the scope of the agency and to provide those records to the principal. These records should include not only a statement of money paid and received, but also the dates, the persons involved, and the nature of the transaction. The agent also has a duty to retain receipts.

Unauthorized Acts An agent must act only as authorized by the principal when acting within the scope of the agency. But what should the agent do if the instructions of the principal are unclear in a particular situation? If the agent knows that the instructions are unclear, he or she should communicate with the principal to clarify them.

If the principal is not available, the agent should try to interpret the principal's instructions in a reasonable manner under the circumstances. If the agent does this, he or she will not be held liable for failure to act only as authorized even if the agent's interpretation turns out to be incorrect.

An agent violates the duty to act only as authorized by doing such things as entering into an unauthorized contract that binds the principal or committing a crime or tort that makes the principal liable. These situations will be discussed in the next two chapters.

Ineffective Acts Limiting the requirement that an agent act only as authorized is another requirement that an agent should not proceed under circumstances in which his or her efforts would be ineffective and would subject the principal to additional expense, and the principal cannot be contacted. For example, if an agent is constructing a building for the principal and discovers that the land on which the building is to stand will not adequately support it, the agent should contact the principal and request instructions as to how to proceed. If the principal cannot be contacted, the agent has a duty not to continue with construction of the building.

Duty to Obey

An agent who has contracted to perform services is under a duty to obey all reasonable instructions of the principal concerning the performance of those services. The primary difficulty in applying this duty arises in determining whether particular instructions by a principal are reasonable.

Some things that should be considered in determining the reasonableness of a principal's instructions are the customs and ethics of the kind of agency involved, the effect that following the instructions will have on the agent, and the closeness of the relationship between the principal and agent. For example, a real estate agent who is hired to sell a principal's property can use standard sales methods to try to sell the property without interference from the principal. On the other hand, a salesman who is hired to work full time for a principal will likely have a duty to use those sales methods required by the principal. In no case, however, will an agent have a duty to obey instructions that are illegal, immoral, or unethical.

Principal's Remedies for Breach of Duty by Agent

Tort Actions In some situations a principal can bring a tort action against an agent who has breached a duty owed to the principal. If the requirements for tort liability discussed in Chapters 5 and 6 are present, the principal will be successful. For example, an agent who negligently or intentionally breaches the duty to exercise care and skill in carrying out the agency and who damages the property of the principal will be liable in tort for the damages caused.

Restitution If an agent benefits from a breach of duty, he or she is liable to the principal to the extent of the benefit received. This remedy is called **restitution**.

For example, an agent who is bribed to disclose confidential information of the principal has breached the duty of loyalty and is liable to pay over to the principal the amount of the bribe. Similarly, if an agent makes a profit by using confidential information of the principal, the agent will be liable to turn over the profit to the principal.

An agent also has to turn property over to the principal that the agent buys in his or her own name under circumstances in which the agent has a duty to buy the property for the principal. This was the remedy provided by the court in the case of *Nye v. Lovelace,* which you read earlier in this chapter. If the agent sells the property that was wrongfully purchased and makes a profit on the sale, the principal may recover the profit.

Contract Actions The duties imposed on agents by agency law are implied terms of the contracts that create most agencies. Therefore, if the agent violates one of the duties, he or she will usually be liable to the principal for breach of contract. When a principal sues an agent for breach of contract, the remedy available will be determined by the rules of contract law (see Chapter 18).

An important determination in such cases is whether the violation of duty by the agent is a material breach of the contract. The agent's breach is material only if it results in a failure by the agent substantially to perform his or her contract with the principal (see Chapter 17). If the breach is not material, the principal's remedy will generally be the collection of money damages from the agent for the foreseeable damages caused by the violation of duty. Sometimes, however, an injunction against the agent will be given by a court in cases in which the agent violates his or her duty by competing with the principal or by using or threatening to disclose confidential information of the principal. If the agent's violation of duty amounts to material breach of contract, the principal will be entitled to a stronger remedy, as discussed in the next section.

Discharge from Employment If the contract creating the agency does not state its duration or if the agency is not created by a contract, the agent is called an **employee at will.** Traditionally, agency law has provided that an employee at will can be discharged at any time for any reason. As you will read later in this chapter, this rule is beginning to change. Nonetheless, there is little doubt that a principal could legally discharge an agent who is an employee at will for a breach of duty by the agent.

If the parties do have a contract of employment that states its duration, the principal only has the right to discharge the agent if the agent's violation of duty is a material breach of the contract, that is, if the agent has failed substantially to perform his or her contract with the principal (see Chapter 17). If the agent's violation is not a material breach of the contract, the principal nonetheless has the *power,* although not the *right,* to discharge the employee, subject to some limitations discussed later in this chapter. A principal who exercises this power, however, will be liable to the agent for breach of contract.

The case that follows involves an agent who was discharged by his principals even though he was working under a contract that had not expired. The agent argued that his discharge was a breach of contract by the principals because he had not violated any duties he owed to them. The principals argued that the agent had violated duties that he owed to them and that the violations of duty were sufficient to constitute a material breach of contract. Therefore, according to the principals, they had the right to discharge the agent.

THOMAS v. BOURDETTE
608 P.2d 178 (Oregon 1980)

[Roy and Fern Bourdette owned an ABC Mobile Breaks (ABC) franchise in Portland, Oregon. They employed James Thomas to manage their business. The employment contract provided that Thomas would manage the business for five years and four months and that his compensation would be $225 a month plus commissions and bonuses based on sales.

The Bourdettes moved to Arizona, but they continued to be actively involved in the business. They did the bookkeeping, paid the bills and payroll, and retained authority to make all decisions regarding the purchase of items costing more than $25 and the purchase of any equipment. Thomas had no check writing authority except for a petty cash account of $100.

The Bourdettes regularly sent instructions to Thomas in Portland. Thomas, however, considered these instructions to be unwarranted interference with his managerial authority and refused to obey some of them. For example, he refused to keep inventory at a certain level and to reduce inventory by $10,000; he purchased a lathe for $900 that he was told not to purchase; he failed to open at the time designated by the Bourdettes; and he failed to have employees fill out time cards and sales reports as directed. Despite the fact that gross sales grew 38 percent during his first years and an additional 30 percent the next year and profit increased substantially, the Bourdettes fired Thomas after two years.

Thomas brought a legal action against the Bourdettes for breach of contract. The Bourdettes defended on the ground that they had been discharged from their duties under the contract because Thomas' failure to obey their instructions had been a material breach of contract by him. The trial court found for the Bourdettes. Thomas appealed.]

TANZER, Presiding Judge

Generally, an employer can discharge an employee at will without incurring liability, but a contract of employment for a definite period continues for that period unless there is a breach, in which case the person in breach cannot enforce the contract. Where, as here, the facts are not in dispute and different inferences from those facts cannot reasonably be drawn, the court must decide as a matter of law whether an employer had good cause to discharge his employee.

Both parties argued based on the Restatement (Second) of Agency, which states that good cause for discharge arises when an employee materially breaches his contract. Whether a breach is material varies with the particular circumstances of each case. Generally, the acts which are sufficient to be good cause for dismissal of a manager are qualitatively and quantitatively distinct from those required to terminate an employee possessing less responsibility and discretion. Comment (b) to Restatement §409(1) suggests that

> . . . a serious violation of the duty of loyalty or of obedience, constitutes an entire breach of contract. A wilful disobedience or a violation of duty of loyalty may constitute a material breach of contract although the harm likely to arise from such breach is very small.

The same breach of the duty to perform may be material or not depending upon whether the behavior is "wilful, negligent or innocent." Here, the refusal to obey is admittedly intentional.

The parties' employment agreement does not expressly allocate power between them. The agreement merely states that plaintiff will be employed "as a Manager." The title "Manager" connotes one in a position of general authority with discretion to exercise that authority. Indeed, unless the parties expressly or impliedly agree otherwise, a contract to manage bestows upon the manager the same authority over the transaction of business as the owner had.

Here, the understanding of the parties of the extent of managerial discretion delegated to plaintiff is demonstrated by the conduct of the parties as they operated under the contract and by plaintiff's admissions at trial. Plaintiff's authority as manager was limited. For example, plaintiff admitted that policy decisions were defendants' prerogative. Moreover, testimony of both parties demonstrates that as a matter of practice defendants retained control of policy decisions and of all significant financial commitments, while giving plaintiff control only over the day-to-day operation of the business. Thus, the record supports the trial court's inference that defendants retained control of business policy.

Once it is established that the delegation to the manager is not complete and an employer has reserved the right to establish certain policy, the trier of fact must determine whether the managerial acts complained of constitute an invasion of the employer's domain or whether they are properly within the manager's operational responsibility. . . .

Plaintiff's purchase of a lathe for over $900 was in direct disobedience of defendants' instruction not to make the purchase. Plaintiff had no authority to buy items for over $25 without first obtaining authorization from defendants. Plaintiff also refused to abide by defendants' specific directives to maintain lower inventory levels and to reduce inventory by $10,000. Moreover, plaintiff regularly failed to open the shop at the time required by defendants, and refused to require employees to fill out time cards and weekly sales reports.

The trial court concluded that the decisions as to equipment purchases, volume of inventory, opening hours, time cards and drivers' sales reports, were policy decisions reserved to defendants. We do not mean to imply that it is insubordination for a manager to manage, or to exercise those powers which his status confers. . . . This record, however, supports the conclusion that plaintiff, by his actions in these matters, invaded defendants' authority.

In this case, plaintiff crossed the line from aggressive management to wilful insubordination contrary to a tacit agreement that defendants would control business policy. Decisions regarding time cards, sales reports and business hours are arguably managerial rather than policy decisions and, therefore, arguably within a contractual delegation of authority to plaintiff as manager. Both the purchase of the lathe and the failure to reduce inventory unquestionably concerned substantial policy questions, so plaintiff's usurpation of defendants' authority in these matters gave rise to just cause for his dismissal. His insubordination in at least these two respects were a material breach of contract . . . which bars him from enforcement of the remainder of the contract.

Affirmed.

CASE REVIEW QUESTIONS

1. Which duties owed by an agent to a principal did Thomas violate?
2. On what basis did Thomas argue that he had not violated any duties that he owed to the Bourdettes?
3. Why were the Bourdettes allowed to discharge Thomas rather than only being allowed to collect damages from him?

DUTIES OF THE PRINCIPAL TO THE AGENT

The duties of the principal to the agent are usually found in the contract that creates the agency relationship. The contract sets out the promises that the principal makes to the agent concerning such things as pay, fringe benefits, and working conditions. When there is no contract or the contract does not state the principal's duties, the duties are implied from any prior relationship between the parties and from the customs of the particular kind of business involved. In addition, state and federal statutes impose certain duties on employers. These duties are discussed in Chapters 52 and 53.

Agency law also imposes certain duties on a principal. It provides that, in exchange for the fiduciary duties owed by the agent, the principal has the duty to provide the agent with the opportunity to work, to act with good conduct, to indemnify the agent for liabilities properly incurred by the agent on behalf of the principal, and to compensate the agent. An important contemporary legal issue is whether the law should also place a duty on principals not to wrongfully discharge agents. These duties are discussed in the following sections of the text.

Providing Opportunity to Work

The duty to provide the agent with an opportunity to work does not exist in all agency relationships. For instance, if the principal can terminate the agency at any time, no such duty exists. Similarly, if the agent is to be paid a fixed salary, the principal need not provide work for the agent to perform.

On the other hand, if the agency agreement indicates that the agent is to benefit from the work itself, a duty on the principal to provide work does exist. For example, if the agent is to serve as an apprentice or is to be compensated only if certain results are accomplished, the principal must give the agent relevant work to perform.

If the principal has a duty to provide work, he or she also has the duty not to interfere with the work of the agent. This duty may require the principal not to withhold information that the agent needs in order to complete the work successfully. In any agency relationship, the principal has a duty to warn the agent of any risks of physical harm or financial loss that may be expected to arise in the performance of the agent's duties and about which the agent is unaware.

Good Conduct

You should recall that the agent owes a duty of good conduct to the principal. The principal owes a similar duty to the agent. Under this duty, the principal must not act in such a way as to harm the agent's reputation or make it impossible for the agent to proceed with the work without risking his or her self-respect or personal safety.

An agent has the right to resign from the employment of an employer who the agent learns is disreputable if the principal's sullied reputation would harm the agent. For example, a sales person for a used car dealer could quit if it were discovered that the dealer was improperly turning back the odometers of the cars to be sold.

Also as a part of the duty of good conduct, the principal may not abuse or humiliate the agent without sufficient cause. Whether this duty is violated will depend on such things as the kind of work being done and the relationship of the parties. For instance, an employer reprimanding a bank teller could breach this duty much more easily than one reprimanding a dock worker.

Reimbursement and Indemnification

A principal is required to reimburse the agent for any payments made by the agent in the course of authorized business on behalf of the principal. For example, a truck driver who buys gas and pays tolls while delivering goods for the principal is entitled to reimbursement from the employer for the expenses.

In addition, the principal must indemnify the agent for any financial losses incurred by the agent on behalf of the principal. For instance, if an agent, on instructions of the principal, enters into a contract in the agent's own name rather than in the principal's name and suffers a financial loss as a result, the principal must indemnify the agent.

On the other hand, if the agent negligently injures a third party or knowingly performs an illegal act and suffers a financial loss as a result of the negligence or the illegal act, the principal has no duty to indemnify the agent. For example, if a truck driver injures a pedestrian and is successfully sued for negligence, the employer does not have to reimburse the negligent truck driver for the amount lost in the law suit.

Compensation

Usually, when a principal asks an agent to do work, there is an express or implied promise to pay for the work. On the other hand, if the agent performs work without the principal's request or consent, no promise to compensate can be implied and there is no duty to pay, even if the agent's services confer a benefit on the principal. Similarly, a promise to pay may not be implied if the services are performed by a close relative, if they are not the kind of services for which people are usually paid, or if they are of a trivial nature.

If an agent performs work without the principal's request or consent, the agent may be able to obtain payment for the work on the basis of quasi-contract. A court will give a person a quasi-contract recovery, even though there is no contract, in cases in which it is determined that the principal has been unjustly enriched (see Chapter 18). For instance, if an agent mistakenly believes that he or she has been requested to perform services for the principal and the principal knows of the agent's mistake, the principal will be required to pay the agent for the fair value of the services rendered.

Amount of Compensation If the principal has promised to pay for the agent's services, how much must be paid? Of course, if the parties have agreed to the amount to be paid, the principal has a duty to pay the amount agreed to. If the parties have not agreed on the amount to be paid, it is implied that the amount to be paid is the market rate or the amount customarily paid for such work. If there is no market or customary rate, the duty of the principal is to pay for the reasonable worth of the services performed. In determining the reasonable worth of services, the amount of work involved, the degree of skill required, the quality of the work performed, and the agent's reputation will all be considered.

Sales Commissions Perhaps the largest single class of agents is salespeople. Salespeople represent a principal to third parties and try to sell either a service or a product. Many salespeople are compensated by the payment of commissions.

A frequent question that arises concerns when a salesperson is entitled to receive a commission.

The general rule is that in the absence of an agreement as to when a commission is due, it is due when a contract of sale is made, even though the contract is never actually performed. For example, if you arrange with a real estate agent to sell your property on a commission basis, and the agent produces a buyer who signs an offer to purchase the property, and you accept the offer, then the agent is entitled to the payment of the sales commission even though the sale is never completed for some reason.

In the case that follows, a salesman made a contract of sale and the contract was later actually performed. Nontheless, the principal refused to pay the salesman's commission because the salesman wasn't present when the contract was performed. Do you think the salesman should receive the commission anyway?

FLOYD v. MORRISTOWN EUROPEAN MOTORS, INC.
351 A.2d 791 (N.J. 1976)

[Floyd brought a legal action against Morristown European Motors, Inc., to collect salesman's commissions from the sale of three automobiles. Floyd won a judgment of $721.25 from the trial court. Morristown European Motors appealed.]

FRITZ, Judge

Plaintiff was employed by defendant as a salesman of foreign automobiles. The verbal contract of employment provided for a weekly draw of $100 against commissions, use of an automobile and "twenty-five percent of the net profit."

Between January 8, 1974 and February 13, 1974 plaintiff "sold" the three automobiles in question. Each of these transactions was sufficiently alike so that the detailing of one would here serve the purposes of all three. At the time of the sale the new model automobiles were not in stock and, in fact, the price was not even yet known. Accordingly, while formal purchase orders were signed and substantial (a little less than 10% of the purchase price) deposits were required, the deposits were said on the orders to be "refundable." The fact of the matter is that none of the deposits had to be refunded; in each case the purchaser paid for and accepted delivery of the car he (or she) ordered.

But in the meantime, and before delivery of the cars, plaintiff, on March 8, 1974, after about one year's ser-

vice, went on a self-proclaimed "vacation." The trial judge reasonably found this to have been within the "expectation" of the employer. Plaintiff overstayed somewhat the anticipated duration of his leave. Plaintiff and defendant agreed that further employment occurred on plaintiff's return, but that plaintiff no longer had the use of an automobile. The trial judge found, also reasonably, that plaintiff "did not leave the employment" and that there was "never any indication that he was fired or that he had voluntarily left the employment."

However, the cars concerned in the purchase orders here in question had been delivered to defendant during plaintiff's absence. Despite the fact that all three purchasers accepted and paid for the automobiles they had ordered from plaintiff, defendant refused to pay plaintiff his commissions because plaintiff "hadn't been there to deliver the cars."

The underlying issue in this case is at what point an automobile salesman's right to his commission vests when the employment contract is silent in this regard. . . .

Considerations of equity and justice cause us to reject defendant's suggestion that the absence of the salesman from the scene at the time of "consummation" of the sale should, of itself, preclude his commission. . . . "[T]he general rule recognized in this and other jurisdictions" not only does not require the presence of the salesman, but protects his commission "notwithstanding the fact that the sale was consummated by the principal personally or through another agent," so long as the salesman is the "procurring cause of [the] sale."

We share this view that the matter should be decided by a determination of whether the salesman seeking the commission was, in fact, the effective cause of accomplishing the sale. If, factually, a salesman effectively produces a sale which ultimately

occurs, then he should be paid his commission, and this irrespective of whether the written memorandum or order, if any, was "enforceable" or whether he was in fact present when the delivery took place.

It is apparent here, as is implicit if not express in the findings of the trial judge, that plaintiff was in fact the effective cause of the sales of the three cars in question. He should not be deprived of his commissions.

Affirmed.

CASE REVIEW QUESTIONS
1. What was the source of Morristown European Motors' duty to compensate Floyd?
2. Had there been no specific agreement between the parties concerning the amount of Floyd's compensation, how would the amount that Morristown European Motors owed Floyd for making the sales have been determined?
3. At what point in time was Floyd entitled to his commission?
4. If Floyd's employment contract had a paragraph stating that it was part of the agent's job to prepare the cars for delivery and that the commission was, in part, payment for this activity, do you think that the result would have been the same? If not, what would have been the result?

Wrongful Discharge

Because an agency relationship is based on the consent of the parties, it has traditionally been the rule that a principal may discharge an agent at any time for any reason without being subject to liability to the agent for doing so. An exception to this rule that has always existed is that if the agent is working under an employment contract and the discharge constitutes a breach of the contract, the principal will be liable to the agent for damages caused by the breach. For example, under most union contracts an employee cannot be discharged except for "good cause."

The federal and state governments have adopted statutes that prohibit the discharge of an agent for such things as engaging in union activities or reporting unsafe working conditions. You are no doubt aware of statutes that prohibit discharging an agent on the basis of race, gender, age, or religious belief (see Chapter 53). Also, civil service laws and court decisions have provided some protection from discharge for government employees.

Nonetheless, many agents are not protected in any of these ways from the traditional rule allowing the principal to discharge the agent at any time for any reason. This rule may not seem harsh when an agency is first created. But after an agent has held the same job or has been with the same company for a long time, certain expectations may arise. Assume, for instance, that a person has worked for an employer for 10 or 15 years and has no employment contract. After this amount of time, there may be an expectation by the employee that he or she will continue to be employed and will be discharged only for just cause. But as you know, this is not the rule.

In one fairly recent case, a salesman for United States Steel Corporation claimed he was discharged for pointing out to his superiors the unsafe nature of a product being sold to the oil and gas industry. The product was subsequently withdrawn from the market by the company. After being discharged, the employee filed a claim against the principal, but the complaint was dismissed. The court recognized no legal duty on the part of the principal to act "reasonably" or in what might be called "the public interest" or in any way other than in its own self-interest.

There is some evidence, however, that the traditional agency rule allowing discharge by the employer at any time for any reason is beginning to change. A few courts have said there is a duty on the employer not to act "unreasonably," and this has been held to mean, generally, that the employer cannot act against the public's best interest. For instance, such a duty has been found in cases where an employer has discharged an employee for disobeying company orders to testify falsely before a state legislative committee or for refusing to alter pollution control reports required by the state. Indeed, at the time of this writing, one court has gone so far as to recognize an implied contractual duty of an employer not to discharge an employee unreasonably. But these cases are the exception, not the rule. The case below is more representative of the law concerning the discharge of employees.

PERCIVAL v. GENERAL MOTORS CORP.
539 F.2d 1126 (Eighth Cir. 1976)

[Worth H. Percival was first employed as an engineer by General Motors in 1947. In 1968, he became head of the General Motors' Mechanical Development Department. In 1973, disagreements arose between Percival and other top management personnel of General Motors. Discussions were held and Percival was offered another position with the company. He was unwilling to accept that position and ultimately resigned.

In 1975, he began a legal action against General Motors for wrongful discharge from his employment. General Motors moved for a summary judgment. The motion was granted and judgment for the defendant was entered. Plaintiff appealed.]

HENLEY, Circuit Judge

Plaintiff contended in the district court and contends here that he was actually discharged from his employment, and that his discharge was wrongful and malicious. However, he does not contend that the alleged discharge was prohibited by any federal or state statute or by any collective bargaining agreement. He denies that his employment was at the will of the defendant, but argues that even if it was his discharge was violative of the public policy of the State of Michigan.

Specifically, plaintiff contends that he was discharged as a result of a conspiracy among his fellow executives to force him out of his employment because of his age and because he had legitimately complained about certain allegedly deceptive practices of General Motors, had refused to give the government false information although urged to do so by colleagues and superiors, and had, on the contrary, undertaken to correct certain alleged misrepresentations made to the government by the defendant. . . .

The record reflects that plaintiff was actually hired on a month to month basis. It appears to us, however, that plaintiff had a right to expect to be continued in employment as long as he performed satisfactorily or until he reached retirement age, and we will assume for purposes of this case that he was employed on those terms. In Michigan such an employment is an employment at will and may be terminated by either party at any time with or without cause. . . . Whether an employee has performed satisfactorily is to be determined by the employer and not by the courts. . . . The district court characterized plaintiff's employment as having been at will, and we are satisfied that it did not err in so doing.

In applying the general rule that a person who is employed at will may be discharged at any time with or without cause and without regard to the motivation of the employer in terminating the employment relationship, the district court took note of a "newly emerging theory" advanced by plaintiff to the effect that the general rule should not be applied to a case in which the discharge violated public policy. The theory is that even if an employer has a general right to discharge an employee without cause or justification, a discharge is wrongful and actionable if it is motivated by the fact that the employee did something that public policy encourages or that he refused to do something that public policy forbids or condemns.

It may be conceded to plaintiff that there are strong policy arguments that can be made in support of the theory which he invokes; there are also strong policy arguments that can be made against it. It should be kept in mind that as far as an employment relationship is concerned, an employer as well as an employee has rights; and it should also be kept in mind that a large corporate employer such as General Motors, except to the extent limited by statute or contractual obligations, must be accorded wide latitude in determining whom it will employ and retain in employment in high and sensitive managerial positions particularly where developments in the field of mechanical engineering are involved. . . .

We conclude that no error was committed when the district court applied the general rule that has been mentioned.

The judgment of the district court will be affirmed.

CASE REVIEW QUESTIONS

1. Under what circumstances would General Motors have been found liable for wrongful discharge?
2. Do you think that the court should have protected Percival from wrongful discharge in this case? Explain.
3. The court says that it assumes that Percival "had a right to expect to be continued in employment as long as he performed satisfactorily. . . ." Why didn't the court protect this right?

Agent's Remedies for Breach of Duty by Principal

The usual remedy available to the agent for the violation of a duty by the principal is damages for breach of contract. For example, if the principal fails to reimburse or indemnify the agent as required by law, the agent can sue for breach of contract to collect the amounts due. If the principal's violation of duty is substantial enough to constitute a material breach of the contract, the agent is discharged from his or her duties, that is, the agent may refuse to continue to perform under the contract (see Chapter 17).

A legal device that helps to protect agents is the agent's lien. A lien is a legal interest in property, the purpose of which is to secure the payment of a debt. For instance, if you borrow money from a bank to buy a house, the bank will require you to give it a lien, called a mortgage, to secure the repayment of the money you borrowed. If you fail to repay the loan, the bank can foreclose on the mortgage. This means that the house will be sold and the proceeds used to pay off your debt to the bank.

An agent has an agent's lien on any goods owned by the principal that are to be dealt with by the agent on behalf of the principal. The agent also has a lien on any proceeds resulting from dealing with such goods on behalf of the principal. The agent's lien secures the payment of amounts due from the principal to the agent as a result of the agency. For example, if a person gives goods to an auctioneer, who sells the goods, the auctioneer has a lien against the money received from the sale of the goods to secure the payment of the amount due for his or her services.

Notice that the lien is restricted to goods that are *dealt with* by the agent for the principal. A truck driver, for instance, would not have a lien on the principal's truck because it is only something to be used by the driver. The driver is not supposed to deal with the truck in the sense of selling or leasing it to third parties.

REVIEW QUESTIONS

1. Give an example of an agency relationship not mentioned in the text and explain why it is an agency using the definition presented in the chapter.
2. Give an example not given in the text of conduct by an agent that would be a breach of duty owed by the agent to the principal. What duty has the agent breached in your example?
3. Under what circumstances may a principal discharge an agent without incurring any liability?
4. Give an example not given in the text of conduct by a principal that would be a breach of duty owed by the principal to the agent. What duty has the principal breached in your example?

CASE PROBLEMS

1. Robert Wilson, Inc., manufactures and sells custom-made shoes. Robert Wilson, the president of the company, hired his grandson, William Wilson, age 17, as a salesman during his summer vacation. William Wilson entered into a contract on behalf of Robert Wilson, Inc., to sell a large order of shoes to Fitright Shoe Stores. Robert Wilson, however, told the general manager of Fitright that the shoes would not be delivered. Fitright brought a legal action against Robert Wilson, Inc., for breach of contract. Robert Wilson, Inc., defended on the grounds that William Wilson did not have the capacity to contract. Who will win the case? Explain.
2. Nancy Dyer, a minor, signed a power of attorney appointing Raymond Dyer her agent "to act for her and in her name in all matters pertaining to her

ownership of 100 shares of stock of Union Electric Company" (Union). Raymond Dyer, using the power of attorney, requested permission to inspect Union's books, a right of shareholders under the law. His request was refused on the grounds that a minor does not have the capacity to appoint an agent. Both Nancy and Raymond Dyer brought a legal action against Union seeking an order from the court that Union treat the power of attorney as valid and allow Raymond Dyer to inspect the books as agent for Nancy Dyer. Who will win the case? Explain.

3. Allen Manufacturing Company (Allen) manufactures screws. Twenty years ago, Allen hired Loika as a drillpress operator, and over the years Loika worked his way up to chief of the Production Engineering Department. In that position, Loika was given permission to adapt a new process for producing screws to Allen's existing production process. Loika, with the help of an outside company and $180,000 of Allen's money, adapted the new process over the course of two years. The diagrams used in accomplishing this were not marked confidential, and the process could be seen in operation by visitors to Allen's plant. It would not be possible, however, to understand the process simply by seeing it in operation. The process gave Allen a competitive advantage, but it could not be patented. Loika was offered a job by a competing screw manufacturer to adapt the new process to the competitor's production process. Loika quit his job with Allen and has begun to work for the competitor. If Allen brings a legal action against Loika, asking the court for an injunction to prohibit Loika from working for the competitor or from disclosing the process, who will win? Explain.

4. Robinson discussed the possibility of buying stock in Ford Motor Company with Braddock, a stock broker with whom he had never done business previously. Braddock discouraged Robinson, and Robinson left Braddock's office without making the purchase. The next day Braddock received information that the Japanese government had told the American government that it would cut back by 10 percent the number of cars it would export to the United States the following year. Braddock knew that this news would have a favorable impact on Ford Motor Company stock, but he did not convey the information to Robinson. The price of the Ford stock did in fact rise as a result of the Japanese decision concerning imports. Robinson has since discovered that Braddock had the information early. If Robinson brings a legal action against Braddock, arguing that Braddock's duty of service to Robinson required that Braddock give him the information, who will win the case? Explain.

5. Chesnut entered into an agreement with Cutcliffe under which Cutcliffe was to purchase stock in Monterey Management Company from Murray and deliver the stock to Chesnut. Cutcliffe purchased the stock in his (Cutcliffe's) own name and for three years failed to transfer the stock to Chesnut. During that three year period, the value of the stock declined substantially. If Chesnut brings a legal action against Cutcliffe, on what grounds can he base his claim? On what grounds can Cutcliffe defend? Who will win? Explain.

6. Upton owned a farm that he leased to Suckow. He asked Suckow to have some excavation work done on the farm. Suckow contracted with Johnson for the job. Johnson billed Suckow $760 for the work, and Suckow forwarded the bill to Upton. Upton paid Johnson only $200. Johnson successfully sued Suckow for the balance due because Johnson's contract had been with Suckow. If Suckow brings a legal action against Upton for indemnification of the $560 paid to Johnson, who will win the case? Explain.

7. McAllister owned a building he wished to sell. He promised Axilbund, a real estate agent, that if Axilbund found a buyer willing to pay $300,000, he (McAllister) would pay the standard commission. Axilbund showed the building to Gross, telling him it was for sale for $300,000. He negotiated with Gross several times concerning purchase of the building, but Gross said the price was too high. McAllister later sold the building to Gross for $295,000. He refused to pay a commission to Axilbund. If Axilbund sues McAllister to collect a commission, who will win the case? Explain.

8. Hepburn was on the audit staff of a large certified public accounting firm. She had been with the firm for six years and was at the level of supervisor. This

position was important in the firm because the supervisor conducted the audit (through subordinates) and was responsible for its accuracy, although a partner in the firm was the one ultimately responsible to the partnership and to the public for the audit. When the audit of Darth Corporation was completed, Hepburn was called into the partner's office. It was explained to her that a few of her qualifying notes would have to be changed. Although her notes were thorough and accurate and changing them was not illegal, the change did not represent what she thought was a fair presentation of the client's business operation. When she refused to make the changes as instructed, she was fired. If Hepburn brings a legal action against the firm because of her discharge from the firm, who will win the case? Explain.

9. Palmater was hired by International Harvester Company in 1962 and at that time he joined the union. In 1966, at the request of International Harvester, he left the union for a nonunion training position. In 1968, he assumed a position in management, foregoing all union contract benefits and protection in reliance on International Harvester's promises to pay him a salary and provide various benefits. Recently Palmater was fired by International Harvester because the company had learned that he had given evidence to a law enforcement agency that an employee of International Harvester might be involved in criminal activity, he had agreed to assist the law enforcement agency in gathering further evidence, and he intended to testify against the employee in court if requested to do so. All of these things were true. If Palmater brings legal action against International Harvester because of his discharge from the company, who will win the case? Explain.

32

CONTRACT LIABILITY TO THIRD PARTIES

In Chapter 31 the first two elements of the agency definition were explained and discussed. They were (1) the agency relationship is fiduciary in nature and (2) it is based upon consent. The remainder of the agency definition stated that the relationship is one in which one person, the agent, acts on behalf of another, the principal, and is subject to the principal's control.

All corporations, partnerships, and governmental units and some individuals employ others to act on their behalf and subject to their control. The last part of the definition of agency implies that agents are used primarily to act for the principal in dealings with persons who are outside of the agency relationship. These people are called "third parties." Indeed, the real heart of agency law is that body of legal principles that creates legal duties between the principal and third parties because of the promises, representations, or acts of the agent. The circumstances under which the agent can create legal duties for the principal—that is, can legally bind the principal to third parties—are the subject of this and the following chapter.

Before proceeding with an analysis of these circumstances, it would be helpful for you to keep in mind a basic distinction between the two central branches of civil law. Civil duties (as opposed to criminal duties) are imposed primarily by the law of torts and the law of contracts. Tort liability arises when a person causes injury to another's person, property, reputation, or some other legally protected interest. The methods the law uses to hold a principal liable to a third party for the torts of an agent are explained in the next chapter. Contract duties or liabilities, on the other hand, arise when one party breaches a promise made to another party. The circumstances under which principals will be liable to third parties based upon a breach of promise made by the agent are presented in this chapter.

Please note, however, that compartmentalizing the law into tort liability and contract liability for purposes of presenting this agency material is not without drawbacks. Some factual patterns do not fit neatly into either category. Nevertheless, we believe that you will be helped in understanding agency law if a factual pattern is read for an understanding of the basic violation of duty, either contract or tort.

When this method of analysis is used, you will find that cases involving a breach of promise are usually resolved by applying legal principles that concern *authority,* and that cases involving torts are usually resolved by applying legal principles that concern the right of the principal to *control* the physical acts of the agent. *Authority* and *control,* then, are the primary distinguishing principles between contract liability and tort liability for the principal.

CONTRACT LIABILITY OF PRINCIPALS TO THIRD PARTIES

Courts will impose liability on a principal for the promises or representations made by an agent to a third party if the court finds that the principal *authorized* the agent to make the promises or representations. There are two broad types of authority: actual authority—either express or implied—and apparent authority. The doctrine of ratification achieves the same result as the application of principles of authority, but it is not usually considered to be a type of authority. Each of the types of authority and the doctrine of ratification are explained and discussed below.

Actual Authority—Express and Implied

Actual authority is authority that the principal intentionally confers on the agent or intentionally or negligently allows the agent to believe he or she possesses. The best example of actual authority is an expression, either written or oral, that another is authorized to accomplish a specific act. This most basic form of authority is also called **express authority.**

Express authority may take the form of a formal document such as a **power of attorney,** which is a sworn statement in writing that another is to act for and in the place of the principal. It may also be manifested in less formal ways, such as a corporate board of directors' resolution or a statement in an employment contract saying that the employee (agent) is to "sell the goods of the employer."

In a commercial transaction of any complexity at all, however, it is impossible for the principal to express all of the authority that may be needed to carry out the job. Therefore, the law recognizes **implied authority,** sometimes called **incidental authority,** as part of an agent's actual authority. Implied authority is that authority that the agent reasonably believes he or she has. Therefore, unless instructed otherwise by the principal, an agent has implied authority to do all of the things necessary to perform the work he or she was instructed to perform and all of the things usually done by a person of the agent's status.

For example, an agent who is called the "manager" of a business usually has the implied authority to hire employees and to buy inventory, even if such authority is not expressly given by the owner (principal) of the store.

The two cases that follow are concerned with whether the agent had express or implied authority to bind the principal to a contract with a third party. As you read these cases, and those that follow in the rest of the material about agency law, it is essential that you clearly understand who the principal, agent, and third party are, who the plaintiff and defendant are, and why the plaintiff believes the defendant is liable. You may find it helpful to draw a diagram for each case to clarify these points. For example, the first case below could be diagramed as follows:

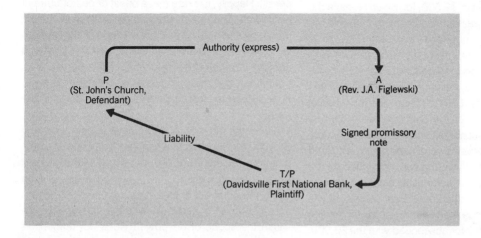

DAVIDSVILLE FIRST NATIONAL BANK v. ST. JOHN'S CHURCH
146 A.102 (Pa. 1929)

[The trial court found for the plaintiff, Davidsville First National Bank, and the defendant, St. John's Church, appeals.]

WALLING, [Judge]

The defendant, St. John's Church, is an unincorporated Roman Catholic Church organization of which Rev. J. A. Figlewski was pastor or priest, and as such gave the plaintiff bank a [promissory] note as follows:

2500.00/100 Davidsville, Pa., Nov. 30, 1925.

On demand after date, we or either of us promise to pay to the order of THE FIRST NATIONAL BANK, DAVIDSVILLE, Pa., at the FIRST NATIONAL BANK,

DAVIDSVILLE, Pa., Two thousand five hundred and no/100—dollars, value received. . . .

WITNESS OUR HANDS AND SEALS

St. John's Church, Windber, Pa. [Seal.]

Rev. J. A. Figlewski, Pastor [Seal.]

In the summer of 1923, the church membership, at a properly convened meeting, decided to repair their school building and erect a convent and to secure a loan of $15,000 for that purpose. Under the rule of the church a parish like the defendant could not incur an indebtedness exceeding $500 without the consent of the bishop of the diocese. Hence, the pastor sought and obtained a permit, as follows:

CHANCERY 1211 Thirteenth St., Altoona, Pa.,
July 7–23

Rev. J. Figlewski:

St. John's Church, Windber.

Dear Father: At a meeting of the Diocesan Consultors you were granted permission to contract a debt of $15,000 for masonry repairs & changes to school & convent.

By Order of the Rt. Rev. Bishop Bernard Conley

Sec'y Consultors.

Some two years and four months after the permit was issued the pastor presented it to the plaintiff and obtained thereon a loan of $2,500, for which he gave the note in suit. There was oral testimony that he told the bank the permit was not nearly exhausted. So far as appears, he made no representations to the bank as to the action taken by the congregation. The evidence for the defendant was that the church had obtained loans to the amount of the $15,000 from two local banks shortly after the date of the permit; with which, and some $10,000 additional raised by the congregation, the specific improvements were made during 1923 and 1924. The loan in suit was the only one made by the pastor from plaintiff for defendant, although he was known to the bank and had previously done business with it. The proof tends to show that soon after making the loan in suit the pastor absconded with the $2,500.

By law the bishop cannot create an indebtedness without the consent of the congregation nor under the canons of the church can it incur an indebtedness exceeding $500 without his permit. Each is a check upon the other.

The trial court erred in treating the mere permit and assurance of the pastor that it was not exhausted as warranting the loan. The age of the permit, nearly two and a half years, was such as to require inquiry of the congregation. The plaintiff bank and the church were close neighbors and slight inquiry by the former would doubtless have disclosed the fact that the improvements stated in the permit had been completed and paid for by funds secured from other banks, to the full amount of the permit and that the congregation had refused to request a further permit. . . .

One who gives credit to a pastor on the faith of an old permit without inquiry from the congregation does so at his peril. Otherwise a pastor might bankrupt the church for his own purposes despite the limit in the permit. Happily, it is rare that a priest or pastor betrays his church. That the pastor had possession of the old permit proved nothing as to its vitality. The money having been secured from different banks, there was nothing strange in his retention of the permit. . . . That it had been fully exhausted shortly after its date, quite clearly appeared by the evidence for the defense. . . .

Here the agency of the pastor was to borrow $15,000 for the church; when that was done and obligations given therefore, the permit was exhausted and the agency terminated. . . . "A person dealing with an agent must not act negligently, but must use reasonable diligence to ascertain whether the agent acts within the scope of his power. He is not authorized under any circumstances blindly to trust the agent's statements as to the extent of his powers." If this loan was valid, one for the entire $15,000 would have been. So the bishop's express limit and the like limit of the congregation would go for nought.

The judgment is reversed.

COBLENTZ v. RISKIN
322 P.2d 905 (Nev. 1958)

[This case involves a consignment agreement. A consignment agreement is one in which the owner of an item gives possession of the item to another person for the purpose of sale. If the item is sold, the seller pays over the proceeds of the sale to the owner and is usually paid a commission for making the sale. If the item is not sold, it is returned to the owner.

In the case, the trial court found for the plaintiff

CONTRACT LIABILITY TO THIRD PARTIES

(Riskin), who was the owner of the consigned item. The defendants (Coblentz and others) appealed.]

MERRILL, Justice

The sole question upon this appeal is whether the record supports the determination of the trial court (sitting without jury) that the acts of the employee in receiving the merchandise and in executing the consignment agreement were on behalf of the defendants and were authorized by them.

Appellants are owners of the Thunderbird Jewel Shop in Clark County, Nevada. Respondent Riskin is a diamond broker and wholesale jeweler of Los Angeles, California. In August, 1955 appellants employed Hyman Davidson for services in connection with their store. In January, 1956 Davidson entered into a consignment agreement with Riskin pursuant to which he received, for purposes of retail sale, two expensive items of jewelry. In his dealings with Riskin, Davidson represented himself as manager of the jewel shop with full authority to receive merchandise on consignment. Riskin did not check these representations with appellants but did check with others in the jewelry trade and satisfied himself as to Davidson's authority. The jewelry pieces were reconsigned by Davidson without Riskin's approval or consent. The person to whom they were reconsigned has disappeared. Riskin demanded of appellants the return of the jewelry or its agreed value pursuant to the terms of the agreement. Upon failure of appellants to comply with his demand this action was brought. Judgment in favor of Riskin was given in the sum of $16,300.

Appellants contend that there is no evidence from which the trial court could have found the essentials of . . . actual . . . authority to exist. . . .

In support of its conclusion of authority the court found,

That during the month of August, 1955 the defendants . . . engaged and employed one Hyman Davidson . . . as manager of the Thunderbird Jewel Shop. . . . That the said Hyman Davidson was and acted as manager of the said Thunderbird Jewel Shop at all times between August, 1955 and the beginning of March, 1956 on behalf of, for the account of and for the benefit of the said defendants and each of them. That the said Hyman Davidson, during the period aforesaid, with the knowledge, consent and approval of the defendants, and each of them, held himself out to the jewelry trade and to persons dealing with the said Thunderbird Jewel Shop as the manager of the said Thunderbird Jewel Shop, with full authority to receive merchandise on behalf of the said Thunderbird Jewel Shop on memorandum and/or consignment.

Although in many respects the evidence is in dispute the record unquestionably provides support for this finding.

Riskin testified that it was the custom in the jewelry trade to take expensive pieces of jewelry on consignment rather than by purchase at wholesale. This testimony is compellingly supported by reason when the nature of consignment transactions and the benefit to retail merchants of this commercial practice are considered. By consignment retail merchants are not financially committed to the purchase of expensive items until they have themselves resold the items. Until resale their only financial commitment is that of safekeeping. . . . It can hardly be questioned that the engaging in consignment transactions would be regarded by those in the jewelry trade as a customary, proper and necessary function of store management.

Davidson testified positively that he had been employed as manager of the store with instructions to run the store as he saw fit; . . .

Actual authority includes . . . implied authority. . . . Implied authority is that which the agent reasonably believes himself to possess as a result of representations by the principal or of acts of the agent permitted by the principal over a course of time in which the principal has acquiesced . . . (or) that which is reasonably necessary, proper and usual to carry into effect the main authority granted. . . .

The trial court has found that Davidson was employed to serve as manager and that he did so serve. The evidence we have recited presents a clear case of . . . implied authority. . . . We conclude that the trial court's determination of actual authority is supported by the record and that appellants are bound by Davidson's actions in their behalf in committing them to the consignment agreement with Riskin.

Affirmed.

CASE REVIEW QUESTIONS

1. What was the express authority of Rev. Figlewski in the *St. John's Church* case?
2. From your reading of the *St. John's Church* case, how would you describe the duty of a third person to ascertain the actual authority of an agent?
3. Diagram the *Coblentz* case, showing who the principal, agent, and third party were and which of them was the plaintiff and which the defendant.
4. What was the express authority of Davidson in the *Coblentz* case?
5. Why did the court in the *Coblentz* case decide that Davidson had implied authority to enter into a consignment agreement with Riskin?

General and Special Agents If you hire an agent and instruct him or her to "manage" your business, what limitations, if any, are placed upon his or her authority to act for you? To help answer this question, some courts recognize a distinction between general and special agents. A **general agent** is one who is employed as a permanent employee to carry out a series of transactions. A general manager is a general agent. Thus, if a person has such a title, he or she can reasonably believe that the position includes the authority that most general managers in that business possess. In the *Coblentz* case, for example, an important element of proof for the plaintiff was the fact that much of the business between jewel owners and jewel sellers or retailers was done on a consignment basis.

A **special agent** is one employed to carry out a specific task. Usually, there is authority to conduct only one transaction. If the circumstances reveal to a third party that an employee is a special agent, the third party should inquire about the precise nature of the authority he or she possesses. In the *St. John's Church* case, the pastor could be labeled a special agent because he was authorized to conduct only one transaction or a very limited number of transactions that varied substantially from his normal, routine activities.

Apparent Authority

Apparent authority is authority that courts sometimes recognize and impose on an agency relationship when an agent does not have actual authority to perform a specific act, but third parties who deal with the agent have been led by the principal to believe that the agent does have authority for the act. A key difference between actual authority and apparent authority is that actual authority is defined by asking what measure of authority was really given to the agent by the principal, whereas apparent authority is defined by asking what measure of authority a third party could reasonably believe the agent to have under the circumstances. The Restatement (Section 8) defines apparent authority as follows:

> Apparent authority is the power to affect the legal relations of another person by transactions with third parties, professedly as agent for the other, arising from and in accordance with the other's manifestations to such third party.

Generally, there are two factual elements that a court must find in order to conclude that an agent was apparently authorized. First, it must find that the principal, referred to in the definition above as the "other person," and not the agent created the circumstances leading the third party to believe that the agent was authorized. Note that the principal, not the agent, must create the appearance of authority that leads the third party to believe that the agent is authorized to act. Second, the court must find that the third party reasonably relied on the appearance of authority created by the principal. If the court finds these two factors present in a case, it will hold the principal liable to the third party even if the principal had expressly forbidden the agent to act.

If an agent with apparent authority enters into a contract with a third party on behalf of the principal, the principal will be bound to the contract and will be liable to the third party for a breach of the contract, just as if the agent had had actual authority to contract. However, if the agent lacked actual authority to enter the contract, the agent has breached the duty to obey the instructions of the principal and will be liable to the principal for damages resulting from the breach of duty. In other words, the apparently authorized agent has the *power* but not the *right* to bind the principal to contracts with third parties.

For example, suppose an owner of a shoe store hires a woman to be the general manager of the store. Usually in the retail shoe business, a store's general manager has the authority to buy inventory for the store. Because of cash flow problems, however, the owner secretly tells the general manager that she does not have the authority to buy inventory, but must instead get approval of all purchases from the owner. Under these circumstances, a shoe seller who did not know of the restrictions could reasonably believe that the general manager had the authority to buy inventory. Therefore, a contract made by the general manager (agent) to purchase shoes for the store would be binding on the store's owner (principal) because the general manager had apparent authority to enter into the contract. If the store owner were harmed because of the failure of the general manager to obey instructions, the owner would have the right to collect damages from the manager.

The concept of apparent authority was created to protect the reasonable expectations of those in commerce who do business with agents. It is one of the more dynamic principles in agency law, and today it occupies a central, almost dominating position, in the agency field. The concept is growing, and it expands a principal's liability for an agent's contracts.

In some instances, a student beginning to study agency law may not understand the distinction between apparent authority and implied authority. As a reminder, to find implied authority, you must find a grant of express authority from which the implied authority can reasonably follow. In the *Coblentz* case, for instance, Davidson was told to "manage" the jewelry store. This grant of express authority carried with it the implied authority to accept consignments. There was no express limitation by the principal on the agent's authority to manage. This authority was then defined by the general practice of jewelers in the area.

The following case is different. Read it with the goal of understanding why the court resolved the conflict in terms of apparent authority rather than implied authority.

HECKEL v. CRANFORD COUNTRY CLUB
117 A.607 (N.J. 1922)

KATZENBACH, Judge

This action was instituted to recover the value of articles of food alleged to have been sold by the plaintiffs – respondents [Heckel and others] to the defendant – appellant [Cranford Country Club]. The articles were purchased between August 1, 1918, and December 10, of the same year. They were ordered by one Roachman, who had been engaged about March 29, 1918, as manager of the club, and was known and is referred to in the testimony as the club manager or steward. Roachman was paid a salary of $200 a month, and also had the restaurant privilege of the club; that is, Roachman was to furnish the members with meals and refreshments to be supplied by him and for which they were to pay him, and the profit, if any, was to supplement his salary. Roachman was the steward during the entire period of the purchases from the plaintiffs. At the time of the first purchase, he introduced himself as the steward of the club. . . . The goods ordered by Roachman were charged by the plaintiffs to the club, delivered to the clubhouse, accompanied by charge slips addressed to the club, with each order delivered. Bills were sent by mail monthly by the plaintiffs, addressed to the club. . . . From these facts the plaintiffs contended that the club was responsible to them for the goods ordered by Roachman, and the defendant contended that Roachman was the plaintiffs' debtor, and no liability to pay the account attached to the club. There was no dispute as to the delivery of the goods or the correctness of the charges made therefor. The one question at issue was that of liability. The trial judge permitted the case to go to the jury, which rendered a verdict for the plaintiffs for the full amount of their claim. From the judgment entered upon the verdict the club has appealed.

The appellant contends that there was no evidence of Roachman's power to bind the club for the payment of the goods ordered by him, and in the absence of such evidence it was the duty of the trial court to grant either the defendant's motion for a nonsuit or for the direction of a verdict in its favor.

Mr. Justice Trenehard . . . stated the law with . . . clearness when he said:

> As between the principal and third persons the true limit of the agent's power to bind the principal is the apparent authority with which the agent is invested. The principal is bound by the acts of the agent within the apparent authority which he knowingly permits the agent to assume, or which he holds the agent out to the public as possessing. And the reason is that to permit the principal to dispute the authority of the agent in such cases would be to enable him to commit a fraud upon innocent persons.
>
> The question in every such case is whether the principal has by his voluntary act placed the agent in such a situation that a person of ordinary prudence, conversant with business usages, and the nature of the particular business, is justified in presuming that such agent has authority to perform the particular act in question, and when the party relying upon such apparent authority presents evidence which would justify a finding in his favor, he is entitled to have the question submitted to the jury.

The difficulty always arises in the application of the law to the facts of the given case. In the present case, did the club place Roachman in such a situation that a person of ordinary prudence, conversant with business usages and the nature of the particular business, would be justified in presuming that Roachman had authority to order provisions for the club? Did the plaintiffs present such evidence of Roachman's apparent authority as to justify the trial court in submitting to the jury the question of his authority to bind the club? We think these two questions should be answered in the affirmative.

It was admitted that the club employed Roachman as manager or steward, and paid him a salary. It is a matter of common knowledge that one of the duties of a steward of a country club is to obtain the supplies necessary to serve the members of the club with meals and refreshments. While it is true that as between Roachman and the club, Roachman was to be responsible for the payment of the supplies ordered by him, yet by his employment as steward the club had apparently clothed Roachman with the powers usually appertaining to the position of steward, of which one was the purchase of supplies for a club. When, therefore, Roachman approached the plaintiffs, informed them of the position he held with the club, ordered provisions, which were charged to the club, delivered to the clubhouse, and bills therefore were mailed to the club monthly, and this course of dealing continued for approximately five months, without either repudiation of Roachman's authority or any intimation from the club that he was without authority to bind it, we feel that such evidence presented a question for the determination of the jury. . . .

The judgment is affirmed.

CASE COMMENT

Some people believe that the doctrine of apparent authority should not be applied in either the *Heckel* case or in the example presented earlier concerning the shoe store manager. They would argue that in both cases it was the agent, not the principal, who misled the third party, and apparent authority requires that the principal be the one who creates the appearance of authority.

These people, however, would come to the same conclusion in both the case and the earlier example. They would do so under a doctrine called **inherent agency power.** A general agent has inherent agency power to do those acts which similar general agents have, even though such acts have been secretly forbidden by the principal. This is so even though the principal does not communicate with the third party in any way. Of course, under both doctrines the agent who does the unauthorized act is liable to the principal for breach of duty.

The courts, however, have not been very careful about distinguishing between apparent authority and inherent agency power. As the *Heckel* case indicates, they tend to use apparent authority to cover both situations. Nonetheless, you should be aware of the principle of inherent agency power and how it differs from apparent authority.

CASE REVIEW QUESTIONS

1. Did Roachman have actual authority to purchase food on behalf of the club? Explain.
2. What did the club do that led Heckel to believe that Roachman had authority to purchase food on behalf of the club?
3. Did Roachman have inherent agency power to purchase food on behalf of the club? Explain.
4. What recourse, if any, did the club have against Roachman following the decision in this case?

Ratification

Ratification is another legal principle applied by courts to hold a principal liable to third parties for acts, including promises, that were not authorized at the time they were performed. The Restatement (Section 82) defines **ratification** in this way:

> Ratification is the affirmance by a person of a prior act, which did not bind him but which was done professedly on his account, whereby the act, as to some or all persons, is given effect as if originally authorized by him.

The definition of ratification contains several important points. First, the agent's act must have been one that was not originally authorized, either actually or apparently. Second, the agent must have indicated in some way that the act was done for the benefit of the principal. Third, the principal must affirm the agent's act by some conduct that indicates that the principal wishes to treat the act as authorized. To affirm, the principal must have knowledge of all material facts concerning the transaction that he or she is ratifying.

Fourth, the ratification relates back to the time of the agent's act and results in the act being treated as if it had been authorized at that time. This means that the act must have been of a kind that could have been authorized originally, but was not. For example, if the principal is a corporation that was not in existence at the time of the agent's act, the corporation cannot ratify the act because a nonexistent corporation would not have the capacity to authorize the agent's act at the time it was originally performed.

Ratification by a principal must be of an entire transaction of the agent. This prevents a principal from ratifying those parts of a transaction that are beneficial while not ratifying those parts that are detrimental. For example, if a sales agent uses fraud to induce a third person to enter a contract that the agent is not authorized to negotiate, the principal cannot repudiate the fraud but ratify the contract. Instead, affirmance by the principal will result in ratification of the entire transaction, that is, of the fraud as well as of the contract.

When ratification occurs, the principal is bound by the agent's act in the same manner and to the same extent as the principal would have been bound if the agent had been authorized when the act was performed. Conversely, ratification releases the agent from liability, either to the principal or to the third person, for having exceeded his or her authority.

A classic application of the principle of ratification is found in the case of *Wilkins v. Waldo Lumber Company.* In this case, Adams, an agent of Waldo Lumber Company, made a contract with a third party, Wilkins, for the purchase of timber. Adams said at the time of the initial agreement, and the contract itself stated, that the contract had to be approved by the principal, Waldo Lumber Company, before it became binding. Before the contract to purchase the wood was approved by the principal, Adams ordered the timber cut and hauled to the mill. The principal was informed of this. For three months, timber was cut and hauled away and sold.

When the agreement began to appear less profitable than it was at first thought to be, Waldo Lumber Company told Wilkins that it was canceling the contract because it had never authorized or approved it. The court held, however, that the Waldo Lumber Company was liable for breach of contract because it knew that Wilkins was acting as if there were a contract and it had affirmed the contract by accepting some of the sale proceeds.

In the case that follows, a third party is attempting to use the doctrine of ratification to hold a principal liable for the acts of his agent. You should keep the requirements of ratification in mind as you read the case.

WING v. LEDERER
222 N.E.2d 535 (Ill. App. 1966)

DAVIS, Justice

Plaintiff, Jacob A. Wing, a licensed tree surgeon, d/b/a [doing business as] Wing's Tree Experts, brought this suit against the defendants, Philip C. Lederer, (herein called Lederer), and Peter Sonza-Novera, (herein called Novera), to recover the sum of $500 for services rendered. The complaint alleged that Novera, who acted as a part time caretaker and yardman for Lederer, either individually, or as Lederer's agent, hired the plaintiff to do certain work at the Lederer residence.

The case was tried before the court without a jury and judgment was entered for the plaintiff against Lederer . . . and for the defendant, Novera. Lederer appealed from the judgment against him. . . .

Lederer contends that the plaintiff did not prove any contractual relationship with him. . . .

Mrs. Lederer testified that in the early spring of 1964 she asked Novera whether a certain maple tree on the Lederer property needed care. He answered that it did, that he knew a man in the business, and that he would send him to her. Novera then contacted the plaintiff, had him come to the property, and showed him this tree, which had some dead branches near its top. Novera testified that he told the plaintiff to talk to the lady of the house about the tree; and that the plaintiff pointed out other tree and shrubbery work which needed to be done.

Plaintiff's version of this conversation is somewhat different. He testified that Novera showed him the maple tree and that he, the plaintiff, told Novera that it, as well as other trees, needed care; that Novera then told him to go ahead and do what was necessary; and that the cost of the work was not discussed.

At the end of June or the first of July, plaintiff sprayed the foliage. Later he came back and pruned the maple tree and root fed several trees. He returned again in the latter part of July and in early September to do more spraying and root feeding. It is undisputed that he neither saw nor talked to either Lederer, Mrs. Lederer or Novera while working on the premises. Sometime during the summer, Novera told Mrs. Lederer that the tree work apparently had been done since the dead branches in the maple tree had been removed. However, the plaintiff did not contact the Lederers and had no conversation with anyone concerning the work, other than that heretofore related between himself and Novera.

No statement was rendered for this work until November of 1964, at which time Lederer received a bill from the plaintiff for $500. Mrs. Lederer did not pay the bill but called the plaintiff on several occasions to discuss it with him. Plaintiff never returned her calls. No further word was received from the plaintiff until October of 1965, at which time another statement was received.

Lederer had unquestionably constituted Novera his agent to recommend someone to take care of the maple tree. There is no issue as to the existence of an agency between Lederer and Novera, but only as to the latter's authority. The authority of the agent may come only from his principal. There is no dispute as to the actual authority conferred upon Novera. He was told to recommend someone to take care of the maple tree and to have that person talk to Mrs. Lederer. Both the principal and the agent understood this to be the extent of the agent's authority. It clearly did not include the hiring of a tree man for any purpose, and under no circumstances could it be parlayed to include the hiring of such man to do whatever he thought was necessary.

Nor can it be said that Lederer clothed Novera with apparent authority to hire plaintiff to do the work which was done. Apparent authority in an agent is such authority as the principal knowingly permits the agent to assume or which he holds his agent out as possessing — it is such authority as a reasonably prudent man, exercising diligence and discretion, in view of the principal's conduct, would naturally suppose the agent to possess. The plaintiff had no contact with Lederer either before or during the time in which the work was done, and Lederer neither did nor failed to do anything which would justify the plaintiff in assuming that Novera had authority to hire him.

Even assuming that the plaintiff's version of his conversation with Novera was correct, he conceded that Novera pointed out to him only the work to be done on the maple tree. It was the plaintiff who mentioned other work which should be done on the trees and shrubbery. Apparently, from the size of the bill, the other work was substantial and, in view of such circumstance, the plaintiff had a duty to confirm that a part time yardman had the authority to direct him to do whatever was necessary.

The plaintiff contends that, absent any original authority on the part of Novera, Lederer, by accepting the work which the plaintiff did, and by retaining the benefit thereof, ratified the acts of his agent in hiring the plaintiff. The rule is that where an agent has acted outside of the scope of his authority, a principal may ratify the act and render it obligatory upon himself; and that subsequent assent and ratification is equivalent to an original authorization and confirms that which originally was an unauthorized act. The ratification may either be express or inferred from the surrounding circumstances, but it must come from the acts or conduct of the principal. However, a principal may not be held to have ratified that which was done unless he acts with full knowledge of all the material facts.

Ratification rests on intention. The mere retention of the benefits of a transaction cannot be held to constitute ratification if the principal does not have the privilege of repudiating the unauthorized act. Absent such choice, the principal's conduct in accepting such benefits does not indicate that he assents to what has been done or intends to confirm it. In all of the cases cited by plaintiff, the ratification by a principal was made when he had full knowledge of the facts and a choice of either accepting or rejecting the benefits of the transaction.

Lederer had no choice! His trees had been pruned and sprayed long before he had knowledge of what had been done. He could not undo that which had then been done and his acceptance of the work was not by choice but by necessity. The fact that he did not stop the plaintiff from doing the work is no evidence of ratification, since it is undisputed that Lederer did not have knowledge of the services during the time they were being rendered. Lederer cannot be held to have ratified the hiring of plaintiff even if it is assumed that Novera hired him to do whatever was necessary.

Reversed.

CASE REVIEW QUESTIONS

1. Why did Novera lack actual authority to hire Wing?
2. Why did Novera lack apparent authority to hire Wing?
3. Why did the court conclude that Lederer had not ratified Novera's act of hiring Wing?
4. Might the outcome of the case have been different if Lederer had watched Wing performing some of his services and had not objected? Explain.
5. Why do you think Wing sued Novera as well as Lederer?

CONTRACT LIABILITY OF THE AGENT TO THIRD PARTIES

There are two ways in which an agent who contracts for a principal may incur liability to the third party. The agent may breach the agent's warranty of authority and he or she may become a party to the contract.

Warranty of Authority

Whenever an agent purports to make a contract on behalf of a principal, the agent warrants (promises) that he or she has the authority or power to bind the principal to the contract. This is called the agent's **warranty of authority.** The agent need not expressly state the warranty because the law implies it in any case in which the agent purports to contract for a principal.

An agent may breach the warranty of authority even if the agent reasonably, though mistakenly, believes that he or she has authority. On the other hand, the warranty is not breached if the third party knows the agent lacks authority. For example, if the third party knew that the principal had died, the agent would not be liable for breach of the warranty of authority.

The warranty of authority does not exist if the parties agree otherwise. Such an agreement may be express, but it may also be implied if the parties contract under circumstances that indicate to the third party that no warranty is being made by the agent. This will occur, for example, if the agent fully discloses the source of authority to the third party and allows the third party to draw his or her own conclusion concerning the agent's authority. For example, if the source of authority is a power of attorney that the agent shows to the third party, there is no warranty of authority by the agent.

If the agent breaches the warranty of authority, but the principal later ratifies the agent's transaction, the liability of the agent to the third person is discharged.

Party to the Contract

Whether an agent becomes a party to a contract he or she makes for the principal is determined primarily by whether, and to what extent, the third party is aware of the existence of and identity of the principal. The Restatement (Section 4) establishes the following classifications:

1. If, at the time of a transaction conducted by an agent, the other party thereto has notice that the agent is acting for a principal and of the principal's identity, the principal is a disclosed principal.
2. If the other party has notice that the agent is or may be acting for a principal but has no notice of the principal's identity, the principal for whom the agent is acting is a partially disclosed principal.
3. If the other party has no notice that the agent is acting for a principal, the one for whom he acts is an undisclosed principal.

Disclosed Principal In most cases the agent discloses both the existence and identity of the principal. One of the most common ways in which the principal is disclosed is by the agent signing the contract in one of the following ways:

Artie Agent for Peter Principal
Peter Principal by Artie Agent
The Principal Corporation by Artie Agent, President

It is not necessary, however, for the agent to be that explicit. Other circumstances, such as the use of letterhead, the use of an office in the same building area as the principal, or even the use of a company car with the company's name on it, may provide notice to the third party that the agent is acting for and on behalf of someone else and may identify that person.

If the principal is disclosed, the agent is not a party to the contract unless the agent is expressly made a party in the contract or the agent signs a negotiable instrument (a promissory note, check, or the like) without the principal's authority and a third party takes it in good faith and pays value for it. (See Chapter 27 for further discussion of the negotiable instrument situation.) If the agent is not a party to the contract, it can only be enforced against the principal.

Partially Disclosed Principal The principal is partially disclosed if the third party knows of the existence of, but not the identity (name) of, the principal. If an agent enters into a contract for a partially disclosed principal, the law usually infers that both the principal and the agent are parties to the contract. The third party, therefore, can enforce the contract against either the principal or the agent. If the third party recovers from the agent, however, the principal must indemnify the agent if the agent acted within the scope of his or her actual authority.

Undisclosed Principal If a principal is undisclosed, the law infers that the agent has personally promised to perform the contract. Therefore, the agent is liable to the third party for any breach of the contract made. The agent, however, will be entitled to indemnification from the principal if he or she acted within the scope of his or her actual authority. But, just as important, the undisclosed principal is also liable for any breach of the contract even though the principal's existence was unknown to the third party when the contract was made. This result may be contrary to your natural instincts. The reason for imposing liability on the undisclosed principal is that it was the principal who initiated the activities of the agent and who had a right to control the agent.

Because the third party may enforce a contract against an undisclosed principal, the law also recognizes the right of the undisclosed principal to enforce the contract against the third party as long as the agent intended that the contract benefit the principal and acted within his or her authority. However, if the agent induced the third party to enter the contract by affirmatively stating that no principal was involved, or if the contract expressly "excludes all principals," then the third party may be granted the remedy of rescission of the contract, thereby escaping liability to the principal. The best course of action for a third party who discovers the existence of an undisclosed principal and who wishes to sue for breach of the contract is to sue both the principal and agent. If either the principal or agent objects, however, the third-party plaintiff must elect to continue against one or the other and may secure a judgment against only the one whom he or she elects to hold.

If the third party knows the identity of the originally undisclosed principal, does not join the principal, and recovers a judgment against the agent, the principal is discharged from liability to the third party. The principal, however, must indemnify the agent if the agent was acting within the scope of his or her actual authority. If the third party does not know the identity of the undisclosed principal at the time of trial and recovers a judgment against the agent, the principal is not discharged from liability to the third party by such a recovery. The third party could, therefore, sue the principal if he or she were unable to collect the judgment against the agent.

In the following case, an agent purchased goods for an undisclosed principal. The principal gave the agent money to pay for the goods, but the agent failed to do so. The third party later learned the identity of the principal and brought a legal action for breach of contract. The principal argued that its liability under the contract had been discharged by its payment to the agent. Note that both the principal and the third party are innocent of any wrongdoing. What do you think the court should do in such a case?

PORETTA v. SUPERIOR DOWEL COMPANY
137 A.2d 361 (Maine 1957)

[Poretta delivered wood worth $2,574.44 to R. H. Young & Son, Inc. (Company). Poretta was not paid by Company, and brought suit against the Superior Dowel Company (Superior), alleging that Superior was the undisclosed principal for Company.

The appellate court affirmed the finding of the trial court which was in favor of the plaintiff and which established that the wood was purchased by Company as agent for Superior and that the Company was within its scope of authority when it purchased the wood. On the final issue before the court, Superior argued that it had paid the agent, Company (presumably insolvent) and had thus discharged its liability.]

DUBORD, Justice

The issue thus raised presents a problem of novel impression in this state. The issue is:

Is an undisclosed principal absolved from liability to his agent's vendor who has sold goods to the agent

upon the credit of the agent who has received payment or advances, or a settlement of accounts from his undisclosed principal, before discovery of the undisclosed principal by the agent's vendor?

There are two different rules bearing upon the issue. The first one, which appears to be supported by the weight of authority, is that an undisclosed principal is generally relieved of his liability for his agent's contracts to the extent that he has settled with his agent prior to the discovery of the agency. The other rule is that an undisclosed principal is discharged only where he has been induced to settle with the agent by conduct on the part of the third person leading him to believe that such person has settled with the agent. . . .

The American Law Institute . . . adopted and promulgated the following rule:

An undisclosed principal is discharged from liability to the other party to the contract if he has paid or settled accounts with an agent reasonably relying upon conduct of the other party, not induced by the agent's misrepresentations, which indicates that the agent has paid or otherwise settled the account. Restatement of Agency, §208.

We are called upon to determine which rule shall become the law in this State.

Manifestly, if we adopt the rule which we have designated as the first rule, as distinguished from the rule laid down in the Restatement of the Law of Agency, then, . . . the exceptions of Superior would have to be sustained. On the other hand, if we adopt the rule laid down in the Restatement, then the decision of the [trial court] was correct and Superior's exceptions should be overruled. . . .

In arriving at his conclusion that the law as now set forth in the Restatement was the correct law, Mr. Mechem had this to say in his Treatise on the Law of Agency,

> If a principal sends an agent to buy goods for him and on his account, it is not unreasonable that he should see that they are paid for. Although the seller may consider the agent to be the principal, the actual principal knows better. He can easily protect himself by insisting upon evidence that the goods have been paid for or that the seller with full knowledge of the facts has elected to rely upon the responsibility of the agent, and if he does not, but, except where misled by some action of the seller, voluntarily pays the agent without knowing that he has paid the seller, there is no hardship in requiring him to pay again. If the other party has the right, within a reasonable time, to charge the undisclosed principal upon his discovery—and this right seems to be abundantly settled in the law of agency—it is difficult to see how this right of the other party can be defeated, while he is not himself in fault, by dealings

between the principal and the agent, of which he had no knowledge, and to which he was not a party.

The Restatement may be regarded both as the product of expert opinion and as the expression of the law by the legal profession.

The Committee on Agency which prepared the Restatement of the Law of Agency was composed of outstanding representatives of the leading law schools of the country. It was headed by Mr. Floyd R. Mechem, who at the time was regarded as the foremost living authority on the subject of agency. Its rule as set forth in §208, expounds the thinking of some of the best legal minds in the country.

The purpose of the Institute in the promotion of clarification of the law can be applied to no more needy situation than that of the question before us for determination. It is our opinion that the reasoning of Mr. Mechem in support of the doctrine promulgated in the Restatement is sound. The adoption of this doctrine by this court will establish a clear cut and explicit rule of law free from the confusion, complications and perplexities which have existed throughout the years.

We, therefore, adopt the rule as laid down in the Restatement of the Law of Agency.

Having already ruled that the Company was the duly authorized agent of Superior and that when it purchased the wood from the plaintiff it was acting within the scope of its authority, we now rule that the [trial court judge] applied the proper law and that his decision was correct and should be affirmed.

Exceptions overruled.

CASE REVIEW QUESTIONS

1. Describe the two rules the court had to choose between in this case. Which did the court choose?
2. Why did the court select the rule it chose? Explain fully.
3. How could Superior have protected itself from liability to Poretta?
4. Would R. H. Young and Son, Inc., have been found liable to Poretta if suit had been brought against them?
5. Would R. H. Young and Son, Inc., be liable to Superior?

REVIEW QUESTIONS

1. What is the difference between express authority and implied authority? Give an example of each that is not presented in the text.
2. What is the difference between actual authority and apparent authority? Give an example of each that is not presented in the text.
3. Give an example of ratification that is not pre-sented in the text. Make sure that your example includes all those things that are necessary for rati-fication to occur.
4. What is the primary factor that determines whether an agent is a party to a contract that the agent enters into on behalf of the principal? Explain.

CASE PROBLEMS

1. Corbus was a sales agent of fertilizer for Pacific Guano Company (Pacific). He entered into a con-tract on behalf of Pacific to sell fertilizer to Ellis. As he had done a number of times before with other customers, Corbus agreed in the contract to have Crumbaker apply the fertilizer to Ellis' fields. It was Pacific's custom when Corbus made such an arrangement to bill the customer for both the fer-tilizer purchased and the application and then to pay Crumbaker for his services. When Crumbaker applied the fertilizer to Ellis' fields, he did so im-properly and damaged Ellis' crops. Corbus' em-ployment contract with Pacific said nothing about the authority to have fertilizer he sold applied to the customer's fields. If Ellis sues Pacific for breach of contract, on what grounds may Pacific defend? Who will win the case? Explain.

2. Pailet owned a vacant building. Guillory ap-proached Abramson, a friend of Pailet, about rent-ing the building. Abramson made it clear to Guil-lory that he did not have authority to lease the building. He did, however, deliver a lease contract proposed by Guillory to Pailet. Pailet approved of the lease and signed it herself. Guillory continued to deal with Abramson on all matters concerning the lease, and had no direct contact with Pailet. Rent checks, made out to Pailet, were delivered to Abramson and Abramson made some minor re-pairs to the leased building. Guillory approached Abramson and asked that the lease be cancelled. Abramson, without Pailet's approval, told Guil-lory that the lease was canceled. When Pailet learned of this, she brought a legal action to collect the rent due under the lease. On what basis may Guillory defend? Who will win? Explain.

3. Peters was in the business of making store fronts and other additions to commercial buildings. Peters hired Anderson to call on the owners of older commercial buildings to promote sales. Peters expressly instructed Anderson that under no condition was he to collect money from any of the customers. Thompson went to Peters' place of business and inquired about a new front for his store. He was directed to Anderson's office. Ander-son negotiated a contract with Thompson and signed the contract on behalf of Peters. Peters' workers began construction of the store front. The contract provided that Thompson was to make periodic payments as the work progressed. He made the periodic payments to Anderson. Because Peters did not keep good financial records, Ander-son was able to pocket a substantial part of Thompson's payments. About the time the work was complete, Anderson disappeared. If Peters brings suit against Thompson to collect payment on the contract, on what basis may Thompson de-fend? Who will win the case? Explain.

4. Pittsburgh Manufacturing Company hired Arm-strong as general manager of its manufacturing plant. Armstrong was instructed to purchase cer-tain materials from specifically named suppliers and no others. Armstrong learned that some of the materials supplied by the designated supplier were inferior and overpriced. Without consulting any-one else within the company, Armstrong con-tracted with other suppliers for better materials at a

lower price. The contracts were typed on plain paper (not letterhead), and Armstrong signed the contracts, in the presence of the new suppliers at Pittsburgh's headquarters, as "Armstrong, general manager for Pittsburgh." Pittsburgh later refused to pay for the supplies delivered under the new contracts, and the suppliers brought suit for breach of contract. Who will win the case? Explain.

5. Vogel, an assistant buyer for the Granite City Department Store, purchased metal art objects from Duval Reproductions. Vogel was totally without express or apparent authority to do so, but he believed that his purchase was a brilliant move likely to get him a promotion. The head buyer of Granite was livid when he learned of Vogel's activities. However, after examining the merchandise and listening to Vogel's pitch, he reluctantly placed the merchandise in the storeroom and put a couple of pieces on display for a few days to see whether they were a "hot item" and a "sure thing" as Vogel claimed. The items were neither "hot" nor "sure" and when they didn't move at all the head buyer ordered the display merchandise repacked and the entire order returned to Duval with a letter that stated the merchandise had been ordered by an assistant buyer who had absolutely no authority to make the purchase. Duval countered with a lawsuit for breach of contract. Who will win the case? Explain. (Adapted from CPA examination question 5a, *Business Law,* May, 1980.)

6. Serges owned a retail meat market. He hired Jones as manager of the market. Jones operated the market on a day-to-day basis. Serges came around to the market about once a month to check the financial records and discuss with Serges the progress of the business and any problems that Serges might have. Jones, as agent for Serges, borrowed $3,500 from First National Bank, telling the bank officer that the money was to be used to expand Serges' market. Soon thereafter, however, Jones disap-

peared, along with the money. When Serges was later notified in person by the bank officer of the loan, about which he had previously known nothing, he was so flustered that he reached in his pocket, pulled out $500, handed it to the bank officer, and said, "I'm sorry this has happened; here's a down payment on paying back the loan." Later, however, Serges notified the bank that he would not repay the loan. If the bank sues Serges to recover the loan, on what basis should Serges defend? Who will win? Explain.

7. Iest owned a farm that he leased to Tadlock. An irrigation pump belonging to Iest was used by Tadlock on the farm. When the pump broke down, Tadlock asked Killinger, an electrician, to take a look at it. Killinger told Tadlock the pump needed extensive repairs that would take a long time to complete. Tadlock then told Killinger that Iest had authorized him (Tadlock) to either repair the old pump or to purchase a new one and that he wanted Killinger to install a new pump. Killinger installed the new pump and sent a bill for $2,048 to Iest. Iest refused to pay the bill. Killinger brought suit against both Tadlock and Iest to collect the amount due. Who will win? Explain.

8. Abbott operates a retail store called Abbott's Gift Shoppe. The store is actually owned by Peterson, although this fact is unknown to anyone except Abbott and Peterson. Peterson instructed Abbott that he was not to sign any contracts without Peterson's approval. Otherwise he could run the store as if it were his own. Abbott signed a contract in his own name to buy inventory for the store from Tracy. He did not get Peterson's approval for the contract, and when Peterson learned of it she called and told Tracy that she was canceling the contract. If Tracy brings a law suit against Abbott and Peterson for breach of contract, who will win? Explain.

33

TORT LIABILITY TO THIRD PARTIES

In the previous chapter, we suggested that it would be useful to divide the discussion of the principal's liability to third persons into two broad categories depending upon the nature of the breach of duty involved. We stated that when the breach of a contract duty is alleged, the courts usually seek to determine whether or not the agent was authorized to contract for the principal. The second category of cases involves a principal's liability to third parties based upon a breach of a tort duty. When breach of a tort duty is alleged, the courts usually seek to determine the degree of control the principal may exercise over the agent's physical conduct. Precisely when and how courts determine that a principal's right of control is sufficient to impose liability on the principal for the torts of the agent is the primary subject of this chapter.

In addition, other situations in which a principal may be held liable to a third person for a tort will be explained and discussed. Finally, the tort liability of agents to third parties will be considered.

TORT LIABILITY

A tort is committed when one person breaches a noncontractual, legal duty owed to another and the breach causes injury to the person or property of the one to whom the duty is owed. A person who commits a tort is called a tortfeasor.

For example, the law imposes a duty on a driver of a car to drive carefully. If the driver drives carelessly, the duty is breached. If someone in another car or a pedestrian is injured as a result, that person may sue the careless driver (the tortfeasor) for compensation for his or her damages.

The subject of torts is treated extensively in Chapters 5 and 6, but we will review it briefly here before discussing principal's and agent's liabilities for torts. It should be noted that neither a principal nor an agent can suffer tort liability unless a tort has been committed.

Torts are generally categorized as negligence, intentional torts, and strict liability. Each of these categories will be discussed in the text that follows.

Negligence

Negligence means carelessness. A difficult problem in determining liability for negligence is determining whether an act was performed carelessly or carefully. To answer this question, a standard of care must be applied against which the particular act in question can be measured.

The standard used is called the reasonable person standard. If the particular act in question was performed as carefully as or more carefully than a reasonably prudent person in the same circumstances would have performed it, negligence has not occurred. If the particular act in question is performed less carefully than a reasonably prudent person in the same circumstances would have performed it, the act has been performed neligently.

When a person is negligent and the negligence is an important cause (i.e., a proximate cause) of injury to another, the victim is entitled to compensation for his or her damages. Negligence is the basis of many of the law suits you will read about in this chapter.

Intentional Torts

Injuries caused by negligence are usually called accidents. This suggests that the person who was careless did not intend to injure the victim. Nevertheless, the careless person is held liable because liability for the tort of negligence does not require intent.

Many other torts, however, require conduct that is performed with the intent to interfere with another's interests. Hence, the term intentional torts. A brief synopsis of the intentional torts mentioned in the text and in the cases in this chapter follows:

Assault — Threatening harmful or offensive conduct. Raising a fist as though to hit someone, for example.

Battery — Touching someone without their consent. Hitting someone with the previously mentioned raised fist would be a battery.

Defamation — Harming another's good name or reputation. Written defamation is called *libel;* spoken defamation is called *slander.*

Fraud — Misleading another by a knowingly false representation for the purpose of inducing the other to act or refrain from acting. A minor who says he or she is an adult in order to be served alcohol is engaged in fraud. This tort is also referred to as deceit.

If the commission of an intentional tort causes injury to another, the tortfeasor will be held liable for the payment of damages.

Strict Liability

Strict liability means liability without fault. This means that the tortfeasor is held liable for damages even though he or she was not careless and did not intend to interfere with the interests of another. Such liability is imposed for reasons of public policy rather than because there was something wrongful about the conduct of the tortfeasor.

An example of strict liability can be found in the area of ultrahazardous activities. Such things as blasting with explosives, spraying crops, and transporting toxic chemicals are beneficial activities for society, so they are not forbidden. Because they are very dangerous, however, strict liability for injuries caused by these activities is imposed on anyone who engages in them.

TORT LIABILITY OF PRINCIPALS TO THIRD PARTIES

If an agent is driving a truck on business for a principal and negligently injures a third party, the agent is liable to the third party. This is so because a fundamental principle of law is that a person is always liable for his or her own torts. The agent, however, may not be as financially well off as the principal. The injured party, therefore, is often interested in finding a way to impute the tort of the agent to the principal so that a judgment can be obtained against the principal. Under what circumstances, then, will a principal be liable for the torts of an agent?

Liability of Principal for Own Torts

Suppose a store owner (principal) instructs a store detective (agent) to attack a customer without justification. If the store detective commits an assault and battery on the customer, both the store detective and the owner are liable to the third party. The owner is liable because the law holds a person causing an act to be performed as responsible as if he or she had personally performed the act. In such a case, both the principal and the agent are tortfeasors, that is, both have committed the torts of assault and battery.

Similarly, a principal will be held liable for negligence if an agent commits a tort and the principal was negligent in hiring or supervising the agent, in entrusting property to the agent, or in any other way, and the negligence of the principal was a proximate cause of the third party's injuries. An example of such direct liability on the principal is found in the following case.

MURRAY v. MADOC STATE BANK
313 P.2d 304 (Kansas 1957)

[On March 9, 1954, Breithaupt, an employee of Madoc State Bank, was sent by the bank to Murray's home. Breithaupt and Murray had argued on previous occasions. While at Murray's home, Breithaupt demanded that Murray do some of his business with the bank in a particular way. When Murray refused, Breithaupt threw him from the porch of the house and assaulted him. Murray was injured as a result.

On March 8, 1956, Murray brought a legal action against Madoc State Bank on the basis of negligence. He alleged in his complaint that the bank's negligence consisted of continuing to employ Breithaupt after having notice of his violent, aggressive, and antagonistic disposition toward Murray and of having Breithaupt transact business with Murray when it knew or should have known that such would reasonably result in an assault on and injury to Murray. In other words, Murray's position was that the bank was negligent because it knew there was bad blood between Murray and Breithaupt and that Breithaupt had a violent temper, but it nontheless allowed Breithaupt to transact business with Murray.

Madoc State Bank moved to dismiss the complaint. It argued that Murray's legal action was actually based on Breithaupt's assault, that under the statute of limitations assault actions had to be brought within one year after the assault occurred, and that Murray had not met this requirement. Murray argued that his legal action was based *directly* on the *bank's negligence* and that the two-year statute of limitations on negligence actions had been met. The trial court denied the bank's motion and the bank appealed.]

SCHROEDER, Justice

The defendant argues that the injury of which the plaintiff complains was occasioned and caused by the assault and battery, and his attempt to change the cause of action into a negligence action by alleging the negligence of the defendant in hiring and retaining a cashier and general manager with known violent, quarrelsome and antagonistic tendencies, is an effort to circumvent the statute of limitations. . . .

This subject has been thoroughly discussed in earlier decisions of this court and the law is now clear that the fundamental distinction between assault and battery, on the one hand, and negligence, on the other, is

that the former is intentional and the latter is unintentional. . . .

The precise point before this court for decision is a matter of first impression. Simply stated, the question is whether [an employer] may be held liable for injuries to a third person proximately resulting from the incompetence or unfitness of his [employee], where the [employer] was negligent in selecting or retaining an incompetent or unfit [employee]. . . .

Construing the pleading most favorably to [Murray], as we must, the issue presented is whether the employer, The Madoc State Bank, was negligent in retaining its managing officer, Breithaupt, who had propensities toward violence. What the evidence will disclose upon trial of the case we are not at liberty to speculate. . . .

Some of the cases in which it was held there was sufficient showing that [an employer] was negligent in keeping his [employee] in employment are: *Duckworth v. Apostalis,* where a guest sued to recover for injuries inflicted by an employee known by the [employer] to have made previous assaults on guests; *Crawford v. Exposition Cotton Mills,* where a customer of a store sued to recover for injuries by [an employee] known by the [employer] to have an unusual and abnormally high temper; *Priest v. F.W. Woolworth Five & Ten Cent Store,* where a customer sought recovery for injuries inflicted by [an employee] while he was engaged in an act of horseplay and who was known by the manager to have been guilty of previous acts; and *Hall v. Smathers,* where a tenant of an apartment house sought to recover as against the [employer] for injuries by [an employee] known by the [employer] to be a drunkard and incompetent and dangerous.

In conclusion, we hold that the plaintiff has alleged a cause of action against the Modoc State Bank on the theory of negligence.

Affirmed.

CASE REVIEW QUESTIONS
1. Why do you think Murray didn't also sue Donald Breithaupt?
2. Carefully define the negligent act that the plaintiff asserts as the basis of the defendant's liability.

Respondeat Superior

In the Murray case, the court said that a third party could sue a principal on the basis of the principal's own tort of negligence. But what can a third party do if the principal has not committed a tort? In this type of case, the third party may seek to have the court impose vicarious liability on the principal. The word "vicarious" means that which is experienced in the place of another. **Vicarious liability** describes a type of legal liability that is imposed on one person for the wrongful acts of another. Vicarious liability may be found in various areas of the American legal system. For example, in many states, parents are vicariously liable for the torts of their minor children.

In agency law, vicarious liability is imposed on the principal for the torts of an agent under the doctrine of **respondeat superior.** Literally translated this Latin phrase means "let the master respond." We will explain this doctrine by first defining it, then by explaining the reasons for it, and finally by examining some important issues under the doctrine in some detail, particularly the concepts of master and servant and scope of employment.

Definition The doctrine of respondeat superior provides that a master is liable for the torts of a servant committed while the servant is acting in the scope of employment. Notice that the doctrine refers to "master" and "servant." These terms will be fully explained later, but for now you only need to know that a master is roughly equivalent to a principal and a servant is roughly equivalent to an agent. Note also that the doctrine of respondeat superior does not say anything about relieving the servant of tort liability. Instead, it makes the master liable as well as the servant.

Suppose, for example, that a truck driver who works for a furniture company negligently hits a pedestrian with the truck while delivering furniture. The pedestrian can seek damages from the truck driver (servant) on the basis of negligence and from the furniture company (master) on the basis of the doctrine of respondeat superior.

Reasons for the Doctrine Respondeat Superior You may think that the doctrine of respondeat superior imposes an unfair burden on the master. However, there are several reasons for the doctrine that may make it seem less unfair. We will briefly mention five of these reasons:*

1. If masters are held liable for the torts of their servants, they will be more apt to take precautions to prevent circumstances in which the servant may cause injury to third parties from occurring. For example, a master can change an agent's pattern of commercial conduct or sales routine or whatever else may contribute to the commission of a tort by the agent.
2. In a similar way, if masters are held liable, they will be more careful in selecting and training their servants.
3. Without this doctrine, the only way to prove a master liable is to prove the master's own negligence in hiring, training, or supervising the servant, as

---

* See W.A. Seavey, "Speculations As To 'Respondeat Superior,'" *Harvard Legal Essays,* 1934.

occurred in the *Murray* case. Even if the master was negligent, however, the task of proving such negligence places a difficult burden on an injured plaintiff who may have to rely on the testimony of other servants of the master to prove the case. Accurate testimony in such cases is apt to be difficult to obtain from the other members of the master's organization.

4. A reason for this doctrine that is not frequently acknowledged by the courts is the so-called "deep pockets" rationale. Simply stated, this rationale suggests that the master should be liable because he or she is likely to be more wealthy than the servant. The objective of the doctrine under this theory is simply to assure that people receive compensation for their injuries. It is believed that masters can afford to pay this compensation as a cost of doing business.

5. Society allows the formation of corporations for the purpose of doing business. When a corporation is formed, it is treated as a legal entity separate from its owners. People who do business with a corporation are dealing with that legal entity, not with the owners. This protects the owners from being held personally liable to people who do business with the corporation. An additional reason for the doctrine of respondeat superior when the master is a corporation is that imposition of liability on the corporation should be a condition for allowing people the advantages of doing business as a corporation.

The Master–Servant Relationship As noted earlier, the doctrine of respondeat superior applies to **master** and **servant** rather than to principal and agent. Although the origin of the terms master and servant dates from centuries past, they are still used today in agency law.

The Restatement (Section 2) defines a master–servant relationship as a subclassification of the principal–agent relationship. More specifically, it provides:

1. A master is a principal who employs an agent to perform service in his affairs and who controls or has the right to control the physical conduct of the other in the performance of the service.
2. A servant is an agent employed by a master to perform service in his affairs whose physical conduct in the performance of the service is controlled or is subject to the right to control by the master.

From these provisions, you can see that the key element in determining the existence of a master–servant relationship is the presence in the master of control or the right to control the physical conduct of the servant. For example, it would be expected that a master carpenter would have the right to control the actions of an apprentice.

At the other end of the control spectrum, we find situations in which one person hires another to perform a task but does not control or have the right to control the physical activities of the person hired to perform the task. In such a situation, the hired person is called an **independent contractor.** The independent contractor may or may not be an agent, but in either case he or she is not a servant. For example, if you hire a plumber to come to your home to fix a broken pipe, the plumber is probably an independent contractor, not a servant, because you neither control nor have the right to control the plumber's physical activities in repairing the broken pipe.

The significance of the distinction between servants and independent contractors is that the doctrine of respondeat superior applies only to situations in which the person committing a tort is a servant. In the case that follows, the court had to determine whether the negligent person was a servant or an independent contractor in order to determine whether the doctrine of respondeat superior was applicable so that the plaintiff could recover damages from the master. Note carefully the factors that the court considers in determining whether the defendant controlled or had the right to control the physical activities of the negligent person.

MASSEY v. TUBE ART DISPLAY, INC.
551 P.2d 1387 (Wash. App. 1976)

[McPherson's Realty Company desired to move an in-ground sign from its previous office location to its new quarters. An agreement was reached with Tube Art Displays, Inc. (Tube Art) to transport and reinstall the sign. Tube Art's employees went to the proposed site for the sign and laid out the exact size and location of the excavation that was necessary to erect the sign. The Tube Art employees marked a 4 by 4-foot square on the ground with yellow paint. The dimensions of the hole, including its depth to 6 feet, were indicated with spray paint inside the square.

Tube Art then hired a backhoe operator, Richard Redford, to dig the necessary hole. Redford began digging in the early evening hours at the location designated by Tube Art. At about 9:30 P.M., the bucket of Redford's backhoe struck a small natural gas pipeline. After examining the pipe and finding no indication of a break or leak, he concluded that the line was not in use and left the site. The following morning, an explosion and fire destroyed the building serviced by the gas pipeline.

Massey had a business in the destroyed building. He brought a legal action against Redford and Tube Art. He argued that Redford was liable for negligence and that Tube Art was liable under the doctrine of respondeat superior. The trial court judge ruled that, as a matter of law, Redford was the servant of Tube Art and instructed the jury accordingly. The jury returned a ver-

dict of $143,000 for Massey against Redford and Tube Art. Tube Art appealed, arguing that the trial court judge had erred in ruling that Redford was Tube Art's servant.]

SWANSON, Judge

Traditionally, servants . . . have been looked upon as persons employed to perform services in the affairs of others under an express or implied agreement, and who, with respect to physical conduct in the performance of those services, are subject to the other's control or right of control.

An independent contractor, on the other hand, is generally defined as one who contracts to perform services for another, but who is not controlled by the other nor subject to the other's right to control with respect to his physical conduct in performing the services.

In determining whether one acting for another is a servant or independent contractor, several factors must be taken into consideration. These are listed in Restatement (Second) of Agency §220(2), as follows:

(a) the extent of control which, by the agreement, the master may exercise over the details of the work;

(b) whether or not the one employed is engaged in a distinct occupation or business;

(c) the kind of occupation, with reference to

whether, in the locality, the work is usually done under the direction of the employer or by a specialist without supervision;

(d) the skill required in the particular occupation;

(e) whether the employer or the workman supplies the instrumentalities, tools, and the place of work for the person doing the work;

(f) the length of time for which the person is employed;

(g) the method of payment, whether by the time or by the job;

(h) whether or not the work is a part of the regular business of the employer;

(i) whether or not the parties believe they are creating the relation of master and servant; and

(j) whether the principal is or is not in business.

All of these factors are of varying importance in determining the type of relationship involved and, with the exception of the element of control, not all the elements need be present. It is the right to control another's physical conduct that is the essential and oftentimes decisive factor in establishing vicarious liability. . . .

In making his ruling that Tube Art was responsible as a matter of law for Redford's actions the trial judge stated,

> I think that under the undisputed evidence in this case they not only had the right to control, but they did control. They controlled the location of the spot to dig. They controlled the dimensions. They controlled the excavation and they got the building permits. They did all of the discretionary work that was necessary before he started to operate. They knew that the method of excavation was going to be by use of a backhoe rather than a pick and shovel which might have made a little difference . . . in this situation. They in effect created

the whole atmosphere in which he worked. And the fact that even though he did not work for them all of the time and they paid him on a piece-work basis for the individual job didn't impress me particularly when they used him the number of times they did. Most of the time they used him for this type of work. So I am holding as a matter of law that Redford's activities are the responsibility of Tube Art.

Our review of the evidence supports the trial court's evaluation of both the right and exercise of control even though Redford had been essentially self-employed for about 5 years at the time of trial, was free to work for other contractors, selected the time of day to perform the work assigned, paid his own income and business taxes and did not participate in any of Tube Art's employee programs. The testimony advanced at trial, which we find determinative, established that during the previous 3 years Redford had worked exclusively for sign companies and 90 percent of his time for Tube Art. He had no employees, was not registered as a contractor or subcontractor, was not bonded, did not himself obtain permits or licenses for his jobs, and dug the holes at locations and in dimensions in exact accordance with the instructions of his employer. In fact, Redford was left no discretion with regard to the placement of the excavations that he dug. Rather, it was his skill in digging holes pursuant to the exact dimensions prescribed that caused him to be preferred over other backhoe operators. We therefore find no disputed evidence of the essential factor — the right to control, nor is there any dispute that control was exercised over the most significant decisions — the size and location of the hole. Consequently, only one conclusion could reasonably be drawn from the facts presented. We find no error.

Affirmed.

CASE REVIEW QUESTIONS

1. Review the reasons for the doctrine of respondeat superior presented earlier in the text. How are those reasons demonstrated by the application of the doctrine in the *Massey* case?

2. Why do you think Massey sued Tube Art as well as Redford?

3. What facts caused the court to conclude that Tube Art had the right to control the physical conduct of Redford?

4. What facts in the case indicate that Redford might have been an independent contractor?

The Scope of Employment Another limitation on the application of the doctrine of respondeat superior is that a master is only liable for the tort of the servant if it is committed within the **scope of employment** of the servant. The Restatement (Section 228) makes the following general statement about the scope of a servant's employment:

1. Conduct of a servant is within the scope of employment if, but only if:
   (a) it is a kind he is employed to perform;
   (b) it occurs substantially within the authorized time and space limits;
   (c) it is actuated, at least in part, by a purpose to serve the master, and
   (d) if force is intentionally used by the servant against another, the use of force is not unexpectable by the master.
2. Conduct of a servant is not within the scope of employment if it is different in kind from that authorized, far beyond the authorized time and space limits, or too little actuated by a purpose to serve the master.

It should be noted that an act can be within the scope of a servant's employment even if the servant has been specifically instructed not to perform the act, if the standard just presented is met. For example, if a truck driver injures someone while delivering goods for an employer, the truck driver is within the scope of employment even though the employer has told the driver, "Drive carefully and don't have any accidents."

There are certain recurring issues that arise in the application of the general statement of what constitutes the servant's scope of employment. These issues are discussed in the following sections of the text.

Incidental Conduct Suppose a landowner hires a person to cut weeds in a field, provides the tools for cutting the weeds, and carefully explains how the weeds are to be cut. Clearly the worker is a servant and the landowner is a master. If the worker negligently injures a guest of the landowner while cutting the weeds, the landowner (master) would no doubt be liable to the guest for the negligence of the worker (servant) under the doctrine of respondeat superior because the worker was acting within the scope of employment when the negligence occurred.

Suppose, though, that the worker builds a fire in the field to heat some coffee. If the worker negligently allows the fire to spread and it destroys a neighbor's crops in an adjacent field, is the landowner liable to the neighbor under the doctrine of respondeat superior? Was the worker's negligence within the scope of his employment?

The answer is that the worker's negligence may have been committed within the scope of employment, and, therefore, the landowner may be liable to the neighbor for the damage caused by the fire. This is so even though one of the requirements of scope of employment set forth in the Restatement is that the servant's conduct must be of "a kind he is employed to perform."

You would be correct in believing that the worker was not employed to build fires to warm coffee. The law, however, has taken the position that some acts by servants, although not acts they were employed to perform, are *incidental* to the employment. Whether conduct by a servant is incidental to the conduct authorized must be determined on a case-by-case basis. There are, however, certain factors that courts consider in making this determination, such as whether the act is one commonly done by such servants; the time, place, and purpose of the act; whether the master had reason to expect the act; and whether it is similar to acts that were authorized. Thus, in this example, if weed cutters commonly make fires to warm coffee, if the fire was built during working hours and in the field where the work was being done, and if the building of the fire could have been anticipated by the landowner, the weed cutter would be within the scope of his employment. The landowner would therefore be liable to the neighbor under the doctrine of respondeat superior.

Doing Personal Business on Company Time In the preceding example, heating coffee was incidental to the main task of the agency because it is usually considered a part of the work. But how would a court resolve the liability issue if the weed cutter built the fire to melt some metal to use in a sculpture he or she was making to be given as a gift?

Many courts would resolve the liability issue in such a case by focusing on the intent of the servant. If the servant is at the place of work but is engaged in an activity intended to benefit only the servant or the servant's family or friends, and a tort is committed while the agent is engaged in this activity, then the tort is not committed within the scope of employment and the master is not liable to an injured third party.

Cases of this type often involve a person hired to drive a motor vehicle who does personal errands on the employer's time. The courts say that the servant is engaged in a "detour" or "frolic." The beginning of a detour or frolic is usually relatively easy to establish. It occurs when the servant substantially departs from the established route with the intent to benefit himself or herself. While some courts have said that deviating a short distance is not a detour, all courts hold that a deviation of several miles or a deviation of considerable proportion is a detour.

What if the tort occurs after the servant has accomplished his or her personal objective and is returning to the established route? In this instance, the courts are divided on whether the servant is within the scope of employment. Some have held that the servant reenters the scope of employment at the moment of turning back, whereas others have said that the servant reenters when he or she is relatively close to the point of departure. Still other courts have allowed recovery from the principal only when the servant is completely back on the authorized road.

In the following case, the court had to decide whether a truck driver was within the scope of employment or had gone off on a frolic of his own.

THOMAS v. McBRIDE EXPRESS COMPANY
266 S.W.2d 11 (Mo. App. 1965)

[McBride Express Company (McBride), a trucking firm, employed Smyser as a driver. Smyser made daily runs for McBride from Maltoon, Illinois, to St. Louis, Missouri. One day, with McBride's permission, Smyser took his 16-year-old son with him. When he arrived in St. Louis, he delivered the freight to the terminal and then put his son on a bus to visit friends while he (Smyser) went to a ball game. He left the game when it began to rain and returned to the terminal to pick up the truck and another load of freight. As he was leaving town, he drove four or five blocks out of his way to pick up his son. Before he picked up his son, he negligently ran into Thomas.

Thomas brought a legal action against McBride on the basis of respondeat superior. Following the presentation of evidence, McBride moved for a directed verdict, arguing that the evidence showed that as a matter of law Smyser had not been within the scope of his employment when the accident had occurred. The trial judge denied the motion. The jury returned a verdict for Thomas. McBride appealed.]

ANDERSON, Presiding Judge

Liability in this case can only be imposed in the event it can be said that Smyser was, at the time of the accident, acting within the scope of his employment. An act of a servant is not within the scope of employment if it is done with no intention to perform it as a part of or incident to a service on account of which the servant is employed.

The solution of the problem presented is not merely a matter of measuring the distance, the time, or the direction of the departure from what may be called the path of authorized conduct. Such circumstances may guide the judgment, but will not control it aside from other circumstances which may characterize the intent of the transaction.

A servant may in certain instances deviate from the most direct or authorized route and still be in the master's service. Thus it may be that one turns aside to avoid heavy traffic, or to seek a smoother route. There may be parallel routes leading in the direction of his ultimate destination, either of which could be said to be within his sphere of service, on the theory that it might be reasonably expected that he would, in the exercise of his best judgment, choose either while in the pursuit of his master's business; or he might turn aside to attend to necessary personal wants which are considered incidental to his employment. But any turning aside from the designated or customary route, where the sole motive is self interest, unmixed with any intent to serve the master, separates the servant from the master's service, regardless of the exent of the deviation. Any other rule would lead to inconsistencies and ultimate confusion in the law.

Smyser, defendant's servant, while making the journey to . . . pick up his son, was performing no service for his master. He was not within his contemplated sphere of service at the time, nor performing an act which could be said to be incidental to his employment. His deviation was not made to facilitate the movement of the freight he was employed to haul. His intent was to serve a private purpose. As a matter of law, Smyser was not within the scope of his employment when the collision occurred.

The trial court should have sustained defendant's motion for a directed verdict. The judgment is reversed.

CASE REVIEW QUESTIONS

1. Once again review the reasons for the doctrine of respondeat superior presented earlier in this chapter. Are they applicable to the situation presented in the *Thomas* case?

2. Review the general statement regarding the scope of a servant's employment presented earlier. How is application of that statement demonstrated in the *Thomas* case?

3. The court's decision does not mention that Smyser had permission from McBride to take his son on the trip to St. Louis. Do you think that this fact should have been considered by the court in deciding the case? Explain.

Intentional Torts Most cases brought by injured third parties against masters under the doctrine of respondeat superior are based on negligence. What if a servant commits an intentional tort such as assault and battery? Is an assault and battery on a third party beyond the scope of employment? You may recall that the Restatement's general statement concerning scope of employment said that if the servant intentionally uses force, it is within the scope of employment if the use of such force could be anticipated by the master.

You may wonder under what circumstances a master could expect a servant to commit an intentional tort. One situation in which the courts have found such an expectation to exist is when a tavern owner employs a bouncer. In the ordinary employment situation, though, a master does not normally expect a servant to be violent.

Court reports show no consistent application of a principle of scope of employment in cases involving intentional torts. The traditional view is that intentional torts are almost always beyond the scope of employment. The modern view is that of the Restatement. The following case illustrates a court holding to the older view, with a dissent representing the more modern view.

SANDMAN v. HAGAN
154 N.W.2d 113 (Iowa 1967)

LARSON, Justice

It appears from the record that on November 7, 1963, the plaintiff Jerry Sandman, employed by the Sioux City Sewer Department, was directed to inspect a job and arrived on the job between 8 and 9 A.M. His duty was to inspect the installation, the hookup, and the backfill of the connection to the city water system being done by Beane Plumbing and Heating Co. [which was owned by Hagan] hereafter referred to as the employer. The defendant Montagne and two other employees of Beane Plumbing and Heating Co., Lloyd Brunssen and Martin Wilde, were doing the actual work. A hole had been dug in the street approximately three to four feet wide, five feet long, and six feet deep. The installation and hookup had been completed and the backfill operation involving the refilling of the hole was awaiting the arrival of Sandman. In this operation a small quantity of dirt is first dumped into the excavation and then this dirt must be firmly tamped beneath the water pipe and main. . . . Inspector Sandman was there to see that the dirt was properly compacted under the main by the installing workmen.

Sandman testified he was observing the backfill operation from above when he noticed that dirt had not been properly compacted under the main, and he brought this to the attention of Brunssen. Not being satisfied with the results of his directions, he jumped down in the hole to show Brunssen that there was a void under the main.

Brunssen testified that Sandman had said nothing to him about improper backfilling, but rather jumped into the hole with him and began shoving dirt into a gap under the main. Both testified that no altercation or abusive language occurred until Sandman had demonstrated to Brunssen that there was indeed a gap between the main and the ground. At this point Sandman testified that Brunssen called him derogatory names, told him to get out of the hole, and said he had no business down there.

Immediately following this name-calling, a fight took place between Sandman and Brunssen. Sandman testified that to the best of his recollection he struck Brunssen only once and that the fight lasted about two minutes. Brunssen testified that he did not strike Sandman, but doubled up to protect himself and that Sandman struck him several times on the face and body, and that the fight lasted about 15 to 30 seconds.

Montagne testified that he did not hear the conversation between Sandman and Brunssen prior to the fight because the noisy air compressor was running at the time, that the first thing he knew Sandman was pounding on Brunssen and he yelled at Sandman to stop but that he did not stop, and that he (Montagne) became scared that Brunssen might be hurt. Montagne then struck Sandman on the back of the head with a shovel. Although Sandman testified he saw Montagne swing the shovel at him, he did not hear Montagne say anything to him before he got hit with the shovel.

The jury returned a verdict for Sandman against all defendants. On motion by the employer, the trial court granted judgment notwithstanding the verdict for it, concluding there was insufficient evidence to sustain a finding that Montagne was acting within the scope of his employment. Plaintiff appeals from the granting of the employer's motion.

The sole issue presented on appeal by appellant Sandman is whether at the time in question employee Montagne was acting within the scope of his [employment] so as to make the defendant employer liable and sustain the jury determination on that issue.

The trial court concluded there was no evidence to sustain a finding that Montagne's authority extended

beyond that of putting in water lines and refilling excavations, or that his duties contemplated conflict with others, or that the assault was done in the furtherance of the employer's business or interests within the scope of his employment. We must agree.

The difficulty encountered by various courts in cases of willful torts committed by servants has resulted in irreconcilable decisions, and unless carefully scrutinized, the authorities seem to be in hopeless confusion. . . . The difficulty is in defining and applying the concept of acts within the course of employment. . . .

It has been said an act is "within the scope of the servant's employment" where such act is necessary to accomplish the purpose of the employment and is intended for such purpose, although in excess of the powers actually conferred on the servant by the master. . . .

It is safe to say that "within the scope of the employment" requires that the conduct complained of must be of the same general nature as that authorized or incidental to the conduct authorized. . . .

As we have pointed out, a deviation from the employer's business or interest to pursue the employee's own business or interest must be substantial in nature to relieve the employer from liability. . . . Here, the employer contends the assault was clearly a deviation substantial in nature, for under no theory advanced would the duty of installing water lines and digging ditches include the exercise of force upon others. It is difficult to see how his employer's business or interest would ever be furthered by such an employee attack, especially on an inspector.

We are aware of the so-called modern trend to find liability in this class of cases on the basis that such wrongs are committed by the employee only because of the employment situation, and that since the employer has the benefit of the enterprise as between two innocent third parties, he is better able to bear the risk of loss. If he cannot altogether avoid such wrongs, he can at least minimize them. In those cases it is argued that a general sense of fairness requires that the employer, as the person interested and benefited by the business, rather than the persons who have no concern in or control over it, should bear the burden of such wrongs as incidental to such business. . . .

If employer liability is to be extended this far, we believe it should come from the legislature, and do not find that this concept has substantial support in judicial decisions.

We are satisfied here that the employee Montagne's assault on Inspector Sandman was a substantial deviation from his duties, that his act was substantially different in nature from that authorized by the employer, and that at the time thereof he was acting outside the scope of his employment. The trial court was correct in granting the employer's motion for judgment notwithstanding the verdict and must be affirmed on appellant Sandman's appeal. . . .

Affirmed.

BECKER, Justice (Dissenting)

I dissent as to plaintiff's appeal from judgment in favor of defendant employer. . . .

In *Carr v. William C. Crowell Co.,* Traynor, J., analyzes the problem in a closely analogous case and sets forth several principles that should govern our consideration here.

> The employer's responsibility for the tortious conduct of his employee extends far beyond his actual or possible control over the conduct of the servant. It rests on the broader ground that every man who prefers to manage his affairs through others remains bound to so manage them that third persons are not injured by any breach of legal duty on the part of such others while acting in the scope of their employment. In the present case, defendant's enterprise required an

> association of employees with third parties, attended by the risk that someone might be injured. The risks of such associations and conditions were risks of the employment. . . . Such associations include the faults and derelictions of human beings as well as their virtues and obediences. Men do not discard their personal qualities when they go to work. Into the job they carry their intelligence, skill, habits of care and rectitude. Just as inevitably they take along also their tendencies to carelessness and camaraderie, as well as emotional makeup. In bringing men together, work brings these qualities together, causes frictions between them, creates occasions for lapses into carelessness, and for fun-making and emotional flareup. Work could not go on if men became automatons repressed in every natural expression. . . . These expressions of human nature are incidents inseparable from working together. They involve risks of injury and these risks are inherent in the working environment.

> If an employee inflicts an injury out of personal malice, not engendered by the employment, the employer is not liable.

Here the employees' duties regularly brought them in contact with the inspector. The inspector and Montagne had had previous altercations. This fight developed over the method of performing the employer's business of laying the pipe. Montagne entered the fray on the side of the fellow employee, if not on his behalf. It is for the jury to decide whether this employee was acting within the scope of his employment or on a venture of his own. I would affirm as to defendant Montagne but would reverse and reinstate the verdict as to [Hagen].

CASE REVIEW QUESTIONS

1. Which opinion, the majority or dissenting, do you believe is most consistent with the reasons for the doctrine of respondeat superior?
2. Which opinion do you believe is most consistent with the Restatement's general statement regarding scope of employment?
3. In the last paragraph of the dissenting opinion, Justice Becker states, "The inspector and Montagne had had previous altercations." Does this suggest another basis on which Sandman might have sued Hagen? Explain.

Liability for Torts of Non-servant Agents

As explained earlier, the distinction between a servant and an independent contractor is essential to the application of the doctrine of respondeat superior. There are, however, certain situations in which courts will impose liability on a principal for a tort committed by an agent, even though the agent is not a servant.

The Restatement (Section 14 N) distinguishes between two types of independent contractors. One type is an independent contractor who is not an agent. For example, if a person hires a contractor to build a house and reserves no right to control the physical activities of the contractor, the contractor is an independent contractor. If, in addition, the contractor has no authority to contract on behalf of the person who hired him or her, the contractor is also not an agent.

The second type of independent contractor is one who is an agent. For example, a company who hires a salesman may have no right to control the salesman's physical activities, thus making the salesman an independent contractor. If, however, the salesman has authority to contract on behalf of the company, he or she is an agent. This type of independent contractor is referred to as a **non-servant agent.**

The reason for distinguishing between the two types of independent contractors is that a principal is held liable for certain torts of a non-servant agent. A principal is not held liable for physical harm caused by the negligent physical conduct of a non-servant agent. A principal is held liable, however, for physical harm to the person or property of another that is caused by a negligent representation by an authorized non-servant agent.

For example, if a wholesale food dealer employs a traveling salesman who owns his or her own car, selects his or her own customers, and is paid on a commission basis, the principal will probably not be liable for the agent's negligent driving on the grounds that the salesman is not a servant. The principal will be liable, however, if the salesman, say, negligently misrepresents certain spoiled food to a grocer as wholesome and a purchaser of the food becomes ill from eating it. This is so because the principal (the wholesale food dealer) is liable for physical harm to another caused by the apparently authorized negligent representation of the non-servant agent (the salesman).

Another situation in which a principal is held liable for the tort of a non-servant agent occurs when an actually or apparently authorized agent commits the tort of fraud. Fraud is an intentional tort, so in the preceding example, in which the salesman was merely negligent, this rule would not apply. If the salesman's misrepresentation was intentional, though, this rule would apply. The wholesale dealer (principal) would then be liable not only for physical harm caused, but also for any economic losses incurred. For example, the wholesale food dealer could be held liable for business lost by the grocer because of the bad publicity resulting from the sale of the spoiled food.

A master is, of course, liable for the defamatory statements of a servant made within the scope of employment under the doctrine of respondeat superior. A principal is also liable, however, for defamatory statements made by a non-servant agent if he or she is actually or apparently authorized. This rule expands the principal's liability for such statements.

Liability for Torts of Apparent Servants or Agents

The doctrine of respondeat superior only applies to situations in which a master–servant relationship exists. If a master–servant relationship does not exist, one party does not have the right to control the physical activities of the other. If the principal lacks the right to control the physical activities of the agent, at least one of the reasons for imposing liability under the doctrine of respondeat superior is not present. This is so because, without the right to control, the principal cannot supervise the agent so as to prevent the commission of a tort.

There are circumstances, however, in which liability is imposed even though a master–servant relationship does not exist. These circumstances arise when a person creates the appearance of the existence of a master–servant relationship and a third person, because of the appearance, relies on the care and skill of the apparent servant and is harmed because of the failure of the care or skill of the apparent servant.

For example, suppose the drivers that work for Ace Taxi Company are independent contractors. Ace, however, advertises that it closely controls its drivers' conduct, creating the impression that the drivers are servants of the company and are careful in their work. Because of the advertising, Smith calls on Ace Taxi. While traveling as a passenger in an Ace Taxi, Smith is injured as a result of the driver's negligence. Ace is liable to Smith because of Smith's reliance. If a pedestrian were also injured in the accident, Ace would not be liable to the pedestrian because the pedestrian did not rely on the appearances created by Ace.

Liability under this doctrine is usually limited to apparent masters because the scope of employment limitation on liability discussed earlier in this chapter is applicable under this rule. An apparent principal would only be held liable for the act of an apparent agent in circumstances in which a principal is liable for the torts of a non-servant agent, as set forth in the previous section of the text.

In the case that follows, the defendant was not the master of the party charged with negligence. The plaintiff, however, based his case on the rule that an apparent master may be liable for the torts of an apparent servant.

ADAMSKI v. TACOMA GENERAL HOSPITAL
579 P.2d 970 (Wash. 1978)

[Adamski injured his finger while playing basketball. He went to Tacoma General Hospital for treatment. He was treated by the physician in charge, Dr. Tsoi. The doctor cleansed the wound and stitched and bandaged it. When Adamski left, he was given a form that said "Tacoma General Hospital Emergency Care" across the top and instructed that the stitches should be removed in 5 to 6 days by the patient's own doctor. It went on to say that if the patient could not contact his or her own doctor, the patient should "feel free to call the Emergency Department" of the hospital.

An infection developed in Adamski's injured finger, and he went to another hospital for medical attention for the finger. Substantial treatment was needed because of the infection. Adamski later brought a legal action against Dr. Tsoi and Tacoma General Hospital. He based his claim against Dr. Tsoi on negligence in the treatment of his finger and against the hospital on the basis that Dr. Tsoi was the hospital's agent.

Tacoma General Hospital moved for a summary judgment. It argued that the doctrine of respondeat superior did not apply because Dr. Tsoi was not a servant. The hospital said it neither controlled nor had the right to control his physical activities. The trial court judge concluded that Dr. Tsoi was an independent contractor, not a servant of the hospital, and granted the summary judgment motion. Adamski appealed.]

REED, Acting Chief Judge

Tacoma General relies upon the law as summarized [as follows]:

> The general principle that the employer of an independent contractor is not liable for the torts of such contractor . . . has frequently been recognized with respect to the liability of a hospital for the negligence or malpractice of a physician or surgeon. In other words . . . the conclusion that, assuming such practitioner was an independent contractor in relation to the hospital, the hospital is not liable for such injury, is supported by many decisions.

Tacoma General argues that the ordinary rules of agency must be applied and that if this is done, Dr. Tsoi must be held to be an independent contractor for whose negligent acts the Hospital is not responsible. We are referred to the case of *Hollingbery v. Dunn,* which adopts the criteria of the Restatement (Second) Agency §220, and holds that the single most important factor to be considered in determining the status of one who performs services for another is the right of the latter to control the former. Tacoma General points out that nowhere in its contract with Dr. Tsoi does it reserve the right to exercise any control over the actual medical treatment rendered to its emergency room patients. Rather, Tacoma General argues, the only contract requirement is that the doctors must be members of Tacoma General's staff and conform to the usual and accepted professional and ethical standards of conduct.

The experience of the courts has been that application of hornbook rules of agency to the hospital–physician relationship usually leads to unrealistic and unsatisfactory results, at least from the standpoint of the injured patient. Consequently, we have seen a substantial body of special law emerging in this area; the result has been an expansion of hospital liability for negligent medical acts committed on its premises.

Where a physician is found not to be the actual agent of the hospital, the latter may still be held responsible for his departures from good medical practice under the so-called "holding out" or "ostensible

agent" theory. Restatement (Second) Agency §267, sets forth the rule as follows:

> One who represents that another is his servant or other agent and thereby causes a third person justifiably to rely upon the care or skill of such apparent agent is subject to liability to the third person for harm caused by the lack of care or skill of the one appearing to be a servant or other agent as if he were such.

Tacoma General argues, however, that there can be no "ostensible agency" or agency by estoppel as it is sometimes called, in the absence of proof of an "affirmative misrepresentation" of Dr. Tsoi's status. The Hospital relies for this point on *Greene v. Rothschild,* in which the Yellow Cab Company was held to have created apparent or ostensible agents of its former employees who had been converted to driver–owners. Liability was predicated on the fact the cab company permitted use of its "colors, markings and name" and failed to give adequate notice to the public of the new relationship. If Tacoma General's position is that before liability may be imposed, the hospital must have informed the patient he is being treated by its employee, we do not agree. On the contrary, a "holding out" or representation may arise when the hospital acts or omits to act in some way which leads the patient to a reasonable belief he is being treated by the hospital by one of its employees.

In the instant case, a jury could find that Tacoma General held itself out as providing emergency care services to the public. A jury could find that plaintiff reasonably believed Dr. Tsoi was employed by the Hospital to deliver that emergency room service. It appears plaintiff was not advised to the contrary and, in fact, he believed he was being treated by the Hospital's agent; in addition, the written instructions provided him after surgery could reasonably be interpreted as an invitation to return for further treatment if plaintiff could not contact his personal physician. The form bearing this instruction also carried the title "Tacoma General Hospital Emergency Care." Clearly, when the facts before the trial court and the fair inferences therefrom are viewed in a light most favorable to plaintiff, a jury could find that the emergency room personnel were "held out" as employees of the Hospital. It was error, therefore, not to submit this issue to the jury.

Reversed and remanded.

CASE REVIEW QUESTIONS

1. Why wasn't the hospital liable to Adamski under the doctrine of respondeat superior?

2. Under what circumstances is an apparent master liable for the torts of an apparent servant? What facts indicated to the court that such circumstances were present in this case?

Tort Liability Based on the Principal's Nondelegable Duty

As stated earlier, a tort is the violation of a legal duty owed to another. Sometimes a principal who owes a duty to another seeks to delegate (transfer) that duty to an independent contractor. If the duty is one which the law says is nondelegable (i.e., may not be transferred) a principal who attempts to delegate the duty to an independent contractor will be held liable if the independent contractor breaches the duty. Similarly, if the duty is nondelegable, the principal is liable for breach of the duty by a servant, even though the servant is outside the scope of the employment when the tort is committed.

Earlier in this chapter, the concept of strict liability was briefly discussed. People and companies that engage in ultrahazardous activities—such as blasting with explosives, spraying noxious solutions on crops, transporting toxic chemicals, and drilling for oil in populated areas—are held strictly liable for injuries that occur as a result of such activities. If a principal who would be subject to strict liability if he or she performed the ultrahazardous activity hires an independent contractor to do the work and a third party is injured, the principal will be liable to the third party. As a matter of public policy, such a duty cannot be delegated.

For example, suppose the General Construction Company has a contract to build a highway. It hires the Dy-No-Mite Company, an independent contractor, to do some blasting as part of the work. A pedestrian is injured by a stone that is sent flying by a blast. General Construction would be liable to the pedestrian for the injuries, even though Dy-No-Mite was an independent contractor, because its duty was nondelegable.

Similarly, there are some duties that cannot be delegated to an independent contractor because a statute prohibits such delegation. For example, the Occupational Safety and Health Act imposes a duty on certain employers to provide a place of work free from recognized danger. If an employer subject to the act hires an independent contractor to make the place of work completely safe, and a worker of the employer is injured because of an unsafe condition, the employer will be liable to the worker. Both the Act and court decisions provide that the duty to maintain a safe and healthy workplace cannot be delegated.

Some contractual duties also may not be delegated (see Chapter 16). In general, a contract duty is not delegable by a promisor if the promisee would be expected to have a particular interest in having the promisor perform the duty. If a contractual duty is nondelegable, but the promisor nonetheless delegates the duty to an independent contractor, the promisor will be liable for any tort of the independent contractor that injures a third party.

For example, suppose you visit a doctor because of his or her reputation and skill as a surgeon. The doctor agrees to perform an operation, but on the day of the surgery, because of the press of other business, the doctor asks another surgeon to perform the operation. You do not know of the change. If the second doctor is negligent in performing the operation, the first doctor will be liable for any damages that occur. This is so because the duty of your doctor to perform the operation carefully is not delegable.

Tort Liability Based on Ratification

Even if there is no other basis for holding a principal liable, a court will allow an injured third party to recover from a principal when someone acting for the principal commits a tort and the principal then accepts the benefits of the action that caused the tort. Courts usually say that the principal has ratified the tort by accepting the benefits. In other words, a principal may ratify a tort just as a principal may ratify a contract.

Ratification is determined by searching for and finding an act of affirmance by the principal. The Restatement (Section 82) says:

> Ratification is the affirmance by a person of a prior act which did not bind him but which was done or professedly done on his account, whereby the act . . . is given effect as if originally authorized by him.

And, Section 83 of the Restatement states:

> Affirmance is either (a) manifestation of an election by one on whose account an unauthorized act has been done to treat the act as authorized, or (b) conduct by him justifiable only if there were such an election.

Most courts would hold that the principal must have general knowledge that a wrong was committed at the time of affirmance. However, specific knowledge of the wrongdoing or its exact dollar damage need not be known.

In a classic case involving the principle of ratification, a coal company demanded payment from a customer who had received a delivery of coal from someone who was not an agent of the owner. This person had voluntarily undertaken to deliver the coal and while doing so had broken a window on the customer's property. The court held that by demanding payment for the coal, with knowledge of the fact that the window had been broken in the process of delivery, the coal company had ratified the negligent act and was liable for the damage. The court stated:

> We have found hardly anything in the books dealing with the precise case, but we are of the opinion that consistency with the whole course of authority requires us to hold that the defendant's ratification of the employment established the relation of master and servant from the beginning, with all its incidents, including the . . . liability for his negligent act. . . . The ratification goes to the relation, and established it *ab initio* [from the beginning]. The relation existing, the master is answerable for torts which he has not ratified specifically, just as he is for those which he has not commanded, and as he may be for those which he has expressly forbidden. . . .

TORT LIABILITY OF AGENTS TO THIRD PARTIES

As noted earlier, in most cases an agent is liable to a third party for a tort committed by the agent, regardless of whether the principal is or is not liable to the third party. An exception to this rule occurs when an agent makes a misrepresentation to a third party based on information from the principal that the principal knows to be false but that the agent believes to be true.

For example, suppose a homeowner tells a real estate agent that her house, which she wants the agent to sell for her, is fully insulated, even though it isn't. If the agent tells a buyer of the house that it is fully insulated, the agent has not committed the tort of fraud, but the homeowner (principal) has. This is so because fraud is an intentional tort, and the agent lacked the requisite intent. The homeowner is liable, however, because she caused the deceit to occur and is as responsible as if she had personally performed the deceit.

Joint and Several Liability

If both the agent and the principal are liable for a tort committed by the agent, the liability is joint and several. This means that the injured third party may sue both the agent and the principal in either the same legal action or separately. Whichever way the third party proceeds, he or she may win judgments against both the agent and the principal. However, once one of the judgments has been satisfied, whether by the principal or the agent, the third party has been fully compensated and may not satisfy the other judgment.

For example, in the *Massey* case presented earlier in this chapter, Massey won a judgment of $143,000 against both Redford, the agent, and Tube Art Display, Inc., the principal, for a tort committed by Redford. Massey could then collect up to $143,000 from either Redford or Tube Art, or he could collect some part of the total amount from each.

If the third party collects any part of the judgment against the principal, the principal then has the right to be reimbursed by the agent. This is so because it is felt that ultimately the loss should fall on the agent, the one who committed the tort. In fact, however, a principal seldom exercises this right of reimbursement against an agent. A principal with a reputation for asserting this right against his or her agents would probably find it difficult to hire employees.

REVIEW QUESTIONS

1. What is the doctrine of respondeat superior and why have the courts chosen to adopt it?

2. What is the key element in determining whether a master–servant relationship exists?

3. What are the key elements in determining whether a servant was acting within the scope of employment when committing a tort?

4. Other than by the application of the doctrine of respondeat superior, under what circumstances will a principal or master be held liable for the torts of an agent or servant?

5. If both a master and a servant are liable for a tort committed by the agent, which of them is ultimately liable? Why?

CASE PROBLEMS

1. Parker owns several parking garages in Cleveland, Ohio. He was approached by Ward, a representative of the Ohio State Prison System, and asked to participate in a social program to employ exconvicts. Parker was not sure he wanted to participate, but he finally agreed to hire one exconvict to work as a collector in one of his garages. As a result, he hired Johnson, who had served ten years in jail for attempted murder. Johnson turned out to be a good employee, always arriving for work on time, treating customers politely, and always turning in all the money he collected. About six months after starting work, however, Johnson came by the garage at which he worked. Although the garage was closed for the night and locked, Johnson was able to get in with a key he had been given by Parker. Johnson stole a car that Allison had parked there. Two blocks away from the garage, he drove the car into a telephone pole and injured himself seriously. He was immediately arrested and is now in jail again. Against whom and on what basis can Allison bring legal action to be compensated for the damage to her car? Who will win the case(s)? Explain.

2. Parker Drilling Company (Parker) drills for oil and employs a number of people on a full- or part-time basis to keep their equipment in good shape. Crouch was one of the people employed by Parker to do welding on the drilling equipment. Crouch owned his own truck and welding equipment, supplied his own welding materials, such as rods and an arc, and maintained his own insurance. He was not on Parker's payroll and was free to take other jobs, but he worked steadily for Parker, submitting invoices for work performed. Parker supplied drawings indicating the type of welding to be done and supplied steel when needed. One of the oil drilling derricks that Crouch welded collapsed because of Crouch's negligence in doing the welding. Flick, a bystander, was killed by the falling derrick. If Flick's estate brings a legal action against Parker, on what basis may Parker defend? Who will win the case? Explain.

3. Harold Watts was employed by Superior Sporting Goods as a route salesman. His territory, route,

and customers were determined by Superior. He was expected to work from 9:00 A.M. to 5:00 P.M., Monday through Friday. He received a weekly salary plus time and a half for anything over 40 hours. He also received a small commission on sales that exceeded a stated volume. The customers consisted of sporting goods stores, department stores, athletic clubs, and large companies that had athletic programs or sponsored athletic teams. Watts used his personal car for making calls and, upon occasion, for making a delivery when the customer was in a rush and the order was not large. Watts was reimbursed for the use of his car for company purposes. His instructions were to assume that the customer is always right and to accommodate the customer where to do so would cost little and would build good will for the company and himself.

One afternoon, while making a sales call and dropping off a case of softballs at the Valid Clock Company, the personnel director told Watts he was planning to watch the company's team play a game at a softball field located on the other side of town, but that his car would not start. Watts said, "Don't worry, it will be my pleasure to give you a lift and I would like to take in a few innings myself." Time was short, and while on the way to the ballpark, Watts ran a light and collided with another car driven by Collins. The other car required $800 of repairs and Collins suffered serious bodily injury. If Collins brings a legal action against Superior, on what basis may Superior defend? Who will win the case? Explain. (Adapted from CPA examination question 3b, *Business Law,* November 1978.)

4. Rapid Delivery Service, Inc., hired Dolson as one of its truck drivers. Dolson was carefully selected and trained by Rapid. He was specifically instructed to obey all traffic and parking rules and regulations. One day, while making a local delivery, Dolson double parked and went into a customer's store. In so doing, he prevented a car legally parked at the curb from leaving. The owner of the parked car, Charles, proceeded to blow the horn of the truck repeatedly. Charles was doing

this when Dolson returned from his delivery. As a result of a combination of several factors, particularly Charles' telling him to "move it" and that he was "acting very selfishly and in an unreasonable manner," Dolson punched Charles in the nose, severely fracturing it. When Charles sought to restrain him, Dolson punched Charles again, this time fracturing his jaw. If Charles brings a legal action against Rapid, on what basis might Rapid defend? Who will win? Explain. (Adapted from CPA examination question 3a, *Business Law,* November 1980.)

5. A Texaco service station operator sold a used car to Gizzi, a regular customer, for $400. As part of the deal, the service station operator agreed to install a new brake system. When the car was ready, Gizzi picked it up. Shortly thereafter, the brakes failed and Gizzi was injured. Gizzi brought a legal action against Texaco, Inc., based on the negligence of the station operator. Texaco presented in evidence the contract between it and the station operator. It showed that the operator was an independent business person who promised to use Texaco products exclusively but who owned the station and was not subject to the control of Texaco in any way in the operation of the station. Gizzi testified that because of the signs at the station, he believed that the station was owned by Texaco. He said that he had relied on Texaco advertising that said, "You can trust your car to the man who wears the Texaco star." On what grounds may Gizzi bring the action against Texaco? On what grounds can Texaco defend? Who will win? Explain.

6. Humphrey was walking across a railroad crossing of the Virginia Railroad Company (VRC) when his foot became wedged between two boards that had become loose. Unable to free himself, Humphrey was severely injured when a train came along shortly thereafter. Humphrey brought a legal action against the railroad company under a statute that provided: "Whenever any railroad shall cross any state road, it shall be required to keep the crossing in proper repair." VRC put into evidence

a contract it had with Safety Maintenance Company (SMC) under which SMC assumed full responsibility for the maintenance of all of VRC's crossings without any right of control for the work being retained by VRC. Therefore, VRC argued, Humphrey should sue SMC. Who will win Humphrey's action against VRC? Explain.

7. The Mutual Creamery Company is engaged in the business of buying eggs from poultry raisers and reselling them. Hanson is the general manager of the business. Sager is an employee who collects eggs from the poultry raisers. One day, Sager was being visited at work by his friend Mecham when Hanson instructed Sager to drive the company's truck to Mrs. Robinson's farm and pick up some eggs. Sager told Mecham that he was too busy with other work to make the trip to Mrs. Robinson's and asked Mecham if he would go instead. Mecham said yes, and unknown to Hanson or anyone else at the company Mecham set out in the company's truck to get Mrs. Robinson's eggs. On the way, Mecham negligently injured Bradford, a pedestrian. After reporting the accident to the police, Mecham continued on, picked up on the eggs and returned to Mutual Creamery. Before Hanson learned about the accident, he sent a check for the eggs to Mrs. Robinson. If Bradford brings a legal action against Mutual Creamery, on what basis may the company defend? Who will win? Explain.

8. Zollers, an employee of Karp Fish Company, negligently injured Hurd while delivering fish for the company. Hurd brought a legal action against Zollers based on negligence and against Karp based on respondeat superior. Hurd won a judgment for $62,000 against both defendants. She collected this amount from Karp. Shortly thereafter, Karp went bankrupt. Cihon was appointed the trustee in bankruptcy of Karp. One of the duties of a trustee in bankruptcy is to collect all money owed to the company. If Cihon, on behalf of Karp, brings a legal action against Zollers to collect the $62,000, who will win? Explain.

34

AGENCY OPERATION AND TERMINATION

In the previous chapters on agency law, you have read about the creation of an agency relationship, the duties of principals and agents to one another, and the contract and tort liability of principals and agents to third parties. This chapter considers some other aspects of the operation of the agency as well as the termination of the agency relationship.

AGENCY OPERATION

In this section, you will read about situations in which a third party wishes to give notification or make payment to a principal by giving the notification or making the payment to an agent of the principal. If the agent fails to pass along the notification or the payment to the principal, the question of the rights of the third party arises. We will then consider to what extent the knowledge of an agent will be imputed to a principal. Also included in this section is an explanation of the law concerning subagents, the delegation of duties by agents, and borrowed servants.

Notification, Payment, and Knowledge

Notification and Payment Sometimes a third party may seek to notify a principal by giving the notification to an agent of the principal. Suppose, for example, that a person is supposed to notify a corporation by a given date as to whether he or she will accept an alteration in a contract with the corporation.

One day before the date, the person calls an officer of the corporation and notifies him or her that the alteration is accepted. The officer leaves that evening on a two-week vacation without telling anyone else of the notification. Has the person successfully notified the corporation? The answer is that notification has been given to the principal (the corporation) if the agent (the officer) was actually or apparently authorized to receive such notification, regardless of whether the agent actually communicated the notification to the principal.

Payment to an agent is treated in the same way. For instance, if a person orders goods from a company through an agent of the company and receives the goods and pays the agent, who then absconds with the money, has payment been made to the principal? Again the answer is yes if the agent was authorized to receive the payment, that is, payment to the agent is treated as payment to the principal. Of course, the principal would be entitled to payment from the agent, if he or she can be found, because the agent has breached a duty to the principal (see Chapter 31).

If the agent is not actually or apparently authorized to receive notification or payment, however, notification or payment to the agent will not be treated as notification or payment to the principal. If the agent misrepresents to the third party that he or she (the agent) has such authority, the agent will be liable to the third party for damages caused by the misrepresentation.

Knowledge As you learned in Chapter 31, an agent's duty of service requires the agent to provide to the principal any information that the agent has and that he or she should expect the principal would want to have or that is relevant to the transactions of the principal with which the agent is involved. If the agent has knowledge of information but fails to disclose that knowledge to the principal, will the principal be treated as having the knowledge? The answer is yes, the agent's knowledge is imputed to the principal.

For example, suppose an agent negotiating a contract on behalf of a principal knows that the third party is making a material mistake of fact in the contract. Suppose further that, after the contract has been formed, the third party seeks to rescind the contract with the principal on the basis of the mistake. Under contract law, if the principal knew of the third party's mistake, the third party may rescind. In such a case the principal will be treated as knowing about the mistake because the agent's knowledge will be imputed to him or her.

The following case concerns an insurance company that is attempting to escape liability under a policy by imputing the knowledge of the agent, who lied on the policy application, to the principal.

BIRD v. PENN CENTRAL CO.
341 F. Supp. 291 (E.D. Pa. 1972)

[An application for a Directors and Officers Liability Insurance Policy (hereinafter referred to as D & O pol-icy) and a Company Reimbursement Insurance Policy was filled out and signed by David C. Bevan, Chairman of the Finance Committee of Penn Central Company. The plaintiffs, the insurance underwriters who issued the policies, brought a legal action to rescind the D & O policy because of fraud contained in the application. The defendants, referred to in the case as "movants," moved for a summary judgment.]

LORD, Chief Judge

The question in this case, [concerns] whether the entire policy is voidable because of an alleged fraudulent act committed in the procurement of the policy.

Item 10 of the application which was the basis for both the Company Reimbursement policy and the D & O policy provides as follows:

> No person proposed for this insurance is cognizant of any act, error, or omission which he has reason to suppose might afford valid grounds for any future claim such as would fall within the scope of the proposed insurance except as follows.

Defendant Bevan's response to this, which is alleged to have been knowingly false, and which is the basis for this rescission action, was "None known." Defendant Bevan, himself, was one of the assureds under the D & O policy. Movants argue that since the answer called for a subjective response, defendant Bevan's answer, if a misrepresentation was made, was a misrepresentation only of his own state of knowledge, but was a true response in his capacity as agent for each individual officer and director (such as movants) who would have truthfully responded "None known" to Item 10.

It is contended that defendant Bevan was acting in three capacities in signing the application: (a) as agent for Penn Central, (b) as principal for his own account as one of the assureds, and (c) as agent for each of the other individual assureds. Recognizing these various capacities, we are asked to consider defendant Bevan's single response to Item 10 as being over sixty separate responses, his own plus one representing the knowledge of each officer and director. Thus, it is urged that plaintiffs should be able to rescind the D & O policy only as to defendant Bevan, for if he answered Item 10 fraudulently it was only in his capacity as principal for his own account. If it was held that the entire D & O policy could be subject to rescission because defendant Bevan happened to be the officer who

signed the insurance application, it would be manifestly unfair to the directors and officers who are completely blameless. . . .

While we sympathize with movants' position, and recognize that innocent officers and directors are likely to suffer if the entire policy is voidable because of one man's fraudulent response, it must be recognized that plaintiff insurers are likewise innocent parties. Defendant Bevan was not plaintiffs' agent. Movants do not deny that he was their agent in completing the application by which the policy was obtained.

The general rule in this type of situation was stated by the Pennsylvania Supreme Court over 100 years ago.

> Where the agent of the insured, in effecting an insurance, makes a false and unauthorized representation, the policy is void. Where one of two innocent persons must suffer by the fraud or negligence of a third, whichever of the two has accredited him, ought to bear the loss. . . .

That the fraud of the agent in inducing a contract is binding on an innocent principal is a well established doctrine of agency law in other jurisdictions as well.

The leading case in Pennsylvania is *Gordon v. Continental Casualty Company.* There a trust company obtained a banker's blanket bond to insure it against any loss due to the dishonesty of its officers and employees. The application which was signed by its secretary and treasurer, Ralph E. Mathews, represented that no losses had been sustained by it during the preceding five years because of employee dishonesty, and that the company had no notice or knowledge of any facts indicating that any of the officers were dishonest or unworthy of confidence. Mathews at that very time, without the trust company's knowledge, was an embezzler of the company's funds to the tune of $26,000, and was of course aware of his own misconduct. The court held that the innocent trust company could not recover on the bond because it was bound by Mathews' misrepresentations. Stated another way, recovery was barred because the knowledge of Mathews' own misdeeds was imputed to the company.

Movants wish to limit the *Gordon* decision strictly to its facts, arguing that the fact that a corporation is an artificial entity and can "know" only through its agents is the reason that the trust company there was bound by the fraudulent knowledge of its agent who completed the insurance application. We do not, however, read the crucial fact in Gordon to be that the principal was a corporation, rather than an individual or a group of individuals. It is rather an application of the usual rule that a principal is bound by the fraud of his agent in procuring a contract.

Therefore, the motions for summary judgment will be denied.

CASE REVIEW QUESTIONS

1. For whom was Bevan an agent?
2. What statement by Bevan did the plaintiffs believe was fraudulent?
3. The plaintiffs' legal action sought to rescind the insurance policies on the basis of fraud. If the principals had answered Item 10 "None known," the statements would have been true. How, then, can the plaintiffs argue that the principals made a fraudulent statement?

Subagents

Appointment of Subagents As part of the operation of an agency relationship, an agent may hire someone else to work directly for the agent in accomplishing tasks for the principal. The person who the agent hires may be a subagent. The Restatement (Section 5[1]) defines a **subagent** as follows:

> A subagent is a person appointed by an agent empowered to do so, to perform functions undertaken by the agent for the principal, but for whose conduct the agent agrees with the principal to be primarily responsible.

Hiring a subagent is not the same as hiring employees for the principal. For example, when a personnel officer for a corporation hires employees for the corporation, they become agents of the corporation, not subagents of the personnel officer. One way to determine whether an agent is a subagent is to look at the work the person was hired to do. If the work primarily involves functions already undertaken by the appointing agent for the principal, the person hired is likely to be a subagent.

Liability for Acts of Subagents A subagent is an agent of both the principal and the appointing agent. As such, the subagent can impose tort and contract liability on both the principal and the appointing agent pursuant to the principles discussed in the two previous chapters. If liability is imposed on both, the appointing agent is held ultimately liable and must reimburse the principal if he or she (the principal) pays a third party for damages suffered. Of course, in the case of a breach of tort duty, ultimate liability falls on the subagent.

As you read the following case, note the possible bases of liability on the appointing agent (Antisdale) and on the principal (Presbytery of San Francisco).

MALLOY v. FONG
232 P.2d 241 (Cal. 1951)

TRAYNOR, Justice

Plaintiff brought this action for damages for personal injuries allegedly caused by the concurrent negligence of defendants Holmes, Fong, and Antisdale. Plaintiff alleged that Fong and Antisdale were acting as agents of defendant Presbytery of San Francisco. The jury exonerated defendant Holmes, but returned a verdict in favor of plaintiff in the amount of $41,500 against defendants Fong, Antisdale, and Presbytery of San Francisco. On motion of defendant Presbytery, the trial court entered a judgment notwithstanding the verdict as to it. . . .

During the summer vacation of 1943, plaintiff Malloy, then a boy of thirteen, attended a vacation Bible school conducted at the San Mateo Presbyterian Church for the children of members of the Church, then a "mission" under the jurisdiction of defendant Presbytery of San Francisco. Defendant Antisdale, pastor of the Church, was in charge of the school and gave the Bible instruction.

Antisdale became ill several days before July 1, 1943, the day plaintiff was injured, and was unable to conduct the school. It was therefore left without an instructor qualified to conduct the Bible classes. Defendant Fong, a 19-year-old divinity student, was at that time vacationing at the home of his guardian, Dr. Jones, a retired Presbyterian minister, in San Mateo. Fong agreed to conduct the Bible instruction in Antisdale's absence so that Antisdale might stay home and rest. In addition to conducting the Bible classes, Fong drove the children to the playground for their recreation period in his guardian's automobile, a Ford station wagon lent to him for that purpose.

Antisdale returned to the Church on the day of the accident, but he was occupied in his office. . . . Antisdale emerged from his office to see the children climbing into Fong's station wagon and several boys, including plaintiff, standing on the running boards. Antisdale then informed the children that he would take some of them in his car to relieve the congestion in the station wagon. . . . The other children remained in Fong's station wagon, plaintiff standing on the left running board and another boy standing on the right running board. . . .

During the trip the children in each vehicle were shouting and challenging the children in the other vehicle to race to the playground. Although the evidence is conflicting on this point, there is testimony that Fong and Antisdale entered into the spirit of the competition and increased the speed of their vehicles. After the vehicles turned west on Twenty-eighth Avenue, Fong pulled out to the left and endeavored to pass Antisdale, who increased the speed of his car to prevent Fong from passing. The two vehicles approached the intersection of Twenty-eighth and Isabelle Avenues in that position, Fong still unsuccessfully attempting to pass Antisdale. Antisdale stopped his car at the intersection, but Fong proceeded out into the intersection at an excessive rate of speed, still on the left-hand side of the road. Defendant Holmes was driving her car north on Isabelle Avenue and had just pulled out into the intersection when Fong drove by her. The vehicles were too close for her to stop in time and, according to her testimony, Fong made no effort to stop. Her right front fender and Fong's station wagon collided, striking plaintiff standing on the left running board.

Plaintiff's complaint was in three counts. In the first count he alleged that Fong was the agent of Antisdale and the Presbytery, that he was a passenger in Fong's car at the time of the accident, and that the accident was caused by the concurrent negligence of defendants Fong and Holmes. In the second count he alleged that Antisdale was the agent of the Presbytery, and that his negligence was a cause of the injuries to plaintiff. . . . In the third count, plaintiff alleged that Antisdale and Fong were negligent in failing to exercise proper care for the safety of the children for whom they were responsible in that they negligently permitted several of them, including plaintiff, to ride on the running boards of the two vehicles, and that such negligence was a proximate cause of plaintiff's injuries. . . .

The verdict against the Presbytery may be supported not only on Antisdale's negligence but on that of Fong as well. Civil Code section 2351 provides: "A subagent, lawfully appointed, represents the principal in like manner with the original agent. . . ." Antisdale was an agent of the Presbytery, i.e., the "original" agent, and he lawfully appointed Fong a subagent.

An agency relationship may be informally created. No particular words are necessary, nor need there be consideration. All that is required is conduct by each party manifesting acceptance of a relationship whereby one of them is to perform work for the other under the latter's direction. . . .

There is ample evidence to support a finding that Antisdale and Fong entered into such a relationship. Antisdale, as pastor of the Church was in charge of the Vacation Bible School. It was his responsibility to supervise and control the instruction and all activities connected with the school. He was in charge of the transportation of the children from the Church to the playground and of their return to the Church. He had authority to direct the activities of the children attending the school. . . .

The evidence that Fong, with Antisdale's knowledge and consent, performed duties for which the latter was responsible, that his performance of those duties was subject to Antisdale's supervision and control, and that his services could be terminated by Antisdale at any time, supports the conclusion that Fong was a subagent acting within the scope of his agency at the time of the accident. This conclusion is not negatived by the fact that Fong was not paid.

The judgment in favor of Presbytery of San Francisco is reversed, and the trial court is directed to enter judgment against Presbytery in accordance with the verdict of the jury.

CASE REVIEW QUESTIONS
1. On what basis was Fong liable to Malloy?
2. It appears from the opinion that Fong was not paid for his work for the Presbytery. How, then, could he have been an agent?
3. On what basis was Antisdale liable to Malloy?
4. On what basis was the Presbytery liable to Malloy?
5. Why wasn't Holmes liable to Malloy?

Delegation of Agency Duties

Closely related to the subagent situation is the delegation by the agent of an entire agency task to someone else. If the principal is aware of the delegation and consents to it, then a new agency relationship is formed. In the absence of this consent, however, an agent's power to delegate is extremely limited. It is generally recognized that an agent cannot delegate to another any task involving the exercise of judgment or discretion in the use of authority held for the principal's benefit.

Just what discretion means must be defined by trade customs and usages. Where the exercise of discretion is minimal and delegation by agents is common, the power to delegate may be inferred. This may be true when a principal employs a corporation for a task that is not generally thought of as involving personal service. However, when a principal deals with a partnership and, in particular, when a principal selects one of the partners to deal with, the agency may not be delegated.

For example, in the case of *W. H. Barber Agency Company v. Co-Operative Barrel Company,* the agent was the principal's exclusive sales representative for the sale of large butter tubs. The agent established a lucrative and growing business selling the tubs. In the fourth year of a five-year contract, the agent decided to change his form of business from a partnership to a corporation. The agent did not change any of the personnel or management but notified the principal of the change in his form of business. The principal claimed that the delegation by the partnership (agent) to a corporation was a breach of the agency contract and refused to do business with the corporation. In affirming a decision that supported the principal's point, the court said:

> The sole question presented and argued is whether Barber could transfer his contract to the plaintiff corporation without the consent of the defendant.
>
> Barber was defendant's sales agent, and the case is controlled by the rules governing agency, . . . The powers conferred upon an agent are based upon the confidence which the principal has in the agent's ability and integrity; and it is the universal rule that an agent cannot transfer to another powers calling for the exercise of discretion skill or judgment. . . . It is held, that, where a principal has authorized a partnership to act as his agent, the subsequent dissolution of the partnership terminates the agency, and that a partner who takes over the business cannot continue to act as such agent unless the principal authorizes him to do so.
>
> In the present case, defendant made Barber its agent. He assumed to transfer to a corporation the powers conferred upon him personally. The corporation is a separate entity controlled by a board of at least three directors, and its stockholders and officers are subject to change at any time. If it acquired Barber's rights under his contract with defendant, it would retain such rights even if Barber should entirely sever his connection with it. To permit a person, employed as an agent, to transfer his duties and powers to a corporation without the consent of his principal would involve a more radical violation of the rules governing the relation of principal and agent than to permit a partnership, employed as an agent, to devolve its powers and duties upon one of its members. Barber could no more substitute plaintiff corporation for himself as defendant's agent, without defendant's consent, than he could so substitute any other corporation or individual.

Borrowed Servants

Sometimes a master will direct or permit the servant to perform services for another. In such a situation, the servant is referred to as a **borrowed servant**. A common example of this occurs when a contractor provides heavy equipment and an operator to another contractor. If the operator commits a tort while working for the other contractor, which contractor is liable?

Liability in such a case is determined by which contractor (master) had the right to control the physical activities being performed by the operator (servant) when the tort was committed, applying the same factors as discussed in the *Massey v. Tube Art Display* case in the previous chapter. In the absence of evidence of direct control by the new contractor, it would be inferred that the operator remained subject to the right of control of the first contractor.

The case that follows involves application of the law concerning liability for the tort of a borrowed servant.

ROCKWELL v. STONE
173 A.2d 54 (Pa. 1961)

[Dr. Stone was an anesthesiologist employed by Graduate Hospital. Dr. Kaplan was a surgeon and Rockwell was his patient. Dr. Kaplan chose to perform surgery on Rockwell at Graduate Hospital and arranged his admission. He told Dr. Stone that Rockwell was to be administered a general anesthetic. Dr. Stone applied the anesthetic sodium pentothal negligently and as a result Rockwell's arm had to be amputated.

Rockwell brought a legal action against both Dr. Stone and Dr. Kaplan. He based his action against Dr. Stone on negligence and against Dr. Kaplan on respondeat superior. The jury returned a verdict against both defendants. Dr. Kaplan moved for a judgment n. o. v., arguing that he could not be held liable under the doctrine of respondeat superior because a master–servant relationship did not exist between the two doctors. The trial court judge denied the motion, and Dr. Kaplan appealed.]

BOK, Justice

As for Dr. Kaplan's responsibility for Dr. Stone's negligence, Dr. Stone testified that a surgeon could use the hospital's anesthesiologist or bring in his own. Dr. Kaplan testified that he was "the boss of the surgical end of it," and that "as long as Dr. Stone had anything to do with the anesthesia I was perfectly satisfied." He chose the hospital in which Dr. Stone worked and chose a general rather than a local anesthetic. Dr. Stone testified that Dr. Kaplan had the authority to ask or tell him what sort of anesthesia he wanted, although it was not the practice at the Graduate Hospital to do so. Dr. Kaplan said that if it was best for his patient's safety he could discontinue the operation and tell the anesthesiologist to stop giving anesthetic, particularly in minor elective surgical procedure. His words were, on the latter point:

Q. Suppose you felt that anesthesia should stop and the anesthetist felt that it should continue, and you felt that continuation would create a critical condition for your patient?

A. I would stop immediately, regardless of what he had to say, if I felt strongly that this should stop, I would stop it.

Q. And you would tell the anesthetist to stop it, wouldn't you?

A. I would.

Q. And he would stop, wouldn't he?

A. I think he would have to.

We think this points clearly to the language concerning borrowed employees in *Mature v. Angelo:* "A servant is the employee of the person who has the right of controlling the manner of his performance of the work, irrespective of whether he actually exercises that control or not."

Nor was there a conflict of evidence on the question of right of control. Dr. Kaplan and Dr. Stone did not disagree in their testimony as it has been condensed above, nor can there be doubt based on common sense that Dr. Stone acted on Dr. Kaplan's business: he had to or the surgeon could not operate. The undisputed evidence clearly shores up the instruction of the trial judge. "And in the eyes of the law, in this case, Dr. Stone was the agent for a step in the operative procedure, the anesthesia step. He was the agent of Dr. Kaplan."

It is clear, . . . that doctors are subject to the law of agency and may at the same time be agent both of another physician and of a hospital, even though the employment is not joint.

Judgment for plaintiff affirmed.

JONES, Justice (Dissenting)

Although alleged, the case at bar in my opinion presents no evidence of any direct negligence on the part of Dr. Kaplan and Dr. Kaplan's liability, if any, must be premised on the theory of vicarious liability. Stated otherwise, is Dr. Kaplan liable for malpractice under the doctrine of respondeat superior for an act of negligence which occurred, outside his presence and without his knowledge, during preoperative procedure involved in the administration of an anesthesia?

Certain factual circumstances must be noted. Dr. Kaplan neither requested nor exercised any choice in the selection of any particular anesthesiologist to administer the anesthesia. Although Dr. Kaplan, as any other surgeon, was at liberty to select any anesthesiologist he so desired, he simply indicated to Dr. Stone, the Chief of the Department of Anesthesiology, that he wanted a general anesthesia administered and relied upon Dr. Stone's professional competency for selection of the type of anesthesia and the person or persons to administer it. Such service was provided by the hospital and the compensation for such service would be billed by the hospital to the patient and would be paid by the latter directly to the hospital. The personnel of the Department were employed by, paid by and under the general control and direction of the hospital which had the sole power to dismiss such personnel.

When the incident occurred, as previously stated, Dr. Kaplan was not present nor was his presence re-

quired at that time and, while the injection and ensuing incident took place at approximately 9:45 A.M., Dr. Kaplan was unaware of it until approximately noon. . . .

In the case at bar, Dr. Kaplan neither prescribed nor was he advised of the use of sodium pentothal; he did not administer it, was not present when it was administered and, in fact, did not know of it until hours later. Moreover, he exercised no direction, control or authority over Dr. Stone . . . while in the induction room and he did not request him to administer this drug. Dr. Kaplan was simply using the hospital facilities and its personnel, a service for which Rockwell would be billed directly.

The sodium pentothal was administered outside of Dr. Kaplan's presence, in the induction room over which. . . "he was not the captain of the ship." . . . [A]t that time *only* Dr. Stone was in command. . . .

Under such circumstances, in my opinion, Dr. Kaplan could not be held liable upon any theory of respondeat superior and the judgment as to Dr. Kaplan should be reversed and judgment . . . entered in his favor.

CASE REVIEW QUESTIONS
1. Dr. Stone was a skilled professional. The court applied the doctrine of respondeat superior, which makes a master liable for the torts of a servant. In what sense can Dr. Stone be called a servant?
2. What factors does the majority opinion point out to support the conclusion that Dr. Kaplan had the right to control the physical activities of Dr. Stone when the negligence occurred?
3. What factors does the dissenting opinion point out to support the conclusion that Dr. Kaplan did not have the right to control the physical activities of Dr. Stone when the negligence occurred?

TERMINATION OF AUTHORITY

The actual authority of an agent can be terminated in two ways. Termination can occur as a result of an act of the agent or the principal or both. It can also occur because of the happening of an event that the law declares terminates the authority. Each of these ways is explained and discussed in this section of the text.

If an agent's actual authority is terminated, what will be the effect of the termination on third parties? Can they continue to rely on the agent's apparent authority? Each of these questions is also considered here.

You should note that if some, but not all, of an agent's actual authority is terminated, the agency relationship continues, but the agent has diminished authority. If all of an agent's actual authority is terminated, the agency itself is also terminated.

Termination by Act of the Parties

Between a principal and his or her agent, authority may be terminated either by the terms of their original agreement or by an act of termination by both or either of them. Authority is terminated by the terms of the original agreement if that agreement includes a condition, the occurrence of which is intended to terminate the agency, and that condition is met. If the condition is expressly included in the agreement, there is usually no problem in determining when the authority terminated.

If the parties say nothing in their original agreement about the termination of authority, it will be implied that the authority is to exist for a reasonable time under all of the circumstances. The primary circumstance to be considered is whether the agent's assignment has been completed. When it has, the agent's authority is terminated. If another person completes the agent's assignment, the agent's authority will generally terminate when the agent receives notice of the other person's performance.

For example, a contract to hire a real estate agent to sell a house may expressly state that the agent's authority will terminate when a buyer for the house has been found. Even if the contract does not expressly state such a condition, it will be implied because the agent would understand that his or her authority would terminate once a buyer was found.

Termination can also occur by an act of termination by both or either of the parties at any time, since agency is a consensual relationship. Of course, if both parties agree to end the agent's authority, the agency terminates. But termination can be accomplished by either party acting alone as well. The agent, for instance, can renounce his or her authority at any time. "I quit" is a phrase available to all agents. If the agent who quits is working under an employment contract, however, he or she may be liable to the principal for breach of contract. In such situations, the agent has the power to terminate but not the right.

The principal can also terminate the agent's authority at any time by revoking it. (Situations in which statutes may prohibit the discharge of an employee are discussed in Chapter 53.) Any act by the principal that indicates that he or she no longer wants the agent's authority to continue will constitute a revocation. The revocation takes effect when the agent receives notice of it. If the agent is working under a contract, however, the principal may be liable to the agent for breach of contract because of the revocation. In other words, as with the agent, the principal may have the power to terminate but not the right. The following case illustrates the application of this principle.

MITCHELL v. VULTURE MINING & MILLING COMPANY
55 P.2d 636 (Ariz. 1936)

McALISTER, Judge

This is an appeal by F. H. Mitchell from a judgment in favor of the Vulture Mining & Milling Company. . . .

The substance of the complaint is that in the summer of 1930 the Vulture Mining & Milling Company, a corporation, hereinafter called defendant, had an authorized capital of one million shares of the par value of one dollar each, six hundred thousand of which were treasury stock it desired to sell for the purpose of raising funds to develop its mining property. F. H. Mitchell, hereinafter called plaintiff, was an experienced mining engineer and salesman who had friends in the eastern section of the United States through whom he felt he could contact prospective purchasers. So, on or about August 10, 1930, he and the defendant entered into an agreement by which he was granted for a reasonable time "the exclusive right to sell in the eastern states of the United States the treasury stock of the defendant." It was agreed that the plaintiff would go to the Eastern States at his own expense and for a reasonable time devote his efforts exclusively to presenting the stock to prospective purchasers and making sales thereof at eighty cents a share and that he should receive as compensation therefor twenty-five per cent of the proceeds of the sales made by or through him. For the purpose of fulfilling this agreement the plaintiff went east on August 21, 1930, and expended large sums of money in an effort to sell the stock, the defendant being kept advised at all times of his activities and prospects.

On the 29th day of October, 1930, while the plaintiff was actively endeavoring to sell the shares and had reasonable prospects of completing a sale, the defendant, without advising him, granted a ten day option on the six hundred thousand shares of treasury stock to the United Verde Extension Mining Company, a corporation . . . having its . . . financial office in the state of New York. It is then averred that the option was granted to a purchaser in the Eastern States, territory in which plaintiff had been given the right to sell, that the option was thereafter exercised by the United

Verde Extension Mining Company, and that the result of this was to disable the defendant from performing its agreement [with plaintiff] and to deprive the plaintiff of the opportunity to fulfill his [agreement with defendant] and to receive compensation for his services and to reimburse himself for the monies expended by him. . . .

The defendant answered, admitting the execution of the option and its exercise by the company. It denied, however, that either act was performed in the East and alleged that the option and the sale of the stock covered thereby was made, exercised and fulfilled within the state of Arizona where the company had been authorized to and had actually carried on business for more than ten years. . . .

The contract being mutual, the giving of an option to United Verde Extension Mining Company and thus placing it beyond the power of the defendant to live up to its terms with Mitchell was just as effectively a breach as a sale by the defendant of the stock in the East, the territory the plaintiff alleged to be exclusively his, would have been. The defendant, it is true, had the power to terminate it any time it saw fit but no right to do so without subjecting itself to liability for whatever damages its act may have caused the plaintiff. It is utterly unthinkable that after he had entered into the agreement, gone east and, at an expense to himself of $2,000, devoted his entire time and effort for two months to selling the stock, the plaintiff's contractual status should have been such that the defendant could, before he had had a reasonable time in which to complete the undertaking, deprive him of the right to do so without rendering itself liable, at least, for the reasonable value of his services and reimbursement for expenditures made or incurred by him. The agreement specified no particular time in which he could make the sale but under all the authorities a reasonable time was implied. . . .

The judgment is reversed and the cause remanded for a new trial.

CASE REVIEW QUESTIONS
1. When did the court believe the agency would terminate by the terms of the agreement between Mitchell and Vulture Mining Company? Were those terms express or implied? Had termination by the terms of the contract occurred before Vulture Mining Company breached their contract with Mitchell?
2. How was the agency terminated?
3. If an agency may be terminated at any time by either party, why did the court hold that Vulture Mining Company was liable to Mitchell?

Agency Coupled with an Interest Suppose that Porter borrows money from Allan. Allan may be concerned that Porter will not pay back the money. If Porter owns property, Allan may ask Porter for a security interest, such as a mortgage, in Porter's land. The security interest will help to protect Allan since, if Porter fails to repay the money owed to Allan, Allan's security interest allows her to have the property sold and to use the proceeds from the sale to pay off Porter's debt.

Another way that Allan can protect herself is by having Porter agree to the creation of an agency relationship in which Allan has the authority to sell Porter's property if he fails to repay the debt. A possible problem with such an arrangement would be that, under the general rule discussed earlier, Porter could terminate Allan's authority at any time by revoking it. This would leave Allan without the security that she sought.

To protect people in a position like Allan's, an exception to the general rule that allows either party to terminate authority at any time has been created. This exception is called an **agency coupled with an interest.** A common situation in which this exception applies occurs when the principal owes a duty to the agent and the agency is created to benefit the agent by securing performance of the principal's duty. In our example, Porter owes Allan a duty to repay the debt and the agency was created to secure the repayment. Therefore, Allan's authority to sell the property if the debt is not paid cannot be revoked by Porter because an agency coupled with an interest has been created.

This exception is not applicable to situations in which the principal's only duty is to pay the agent for services rendered. For example, if Adams is a commission salesman for Powers and is to be paid out of the proceeds of a sale he makes, there is not an agency coupled with an interest. This is so because the agency was created for the purpose of selling Powers' goods, not to protect Adams. Therefore, Powers can terminate Adam's authority at any time, subject, of course, to the possibility of a suit for breach of contract by Allan.

Termination by Operation of Law

The occurrence of certain events can cause termination of an agent's authority. Specific events having this effect are the loss of the principal's capacity to contract (e.g., when the principal is legally declared bankrupt or insane) and the death of either the principal or the agent.

More generally, authority is terminated when there is such a change in the circumstances that were expected when the agency was created that the agent should realize that the principal no longer wishes him or her to act. For example, if an agent learns of a change in the law that would make performance of his or her authority illegal, the authority is terminated. Similarly, if a change in business climate greatly decreased the value of the principal's property, a selling agent should realize that the authority to sell the property is terminated.

Another change in circumstances that will terminate authority is the destruction of the subject matter of the agency. A difficult determination for a court can arise when there has been only a partial destruction of the subject matter. The usual test is that there must be such an alteration in the subject matter that it creates a material change in the agency. That is, the subject matter must be so altered that it is not the same as it was when the agency was created.

For example, suppose a home owner hires a realtor to sell her house and land. The realtor finds a willing buyer, but before a contract of sale is entered into, the house is totally destroyed by fire. Later, the home owner sells the land on which the house previously stood to the same buyer. Under these circumstances the realtor would not be entitled to a commission for the sale because the authority to sell the house and land was terminated when the subject matter of the agency (the house and land) was materially altered (the house was destroyed by fire). The agency was materially altered because undeveloped land does not have the same value and is not subject to the same uses as land on which there is a house. On the other hand, if the house had only been slightly damaged by the fire and had then been sold to the same buyer, the realtor would be entitled to a commission. In this case, there would not have been a sufficient enough change in the subject matter of the agency to cause a material change in the agency.

The Effect of Termination on Third Parties

Termination of authority by an act of both or either of the parties or by the operation of law deprives the agent only of actual authority (i.e., the authority actually given to the agent by the principal). The agent's apparent authority, however, continues until a third party knows or should know of the termination. This means that, under certain circumstances, the agent can bind the principal to a contract with a third party even though the agent's actual authority has been terminated.

Most states and the Restatement take the position that death or incapacity of the principal are events of such notoriety that it can be assumed that all third parties will know of the termination of the agent's authority. Thus, if a principal dies, and the agent afterwards contracts with a third party on behalf of the principal, the third party cannot enforce the contract against the principal even though neither the agent nor the third party had heard about the death. The unsuspecting agent, however, would be liable to the third party for breach of the warranty of authority (see Chapter 32).

If the agent's actual authority is terminated in a way other than by the death or incapacity of the principal, the principal is required to notify third parties of the termination in order to terminate the agent's apparent authority. With respect to third parties with whom the agent had not dealt prior to the termination of authority, notice of the agent's termination of authority may be given by advertising the fact in a newspaper of general circulation in the place where the agency operates or by some other manner reasonably calculated to give notice to such third parties.

A third party who had previously dealt with or had begun to deal with the agent, however, must be given actual notice of termination of the agent's authority. This means that the notice must be given to the third party personally, mailed to his or her business, or posted in a place where, in view of the business customs between the parties, the third party could reasonably be expected to look for such notice. If the principal fails to give notice of the termination and a third party who had previously dealt with the agent enters into a contract with the principal through the agent without otherwise having had notice of the termination, the principal is bound to the contract. Although the following case is old, it accurately reflects the law on this issue today.

BURCH v. AMERICAN GROCERY COMPANY
53 S.E. 1008 (Ga. 1906)

EVANS, Judge

The American Grocery Company sued J. B. Burch for a balance alleged to be due. . . . The only item in dispute was one of May 8, 1903, for a certain quantity of tobacco. The defendant contended that this item was purchased by his clerk, Mike Burch, after he had left his employment, and that he neither authorized nor ratified the purchase nor received the tobacco. On the other hand, the plaintiff insisted that Mike Burch was the general agent of the defendant in the management of his store, and as such, on previous occasions, had ordered goods of plaintiff on defendant's account, and that the plaintiff, without notice that Mike Burch was no longer employed by the defendant, took the order in the defendant's name and shipped the goods to the defendant, as was usual in the past transactions. . . .

The plaintiff's salesman called at the commissary of the defendant and asked for Mike Burch, as he had always done, and was informed that Mike Burch was about three miles away, superintending the putting down of a sawmill. There he found him and took the order for the merchandise. It was shipped to the defendant. The defendant testified that the goods were never received by him, but were taken possession of

by Mike Burch without his knowledge. Upon these facts the jury returned a verdict in favor of the plaintiff for the value of the goods, which verdict the trial judge refused to set aside. . . .

[The applicable law for this case has been stated as follows:]

> Whenever a general agency has been established for any purpose, all persons who have dealt with such agent, or who have known of the agency and are apt to deal with him, have a right to presume that such authority will continue until it is shown to have been terminated in one way or another; and they also have a right to anticipate that if the principal revokes such authority, they will be given due notice thereof. It is a general rule of law, therefore, upon which there seems to be no conflict of authorities, that all acts of a general agent within the scope of his authority, as respects third persons, will be binding on the principal, even though done after revocation, unless notice of such revocation has been given to those persons who have had dealings with and who are apt to have other dealings with the agent upon the strength of his former authority.

In the present case no express notice was shown, and the controlling issue was whether or not the plaintiff had "implied notice" that there had been a revocation of the agency. . . . The only circumstance upon which the defendant could rely as suggesting the necessity of making inquiry whether the agency had been terminated was that the order for the goods was given to the plaintiff's salesman three miles from the defendant's store, where the agent had been employed. The defendant was engaged in the sawmill business, and his "commissary" was run in connection with that business, as an adjunct to it, and not as a wholly independent enterprise. When the order for the goods was taken, Mike Burch, who still assumed to act as the defendant's agent, was superintending the erection of a sawmill. That it did not belong to the defendant or was not to be used in connection with his business was not self-apparent, nor was the fact that Mike Burch was not at the time engaged in his customary duties at the commissary calculated to put the plaintiff's salesman on notice that he had left the service of the defendant. Moreover, the salesman had first driven by the store of the defendant and inquired for Mike Burch, who had theretofore been in charge of it. Instead of being notified that Mike Burch was no longer in the defendant's employ, the salesman was told where Mike Burch could be found. . . .

The jury, after considering all facts and circumstances brought to light at the trial, found against the contention of the defendant that due caution and prudence on the part of the plaintiff's salesman . . . ought to have suggested to him the propriety of making inquiry, if he did not divine the truth. . . . The defendant was admittedly at fault, having failed to take any steps to give notice to the plaintiff, whereas the plaintiff had not omitted to perform any legal duty owing to the defendant, and the plaintiff's salesman admittedly acted in entire good faith. . . .

Justice to parties dealing with agents requires that the rule requiring notice in such cases should not be departed from on slight grounds, or dubious or equivocal circumstances substituted in place of notice. If notice was not in fact given, and loss happens to the defendant, it is attributable to his neglect of a most usual and necessary precaution. The verdict of the jury appears to be in accord both with the strict law and the common justice of the case. . . .

Judgment affirmed.

CASE REVIEW QUESTIONS

1. If Mike Burch's authority had terminated because of the death of J. B. Burch, what would have been the outcome of the case?
2. What action should J. B. Burch have taken when Mike Burch left his employment in order to protect himself from being bound to contracts by Mike Burch?
3. If the salesman had known that Mike Burch was no longer employed by J. B. Burch, why would that knowledge have affected the rights of American Grocery Company?
4. After the decision in this case, what rights, if any, does J. B. Burch have against Mike Burch?

REVIEW QUESTIONS

1. Give examples not presented in the text in which notification or payment to an agent would be treated as notification or payment to the principal.
2. If a student is hired by the manager of a dining hall to work as a dishwasher and is paid by the university, is the student an agent or a subagent of the university? What difference might it make?
3. What is the legal standard the courts use for determining which master is liable in a borrowed servant situation?

4. What is meant when it is said that in some situations a principal or agent has the power but not the right to terminate the agent's authority?

5. Local newspapers usually print obituaries of people in the area who have recently died. In the context of this chapter, of what use could the obituaries be to a person who operates a business?

CASE PROBLEMS

1. Jackson wished to rent a car from Firstrate Truck Rental Company In discussing the rental with Hart, Firstrate's agent, Jackson said that he could only return the truck on Sunday. Hart said that trucks could not be returned on Sunday because Firstrate was closed on that day and the fenced-in lot in which they kept their trucks would be locked. Hart, however, said he would ask Miller, who lived next door to Firstrate, if he would park the truck in his driveway overnight if Jackson returned it on Sunday. Miller said he would, and Hart instructed Jackson to return the truck to Miller. Jackson brought the truck to Miller as arranged. Miller, however, stole the truck and has disappeared. If Firstrate brings a legal action against Jackson based on his failure to return the truck to Firstrate, on what basis can Jackson defend? Who will win the case? Explain.

2. Beech Aircraft Corporation (Beech) designs, manufactures, and sells aircraft and supporting systems. It has a government contract for the design of fuel systems for the Titan II rocket program. The Titan II is a liquid-fueled rocket and the propellant used is extremely toxic and corrosive. Killian, an agent of Beech, met with Frabbe, an agent of Flexible Tubing Corporation (Flexible), to discuss the purchase by Beech of tubing that could be used in the rocket. At this meeting, Killian informed Frabbe of the specific standards the hose would have to meet. Frabbe responded that Flexible produced a hose that would meet those standards. When the contract of sale was drawn up between Beech and Flexible and signed by Killian and Frabbe on behalf of their companies, it described the hose to be sold but did not mention the standards the hose would have to meet.

When Beech received the hoses, it tested them. They were not able to meet the standards that Killian had told Frabbe about. Beech brought a legal action against Flexible to rescind the contract. Flexible argued that Beech had received the hoses described in the contract and that it (Flexible) had not known anything about the statements of Frabbe when he negotiated the contract. Who will win the case? Explain.

3. Thormyer is Director of the Department of Highways for the state of Ohio. Ohio law provides that the director of a department has sole authority to hire, suspend, or discharge civil service employees. Reiners has been authorized by Thormyer to handle all civil service matters within the Department and to sign Thormyer's name to any document concerning any matter within Reiners' authority. Reiners wrote a letter to Kendrick, a civil service employee in the Department, suspending him from employment for 30 days. Reiners signed Thormyer's name to the letter. Thormyer had not told Reiners to send the letter and, in fact, knew nothing about it. On what grounds can Kendrick bring a legal action against Thormyer seeking to have his suspension declared void? How might Thormyer defend? Who will win the case? Explain.

4. Dixie-Ohio Express Company (D.O.X.), a common carrier, had a contract with Aluminum Company of America (Alcoa) to load and transport aluminum. Wilson, a driver for D.O.X., was instructed to pick up a load of aluminum from Alcoa's plant in Tennessee and deliver it to points in Ohio. At the Alcoa plant, the truck was loaded by employees of Alcoa who were supervised by an Alcoa foreman. Wilson was also present and advised the Alcoa employees how to place the aluminum in the truck. The aluminum was placed in the truck negligently. As a result, the load shifted while Wilson was driving to Ohio, causing the truck to crash. Wilson was killed. If his estate brings a legal action against Alcoa, on what basis can Alcoa defend? Who will win the case? Explain.

5. Foremost Realty, Inc., is a real estate company that also buys and sells real property for its own account. Hobson purchased a ranch from Foremost. The terms were 10 percent down with the balance payable over a 25-year period. Foremost held a mortgage to secure Hobson's payments. After several years of profitable operation of the ranch, Hobson had two successive bad years. As a result, he defaulted on his mortgage. Foremost did not want to foreclose, so it offered to allow Hobson to remain on the ranch and suspend the payment schedule until Foremost could sell the property at a reasonable price. However, Foremost insisted that it be appointed as the irrevocable and exclusive agent for the sale of the property. Although Hobson agreed, he subsequently became dissatisfied with Foremost's efforts to sell the ranch and gave Foremost notice in writing terminating the agency. Foremost then entered into a contract on behalf of Hobson to sell the ranch to Williams. When Hobson refused to honor the contract, Williams brought a legal action for breach of contract. On what basis may Hobson defend? Who will win the case? Explain. (Adapted from CPA Examination Question 5b, *Business Law,* May 1980.)

6. Margaret Berry gave a power of attorney to her niece, Irene Montanye, giving the niece authority to handle Berry's financial affairs. Shortly thereafter, Berry suffered a stroke which caused her to go into a coma. The day after Berry was admitted to the hospital in a coma, Montanye entered into a substantial financial transaction on behalf of Berry that benefitted Ann Scully. Berry never regained consciousness and died about two months later. People interested in her estate brought a legal action seeking to rescind the transaction made by Montanye that had benefitted Scully. Who will win the case? Explain.

7. Osborne owned and operated a small plastics manufacturing business which served businesses in the north central Indiana area where Osborne was located. He employed a traveling salesman, Seimer, who was authorized not only to make sales but also to collect up to $500 in payments from customers. After two years, Osborne fired Seimer. He ran an advertisement in a local newspaper the same day which read:

> Seimer, general sales agent of Osborne Plastics, was discharged from his employment as of this date.

Seimer was angry was Osborne. He was also desperate for money, so he went to Chestertown, a good customer of Osborne, and made a sale in the amount of $450. As he had done many times in the past, Chesterton paid cash to Seimer on the spot. Seimer was never heard from again, and Osborne refused to deliver the order that Chesterton had given to Seimer. If Chesterton brings legal action against Osborne, who will win? Explain.

PART VII

PARTNERSHIP LAW

35

PARTNERSHIP CREATION

In this chapter, we will discuss the circumstances in which the courts will find that a partnership has been created and will therefore impose certain rights and duties on the partners. In partnership law, as well as in some other areas of the law, uniformity among the states is desirable. Many partnerships do business in more than one state. If they were subject to different laws in each state, an unnecessary element of complexity would exist. To promote uniformity in state laws, the National Conference of Commissioners on Uniform State Laws — a body of lawyers, judges, and law professors — meets yearly to draft uniform laws in a variety of legal areas and make them available for adoption by state legislatures. Today, almost all 50 states have adopted the Uniform Partnership Act with few changes in the language originally proposed in 1914. Throughout the next two chapters, we will use the Uniform Partnership Act, which we will refer to as the UPA, in our presentation of material. The UPA is reproduced in Appendix C.

As you read this chapter and the next, you should note that, even though partnership law is mostly statutory, case law is very important for interpreting the statutory language. Appellate cases, better than any other source, provide an understanding of the circumstances in which the legal system will act to enforce the duties of partners and partnerships.

PARTNERSHIP CREATION

A Partnership As A Separate Legal Entity

A **partnership** is defined in §6 of the UPA as follows:

> A partnership is an association of two or more persons to carry on as co-owners a business for profit.

One of the difficult issues in partnership law arises from the use of the word "association" in the definition of a partnership. The issue is whether a partnership is a legal entity that exists separate from the partners themselves. Is it like a corporation, which is a distinct legal entity, or is it like a proprietorship, in which the business and personal assets of the owner are not separated?

The UPA does not answer this question, but as a general rule, a partnership is recognized by most courts today as a separate legal entity for limited purposes. More specifically, a partnership can contract, can own both personal and real property, and can sue and be sued in its own name. Also, the Internal Revenue Code requires that partnerships file income tax returns (for information purposes only), and the bankruptcy statutes treat partnerships as separate legal entities.

A very important exception to the treatment of a partnership as a separate legal entity is that a partner may not shield his or her personal assets — savings accounts, home, automobile, and so forth — from the business creditors of the partnership. Thus, if a partnership is unable to pay its debts, the creditors of the partnership may sue and collect from the individual partner as well as from the partnership. Indeed, most suits against partnerships also join the partners as individuals so that any judgment won may be recovered against either.

The Legal Character of a Partner

The UPA definition states that a partnership "is an association of . . . persons." Section 2 the UPA states that the word "person" includes "individuals, partnerships, corporations, and other associations." Thus, the UPA permits people to be partners with other people or with any other legal form of business association.

In the nineteenth century, some state legislatures would not permit a corporation to become a partner. Their position was that a corporation must be managed by a board of directors that is responsible to the shareholders. This requirement was thought to be incompatible with the fact that a corporation-partner would be subject to the control of the other partners.

Today, many legislatures and courts will allow a corporation to be a partner, especially when the purpose of the partnership is narrow enough to limit the power of the other partners to control the corporation-partner or when the corporation's authority to act for the partnership is eliminated as part of the partnership agreement. The point to be remembered is that state partnership law does not preclude corporations from becoming partners; state corporation law, however, may not permit a corporation to become a partner because control of the corporation would then be held by its partners rather than by its own board of directors.

Legal Capacity of a Partner

To be a **partner**, a party must have the legal capacity to contract (see Chapter 14). Generally, minors, persons declared insane, or persons deprived of their civil rights, such as those in prison for a felony, lack the legal capacity to contract. Minors' contracts, however, are treated differently from those of insane persons or others lacking capacity to contract in many jurisdictions. Minors' contracts are usually voidable at the option of the minor, whereas the contracts of insane persons are usually void and unenforceable by either party. Therefore, although a minor may sometimes become a partner if he or she wishes, his or her obligations to the partnership and its creditors may be repudiated at his or her option in most jurisdictions.

In some jurisdictions, cases in the early twentieth century held that husband – wife partnerships were not permitted because the potential for disagreement and consequent litigation was considered to be incompatible with the family relationship. It is doubtful, though, that these courts would take a similar stand today. Similarly, older cases held it improper for a trustee to invest in a partnership because it was too risky. Today, such an investment by a trustee will be allowed as long as it is reasonably prudent.

The Meaning of "Co-Owners"

The definition of a partnership also states that partners must carry on their business "as co-owners." Although one partner may act for or under the control of another partner, a partnership exists if there is an intent to do business as co-owners, that is, if there is an intent to co-own.

What is meant, though, by the phrase "intent to co-own"? An important element of ownership is the power of ultimate control of that which is owned. To be a co-owner, then, means to have the power of ultimate control but to share it with one or more co-owners. Control of a business means the right to make management decisions. Therefore, a partner will usually have the ultimate, though shared, right to make management decisions. Although the shared right to control is not an essential element of co-ownership, its presence is an important indication that co-ownership was intended. The courts often look for such a shared right in determining whether or not a partnership exists.

Another important factor in determining intent to co-own is the sharing of profits. Section 7(4) of the UPA states:

> The receipt by a person of a share of the profits of a business is prima facie evidence that he is a partner in the business, but no such inference shall be drawn if such profits were received in payment:
> (a) As a debt by installments or otherwise,
> (b) As wages of an employee or rent to a landlord,
> (c) An an annuity . . . ,
> (d) As interest on a loan, though the amount of payments vary with the profits of the business,
> (e) As the consideration for the sale of good-will of a business. . . .

In addition to sharing control and profits, other evidence of an intent to co-own may be found in the joint ownership of property and in the joint obligation to contribute capital to the enterprise.

Business Association for Profit

The UPA requires that a partnership be a business carried on for profit. This means that associations created primarily for charitable, religious, fraternal, or social purposes are not partnerships even though they may share in the revenue of a fund-raising project or devote this revenue to furthering their purposes.

Need for a Written Partnership Agreement

In most instances, partnerships are created by a document, called a *partnership agreement* or *articles of partnership,* that clearly states the intent of the partners to co-own the enterprise. But even if there is no writing, a partnership exists in the eyes of the law where the circumstances surrounding an association meet the requirements of the UPA definition.

In a few instances, a contract or a writing of some kind is required by the Statute of Frauds (see Chapter 13). The Statute of Frauds requires contracts for the sale of an interest in real estate or agreements that cannot be performed in less than one year to be in writing. So, if a partnership confers authority on a partner to buy or sell real property, the authority should be put in writing. If it is not and the partner contracts with a third person to buy or sell real property, the contract may not be enforced by or against the partnership. Also, if the partners intend the partnership to exist for longer than one year, they should put their agreement in writing.

Whether or not a written agreement is required by the Statute of Frauds, it is always best for the partners to put their agreement in writing. By so doing, they can consider and plan for events that may occur in the future. For instance, what will happen to the partnership if a partner dies? What will happen if business goes bad and losses are incurred? These types of issues should be resolved before a partnership is formed and the agreements about them should be put in writing.

Two cases follow in which courts had to decide whether a partnership existed. In the first case, there was no written agreement, but the court decided that a partnership existed. In the second case, there was a written agreement, but the court nonetheless concluded that no partnership existed. See if you can determine why the courts decided as they did in each case.

ZAJAC v. HARRIS
415 S.W.2d 593 (Ark. 1967)

[George Harris brought a legal action against Carl Zajac to have Zajac account for the profits and assets of a partnership that Harris alleged existed between them for two years. Zajac denied that a partnership existed, arguing instead that Harris was merely an employee in a business owned by Zajac. The trial court agreed with Harris that a partnership existed. Zajac appealed.]

SMITH, Justice

The business association that is known in the law as a partnership is not one that can be defined with precision. To the contrary, a partnership is a contractual relationship that may vary, in form and substance, in an almost infinite variety of ways. The draftsmen of the controlling statute, the Uniform Partnership Act, tacitly acknowledged that fact by stating only in the most general language an assortment of rules that are to be considered in determining whether a partnership exists. . . .

In the case at bar there is the . . . consideration that these two laymen went into business together without consulting a lawyer or attempting to put their agreement into writing. It is apparent from the testimony that neither man had any conscious or deliberate intention of entering into a particular legal relationship. Our problem is that of determining from the record as a whole whether the association they agreed upon was a partnership or an employer-employee relationship.

In the salvage operation now in controversy the parties bought wrecked automobiles from insurance companies and either rebuilt them for resale or cannibalized them by reusing or reselling the parts. Harris, the plaintiff, testified that he and Zajac agreed to go into business together, splitting the profits equally— except that Harris was to receive one fourth of the proceeds from any parts sold by him. Harris borrowed $9,000 from a bank, upon the security of property that he owned, and placed the money in a bank account that he used in buying cars for the firm. The profits were divided from time to time as the cars were resold, so that Harris's capital was used and reused. He identified checks totalling more than $73,000 that he signed in making purchases for the business.

Zajac, by contrast, took the position that Harris was merely an employee working for a commission of one half the profits realized from cars that Harris himself had bought. Zajac denied that he had ever agreed that Harris would spend his own money in buying cars. ''I told him, when you go out there, when you bid on a car, make a note that I will pay for it.'' We have no doubt, however, that Harris did use his own money in the venture and that Zajac knew that such expenditures were being made.

Counsel for Zajac put much stress on their client's controlling voice in the management of the business. Zajac and his wife and their accountant had charge of the books and records. No partnership income tax return was ever filed. Harris was ostensibly treated as an employee, in that federal withholding and Social Security taxes were paid upon his share of the profits. The firm also carried workmen's compensation insurance for Harris's protection. In our opinion, however, any inferences that might ordinarily be drawn from these bookkeeping entries are effectively rebutted by the undisputed fact that Harris, apart from being able to sign his name, was unable to read or write. There is no reason to believe that he appreciated the significance of the accounting practices now relied upon by Zajac.

We attach much weight to Zajac's candid admissions . . . that Zajac paid Harris one half of the profits derived from cars that Zajac bought with his own money and sold by his own efforts. Zajac had insisted from the outset that Harris was working upon a commission basis, but that view cannot be reconciled with Harris's admitted right to receive his share of the profits derived from business conducted by Zajac alone.

There is no real dispute between the parties about the governing principles of law. The ultimate question is whether the two men intended to become partners, as that term is used in the law. . . . Harris's receipt of a share of the net profits is prima facie evidence that he was a partner, unless the money was paid to him as wages. . . . He invested, as we have seen, substantial sums of his own money in the acquisition of cars for the firm. Zajac concedes that Harris was entitled to a share of the profits from transactions that Harris certainly did not handle on a commission basis. . . . [It] does not appear that the [trial court judge] was wrong in deciding that a partnership existed.

Affirmed.

SHELDON v. LITTLE
15 A.2d 574 (Vt. 1940)

[Adelaide Sheldon, the plaintiff, brought a legal action against Russell Little, the defendant, seeking a judgment for money allegedly owed to her. Little moved to dismiss the complaint on the grounds that the legal action brought by Sheldon should not be for money owed but should, instead, be for a "formal account," that is a legal action seeking a settlement of accounts between Sheldon and Little as partners. Sheldon argued that Little's motion should be denied because no partnership had been formed between the two. The trial court denied the motion. Little appealed.]

BUTTLES, Justice

On March 5, 1925, the parties executed a written agreement providing for the consolidation of their two insurance agencies. Thereafter the consolidated business was conducted in accordance with such agreement until October 1, 1932, when the parties ceased to do business together under such agreement or in any other way. During all of the time that the business was so conducted it was actively managed by the defendant [Little] who took general charge of the same, kept the books and handled the finances. Meanwhile the plaintiff [Sheldon] was away much of the time and took no active part in the business except that during the year 1932 she gave it some attention and participated in its management. At the end of each year except 1932 the defendant submitted to the plaintiff a written report or statement purporting to give certain data regarding the business for that year. . . .

[The parties'] written agreement provided that the agencies, after being consolidated, should be run as the property of the plaintiff and under the name of the Sheldon Agency; that the defendant should have the supervision and management of said agency, bringing to the Sheldon office the books, files, papers, and other personal property previously used by him in his own agency and continue there the general business of the consolidated agencies, devoting his entire working time to the management and development thereof; that the plaintiff might give such time to the management of the business as she cared to give from time to time, but should be under no obligation at any time to give the same her personal attention and care; that from the gross income of the business there should be paid the running expenses including rent, heat, light, office supplies, stenographer and other incidental expenses usual in the conduct of such a business, and that the net profits after the payment of such expenses

should be equally divided between the parties to the agreement.

The question for determination is whether the plaintiff and defendant were partners or sustained some other relation to each other. Where the rights of the parties . . . are concerned, and no question as to third parties is involved, the criterion to determine whether the contract is one of partnership or not must be: What did the parties intend by the contract which they made as between themselves? . . . This intention may be shown by their express agreement or inferred from their conduct and dealings with one another. But we have here no indication of the intention of the parties other than their written agreement, so that their intention is to be ascertained by a construction of that writing.

This Court has recently said that the indispensable constituent of a partnership is that the parties shall be jointly interested in the profits and affected by the losses of the business. . . . Such joint interest may result even though one party furnishes the capital or stock and the other contributes labor and skill. . . . But there is a clear distinction between agreements whereby the parties have a specific interest in the profits themselves as profits, and agreements which give to the person sought to be charged not a specific interest in the business or profits but a stipulated proportion of the proceeds as compensation for his labor and services. The former constitute a partnership but the latter do not. . . .

In the case we are considering by the terms of the agreement the business was to be run as the property of the plaintiff; no substantial increase in expenses of management could be incurred by the defendant as manager except with the approval of the plaintiff; the plaintiff could terminate the agreement at any time, resume control of the business and discharge the defendant as manager by paying him a sum equal to one half of the earnings for another year; the plaintiff could sell the business at any time, but before selling to another she was required to offer it to the defendant at a price to be based on the business done by the agency during the year 1924; in case of plaintiff's death the defendant was to have a similar option to purchase the business from plaintiff's personal representatives. Clearly it was the intent of the parties that the plaintiff should have the sole proprietary interest in the business and in the profits resulting therefrom before they were divided. The defendant received a portion of the profits not as profits, but as compensation for his services as manager of the plaintiff's business. We hold that the parties were not partners and there was no error in the denial of the defendant's motion as made.

Affirmed.

CASE COMMENT

You should have noticed that the plaintiff in the *Zajac* case was seeking a formal account from the defendant and that the defendant in the *Sheldon* case was arguing that the plaintiff should have sought a formal account. As used in partnership law, a formal account (sometimes called an accounting) is a remedy that may be given by a court by which the court orders that a comprehensive investigation of the transactions of the partnership and a complete statement of the partnership accounts be made. The circumstances in which a partner is entitled to a formal account will be discussed later in this chapter.

CASE REVIEW QUESTIONS

1. In the *Zajac* case, what facts did the court rely on in reaching its conclusion that a partnership existed?
2. Why do you think it was advantageous for Harris to establish that a partnership existed between him and Zajac?
3. In the *Sheldon* case, what facts did the court rely on in reaching its conclusion that a partnership did not exist?
4. Do you think the decisions in the *Zajac* case and the *Sheldon* case are consistent with one another? Explain.

The most conventional way to establish a partnership is for the parties to sign a contractual agreement declaring their intent to form a partnership. This agreement, customarily referred to as a *partnership agreement* or *articles of partnership,* may be as simple or complex as the parties desire. We have reproduced a rather simple partnership agreement in Figure 35-1. You should read it carefully. Reference to this agreement will be made throughout the remaining discussion of partnership law.

RIGHTS AND DUTIES OF PARTNERS

If a partnership exists, certain rights and duties are imposed on the partners by the UPA. Rights and duties can also be created by agreement among the

Partnership Agreement

AGREEMENT made June 4, 1973, between John O'Connell and Harry Jones, both of New York, New York.

1. Name and business. The parties hereby form a partnership under the name of Ace Advertising Co. to conduct a general advertising business. The principal office of the business shall be in New York, New York.
2. Term. The partnership shall begin on June 4, 1973, and shall continue until terminated as herein provided.
3. Capital. The capital of the partnership shall be contributed in cash by the partners as follows:

John O'Connell	$20,000
Harry Jones	$20,000

   A separate capital acount shall be maintained for each partner. Neither partner shall withdraw any part of his capital account. . . .

   Upon the demand of either partner, the capital accounts of the partners shall be maintained at all times in the proportions in which the partners share in the profits and losses of the partnership.
4. Profit and loss. The net profits of the partnership shall be divided equally between the partners and the net losses shall be borne equally by them. A separate income account shall be maintained for each partner. Partnership profits and losses shall be charged or credited to the separate income account of each partner. If a partner has no credit balance in his income account, losses shall be charged to his capital account.
5. Salaries and drawings. Neither partner shall receive any salary for services rendered to the partnership. Each partner may, from time to time, withdraw the credit balance in his income account. No additional share of profits shall inure to either partner by reason of his capital or income account being in excess of the capital or income account of the other.
6. Interest. No interest shall be paid on the initial contributions to the capital of the partnership or on any subsequent contributions of capital.
7. Management, duties, and restrictions. The partners shall have equal rights in the management of the partnership business, and each partner shall devote his entire time to the conduct of the business. . . . Without the consent of the other partner neither partner shall on behalf of the partnership borrow or lend money, or make, deliver or accept any commercial paper, or execute any mortgage, security agreement, bond, or lease, or purchase or contract to purchase, or sell or contract to sell any property for or of the partnership other than the type of property bought and sold in the regular course of its business. Neither partner shall, except with the consent of the other partner, assign, mortgage, grant a security interest in, or sell his share in the partnership or in its capital assets or property, or enter into any agreement as a result of which any person shall become interested with him in the partnership, or do any act detrimental to the best interests of the partnership or which would make it impossible to carry on the ordinary business of the partnership.
8. Banking. All funds of the partnership shall be deposited in its name in such checking account or accounts as shall be designated by the partners. All withdrawals therefrom are to be made upon checks signed by either partner.
9. Books. The partnership books shall be maintained at the principal office of the partnership,

FIGURE 35-1

A Partnership Agreement

and each partner shall at all times have access thereto. The books shall be kept on a fiscal year basis, commencing July 1 and ending June 30, and shall be closed and balanced at the end of each fiscal year. An audit shall be made as of the closing date.

10. Voluntary termination. The partnership may be dissolved at any time by agreement of the partners, in which event the partners shall proceed with reasonable promptness to liquidate the business of the partnership. The partnership name shall be sold with the other assets of the business. The assets of the partnership business shall be used and distributed in the following order: (a) to pay or provide for the payment of all partnership liabilities and liquidating expenses and obligations; (b) to equalize the income accounts of the partners; (c) to discharge the balance of the income accounts of the partners; (d) to equalize the capital accounts of the partners, and (e) to discharge the balance of the capital accounts of the partners.

11. Retirement. Either partner shall have the right to retire from the partnership at the end of any fiscal year. Written notice of intention to retire shall be served upon the other partner at the office of the partner at the office of the partnership at least three months before the end of the fiscal year. The retirement of either partner shall have no effect upon the continuance of the partnership business. The remaining partner shall have the right either to purchase the retiring partner's interest in the partnership or to terminate and liquidate the partnership business. If the remaining partner elects to purchase the interest of the retiring partner, he shall serve notice in writing of such election upon the retiring partner at the office of the partnership within two months after receipt of his notice of intention to retire.

(a) If the remaining partner elects to purchase the interest of the retiring partner in the partnership, the purchase price and method of payment shall be the same as stated in paragraph 12 with reference to the purchase of a decedent's interest in the partnership.

(b) If the remaining partner does not elect to purchase the interest of the retiring partner in the partnership, the partners shall proceed with reasonable promptness to liquidate the business of the partnership. The procedure as to liquidation and distribution of the assets of the partnership business shall be the same as stated in paragraph 10 with reference to voluntary termination.

12. Death. Upon the death of either partner, the surving partner shall have the right either to purchase the interest of the decedent in the partnership or to terminate and liquidate the partnership business. If the surviving partner elects to purchase the decedent's interest, he shall service notice in writing of such election, within three months after the death of the decedent, upon the executor or administrator of the decedent, or, if at the time of such election no legal representative has been appointed, upon any one of the known legal heirs of the decedent at the last known address of such heir.

(a) If the surviving partner elects to purchase the interest of the decedent in the partnership, the purchase price shall be equal to the decedent's capital account as at the date of his death plus the decedent's income account as at the end of the prior fiscal year, increased by his share of partnership profits or decreased by his share of partnership losses for the period from the beginning of the fiscal year in which his death occurred until the end of the calendar month in which his death occurred, and decreased by withdrawals charged to his income account during such period. No allowance shall be made for goodwill, trade name, patents, or other intangible assets, except as those assets have been reflected on the partnership books immediately prior to the decedent's death; but the survivor shall nevertheless be entitled to use the trade name of the partnership. The purchase price shall be paid without interest in four semi-annual installments beginning six months after the end of the calendar month in which the decedent's death occurred.

(b) If the surviving partner does not elect to purchase the interest of the decedent in the partnership, he shall proceed with reasonable promptness to liquidate the business of the partnership. The surviving partner and the estate of the deceased partner shall share equally in the profits and losses of the business during the period of liquidation, except that the decedent's estate shall not be liable for losses in excess of the decedent's interest in the partnership at the time of his death. No compensation shall be paid to the surviving partner for his services in liquidation. Except as herein otherwise stated, the procedure as to liquidation and distribution of the assets of the partnership business shall be the same as stated in paragraph 10 with reference to voluntary termination.

In witness whereof the parties have signed this agreement.

s/ ....

John O'Connell

s/ ....

Harry Jones

Source: *Current Legal Forms with Tax Analyses,* Vol. 1, Matthew Bender, 1975, p. 1-1004 Form 1.01. Copyright © 1975 by Matthew Bender & Co., Inc., and reprinted from Rabkin & Johnson *Current Legal Forms* with permission from the publisher.

---

partners. Most of the rights and duties imposed by the UPA can be altered by agreement among the partners, but some cannot. As you read the remaining sections of this chapter, you should note which rights and duties are subject to contrary agreement by the partners and which are not.

The first three sections that follow explain three *property* rights of partners. Section 24 of the UPA provides:

The property rights of a partner are (1) his rights in specific partnership property, (2) his interest in the partnership, and (3) his right to participate in the management.

In the last two sections, other rights and duties of partners are discussed.

Rights in Partnership Property

Partnership Property The initial capital of a partnership consists of the property contributed to the partnership by the partners. These contributions may take the form of cash or other personal or real property. Not all the partners need make a contribution, however. It is not necessary to contribute capital to the partnership in order to become a partner.

All property originally contributed to and all property subsequently contributed to or acquired by the partnership is **partnership property** [UPA §8(1)]. If there is a dispute over whether an individual partner or the partnership owns certain property, the intent of the partners controls. It is sometimes difficult, however, to ascertain this intent.

The best evidence of the partners' intent, at least with regard to the original capital contributions, is the partnership agreement. If the partnership agreement does not provide an answer, other evidence will be looked to. For example, if partnership funds were used to acquire property, the law presumes that it belongs to the partnership even though it may be held in the name of one of the partners rather than the partnership [UPA §8(2)]. Property held in the name of the partnership is presumed to be partnership property [UPA §8(4)].

A Partner's Rights The UPA [§24(1)] provides that a partner has "rights in specific partnership property." This phrase may be somewhat misleading, however. A partner has no "individual" right to specific partnership property. Rather, subject to contrary agreement by the partners, a partner has only an equal right, shared with the other partners, to possess partnership property for the purpose of carrying out partnership business [UPA §25(2)(a)]. This includes property that the partner originally contributed to the partnership. The right to possess or control property to the exclusion of the other partners is lost once the property becomes partnership property.

A partner's rights in partnership property cannot be sold, given away, or otherwise transferred to someone else without the consent of all the partners [UPA §25(2)(b)]. Nor may a creditor of a partner, called an *individual creditor,* reach these rights [UPA §25(2)(c)]. This means that a partner may shield personal assets from individual creditors by transferring them to the partnership. To this extent, a partnership is a legal entity separate from the partners. Of course, partnership property is subject to the claims of *partnership creditors.*

The following case illustrates some of the legal implications of the rather unique concept of partnership property.

STATE v. ELSBURY
175 F.2d 430 (Nev. 1946)

McKNIGHT, District Judge

Appellant [Elsbury] was convicted of the crime of grand larceny. He has appealed from the judgment.

The [State] charged appellant with having stolen the sum of $1,000 from one S.L. Corsino.

The evidence shows that at the time of the alleged theft appellant and S.L. Corsino were general partners, engaged as such in operating a cafe, under written articles of partnership; that the sum of $1,000, admittedly taken and retained by appellant, constituted part of the proceeds from the business on deposit in the

bank in a checking account in the firm name; and that the partnership was heavily in debt. It also shows that S.L. Corsino originally furnished the largest amount of the firm's capital.

The statute defining grand larceny reads as follows:

Every person who shall . . . steal, take, and carry away, lead or drive away, the personal goods or property of another, of the value of fifty dollars or more, shall be deemed guilty of grand larceny. . . .

Under this statute, it is essential that money which

has been unlawfully taken and retained must be the "property of another."

But the State relies upon section 10339, N.C.L. which provides that:

It shall be no defense to a prosecution for larceny . . . that the money or property appropriated was partly the property of another and partly the property of the accused.

The important question to be decided, therefore, is whether this statute is applicable to a general partner who takes and retains partnership property during the existence of a partnership.

Section 24 of the Uniform Partnership Act reads:

The property rights of a partner are (1) his rights in specific partnership property, (2) his interest in the partnership, and (3) his right to participate in the management.

By the statement that one of the property rights of a partner is his right in specific partnership property is meant simply that a partner, subject to any contrary agreement, has an equal right with his copartners to use or possess any partnership property for any proper partnership purpose. . . .

Under Section 25 of the Uniform Partnership Act, a partner is co-owner with his partners of specific partnership property holding as a tenant in partnership. The incidents of this tenancy are such that: A partner, subject to the provisions of the act and to any agreement between the partners, has an equal right with his partners to possess specific partnership property for partnership purposes, but cannot otherwise possess same without the consent of his partners. His rights in specific partnership property are not assignable except in connection with the assignment of rights of all the partners in the same property, nor are they subject to [remedies of a creditor] upon a personal claim against him.

Section 26 of the same statute specifically provides:

A partner's interest in the partnership is his share of the profits and surplus, and the same is personal property.

A partner has no individual property in any specific assets of the firm. . . .

Instead, the interest of each partner in the partnership property is his share in the surplus, after the partnership debts are paid and the partnership accounts have been settled. . . .

Until that time arrives, it cannot be known what property will have to be used to satisfy the debts and, therefore, what property will remain after the debts are paid. . . .

The amounts of money invested by the partners respectively in the firm would be no criterion in determining their ownership of the partnership property, for the partner who furnished in the first instance the largest amount of capital, on final settlement might be found to have no interest whatever in the assets then on hand. . . .

When a partnership is admittedly insolvent, as was the partnership in the case at bar at the time of the alleged larceny, neither of the partners can possibly have any separate interest in the firm property. . . .

As each partner is the ultimate owner of an undivided interest in all the partnership property, none of such property "Can be said, with reference to any partner, 'to be the property of another.'" [Citation omitted.]

Therefore, it seems plain that the statute relied upon by the State does not apply where, as in this case, partnership property is appropriated by one of the partners during the existence of the partnership.

The judgment of conviction and the order . . . are reversed. . . .

CASE REVIEW QUESTIONS

1. If the $1,000 did not belong to Corsino, then it also did not belong to Elsbury. To whom did it belong?
2. Suppose you were asked by a Nevada state legislator to propose a change in the larceny statute that would lead to the conviction of people who did what Elsbury did. What change or changes would you propose?

Interest in the Partnership

The second property right of a partner is an "interest in the partnership," which is sometimes referred to as a **partnership interest** [UPA §24(2)]. Section 26 of the UPA states: "A partner's interest in the partnership is his share of the profits and surplus."

Unless they agree otherwise, profits and losses are shared equally by all of the partners, regardless of the type or amount of capital contribution each originally made [UPA §18(a)]. At the same time, none of the partners are entitled to any other compensation for participating in partnership business, unless they otherwise agree [UPA §18(f)]. Also, a partner is not entitled to interest on capital contributions [UPA §18(d)], although interest is payable by the partnership to a partner who advances funds in excess of the capital that the partner agreed to contribute [UPA §18(c)].

Unlike a partner's right in partnership property, a partner's interest in the partnership's profits and surplus can be sold, given away, or otherwise transferred by the partner to someone else. Such a transfer does not result either in the transferor no longer being a partner or in the dissolution of the partnership [UPA §27(1)]. Also, a partner's right to profits and surplus can be reached by an individual creditor of that partner. The individual creditor can obtain a judgment against the partner and a court order, called a **charging order,** that directs the partner's profits and surplus to be paid to the creditor [UPA §28].

Right to Participate in Management

The third property right of a partner is the right to participate in the management of the partnership [UPA §24(3)]. The partners can delegate the authority to manage all or a specified part of the business to one or more of the partners. If they do not, each of the partners has the authority to make independent decisions concerning the day-to-day operation of the partnership [UPA §9(1)].

When the partners confer with each other concerning the ordinary operation of the business and there has been no delegation of authority, decisions are made by a *majority vote of the partners* [UPA §18(h)]. Note that each partner has equal voting power, regardless of the type or amount of his or her capital contribution, unless the partners have agreed otherwise [UPA §18(e)]. Votes on matters that would constitute a violation in the partnership agreement are treated differently. Such votes require a unanimous vote, that is, the approval of all the partners [UPA §18(h)].

Section 18 of the UPA has been criticized because it may allow a majority of the partners to exploit dissenting partners. Section 18 states:

> The rights and duties of the partners in relation to the partnership shall be determined, *subject to any agreement between them,* by the following rules: . . . [Emphasis added.].

Then, paragraph (h) states:

> no act in contravention of [in opposition to] any agreement between the partners [such as changing the nature of the partnership business or adding or expelling partners for reasons not mentioned in the agreement] may be done rightfully without the consent of all the partners.

Because "subject to any agreement between them" qualifies paragraph (h), a possible interpretation of Section 18 is that a majority vote of the partners may determine any issue, including a change in the agreement, if the partnership agreement so provides. This could lead to a rather abrupt change in partnership affairs that might work to the disadvantage of a minority of the partners who may not want the change. One court that considered this issue did not interpret Section 18(h) in this way. It held that any "fundamental change" in the partnership agreement requires a unanimous vote even when the partnership agreement provides for amendment by a majority vote of the partners. Other courts, however, may decide that a majority vote of the partners will be sufficient to determine any partnership decision if the partnership agreement so provides.

Other Rights of Partners

In addition to the property rights just discussed, the UPA and most partnership agreements provide that partners have the following rights:

1. The right to be repaid for capital contributions or loans to the partnership, if there are funds available at dissolution [UPA §18(a)]. (This right is discussed more fully in the next chapter.)
2. The right to be repaid for payments made and liabilities incurred in the ordinary course of business [UPA §18(b)].
3. The right to copy the firm's books [UPA §19].
4. The right to a formal account of partnership affairs [UPA §22].

The first two of these rights can be altered or eliminated if the partners so agree, but the other two cannot.

Section 22 of the UPA provides that any partner shall have the right to a formal account of partnership affairs:

1. If he or she is wrongfully excluded from the partnership business or possession of its property by his or her copartners.
2. If the right exists under the terms of any agreement.
3. As provided in UPA §21 (which deals with a partner receiving a partnership benefit without the consent of the other partners).
4. Whenever other circumstances render it just and reasonable.

Duties of Partners

A partner is an agent of the partnership. This means that the law imposes on a partner the fiduciary duties of loyalty, service, and obedience (see Chapter 31). These duties are owed to the partnership and, through the partnership, to the other partners. Some of the duties thus imposed on a partner are as follows:

1. To avoid or to reveal to the other partners any conflicts of interest with the partnership.
2. Not to benefit personally from the use of partnership property.
3. To act in the best interest of the partnership.

4. To render true and full information concerning all things affecting the partnership business.

5. To keep accurate records concerning partnership business.

6. Not to commingle partnership property with his or her personal property.

These duties cannot be altered or eliminated by any agreement among the partners.

In the case that follows, the court had to decide whether one partner had breached his fiduciary duties to the partnership.

CLEMENT v. CLEMENT
260 A.2d 728 (Pa. 1970)

ROBERTS, Justice

Charles and L.W. Clement are brothers whose forty-year partnership has ended in acrimonious litigation. The essence of the conflict lies in Charles' contention that L.W. has over the years wrongfully taken for himself more than his share of the partnership's profits. Charles discovered these misdeeds during negotiations with L.W. over the sale of Charles' interest in the partnership in 1964. He then filed an action asking for dissolution of the partnership . . . and an accounting. Dissolution was ordered. . . . After lengthy hearings on the issue of the accounting the court decided that L.W., who was the brighter of the two and who kept the partnership books, had diverted partnership funds. The judge awarded Charles a one-half interest in several pieces of property owned by L.W. and in several insurance policies on L.W.'s life on the ground that these had been purchased with partnership assets.

The [intermediate appellate] court . . . then heard the case and reversed the lower court's decree in several material respects. The reversal was grounded on two propositions: that Charles' recovery could only be premised on a showing of fraud and that this burden was not met. . . .

There is a fiduciary relationship between partners. Where such a relationship exists actual fraud need not be shown. There was ample evidence of self-dealing and diversion of partnership assets on the part of L.W.

—more than enough to sustain the [trial] judge's conclusion that several substantial investments made by L.W. over the years were bankrolled with funds improperly withdrawn from the partnership.

The [Partnership] Act of 1915 very simply and unambiguously provides that partners owe a fiduciary duty one to another. One should not have to deal with his partner as though he were the opposite party in an arms-length transaction. One should be allowed to trust his partner, to expect that he is pursuing a common goal and not working at cross-purposes.

It would be unduly harsh to require that one must prove actual fraud before he can recover for a partner's derelictions. Where one partner has so dealt with the partnership as to raise the probability of wrongdoing it ought to be his responsibility to negate that inference. It has been held that "where a partner fails to keep a record of partnership transactions, and is unable to account for them, every presumption will be made against him." Likewise, where a partner commingles partnership funds with his own and generally deals loosely with partnership assets he ought to have to shoulder the task of demonstrating the probity of his conduct.

In the instant case L.W. dealt loosely with partnership funds. At various times he made substantial investments in his own name. He was totally unable to explain where he got the funds to make these investments. The court . . . held that Charles had no claim on the fruits of these investments because he could not trace the money that was invested therein dollar for dollar from the partnership. Charles should not have had this burden. He did show that his brother had diverted substantial sums from the partnership funds under his control. The inference that these funds provided L.W. with the wherewithall to make his investments was a perfectly reasonable one for the [trial judge] to make and his decision should have been allowed to stand.

The decree is vacated and the case remanded for further proceedings consistent with this opinion.

EAGEN, Justice (dissenting)

In 1923, L.W. Clement and his younger brother, Charles, formed a partnership for the purpose of engaging in the plumbing business under the name of Clement Brothers. They agreed to share the profits of the business equally after payment of the debts. L.W. was the more alert and aggressive of the two. He attended special training schools to upgrade his plumbing skills and became a master plumber. He alone conducted the business here involved and had complete control of its finances. He frequently worked nights, Sundays and holidays. Charles, on the other hand, refused to be "bothered" with the administration of the business or its finances. He insisted also on limiting his work to a regular eight-hour shift and confining his

contribution to the business to the performance of various plumbing jobs assigned to him.

Over the years, L.W. accumulated assets which eventually became quite valuable. For instance, in 1945 he purchased two lots of land for $5,500, and subsequently constructed a commercial building thereon. This construction was financed in most part by money secured through placing a mortgage on the property. In 1951 he purchased another piece of real estate for $3,500, and in 1927, 1936, 1938, 1945, 1947, 1955, and 1965 purchased policies of life insurance on his own life. There are presently existing substantial loans against some of these policies.

In 1964, Charles for the first time accused his brother, L.W., of misusing partnership funds to gain the assets he had accumulated. Charles did not have any evidence to substantiate the accusation, but surmised something must be wrong since L.W. had so much while he had so little.

At trial, not a scintilla of evidence was introduced to establish that L.W. diverted any partnership funds to purchase any of his personal assets. In view of this, a majority of the [intermediate appellate] court . . . ruled that Charles failed to establish that he had any interest or property rights therein. With this I agree. The majority of this Court now rule, in effect, that, because of the fiduciary relationship existing, it is L.W.'s burden to prove that he did not misuse partnership funds. This I cannot accept.

I dissent and would affirm the decree of the [intermediate appellate] court. . . .

CASE REVIEW QUESTIONS

1. What duties owed to Charles did L.W. violate?
2. What did L.W. do that the court considered to be a breach of the duties owed to Charles?
3. What evidence was there that L.W. did the things that the court considered to be a breach of the duties owed to Charles?
4. Why was the court satisfied that the evidence of a breach of duty was sufficient?
5. What is the relevance of the facts that L.W. was brighter and worked harder than Charles?

REVIEW QUESTIONS

1. What are the elements necessary for the creation of a partnership?
2. What are the primary factors to be considered in determining whether people who operate a business together are co-owners of the business?
3. What are the three property rights of a partner? Explain what each of these rights means.

4. In which of the property rights of a partner would an individual creditor of a partner be primarily interested?
5. Why does a partner owe fiduciary duties to the partnership?

CASE PROBLEMS

1. Potter told Childs that he had contracted to buy two carloads of hogs from Harvey. The hogs were to be delivered the next day, but he did not have enough money to pay for them. Potter proposed that if Childs would loan him the money to buy the hogs, he would give Childs half of the profits when he resold the hogs. He also said that he would give Childs a security interest in the hogs that would allow Childs to take possession of the hogs and sell them if Potter failed to repay the money loaned to him. Finally, Potter promised that under no circumstances would Childs suffer any loss. Childs accepted this proposition and loaned Potter $2,500. Potter took delivery of the hogs but did not pay for them. He was then unable to resell the hogs. Childs took possession of the hogs and had them resold. The sale price, however, did not amount to $2,500. Potter then paid Childs the balance due. Meanwhile, Harvey has not been paid for the hogs. If Harvey brings a legal action against Childs for payment of the amount due on the original sale of the hogs, arguing that Potter and Childs were partners, who will win the case? Explain.

2. Ostover wanted to open a restaurant. He entered into an oral agreement with Barbet, a chef, under which Ostover would provide the money necessary to open the restaurant and both of them would participate actively in the business. It was further agreed that profits, as they came in, would be used first to repay Ostover, with interest, for the funds used to open the restaurant. After Ostover had been repaid, all future profits would be divided equally between the two parties. When Ostover and Barbet rented space for the restaurant, they signed the lease as partners. Subsequently, the two men had a falling out. Barbet brought a legal action seeking an accounting. Ostover defended on the grounds that a partnership did not exist. Instead, he argued, there was only an agreement to become partners after Ostover had been repaid the money he had used to start the business. Who will win the case? Explain.

3. Elwynn, Mitchell, and Grady formed a partnership to assemble and market lamps. After renting delivery trucks for several years, the partnership was able to accumulate enough cash to purchase three delivery trucks. The titles to the trucks were placed in the name of the partnership. Six months after the trucks were purchased, Grady sold one of the trucks and retained the proceeds, saying that one of the three trucks belonged to him. The other partners disagreed with Grady and have brought a legal action against him for an accounting. Who will win the case? Explain. [Adapted from CPA examination question 5a, *Business Law,* May 1977.]

4. Corn and Gauldin orally agreed to operate a business raising cattle and hogs as partners and to split the profits evenly between them. The business was operated on property owned by Corn, and Corn alone paid taxes on the property. Some of the income from the business was used to build two

buildings on the property to be used in the business. Does Gauldin have any rights in the property or in the buildings? Explain.

5. The Minlow, Richard, and Jones partnership agreement is silent on whether the partners may transfer all or part of their partnership interests to an outsider. Richard has assigned his interest in the partnership to Smith, a personal creditor, and as a result, the other partners are furious. They are particularly upset because Smith has sent a letter to the partnership claiming to be a partner and demanding access to the firm's books. Is Smith entitled to see the books? Explain. [Adapted from CPA examination question 5b, *Business Law,* May 1977.]

6. Donnell and Metzger formed a partnership to develop and produce new applications of plastic to metal surfaces in heavy industrial machines to reduce friction. Donnell is very wealthy and contributed $50,000 to the partnership's capital. It was agreed that Donnell would not take part in the day-to-day operation of the business but would be available for consultation and would vote on important partnership matters. Metzger is very bright but penniless. It was agreed that Metzger would contribute his technical knowledge and would manage the business. Recently, Metzger proposed to Donnell that the firm hire Richards as a salesman. Donnell objected, claiming that Richards was incompetent. Metzger demanded a formal vote on the matter. Metzger voted in favor of hiring Richards and Donnell voted against. Does Metzger have authority to hire Richards? Explain.

7. Hartzler and Allan operate a tavern as partners. The partnership leases the building in which the business is conducted, and the lease expires on the same day that the partners have agreed to terminate their partnership. The partnership has spent a large amount of money improving the property. Over one year before the lease is due to expire, Hartzler went to the owner of the property and obtained a lease in his own name to begin when the present lease and partnership are terminated. When Allan learned of this, he brought a legal action against Hartzler, claiming that Hartzler had breached a duty owed to the partnership and seeking to have the new lease declared partnership property. Who will win the case? Explain.

36

PARTNERSHIP OPERATION AND DISSOLUTION

This chapter considers two topics of partnership law. The first, partnership operation, deals with that portion of partnership law concerned with the liabilities of the partners and the partnership. The second, partnership dissolution, deals with the ways in which a partnership can be ended and the resulting duties of the partners.

For discussing the liabilities of the partners and the partnership to third parties, we believe it is convenient to divide them into two categories: contract liability and tort liability.

PARTNERSHIP OPERATION: CONTRACT LIABILITY

The law of agency is applicable to partnerships. That is, conflicts among partners, between partners and the partnership, or between the partnership and third parties are resolved by the direct application of the same principles of agency law that were discussed in Chapters 31 through 34. Indeed, much of partnership law is really just a special application of agency law. For instance, when a partner enters into a contract on behalf of a partnership, the partnership is the principal and the partner acting for it is the agent. Thus, a partnership (the principal) is generally deemed to be on notice of or to have knowledge of those matters that the partners (agents) are on notice of or know [UPA §12].

A partner can bind the partnership contractually when he or she has the actual or apparent authority to act. This is expressed in §9 of the UPA:

> Every partner is an agent of the partnership for the purpose of its business, and the act of every partner, . . . for apparently carrying on in the usual way the business of the partnership . . . binds the partnership. . . .

The articles of partnership usually state the actual limits to the authority granted to the partners. (See, for example, paragraph 7 of the partnership agreement presented in Figure 35-1 in the previous chapter.) The authority granted by the articles may include the right to perform any business act that may be lawfully delegated.

In addition, partners have the apparent authority to carry on the partnership's business in the usual way. This apparent authority of a partner is determined by considering the business purpose or nature of the partnership, the methods of doing business ordinarily used by similar businesses, and the reasonable expectations of third parties. According to §9(3) of the UPA, a partner's apparent authority does not include the authority to perform extraordinary acts — such as assigning partnership property in trust for creditors, disposing of the firm's good will, or submitting a partnership claim to arbitration — or any other act that would make it impossible for the partnership to carry on its ordinary business.

Trading and Nontrading Partnerships

Some courts have developed a useful analytical device for determining the liability of a partnership when the evidence shows that no express authority existed for a particular act performed by a partner. In cases that involve borrowing money or executing a negotiable instrument, these courts have distinguished between trading and nontrading partnerships.

A *trading partnership* is organized primarily to buy and sell goods for profit. Conversely, a partnership that is organized primarily to offer a service and in which the passage of title to goods is not the central means of making a profit is a *nontrading partnership*. Examples of nontrading partnerships include professional partnerships (such as those formed by doctors, lawyers, and accountants) and partnerships formed to provide a service (such as the operation of a theater or the selling of insurance). If a partnership is a trading partnership, some courts will presume the existence of implied or circumstantial authority to obligate the partnership on a loan or some other negotiable instrument. If the partnership is a nontrading partnership, these courts may require the existence of actual authority before a partner can bind the partnership to loan obligations or on negotiable instruments.

Whether this distinction would be used by most courts today is questionable. Given the growing diversity of activities in which a single business is likely to engage and the increasing variety of financing methods, this rather simplistic approach for establishing implied or circumstantial authority may not be as useful as it once was. Furthermore, one may question the logic of connecting buying and selling with borrowing. The best approach, therefore, is to think of the partnership as the principal, the contracting partner as the agent, and the other contracting party as the third party, and then to search the facts for evidence of actual authority, apparent authority, or ratification, as discussed in Chapter 32.

The case that follows reveals how complex the issue of authority can become when a partnership engages in several types of business.

HODGE v. GARRETT
614 P.2d 420 (Idaho 1980)

BISTLINE, Justice

Hodge and defendant-appellant Rex E. Voeller, the managing partner of the Pay-Ont Drive-In Theatre, signed a contract for the sale of a small parcel of land belonging to the partnership. That parcel, although adjacent to the theater, was not used in theater operations except insofar as the east 20 feet were necessary for the operation of the theater's driveway. The agreement for the sale of land stated that it was between Hodge and the Pay-Ont Drive-In Theatre, a partnership. Voeller signed the agreement for the partnership, and written changes as to the footage and price were initialed by Voeller. . . .

The trial court found that Voeller had actual and apparent authority to execute the contract on behalf of the partnership, and that the contract should be . . . enforced. The partners of the Pay-Ont Drive-In Theatre appeal, arguing that Voeller did not have authority to sell the property and that Hodge knew that he did not have that authority.

At common law one partner could not, "without the concurrence of his copartners, convey away the real estate of the partnership, bind his partners by a deed, or transfer the title and interest of his copartners in the firm real estate." . . . This rule was changed by the adoption of the Uniform Partnership Act. The relevant provisions are as follows:

> Every partner is an agent of the partnership for the purpose of its business, and the act of every partner, including the execution in the partnership name of any instrument, for apparently carrying on in the usual way the business of the partnership of which he is a member binds the partnership, unless the partner so acting has in fact no authority to act for the partnership in the particular matter, and the person with whom he is dealing has knowledge of the fact that he has no such authority.

Thus this contract is enforceable if Voeller had the actual authority to sell the property, or, even if Voeller did not have such authority, the contract is still enforceable if the sale was in the usual way of carrying on the business and Hodge did not know that Voeller did not have this authority.

As to the question of actual authority, such authority must affirmatively appear, "for the authority of one partner to make and acknowledge a deed for the firm will not be presumed. . . ." Although such authority may be implied from the nature of the business or from similar past transactions, nothing in the record in this case indicates that Voeller had express or implied authority to sell real property belonging to the partnership. There is no evidence that Voeller had sold property belonging to the partnership in the past, and obviously the partnership was not engaged in the business of buying and selling real estate.

The next question, since actual authority has not been shown, is whether Voeller was conducting the partnership business in the usual way in selling the parcel of land, . . . i.e., whether Voeller had apparent authority. Here the evidence showed, and the trial court found:

> That at the inception of the partnership, and at all times thereafter, Rex E. Voeller was the exclusive, managing partner of the partnership and had the full authority to make all decisions pertaining to the partnership affairs, including paying the bills, preparing profit and loss statements, income tax returns and the ordering of any goods or services necessary to the operation of the business.

The court made no finding that it was customary for Voeller to sell real property, or even personal property, belonging to the partnership. Nor was there any evidence to this effect. Nor did the court discuss whether it was in the usual course of business for the managing partner of a theater to sell real property. Yet the trial court found that Voeller had apparent authority to sell the property. From this it must be inferred that the trial court believed it to be in the usual course of business for a partner who has exclusive control of the partnership business to sell real property belonging to the partnership, where that property is not being used in the partnership business. We cannot agree with this conclusion. For a theater, "carrying on in the usual way the business of the partnership," means running the operations of the theater; it does not mean selling a parcel of property adjacent to the theater. Here the contract of sale stated that the land belonged to the partnership, and, even if Hodge believed that Voeller as the exclusive manager had authority to transact all business for the firm, Voeller still could not bind the partnership through a unilateral act which was not in the usual business of the partnership. We therefore hold that the trial court erred in holding that this contract was binding on the partnership.

Judgment reversed.

SHEPARD, Justice (dissenting)

The majority, and I am sure inadvertently, neglects to include certain uncontroverted facts. . . . Some considerable time elapsed between the signing of the instrument and the decision of Voeller not to honor the contract on behalf of the partnership. During that period of time, Hodge was placed in possession of the property in question, made extensive improvements thereon, including the placement of a commercial office structure thereon which Hodge rented to a third party for the sum of $75.00 per month. . . . The majority's reversal with directions to enter judgment for the defendant effectively prevents Hodge from ever recovering any of his uncontroverted damages resulting from Voeller's breach of the contract.

It should be remembered that Voeller clearly admitted the execution of the contract of sale on behalf of the partnership. Such was not denied by the other partners. . . . It is uncontroverted that, as Hodge stated, the property involved has undergone an enormous increase in value since the execution of the contract. Undoubtedly, the trial court viewed the defense protestations of Voeller's lack of authority in that light. Indeed, Voeller testified that the sole reason the transaction was not consummated was that he later came to believe that such a sale would amount to a subdivision of the theatre property and hence result in the partnership property being brought into the city limits with a resultant increase in taxes. . . .

Contrary to the assertions of the majority, the record reveals that the partnership had not too long before the instant transaction sold real estate in Emmett, including the entire theatre business located thereon.

I am indeed startled at the following assertion of the majority: ". . . and obviously the partnership was not engaged in the business of buying and selling real estate." The murky and complicated history of the partnership clearly demonstrates to the contrary. As revealed in the record, what had been originally partnership property (such as three theatres in Burley, Idaho) had been somehow converted into corporate assets. . . . However, the record is clear that the partnership did purchase real property, that the partnership did sell real property, and that Voeller himself, on behalf of the partnership, engaged in the rental of property to other persons, including the leasing of the theatre operation in Lovelock, Nevada. On the basis of the above, I cannot agree with the majority's characterization of this partnership, but again would agree with the trial judge in his undoubted conclusion, albeit unstated, that the partnership failed to carry its burden of proof that the transaction in question here was outside the authority of Voeller and outside the usual and ordinary course of business of the partnership.

CASE REVIEW QUESTIONS

1. What is the basis of the disagreement between the majority opinion and the dissenting opinion concerning the outcome of the case?
2. Reread §9 of the UPA and apply it to the facts of the case. What conclusion do you reach concerning the outcome of the case:? Is your conclusion in agreement with the majority opinion or with the dissenting opinion?

PARTNERSHIP OPERATION: TORT LIABILITY

The liability of a partnership to damaged third parties for the torts of a partner is based upon the same reasoning that supports the doctrine of respondeat superior in agency law (see pages 695–704). The principle of a partnership's vicarious liability is clearly stated in §13 of the UPA:

> Where, by any wrongful act or omission of any partner acting in the ordinary course of the business of the partnership or with the authority of his copartners, loss or injury is caused to any person, not being a partner in the partnership, or any penalty is incurred, the partnership is liable therefor to the same extent as the partner so acting or omitting to act.

The key words here are "acting in the ordinary course of business of the partnership or with the authority of his co-partners." The basic issue, then, is whether a tort occurred within the ordinary course of business or was authorized.

In the discussion of the doctrine of respondeat superior, we stated that intentional torts are almost always beyond the scope of an agent's employment (see page 702). In the case that follows, the plaintiff alleged that a partner committed an intentional tort for which the defendant partnership was liable. The court rejected the plaintiff's argument that the partner was acting in the ordinary course of the partnership's business or within his authority when he committed the alleged tort. Nonetheless, the court believed that the partnership could be held liable for the damage caused by the intentional tort of the partner. As you read the case, see if you can understand the basis of the court's belief.

KELSEY-SEYBOLD CLINIC v. MACLAY
466 S.W.2d 716 (Texas 1971)

[Maclay brought a legal action against Dr. Brewer and the Kelsey-Seybold Clinic, a medical partnership with which Dr. Brewer was associated. Maclay alleged that Dr. Brewer had alienated the affections of his wife. "Alienation of affections" means taking from a married person the affection, fellowship, and comfort that inheres in a normal marriage. Maclay also argued that the clinic was liable for Dr. Brewer's wrongdoing.

The Clinic moved for a summary judgment. The trial court judge granted the motion. Maclay appealed. An intermediate appellate court reversed the decision of the trial court. The Clinic then appealed from the deci-

sion of the intermediate appellate court to the Texas Supreme Court.]

WALKER, Justice

Plaintiff alleged that Dr. Brewer and the Clinic had treated him, his wife and their children for several years; that Dr. Brewer, who is a pediatrician and one of the partners in the Clinic, was the doctor to whom his wife had taken their children; that beginning in late 1966, Dr. Brewer conceived and entered into a scheme to alienate the affections of plaintiff's wife, Mrs. Maria Maclay; that he showered his attentions and gifts upon her until April or May, 1967, when her affections were alienated as a direct result of his actions, causing her to separate from plaintiff on or about July 25, 1967.

Plaintiff further alleged that Dr. Brewer's actions designed to alienate Mrs. Maclay's affections occurred while he was acting as a medical doctor for plaintiff's family and in the course and scope of his employment as a partner in the Clinic; that various acts of undue familiarity occurred both on and off the premises of the Clinic; that prior to April, 1967, the Clinic, through Dr. Mavis Kelsey, one of the senior partners, had knowledge of Dr. Brewer's actions; that at the time this knowledge was acquired, the Clinic was providing medical treatment for plaintiff and his entire family; and that "the partnership approved of, consented to, and ratified and condoned such conduct of its partner, Brewer, and refused to come to the aid of the plaintiff or in any way attempt to halt or disapprove the actions of Brewer." . . .

At some time in the Spring of 1967, plaintiff complained to Dr. Kelsey that Dr. Brewer was having an affair with Mrs. Maclay. According to Dr. Kelsey's recollection of this conversation, plaintiff stated that he and his wife had separated. . . .

It was Dr. Kelsey's impression that the purpose of plaintiff's two telephone calls was to seek sympathy. Plaintiff did not ask him to do anything, and he had done nothing. He did not talk with Dr. Brewer about the matter until after this suit was filed. . . .

Plaintiff countered with an affidavit in which he stated that in his telephone conversation with Dr. Kelsey, he inquired whether the latter was aware that Dr. Brewer had a romantic interest or involvement with his wife. . . .

The bases of liability alleged in the petition are: (1) that Dr. Brewer's wrongful conduct was in the course and scope of the partnership business and was approved, consented to, ratified and condoned by the Clinic; and (2) that the Clinic, after notice of the alleged relationship between Dr. Brewer and Mrs. Maclay, failed to take any action. Plaintiff is thus relying upon the vicarious or partnership liability of the Clinic for the acts of one of the partners and also its liability for breach of a duty owed by the Clinic when it learned of Dr. Brewer's relationship with Mrs. Maclay.

We assume for the purpose of this opinion that Dr.

Brewer was not acting in the ordinary course of the Clinic's business and that his conduct was neither authorized nor ratified by the partnership. . . .

We are unwilling to believe that plaintiff seriously expects to prove in a conventional trial that the acts alleged to have been committed by Dr. Brewer were in the course and scope of the partnership business or were either authorized or ratified by the Clinic.

The Clinic was under a duty, of course, to exercise ordinary care to protect its patients from harm resulting from tortious conduct of persons upon the premises. A negligent breach of that duty could subject the Clinic to liability without regard to whether the tortious conduct immediately causing the harm was that of an agent or servant or was in the ordinary scope of the partnership business. For example, it might become liable, as a result of its own negligence, for damage done by a vicious employee while acting beyond the scope of his authority. . . .

We are also of the opinion that the Clinic owed a duty to the families of its patients to exercise ordinary care to prevent a tortious interference with family relations. It was not required to maintain constant surveillance over personnel on duty or to inquire into and regulate the personal conduct of partners and employees while engaged in their private affairs. But if and when the partnership received information from which it knew or should have known that there might be a need to take action, it was under a duty to use reasonable means at its disposal to prevent any partner or employee from improperly using his position with the Clinic to work a tortious invasion of legally protected family interests. This duty relates only to conduct of a partner or employee on the premises of the Clinic or while purportedly acting as a representative of the Clinic elsewhere. Failure to exercise ordinary care in discharging that duty would subject the Clinic to liability for damages proximately caused by its negligence.

The rather meager information in the present record does not necessarily indicate that the Clinic was under a duty to act or that it could have done anything to prevent the damage when Dr. Kelsey first learned of the situation. On the other hand, it does not affirmatively and clearly appear that the Clinic could or should have done nothing. Mrs. Maclay's affections may have been alienated from her husband before anyone talked with Dr. Kelsey, but the facts in that respect are not fully developed. There is no proof as to when, where or under what circumstances the misconduct, if any, on Dr. Brewer's part occurred. Dr. Kelsey testified that he did not believe anything improper occurred at the Clinic, but the proofs do not establish as a matter of law that he was justified in not making further inquiry after his conversations with plaintiff. . . . The record does not show whether there is a partnership agreement that might have a bearing on the case, and we have no way of knowing the extent to which the Clinic might have determined which patients were to be seen by Dr. Brewer or controlled his actions while on duty. Dr. Kel-

sey's testimony suggests that the partners might have been in a position to prevent improper conduct by one of their number on the premises of the Clinic. In our opinion the Clinic has failed to discharge the heavy, and in a case of this character virtually impossible, burden of establishing as a matter of law at the summary judgment stage that it is not liable under any theory fairly presented by the allegations of the petition.

[The decision of the intermediate appellate court is affirmed.]

CASE REVIEW QUESTIONS

1. What tort did the court believe Maclay might be able to prove had been committed by one of the partners of the clinic?
2. Which partner or partners did the court believe Maclay might be able to prove had committed a tort that had caused him damage?

Partnership Liability for the Negligent Operation of an Automobile

An area of frequent litigation involves the liability of a partnership for the negligence of a partner when he or she is traveling by automobile on partnership business. In such cases, two facts are very important. The first is the ownership of the auto, and the second is the nature of the partnership's business. If the auto is owned by the partnership and the partner is traveling on partnership business, the partnership is usually liable. However, if the partner personally owns the auto and it is under his or her control, liability usually depends on the nature of the business of the partnership. There is some conflict among the court decisions in this area. We believe that the partnership should not be held liable for the partner's negligence in the operation of an auto unless the business of the partnership inherently involves the delivery of goods or services. Thus, in the case of professional partnerships, such as those formed by attorneys, physicians, and accountants, no partnership liability should result when a partner negligently drives his or her own car when traveling from one business site to another.

One of the best cases illustrating the circumstances under which a court will hold a partnership liable for a partner's negligent operation of an auto is the *Phillips v. Cook* case, which follows. When reading this case, try to discern the facts that the court thought important in deciding to impose liability on the partnership.

PHILLIPS v. COOK
210 A.2d (Md. 1965)

[Delores Cook and Marshall Cook, her husband, brought a legal action against Daniel Phillips and Isadore Harris, individually and as copartners of Dan's Used Cars. They sought to recover damages for injuries sustained as a result of a collision involving a partnership automobile operated by Harris and bearing dealer plates issued to Dan's Used Cars by the Department of Motor Vehicles.

After the presentation of evidence, Phillips moved for a directed verdict in so far as he was being sued as a copartner of Dan's Used Cars. He argued that there was no evidence from which the jury could find that Harris was acting within the scope of the partnership business or was benefitting the partnership at the time of the accident. The trial court denied the motion. The jury found Phillips liable to the Cooks as a copartner. Phillips appealed, arguing that his motion for a directed verdict should have been granted.]

MARBURY, Judge

The accident in question occurred on January 7, 1960, at about 6:50 P.M., when a partnership automobile operated by Harris struck the rear of a vehicle driven by one Smith, which in turn hit an automobile operated by Delores Cook. . . . Harris was on his way home from the used car lot when the accident occurred. He was using the most direct route from the partnership lot and was only five blocks from his home at the time of the incident.

In October 1959, Harris and Phillips entered into a partnership on an equal basis under the name of "Dan's Used Cars" for the purpose of buying and selling used automobiles. Phillips owned the lot and a gas station adjacent to it. He went into the partnership with Harris because the latter had the experience and money which he did not have to put into the business. This partnership agreement was oral and it was agreed

between the partners that each would have an equal voice in the conduct and management of the business.

Neither of the partners owned a personal automobile or had one titled in his individual name. It was agreed as a part of the partnership arrangement that Harris would use a partnership vehicle for transportation to and from his home. Under this agreement, he was authorized to demonstrate and sell such automobiles, call on dealers for the purpose of seeing and purchasing used cars, or go to the Department of Motor Vehicles on partnership business after leaving the lot in the evening and before returning the next day. Both Harris and Phillips could use a partnership automobile as desired. Such vehicles were for sale at any time during the day or night and at various places they had "for sale" signs on the windshields. Harris had no regular hours to report to the used car lot but could come and go as he saw fit. . . .

If there was any evidence, no matter how slight, viewed in the light most favorable to appellees, that Harris, in using the partnership vehicle, was acting within the scope of the partnership agreement and business, i.e., the use was of some benefit or incidental to the partnership arrangement, then the question was for the jury's determination. Appellant contends that because Harris was on his way home from the used car lot at the time of the accident, the evidence was insufficient to support a finding by the jury that he was acting within the scope of the partnership arrangement or that such use of the vehicle was of benefit to the partnership. . . .

The test of the liability of the partnership and of its members for the torts of any one partner is whether the wrongful act was done within what may reasonably be found to be the scope of the business of the partnership and for its benefit. The extent of the authority of a partner is determined essentially by the same principles as those which measure the scope of an agent's authority. . . . Partnership cases may differ from principal and agent and master and servant relationships because in the non-partnership cases, the element of control or authorization is important. This is not so in the case of a partnership for a partner is also a principal, and control and authorization are generally within his power to exercise. . . .

Here, the fact that the defendant partners were in the used car business; that the very vehicle involved in the accident was one of the partnership assets for sale at all times, day or night, at any location; that Harris was on call by Phillips or customers at his home — he went back to the lot two or three times after going home; that he had no set time and worked irregular hours, coupled with the fact that he frequently stopped to conduct partnership business on the way to and from the lot; . . . requires that the question of whether the use of the automobile at the time of the accident was in the partnership interest and for its benefit be submitted to the jury. We find that the lower court did not err in refusing to grant appellant's motions for a directed verdict as to him in the capacity of a co-partner trading as Dan's Used Cars.

Judgment affirmed.

HAMMOND, Judge (dissenting)

I dissent because I think the evidence conclusively rebutted the presumption that the operator of a motor vehicle owned by another is the agent or servant of the owner, acting within the scope of the owner's business, and left no room for the jury to find the partnership liable. . . .

There was no contradiction or impeachment of, or reason to doubt, the testimony that Harris had left the used car lot on the evening of the accident for the day and was driving home to eat supper and spend the evening. He planned to remain at home and to drive back to the used car lot the next morning. It is undis-

puted that both Harris and Phillips were free to treat vehicles owned by the partnership as their own for personal trips and uses. In the months that the partnership had existed, Harris had returned to the used car lot, after he had gone home, only two or three times. He never kept a car at home for sale, always on the partnership lot. The car he drove he had paid for although it was titled in the name of the partnership. He did not solicit business away from the lot and apparently had not sold a car away from there, but if some one had asked him to sell the car he was driving he would have done so at the right price. . . .

The test is not whether the servant on another occasion or at another time might use the instrumentality in furtherance of the master's business or interests or within the scope of the business of the partnership, it is whether at the time the servant causes harm he then reasonably could be found to be so acting. If the servant's activities at the time of the infliction of the harm were for his own purposes, or in his own behalf, the master is not liable. It matters not that earlier he had acted for his master or that later he would again act for him; at the time of the harm the immediately predominating purpose of the servant must have some significant relation to the business of the master, if the master is to be held liable. . . .

The fact that Harris would have sold the car for a price if some purchaser had flagged him down while he was en route home or telephoned him at home, does not make his purpose in driving home to supper and an evening of television and sleep less predominantly personal and unmixed with business than that of a lawyer driving home from his office with a briefcase full of files (which he may or may not open). If the lawyer negligently injures someone while driving home, his partners certainly would not be liable because of the briefcase or because a client involved in a street accident might flag him down en route or another client call him at home for advice. . . .

The defendant's prayer for [a directed] verdict should have been granted.

CASE COMMENT

In *Phillips v. Cook,* the majority thought the ordinary course of the business involved — selling autos — could be conducted anywhere. Therefore, even though one of the partners was on his way home for the evening, there was still a potential to conduct business. Usually, the "ordinary course of business" is easier to define. It should be obvious that the negligent preparation of an audit by a partner will subject a CPA partnership to liability, even though the other partners did not participate. The same would be true of a partnership of physicians if one of them were to be negligent in the treatment of a patient.

CASE REVIEW QUESTIONS

1. Does this case reflect the legal principle that whenever a partner commits a tort while on partnership business, the partnership will be held liable? Explain.
2. List the facts that caused the court to conclude that the plaintiff's case against the partnership should not have been subject to a directed verdict. That is, what circumstances establish the conclusion that the negligent partner was operating the vehicle in the ordinary course of business?
3. Do you agree with the majority or with the dissent? Shouldn't the majority have focused upon the intent and purpose of the particular trip involved? Wasn't the partner going home for the evening? Explain.

Partnership Liability for Intentional Torts

As noted earlier, a partnership is generally not liable for the intentional torts of its partners because intentional torts are not usually authorized or committed in the ordinary course of the business of the partnership. Before liability will be imposed on the partnership, a strong connection between the partner's motive in committing the tort and the partnership business must be shown. If the partner's motive in committing the intentional tort was to further the business of the partnership, liability may be imposed. This is the issue considered by the court in the following case.

VRABEL v. ACRI
103 N.E.2d 564 (Ohio 1952)

[Vrabel brought a legal action against Mrs. Florence Acri as a partner of the Acri Cafe for reasons set out in the court's opinion. Following the presentation of the evidence, Acri moved for a directed verdict. The trial court judge denied the motion. Acri appealed.]

ZIMMERMAN, [Judge]

The evidence presented on the trial supports the claim [of the plaintiff] as to the manner in which plaintiff was injured. It shows that, while plaintiff and his companion were sitting quietly at the bar of the Acri Cafe on the night of February 17, 1947, partaking of alcoholic beverages, Michael Acri, for no apparent cause, shot and killed plaintiff's companion and afterwards viciously attacked plaintiff. Evidence was also introduced which might justify the conclusion that at the time of plaintiff's injuries Michael Acri and the defendant, then husband and wife, were joint proprietors of the Acri Cafe which had been started in 1933, although defendant herself denied any such relationship. . . .

It also appears from the evidence that plaintiff secured a judgment for $10,000 against Michael Acri for the injuries received at Acri's hands, and that Acri is now serving a life sentence in the Ohio Penitentiary for killing plaintiff's companion.

For the purpose of the discussion which follows, we shall accept plaintiff's claim, supported by some evidence, that defendant and Michael Acri were joint proprietors of the Acri Cafe at the time plaintiff was assaulted by Acri. . . .

[W]here a partnership . . . is shown to exist, each member of such project acts both as principal and agent of the others as to those things done within the apparent scope of the business of the project and for its benefit. . . .

However, it is equally true that where one member of a partnership . . . commits a wrongful and malicious tort not within the actual or apparent scope of the agency or the common business of the particular venture, to which the other members have not assented, and which has not been concurred in or ratified by them, they are not liable for the harm thereby caused. . . .

We cannot escape the conclusion, therefore, that the above rules, relating to the nonliability of a partner . . . for wrongful and malicious torts committed by an associate outside the purpose and scope of the business, must be applied in the instant case. The willful and malicious attack by Michael Acri upon the plaintiff in the Acri Cafe cannot reasonably be said to have come within the scope of the business of operating the cafe, so as to have rendered the absent defendant, assuming her joint proprietorship of the cafe, accountable.

Since the liability of one partner . . . for the acts of his associates is founded upon the principles of agency, the statement is in point that an intentional and willful attack committed by an agent or employee, to vent his own spleen or malevolence against the injured person, is a clear departure from his employment and his principal or employer is not responsible therefor. . . .

Therefore, under the evidence in this case, we entertain the view that the trial court should have directed a verdict for the defendant at the close of the evidence, in response to her motion. . . .

Judgment reversed.

CASE REVIEW QUESTIONS

1. On what other theory of tort liability could Vrabel have based his claim against Florence Acri? (See *Kelsey-Seybold Clinic v. Maclay,* page 755.)
2. Under what different circumstances might Florence Acri have been held liable as a partner for the intentional tort committed by Michael Acri?

A Note on the Joint and Several Liability of Partners The treatment of tort liability of a partnership is procedurally different from the treatment of contract liability. Section 15 of the UPA provides that partners are jointly and severally liable for all wrongful acts, omissions, and breaches of trust, but that they are only jointly liable for all contractual debts. **Joint and several liability** means that, as a procedural matter, any partner may be sued alone for the tortious acts of another partner and that the other partners need not be joined. In addition, judgment against any one partner, if it remains uncollected, is not a bar to a subsequent law suit against another partner for the same negligent act. The law here seeks to protect an injured third party by providing a remedy against any one of the partners once it has been determined that a tort was authorized or was committed in the ordinary course of the partnership's business.

If a tort judgment is recovered against the partnership or against a partner who did not in fact cause the tort, then the partner who did in fact cause the tort must indemnify the partnership or the other partners for their loss. This assumes, of course, that it is possible to establish clearly which partner committed the tort.

On February 3, 1982, the *Wall Street Journal* reported that a federal jury in New York had ordered the partnership of Arthur Andersen & Company, one of the "Big Eight" accounting firms, to pay $80 million to the shareholders of a firm because partners of Andersen had committed the tort of fraud. The plaintiffs alleged that the partners failed to disclose a fraudulent scheme of intentionally undervaluing property that they knew about or should have known about. If this verdict stands after appeal and the partnership is not insured against such a large award, the partners of Andersen will be individually liable for the judgment. Establishing which of the more than 1,400 partners of Andersen should be ultimately responsible and should therefore indemnify the other partners for their loss may be extremely difficult, however.

Joint liability for contractual obligations means that all partners must be joined (named) in a suit. If they are not, then a judgment recovered against fewer than all of the partners cannot be enforced against those not joined. Practically speaking, then, all of the partners must be made individual defendants so that the court will have jurisdiction over all of them whenever a judgment against individual partners having joint liability is sought. If the partnership is joined as a defendant, a successful plaintiff may attach partnership assets.

Criminal Liability of a Partnership and a Partner

If a partner commits a crime, the state may prosecute the partner as an individual. The difficult issue here is whether a partnership itself can be held criminally liable. A clear statement about the criminal liability of a partnership is not possible because not all state courts have decided that a partnership is a distinct and separate entity from the partners for the purposes of establishing criminal liability. Some courts have recognized partnership as separate legal entities, however. Where this has occurred and when there are compelling societal needs for the establishment of criminal liability, a court may decide that a partnership is criminally liable. The following case presents the modern view that the courts should hold a partnership potentially liable for a crime committed by one of its partners when the public is threatened.

PEOPLE v. SMITHTOWN GENERAL HOSPITAL
399 N.Y.S.2d 993 (N.Y. 1977)

[A criminal indictment was filed against Smithtown General Hospital for reasons set forth in the court's opinion. The hospital moved to dismiss the indictment on the grounds that, as a partnership, it was not an entity separate and apart from the aggregate of the individuals who were members of the partnership. It argued that the doctrine of respondeat superior did not apply and that, therefore, the partnership could not be indicted unless each of the 42 partners had the necessary criminal intent.]

JASPAN, Judge

The defendant [partnership] operates a hospital and is charged, in effect, with permitting an unauthorized person to participate in a surgical procedure upon an uninformed, nonconsenting patient and falsifying its records to conceal that crime. The indictment is couched in terms appropriate to Penal Law Section 120.05(5) and Penal Law Section 175.10 which respectively provide as follows:

P.L. Section 120.05:

A *person* is guilty of assault in the second degree when:

5. For a purpose other than lawful therapeutic treatment, he intentionally causes stupor, unconsciousness or other physical impairment or injury to another person by administering to him, without his consent, a drug, substance or preparation capable of producing the same. . . . [Emphasis added.]

P.L. Section 175.10:

A *person* is guilty of falsifying business records in the first degree when he commits the crime of falsifying business records in the second degree, and when his intent to defraud includes an intent to commit another crime or to aid or conceal the commission thereof. [Emphasis added.]

Person is defined in P.L. Section 10.00, subd. 7, as a "human being, and *where appropriate,* a public or private corporation . . . [or] a *partnership.* . . ." [Emphasis added.]

While the criminal liability of corporations and of individuals acting in the name of a corporation is expressly set forth in the Penal Law no similar provision is found with respect to partnerships and no reported case has been found in this State which deals directly with this issue.

The legislative pattern is probably grounded upon common law concepts of a partnership as opposed to that of the entity known as a corporation. But the definition of "person" in the Penal Law and the mandate of that law . . . that it be liberally construed provide an opportunity for rationalization in the interests of promoting justice and effecting the objects of the law.

The partnership can be either an entity or an aggregate of its members depending upon the nature of its activities and in the case of criminal law depending also upon the nature of the infraction. . . .

The concept of a partnership as an entity liable for certain of its criminal activities independent of culpability by its respective members was expressly considered in *United States v. A & P Trucking Co.* Two partnerships were charged, as entities, with violations [of a section of the United States Code] which makes it a crime to knowingly violate some Interstate Commerce Commission regulations. . . .

The Supreme Court, relying upon a definition of person similar to that found in P.L. Section 10.00, subd. 7, held that impersonal entities can be guilty of knowing or wilful violations of regulatory statutes through the doctrine of respondeat superior and that a partnership may be considered an entity separate and apart from the aggregate of its members.

The operation of a hospital is so intertwined with the public interest as to legally justify the imposition of extensive controls by all levels of government. The applicable regulatory statutes and implementing regulations not only involve care and services, but relate to the creation and ownership of those institutions and to every aspect of its internal affairs including limitations as to costs and charges.

The counts in the respective indictments relating first to the anesthetization of a patient without his consent for a purpose other than lawful medical or therapeutic treatment and secondly to the records maintained with respect thereto have that apparent nexus to the regulatory provisions controlling a hospital as to bring this case within the orbit of the principles enunciated in *United States v. A & P Trucking, supra.* . . .

In civil law, two or more persons conducting a partnership may sue or be sued in the partnership name. I now hold that this defendant may be charged in an indictment as an entity with the commission of crimes related to the discharge of its primary obligations as a general hospital even though there is no showing of culpability on the part of the individual's partners.

The motion to dismiss the indictment against Smithtown General Hospital is denied.

CASE REVIEW QUESTIONS

1. Given the reasoning of this court, are partnerships now indictable in New York, or is the holding narrower and limited to such activities as the operation of hospitals? Explain.
2. Did the court hold that the partnership of all 42 of its partners are liable for the criminal conduct alleged, or did it hold that a criminal trial with the partnership as a defendant is proper? Explain.

PARTNERSHIP DISSOLUTION

Partnership **dissolution** is defined as "the change in the relation of the partners caused by any partner ceasing to be associated in the carrying on . . . of the business" [UPA §29]. When dissolution occurs, the remaining partner or partners may continue operating the business under some circumstances. If the business is not continued, it is necessary to wind up the business by liquidating the partnership's assets and paying the partnership's obligations. When the winding up is completed, **termination** of the partnership occurs. You should be careful to distinguish the three legal terms *dissolution, winding up,* and *termination.* The first two describe the two-step process that accomplishes the third.

Causes of Dissolution

Section 31 of the UPA provides that dissolution of a partnership may be caused by any of the following:

1. The termination of the definite term or particular undertaking of the partnership specified in the articles of partnership [UPA §31(1)(a)].
2. The express will of any partner if no definite term or particular undertaking is specified [UPA §31(1)(b)].
3. The express will of all the partners [UPA §31(1)(c)].
4. The expulsion of any partner pursuant to the terms of the articles of partnership [UPA §31(1)(d)].
5. An event that causes the partnership's business to be illegal [UPA §31(3)].
6. The death of a partner [UPA §31(4)].
7. The bankruptcy of a partner or the partnership [UPA §31(5)].

Dissolution by Court Decree Any of the occurrences just listed will cause the dissolution of a partnership without further action by the partners. Section 32 of the UPA provides for dissolution of a partnership by a decree of a court. Under this provision, a court is directed to declare the dissolution of a partnership if a partner applies for dissolution and can prove that any of the following conditions exist:

1. A partner has been legally declared insane or is shown to be of unsound mind [UPA §32(1)(a)].
2. A partner is otherwise incapable of performing his or her part of the partnership contract [UPA §32(1)(b)].

3. A partner has been guilty of conduct that tends to affect prejudicially the carrying on of the business [UPA §32(1)(c)].
4. A partner has wilfully or persistently breached the partnership agreement or has otherwise acted in such a way in matters relating to the business that it is not reasonably practicable to remain in partnership with him or her [UPA §32(1)(d)].
5. The business can only be carried on at a loss [UPA §32(1)(e)].
6. Other circumstances render a dissolution equitable [UPA §32(1)(f)].

In addition, a person who has obtained a partner's interest or a charging order, as discussed in the previous chapter, is entitled to a court decree dissolving the partnership if he or she applies for dissolution and can prove either of the following:

1. The specified term or particular undertaking of the partnership has been completed [UPA §32(2)(a)].
2. The partnership was a partnership at will when the interest or the charging order was obtained [UPA §32(2)(b)].

Dissolution in Violation of Partnership Agreement In addition to the causes of dissolution just set forth, the UPA provides that a partnership may be dissolved by the express will of *any* partner at *any* time [UPA §31(2)]. This cause for dissolution can be used by a partner even if by using it he or she will be violating the partnership agreement. It could be used, for instance, when a partnership agreement provides that the term of the partnership is to be for ten years, but one of the partners wants to dissolve the partnership prior to the completion of the ten-year period. Such a dissolution is called a *dissolution in violation of the partnership agreement.*

Although a dissolution in violation of the partnership agreement can be used, it constitutes a breach of the partnership agreement by the partner who uses it. The other partners therefore have the right to collect damages for the breach of contract from that partner. The other partners may also continue to operate the business for the term specified in the agreement. If the business is wound up instead of being continued, the partner who has breached the partnership agreement may not participate in the winding up process.

In the case that follows, a partner brought a legal action under UPA §32 seeking dissolution of a partnership by court decree. The other partner argued that bringing such a legal action constituted a breach of the partnership agreement, which entitled him to certain rights. The court had to decide whether a breach had occurred.

COOPER v. ISAACS
448 F.2d 1202 (D.C. Circuit 1971)

[Cooper and Isaacs were partners in the janitorial supply business. Their partnership agreement stated that the partnership was to continue "until terminated as provided herein." The agreement also contained express provisions for termination of the partnership by sale, mutual consent, and the retirement, death or incompetence of one of the partners.

Cooper brought a legal action to have the partnership dissolved. He argued that "irreconcilable differences" between him and his partner entitled him to a court decree dissolving the partnership. Isaacs counterclaimed on the basis that Cooper's legal action was a breach of the partnership agreement, which entitled him (Isaacs) to damages for breach of contract and allowed him to continue the business. Both Cooper and Isaacs moved for a temporary remedy prior to the trial in which a final determination of their rights would be made. The trial court granted Cooper's motion and denied Isaacs' motion. Isaacs appealed.]

TAMM, Circuit Judge

[W]e must first decide whether appellee Cooper's filing of his complaint requesting dissolution of the partnership on the ground of irreconcilable differences regarding business policy was itself a wrongful dissolution of the partnership in contravention of the partnership agreement. If it was, then appellant Isaacs was entitled to relief under [§38(b)(2)]. . . .

Turning to [§32], we find the following provisions:

(1) On application by or for a partner the court shall decree a dissolution whenever: . . . .

   (c) a partner has been guilty of such conduct as tends to affect prejudicially the carrying on of the business,
   (d) a partner wilfully or persistently commits a breach of the partnership agreement, or otherwise so conducts himself in matters relating to the partnership business that it is not reasonably practicable to carry on the business in partnership with him, . . .
   (f) other circumstances render a dissolution equitable.

Courts interpreting these provisions have consistently held that serious and irreconcilable differences between the parties are proper grounds for dissolution by decree of court. Since the Act provides for dissolution for cause by decree of court and Cooper has alleged facts which would entitle him to a dissolution on this ground if proven, his filing of his complaint cannot be said to effect a dissolution, wrongful or otherwise, under the Act; dissolution would occur only when decreed by the court or brought about by other actions.

A partnership agreement can presumably change this result, but the terms of the agreement must be quite specific to effect such a change. This is so because the provisions of the Act regarding dissolution by decree of court were clearly designed to allow partners to extricate themselves from business relationships which they felt had become intolerable without exposing themselves to liability in the process. . . .

We do not believe it can be said at this time, with the case in its present posture, that the partnership agreement involved here was clearly meant to exclude the possibility of dissolution of the partnership by decree of court under section [32]. True, the partnership agreement does discuss certain ways by which the partnership can be terminated and states that the partnership "shall continue until terminated as herein provided." However, it may well be that the parties did not consider the possibility that serious disagreements would arise at the time they made the agreement; the language limiting the methods of terminating the partnership may have been intended only to prevent a partner from dissolving the partnership voluntarily and without good cause. We thus conclude that without further inquiry into the partnership agreement and the claims made by the parties, it is impossible to say that the mere filing of the complaint by Cooper constituted a wrongful dissolution.

Affirmed.

CASE REVIEW QUESTIONS

1. If Cooper can prove that there are irreconcilable differences between him and Isaacs, will he necessarily be entitled to a court decree ordering dissolution of the partnership? Explain.
2. Explain in your own words why the court did not agree with Isaacs' argument that

Cooper's legal action to dissolve the partnership was a breach of the partnership agreement.

3. If it were determined that Cooper's legal action to dissolve the partnership was a breach of the partnership agreement, what rights would Isaacs have?

Continuing the Business

When a partner dies, retires, or withdraws from a partnership, the other partners often prefer to continue the business rather than to wind up and terminate it. Many large law and accounting partnerships, for example, have over 100 partners, and the withdrawal of one or another of them from the partnership occurs frequently. Each time this happens, there is a technical dissolution of the partnership because there is a "change in the relation of the partners caused by [the] partner ceasing to be associated in the carrying on . . . of the business." The partnership seldom ends its business activity, however. Indeed, if the partners are prudent, dissolution in which the business is continued after a change in partners will be one of the most important items covered in the articles of partnership.

Rights of Partnership Creditors The dissolution of a partnership does not affect the liability of the partners or the partnership. Even if the business is continued, both the noncontinuing and continuing partners are liable for all partnership liabilities incurred prior to dissolution.

In addition, if the business is continued, the creditors of the old partnership become creditors of the new partnership on an equal basis with new creditors of the new partnership [UPA §41]. In this situation, a noncontinuing partner can be discharged from his or her liability for obligations incurred prior to the dissolution by an agreement to that effect among the noncontinuing partner, the continuing partners, and the creditors [UPA §36(2)]. An agreement between the noncontinuing and continuing partners alone, however, will not discharge the noncontinuing partner from his or her liabilities to third-party creditors incurred prior to the dissolution.

The UPA also provides that, when a partnership is continued after a partner retires or dies, the old partnership creditors have priority over the individual creditors of the retiring or deceased partner with respect to his or her interest in the partnership [UPA §41(8)].

Rights of a Noncontinuing Partner with Prior Agreement Generally, articles of partnership provide for the valuation of a partner's interest in the partnership upon his or her retirement or death. (See paragraphs 11 and 12 of the partnership agreement presented in the previous chapter in Figure 35-1.) A partner's interest in the partnership consists of the right to the return of property in exchange for that brought into the partnership, the right to a share of the profits if there are any, and the right to a payment for the partner's contribution to the good will of the firm if the partnership agreement so provides. The entire interest is valued, usually by a preset formula, and the partner is paid this value.

We are assuming here that the partnership is a solvent, on-going enterprise at the time of dissolution. In those cases where the partnership is insolvent and does not have the funds to pay its creditors, the noncontinuing partner or his or her estate may have to contribute more capital to the partnership in order to pay the creditors.

Rights of a Noncontinuing Partner without Prior Agreement If one partner retires or dies and the other members of the partnership wish to continue the business but there has been no prior agreement concerning the matter, the continuing partners may negotiate an agreement with the retired partner or the deceased partner's estate concerning the value of his or her interest in the partnership. This amount is then paid to the retired partner or to the deceased partner's estate.

If no agreement can be reached, §42 of the UPA provides that the retiring partner or the estate of the deceased partner:

> may have the value of his interest at the date of dissolution ascertained, and shall receive as an ordinary creditor an amount equal to the value of his interest in the dissolved partnership. . . .

In addition to the value of his or her partnership interest, the noncontinuing partner has the choice of either receiving interest on the amount due from the time of dissolution until the time of payment or receiving profits attributable to the use of his or her interest in the partnership from the time of dissolution until the time of payment.

In the following case, the partnership agreement provided a formula for valuing a deceased partner's interest in the partnership. It also provided that the source of payment of the partner's interest was to be in part earnings of the partnership prior to the partner's death and in part earnings of the partnership subsequent to the partner's death. The issue that the court had to decide was whether that part of the deceased partner's interest in the partnership that was to be paid out of earnings of the partnership subsequent to the partner's death was a part of the deceased partner's estate at the time of his death.

McCLENNEN v. COMMISSIONER OF INTERNAL REVENUE
131 F.2d 165 (1st Circuit 1942)

MAGRUDER, Circuit Judge

George R. Nutter had been a partner in the firm of Nutter, McClennen & Fish, practicing law in Boston, Massachusetts. The firm kept its accounts on the cash receipts and disbursements basis. Its receipts were derived solely from personal services. Under the partnership agreement Mr. Nutter's share of the firm's net profits was 8 percent. The agreement also contained the following provision:

> On the retirement of a partner or on his death . . . the retiring partner or his estate in the case of his death shall, in addition to his percentage of net profits of the Firm received by it in cash up to the date of such death or retirement, also receive the same percentage of net profits of the Firm received by it in cash until the expiration of the eighteen (18) calendar months next after such retirement, or death, and this shall be in full payment of the retiring or deceasing member's interest in the capital, the assets, the receivables, the possibilities of the Firm. The continuing members shall have the right to the good will and the use of the Firm name except that the deceasing or retiring member's name shall not be used without his written consent or that of his estate. . . .

After the death of George R. Nutter the other partners continued the business. Eight percent of the net profits of the firm for the 18 calendar months next after the death, computed on the basis of cash receipts and disbursements, amounted to $34,069.99, which amount was paid over to the petitioners as executors.

Petitioners filed an estate tax return with the Collector of Internal Revenue at Boston, and paid the tax thereon shown to be due. . . . The sum of $6,136.21, which had been received by the executors as representing the decedent's share of the undistributed profits as of the date of the death, was included in the estate tax return as part of the decedent's gross estate. But beyond this nothing was included on account of the value of the decedent's interest in the partnership.

In his notice of deficiency the Commissioner determined that $34,069.99 should have been included in the gross estate as the value of decedent's "interest in partnership Nutter, McClennen & Fish." The Board [of Tax Appeals] has upheld the Commissioner in this determination. We think the Board was right.

In the absence of a controlling agreement in the partnership articles the death of a partner dissolves the partnership. The survivors have the right and duty, with reasonable dispatch, to wind up the partnership affairs, to complete transactions begun but not then finished, to collect the accounts receivable, to pay the firm debts, to convert the remaining firm assets into cash, and to pay in cash to the partners and the legal representative of the deceased partner the net amounts shown by the accounts to be owing to each of them in respect of capital contributions and in respect of their shares of profits and surplus. The representative of a deceased partner does not succeed to any right to specific partnership property. In substance the deceased partner's interest, to which his representative succeeds, is . . . a right to receive in cash the sum of money shown to be due him upon a liquidation and accounting. . . . The same substantive results are reached under the Uniform Partnership Act. . . . That act . . . conceives of the partner as a "co-owner with his partners of specific partnership property holding as a tenant in partnership"; but provides that on the death of a partner "his right in specific partnership property vests in the surviving partner or partners." Another enumerated property right of a partner, "his interest in the partnership," is described as "his share of the profits and surplus, and the same is personal property. . . ."

This [right] to which the representative of the deceased partner succeeds, the right to receive payment of a sum of money shown to be due upon a liquidation and accounting, is of course a part of the deceased partner's wealth, and includable in the decedent's gross estate, for purposes of computing the estate tax. . . . This is none the less true even though the net amount thus shown to be due to the estate is derived in whole or in part from past earnings or profits of the partnership resulting from personal services — profits which the decedent, if he had lived, would have had to report as income. . . .

In the case at bar, if there had not been the controlling provision in the partnership articles, above quoted, or if the survivors had not come to some agreement otherwise with the executors of Mr. Nutter, the survivors would have had to proceed to wind up the affairs of the partnership, to conclude all unfinished legal business on hand at the date of the death, to realize upon all of the assets of the firm, tangible or intangible, to pay the debts, to return to Mr. Nutter's estate his contribution of capital, if any, and to pay to his estate in cash the amount shown to be due in respect of his "interest in the partnership," that is, his "share of the profits and surplus," as determined upon an accounting. Among other things to be taken into account, "the earned proportion of the unfinished business" would have had "to be valued to determine the decedent's interest in the partnership assets."

To obviate the necessity of a liquidation, or to eliminate accounting difficulties in determining the value of the deceased partner's interest, partners often make specific provision in the partnership articles. . . .

In the case at bar the partnership agreement contains [a] familiar arrangement, whereby no liquidation and final acounting will ever be necessary in order to satisfy the claim of the deceased partner. In place of . . . a right to receive payment in cash of the amount shown to be due the deceased partner upon a complete liquidation and accounting, a different right is substituted, a right of the estate to receive a share of the net profits of the firm for 18 calendar months after the partner's death. . . .

In the present case the Commissioner valued Mr. Nutter's interest in the partnership at the sum of $34,069.99, which happened to be the exact amount received by the executors from the survivors as representing 8 percent of the net profits of the partnership for the 18 calendar months after the death. There is no contention that this was an overvaluation. . . .

The decision of the Board of Tax Appeals is affirmed.

CASE REVIEW QUESTIONS

1. What action taken by the original partnership made a winding up and termination of the partnership unnecessary?
2. What argument did McClennen's estate make for omitting the $34,069.99 from the estate's tax return? Why did the court reject this argument?
3. Reread paragraph 12a of the partnership agreement that is presented in Figure 35-1 in the previous chapter. How do the provisions in that agreement for valuing the interest of a retiring or deceased partner differ from the provisions in the agreement in this case?

Winding up the Business

If the surviving partner or partners do not wish to continue the business, the authority of the partners to act for the partnership in the ordinary course of business ends at dissolution [UPA §33]. The partners continue to have the authority necessary to wind up the business, however. **Winding up** involves selling the firm's assets, paying off the firm's obligations to third parties, and distributing the amounts remaining to the partners. During the period of winding up, the partners continue to owe fiduciary duties to each other.

When dissolution occurs because all of the partners agree to it, they all have the right to participate in the winding up of the business [UPA §37]. If, on the other hand, the dissolution occurs because of the bankruptcy or death of one of the partners, the bankrupt partner or the estate of the deceased partner does not have the right to participate in the winding up. When dissolution occurs as a result of a court decree, the court will usually appoint a receiver to wind up the business.

Notice of Dissolution As just noted, dissolution ends the actual authority of the partners to act for the partnership, except for the purpose of winding up. However, third parties who have dealt with the partnership prior to dissolution and who deal with a partner after dissolution without notice of the dissolution may be able to hold the partnership liable on the basis of the partner's apparent authority.

Apparent authority may be terminated only by notice to the third parties. More specifically, §35(1)(b)(I) of the UPA requires that a third party who has given credit to the partnership prior to dissolution be given actual notice of the dissolution. This notice must be communicated directly to the third party or its agent. If notice is not given, and the third party does not otherwise have knowledge of the dissolution, then a partner acting in the ordinary course of business (as established before the dissolution) binds the partnership.

If a third party has not previously extended credit to the partnership but only knew of the partnership, then constructive notice is sufficient to terminate the partners' apparent authority. Constructive notice does not require that notice be given directly to the third party. Instead, it only requires that the information be made available in such a way that the third party could discover it by due diligence. Constructive notice might be given, for instance, by publishing the fact of dissolution in a newspaper of general circulation in the place where the partnership's business was regularly carried on.

Section 35(3) of the UPA provides that no notice is needed when dissolution is caused by the partnership's business being declared illegal or by the bankruptcy of a partner. Note, however, that the UPA differs from the Restatement of Agency concerning the requirement of notice in the case of death. Remember that in agency law, no notice to third parties who have dealt with an agent is required when the principal dies (see page 724). In contrast, the UPA does not consider dissolution caused by the death of a partner to be notorious enough to negate the necessity of notice.

The following is an old case that illustrates some basic concepts about the nature of partnerships and the notice requirements that must be met by a partnership upon dissolution. These concepts have been incorporated into the UPA.

SOLOMON v. KIRKWOOD
55 Mich. 256 (1884)

[Solomon and others were dealers in jewelry in Chicago. They brought a legal action against Kirkwood and Hollander, as partners, to collect on a promissory note for $791.92, dated November 9, 1882, and signed "Hollander & Kirkwood." The note had been given by Hollander. Kirkwood's defense to the legal action was that no partnership existed between the defendants on the date the note was given.

The trial court found for the defendant, Kirkwood. Plaintiffs appealed from the judgment for Kirkwood.

The appellate court affirmed the trial court's decision on the two issues discussed in the following opinion. The appellate court reversed the trial court's decision on an issue not included here.]

COOLEY, Chief Judge

The evidence on the trial tends to show that on July 6, 1882, Hollander & Kirkwood entered into a written agreement for a partnership for one year from the first day of the next ensuing month, in the business of buying and selling jewelry, clocks, watches, etc., and in repairing clocks, watches, and jewelry, at Ishpeming, Michigan. Business was begun under this agreement, and continued until the latter part of October, 1882, when Kirkwood, becoming dissatisfied, locked up the goods and excluded Hollander altogether from the business. He also caused notice to be given to all persons with whom the firm had had dealings that the partnership was dissolved, and had the following inserted in the local column of the paper published at Ishpeming: ''The copartnership heretofore existing between Mr. C. H. Kirkwood and one Hollander, as jewelers, has ceased to exist, Mr. Kirkwood having purchased the interest of the latter.'' This was not signed by any one.

A few days later Hollander went to Chicago, and there, on November 9, 1882, he bought, in the name of Hollander & Kirkwood, of the plaintiffs goods in their line amounting to $791.92, and gave to the plaintiffs therefor the promissory note now in suit. The note was made payable December 15, 1882, at a bank in Ishpeming. When the purchase was completed Hollander took away the goods in his satchel. The plaintiffs had before had no dealings with Hollander & Kirkwood, but they had heard there was such a firm, and were not aware of its dissolution. They claim to have made the sale in good faith, and in the belief that the firm was still in existence. . . .

The questions principally contested on the trial were — First, whether the acts of Kirkwood amounted to a dissolution of the partnership; and second, whether sufficient notice of dissolution was given. . . . The trial judge, in submitting the case to the jury, instructed them that Kirkwood, notwithstanding the written agreement, had a right to withdraw from the partnership at any time, leaving matters between him and Hollander to be adjusted between them amicably or in the courts; and for the purpose of this case it made no difference whether Kirkwood was right or wrong in bringing the partnership to an end: if wrong, he might be liable to Hollander in damages for the breach of his contract. Also, that when partners are dissatisfied, or they cannot get along together, and one partner withdraws, the partnership is then at an end as to the public and parties with whom the partnership deals, and neither partner can make contracts in the future to bind the partnership, provided the retiring partner gives the proper notice. Also, that if they should find from the evidence that there was trouble between Hollander and Kirkwood prior to the sale of the goods and the giving of the note; that Kirkwood informed Hollander, in substance, that he would have no more dealings with him as partner; that he took possession of all the goods and locked them up, and from that time they ceased to do business — then the partnership was dissolved. Further, that whether sufficient notice had been given of the dissolution was a question for the jury. Kirkwood was not bound to publish notice in any of the Chicago papers; he was only bound to give actual notice to such parties there as had dealt with the partnership. But Kirkwood was bound to use all fair means to publish as widely as possible the fact of a dissolution. Publication in a newspaper is one of the proper means of giving notice, but it is not absolutely essential; and on this branch of the case the question for the jury was whether Kirkwood gave such notice of the dissolution as under the circumstances was fair and reasonable. If he did, then he is not liable on the note: if he did not, he would still continue liable. . . .

We think the judge committed no error in his instructions respecting the dissolution of the partnership. The rule on this subject is thus stated in an early New York case. The right of a partner to dissolve, it is said,

> is a right inseparably incident to every partnership. There can be no such thing as an indissoluble partnership. Every partner has an indefeasible right to dissolve the partnership as to all future contracts by publishing his own volition to that effect; and after such publication the other members of the firm have no capacity to bind him by any contract. Even where partners covenant with each other that the partnership shall continue seven years, either partner may dissolve it the next day by proclaiming his determination for that purpose; the only consequence being, that he thereby subjects himself to a claim for damages for a breach of the covenant. The power given by one partner to another to make joint contracts for them both, is not only a revocable power, but a man can do no act to divest himself of a capacity to revoke it.

. . . When one partner becomes dissatisfied there is commonly no legal policy to be subserved by compelling a continuance of the relation, and the fact that a contract will be broken by the dissolution is no argument against the right to dissolve. Most contracts may be broken at pleasure, subject however to responsibility in damages. And that responsibility would exist in breaking a contract of partnership as in other cases.

The instruction respecting notice was also correct. No court can determine for all cases what shall be sufficient notice and what shall not be: the question must necessarily be one of fact. Publication of notice of dissolution in a local newspaper is common, but it is not the only method in which notice can be given. The purpose of the notice is to make notorious in the local community the fact that a dissolution has taken place; and publication of a notice may or may not be the most effectual means for that purpose. Very few persons in any community probably read all the advertisements published in the local papers; and matters of local im-

portance which are advertised are quite as likely to come to them from other sources as from the published notices. . . .

One who derives knowledge of the fact from public notoriety is sufficiently notified; . . . and probably in many small communities a fact would sooner be made notorious by a notice in the local column of the county or village paper than in any other way. In a large city it might be otherwise. But all that can be required in any case is that such notice be given as is likely to make the fact generally known locally. . . . When that is done the party giving the notice has performed his duty, and any one contemplating for the first time to open dealings with the partnership must at his peril ascertain the facts. This, in effect, was the instruction given. . . .

[Reversed on other grounds.]

CASE REVIEW QUESTIONS

1. Earlier in the chapter, the causes of dissolution set forth in the UPA were discussed. If the UPA had been in effect at the time of the Hollander & Kirkwood partnership, which of the causes of dissolution set forth in it would have been applicable?
2. Solomon did not know of the dissolution of the Hollander & Kirkwood partnership. Why, then, couldn't he hold the partnership liable on the grounds of apparent authority?
3. Under what different circumstances could Solomon have been successful in holding the partnership liable on the grounds of apparent authority?

Distribution of Assets The final step in winding up a dissolved partnership is the distribution of assets. Section 40 of the UPA provides for the distribution of the partnership's assets in the following order:

1. Those owed to creditors other than the partners.
2. Those owed to partners other than for capital and profits, that is, for advances or loans.
3. Those owed to partners with respect to capital.
4. Those owed to partners with respect to profits.

Insolvent Partnership If the partnership is solvent at the time of dissolution, there should be no problems in distributing the partnership's assets as §40 provides. If the partnership is insolvent at the time of dissolution, however, §40(d) requires that "[t]he partners shall contribute . . . the amount necessary to satisfy the liabilities." In other words, the partners are personally liable for the debts of an insolvent partnership and must contribute sufficient funds to pay off those debts.

Unless the partnership agreement provides otherwise, partnership profits and losses are divided equally among the partners. Consider, for example, Figure 36-1. Suppose that the partners have contributed $10,000 to capital in the amounts indicated in the figure and are to share profits and losses equally. During the winding up of the partnership, the assets are sold for $6,700. The partnership has thus suffered a loss of $3,300. Because the loss is to be shared equally by the three partners, partner C will have to contribute $100 more to the partnership.

Insolvent Partners Suppose that one or more of the partners of an insolvent partnership is also insolvent. What affect does this have on the personal liability of the partners who are solvent? Section 40(d) of the UPA states that:

> [I]f any, but not all, of the partners are insolvent . . . the other partners shall contribute their share of the liability. . . .

This means that partnership creditors will be paid if any of the partners are able to pay.

Partnership versus Individual Creditors As a general rule, the creditors of a partnership have first claim against the partnership's assets, and the individual creditors of a partner have first claim against the partner's individual assets. Under the federal Bankruptcy Act, however, a trustee in bankruptcy of a *partnership* has a claim equal to the claims of the unsecured individual creditors of the partners against the individual assets of the partners.

The case that follows illustrates several issues that can arise in the dissolution, winding up, and termination of a partnership.

MAHAN v. MAHAN
489 P.2d 1197 (Ariz. 1971)

CAMERON, Justice

Plaintiff brought this action individually and as executrix [legal representative] of the estate of her deceased husband. She sought an accounting and division of properties of a partnership in which her husband had been a partner. From a decision of the Superior Court of Coconino County granting her what she considered inadequate relief, she appeals.

We are called upon to consider the following questions:

1. Did the court err in determining that plaintiff's husband's partnership share should be measured by his capital account?
2. Did the court err in accepting the book value as the proper valuation of the property?
3. Did the court err in failing to direct the liquidation and sale of the remaining partnership assets?

Plaintiff is the widow of Terrell B. Mahan, who died 15 July 1966, in Prescott, Arizona. . . . When plaintiff

Capital Contributed	Profit or Loss	Individual Loss
A:$ 5,000	$10,000 owed to partners	$3,300 divided
B:$ 4,000	6,700 available to pay	by 3, equals
C:$ 1,000	partners	$1,100
$10,000	$ 3,300 (loss)	
	Distribution of Assets	

Payment to A—$5,000 minus $1,100—is $3,900.

Payment to B—$4,000 minus $1,100—is $2,900.

C paid only $1,000 and must contribute $100 more to suffer loss of $1,100.

FIGURE 36-1

Distribution of Assets upon Dissolution of an Insolvent Partnership

married Terrell Mahan in 1948, a construction and agriculture partnership existed between Terrell and his brothers, Gordon and Merwin. (Merwin withdrew from the partnership in 1962 and is not involved in the lawsuit.) The partnership was an equal one in the sense that the profits were divided on an equal basis, first three ways, and then two.

In 1964 the partnership traded one of the partnership properties for a home into which Terrell and his wife moved. The property was taken in the name of Terrell and his wife. The bookkeeper reduced the capital account of Terrell and his wife by $23,000. In short, Terrell and his wife received a house worth $23,000, more or less, in exchange for reducing their capital account to $23,000 less than Gordon's.

At about this time (1964–1965), the partnership became inactive, and it remained inactive through Terrell's death in 1966 and the bringing of the present lawsuit in 1969. Gordon, the surviving partner, did nothing toward settling the affairs of the partnership and accounting to the executrix until Terrell's widow brought this suit.

The principal partnership asset at Terrell's death and the time of the lawsuit was the remainder of a block of Coconino County land bought in 1950 and known as the Red Lake Ranch. In 1960, the partnership sold a portion of the ranch for $80,000 leaving 1,752.34 acres of [owned] land, plus 1,843 acres of leased land. In December, 1961, the partnership made an aborted sale of practically the same block owned at Terrell's death. The sale, for $284,200, fell through in 1963, and the Mahan brothers regained the land. In 1963, an appraiser valued the land at $43,868.44, and in 1965 an accountant, for federal tax purposes, lowered the value on the partnership books to $15,622.61.

The balance sheet of the partnership as of 31 December 1965 showed $33,274.61 worth of assets. The principal components of this amount were $15,622.61 for the Red Lake Ranch, two investments with a total book value of $9,150, but market values of $900 and $0 respectively, and an oil lease listed at $4,000 but actually worthless.

The defendant advanced, and the trial court accepted, the contention that since Terrell's capital account was reduced by $23,000 to $4,005.45 and was one-eighth of the value of the total capital account ($31,308.06), Terrell's widow should receive in distribution, one-eighth of $33,274.31 or $4,159.29.

Plaintiff contends that after payment of the partnership debts, she should share with Gordon on a 50–50 basis. We agree with plaintiff as long as it is understood that the capital account, as used by the bookkeeper in this case, represents a debt of the partnership.

Upon liquidation, the rules of payment are governed by [UPA §40] which decrees that the liabilities of the partnership shall rank in the following order of payment:

(a) Those owing to creditors other than partners.
(b) Those owing to partners other than for capital and profits.
(c) Those owing to partners in respect of capital.
(d) Those owing to partners in respect of profits.

"The capital of the partnership is the amount specified in the agreement of the partners, which is to be contributed by the partners for the purpose of initiating and operating the partnership business." Thus, ordinarily we would look to the initial contributions for a determination of the amounts "owing to partners in respect of capital." While the general rule is that the amount of capital may not be changed absent consent of all the partners, the partners in this case have apparently conceded to adjustments in their capital accounts. Thus, we accept, for purposes of this case, adjustments in plaintiff's and defendant's capital accounts to $4,005.45 and $27,302.61 respectively.

> The distribution of partnership assets in the course of winding up consists, first of all, in the payment of creditors other than partners. Then come the claims of partners other than those for repayment of capital contributions or profits, such as claims for advancements made by partners. After this, partners are entitled to return of their respective capital contributions. Finally, any remaining balance of partnership property is distributable as profits.

Therefore, whether the money left after satisfaction of creditor's claims and recoupment of partnership capital is termed profits or surplus, the clear mandate of the authorities is that, absent agreement to the contrary, it is divided equally as profits.

As mentioned earlier, the defendant in this case has placed reliance on [UPA §42] relating to continuation of the business when a partner dies. In the instant case, the business was not continued by the surviving partner. Quite the contrary. The partnership remained dormant and nothing was done until suit was brought by the plaintiff to compel an accounting. Where the efforts of one partner in the production of profits in an active partnership cease, it is apparent that he no longer bears full entitlement to his respective share of the profits. In this case, however, where the partnership has been and continues to be inactive, any appreciation or worth is due to the nature of the partnership property rather than the effort of the surviving partner. Thus, we hold that any profit or surplus resulting shall be shared equally.

This conclusion is buttressed by the situation confronting plaintiff and her husband Terrell when they gave up $23,000 of their capital account for a $23,000 home. They knew that the partnership had few or no debts and owned a piece of property that had sold for $284,200 a few years previous. If the value of the land had stayed reasonably constant in the interim, the partnership would have been worth over $300,000. It is highly unlikely that the plaintiff and her husband intended, when they gave up $23,000 of their capital account for a $23,000 house, that they were actually giving up not $23,000 but well over $100,000.

The answer to the question of whether the court erred in accepting the book value of the assets can be answered by looking at the figures we have reconstructed. Every single component of the $33,274.61 book value has been strongly contested. The Red Lake Ranch, for example, was sold in 1961 for over $28,000, but has an arbitrary book value of $15,622.61. An "investment" valued at $9,150 is made up of two investments, one worthless and the other worth only $900. In short, the book values are completely arbitrary and should not have been used.

Our determination that the trial court erred in accepting book value is in accord . . . with general principles of partnership accounting. The normal rule is that book value is only used in ascertaining the respective shares when there is an explicit contractual provision to that effect, and even then is not used where the facts of the case make it inequitable to do so. Here there was no contractual provision mandating the use of book value, and even if there were, the facts show book value in this case to be so disproportionate to possible real values that it would be inequitable for it to be used anyway.

Having decided that book value should not be used in valuing the partnership assets, we are forced to conclude that the trial court should have granted plaintiff's wish to have the assets liquidated. . . .

We hold that the partnership assets must be liquidated, and that the general creditors be paid first. If the assets are insufficient for this purpose, the estate and Gordon should be charged equally for the losses. If the assets are more than sufficient, then the surviving partner should be paid first up to the amount of $23,297.16 to set off the withdrawal from the capital account by Terrell. Any amount left over should be equally divided between Terrell's estate and the surviving partner, Gordon Mahan.

Reversed and remanded.

CASE REVIEW QUESTIONS

1. Explain the following statement made by the court: "Plaintiff contends that after payment of the partnership debts, she should share with Gordon on a 50–50 basis. We agree with plaintiff as long as it is understood that the capital account . . . represents a debt of the partnership."

2. The court decided that plaintiff should share equally in the profits of the partnership. On what basis did the defendant argue that the plaintiff was not entitled to an equal share of the profits prior to the death of Terrell? On what basis did the defendant argue that the plaintiff was not entitled to an equal share of the profits after Terrell's death? Why did the court reject each of these arguments?

REVIEW QUESTIONS

1. What is the relationship between agency law and partnership law?

2. How should you determine whether or not a partner has the authority to contract with third persons on behalf of the partnership?

3. Give an example not given in the text in which a partnership would be held liable for an intentional tort committed by a partner.

4. What do *dissolution, winding up,* and *termination* mean in partnership law? How are the three concepts related to one another?

5. May a partner dissolve a partnership if doing so will constitute a violation of the partnership agreement?

6. What is the order of distribution of the assets of a partnership in the process of winding up a partnership?

CASE PROBLEMS

1. Williams, Watkins, and Glenn is a general partnership engaged primarily in the real estate brokerage business; however, in addition, it buys and sells real property for its own account. Williams and Watkins are almost exclusively responsible for the brokerage part of the business, and Glenn devotes almost all of his time to partnership acquisitions and sales of real estate. The firm letterhead makes no distinction along these functional lines and all members are listed as licensed real-estate brokers. Normally, acquisitions are made in the firm's name, although for convenience or other reason, Glenn occasionally takes title in his own name for and on behalf of the firm.

   The partnership agreement contains, among other provisions, the following:

   No partner shall reduce the standard real estate commission charged (6%) without the consent of at least one other partner.

   No partner shall purchase or sell real property for or on behalf of the partnership without the consent of all other partners. Title to real property so acquired shall be taken exclusively in the partnership name, unless otherwise agreed to by all the partners.

   All checks received which are payable to the partnership and all checks and cash received for or on behalf of the partnership shall be deposited intact in one of the partnership's bank accounts.

   Watkins showed a magnificent $350,000 ranch estate, listed for over a year with the firm by John Foster, to numerous prospective purchasers. The firm's exclusive listing had recently expired, and Watkins was afraid the firm would lose the sale. Foster's price was firm, and he had repeatedly refused to negotiate with interested parties or to accept an offer below $350,000. The most recent prospective buyer offered $340,000 but would not budge from that price. Watkins, fearing that a rival broker might obtain a buyer and cause him to lose the commission, agreed to lower the commission to $11,000, which was acceptable to Foster. Watkins did this without the consent of either of the other partners. Can Williams, Watkins, and Glenn or Williams and Glenn recover from Foster the $10,000 reduction in the commission granted by Watkins to Foster? Explain. What recourse does the partnership or the other partners have against Watkins? Explain. [Adapted from CPA examination question 7, *Business Law,* November 1975.]

2. During the annual examination of the financial statements of the Williams, Watkins, and Glenn partnership, the auditor discovered that Glenn had recently engaged in a series of questionable transactions affecting the firm's financial position. Following is a description of these transactions.

First, Glenn sold a tract of land to Bill Sparks for $18,500. Title to the land was held in the name of the partnership. Spark's check was payable to the partnership and was cashed by Glenn at the First City Bank, which handled the firm's checking account. Glenn indorsed the firm name "Per Donald Glenn, Partner" and took the cash. Obtaining this amount of cash at the First City Bank was not an uncommon practice for the partnership because the firm paid its substantial weekly payroll and commissions in cash.

Glenn's second series of transactions involved the sale of the firm's former office building for $38,000 to Charles Whitmore. Whitmore was formerly associated with the firm but had left to establish his own real-estate business and was a tenant in the firm's old offices. Whitmore was cognizant of the express limitations on the partners' authority contained in the Williams, Watkins, and Glenn partnership agreement. However, Whitmore was assured by Glenn that the requisite consent for his individual actions had been obtained from the other partners regarding the sale in question. Glenn also persuaded Whitmore, "for convenience sake," to make the check payable to

his individual order. Glenn cashed the check at one of the savings banks in which the firm had a balance in excess of $50,000.

Glenn's third series of transactions began when he acquired a tract of land for $55,000 from Arthur Douglas. Glenn paid for the land with a partnership check but took record title in his own name. A few days later, two days before leaving for vacation, Glenn closed the sale of this property to Frank Carlson and received a certified check for $58,500 payable to his own order. The proceeds of this sale were not deposited in any of the firm's bank accounts. It was subsequently learned that he cashed the check and retained the funds for his personal use. Glenn has not returned from his vacation. In fact, he is five days overdue and has not communicated with the firm.

What rights, if any, does the partnership or Williams and Watkins have against Bill Sparks, First City Bank, Charles Whitmore, Frank Carlson, and Glenn? Explain. [Adapted from CPA examination question 7, *Business Law,* November 1975.]

3. Plushkin owned a small farm, part of which he leased to Edwards and Franks, who operated a pig-raising business. Edwards and Franks split profits and jointly managed the business. After the business had been in operation for about a year, the county in which the farm was located passed legislation that prohibited the use of the land for such purposes. Edwards subsequently went to the premises, intending to remove some lumber, some fencing, and the pigs. Upon entering, Edwards failed to close the gate, which allowed most of the pigs to escape into Plushkin's cornfield, where they trampled and ate some of Plushkin's crop. Edwards and Plushkin argued about Edward's right to remove the lumber and the fencing, and Edwards intentionally struck Plushkin, injuring him. A few days after the altercation, while Plushkin was still in the hospital, Edwards returned to the farm and removed the lumber, the fencing, and the pigs. If Plushkin sues Edwards and Franks, as partners, for the bodily injury caused by Edwards and the damage to his crops, who will win the case? Explain. If Plushkin presses criminal charges against Edwards and Franks, as partners, for assault and battery,

will a criminal prosecution against them be successful? Explain.

4. Dowling, a partner of Lazor, Bassett, Dowling & Lamb, died on February 2, 1976. The four partners were equal partners in all respects (i.e., capital accounts, profit and loss sharing, etc.). The partnership agreement was silent on the question of the rights of a deceased partner on his death. Dowling's will bequeathed his entire estate to his "beloved wife." His widow is now claiming the right to 25 percent of all partnership property. What rights does Dowling's widow have with respect to specific partnership property or against the partnership or the surviving partners? Explain. [Adapted from CPA examination question 6c, *Business Law,* May 1976.]

5. Able, Baker, and Carey each contributed $75,000 in capital to their partnership when it was created. It was agreed that each partner was to share equally in the profits and losses of the partnership. Able elected to withdraw from the partnership because his personal assets were depleted. An accounting was ordered, and it was found that Able had advanced an additional $10,000 to the partnership several years before the dissolution. This amount remained unpaid. Baker had drawn out $25,000 of his capital before dissolution, and Carey had drawn out all of his capital. In addition, Carey owed a $2,000 debt to the partnership. When the partnership assets were liquidated, $141,000 was received. The partnership owed $18,000 to creditors and $2,000 to Baker for services rendered in winding up the business. What amounts, if any, should be distributed to each of the partners? Explain.

37

OTHER FORMS OF PARTNERSHIP

In the previous two chapters, you have learned about the law that affects the creation, operation, dissolution, and termination of the usual form of partnership. In this chapter, you will learn about some other forms of partnership: *partnership by estoppel, joint venture, mining partnership,* and *limited partnership.* The most common and most important of these is the limited partnership. As you read about each of these forms of partnership, you should note the ways it differs from the ordinary form.

PARTNERSHIP BY ESTOPPEL

Generally, a partnership is created only if all of the partners agree to its creation, and only those who are parties to the agreement are partners. Sometimes, however, a court will recognize the existence of a partnership even though one does not actually exist or will impose the duties of a partner on a person who is not actually a partner. This is done to provide a remedy for a third party who has been led to believe that a partnership exists or that a person is a partner. When a court takes this action, it is said to create a **partnership by estoppel** or **partner by estoppel**, a doctrine that protects the reasonable expectations of third parties.

Section 16 of the Uniform Partnership Act (UPA) imposes the liability of a partner on a person by estoppel in two circumstances:

1. When a person represents himself or herself as a partner in a partnership, he or she is liable to any person to whom such representation has been made and who has given credit to the actual or apparent partnership.

2. When a person has been represented to be a partner in a partnership, he or she is an agent of the persons consenting to such representation, with respect to persons who have relied upon the representation, to the same extent and in the same manner as though he or she were a partner in fact.

For example, if Smith represented herself to be a partner in the Olympus Associates partnership, even though in reality she was not, and Jones extended credit to the partnership, Smith would be treated as a partner by estoppel under point 1. Under point 2, members of the Olympus Associates partnership who knew that Smith was representing that she was a partner would be liable to Jones. If all of the partners of Olympus Associates knew of Smith's representation, then the partnership would also be liable to Jones.

Although a person may be held liable to an injured third party as a partner under the doctrine of estoppel, you should note that this is done solely for the purpose of providing a remedy to the third party. In fact, no real partnership is created, and the persons who are treated as partners by estoppel cannot enforce the other duties of partners against one another.

JOINT VENTURE

A **joint venture**, or **joint adventure** as it is sometimes called, is a business association that is essentially a partnership with a narrow purpose. Usually, a joint venture is formed for a single undertaking or a series of related undertakings of fairly short duration that do not require the complete attention of the members. For example, an association created for the purpose of subdividing and selling lots in a real estate development has been categorized as a joint venture. Because a joint venture is a form of partnership, it and its members are subject to the UPA.

There is one particularly significant reason for distinguishing between a partnership and a joint venture. In the few states that prohibit corporations from being general partners, the courts are likely to allow them to be participants in a joint venture. The different treatment is based upon the theory that there is less of a surrender of managerial authority to a joint venture by a corporation's board of directors than there is to an ordinary partnership because of the limited nature of the undertakings of a joint venture.

MINING PARTNERSHIP

Some states recognize a form of partnership called a **mining partnership**. The creation of a mining partnership requires that the partners co-own land, jointly operate a mining claim (including oil and gas claims) on the land, and share in the operation's profits and losses.

A mining partnership differs from an ordinary partnership in two important ways. First, any partner can transfer his or her interest in a mining partnership without the consent of the other partners and without terminating the partnership. Second, dissolution of a mining partnership only occurs by the express agreement of the partners, by the expiration of the time period for the partnership agreed to by the partners, by the purchase of the interests of all the partners by a single individual, or by judicial decree.

LIMITED PARTNERSHIP

As you learned in the previous chapter, a partner has unlimited personal liability for the debts of a partnership. Because of this rule of partnership law, a person who does not want to be exposed to the risk of unlimited personal liability will avoid becoming involved in a partnership.

In the early part of the nineteenth century, states began to authorize the creation of a different form of partnership in which some of the partners could be protected from unlimited personal liability. This new form of partnership, called a **limited partnership,** was developed to attract more capital to partnerships. More capital is attracted because the amount of risk is reduced for some of the partners, called **limited partners,** by limiting their liability to the amount of their contribution of capital to the partnership.

In order to provide uniformity in limited partnership law among the states, the National Conference of Commissioners on Uniform State Laws drafted the Uniform Limited Partnership Act (ULPA) in 1916. The ULPA or similar laws were subsequently adopted by all the states. In 1976, the ULPA was substantially revised. Only a few states have thus far adopted the Revised Uniform Limited Partnership Act (RULPA), however, because the Internal Revenue Service delayed giving approval of some of its provisions. The Internal Revenue Service has now approved of the revised act and its widespread adoption is anticipated. In this chapter, we will refer to both the ULPA and the RULPA. These acts are reproduced in Appendices D and E.

Formation of a Limited Partnership

Section 1 of the ULPA defines a limited partnership as

> a partnership formed by two or more persons . . . having as members one or
> more general partners and one or more limited partners.

One of the important differences between a limited partnership and a general partnership is that to create a limited partnership it is necessary to file a certificate of limited partnership in a designated public office [ULPA §2]. The primary purpose of this filing requirement is to put those who do business with the partnership on notice of the limited liability of the limited partners.

The certificate of limited partnership must include:

1. The limited partnership's name, general character, and address.
2. The name and business address of each partner.
3. Identification of each partner as a general partner or a limited partner.
4. Information concerning the contributions to the capital of the partnership by the partners, the power of a limited partner to assign his or her partner-

ship interest, and the rights of partners to receive distributions from or to withdraw from the partnership.

5. Any right of the remaining general partners to continue the business if a general partner withdraws.

6. The causes for the dissolution and winding up of the affairs of the partnership.

The limited partnership's existence begins when the certificate of limited partnership is properly filed or at a later time specified in the certificate [RULPA §201(b)]. Failure to file the certificate properly may result in the partnership being treated as a general rather than limited partnership. Consequently, the partners may be subject to unlimited individual liability to the partnership's creditors. Section 11 of the ULPA, however, provides that a person who erroneously believes himself or herself to be a limited partner will not be treated as a general partner as long as he or she promptly renounces his or her interest in the profits of the partnership or in other compensation from the partnership after learning of the improper filing. The RULPA provides similar protection in §304.

Limited Personal Liability

The most significant difference between a general partnership and a limited partnership is that the limited partners of a limited partnership are not subject to unlimited personal liability for partnership debts. In other words, the creditors of a limited partnership may look to the partnership assets and the individual assets of the general partners for payment, but they may not look to the individual assets of the limited partners.

Section 7 of the ULPA provides:

A limited partner shall not become liable as a general partner unless, in addition to his rights and powers as a limited partner, he takes part in the control of the business.

Note that, in order to maintain limited liability, a limited partner must not take part in the control of the partnership's business. The privilege of controlling the business is restricted to the general partners. In the following case, the court had to determine whether two of the members of a partnership were general partners or limited partners. To make this determination, the court had to decide whether the two partners took part in the control of the business.

HOLZMAN v. DE ESCAMILLA
195 P.2d 833 (Cal. App. 1948)

MARKS, Justice

This is an appeal by James L. Russell and H. W. Andrews from a judgment decreeing they were general partners in Hacienda Farms, Limited, a limited partnership, from February 27, to December 1, 1943, and as such were liable as general partners to the creditors of the partnership.

Early in 1943, Hacienda Farms, Limited, was organized as a limited partnership . . . with Ricardo de Escamilla as the general partner and James L. Russell and H. W. Andrews as limited partners.

The partnership went into bankruptcy in December, 1943, and Lawrence Holzman was appointed and qualified as trustee of the estate of the bankrupt. On November 13, 1944, he brought this action for the purpose of determining that Russell and Andrews, by taking part in the control of the partnership business, had become liable as general partners to the creditors of the partnership. The trial court found in favor of the plaintiff on this issue and rendered judgment to the effect that the three defendants were liable as general partners.

The findings supporting the judgment are so fully supported by the testimony of certain witnesses, although contradicted by Russell and Andrews, that we need mention but a small part of it. . . .

De Escamilla was raising beans on farm lands near Escondido at the time the partnership was formed. The partnership continued raising vegetable and truck crops which were marketed principally through a produce concern controlled by Andrews.

The record shows the following testimony of de Escamilla:

Q. Did you have a conversation or conversations with Mr. Andrews or Mr. Russell before planting the tomatoes?

A. We always conferred and agreed as to what crops we would put in. . . .

Q. Who determined that it was advisable to plant watermelons?

A. Mr. Andrews. . . .

Q. Who determined that string beans should be planted?

A. All of us. There was never any planting done — except the first crop that was put into the partnership as an asset by myself, there was never any crop that was planted or contemplated in planting that wasn't thoroughly discussed and agreed upon by the three of us; particularly Andrews and myself.

De Escamilla further testified that Russell and An-

drews came to the farms about twice a week and consulted about the crops to be planted. He did not want to plant peppers or egg plant because, as he said "I don't like that country for peppers or egg plant; no sir," but he was overruled and those crops were planted. The same is true of the watermelons.

Shortly before October 15, 1943, Andrews and Russell requested de Escamilla to resign as manager, which he did, and Harry Miller was appointed in his place.

Hacienda Farms, Limited, maintained two bank accounts, one in a San Diego bank and another in an Escondido bank. It was provided that checks could be drawn on the signatures of any two of the three partners. It is stated in plaintiff's brief, without any contradiction (the checks are not before us) that money was withdrawn on twenty checks signed by Russell and Andrews and that all other checks except three bore the signature of de Escamilla, the general partner, and one of the other defendants. The general partner had no power to withdraw money without the signature of one of the limited partners.

[ULPA §7] provides as follows:

> A limited partner shall not become liable as a general partner, unless, in addition to the exercise of his rights and powers as a limited partner, he takes part in the control of the business.

The foregoing illustrations sufficiently show that Russell and Andrews both took "part in the control of the business." The manner of withdrawing money from the bank accounts is particularly illuminating. The two men had absolute power to withdraw all the partnership funds in the banks without the knowledge or consent of the general partner. Either Russell or Andrews could take control of the business from de Escamilla by refusing to sign checks for bills contracted by him and thus limit his activities in the management of the business. They required him to resign as manager and selected his successor. They were active in dictating the crops to be planted, some of them against the wishes of de Escamilla. This clearly shows they took part in the control of the business of the partnership and thus became liable as general partners. . . .

Judgment affirmed.

CASE REVIEW QUESTIONS

1. What standard did the court use to determine whether Russell and Andrews were general partners or limited partners?
2. What were the facts that were relevant to the determination of whether Russell and Andrews were general partners or limited partners?
3. Suppose all of the creditors of Hacienda Farms, Limited (the limited partnership) knew that Russell and Andrews were supposed to be limited partners. Do you think this would have changed the outcome of the case? Explain.

What Constitutes "Control of the Business"? Uncertainty as to the circumstances in which a limited partner may be considered to take part in the "control of the business" and thereby become liable as a general partner is probably the greatest drawback to the use of the limited partnership form. In the case of *Holzman v. de Escamilla,* the partners took part in some important day-to-day business decisions of the partnership and, as a result, were treated as general partners. But what if a limited partner only participates in major partnership policy decisions?

Some states and the RULPA have dealt with this problem by stating specifically what activities and decisions a limited partner can be involved in without losing his or her status as a limited partner. Section 303(b) of the RULPA provides that a limited partner does not participate in the control of the business through any of the following:

1. Being a contractor for or an agent or an employee of the limited partnership or of a general partner.
2. Consulting with and advising a general partner concerning the partnership's business.
3. Acting as a surety (one who guarantees payment of a debt) for the limited partnership.
4. Approving or disapproving an amendment to the partnership agreement.
5. Voting on one or more of the following:
   a. Dissolving and winding up the limited partnership.
   b. Transferring all or substantially all of the limited partnership's assets other than in the ordinary course of business.
   c. Incurring indebtedness other than in the ordinary course of business.
   d. Changing the nature of the business.
   e. Removing a general partner.

Section 303(c) of the RULPA states that participation in activities and decisions of a limited partnership other than those listed in §303(b) does not necessarily constitute taking part in the control of the business. Thus, although it is clearer under the RULPA what *does not* constitute taking part in the control of the business, it is still not clear what *does* constitute taking part in control.

Is Reliance Necessary? Suppose that a limited partner takes some part in the control of the business, but a third party dealing with the limited partnership does not know that the limited partner is doing this. In such a situation, there is no reliance by the third party — based on the limited partner's exercise of control — that the limited partner is a general partner. May the third party nevertheless hold the limited partner individually liable for the debts of the partnership? In other words, should the limited partner lose his or her limited liability and be treated as a general partner?

Section 7 of the ULPA says nothing about the need for reliance by the third party. The RULPA provision, which is not especially clear, states:

> [I]f the limited partner's participation in the control of the business is not substantially the same as the exercise of the powers of a general partner, he is liable only to the persons who transact business with the limited partnership with actual knowledge of his participation in control [RULPA §303(a)].

Presumably, this provision means that a limited partner who takes some part in the control of the partnership's business, but does not participate fully, will only lose his or her limited liability if the third party actually knows of the participation. Indeed, a few courts, including one in a case you will read later in this chapter, have taken this stance. Nonetheless, the lack of clarity concerning the need for reliance, like the lack of clarity on the issue of what constitutes taking part in the control of the business, causes some people who might otherwise become limited partners to choose not to do so. They fear that, without realizing it or intending it, they might do something that would cause them to lose their limited liability status.

Corporate General Partner An advantage of doing business as a partnership rather than as a corporation is that only the partners, not the partnership, must pay taxes on partnership income. In contrast, a corporation must pay taxes on corporate income and then the shareholders must also pay taxes on that corporate income distributed to them as dividends. In other words, the use of the partnership form can avoid the double taxation of income that occurs to some extent when the corporate form is used.

A disadvantage of doing business as a partnership is that partners are individually liable for the debts of the partnership. If the corporate form is used, the corporation is treated as a separate legal entity, and the shareholders cannot be held individually liable for the debts of the corporation.

Limited liability for some partners can be achieved through the use of the limited partnership form of business, as you have seen earlier in this chapter. However, even when the limited partnership form is used, there must be at least one general partner. This means that at least one partner must expose himself or herself to the risk of unlimited individual liability for the debts of the limited partnership.

One possible way to avoid placing this risk on any of the individuals who are members of the partnership would be to have the general partner be a corporation. If this could be done, the corporation would be liable for the debts of the limited partnership, but the limited partners and the shareholders of the corporation would not be. If the limited partners were also the directors of the corporation, they could then control the limited partnership through the corporation.

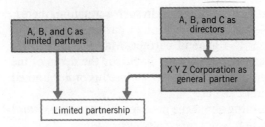

FIGURE 37-1

Use of a Corporate General Partner in the Formation of a Limited Partnership

For instance, suppose three people — A, B, and C — wish to form a partnership, but they all want to be limited partners. They therefore form the XYZ Corporation and elect themselves directors. They then form a limited partnership, making themselves limited partners and the XYZ Corporation the general partner. (See Figure 37-1.)

If A, B, and C control the activities of the limited partnership through their positions as directors of XYZ, should they be subject to individual liability for the debts of the limited partnership — that is, should they be treated as general partners? This is the question that confronted the courts in the following two cases. As you read the cases, see if you can understand what led the courts to give different answers.

DELANEY v. FIDELITY LEASE LIMITED
526 S.W.2d 543 (Texas 1975)

[Delaney and others entered into an agreement with Fidelity Lease Limited (Fidelity), a limited partnership composed of 22 individual limited partners and a corporate general partner, Interlease Corporation, to lease a fast-food restaurant to the partnership. The plaintiffs then built the restaurant, but Fidelity failed to take possession or pay rent.

Delaney and others brought suit for damages for breach of the lease agreement against Fidelity, Interlease Corporation as general partner, and the 22 limited partners. The trial court dismissed the plaintiff's legal action against the limited partners on the basis that they were not personally liable for the debts of the partnership. The plaintiffs appealed the trial court's dismissal as to three of the limited partners — Crombie, Kahn, and Sanders. The plaintiffs argued that these three defendants had taken part in the control of the business of Fidelity because they were the officers, directors, and shareholders of the general partner, Interlease Corporation. An intermediate court of appeals affirmed the trial court's decision, and the plaintiffs appealed to the Texas Supreme Court.]

DANIEL, Justice

The question here is whether limited partners in a limited partnership become liable as general partners if they "take part in the control of the business" while acting as officers of a corporation which is the sole general partner of the limited partnership.

Pertinent portions of the Uniform Limited Partnership Act provide:

A limited partner shall not become liable as a general partner unless, in addition to the exercise of his rights and powers as a limited partner, he takes part in the control of the business.

It was alleged by plaintiffs, and there is evidence, that the three limited partners controlled the business of the limited partnership, albeit through the corporate entity. The defendant limited partners argue that they acted only through the corporation and that the corporation actually controlled the business of the limited partnership. In response to this contention, we adopt the following statements in the dissenting opinion of Chief Justice Preslar in the court of civil appeals:

> I find it difficult to separate their acts for they were at all times in the dual capacity of limited partners and officers of the corporation. Apparently the corporation had no function except to operate the limited partnership and Appellees were obligated to their other partners to so operate the corporation as to benefit the partnership. Each act was done then, not for the corporation, but for the partnership. Indirectly, if not directly, they were exercising control over the partnership. . . .

Thus, we hold that the personal liability, which attaches to a limited partner when "he takes part in the control and management of the business," cannot be evaded merely by acting through a corporation.

The defendant limited partners also contend that the "control" test enumerated in [the ULPA] for the purpose of inflicting personal liability should be coupled with a determination of whether the plaintiffs relied upon the limited partners as holding themselves out as general partners. Thus, they argue that, before personal liability attaches to limited partners, two elements must coincide: (1) the limited partner must take part in the control of the business; and (2) the limited partner must have held himself out as being a general partner having personal liability to an extent that the third party, or plaintiff, relied upon the limited partners' personal liability. They observe that there is no question in this case but that the plaintiffs were in no way misled into believing that these three limited partners were personally liable on the lease, because the lease provided that the plaintiffs were entering into the lease with "Fidelity Lease, Ltd., a limited partnership acting by and through Interlease Corporation, General Partner."

We disagree with this contention. [The ULPA] simply provides that a limited partner who takes part in the control of the business subjects himself to personal liability as a general partner. The statute makes no mention of any requirement of reliance on the part of the party attempting to hold the limited partner personally liable.

It is quite clear that there can be more than one general partner. Assuming that Interlease Corporation was a legal general partner, this would not prevent Crombie, Kahn, and Sanders from taking part in the control of the business in their individual capacities as well as their corporate capacities. In no event should they be permitted to escape the statutory liability which would have devolved upon them if there had been no attempted interposition of the corporate shield against personal liability. Otherwise, the statutory requirement of at least one general partner with general liability in a limited partnership can be circumvented or vitiated by limited partners operating the partnership through a corporation with minimum capitalization and therefore minimum liability. We hold that the trial court erred in granting . . . judgment for the defendants, Crombie, Kahn, and Sanders. If, upon trial on the merits it is found from a preponderance of the evidence that either of these three limited partners took part in the control of the business, whether or not in his capacity as an officer of Interlease Corporation, he should be adjudged personally liable as a general partner.

Reversed and remanded.

FRIGIDAIRE SALES CORPORATION v. UNION PROPERTIES, INC.
562 P.2d 244 (Wash. 1977)

HAMILTON, Associate Justice

Petitioner, Frigidaire Sales Corporation, sought review of a Court of Appeals decision which held that limited partners do not incur general liability for the limited partnership's obligations simply because they are officers, directors, or shareholders of the corporate general partner. Petitioner entered into a contract with Commercial Investors (Commercial), a limited partnership. Respondents, Leonard Mannon and Raleigh Baxter, were limited partners of Commercial. Respondents were also officers, directors, and shareholders of Union Properties, Inc., the only general partner of Commercial. Respondents controlled Union Properties, and through their control of Union Properties they exercised the day-to-day control and management of Commercial. Commercial breached the contract, and petitioners brought suit against Union Properties and respondents. The trial court concluded that respondents did not incur general liability for Commercial's obligations by reason of their control of Commercial, and the Court of Appeals affirmed.

We first note that petitioner does not contend that respondents acted improperly by setting up the limited partnership with a corporation as the sole general partner. Limited partnerships are a statutory form of organization, and parties creating a limited partnership must follow the statutory requirements. In Washington, parties may form a limited partnership with a corporation as the sole general partner.

Petitioner's sole contention is that respondents should incur general liability for the limited partnership's obligations because they exercised the day-to-day control and management of Commercial. Respondents, on the other hand, argue that Commercial was controlled by Union Properties, a separate legal entity, and not by respondents in their individual capacities.

Petitioner cites *Delaney v. Fidelity Lease Ltd.* as support for its contention that respondents should incur general liability for the limited partnership's obligations. That case also involved the issue of liability for limited partners who controlled the limited partnership as officers, directors, and shareholders of the corporate general partner. The Texas Supreme Court reversed the decision of the Texas Court of Civil Appeals and found the limited partners had incurred general liability because of their control of the limited partnership.

We find the Texas Supreme Court's decision distinguishable from the present case. In *Delaney,* the corporation and the limited partnership were set up contemporaneously [at the same time], and the sole

purpose of the corporation was to operate the limited partnership. The Texas Supreme Court found that the limited partners who controlled the corporation were obligated to their other limited partners to operate the corporation for the benefit of the partnership. This is not the case here. The pattern of operation of Union Properties was to investigate and conceive of real estate investment opportunities and, when it found such opportunities, to cause the creation of limited partnerships with Union Properties acting as the general partner. Commercial was only one of several partnerships so conceived and created. Respondents did not form Union Properties for the sole purpose of operating Commercial. Hence, their acts on behalf of Union Properties were not performed merely for the benefit of Commercial.

For us to find that respondents incurred general liability for the limited partnership's obligations would require us to apply a literal interpretation of the statute and totally ignore the corporate entity of Union Properties, when petitioner knew it was dealing with that corporate entity. There can be no doubt that respondents, in fact, controlled the corporation. However, they did so only in their capacities as agents for their principal, the corporate general partner. Although the corporation was a separate entity, it could only act through its board of directors, officers, and agents. Petitioner entered into the contract with Commercial. Respondents signed the contract in their capacities as president and secretary-treasurer of Union Properties, the general partner of Commercial. In the eyes of the law it was Union Properties, as a separate corporate entity, which entered into the contract with petitioner and controlled the limited partnership.

Further, because respondents scrupulously separated their actions on behalf of the corporation from their personal actions, petitioner never mistakenly assumed that respondents were general partners with general liability. Petitioner knew Union Properties was the sole general partner and did not rely on respondents' control by assuming that they were also general partners. If petitioner had not wished to rely on the solvency of Union Properties as the only general partner, it could have insisted that respondents personally guarantee contractual performance. Because petitioner entered into the contract knowing that Union

Properties was the only party with general liability, and because in the eyes of the law it was Union Properties, a separate entity, which controlled the limited partnership, there is no reason for us to find that respondents incurred general liability for their acts done as officers of the corporate general partner.

The decision of the Court of Appeals is affirmed.

CASE REVIEW QUESTIONS

1. Which of the two decisions do you think is most consistent with §7 of the ULPA? Explain.
2. Do you think that the Washington court in the *Frigidaire Sales* case was correct in the way it distinguished the case it was deciding from the *Delaney* case? Explain.
3. Which of the two decisions applies the reliance requirement found in the RULPA? What arguments can be made for and against imposing the reliance requirement?
4. Which of the two decisions most protects the creditors of limited partnerships? Which decision most protects the limited partners? Which do you think is the better decision? Why?

Other Rights of Limited Partners

Limited partners have the right to inspect the partnership's books and records, to bring a legal action on behalf of the partnership, and to sue for a partition and an accounting. A limited partner also has the right to assign his or her interest in the partnership and to veto the admission of new general or limited partners.

Dissolution of a Limited Partnership

Section 801 of the RULPA lists the events that will cause the dissolution of a limited partnership. For the most part, they are the same as the events that will cause the dissolution of an ordinary partnership, which were discussed in the previous chapter. However, the withdrawal of a *limited partner* does not result in the dissolution of a limited partnership. Furthermore, the withdrawal of a *general partner* from a limited partnership does not necessarily result in dissolution if the certificate of limited partnership so provides or if the remaining partners agree to continue the business of the limited partnership.

Section 802 of the RULPA provides a much simpler standard for determining when dissolution can be obtained by court decree than the standard applied to ordinary partnerships. It states that dissolution may be decreed if the court determines that "it is not reasonably practicable to carry on the business in conformity with the partnership agreement."

The general partners who have not wrongfully dissolved the limited partnership have the right to wind up its affairs. If there are no such general partners, the limited partners may wind up. Either of these rules, however, may be changed by provision in the partnership agreement [RULPA §803].

The ULPA (§23) and the RULPA (§804) differ as to the way assets are to be distributed when the winding up of the affairs of the partnership is completed. Both acts provide for the partnership's creditors to be paid first. Under the ULPA, the claims of the limited partners to profits and capital contributions are paid prior to the claims of the general partners. The RULPA provides that general partners' and limited partners' claims to profits and capital contributions are to be treated equally, unless the partnership agreement provides otherwise.

REVIEW QUESTIONS

1. What forms of partnership other than the ordinary form are there? In what important ways does each of these forms differ from the ordinary form of partnership?

2. In a limited partnership, what is the difference between a general partner and a limited partner?

3. Under what circumstances may a limited partner be treated by the courts as a general partner?

CASE PROBLEMS

1. Bramble leased land from Flectheer, on which he conducted a fruit-farm and nursery business. For a three-month period, he advertised the business in the newspaper under the name "Flectheer & Bramble." He had prepared the advertisements without Flectheer's consent. When Flectheer saw one of the ads, he instructed Bramble to stop immediately, which Bramble did. Pullen was in the business of selling fruit trees. He did business with Bramble and received documents from Bramble from time to time that were signed "Flectheer and Bramble." Flectheer had no knowledge of these documents, but Pullen believed that Flectheer and Bramble were co-owners of the business. When Bramble died, there was an unpaid bill owed to Pullen for trees. If Pullen sues Flectheer as a partner of Bramble, who will win the case? Explain.

2. Stanley Livingston was a young college graduate who returned to his hometown to start his own business. He had never been exceptionally bright. Stanley was relatively unknown compared with his father, Fred Livingston, who was the recently retired football coach of the local high school. Stanley founded a small insurance business and, with his father's permission, called it "Fred Livingston & Son Insurance." Between Fred and Stanley, it was agreed that Stanley was the owner and would make all the decisions in the business. Fred was employed to greet potential clients from time to time and to seek out business in the community. He was paid a straight hourly wage and only worked a few days each week. When Stanley was purchasing office furniture from Porter, Porter came to Stanley's place of business. Porter recognized Fred, who happened to be there, and primarily on the strength of Fred's reputation in the community as a leader and a man of his word, sold $5,000 worth of furniture to "Fred Livingston & Son Insurance" on credit. Stanley signed the purchase agreement. When Stanley failed to pay for the furniture, Porter brought a legal action against Fred Livingston to collect. What arguments will each of the parties make? Who will win the case? Explain.

4. Fletcher, Dry, Wilbert, and Cox selected the limited partnership as the form of business entity most suitable for their purpose of investing in mineral leases. Fletcher, the general partner, contributed $50,000 in capital. Dry, Wilbert, and Cox each contributed $100,000 capital and became limited partners. The necessary limited-partnership pa-

pers were duly prepared and filed, clearly indicating that Fletcher was the sole general partner and that the others were limited partners.

Fletcher managed the partnership during the first two years. During the third year, Dry and Wilbert overruled Fletcher as to the type of investments to be made, the extent of the commitments, and the major terms contained in the leases. They also exercised the power to draw checks on the firm's bank account. Finally, Fletcher withdrew and was replaced by Martin, a new and more receptive general partner. Cox did not join his follow partners in these activities. However, his name was used on the partnership stationery as part of the firm's name without qualification and with his general knowledge and consent. What is the legal liability of Martin, Dry, Wilbert, and Cox as individuals to creditors of the partnership? [Adapted from CPA examination question 6b, *Business Law*, May 1976.]

4. Anderson, Baker, and Cook formed a corporation, ABC, Inc., to be the general partner in a limited partnership in which they were limited partners. Each of them contributed $10,000 to the corporation in exchange for voting stock. They elected themselves to the board of directors and then appointed themselves officers of the corporation. The partnership borrowed $500,000 from First National Bank. When the partnership defaulted on the loan, the amount owed to First National Bank exceeded the value of the assets of the partnership and the corporation. If First National Bank brings a legal action against Anderson, Baker, and Cook as individuals, on what basis may they defend? Who will win the case? Explain.

PART VIII

CORPORATION LAW

38

FORMING AND FINANCING THE CORPORATION

Thinking and studying about corporations is difficult for at least two reasons. The first is that corporations are an extremely diverse group of enterprises. Consider just the element of size. In some states, one person may incorporate a business and be the only shareholder, the only director, the only officer, and the only employee. Contrast this with the very large corporations that have millions of shareholders and hundreds of thousands of employees and that sell goods worth billions of dollars every year. These very large corporations are one of the dominating forces in the economies of both the nation and the world. Indeed, like our laws creating and protecting property rights, corporations are a major tool of capitalism; they are one of the most significant legal innovations in the development of the Western political system.

Each very large corporation is certainly a powerful and significant element of our commercial society, but when these large corporations are considered as a group, their impact is even more awesome. In 1980, the 200 largest manufacturing companies had total assets that were just short of 60 percent of the assets of all manufacturing corporations combined,[1] and according to *Forbes* magazine, total sales that amounted to 64.13 percent of the American gross national product and total profits that were 90.25 prcent of all corporate profits.

Besides being diverse in size, corporations engage in every conceivable type of activity. Not only businesses, but also towns and villages, churches, schools, and such organizations as the YMCA and the Girl Scouts may be incorporated.

[1] U.S. Department of Commerce, *Statistical Abstract of the United States,* 1981, Figure No. 917, p. 541.

This diversity necessarily makes any discussion of corporations very general and subject to numerous exceptions.

The second reason that thinking and studying about corporations is difficult is that there exists no tradition of systematic inquiry, analysis, and evaluation of corporations, despite their being so significant and powerful in our world. Unlike the other power centers in our society—government and organized religion—large corporations do not normally receive formalized study. By "formalized study," we mean a systematic course of instruction in high schools and universities of the type devoted to government and its operation.

The major reason there is little formalized study of large corporations and their impact on our society is that American social science (and a large part of Western philosophy as well) is premised on individual action rather than group action. Because our traditions and our ideology of individualism define how we see and understand complex social phenomena, we often assume that the large corporation acts as a rational individual would. This view ignores the collective, group-oriented nature of the large corporation.

CORPORATION STATUTES

The Focus of State Corporation Statutes

When you study corporation law, it is important that the image of the corporation you have in mind be roughly equivalent to that contemplated by state legislatures when they adopt and amend state corporation statutes. If you can imagine a continuum with one-person corporations at one end and giant corporations at the other, the proper focus for understanding state corporation statutes is on the nine-tenths of the continuum that stretches out from the one-person corporation (see Figure 38-1). In 1977, there were about 2.25 million corporations in this country, so this focus encompasses something over two million of them.

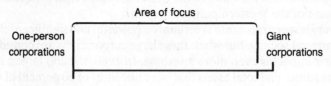

FIGURE 38-1
The Focus of State Corporation Statutes

The Nature of Corporation Law

Corporation law consists mainly of the various state statutes that pertain to corporate structure. It prescribes, for instance, how the shareholders relate to one another, to the directors of the corporation, and to the corporation itself. Corporation law also governs shareholders' and board of directors' meetings, and it defines how the powers of corporations are allocated and limited.

Ideally, the material discussed in this section would apply to all corporations, but the reality is that it applies to some corporations more than to others. Although very large corporations are supposedly subject to the same laws as all other corporations, the larger a corporation is, the more complex its structure is and the more difficult applying the laws of any single state to it becomes. Also, the larger a corporation, the greater the likelihood that the rights of its shareholders will be affected by federal law—primarily, the federal securities laws. Therefore, to round out our presentation of the law that applies to corporations, material on the federal securities laws is included in this book in Chapter 51.

Historical Background

Method of Incorporation Prior to the middle of the nineteenth century, corporations were created by specific legislative act. The key distinctive features of the corporation—limited liability for the owners and unlimited life (perpetual existence) for the corporation—were thought to be privileges that should be bestowed only when the recipients could convince the legislature that a public purpose would be served in exchange for these privileges. Thus, most of the early corporations were such businesses as toll road companies and railroads, although a few were manufacturing companies.

There were several problems with the practice of granting corporate charters by specific legislative act. Foremost was the complaint that some of these grants essentially awarded monopolies. Another was that those who wished to form a corporation might not have the necessary political power or knowledge to obtain a legislative grant of a charter. In short, the system of granting corporate charters by specific legislative act was a matter of intense political debate.

By the time of the election of Andrew Jackson in 1829, the political debate about corporate charters was focused on whether the corporate form of doing business should be abolished altogether or should be made freely available to everyone. This debate was resolved in favor of "General Incorporation Laws," which set out basic criteria and required that a corporate charter be granted to anyone who applied who met these criteria. These general laws were first adopted on the East Coast; and by the 1850's they had spread to the Midwest.

Attracting Corporations As manufacturing grew in importance and corporations began doing business in states other than the one in which they were chartered, they realized that some states treated them more favorably than others. So businesses began to shop around for the most convenient state in which to incorporate.

New Jersey was the first state to attempt to attract corporations by enacting favorable corporation laws. In the 1890's New Jersey was experiencing a severe financial crisis, so it went into the "business" of chartering corporations. First, the state repealed its antitrust laws, and then it passed the General Revision Act, which contained the basic provisions found in most twentieth-century state corporation statutes. In retrospect, these provisions do not seem overly attractive, but against a historical background characterized by suspicion and extreme legislative caution in the chartering of corporations, these "revisions" were radical.

New Jersey's approach worked. As a consequence, there was intense competition among the eastern states for the incorporation of businesses during the early twentieth century. The ultimate winner was the state of Delaware, which expanded and liberalized the most attractive features of the New Jersey law. As one scholar put it, "What began as a tragedy in New Jersey was institutionalized as a farce in Delaware."[2]

From time to time, other states have tried to "out-Delaware" Delaware, but none have succeeded. Delaware corporation law is so favorable to management (usually at the expense of the shareholders and the public) that, as of 1974, it had chartered 448 of the 1,000 largest American corporations, including 52 of the largest 100 and 251 of the largest 500.[3] In 1974, these 448 corporations accounted for over 52 percent of the sales of the 1,000 largest corporations. However, most of the approximately two million corporations that are the focus of this part of the book cannot afford to or are not inclined to incorporate in Delaware. All states have general incorporation laws that apply to these small and medium-sized corporations, and it is to these laws that we now turn our attention.

The Model Business Corporation Act

The Model Business Corporation Act (MBCA) was first published in 1950 by the section on Corporation, Banking, and Business Law of the American Bar Association. Since that time, 28 states have adopted the MBCA more or less in whole and 10 additional states have adopted substantial parts of it. This act appears in Appendix F of this book. Because of the widespread recognition of the MBCA, we will use it as the primary source for our discusion of corporation law. Unlike Delaware law, the MBCA attempts to balance the interests of the shareholders, corporation management, and the public.

As you study corporation law, you should be aware that most states have entirely separate statutory schemes that apply to nonprofit corporations, banks, insurance companies, cooperatives, and the various governmental units that incorporate. Therefore, these types of corporations are excluded from the principles discussed in the following materials.

FORMATION OF A CORPORATION

Advantages and Disadvantages of Incorporation

An entrepreneur can operate a business alone as a sole proprietorship, with others as a partnership, or as a corporation. The primary advantage of the corporate form over the sole proprietorship form or the partnership form is the *limited liability* that is extended to the shareholders of a corporation. A shareholder's liability to creditors of the corporation is limited to the amount of his or her investment in the corporation. This limitation on the liability of the share-

---

[2] R. Nader, M. Green, and J. Seligman, *Taming the Giant Corporation,* 1976, p. 50. New York: Norton.

[3] *Ibid.,* at p. 57.

holders of a corporation is provided for in §25 of the MBCA, which states in part:

> A holder of or subscriber to shares of a corporation shall be under no obligation to the corporation or its creditors with respect to such shares other than the obligation to pay to the corporation the full consideration for which such shares were issued or to be issued.

Consider a simple example. Suppose A, B, and C decide to incorporate, and each contributes $5,000 to the enterprise, which is incorporated as the ABC Corporation. In the first month of its existence, an employee of ABC is negligent and injures D. D sues ABC and recovers a judgment of $25,000. The *judgment* can be for more than the corporation is worth because it reflects the extent of D's damages, but recovery of the judgment will be limited to the value of the assets of the corporation ($15,000). That is, the judgment may be for $25,000 but only $15,000 of it will be collectible. The personal assets of the shareholders cannot be reached by the corporation's creditors to pay the corporation's debts.[4] On the other hand, if A, B, and C had formed a partnership rather than a corporation, D would have been able to collect the judgment not only from the partnership's assets but also from the personal assets of A, B, and C (see Chapter 36).

Other advantages of incorporating a business rather than operating it as a partnership are the *continuity of existence* of the corporation, regardless of increases or decreases in the number of owners, and the ease with which ownership interests can be transferred (see Chapters 35 and 36).

The greatest potential disadvantage of incorporating has to do with taxes. A corporation pays tax on its profits; when, in turn, those profits are distributed to the shareholders in the form of dividends, they constitute taxable income to the shareholders. Thus, there are two levels of taxes on the income received by shareholders, which result in a form of double taxation.

The corporate form also offers certain tax advantages, however. For instance, reasonable salaries paid to employee-shareholders are deductible from corporate gross income, and a corporation may accumulate a reasonable amount of earnings rather than distribute them to the stockholders as dividends. A partnership may not deduct the partners' salaries as a business expense, and a partner is taxed on his or her share of the partnership profits whether or not they are distributed.

Another disadvantage of the corporate form is that the necessary corporate formalities, such as board of directors' meetings and shareholders' meetings, are more cumbersome and restrictive than are the operating procedures of a partnership.

A final disadvantage of the corporate form is the expense of creating it. Proprietorships cost very little to form; partnerships cost more because an attorney is usually paid to draw up the contractual agreement of the parties.

---

[4] Exceptions to the limited liability of corporate shareholders will be discussed later in this chapter.

Corporations cost the most to form because fees must be paid to the state (the amount varies according to the number of shares that are authorized) as well as to an attorney. The attorney usually buys a corporate minute book and arranges for the printing of stock certificates and the purchase of a seal. At the minimum, it costs $400 to $600 to form a corporation.

Special Tax Provisions One method for minimizing the double taxation disadvantage of the corporate form as well as for securing other tax advantages is provided by Subchapter S of the Internal Revenue Code (Sections 1371–1379). The code allows corporations that have 35 or fewer shareholders who are individuals or estates (not partnerships or corporations), that have only one class of stock, and that meet certain other requirements to qualify as a *Subchapter S corporation* (called simply an *S corporation* by the Internal Revenue Service) for special tax treatment. This special status generally allows the shareholders to treat the profit or loss of an S corporation as their own personal profit or loss. For example, the owners of an S corporation may offset their share of corporate losses, to the extent of their capital contributions and loans, against their personal incomes, which results in a lower personal income tax liability. If a corporation elects to file under Subchapter S, the tax treatment of the corporation's profit or loss is very similar to that of a partnership.

Section 1244 of the Internal Revenue Code offers further tax advantages to small corporations that qualify. Generally, §1244 provides that a qualifying corporation may issue stock pursuant to a plan that meets its requirements. Any loss sustained by an individual shareholder upon the sale of this stock may be treated as an ordinary loss by the shareholder, which means that it can be deducted from the shareholders' ordinary income up to a maximum amount of $25,000.

Thus, for instance, Subchapter S and §1244 could permit a doctor with an individual income of $75,000 a year to buy a small cattle ranch and incorporate it. The ranch would be the chief asset of the S corporation. By paying ranch hands salaries that just equal the ranch's income and by taking depreciation on the ranch buildings, the ranch could be run at a paper loss of, say, $5,000 a year. This loss could be transferred through the corporation to the doctor and deducted from his or her individual income, resulting in a $5,000 deduction before taxable income is determined. This would result in a reduction of the cost basis on the buildings for capital gains purposes if they are later sold, but it would still result in a substantial current tax savings. Also, if the doctor should sell his or her corporate shares at a loss, the loss may be used to offset as much as $25,000 in individual income.

Do not confuse the privilege of offsetting S corporation losses against individual income with limited liability. S corporations still offer limited liability in that the shareholders cannot be made to pay for corporate debts. What shareholders are offered under Subchapter S is the privilege of offsetting corporate losses against their individual incomes to reduce their personal income tax liabilities.

Professional Corporations As stated before, an important advantage of the corporate form is the limited liability it affords to the owners of the corporation. Limited liability is a legal privilege bestowed by the state; it may also be withheld by the state. Until recently, individuals offering a professional service, such as doctors, lawyers, dentists, and optometrists, were forbidden from incorporating by most states. Being able to separate personal assets from business assets was believed to be inappropriate for individuals who offer professional services. Patients or clients rely on the personal skill and judgment of a professional in the rendering of his or her service; therefore, the professional should not be able to shield his or her personal assets from the risks of his or her profession. Another reason for denying professionals the use of the corporate form was that, by law, the business of a corporation must be managed by a board of directors. It was considered inappropriate for a professional's actions and judgments to be subject to the direction of a board of directors.

Within the last decade, however, many states have passed special statutes that allow the formation of *professional corporations.* These statutes have been enacted in response to pressure from professionals to allow them to share in some of the special tax benefits offered by the corporate form. Although the owners of a professional corporation are subject to double taxation if they pay themselves dividends, the tax advantages with regard to their retirement plans and insurance programs are considerable and more than offset the double taxation disadvantage.

For example, if a professional is a partner and the partnership decides to use some of its income to contribute to a retirement plan or to pay for insurance premiums on the life of a partner, these payments or premiums are taxed as income to the partner in the year in which they are made. However, if the professional is an employee of a corporation, any contributions the corporation makes to the employee's retirement plan or insurance program can be deducted as a business expense by the corporation, and they are not taxed as income to the employee in the year they are made. The shareholder-employee will, of course, have to pay income tax on the benefits of the retirement plan or insurance program when they are distributed. Thus, corporate retirement plans and insurance programs generally allow the professional to postpone taxation on a portion of his or her income. During an individual's peak income years, it is often advantageous for the individual to postpone some current income to later years when his or her annual income will presumably be lower. The individual thereby has a lower current tax liability, and, hopefully, a lower total tax liability. A lower tax liability, then, is the chief advantage of the professional corporation.

The Internal Revenue Service has argued that for a professional corporation to be taxed as a regular corporation, the professional's potential liability to third parties can be no greater than that of a shareholder in a regular corporation. This view has not prevailed, however, and most state laws pertaining to professional corporations do not allow professionals to limit their personal liability for their own acts or the acts of their associates. Thus, the potential liability of a shareholder in a professional corporation to third parties is much greater than that of a shareholder in a regular corporation. Still, the courts have overruled the IRS and have allowed professionals to enjoy the tax benefits just described. In short, many states have allowed the creation of a hybrid form of corporation that permits professionals to incorporate for tax purposes but not for the purpose of limiting personal liability.

Where to Incorporate

A corporation can be incorporated in any state. Furthermore, the corporate headquarters or primary place of business need not be in the state of incorporation. The corporation need not even do any business in the state of incorporation, although it must have a registered agent and office located in that state. Usually, small and medium-sized corporations find it most practical to incorporate in the state where they do most of their business. Different considerations exist for larger corporations, however, which often have complex capital structures and engage in business in many states.

The decision of where to incorporate is based on the corporation's self-interest. Businesses select the location that is most favorable to them. Corporation statutes can vary in important respects from state to state. Certain features of one state's law might be unattractive, such as Illinois' prohibition against nonvoting stock. Another state may permit a type of management flexibility that is inviting. The taxes and fees imposed, the degree of management flexibility allowed, the powers granted to shareholders, and the limitations placed on anyone attempting a corporate takeover are some of the aspects of a state's corporation laws that are weighed. What is an important aspect to one group considering incorporation may be relatively unimportant to another group with different needs and interests.

Foreign Corporations A corporation that operates within the state in which it is incorporated is called a **domestic corporation** [MBCA §2(a)]. In all other states and countries, it is called a **foreign corporation** [MBCA §2(b)]. Each state has the power to regulate foreign corporations that do business within its borders. Therefore, a corporation must qualify to do business as a foreign corporation before it commences doing business in a state other than its state of incorporation. Qualification usually involves filing certain routine information with the state's secretary of state and paying a fee.

The primary purpose of the qualification requirement for foreign corporations is to facilitate the assessment and collection of various taxes. Failure to qualify can result in the imposition of monetary penalties, the prohibition of further business activity in the state, and the filing of criminal misdemeanor charges. Also, some states deny any corporation that has failed to qualify properly access to their courts, which makes the enforcement of contracts by that corporation impossible.

A person who wishes to bring a legal action against a corporation will always be able to bring the action in the state in which the corporation is incorporated.

A state's courts have jurisdiction over all persons and corporations domiciled within that state, and a corporation is considered to be domiciled in the state in which it is incorporated. A state's courts also have jurisdiction over any foreign corporation that is doing business within the state, unless that foreign corporation does not have sufficient minimal contact with the state. (The issue of jurisdiction over corporations is discussed fully on pages 18–25.)

"Runaway" Corporations New York and California have adopted statutes that subject certain foreign corporations—referred to as *"runaway" corporations*—to those parts of New York or California corporation law that protect the shareholders and creditors of domestic corporations. The foreign corporations that are subject to these statutes are those that have a high percentage of shareholders living within the state or that do a substantial amount of business within the state. The exact percentage of in-state shareholders and the exact amount of in-state business necessary for the law to apply are specified by the respective statutes. These statutes are an attempt to prevent what are essentially local corporations from "running away" and avoiding the corporation law of New York or California by incorporating in another state. The statutes may be unconstitutional, however.

Promoters

A corporation doesn't simply blossom into existence by itself. Someone must do the planning and other work necessary for filing the required incorporation documents. The design of the corporation must be formulated, subscriptions for shares of stock must be properly solicited and acquired, employees must be hired, and all the other items necessary for incorporating a business must be taken care of. An individual who does these things is called a **promoter**.

The process of promoting a corporation usually requires that the promoter spend money. Naturally, the promoter will want to be reimbursed for these expenses and, possibly, to be compensated for his or her services after the business has been incorporated. The promoter will be paid if the state's corporation statute's make the corporation responsible for the reasonable expenses of its promotion, if the articles of incorporation specify that payment be made, or if the corporation, once formed, agrees to pay. Usually obtaining reimbursement for promotion expenses is not a problem for a promoter because, typically, he or she is also an influential incorporator, shareholder, and director of the corporation that has been created.

Preincorporation Contracts Often, a promoter has to make contracts during the promotion process. The corporation, however, is not liable for these *preincorporation contracts* because it was not in existence when they were made. Although the promoter entered into the contracts for the future benefit of the corporation, he or she was not acting as an agent for the corporation because a person cannot be an agent for a principal that does not exist.

A corporation may, however, incur liability for preincorporation contracts after it has been incorporated. For example, the board of directors might pass a resolution accepting the contract, the corporation might make payments under the contract, or the corporation might accept benefits from the contract. In such instances, the corporation is said to have "adopted" the contract. *Adoption* is the functional equivalent of ratification in agency law (see page 681).

What about the promoter's personal liability for preincorporation contracts? The promoter is not necessarily relieved of this liability even if the corporation adopts the contract. Indeed, the promoter remains liable for any preincorporation contracts unless (1) the parties did not intend the promoter to be liable under the contract when they entered into it or (2) the promoter, the corporation, and the third party make an agreement, called a *novation,* to the effect that the promoter is not liable under the contract.

In the following case, the court had to determine whether a promoter was liable to a third party under a preincorporation contract.

H.F. PHILIPSBORN & CO. v. SUSON
322 N.E.2d 45 (Ill. 1974)

[H.F. Philipsborn & Co. (Philipsborn) is an Illinois corporation engaged in the business of mortgage banking. Suson, a real estate developer, negotiated with Philipsborn concerning financing for a proposed real estate development. Philipsborn pepared an application for a loan of $5,488,000, naming North Shore Estates, Inc. (Estates) as the applicant. Where the form read "Title to be in the name of————," Philipsborn inserted "Trust to be formed." (A trust is a form of business organization.) The application provided that acceptance of the application by Philipsborn within 60 days would "constitute a binding contract" and that in "such event we [the applicant] agree to pay [Philipsborn] a commission equal to 2 percent of the loan."

Suson signed the application "North Shore Estates, Inc., by Morris Suson Pres." He also added the words "or corporation to be formed" after the words "Trust to be formed" on the application. Sometime thereafter, Philipsborn accepted the application and sent mortgage documents and a promissory note to Estates to be signed. However, the documents and the note were returned to Philipsborn unsigned because Suson had obtained a mortgage loan elsewhere.

Philipsborn then brought a legal action against Suson and Estates to collect the 2 percent commission. The trial court gave judgment to the plaintiff (Philipsborn) against both defendants (Suson and Estates). Suson appealed to an intermediate appellate court, which reversed the trial court's judgment against Suson. Philipsborn then appealed to the Illinois Supreme Court.]

GOLDENHERSH, Justice

Plaintiff concedes that it intended Estates to be the obligor on the loan application and that the application, of itself, imposed no individual liability on Suson for the payment of its commission. It contends, however, that Estates, which purportedly applied for the loan, did not, at the time of the application, exist as a corporate entity, and that plaintiff, at that time, was not aware of that fact. The record shows that on September 17, 1963, when the application was signed, there was no corporate entity named North Shore Estates, Inc. It was incorporated on November 12, 1963, with Suson as the sole shareholder and director. The corporate minutes reflect that the Board of Directors "approved and adopted all acts of Morris Suson to date and assumed liability therefor."

It is plaintiff's theory "that in the absence of a knowing agreement to the contrary" Suson, as a promoter of Estates, "is personally liable on a pre-incorporation contract and is not released by subsequent incorporation and ratification of the contract." It argues that "the general rule concerning promoters' contracts is that the promoter will be personally liable on contracts on behalf of a nonexistent corporation unless the contract provides to the contrary." The record shows that the [trial] court admitted testimony on the question whether plaintiff knew that Estates was not in existence when the application was executed. . . . Plaintiff contends that the question whether it was unaware of the nonexistence of Estates was properly submitted to the jury and that the appellate court erred in [reversing the trial court's decision].

The parties to this appeal appear to be in agreement that, unless the parties to the transaction agree otherwise, an individual who conducts the ordinary affairs of a business in the name of a nonexistent corporation is personally liable on contracts made in connection with the business. A number of the decisions of the courts of other jurisdictions state that where a promoter had become liable on a preincorporation contract, he was not, in the absence of an agreement to that effect, discharged from liability merely because the corporation was later organized and ratified the contract.

We find the facts of *Whitney v. Wyman* similar to those of this case and the reasoning persuasive. In that case a letter was sent to Baxter Whitney stating, "Our company being so far organized, by direction of the officers, we now order from you" certain machinery and was signed "Charles Wyman, Edward P. Ferry, Carlton L. Storrs, Prudential Committee Grand Haven Fruit Basket Co." Baxter, in a letter addressed to the Grand Haven Fruit Basket Co., accepted the order for the machinery. The machinery was delivered. The letters of order and acceptance were dated February 1, 1869, and February 10, 1869, respectively, which was before the articles of incorporation were filed with the Secretary of State and the county clerk and, therefore, before the corporation was authorized to do business. Whitney filed an action against Wyman, Ferry and Storrs, individually, to recover the value of the machinery.

The rule applied by the court was that whether liability will be imposed upon the promoter depends upon the intent of the parties. It found from the exchange of letters "that both parties understood and meant that the contract was to be and, in fact, was with the corporation and not with the defendants individually." In response to the argument that his intent could not be given effect because the corporation was forbidden to do any business when the letters were written, the court said: "The corporation subsequently ratified the contract by recognizing and treating it as valid. This made it in all respects what it would have been if the requisite corporate power had existed when it was entered into."

In our opinion, insofar as the loan commission executed by Suson [was] concerned, the question whether there was acceptance of the loan application . . . [was] the only [issue] of fact for determination by the jury. A contract is to be construed to give effect to the intent of the parties, and effect must be given to the contract as written. . . . Estates was organized within 60 days of the execution of the loan application, and upon its approval and adoption of Suson's acts to date, and its assumption of liability for those acts, plaintiff had received everything for which it had bargained. The record shows that when the loan application was signed Suson had an option to acquire, but did not own, the land on which the proposed project was to be built, and that upon acquisition title was to be taken in either a trust or corporation, in either event, not in existence, but "to be formed." Clearly, under these circumstances, plaintiff looked only to Estates for its commission, and the fact that Estates had not at that time been formed furnished no basis for the imposition of personal liability on Suson for the payment of the loan commission. On this record we hold that whether or not Estates existed as a corporate entity at the time the application was executed, or whether plaintiff knew that it was not, was not controlling, and that the appellate court correctly reversed the judgment entered against Suson.

Affirmed.

CASE REVIEW QUESTIONS

1. Why was North Shore Estates, Inc., which did not exist when the application was signed, liable to Philipsborn?
2. Suppose that the application had made no reference to North Shore Estates, Inc. Would Suson have been liable to Philipsborn for performance of the promises contained in the application? Explain.
3. Suppose that North Shore Estates, Inc., had not been created. Would Suson have been liable to Philipsborn for performance of the promises contained in the application? Explain.
4. Suppose that North Shore Estates, Inc., had not adopted the application. Would Suson have been liable to Philipsborn for performance of the promises contained in the application? Explain.

Articles of Incorporation

To incorporate a business, the incorporators must comply with the statutory formalities of the particular state in which they wish to incorporate. A document referred to variously as the **articles of incorporation** [MBCA §2(a)], the **certificate of incorporation,** or **the corporate charter** is filed with the secretary of state of the state of incorporation. This document is signed by the incorporators [MBCA §53]. Often the promoters will also be the incorporators.

The information required in the articles of incorporation is generally the same regardless of the state of incorporation. Section 54 of MBCA requires that the articles of incorporation include the following:

1. The name of the corporation, which under MBCA §8 must contain the word "corporation," "company," "incorporated," or "limited" or an abbreviation of one of these words.
2. The period of duration of the corporation, which may be and usually is perpetual.
3. The purpose or purposes for which the corporation is being organized.
4. Information concerning the corporation's capital structure.
5. The address of the corporation's initial registered office and the name of its initial registered agent at that address. (The purpose of this requirement is to provide a person who wants to begin a lawsuit against the corporation with a place to serve the necessary legal papers.)
6. The number of directors and the names and addresses of the persons who will serve as directors until the shareholders elect directors.
7. The names and addresses of the incorporators.

Figure 38-2 presents an example of a form that could be filled out and signed by incorporators in order to fulfill the requirements of the Illinois corporation law concerning the articles of incorporation. Forms of this type are often used by lawyers when they prepare legal documents.

ARTICLES OF INCORPORATION

The undersigned,

| | | | Address | |
| Name | Number | Street | City | State |

....

....

....

....

being one or more natural persons of the age of twenty-one years or more or a corporation, and having subscribed to shares of the corporation to be organized pursuant hereto, for the purpose of forming a corporation under "The Business Corporation Act" of the State of Illinois, do hereby adopt the following Articles of Incorporation:

Article One

The name of the corporation hereby incorporated is: ....

....

Article Two

The address of its initial registered office in the State of Illinois is: ....

.... Street, in the .... of ....

.... (.......................................) County of ....
(Zip Code)

and the name of its initial Registered Agent at said address is: ....

....

Article Three

The duration of the corporation is: ....

Article Four

The purpose or purposes for which the corporation is organized are:

Article Five

Paragraph 1: The aggregate number of shares which the corporation is authorized to issue is ...., divided into .... classes. The designation of

FIGURE 38-2
Articles of Incorporation

each class, the number of shares of each class, and the par value, if any, of the shares of each class, or a statement that the shares of any class are without par value, are as follows:

Class	Series (If any)	Number of Shares	Par value per share or statement that shares are without par value

Paragraph 2: The preferences, qualifications, limitations, restrictions and the special or relative rights in respect of the shares of each class are:

Article Six

The class and number of shares which the corporation proposes to issue without further report to the Secretary of State, and the consideration (expressed in dollars) to be received by the corporation therefor, are:

Class of shares	Number of shares	Total consideration to be received therefor:
		$ ....
		$ ....

Article Seven

The corporation will not commence business until at least one thousand dollars has been received as consideration for the issuance of shares.

Article Eight

The number of directors to be elected at the first meeting of the shareholders is:

....

Article Nine

Paragraph 1: It is estimated that the value of all property to be owned by the corporation for the following year wherever located will be $ ....
Paragraph 2: It is estimated that the value of the property to be located within the State of Illinois during the following year will be $ ....
Paragraph 3: It is estimated that the gross amount of business which will be transacted by the corporation during the following year will be $ ....
Paragraph 4: It is estimated that the gross amount of business which will be transacted at or from places of business in the State of Illinois during the following year will be $ ....

NOTE: If all the property of the corporation is to be located in this State and all of its business is to be transacted at or from places of business in this State, or if the incorporators elect to pay the initial franchise tax on the basis of its entire stated capital and paid-in surplus, then the information called for in Article Nine need not be stated.

....

....

Incorporators

....

....

NOTE: There may be one or more incorporators. Each incorporator shall be either a corporation, domestic or foreign, or a natural person of the age of twenty-one years or more. If a corporation acts as incorporator, the name of the corporation and state of incorporation shall be shown and the execution must be by its President or Vice-President and verified by him, and the corporate seal shall be affixed and attested by its Secretary or an Assistant Secretary.

OATH AND ACKNOWLEDGMENT . . .

The following fees are required to be paid at the time of issuing the certificate of corporation: Filing fee, $75.00; Initial license fee of 50¢ per $1,000.00 or 1/20th of 1% of the amount of stated capital and paid-in surplus the corporation proposes to issue without further report (Article Six); Initial franchise tax of 1/10th of 1% of the issued, as above noted. However, the minimum initial franchise tax is $100.00.

The Beginning of Corporate Existence

When the articles of incorporation are sent to the secretary of state by the incorporators, they are checked to determine whether they comply with all of the statutory requirements of the state's corporation laws. If they do, and if all the required fees have been paid, the secretary files one copy and returns the other copy to the incorporators along with a certificate of incorporation [MBCA §55]. Many states also require the incorporators to file a copy of both the articles of incorporation and the certificate of incorporation in the county where the corporation has its principal place of business.

Organization Meetings

After the articles of incorporation are filed with the secretary of state, §57 of the MBCA requires that an organization meeting of the directors named in the articles of incorporation be held. In some states, the first organization meeting is held by the incorporators or by the incorporators and the persons who have subscribed to shares of the corporation. Where this procedure is used, the initial meeting is held to elect the corporate directors. Then the directors must hold a meeting of their own.

At the initial directors' meeting, several important organizational acts are completed. One of the most important of these is the adoption of bylaws [MBCA §57]. The articles of incorporation set forth the general information about a corporation. The **bylaws,** on the other hand, contain specific and detailed provisions about how the corporation will be governed. For example, the articles of incorporation will state the number of directors, but they might not say anything about the directors' qualifications, term of office, or compensation. These matters will be contained in the bylaws. The bylaws will also cover such items as the time and place of shareholders' and directors' meetings, notice and quorum requirements for meetings, the percentage of affirmative votes needed to approve matters that are voted upon, the processes for selecting and removing directors and officers, and the titles and duties of the corporate officers. If there is any conflict among the provisions of the state corporation law, the articles of incorporation, and the bylaws, the bylaws are subordinate to the articles, which are in turn subordinate to the state corporation law. Other important business that may be transacted at the initial directors' meeting includes the election of officers and the adoption of preincorporation contracts.

Failure to Comply with Incorporation Requirements

Corporation de Jure If all of the requirements for incorporation in the applicable state's corporation law are met, a **corporation de jure** is formed. Even if there is a minor deviation from the statutory requirements, a corporation de jure is formed as long as there has been substantial compliance with the requirements. For instance, the misspelling of an incorporator's name would not prevent the formation of a corporation de jure. If a corporation de jure is formed, no one will be able to question its existence successfully.

If, on the other hand, there has not been substantial compliance with the statutory requirements for incorporation, a corporation de jure is not formed. In this situation, the state may bring a legal action, called a **quo warranto proceeding,** to challenge the existence of the corporation. (The Latin term *quo warranto* means "by what authority.") The state can force the corporation to comply with the law or, if the corporation refuses to comply, force it to cease doing business as a corporation.

Corporation de Facto Sometimes, people who have dealt with a corporation that has not complied with all incorporation requirements or such a corporation itself may challenge the corporation's existence. This might be done, for instance, in an attempt to avoid a contract made in the corporation's name. Of course, such a challenge will be unsuccessful if it is made against a corporation de jure. It will also be unsuccessful if the corporation qualifies as a corporation de facto, which sometimes occurs even when there has not been substantial compliance with the requirements for incorporation.

For a corporation to qualify as a **corporation de facto,** the courts have traditionally held that three requirements must be met:

1. There must be a state statute under which the corporation could have been formed.
2. The incorporators must have made a good-faith attempt to meet the statutory requirements.
3. The corporation must have conducted business as a corporation.

If these requirements have been met and a corporation de facto has been formed, no one, other than the state government in a quo warranto proceeding, will be able to question the corporation's existence successfully.

MBCA Provision Section 56 of the MBCA provides:

> Upon the issuance of the certificate of incorporation, the corporate existence shall begin, and such certificate of incorporation shall be conclusive evidence that all conditions precedent required to be performed by the incorporators have been complied with and that the corporation has been incorporated under this Act, except as against [the] State in a proceeding to cancel or revoke the certificate of incorporation or for involuntary dissolution of the corporation.

In states that have adopted this provision, the issuance of a certificate of incorporation creates a corporation de jure. Some courts have held that under this provision either a corporation de jure is formed or no corporation is formed at all. In other words, these courts believe that there cannot be a corporation de facto or a corporation by estoppel in a state that has adopted §56 of the MBCA. (Corporation by estoppel is discussed in the following section.)

Liability When No Corporation Exists If a corporation that has not complied with all incorporation requirements does not qualify as either a corporation de jure or a corporation de facto, no corporation exists and someone will be held personally liable as a partner for the debts of the nonexistent corporation. In some states, this liability is imposed on anyone who holds stock in the nonexistent corporation. More frequently, however, this liability is imposed only on those who are actively engaged in the management of the business or who are responsible for the defects in the formation of the corporation.

On the other hand, anyone who has represented a business as being a corporation will be estopped (prevented) from denying that the corporation exists, even if the business is neither a corporation de jure nor a corporation de facto, if by those representations he or she has induced others to do business with the nonexistent corporation. For instance, suppose Jones does business under the name "Jones Co., Inc." even though she has met none of the statutory requirements for incorporating. If Smith enters into a contract with the "corporation" and later sues the "corporation" for breach of contract, Jones will be estopped from arguing that Smith's lawsuit should be dismissed because the corporation does not exist. In a sense, a *corporation by estoppel* is considered to exist even though a corporation does not in fact exist.

Disregarding the Corporate Entity

There are some circumstances under which a court will disregard the corporate entity and hold the shareholders personally liable for the debts of the corporation even though the corporation legally exists. Called *piercing the corporate veil,* this is done to prevent the evasion of statutory obligations, the perpetration of frauds, or any other activity that violates public policy.

The circumstances in which courts may pierce the corporate wall can be conveniently divided into four categories. These categories are not rigid, and a particular situation may come under more than one category. Nevertheless, these categories provide an overview of this important exception to the doctrine of limited liability. The four categories are discussed in the following sections.

Suits Against Individuals Who Are Shareholders The typical case of piercing the corporate veil involves a suit by a creditor against the shareholders of a corporation for debts not paid by the corporation. To be successful, the creditor must prove either that the corporate entity was used as a mere appendage or "alter ego" of the shareholders and was not in fact treated as a separate entity or that the corporation was undercapitalized at the time the debt was incurred.

The "alter ego" approach is usually found in cases involving a corporation with very few shareholders. Some of the kinds of evidence that can be used to show that a corporation was used as an "alter ego" of the shareholders rather than as a separate entity are as follows:

1. The commingling of shareholder and corporate assets—for example, using corporate funds to pay individual debts and using corporate assets for private purposes or vice versa.
2. A lack of observance of basic corporate formalities, such as issuing stock, failing to elect directors or to appoint officers, failing to hold shareholders' or directors' meetings, or not keeping separate corporate records.
3. Any other evidence that tends to show that, in the everyday operation of the corporation, the shareholders treated the corporate entity as their business "conduit, instrumentality, or agency" (a phrase used frequently by the courts) rather than as a separate entity.

If a creditor attempts to pierce the corporate veil by showing that the corporate debtor was undercapitalized at the time the debt was incurred, he or she must prove that the shareholders could reasonably have anticipated that the corporation would be unable to pay the debts it was incurring. In some states, undercapitalization is treated merely as another kind of evidence for showing that a corporation was used as an "alter ego" of the shareholders; in other states, the fact of undercapitalization alone may be sufficient to pierce the corporate veil.

Suits Against a Corporation that Is a Shareholder Another situation in which a plaintiff may seek to pierce the corporate veil occurs when a creditor sues a parent corporation for the debts of a subsidiary corporation. A **subsidiary corporation** is a corporation that has a majority of its stock owned by another corporation, called the **parent corporation**. If the parent corporation owns 100 percent of the stock of the subsidiary, the subsidiary is said to be a *wholly owned subsidiary*.

Subsidiaries are very common, and they are usually formed for legitimate business purposes. For instance, a corporation may want to engage in a very risky speculative venture and simultaneously limit its liability. It can do this by forming a subsidiary to conduct the venture. Or, a corporation may export raw materials from other countries, one of which levies a higher tax on exports by foreign corporations. The corporation may therefore incorporate a subsidiary in that country to export the raw materials in order to qualify for the lower tax rate.

Frequently, the directors and officers of the parent corporation will serve in the same capacity for the subsidiary. The respective corporate headquarters may be in the same building or even in the same office. These facts, in and of themselves, do not automatically make the parent corporation liable for the debts of its subsidiary. Instead, the courts examine the degree to which corporate formalities have been honored and the manner in which the parent controls the subsidiary.

Generally, the evidence a creditor must present in a suit against a corporation that is a shareholder is the same as for a suit against individuals who are shareholders, but the reason that the courts impose liability is somewhat different. In suits against individuals, liability is imposed because a creditor was somehow unjustly misled as to the true character of the corporation that caused the damage to the creditor. In a suit against a corporation that is a shareholder, the reason for imposing liability is that a corporation should not be allowed to artificially fragment its business in such a way that an injustice to a creditor results.

Before we move on to the final two categories in which shareholder liability is imposed, we present two cases. In one, the court pierced the corporate veil; in the other, it did not. By contrasting these two cases, you will better understand when courts will and when they will not pierce the corporate veil.

CONSOLIDATED SUN RAY, INC. v. OPPENSTEIN
335 F.2d 801 (Eighth Cir. 1964)

VOGEL, Circuit Judge

This suit sought a declaratory judgment by Michael Oppenstein against appellant Consolidated Sun Ray, Inc. (Consolidated) and Berkson Brothers, Inc. (Berkson), with respect to a lease entered into on December 4, 1939, by Oppenstein and his since deceased brothers as Lessors and Berkson as Lessee. Oppenstein asked judgment declaring Consolidated liable under the lease on the theory that Berkson was the wholly owned subsidiary of Consolidated, under its complete domination and control beginning in June 1955 and continuing thereafter, and was accordingly the alter ego of Consolidated, and as a result thereof Consolidated was liable on the lease as though it were in fact a named lessee.

On April 5, 1963, the [trial] court entered a declaratory judgment holding Consolidated also liable on the lease. Such judgment was entered on that date against both Berkson and Consolidated. On October 24, 1963, the case (as to damages) went to trial before a jury and the jury returned a verdict in favor of Oppenstein and against Consolidated and Berkson in the sum of $102,674.73 as appellee's damages. Judgment was entered thereon, from which judgment Consolidated and Berkson noticed appeals to this court.

Appellant Consolidated bases this appeal upon the following grounds.

1. The District [trial] Court erred in holding that the

separate corporate entity of Berkson should be disregarded and that Berkson was the alter ego of Consolidated.

2. . . . .

The District Court found that all of the stock of Berkson was owned by Consolidated; that on December 4, 1939, Oppenstein leased certain property to Berkson for a term of 26 years and 11 months ending June 30, 1967; that after June or July 1955 Consolidated made certain changes in its dealings with its wholly owned subsidiary Berkson, such as (a) eliminated Berkson's control of money received from its retail store which was operated at the leased premises and reserved to Consolidated alone the right to issue checks on the bank account deposited in the Commerce Trust Company in Kansas City; (b) in 1959 closed the bank account, opening a new one in Consolidated's name so that thereafter Berkson operated without an account in its own name; (c) pledged Berkson's accounts receivable as security for a loan Consolidated negotiated for itself; (d) took from Berkson its former independent buying discretion and merchandising policies, buying merchandise for Berkson in New York and warehousing it in its own building in New York and directed complete retail price details; (e) changed fire and liability insurance on the leased premises from the name of Berkson to Consolidated; (f) prepared in New York and completely controlled all advertising; (g) arranged so that the directors and officers of Berkson were persons employed by Consolidated and were the same persons who were directors or officers of Consolidated, and no director or officer of Berkson lived in the Kansas City, Missouri trade area, and the local store manager was not a director or officer of Berkson; (h) charged against Berkson a share of the cost of Consolidated's accounting and warehousing operations; . . . (k) Many of the corporate minutes of Berkson were printed forms apparently used by Consolidated for all of its subsidiaries, with the name "Berkson's" typed in; (l) all correspondence pertaining to the business of the lessee under the lease, whether written to the lessor, to third parties or to agent of Consolidated, was on Consolidated's letterhead and was for the most part signed "Consolidated Retail Stores by"; in such correspondence Consolidated referred to the lease as "its lease," . . . ; (n) in

October 1961 the retail store on the leased premises was closed and the inventory was sold to Macy's; the consideration therefor was paid to and kept by Consolidated, no part being made available to apply on the rent due Oppenstein for November 1961 or thereafter; (o) Consolidated operated Berkson the same as if it were one of the division stores of Consolidated rather than a wholly-owned subsidiary; (p) Consolidated did maintain substantially all the legal formalities required of Berkson as a separate corporation, such as filing necessary papers, reports and corporate tax returns.

The court also found there was a default in the payment of rent beginning November 1961. From these findings the District Court made its Conclusions of Law.

1. That Consolidated had complete and absolute control over the actions and rights of Berkson from and after July 1955; that Consolidated used its power and control for the benefit of Consolidated and not for the benefit of Berkson;

2. That from June or July 1955 Consolidated did not respect the separateness of the corporate entity of Berkson, treating Berkson as a division, department, or adjunct of Consolidated; caused Berkson's assets to be intermingled with its own, making Berkson the alter ego of Consolidated;

3. That the use by Consolidated of Berkson as a division, conduit or instrumentality of Consolidated and Berkson's loss of control of its own destiny and inability to protect its own assets and the imposition of excessive financial burdens on Berkson was an injustice to Oppenstein, who sustained damage thereby;

4. That Consolidated should be held liable for the actions and obligations of Berkson, the same as though they were the acts and obligations of Consolidated.

From the evidence in this case there can be no reasonable doubt but that Consolidated did completely control and use Berkson as a mere conduit, instrumentality or adjunct of Consolidated itself. The ultimate fact question for determination, then, was Consolidated's purpose in so doing. If that purpose was unlawful or improper or for some illegitimate purpose which might result in damage to Oppenstein, then the court has the power to look behind Berkson, the alter ego, and hold Consolidated liable for Berkson's obligations. This necessitates a determination by the trier of the facts. Here the [trial] court found against Consolidated on that issue. The law of Missouri is that, where the subsidiary is a mere conduit, instrumentality, or adjunct through which the parent corporation achieves some improper end, its own corporate entity will be disregarded.

We hold here that Consolidated's complete and absolute control over Berkson, making Berkson a sup-

plemental part of Consolidated's economic unit, and operating Berkson without sufficient funds to meet its obligations to its creditors, constituted circumstantial evidence from which the court could reasonably draw the inference that Consolidated's purpose was improper and was detrimental to Oppenstein. Such inference is sustained by substantial evidence. It may not be disturbed here on appeal.

As to the first issue . . . this case is affirmed. . . .

BERGER v. COLUMBIA BROADCASTING SYSTEM
453 F.2d 991 (Fifth Cir. 1972)

[The plaintiff, Berger, entered into a contract with CBS Films, Inc. (Films), a wholly owned subsidiary of the defendant, Columbia Broadcasting System, Inc. Under the contract, Films was to acquire and distribute film footage of the plaintiff's International Fashion Festival for the year 1965. The festival was never broadcast by CBS. Berger sued the parent company, Columbia Broadcasting System, Inc., for breach of contract alleging that the much smaller corporate unit, Films, was an alter ego of the parent company. The trial court found in favor of Berger and awarded a judgment of $200,000 against CBS. On appeal, CBS argued that piercing the corporate veil was not proper.]

GOLDBERG, Circuit Judge

It is elemental that a corporation is a creature of the law, endowed with a personality separate and distinct from that of its owners, and that one of the principal purposes for legal sanctioning of a separate corporate personality is to accord stockholders an opportunity to limit their personal liability. There does exist, however, a large class of cases in which the separateness of a corporate entity has been disregarded and a parent corporation held liable for the acts of its subsidiary because the subsidiary's affairs had been so controlled as to render it merely an instrument or agent of

its parent. But the dual personality of parent and subsidiary is not lightly disregarded, since application of the instrumentality rule operates to defeat one of the principal purposes for which the law has created the corporation. Therefore, to justify judicial derogation of the separateness of a corporate creature, an aggrieved party must prove something more than a parent's mere ownership of a majority or even all of the capital stock and the parent's use of its power as an incident of its stock ownership to elect officers and directors of the subsidiary.

In *Lowendahl v. Baltimore & O. R.R.,* a New York court analyzed the various terms and legal theories [for holding a parent corporation liable for the acts of its subsidiary] and concluded that the instrumentality rule furnished the most practical theory for toppling a parent corporation's immunity. The court in *Lowendahl* then postulated the following three elements as the quantum of proof necessary to sustain application of the instrumentality rule:

(1) Control, not mere majority or complete stock control, but complete domination, not only of finances, but of policy and business practice in respect to the transaction attacked so that the corporate entity as to this transaction had at the time no separate mind, will or existence of its own; and

(2) Such control must have been used by the defendant to commit fraud or wrong, to perpetrate the violation of a statutory or other positive legal duty, or a dishonest and unjust act in contravention of plaintiff's legal rights; and

(3) The aforesaid control and breach of duty must proximately cause the injury or unjust loss complained of.

Applying these three elements to the relationship between the defendant and Films in the case at bar, we first turn to the lower court's factual determinations. The [trial] court held that at all relevant times Films was merely an instrumentality of the defendant based on the following findings: (1) the board of directors of Films consisted solely of employees of the defendant; (2) the organization chart of CBS, Inc. included Films; and (3) all lines of employee authority from Films passed through employees of the defendant and other subsidiaries to the chairman of the board of CBS, Inc. In addition, the trial judge was greatly influenced by the fact that several witnesses, including a comptroller of one of the defendant's subsidiaries, testified that Films was a "division" of CBS, Inc. Comparing these several facts to the requisite quantum of proof necessary to satisfy *Lowendahl's* "control" element, we think it is obvious that these factual determinations, standing alone, are insufficient to sustain application of the instrumentality rule. Moreover, an independent examination of the record in this case convinces us that the evidence adduced below concerning the relationship between the defendant and Films could not sustain any finding that the defendant completely dominated not only the finances, but the policy and business practice of Films.

In our opinion complete stock ownership, common officers and directors, and the use of organizational charts illustrating lines of authority are all business practices common to most parent-subsidiary relationships, and such proof of a parent's potential to dominate its subsidiary is precisely the kind of evidence that New York courts have consistently rejected as insufficient in proving a community of management between corporations.

The only evidence concerning the corporate relationship during the period in which the transaction involved herein occurred negates any assertion that Films was being operated as the alter ego of the defendant. The uncontradicted testimony of Mr. Sam

Cook Digges, former administrative vice president of Films, is as follows:

Q What was the relationship of CBS Films, Inc. to CBS Television Network?

A Many of the programs that were telecast on the CBS Television Network eventually went into distribution through CBS Films. . . .

Q For what period of time did you act as the administrative vice-president or operational head of CBS Films, Inc.?

A From 1959 to 1967.

Q In this eight-year period, Mr. Digges, did you ever sell a program from CBS Films, Inc., to CBS for network broadcast?

A Yes, we did. We sold many of the Terry-Toon products in the Saturday morning kid block.

We also sold a program when we were in the production end of the business also producing shows called Angel. This was a program that was produced by Jess Oppenheimer, who developed the Lucy series. Angel was on the CBS Television Network for one year. . . .

Q Did you make any sales to CBS?

A Not except for the Angel show.

Q Did you make any sales to any other network?

A Yes. The sale was made prior to the time I joined CBS, but the show was still running when I was there. That was a program called Navy Log, which was sold to ABC.

We also sold a show called the Children's Doctor, which is a five-minute medical series, a pediatrician, to the ABC Television Network.

Q Is there any contractual commitment for the network to broadcast any product that is produced by CBS Films, Inc.?

A No, there isn't. My life would have been easier if there had been such an arrangement.

Q Of the properties that CBS Films, Inc., would be distributing, was there any obligation on the part of CBS Films, Inc., to sell it to the CBS Television Network?

A No, there was not.

Faced with both this testimony and the total absence of any evidence showing the defendant's actual domination of its subsidiary Films during the period in which the plaintiff's contract was executed and allegedly breached, this court has no alternative but to reverse the decision of the district court on the simple basis that plaintiff has failed to prove, in accordance with New York law, that Films was the alter ego of the defendant.

Reversed.

CASE REVIEW QUESTIONS

1. In view of the high degree of control that Consolidated executed over Berkson, why do you think it bothered to keep Berkson as a separate corporate subsidiary rather than simply operating it as a part of Consolidated?

2. Are the decisions in the *Oppenstein* case and the *Berger* case consistent with each other or are they contradictory? Explain.

Suits to Prevent Evasion of Corporate Obligations Another category of cases in which a court may pierce the corporate veil includes those cases in which a corporation has attempted to evade a statutory, a court imposed, or a contractual obligation by having its shareholders, rather than the corporation itself, violate the obligation. For example, if it would be a violation of the antitrust laws for a particular corporation to buy the assets of a competitor, it would also be a violation for the shareholders to buy the competitor's assets and then transfer them to their corporation. In such cases, the courts will ignore the separate legal status of the corporation and the shareholders and will impose the obligations of the corporation on the shareholders as well.

Subordination of Shareholder Debts The final category of cases in which a corporation and its shareholders may be treated as one rather than as separate involves situations in which a corporation has become insolvent and owes debts to both ordinary business creditors and its shareholders. If there is evidence of bad faith in the creation of the debt to the shareholders or of conscious undercapitalization that adversely affected the corporation's ability to pay the outside creditors, the debts of the shareholders may be subordinated to those of the outside creditors. This means that the court will order that the debts to the outside creditors be paid first, and only after these payments are made are the debts to the shareholder creditors to be paid. If the assets of the corporation are not sufficient to pay all the creditors, the shareholder creditors will not receive full payment.

FINANCING THE CORPORATION

There are two methods of financing a corporation — debt financing and equity financing. Debt financing is accomplished by the issuance of debt securities, such as bonds and debentures. Equity financing is accomplished by the issuance of equity securities, called shares or stock. Who controls the business decisions of the corporation, who is entitled to share in the corporation's profits, and who participates in the distribution of assets if the corporation is dissolved (terminated) will be determined by the way in which the debt securities and equity securities are allocated among those who invest in the corporation.

Debt Financing

Debt financing is essentially long-term borrowing. Usually, it is available only to large corporations. The most common type of corporate debt financing is the bond. When a corporation issues a bond, it is borrowing money from the bondholder. The **bond** is a promise to the bondholder to repay the principal (the amount borrowed) at the maturity date (the date designated for repayment) and to pay interest periodically until then. Bonds are sometimes referred to as *debt securities.* Usually, a corporation will reserve the right to *redeem* (buy back) a bond prior to its maturity date.

A bondholder is a creditor of the corporation. As such, he or she has no right to participate in the control of the corporation or to share in its profits. If the corporation is dissolved, however, bondholders participate in the distribution of the corporation's assets before shareholders do. The subject of corporate dissolution is discussed fully in Chapter 41.

Bonds can take a variety of forms. Usually, they will be secured by a lien or a mortgage on the assets of the corporation, which makes the bondholder a secured creditor. A debt security that is unsecured is called a **debenture.** A bond also can be made *convertible* (exchangeable) into shares of stock of the corporation.

Equity Financing

The only method of raising capital available to most corporations is the sale of shares or stock. A contract by a corporation to sell stock is called a stock subscription agreement.

Preincorporation stock subscription agreements are sometimes used by a promoter to finance a corporation that is to be created. After the corporation is formed, the board of directors may choose to accept or to reject preincorporation stock subscriptions. If they are accepted, the corporation will collect payment and issue the shares. A number of states have passed statutes providing that a preincorporation stock subscription is irrevocable by the subscriber for a stated period unless the subscription agreement provides otherwise. Section 17 of the MBCA, for instance, sets this period of irrevocability at six months. Thus, a promoter can rely on the fact that a subscription can be enforced by the corporation against the subscriber as long as the subscription is accepted within the period of time during which it is irrevocable.

Under §19 of the MBCA, shares may be issued by a corporation in return for money, tangible or intangible property, or labor or services actually performed for the corporation. This means that shares cannot be issued in return for promissory notes or for services to be performed in the future. Under the Delaware corporation law, however, corporate shares may be issued in return for promissory notes.

A shareholder is an owner of the corporation, not a creditor. A shareholder's ownership interest, which is represented by a stock certificate (see Figure 38-3), can be transferred by transferring the stock certificate to the new owner, unless a transfer restriction is noted on the certificate. However, restrictions are usually only imposed on the shareholders of "close corporations," which will be dis-

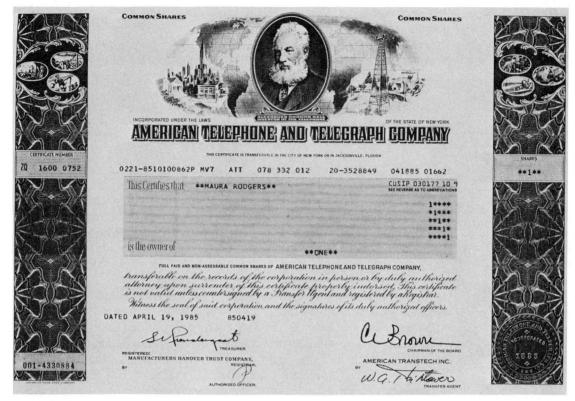

FIGURE 38-3
Stock Certificate

cussed in the next chapter. Unlike a partnership, a corporation is not dissolved when ownership is transferred; rather, it continues to exist. This is an advantage of the corporate form of doing business over the partnership form.

Terminology **Authorized shares** are the number of shares that the articles of incorporation permit the corporation to issue [MBCA §2(g) and §15]. The articles may also divide authorized shares into two or more *classes* of shares, each class having different rights, preferences, and limitations [MBCA §15].

Issued shares are shares that the corporation has sold to shareholders. **Treasury shares** are shares that were issued and have subsequently been reacquired by the corporation. Although they belong to the corporation, they cannot be voted by management at shareholders' meetings, dividends are not paid on them, and they are not listed on the corporate balance sheet as shares "outstanding."

Par Value versus No Par Value Shares **Par value shares,** also called *par shares,* are shares that have had a stated money value, such as $100, placed on them in the articles of incorporation. Generally, the par value is also stated on the stock certificate. When par value shares are issued, the corporation must receive payment for them that is not less than their par value. For instance, if 100 shares of $100 par value stock are issued by the corporation, the corporation must receive at least $10,000 for them. The market value of par shares, however, is not necessarily the same as the par value of those shares.

No par value (or no par) *shares* are shares that do not have a stated money value placed on them in the articles of incorporation. Nonetheless, the corporation must receive some payment when it issues no par shares. Once issued, no par shares are bought and sold at their market value.

Common versus Preferred Shares The two basic classes of stock are common stock and preferred stock. *Common stock* is the type of stock most frequently issued. The common shareholders usually have the right to control the corporation because common stock is traditionally voting stock. Common shareholders also usually have the right to receive a portion of the corporate profits in the form of dividends. Upon the dissolution of the corporation, they share in any assets that remain after all the creditors, including bondholders, have been paid.

Preferred shareholders are entitled to certain preferences (advantages) over the common shareholders. Generally, they enjoy the right to receive dividends at a specified rate before any dividends can be distributed to common shareholders. In practice, this sometimes means that the preferred shareholders will receive dividends and the common shareholders will not. Preferred shareholders are also given preference over common shareholders to the assets of the corporation upon the dissolution of the corporation. Preferred shareholders are usually denied voting privileges, and they therefore do not normally participate in control of the corporation. Sometimes, however, preferred shareholders are allowed to vote if no dividends have been paid to them for a certain number of years.

One class of preferred stock may enjoy a preference over other classes of preferred stock in certain matters, such as sharing in the assets upon dissolution. If the difference is in the amount of dividends, the preferred stock is said to be issued in series. For example, Series A might pay eight percent dividends whereas Series B might pay only six percent dividends.

It is also possible to have *convertible* preferred shares [MBCA §15]. This allows a preferred shareholder to convert his or her preferred stock into common stock. The rate at which the preferred shares can be converted and the conditions under which they can be converted are specified when the stock is issued.

Cumulative versus Noncumulative Preferred Shares Preferred stock can also be either *cumulative* or *noncumulative* [MBCA §15]. If dividends are not paid on *cumulative* preferred stock in a given year, those dividends cumulate. This means that the preferred shareholders are entitled to the payment of all past and present dividends owed to them before any dividends can be paid to the common shareholders. With *noncumulative* stock, dividends not paid in a given year are forever lost. The next year, the corporation need only pay the current dividend to the preferred shareholders in order to be able to pay dividends to the common shareholders. Unless specifically noted otherwise, preferred stock is usually cumulative.

Participating versus Nonparticipating Preferred Shares Preferred stock is also either participating or nonparticipating. Once the required dividends have been paid on *nonparticipating* preferred stock, any remaining surplus may be distributed among only the common stockholders. However, once the required dividends have been paid on *participating* preferred stock and equal dividends have been paid on the common stock, both the preferred stockholders and the common stockholders may share in the distribution of any remaining surplus. For preferred stock to be participating, it must be explicitly noted as such on the stock certificate.

Preemptive Rights In some circumstances, a shareholder has the right to purchase a pro rata share of any newly authorized and issued shares of a corporation. This right, called the **preemptive right,** was developed by the common law to enable a shareholder to maintain a proportionate interest in the corporation. The new shares must be offered to the shareholder before they can be offered to other prospective purchasers. It is the shareholders' choice whether to exercise this right.

The preemptive right doctrine is easily applied in a small corporation that has only one class of common stock. Indeed, shareholders in small corporations are normally concerned that their voting and financial interests not be diluted by the issuance of new shares to other individuals. The situation is quite different, however, in a large, publicly held corporation. The typical shareholder of a large corporation has only a small fractional ownership interest in the corporation and is therefore usually not concerned about the small dilution to his or her proportionate voting and dividend rights brought about by the issuance of new stock. Further, the administrative burden and the expense involved when a large number of shareholders have peemptive rights can be substantial.

Preemptive rights can also result in a delay in securing financing. Shareholders are entitled to a reasonable period of time to consider and accept the opportunity to buy shares. In the interim, the public market for the securities may decline. Finally, a publicly held corporation may have several different classes of both common and preferred shares, each of which may entitle the shareholder to different legal rights. This situation can make determining which shareholders are entitled to preemptive rights and in what amounts a legal morass.

Since preemptive rights can prove to be troublesome, may a corporation dispense with them? Yes. The states take two approaches. One is to eliminate preemptive rights unless the articles of incorporation specifically call for them [MBCA §26]. The other is to permit preemptive rights unless they are limited or denied in the articles of incorporation. In actual practice, therefore, preemptive rights tend to be confined to close corporations.

REVIEW QUESTIONS

1. For what reasons might a state adopt corporation law statutes that are more protective of the interests of corporate managers than the interests of corporate shareholders?

2. What are the advantages and disadvantages of doing business as a corporation?

3. What things might promoters consider when deciding in what state to incorporate a business?

4. Under what circumstances will a promoter be held liable on a preincorporation contract? When will a corporation be held liable on a preincorporation contract?

5. What information must be included in the articles of incorporation?

6. What is the difference between a corporation de jure and a corporation de facto? Under what circumstances might it make a difference whether a corporation is categorized as one or the other?

7. Under what circumstances will a court pierce the corporate veil?

8. What are the various choices a corporation must make in determining its capital structure?

CASE PROBLEMS

1. Jackie Armstrong is a young certified public accountant who works for a large, international accounting firm in New York City. She has decided that she is tired of working for a large firm in a big city, and she is soon going to return to her hometown, Springfield, Illinois, and open up her own CPA firm. One of the things she has wondered about is whether her new firm should be incorporated or operated as a sole proprietorship. What things should Armstrong consider in making her decision? What additional facts would you want to know before advising her as to whether she should incorporate her firm?

2. Seon Cab Corporation owns two taxicabs and carries only the legally required minimum liability insurance ($10,000) on each cab. Walkovszky was severely injured in an accident involving one of Seon's cabs. The accident occurred because of the negligence of Seon's driver. Walkovszky brought a legal action to collect damages for his injuries against Carlton, a shareholder in Seon. Carlton is also a shareholder in nine other corporations, each of which owns two cabs and carries only the minimum amount of insurance. Walkovszky argued that the shareholders of Seon should be held personally liable for the damages due to him because the multiple corporate structure constitutes an unlawful attempt to defraud members of the general

public injured by the cabs. What arguments can Carlton make in his defense? Who will win the case? Explain.

3. Terminal Transportation, Inc. (Terminal) is owned by three shareholders. These same shareholders also own four taxicab corporations. Although Terminal is not a shareholder in any of the four taxicab corporations, it services, inspects, repairs, and dispatches all of the taxis of the four corporations. Also, the name Terminal is conspicuously displayed on all of the taxis. Mangen was injured as a result of the negligence of one of the taxi drivers. In addition to suing the driver and the corporation that owned the taxi, Mangen sued Terminal. On what ground can Mangen argue that Terminal is liable for the taxi driver's negligence? How will Terminal defend itself? Who will win the case? Explain.

4. Grace Dawson was actively engaged in the promotion of a corporation to be known as Multifashion Frocks, Inc. On January 3, 1978, she obtained written commitments for the purchase of shares totaling $600,000 from a group of 15 potential investors. She was also assured orally that she would be engaged as the president of the corporation upon the commencement of business. Dawson immediately began work on the incorporation of Multifashion. She made several contracts for and

on its behalf and made cash expenditures of $1,000 on accomplishing these goals. At the first shareholders' meeting on April 5, 1978, the day the corporation came into existence, the shareholders elected a board of directors. With shareholder approval, the board took the following actions:

(a) It adopted some but not all of the contracts made by Dawson.

(b) It declined to engage Dawson in any capacity.

(c) It agreed to pay Dawson $750 for those cash outlays that were deemed to be directly beneficial to the corporation and rejected the balance.

Discuss the legal implications of the actions taken by the board. [Adapted from CPA examination question 4, *Business Law,* May, 1978.]

5. Otis Corporation (Otis) incorporated in 1983. Ninety-four percent of its shares are owned by James T. Parker, President; 1 percent, by his wife; and 5 percent, by Wilbur Chumley. These three individuals were the incorporators and are the officers and directors of the corporation. Otis manufactures and sells telephone equipment. In 1983, it had sales of approximately $350,000 almost exclusively in the state of its incorporation. In 1984, Otis began to branch out. It had sales of about $550,000 in its home state and of about $50,000 in a neighboring state. Otis expanded rapidly, and 1985 was a banner year, bringing sales of $1,250,000 and profits of $175,000. Otis constructed a small office building on a tract of land it had purchased for expansion purposes in the neighboring state. It used the top floor to establish a regional sales office and rented the balance of the building.

During the course of an audit of Otis for the year 1985, it was discovered that Parker had commingled his personal funds with those of the corporation, had kept very few records of board and shareholder meetings, and at his convenience had disregarded corporate law regarding separateness of personal and corporate affairs. The corporation had 1985 sales in excess of $300,000 in the neighboring state. The corporation has not filed any papers with the secretary of state of that state in connection with these operations.

In light of these discoveries, the original incorporation papers that were filed by Parker in 1983 were examined. The following irregularities were discovered: the purpose clause of the articles of incorporation states that the newly created corporation will do business only in the state of incorporation; a certified copy of the corporate charter was not obtained and filed in the county in which the corporation's principal place of business is located, as required by state law; Mr. Chumley and Mrs. Parker did not sign the articles of incorporation; and prior to the effective date of incorporation, a lease was taken out and a car was purchased in the corporate name.

Is Otis a valid corporate entity? What could be the effect of doing business in the neighboring state without having first qualified to do business there? What is the effect of doing business outside the state of incorporation when the corporate charter does not permit business outside the state? [Adapted from CPA examination question 6a, *Business Law,* November, 1977.]

6. Seminole, Inc., is a California corporation that operates a swimming pool, which it leases from Edwards. Seminole was formed by Cavaney, a lawyer, at the request of Edwards. However, after the corporation was formed, no shares of stock were ever issued, no shareholders' or directors' meetings were ever held, and the corporation owned no assets. Edwards actually runs the pool, and Cavaney's office is used to keep records and receive mail for the corporation. After his daughter drowned in the pool, Minton brought a legal action against Seminole to collect damages for negligence. Minton won a verdict of $100,000 but was unable to collect any of it from Seminole. Minton has now brought a legal action against Edwards and Cavaney to collect the $100,000 judgment, asking the court to pierce the corporate veil and hold the two defendants personally liable for the debts of Seminole. On what basis will Edwards and Cavaney defend themselves? Who will win the case? Explain.

7. Blackhawk Corporation issued two classes of shares. The Class A common shares carry the right to vote, the right to dividends, and the right to participate in the distribution of assets upon disso-

lution of the corporation. The Class B common shares, however, carry only the right to vote; they do not carry any right to share in the corporation's profits or in the distribution of assets upon dissolution. The Class A shareholders brought a legal action against Blackhawk Corporation, requesting the court to deny the Class B shareholders the right to vote at a shareholders' meeting. The Class A shareholders argued that the Class B shares are not equity securities, so the Class B shareholders are not entitled to vote. Who will win the case? Explain.

8. Lavine and Cacolides are considering forming a corporation to run a laundry business. They will not need to borrow any money because Lavine has $10,000 in cash to contribute to the business. Lavine, however, will not work for the business. Cacolides has no funds to contribute, but she has 10 years experience in managing a laundry business and will be the full-time manager of the business. Lavine and Cacolides agree that they should share equally in the control of corporate policy and should split the profits evenly. They further agree that Lavine should be protected against the loss of her investment as much as possible. How would you recommend that Lavine and Cacolides structure the capital of their corporation?

39

CORPORATE POWERS AND GOVERNANCE

This chapter considers the topics of the powers of corporations and how those powers are governed within the corporation. Both of these topics are important issues of public policy. From society's viewpoint, it is important for corporations to have enough power to carry out their socially beneficial functions; but it is likewise important for corporate power to be restricted if restrictions are necessary to protect society. It is similarly important for the governance of corporations to be structured in such a way that corporate powers will be used for the greatest good of society. As you read this chapter, you should consider what changes, if any, you would recommend in corporation law as it affects corporate powers and their governance in order to insure the greatest social good is derived from corporations.

CORPORATE POWERS

One of the items that must be included in the articles of incorporation when a corporation is created is a statement of the purpose or purposes for which the corporation is being formed (see page 808). At one time, these purposes had to be stated quite precisely. Today, however, it is permissible in many states for the purpose clause of the articles to provide merely that the corporation is being formed for "any lawful purpose" [MBCA §3].

The statement of corporate purposes in the articles provides the basis for determining the powers of the corporation. Traditionally, the courts have said that a corporation has only the power to perform those acts that are legal, that are reasonably necessary for the accomplishment of corporation's purposes, and that are not withheld from the corporation by the articles of incorporation. Those acts that a corporation has the power to perform are said to be *intra vires* (within the power of) the corporation, whereas those acts that a corporation does not have the power to perform are said to be *ultra vires* (beyond the power of) the corporation.

The Effect of *Ultra Vires* Acts

Suppose that a corporation does something, such as entering a contract, that is *ultra vires* the corporation. What effect will the fact that entering the contract is *ultra vires* have on enforcement of the contract? At one time, some courts said that an *ultra vires* contract was void and not enforceable by either party. Other courts distinguished between *ultra vires* contracts that were executory (not yet performed by either party), partially executed (performed by one party but not the other), and fully executed (performed by both parties). If the contract was executory, either party could use the fact that the contract was *ultra vires* to prevent its enforcement by a court. If the contract was fully executed, neither party could use the fact that the contract was *ultra vires* to prevent enforcement of it. If the contract was partially executed, the party who had received benefits because of the other party's performance could not use *ultra vires* to prevent performance of the contract, but the party who had performed could.

Today, the issue of whether a particular corporate act is *ultra vires* does not arise very often because, as noted earlier, the purpose clause of the articles of incorporation in many states may now provide that a corporation is being formed for *any lawful purpose.* In addition, many state corporation laws now list many powers that all corporations formed under those laws have and expressly limit the use of the doctrine of *ultra vires* (see MBCA §4 and §7). Consequently, *ultra vires* questions arise today in only a few situations. One of those situations, discussed in Chapter 35, concerns whether a corporation can be a member of a partnership (see page 734). Many corporation laws now expressly provide that a corporation has the power to be a partner.

Another corporate act that may be *ultra vires* today is cosigning or guarantying as an accommodation party (which means that the corporation receives no payment for cosigning or guarantying) a loan for someone with whom the corporation does not have a business relationship. In some states, this act will be *ultra vires* unless the power to perform it is expressly provided for in the articles of incorporation. The MBCA, however, expressly empowers corporations to make guarantees and to incur liabilities [MBCA §4(h)].

One final corporate act that has been attacked upon occasion as being *ultra vires* is the making of contributions to charity or to the public welfare. In the case that follows, shareholders brought a legal action against their corporation on the grounds that a donation made by the corporation to a university was *ultra vires.*

A.P. SMITH MFG. CO. v. BARLOW
98 A.2d 581 (N.J. 1953)

JACOBS, [Judge]

The [trial court] determined that a donation by the plaintiff The A.P. Smith Manufacturing Company to Princeton University was *intra vires.* Because of the public importance of the issues presented, the appeal duly taken to the [intermediate appellate court] has been certified directly to this [highest] court.

The company was incorporated in 1896 and is engaged in the manufacture and sale of valves, fire hydrants and special equipment, mainly for water and gas industries. Its plant is located in East Orange and Bloomfield and it has approximately 300 employees. Over the years the company has contributed regularly to the local community chest and on occasions to Upsala College in East Orange and Newark University, now part of Rutgers, the State University. On July 24, 1951 the board of directors adopted a resolution which set forth that it was in the corporation's best interests to join with others in the 1951 Annual Giving to Princeton University, and appropriated the sum of $1,500 to be transferred by the corporation's treasurer to the university as a contribution towards its maintenance. When this action was questioned by stockholders the corporation instituted a [legal] action and trial was had in due course.

Mr. Hubert O'Brien, the president of the company, testified that he considered the contribution to be a sound investment, that the public expects corporations to aid philanthropic and benevolent institutions, that they obtain good will in the community by so doing, and that their charitable donations create favorable environment for their business operations. In addition, he expressed the thought that in contributing to liberal arts institutions, corporations were furthering their self-interest in assuring the free flow of properly trained personnel for administrative and other corporate employment. Mr. Frank W. Abrams, chairman of the board of the Standard Oil Company of New Jersey, testified that corporations are expected to acknowledge their public responsibilities in support of the essential elements of our free enterprise system. He indicated that it was not "good business" to disappoint "this reasonable and justified public expectation," nor was it good business for corporations "to take substantial benefits from their membership in the economic community while avoiding the normally accepted obligations of citizenship in the social community." Mr. Irving S. Olds, former chairman of the board of the United States Steel Corporation, pointed out that corporations have a self-interest in the maintenance of liberal education as the bulwark of good government. He stated that "Capitalism and free enterprise owe their survival in no small degree to the existence of our private, independent universities" and that if American business does not aid in their maintenance it is not "properly protecting the long-range interest of its stockholders, its employees and its customers."

The objecting stockholders have not disputed any of the foregoing testimony nor the showing of great need by Princeton and other private institutions of higher learning and the important public service being rendered by them for democratic government and industry alike. Nevertheless, they have taken the position that the plaintiff's certificate of incorporation does not expressly authorize the contribution and under common-law principles the company does not possess any implied or incidental power to make it.

In his discussion of the early history of business corporations Professor Williston refers to a 1702 publication where the author stated flatly that "The general intent and end of all civil incorporations is for better government." And he points out that the early corporate charters . . . furnish additional support for the notion that the corporate object was the public one of managing and ordering the trade as well as the private one of profit for the members. However, with later economic and social developments and the free availability of the corporate device for all trades, the end of private profit became generally accepted as the controlling one in all businesses other than those classed broadly as public utilities. As a concomitant the common-law rule developed that those who managed the corporation could not disburse any corporate funds for philanthropic or other worthy public cause *unless* the expenditure would benefit the corporation. During the 19th Century when corporations were relatively few and small and did not dominate the country's wealth, the common-law rule did not significantly interfere with the public interest. But the 20th Century has presented a different climate. Control of economic wealth has passed largely from individual entrepreneurs to dominating corporations, and calls upon the corporations for reasonable philanthropic donations have come to be made with increased public support. In many instances such contributions have been sustained by the courts within the common-law doctrine upon liberal findings that the donations tended reasonably to promote the corporate objectives.

Over 20 years ago Professor Dodd, . . . cited the views of Justice Letton in *Sorensen v. Chicago B. & Q. R. Co.,* . . . with seeming approval and suggested the doctrine that corporations may properly support charities which are important to the welfare of the communities where they do business as soundly representative of the public attitude and actual corporate practice. Developments since he wrote leave no doubts on this score.

When the wealth of the nation was primarily in the hands of individuals they discharged their responsibilities as citizens by donating freely for charitable purposes. With the transfer of most of the wealth to corporate hands and the imposition of heavy burdens of individual taxation, they have been unable to keep pace with increased philanthropic needs. They have therefore, with justification, turned to corporations to assume the modern obligations of good citizenship in the same manner as humans do. In actual practice corporate giving has correspondingly increased. Thus, it is estimated that annual corporate contributions throughout the nation aggregate over 300 million dollars, with over 60 million dollars thereof going to universities and other educational institutions. Similarly, it is estimated that local community chests receive well over 40 percent of their contributions from corporations.

More and more they have come to recognize that their salvation rests upon a sound economic and social environment which in turn rests in no insignificant part upon free and vigorous nongovernmental institutions of learning. It seems to us that just as the conditions prevailing when corporations were originally created required that they serve public as well as private interests, modern conditions require that corporations acknowledge and discharge social as well as private responsibilities as members of the communities within which they operate. Within this broad concept there is no difficulty in sustaining, as incidental to their proper objects and in aid of the public welfare, the power of corporations to contribute corporate funds within reasonable limits in support of academic institutions. But even if we confine ourselves to the terms of the common-law rule in its application to current conditions, such expenditures may likewise readily be justified as being for the benefit of the corporation; indeed, if need be the matter may be viewed strictly in terms of actual survival of the corporation in a free enterprise system.

We find that it was a lawful exercise of the corporation's implied and incidental powers under common-law principles. . . . Clearly then, the appellants, as individual stockholders whose private interests rest entirely upon the well-being of the plaintiff corporation, ought not be permitted to close their eyes to present day realities and thwart the long-visioned corporate action in recognizing and voluntarily discharging its high obligations as a constituent of our modern social structure.

Affirmed.

CASE REVIEW QUESTIONS

1. If you had been a corporate manager in New Jersey prior to the decision in the *Barlow* case and you were trying to determine whether a contribution your corporation was considering making was *intra vires* or *ultra vires,* what standard would you have applied in making your decision?

2. After the decision in the *Barlow* case, if you were a corporate manager in New Jersey who was trying to determine whether a contribution that your corporation was considering making was *intra vires* or *ultra vires,* what standard would you apply in making your decision?
3. If your answer to Question 2 is different from your answer to Question 1, how do you explain the difference?

CORPORATE GOVERNANCE

In this part of the chapter, we will consider the ways in which corporation law allocates the power to operate a corporation. In general, corporation law provides that the ultimate control of a corporation is allocated to the shareholders, who elect a board of directors. The board of directors manages the business of the corporation. The board of directors also selects the corporate officers, who are responsible for implementing the management decisions of the board. This is the orthodox theory of corporation law. There is another theory, however, that regards the theory of shareholder control and shareholder democracy — that is, the theory that shareholders control corporate affairs through the election of directors — as a fiction.

In 1932, A. Berle and G. Means published a classic book, *The Modern Corporation and Private Property.* In it, they noted that ownership was being separated from control within the realm of corporations. Control was shifting out of the hands of the shareholders into the hands of professional managers. Some people believe this shift has been completed and that management is now able to perpetuate itself in office and to dominate corporate affairs.

Where does the truth lie? Probably somewhere in between, depending on the size of corporation involved. In small corporations, shareholder democracy is alive and working. The shareholders of small corporations will either be the managers themselves, or they will carefully follow and control the details of the corporation's operation. These small corporations comprise a large percentage of the total 2.25 million corporations.

In the middle of the corporate spectrum are those corporations that, while not small, are not giants either. These mid-sized corporations are also substantial in number. It is difficult to generalize about them, however. One of these corporations might have a relatively small number of shareholders who take an active interest in corporate affairs. Under these circumstances, management is probably directly responsible to the shareholders. Yet, a similar sized corporation could have a substantial number of disinterested shareholders who merely rubber stamp all of management's proposals.

With very large corporations, it is a virtual certainty that ownership and control will be separated. The large number of shareholders of these corporations (in some cases, more than one million) and their wide geographic distribution make it impossible for them to exercise their voting power so as to control the corporation. Therefore, control devolves to the managers who determine and implement corporate policy on a day-to-day basis.

It is important to understand the way in which corporation law allocates the power to operate a corporation because all corporations, from the smallest to the largest, are legally bound to act in accordance with this allocation of power. And in the case of the millions of corporations in which ownership and control are not separated, the allocation of powers imposed by corporation law does in fact determine the way in which decisions are made and implemented.

Shareholders' Powers

Corporation law attempts to place the *shareholders,* sometimes called *stockholders,* in ultimate control of the power of a corporation by giving them the following powers:

1. The power to elect and remove directors.
2. The power to adopt, repeal, and amend bylaws.
3. The power to vote on extraordinary corporate changes.
4. The power to adopt resolutions.

Each of these powers of the shareholders is discussed in the following sections.

Election and Removal of Directors As you read in the previous chapter, the initial directors of a new corporation are usually either named in the articles of incorporation [MBCA §54] or are elected at an organizational meeting by the incorporators or by the incorporators and the preincorporation share subscribers. Thereafter, the directors are elected by the shareholders [MBCA §36]. This power to elect the directors is the most fundamental of the powers of the shareholders. Through it, the shareholders are expected to exercise their ultimate control over the power of the corporation.

Shareholders also have the power to remove directors, but in most states removal may only be for "cause." What constitutes "cause" is not especially clear because the courts have not had to decide many cases in which the issue has arisen. However, there is little doubt that a director who engages in misconduct that interferes with his or her performance as a director or that is contrary to the best interests of the corporation can be removed for cause.

Section 39 of the MBCA provides that the shareholders may remove directors either with or without cause. Although they do not yet comprise a majority, there seems to be a movement among the states toward providing for removal of directors with or without cause.

Adoption, Amendment, and Repeal of Bylaws The bylaws of a corporation determine the legal relationships of the shareholders, the directors, and the officers to the corporation and to each other. Although the initial bylaws may be adopted by the incorporators or the directors at an organizational meeting, as was discussed in the previous chapter, one of the ways in which the shareholders can exercise their ultimate right to control the corporation is through their power to adopt, repeal, and amend the bylaws. In some states and under §27 of the MBCA, however, the shareholders only have these powers if they are given them in the articles of incorporation.

Extraordinary Corporate Changes A shareholder who invests in a corporation is considered to do so with the expectation that the articles of incorporation define the corporation in which he or she is investing. If the corporation wants to change in an extraordinary way, the shareholders must be given the opportunity to vote on whether they approve of the extraordinary change. Extraordinary changes include amendments of the articles of incorporation, mergers, consolidations, sales or leases of corporate assets not in the ordinary course of business, and dissolutions. These matters are the subject of Chapter 41.

Shareholder Resolutions Shareholders may also adopt resolutions concerning the corporation. However, as you will read later, the power to adopt resolutions does not give the shareholders the power to tell the directors and officers of the corporation how to operate the business. Instead, shareholder resolutions are used for the most part to ratify actions already taken by directors and officers.

Because the shareholders may not tell the directors and officers how to operate the business, the shareholders' ultimate control over the corporation is exercised by electing and removing directors; adopting, amending and repealing bylaws; and voting on extraordinary corporate changes.

Shareholders' Meetings

The powers of the shareholders can only be exercised at a properly called shareholders' meeting. The bylaws usually provide for the time and place of the *annual meeting* of the shareholders, and the state corporation statute provides for the content and the timing of the notice of the meeting that must be given to the shareholders [MBCA §29].

In addition to an annual meeting, shareholders may also hold *special meetings.* Usually, a corporation's bylaws provide that a special shareholders' meeting can be called by the corporation's president or board of directors. Some states also allow the holders of a specified percentage of a corporation's outstanding shares to call a special meeting. For instance, §28 of the MBCA provides that the holders of not less than 10 percent of all of the shares entitled to vote at a shareholders' meeting may call a special meeting.

If a special meeting is called, notice of the meeting specifying its time, place, and purpose must be given to the shareholders. The business transacted at a special meeting will be limited to those matters related to the stated purpose of the meeting contained in the notice.

In the case that follows, some of the shareholders of a corporation wanted to hold a special shareholders' meeting in order to exercise their powers. Their request for the meeting was ignored by the corporation's president, however. The shareholders then brought a legal action asking the court to order the president to call the requested meeting.

AUER v. DRESSEL
118 N.E.2d 590 (N.Y. 1954)

[Joseph L. Auer owned class A stock of R. Hoe & Co., Inc. (Hoe). Auer and other class A stockholders requested Dressel, the president of Hoe, to call a special stockholders' meeting. When Dressel ignored their request, Auer and the others petitioned the court to order Dressel to call the meeting. The trial court issued the order, and Dressel appealed.]

DESMOND, Judge

Section 2 of article 1 of [the] by-laws [of Hoe] says that "It shall be the duty of the President to call a special meeting whenever requested in writing to do so by stockholders owning a majority of the capital stock entitled to vote at such meeting." [P]etitioners submitted to the president written requests for a special meeting of class A stockholders, which writings were signed in the names of the holders of slightly more than 55% of the class A stock. The president failed to call the meeting and, after waiting a week, the petitioners brought the present proceeding.

There was no discretion in this corporate officer as to whether or not to call a meeting when a demand therefor was put before him by owners of the required number of shares. The important right of stockholders to have such meetings called will be of little practical value if corporate management can ignore the requests, force the stockholders to commence legal proceedings, and put the stockholders to lengthy and expensive litigation.

The [plaintiff's] petition was opposed on the alleged ground that none of the four purposes for which petitioners wished the meeting called was a proper one for such a class A stockholders' meeting. Those four stated purposes were these: (A) to vote, upon a resolution indorsing the administration of Joseph L. Auer, who had been removed as president by the directors, and demanding that he be reinstated as such president; (B) voting upon a proposal to amend the charter and by-laws to provide that vacancies on the board of directors, arising from the removal of a director by

stockholders or by resignation of a director against whom charges have been preferred, may be filled, for the unexpired term, by the stockholders only of the class theretofore represented by the director so removed or so resigned; (C) voting upon a proposal that the stockholders hear certain charges preferred against four of the directors, determine whether the conduct of such directors or any of them was inimical [hostile] to the corporation and, if so, to vote upon their removal and vote for the election of their successors; and (D) voting upon a proposal to amend the by-laws so as to provide that half of the total number of directors in office and, in any event, not less than one-third of the whole authorized number of directors constitute a quorum of the directors.

The Hoe certificate of incorporation provides for eleven directors, of whom the class A stockholders, more than a majority of whom join in this [legal action], elect nine and the common stockholders elect two. The obvious purpose of the meeting here sought to be called (aside from the indorsement and reinstatement of former president Auer) is to hear charges against four of the class A directors, to remove them if the charges be proven, to amend the by-laws so that the successor directors be elected by the class A stockholders, and further to amend the by-laws so that an effective quorum of directors will be made up of no fewer than half of the directors in office and no fewer than one third of the whole authorized number of directors. No reason appears why the class A stockholders should not be allowed to vote on any or all of those proposals.

The stockholders, by expressing their approval of Mr. Auer's conduct as president and their demand that he be put back in that office, will not be able, directly, to effect that change in officers, but there is nothing invalid in their so expressing themselves and thus putting on notice the directors who will stand for election at the annual meeting. As to purpose (B), that is, amending the charter and by-laws to authorize the stockholders to fill vacancies as to class A directors who have been removed on charges or who have resigned, it seems to be settled law that the stockholders who are empowered to elect directors have the inherent power to remove them for cause. Of course, there must be the service of specific charges, adequate notice and full opportunity of meeting the accusations, but there is no present showing of any lack of any of those in this instance. Since these particular stockholders have the right to elect nine directors and to remove them on proven charges, it is not inappropriate that they should use their further power to amend the by-laws to elect the successors of such directors as shall be removed after hearing, or who shall resign pending hearing. Quite pertinent at this point is *Rogers v. Hill* which made light of an argument that stockholders, by giving power to the directors to make by-laws, had lost their own power to make them; quoting a New Jersey case, the United States Supreme Court said: " 'It would be preposterous to leave the real owners of the corporate property at the mercy of their agents, and the law has not done so.' " Such a change in the by-laws, dealing with class A directors only, has no effect on the voting rights of the common stockholders, which rights have to do with the selection of the remaining two directors only. True, the certificate of incorporation authorizes the board of directors to remove any director on charges, but we do not consider that provision as an abdication by the stockholders of their own traditional, inherent power to remove their own directors. Rather, it provides an additional method. Were that not so, the stockholders might find themselves without effective remedy in a case where a majority of the directors were accused of wrong-doing and, obviously, would be unwilling to remove themselves from office.

We fail to see, in the proposal to allow class A stockholders to fill vacancies as to class A directors, any impairment of any violation of paragraph (h) of article Third of the certificate of incorporation, which says that class A stock has exclusive voting rights with respect to all matters "other than the election of directors." That negative language should not be taken to mean that class A stockholders, who have an absolute right to elect nine of these eleven directors, cannot amend their by-laws to guarantee a similar right, in the class A stockholders and to the exclusion of common stockholders, to fill vacancies in the class A group of directors.

There is urged upon us the impracticability and unfairness of constituting the numerous stockholders a tribunal to hear charges made by themselves, and the incongruity of letting the stockholders hear and pass on those charges by proxy. Such questions are really not before us at all on this appeal. The charges here are not, on their face, frivolous or inconsequential, and all that we are holding as to the charges is that a meeting may be held to deal with them. Any director illegally removed can have his remedy in the courts.

Affirmed.

CASE REVIEW QUESTIONS

1. What remedy did the shareholders seek from the court? Why was it necessary for the shareholders to obtain that remedy?
2. What shareholders' powers discussed earlier in the chapter did the class A stockholders want to exercise?
3. What would be the effect of the adoption at a special shareholders' meeting of a resolution indorsing the administration of Joseph L. Auer and demanding that he be reinstated as president? Explain.
4. Does it appear from the case that the class A stockholders had the power to remove directors for cause? Explain.

Waiver of Notice If the notice requirements for either an annual or a special shareholders meeting are not met, actions taken at the meeting are a nullity [of no effect]. The notice requirements, however, may be waived by shareholders before, during, or after the meeting; if this is done, failure to meet the notice requirements will not affect the actions taken at the meeting. To be effective, waiver must be made by all of the shareholders who do not receive proper notice.

Quorum Requirement The state corporation law will state the percentage of shares that constitute a quorum, which means the number of shares that must be represented at the meeting before business can be validly transacted. Most states, however, allow the corporation to alter, within limitations, the quorum requirement stated in the corporation law. For instance, §32 of the MBCA allows a corporation to state its own quorum requirement in the articles of incorporation, provided that the quorum requirement is not less than one-third of the shares entitled to vote at the meeting.

Action Without a Meeting In many states today and under §145 of the MBCA, the shareholders can take action without a meeting. Under the MBCA, this can be done if specified actions are consented to in writing by all of the shareholders. Of course, obtaining unanimous written consent will only be possible when the number of shareholders is relatively small.

Voting Generally, each share of the corporation outstanding is entitled to one vote on each matter that is put to a shareholder vote [MBCA §33]. This means that when a vote is taken, a shareholder who owns 100 shares may cast 100 votes, a shareholder with 500 shares may cast 500 votes, and so on. The usual rule is one share, one vote, not one shareholder, one vote. This method of voting is called *straight voting*.

Nonvoting Shares In some states, a corporation may issue shares that do not have voting rights. Section 33 of the MBCA, for instance, provides that nonvoting shares may be issued if they are provided for in the articles of incorporation. Nonvoting shares are a device that is used to secure equity financing for the corporation while keeping control of the corporation within the hands of the group that holds the voting shares. A few states will not permit the issuance of nonvoting shares on the grounds that all shareholders should have a voice in corporate affairs.

In certain circumstances, nonvoting shares have voting power. Generally, the holders of nonvoting shares may vote when they will be adversely affected by a proposed change in the articles of incorporation or the bylaws or by any other extraordinary corporate change. In such instances, the holders of the nonvoting shares vote as a class—which means that their votes are counted separately from the votes of other classes of shares—on the proposed change in their shareholder status. If a majority of the nonvoting shares opposes the proposed change, it cannot be made. In this way, the holders of the nonvoting shares are protected from harmful actions by the holders of the voting shares.

Cumulative Voting The most important item of business at an annual share-holders' meeting is usually the election of directors. If this election were to be presented to the shareholders as an ordinary business item and if the bylaws provided that ordinary business items were to be decided by a majority vote, then the holders of a majority of the shares could elect the entire board, closing out any minority-shareholder representation.

For example, assume that Corporation X has 3,000 shares outstanding; 2,400 are present at a shareholders' meeting, 1,500 are owned by a group that is or is associated with management, and 900 are owned by nonmanagement interests. If five directors are to be elected by straight voting (one vote per share) and if the election for each position is a separate business item, the candidates might be represented as follows:

Management Nominees					Nonmanagement Nominees				
A	B	C	D	E	F	G	H	I	J

In the first election, A would stand against F and would win by a vote of 1,500 to 900. The next election, B versus G, would proceed the same way. A, B, C, D, and E would thus be elected.

Cumulative voting is designed to enable a minority group of shareholders to gain representation on the board of directors. The representatives of the majority shareholders will still dominate board affairs, but the minority shareholders will have representation on the board and will thereby have access to first hand knowledge of corporate affairs. Typically, management opposes cumulative voting. The stated reason for the opposition is usually that the duty of the board is to represent the best interests of all shareholders, so the representatives of special interests who could be elected through cumulative voting have no place on the board. The real reason for the opposition, however, may be management's desire to avoid having its policies vigorously questioned by board members who represent minority interests.

Cumulative voting allows a shareholder to multiply the number of shares he or she owns by the number of directors to be elected. The shareholder can then cast all of his or her votes for a single candidate or allocate them among several candidates. From a tactical standpoint, the minority shareholders will desire to use their votes so as to elect the largest possible number of directors.

How is this achieved? The following formula can be used to determine the most advantageous distribution of votes.

$$X = \frac{Y \times N^1}{N + 1} + 1$$

In the formula, X is the number of shares needed to elect a given number of directors, Y is the total number of shares to be voted at the meeting, N^1 is the number of directors an individual or group wants to elect, and N is the total number of directors to be elected.

Let us now examine the formula in operation. Using the same example as before and assuming that the group of minority shareholders wants to elect one director to the board, how many shares will they need?

$$X = \frac{2400 \times 1}{5 + 1} + 1$$

$$X = 401 \text{ shares}$$

Thus, the minority shareholders will need 401 shares to elect one person to the board of directors. To elect two directors will require 801 shares. Since the minority shareholders own 900 shares, they will be able to elect two of the five board members by cumulating their votes and casting them for their two nominees.

Classifying the board and staggering the terms of each of the classes of directors is a method sometimes used by management to frustrate the purpose of cumulative voting. For example, if a corporation's board is composed of three members divided into three classes serving staggered three-year terms, only one board member will be elected annually. As a result, the majority shareholders will be able to elect their nominee each year. Some states that mandate cumulative voting have therefore prohibited staggered terms for directors. Section 37 of the MBCA permits classification of the board and staggered terms for directors only if the board consists of nine or more members and the directors are divided into only two or three classes. This means that at least three directors must be elected each year.

Generally, the larger the corporation, the less likely it is that cumulative voting is used. Very large corporations usually choose to incorporate in states that do not require cumulative voting. Indeed, estimates are that approximately 90 percent of all large industrial corporations do not require cumulative voting. Furthermore, in their efforts to lure corporations, many states are moving away from requiring cumulative voting. Today, Delaware and 32 other states do not require cumulative voting, but they permit it if the articles of incorporation provide for it (see MBCA §33).

Proxies Usually, only a very few shareholders actually attend the annual meeting of a large corporation because the time and expense it requires can be substantial. This lack of attendance raises two potential problems. First, the shareholders who are unable to attend could be denied their right to vote. Second, the quorum that is necessary to hold the meeting might not be assembled.

These potential problems are avoided by the use of the proxy system. A proxy is the shareholder's equivalent of the absentee ballot. By using a proxy, a shareholder can vote his or her shares without attending the meeting and, at the same time, those shares can be counted toward satisfying the quorum requirement.

Under the proxy system, a shareholder appoints an agent, called a proxy, to attend the meeting and to vote his or her shares. The shareholder can limit the authority of the proxy to voting the shares in a specified manner, or the shareholder can delegate general authority permitting the proxy to vote as the proxy believes best. However, the proxy cannot vote for fundamental corporate changes—mergers, dissolution, amendments to the articles, and the like—unless the shareholder specifically delegates the authority to do so.

Proxies are governed by the law of agency. Thus, a proxy is revocable by the shareholder-principal. The shareholder may revoke his or her proxy by attending the meeting and voting the shares personally. Also, granting a subsequent proxy to another agent revokes any previous proxy. A proxy coupled with an interest is irrevocable, however. For example, if A sells her shares to B after the record date for the shareholder's meeting—the date, prior to the meeting, on which the eligibility of shareholders to vote is determined from the corporation's records of share ownership—and, in addition, A gives her proxy to B, that proxy is irrevocable because it is coupled with B's interest in the shares.

The Securities Exchange Act of 1934 subjects the solicitation of proxies to vigorous regulation, and soliciting proxies without complying with the requirements of that act is unlawful. These requirements are discussed in detail in Chapter 51.

Voting Trusts A voting trust is created when some or all of the shareholders of a corporation transfer their shares to a trustee for voting purposes. The terms and conditions of the trust are set out in a voting trust agreement. Typically, this agreement will be limited by statute to a duration of ten years. Unlike a proxy, which is revocable, a voting trust is irrevocable once it has been established. Legal title to the shares, accompanied by voting rights, is vested in the trustee, who issues "voting trust certificates" to the shareholders to indicate their respective proportionate interests in the trust. The shareholders are the beneficiaries of the trust, and the trustee forwards any dividends to them. (See §34 of the MBCA.)

Directors' Powers

The power of the shareholders to control the operation of the corporation's business is quite indirect and is virtually exhausted once the shareholders have elected the board of directors. The power of the directors to control the operation of the corporation's business, on the other hand, is very direct. It includes both the general power to manage the corporation as well as specific powers to do certain things. These powers are explained in the following sections.

General Management Power Section 35 of the MBCA provides that:

All corporate powers shall be exercised by or under the authority of, and the business and affairs of a corporation shall be managed under the direction of, a board of directors. . . .

The corporation laws of almost all the states include either this provision or a similar one allocating the general power to manage a corporation to the board of directors.

Specific Management Powers The MBCA expressly allocates specific management powers to do the following things to the board of directors:

1. Adopt, amend, and repeal bylaws [MBCA §38].
2. Fill vacancies on the board of directors between shareholders' meetings [MBCA §38].
3. Delegate some or all of the authority of the board of directors to committees of the board [MBCA §42].
4. Declare dividends [MBCA §45].
5. Select, supervise, and remove officers [MBCA §§50 and 51].
6. Propose amendments to the articles of incorporation [MBCA §59].
7. Propose extraordinary corporate changes to the shareholders [MBCA §§71, 72, 79, and 84].

The board possesses some of these powers only if those powers are expressly given to the board in the articles of incorporation or the bylaws of the corporation. The board has others of these powers unless those powers are expressly denied to the board in the articles or the bylaws. Lastly, the board has some of these powers inherently, so those powers cannot be denied to the board.

Declaration of Dividends One of the inherent powers of a board of directors is the power to declare dividends. A **dividend** is a distribution of the corporations' assets to the shareholders on the basis of the number of shares each shareholder owns.

State corporation laws are not in agreement concerning the circumstances in which a dividend may be declared by a board of directors. Generally, however, the states prohibit dividends in the following situations:

1. *When the corporation is insolvent or would become insolvent as a result of the payment of the dividend* [MBCA §45]. Insolvent may mean either that the corporation is unable to pay its debts as they become due in the usual course of its business or that the corporation lacks sufficient assets to pay its outstanding liabilities.
2. *When the corporation cannot pay the dividend from the source specified in the corporation law of its state of incorporation.* The source specified may be *earned surplus,* which is income derived from the corporation's business; *surplus,* which is income derived not only from the corporation's business but also from the corporation's sales and purchases of its own stock; or *current net earnings,* which are the profits for the year for which the dividend is declared.

Usually, dividends are paid in cash, but they may also be paid in other kinds of property, such as shares of a subsidiary corporation.

In another popular type of distribution, called a **stock dividend,** a corporation distributes shares of its own stock to its shareholders. Actually, a stock dividend is not a dividend at all because no assets are distributed to the shareholders. To illustrate, suppose that X Corporation has issued 1,000 shares of stock and A owns 100 of them. The directors then declare and pay a 20 percent stock dividend. X Corporation now has 1,200 issued shares, and A owns 120 of them. Although A now owns more shares, so do all the X Corporation shareholders, so A's proportionate interest in X is exactly the same as it was before the stock dividend. As you can see, there has been no distribution of X's assets to A or to any of the other shareholders.

Directors' Meetings

The directors of a corporation have no power to act on behalf of the corporation as individuals; they can only act as a board. Regular meetings of the board of directors can normally be held only after notice of the meeting is given to all of the directors as provided in the bylaws. Usually, the time and place of regular meetings are specified in the bylaws. However, under §43 of the MBCA, the bylaws can provide that regular meetings may be held without notice. All special directors' meetings and all meetings of the board's committees require notice.

Attendance at a meeting for which notice is required constitutes a waiver of the notice requirement, unless a director attends the meeting for the express purpose of protesting the fact that he or she did not receive notice [MBCA §43]. A director may also waive the notice requirement in writing before, during, or after the meeting.

Generally, business can be transacted at a board of directors' meeting only when a quorum of the directors is present. Under §40 of the MBCA, a quorum is a majority of the total number of directors, unless the articles of incorporation or the bylaws provide that a larger percentage of the total number of directors is necessary. Normally, action can be taken by the board only after it is approved by the vote of the majority of the directors present at a meeting that has a quorum, unless the articles or bylaws require approval by the vote of a larger percentage of the directors present.

Suppose, for example, that the articles and bylaws of XYZ Corporation provide for eleven directors and say nothing about quorum or vote requirements for board of directors' meetings. Proper notice of a meeting is given, and six of the directors attend. A quorum is present, so the board can transact business. A vote to appoint Smith president of XYZ is taken. If three or fewer of the directors present — that is, less than a majority of those present — vote to approve the appointment, Smith will not become president. If four or more of the directors present vote to approve the appointment, Smith will become president.

Exceptions to the Meeting Requirement The MBCA provides for two exceptions to the basic requirement that the directors may only take action at a meeting at which a quorum is physically present. The first exception is that the directors may take action by means of a conference telephone hook-up or similar communications process, as long as everyone involved can hear what all the others are saying [MBCA §43]. The second exception is that the directors may take action without a meeting if all of the directors sign a written consent that sets forth the action taken [MBCA §44]. Under the MBCA, a corporation's directors may use these two exceptions unless the articles of incorporation or the bylaws provide otherwise.

In the case that follows, the plaintiff argued that an action taken by a board of directors was invalid because it had not been taken at a properly called meeting of the board.

STONE v. AMERICAN LACQUER SOLVENTS COMPANY
345 A.2d 174 (Pa. 1975)

EAGEN, Justice

The plaintiff-appellant, Rachel Stone, is the widow of Harold E. Stone, deceased, who was the Chairman of the Board of Directors of defendant-appellee, the American Lacquer Solvents Company [American], a Pennsylvania corporation, on December 7, 1967, and continuously thereafter until his death on November 1, 1968. On December 7, 1967, the Board of Directors of American, in consideration for services rendered the company by Harold E. Stone, adopted a Resolution providing that in the event of Harold E. Stone's death prior to that of his wife (Rachel Stone), American was to pay an annual pension of $8,000 to said wife until her death or remarriage. The Resolution further provided that it could not be revoked without Harold E. Stone's consent.

On March 2, 1968, Stone and his wife suffered a marital dispute while residing in Coral Gables, Florida. Following this Stone contacted his son-in-law Robert Shaw, President and General Manager of American, who was visiting Florida at the time, and told him he wanted the Resolution providing a pension for his wife cancelled. Shaw contacted the company's counsel and, acting in accordance with his advice as to the procedure to be followed, prepared a letter from Stone to the Board of Directors of American saying, "It is my wish that the Resolution dated December 7, 1967 concerning a pension for my wife Rachel be rescinded." Stone signed and personally delivered the letter to Shaw on March 3rd.

On March 11, 1968, Shaw convened a special meeting of the Board of Directors of American. Five of the seven members of the Board attended the meeting and when Stone's letter was brought to their attention,

they voted unanimously to rescind the Resolution of December 7, 1967. Stone was not notified the meeting was to be held and did not attend.

Stone died on November 1, 1968, and when American refused to pay his widow, Rachel Stone, the pension provided for in the Resolution of December 7, 1967, she instituted this action seeking specific performance. The trial court ruled the Resolution, providing for the payment of the pension, had been validly rescinded by the Board at the meeting of March 11, 1968, and hence, the plaintiff had no cause of action. The correctness of this ruling is challenged by this appeal.

As a general rule the directors of a corporation may bind a corporation only when they act at a legal meeting of the board. If they purport to act at a meeting which is not a legal meeting, their action is not that of the corporation, and the corporation . . . is not bound.

As to special meetings of the board of directors of a corporation, the general rule in Pennsylvania is that such a meeting held without notice to some or any of the directors and in their absence is illegal, and action taken at such a meeting, although by a majority of the directors, is invalid. . . . However, this notice requirement may be waived by a director either prior or subsequent to the special meeting, provided such waiver is in writing. Additionally, any action which may properly be taken at a meeting of a board of directors of a corporation may be effected and is binding without a meeting, if a consent in writing setting forth the action so taken is signed by each and every member of the board and filed with the secretary of the corporation.

A reading of the trial court's opinion filed in support of its decree upholding the legality of the Board's action of March 11, 1968, rescinding the Board's prior Resolution providing for the payment of the pension to the plaintiff was based on three grounds, any one of which, if correct, would warrant its ruling. [Only two grounds are included in this edited version of the case.]

First, the court concluded that Stone's letter of March 3, 1968, constituted a consent to the Board's subsequent action rescinding the pension Resolution. The difficulty with this position is that the applicable statute requires that such a consent be executed after the meeting and that it specifically set forth the action taken, and that it be filed with the secretary of the corporation. Stone's letter does not meet these requirements.

Secondly, the court concluded Stone's letter of March 3, 1968, constituted a waiver of receipt of notice of the meeting of March 11, 1968. The difficulty with this position is that the letter does not refer to the meeting or indicate in any way that notice thereof is waived. The letter amounts to no more than an expression of desire or consent to rescind the pension Resolution.

In connection with its conclusion that Stone's letter constituted a waiver of notice of the meeting, the court reasoned that no purpose would be served by Stone's presence at the meeting since the other Directors were merely acceding to Stone's wishes and request. This analysis overlooks the rationale for the salutory rule that all directors receive notice of special meetings. The rationale is that

> each member of a corporate body has the right of consultation with the others, and has the right to be heard upon all questions considered, and it is presumed that if the absent members had been present they might have dissented, and their arguments might have convinced the majority of the unwisdom of their proposed action and thus have produced a different result.

We agree with this rationale and, in view of the presumption embodied therein, we cannot concur in the trial court's premise that Stone and the other Directors were of one mind as regards the pension recission. In relation to this, we specifically note that another member of the Board of Directors failed to attend the meeting of March 11, 1968, and there is nothing in the record to show if he received notice of the meeting, or ever consented to the action taken at the meeting.

Reversed.

CASE REVIEW QUESTIONS

1. Which of the directors' powers discussed in the text preceding the case did the board of directors attempt to exercise?
2. Why did the board of directors fail in their attempt to exercise this power?
3. Was there a quorum of the directors present at the March 11 meeting of the board? Explain.
4. Why did the court decide that Stone had not waived his right to notice of the meeting?
5. Why did the court decide that Stone's letter did not constitute a consent to the board's action?
6. How does Pennsylvania's law concerning directors' consent to actions taken by a board of directors apparently differ from §44 of the MBCA, which was discussed in the text immediately preceding the case?
7. In your own words, present a justification of the court's decision.

Delegation of Directors' Powers Most corporation law statutes allow a board of directors to delegate some of its authority to committees. Section 42 of the MBCA provides that authority can be delegated to an executive committee and one or more additional committees, the members of which must all be directors, if the power to delegate authority is given to the board in the articles of incorporation or the bylaws. However, the authority delegated to committees generally may not include the most important of the powers of the directors, such as the power to declare dividends, to propose amendments to the articles of incorporation to the shareholders, to fill vacancies on the board, to amend bylaws, or to propose extraordinary corporate changes to the shareholders [MBCA §42].

An executive committee is a committee with general jurisdiction over corporate matters. It is, in a sense, a mini-board of directors. As such, it is likely to be used to act on matters that require action by the board of directors between regular meetings of the board, subject to the limitations discussed in the previous paragraph.

Other committees are usually more specialized, concerning themselves with particular areas of board interest. These often include audit, finance, compensation, and nominating committees. Here, we will discuss two of the more important board committees—audit committees and nominating committees.

Audit Committees In 1974, the Securities and Exchange Commission (SEC) began to require that each corporation under its jurisdiction form an audit committee of the board of directors and disclose the names of the committee's members to its shareholders. In 1977, the New York Stock Exchange adopted a requirement that all corporations listed on that exchange have audit committees. In 1978, the Special Committee on Audit Committees of the American Institute of Certified Public Accountants indorsed the creation of audit committees.

An audit committee's basic functions are to choose independent financial auditors, review the findings of those auditors, and report the findings to the board of directors. All members of the audit committee must be *outside directors*—that is, they must be directors who are not officers of the corporation or relatives of officers of the corporation. The purpose of this requirement is to prevent *inside directors*—that is, directors who are or are related to officers of the corporation—from controlling the collecting and reporting of corporate financial information.

Nominating Committees A main function of a nominating committee is to select the slate of nominees that will be submitted to the shareholders for election to the board of directors. As with audit committees, the SEC and others have encouraged that nominating committees be composed primarily of outside directors so that the power to control the selection of who will serve on the board of directors is not held by the corporation's officers.

Officers' Powers

Under §50 of the MBCA, the officers of a corporation are the president, one or more vice presidents, a secretary, a treasurer, and any other officers that are deemed necessary by the board of directors. These officers are chosen by the board of directors, and they, in turn, usually appoint lower-level officers and other employees of the corporation. All officers and employees can normally be removed from office by the board of directors, either with or without cause, even if the removal constitutes a breach of the corporation's employment contract with the officer or employee.

The powers given to the various officers to conduct activities that are internal to the operation of the corporation's business, such as managing a corporate division, supervising internal accounting, or assisting the president, are of no concern to the law. The courts become concerned with the acts of officers only when they affect third parties. In such cases, the courts apply the rules of agency law discussed in Chapters 31 through 34. Here, we will review those rules insofar as they commonly affect the powers of corporate officers.

Actual Authority The actual authority of a corporate officer is that authority actually conferred on him or her (see page 674). Actual authority may be expressly conferred by the state corporation law or by the articles of incorporation, although this rarely occurs. More frequently, *express actual authority* is conferred by the corporation's bylaws and by board of directors' resolutions.

Actual authority may also be impliedly conferred on a corporate officer. *Implied actual authority* is the authority that an officer reasonably believes he or she has. One way in which this belief might arise is from the acquiescence of the board of directors in the exercise of certain authority. For instance, a corporate officer without express actual authority to hire employees who nonetheless hires employees regularly with the knowledge of and without objection by the board of directors has the implied actual authority to hire employees.

Implied actual authority might also arise "by virtue of office." In other words, an officer may believe that any person who holds a particular office has certain powers. But is such a belief reasonable? There has been a good deal of litigation concerning the implied authority possessed by an officer by virtue of office, and the courts of the different states have not agreed on this matter. Some courts have held that appointment to an office, in and of itself, bestows no authority. However, there is a trend in the courts today toward the position that a corporate president has implied authority to enter into contracts on behalf of the corporation in the ordinary course of business. (Determining whether a contract has been entered into in the ordinary course of business requires the consideration of such factors as the custom and practice in the industry, the dollar amount of the transaction relative to the corporation's financial status, and whether or not an emergency situation exists.) At the same time, the courts generally agree that vice-presidents, treasurers, and secretaries have no implied authority by virtue of office.

Apparent Authority The apparent authority of a corporate officer is the authority that a third party reasonably believes the officer to have as a result of appearances created by the corporation (see page 678). However, the courts have usually said that a third party dealing with a corporate officer has the duty to inquire of the corporation as to the officer's authority. This means that the third party has the duty to refer to the bylaws and to board resolutions when forming a belief as to an officer's authority.

Nonetheless, a corporate officer may sometimes have apparent authority. Suppose, for instance, that the bylaws of XYZ, Inc., authorize the vice-president of purchasing to enter into contracts on behalf of the corporation in order to purchase inventory. The president of XYZ, however, secretly instructs the vice-president of purchasing not to purchase any inventory from Smith Supply. Contrary to these instructions, the vice-president enters into a contract with Smith Supply on behalf of XYZ. The vice-president has apparent authority to enter the contract because, under these circumstances, Smith Supply could reasonably believe such authority exists. Therefore, Smith Supply can enforce the contract even though the vice-president did not have actual authority to enter into it.

Another situation in which an officer may have apparent authority occurs when the board of directors acquiesces in that officer's unauthorized acts. Suppose, for instance, that the bylaws of XYZ, Inc., do not authorize the purchase of inventory by the vice-president of purchasing. Despite this, the vice-president has been telling suppliers that he has such authority and has been purchasing inventory for several years. The board of directors has done nothing to stop the purchases even though it has been aware of them. Under these circumstances, the corporation may not be successful if it subsequently attempts to withdraw from an inventory purchase contract made by the vice-president with Smith Supply on behalf of XYZ on the grounds that the vice-president did not have authority to enter into the contract for XYZ. If Smith Supply knew of the vice-president's prior purchases and of the board's acquiescence in them, then the vice-president had apparent authority to enter into the contract for XYZ because Smith Supply could have reasonably believed that such authority existed.

In the following case, a third party tried to enforce a contract against a corporation. The corporation's defense was that the officer who was representing the corporation in the formation of the contract lacked authority to bind the corporation to such a contract.

GOLDENBERG v. BARTELL BROADCASTING CORPORATION
262 N.Y.S.2d 274 (N.Y. 1965)

[Goldenberg entered into a written contract with Bartell Broadcasting Corporation wherein Goldenberg was hired as an assistant to Gerald A. Bartell (Bartell), the president of Bartell Broadcasting Corporation. The contract, which was for a period of three years, provided for the payment of a monthly salary and the delivery of 12,000 shares of Bartell Broadcasting Corporation to Goldenberg.

The contract was signed by Goldenberg and by Gerald A. Bartell, in his capacity as president of Bartell Broadcasting Corporation. When Bartell Broadcasting Corporation stopped paying the monthly salary and failed to deliver the shares as provided in the contract, Goldenberg (the plaintiff) brought a legal action for breach of contract against Bartell Broadcasting Corporation (the defendant). Bartell Broadcasting Corporation moved to dismiss the complaint on the grounds that Gerald A. Bartell did not have the authority to bind it to the contract in question.]

WALTEMADE, Justice

A corporation can only act through its directors, officers and employees. They are the conduit by and through which the corporation is given being and from which its power to act and reason springs. Therefore in every action in which a person sues a corporation on a contract executed on behalf of the corporation by one of its officers, one of the issues to be determined is whether the officer had the express, implied or apparent authority to execute the contract in question.

There has been no proof offered in this case indicating that Gerald A. Bartell, as president of the defendant Bartell Broadcasting Corporation, had express authority to enter into the agreement, which is the subject of the first cause of action. Did Gerald A. Bartell then have either implied or apparent authority to execute the contract?

Implied authority is a species of actual authority, which gives an officer the power to do the necessary acts within the scope of his usual duties. Generally, the president of a corporation has the implied authority to hire and fire corporate employees and to fix their compensation. However the president of a corporation does not have the implied power to execute "unusual or extraordinary" contracts of employment.

The agreement not only provides for the payment of a substantial monthly compensation, but also requires the delivery of 12,000 shares of stock of the defendant Bartell Broadcasting Corporation. While the payment of the monthly compensation would not make the con-

tract "unusual or extraordinary," the Court is of the opinion that the inclusion in the contract of the provision requiring the delivery to plaintiff of 12,000 shares of stock does bring the agreement within the category of being an "unusual and extraordinary" contract.

The reason for [this] rule is easily discernible. Corporate stock is the sinew, muscle and bone upon which the financial structure of a corporation is constructed. Corporate stock is sold, traded or disposed of in exchange for money, labor, services or other property. Thus in this manner a corporation acquires the necessary assets needed for the fulfillment of the corporate purposes.

To permit the president of a corporation, without the express authority and approval of the corporation's Board of Directors, to barter or contract away the corporation's unissued stock, would not only be an express violation of the statutes, but would also make possible the denudation of a corporation's assets, and the dilution of the value of the stock already issued to the detriment and disadvantage of the corporate stockholders.

Apparent authority is the authority which the principal permits the agent to represent that he possesses. Generally, persons dealing with officers of a corporation are bound to take notice that the powers of an officer are derived from statutes, by-laws and usages which more or less define the extent of the officer's authority. In a doubtful case one must at his peril acquaint himself with the exact extent of the officer's authority. The right of a third party to rely on the apparent authority of a corporate officer is subject to the condition that such third person has no notice or knowledge of a limitation in such authority.

The plaintiff is not a naive person, uninitiated in the business world, nor is he without knowledge of corporate financing or business practices. By his own testimony he is and was a stockholder, officer and director of several corporations. There is testimony that the plaintiff has engaged in the sale of securities to the general public.

It is reasonable to infer that the plaintiff was aware, or at the least, had reason to be aware, that the authority for the issuance of corporate stock rests solely within the powers of the Board of Directors of the corporation, and that in the absence of express authority, the president of a corporation does not have the implied or apparent authority to enter into an employment contract which provides for the issuance of corporate stock as compensation.

Accordingly, the motion of the defendant to dismiss the complaint is granted.

CASE REVIEW QUESTIONS
1. Why didn't Bartell have express actual authority to enter into the contract with Goldenberg on behalf of the corporation?
2. Why didn't Bartell have implied actual authority to enter into the contract with Goldenberg on behalf of the corporation?
3. Why didn't Bartell have apparent authority to enter into the contract with Goldenberg on behalf of the corporation?
4. How could Goldenberg have protected himself from the outcome of this case when he entered into the contract?

Ratification Even though a corporate officer lacks actual or apparent authority to bind a corporation to a contract, the corporation will be liable under the contract if it ratifies the officer's unauthorized act. Ratification occurs when the corporation does something that indicates that it approves of the officer's act even though it was an unauthorized act. If the act is ratified, the law treats it as though it was authorized when it was done by the officer (see page 681).

It is not unusual for a board of directors to ratify the acts of the corporation's officers. An officer who without authority takes advantage of an opportunity that benefits the corporation can generally be assured that his or her actions will be ratified. Ratification may be express, such as by a resolution of the board of directors, or it may be implied, such as by the acceptance by the corporation of the benefits of the unauthorized contract.

CLOSE CORPORATIONS

Thus far in this chapter, you have read about the typical governance structure of corporations. The shareholders, directors, and officers all have certain powers in determining and implementing the operation of the corporation's business. The ways in which these powers are usually allocated and exercised are referred to as *corporate norms*.

There are some situations, however, in which the participants in a corporation may find corporate norms undesirable. This most often happens in connection with a **close corporation,** which is a corporation that has a small number of shareholders, all of whom want to retain that amount of control over the operation of the business they would have if they did business as a partnership (see Chapter 35), but all of whom also want to obtain some particular advantages they would have if they did business as a corporation — limited liability, continuity of existence if a shareholder dies, and tax benefits, for example (see page 800).

Until 1950, attempts by shareholders to structure a corporation so as, for instance, to give themselves rather than the directors control of the operation of the corporation's business, was looked on unfavorably by the courts. Since then, however, the courts have become more sympathetic to attempts by shareholders to alter corporate norms. Today, they generally allow shareholders to structure the governance of a corporation as they please, so long as public policy is not violated. Furthermore, many state legislatures have enacted statutes that expressly permit alternative structures.

The case that follows reflects the contemporary attitude of the courts. It also illustrates the types of circumstances in which shareholders may want to retain control of the corporation's operation and the means they may try to use.

GALLER v. GALLER
203 N.E.2d 577 (Ill. 1964)

UNDERWOOD, Justice

Plaintiff, Emma Galler, sued for specific performance of an agreement made between plaintiff and her husband and defendants, Isadore A. Galler, and his wife, Rose. Defendants appealed from a decree of the [trial] court granting [specific performance]. The [intermediate] appellate court reversed the decree and denied specific performance. [Plaintiff appealed.]

There is no substantial dispute as to the facts in this case. From 1919 to 1924, Benjamin and Isadore Galler, brothers, were equal partners in the Galler Drug Company, a wholesale drug concern. In 1924 the business was incorporated under the Illinois Business Corporation Act, each owning one half of the outstanding 220 shares of stock. In 1945 each contracted to sell 6 shares to an employee, Rosenberg, at a price of $10,500 for each block of 6 shares, payable within 10 years.

In March, 1954, Benjamin and Isadore, on the advice of their accountant, decided to enter into an agreement for the financial protection of their immediate families and to assure their families, after the death of either brother, equal control of the corporation. Between the execution of the agreement in July, 1955, and Benjamin's death in December, 1957, the agreement was not modified.

It appears from the evidence that some months after the agreement was signed, defendants Isadore and Rose Galler and their son, the defendant, Aaron Galler sought to have the agreements destroyed. The evidence is undisputed that the defendants had decided prior to Benjamin's death they would not honor the agreement, but never disclosed their intention to plaintiff or her husband.

The essential features of the contested portions of the agreement are substantially as set forth in the opinion of the Appellate Court: that the bylaws of the corporation will be amended to provide for a board of four directors; that the necessary quorum shall be three directors, and that no directors' meeting shall be held without giving ten days notice to all directors; the shareholders will cast their votes for the above named persons (Isadore, Rose, Benjamin, and Emma) as directors at said special meeting and at any other meeting held for the purpose of electing directors; in the event of the death of either brother his wife shall have the right to nominate a director in place of the decedent; certain annual dividends will be declared by the corporation providing a $500,000 surplus is maintained; the certificates evidencing the said shares of Benjamin Galler and Isadore Galler shall bear a legend that the shares are subject to the terms of this agreement; a salary continuation agreement shall be entered into by the corporation which shall authorize the corporation upon the death of Benjamin Galler or Isadore Galler, or both, to pay a sum equal to twice the salary of such officer [to the officer's widow] payable monthly over a five year period; in the event either Benjamin or Isadore decides to sell his shares he is required to offer them first to the remaining shareholders and then to the corporation at book value, according each six months to accept the offer.

The Appellate Court found the 1955 agreement void because [of] "the undue duration, stated purpose and substantial disregard of the provisions of the Corporation Act. . . ." and held that "the public policy of this state demands voiding this entire agreement."

At this juncture it should be emphasized that we deal here with a so-called close corporation. Various attempts at definition of the close corporation have been made. For our purposes, a close corporation is one in which the stock is held in a few hands, or in a few families, and wherein it is not at all, or only rarely, dealt in by buying or selling. Moreover, it should be recognized that shareholder agreements similar to that in question here are often, as a practical solution, quite necessary for the protection of those financially interested in the close corporation. While the shareholder of a public-issue corporation may readily sell his shares on the open market should management fail to use, in his opinion, sound business judgment, his counterpart of the close corporation often has a large total of his entire capital invested in the business and has no ready market for his shares should he desire to sell. He feels, understandably, that he is more than a mere investor and that his voice should be heard concerning all corporate activity. Without a shareholder agreement, specifically enforceable by the courts, insuring him a modicum of control, a large minority shareholder might find himself at the mercy of an oppressive or unknowledgeable majority. Moreover, as in the case at bar, the shareholders of a close corporation are often also the directors and officers thereof. With substantial share-

holding interests abiding in each member of the board of directors, it is often quite impossible to secure, as in the large public-issue corporation, independent board judgment free from personal motivations concerning corporate policy. For these and other reasons too voluminous to enumerate here, often the only sound basis for protection is afforded by a lengthy, detailed shareholder agreement securing the rights and obligations of all concerned.

[T]here has been a definite, albeit inarticulate, trend toward eventual judicial treatment of the close corporation as *sui generis* [in a separate class]. Several shareholder-director agreements that have technically "violated" the letter of the Business Corporation Act have nevertheless been upheld [by courts] in the light of the existing practical circumstances, i.e., no apparent public injury, the absence of a complaining minority interest, and no apparent prejudice to creditors.

Courts have long ago quite realistically, we feel, relaxed their attitudes concerning statutory compliance when dealing with close corporate behavior, permitting "slight deviations" from corporate "norms" in order to give legal efficacy to common business practice.

Numerous helpful textual statements and law review articles dealing with the judicial treatment of the close corporation have been pointed out by counsel. One article concludes with the following:

> New needs compel fresh formulation of corporate "norms." There is no reason why mature men should not be able to adapt the statutory form to the structure they want, so long as they do not endanger other stockholders, creditors, or the public, or violate a clearly mandatory provision of the corporation laws. In a typical close corporation the stockholders' agreement is usually the result of careful deliberation among all initial investors. In the large public-issue corporation, on the other hand, the "agreement" represented by the corporate charter is not consciously agreed to by the investors; they have no voice in its formulation, and very few ever read the certificate of incorporation. Preservation of the corporate norms may there be necessary for the protection of the public investors.

We now, in the light of the foregoing, turn to specific provisions of the 1955 agreement.

The Appellate Court correctly found many of the contractual provisions free from serious objection, and we need not prolong this opinion with a discussion of them here. That court did, however, find difficulties in the stated purpose of the agreement as it relates to its duration, the election of certain persons to specific offices for a number of years, the requirement for the mandatory declaration of stated dividends (which the Appellate Court held invalid), and the salary continuation agreement.

Since the question as to the duration of the agreement is a principal source of controversy, we shall consider it first. The parties provided no specific termination date. In view of the history of decisions of this court generally upholding, in the absence of fraud or prejudice to minority interests or public policy, the right of stockholders to agree among themselves as to the manner in which their stock will be voted, we do not regard the period of time within which this agreement may remain effective as rendering the agreement unenforceable.

The clause that provides for the election of certain persons to specified offices for a period of years likewise does not require invalidation. In *Kautzler v. Bensinger,* this court upheld an agreement entered into by all the stockholders providing that certain parties would be elected to the offices of the corporation for a fixed period. In *Faulds v. Yates,* we upheld a similar agreement among the majority stockholders of a corporation, notwithstanding a minority that was not before the court complaining thereof.

We turn next to a consideration of the effect of the stated purpose of the agreement upon its validity. The pertinent provision is: "The said Benjamin A. Galler and Isadore A. Galler desire to provide income for the support and maintenance of their immediate families." Obviously, there is no evil inherent in a contract entered into for the reason that the persons originating the terms desired to so arrange their property as to provide post-death support for those dependent upon them.

The terms of the dividend agreement require a minimum annual dividend of $50,000, but this duty is limited by the subsequent provision that it shall be operative only so long as an earned surplus of $500,000 is maintained. It may be noted that in 1958, the year prior to commencement of this litigation, the corporation's net earnings after taxes amounted to $202,759 while its earned surplus was $1,543,270, and this was increased in 1958 to $1,680,079 while earnings were $172,964. The minimum earned surplus requirement is designed for the protection of the corporation and its creditors, and we take no exception to the contractual dividend requirements as thus restricted.

The salary continuation agreement is a common feature, in one form or another, of corporate executive employment. It requires that the widow should receive a total benefit, payable monthly over a five-year period, aggregating twice the amount paid her deceased husband in one year.

Accordingly, the judgment of the Appellate Court is reversed.

CASE REVIEW QUESTIONS

1. What things were the Gallers trying to achieve by their agreement?
2. What corporate norms were "violated" by the Galler's agreement?
3. Why did the court enforce the Galler's agreement rather than uphold the corporate norms?
4. The court's decision refers to "public policy." Didn't the Illinois legislature establish the state's public policy concerning corporations when it enacted the Business Corporation Law? Why, then, does the court say that the Galler's agreement doesn't violate public policy?

Close Corporation Legislation

In the *Galler* case, the court upheld a shareholders' agreement even though it was inconsistent with the norms of the Illinois Business Corporation Law. Today, Illinois and many other states have statutes that expressly provide for the needs of close corporations. Some states have a separate part of the corporation law that contains provisions applicable only to close corporations. Other states either include special close corporation provisions as part of their general corporation law or provide for deviations in corporate norms without express reference to close corporations. The Model Business Corporation Act that appears in Appendix F is an example of the latter type.

What is a Close Corporation? In those states that have corporation law provisions that apply only to close corporations, the law must also identify those corporations that can use the provisions. The states have not agreed on a single definition of a close corporation, but they generally agree on the types of things that should be considered in the definition, which are as follows:

1. *The number of shareholders.* The number of shareholders is limited; it seldom is over 50 and most often is between one and ten.
2. *Whether there is a restriction on the right of the shareholders to transfer their shares.* Only corporations with restrictions on the transfer of shares will be considered close corporations.
3. *Whether the corporation's shares are listed on a stock exchange or in an organized over-the-counter market.* Corporations whose shares are listed will not be considered close corporations.

The purpose of these requirements is to limit the use of the close corporation provisions to situations in which all of the shareholders are likely to be fully aware of the unusual governance structure being used by their corporation.

Close Corporation Provisions Corporation law provisions that are often used by close corporations include the following:

1. Management of the business and affairs of the corporation may be placed in the hands of the shareholders rather than the board of directors [MBCA §35].
2. Voting and quorum requirements for shareholders' and directors' meetings may be set at more than a majority. By requiring unanimity or near unanimity in decisions, each participant in the close corporation has a veto power over proposed corporate actions [MBCA §§32 and 40].
3. Agreements among shareholders concerning future corporate officers, directors, dividends, and policies may be enforceable [MBCA §34].
4. Agreements restricting the transfer of shares by shareholders are enforceable.
5. A court may order liquidation of a corporation if a dispute among the shareholders results in a voting deadlock that prevents the shareholders from electing directors or the directors from making decisions [MBCA §97].

By using corporation law provisions such as these, the shareholders of a close corporation are able to take advantage of the limited liability, continuity of existence, and tax benefits of doing business as a corporation, while at the same time, they are able to retain the control over the operation of the business they would have if they did business as a partnership.

REVIEW QUESTIONS

1. What do the legal concepts *ultra vires* and *intra vires* mean? What are their significance for corporation law?
2. How can it be determined whether a particular corporation has the power to perform a particular act?
3. What powers do corporate shareholders have?
4. What steps must shareholders take in order to exercise their powers?
5. What powers do corporate directors have?
6. What steps must directors take in order to exercise their powers?
7. What types of authority do corporate officers have?
8. In what ways may the shareholders of close corporations want to deviate from the norms of corporate governance?

CASE PROBLEMS

1. The Chicago Cubs are the only major league baseball team that does not have lights around its field. Consequently, the Cubs play only day games, unlike all other teams, which play the majority of their games at night. Shilensky, a shareholder in the corporation that owns the Cubs, brought a legal action asking the court to order the corporation to install lights and to play night games. Shilensky argues that it is clear from the action of all the other teams that the Cubs would make a greater profit if they played night games. The management of the corporation defends that playing night games would damage the neighborhood surrounding the ballpark. On what basis might Shilensky argue that management's defense should not be allowed? Who will win the case? Explain.

2. Control of Loew's Incorporated (Loew's) was contested by two groups, one headed by Loew's president, Vogel, and the other headed by Tomlinson. A compromise was worked out between the two groups whereby six members of the Vogel group, six members of the Tomlinson group, and one neutral party were elected to the board of directors at the annual shareholders' meeting. A few months later, however, two of the Vogel directors, one of the Tomlinson directors, and the neutral director resigned. Shortly thereafter, the remaining five Tomlinson directors attended a properly called meeting of the board of directors and elected four additional Tomlinson directors to fill the vacancies on the board. The next day Vogel, as president, sent out a notice calling a special shareholders' meeting to (1) fill director vacancies, (2) increase the board of directors from 13 to 19 and the quorum requirement from seven to ten, and (3) remove and replace two Tomlinson directors.

   Was the action of the five Tomlinson directors at the board meeting valid? Has the special shareholders' meeting been properly called? Explain your answers. [You may assume that the provisions of the Model Business Corporation Act (Appendix F) are in effect.]

3. In 1940, William Feahndrich founded a business that manufactures, imports, and markets cheeses. The business was incorporated as William Feahndrich, Inc., and the articles of incorporation authorized 1,000 shares of $100 par value common stock. Fifty shares were issued to and paid for by

William Feahndrich at the time of incorporation. In 1985, 100 additional shares of stock were issued to and paid for by William and 151 shares were issued to and paid for by William's son, Rudolph. William and Rudolph then voted their shares at a shareholders' meeting to elect themselves to the two positions on the board of directors. Then at a directors' meeting they elected Rudolph president and William secretary-treasurer of the corporation. As directors they also hired William as a paid consultant to the corporation.

A short time later, William and Rudolph had a falling out. Because of this, Rudolph as president, caused a notice to be sent to his father advising him of a special shareholders' meeting. The notice stated:

> Please take notice that a meeting of the shareholders of William Feahndrich, Inc., will be held in the office of the corporation, 11 Harrison Street, New York, New York, on the 9th day of January, 1986, at 4:00 P.M. for the purpose of removing and replacing a director of the corporation.

William did not attend the meeting. Rudolph did attend and voted his shares to remove William as a director. Rudolph then voted his shares to elect his wife, Denise, to replace William as a director. Rudolph and Denise immediately held a directors' meeting, voted to remove William as secretary-treasurer, elected their son George as secretary-treasurer, and terminated William's employment with the corporation.

Was the removal of William as a director valid? Was the election of Denise as a director valid? Was the removal of William as secretary-treasurer valid? Was the election of George as secretary-treasurer valid? Was the termination of William's employment with the corporation valid? Explain your answers. [You may assume that the provisions of the Model Business Corporation Act (Appendix F) are in effect.]

4. The Corelle Elevator Corporation's articles of incorporation require cumulative voting. There are 2,400,000 shares of common voting stock issued and outstanding. Orkin heads a group of share-

holders that intends to oppose management's nominees for the seven director positions at the annual shareholders' meeting next week. Orkin's group controls 300,000 shares. Management controls 1,600,000 shares by ownership or proxy. It is highly unlikely that any shares not controlled by the Orkin group or by management will be voted at the meeting. How many directors do you think will be elected by the Orkin group and by management, respectively? Will it make any difference if shares other than those controlled by the Orkin group and management are voted? Explain your answers.

5. The bylaws of Liberty Leasing Company, Inc. (Liberty) provide that there will be five directors. A short time ago one of the directors resigned. The bylaws of Liberty also provide that the filling of vacancies on the board of directors shall be done "at a special meeting of the board of directors called for that purpose." A notice of a special meeting of the board was sent out by the president of Liberty, but it did not state the purpose of the meeting. All four of the remaining directors attended the meeting and unanimously elected a new director to fill the vacancy. Later, however, three of the four directors who elected the new director claimed that the election was invalid because the bylaws concerning the filling of vacancies had not been followed. Are they correct? Explain.

6. Chester Gusick, Charles Gusick, and Milton Lubow organized the Granite Lake Camp Corporation (Granite) to operate a summer resort business, and they were the corporation's only shareholders, directors, and officers. As directors, the three men elected Lubow as treasurer of the corporation, but no actual authority was conferred on the treasurer by either the bylaws or by resolutions of the board. Lubow, without the knowledge of the Gusicks, sent a letter to all those firms with which Granite might do business stating that he had authority to purchase supplies for the corporation. For three years, Lubow purchased and paid for supplies for Granite, and the Gusicks were aware of this. Subsequently, however, Granite refused to pay a substantial bill to Cote Bakery on the

grounds that Lubow did not have authority to purchase supplies for Granite. Cote Bakery has now brought a legal action against Granite to collect the bill. Who will win the case? Explain.

7. Comerford was president, treasurer, and one of the two directors of Citizens Finance, Inc. (Citizens). A shareholder of Citizens brought a legal action against the corporation requesting the court to terminate Citizens as a corporation. Comerford entered into an agreement with an attorney named Kelly to have Kelly defend the action against Citizens, which had never before been sued. Shortly thereafter, however, Citizens notified Kelly that he was discharged as the corporation's attorney in the matter of the shareholder's lawsuit. Kelly has now brought a lawsuit against Citizens for breach of the contract with him to serve as attorney. Citizens is defending on the grounds that Comerford did not have authority to hire Kelly on behalf of the corporation. Both parties agree that there is no bylaw or resolution of the board granting such authority to Comerford. Who will win the case? Explain.

8. Toscano, Rosenthal, and Groff have decided to incorporate their small carpeting business, which they have until now operated as a partnership. Each of the three women will own one-third of the shares of the corporation. Their lawyer has recommended that the following three provisions be included in the articles of the incorporation:

The business and affairs of the corporation shall be managed by the shareholders.

At all meetings of the shareholders, there shall be present in person or by proxy shareholders owning all of the shares entitled to vote in order to constitute a quorum.

A unanimous vote of the shareholders owning all of the shares entitled to vote shall be necessary to adopt any resolution voted upon by shareholders.

The lawyer has also recommended that the three women enter into a contract by which each of them agrees to vote her shares at each year's annual shareholders' meeting to elect Toscano as president, Rosenthal as vice president, and Groff as secretary-treasurer of the corporation.

Why do you think that the lawyer made each of the recommendations? Are each of the recommendations legally valid? Explain. [You may assume that the provisions of the Model Business Corporation Act (Appendix F) are in effect.]

40

INTERNAL CORPORATE CONFLICT

Most of the time shareholders, directors, and officers carry out their respective corporate roles in accordance with corporate norms and without conflict. Sometimes, however, conflicts arise, generally because of complaints by shareholders that the directors and officers have engaged in or are presently engaging in some form of wrongdoing. Sometimes, especially in close corporation situations, conflicts also arise between the majority shareholders and the minority shareholders.

To understand how the law resolves corporate conflicts, you must learn about the duties of directors, officers, and majority shareholders. These duties are discussed in the first two sections of this chapter. To understand how these duties are enforced, you must learn about the enforcement mechanisms that are available to shareholders. These mechanisms are the subject of the final section of the chapter.

THE DUTIES OF CORPORATE EXECUTIVES

When a shareholder invests in a corporation, he or she entrusts that investment to the directors and officers of the corporation who determine and implement the policies that the corporation follows. Thus, when directors and officers make decisions and take action, the primary impact of those decisions and actions is on the shareholders. The wisdom of those decisions and actions determines the success of the shareholders' investments.

Because corporate executives, meaning both directors and officers, control the property of other people, they are in a position similar to that of a trustee of a trust. The law categorizes a trustee as a *fiduciary,* which is a person who is vested with a special form of trust and who is required to display scrupulous good faith and candor (see page 655).

In some of the cases you will read in this section, you will see that the courts sometimes call corporate executives fiduciaries. Nevertheless, executives are not in fact fiduciaries, and some acts that would be a breach of duty by a trustee would not be treated as a breach if performed by an executive.

In this section, you will read about the duty of care, the duty of loyalty, and the statutory duties that are imposed by law on corporate executives. You will also read about the defenses that may be used by an executive who has been charged with a breach of duty and about the possibility that an executive who has been so charged may be reimbursed for the expenses that result.

Duty of Care

One of the duties that an executive owes to the corporation is the duty to carry out his or her job "with such care as an ordinarily prudent person in a like position would use under similar circumstances" [MBCA §35]. You may recognize this duty as the same duty of care that all of us owe to others, which is imposed by the law of torts (see page 83). Breach of the duty of care is called *negligence.*

The primary work of corporate directors and officers is making business decisions. If an executive makes a decision that an ordinarily prudent person would not make under similar circumstances — that is, if he or she makes a negligent decision — and that negligent decision causes damage to the corporation, it would seem logical for the executive to be liable to the corporation for the damage. In fact, however, liability for negligent business decisions is hardly ever imposed on corporate executives.

The Business Judgment Rule Normally, liability for negligent business decisions is imposed on corporate executives only in extreme circumstances. One reason for this is that the courts have been reluctant to second-guess, with the benefit of hindsight, the decisions of executives. This reluctance has led to the development of the business judgment rule by the courts.

The **business judgment rule,** which is now included in many state corporation statutes, provides that decisions that are made *in good faith* will not subject executives to liability even if they are made negligently. In other words, an executive's decision that is negligent and that causes damage to the corporation will not necessarily result in the liability of the executive who made the decision as long as the decision was made in good faith.

Note that this type of limitation on the liability of executives for their negligence is not found in ordinary tort law. For instance, when you drive your car, you have a duty of care to drive as a reasonably prudent person would drive under similar circumstances. You cannot escape liability for negligent driving by showing that you *honestly believed* you were acting as a reasonably prudent person. Generally, the courts have explained their application of the business judgment rule on the grounds that capable people will refuse to serve as corporate executives unless a limit is placed on executive liability for negligence.

In the case that follows, certain shareholders of AT&T brought a legal action on behalf of the corporation, which is called a derivative suit, against all but one of the directors of the corporation on the grounds that the directors had breached their duty of care. The directors argued that they could not be held liable because of the business judgment rule. For reasons stated in the decision, the court said the business judgment rule was not applicable to the case.

MILLER v. AMERICAN TELEPHONE & TELEGRAPH COMPANY
507 F.2d 759 (Third Cir. 1974)

SEITZ, Chief Judge

Plaintiffs, stockholders in American Telephone and Telegraph Company ("AT&T"), brought a stockholders' derivative action against AT&T and all but one of its directors. The suit centered upon the failure of AT&T to collect an outstanding debt of some $1.5 million owed to the company by the Democratic National Committee ("DNC") for communications services provided by AT&T during the 1968 Democratic national convention.

Plaintiffs' complaint alleged that "neither the officers or directors of AT&T have taken any action to recover the amount owed" from August 20, 1968, when the debt was incurred, until May 31, 1972, the date plaintiffs' complaint was filed. The failure to collect was alleged to have involved a breach of the defendant directors' duty to exercise diligence in handling the affairs of the corporation, to have resulted in affording a preference to the DNC in collection procedures in violation of the Communications Act of 1934, and to have amounted to AT&T's making a "contribution" to the DNC in violation of a federal prohibition on corporate campaign spending.

Plaintiffs sought permanent relief in the form of an injunction requiring AT&T to collect the debt, an injunction against providing further services to the DNC until the debt was paid in full, and a surcharge for the benefit of the corporation against the defendant directors in the amount of the debt plus interest from the due date.

On motion of the defendants, the district [trial] court dismissed the complaint for failure to state a claim upon which relief could be granted. The court stated that collection procedures were properly within the discretion of the directors whose determination would not be overturned by the court in the absence of an allegation that the conduct of the directors was "plainly illegal, unreasonable, or in breach of a fiduciary duty . . . ." Plaintiffs appeal from dismissal of their complaint.

A complaint should not be dismissed unless it appears that the plaintiffs would not be entitled to relief under any facts which they might prove in support of their claim. Judging plaintiffs' complaint by these standards, we feel that it does state a claim upon which relief can be granted.

The pertinent law on the question of the defendant directors' fiduciary duties in this action is that of New York, the state of AT&T's incorporation. The sound business judgment rule, the basis of the district court's dismissal of plaintiffs' complaint, expresses the unanimous decision of American courts to eschew intervention in corporate decision-making if the judgment of directors and officers is uninfluenced by personal considerations and is exercised in good faith. Underlying the rule is the assumption that reasonable diligence has been used in reaching the decision which the rule is invoked to justify.

Had plaintiffs' complaint alleged only failure to pursue a corporate claim, application of the sound business judgment rule would support the district court's ruling that a shareholder could not attack the directors' decision. Where, however, the decison not to collect a debt owed the corporation is itself alleged to have been an illegal act, different rules apply. When New York law regarding such acts by directors is considered in conjunction with the underlying purposes of the particular statute involved here, we are convinced that the business judgment rule cannot insulate the defendant directors from liability if they did in fact breach [the law prohibiting corporate campaign contributions], as plaintiffs have charged.

Roth v. Robertson illustrates the proposition that even though committed to benefit the corporation, illegal acts may amount to a breach of fiduciary duty in New York. In *Roth,* the managing director of an amusement park company had allegedly used corporate funds to purchase the silence of persons who threatened to complain about unlawful Sunday operation of the park. Recovery from the defendant director was sustained on the ground that the money was an illegal payment:

> For reasons of public policy, we are clearly of the opinion that payments of corporate funds for such purposes as those disclosed in this case must be con-
> demned, and officers of a corporation making them held to a strict accountability, and be compelled to refund the amounts so wasted for the benefit of stockholders. . . . To hold any other rule would be establishing a dangerous precedent, tacitly countenancing the wasting of corporate funds for purposes of corrupting public morals.

The plaintiffs' complaint in the instant case alleges a similar "waste" of $1.5 million through an illegal campaign contribution.

The alleged violation of the federal prohibition against corporate political contributions not only involves the corporation in criminal activity but similarly contravenes a policy of Congress clearly enunciated: (1) to destroy the influence of corporations over elections through financial contributions and (2) to check the practice of using corporate funds to benefit political parties without the consent of the stockholders.

Since plaintiffs have alleged actual damage to the corporation from the transaction in the form of the loss of a $1.5 million increment to AT&T's treasury, we conclude that the complaint does state a claim upon which relief can be granted sufficient to withstand a motion to dismiss.

The order of the district court will be reversed and the case remanded for further proceedings consistent with this opinion.

CASE REVIEW QUESTIONS

1. What duty did the plaintiffs believe that the defendants had breached? What acts of the AT&T directors did the plaintiffs believe constituted a violation of that duty?
2. Did the defendants defend themselves on the grounds that they did not commit the acts alleged by the plaintiffs? If not, on what grounds did the defendants defend themselves against the plaintiffs' claim?
3. To what extent did the appellate court reject the defendants' defense?
4. Is the court's decision consistent with the explanation of the business judgment rule in the text prior to the case? Explain.

The Causation Requirement If it is alleged in a lawsuit that an executive has been negligent, the plaintiff must not only prove that the executive breached his or her duty of care to the corporation, which as explained earlier can be very difficult because of the business judgment rule, but the plaintiff must also prove that the executive's negligence *caused damage* to the corporation. Even if a corporation has lost money or failed, proving a definite causal relationship between an executive's negligence and the corporation's losses can be very difficult.

For example, in a case in which a company had gone into receivership—a legal procedure in which a receiver is appointed to operate a business during a lawsuit—the receiver proved that one of the directors had failed to attend board meetings or otherwise to keep himself informed about corporate affairs. The court decided that the director had breached his duty of care, but nonetheless, it decided that the director was not liable to the corporation for the breach because the receiver had failed to show a causal relationship between the director's negligence and the corporation's collapse. The judge said:

> The plaintiff must go further than to show that [the director] should have been more active in his duties. The cause of action rests upon a tort. . . . The plaintiff must accept the burden of showing that the performance of the defendant's duties would have avoided loss, and what loss it would have avoided. I pressed [the plaintiff] to show me a case in which the courts have held that a director could be charged generally with the collapse of a business in respect of which he had been inattentive, and I am not aware that he has found one . . . .

The Duty of Loyalty

Although the courts seldom find corporate executives liable for breach of the duty of care, they more frequently hold executives liable for breach of the duty of loyalty. The duty of loyalty requires corporate executives to apply their undivided attentions to the best interests of the corporation. Common situations in which an executive's duty of loyalty is called into question involve (1) transactions between an executive and his or her corporation, (2) transactions between corporations that share the same executive, and (3) transactions in which an executive takes advantage of an opportunity that may properly belong to the corporation.

Self-Dealing Self-dealing refers to a situation in which a business transaction is entered into between a corporate executive and his or her corporation. When the courts were first confronted with cases involving self-dealing, they decided that all such transactions were voidable by the corporation. For instance, if a corporation bought land from one of its executives, it could later avoid the transaction. In other words, it could get its money back from the executive by returning the land to him or her.

In time, however, it was recognized that there are situations in which it can be to a corporation's benefit to deal with its executives. For instance, a corporation may be unable to borrow money to buy land that it needs. An officer of the corporation, however, might be willing to sell land to the corporation in return for the corporation's promise to pay for the land in the future. The ability to enter into a binding contract with the officer would therefore be beneficial to the corporation.

Because an executive is now allowed to deal with his or her corporation, the risk exists that the executive will take advantage of the fact that he or she is involved in both sides of the transaction — as an individual on one side and as a representative of the corporation on the other — and treat the corporation unfairly. The courts have therefore imposed certain duties on executives who deal with their own corporations. If these duties are not met, the transaction with the executive is voidable by the corporation.

In order to be fully assured that a contract with his or her corporation is binding, an executive should disclose the material facts of his or her conflict of interest to the corporation, refrain from voting on the corporation's decision to enter into the transaction, obtain ratification of the transaction from the shareholders, and make sure that the terms of the transaction are fair to the corporation. If all of these precautions are taken, the corporation will not be able to avoid the contract at a later time.

The states are not in agreement, however, as to whether a corporation can avoid a contract if some, but not all, of the above precautions are taken. Section 41 of the MBCA provides that a contract between an executive and his or her corporation is binding if it is approved by a disinterested majority of the board of directors *or* if it is approved by the shareholders *or* if it is fair to the corporation. In other words, under the MBCA, an executive can enter into a binding contract with his or her corporation by fulfilling any *one* of these requirements.

Executive Compensation One matter in which there is commonly self-dealing is executive compensation. An officer who is also a director will be involved in compensation decisions both as recipient of the compensation and as one of the persons who determines the amount of compensation.

The courts are reluctant to overrule executive compensation decisons when they are questioned. Boards of directors are generally careful to follow procedures that reduce the appearance of self-dealing. Usually the conflict of interest is disclosed, officers who are board members leave the meeting while their salaries are discussed and voted on, and shareholder ratification is later secured. As to the question of fairness, the courts will rule that executive compensation is not excessive as long as the amount paid relates to some degree to the services rendered.

Executive Loans Another matter in which self-dealing may exist concerns loans by a corporation to its executives. Corporation laws usually deal specifically with loans to executives. Section 47 of the MBCA, for instance, permits loans to directors if the loans are approved by the shareholders, and it permits loans to officers who are also directors if the board decides that the loan will benefit the corporation. Some states expressly prohibit corporate loans to directors and officers, however.

Dividend Policies In a close corporation, the issue of self-dealing can arise in the context of dividend policies. The people in control of a close corporation may prefer that the corporation distribute its income in the form of salaries paid to themselves, whereas the minority shareholders may prefer that the corporation pay lower salaries and higher dividends on its stock.

Sometimes those in control will try to withhold dividends in order to "squeeze out" the minority shareholders. The idea is that, if no dividends are paid, the minority shareholders may be forced to sell their shares to those in control at bargain prices. In an attempt to deter squeeze-outs, some states have provisions in their corporation laws that regulate the distribution of dividends in close corporations. California, for instance, requires the board of directors of a close corporation to justify any decision to pay less than one third of the annual net profits in dividends if holders of 20 percent or more of the corporation's shares complain.

In the following case, the minority shareholders believed that those in control were trying to squeeze them out by withholding dividends. The minority shareholders brought a legal action alleging self-dealing by the defendants and seeking to have the court compel the distribution of dividends. As you read the case, you should also note the court's treatment of executive compensation and loans.

GOTTFRIED v. GOTTFRIED
73 N.Y.S.2d 692 (N.Y. 1947)

[Gottfried Baking Corporation (Gottfried) is a closely held corporation. All of its shareholders are children of the founder of the business, Elias Gottfried. During the period with which the case is concerned, Gottfried purchased all the shares of Hanscom Baking Corporation and operated it as a wholly owned subsidiary.

The minority shareholders of Gottfried brought a legal action to compel the board of directors to declare dividends on its common stock. The directors moved to dismiss the complaint.]

CORCORAN, Justice

The action is predicated upon the claim that the policy of the Board of Directors with respect to the declaration of dividends is animated by considerations other than the best welfare of the corporations or their stockholders. The plaintiffs claim that bitter animosity on the part of the directors, who own the controlling stock, against the plaintiff minority stockholders, as well as a desire to coerce the latter into selling their

stock to the majority interests at a grossly inadequate price, and the avoidance of heavy personal income taxes upon any dividends that might be declared, have been the motivating factors that have dominated the defendants. Plaintiffs contend, moreover, that the defendants by excessive salaries, bonuses and corporate loans to themselves or some of them, have eliminated the immediate need of dividends insofar as they were concerned, while at the same time a starvation dividend policy with respect to the minority stockholders — not on the payroll — operates designedly to compel the plaintiffs to sacrifice their stock by sale to the defendants.

There is no essential dispute as to the principles of law involved. If an adequate corporate surplus is available for the purpose, directors may not withhold the declaration of dividends in bad faith. But the mere existence of an adequate corporate surplus is not sufficient to invoke court action to compel such a dividend. There must also be bad faith on the part of the directors.

There are no infallible distinguishing earmarks of bad faith. The following facts are relevant to the issue of bad faith and are admissible in evidence: Intense hostility of the controlling faction against the minority; exclusion of the minority from employment by the corporation; high salaries, or bonuses or corporate loans made to the officers in control; the fact that the majority group may be subject to high personal income taxes if substantial dividends are paid; the existence of a desire by the controlling directors to acquire the minority stock interests as cheaply as possible. But if they are not motivating causes they do not constitute "bad faith" as a matter of law.

The essential test of bad faith is to determine whether the policy of the directors is dictated by their personal interests rather than the corporate welfare. Directors are fiduciaries. Circumstances such as those above mentioned and any other significant factors, appraised in the light of the financial condition and requirements of the corporation, will determine the conclusion as to whether the directors have or have not been animated by personal, as distinct from corporate, considerations.

The court is not concerned with the direction which the exercise of the judgment of the Board of Directors may take, provided only that such exercise of judgment be made in good faith. It is axiomatic that the court will not substitute its judgment for that of the Board of Directors.

It must be conceded that closely held corporations are easily subject to abuse on the part of dominant stockholders, particularly in the direction of action designed to compel minority stockholders to sell their stock at a sacrifice. But close corporation or not, the court will not tolerate directorate action designed to achieve that or any other wrongful purpose. Even in the absence of bad faith, however, the impact of dissention and hostility among stockholders falls usually with heavier force in a closely held corporation. In many such cases, a large part of a stockholder's assets may be tied up in the corporation. It is frequently contemplated by the parties, moreover, that the respective stockholders receive their major livelihood in the form of salaries resulting from employment by the corporation. If such employment be terminated, the hardship suffered by the minority stockholder or stockholders may be very heavy. Nevertheless, such situations do not in themselves form a ground for the interposition of a court.

There is no doubt that in the present case bitter dissension and personal hostility have existed for a long time between the individual plaintiffs and defendants. The plaintiffs Charles Gottfried and Harold Gottfried have both been discontinued from the corporate payrolls.

It is true too that several of the defendants have in recent years received as compensation substantial sums. In the case of Maurice K. Gottfried this has taken the form of ten percent of the gross annual profits of Hanscom before corporate income taxes. The evidence in this connection discloses, however, that he has been the chief executive officer of Hanscom since its acquisition by Gottfried. The stock of Hanscom had been purchased at a cost of $10,000 plus the assumption of liabilities amounting to $18,000. At that time Hanscom had 12 retail stores, a basement bakery, and volume of sales around $300,000. By way of contrast, for the year 1945 its net sales aggregated $4,614,000. For the year 1946, they had increased to $5,907,500. The number of stores had grown to 63, and operations had been expanded from the Washington Heights district of Manhattan to all the boroughs of the City of New York except Richmond.

The evidence also discloses that substantial advances or loans have been made from time to time to several of the defendants, part of which still remain outstanding. Advances and loans of this character in varying amounts likewise had been made for many years to stockholders and directors. Without passing upon the propriety or legality of these transactions, the evidence does not sustain an inference that they were made with a view to the dividend policy of the corporation. They were incurred, in large part, long before any controversy arose with respect to dividends, nor is the aggregate amount thereof of sufficient magnitude to affect in a material way the capacity of Gottfried to pay dividends.

The testimony discloses that many general considerations affected the policy of the Board of Directors in connection with dividend payments. Some of the major factors were as follows: The recognition that earnings during the war years might be abnormal and not representative of normal earning capacity; the pressing need for heavy expenditures for new equipment and machinery, replacement of which had been impossible during the war years; heavy expenditures required to finance the acquisition and equipment of new Hanscom stores in harmony with the steady growth of the business; the increased initial cost of opening new stores because, under present conditions, it has been difficult to lease appropriate sites necessitating actual acquisition by ownership of locations; the erection of a new bakery for Hanscom at a cost of approximately $1,000,000 inasmuch as the existing plant is incapable of producing the requirements of Hanscom sales which are running at the rate of approximately $6,000,000 per annum; unstable labor conditions with actual and threatened strikes; several pending actions involving large sums of money under the Federal Fair Labor Standards Act; a general policy of financing expansion through earnings requiring long-term debt.

The plaintiffs oppose many of these policies of expansion. There is no evidence of any weight to the effect that these policies of the Board of Directors are actuated by any motives other than their best business judgment. If they are mistaken, their own stockholdings will suffer proportionately to those of the plaintiffs. With the wisdom of that policy the court has no concern. It is this court's conclusion that these policies and the expenditures which they entail are undertaken in good faith and without relation to any conspiracy, scheme or plan to withhold dividends for the purpose of compelling the plaintiffs to sell their stock or pursuant to any other sinister design.

The plaintiffs have failed to prove that the surplus is unnecessarily large. They have also failed to prove that the defendants recognized the propriety of paying dividends but refused to do so for personal reasons.

The complaint is dismissed and judgment directed for the defendants.

CASE REVIEW QUESTIONS

1. What duty did the plaintiffs believe that the defendants had breached? In what sense were the defendants involved in self-dealing?
2. On what grounds did the defendants defend themselves against the plaintiffs' claim? In what way does this defense relate to §41 of the MBCA, which was discussed in the text prior to the case?
3. Did the plaintiffs argue that the compensation paid to Maurice K. Gottfried or the loans made to some of the defendants constituted breaches of duty by the directors? If not, what was the relevance of these matters to the case?

Interlocking Directorates A transaction between corporations that share one or more officers or directors may be similar to transactions involving self-dealing, especially if the interest of a shared executive is substantial in one corporation and small in the other. There is a risk in such situations that an executive will take advantage of the fact that he or she is involved on both sides of the transaction — as a decision maker for each corporation — and treat one of the corporations unfairly. Usually, the shared executive in such transactions is a director. When corporations share one or more directors, an **interlocking directorate** is said to exist.

If corporations with shared directors transact business with each other, the safest procedure is for them to meet all of the precautions previously recommended for self-dealing situations: full disclosure of the executives' conflicts of interest, nonparticipation by the shared executives in the corporate decisions, shareholder ratification, and fairness in the transaction. The courts, however, have placed the greatest emphasis on the fairness of the transaction when deciding whether one of the corporations in this situation can avoid a contract. Generally, a contract between corporations with shared executives is only voidable if the contract is unfair. Still, if the recommended procedural precautions are taken, a court is more likely to find the resulting contract to be fair.

Corporate Opportunities The third situation in which an executive's duty of loyalty may be called into question involves transactions in which an executive takes personal advantage of an opportunity that may properly belong to the corporation. For instance, if a corporate oil company is presented with the opportunity to buy valuable oil fields at a bargain price, the corporate president would breach the duty of loyalty if he or she purchased the oil fields for his or her personal benefit rather than for the benefit of the corporation.

When an executive is accused of taking personal advantage of a corporate opportunity, he or she may defend on two different bases. First, the executive may argue that the opportunity was not one that belonged to the corporation; that is, he or she may argue that it was not a *corporate* opportunity. Second, the executive may argue that he or she fulfilled his or her duties to the corporation before taking personal advantage of the corporate opportunity. We will now discuss each of these defenses in more detail.

Did a Corporate Opportunity Exist? An executive who takes advantage of a business opportunity breaches his or her duty of loyalty to the corporation only if the business opportunity properly belongs to the corporation. In some situations, the opportunity clearly belongs to the corporation. For instance, if the corporation has a legally enforceable right to the opportunity (such as an option to buy), if corporation funds have been used to develop the opportunity, if the opportunity has been offered directly to the corporation, or if the corporation has been seeking such an opportunity, the opportunity clearly belongs to the corporation.

But what if the executive learns of an opportunity that the corporation knows nothing about and has not been specifically seeking? In such instances, the courts of the various states are not in agreement as to whether a corporate opportunity exists. Although some courts take the position that a corporate opportunity exists only under the types of circumstances discussed in the previous paragraph, the more common approach is for the courts to apply a "line of business" test. Under this test, a court first defines the opportunity, then it defines the corporation's line of business, and finally, it compares the opportunity to the line of business. If the opportunity relates closely to the line of business, the opportunity is determined to be a corporate opportunity.

Suppose, however, that the corporation does not have sufficient funds to take advantage of an opportunity, that the opportunity is *ultra vires* (outside the power of) the corporation, or that the corporation is otherwise incapable of taking advantage of the opportunity. In such circumstances, the courts have generally said that a corporate opportunity does not exist. In situations involving the lack of sufficient corporate funds, however, an executive must make a good faith effort to help the corporation raise the necessary funds before he or she takes personal advantage of the opportunity.

In the case that follows, an executive was accused by a shareholder of taking personal advantage of a corporate opportunity. The executive argued that the opportunity was not one that properly belonged to the corporation. The facts of the case are somewhat complex, so read the beginning of the case carefully so that you will understand the relationships among the various individuals and corporations involved in it.

JOHNSTON v. GREENE
121 A.2d 919 (Del. 1956)

[Airfleets, Inc., is a corporation that was organized to finance the purchase of airplanes by airlines. However, after a successful business venture unrelated to that purpose, its only assets were cash and marketable securities and it was looking for investments of any kind. Airfleets' largest shareholder was Atlas Corporation, an investment company. Odlum was the president of both Airfleets and Atlas.

Nutt-Shel Company, a corporation, was in the business of manufacturing self-locking nuts used in aircraft. Lester Hutson owned all of the shares of Nutt-Shel, and he also owned the patents on the self-locking nuts made by Nutt-Shel. Hutson, who did not know of the existence of Airfleets, offered Odlum the opportunity to buy the patents and the shares of Nutt-Shel. Hutson suggested, however, that for tax purposes it would be best if the same person or corporation did not own both the patents and the shares of Nutt-Shel.

Odlum decided to purchase both the patents and the shares. He was advised, however, that the acquisition of Nutt-Shel might help solve some tax problems of Airfleets. He thus submitted Hutson's offer to the board of directors of Airfleets, which decided, under Odlum's influence, that Airfleets would purchase the shares of Nutt-Shel but not the patents. Odlum then arranged for the purchase of the patents by 37 different persons and corporations, including himself.

A legal action was then brought against Odlum by Greene, a shareholder of Airfleets, on the grounds of breach of his duty of loyalty to Airfleets. (Also named as defendants were the other directors of Airfleets, one of whom was Johnston.) Greene claimed that the patents were a corporate opportunity of Airfleets that had been rejected only because of the influence and domination of Odlum. One of Odlum's defenses, discussed in the court's opinion, was that the opportunity to purchase the patents was not a corporate opportunity. The trial court found for the plaintiff. Odlum appealed.]

SOUTHERLAND, Chief Justice

The case made by the complaint is one of the unlawful diversion of a corporate opportunity for the benefit of the president and dominating director of a corporation.

The general principles of the law pertaining to corporate opportunity are settled in this state. Speaking for the Supreme Court [of Delaware], Chief Justice Layton said [in *Guth v. Loft*]:

> It is true that when a business opportunity comes to a corporate officer or director in his individual capacity rather than in his official capacity, and the opportunity is one which, because of the nature of the enterprise, is not essential to his corporation, and is one in which it

has no interest or expectancy, the officer or director is entitled to treat the opportunity as his own, and the corporation has no interest in it, if, of course, the officer or director has not wrongfully embarked [invested] corporation's resources therein.

On the other hand, it is equally true that, if there is presented to a corporate officer or director a business opportunity which the corporation is financially able to undertake, is, from its nature, in the line of the corporation's business and is of practical advantage to it, is one in which the corporation has an interest or a reasonable expectancy, and, by embracing the opportunity, the self-interest of the officer or director will be brought into conflict with that of his corporation, the law will not permit him to seize the opportunity for himself.

The first important fact that appears is that Hutson's offer came to Odlum, not as a director of Airfleets, but in his individual capacity. The second important fact is that the business of Nutt-Shel — the manufacture of self-locking nuts — had no direct or close relation to any business that Airfleets was engaged in or had ever been engaged in, and hence its acquisition was not essential to the conduct of Airfleets' business. The third fact is that Airfleets had no interest or expectancy in the Nutt-Shel business, in the sense that those words are used in the decisions dealing with the law of corporate opportunity. For the corporation to have an actual or expectant interest in any specific property, there must be some tie between that property and the nature of the corporate business. No such tie exists here.

At the time when the Nutt-Shel business was offered to Odlum, his position was this: He was the president of Airfleets. He was also president of Atlas — an investment company. He was a director of other corporations and a trustee of foundations interested in making investments. If it was his fiduciary duty, upon being offered any investment opportunity, to submit it to a corporation of which he was a director, the question arises, which corporation? Why Airfleets instead of Atlas? Why Airfleets instead of one of the foundations? So far as appears, there was no specific tie between the Nutt-Shel business and any of these corporations or foundations. Odlum testified that many of his companies had money to invest, and this appears entirely reasonable. How, then, can it be said that Odlum was under any obligation to offer the opportunity to one particular corporation? And if he was not under such an obligation, why could he not keep it for himself?

It was unnecessary to labor the point further. We are of opinion that the opportunity to purchase the Nutt-Shel business belonged to Odlum and not to any of his companies.

Reversed.

CASE REVIEW QUESTIONS

1. What duty did the plaintiff believe that Odlum had breached? What acts by Odlum did the plaintiff believe constituted a violation of that duty?
2. On what grounds did Odlum defend himself against the plaintiff's claim?
3. What standard did the court use to determine whether a corporate opportunity existed?

Did the Executive Fulfill the Duty of Loyalty? Even if it is determined that an opportunity that an executive has taken personal advantage of was a corporate opportunity, the executive can still defend on the grounds that he or she fulfilled the duty of loyalty before accepting the opportunity. If the executive can prove that the opportunity was voluntarily rejected for the corporation by other executives of the corporation who had full knowledge of and no personal interest in the opportunity, most courts will decide that the duty of loyalty has not been breached. In proving that the rejection of the opportunity by the corporation was voluntary, it is helpful if a reason or reasons for the rejection —such as a general business policy of the corporation that is opposed to the kind of opportunity involved—can be shown.

Statutory Duties

In addition to corporate executives' general duties of care and loyalty, corporation law statutes impose specific duties on executives that are applicable to particular transactions. For example, a director is liable for breach of statutory duty if he or she approves (1) the declaration of an improper dividend [MBCA §48], (2) the improper purchase by the corporation of its own shares [MBCA §6], or (3) the beginning of business before the corporation has received the minimum required consideration for its shares [MBCA §9].

A director is not liable for breach of statutory duty if he or she voted against the prohibited action when it was approved by the board. However, if the director was present at the meeting at which the prohibited action was approved, it is presumed that he or she voted in favor of the action unless his or her negative vote is recorded in the minutes of the meeting or he or she filed a dissent with the corporate secretary.

Defenses of Executives

The most direct defense to a legal action alleging breach of duty by an executive is that no duty was breached. When this defense is used, the application of the business judgment rule increases the probability that a court will agree that there was no breach of duty by the executive. Even if there appears to be a breach of duty, however, there are other defenses that may be helpful to an executive.

Articles of Incorporation Provisions Sometimes, a corporation's articles of incorporation will state that transactions between the corporation and its executives are not to have the "adverse inferences that might be drawn from them." Although a court may give some weight to such a provision, the court will still carefully scrutinize any transactions that involve self-dealing. Certainly, such a provision in the articles would not exonerate an executive from liability for fraudulent or grossly unfair dealings with the corporation.

Shareholder Ratification As indicated earlier, a possible defense an executive can use against an allegation of self-dealing is that the transaction in question was ratified (approved) by the corporation's shareholders. The courts have held, however, that not all such transactions can be ratified by a simple majority vote of the shareholders. Transactions involving fraud or the waste of corporate assets may only be ratified by a unanimous vote. The purpose of this requirement is to prevent the majority shareholders from approving grossly unfair transactions to the detriment of the minority shareholders.

Reliance on Information Another defense an executive may use is that the alleged breach occurred only because he or she relied on information provided by the corporation. Section 35 of the MBCA states that a director may justifiably rely on such information so long as he or she does not have actual knowledge that would cause such reliance to be unwarranted.

For example, suppose that a corporation provides its directors with financial information indicating that it would be proper for the board to declare a dividend, which the board proceeds to do. Later, the information provided turns out to be false, so the declaration of the dividend was improper. If a legal action is brought against the directors for improperly declaring the dividend, they may defend themselves on the grounds that they properly relied on information provided by the corporation. Unless the plaintiff can show that the directors had knowledge that made their reliance unwarranted, their defense would be successful.

Indemnification of Executives

If a legal action alleging breach of duty is brought against a corporate executive, the executive may be reimbursed by the corporation for the cost of defending against the action and, perhaps, for any amounts paid to settle the action or to satisfy a judgment against the executive. Such reimbursement is called *indemnification.*

The MBCA provides that an executive *must* be indemnified by the corporation in cases in which the executive's defense to the legal action is successful [MBCA §5(d)(1)]. If the executive does not successfully defend against the legal action, he or she *may* be indemnified by the corporation, but only if he or she acted in good faith and reasonably believed that his or her conduct was in the corporation's best interests or was at least not opposed to the best interests of the corporation [MBCA §5(b)]. The determination of whether the executive's actions should be so characterized must be made by the directors not involved in the legal action, by an independent legal counsel, or by the shareholders [MBCA §5(e)].

The MBCA does not require indemnification in cases in which an executive has not successfully defended against a legal action. However, many corporations provide in their articles of incorporation that the corporation *must* indemnify its executives in such cases "to the full extent permitted by law."

Many corporations also purchase directors' and officers' liability insurance —referred to as *D & O insurance*—to protect themselves against the risk of having to indemnify their executives. This insurance also assures executives that indemnification will be made whether or not the corporation itself is financially able to make payment.

DUTIES OF CONTROLLING SHAREHOLDERS

Generally, shareholders are free to use their shares, which are their private property, in the pursuit of their own interests. They can vote their shares as they please and sell them if they wish, and in so doing they owe no duties to anyone.

There are some circumstances, however, in which the law imposes certain duties on a *controlling shareholder,* which is a shareholder who owns a large enough percentage of the shares of the corporation that he or she can effectively control the corporation's policies and operations. One of these circumstances occurs when a controlling shareholder is voting on extraordinary corporate matters that require shareholder approval. The duties of a controlling shareholder in this circumstance will be discussed in the next chapter.

Sale of Control

Another situation in which duties are imposed on a controlling shareholder occurs when he or she sells his or her controlling interest in the corporation. A shareholder need not own a majority of a corporation's shares in order to control its policies and operations. Someone holding as little as 10 percent of the shares of a corporation may be able to elect a majority of the board of directors if the other shareholders are not interested in the corporation's affairs. Such a shareholder is said to have "working control" of the corporation.

When a controlling shareholder sells all of his or her shares, he or she can expect to receive more money per share than an ordinary shareholder would because the purchaser is acquiring not only the shares but also the control of the corporation. The extra amount the controlling shareholder receives for his or her shares is called a *control premium.* Normally, the seller of a controlling block of shares may retain the control premium. When selling control, however, the controlling shareholder owes both a duty of care and a fiduciary duty to the corporation. If the controlling shareholder breaches either of these duties, he or she will be liable for any damages that result from the breach.

Duty of Care A controlling shareholder's duty of care requires that he or she not be negligent in choosing the person or persons to whom he or she sells control of the corporation. This means that the controlling shareholder must make a reasonable investigation of prospective purchasers and must not transfer control if the investigation indicates that the purchasers plan to "loot" the corporation's assets. "Looting" involves selling the corporation's assets for cash and then distributing the cash to the shareholders.

Fiduciary Duty A controlling shareholder's fiduciary duty requires that he or she treat the power to control the corporation as a power held in trust for the benefit of the corporation and the other shareholders and not as a power to be used for his or her own personal benefit. Thus, the power to control cannot be sold in any way the controlling shareholder wishes; the continued welfare of the corporation and the other shareholders must be given precedence. In the case that follows, minority shareholders argued that the controlling shareholder breached his fiduciary duty to them.

PERLMAN v. FELDMANN
219 F.2d 173 (Second Cir. 1955)

CLARK, Chief Judge

This is an action brought by minority stockholders of Newport Steel Corporation to compel accounting for, and restitution of, allegedly illegal gains which accrued to defendants as a result of the sale in August, 1950, of their controlling interest in the corporation. The principal defendant, C. Russell Feldmann, who represented and acted for the others, members of his family, was at that time not only the dominant stockholder, but also the chairman of the board of directors and the president of the corporation. Newport operated mills for the production of steel sheets for sale to manufacturers of steel products. The buyers, Wilport Company, a corporation, consisted of end-users of steel who were interested in securing a source of supply in a market becoming ever tighter in the Korean War. Plaintiffs contend that the consideration paid for the stock included compensation for the sale of a corporate asset, a power held in trust for the corporation by Feldmann as its fiduciary. This power was the ability to control the allocation of the corporate product in a time of short supply, through control of the board of directors; and it was effectively transferred in this sale by having Feldmann procure the resignation of his own board and the election of Wilport's nominees immediately upon consummation of the sale. Plaintiffs argue here, as they did in the court below, that in the situation here disclosed the vendors must account to the non-participating minority stockholders for that share of their profit which is attributable to the sale of the corporate power. [The trial court judge] denied the validity of the premise, holding that the rights involved in the sale were only those normally incident to the possession of a controlling block of shares, with which a dominant stockholder, in the absence of fraud or foreseeable looting, was entitled to deal according to his own best

interests. Plaintiffs appeal from [this ruling] of law which resulted in the dismissal of their complaint.

Both as director and dominant stockholder, Feldmann stood in a fiduciary relationship to the corporation and to the minority stockholders as beneficiaries thereof. [T]he responsibility of the fiduciary is not limited to a proper regard for the tangible balance sheet assets of the corporation, but includes the dedication of his uncorrupted business judgment for the sole benefit of the corporation, in any dealings which may adversely affect it. Although [this rule] is particularly relevant to Feldmann as a director, the same rule should apply to his fiduciary duties as majority stockholder, for in that capacity he chooses and controls the directors and thus is held to have assumed their liability. This, therefore, is the standard to which Feldmann was by law required to conform in his activities here under scrutiny.

It is true, as defendants have been at pains to point out, that this is not the ordinary case of breach of fiduciary duty. We have here no fraud, no misuse of confidential information, no outright looting of a helpless corporation. But on the other hand, we do not find compliance with that high standard which we have just stated and which we and other courts have come to expect and demand of corporate fiduciaries. The actions of defendants in siphoning off for personal gain corporate advantages to be derived from a favorable market situation do not betoken the necessary undivided loyalty owed by the fiduciary to his principal.

We do not mean to suggest that a majority stockholder cannot dispose of his controlling block of stock to outsiders without having to account to his corporation for profits or even never do this with impunity when the buyer is an interested customer, actual or potential, for the corporation's product. But when the sale necessarily results in a sacrifice of [an] element of corporate good will and consequent unusual profit to the fiduciary who has caused the sacrifice, he should account for his gains. So in a time of market shortage, where a call on a corporation's product commands an unusually large premium, in one form or another, we think it sound law that a fiduciary may not appropriate to himself the value of this premium. Such personal gain at the expense of his coventurers seems particularly reprehensible when made by the trusted president and director of his company.

Hence to the extent that the price received by Feldman and his codefendants included such a bonus, he is accountable to the minority stockholders who sue here. And plaintiffs, as they contend, are entitled to a recovery in their own right, instead of in right of the corporation, since neither Wilport nor their successors in interest should share in any judgment which may be rendered. Defendants cannot well object to this form of recovery, since the only alternative, recovery for the corporation as a whole, would subject them to a greater total liability.

The case will therefore be remanded to the district [trial] court for a determination of the value of defendants' stock without the appurtenant control over the corporation's output of steel. Judgment should go to these plaintiffs and those whom they represent for any premium value so shown to the extent of their respective stock interests.

Reversed.

CASE REVIEW QUESTIONS

1. What duty did the plaintiffs believe that Feldman had breached? What acts by Feldman did the plaintiffs believe constituted a violation of that duty?
2. On what grounds did the trial court determine that Feldman had not breached the duty he was charged with violating? Why did the appellate court disagree with the trial court?

ENFORCEMENT OF DUTIES BY SHAREHOLDERS

In this section, we consider two mechanisms for enforcing the duties discussed in this chapter that are available to shareholders. The first, inspection of books and records, can lead to the discovery of wrongdoing. The second, shareholder lawsuits, can be used to remedy wrongdoing.

Inspection of Corporate Books and Records

By law, corporations are required to keep correct and complete financial records, minutes of shareholders' and board of directors' meetings, and a record of its shareholders [MBCA §52]. By choice, corporations also keep many other kinds of books and records of their activities.

Generally, the executives are the ones who are interested in the various corporate books and records. Sometimes, however, a shareholder may want to inspect these materials. If a corporation denies a shareholder access to its books and records, the law has to decide whether the shareholder has a legal right to inspect them. If the shareholder is determined to have this right in a particular case, the corporation must allow the shareholder to inspect those books and records that are relevant to the shareholders' purpose for wanting to inspect them.

Who May Inspect? The specific shareholders who are entitled to inspect a corporation's books and records varies among the states. However, the principles applied to the determination of who may inspect corporate books and records are generally the same. The specific requirements discussed here are those set forth in §52 of the MBCA.

First, a shareholder wishing to inspect the corporation's books and records must make a written demand for inspection. Second, the shareholder must have been a shareholder for at least six months prior to making the demand or must own at least five percent of all the shares of the corporation outstanding. Third, the shareholder must wish to inspect for a proper purpose. If a shareholder who meets these requirements is refused access to the corporation's books and records, the corporate officer or agent responsible for the refusal is subject to a penalty equal to ten percent of the value of the shareholder's shares.

Whether a shareholder meets the first two requirements is usually easy to determine. Whether the shareholder's demand is for a proper purpose is not always easy to determine, however. The courts have held that a proper purpose is one intended to obtain information that concerns or seeks to protect the interests of all the shareholders of the corporation.

For instance, if the inspection is being sought to determine the corporation's true financial position or its ability to pay dividends or to expose mismanagement by corporate executives, it is being sought for a proper purpose. On the other hand, the shareholder's purpose is not proper if the inspection is being sought to harass management, to obtain trade secrets, or to satisfy the shareholder's curiosity. If the purpose for the inspection is not proper, the corporation can rightfully deny the shareholder's demand.

In the case that follows, a shareholder and a corporation disagreed as to whether the shareholder's demand to inspect certain books and records was for a proper purpose.

PILLSBURY v. HONEYWELL, INC.
191 N.W.2d 406 (Minn. 1971)

[Pillsbury, who was opposed to the Vietnam war, was upset when he learned that Honeywell, Inc., a corporation that had its headquarters in Pillsbury's home town, had a large government contract to produce bombs used in that war. Pillsbury purchased one share of Honeywell stock and then submitted a written demand to inspect the corporation's shareholder list and all records dealing with the manufacture of weapons and munitions. Honeywell denied his demand.

Pillsbury brought a legal action seeking an order from the court requiring Honeywell to produce the demanded records for inspection. Honeywell answered Pillsbury's complaint and then took Pillsbury's deposition. In the deposition, Pillsbury stated that his reason for demanding inspection was his concern about the war; he wanted to communicate with other shareholders and convince them to change Honeywell's board of directors and thereby its policy.

Honeywell moved that Pillsbury's legal action be dismissed on the grounds that he was not seeking to inspect the corporation's books for a proper purpose. The trial court granted Honeywell's motion, and Pillsbury appealed.]

KELLY, Justice

This court has had several occasions to rule on the propriety of shareholders' demands for inspection of corporate books and records. While inspection will not be permitted for purposes of curiosity, speculation, or vexation, adverseness to management and a desire to gain control of the corporation for economic benefit does not indicate an improper purpose.

Several courts agree with petitioner's contention that a mere desire to communicate with other shareholders is, *per se,* a proper purpose. This would seem to confer an almost absolute right to inspection. We believe that a better rule would allow inspections only if the shareholder has a proper purpose for such communication. This rule was applied in *McMahon v. Dispatch Printing Co.* [a New Jersey case], where inspection was denied because the shareholder's objective was to discredit politically the president of the company, who was also the New Jersey secretary of state.

The act of inspecting a corporation's shareholder ledger and business records must be viewed in its proper perspective. In terms of the corporate norm, inspection is merely the act of the concerned owner checking on what is in part his property. In the context of the large firm, inspection can be more akin to a weapon in corporate warfare.

That one must have proper standing to demand inspection has been recognized by statutes in several jurisdictions. Courts have also balked at compelling inspection by a shareholder holding an insignificant amount of stock in the corporation.

Petitioner's standing as a shareholder is quite tenuous. He only owns one share in his own name, bought for the purposes of this suit. Petitioner had utterly no interest in the affairs of Honeywell before he learned of Honeywell's production of fragmentation bombs. Immediately after obtaining this knowldge, he purchased stock in Honeywell for the sole purpose of asserting ownership privileges in an effort to force Honeywell to cease such production.

But for his opposition to Honeywell's policy, petitioner probably would not have bought Honeywell stock, would not be interested in Honeywell's profits and would not desire to communicate with Honeywell's shareholders. His avowed purpose in buying Honeywell stock was to place himself in a position to try to impress his opinions favoring a reordering of priorities upon Honeywell management and its other shareholders. Such a motivation can hardly be deemed a proper purpose germane to his economic interest as a shareholder.

We do not mean to imply that a shareholder with a bona fide investment interest could not bring this suit if motivated by concern with the long- or short-term economic effects on Honeywell resulting from the production of war munitions. Similarly, this suit might be appropriate when a shareholder has a bona fide concern about the adverse effects of abstention from profitable war contracts on his investment in Honeywell.

In the instant case, however, the trial court, in effect, has found from all the facts that petitioner was not interested in even the long-term well-being of Honeywell or the enhancement of the value of his shares. His sole purpose was to persuade the company to adopt his social and political concerns, irrespective of any economic benefit to himself or Honeywell. This purpose on the part of one buying into the corporation does not entitle the petitioner to inspect Honeywell's books and records.

Affirmed.

CASE REVIEW QUESTIONS

1. What standard does the court use for determining whether Pillsbury's demand to inspect Honeywell's books and records was for a proper purpose?

2. If the state of Minnesota had enacted §52 of the MBCA as part of its corporation law prior to Pillsbury's demand to inspect Honeywell's books and records, could Honeywell have properly rejected the demand? Explain.

Lawsuits by Shareholders

If a shareholder believes that corporate executives have committed a legal wrong, he or she may choose to bring a lawsuit to correct that wrong or to obtain compensation for it. A lawsuit by a shareholder may be categorized as a direct action, a class action, or a derivative action.

Shareholder's Direct Action A *direct action* is a lawsuit in which a shareholder seeks to correct or obtain compensation for a wrong done directly to him or her as a shareholder. For instance, a suit to require the granting of a demand to inspect books and records such as in the immediately preceding case, *Pillsbury v. Honeywell, Inc.,* would be a shareholder's direct action. In such cases, the shareholder is alleging that the corporation has harmed him or her by breaching its contract with him or her.

Shareholders' Class Action A *class action* is a lawsuit in which a large group of people have similar legal claims that could be brought by each of them individually, but even though the total of the claims is large, each individual claim is so small that it is unlikely to be pursued. In such circumstances, a member of the group may bring a class action on his or her own behalf and on behalf of all of the members of the group.

A shareholder may be able to bring a class action lawsuit when he or she claims that the corporation has not only committed a wrong against him or her but has also committed a wrong against other shareholders of a certain class as well. For instance, a preferred shareholder might bring an action to compel a dividend payment not only to himself or herself but to all the other preferred shareholders as well.

Shareholder's Derivative Action A **derivative action** differs from a direct action or a class action in that the shareholder is not claiming that a wrong was committed directly against him or her but is instead claiming that a wrong was committed against the corporation. Thus, the shareholder is seeking to correct or obtain compensation for the wrong on behalf of the corporation rather than on his or her own behalf. If damages are awarded by the court in a derivative action, the payment is made to the corporation, not to the shareholder-plaintiff.

For example, an action by a shareholder to recover funds that have been embezzled from the corporation by an executive would be a derivative action. Similarly, an action by a shareholder to require the corporation to collect money that is owed it by a third party would be a derivative action. *Miller v. American Telephone & Telegraph Company,* which you read earlier in this chapter, was a derivative action.

In federal courts and in many states, certain requirements must be met by a shareholder before he or she can bring a derivative action. These requirements are contemporary ownership, demand on directors, and approval of shareholders.

Contemporary Ownership The shareholder bringing a derivative action must have owned his or her shares at the time the alleged wrong to the corporation took place. This requirement prevents a person from buying shares in a corporation solely for the purpose of bringing a derivative action concerning previous wrongdoing.

Demand on Directors Before a shareholder can bring a derivative action, he or she must make a good faith effort to have the corporation bring the legal action itself, which is usually done by making an express demand on the directors to bring the lawsuit. This requirement is excused only if the shareholder can show that such a demand would be useless, as would be the case, for instance, if all of the directors were themselves involved in the alleged wrongdoing. If the demand to the board of directors is made and the board refuses to bring the lawsuit, the shareholder can only bring the derivative action if he or she can show that the board's decision violates the directors' duties to the corporation.

Approval of Shareholders Before a shareholder can bring a derivative action, he or she must also obtain the approval of a majority of the shareholders. This requirement is usually referred to as a *demand on shareholders*. If a majority of the shareholders vote against bringing the derivative action, the vote is in fact a ratification (approval) by the shareholders of the alleged wrongdoing, which means that the parties charged have not committed a wrong against the corporation.

A shareholder is excused from meeting this requirement if he or she can provide an adequate reason for not getting shareholders' approval of the derivative action. For instance, shareholder approval would be excused if the alleged wrongdoers own a majority of the corporation's shares. In the case that follows, the shareholder-plaintiff provided the trial court with another reason for not seeking shareholder approval. The trial court did not accept the reason, and the shareholder-plaintiff appealed.

MAYER v. ADAMS
141 A.2d 458 (Del. 1958)

SOUTHERLAND, Chief Justice

The case concerns Rule 23 (b) of the [Delaware] Rules of [Procedure] relating to stockholders' derivative suits. The second sentence of paragraph (b) provides:

> The complaint shall also set forth with particularity the efforts of the plaintiff to secure from the managing

directors and, if necessary, from the shareholders such action as he desires, and the reasons for his failure to obtain such action or the reasons for not making such effort.

The question is: Under what circumstances is a preliminary demand on shareholders necessary?

Plaintiff is a stockholder of the defendant Phillips Petroleum Company. She brought an action to redress alleged frauds and wrongs committed by the defendant directors upon the corporation. They concern dealings between Phillips and defendant Ada Oil Company, in which one of the defendant directors is alleged to have a majority stock interest.

The complaint set forth reasons why demand on the directors for action would be futile and the sufficiency of these reasons was not challenged. It also set forth reasons seeking to excuse failure to demand stockholder action. The principal [reason was] that fraud was charged, which no majority of stockholders could ratify.

In the view we take of the case, the issue between the litigants narrows itself to this: If the ground of the derivative suit is fraud, is demand for stockholder action necessary under the rule?

When it is said that a demand on stockholders is necessary in a case involving fraud, the inquiry naturally arises: demand to do what?

Let us suppose that the objecting stockholder submits to a stockholders' meeting a proposal that a suit be brought to redress alleged wrongs. He may do so either by attending the meeting, or, if the regulations of the Securities and Exchange Commission are applicable, by requiring the management to mail copies of the proposal to the other stockholders.

Let us suppose that the proposal is disapproved by the majority stockholders—as common knowledge tells us it will ordinarily be. What of it? They cannot ratify the alleged fraud.

If the foregoing is a correct analysis of the matter, it follows that the whole process of stockholder demand in a case of alleged fraud is futile and avails nothing.

We hold that if a minority stockholders' complaint is based upon an alleged wrong committed by the directors against the corporation, of such a nature as to be beyond ratification by a majority of the stockholders, it is not necessary to allege or prove an effort to obtain action by the stockholders to redress the wrong.

The question may be asked: In what circumstances is such demand necessary? Obviously the rule contemplates that in some cases a demand is necessary; otherwise, it would have not been adopted.

We are not called upon in this case to attempt to enumerate the various circumstances in which demand on stockholders is excused; and likewise we do not undertake to enumerate all the cases in which demand is necessary. It seems clear that one instance of necessary demand is a case involving only an irregularity or lack of authority in directorate action.

[Reversed and remanded.]

CASE COMMENT

You may wonder why Phillips Petroleum Company, the corporation on whose behalf the derivative action was brought, is referred to as a "defendant" in the court's opinion. The reason is that the corporation must be a party to a derivative suit. Phillips had refused to participate as a plaintiff, so it was made a party to the suit by being named a defendant. Nonetheless, as mentioned before, any damages paid by a defendant who has harmed the corporation will usually be paid to the corporation.

CASE REVIEW QUESTIONS
1. What duty did the plaintiff believe that the defendants had breached?
2. At the beginning of the lawsuit, on what grounds did the defendants defend themselves against the plaintiff's claim?

3. On what grounds did the appellate court reject the defendants' defense?
4. What reason do you think the plaintiff gave for not making a demand on the directors to bring a lawsuit?

Shareholder's Strike Suit A derivative action that is brought by a shareholder not to correct or obtain compensation for a wrong done to the corporation but rather to obtain a settlement that is personally profitable to the shareholder and his or her attorney is called a *strike suit.* The law has attempted to prevent strike suits (1) by adopting security-for-expenses statutes and (2) by prohibiting private settlements.

Security-for-Expenses Statutes Security-for-expenses statutes require certain shareholders who are bringing a derivative action to provide security for the reasonable expenses, including attorney's fees, that the corporation and the alleged wrongdoers may incur in defending against the lawsuit. In some states, security must be given in all derivative actions. In others, security-for-expenses is only required when the court feels that the shareholder's suit is groundless and is therefore a strike suit.

If the shareholder's lawsuit is unsuccessful, the court may award the defendants payment for their expenses from the security provided by the shareholder. This means that an unsuccessful shareholder may have to pay for both his or her own expenses and the defendants' expenses. Needless to say, this possibility serves as a strong deterrent to the bringing of strike suits.

Prohibition of Private Settlements The success of a strike suit depends on the desire of the alleged wrongdoers to settle the case by making a payment directly to the shareholder-plaintiff in return for his or her voluntary withdrawal of the suit. A settlement will sometimes be made because the alleged wrongdoer prefers to settle rather than incur the expenses of defending against the suit. At other times, the settlement may be nothing more than a payoff to the shareholder for disregarding the wrongdoing involved.

Today, a derivative suit usually cannot be settled until all shareholders have been advised of the proposed settlement and have been given a chance to object to it and a court approves the settlement. A court will not approve of a settlement that benefits the shareholder-plaintiff to the detriment of the corporation and the other shareholders.

REVIEW QUESTIONS

1. Explain in your own words the duties that corporate officers and directors owe to their corporations.

2. What effect does the business judgment rule have on the duty of care that a corporate executive owes to his or her corporation?

3. What are the three common situations in which a corporate executive's duty of loyalty may be called into question?
4. What steps can a corporate executive take to fulfill his or her duty of loyalty?
5. What duties does a controlling shareholder owe when he or she sells the controlling interest in a corporation?
6. Under what circumstances is a shareholder enti-

tled to inspect the books and records of a corporation?
7. Under what circumstances is a shareholder entitled to bring a derivative suit on behalf of a corporation?
8. Categorize each of the cases in this chapter in terms of whether it was a direct action, a class action, or a derivative action.

CASE PROBLEMS

1. Allis-Chalmers Manufacturing Company, a corporation, has 24 plants, 145 sales offices, 5,000 dealers and distributors, more than 31,000 employees, and annual sales in excess of half a billion dollars. Its operating policy is to decentralize decision making by delegating authority to the lowest possible management level. Two years ago, four middle-level managers pleaded guilty to antitrust violations involving price fixing. Subsequently, Allis-Chalmers has paid out substantial sums to its customers as damages in civil lawsuits based on the same antitrust violations. A shareholders' derivative action has been brought against the directors claiming that they were negligent in failing to take action designed to learn of and prevent antitrust violations by Allis-Chalmers' employees. There is, however, no evidence that the directors had actual knowledge of any facts that would have put them on notice of the price-fixing. Who will win the case? Explain.
2. Clayborn is the president and director of Marigold Corporation. He currently owns 1,000 shares of Marigold, which he purchased several years ago when he joined the company and assumed the presidency. At that time, he received a stock option for 10,000 shares of Marigold at $10 per share. The option is about to expire, but Clayborn does not have the money to exercise his option. Credit is very tight at present, and most of his assets have already been used to obtain loans. Clayborn spoke to the chairman of Marigold's board about his plight, and he told the chairman that he is going to

borrow $100,000 from Marigold in order to exercise his option. The chairman was responsible for Clayborn's being hired as the president of Marigold and is a close personal friend. Fearing that Clayborn will leave unless he is able to obtain a greater financial interest in Marigold, the chairman told Clayborn: "It is okay with me and you have a green light." Clayborn authorized the issuance of a $100,000 check payable to his order. He then negotiated the check to Marigold in payment for the shares of stock. What are the legal implications raised by these circumstances? [Adapted from CPA examination question 3b, *Business Law,* May, 1979.]
3. Towne is a prominent financier, the owner of one percent of the shares of Toy, Inc., and one of Toy's directors. He is also the chairman of the board of Unlimited Holdings, Inc., an investment company in which he owns 80 percent of the stock. Toy needs land on which to build additional warehouse facilities. Toy's president, Arthur, surveyed the feasible land sites. In Arthur's opinion, the best location from all standpoints, including location, availability, access to transportation, and price, is an eight-acre tract of land owned by Unlimited. Neither Arthur nor Towne wishes to create any legal problems in connection with the possible purchase of the land. What are the legal parameters within which this transaction may be legally consummated? What would be the legal ramifications if there were a $50,000 payment "on the side" to Towne so he would use his efforts to "smooth the

way" for the proposed purchase? [Adapted from CPA examination question 3c, *Business Law,* May, 1979.]

4. Acoustic Corporation manufactures radios. In order to produce a new line of radios, it needed to obtain patents from DeForest Radio, Inc. Bell, a director of Acoustic, was assigned the job of negotiating the purchase of the patents from DeForest. Although Bell was not successful in negotiating the purchase of the patents, he did obtain from DeForest a written offer to sell a substantial number of DeForest's shares for $500,000, which would give Acoustic access to the patents. The offer to sell was directed to Bell personally, "subject to approval of your board of directors." The board of directors considered the offer, but hesitated to approve it because the directors were unsure that Acoustic could afford the purchase. The directors instructed Deutsch, Acoustic's president, to try to borrow the necessary funds to buy the DeForest shares. The directors also agreed that, if Deutsch was unsuccessful, they would purchase the shares with their own money on behalf of Acoustic. Deutsch did not attempt to borrow the necessary funds. Instead, he and Bell accepted DeForest's offer for themselves. After buying the DeForest shares, Bell and Deutsch resold them at a substantial profit. When a derivative action was brought on behalf of Acoustic against Bell and Deutsch, they defended on the grounds that (1) DeForest's contract to sell had been with Bell personally and (2) Acoustic had not been financially capable of making the purchase itself. Who will win the case? Explain.

5. The United States Justice Department commenced a criminal action against Sky Manufacturing Corporation and its president, Masterson, for conspiring to fix prices on the sale of certain heavy industrial machinery. Both the corporation and Masterson denied the allegations. After a lengthy trial, the jury found that although an illegal conspiracy did exist among certain manufacturers, neither Sky nor Masterson were parties to it. The cost to the corporation for defending the action against it was $500,000. Masterson's individual legal fees and expenses amounted to $250,000, of which Sky has paid $50,000 directly. Masterson seeks indemnification for the remaining $200,000.

Heinz, a dissenting shareholder of Sky, advised the board of directors that the payment of any of Masterson's expenses by the corporation was improper. In the event that no action is taken to recover the $50,000 already advanced, Heinz has threatened to commence a shareholder's derivative action against Masterson. Furthermore, unless the board unequivocally promises not to indemnify Masterson for the unpaid balance of his legal expenses, Heinz says he will seek a court order ruling that Masterson's legal expenses not be paid. What rights and limitations apply to Sky's payment of Masterson's legal fees and expenses? [Adapted from CPA examination question 2c, *Business Law,* May, 1976.]

6. Yates owns enough shares of Republic Pictures Corporation to have working control of the corporation. He recently received an offer to buy his shares from Essex Corporation. One of the provisions of the offer is the following:

6. Resignations

Upon and as a condition to the closing of this transaction if requested by Buyer at least ten (10) days prior to the date of the closing:

(a) Seller will deliver to Buyer the resignations of the majority of the directors of Republic.

(b) Seller will cause a special meeting of the board of directors of Republic to be held, legally convened pursuant to law and the by-laws of Republic, and simultaneously with the acceptance of the directors' resignations set forth in paragraph 6(a) immediately preceding will cause nominees of Buyer to be elected directors of Republic in place of the resigned directors.

What precautions should Yates take before accepting the offer of Essex?

7. Ormand Industries, Inc. (Ormand) is in the outdoor advertising business in California. Its controlling shareholder and president is Jarrell Ormand. H.P. Skoglund is a minority shareholder. Based on Ormand's financial statements and on conversa-

tions with Robert Brunson, a former officer of Ormand, Skoglund believes that the corporation is being mismanaged and defrauded by Jarrell Ormand. Consequently, Skoglund wants to gain control of Ormand and oust its present management. Skoglund recently submitted to Ormand a written demand to inspect certain books and records that will enable him to determine whether mismanagement and fraud have occurred. Ormand refused the demand, and Skoglund then brought a legal action seeking a court order requiring Ormand to produce the demanded books and records for inspection. Ormand defends its refusal to allow inspection on the grounds that (1) Skoglund owns an outdoor advertising business in Seattle, Washington; (2) Brunson's allegations against Jarrell Ormand are motivated by bad blood between them over a personal matter; and (3) Skoglund's real purpose in making the demand to inspect is to help him gain control of Ormand. Who will win the case? Explain.

8. Maldonado, a shareholder of Zapata Corporation (Zapata), began a derivative action on behalf of Zapata against ten officers and directors, alleging breaches of fiduciary duties. Maldonado did not first demand that the board of directors bring the action. Instead, he stated in his complaint that such a demand would be futile because all of the directors had participated in the acts that constituted the breaches of fiduciary duties and were named as defendants in the suit. After the suit was begun, two of the defendant-directors resigned from the board, and the remaining directors appointed two new outside directors to replace them. The board then created an "Independent Investigation Committee" (Committee), composed solely of the two new directors, to investigate Maldonado's derivative action and to determine whether the corporation should continue the litigation. The board's resolution stated that the Committee's determination would be "final, not subject to review by the Board of Directors, and in all respects binding on the Corporation." Following an investigation, the Committee concluded that the derivative action should "be dismissed forthwith, as its continued maintenance is harmful to the corporation's best interests." Consequently, Zapata moved for dismissal of Maldonado's derivative action. Should the motion be granted or denied? Explain.

41

EXTRAORDINARY CORPORATE CHANGES AND DISSOLUTION

In Chapters 38 through 40, you have read about those activities that occur in the ordinary course of corporate business. These corporate business activities are generally managed by the board of directors and the corporate officers on whom the board has conferred authority.

In this chapter, you will read about extraordinary corporate activities that occur outside of the ordinary course of business. These activities are amending the articles of incorporation, merging and consolidating, selling or otherwise disposing of all or substantially all assets, purchasing shares to gain working control, and dissolving the corporation. Because these activities are extraordinary, they generally require shareholder approval. In addition, with some of them, shareholders who oppose the activity are entitled to have their shares purchased by the corporation.

EXTRAORDINARY CORPORATE CHANGES

Amending the Articles of Incorporation

In Chapter 38, you learned that a corporation is created by the filing of articles of incorporation with the secretary of state of the state of incorporation. The articles describe certain basic characteristics of the corporation, such as its name, the period of its duration, its purpose, and its capital structure (see page 808). After a corporation has been created, people associated with it may decide that a change in one or more of its basic characteristics is desirable. To accomplish such a change, the articles of incorporation must be amended.

The articles of incorporation may be amended to include any provision that can be included in the articles of a new corporation at the time the amendment is made [MBCA §58]. For an amendment to be valid, however, the procedure required by the corporation law of the state of incorporation must be followed. Here we will outline the procedure required by the MBCA.

Procedure for Amending Articles The amendment process begins when the board of directors adopts a resolution setting forth the proposed amendment and directing that it be submitted to a vote of the shareholders at an annual or a special meeting [MBCA §59(a)]. Notice of the proposed amendment must then be given to each shareholder who is entitled to vote on the amendment at the meeting [MBCA §59(b)].

At the shareholders' meeting, the proposed amendment must receive the affirmative vote of the holders of at least a majority of the shares entitled to vote on the amendment in order to be adopted [MBCA §59(c)]. Note that a majority of all the shares *entitled to vote,* not just those shares represented at the meeting, is required. In some states, a two-thirds majority of the shares entitled to vote is required.

If the holders of a certain class of shares will be affected by the adoption of a proposed amendment, they are entitled to vote on it as a class [MBCA §60]. For instance, if a proposed amendment would eliminate the preemptive rights of a class of shares, the holders of those shares are entitled to vote on the proposal as a class. The proposed amendment must receive the affirmative vote of the holders of at least a majority of the shares of each class entitled to vote as a class as well as a majority of all the shares entitled to vote.

If the required shareholder approval is given, the adopted amendment is then filed with the secretary of state in a document called the *articles of amendment* [MBCA §61 and §62]. If the articles of amendment are properly filed, the secretary of state issues a *certificate of amendment.* The amendment becomes effective when the certificate is issued [MBCA §63].

Merger and Consolidation

Sometimes two or more corporations are combined to form one corporation through either a merger or a consolidation. In a **merger,** one or more corporations are merged into another corporation. After the merger, the merged corporations cease to exist and the surviving corporation takes title to their assets and assumes responsibility for their liabilities. For instance, Corporation A may merge into Corporation B. A then ceases to exist, and B takes over A's assets and liabilities.

In a **consolidation,** two or more corporations combine to form a new corporation. For instance, Corporation A and Corporation B may consolidate to form Corporation C, which then takes over the assets and liabilities of both A and B.

Traditionally, when a merger or a consolidation was completed, the shareholders in a corporation that no longer existed would hold shares in the surviving corporation. In the last 25 years, however, forms of mergers and consolidations have been devised in which some shareholders involved do not end up owning shares in the surviving corporation. Instead, they may receive shares in another corporation, cash, or other property [MBCA §71(c)].

Procedure for Merger or Consolidation The process of combining corporations by merger or consolidation begins with the approval of the boards of directors of the corporations involved [MBCA §71 and §72]. Generally, proper notice to and approval by the shareholders of the corporations involved is also required. In some states, even the holders of nonvoting shares are allowed to vote on a merger or a consolidation. In most states, the required shareholders' approval is two-thirds of the shares entitled to vote, although some states and the MBCA (§73) require only majority approval.

There are two situations in which shareholder approval of a merger or a consolidation is not required. First, shareholder approval is not necessary if the acquiring corporation owns 90 percent of the shares of the corporation to be merged [MBCA §75]. This is called a *short-form merger.* Second, shareholder approval is not necessary if a merger will have only a small impact on the affairs of the surviving corporation. Under the MBCA (§73(d)), there is only a small impact if the name of the surviving corporation does not change, if its shareholders have the same number of shares before and after the merger, and if the issued shares of the corporation do not increase by more than 20 percent.

If shareholder approval is unnecessary or has been given, *articles of merger* or *articles of consolidation* are filed with the secretary of state. The merger or consolidation takes effect when the secretary of state issues a *certificate of merger* or a *certificate of consolidation* [MBCA §74].

Sale or Other Disposition of All Assets

In some situations, one corporation may find it preferable to purchase all or substantially all of the assets of another corporation rather than go through a merger or a consolidation. One reason that purchasing the assets of another corporation may be preferable is that approval of the transaction by the buying corporation's shareholders is unnecessary. Only the approval of the buyer's directors and the seller's directors and shareholders need be obtained. Approval by the shareholders of the selling corporation is required because a sale or other disposition (including a lease) not in the regular course of business of all or substantially all of the assets of a corporation is one of the extraordinary activities that requires shareholder approval [MBCA §79].

When two firms merge or consolidate, the surviving or new corporation assumes responsibility for the liabilities of the corporation or corporations that cease to exist. Another reason why the purchase of assets may be preferable to a merger or a consolidation is that the corporation that buys assets does *not*, as a general rule, assume the liabilities of the selling corporation. There are, however, four usual exceptions to this general rule. The buying corporation is responsible for the liabilities of the selling corporation when any of the following occur:

1. The buyer agrees to assume the liabilities.

2. A court decides that the combining of the corporations was actually a merger or a consolidation.
3. The buying corporation is really nothing more than a continuation of the selling corporation.
4. The purchase of assets was made in order to allow the selling corporation to escape liability for its debts.

In the case that follows, a corporation that had bought substantially all of the assets of another corporation was sued by a person who was injured by a product that had been manufactured by the selling corporation. The buying corporation argued that it was not liable to the injured person because it was not responsible for the selling corporation's liabilities. The court decided that none of the four usual exceptions to the rule that a buying corporation is not responsible for the liabilities of a selling corporation were applicable. Nonetheless, the court imposed liability on the buying corporation. See if you can understand the court's reasons for doing so.

RAY v. ALAD CORPORATION
560 P.2d 3 (Cal. 1977)

[Herbert Ray was injured while using a ladder that had been manufactured by Alad Corporation (Alad I). Subsequent to Ray's purchase of the ladder but prior to his injury, Alad I sold all of its assets except its cash, accounts receivable, unexpired insurance, and prepaid expenses to Lightning Maintenance Corporation (Lightning). As part of the transaction, Alad I agreed to dissolve its corporate existence and to help Lightning form a *new* corporation under the name Alad Corporation (Alad II). Lightning did not agree to assume the liabilities of Alad I. Subsequently, Alad I was dissolved and Alad II was formed. Alad II continued the operation of Alad I's business without interruption.

Ray brought a legal action based on strict liability in tort (see pages 125–130) against Alad II. Alad II defended on the grounds that it was not responsible for the liabilities of Alad I. The trial court found for Alad II, and Ray appealed.]

WRIGHT, Associate Justice
Our discussion of the law starts with the rule ordinarily applied to the determination of whether a corpo-

ration purchasing the principal assets of another corporation assumes the other's liabilities. As typically formulated the rule states that the purchaser does not assume the seller's liabilities unless (1) there is an express or implied agreement of assumption, (2) the transaction amounts to a consolidation or merger of the two corporations, (3) the purchasing corporation is a mere continuation of the seller, or (4) the transfer of assets to the purchaser is for the fraudulent purpose of escaping liability for the seller's debts.

If this rule were determinative of Alad II's liability to plaintiff it would require us to affirm the [trial court's decision]. None of the rule's four stated grounds for imposing liability on the purchasing corporation is present here. There was no express or implied agreement to assume liability for injury from defective products previously manufactured by Alad I. Nor is there any indication or contention that the transaction was prompted by any fraudulent purpose of escaping liability for Alad I's debts.

With respect to the second stated ground for liability, the purchase of Alad I's assets did not amount to a consolidation or merger. This exception has been invoked where one corporation takes all of another's assets without providing any consideration [payment] that could be made available to meet claims of the other's creditors or where the consideration consists wholly of shares of the purchaser's stock which are promptly distributed to the seller's shareholders in conjunction with the seller's liquidation. In the present case the sole consideration given for Alad I's assets was cash in excess of $207,000. Of this amount Alad I was paid $70,000 when the assets were transferred and at the same time a promissory note was given to Alad I for almost $114,000. Shortly before the dissolution of Alad I the note was assigned to the Hambly's, Alad I's principal stockholders, and thereafter the note was paid in full. The remainder of the consideration went for closing expenses or was paid to the Hamblys for consulting services and their agreement not to compete. There is no contention that this consideration was inadequate or that the cash and promissory note given to Alad I were not included in the assets available to meet claims of Alad I's creditors at the time of dissolution. Hence the acquisition of Alad I's assets was not in the nature of a merger or consolidation for purposes of the aforesaid rule.

Plaintiff contends that the rule's third stated ground for liability makes Alad II liable as a mere continuation of Alad I in view of Alad II's acquisition of Alad I's operating assets, its use of those assets and of Alad I's former employees to manufacture the same line of products, and its holding itself out to customers and the public as a continuation of the same enterprise. However, California decisions holding that a corporation acquiring the assets of another corporation is the latter's mere continuation and therefore liable for its debts have imposed such liability only upon a showing of one or both of the following factual elements: (1) no adequate consideration was given for the predecessor corporation's assets and made available for meeting the claims of its unsecured creditors; (2) one or more persons were officers, directors, or stockholders of both corporations. There is no showing of either of these elements in the present case.

We therefore conclude that the general rule governing succession to liabilities does not require Alad II to respond to plaintiff's claim. [However,] we must decide whether the policies underlying strict tort liability for defective products call for a special exception to the rule that would otherwise insulate the present defendant from plaintiff's claim.

The purpose of the rule of strict tort liability "is to insure that the costs of injuries resulting from defective products are borne by the manufacturers that put such products on the market rather than by the injured persons who are powerless to protect themselves." However, the rule

> "does not rest on the analysis of the financial strength or bargaining power of the parties to the particular action. It rests, rather, on the proposition that '[t]he cost of an injury and the loss of time or health may be an overwhelming misfortune to the person injured, and a needless one, for the risk of injury can be insured by the manufacturer and distributed among the public as a cost of doing business.' "

Thus, "the paramount policy to be promoted by the rule is the protection of otherwise defenseless victims of manufacturing defects and the spreading throughout society of the cost of compensating them." Justification for imposing strict liability upon a successor to a manufacturer under the circumstances here presented rests upon (1) the virtual destruction of the plaintiff's remedies against the original manufacturer caused by the successor's acquisition of the business, (2) the successor's ability to assume the original manufacturer's risk-spreading rule, and (3) the fairness of requiring the successor to assume a responsibility for defective products that was a burden necessarily attached to the original manufacturer's good will being enjoyed by the successor in the continued operation of the business. [The court then considered each of these factors in the context of the case before it.]

We therefore conclude that a party which acquires a manufacturing business and continues the output of its line of products under the circumstances here presented assumes strict tort liability for defects in units of the same product line previously manufactured and distributed by the entity from which the business was acquired.

The judgment is reversed.

CASE REVIEW QUESTIONS

1. Which corporation's shareholders had to approve the sale of substantially all of the assets of Alad I to Lightning? Explain.
2. What are the usual exceptions to the general rule that a corporation that buys all or substantially all of the assets of another corporation does not assume the liabilities of the selling corporation?
3. Explain in your own words why Alad II was held responsible for the liability of Alad I to Ray.

Purchase of Shares to Gain Working Control

Another method of combining two corporations is for one corporation to purchase enough of the shares of another corporation to gain working control of it. As noted earlier, owning a majority of a corporation's shares is usually not necessary to have working control of the corporation. If control can be obtained, the acquiring corporation votes its shares to gain a majority on the board of directors of the acquired corporation. The new board then proposes a merger with the acquiring corporation. Finally, the acquiring corporation votes its shares to provide shareholders' approval of the merger.

This process is called a **takeover.** It allows the acquiring corporation to take over another corporation without having to get the approval of the acquired corporation's original board of directors, as is necessary when a merger, a consolidation, or a purchase of assets takes place. Also, a takeover is usually less costly than a merger, a consolidation, or a purchase of assets because the acquiring corporation need purchase only enough shares to gain working control; it need not buy the whole acquired company.

Usually, the purchase of the acquired corporation's shares is accomplished by means of a **tender offer,** which is a public offer to purchase shares at a specified price for a specified period of time. The Securities Act of 1934 and the Securities and Exchange Commission's rules closely regulate tender offers. These laws and rules are explained in Chapter 51 (see pages 1145–1148).

Rights of Dissenting Shareholders

As you have read, the law provides that amending the articles of incorporation or consummating a merger, a consolidation, or the sale of all or substantially all corporate assets outside the ordinary course of business generally requires the approval of a corporation's shareholders. The law also provides that shareholders who dissent from any of these extraordinary corporate changes may, under certain circumstances, have their shares appraised (i.e., have the value of their shares determined) and purchased by the corporation if they do not wish to continue as investors in the corporation [MBCA §80(a)]. This right is called the shareholder's **appraisal right.** The reason for giving a shareholder an appraisal right is that when an extraordinary corporate change occurs, the shareholder's investment is no longer in the same type of corporation, so the corporation should buy back the shareholder's investment.

Under the MBCA, a shareholder who dissents from an amendment to the articles of incorporation will have a right of appraisal if the amendment has a material and adverse effect on the rights attached to the shareholder's shares, such as abolishing a preference of the shares or eliminating a preemptive right [MBCA §80 (a)(4)]. In some states, a dissenting shareholder has a right of appraisal if the purpose or duration clauses are amended or if the capital structure is amended in any way.

The MBCA (§80(c)) provides that there is no right of appraisal for a shareholder of the surviving corporation in a merger if shareholder approval of the merger was not necessary. You will recall that approval by the shareholders of a surviving corporation in a merger is not necessary for a short-form merger or when the merger will have only a small impact on the surviving corporation.

In some states, there is no appraisal right for a shareholder who dissents from a merger, a consolidation, or the sale of all or substantially all assets outside the ordinary course of business if the corporation's shares are listed on a national securities exchange such as the New York Stock Exchange. The rationale for this exception is that a dissenting shareholder who holds shares that are listed on a securities exchange does not need the appraisal right because he or she can just as easily sell his or her shares in the stock market.

In the case that follows, the court had to decide whether a shareholder in a corporation that transferred some of its assets to a subsidiary corporation was entitled to a right of appraisal.

CAMPBELL v. VOSE
515 F.2d 256 (Tenth Cir. 1975)

[Southwestern Cotton Oil Company (Southwestern) is a corporation engaged in the cotton oil business. Over the years it accumulated a large amount of earnings, which it invested in various ways. Management decided that for tax purposes all of the assets of Southwestern used in the cotton oil business should be transferred to a subsidiary corporation while all the nonoperating assets (bank accounts, promissory notes, and investments) should be retained by Southwestern. A subsidiary corporation, Machine Works, Inc., was formed and all of the operating assets of Southwestern were transferred to it in return for shares and debentures in Machine Works.

Campbell, a shareholder of Southwestern, brought a derivative action against Vose and other directors of Southwestern. One of his claims, referred to in the case as the Third Cause of Action, was that he was entitled to a shareholder's appraisal right because Southwestern had sold substantially all of its assets to Machine Works. The trial court denied Campbell's claim, and he appealed.]

SETH, Circuit Judge

The Third Cause of Action in the complaint is directed to the rights of minority stockholders when the corporation sells "all" or "substantially all" of its assets. The trial court concluded that the creation of a wholly owned subsidiary corporation, and the transfer to it of the land and plant of the Cotton Oil Company without a stockholders' vote, was not an event under Oklahoma law which would give rise to rights [of appraisal] in the dissenting stockholders.

The figures used by the trial court and in the corporate balance sheet at the time of transfer show that about one-third of all corporate assets were transferred to the subsidiary in exchange for stock and for debentures. The book value of the tangibles transferred was about $495,000, and the assets retained had a value at cost of $981,095, using the figures in the corporate resolutions. These figures are characterized as "cost" figures or as the corporate "investment" in certain assets. Apparently no attempt was made to relate the numbers to current values. Some testimony places the actual value of the land much higher but with no definite figures used. The record shows that the land, buildings, machinery, inventory, and all tangibles of the company were transferred. The assets retained were bank balances, promissory notes, and the investment portfolio, consisting of common stocks. Thus all the operating property and tangibles that remained of the old cotton oil business were transferred. The surpluses and accumulated earnings were retained as represented in the investments and bank accounts. The record shows that the tangibles were instrumental in creating the current income of the corporation which had been a problem to management. This was removed by the transfer and creation of the debt.

The appellees argue that the transfer was not a "sale" as urged by appellant. Appellees state in their brief that since the transferee was a wholly-owned subsidiary, the parent corporation still had enough "control" over the assets to prevent the transaction from being a sale. Thus the appellees in their brief say:

> In this case, the property which was transferred is still subject to the Company's use, possession and control since Machine Works is a wholly owned subsidiary of the Company.

It is difficult to see how there could be any real corporate entity for the subsidiary for any purpose if the assets transferred are in the present corporation's "possession," and within its control. Perhaps no transfer was actually made if the assets remain in the transferor's "possession" as the appellees urge. If this is the case, we may have no problem, but if the parent company has the usual relationship with the subsidiary and an actual transfer was made, which we assume on the basis of the trial court's findings, then the parent divested itself of possession and title to [ownership of] the assets, and placed them in the possession and control of the subsidiary. Thus it looks more like a sale or "other disposition" under the statute than anything else. An exchange for stock and for evidence of indebtedness was made, and the indicia of ownership were held by the subsidiary. We must hold that the transaction did bring into play the statutory rights of dissenting shareholders, contrary to the trial court's conclusion.

The "all" or "substantially all" of the assets presents another issue, and is also a condition which must exist before the statute comes into play. The statute is in purely quantitative terms, but the appellant urges that other considerations exist because the assets transferred were all the "operating assets," and only money or investments remained. The record shows that the Cotton Oil Company had engaged in dual activities for several years, the plant operations (storage and machine shops) on one hand, and investments of the accumulated earnings on the other hand.

In the corporate resolution relating to the transfer, the recitation is made that the desire was to separate the "operating business activities from its investment activities." Such a change was substantial. Thus the corporate changes surrounding the creation of the subsidiary, the separation of the business activities with the result that the parent corporation has only investments, makes the transfer of assets have much different implications than it would ordinarily have. The consequences of the creation of the subsidiary discussed above with the fact all operating assets were transferred to it makes the transaction a sale and results in a situation where for all practical purposes, "substantially" all of the assets were sold. All the effective operating assets were sold. The investment segment remaining was large in dollars but was the last and a large step in the change in the nature of corporate activity. In these circumstances, more than dollar values must be considered. It was another significant step also in the prevention of current income which was another aspect of the change in corporate purpose. The transaction was thus one which required consideration by the stockholders, and gives rise to the rights of dissenting shareholders under the Oklahoma statutes.

The judgment is reversed.

CASE REVIEW QUESTIONS

1. On what grounds did the defendants argue that there had not been a sale or other disposition of assets from Southwestern to Machine Works? Why did the court disagree?

2. On what grounds do you think the defendants argued that substantially all of the assets of Southwestern had not been transferred to Machine Works? Why did the court disagree?

Appraisal Right Procedure The procedure for carrying out the shareholder's right of appraisal is extremely complex [MBCA §81]. Basically, the shareholder must file a written objection to the extraordinary action being taken by the corporation prior to the shareholder vote, must either refrain from voting or must vote against the corporate action, and must demand payment for his or her shares if the action receives the necessary shareholders' approval. If these steps are taken, the shareholder is entitled to receive the fair value of his or her shares in cash. If the shareholder and the purchasing corporation cannot agree on the fair value of the shares, the fair value will be determined by a court. The judge may appoint an appraiser to help with the valuation of the shares.

If enough shareholders exercise their right of appraisal, the corporation may not be able to complete a merger, a consolidation, or the sale of substantially all of its assets even though the required percentage of shareholders approve of the transaction. This will happen if the purchasing corporation does not have sufficient cash to purchase the shares of the stockholders who assert their appraisal rights.

Fiduciary Duties

In Chapter 40, you read about the various duties of corporate directors, officers, and majority shareholders. These duties also apply when extraordinary changes occur in a corporation. For instance, directors owe fiduciary duties to the corporation when they vote on extraordinary corporate changes. Similarly, a controlling shareholder owes a fiduciary duty to the minority shareholders when he or she votes on extraordinary corporate changes that require shareholder approval.

One situation in which the existence of these duties is important occurs when controlling shareholders want to freeze out (eliminate) the minority shareholders from the corporation. In the following case, which involves a freeze out, the controlling shareholder argued that, because the statutory requirements for a merger had been met, a dissenting shareholder's only remedy was to exercise his or her right of appraisal. The court disagreed, however, and held that the controlling shareholder owed a fiduciary duty to minority shareholders and that the minority shareholders could seek a remedy for breach of that duty rather than exercise their appraisal right.

SINGER v. MAGNAVOX CO.
380 A.2d 969 (Del. 1977)

[North-American Philips Corporation (North American) formed North American Philips Development Corporation (Development) for the sole purpose of having Development make a tender offer for the common shares of The Magnavox Company (Magnavox). Development offered to buy all of the outstanding Magnavox shares at a price of $9.00 per share. Development purchased the 84.1% of the Magnavox shares that were tendered to it. Then, in order to obtain the rest of the Magnavox shares, North American, which controlled both Development and Magnavox, arranged for a merger of Magnavox into T.M.C. Development Corporation (T.M.C.), which was wholly owned by Development. Under the terms of the merger, each shareholder of Magnavox would receive $9.00 for each share of Magnavox that he or she owned. The merger was approved by the Magnavox directors and shareholders (84.1% of the shares being held by Development), and the merger was accomplished.

Singer and other minority shareholders of Magnavox sued Development, North American, and others on the grounds, among others, that the defendants breached their fiduciary duties to the minority shareholders in approving the merger at a cash price they knew to be grossly inadequate. The defendants moved to dismiss the complaint. The trial court granted the motion, and plaintiffs appealed.]

DUFFY, Justice

We turn, first, to what we regard as the principal consideration in this appeal; namely, the obligation owed by majority shareholders in control of the corporate process to minority shareholders, in the context of a merger, under Delaware Corporation Law §251, of two related Delaware corporations.

To state the obvious, under §251 two (or more) Delaware corporations "may merge into a single corporation." Generally speaking, whether such a transaction is good or bad, enlightened or ill-advised, selfish or generous—these considerations are beside the point. Section 251 authorizes a merger, and any judicial consideration of that kind of togetherness must begin from that premise.

Section 251 also specifies in detail the procedures to be followed in accomplishing a merger. Briefly, these include approvals by the directors of each corporation and by "majority [vote] of the outstanding stock of" each corporation, followed by the execution and filing of formal documents. The consideration given to the shareholders of a corporation in exchange for their stock may take the form of "cash, property, rights or securities of any other corporation." A shareholder who objects to the merger and is dissatisfied with the value of the consideration given for his shares may seek an appraisal.

In this appeal it is uncontroverted that defendants complied with the stated requirements of §251. Thus there is both statutory authorization for the Magnavox merger and compliance with the procedural requirements. But, contrary to defendants' contention, it does not necessarily follow that the merger is legally unassailable. We say this because, (a) plaintiffs invoke the fiduciary duty rule which allegedly binds defendants; and (b) Delaware case law clearly teaches that even complete compliance with the mandate of a statute does not, in every case, make the action valid in law.

From this premise we must now analyze the encounter between the exercise of a statutory right and the performance of the alleged fiduciary duty. As we have noted, §251, by its terms, makes permissible that which the North American side of this dispute caused to be done: the merger of Magnavox into T.M.C. We must ascertain, however, what restraint, if any, the duty to minority stockholders placed on the exercise of that right.

It is a settled rule of law in Delaware that Development, as the majority stockholder of Magnavox, owed to the minority stockholders of that corporation a fiduciary obligation in dealing with the latter's property. The fiduciary obligation is the cornerstone of plaintiff's rights in this controversy and the corollary, of course, is that it is likewise the measure of the duty owed by defendants.

Delaware courts have long announced and enforced high standards which govern the internal affairs of corporations chartered here, particularly when fiduciary relations are under scrutiny. It is settled Delaware law, for example, that corporate officers, directors, and controlling shareholders owe their corporation and its minority shareholders a fiduciary obligation of honesty, loyalty, good faith and fairness.

Defendants concede that they owe plaintiffs a fiduciary duty but contend that, in the context of the present transaction, they have met that obligation by offering fair value for the Magnavox shares. And, say defendants, plaintiff's exclusive remedy for dissatisfaction with the merger is to seek an appraisal. We disagree. In our view, defendants cannot meet their fiduciary obligations to plaintiffs simply by relegating them to a statutory appraisal proceeding.

We agree that, because the power to merge is conferred by statute, every stockholder in a Delaware corporation accepts his shares with notice thereof. Beyond question, the common law right of a single stockholder to simply veto a merger is gone. But it by no means follows that those in control of a corporation may invoke the statutory power conferred by §251 when their purpose is simply to get rid of a minority. On the contrary, just as a minority shareholder may not thwart a merger without cause, neither may a majority cause a merger to be made for the sole purpose of eliminating a minority.

We hold the law to be that a Delaware Court will not be indifferent to the purpose of a merger when a freeze out of minority stockholders is alleged to be its sole purpose. In such a situation, if it is alleged that the purpose is improper because of the fiduciary obligation owed to the minority, the Court is duty-bound to closely examine that allegation even when all of the relevant statutory formalities have been satisfied.

[Reversed.]

CASE COMMENT

In 1983, the Delaware Supreme Court overruled *Singer v. Magnavox Co.* In *Weinberger v. UOP, Inc.,* the court held that a minority shareholder who brings a suit on the grounds of breach of fiduciary duty must do more than allege in his or her complaint that the only purpose of the merger was to freeze out the minority shareholders. The minority shareholder must also allege specific acts by the controlling shareholder that constitute a breach of fiduciary duty, such as fraud, misrepresentation, or other misconduct that demonstrates the unfairness of the merger to the minority. In other words, controlling shareholders, directors, and officers in Delaware continue to owe fiduciary duties when extraordinary corporate changes occur, but the standard for proving a breach of those duties has been raised.

CASE REVIEW QUESTIONS

1. Trace the series of events that resulted in the merger of Magnavox into T.M.C. What procedures had to be followed to accomplish each of these steps?
2. As a result of the court's decision, are the defendants liable to the plaintiffs for breach of fiduciary duty? If not, what did the court decide?

DISSOLUTION

Dissolution is the legal process by which a corporation's status as a legal entity is terminated. If the period of duration that is stated in the corporation's articles of incorporation expires, dissolution occurs automatically. Otherwise, dissolution may occur either as a voluntary action taken by the corporation or as an involuntary action imposed on the corporation.

Voluntary Dissolution

There are three ways in which a *voluntary dissolution* of a corporation can occur. Two of these are relatively simple. First, a corporation that has not begun business and has not issued any shares may be dissolved if a majority of the incorporators file *articles of dissolution* with the secretary of state [MBCA §82]. Second, a corporation may be dissolved if all of the shareholders consent in writing to the dissolution [MBCA §83].

The third method of voluntary dissolution is somewhat more complex and resembles the procedure that is followed with other extraordinary corporate changes that was discussed earlier in this chapter [MBCA §84]. The process begins with the adoption by the board of directors of a resolution recommending dissolution. The shareholders are then notified that dissolution will be considered at a shareholders' meeting. Under the MBCA, shareholder approval of a voluntary dissolution recommended by the board of directors requires the affirmative vote of a simple majority of the shares entitled to vote on the matter; in many states, though, a two-thirds majority is required. A *statement of intent to dissolve* is then filed with the secretary of state [MBCA §85].

Involuntary Dissolution

There are three ways in which an *involuntary dissolution* of a corporation can occur. First, the attorney general of the state of incorporation can obtain a court decree of dissolution by proving that the corporation has (1) failed to file its annual report or pay its franchise fee when due, (2) used fraud in procuring its articles of incorporation, (3) continues to exceed or abuse its authority, or (4) failed for thirty days to appoint and maintain a registered agent or to notify the state of a change in its registered office or agent [MBCA §94]. These provisions are seldom used. They tend to be used only when the offense involved is flagrant.

Second, a creditor can obtain a court decree of liquidation (a concept that will be explained later) that will result in involuntary dissolution by proving that (1) the creditor has a judgment against the corporation that has not been paid and the corporation is insolvent or (2) the corporation has admitted in writing that it owes money to the creditor and the corporation is insolvent [MBCA §97(b)].

Third, a shareholder can obtain a court decree of liquidation that will result in involuntary dissolution by proving (1) that there is an unbreakable decision-making deadlock among the directors that threatens irreparable harm to the corporation; (2) that there is illegal, oppressive, or fraudulent conduct by those in control of the corporation; (3) that there is a deadlock among the voting shareholders that has resulted in a failure to elect new directors for two years; or (4) that corporate assets are being misapplied or wasted [MBCA §97(a)].

Generally, the courts are hesitant to grant to a shareholder a decree of liquidation that will result in involuntary dissolution. Usually, only when there is substantial evidence of actual abuse or harm by those in control of the corporation will a court rule that liquidation and dissolution is necessary. In most cases, a shareholder will be successful in obtaining a court decree of dissolution only when the provision that allows dissolution if there is a shareholder deadlock and a failure to elect directors for two years—a matter that is subject to objective proof—is used. The following case illustrates the reluctance of the courts to decree dissolution even though there is substantial strife among the shareholders.

CALLIER v. CALLIER
378 N.E.2d 405 (Ill. 1978)

WINELAND, Justice

All Steel Pipe and Tube (All Steel) is a close corporation formed in 1969 to engage in the business of selling steel pipes and tubes. The two equal shareholders, plaintiff-appellee Leo Callier and defendant-appellant Scott Callier, each made an initial investment of $500 in the corporation. Scott is Leo's uncle. Defendant-appellant Felix Callier, one of the two directors of the corporation, is Scott's father and Leo's grandfather. It is undisputed that Felix, who is in his 80's, is the "nominee" of Scott on the board of directors, and that he has never taken an active role in the day-to-day management of the business. Leo is the other director, and is president of the corporation. Scott's title is general manager; he was appointed to that position by unanimous resolution of the board, and can only be removed by the board.

Increasingly over the years of their business association, Scott and Leo had differences of opinion about various aspects of the operation of the company. Despite the steady deterioration of the owners' relationship, the company flourished. From about $200,000 in 1970, gross sales had increased to $25,000,000 a year in 1974.

In early 1975, the series of events leading to this litigation took place. Scott was involved in preparing and sending to each employee of the corporation, and each employee's spouse, a letter warning that "social and/or emotional and/or physical relationships between male and female employees for other than business purposes" would thenceforth be grounds for immediate dismissal. This so called "fraternization letter" created a furor within the company, and resulted in Leo's informing Scott that he no longer wanted to be associated with him.

Negotiations looking towards the redemption of Scott's shares by Leo began immediately, but despite the diligent efforts of their attorneys the parties could not reach an agreement. In April 1975, the discussion turned to voluntary dissolution and liquidation of the corporation, but still no agreement could be reached.

On April 30, 1975, Leo sent a telegram to Scott purporting to fire him as general manager. On the next day, without any prior notice, Leo called all the employees together and announced that the business was being closed down immediately. During the next month, Leo began to wind down the business of All Steel. On May 5 he formed a new Delaware corporation, Callier Steel Pipe and Tube, Inc. On May 30, all operations at All Steel ceased. Callier Steel opened for business on June 2, employing about 40 of All Steel's previous employees.

[On June 11, Leo began a legal action seeking liquidation that would result in involuntary dissolution under a corporation law provision that is quoted below by the court. The court issued a decree of liquidation. Scott appealed on the grounds that Leo had failed to prove the elements required under the statute for dissolution.]

Corporations, which are creatures of statute, can only be dissolved according to statute. As our Supreme Court said in the *Davis* case, "Corporate dissolution is a drastic remedy, and the teachings of generations of [judges] admonish us that it must not be lightly invoked."

The statute at issue here is as follows:

Circuit courts have full power to liquidate the assets and business of a corporation:
(a) In an action by a shareholder when it appears:
(1) That the directors are deadlocked in the management of the corporate affairs and the shareholders are unable to break the deadlock, and that irreparable injury to the corporation is suffered or threatened by reason thereof . . . .

This section has not been a frequently used basis for dissolution, presumably because of the "substantial problems of interpretation" connected with its provisions. The terms deadlock and irreparable injury are both undefined and troublesome. It has been said that mere dissention among stockholders is not a ground for dissolution unless it is of such serious proportions as to defeat the end for which the corporation is organized. This formulation would seem consistent with the dictionary definition of the word deadlock:

A counteraction of things producing entire stoppage; hence, *a state of inaction* or of neutralization caused by the opposition of persons or of factions, as in a government or in a voting body. (Webster's New International Dictionary, Unabridged 674, 2d ed. 1956.) [Emphasis added by the court.]

After a careful review of the entire record, we have concluded that plaintiff's proof was insufficient to show either deadlock in the management of corporate affairs or the threat of irreparable injury to the corporation. What the evidence shows, instead, is two equal shareholders who were unable to get along and unable to reach agreement within a four-month period as to the redemption of one's shares by the other or to the terms of voluntary dissolution. This is not equivalent to an inability of the corporation to perform the functions for which it was created. Without adopting the position of defendants that the threat of irreparable injury can never be shown under this statute so long as a corporation is making a profit, we must agree with defendants that such a threat was not proved here.

It appears to us that Leo Callier simply decided that he was not going to have anything more to do with Scott Callier, and when their redemption–liquidation negotiations stalled, he made a unilateral decision—without consulting the other director and shareholder—to shut down the corporation. On the day that he informed the employees of the closing of the corporation, corporate affairs were being managed, and quite successfully. In fact, the company appeared on its way to the second best year in its history, despite a general downturn in the pipe industry. Neither Scott nor Felix Callier was interfering with the management of the corporation; Scott had in fact intentionally stayed away from the company and allowed Leo to run things alone while the redemption discussions were going on.

Thus, absent sufficient proof of the facts of deadlock and irreparable injury, the court below erred in ordering liquidation of the corporate assets.

A further consideration impels us towards reversal of the trial court's decision. At the time that he was winding down the affairs of All Steel, Leo Callier was in the process of forming another company to carry on the same kind of business, with many of the same employees and the same customers. That company is now doing business; All Steel is not. Should we sanction what appears to be a flagrant breach of Leo's fiduciary duty as a director of All Steel, we would be permitting him to siphon off the going-concern value of All Steel, leaving the 50 percent shareholder who was opposed to dissolution with only half of whatever assets are in the control of the receiver. This, we think, would be manifestly unfair.

We realize, of course, that merely by reversing the order of the court below we cannot revivify All Steel Pipe and Tube in this appeal. We cannot, however, sustain a judgment which is not founded on proof of the statutory requirements for dissolution and which permits one owner of a corporation to deprive one who is an equal owner of his equal share of the corporate assets by means of self-help.

Appellants in their brief would have us take certain steps in order to revitalize the corporation. There is little doubt that a court has power to achieve a just result in such cases. We remain content at this time however to reverse the judgment of the trial court,

leaving it to the further pleadings of the parties, and to the trial court to determine what further action should be decreed to fashion a fair and equitable remedy for the redress of the wrong done to appellants. Trial courts are ordinarily much better equipped to deal with such matters, than are courts of appeal.

The judgment is reversed, and this cause is remanded to [the trial] court for further proceedings consistent with this opinion.

CASE REVIEW QUESTIONS

1. In light of the fact that All Steel had stopped doing business, why didn't the court grant a decree of dissolution under the statute quoted in the case?
2. Why didn't the court grant a decree of liquidation for any of the other reasons for which a shareholder may obtain such a decree? (These reasons are discussed in the text prior to the case.)
3. Why do you think the courts are reluctant to grant to a shareholder a decree of liquidation that will result in the involuntary dissolution of a corporation?

Liquidation

Before the secretary of state will issue a certificate of dissolution or a court will enter a final decree of dissolution, liquidation of the corporation must be completed. **Liquidation** is the process by which all a corporation's uncompleted contracts are performed or terminated, all the corporate assets are collected and reduced to cash, all creditors are paid, and the remaining funds are distributed to the shareholders according to their liquidation preferences.

If dissolution is voluntary, liquidation is generally carried out by management. A creditor who remains unpaid after liquidation may, for a period of two years following final dissolution, seek payment from the corporation, the shareholders, or the directors who approved the improper distribution of assets to the shareholders.

If the dissolution is involuntary or if management requests it even when the dissolution is voluntary, liquidation will be supervised by a court. When this occurs, creditors file their claims with the court, and a person, called a *receiver,* is then appointed by the court to carry out the liquidation process.

REVIEW QUESTIONS

1. What is the procedure that a corporation must follow to amend its articles of incorporation?

2. What is the difference between a merger and a consolidation?

3. Under what circumstances is shareholder approval of a merger not required?
4. Why might a corporation purchase the assets of another corporation rather than combine with the other corporation through a merger or a consolidation?
5. Why might a corporation purchase the shares of another corporation rather than combine with the other corporation through a merger or consolidation?
6. What is a shareholder's appraisal right?
7. Describe all of the ways in which corporate dissolution may occur.

CASE PROBLEMS

1. Burhyte, Murphy, and Brandano each own one-third of the shares of BMB, Inc. (BMB). The articles of incorporation of BMB state that its purpose is to engage in the business of catering private parties in people's homes. Burhyte and Murphy want to have the corporation open up a restaurant. They have been advised by a lawyer, however, that this would be *ultra vires* (outside the power of) the corporation unless the purpose clause of the articles is amended. Brandano opposes the idea of having the corporation open a restaurant. Will Burhyte and Murphy be able to amend BMB's articles of incorporation without Brandano's cooperation? Explain.

2. Altes operated a quarry on property that he owned. He granted to OMR, Inc. (OMR) the right to run a pipeline across the property. After OMR had installed the pipeline, one of Altes' quarry workers punctured it. Subsequent to the damage to the pipeline, OMR was merged with Sun Pipe Line Company (Sun), and Sun was the surviving corporation. When Sun sued Altes to recover for the damage to the pipeline, Altes argued that the claim for damages belonged to OMR not to Sun and thus Sun did not have standing to sue. Who will win the case? Explain.

3. Rath Packing, Inc. (Rath) entered into an agreement to purchase all of the assets of Needham Corporation (Needham). Under the terms of the agreement, Rath was to pay for the assets with shares of Rath stock. According to the applicable state corporation law, a merger requires the affirmative vote of two-thirds of the shares of a corporation, while amendments to the articles of incorporation require only the affirmative vote of a majority of the shares of the corporation. Rath's shareholders were asked to vote on several amendments to the articles, including a change of the corporation's name to Rath-Needham Corporation and a change in the corporation's capital structure, but they were not asked to vote on a merger. The amendments were approved by 60 percent of the corporation's outstanding shares and by 77 percent of those shares that were voted. Howard, a shareholder of Rath, has brought a legal action against Rath to prevent what he argues is a merger between Rath and Needham that had not been approved by Rath's shareholders. Who will win the case? Explain.

4. Wyndham Gabhart, his father, his two brothers, and Jerome Walker formed Washington Nursing Center, Inc. (Nursing) to operate a nursing home. Each of the five men received 100 of the 500 outstanding shares and each was elected to fill one of the five positions on the board of directors. About a year ago, Wyndham resigned from the board of directors because travel related to his primary employment made it difficult for him to attend directors' meetings. The five corporate participants then negotiated concerning the sale and purchase of Wyndham's shares, but the negotiations were not successful. The four other shareholders then formed a new corporation, Washington Health Services, Inc. (Health), in which they held all the stock. After approval by the directors and shareholders of both Nursing and Health, Nursing was merged into Health following the procedures required by corporation law. Each Nursing shareholder received a bond from Health in place of his shares in Nursing. Wyndham brought a legal ac-

tion against the other four men on the grounds of breach of fiduciary duty because the only purpose of the merger was to deprive him of his interest in Nursing. If Wyndham can prove his allegations, who will win this case? Explain.

5. Radom & Neidorff, Inc., has for many years and with great success conducted the business of printing musical compositions. For thirty years after its incorporation, Henry Neidorff and David Radom each owned half of the corporation's shares and operated the business together. Last year, Neidorff died and left his shares to his wife, Anna Neidorff, who is Radom's sister. Although they are brother and sister, Anna and David were unfriendly before Neidorff's death and their hostility has continued.

   Radom brought a legal action to obtain a court decree of liquidation and dissolution of the corporation. The evidence shows that there were no directors elected at this year's annual shareholders' meeting; that the corporation is solvent; that David has offered to buy Anna's shares, but she has rejected the offer; that Anna has not interfered with David's conduct of the business since her husband's death; that Anna has refused to sign David's salary checks because she has brought a derivative suit claiming that David is enriching himself at the corporation's expense; and that since Neidorff's death, the business has operated very successfully. Should the court grant the decree of liquidation and dissolution? Explain. If the court does not grant the decree, what would you advise David to do?

6. Victor Gidwitz and his brother Joseph each own half of the shares of Lanzit Corrugated Box, Inc. Victor controls two of the corporation's four direc-

tors and Joseph controls the other two. Joseph, however, is the president of the corporation and has broad management authority under the bylaws. Victor is the secretary-treasurer, an office that carries virtually no management authority at all.

   Victor has brought a legal action seeking a court decree of liquidation that will result in the dissolution of the corporation. He argues that Joseph is engaging in oppressive conduct. His evidence, which is uncontradicted, shows that no annual meeting of shareholders has been held for ten years; that Victor proposed increasing the number of directors from four to five at a special shareholders' meeting, but Joseph ruled the proposal out of order; that at the few directors' meetings that have been held during the past ten years, Joseph has presented no matters of business policy for action, discussion, or approval; and that Joseph, contrary to the bylaws, has failed to make reports to the shareholders or directors. Should the court grant the decree of liquidation and dissolution? Explain.

7. Leroy Corporation (Leroy) purchased all of the assets of NLM, Inc. (NLM). Leroy paid for the assets with Leroy shares. Although the assets had a value of only $165,000, the shares paid to NLM for them were worth $700,000. NLM then voluntarily dissolved and in liquidation distributed the Leroy shares to its shareholders. At the time of dissolution, Leroy failed to pay a creditor named Lamb a $15,000 debt that it owed. Against whom and on what bases may Lamb seek payment of the debt? Explain.

PART IX

PROPERTY LAW

42

PERSONAL PROPERTY

THE CONCEPT OF PROPERTY

In common usage, the word *property* usually refers to some tangible item such as a chair, a ring, or a parcel of land. From a legal perspective, however, property is not the item itself but the grouping or "bundle" of rights that attach to the item. This bundle of rights includes the rights to use the item to exclude others from it, and to dispose of it.

The famous English writer Blackstone referred to property as "an absolute right." William Pitt declared that not even the king could cross the poorest man's threshold without an invitation. The language of these writers is reassuring to those of us who are property owners, but it fails to capture reality either then or now. The rights to use, to exclude others from, and to dispose of property have always been qualified. For example, owners cannot use their land in a way that unreasonably interferes with the reasonable use of neighboring land. Nor can an urban homeowner exclude firemen from entering his or her land to put out a house fire. Property rights, like all other rights, have limitations.

The distinction between property as a tangible item and property as a group of legal rights is important for several reasons. For instance, property rights are recognized in things other than tangible items. Intangible property in the form of investment securities (e.g., corporate stock), security interests (e.g., mortgages), municipal bonds, writers' copyrights, and inventors' patents comprise a significant share of our wealth and are things that give rise to property rights. They can be used to the exclusion of others and can be disposed of when desired.

Furthermore, though tangible items such as the chair, the ring, and the land may not have changed physically since Blackstone's pronouncement, legal rights in these items have changed. The ring cannot be sold by a merchant unless he or she charges a federal excise tax. The excise tax is a hindrance to or limitation on the merchant's right to dispose of the ring. Similarly, the twentieth-century owner of land cannot build a house on it until public officials are satisfied that the house is permitted under the zoning code and that the water supply, sewers, and utility hookups are all adequate. Each of these requirements is an encumbrance on the owner's unfettered use of the land.

The bundle of property rights may be enhanced or diminished over time by government, depending on current perceptions of social needs. A landowner's property rights are diminished, for example, when the legislature prohibits him or her from discriminating racially when selling a house. Society, or at least the legislature, has decided that the civil right of racial equality in housing is more important than the right of being able to sell property to whomever you wish. In other words, property, or the bundle of property rights, is a dynamic, continually changing concept.

Personal Property and Real Property

Property is divided into two basic categories—real property and personal property. **Real property** (realty) is land and those things permanently affixed to the land. **Personal property** (personalty) encompasses all other forms of property. Real property tends to be immobile, whereas personal property tends to be mobile. Moreover, objects can be personalty at one time and realty at another. For example, the cement blocks in the inventory of a lumber yard are personalty. When the same blocks become part of a house, they become realty. Fifty years later, when the blocks are carted away by a wrecking crew that has demolished the old house, they are again personalty.

The legal rules that are applied to personalty and to realty vary. For example, transactions involving the disposal of real property must generally be in writing, whereas there may not be such legal requirements for similar dealings with personal property. In addition, taxes are often imposed on one type of property but not on the other, and the rules for inheriting when the owner dies also depend upon the type of property. One can debate whether the differences in the rules for personal property and real property are necessary, but that they exist and must be contended with is a fact of life.

This chapter will discuss some of the methods of acquiring ownership of personal property. Most often, ownership of personalty is obtained through a purchase. In some instances, acquisition results from possession, as when property is found or is received as a gift. A person can sometimes increase the value of existing personal property through the concept of "adding to" or *accession.* Ownership of the intermingled property of several owners—grain in a silo, for example—may become ownership in common through the concept of *confusion.* Also, situations may arise in which an owner surrenders possession without relinquishing ownership. This area of the law is called *bailments.* Finally, under the concept of *fixtures,* personal property may legally become real property when it is attached to real property. Each of these legal concepts will be discussed in this chapter.

POSSESSION

One of the primary factors considered in determining the relative rights of competing parties to personal property is possession. **Possession** has two essential requirements: (1) the possessor must have physical control over the property and (2) the possessor must intend to control the property to the exclusion of others. For example, a young boy is not in possession of the popular video game in a store window regardless of how much he yearns to have it because he lacks the requisite physical control. Similarly, the college student is not in possession of a notebook that has fallen, accidentally and unbeknownst to her, from the bookstore shelf into her shoulder bag because she has no intent to control or possess the notebook.

Due to the size, weight, or nature of some personal property, actual possession in the traditional sense of having physical control of it is not practical. For instance, a large safe cannot be held or carried. In such situations, the courts will look to see if there is some type of *constructive possession.* A person may have constructive possession of the safe when it is located on his or her real property. The sole person with the combination to the safe may have constructive possession of the safe, however. There is no difference in legal effect between a person who has constructive possession and one who has actual possession.

In earlier times, obtaining possession was the primary method of acquiring ownership to personal property. In some areas of the law, such as that dealing with the ownership of wild animals, possession continues to be the primary factor considered in determining ownership. For example, a trout swimming free in a stream is owned by no one. Somewhere between hooking the trout and placing it in his or her creel, actual control, and with it ownership via possession of the trout, is obtained by the fisherman. Should the trout slip from the creel back into the water and swim away, possession, and with it ownership, is lost.

Found Property

An old grammar school adage says "finders keepers, losers weepers." As with many old sayings, there is a grain of truth in this one. Finders are sometimes keepers. However, losers are rarely weepers, legally speaking. The courts, for sound reasons, have made the matter of determining the rights to found property a great deal more complicated than the old saying implies.

To qualify as a finder, a person must take possession of the property found; that is, he or she must obtain physical control of the property with the intent to possess it. In contrast to situations involving unowned wild animals, found property is usually property that is owned by someone other than the finder. Traditionally, the law has not allowed a finder to keep found property if the owner has shown up and claimed it. In other words, the original owner's rights to found goods are generally superior to those of a finder. There is no need, then, for the loser to weep.

If the original owner does not come forward and claim the found property, the finder may still become involved in a conflict with the owner of the place where the property was found over who may keep it. The place where property is found is sometimes called the *locus*. Generally, the courts resolve conflicts between the finder and the owner of the locus by categorizing the property as either lost property or mislaid property.

Lost property is property with which the owner has involuntarily or unconsciously parted possession. For example, a $20 bill found on a sidewalk would be categorized as lost property. Given the value of the bill and the place where it was found, the owner would be assumed to have parted with possession of the bill involuntarily. If property is categorized as lost, the finder is entitled to keep it unless the original owner returns to claim it.

If the same $20 bill were found neatly placed between the mattress and the box spring of a bed, it would be difficult to believe that the owner parted with the bill involuntarily. In this situation, the bill would be categorized as mislaid property. **Mislaid property** is property that has been intentionally placed somewhere and then unintentionally left or forgotten. Possession of mislaid property does not go to the finder; rather, it generally goes to the owner of the place where the property was found. In other words, the owner of the locus has better rights to mislaid property than anyone except the original owner. Legally, the owner of the locus becomes the indefinite, gratuitous bailee for the original owner. A *gratuitous bailee* is a person who holds property solely for the benefit of another, called the *bailor,* who in this case would be the actual owner of the property.

Traditionally, legal disputes between the finder and the owner of the locus have involved only *possessory* rights, that is, which of them may keep possession of the property. This has been the case because the law has given neither the finder nor the owner of the locus *ownership* rights in found property that are superior to those of the original owner. Therefore, the finder or the owner of the locus has had to hold the property indefinitely and has not been allowed to use it as his or her own because of the possibility that the original owner might show up and claim the property. Some states have changed the traditional rules by adopting statutes, called *estray statutes,* that provide a procedure by which the finder or the owner of the locus can obtain ownership rights superior to those of the original owner.

The reason for differentiating between lost property and mislaid property is a practical one. Since the original owner has parted with the possession of mislaid property voluntarily, there is a significant likelihood that he or she will return to the place where the property was mislaid to claim it. Reuniting the owner and mislaid property is facilitated by placing the property in the hands of the owner of the locus. Conversely, when property has been parted with involuntarily, the chance that the owner will return to the place where the property was lost is less probable. Admittedly, there is some chance of return, and recovery would be facilitated by having the property remain with the owner of the locus. However, the finder is given superior rights to lost property, perhaps because finders are sentimental favorites with the courts or, more likely, because the courts want to encourage the finding of lost property.

There is a third category of found property. In some situations, an owner may simply throw property away, that is, abandon it. **Abandoned property,** then, is property in which the owner has intentionally surrendered his or her interests. Since prior ownership has been intentionally relinquished, the finder of property that is determined to be abandoned obtains actual ownership by taking possession of the property.

The following case illustrates the common law rules just discussed. The state involved, Illinois, has an estray statute that attempts to circumvent the common law problem of having the finder or owner of the locus continue indefinitely as a holder of property for another. The statute frees the parties from this legal limbo by providing a procedure for obtaining ownership rights superior to those of the original owner.

PASET v. OLD ORCHARD BANK & TRUST COMPANY
378 N.E.2d 1264 (Ill. 1978)

SIMON, Justice

On May 8, 1974, the plaintiff, Bernice Paset, a safety [deposit] box subscriber at the defendant Old Orchard Bank (the bank), found $6,325 in currency on the seat of a chair in an examination booth in the safety deposit vault. The chair was partially under a table. The plaintiff notified officers of the bank and turned the money over to them. She then was told by bank officials that the bank would try to locate the owner, and that she could have the money if the owner was not located within 1 year.

The bank wrote to everyone who had been in the safety deposit vault area either on the day of, or on the day preceding, the discovery, stating that some property had been found and inviting the customers to describe any property they might have lost. No one reported the loss of currency, and the money remained unclaimed a year after it had been found. However, when the plaintiff requested the money, the bank refused to deliver it to her, explaining that it was obligated to hold the currency for the owner.

The safety deposit vault area of the bank was located on a lower floor of the bank. This area was separated from a lobby by a gate, and, according to an affidavit filed by the bank, entrance to the safety deposit vault area was restricted to bank employees and customers maintaining safety deposit boxes in the vault. The affidavit stated that no customer could enter

this vault without the consent of a bank guard or employee stationed at the gate, and that customers were allowed to enter only after their signatures were verified. When a customer entered, a bank employee would accompany the customer to the safety deposit vault to obtain the box and then escort him to one of the 16 examination booths maintained in the area.

The plaintiff sought a declaratory judgment that the Illinois estray statute was applicable to her discovery and granted her ownership of the $6,325. The [trial] court judge, however, found that the money was "deemed mislaid," and concluded that despite the plaintiff's compliance with the requirements of the estray statute, that statute was not applicable.

The bank's position is that the estray statute is not applicable because the money was not lost in the sense the word "lost" is used in that statute. The bank contends that the money was mislaid by its owner rather than lost, and that the estray statute does not apply to mislaid property. In the alternative, the bank argues that the money was discovered not in a public place, but in a private area with access restricted to safety deposit box subscribers. The bank claims, therefore, that the money always was in its constructive possession or custody, either as owner of the premises or as bailee for an unknown and unidentified safety deposit box subscriber, and that property in someone's constructive possession or custody cannot be lost. As against the plaintiff, the bank claims to have the superior right to hold the money indefinitely, and in fact is required to do so until the true owner puts in his appearance.

This appeal, then, requires a determination of whether a finder of cash in an examining booth in a safety deposit vault may be a keeper under the Illinois estray statute and an analysis of the extent to which the common law concepts of lost and mislaid property apply to the statute.

The Illinois estray statute's principal purposes are to encourage and facilitate the return of property to the true owner, and then to reward a finder for his honesty if the property remains unclaimed. The statute provides an incentive for finders to report their discoveries by making it possible for them, after the passage of the requisite time, to acquire legal title to the property they have found. By directing the county clerk to publicize and advertise the property, the statute further enhances the opportunity of the owner to recover what he has lost.

Traditionally, the common law has treated lost and mislaid property differently for the purposes of determining ownership of property someone has found. Mislaid property is that which is intentionally put in a certain place and later forgotten; a finder acquires no rights to mislaid property. The element of intentional deposit present in the case of mislaid property is absent in the case of lost property, for property is deemed lost when it is unintentionally separated from the dominion of its owner. We are not concerned in this case with abandoned property where the owner, intending to relinquish all rights to his property, leaves it free to be appropriated by any other person. Although the finder is entitled to keep abandoned property, the plaintiff has not taken the position that the money was abandoned.

Our conclusion is that the estray statute should be applied, and ownership of the money vested in the plaintiff finders. Thus, we do not accept the bank's initial argument that the money was mislaid rather than lost. It is complete speculation to infer, as the bank argues, that the money was deliberately placed by its owner on the chair located partially under a table in the examining booth, and then forgotten. If the money was intentionally placed on the chair by someone who forgot where he left it, the bank's notice to safety deposit box subscribers should have alerted the owner. The failure of an owner to appear to claim the money in the interval since its discovery is affirmative evidence that the property was not mislaid.

Because the evidence, though ambiguous, tends to indicate that the money probably was not mislaid, and because neither party contends that the money was abandoned, we conclude that the ambiguity should, as a matter of public policy, be resolved in favor of the presumption that the money was lost. This conclusion is in harmony with the above mentioned purposes of the estray statute, for it construes the statute liberally rather than technically, with the result that the statute is brought into play rather than rejected. Such an application of the statute better effectuates the legislature's goal of restoring property to a true owner; it provides incentive for a finder to report his discovery by rewarding him if the true owner does not appear within the statutorily-determined time limit. Accordingly, we reject the bank's first contention that the money was mislaid and the estray statute irrelevant, and conclude that the money was "lost," and so encompassed by the Illinois estray statute.

We also reject the bank's alternative argument that the money, having been found in a place from which the general public was excluded, was always in the bank's constructive custody or possession, and therefore could not have been "lost," as that word is used in the estray statute. In Illinois the relationship of a safety deposit company to the box owner is that of bailor and bailee. As bailee a company has possession of a box and its contents even though the company has no knowledge of the character or quantity of the box's contents. This relationship applies, however, only to a box and to any property in the box; it does not apply to property which never was deposited in a box. In this case, it is impossible for any court to determine how the money was brought into the safety deposit vault area, whether the money was ever placed in a safety deposit box, who carried the money into the vault area, or who was the money's owner. Consequently, any rights or duties the bank had with respect to the money would have to be based on the untenable fiction that the bank had constructive possession or custody of all property in its vault premises, no matter how that property arrived there.

Further, whether the property was discovered in a public or private place should not be permitted to preclude the application of the estray statute. The statute itself makes no distinction between "public" and "private" places of finding.

Accordingly, the judgment of the [trial] court is reversed and the case is remanded with directions to enter judgment in favor of the plaintiff finder.

CASE REVIEW QUESTIONS

1. After the decision in this case, what happens if the original owner of the $6,325 shows up, declaring that the money was placed on the chair while he or she was examining other contents of a safety deposit box and that he or she simply forgot to put it back in the box?
2. If the question of the type of property had been sent to a jury and the jury had determined it to be mislaid, who would have won the case? Explain.
3. If there had not been an estray statute in Illinois, to whom would the $6,325 have belonged?

Inter Vivos Gifts

There are occasions when an owner of personal property voluntarily transfers possession of the property without receiving compensation and without intending to reclaim the property. Giving a gift is an example of such a transfer.

For a **gift inter vivos,** meaning a gift "among the living," to take effect, three essential conditions must be met:

1. The donor must deliver the personal property to another person and thereby place it beyond the donor's control.
2. The donor must have a donative intent.
3. The donee must accept the property as a gift.

To make delivery, the donor must surrender physical control over the property. Surrendering control should be a familiar concept to you by this time. It requires that the donor give up possession of the property to another. However, the donee need not be the one who takes possession of the gift. Delivery may occur if the donor relinquishes control to a third person, not the donee, so long as that person is not likely to return the property to the donor upon request. For example, if Ellen gives her diamond bracelet to her husband, Marco, to deliver to their daughter, Janice, when she comes home from college, a delivery would take place only if Marco would not return the bracelet to Ellen upon her request, which is unlikely.

If Ellen delivers the bracelet to her friend and attorney, Alice, a more difficult question is raised. As an attorney, Alice should realize that the delivery is only effective if she would not return the bracelet to Ellen upon her request. On the other hand, Alice may value Ellen's friendship so much that she would return the bracelet if asked to. Thus, whether this delivery put the bracelet beyond Ellen's control raises a question of fact that must be decided at trial.

Delivery may sometimes occur without the donor physically relinquishing possession of the property. For instance, a husband may want to make a gift to his wife of his piano that is sitting in the family living room. A typical delivery involving surrender of possession is not practical under these circumstances. Therefore, in this type of situation, the law will recognize a symbolic delivery or a constructive delivery. The husband can make a *symbolic delivery* by announcing the gift and giving his wife the original bill of sale for the piano at a family ceremony. A constructive delivery occurs when the means of attaining possession of the property, rather than the property itself, is transferred from the donor to the donee. For example, the husband may deliver the key to the piano cover to his wife, thereby providing her with access to the keyboard.

The second requirement to effectuate a gift is that the donor must have a donative intent; that is, he or she must have the present intent to give a gift. Frequently, donative intent is made clear by the words used by the donor at the time the gift is given. Where clear words are not used, the existence of a donative intent will be determined by examining the surrounding facts. Some relevant considerations are the words that were spoken or deeds that were performed at the time the gift was given, the relationship between the parties, and the conduct of the donor toward the property afterward. For example, suppose Fred delivers his lawn mower to his friend and neighbor, Alex, and simply says, "Here, use it in good health." Some doubt may exist as to whether a gift or merely the temporary loan of the mower was intended. If, however, Fred goes out that afternoon and buys a new mower and if he tells another neighbor that he got rid of the old one, these facts, along with his friendship with Alex, would indicate that Fred had a donative intent when he delivered the lawn mower to Alex.

The third element needed to effectuate a gift inter vivos is acceptance by the donee. Generally, acceptance of a gift is presumed by the court. A donee does, however, have the right to refuse a gift. For instance, Alex may not want Fred's lawn mower. He may reject the gift by returning the mower to Fred and disclaiming any rights to it. To avoid the situation of having a gift forced upon a donee, acceptance, though presumed, is required.

The following case raises the issue of the existence of an inter vivos gift. Two additional issues—estoppel and tenancy by the entireties—are discussed by the court. An *estoppel* arises when a party is legally prohibited from alleging certain facts in court because of prior action or inaction by the party that misled a second party to the second party's detriment. A *tenancy by the entireties* is a form of joint ownership of property between a husband and wife in which the property becomes wholly owned by the survivor at the death of one of the spouses. Generally, when the property involved is real property, a tenancy by the entireties is indestructible, unless its destruction is agreed to by both parties. Estoppel and tenancy by the entireties are discussed in more detail in other sections of the text.

McENTIRE v. ESTATE OF J.L. McENTIRE
590 S.W.2d 241 (Ark. 1979)

TURNER, Special Chief Justice

Prior to December 18th, 1975, J.L. McEntire maintained a checking account in Pine Bluff National Bank in his individual name with sole authority in the owner to withdraw funds from the account. On December 18, 1975, a new signature card for the account was executed by McEntire and his wife, Vera E. McEntire, permitting either to withdraw funds from the account but retaining the acount in the sole name of J.L. McEntire. Thereafter, both Mr. and Mrs. McEntire did, on occasion, withdraw funds from the account on their individual signature. On January 6, 1977, J.L. McEntire caused a new signature card to be issued in his sole name withdrawing the authority of Mrs. McEntire to draw funds from the account.

Both signature cards contained the following identical language:

> You are authorized to recognize either of the signatures subscribed below in the payment of funds or the transaction of any business for this account. . . . The below-signed, joint depositors, hereby agree each with the other and with you that all sums now on deposit or herebefore or hereafter deposited by either or both of said joint depositors with you to their credit as such joint depositors with all accumulations thereon are and shall be owned by them jointly, with right of survivorship, and be subject to the check or receipt of either of them or the survivor of them. . . .

> Your rights or authority under this agreement shall not be changed or terminated by us or either of us except by written notice to you which shall not affect transactions therebefore made.

J.L. McEntire died subsequent to January 6, 1977. Vera McEntire brought this action against the Estate of her deceased husband and Pine Bluff National Bank to recover the funds on deposit in the account. Thereafter, both parties moved for summary judgment which was granted in favor of the estate and the Bank. From that Judgment, this appeal is taken.

Appellant urges that she is entitled to Summary Judgment because a tenancy by the entireties was created in the bank account on December 18, 1975, which could not be destroyed by the unilateral act of J.L. McEntire in removing the cotenant's name from the account. Appellant further urges that the Bank is estopped to deny appellant's absolute right to the balance in the account because checks executed by appellant and drawn on the account were honored by the bank subsequent to January 6, 1977.

The Complaint alleges (1) that a gift was made; (2) estoppel by the Bank; and (3) the creation of a tenancy by the entireties in the account.

In order to establish a completed inter vivos gift, there must be clear and convincing evidence that there was an actual delivery of the subject matter of the gift with a clear intent to make an immediate, present and final gift beyond recall, accompanied with an unconditional release of all future dominion and control by the donor over the property delivered.

The affidavits of Vera McEntire and Aileen Ezell filed by appellant in support of her Motion for Summary Judgment clearly establish an intent other than to make an immediate, present and final gift beyond recall. To the contrary, Mrs. McEntire stated that "it (the account) was created in order that both of us could write checks on the account for whatever we needed, and my husband informed me that the balance would be to me upon his death." The affidavit of Ms. Ezell asserts that it was her understanding that the involved checking account was to be the property of Mrs. McEntire upon the death of Mr. McEntire.

The affidavits produced by appellant leave no issue of fact relating to inter vivos gift and the establishment of the account did not constitute a gift, as a matter of law.

The assertion that Pine Bluff National Bank is estopped by its conduct in honoring checks drawn against the account after January 6, 1977, is without merit. The uncontroverted facts in the record before us are that at the time the bank honored the checks, the authority of Mrs. McEntire to draw funds from the account had already been terminated.

Equitable estoppel is available only to one who has in good faith relied upon the conduct of another and has been led thereby to a change of position for the worse, acted to his injury, or gave up or abandoned a legal right upon the representations or conduct constituting the estoppel.

Applying the facts of this case to the estoppel rule, it is immediately apparent that the appellant neither alleged or in fact changed her legal position or status because the checks were honored; she has not acted to her injury; and lastly, she gave up no legal right as a result thereof. . . .

The remaining question relates to the estate created between this husband and wife upon execution of the account signature card on December 18, 1975. The account, as it existed subsequent to December 18, 1975, and prior to January 6, 1977, was a tenancy by the entireties. Having previously disposed of the inter vivos gift and the estoppel arguments, this leaves only the question of the rights of the parties under a tenancy by the entireties in a bank account—those rights being the subject of established law.

An estate by the entireties in a bank account differs in one significant aspect from such an estate in real property in that the estate exists in the account only until one of the tenants withdraws such funds or dies leaving a balance in the account. Funds withdrawn or otherwise diverted from the account by one of the tenants and reduced to that tenant's separate possession ceases to be a part of the estate by the entireties. This does not mean that in a proper case under timely allegations of fraud or other such remedy, that one of the cotenants could not sustain an action to recover all or a part of the funds diverted or withdrawn by the other. No such allegation or proof exists in this case.

The decree of the Chancellor is in all things affirmed.

CASE REVIEW QUESTIONS

1. What prevents the money placed in the joint account by Mr. McEntire from being a gift inter vivos when he apparently stated that he wanted the balance to go to Mrs. McEntire at his death?
2. If Mr. McEntire put all of the money into the joint account, what, legally speaking, is the status of the money withdrawn by Mrs. McEntire prior to Mr. McEntire's death and used for her own benefit?

Accession

A person may augment the value of personal property, which is called **accession,** with either labor or materials. When the person adding the value to the property does so without the consent of the owner, a problem may arise as to who is entitled to the augmented property.

For instance, suppose that Juan comes into possession of a written outline for a short story. Following the outline, Juan completes the story and sells it to a publisher for $100,000. Deborah, who wrote the outline, realizes that it has been used when she reads the short story. She then demands that Juan hand over the $100,000.

A critical question in resolving this dispute is how Juan came into possession of the outline. If he obtained the outline while burglarizing Deborah's house, the law will probably favor Deborah. The general rule is that when the improver of the property gets possession of it wrongfully or in bad faith, the owner is entitled to the property and to the value added.

On the other hand, if Juan found the outline on a crumpled piece of paper in a pasture and erroneously assumed that it had been thrown away, the result may be different. Although the improvement to the outline was done without the owner's permission, it was done in the good-faith belief that the property had been abandoned. When the improver acts in good faith, the right to the personalty will depend upon the extent of the value added by the improver. If the improvement is a significant part of the value of the property, the courts will favor the improver. If the improvement is not significant, the owner will retain the property. In either case, the person who gets the personal property must reimburse the other party for the value of the other's interest. If the value of the short story is predominantly due to Juan's work, he will be able to retain the rights to the story, but he must reimburse Deborah for the value of the outline. Conversely, if the value of the short story is predominantly due to the thoroughness of Deborah's outline, she will obtain the right to the short story and the $100,000, minus the value added by Juan.

Confusion

A farmer may store his corn crop in a silo at the cooperative to which he belongs. When his corn is mixed with corn of a similar grade belonging to fellow members of the cooperative, the commingling is called **confusion**. The farmer can never recover the exact kernels of corn he stored in the silo because they are indistinguishable from those of the other farmers. He is still the owner of the corn, though, as a tenant in common with the other farmers who have stored corn in that silo. If one-third of the corn in the silo is our farmer's, he has an undivided one-third interest in the contents of the silo. He can remove his share of the corn at any time, thereby severing his interests in the common ownership of the contents of the silo.

The problem with commingled goods arises when there is a loss of part or all of the property. If the loss is not due to the wrongdoing of one of the owners of the commingled goods, any loss is apportioned according to each person's share of the goods. If the loss is caused by the wrongdoing of one of the owners, however, that person must bear the entire loss, up to the point that his or her share is exhausted. If our farmer carelessly fails to lock the access way to the silo and someone steals 50 percent of the corn, he must absorb the loss of his entire one-third interest in the corn. The remainder of the loss (17 percent) is borne proportionately by the other owners of the corn in the silo.

BAILMENTS

There are times when a person in possession of personal property surrenders possession with the intent of reclaiming the property at a later time. This type of arrangement is called a bailment. A **bailment** occurs when a person in rightful possession of personal property (the **bailor**) delivers possession of that property to another (the **bailee**) with the expectation that the bailee is under a duty to return the goods to the bailor. For example, your delivery of soiled clothes to a dry cleaner creates a bailment situation.

The law sometimes imposes a bailment even though there is no agreement or contract between the parties. For example, in the preceding section, you learned about lost and mislaid property. Unless there is an estray statute, such property is considered a bailment when it is in the hands of the finder or the owner of the place where the property was found. The law implies an agreement of bailment in order to protect the interest of the original owner. As you can see, then, the law sometimes imposes a bailment upon parties regardless of the bailee's intent.

Most bailments arise from an agreement or contract between the parties involved. Generally, the bailee accepts delivery of possession knowing that he or she has a duty to return the goods to the bailor. The dry cleaner accepts possession of your laundry with the mutual expectation that the laundry will be cleaned and then returned to you. The fact that neither the dry cleaner nor you think in terms of creating a bailment nor expressly discuss the return of the laundry does not defeat the existence of the bailment. Implicit within the transaction is the presumption that the transfer of possession is temporary and that, upon your payment of a fee for the cleaning, the laundry will be returned to you.

For a bailment to exist, the bailor must surrender possession of the bailed property and the bailee must accept it. Possession, as you read earlier, means acquiring of physical control over property with the intent to control it. When a woman hands her coat to a companion to hold while she tries on a dress in a store, there is no *intent* to give up the right to physical control of the coat. The coat is merely in the custody of the companion and, therefore, a bailment is not created.

The following case illustrates the impact of the method of operating a parking lot on the creation or the failure to create a bailment.

ALLRIGHT AUTO PARKS, INC. v. MOORE
560 S.W.2d 129 (Texas, 1977)

[The plaintiff, Richard Moore, brought a legal action against Allright Auto Parks, Inc., to collect $2,600 for the value of his automobile, which was stolen from a parking lot operated by Allright. The parking lot was located at the San Antonio International Airport. The trial court gave a judgment in favor of the plaintiff for the amount requested.]

MURRAY, [Judge]

On February 28, 1974, plaintiff drove a 1972 Ford LTD convertible to a short term parking lot at the San Antonio Municipal Airport. Upon entering the lot, plaintiff received a ticket from a machine that controls the entrance gate and which causes the gate arm to raise and close automatically. Mr. Moore chose his own parking place and parked the car, locked it, and took the keys with him when he departed on a flight to Cleveland, Ohio. The machine receipt ticket was left in the automobile above the sunvisor. The short term lot is enclosed by a fence, with the exception of the entrances and exit. Upon exiting the lot, the driver presents the ticket he received from the entrance gate to the cashier for the purpose of calculating the fee owed for the particular length of time parked. The parties agreed that the car was stolen by an unknown third party sometime between February 28, 1974 through March 5, 1974.

In order to constitute a bailment transaction there must be a contract, express or implied, delivery of the property to the bailee, and acceptance of the property by the bailee. An essential element of a bailment is delivery of the property by the bailor to the bailee, and without such delivery there can be no bailment.

The very essence of a contract of bailment is that after its purpose has been fulfilled the bailed property shall be redelivered to the bailor.

The creation of a bailment requires that possession and control over an object pass from the bailor to the bailee. We hold that a relationship of bailment has not been established, and control over the automobile did not pass from the bailor to the bailee.

In a similar case, involving a theft of an automobile from a parking lot at O'Hare Airport in Chicago, in holding that there was no bailment, the Court stated:

> While it is true . . . defendant could have restrained Wall from exiting the lot without paying the parking charges, this in no way related to any possession or control which defendant may have exercised over the automobile, but merely relates to the power of defendant to enforce its lien for the parking charges. While there need not be a delivery of the property in the technical sense, there must be an actual change of possession of the property from the bailor to the bailee.

In the present case the facts indicate that control did not pass from Mr. Moore to Allright Auto Parks, Inc. Mr. Moore chose his own parking space; locked the car; took the keys with him; and obtained a ticket from an automatic machine, issued not for the purpose of identifying the automobile, but rather for determining time in computing the fee.

The judgment of the trial court is reversed and judgment is rendered for appellant.

CASE REVIEW QUESTIONS
1. Would the result of the case have been different if Mr. Moore had driven his car only up to the entrance to the parking lot and an attendant had driven the car to the parking space and had kept the keys until Mr. Moore returned? Explain.
2. In terms of the concept of possession, why was there no bailment in the Allright case?

Duties of the Bailee
When a bailment is created, the bailee assumes two basic legal responsibilities or duties:

1. To take appropriate care of the property while it is in his or her possession.
2. To return the goods to the bailor at the end of the bailment.

Bailee's Duty of Care The standard of care the bailee must exercise may vary in different situations. For example, in a gratuitous bailment, the bailee can be held liable only for gross negligence. A *gratuitous bailment* is one that is entered solely for the benefit of the bailor. For instance, a homeowner who is planning a vacation may ask a neighbor, as a favor, to pick up any mail or newspapers delivered while he or she is away. The neighbor becomes a gratuitous bailee and is only liable for loss or damage to the items delivered if he or she acted recklessly — that is, with gross negligence — in handling those items.

If the bailment is for the mutual benefit of both the bailor and bailee, the bailee must exercise reasonable care while he or she has possession of the property. The dry cleaner cleans your clothes for an agreed upon fee. Since this is a bailment for the mutual benefit of the parties, the dry cleaner must use reasonable care in handling your clothes.

If the bailment is solely for the benefit of the bailee, the bailee is liable for even slight negligence. The neighbor who borrows a snowblower to clean her walks and driveway, for instance, is liable for any negligently caused damage to the snowblower while it is in her possession.

Generally, a bailment is the product of a contract, and the parties involved are free to determine the terms of their agreement. They may decide to vary the standard of care normally required of the bailee. As a rule, courts do not favor a lessening of the standard of care unless the reduction was clearly part of the parties' agreement. For example, the dry cleaner's sign denying responsibility for clothing left beyond 30 days is not likely to be enforceable, unless the sign is called to the customer's attention. Even then, the limitation is not likely to be enforced unless the court determines that the requirement for the clothes to be picked up within 30 days was an expressed part of the bargain.

Bailee's Duty to Return the Property The second duty of the bailee is to redeliver the property to the bailor upon request or at the agreed upon time. The property must be redelivered in the same undamaged condition it was in when it was received. The bailee will be liable for any damage, except when the damage occurred in spite of the bailee's use of the proper standard of care as discussed above.

Duties of the Bailor

Depending on the type of bailment agreed to by the parties, the bailor may have certain legal responsibilities to the bailee. The two duties that most often arise are

1. To compensate the bailee.
2. To notify the bailee of any defects in the bailed property.

Bailor's Duty to Compensate If the bailment is for the mutual benefit of the parties involved, the bailor must pay the bailee for the services provided. For example, the service department at a car dealership is entitled to be paid for repair work it did prior to redelivering a car. The amount of compensation is normally set by the agreement between the parties. Failure to specify an amount entitles the bailee to reasonable value for the services performed. If the bailment is for the sole benefit of either party, however, no compensation is involved.

Bailor's Duty to Notify of Defects When an owner lends her lawn mower to a neighbor to cut the grass, she is generally considered to implicitly warrant that the mower is fit for that purpose. If a bailment is solely for the benefit of the bailee, a defect making the property unfit must be known to the bailor in order for the warranty obligation to attach. In other instances, the bailor must use reasonable care to learn of any defects in the property and to report them to the bailee.

The following case discusses the duty of the bailee to return the property to the bailor.

SPENCER v. GLOVER
412 N.E.2d 870 (Ind. 1980)

NEAL, Judge

On June 6, 1978, Glover agreed to purchase a truck from Spencers at a price of $5,500. Under the sales agreement Spencers were obligated to install a winch on the vehicle. Glover paid $5,000 and took possession; the balance was to become due upon installation of the winch.

Sometime later Robert Spencer came to Glover and took possession of the truck for the purpose of taking it to Flat Rock, Michigan, to have the winch installed. At that time a conversation took place between Glover and Robert Spencer. Glover's version of the conversation is as follows:

Q. Okay. Was anything said at the time Bob came to pick the wrecker up regarding when it would be fixed and how?

A. Well, he said it would be a week or so and that he would take good care of it and if anything happened to it that he would, you know, stand behind it and take care of it.

Q. Was anything said by Bob about redelivering it in good condition?

A. Yea, he said he would bring it back, just like, you know, just like he got it.

Robert Spencer presented the following version of the conversation:

Q. Did you say anything to Ed then about that if anything happens to it, you would make it good?

A. I can't recall saying anything like that. But I'm sure we had that understanding, you know, about the business we had taken care of before on the truck deal.

Q. Had you operated in that manner before or how would you have this understanding?

A. Well, for one thing, I have known Ed for a while and maybe I wouldn't have to say that with him.

Q. Well, was there any agreement between the two of you made regarding that you would redeliver the wrecker to him in as good condition as you took it from him?

A. Yes, I think there was something said about that if I remember right.

Q. Where did that conversation take place—at Ed's?

A. Yes.

Q. When you picked it up?

A. Yes, that morning.

Q. O.K. That's all.

A. I think I remember telling him not to worry about his truck. Something like that.

Robert Spencer drove the truck to Flat Rock, Michigan, and parked it in a well-lighted area in front of a reputable motel which was adjacent to other businesses. During the night the truck was stolen. Spencer was unable to recall whether he locked the truck, but he did recall that he kept the key in his possession.

When Spencer failed to return his truck, Glover commenced this action. The complaint proceeded with a theory of absolute liability under the contract of bailment. The trial court entered judgment for Glover for the value of the truck.

The parties agree the transaction created a bailment.

It is the law in this state that in an action based upon breach of a bailment contract, a showing that the goods were received by the bailee in good condition and that they were in damaged condition when returned to the bailor, gives rise to an inference that the damage was caused through the fault or neglect of the bailee. Such an occurrence places upon the bailee the burden of producing evidence to show that the damage was caused without fault or neglect on his part.

However, this rule may be altered by contract. Two Indiana cases exist in which the court imposed liability regardless of fault where the bailee had agreed to return the goods in as good a condition as he had received them. The first is *Morrow, Inc. v. Paugh,* a case in which a truck lease contained a provision whereby the lessee agreed to return the truck to the lessor "in as good condition as when received, ordinary wear and tear excepted." The truck was destroyed by collision without fault on the part of the lessee. The court held that the rights and liabilities of the parties were to be determined by the terms of the contract. The court quoted the following proposition:

[W]here one, at the time of making his contract, must have known or could have reasonably anticipated,

and in his contract could have guarded against, the possible happening of the event causing the impossibility of his performance, and nevertheless he makes an unqualified undertaking to perform, he must do so or pay damages for his failure.

The court then, in ruling for the lessor, concluded:

Surely it cannot be asserted it was unreasonable to assume the parties had in mind the performance of this contract such an accident might happen. Therefore, the accident by which [the lessor's] vehicle was destroyed did not relieve [the lessee] of the obligation it assumed by reason of the unequivocal provision of Clause 4 of the contract.

In *Light v. Lend Lease Transportation Co.,* a leased vehicle was stolen while in the possession of the lessee. The lease contained a provision similar to that in *Morrow;* the lessor based his complaint upon the bailment contract, without regard to fault. Following *Morrow,* the court held that where the contract of bailment contained an enlarging provision to restore possession of the vehicle to the lessor, the lessee was not relieved of his obligation although the vehicle was stolen by a third party without fault on the lessee's part.

Spencer attempts to distinguish *Morrow,* and *Light,* on the basis that the bailment contracts were in writing. We disagree. In *Weddington v. Stolkin,* the court quoted with approval:

In order to establish a bailment there must ordinarily be an acceptance of the article bailed, it being necessary to show either an express contract to take the article and later redeliver it, or circumstances from which such a contract can be implied. . . .

The validity of a bailment is governed by the rules of validity of contracts generally. A bailment is a delivery of goods by an owner to another for some purpose, upon a contract, express or implied, that after the purpose has been fulfilled, the goods shall be redelivered to the owner. Subject to statutory regulations, a bailment may be written or oral, and no formal language is required for its creation. The contract may be express or implied.

We are of the opinion that sufficient evidence was presented from which the trial court could find that the parties had entered into a bailment contract which unequivocally obligated Spencers to return the truck in the same condition as they received it. As in *Light,* the possibility of the truck being stolen was reasonably foreseeable. Having entered into such an agreement, Spencers are bound by the obligations thereby created.

To rule otherwise would strain the law of contracts. At the time of entering into a bailment contract, it may be that, absent absolute guarantees, a bailor may be unwilling to expose his property to loss or damage from any cause. At the same time, the bailee, for the purpose of effecting the bailment, may be willing to extend such guarantees as will satisfy the bailor. If they agree to some mutually satisfactory guaranty provision in their bailment contract, we see no reason why such an agreement should not be enforced.

For the above reasons, the decision of the trial court is affirmed.

CASE REVIEW QUESTIONS
1. Did the outcome in the case in favor of the plaintiff, Glover, result from the court's conclusion that Spencer, as bailee, had failed to exercise reasonable care as required by law? Explain.
2. The testimony of the defendant, Spencer, appears quite favorable to Glover's case. It would have been considerably cheaper just to pay up at the start. Why did he bother to incur the expense of the trial and the appeal?

FIXTURES

Real property is land and things permanently attached to the land. Personal property is all other types of property. However, items of personal property can change their "legal spots" and become real property. Some items, like the boards used in building a house, lose their separate identity completely and become part of the realty under the doctrine of accession, which was discussed earlier in this chapter. When objects are attached to the realty but retain their separate identity, they are called **fixtures.** Objects that become fixtures are no longer personalty and are governed by the laws of realty.

Generally, an item becomes a fixture when

1. It is annexed to the realty.
2. It is adapted to the use to which the land is being put.
3. The intent of the annexor is to have it become part of the realty.

Annexation

Annexation to the realty requires that the property be attached to the land itself or to other items of realty, such as a building. For example, coolers attached to a supermarket building by bolts, plumbing, and wiring are actually annexed to the realty. A large, heavy statue on the lawn of an estate house, though not actually attached, is constructively annexed to the realty by its sheer weight. The degree of attachment required for personal property to become fixtures varies among the states. Courts in some states examine the facts closely to assure themselves that annexation has occurred. In other states, the courts are more lenient and require evidence of only some slight actual or constructive annexation.

Adaptation

The element of **adaptation** requires the existence of a close relationship between the use of the land and the property in question. An attached pipe organ in the loft of a church is peculiarly adapted to the use for which the land is being put. The same organ in a private residence is not peculiarly adapted to the lands' use as a dwelling house. The former is a fixture; the latter is not. As with annexation, the importance of the element of adaptation varies from state to state.

Intent of the Annexor

The intent of the annexor to make an item a fixture is a critical element in all states. Intent here refers to the objective (apparent) intent of the annexor, not to any secret intent that may be in his or her mind. Objective intent is gleaned from the numerous facts surrounding the attachment of personal property to realty. The expressed intention of the annexor, the nature of the item, the manner of attachment, the relationship between the parties involved, and local custom are just a few of the facts that may be considered in ascertaining the annexor's intent.

It should be noted that there are no universal rules for some items. A refrigerator, for example, may be a fixture in some localities, whereas it may remain personalty in others. It is, therefore, very important for the buyer and seller of realty to stipulate clearly whether such doubtful items are part of a sales transaction.

If an owner of land attaches property to the land that would appear to be a fixture, the presumption is that it is a fixture. When a tenant attaches the same object, however, the presumption is that it remains personalty. These presumptions are based upon the notion that the owner's usual intent is to attach the property permanently but the tenant's usual intent is to take the property with him or her at the conclusion of the lease.

The case that follows deals with property used in the strip-mining of coal. As you read the case, notice that surface rights and subsurface rights to land can be, and often are, owned by different parties. The case also mentions *trade fixtures,* which are personalty that has been attached to realty by a tenant business for specific use in the business. Trade fixtures can be removed by the tenant at or before the termination of the lease.

MILFORD v. TENNESSEE RIVER PULP AND PAPER COMPANY
355 So.2d 687 (Ala. 1978)

[Wood-Burleson Coal Company (Wood) installed a coal washing operation on the surface of certain lands that it owned. The washer operation consisted of a washer, tipple, scales, two settling ponds, and various other items. Subsequently, in 1960, Wood sold all surface rights to the land to Tennessee River Pulp and Paper Company (Tennessee River). In 1962, Wood sold the rights to the minerals under the surface and the coal washing operation to May. May used the washer operation in conjunction with his coal mining activities. In 1968, May sold the washing operation to Beasley and leased the mineral rights to him. In 1969, Beasley sold the washing operation to Milford. The settling ponds have been used in the coal mining operation since the ownership of Wood, but they were never mentioned in the sales of the washer operation or the surface rights or mineral rights to the land.

Milford used the washing operation to clean coal mined elsewhere. He viewed the land as "lost land," and never inquired as to the ownership of the surface rights. He did not pay rent to Tennessee River, the owner of the surface rights, though Tennessee River's agents requested an agreement to pay rent. In 1972, Milford became physically infirm and discontinued his activities on the land. A few years later, Beasley and Lee West entered the picture by leasing the surface rights from Tennessee River.

When Beasley began removing the coal from the settling ponds, Milford brought a suit alleging that the coal and the washing operation equipment were his property. The trial court held that Milford could recover certain unattached personalty located on the land. It held further that Beasley and West were entitled to the coal and that the equipment attached to the realty were fixtures belonging to Tennessee River, the owner of the surface rights. The case was appealed to the Alabama Supreme Court.]

JONES, [Judge]

Milford raises two primary contentions on this appeal. First, he asserts that the coal in the settling ponds is personalty and, as such, belongs to him. Secondly, he insists that the washer, tipple, and scales are not fixtures but are merely personalty. Even should this Court hold such property to be fixtures, he contends, they should be deemed trade fixtures which should also be recoverable.

It is well settled that minerals unsevered from the soil, lying in place, are part of the [realty]. When such minerals are severed from the soil, however, they become personalty. Therefore, the coal processed through this washer operation had become the personalty of the mineral estate owner.

Milford contends that it is inconsistent to allow him to recover his other personalty, while not permitting

recovery of the coal refuse. This, however, is fallacious because, whereas there was no abandonment of his other personal property, the refuse is merely abandoned personalty.

A determination whether certain personalty is abandoned stems from a consideration of the nature of the particular property, the intent to abandon, and some external act evidencing this intent. It is from the party's conduct, then, that his intent may be discerned.

Though ordinarily there exists a presumption that one does not intend to abandon his property, this presumption is not attendant where the article claimed to have been abandoned is generally considered valueless. In the case at bar, Milford admits he considered the coal valueless and that all purchasers had refused future shipments of it. Moreover, prior to Beasley's and West's occupancy, no one had used the ponds for several years. (Unlike the coal refuse, the washing operation and equipment were locked and obviously not abandoned.) Therefore, the Court properly held that the coal refuse was abandoned property. As such, it could be legally appropriated by Tennessee River.

Appellant's second contention is also without merit. A "fixture" is "an article which was once a chattel, but which by being physically annexed or affixed to the realty, has become accessory to it and part and parcel of it." It is only from an examination of the circumstances of each case that doubt may be resolved as to whether a certain item is a fixture. Criteria for this determination include:

(1) Actual annexation to the realty or to something appurtenant thereto; (2) Appropriateness to the use or purposes of that part of the realty with which it is connected; (3) The intention of the party making the annexation of making permanent attachment to the freehold. This intention of the party making the annexation is inferred: (a) From the nature of the articles annexed; (b) The relation of the party making the annexation; (c) The structure and mode of annexation; (d) The purposes and uses for which the annexation has been made.

In the case before us, the first two requirements have obviously been fulfilled. The washer equipment is set into concrete and permanently attached to the realty. The process is particularly appropriate for this land in that the property itself is coal producing. Furthermore, extensive stripmining is conducted in the area.

The final requirement, however, is in dispute. Intent to affix property to the realty may be express or implied; but where a building or other structure has been voluntarily erected, such intent is presumed.

Though the determination of whether an article is a chattel or a fixture is a mixed question of fact and law the trial Court clearly ruled correctly in this case. The property is of such nature that permanent affixment must certainly have been originally intended. Furthermore, the equipment has been attached and in place for well over twenty years. The only inference properly drawn from this evidence is that the pieces of equipment, so annexed to the realty, are fixtures.

Thus viewed, we must now determine one final point in controversy. Milford contends that he was either a licensee or a tenant at will and, as such, is entitled to remove trade fixtures attached during his tenancy. If we hold that Milford attained such status, his assertion is correct. It is this assertion as to Milford's status, however, with which we disagree.

Milford was under no lease or sale agreement with Tennessee River. He neither sought nor obtained permission to remain on the land. Furthermore, Tennessee River, through its agents, consistently opposed his rent-free possession. Therefore, because occupancy must be permissive before one may be considered a licensee, Milford cannot be deemed to have attained this status. The mere fact that no suit is brought by the true owner does not create a tenancy relationship, nor elevate a trespass to a tenancy at will. From the evidence presented, Milford must be deemed a trespasser.

As a trespasser, one has no claim to fixtures attached to the realty of another.

It is . . . true generally, that if there is a tortious entry upon lands, and the tortfeasor makes improvements upon them, annexed to the soil, for the better use and enjoyment of the lands, such improvements become a part of the realty; all property in them is vested in the proprietor of the soil, who is under no legal or equitable obligation to make compensation for them, or to suffer them dissevered and removed.

Both questions raised concern a mixture of fact and law. As such, a presumption of correctness attends the decision of the trier of fact. Because no error is manifest upon the record, the judgment of the trial Court is due to be affirmed.

Affirmed.

CASE REVIEW QUESTIONS

1. What facts led the courts to the conclusion that Wood-Burleson Coal Company, the annexor, intended the attachment of the washing equipment to be permanent?
2. If Milford thought it economically beneficial to do so, could he have removed the coal from the settling ponds prior to discontinuing his business in 1972? Explain.

Fixtures under the Uniform Commercial Code

The Uniform Commercial Code (UCC) deals primarily with personal property. It has, however, a vital role in the law pertaining to fixtures. Generally, a seller of goods on credit wishes to retain a security interest in the goods until payment is completed. If those goods are attached to realty and become fixtures, questions arise as to the relative rights of the creditor and other parties with an interest in the realty. The UCC attempts to resolve these questions in §9-313.

Two concepts are critical for determining the priority rights of the creditor. The first is **attachment**, which is the process by which the creditor acquires a security interest in the goods. A security interest attaches when the buyer and seller enter into a security agreement. Generally, the seller (the secured party) provides the buyer (the debtor) with a standard form containing the terms of the security arrangement for signature. Once the form is signed, the security interest attaches.

The second important concept is **perfection,** which is the process by which the creditor makes a public filing of either the security agreement or a form called a *financing statement.* The purpose of the filing is to give notice to third parties of the seller's outstanding credit interest in the property. Its effect is to give the seller-creditor priority over interest holders in the realty to which the goods are attached. The filing normally takes place in the office where liens on the realty are recorded. The filing will be notice to anyone who is seeking information regarding liens on the realty.

If the security interest attaches and is perfected prior to the time the goods become fixtures, the seller-creditor has priority over all other creditors. If the security interest attaches but the seller-creditor fails to perfect, *subsequent* bona fide purchasers for value, mortgagees, and judgment creditors will have better rights than the seller-creditor. The seller-creditor will continue to prevail over prior lien holders only if the security interest attached before installation and the interest was perfected within ten days of installation.

The prevailing creditor may remove the fixtures from the realty in the event of default by the debtor. The creditor must reimburse interest holders in the realty for physical injury to the realty during the removal. In fact, a party entitled to reimbursement may require that a performance bond be provided by the creditor prior to the removal of the fixtures.

There are variations in the rules adopted by individual states regarding fixtures and the rights of interested parties. Particular state laws should be consulted to determine the rules in your state.

REVIEW QUESTIONS

1. Discuss the common thread that runs through each of the areas of personal property described in the chapter.
2. In which areas of law is delivery important? Why is it a necessary element?
3. What distinguishes personal property from real property?
4. Discuss the statement, "Once personalty, always personalty."

CASE PROBLEMS

1. Dombrowski went rabbit hunting with his beagle hound. In a patch of woods, the dog came on the scent of a rabbit. It began to bark and to trail the rabbit. Dombrowski stopped and waited for the dog to bring the rabbit around in a circle, as the dog was trained to do, so that he could get a shot. However, with the dog in hot pursuit, the rabbit passed in front of Chauncey, another hunter, and was shot dead. Upon Chauncey's refusal to turn the rabbit over to him, Dombrowski brought suit in small

claims court for the value of the rabbit. What will be the outcome of the case? Explain.

2. Jackson, a chambermaid, found eight $100 bills in the dresser drawer of a room that she was cleaning for her employer. The bills were concealed beneath the lining in the drawer. Jackson turned the bills over to her employer, Steinberg, who has unsuccessfully sought the owner. After one year Jackson sues Steinberg to recover the $800. Who will win the case? Explain.

3. Three small boys found a bottle partially buried in some loose soil in a salvage yard. The bottle contained $12,590. The money was delivered to the police for safekeeping, and attempts to locate the owner of the money were unsuccessful. The salvage yard was owned by Bishop, and the three boys were playing on Bishop's property without permission. Bishop sued the three boys to get a judicial determination as to whether he or the boys were entitled to the cash. What will be the outcome of the case? Explain.

4. McNamee was a guest at the Hotel Eldorado. Upon learning that Franklin, a noted jeweler, was staying at the hotel, she left her ring with the hotel cashier to be given to Franklin when he returned. The cashier placed the ring in an envelope, wrote Franklin's name on it, and placed it in her desk drawer. The ring somehow disappeared from the drawer and was never delivered to Franklin. McNamee sues the hotel for failure to return the ring. The hotel's defense is that they had no idea that the ring was so valuable and thus no bailment existed. The ring was worth $5,000. Who will win the case? Explain.

5. Rothchild became engaged to be married to Cohen. Rothchild gave her an expensive diamond engagement ring. Prior to the marriage, Rothchild was killed in an automobile accident. The estate of Rothchild sues Cohen to recover the engagement ring. Who will win the case? Explain.

6. Prior to a trip to Europe, Otis Robinson delivered a family heirloom gold piece to his friend and attorney, Rogers. He asked Rogers to give the gold piece as a gift to his son, Barnabas, upon his return home from college in the spring. Rogers agreed to do this, put the gold piece in his office safe, and forgot about it. In the summer when Otis returned from Europe, he had an argument with Barnabas. During their argument, both came to realize that Rogers had never delivered the gold piece to Barnabas as requested by Otis. Thereafter, Otis demanded that Rogers return the gold piece to him. Barnabas brings a lawsuit seeking to enjoin Rogers from returning the gold piece to Otis and requesting that he be declared the donee of a gift inter vivos. Will Barnabas' suit be successful? Explain.

7. Cruz, a tenant, purchased a window air conditioner and installed it in a window in her apartment. Subsequently, Cruz decided to leave the apartment at the end of her lease. The landlord, Bettlemeir, upon receiving notice of her intent to leave, notified Cruz that the air conditioner must remain as it is a fixture. If Cruz removes the air conditioner and Bettlemeir brings suit against her as a result, who will win the case? Explain.

43

REAL PROPERTY

Real property is land and those things permanently attached to the land. Buildings, trees or shrubs, and underground minerals are all real property because they are all permanently attached to land. Of course, the idea of permanent attachment is a relative one. At some point in time, buildings may be razed, trees or shrubs may be cut down, and minerals may be extracted. When such things are detached from the land and become movable, they cease to be realty and become personal property.

The law of real property is steeped in the past. Much of the language and some of the rules reflect their common law origins despite modern changes. The focus in this chapter will be on the various types of ownership of real property and on various ways real property is transferred from one owner to another.

INTERESTS IN REAL PROPERTY

Estates in Land

The concept of the **estate in land** arose from the system of feudalism that existed in England from the eleventh through the fourteenth centuries. Under feudalism, the basic principle governing land transfers was *tenure,* which held that each transferee of land *indefinitely* owed certain duties and services to the transferor in exchange for the land. These duties and services commonly involved providing a share of the agricultural crops grown on the land and military service, when needed, to the transferor.

Under the tenure system, great lords conveyed parts of their lands to lesser lords, lesser lords conveyed parts of this land to others, and so on down the line. These conveyances were not outright grants of ownership but, rather, of "tenancy." If a tenant died without heirs, the estate would revert to the transferor. The concept of tenure was used in a few states during Colonial times, but for the most part, it did not become a formal part of American law.

Tenure did create the underpinnings of the concept of estates in land, however, by providing for the separation of the real property itself from the interests of people in that property. As a result, several persons can today have interests in the same piece of land. For instance, one person may hold legal title to a parcel of land, whereas another may have the right to possess the land for a stated period of time, and a third may have the right to use the land to gain access to another parcel of land. As you can see, the property rights in the same piece of land have been divided among several persons, each having a different estate in the land. In the following sections, you will read about some of the most common estates in land and the rights that holders of these estates possess.

Fee Simple A person who owns a **fee simple** estate in land possesses all the rights commonly associated with land ownership. The fee simple holder has the right to possess and to use the property, to exclude others from it, and to dispose of it. All of these rights are held by the fee simple owner until he or she conveys the property or dies. If the fee simple owner dies, the estate passes to his or her heirs or to those persons designated in his or her will. Most land in the United States is owned in fee simple.

The grant of a fee simple estate is most commonly made by the use of specific language—"to [name of grantee] and his heirs forever" or "to [name of grantee] and her heirs forever," the word *forever* indicating the indefinite duration of the interest. In most states today, however, any words that indicate an intent to convey a fee simple are usually acceptable. For instance, a grant simply "to [name of grantee]" will normally convey a fee simple estate.

Several types of *conditional fee simple estates* were created by common law. These estates are said to be conditional because the owner of the estate may lose his or her ownership under certain circumstances. For example, a grant of realty to Mary Jones "so long as she does not marry" is a conditional fee simple estate. Other examples include the *fee tail,* the *fee simple determinable,* and the *fee simple subject to condition subsequent.* Although each of these conditional fee simple estates has its own special characteristics, they are so seldom used today that they will not be discussed here.

Life Estates A **life estate** is an estate of limited time span, the duration of which is measured by the life of the life tenant or some third person. For instance, a grant might be made "to Prancer for life and then to Donner" or "to Prancer for the life of Dancer, and then to Donner." In each of these grants, Prancer receives a life estate.

A life estate is a possessory interest in land, which means that the life tenant has possession of the land and can use, convey, or encumber (e.g., mortgage) it for as long as he or she has the life interest. The life tenant has a duty, however, not to use the land in a way that will permanently reduce its market value. If this duty is violated, the fee simple owner can bring a legal action, called an **action for waste,** against the life tenant. The life tenant also had the duties to pay taxes on the property and to keep it in repair.

Life estates are usually created by the land owner, that is, by the owner of the fee simple estate. In certain situations, however, a life estate is created by law. In some states, for instance, a widow obtains a dower interest in her husband's real property. **Dower** is a life estate for the widow in one-third of all real property owned by her husband during the marriage. The life estate begins immediately upon his death. While the husband is alive, the wife has a potential estate. A wife can release her potential dower interest by signing, along with her husband, a deed conveying the land to another.

At common law, a husband had a similar, but somewhat different, potential estate called **curtesy.** In states where dower exists today, the potential interests of husband and wife have been made uniform; that is, the differences between dower and curtesy have been abolished.

Leasehold Estates A **leasehold estate** is created when the owner of a fee simple or a life estate, called the *landlord* or *lessor,* conveys to another, called the *tenant* or *lessee,* a possessory interest in real property in exchange for rent. During the period of this estate, the tenant has the sole right to possession of the property, exclusive of everyone else including the landlord.

A legal duty on the tenant to pay rent arises from the right to possession of the leasehold estate. The duty to pay rent and the amount of the rent do not need to be expressly stated in the lease, although they usually are. In other words, even if the amount of rent is not stated, a reasonable rent is nonetheless due.

There are four types of leasehold estates. As you read about them, note particularly how each type is created, how long it exists, and how it is terminated.

Term Tenancy A term tenancy is created by an oral or written agreement between the landlord and tenant. The distinguishing characteristic of a **term tenancy** is that it has specific beginning and ending dates. When the ending date arrives, the tenancy is usually terminated automatically. This means that the landlord generally does not have to give notice to the tenant in order to terminate the tenancy. However, if the terms of the lease stipulate that notice must be given or that other conditions must be met in order to terminate the tenancy, these terms supersede the usual rule that the tenancy terminates automatically.

Periodic Tenancy A **periodic tenancy** continues from period to period, usually from month to month or year to year, unless terminated by timely notice from either the landlord or the tenant. Periodic tenancies usually arise by express agreement between the parties involved. They can also arise by implication when a tenant continues in possession of property after a term tenancy expires and the landlord chooses to continue to accept rent payments rather than to evict the tenant.

If the periods of the tenancy are not expressly agreed upon, the periods when rent payments are due are a good indicator of what they are. For example, if the rent is paid monthly but the periods are otherwise uncertain, the tenancy will probably be construed to be a month-to-month tenancy. A common exception to this rule occurs when the rent is stated in annual terms. The lease will be construed to be a year-to-year lease even if the payments are made monthly.

Unless the parties agree otherwise, a periodic tenancy can only be terminated at the end of one of the periods. Traditionally, the law has required that notice of termination must reach the other party at least one full period in advance of the desired termination date. Suppose, for instance, that a tenant wishes to terminate a month-to-month lease on April 30. The tenant would have to give notice of termination by March 31 in order for the notice to be timely. In no case, however, is more than six months' notice required. Thus, if a periodic tenancy is from year to year, only six months' notice of termination is necessary for the notice to be timely. In any case, these notice requirements can be varied by agreement between the parties.

Tenancy at Will A tenancy at will is a leasehold estate that does not have a fixed term. It is usually created by an express agreement between the parties involved. For example, a lease that exists "so long as both parties agree" creates a tenancy at will.

Sometimes, a tenancy at will is created by implication. For instance, leases for a period longer than one year, or longer than three years in some states, must be in writing. Suppose A orally leases Blackacre to B for five years in a state that requires leases longer than one year to be in writing. B becomes a tenant at will by implication after the first year of the lease.

A tenancy at will continues to exist until one of the parties elects to terminate it. At common law, either party could terminate such a tenancy without notice. Today, however, many states have statutes that establish a minimum notice period for termination.

Tenancy at Sufferance A tenancy at sufferance is created when a tenant who originally gained possession of property legally continues to possess the property wrongfully. This most commonly occurs when a legal tenant under a term tenancy wrongfully retains possession after the termination of the tenancy. Such a tenant is called a *holdover tenant*. A holdover tenant remains a tenant at sufferage until the landlord either creates a periodic tenancy by accepting rent from the tenant or evicts the tenant.

THE LANDLORD–TENANT RELATIONSHIP

As stated earlier, a leasehold estate is created when the owner of a fee simple or a life estate, called the landlord or lessor, conveys to another, called the tenant or lessee, a possessory interest in real property in exchange for rent. Whenever a leasehold estate is created, the law imposes certain duties on the landlord and on the tenant. These duties, and the remedies available to the parties if the duties are violated, are discussed in this section of the chapter.

The Landlord's Duties

A landlord's primary duties are to give possession of the premises (called the landlord's *warranty of possession*) to the tenant and not to interfere with that possession during the term of the lease (called the landlord's *covenant of quiet enjoyment*).

At common law, the landlord had no duty to repair the premises. In other words, the tenant accepted the premises "as is" upon entry. The tenant was responsible for making any repairs he or she desired during the term of the lease. In recent years, however, most states have abandoned the "no duty to repair" rule to some degree. By judicial decision or legislation, these states have imposed a **warranty of habitability** on the landlord. Under this warranty, the landlord has the duty to assure that the residential property that he or she leases is safe, sanitary, and fit for living during the entire period of the tenancy.

The Tenant's Duties

A tenant's primary duty is to pay the required rent. A tenant is also obligated not to use the premises unreasonably and to return the premises to the landlord upon the expiration of the lease in the same condition as when it was received, except for normal wear and tear. The tenant has no duty to repair, except to protect the premises from the natural elements, nor does he or she have a duty to insure the premises.

The Landlord's Remedies

The most common remedies used by landlords when there has been a breach of duty by a tenant are eviction and action for rent. **Eviction** is a legal action brought by a landlord seeking to have a tenant removed from the premises because of a breach of duty by the tenant. At common law, a breach of duty by the tenant entitled the landlord only to money damages. Today, however, under the laws of many states and under the terms of most leases, a breach by the tenant entitles the landlord to bring an eviction action. An eviction action terminates the obligation of the tenant to pay rent, unless the lease contains a "survival clause" that continues the obligation after eviction.

An action for rent can be brought by a landlord when a tenant has failed to make the agreed upon rent payments. At common law, an action for rent could not be started until the period of the lease expired. Today, however, most leases contain a clause that permits such actions prior to expiration of the lease.

If a tenant abandons the property before the end of the lease, the landlord has no legal remedy to recover possession of the property until the expiration of the lease. A nonjudicial remedy available to the landlord, however, is to simply reenter the property and thereby accept the surrender of the property by the tenant. Unless there is a survival clause in the lease, however, reentry by the landlord will discontinue the tenant's obligation to pay future rents because it constitutes acquiescence in the abandonment of the property by the tenant.

The Tenant's Remedies

When a tenant is wrongfully evicted by a landlord, he or she may sue to recover possession of the property or to collect damages caused by the landlord's breach of the lease. If the landlord fails to repair the premises, and is required to do so either by the lease or by a warranty of habitability, the tenant has other remedies available. The tenant may make the repairs and sue the landlord for the expenses incurred. Alternatively, the tenant may seek reformation or rescission of the contract. For instance, the court can reduce the rent because of the landlord's failure to repair and thereby reform the contract. The court can also completely negate or rescind the lease if that remedy is appropriate.

In an action by a landlord for unpaid rent, the tenant may be able to assert a defense of **constructive eviction**. This means that the tenant takes the position that the premises have become uninhabitable because of the landlord's failure to keep them repaired. To prove constructive eviction, the tenant must show that the premises are in fact uninhabitable, that the landlord was notified of the problems and failed to remedy them within a reasonable time, and that the tenant has actually vacated the premises. The tenant's obligation to pay rent ceases at the point the constructive eviction occurs.

Sometimes a tenant in conflict with a landlord will simply choose to withhold rent payments as a way of dealing with the problem. Rent withholding, however, is a remedy that should be used carefully, if at all. Only a few states permit it as a legal remedy. Therefore, prior to withholding rent, the tenant should check carefully to make sure it is permitted under state or local law where he or she lives. If it is, care should be taken to comply strictly with the law. If rent withholding is not allowed or if it is done improperly, it will constitute a breach of duty by the tenant, entitling the landlord to the legal remedies discussed earlier. In the case that follows, the landlords are pursuing such remedies because their tenants have withheld rent.

KLINE v. BURNS
276 A.2d 428 (N.H. 1971)

[Fred Daggett leased an apartment at 28 Tanner Court from Samuel and Gertrude Kline. Martin S. Burns leased an apartment at 26 Tanner Court from the Klines. Both of the leases were oral, were for an unstated duration, and called for the payment of $50 per month in rent. A few months after Daggett and Burns took possession of their respective apartments, both premises were inspected by a city building inspector who found certain violations of the city building code.

The Klines were notified of the violations but did not make any repairs. Daggett and Burns began to withhold their rent payments. In addition, Burns brought a legal action against the Klines to recover all rent payments he had previously made on the grounds that the lease was in violation of the city building code. The Klines brought an action for eviction and an action for rent against both Daggett and Burns. All of the legal actions were tried together.

The trial court ordered the eviction of both Daggett and Burns, and this judgment was not appealed. The trial court also dismissed Burns' action to recover rent payments previously made and granted judgment for the Klines in their actions for unpaid rent against Daggett and Burns. Daggett and Burns appealed from the trial court's judgment in favor of the Klines for the unpaid rent, and Burns appealed from the trial court's dismissal to recover rent payments previously made.]

LAMPRON, Justice

It is evident that the trial court's verdicts for the landlords for unpaid rent, and the dismissal of tenant Burns' action to recover the rent paid during his tenancy because the premises did not comply with the housing code, were based on the following common law principles governing the rights and duties of landlords and tenants which still prevail in this jurisdiction. "There is no warranty implied in the ordinary contract of letting that the premises are reasonably safe or suitable for the uses intended." The only duty the law imposes on a landlord for the benefit of his tenants, insofar as the leased premises are concerned, is a limited duty not to deceive the tenants as to the dangers incident to their use of which the landlord knows and they do not. In other words, the "rule of caveat emptor [let the buyer beware] applies the same as between buyer and seller." The landlord is under no legal duty to repair the leased premises unless he is so obligated by the express terms of the tenancy. The landlord's breach of an express covenant to repair does not excuse, nor is it a defense to, the failure of the tenant to pay rent.

The brief, submitted on behalf of Burns and Daggett, takes the position that the trial court erred in ruling that violations of the housing code by the landlords were not determinative of the rights of the parties. They contend that the duty to comply with the code was a contractual obligation of the landlords to the tenants and that their obligation to pay rent was dependent on the landlords' performance of their obligation. They maintain also that the common law principles of landlord and tenant relied on by the trial court; that is (1) the doctrine of caveat emptor by which the tenants take the premises as they are in the absence of fraudulent concealment of defects; (2) the lack of duty on the landlords to keep the premises in repair; (3) the absence of mutual dependency between the obligations of the landlords and those of the tenants, are all remnants of an ancient feudal system and anachronisms in our present society.

Under the tenurial system a lease was considered primarily as a conveyance of lands for a certain term or at will. The tenant was considered both an owner and occupier in order to provide him with the remedies with which to protect his interest against the landlord and others. Furthermore, in the agrarian society then existing, the value of the lease to the tenant was the land itself which would often yield the rent. Also the buildings on the land were mostly incidental to the lease. They were constructed simply without modern conveniences and could be easily kept in repair by the tenant. Because the lease was primarily a conveyance of land, the covenants of the parties were considered to be mutually independent of each other.

Nowadays the value to the tenant of his lease of an apartment is not in the land itself, but rather, in the right to enjoy the building thereon as a place in which to live. He is more concerned with habitability than with the possibility of the landlord's interference with his possession. Keeping the apartment in a livable state is much more complex and costly than it was in the agrarian society which gave birth to the feudal system and the ensuing common law of landlord and tenant. The importance of a lease of an apartment today is not to create a tenurial relationship between the parties, but rather, to arrange the leasing of a habitable dwelling.

Our legislature, like those of many other states, recognized the need and desirability of insuring adequate housing by adopting legislation granting to municipalities the power to establish and enforce minimum standards for use and occupancy of dwellings. In order to help insure the desired adequate housing, "(c)ourts have a duty to reappraise old doctrines in the light of the facts and values of contemporary life—particularly old common law doctrines which the courts themselves created and developed."

The following are factors to be considered in the appraisal of the legal principles to be applied to the present day relationship of landlord and tenant: (1) Our legislature has recognized that the public welfare requires that dwellings offered for rental be at the beginning, and continue during the tenancy to be, in a safe condition and fit for human habitation. (2) Common experience demonstrates that the landlord has a much better knowledge of the conditions of the premises than the tenant. Furthermore housing code requirements and violations are usually known or made known to the landlord. It follows that the landlord is in a better position to know of latent defects, such as some of those involved in this case, which might go unnoticed by the tenant who rarely has sufficient knowledge or expertise to see or discover defects in wiring, fusing, or venting of gas appliances or furnaces. It is appropriate that the landlord who will retain ownership of the premises and any permanent improvements should bear the cost of repairs necessary to make the premises safe and fit for human habitation. In today's housing market, the landlord is usually in a much better bargaining position than the tenant, which results in rental of poor housing in violation of public policy.

In our opinion the above considerations demonstrate convincingly that in a rental of an apartment as a dwelling unit, be it a written or oral lease, for a specified time or at will, there is an implied warranty of habitability by the landlord that the apartment is habitable and fit for living. This means that at the inception of the rental there are no latent defects in facilities vital to the use of the premises for residential purposes and that these essential facilities will remain during the entire term in a condition which makes the property livable. The very object of the letting was to furnish the defendant with quarters suitable for living purposes. This is what the landlord at least impliedly (if not expressly) represented he had available and what the tenant was seeking. The warranty of habitability which we hold exists in such a case is imposed by law on the basis of public policy. It arises by operation of law because of the relationship of the parties, the nature of the transaction, and the surrounding circumstances.

Adoption of this view makes available to the tenant the basic contract remedies of damages, reformation, and rescission. The tenant can obtain relief by instituting an action for breach of warranty or by offsetting his damages against a claim made against him by the landlord.

In order to constitute a breach of the implied warranty of habitability the defect must be of a nature and kind which will render the premises unsafe or unsanitary and thus unfit for living therein. The nature of the deficiency, its effect on habitability, the length of time for which it persisted, the age of the structure, the amount of the rent, the area in which the premises are located, whether the tenant waived the defects, whether the defects resulted from malicious, abnormal, or unusual use by the tenant, are among the factors to be considered in deciding if there has been a breach of the warranty of habitability. The existence of a breach is usually a question of fact to be determined by the circumstances of each case.

If a material or substantial breach of the implied warranty of habitability is found, the measure of the tenant's damages is the difference between the agreed rent and the fair rental value of the premises as they were during their occupancy by the tenant in the unsafe, unsanitary or unfit condition. In other words, the tenant's rent liability will be limited to the difference between the agreed rent and the reasonable rental value of the premises in their condition while occupied.

Remanded.

CASE REVIEW QUESTIONS

1. What type of leasehold estate existed between Burns and the Klines?
2. What duty did the Klines argue had been breached by Burns and Daggett? What remedies did they seek?
3. On what basis did Burns and Daggett defend against the action for rent brought by the Klines?
4. The case was remanded (returned) by the appellate court to the trial court. Why was this done?

Sublease and Assignment

Upon occasion, a tenant may seek to transfer a leasehold estate to a third party. Such a transfer may be either a **sublease** or an **assignment**. The transaction is a sublease if the tenant retains a *reversionary interest* in the property — that is, if he or she transfers less than the full leasehold estate. For example, if a tenant agrees to give possession to a third party until June 30 but the original lease does not expire until December 31, the transaction is a sublease because the tenant has retained a reversionary interest. Conversely, in an assignment the tenant transfers all the leasehold interest he or she has to the third person. In other words, the tenant does not retain a reversionary interest.

The difference between a sublease and an assignment can be an important one. If the transfer is a sublease, the subleasee owes all obligations under the lease to the tenant-subleasor, not to the original landlord. The rent and all other responsibilities are owed to the tenant, and the tenant must continue to observe his or her promises to the landlord. In short, the obligations under the original lease agreement are unaltered.

On the other hand, if the transfer is an assignment, the assignee stands in the same legal position as the tenant in relationship to the landlord. Thus, the assignee is the person primarily obligated to pay rent directly to the landlord. This is so because a transfer of an entire leasehold estate is said to create *privity of estate* between the assignee and the original landlord, and privity of estate carries with it the duty to pay rent. Though the primary responsibility to pay rent shifts to the assignee, the assignment does not relieve the original tenant of his or her obligations under the initial lease. If the assignee defaults, the tenant-assignor can still be held liable by the landlord.

Unless the lease prohibits it, a tenant is free to sublease or assign the premises. Most leases today, however, contain a clause requiring the approval of the landlord to do either. The lease in the case that follows required such approval by the landlords. Although the landlords granted their approval, they later became involved in a conflict with the transferee of the lease over whether the transfer was a sublease or an assignment.

ERNST v. CONDITT
360 S.W.2d 703 (Tenn. 1964)

[B. Walter Ernst and Emily Ernst entered into a written lease with Rogers to lease land they owned. The term of the lease was for one year and seven days, commencing on June 23, 1960, and rent was to be paid monthly. Rogers constructed a go-cart track on the leased premises and operated a go-cart track business there for a short time. In July 1960, Rogers began negotiations with A.K. Conditt concerning the sale of the business. During the negotiations, Conditt stated that he wanted to have a two-year lease of the property.

The original lease between the Ernsts and Rogers

provided that:

> Lessee shall have no right to assign or sublet the leased premises without prior approval of the lessors. In the event of any assignment or sublease, lessee is still liable to perform the covenants of this lease, including the covenant to pay rent. . . .

Conditt and Rogers went to the home of the Ernsts and requested them to extend the lease and to approve the transfer of the lease from Rogers to Conditt. The Ernsts agreed to these two requests in a written amendment to the lease that they signed. The amendment expressly referred to the transfer of the lease as a "subletting." In the same document Rogers agreed to "sublet" the premises to Conditt. The amendment also provided that Rogers would still be liable for the performance of all of the tenant's duties under the original lease and the amendment.

Conditt operated the go-cart track and paid the rent for a few months. Later, however, he failed to make the required rent payments. In August 1962, the Ernsts, referred to as the complainants in the case, brought an action for rent against Conditt. Conditt defended on the grounds that he was not liable to the Ernsts because the transfer of the lease to him was a sublease, not an assignment. The trial court entered a judgment for complainants. Conditt, the defendant, appealed.]

CHATTIN, Judge

To support his theory the instrument is a sublease, the defendant insists the amendment to the lease entered into between Rogers and complainants was for the express purpose of extending the term of the lease and obtaining the consent of the lessors to a "subletting" of the premises to defendant. That by the use of the words "sublet" and "subletting" no other construction can be placed on the amendment. . . .

Further, [the defendant argues that] since complainants agreed to the subletting of the premises to defendant "upon the express condition and understanding that the original lessee, Frank D. Rogers, will remain personally liable for the faithful performance of all the terms and conditions of the original lease and this amendment to the original lease," no construction can be placed upon this language other than it was the intention of complainants to hold Rogers primarily liable for the performance of the original lease and the amendment thereto.

As stated in complainants' brief, the liability of defendant to complainants depends upon whether the transfer of the leasehold interest in the premises from Rogers is an assignment of the lease or a sublease. If the transfer is a sublease, no privity of contract exists between complainants and defendant; and, therefore, defendant could not be liable to complainants on the covenant to pay rent. . . . But, if the transfer is an assignment of the lease, privity of contract [i.e., a contractual relationship] does exist between complainants and defendant; and defendant would be liable directly and primarily for the amount of the judgment.

The general rule as to the distinction between an assignment of a lease and a sublease is an assignment conveys the whole term, leaving no interest nor reversionary interest in the grantor or assignor. Whereas, a sublease may be generally defined as a transaction whereby a tenant grants an interest in the leased premises less than his own.

The fact that Rogers expressly agreed to remain liable to complainants for the performance of the lease did not create a reversion nor a right to re-enter in Rogers either express or implied. The obligations and liabilities of a lessee to a lessor, under the express covenants of a lease, are not in anywise affected by an assignment or a subletting to a third party, in the absence of an express or implied agreement or some action on his part which amounts to a waiver or estops him from insisting upon compliance with the covenants. This is true even though the assignment or sublease is made with the consent of the lessor. By an assignment of a lease the privity of estate between the lessor and lessee is terminated, but the privity of contract between them still remains and is unaffected. Neither the privity of estate or contract between the lessor and lessee are affected by a sublease.

Thus, the express agreement of Rogers to remain personally liable for the performance of the covenants of the lease created no greater obligation on his part or interest in the leasehold, other than as set forth in the original lease.

The argument that since the agreement between Rogers and defendant contains the words, "sublet" and "subletting" is conclusive the instrument is to be construed as a sublease is, we think, unsound.

Prior to the consummation of the sale of the Go-Cart business to defendant, he insisted upon the execution of the amendment to the lease extending the term of the original lease. For value received and on the promise of the defendant to perform all of the conditions of the lease as amended, Rogers parted with his entire interest in the property. Defendant went into possession of the property and paid the rent to complainants. He remained in possession of the property for the entire term. By virtue of the sale of the business, defendant became the owner of the improvements with the right to their removal at the expiration of the lease.

Rogers reserved no part or interest in the lease; nor did he reserve a right of re-entry in event of a breach of any of the conditions or covenants of the lease on the part of defendant.

It is our opinion the defendant, under the terms of the agreement with Rogers, had a right to the possession of the property for the entire term of the lease as amended. . . . Rogers merely agreed to become personally liable for the rent . . . upon the default of defendant. He neither expressly, nor by implication, reserved the right to re-enter for a condition broken by defendant.

Thus, we are of the opinion the use of the words, "sublet" and "subletting" is not conclusive of the construction to be placed on the instrument in this case.

The decree of the [trial court] is affirmed.

CASE REVIEW QUESTIONS
1. On what basis did Conditt argue that the transfer of Rogers' leasehold interest to him was a sublease and not an assignment?
2. Why did Conditt make this argument?
3. Why did the court reject Conditt's argument?

CO-OWNERSHIP

Real property can be owned by two or more persons at the same time. Such co-ownership will take one of the forms discussed in the sections of the text that follow. As you read these sections, you should note especially how each form of co-ownership is created, how each is terminated, and what happens to the ownership of the property if one of the co-owners dies.

Under all of the forms of co-ownership, the co-owners have a unity of possession. This means that each has an equal right of possession in all of the property. In other words, if there are two co-owners, each of them does not have the exclusive right to possess half of the property. Consequently, they must either arrange to share the benefits of the property or sever (terminate) the co-ownership.

Joint Tenancy

To create a **joint tenancy,** four unities — time, title, interest, and possession — must exist. The unities of time and title mean that the joint tenants must receive their interests at the same time and through the same instrument (e.g., the same deed). The unity of interest requires that each joint tenant acquire a same estate (e.g., a fee simple). The unity of possession requires that each tenant have an undivided right to possession, as explained earlier. Since joint tenancies are not favored in some states, parties who wish to create a joint tenancy should be careful to indicate expressly that one is being created.

A joint tenancy is severed (terminated) if any of the requisite unities is destroyed. For example, suppose Johnson and Clark own Blackacre as joint tenants. If Johnson conveys her interest to Ruiz, the unities of time and title do not exist between the new co-owners, Clark and Ruiz. Instead, Clark and Ruiz own as tenants in common, a form of co-ownership that will be discussed later in the chapter.

The most significant attribute of a joint tenancy is the right of survivorship. Upon the death of one of the joint tenants, the surviving joint tenant (or tenants) automatically receives the decedent's interest in the real property. For example, suppose Norman and his brother Malcolm are joint tenants of Blackacre. If Norman dies first, Malcolm will become the sole owner of Blackacre.

The right of survivorship only exists, however, if the joint tenancy has not been severed. In the case that follows, the court had to determine whether a joint tenancy still existed at the time of the death of one of the co-owners.

ESTATE OF ESTELLE v. ESTELLE
593 P.2d 663 (Ariz. 1979)

STRUCKMEYER, Vice Chief Justice

There is no dispute as to the facts of this case. In March, 1955, John and Elizabeth Estelle acquired title to a house and lot at 318 West State Avenue, Phoenix, Arizona. Title was taken in joint tenancy with right of survivorship. On January 21, 1974, the parties were divorced. The [divorce] decree incorporated by reference a property settlement agreement which provided that their jointly held residence on State Avenue was to be listed with a real estate broker within one week of the signing of the agreement and that it was to be sold to the first person who made an offer within $1,500 of the appraised value. The proceeds of the sale were to be divided equally between the two.

After the divorce, John established his residence at Sun City, Arizona, but Elizabeth continued to reside at the State Avenue property. Approximately two years after the divorce, John Estelle died intestate [without a will]. There had been an appraisal of the property prior to John's death; however, it had never been listed for sale with a real estate broker.

Elizabeth filed a claim against the estate, asserting full ownership of the home as the survivor of the joint tenancy. [A motion for a summary judgment by the estate was granted. Elizabeth appealed, seeking to have the appellate court] declare her sole owner of the property.

The first point in dispute is whether either the property settlement agreement or the decree severed the joint tenancy as a matter of law.

A joint tenancy is an estate held by two or more persons jointly, each having an equal right to its enjoyment during his or her life. The distinguishing feature of a joint tenancy is the right of survivorship by which the survivor takes the estate free of any claim of a deceased joint tenant. Joint tenancy requires the presence of the four unities: time, title, possession, and interest. Severance or destruction of one or more of these unities results in a destruction of the joint tenancy and the failure of the right of survivorship. The inquiry is directed to determining whether one or more of the four unities were destroyed or severed when the parties executed the property settlement agreement.

As a general rule, a joint tenancy may be severed or destroyed either by a direct provision in a contract or by implication if a provision of the contract is inconsistent with the continued existence of the joint tenancy. In *Naiburg v. Hendriksen* the court said:

> We have been unable to find any cases from this jurisdiction on the question of whether a contract to convey operates . . . as a severance of the joint tenancy.

While the foregoing was said about a contract to convey to a third party, we can think of no reason it should not have application to a contract between joint tenants.

In *Wardlow v. Pozzi,* the California Court of Appeals addressed the issue of whether a property settlement agreement could sever a joint tenancy by implication. There, Nellie and Walter Pozzi acquired title to certain real property as joint tenants. They subsequently leased the property to one Wilson for five years with an option to renew if the lessors did not desire the property for their own use. The Pozzis separated, and Nellie commenced an action for divorce. Prior to the commencement of the divorce action, the parties executed a property settlement agreement which provided in part:

> It is . . . agreed that said party of the first part [Walter] and the party of the second part [Nellie] shall continue to hold as joint tenants the ranch owned by them as such joint tenants, located near Fulton, Sonoma County, California; that said joint tenancy real property is now leased to one Wilson, and that all rents received shall be deposited in First National Bank of San Rafael, at Novato, California, and out of said fund shall be paid all interest, principal and taxes due in and about said property. That at the expiration of the Wilson lease (or before) each of said parties shall have the option to purchase the other's one-half interest at an appraisal valuation or that the said property shall be sold and the net proceeds divided equally between the said parties. . . .

[Walter Pozzi died, and the legal representative of his estate brought a legal action against Nellie, claiming that Nellie did not have a right of survivorship in the property because] the property settlement agreement terminated the joint tenancy. The court stated:

> There can be no question but that a joint tenancy may be terminated by express agreement between the joint tenants and an agreement between the tenants which, although it does not expressly terminate the tenancy, is inconsistent by its terms with one or more of the four essential unities of a joint tenancy will also be adjudged to be a severance thereof. Therefore, any interference with the right of survivorship by the terms of the agreement will sever the joint tenancy relationship.

In the instant case, the agreement provided that the property was to be sold and the proceeds divided equally. This provision is patently inconsistent with the continued right of survivorship. The parties no longer viewed themselves as holding the same "undivided possession." In order to find the provision for sale compatible with joint tenancy, it would be necessary to assume that the parties intended to continue a joint tenancy in the proceeds of the sale. As the court stated in *Pozzi,*

> . . . it is hard to see how two persons in domestic difficulties, and desirous of settling their domestic problems as well as those relating to property, would have intentionally entered into an agreement such as the one before us which would have left the bulk of his or her estate to the other.

We think that the right of survivorship did not continue in their joint property after the execution of the property settlement agreement.

For the foregoing reasons, the judgment is affirmed.

CASE REVIEW QUESTIONS
1. Were John and Elizabeth Estelle ever joint tenants? Explain.
2. Why didn't the court believe that John and Elizabeth were joint tenants at the time of John's death?
3. What was the effect of the court's decision that John and Elizabeth were not joint tenants at the time of John's death?

Tenancy by the Entirety

Tenancy by the entirety is a specialized form of joint tenancy. It is distinguishable from a regular joint tenancy in that it can only exist between a husband and wife and it cannot be terminated by one party without the consent of the other. If Ted and Alice, who are both single, want to purchase a house and own it as tenants by the entirety, they must wait until after they are married. If their marriage should end in divorce, the tenancy by the entirety will cease to exist upon the effective date of the divorce and they will own the house as tenants in common, a form of co-ownership discussed in the next section of the text.

During their marriage, neither Ted nor Alice will be able to sell or encumber the house without the agreement of the other. A deed signed by both of them is necessary to convey the property. Tenancy by the entirety, like joint tenancy, includes the right of survivorship.

The tenancy by the entirety form of co-ownership is not recognized in all states. This is why the court in the *Estelle* case, which you read earlier, categorized the co-ownership between John and Elizabeth Estelle as a joint tenancy rather than a tenancy by the entirety.

Tenancy in Common

Tenancy in common is a form of co-ownership in which each owner has an undivided interest in the property. A key difference between it and a joint tenancy or a tenancy by the entirety is that there is no right of survivorship. Upon the death of one co-tenant, the deceased's interest passes to his or her heirs. The heirs take as tenants in common with the other co-tenant(s).

Only the unity of possession needs to exist to create a tenancy in common. The co-tenants need not take title to the property at the same time or through the same instrument or have similar estates. Unlike tenancy by the entirety, one co-tenant's interest in the property can be conveyed at any time without the agreement of the other co-tenant(s).

When the courts have doubts as to whether a joint tenancy or a tenancy in common was intended by the parties, they generally conclude that a tenancy in common was created.

Community Property

Several states have passed community property statutes. These statutes vary as to specifics, but they all operate under the assumption that a husband and wife are to be regarded as partners. As a result, each spouse is a co-owner of all property acquired during the marriage, except for property received by gift or inheritance. Who earned or acquired the property or in whose name the property is recorded is immaterial; all property is owned jointly as community property.

ADVERSE POSSESSION

The concept of **adverse possession** provides that a person who wrongfully enters the land of another may in time acquire ownership of that land. Several elements must be proved by the adverse possessor to attain title to land by adverse possession. He or she must prove that the possession was

1. Actual
2. Exclusive
3. Open and notorious
4. Continuous
5. Hostile and adverse

In addition, the person must prove that each of the elements existed for a period mandated by state statute, which may vary from 5 to 20 years depending on the state. After all the elements have existed for at least the designated period, a lawsuit by the original owner to recover the land from the person who originally entered the land wrongfully is barred.

The element of actual possession requires that the wrongful possessor must exercise dominion over the land. What constitutes the exercise of dominion will depend on the location, the condition, and the reasonable uses that can be made of the property.

Exclusive possession requires that the possessor be the sole possessor of the land. Occasional use by others does not result in a failure to meet this requirement, however.

The possession is open and notorious if the land is occupied in such a way that the possession would be visible to the owner of the property if he or she chose to look. In other words, the acts of the possessor that assert his or her dominion over the land must be such as to put a reasonably prudent owner on notice that the possessor is claiming the land as his or her own.

Continuous possession means that the possessor's occupancy of the land must be uninterrupted during the designated period. Possession is interrupted if the possessor leaves the property for an unreasonable period of time or is physically evicted by the owner or if the owner begins a legal action to evict the possessor.

The requirement of hostile and adverse possession means that the possessor must actually claim he or she owns the land during the period of wrongful possession. Sometimes the claim is made because the possessor has a deed to the land that he or she believes to be valid but is in fact invalid because the person who gave the deed to him or her did not own the land. A claim of this sort is said to be made under "color of title." At other times, the possessor does not have a deed for the property in question but claims ownership either expressly or impliedly through use of the property. A claim of this sort is called a "claim of right."

In the case that follows, the plaintiff claimed to have become the owner of certain property by adverse possession. The defendant argued that the plaintiff had only used the property because of the mistaken belief that it belonged to him and that the possession was not, therefore, hostile and adverse.

SOMON v. MURPHY FABRICATION AND ERECTION COMPANY
232 S.E.2d 524 (W.Va. 1977)

[Somon bought some land in 1953. Before the sale, the seller showed Somon what the seller believed to be the boundaries of the property being sold. The seller stated that one boundary was marked by an old fence. In fact, however, the boundary line was some distance in front of the fence, and the fence was actually located on property owned by Murphy Fabrication and Erection Company (Murphy).

Somon used the property he had purchased, including the portion up to the fence, primarily for grazing cattle and occasionally for cutting timber and hunting. In 1974 Murphy, through its attorney, advised Somon for the first time that the old fence was on Murphy's property. Somon then brought a legal action against Murphy to establish the boundary line, claiming that he had obtained ownership of all the land up to the fence by adverse possession. The trial court held that Somon had obtained the property by adverse possession. Murphy appealed.]

MILLER, Justice

Murphy's attack to Somon's claim of adverse possession rests upon a broad front with the initial contention that none of the elements were proven.

We do not believe that this position can be sustained under the facts. It appears that for the statutory period . . . [t]here was an enclosure coupled with the grazing of cattle and cutting of timber, which has been held to be sufficient to establish necessary elements of adverse possession.

The one challenge that appears of merit is Murphy's assertion that since Somon thought the boundary line was the old fence line, he did not intend to possess the disputed area adversely or hostilely. The argument is

advanced that Somon, being mistaken in believing that his deed description carried to the fence line . . . when in fact it did not, never intended to lay adverse claim to the disputed area. In effect he could not claim adversely as he had a bona fide belief that he owned the area.

The doctrine of mistake as to boundaries in adverse possession centers on the element of adversity or hostility. This principle is stated . . . as follows:

> The solution of the question whether adverse possession can be established, although there has been a mistake in or ignorance of boundary lines, is controlled by whether possession under such circumstances, all other factors being present, can be considered hostile.

We are not aware of any case in which this Court has been asked to consider whether, if it is shown that one holds property under the mistaken belief it is within his deed, this fact destroys his right to claim that he held it hostilely or adversely.

It is, perhaps, sufficient to comment briefly on the two major and opposite views that have evolved in this area. One advances a subjective test; the other an objective one. Those courts that follow the subjective test reason that the element of hostile and adverse connotes a mental intent and therefore if one entertains a belief that he holds the disputed area by virtue of his title document, he does not possess it with the requisite adverse or hostile intent. The other view looks on the physical acts and concludes that if physical dominion has been exercised over the disputed area, this is sufficient to satisfy the adverse or hostile element. We favor this latter theory.

The reasons for such selection may be at best arbitrary, but it does appear that proof is more certain if limited to objective evidence. The physical evidence of possession should alert the true owner that an adverse claim is made, at which point he has ten years [the designated statutory period in West Virginia] to end the problem.

Affirmed.

CASE REVIEW QUESTIONS

1. State the elements of adverse possession that Somon had to prove in order to win his legal action. With reference to the facts of the case, how was each element satisfied?
2. Why was there a question of whether Somon had proved the element of hostile and adverse possession?
3. Why did the court decide that Somon's possession was hostile and adverse?

EASEMENTS

An **easement** is a nonpossessory interest in real property. The key difference between an easement and the property interests discussed previously in this chapter is that an easement does not include the right of possession. Instead, the recipient of an easement has only a right to use the property for limited purposes. For instance, an easement may be used by a public utility to string lines, by a municipality to ensure that drainage facilities remain in place, or by a landowner to permit a neighbor to use the landowner's driveway.

The jargon in this area of law is unusual. The land subject to the easement is referred to as the **servient tenement.** If the easement is **appurtenant** — that is, if it directly benefits a nearby parcel of land — the parcel that is benefited is referred to as the **dominant tenement.** In other words, the dominant tenement is served by the servient tenement.

Easements can be created by a written instrument or by implication of law. When an easement is granted by a writing, the easement maker may grant it to another or reserve it to himself or herself when conveying the title to the land to another. For example, Harding, a landowner, could grant a conservation easement to a private group, permitting the group to use her land for the purpose of nature studies. Alternatively, Harding could sell her land to the private group but reserve to herself an easement for access to a river that flows through her property.

Regardless of how the easement is created, it is said to "attach to" or "run with" the land. This means that a conveyance by either the owner of the dominant or servient tenement will not alter the existence of the easement.

Easement by Prescription

An **easement by prescription** is created in much the same way as ownership of property is obtained by adverse possession. The party claiming an easement by prescription must meet most of the same requirements as an adverse possessor with regard to the servient parcel. More specifically, the claimant must show use of the servient parcel that is open and notorious, continuous, and hostile and adverse for the designated statutory period. These requirements are explained more fully in the preceding section of the text.

In most cases, an easement by prescription will not be found if the land involved is open and unfenced or if many persons use the land nonexclusively. For instance, if a number of schoolchildren use a path through a farmer's unfenced field to get to and from school, an easement by prescription will not be created.

Express Easement

An *express easement* is created by a written document that is similar to a deed that conveys ownership of property. It uses language similar to that found in a deed, and it is placed on public record as is a deed.

Easement by Implication

An *easement by implication* is an easement that is not expressly agreed to by the parties but is, instead, imposed on them by law under certain circumstances. For instance, the law will sometimes impose an **easement by necessity,** which is a form of easement by implication. For example, suppose that Sanders owns a large tract of land and sells a portion of it to Daniels. The portion that Daniels purchases is landlocked, meaning that it is not accessed by any roads. Under these circumstances, the law will give an easement to Daniels to allow her to travel over Sanders' property to get to her own property.

In order for a court to impose an easement by necessity, the person claiming the easement must show two things. First, he or she must show that the two parcels involved were at one time part of a single unit. Second, he or she must show that there is no existing access to his or her property. Generally, the servient parcel owner, over whose land the easement will be given, is allowed to select the route the easement will take across his or her land.

In the case that follows, two people argued that they had easements by implication over the property of the party from whom they had purchased their land. Note the primary argument they made concerning why the court should impose such an easement.

JONITA, INC., v. LEWIS
368 So.2d 114 (Fla. 1979)

[Jonita, Inc., owns a residential development called Lake Lorraine Estates. On November 21, 1967, John W. Boyce, president of Jonita, filed a plat to Lake Lorraine Estates in the public records of the county in which the development is located. A plat is a map that shows how land is to be subdivided into lots, streets, parks, and so forth. The plat showed the entrance to the development to be Country Club Road.

Subsequently, Lewis and Gillespie purchased lots in Lake Lorraine Estates from Jonita. The deeds that conveyed the lots to them referred to the plat, but the two purchasers had never looked at the plat. Instead, prior to the time of their respective purchases, Lewis and Gillespie had seen maps of Lake Lorraine Estates showing the entrance to the development to be Entrance Road. In fact, Entrance Road was used as the entrance to the development for some years.

Later, however, Jonita closed Entrance Road and made Country Club Road the entrance to the development. Lewis and Gillespie brought a legal action asking the court to require Jonita to keep Entrance Road open. They argued that they had obtained a permanent easement by implication over Entrance Road. The trial court found for the plaintiffs, Lewis and Gillespie. Jonita appealed.]

MILLS, Judge

Lewis and Gillespie testified that they were given copies of a map when they visited Jonita's office and indicated an interest in the property. A large copy of the map was located on a wall behind the secretary in Boyce's office, the office from which all sales were made. The plat and the map indicate different entrances to the subdivision. The plat indicated the entrance to be by Country Club Road. The map indicated the entrance to be by Entrance Road.

Gillespie testified that at the time he purchased his property and later at the time he finished and moved into his house in November 1968, there was no practical access to his property by regular passenger vehicle other than the bay approach by Entrance Road. Lewis testified that at the time he moved into his house in December 1971, the only paved access to his property was over Entrance Road, the route by the bay.

Both witnesses testified that Country Club Road, at the north of the development, was later extended to the west and then south to the point where it connected with Entrance Road leading from Fourth Avenue. Gillespie testified that his first knowledge of any map showing plans for the extension of Country Club

Road west and south was a newspaper ad appearing in October 1968.

Boyce testified that Entrance Road came about as a means of access to the country club, that he originally planned to build a commercial lodge in the area of the disputed road segment, and that the road was not constructed as a permanent road. Boyce also testified that the disputed road section was closed in June 1973 due to extreme erosion.

The segment of Entrance Road in question, the part traversing the area between the clubhouse and Choctawhatchee Bay, was not reflected on the recorded plat to Lake Lorraine Estates. Lewis and Gillespie contend that they purchased their lots relying upon the location of Entrance Road as shown on the map, therefore, they are entitled to an easement to this roadway.

Assuming the trial court found that Lewis and Gillespie relied upon the map as an inducement to purchase their properties, a lawful and proper basis for implying an easement has not been demonstrated. An easement can be created in only three ways: by express grant, by implication, or by prescription. The theory of this case is that certain easement rights arose by implication.

In *McCorquodale v. Keyton,* our Supreme Court upheld the right of subdivision property owners to enjoin the obstruction of an area labeled "Sunnyside Park" on a recorded plat. The question in the case at bar is whether the *McCorquodale* rule can be extended to create private easement rights based upon pictorial representations appearing in the developer's advertising material and general layout maps but not referenced in the conveying instrument itself or in a recorded plat referred to in the conveying instrument.

In *Owen v. Yount,* the Court stated that an easement can be impressed only by specific written grant or reservation, by dedication and acceptance or by prescription, and cannot be impressed solely by conversation or by advertising and selling. In *Brooks-Garrison Hotel Corp. v. Sarah Investment Company,* the Court held that an implied easement did not result from an unfiled and unrecorded plat which reflected that a strip of land was dedicated to the public for a street. Thus, the traditional theory of an implied easement is not available to sustain the conclusion of the trial court.

Further, the appellees did not acquire an easement of necessity. A "way of necessity" may have existed in the developmental stages of the subdivision to afford access to subdivision purchasers along the bay, however, this right terminated upon completion of the Country Club Road extension which provided public road access to the lots in question.

The final judgment appealed is reversed.

CASE REVIEW QUESTIONS

1. Which property in the case did Lewis and Gillespie argue was a servient tenement? Which property did they argue was the dominant tenement?
2. Why do you think Lewis and Gillespie did not argue that they had an express easement or an easement by prescription?
3. On what basis did Lewis and Gillespie argue that they had an easement by implication?
4. Why did the court reject the argument of Lewis and Gillespie?

TRANSFER OF REAL PROPERTY

Real property can be transferred from one person to another in many different ways. On the death of the owner, it may be transferred to heirs by inheritance or to a co-owner by right of survivorship. It may be acquired by adverse possession, as described earlier in this chapter. It can also be transferred as a gift, though some formalities are needed. The most common method of transferring land, however, is through a sale. A sale of real property generally follows the pattern that is described in the following sections of the text.

The Contract of Sale

A contract of sale is an agreement between a seller, who promises to convey the property by deed, and a buyer, who agrees to accept the conveyance and to pay a specified price. A contract of sale must include all of the essential elements of a contract. The initial offer may be made by either the buyer or seller, depending on local custom or the individual situation.

Generally, contracts involving real property must be in writing. This requirement can be met either by having the contract of sale itself be in writing or by having a written memorandum signed by the party held responsible under the contract. The written memorandum need not contain the total agreement between the parties, but it must, at the minimum, describe the property and state the essential terms of the agreement.

A contract of sale for real estate usually contains the following: the date, the names of the parties, the amount of the down payment, a description of the property, the way in which taxes and insurance on the property are to be prorated, the type of deed to be used to effect the conveyance, and the signatures of the parties. It may also contain contingency clauses. For example, performance of the contract may be made contingent (dependent) on the ability of the buyer to secure a mortgage.

The Title Search

Subsequent to the signing of the contract of sale, a **title search** is performed to obtain the chain of title of the land involved, which is the recorded history of events that have affected the parcel of land. The purpose of the title search is to verify that the seller actually has the title to—that is, owns—the property and to discover whether there are any restrictions or liens on the seller's title. Depending on local practice, either the buyer or seller will provide the title search.

The title search will reveal any conveyances made by the seller or the seller's predecessors that affect the title. It will also disclose any liens on the property, such as an unpaid mortgage, an unsatisfied judgment, pending litigation, a mechanic's lien for labor and supplies used in construction, or any other lien that encumbers the title to the land.

Once the title search has been performed, the buyer will be deemed to have constructive notice of all matters that appear in the chain of title. This means that the buyer will be deemed to know the contents of all documents pertaining to the property that have been properly recorded regardless of whether he or she actually checks the chain of title. If the buyer discovers that the seller's title is clouded by conveyances that limit the title, the buyer will not be required to go through with the transaction. If the title search discloses liens on the property, they must be satisfied by the seller prior to the conveyance of the property.

The Deed

A conveyance of land must be in writing, the usual form of which is a deed. A **deed,** then, is an instrument through which a grantor (seller) conveys real property to a grantee (buyer). A valid deed must contain identification of the grantor and grantee, words of conveyance, a description of the property, and an acknowledged signature of the grantor. To effectuate the conveyance, the deed must also be delivered and accepted.

The words of conveyance appear in the granting clause of a deed. No particular words are necessary as long as the intent of the grantor to convey the property is clear. However, most deeds contain the language "grants, bargains, sells, and conveys" or something similar. This language transfers a fee simple to the grantee.

The grantor's signature, which is customarily placed at the end of the deed, must be acknowledged before the deed can be recorded. An **acknowledgment** is a written declaration made before a public official, usually a notary public, assuring that the deed is genuine and is being executed voluntarily. The purpose of the acknowledgment is to prevent fraudulent deeds from being recorded.

Types of Deeds There are several types of deeds. A **warranty deed** is an instrument by which a grantor conveys title to property and warrants (promises) that the title is free of any encumbrances. There are two forms of warranty deeds. In a **general warranty deed,** the grantor warrants that title is clear of any encumbrances anywhere in the chain of title. A **special warranty deed** is more limited. In it, the grantor promises only that the title is free of any encumbrances arising during his or her ownership, not during the entire chain of title.

A **quitclaim deed** is a type of deed by which the grantor conveys whatever interest he or she has in a piece of property. The grantor neither promises that he or she has title to the property nor gives any warranties as to the title. Quitclaim deeds are not commonly favored by grantees. They are mainly used to clear up defective titles. For example, if the recorded title to a parcel of land is clouded because of faulty boundary descriptions in earlier deeds, one possible owner may seek a quitclaim deed from the other possible owner for the disputed portion in order to remove the cloud from the title.

Recording a Deed Deeds and other conveyances of land are customarily recorded at a county government office in the county in which the property is located. The purpose of recording is to give notice of the conveyance to anyone who may subsequently have an interest in the property. For example, suppose Franklin enters a contract of sale with Stein for Greenacre. Stein can check the county records to assure herself that Franklin owns the property. If Stein has contacted a bank about obtaining a mortgage on the property, the bank can also check the county records to see if there are any liens outstanding against the property that would have priority over their mortgage.

Delivery of the Deed To effectuate a conveyance of real property, there must be a delivery of the deed by the grantor and an acceptance of the deed by the grantee. Delivery requires that the grantor intends to pass title to the land and that he or she surrenders control of the deed.

In the case that follows, the grantor had surrendered control of the deed to the grantee, but she claimed that she had not intended to pass title to him. In order to prove this, she wanted to put into evidence an oral agreement between the parties concerning when the deed was to take effect. The court had to decide whether such evidence was admissible.

PAOLI v. ANDERSON
208 So.2d 167 (Miss. 1968)

ETHRIDGE, Chief Justice

This case involves a conditional delivery of a deed dated November 22, 1961, from appellant, Mrs. Bessie Stockstill Paoli, to her brother, James R. Stockstill, who died March 30, 1965. After Stockstill's death the deed was found in his lock [safe deposit] box at the bank. Mrs. Paoli filed a [legal action] against Janie Anderson and others, heirs at law . . . of her deceased brother, James R. Stockstill. She sought to cancel as a cloud on her title the deed from her to her brother of November 22, 1961. The [trial] court dismissed the [legal action], and we affirm.

On November 1, 1961, James R. Stockstill conveyed by warranty deed to Mrs. Paoli the west 135 feet of the south 65 feet of Lot 2, Block H, in the City of Picayune. This deed was filed for record on November 22, 1961. It recited no conditions.

On November 22, 1961, Mrs. Paoli signed a warranty deed to Stockstill conveying the same property to him. This deed contained no restrictions or conditions. It was acknowledged by Mrs. Paoli before a notary public, and stated that she had "signed, delivered and executed" it on the date of the instrument. The deed was filed for record by the administrator of [Stockstill's] estate on June 15, 1965, after Stockstill's death, when it was found in his lock box at the bank.

On May 23, 1962, Mrs. Paoli executed a warranty deed to Stockstill conveying to him the west 75 feet of the south 65 feet of Lot 2, Block H, of the City of Picayune. This deed was filed for record the day after its execution.

The originals of these three deeds were found in the lock box at the bank which had been rented by Stockstill. He had its exclusive use. Moreover, the record supports a finding by the [trial] court, implied from its decree against appellant, that Stockstill dealt with the property as his own. He rented part of it, and a part was blacktopped and used for a parking lot. The lessees paid Stockstill the rent and the cost of the blacktopping.

Fire insurance policies on the improvements listed Mrs. Paoli as the insured. The evidence indicated that she paid the taxes on this property for the years 1962–1964.

Mrs. Paoli offered to testify that she had an oral agreement with her brother that the deed from her to him (November 22, 1961) was not to take effect on that date, but was to become effective only if she predeceased him. The trial court sustained appellees' objection to this testimony, on the ground that the grantor could not testify as to any oral agreement which she might have had with the grantee concerning the purpose of the deed and oral conditions or restrictions on its effect.

A presumption of delivery of a deed arises from its possession by the grantee. This presumption may be rebutted by showing that there was in fact no delivery. However, this must be done by clear and convincing evidence, and there was none here.

The general rule on conditional delivery to the grantee is summarized [as follows]:

> When a grantor "delivers" his deed directly to the grantee but annexes to such delivery some oral condition, the great weight of authority finds ownership located in the grantee and the oral condition completely ineffective. A relatively small group of states treat the majority rule as an excess of formalism and permit oral conditions attached by the grantor to a delivery made directly to the grantee, to be enforced. . . . In view of the readily available and permissible device of a delivery in escrow [i.e., delivery to a third person who is to deliver the deed when the required condition occurs], when the grantor wishes to make his delivery conditional, this writer believes the majority rule to be the sound one and not a mere anachronistic survival of primitive formalism, as has been charged.

The instrument contained no conditions or restrictions on its effectiveness. To permit Mrs. Paoli to set up a condition by parol [oral] evidence would contradict her deed, which is unambiguous on its face. Thus such parol evidence as to a conditional delivery is generally held to be inadmissible. This view has been consistently applied in this jurisdiction. Parol evidence is not admissible to vary the terms of a plain and unambiguous deed. In short, delivery to the grantee of a deed absolute on its face will pass complete title to him regardless of any oral condition or contingency upon which its operative effect is made to depend. Because of the importance of stability of titles, we think this rule is a sound one and not a mere formalism.

In summary, the grantee had exclusive possession of an unqualified deed, and was exercising control over the property as his own. Although some of the evidence indicated a possible contemporaneous oral condition, that is, the payment of taxes by Mrs. Paoli and designating her as the insured, these circumstances alone are insufficient. They may well have been the result of a brother's undertaking to help his sister. The presumption of delivery and the parol evidence rule preclude this attack on the deed.

Affirmed.

CASE REVIEW QUESTIONS
1. What kind of deed did the grantor give to the grantee?
2. On what basis did Paoli argue that delivery of the deed had not been effective to convey title to the property? Why did the court reject her argument?

REVIEW QUESTIONS

1. What important role does the ancient concept of tenure play in modern real property law? Give an example of this role that is not presented in the text.
2. What is the basic difference between a term tenancy and a periodic tenancy? Under what circumstances may a term tenancy become a periodic tenancy?
3. What are the primary duties of a landlord and of a tenant? What remedies are available to a landlord or a tenant if the other breaches his or her duties?
4. What is the difference between a sublease and an assignment of a lease? In what way can this difference be of importance in some situations?
5. Compare and contrast the three forms of co-ownership of real property.
6. State and explain the five elements of adverse possession.
7. How do easements differ from other estates in land?
8. Compare and contrast a warranty deed and a quitclaim deed.

CASE PROBLEMS

1. Irene Kern leased an apartment from Colonial. She was constantly annoyed by loud parties and other late-night noises emanating from the apartment beneath her. She notified Colonial of the problem and reminded them that they had assured her that the apartment was quiet. Colonial warned the downstairs tenants that they would be evicted unless they quieted down. After a period of quiet, the noises from below began disturbing Kern again. What remedies might be available to Kern? What must she prove to be entitled to these remedies?
2. Jon Karen purchased Greenacre in fee simple. Subsequently, Jon was married to Ann. After the marriage Jon had a deed prepared and recorded that stated, "I, Jon Karen, do hereby grant and convey Greenacre to Jon Karen and Ann Karen, as joint tenants with right of survivorship." Two years later Jon died leaving his son, Arthur, as his legal heir. Who is the owner of Greenacre? Explain.
3. Horst took possession of Greenacre though he did not have title to it. The recorded title was in the name of Brock. Horst did all the things necessary to become an adverse possessor for the required statutory period. Sometime thereafter, Brock found Horst on the land and physically ousted him from it. Two weeks after the ouster, Brock sold the land to Cranston, who had done a title search that revealed that Brock had recorded title to the land and that there were no encumbrances against it. Horst then brought an action to eject Cranston from the premises. Who will win the case? Explain.
4. Homer owned a one-acre lot. He conveyed one-half of the lot to McNamee. The deed stated that an easement for "driveway purposes" across the conveyed lot was retained by the grantor. Later, Homer conveyed the remaining one-half acre to

Snyder. Snyder parks his car in the driveway despite the objections of McNamee. McNamee has brought a legal action against Snyder, seeking to have the court stop Snyder from parking in the driveway. Snyder claims rights under the easement contained in the deed from Homer to McNamee. Who will win the case? Explain.

5. Warner owned Greenacre in fee simple. During the process of negotiating a sale to Blackledge for cash, he prepared a deed to Greenacre for Blackledge, signed it, and had the signature acknowledged. Following one negotiating session, Warner handed the deed to Blackledge and told him, "This is the deed you will receive when you pay the $22,000 purchase price." Blackledge responded, "Fine! I'll take it home to look it over and make up my mind." On the way home, Blackledge had the deed recorded at the Recorder of Deed's office. If Blackledge brings suit to eject Warner from Greenacre, contending that he has title through a valid, signed, and recorded deed, who will win the case? Explain.

6. Zollers is the owner of an apartment building. She leased apartment 1C to Arones for a term of one year beginning May 1 and ending April 30. In January, Arones was transferred by her employer to another city. Arones paid January's rent, and with the consent of Zollers, entered into agreement with Ruebhausen by which Ruebhausen would take over the lease through April 30. Ruebhausen occupied apartment 1C and paid the rent for the month of February. Ruebhausen then disappeared and has not been seen since February 28. In May, Zollers brought a legal action against Arones for the rent for the months of March and April. Who will win the case? Explain.

44

WILLS, ESTATES, AND TRUSTS

In Chapter 42, we stated that, from a legal perspective, property is a "bundle" of rights. One of these rights is the right to dispose of property by transferring ownership of it to another person. Earlier in this book, several chapters were devoted to the law of the sale of goods, which is one way ownership of property is transferred from one person to another person (see Chapters 19–24). In Chapters 42 and 43, some additional ways a person can transfer ownership of property to another were explained. Two of the most common methods of transfer are by *inter vivos gift* (a gift among the living; see pages 909–912) and by conveyance of real estate (see pages 944–948).

In this chapter, you will learn about another common way in which ownership of property is transferred: by testamentary gift. A *testamentary gift* is a gift that does not take effect until after the death of the person making it. This kind of gift is accomplished through the use of a will, although, as you will see, the property of a deceased person is transferred to others whether or not he or she leaves a will. The legal procedure through which the transfer of the property of a deceased person is accomplished is discussed in this chapter.

Later in the chapter, you will learn about a special type of transfer in which property is transferred from one person to another *for the benefit of* a third person. An arrangement in which one person owns property for the benefit of another is called a *trust*.

WILLS

A **will** is a declaration by a person of the way in which his or her property is to be distributed after he or she dies. A will can also be used to appoint a particular person to administer and distribute the property and to appoint a person to be the guardian of minor children. A man who makes a will is called a **testator**, whereas a woman who makes a will is called a **testatrix**.

Making a Valid Will

Every state has statutes that prescribe the requirements for making a valid will. Although the specifics of these statutes vary among the states, they all require that the person making the will have testamentary capacity and that certain formal steps be taken in executing (signing) the will. A will is invalid if these requirements are not met. In addition, a will is invalid if the declarations in it were made by the testator or testatrix as a result of fraud, duress, or undue influence by another person.

Testamentary Capacity In order to have *testamentary capacity,* which means the capacity to make a will, a person must have reached the age (usually 18) required by the state in which the will is executed before signing the will and must be of sound mind. To be of sufficiently sound mind to sign a will, a person must (1) understand who the people are to whom he or she would most naturally want to distribute his or her property, (2) understand how much and what kind of property will be distributed after his or her death, and (3) be able to make a plan for distributing the property.

Generally, a person making a will does not have to have the same degree of mental capacity as he or she would have to have to make a contract. A court will usually find that a person who has made a will had sufficient testamentary capacity unless it is clear that he or she did not meet each of the three requirements discussed in the previous paragraph. The case that follows exemplifies this point.

ESTATE OF ROSEN
447 A.2d 1220 (Maine 1982)

[A trial court called a probate court determined that Seymour M. Rosen had testamentary capacity when he signed his will. His wife and son appealed the court's decision.]

GODFREY, Justice

Decedent, a certified public accountant, had an accounting practice in New York City, where he had been married to Phoebe [Rosen] for about thirty years. Their son, Jeffrey, works in New York City. In 1973, the decedent was diagnosed as having chronic lymphatic leukemia, a disease that, as it progresses, seriously impairs the body's ability to fight infection. From 1973 on, he understood that he might die within six months. In June, 1978, he left his home and practice and moved to Maine with his secretary of two months, Robin Gordon. He set up an accounting practice in Camden.

The leukemia progressed. The decedent was on medication and was periodically hospitalized for infections, sometimes involving septic shock, a condition described by the treating physician as akin to blood poisoning. The infections were treated with antibiotics with varying degrees of success. Despite his medical problems, the decedent continued his accounting practice, working usually three days a week, until about two months before his death on December 4, 1980. Robin Gordon lived with him and attended him until his death.

While living in New York, the decedent had executed a will leaving everything to his wife or, if she should not survive him, to his son. In November, 1979, decedent employed the services of Steven Peterson, a lawyer whose office was in the same building as the decedent's, to execute a codicil [amendment] to the New York will leaving all his Maine property to Robin. At about this time, decedent negotiated a property settlement with his wife, who is now living in Florida. He executed the will at issue in this proceeding on July 25, 1980, shortly after a stay in the hospital with a number of infections, and shortly before a hospitalization that marked the beginning of the decedent's final decline. This will, which revoked all earlier wills and codicils, left all his property, wherever located, to Robin, or to Jeffrey if Robin did not survive him.

The Probate Court applied the standard heretofore declared by this Court [in the case of In re Leonard] for determining whether a decedent had the mental competence necessary to execute a valid will:

> A "disposing mind" involves the exercise of so much mind and memory as would enable a person to transact common and simple kinds of business with that intelligence which belongs to the weakest class of sound minds; and a disposing memory exists when one can recall the general nature, condition and extent of his property, and his relations to those whom he gives, and also to those from whom he excludes, his bounty. He must have active memory enough to bring to his mind the nature and particulars of the business to be transacted, and mental power enough to appreciate them, and act with sense and judgment in regard to them.

Appellants portray the decedent as "a man ravaged by cancer and dulled by medication," and it is true that some evidence in the record tends to support this characterization. However, the law as set out in In re Leonard requires only a modest level of competence ("the weakest class of sound minds"), and there is considerable evidence of record that the decedent had at least that level of mental ability and probably more:

1. The three women who witnessed the will all testified that decedent was of sound mind. They worked in the same building as the decedent, knew him, and saw him regularly.
2. Lawyer Peterson, who saw the decedent daily, testified that he was of sound mind. Peterson used the decedent as a tax adviser, and the decedent did accounting work for Peterson's clients. Peterson had confidence in the decedent's tax abilities and left the tax aspects of the will to the decedent's own consideration.
3. Dr. Weaver, the treating physician, testified that although the decedent would be mentally deadened for a day or two while in shock in the hospital, he would then regain "normal mental function." Though on medication, the decedent was able to conduct his business until soon before his death. Dr. Weaver testified without objection that on one occasion he had offered a written opinion that the decedent was of sound mind.

Appellant's principal objection to the will is that the decedent lacked the necessary knowledge of "the general nature, condition and extent of his property." The record contains testimony of Robin Gordon and lawyer Peterson that decedent did not know what his assets were or their value. However, there is other evidence, chiefly Peterson's testimony about his discussions with the decedent preliminary to the drafting of the 1980 will and, earlier, when the 1979 codicil to the New York will was being prepared, that the decedent did have knowledge of the contents of his estate. He knew that he had had a Florida condominium, although he was unsure whether this had been turned over to his wife as part of the recent property settlement; he knew that he had an interest in an oil partnership, and, although he was unable to place a value on that interest, he knew the name of an individual who could supply further information about it; he knew he had stocks and bonds, two motor vehicles, an account at the Camden National Bank, and accounts receivable from his accounting practice.

The law does not require that a testator's knowledge of his estate be highly specific in order for him to execute a valid will. It requires only that the decedent be able to recall "the general nature, condition and extent of his property." Such knowledge of one's property is an aspect of mental soundness, not an independent legal requirement as the appellants seem to suggest. Here, there was competent evidence that the decedent had a general knowledge of his estate. The Probate Court was justified in concluding that, in the circumstances, the decedent's ignorance of the precise extent of his property did not establish his mental incompetence. The decedent's uncertainty about his property was understandable in view of the fact that some of his property had been transferred to his wife in the recent property negotiations in circumstances rendering it possible that the decedent might have wanted to put the matter out of his mind. Also, there was evidence from which the court could have inferred that much of the property was of uncertain or changing value.

On the evidence of record, this Court cannot hold that the findings of the Probate Court were erroneous.

Judgment affirmed.

CASE REVIEW QUESTIONS

1. What things had to be shown in order for the probate court to determine that Seymour Rosen had testamentary capacity?
2. On what grounds did Phoebe and Jeffrey Rosen argue that Seymour Rosen lacked testamentary capacity?
3. Why do you think that Phoebe and Jeffrey Rosen argued that Seymour Rosen lacked testamentary capacity?
4. Why did the court disagree with the argument of Phoebe and Jeffrey Rosen?

Formal Steps in Executing a Will The formal steps that must be followed when a will is executed vary from state to state. In every state, however, the purpose of requiring certain steps is to prevent fraud. The courts usually interpret the statutes that require particular steps very strictly, and they will declare a will invalid if the required steps have not been taken, even if the desires of the person who made the will are perfectly clear. It is therefore important that a person who makes a will take all of the formal steps for executing a will that are required by the state in which the will is executed. Generally, the requirements are that a will must be

1. In writing.
2. Signed by the person who is making the will or at his or her direction in the presence of two or three witnesses.
3. Signed in the presence of the person who is making the will by two or three witnesses, who also sign in the presence of each other and who will not receive any property under the terms of the will.

Exceptions to Formal Requirements There are two situations in which a will may be valid even though the required formal steps were not followed when it was executed. These situations involve holographic wills and nuncupative wills.

Holographic Will A holographic will is a will that is written and signed entirely in the handwriting of the person making the will. In some states, a holographic will is valid even if the formal steps for executing a will are not taken. Occasionally, however, a document that appears to have been intended by its maker to be a holographic will fails to indicate that it is to take effect only at death. For instance, it may simply say, "I give everything to my husband." In such a case, a probate court will allow evidence to be submitted to prove that the document was intended to be a will.

Nuncupative Will A nuncupative will is an oral will spoken to witnesses. In some states, a noncupative will is valid if it is made by a person during his or her last illness before death or by a member of the military on active duty. In either case, a noncupative will can only be used to dispose of personal property, not real property.

Fraud, Duress, and Undue Influence For a will to be valid, the person making the will must intend to make a will. If the testator or testatrix is induced to make the will by fraud, duress, or undue influence, then the will does not represent his or her true intent. Under such circumstances, the will, or any part of it that was induced by fraud, duress, or undue influence, is invalid. A will induced by *fraud* is one that is made as a result of intentional lies told by another person. A will induced by *duress* is one that is made because of the wrongful threats or acts of another person, such as the threat or use of violence.

What constitutes a will made as a result of *undue influence,* which means unfair persuasion, can be difficult to decide. Generally, two things are considered in determining whether there has been unfair persuasion.

1. Whether the testator or testatrix failed to distribute his or her property to the people who would be expected to receive it.
2. Whether the property was distributed to a person who was in a confidential relationship with the testator or testatrix that allowed for the use of undue influence and who used the relationship to influence improperly the testator or testatrix.

In the case that follows, the court found that even if influence was used, it was not improper.

IN RE ESTATE OF WEIR
475 F.2d 98 (D.C. Cir. 1973)

[Paul Weir was a lifelong bachelor. He met Elizabeth Holmead, a widow of approximately the same age as Weir, shortly after World War II, and they became close friends. Although Weir and Holmead had separate apartments, they shared each other's company, traveled together, and took their meals together. In short, they became constant companions until Weir's death, at the age of 80, on February 19, 1971.

On June 6, 1966, Weir executed a will in which he left $10,000 each to his nephew and niece and the rest of his estate, which was quite large, to Holmead. After Weir's death, the niece, Margaret Weihs, challenged the validity of the will on the grounds that it was made as a result of undue influence by Holmead. After trial, the trial court judge decided that, because no evidence of undue influence had been presented by Weihs, the issue of undue influence should not be given to the jury for decision. The judge therefore granted a directed verdict upholding the validity of the will. Weihs appealed.]

PER CURIAM

[T]he evidence presented as to undue influence was insufficient to allow the jury to take that issue. All the witnesses testified without qualification that testator and Mrs. Holmead had great affection for each other, and with the exception of Mrs. Holmead, testator had no close friends. He saw his niece and nephew very infrequently, and only rarely spoke with them on the phone. Although testator's nephew testified that he believed Mrs. Holmead exercised a "wifely" influence on his uncle, neither nephew or niece could recite anything in particular that Mrs. Holmead ever did or said to unduly influence their uncle.

Unfortunately for [Weihs], influence gained by years of mutual affection is not sufficient in law to establish undue influence. Undue influence is influence gained by improper means. As this court stated in *MacMillan v. Knost:*

> Influence gained by kindness and affection will not be regarded as "undue," if no imposition of fraud be practiced, even though it induces the testator to make an unequal . . . disposition of his property in favor of those who have contributed to his comfort, . . . if such disposition is voluntarily made. Confidential relations existing between the testator and beneficiary do not alone furnish any presumption of undue influence. . . . One has the right to influence another to make a will in his favor. He may . . . lay his claims for preferment before the testator. They may be based on kinship or friendship or kindness or service or need or any other sentimental or material consideration. One can use argument and persuasion so long as it is fair and honest

and does not go to an oppressive degree where it becomes coercive.

The court then added that the "possibility or suspicion of undue influence is not enough."

In rejecting a contention that undue influence was exerted by testatrix's daughter, this court, in *Brooke v. Barnes,* stated:

> It is no ground of criticism that others might have made a different will. . . . It will be remembered that it is not influence, but undue influence, that is charged, and is necessary to overthrow a will.

The court emphasized that the fact one requests the testator to make a will a particular way does not establish undue influence.

The cases cited by appellant are completely inapposite, and the distinguishing facts of each only serve to illustrate the lack of any evidence of undue influence in this case. Where the issue of undue influence had been permitted to go to the jury in the cases cited by appellant, there had been testimony which strongly indicated that the testator was peculiarly in a position to be coercively influenced. For example, the testatrix was extremely ill and prevented, by false representations of a nurse, from seeing her relatives, or the testatrix was subject to threats of physical abuse while under sedation to compel her to execute a will. In contrast, there was absolutely no testimony in this case indicating any coercion exercised by Mrs. Holmead, or anyone else. If [she] exercised any influence whatsoever over testator, it was the influence that arises from genuine mutual affection. And, as noted above, "influence gained by kindness and affection" is not regarded as undue.

If the long-standing salutary policy of our law favoring free and untrammeled disposition of one's property means anything, it means that the [trial court] would have erred in allowing this case to go to the jury. Only through sheer speculation could the jury have found undue influence.

Affirmed.

CASE REVIEW QUESTIONS

1.   What would Wiehs have had to show in order to prove that her uncle's will was executed as the result of undue influence?

2. Why did the court believe that Wiehs had failed to prove that her uncle's will was executed as the result of undue influence?

Types of Dispositions of Property

A disposition of real property under a will is called a **devise;** a disposition of personal property is called a **bequest.** A devise or a bequest may be specific, general, demonstrative, or residuary.

A *specific* devise or bequest is one that makes specific reference to particular property. For example, "I give my 1985 Chevrolet Corvette to my daughter, Tina," is a specific bequest. If the specified property is not owned by the deceased at the time of his or her death, an **ademption** occurs, meaning that the specific devise or bequest fails and the person named to receive the property receives nothing.

A *general* devise or bequest does not specify particular property. For example, "I give $10,000 to my daughter, Tina," is a general bequest. A *demonstrative* bequest is one that designates a particular source from which the bequest is to be paid but also provides that the bequest is to be treated as a general bequest if the designated source no longer exists or is insufficient to pay the bequest. For example, "I give $10,000 to my daughter, Tina, to be paid from the funds received from the sale of my 1985 Chevrolet Corvette; but if I do not own the Corvette at the time of my death or the funds received for it are insufficient, the $10,000 is to be paid from my other assets," is a demonstrative bequest. A *residuary* devise or bequest is one that disposes of the property that remains after the specific, general, and demonstrative dispositions in the will have been made. For example, "I give to my daughter, Tina, all the rest of my property," is a residuary bequest.

Limitations on the Use of Wills

The statutes that allow for the disposition of property by will also limit the extent to which a person can use a will to avoid having property go to his or her surviving spouse. The purpose of these statutes is to protect the surviving spouse from being disinherited. In most states, a surviving spouse can choose to receive a certain proportion of the deceased spouse's property — often one-third — rather than the amount, if any, given to him or her in the deceased spouse's will. The surviving spouse's right to renounce the will and to receive a proportion of the deceased's property is called the spouse's *forced share* or *elective share*. If the surviving spouse elects to take the forced share, he or she is paid his or her share of the estate first. The will is otherwise effective as written except for any devises or bequests made to the spouse.

Surviving children have much more limited protection from disinheritance. It is legal for a person who makes a will to disinherit his or her children intentionally. However, the intent to disinherit must be evident from the will itself. It can be shown by mentioning a child by name but giving him or her either nothing or merely a token bequest. If intent to disinherit is not found in the will, the child is said to be pretermitted. **Pretermission** most frequently occurs when a child is born after a will has been made and no new will is made subsequent to the child's birth. A pretermitted child is entitled to the payment of that share of the deceased parent's estate that he or she would have received if the parent had died without a will. The will is otherwise effective as written.

Amendment and Cancellation

A person may amend a valid will at any time before his or her death by making a valid **codicil** to the original will. A codicil must meet all of the requirements for making a valid will that were discussed earlier.

A person may cancel a valid will at any time before his or her death by *revoking* it. A will that has been revoked cannot become effective again unless a valid codicil is added to it. Revocation of a will may occur either by operation of law or because of an action taken by the maker of the will.

Revocation by Operation of Law Certain changes in the relationships with others of a person who has made a will may revoke the will by operation of law. For instance, in some states the marriage of a testator or testatrix will revoke a will made before the marriage. Likewise, a divorce may revoke a disposition made in a will to the former spouse. This kind of will revocation is said to occur by operation of law because it occurs automatically and is not dependent on the *intent* to revoke the will of the person who made it.

Revocation by Action Taken by the Maker of the Will One way in which a testator or testatrix may revoke a will is by executing a new valid will or a codicil that expressly revokes an earlier will or is inconsistent with it. The best practice is to revoke old wills expressly in any new will that is made.

Another way in which a testator may revoke a will is by physically burning, tearing, obliterating, or destroying it. To be effective as a revocation, the physical change in the document must be made with the intent to revoke. A will may be partially revoked by physically changing only that part of the document the maker of the will intends to cancel. No witnesses are required to make either a full or partial revocation valid.

In the following case, a testatrix who may have tried to revoke her will failed to do so because she did not use one of the accepted methods of revocation.

ESTATE OF EGLEE
383 A.2d 586 (R.I. 1978)

[Lisbeth Eglee died November 11, 1973. A document dated and executed March 7, 1966, was found among her belongings. The document had been executed as the decedent's will in full compliance with the law. However, when it was found after her death, the will had red pencil lines through every word in it and through the signature. Also, Eglee's initials, the word "obliterated," and the date September 19, 1973, had been written in red pencil across each clause of the will. Despite this defacement, however, the entire document could be read.

Milton Haller, a nephew of Eglee, argued in the trial court that the will had been revoked. The trial court, however, found that the will had not been revoked. Haller appealed.]

BEVILACQUA, Chief Judge

The issue before us is whether the decedent's actions constituted a sufficient revocation of her will. It is well settled that a will may be validly revoked if the testator, or some third person acting under the testator's direction and in his presence, performs a prescribed physical act with the specified intent of revoking the will. The revocation procedure in Rhode Island is set forth in §33-5-10, which reads:

> No will or codicil or any part thereof shall be revoked otherwise than . . . by *burning, tearing, or otherwise destroying* the same by the testator, or by some person in his presence and by his direction, with the intention of revoking the same. [Emphasis added by the court.]

Thus, revocation of a validly executed will under §33-5-10 requires the intent to revoke coupled with the act of "burning, tearing, or otherwise destroying" the will.

The plaintiff contends that the phrase "otherwise destroying" in §33-5-10 should be construed so as to include the acts of cancelling and obliterating. However, in interpreting such provisions our duty is very narrowly described. We must construe statutes, not redraft them. In so doing, we are bound to ascertain the intent of the Legislature and to effectuate that intent when it is lawful and within legislative competence. Specifically, where a statute prescribes the methods and acts by which a will may be revoked, as does §33-5-10, no acts other than those mentioned in the statute can operate as a revocation, because statutes governing revocation are mandatory and must be strictly construed. The rationale for making statutory formalities governing revocation of a will mandatory is to prevent mistake, misrepresentation, and fraud.

Examining the legislative history of §33-5-10, we find that prior to 1896, our revocation statute omitted the phrase "otherwise destroying" and provided that a will could be revoked by "cancelling" or "obliterating" as well as by other enumerated methods. When the Legislature amended the revocation statute in 1896, it deleted the words "cancelling" and "obliterating" and inserted the phrase "otherwise destroying." Generally, the omission from a revocation statute of one of the modes of revocation previously included renders it impossible to revoke a will by the omitted method. It is obvious that if, as plaintiff argues, the Legislature had intended that the term "otherwise destroying" were to include revocation by cancellation or obliteration, it would have framed the pertinent clause to read "or by burning, tearing, cancelling, obliterating, or otherwise destroying." To adopt plaintiff's construction would contravene both the mandatory method of revocation delineated by §33-5-10 and the obvious intent of the Legislature in drafting that statute.

Courts that have considered statutes identical to §33-5-10 have held that when the Legislature, after mentioning specific acts such as "burning" and "tearing" as sufficient to revoke a will, speaks of "otherwise destroying" a will, it must be understood as intending by the latter some mode of destruction of the same kind or nature as by the methods previously mentioned. Therefore, we believe that the phrase "otherwise destroying" imports a destruction of both the substance and contents of the will. Anything short of a destruction of this degree is entirely ineffectual as a revocation, particularly where the original writing remains legible as in the instant case.

Because §33-5-10 cannot be construed so as to include cancelling and obliterating as appropriate methods of revocation, and because the acts of the testator in this case did not constitute "otherwise destroying" the will, we must agree with the trial justice that despite the testator's obvious intent to revoke, the will was not validly revoked according to §33-5-10.

Affirmed.

CASE REVIEW QUESTIONS

1. How did the legislative history of §33–5–10 help the court to conclude that obliteration and cancellation are not effective means for revoking a will in Rhode Island?
2. Some people would think it unjust that the court decided that Eglee had not revoked her will even though, as the court admits, she intended to do so. Can you think of any justification why the legislature excluded obliteration and cancellation as means of effectively revoking a will?

Dying Without a Valid Will

A person who dies without having a valid will at the time of death is called an **intestate,** which means simply that the person died without a will. Because the deceased has not declared the way in which his or her property is to be disposed of after he or she dies, state statutes, called *intestacy laws,* provide for how the property will be distributed. The people who receive the property of an intestate are called **heirs.**

Intestacy Laws The details of intestacy laws vary among the states. However, first consideration under these laws is given to the surviving spouse. If there is a surviving spouse and also surviving children, grandchildren, father, mother, brothers, sisters, nieces, or nephews, the surviving spouse inherits a specified percentage of the intestate's property. If none of these relatives survives the deceased, the surviving spouse receives all of the property of the intestate.

After the surviving spouse's share has been paid, any remaining property (surplus) of the intestate, or all of the property if there is no surviving spouse, is distributed to the surviving children and grandchildren. If there are no surviving children or grandchildren, it is distributed to the surviving mother and father. If there are no children, grandchildren, mother, or father surviving, it is distributed to brothers and sisters and their descendants who are surviving.

If there are no surviving spouse, children, grandchildren, father, mother, brothers, sisters, nieces, or nephews, the property of the intestate is distributed to more distant relatives, such as uncles, aunts, cousins, and grandparents. Finally, if there are no surviving relatives that are included in the intestacy laws, the intestate's property **escheats,** which means that it is distributed to the state.

General Principles of Intestacy Laws You should note two general principles of the intestacy laws. First, only a person with a blood relationship to the intestate can generally inherit the intestate's property. Except for a spouse, people who are only related by marriage cannot inherit property. Second, to inherit property from an intestate, a person must survive the intestate, which means that he or she must be alive when the intestate dies. The only exception to this principle concerns children of an intestate who are born after the intestate's death; they inherit as though they were alive at the time the intestate died.

Per Capita and Per Stirpes Distribution The distribution of an intestate's property to children and to brothers and sisters is made on a *per capita* basis, meaning that each child or each brother and sister receives an equal share. However, if a child, brother, or sister who would have inherited a share of the intestate's property did not survive the intestate, distribution is generally made to the descendants of that person on a *per stirpes* basis, meaning that they divide the share equally among them.

Suppose, for example, that Jones dies intestate and leaves no surviving spouse, one surviving child, and three surviving grandchildren who are the children of a child of Jones who died before Jones. If both of Jones' children had survived him, his property would have been distributed equally between them. However, even though only one child survives Jones, that child still receives only half of Jones' property (a per capita share). The other half goes to the three surviving grandchildren, each of whom receives one-sixth of the property (a per stirpes share). In other words, although there are four surviving heirs, each does *not* receive one-fourth of Jones' property. (This example is illustrated in Figure 44-1.)

Who is a Child? Throughout this discussion of intestacy laws, reference has been made to children. Generally, whether or not a person is a child of an intestate is clear. In some situations, however, a question arises as to whether a particular person is a child of an intestate with regard to the application of the intestacy laws.

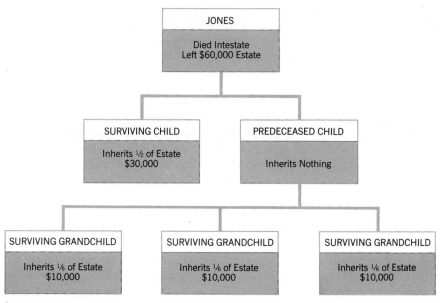

FIGURE 44-1
Example of Per Capita and Per Stirpes Distribution

In most states, a child who has been adopted by the intestate is considered a child of the intestate under the intestacy laws. Conversely, an adopted child has no right to inherit from his or her natural parents. Also, stepchildren are usually treated as the children of their stepparents under the intestacy laws.

Illegitimate children inherit from their mothers just as legitimate children do. However, an illigitimate child is generally treated as a child of his or her father under the intestacy laws only if the parent–child relationship has been acknowledged in some way by the father.

ESTATES

When a person dies, some of the property in which he or she had a legal interest may immediately become the property of another person. For instance, in Chapter 43 you read about certain interests in real property, such as the life estate (see page 926) and the joint tenancy (see page 935), that are transferred automatically upon the death of people who have these interests. Similarly, when a person who has life insurance that names a beneficiary dies, the beneficiary immediately has a claim against the insurance company.

Other property interests do not automatically become the property of another when a person dies, however. For example, if a person owns land individually in fee simple (complete ownership), the land does not automatically become the property of anyone else when the owner dies. Instead, the land becomes an asset of the *estate* of the deceased. It is therefore necessary to have procedures whereby someone represents and administers the deceased's estate, gathers together the property that becomes the property of the estate, pays or otherwise settles the outstanding debts of the deceased, and distributes the remaining property to those who should receive it according to the terms of a valid will or to the terms of the intestacy laws.

Probate

The legal process whereby the validity of a will is determined, a person is appointed to administer the estate, and the estate is administered is called **probate**. The court in which this process takes place is called a *probate court* in most states. In situations involving estates having only a small amount of personal property and no real property, a simple alternative to probate called a *summary procedure* is sometimes available for administering the estate.

Admission of a Will to Probate A will has no legal effect until its validity has been proved to the probate court. Proof is made through the testimony of the witnesses to the will that the deceased had sufficient mental capacity to execute the will, that the necessary steps for the legal execution of the will were taken, and that the deceased intended the document presented to the court to be his or her will. If anyone opposes the validity of the will, he or she may present evidence indicating that the will is not valid. If the probate court determines that the will is valid, as occurs in most probate proceedings, the will is *admitted to probate.* If the court decides that the will is not valid, it is not admitted to probate. Unless another will is submitted to the court and is determined to be valid, the deceased is then treated as having died intestate.

Appointment of an Estate Representative If a person dies intestate, the person that the court appoints to represent the estate is called an **administrator** (male) or an **administratrix** (female). If a person dies leaving a valid will, the person that the court appoints to represent the estate is called an **executor** (male) or an **executrix** (female). Sometimes, the appointed representative may be an institution such as a bank. Often a person states in a will who he or she prefers to be appointed to represent the estate. Although the probate court is not bound to follow the recommendation in the deceased's will, most of the time the person named in the will is appointed as the estate's representative. Frequently, the representative is the spouse or some other close relative of the deceased. An estate representative is entitled to the payment of a fee by the estate for services rendered, but the fee is often waived if the representative is a member of the deceased's family.

Administering the Estate The first task of the representative of an estate is to inventory (make a list of) and take control of the deceased's assets. If the deceased had any claims outstanding, such as accounts receivables, at the time of his or her death, the representative collects them. The representative also gives notice to creditors and pays any valid claims owed by the deceased as well as any state or federal taxes owed by the estate. When the claims and taxes have been paid, the remainder of the estate is distributed to those who are entitled to receive it under the will admitted to probate or under the intestacy laws.

Fiduciary Duties of an Estate Representative An estate representative is considered by the law to be a **fiduciary,** which is a person who is vested with a special form of trust and who is required to display scrupulous good faith and candor. As a result, a representative has a duty to act with care, to act only in the best interests of the estate, and not to take any personal advantage from his or her administration of the estate. If a representative breaches these fiduciary duties and the estate is financially damaged, he or she is personally liable for those damages. When the representative is appointed by the probate court, he or she may be required to post a bond that insures the payment of any liability the representative may incur to the estate.

TRUSTS

When a person dies, the property in his or her estate may be subject to the federal estate tax and to a state inheritance tax. One way a person can avoid estate and inheritance taxes is by disposing of his or her property through *inter vivos* gifts (gifts among the living) while he or she is still alive. However, the extent to which a person can avoid taxes by disposing of property while he or she is still alive is limited by the federal and state gift taxes that are levied on *inter vivos* gifts. In some situations, though, a person may not wish to transfer property directly to another person. For example, a parent with a young child would certainly not want to give a large amount of property to the child. In a situation such as this, a useful device called a trust can be used.

A **trust** is a legal device by which a person with *legal title* to property holds it for the benefit of another person, who is said to have *equitable title* to the property. The person who creates a trust is called the **donor** or the **settlor**, the person who holds the property is called the **trustee**, and the person for whose benefit the property is held is called the **beneficiary**. The property that is held by the trustee is sometimes referred to as the **res** or the **corpus**.

For example, suppose that Donald Jones transfers 1,000 shares of AT&T stock to the Third National Bank & Trust Company for the benefit of his daughter, Barbara. A trust has been created in which Donald is the donor, Third National is the trustee, Barbara is the beneficiary, and the 1,000 shares of stock is the res.

This example involves an express trust because it was created by the express intent of the donor. If the donor creates an express trust during his or her lifetime, it is called an *inter vivos trust.* If the donor creates an express trust by a provision in a will so that it will only take effect after his or her death, it is called a *testamentary trust.* Another form of trust, which is created by operation of law rather than by the donor's express intent, is called an *implied trust.*

Creation of an Express Trust

In order for a donor to create a valid express trust, the following six things must be true:

1. The donor must have the necessary legal capacity to convey property if the trust is *inter vivos* or to make a valid will if the trust is testamentary.
2. The donor must expressly intend to create a trust.
3. The donor must have the legal right to transfer the property that is put in the trust.
4. The donor must follow the formal steps required by law to convey property or to make a valid will.
5. The beneficiary must be identified.
6. The trust must be created for a purpose that is legal and does not violate public policy.

You might have noticed that the donor does *not* have to designate a trustee in order to create an express trust. Although a trustee is almost always named by the donor, should the donor fail to name a trustee or should a named trustee be or become imcompetent or resign, a court will appoint a trustee.

Creation of an Implied Trust

There are circumstances in which a court will find that a trust, called an *implied trust,* has been created even though the donor had no intent to create a trust. One type of implied trust is the constructive trust and the other is the resulting trust.

Constructive Trust A court will find that a **constructive trust** has been created under circumstances in which the imposition of a trust will prevent unjust enrichment. Situations in which constructive trusts are typically imposed include cases in which a corporate executive, an agent, an estate representative, or a trustee breaches a fiduciary duty and thereby personally enriches himself or herself. A court will order the party who has breached the duty to hold any personal gain that he or she possesses as a result of the breach in trust for the benefit of the person to whom the duty was owed. For example, if a corporate executive who works for an oil company purchases an oil field at a bargain price for his or her own benefit rather than for the company, he or she breaches the duty of loyalty owed to the company. In such a case, the court will impose a constructive trust as of the time of purchase and will require the executive to hold the oil field in trust for the benefit of the company until such time as the executive transfers it to the company. Consequently, any profit from the oil field made by the executive while he or she owns it will also he held in trust for the company.

Resulting Trust A court will find that a **resulting trust** has been created under circumstances in which the imposition of the trust will carry out the apparent intent of the donor to create a trust even though the intent has not been made expressly clear. In such a situation, the donor's intent is implied from the conduct of the parties.

For example, suppose Donald Jones transfers ownership of 1,000 shares of AT&T stock to the Third National Bank & Trust Company and mails the shares to the trust department. The bank is now the legal owner of the shares, but even if Jones has not yet made out a written trust instrument, the bank holds the shares in trust — a resulting trust — for the benefit of Jones.

Other Forms of Trusts

Some trusts are categorized by the particular purpose for which they are created and have special rules applied to them. Three of these are the charitable trust, the spendthrift trust, and the totten trust.

Charitable Trust A **charitable trust** is one that is created for a charitable purpose, meaning a purpose that is beneficial to society. For example, the purpose of a charitable trust might be to benefit a religious order, a university, a museum, or a park. If the purpose of the trust is entirely charitable, but the specified purpose becomes impossible or illegal after the trust is created, a court will redirect the particular purpose of the trust to one that is possible and legal and that falls within the general intent of the donor.

Spendthrift Trust A **spendthrift trust** is one that is created for the purpose of preventing the beneficiary from impairing his or her rights in the trust. This is accomplished by including a clause in the document creating the trust that prevents the beneficiary from voluntarily or involuntarily assigning his or her rights in the trust. For example, a beneficiary of a spendthrift trust cannot borrow money and assign his or her right to future income from the trust as security for the loan. Similarly, a creditor of a spendthrift trust beneficiary cannot obtain a court order attaching the beneficiary's right to future income from the trust. Without the spendthrift trust clause, both of these things could be done. However, once payment is made by the trustee to the beneficiary, creditors may attach the property that belongs to the beneficiary.

Generally, spendthrift trusts are valid and are enforced by the courts. However, there are limitations on the use of spendthrift trusts. For instance, a spendthrift trust will not be enforced (1) if a donor makes himself or herself the beneficiary of the spendthrift trust in order to put property outside the reach of his or her own creditors, (2) if a divorced spouse or child seeks to attach the beneficiary's right to future income in order to secure alimony and child support payments, or (3) if a creditor seeks to attach the beneficiary's right to future income in order to obtain payment for necessaries (important items).

Totten Trust A totten trust is created when one person deposits money in a bank account and names himself or herself as the trustee for the benefit of another person. The courts have decided that this arrangement is only a tentative trust. Thus, the donor-depositor may withdraw any amount of the funds from the account at any time for any purpose without breaching his or her fiduciary duties to the beneficiary. The totten trust continues until the donor-depositor either makes an *inter vivos* gift of the account to the beneficiary or dies. When the gift is made or the donor dies, the money in the account belongs to the beneficiary.

Powers of a Trustee

State statutes provide for the powers a trustee can exercise in carrying out the donor's purpose in creating the trust. Generally, these statutes conservatively restrict the powers of trustees. For example, they may provide what kinds of investments a trustee can and cannot make. It is therefore common for a donor to expand the powers of the trustee in the document that creates the trust. A donor may, for instance, give the trustee the power to make more risky investments than those allowed by statute. The donor is permitted by law to expand a trustee's powers in this way.

Fiduciary Duties of a Trustee

The job of the trustee is to carry out the donor's purpose in creating the trust. In doing this work, a trustee is considered to be a fiduciary whose fiduciary duties are the same as those of an estate representative, which were discussed earlier in the chapter. The trustee must act with care, must act only in the best interests of the beneficiary, and must not take personal advantage of his or her position as trustee. If a beneficiary is financially damaged as a result of a breach of fiduciary duty by the trustee, the trustee is personally liable to the beneficiary for the damages. Even if no damage is caused, a breach of fiduciary duty can be grounds for a legal action to have a trustee removed from that position.

In the following case, the beneficiaries of a trust sought both to collect damages for breach of fiduciary duty by the trustee and to have the trustee removed.

WITMER v. BLAIR
588 S.W.2d 22 (Missouri 1979)

WELBORN, Special Judge

Plaintiffs, beneficiaries of a testamentary trust, filed [an] action against defendant trustee, seeking removal of the trustee and damages for breach of fiduciary duties. After trial to the court, the court ordered removal of the defendant as trustee but found against plaintiffs on their claim for damages for breach of fiduciary duties. Plaintiffs appeal from this portion of the decree. [The defendant is referred to as the respondent.]

By his Last Will and Testament, Henry F. Nussbaum made a residual bequest and devise of his estate to his niece, Jane Ann Blair, as trustee, "in Trust however, for the education of my grandchildren (children of my daughter, Dorothy Janice Witmer) living at the time of my decease, or born within a period of nine months thereafter." In the event that none of his grandchildren survived to inherit the estate, the residue would revert to plaintiff Dorothy Janice Witmer, his daughter and first cousin of defendant trustee.

Nussbaum died in 1960. The trust estate came into the hands of the trustee in 1961. It consisted of $1,905 in checking and savings accounts, $5,700 in certificates of deposit and a house valued at $6,000.00. The house was sold in 1962, netting $4,467 to the trust estate. That amount was deposited in a trust checking account. In 1963, $2,000 in certificates of deposit were acquired by the trust and $500 was so invested in 1964. As of December 31, 1970, the trust fund assets consisted of $5,847 in checking account, $506 in savings account and $8,200 in certificates of deposit. In 1971 and 1972, the checking account balance was reduced by transfers to the savings account and on December 31, 1975, the trust assets consisted of $2,741 checking account, $5,474 savings account and $8,200 certificates of deposit.

Plaintiff-appellant Marguerite Janice Witmer was the only grandchild of the testator who became a beneficiary of the trust. She was born September 3, 1953. At the time of the trial, she was 23 years of age. She had not attended a college or university. However, various sums of money had been expended from the trust for her benefit, including a typewriter, clothes, glasses, modeling school tuition and expenses and a tonsillectomy. These expenditures totalled some $1,225.00. The trust also provided $350 for dentures for the mother, Dorothy Witmer.

The trust was handled by appellant rather informally. She kept no books for the trust. The expenditures above mentioned were in most cases advanced by her from her personal account and she reimbursed herself from the trust income. In 1965, the bank erroneously credited the trust account with $560 which should have gone to the trustee's personal account. The mistake was not corrected and that amount remained in the trust account. The trustee received no compensation for her services. Asked at the trial whether she had ever been a trustee before, she responded negatively, adding: "And never again." She explained the large checking account balances in the trust account by the fact that college for Janice "was talked about all the way through school. . . . [I]n my opinion it was the sensible way to keep the money where I could get it to her without any problems at all in case she needed it quickly."

An accountant testified for plaintiffs that if the sum of $800 had been kept in the checking and savings accounts (the $800 was based upon the maximum disbursement in any year) and the balance of the trust placed in one-year certificates of deposit, $9,138 more interest would have been earned as of September 30,

1976, from the trust estate than had been received under respondent's handling of the trust.

In this court, appellants contend that the respondent as trustee was bound to comply with the directions of the trust that she "invest the principal and re-invest the same" and that her failure to invest the trust corpus constituted a breach of her fiduciary duty for which she is liable. The respondent answers that inasmuch as the will failed to specify when and what investments were to be made, such matters were left to the discretion of the trustee and that she exercised such discretion honestly, with ordinary prudence and within the limits of the trust and is not liable for damages.

[T]here has been a breach of trust by the trustee in this case and her good faith is not a defense to appellant's claim. When the respondent came into possession of the trust estate in 1962, appellant Marguerite was some nine years of age. Respondent was acquainted with her and was aware of her age. Obviously there was no prospect of the beneficiary's attending college for a number of years. Respondent's failure to invest a large portion of the trust corpus during such time may not be justified on the grounds that during such time she acceded to requests of the beneficiary's mother to provide small sums for the beneficiary or her mother. Respondent's brief acknowledges that such expenditures were not authorized under the trust. A breach of duty by the trustee in that regard cannot justify her further breach of duty to invest the trust corpus.

However, when Marguerite became of college age and was considering a college education, the respondent should not be faulted for keeping readily available a sum of money which would permit the use of the trust fund for such purpose. Marguerite was somewhat less than candid regarding her college plans. She stated that in 1972 when she went to the modeling school, ". . . we had talked about [going to college]

but . . . I wasn't sure what I wanted to do. There was a chance I could have gone to college and a chance I couldn't have. There was no definite talk either way." However, her mother, in a letter dated February 6, 1972, had told respondent:

> Jan (Marguerite) has still been inquiring about C.U. Extension and Denver University and Arapahoe Jr. College with the idea of possibly starting this fall semester. She still wants more schooling. For this I am so thankful.

It may be conceded that at sometime thereafter respondent should have become aware that college was not realistically in Marguerite's plans and should have handled the Trust accordingly. However, in 1971 and 1972 she did substantially reduce the trust checking account by transfer to the interest-bearing savings account.

The accountant who testified for appellants calculated that between the opening of the Trust and 1971, when college for Marguerite would have been a realistic possibility, had the trust funds, in excess of $100 checking account and approximately $800–1,000 savings account, been invested in one-year certificates of deposit, the trust would have earned additional interest of $2,840.00. In view of the trustee's transfer of a substantial portion of the checking account balance to savings in 1971 and 1972 and in view of the relatively small difference between the return from savings and what might have been earned from certificates of deposit (½% to 1-½%), no damages should be assessed against the trustee for the handling of the estate during that period. However, the trustee should be held liable for the $2,840 which, according to the measure of damages, invoked by appellants, might have been earned by investment of the trust between 1962 and 1971.

Judgment reversed insofar as it denied plaintiff's claim for actual damages. Remanded with directions to enter judgment for plaintiffs for $2,840 actual damages.

CASE REVIEW QUESTIONS

1. As a trustee, what fiduciary duties did Blair owe to the beneficiaries of the trust?
2. What fiduciary duty did Blair breach and how did she breach it?

3. What remedies did the court provide to the beneficiaries as a result of Blair's breach of fiduciary duty?

Modification and Termination

Generally, a donor may not modify or revoke a trust unless the power to do so has been provided for in the document that created the trust. However, even if this power has not been provided for, a trust can be modified or terminated by court order if the donor and all of the beneficiaries consent. If the donor has died, as is always true in the case of a testamentary trust, a court may order modification or termination of a trust if all of the beneficiaries consent and if the action requested of the court will not defeat the donor's purpose in creating the trust.

A trust will terminate automatically when the term of the trust stated in the document that created the trust is completed. For instance, a trust established by Donald Jones for his minor daughter, Tina, that provides for its termination when Tina becomes 21 years old will automatically terminate when Tina reaches the age of 21.

REVIEW QUESTIONS

1. What are the usual requirements for executing a valid will?
2. State the various types of dispositions that may be contained in a will and give an example of each that is not given in the text.
3. Explain in your own words how the property of an intestate is distributed.
4. Explain in your own words the legal process that is called probate.
5. What is a trust and how does it differ from other situations in which ownership of property is transferred from one person to another?
6. What are the requirements for the creation of an express trust?
7. How is an implied trust created?

CASE PROBLEMS

1. Lena Unger died at the age of 78, leaving a will. When the will was submitted for probate, close relatives of the deceased objected to probate of the will on the grounds that Unger did not have sufficient mental capacity to execute a will. The two witnesses who signed the will, who met Unger only at the time the will was executed, testified that they believed she had sufficient mental capacity to execute a will. Unger's nephew, the primary beneficiary under the will, also testified that Unger's mental capacity to make a will was sufficient. However, Unger's doctor and four nurses on the staff of the nursing home in which Unger resided at the time the will was executed testified that they believed she did not have the mental capacity to make a will. The doctor testified that Unger suffered from a mental disorder that made her incapable of orienting herself as to time or place and left

her without short term memory and with very poor long term memory. The nurses testified that, among other things, Unger could not distinguish her room and possessions from those of other patients. Should the probate court admit the will to probate? Explain.

2. Boyd Ruff was married to Modene Ruff, with whom he lived and got along well, for many years. He knew he had a serious heart condition that might cause his death at any time. After a severe heart attack, which he survived, he wrote the following words on the back of a blank check:

> I Boyd Ruff request that all I own in the way of personal or real property to be my wife Modene.
>
> Boyd Ruff

Following Boyd's death, the check was found in his wallet by Modene. She submitted it to a probate court for probate as a will. Who might object to the admission of the document to probate as a will? On what grounds might that person or those persons object? Should the document be admitted to probate as a will? Explain.

3. Matilda Manchester died recently. After her death, a document written entirely in her own handwriting was found in her house. It read:

> I, Matilda Manchester, leave and bequeath all my estate, after payment of legal and funeral expenses, to the following people: [There followed a list of devises and bequests.]
> Whereunto I hereby set my hand this 14th day of January, 1984.

The name of the deceased does not appear anywhere on the document except in the opening clause. The document was found in an envelope on which was written, "My Will, Matilda Manchester," in the deceased's handwriting. If this document is submitted for probate, on what basis might there be objection to its admission to probate? Should the court admit the document to probate? Explain.

4. In April 1981, Grace Peterson, a spinster then aged 74, asked Chester Gustafson, an attorney, to draw a will for her. Gustafson drew this first, as well as

six subsequent wills and a codicil, free of charge because Peterson had no money to pay for his services. The beneficiaries of the first will were various cousins and close friends. In this will, as well as in all subsequent wills except the last, Peterson bequeathed to each beneficiary specific household goods, wearing apparel, or personal effects and named Howard Rhedin, a cousin, as the residuary beneficiary. In December 1982, and in January 1983, Gustafson drew new wills for Peterson, each containing several changes in her bequests and in the beneficiaries. In May 1984, Gustafson drew a fourth will for Peterson. In this will, Peterson for the first time included Gustafson's children, then aged 20 and 18, as beneficiaries. She left each a diamond ring.

Subsequent to this fourth will, Gustafson drew two more wills and a codicil, each will increasing the specific bequests of household articles to his children. In October 1984, he drew a seventh will in which Peterson left all of her property, which at her death included a homestead valued at $10,000 and personal property valued at $1,459, to the Gustafson children.

The only contacts Peterson ever had with Gustafson's children were several chance encounters between five and ten years before in the offices where she worked, when the children delivered some produce to one of Peterson's employers. She never saw the children after that time. When she died, they neither attended her funeral nor appeared or testified in probate court.

During the last four years of her life, Peterson often visited Gustafson in his office, where he kidded and flattered her. He sent her flowers, brought her vegetables, visited in her home but never entertained her in his, was given a key to her house, and arranged a $1,000 loan for her. Grace V. Peterson died on February 1, 1985, without ever changing the will of October 1984. Gustafson, who was named as executor, sought to have it admitted to probate. On what grounds might there be objection to admission of the will to probate? Should the court admit the will to probate? Explain.

5. Michael Nakonezny died recently. In a valid will that he left, he made a specific devise of property at

3039 Preble Avenue to his son Paul. However, before his death, Michael had sold the property at 3039 Preble Avenue. Paul presented evidence to the executor of his father's estate that showed without question that the funds his father had received from the sale of the Preble Avenue property had been used to buy government bonds. The bonds were a part of the estate of Michael Makonezny. Should the executor transfer ownership of the bonds to Paul? Explain.

6. In June 1985, Leonard Wolfe was involved in a fatal automobile accident while he was driving his 1984 Buick Electra. The car was a total loss and decedent's insurance carrier paid the executor of his estate $6,500 for damage to the automobile. Wolfe's will includes a specific bequest of the car to his brother David. The residuary bequest in the will gives any property remaining after the payment of all other bequests to Wolfe's daughter Carol. Assuming there is enough property in the estate to pay all other bequests and devises, what argument can Carol make that she is entitled to the $6,500 paid by the insurance company? What argument could David make that he is entitled to the $6,500? Who do you think should receive the $6,500? Explain.

7. Charles Uhl died in 1985 at the age of 96. After his death, a will was found that Uhl had executed in 1935. Throughout the will, there were notations in the margins that indicated changes that Uhl had thought about making or had wanted to make during the 50 years since he executed the will. On the first page there was a large marginal notation that said, "REVISE WHOLE MESS." Did any of these notations constitute a revocation of Uhl's will? Explain.

8. Rodney Sharp is a dairy farmer with only an eighth grade education. After his wife died a few years ago, Sharp, 56 years old at the time, developed a very close relationship with Jean Kosmalski, who

was 40. In time, Sharp became dependent on Kosmalski's companionship and proposed marriage to her. She refused his proposal but continued her relationship with him. Sharp began to shower her with gifts. Among other things, he named Kosmalski the sole beneficiary of his will and transferred ownership of his farm to her. Recently, the relationhip ended abruptly when Kosmalski ordered Sharp to move off the farm and took possession of the house, farm, buildings, and equipment. Sharp is now left with assets of $300. On what grounds might Sharp be able to argue to a court that Kosmalski holds the farm in trust for him? Would the court agree with Sharp? Explain.

9. Sidney Graves is the beneficiary of a testamentary trust created by his deceased wife, who died in 1982. When the will was probated, Graves could have renounced the will and chosen instead to receive the amount he would have received had his wife died intestate. Had he done so, he would have become owner of the property he received from the estate. He did not elect to take his forced share, however, and instead became the beneficiary of the trust created in the will. This trust contained a spendthrift provision.

In 1984, a creditor who had loaned money to Graves for a trip to London but who had not been repaid brought a legal action against Graves to collect the money due. After obtaining a judgment, the creditor sought a court order attaching Graves' right to income from the trust. The trustee, however, argued that the court should not give the creditor an order of attachment because of the spendthrift provision in the trust. What argument could the creditor make to try to convince the court that an order of attachment would be proper despite the spendthrift provision in the trust? Should the court grant the order of attachment? Explain.

PART X

THE REGULATORY ENVIRONMENT OF BUSINESS

45

INTRODUCTION TO GOVERNMENT REGULATION

In response to the deaths of several infants who had slid through the slats on the sides of their cribs, the Consumer Product Safety Commission undertook a study of the problem. The Commission, a federal agency charged with regulating the safety of consumer products, found that the children's furniture industry used a standard spacing of 3.5 inches for the slats on the sides of cribs. The Commission also found that some infants could slide their bodies between the slats, though their heads would get caught. These infants were sometimes strangled by the pressure of the slats against their necks.

A further study of infant body measurements indicated that a slat spacing of 2.375 inches would prevent 95 percent of all infants from sliding between the slats. The Commission then published a notice in the *Federal Register,* a daily chronicle of all federal regulatory activities, mandating that all new cribs sold must have a maximum spacing of 2.375 inches between the slats. Firms that did not comply with this standard could be subject to legal proceedings, which might result in the recall of their products, the seizure of offending products, or the imposition of fines.

This action by the Consumer Product Safety Commission is but one example of how government administrative agencies regulate business conduct. These agencies are the primary means by which governments — state, federal, and local — attempt to direct and control business behavior. In their regulatory activities, these agencies exercise a number of different functions. They investigate problems, develop and promulgate legally binding rules, prosecute viola-

975

tors of those rules, and adjudicate claims of violations. In short, the agencies act legislatively in developing rules, judicially in deciding disputes involving those rules, and executorily in administering and enforcing those rules.

This chapter will focus on the rationale for regulating business and the jurisdictions of both federal and state governments. We will discuss why administrative agencies are used and how far state and federal agencies may go in regulating business activity. The following chapter will focus on how agencies operate. In it, we will discuss agency procedures and the legal controls and limitations placed upon agencies.

REGULATION BY ADMINISTRATIVE AGENCIES

Our government is a liberal democracy. We recognize individual rights, and we hold that the power of government over its citizens should be limited. One of the most fundamental individual rights is the right to own and use property.

Business activities involve individuals — be they entrepreneurs or corporate officials — using property to produce economic benefits. With individuals free to pursue their choice of activities to promote their own interests, the role of government becomes to ensure that the pursuit of individual interests does not undermine the general welfare of society. Individuals engaged in economic activities interact in the marketplace. The purpose of government regulation is to ensure that the results of these interactions are compatible with the interests of the general public as these interests are defined by our society.

Rather than controlling all economic activity through government ownership of property, as is the case in some societies, we choose to use regulation. This practice allows individual economic activity while, at the same time, it promotes and protects the interests of the public. Even in our society, though, the government engages directly in economic activity to some extent through its ownership or control of such enterprises as the Tennessee Valley Authority or the National Rail Passenger Corporation (Amtrak). The government also uses its influence as a major purchaser of vast quantities of services, products, and supplies to influence business conduct. These methods of influencing economic activity pale in significance, however, when they are compared to our overwhelming reliance upon administrative agencies to regulate business activity.

The regulatory schemes administered by agencies at all levels of government constitute a substantial portion of the legal environment in which any business operates. The way a firm raises capital may be regulated by the Securities and Exchange Commission, its production process may be subject to the regulations of the Environmental Protection Agency, its hiring practices are scrutinized by the Equal Employment Opportunity Commission, its dealings with employees may be regulated by the National Labor Relations Board, its working conditions are subject to the regulations of the Occupational Safety and Health Administration, its marketing practices may be regulated by the Federal Trade Commission, and the design of its products must conform to standards set by the Consumer Product Safety Commission. All of these are federal agencies; they are joined by state and local counterparts.

Reasons for the Use of Administrative Agencies

Administrative agencies are ideal for carrying out the complex and detailed functions involved in regulation. They have the expertise and procedural flexibility to deal effectively with regulatory issues. At the same time, the various branches of government retain enough control over administrative agencies to ensure that they act appropriately.

Agency Actions in Regulation Regulatory actions are often quite involved. For example, determining the maximum allowable spacing between the slats of a child's crib involves a number of specialized investigations. Anthropomorphic studies that statistically analyze the sizes and shapes of infants' bodies must be undertaken. There should be consultations with industry groups to ensure that proposed standards are acceptable to the industry and are not an unreasonable economic burden. The Commission should also study the extent of the crib-slat problem to determine whether it really requires regulatory action. Lastly, the Commission should analyze the costs of a new crib-slat spacing standard versus the benefits the standard would produce. If the benefits outweigh the costs, the Commission should adopt the new spacing requirement.

We can see, then, that the activities involved in regulation, even for a relatively simple matter like the spacing between crib slats, require specialized and technical skills. When the regulatory problem being considered concerns the design of safety controls on nuclear reactors or the maximum allowable levels of employee exposure to toxic chemicals such as benzene or the rates that can be charged by electrical power companies, the need for expertise and flexible procedures is all the greater.

Agencies and the Courts Complex and technical regulatory problems require detailed expertise that the courts do not have. They may also require extensive investigations that cannot be undertaken by the courts. Courts are limited to deciding adversarial disputes between two parties in which there must be a winner and a loser. Judicial procedure does not allow for the consideration of a whole range of alternative approaches to a problem or the consideration of the interests and positions of a number of involved parties. Agencies must negotiate, consult, mediate, and compromise. Because they offer the advantages of expertise and procedural flexibility, agencies, rather than the courts, have been entrusted with the task of carrying out the regulation of business.

The courts have not been totally removed from the regulatory process, however. They are charged with overseeing the operations of administrative agencies through the judicial review of agency actions. In other words, the courts have a supervisory role. Their purpose is not to "second-guess" agency expertise; rather, it is to ensure that agencies do not abuse their legal authority and that they use fair procedures that respect the rights of all the parties involved. Judicial review of agency actions will be discussed in detail in the next chapter.

Agencies and the Legislature Administrative agencies also act as surrogates (substitutes) for the legislature in formulating regulatory policies. While the legislature must initially pass the legislation that establishes an agency and authorizes it to act, the detailed, day-to-day problems of regulating industry are beyond its competence. The large number of issues that require legislative attention make it impossible for the legislature to discuss such detailed techni- cal issues as whether crib slats should be spaced 3.25 or 2.375 inches apart. The partisan nature of legislative debates also restricts the ability of the legislature to deal with complex regulatory problems.

The legislature is, however, suited to determine whether certain activities or industries should be regulated. In addition, through its power to create or dismantle agencies and to expand or restrict their authority, the legislature retains control over the actions of those agencies. The legislature is also well equipped to determine the general direction regulatory policy should take. By creating administrative agencies and delegating to them the authority to deal with complex regulatory details, the legislature can ensure that important regu- latory issues will be appropriately considered.

Agencies and the Executive Branch Lastly, an agency exercises some of the powers of the executive branch of government by enforcing and administering regulatory statutes. The president, or the governor at the state level, has far too many matters competing for his or her attention to allow time for considering whether the spacing of crib slats requires regulation. An administrative agency, on the other hand, is created expressly to consider such matters. The executive branch retains control over agency action, however, through its power to ap- point and remove agency officials. The executive branch also has the power to veto the legislation that creates agencies or that expands or restricts their au- thority.

FEDERAL VERSUS STATE REGULATION OF BUSINESS

Because administrative agencies exist at all levels of government, it is impor- tant to understand the limits of the authority of the various levels of govern- ment to regulate business activity. The main source of legal authority for the federal regulation of business is the Commerce Clause of the U.S. Constitution. The states rely upon their inherent "police powers" to regulate matters affecting the health, safety, welfare, and morals of their residents. County and municipal governments derive their authority from power delegated to them by the state governments. The material that follows will examine the scope of both federal and state authority to regulate business activity.

Federal Jurisdiction over the Regulation of Business

As we have noted, the Commerce Clause, found in Article I, Section 8 of the U.S. Constitution, is the main source of federal regulatory authority. That clause states:

Congress shall have Power . . . To regulate commerce with foreign Nations, and among the several States, and with the Indian Tribes. . . .

We can see from the wording of the Commerce Clause that the federal government can regulate trade activities among the states, which is referred to as **interstate commerce.** Federal power over interstate commerce extends beyond those activities that cut across states lines, however. The Supreme Court has interpreted the federal power to regulate interstate commerce to include wholly **intrastate commerce** — that is, trade activities that do not cross state lines — that may have an *effect* upon interstate commerce.

For example, the Supreme Court held that wheat grown by a farmer in Ohio for his own use was subject to federal agricultural regulations because it affected the demand for wheat marketed in interstate commodity trading. The Supreme Court also held that the sale of real estate in Virginia was subject to federal antitrust laws because the money used to finance the mortgages for the real estate was provided through the interstate banking activities of the Federal Reserve Banks. In both cases, the Supreme Court decided that an intrastate activity was subject to federal regulation because of its *effect* on interstate commerce.

Federal jurisdiction over activities under the Commerce Clause is far reaching; it can even extend to such activities as racial discrimination in employment or accommodations. The following case indicates the scope of federal Commerce-Clause power and illustrates the legal test used to determine whether an activity is subject to the Commerce Clause.

HEART OF ATLANTA MOTEL, INC. v. UNITED STATES
379 U.S. 241 (U.S. Supreme Ct. 1964)

[The Heart of Atlanta Motel is located in downtown Atlanta; it is readily accessible from Interstate highways 75 and 95. Approximately 75 percent of its registered guests are from outside the state of Georgia. Prior to the decision in this case, the motel followed a practice of refusing to rent rooms to blacks. Title II of the Civil Rights Act of 1964 prohibits racial discrimination in places of public accommodation when their operation affects interstate commerce. Heart of Atlanta filed suit to have Title II of the Civil Rights Act declared unconstitutional, claiming, among other things, that Congress exceeded its power under the Commerce Clause in passing the act. The district court upheld the act and enjoined Heart of Atlanta from discriminating on the basis of race or color in making accommodations available. Heart of Atlanta appealed to the Supreme Court.]

CLARK, Justice

It is admitted that the operation of the motel brings it within the provisions of the Act and that appellant refused to provide lodging for transient Negroes because of their race or color and that it intends to continue that policy unless restrained.

The sole question posed is, therefore, the constitutionality of the Civil Rights Act of 1964 as applied to these facts. The legislative history of the Act indicates that Congress based the Act on . . . its power to regulate interstate commerce under Art. I, §8, cl. 3, of the Constitution [the Commerce Clause].

The Senate Commerce Committee made it quite clear that the fundamental object of Title II [of the Civil Rights Act of 1964] was to vindicate "the deprivation of personal dignity that surely accompanies denials of equal access to public establishments." At the same time, however, it noted that such an objective has been and could be readily achieved "by congressional action based on the commerce power of the Constitution." Our study of the legislative record, made in the light of prior cases, has brought us to the conclusion that Congress possessed ample power in this regard. . . .

While the Act as adopted carried no congressional findings, the record of its passage through each house is replete with evidence of the burdens that discrimination by race or color places upon interstate commerce. This testimony included the fact that our people have become increasingly mobile with millions of people of all races travelling from State to State; that Negroes in particular have been the subject of discrimination in transient accommodations, having to travel great distances to secure the same; that often they have had to call upon friends to put them up overnight, and that these conditions have become so acute as to require the listing of available lodging for Negroes in a special guidebook which was itself "dramatic testimony to the difficulties" Negroes encounter in travel. These exclusionary practices were found to be nationwide, the Under Secretary of Commerce testifying that there is "no question that this discrimination in the North still exists to a large degree" and in the West and Midwest as well. This testimony indicated a qualitative as well as quantitative effect on interstate travel by Negroes. The former was the obvious impairment of the Negro traveler's pleasure and convenience that resulted when he continually was uncertain of finding lodging. As for the latter, there was evidence that this uncertainty stemming from racial discrimination has the effect of discouraging travel on the part of a substantial portion of the Negro community. This was the conclusion not only of the Under Secretary of Commerce but also of the Administrator of the Federal Aviation Agency who wrote the Chairman of the Senate Commerce Committee that it was his "belief that air commerce is adversely affected by the denial to a substantial segment of the traveling public of adequate and desegregated public accommodations." We shall not burden this opinion with further details since the voluminous testimony presents overwhelming evidence that discrimination by hotels and motels impedes interstate travel.

The power of Congress to deal with these obstructions depends on the meaning of the Commerce Clause. [T]he determinative test of the exercise of power by the Congress under the Commerce Clause is simply whether the activity sought to be regulated is "commerce which concerns more States than one" and has a real and substantial relation to the national interest.

[The Court then considered several cases that had held that the movement of persons through states was commerce.]

Nor does it make any difference whether the transportation is commercial in character.

The same interest in protecting interstate commerce which led Congress to deal with segregation in interstate carriers and the white-slave traffic has prompted it to extend the exercise of its power to gambling, to criminal enterprises, to deceptive practices in the sale of products, to fraudulent security transactions, to misbranding of drugs, to wages and hours, to members of labor unions, to crop control, to discrimination against shippers, to the protection of small business from injurious price cutting, to resale price maintenance, to professional football, and to racial discrimination by owners and managers of terminal restaurants.

That Congress was legislating against moral wrongs in many of these areas rendered its enactments no less valid. In framing Title II of this Act Congress was also dealing with what it considered a moral problem. But that fact does not detract from the overwhelming evidence of the disruptive effect that racial discrimination has had on commercial intercourse. It was this burden which empowered Congress to enact appropriate legislation, and, given this basis for the exercise of its power, Congress was not restricted by the fact that the particular obstruction to interstate commerce with which it was dealing was also deemed a moral and social wrong.

We, therefore, conclude that the action of the Congress in the adoption of the Act as applied here to a motel which concededly serves interstate travelers is within the power granted it by the Commerce Clause of the Constitution, as interpreted by this Court for 140 years. It may be argued that Congress could have pursued other methods to eliminate the obstructions it found in interstate commerce caused by racial discrimination. But this is a matter of policy that rests entirely with the Congress not with the courts. How obstructions in commerce may be removed—what means are to be employed—is within the sound and exclusive discretion of the Congress. It is subject to only one caveat—that the means chosen by it must be reasonably adapted to the end permitted by the Constitution. We cannot say that its choice here was not so adapted. The Constitution requires no more.

Affirmed.

CASE REVIEW QUESTIONS

1. When is an activity subject to federal regulation under the Commerce Clause?
2. What is the relationship of a motel located in downtown Atlanta to interstate commerce?
3. How does racial discrimination in public accommodations affect interstate commerce?
4. Considering the decision in this case, do you think there are any local activities to which the federal commerce power does not extend? Explain.

Limitations on Federal Commerce-Clause Jurisdiction Although the scope of federal jurisdiction under the Commerce Clause appears to be vast, there are some limitations. The courts have held that some activities are not commerce. The most notable of these exceptions is professional baseball, which the Supreme Court has repeatedly held to be a "sport" and not a business. The accreditation of institutions of higher learning is also excluded.

In addition to these judicially created limitations, the federal commerce power is subject to limits that have been legislatively imposed by Congress. For example, the insurance industry is not subject to any federal regulations that deal specifically with the business of insurance because of federal legislation that gives the states exclusive jurisdiction over such matters.

The federal power to regulate activity under the Commerce Clause is also limited by other provisions of the Constitution. The Due Process Clause of the Fifth Amendment requires that government actions that affect the property rights of businesses must follow "fair" procedures. These procedures include advance notice of any action and the right to be heard before an unbiased adjudicator. The First Amendment protection of freedom of speech limits government regulation of commercial speech—that is, advertising—provided that it is truthful and does not promote illegal transactions.

The Tenth Amendment also limits the power of the federal government to regulate business. The Tenth Amendment provides:

The powers not delegated to the United States by the Constitution, nor prohibited by it to the States, are reserved to the States respectively, or to the people.

The Supreme Court has interpreted the Tenth Amendment to prohibit federal regulation of state and local government activities where such regulation would undermine the sovereignty or impair the functioning of the state or local government. Activities that have traditionally been functions of state or local government or that are necessary for carrying out traditional functions may not be regulated by the federal government. For example, the Supreme Court has held that federal regulation of the wages and hours of state and local government employees violates the Tenth Amendment. The Tenth Amendment does not, however, prevent federal legislation from prohibiting race discrimination or age discrimination in employment by state or local governments. The following case involves the question of whether the state operation of a railroad is immune from federal regulation because of the Tenth Amendment.

UNITED TRANSPORTATION UNION v. LONG ISLAND RAILROAD COMPANY
455 U.S. 678 (U.S. Supreme Ct. 1982)

[The Long Island Railroad (LIRR) provides both freight and passenger service to Long Island; it operates entirely within the state of New York. The LIRR was privately owned at one time, but it was acquired by New York State through its Metropolitan Transportation Authority in 1966. After the state acquired it, the LIRR and the United Transportation Union (UTU) continued to conduct collective bargaining under the procedures set forth in the federal Railway Labor Act.

In 1978, the UTU and the LIRR entered into negotiations to renew their collective-bargaining agreement. They failed to reach an agreement and sought help from the National Mediation Board. Seven months of mediation also failed to produce an agreement, and the union prepared to go on strike, as permitted under the Railway Labor Act. New York believed that the state's acquisition of the railroad would remove it and its employees from the coverage of the Railway Labor Act and place them under New York State's Taylor Law, which prohibited strikes.

The LIRR then filed suit under the Taylor Law to enjoin the pending strike. The UTU filed a countersuit for a declaration that the LIRR was subject to the Railway Labor Act rather than the Taylor Law. The trial court held that the operation of a railroad in interstate commerce is not an integral part of state government activity, and that the Railway Labor Act could be applied to the state-owned railroad. The Court of Appeals reversed, holding that the operation of the railroad was an integral state governmental function and was therefore not subject to federal regulation. The UTU appealed to the Supreme Court.]

BURGER, Chief Justice

We granted [this appeal] to decide whether the Tenth Amendment prohibits application of the Railway Labor Act to a state-owned railroad engaged in interstate commerce. . . .

The determination of whether a federal law impairs a state's authority with respect to "areas of traditional [state] functions" may at times be a difficult one. In this case, however, we do not write on a clear slate. . . . It is . . . clear that operation of a railroad engaged in interstate commerce is not an integral part of traditional state activities generally immune from federal regulation. The Long Island is concededly a railroad engaged in interstate commerce [because it affects interstate commerce]. Operation of passenger railroads, no less than operation of freight railroads, has traditionally been a function of private industry, not state or local governments. It is certainly true that some passenger railroads have come under state control in recent years, as have several freight lines, but that does not alter the historical reality that the operation of railroads is not among the functions *traditionally* performed by state and local governments. Federal regulations of state-owned railroads simply does not impair a state's ability to function as a state. This Court's emphasis on traditional governmental functions and traditional aspects of state sovereignty was not meant to impose a static historical view of state functions generally immune from federal regulation. Rather it was meant to require an inquiry into whether the federal regulation affects basic state prerogatives in such a way as would be likely to hamper the state government's ability to fulfill its role in the Union and endanger its "separate and independent existence."

Just as the Federal Government cannot usurp traditional state functions, there is no justification for a rule which would allow the states, by acquiring functions previously performed by the private sector, to erode federal authority in areas traditionally subject to federal statutory regulation. Railroads have been subject to comprehensive federal regulation for nearly a century. The Interstate Commerce Act—the first comprehensive federal regulation of the industry—was passed in 1887. The first federal statute dealing with railroad labor relations was the Arbitration Act of 1888. . . . Federal mediation of railroad labor disputes was first provided by the Erdman Act of 1898 and strengthened by the Newlands Act of 1913. In 1916, Congress mandated the eight-hour-day in the railroad industry. . . . Finally, in 1926, Congress passed the Railway Labor Act, which was jointly drafted by representatives of the railroads and the railroad unions. The Act has been amended a number of times since 1926, but its basic structure has remained intact. The Railway Labor Act thus has provided the framework for collective bargaining between all interstate railroads and their employees for the past 56 years. There is no comparable history of longstanding state regulation of railroad collective bargaining or of other aspects of the railroad industry.

Moreover, the Federal Government has determined that a uniform regulatory scheme is necessary to the operation of the national rail system. In particular, Congress long ago concluded that federal regulation of railroad labor relations is necessary to prevent disruptions in vital rail service essential to the national economy. A disruption of service on any portion of the interstate railroad system can cause serious problems throughout the system. Congress determined that the most effective means of preventing such disruptions is by way of requiring and facilitating free collective bargaining between railroads and the labor organizations representing their employees. To allow individual states, by acquiring railroads, to circumvent the federal system of railroad bargaining, or any of the other elements of federal regulation of railroads, would destroy the uniformity thought essential by Congress and would endanger the efficient operation of the interstate rail system.

In addition, a state acquiring a railroad does so knowing that the railroad is subject to this longstanding and comprehensive scheme of federal regulation of its operations and its labor relations. Here the State acquired the railroad with full awareness that it was subject to federal regulation under the Railway Labor Act.

The parties proceeded along those premises for the next 13 years, with both sides making use of the procedures available under the Railway Labor Act, and with Railroad employees covered by the Railroad Retirement Act, the Railroad Unemployment Insurance Act and the Federal Employers' Liability Act. Conversely, Railroad employees were not eligible for any of the retirement, insurance or job security benefits of state employees.

The State knew of and accepted the federal regulation; moreover, it operated under federal regulation for 13 years without claiming any impairment of its tradition sovereignty. Indeed, the State's initial response to this suit was to acknowledge that the Railway Labor Act applied. It can thus hardly be maintained that application of the Act to the State's operations of the Railroad is likely to impair the State's ability to fulfill its role in the Union or to endanger [its] "separate and independent existence. . . ."

Reversed and remanded.

CASE REVIEW QUESTIONS
1. In what way is a railroad located entirely in the state of New York involved in interstate commerce?
2. What state activities are immune from federal regulation under the Tenth Amendment?
3. What is the policy rationale behind the limitations imposed upon federal regulation by the Tenth Amendment?

State Jurisdiction Over the Regulation of Business

Because federal jurisdiction under the Commerce Clause is so vast, it is important to determine what areas of business activity are left for state regulation. The Tenth Amendment, as we have noted, reserves for the states any powers not expressly given to the federal government or expressly prohibited to the states. Since the Constitution does not expressly prohibit state regulation of commerce, the courts have held that some state power over interstate commerce is compatible with federal Commerce-Clause power. The courts have also held that the states, under the Tenth Amendment's residual grant of power, are granted police power— that is, the power to legislate on matters concerning the health, safety, welfare, and morals of their residents. For instance, criminal law, which is almost entirely state law, is a product of the states' police power. Police power is also the basis of authority for state regulation of business activity.

A state may regulate an activity that is also subject to federal regulation. This occurs when the activity is involved in or affects interstate commerce and, hence, is subject to federal regulation. The states may also regulate such an activity if the regulation is related to a valid purpose under the states' police power. For example, states can set speed limits on state and local highways even though those highways may be used by persons engaged in interstate commerce. The setting of speed limits is not directed specifically against interstate commerce, and it is related to the states' police power to ensure the safety of their residents.

As a practical matter, most business activity is subject to both federal and state regulation. Examples abound: the banking industry is heavily regulated by both state and federal governments; the issuance and sale of securities is subject to both federal and state regulation; most states have legislation that prohibits racial and sexual discrimination in employment, which is also prohibited under federal law; and both state and federal regulations deal with occupational safety and health matters.

The states may not use their regulatory powers to discriminate against interstate activities, however. For example, regulations aimed at excluding out-of-state businesses or that have the effect of imposing an undue burden on them are unconstitutional.

A state may tax the activities of an out-of-state business if the tax is based upon activities related to the state. In the following case, Mississippi applied its corporate tax to the in-state activities of an interstate business. The firm, Complete Auto Transit, argued that its activities were in interstate commerce and were therefore beyond the legal reach of Mississippi. Complete Auto Transit characterized the tax as simply on the "privilege" of doing business within Mississippi. Taxes on the "privilege" of doing business in a state cannot be applied to out-of-state corporations. Mississippi argued that the tax, which was applied only to those activities of the firm that took place within Mississippi, was a valid exercise of state power.

COMPLETE AUTO TRANSIT v. BRADY
430 U.S. 274 (U.S. Supreme Ct. 1976)

[Complete Auto Transit is a Michigan corporation engaged in transporting vehicles for General Motors. Vehicles destined for dealers in Mississippi are shipped by rail to Jackson and are then trucked by Complete Auto Transit to the dealers' locations. The Mississippi Tax Commission assessed taxes against Complete Auto Transit for the operation of a transportation business within the state.

Complete Auto Transit challenged the assessment of the taxes against it, arguing that they were unconstitutional in that they were being applied to operations in interstate commerce. A Mississippi State trial court upheld the assessment of the taxes, and the Mississippi Supreme Court affirmed the decision. Complete Auto Transit then appealed to the U.S. Supreme Court. Defendant Brady is the chairman of the Mississippi Tax Commission.]

BLACKMUN, Justice

Appellant's attack is based solely on decisions of this Court holding that a tax on the "privilege" of engaging in an activity in the State may not be applied to an activity that is part of interstate commerce. This rule looks only to the fact that the incidence of the tax [the

activity upon which the tax is based] is the "privilege of doing business"; it deems irrelevant any consideration of the practical effect of the tax. The rule reflects an underlying philosophy that interstate commerce should enjoy a sort of "free trade" immunity from state taxation.

Appellee, in its turn relies on decisions of this Court stating that "[i]t was not the purpose of the commerce clause to relieve those engaged in interstate commerce from their just share of state tax burden even though it increases the cost of doing the business." These decisions have considered not the formal language of the tax statutes but rather its practical effect, and have sustained a tax against Commerce Clause challenge when the tax is applied to an activity with a substantial nexus [connection] with the taxing State, is fairly apportioned, does not discriminate against interstate commerce, and is fairly related to the services provided by the State.

The prohibition against state taxation of the "privilege" of engaging in commerce that is interstate was reaffirmed in *Spector Motor Service* v. *O'Connor,* a case similar on its facts to the instant case. The taxpayer there was a Missouri corporation engaged exclusively in interstate trucking. Some of its shipments originated or terminated in Connecticut. Connecticut imposed on a corporation a "tax or excise upon the privilege of carrying on or doing business within the state," measured by apportioned net income [that portion of net income produced by operations within the taxing state]. Spector brought suit in federal court to enjoin collection of the tax as applied to its activities. The District Court issued the injunction. The Second Circuit reversed. This Court, with three Justices in dissent, in turn reversed the Court of Appeals and held the tax unconstitutional as applied.

The Court recognized that

> where a taxpayer is engaged both in intrastate and interstate commerce, a state may tax the privilege of carrying on intrastate business and, within reasonable limits, may compute the amount of the charge by applying the tax rate to a fair proportion of the taxpayer's business done within the state, including both interstate and intrastate.

It held, nevertheless, that a tax on the "privilege" of doing business is unconstitutional if applied against what is exclusively interstate commerce.

The unsatisfactory operation of the *Spector* rule is well demonstrated by our recent case of *Colonial Pipeline Co.* v. *Traigle*. Colonial was a Delaware corporation with an interstate pipeline running through Louisiana for approximately 258 miles. It maintained a work force and pumping stations in Louisiana to keep the pipeline flowing, but it did no intrastate business in that State. In 1962, Louisiana imposed on Colonial a tax for "the privilege of carrying on or doing business" in the State. The Louisiana Court of Appeal invalidated the tax as violative of the rule of *Spector*. The Supreme Court of Louisiana refused review. The Louisiana Legislature, perhaps recognizing that it had run afoul of a rule of words rather than a rule of substance, then redrafted the statute to levy the tax on the "qualification to carry on or do business in this state or the actual doing of business within this state in a corporate form." Again, the Court of Appeal held the tax unconstitutional as applied to the appellant. But this time the Louisiana Supreme Court upheld the new tax.

By a 7-to-1 vote, this Court affirmed. No question had been raised as to the propriety of the apportionment of the tax, and no claim was made that the tax was discriminatory. The Court noted that the tax was imposed on that aspect of interstate commerce to which the State bore a special relation, and that the State bestowed powers, privileges, and benefits sufficient to support a tax on doing business in the corporate form in Louisiana. Accordingly, the tax was held to be constitutional. The court distinguished *Spector* on the familiar ground that it involved a tax on the privilege of carrying on interstate commerce, while the Louisiana Legislature, in contrast, has worded the statute at issue "narrowly to confine the impost to one related to appellant's activities within the State in the corporate form."

In this case, of course, we are confronted with a situation like that presented in *Spector*. The tax is labeled a tax "for the privilege of . . . doing business" in Mississippi, and the activity taxed is, or has been assumed to be, interstate commerce. We note again that no claim is made that the activity is not sufficiently connected to the State to justify a tax, or that the tax is not fairly related to benefits provided the taxpayer, or that the tax discriminates against interstate commerce, or that the tax is not fairly apportioned.

The view of the Commerce Clause that gave rise to the rule of *Spector* perhaps was not without some substance. Nonetheless, the possibility of defending it in the abstract does not alter the fact that the Court has rejected the proposition that interstate commerce is immune from state taxation. . . .

Not only has the philosophy underlying the rule been rejected, but the rule itself has been stripped of any practical significance. If Mississippi had called its tax one on "net income" or on the "going concern value" of appellant's business, the *Spector* rule could not invalidate it. There is no economic consequence that follows necessarily from the use of the particular words, "privilege of doing business," and a focus on the formalism merely obscures the question whether the tax produces a forbidden effect. Simply put, the *Spector* rule does not address the problems with which the Commerce Clause is concerned. Accordingly, we now reject the rule of *Spector Motor Service, Inc.* v. *O'Connor*, that a state tax on the "privilege of doing business" is *per se* unconstitutional when it is applied to interstate commerce, and that case is overruled.

There being no objection to Mississippi's tax except that it was imposed on nothing other than the "privi-lege of doing business" that is interstate, the judgment of the Supreme Court of Mississippi is affirmed.

It is so ordered.

CASE REVIEW QUESTIONS

1. In what way is the transportation of autos from Jackson, Mississippi, to dealers within the state an activity involving interstate commerce?
2. Does the tax involved here apply to all businesses operating in Mississippi or only to interstate businesses that operate in Mississippi? Should this make a difference regarding the legality of the tax?
3. When can a state regulate an interstate activity?

Limitations on State Jurisdiction There are some limitations that apply to state regulation of business. Just as with federal regulations, state regulations must not violate the safeguards of the Constitution. State regulations are also subject to the provisions of the respective state constitutions. In addition, state regulations must not place an undue burden on interstate commerce, cannot conflict with federal law, and must not involve activities where pervasive federal regulation has preempted any state regulation. We will now discuss each of these limitations.

Undue Burden on Interstate Commerce As discussed earlier, a state may use its police powers to impose restrictions upon certain activities in order to promote local safety or welfare concerns. For example, a state may require that all soft drink or beer containers sold in the state be subject to a deposit to discourage littering. While the regulation promotes a valid state concern — stopping litter — it also imposes a burden on soft drink or beer producers who market their products in several states.

In determining whether a state regulation imposes an *undue burden* upon interstate commerce and is therefore unconstitutional, the courts consider whether the regulation is directly related to a valid state purpose and to what degree that purpose is promoted by the regulation. Against those considerations, the courts assess the extent of the burden imposed upon interstate commerce. If the burden of the regulation outweighs its benefits, the regulation is normally held to be invalid. If the burden is slight, the regulation is normally held to be valid.

State "Bottle Bills," which require a deposit on all soft drink and beer containers sold in the state, have been upheld by the courts. State limits on the length of freight trains and double-trailer trucks, on the other hand, have been struck down for burdening interstate commerce more than is warranted by any safety benefits they may promote.

Conflict with Federal Laws Under the Constitution, federal laws are held to be supreme over state laws in the event that there is a conflict between them. Therefore, state regulatory provisions that conflict with federal laws are unconstitutional. The courts will hold state law to conflict with federal law when the two laws are irreconcilable; that is, when it is impossible to comply with one law without violating the other. Generally, the courts are reluctant to hold laws in conflict unless they are truly irreconcilable. If compliance with both laws is possible despite the fact that one law imposes stricter requirements, both laws will be valid.

For example, both New York State law and federal law forbid age discrimination in employment. The federal Age Discrimination in Employment Act protects employees between the ages of 40 to 70 from any discrimination in terms or conditions of employment because of age. The New York State Human Rights Law protects workers between the ages of 18 to 70 from age discrimination in employment. Since an employer can comply with both laws by refraining from age discrimination for all workers between 18 and 70, the laws are not in conflict. However, if the New York law were to require that workers *must* be retired at age 65 and the federal law were to prohibit involuntary retirement before 70, the employer would not be able to comply with both laws. In that case, the New York law would be unconstitutional, and therefore void, because it would conflict with federal law.

Federal Preemption and the Need for National Uniformity When an activity is subject to pervasive federal regulations or when national uniformity in the regulation of an activity is essential, the states may be precluded from regulating an activity even though there is no express prohibition against state regulation. Because federal regulation of some activities is so extensive, the federal government is said to have "occupied the field" and to have "preempted" any state regulation. There is simply no room left for state regulation of these activities. For example local regulations that limited the hours aircraft could take off and land at Los Angeles International Airport were held to be invalid because federal aviation regulations had preempted the field.

Closely related to the idea of preemption is the concern with the need for national uniformity in the regulation of some activities. When national uniformity in the regulation of an activity is held to be essential by the courts, the states are precluded from regulating that activity. Unlike preemption, though, state regulation may be precluded in these situations even when the federal government has not regulated the activity, because regulations by the individual states could not meet the need for national uniformity. The regulation of nuclear power and atomic energy is an area where national uniformity is essential. Local restrictions on the transportation of radioactive wastes have therefore been held to be invalid.

The following case involves a challenge to a city ordinance designed to protect city residents from the sale of improperly processed milk.

DEAN MILK COMPANY v. CITY OF MADISON
340 U.S. 349 (U.S. Supreme Ct. 1951)

[The city of Madison, Wisconsin, adopted an ordinance making it unlawful to sell milk unless it had been pasteurized and bottled at a city-approved plant located within five miles of Madison. Madison is located in Dane County, which contains 5,600 dairy farms; Dane County supplies large quantities of milk to Chicago, Illinois, and other areas.

Dean Milk Company is an Illinois corporation that distributes milk and dairy products in Wisconsin and Illinois. It sued the city of Madison, challenging the ordinance as violating the Commerce Clause of the Constitution because it discriminated against interstate commerce and imposed an undue burden on interstate commerce. The Supreme Court of Wisconsin upheld the ordinance as a valid exercise of police power on the grounds that it promoted the convenient, economical, and efficient inspection of milk plants by municipal inspectors. Dean Milk appealed to the U.S. Supreme Court.]

CLARK, Justice

It is conceded that the milk which appellant seeks to sell in Madison is supplied from farms and processed in plants licensed and inspected by public health authorities of Chicago, and is labeled "Grade A" under the Chicago ordinance which adopts the rating standards recommended by the United States Public Health Service. Both the Chicago and Madison ordinances, though not the section of the latter here in issue, are largely patterned after the Model Milk Ordinance of the Public Health Service. However, Madison contends and we assume that in some particulars its ordinance is more rigorous than that of Chicago.

Upon these facts we find it necessary to determine only the issue raised under the Commerce Clause, for we agree with appellant that the ordinance imposes an undue burden on interstate commerce.

This is not an instance in which an enactment fails because of federal legislation which, as a proper exercise of paramount national power over commerce, excludes measures which might otherwise be within the police power of the states. There is no pertinent national regulation by the Congress.

It is not contended, however, that Congress has authorized the regulation before us.

Nor can there be objection to the avowed purpose of this enactment. We assume that difficulties in sanitary regulation of milk and milk products originating in remote areas may present a situation in which "upon a consideration of all the relevant facts and circumstances it appears that the matter is one which may appropriately be regulated in the interest of the safety, health and well-being of local communities. . . ." We also assume that since Congress has not spoken to the contrary, the subject matter of the ordinance lies within the sphere of state regulation even though interstate commerce may be affected.

But this regulation, in practical effect, excludes from distribution in Madison wholesome milk produced and pasteurized in Illinois. . . .

In thus erecting an economic barrier protecting a major local industry against competition from without the State, Madison plainly discriminates against interstate commerce. This it cannot do, even in the exercise of its unquestioned power to protect the health and safety of its people, if reasonable nondiscriminatory alternatives, adequate to conserve legitimate local interests, are available. A different view, that the ordinance is valid simply because it professes to be a health measure, would mean that the Commerce Clause of itself imposes no limitations on state action . . . save for the purpose to discriminate against interstate goods. Our issue then is whether the discrimination inherent in the Madison ordinance can be justified in view of the character of the local interests and the available methods of protecting them.

It appears that reasonable and adequate alternatives are available. If the City of Madison prefers to rely upon its own officials for inspection of distant milk sources, such inspection is readily open to it without hardship, for it could charge the actual and reasonable cost of such inspection to the importing producers and processors. Moreover, appellee Health Commissioner of Madison testified that as proponent of the local milk ordinance he had submitted the provisions here in controversy and an alternative proposal based on §11 of the Model Milk Ordinance recommended by the United States Public Health Service. The model provision imposes no geographical limitation on location of milk sources and processing plants but excludes from the municipality milk not produced and pasteurized conformably to standards as high as those enforced by the receiving city. In implementing such an ordinance, the importing city obtains milk ratings based on uniform standards and established by health authorities in the jurisdiction where production and processing occur. The receiving city may determine the extent of enforcement of sanitary standards in the exporting area by verifying the accuracy of safety ratings of specific plants of the milkshed in the distant jurisdiction through the United States Public Health Service, which routinely and on request spot checks the local ratings. The Commissioner testified that Madison consumers "would be safeguarded adequately" under either proposal and that he had expressed no preference. The

milk sanitarian of the Wisconsin State Board of Health tesitifed that the State Health Department recommends the adoption of a provision based on the Model Ordinance. Both officials agreed that a local health officer would be justified in relying upon the evaluation by the Public Health Service of enforcement conditions in remote producing areas.

To permit Madison to adopt a regulation not essential for the protection of local health interests and placing a burden on interstate commerce would invite a multiplication of preferential trade areas destructive of the very purpose of the Commerce Clause. Under the circumstances here presented, the regulation must yield to the principle that "one state in its dealings with another may not place itself in a position of economic isolation."

For these reasons we conclude that the judgment below sustaining the five-mile provision as to pasteurization must be reversed.

It is so ordered.

CASE REVIEW QUESTIONS

1. What is the stated purpose of the Madison city ordinance involved here? Do you suspect that there may be another, unspoken, purpose behind the ordinance?
2. What is the effect of this ordinance upon interstate commerce? Explain.
3. Does this ordinance conflict with federal law, or is it preempted by federal regulation? Explain.
4. What alternatives are available to the city of Madison to meet the stated purpose of the ordinance? How could you redraft the ordinance so that it would be upheld by the Supreme Court?

REVIEW QUESTIONS

1. Why are administrative agencies used for regulation? What advantages do they offer over the use of courts? What advantages do they offer over legislatures? What are the disadvantages of using agencies for regulation?

2. What controls does the legislature exercise over administrative agencies? What controls does the executive branch (president or governor) exercise over agencies?

3. What is meant by the federal Commerce-Clause

power? To what activities does this federal power extend?

4. What is meant by the states' "police powers"? To what activities does this power extend?

5. Can states ever regulate interstate activity? Explain. Can the federal government regulate activities that are only local or intrastate? Explain.

6. What are the specific legal limitations upon the ability of states to regulate commerce?

CASE PROBLEMS

1. Blackburn operates a grocery store on an Indian reservation in Arizona. The state of Arizona passed a law requiring that all firms doing business on Indian reservations within the state be licensed by the State Commerce Department. The license requirement is intended to ensure that the firms are not engaged in deceptive or unfair trade practices. Blackburn refuses to get a license, and Arizona brings a suit to force him to get a license or to stop doing business on the reservation. Who will win the case? Explain.

2. The state of South Dakota owns and operates a cement plant. During times when cement is in short supply, the plant will sell its cement only to residents of South Dakota. Classic Construction Company, located in North Dakota, wished to purchase cement from the South Dakota plant because it is the closest supplier. The plant refused to sell to Classic. If Classic sues the state, asking the court to require South Dakota to sell cement to it, who will win the case? Explain.

3. The state of Alaska requires that all employers within the state that are engaged in the business of producing, refining, processing, transporting, distributing, or selling petroleum products produced from oil extracted from state oil leases must give priority to Alaskan residents when hiring employees. Brown, a resident of Washington, is refused employment by Anchorage Pipeline Company because it only hires Alaskan residents. If Brown brings a legal action against Anchorage Pipeline, who will win the case? Explain.

4. Austin, a resident of Maine, works at a factory located in New Hampshire. New Hampshire, which does not have a state income tax, enacted a "Commuter Income Tax" that applies only to nonresidents who work in New Hampshire. Austin brings a suit challenging the tax. Who will win the case? Explain.

5. The state of Wyoming requires that its game wardens retire at age 60. The federal Age Discrimination in Employment Act prohibits employers from requiring employees to retire prior to the age of 70. The federal act also applies to state and local governments in their role as employers. The Equal Employment Opportunity Commission filed suit against Wyoming to stop the practice. Wyoming defended on the grounds that the EEOC is prohibited by the Tenth Amendment from enforcing the act against a state. Who will win the case? Explain.

6. The New York State Human Rights Law prohibits employment discrimination on the basis of race, religion, color, sex, or national origin. The law recognizes, however, that in some instances employers may hire persons of a specific sex, religion, or race when the characteristic is a "bona fide occupational qualification." Title VII of the federal Civil Rights Act of 1964, as amended, also prohibits employment discrimination by race, color, religion, sex, or national origin. The federal law says that only religion, sex, or national origin may be used as bona fide occupational qualifications. Skin-Tone, Inc., produces cosmetics for black women. Worthington, a white, is refused a job as salesperson at Skin-Tone's New York City store because Skin-Tone will only hire blacks for sales positions. Worthington files suit against Skin-Tone's hiring practices; Skin-Tone defends on the grounds that New York State law permits them to use race as a bona fide occupational qualification. Who will win? Explain.

46

ADMINISTRATIVE AGENCY PROCEDURES

As discussed in the previous chapter, administrative agencies combine legislative, executive, and judicial functions. Like legislatures, agencies engage in rulemaking when they set procedures or develop rules as part of their regulatory duties. Like the executive branch of government, agencies enforce and administer the statutes that created them and define their regulatory authority. Lastly, like courts, agencies adjudicate disputes involving the application of their regulations. Also like courts, their decisions affect the rights and liabilities of the various parties involved.

This combination of legislative, executive, and judicial functions provides a practical approach to the problems inherent in attempting to regulate complicated or technical activities. An agency can apply its expertise on the subject involved to full advantage within a framework that safeguards the rights of the various parties affected.

In order to ensure that agencies exercise their broad powers responsibly, legal checks are imposed upon their actions. The primary legal check is judicial review. The courts will review agency action when a party involved in or affected by such action requests it. The reviewing court will not attempt to substitute its own judgment for that of the agency, but it will make sure that the agency followed fair and proper procedures in taking the action. Another legal check on agencies is legislation, which may require that certain procedures be followed in specific situations.

This chapter will focus upon the procedures used by administrative agencies in carrying out their regulatory duties. We will concentrate on federal agencies and the **Administrative Procedure Act,** the federal law that sets certain procedural requirements for federal agency action. State and local agencies use similar procedures and often operate under specific legislation similar to the Administrative Procedure Act. This chapter will also examine the judicial review of administrative agency actions.

ADMINISTRATIVE RULEMAKING

In carrying out their regulatory functions, agencies often engage in rulemaking. They may formulate **procedural rules** (which set forth the procedures by which the agencies carry out their duties), **interpretive rules** (which act as guides to the administration and interpretation of the statutes enforced by the agency), and **substantive rules** (which may require specific standards of conduct, may impose sanctions upon violators, and have the force of law). These various kinds of rules are made through different procedures. They are also accorded differing degrees of deference by the reviewing courts, which means that the courts use different approaches in determining the validity of the different types of rules.

No specific requirements are set by the Administrative Procedure Act for the development of agency procedural rules and interpretive rules, because such rules generally have a less substantial impact on the rights of private parties than do substantive rules. An administrative agency may simply issue such a rule. No public participation in their development is required. Agencies usually have discretion in determining whether or not they will clarify their procedures or policies by issuing procedural or interpretive rules. However, because these rules have not been developed with public examination and participation, they are generally scrutinized very closely by the courts if they are ever called into question through judicial review.

Substantive rules, which are also known as **legislative rules,** generally have a more substantial impact upon the rights of interested parties than do procedural or interpretive rules. They specify standards of conduct and may impose sanctions for violations.

Administrative agencies are making increasing use of substantive rules because such rules tend to simplify adjudicatory and regulatory functions. Additionally, they give a clear definition of the standard of conduct called for, and they ensure equal treatment of all cases involving such activities. The procedures used in creating substantive rules require that the agency give notice to all interested parties and afford them the opportunity of participating in the process.

For example, the Federal Trade Commission (FTC) may decide that certain door-to-door sales practices are deceptive and unfair to consumers. It therefore decides to develop a rule outlawing such practices. Through the rulemaking procedures, interested parties—both firms that sell door-to-door and consumer groups—can give evidence about the effects of such practices. Once the FTC adopts a rule declaring such practices illegal, the validity of the rule cannot be questioned as a defense to a charge of violating the rule. Therefore, if a firm is subsequently charged with engaging in such practices, the FTC need only determine whether the practices actually took place and whether the rule should apply in the particular case. It need not reestablish the fact that such practices have a deceptive and unfair effect upon consumers. This simplification of the adjudicatory process saves both the FTC and the parties involved time, effort, and money.

The Administrative Procedure Act provides two different sets of procedures for the development of substantive rules by federal agencies. These sets of procedures are *notice and comment rulemaking,* also known as **informal rulemaking,** and *rulemaking through a hearing process,* also known as **formal rulemaking.** Unless the statute empowering the agency specifically requires formal rulemaking, the choice of the procedure used is up to the agency. Because formal rulemaking is a costly and time-consuming affair, an agency generally opts for informal rulemaking whenever possible.

Informal Rulemaking

The procedures for informal rulemaking are spelled out in §4 of the Administrative Procedure Act. To begin, an agency must give public notice that it intends to develop a rule. The notice must contain the terms and substance of the proposed rule or a description of the subjects and issues involved. This notice is usually published in the *Federal Register,* a daily chronicle of all federal regulatory activity. The agency may also send notices to industry and consumer groups who are likely to be interested.

After notice is given, the agency must allow interested persons the opportunity to participate in the rulemaking process through the submission of written comments containing data, arguments, or views on the issues involved. The agency is not required to hold any public hearings, however. After the agency has considered and analyzed the public comments it has received, it must issue the final rule along with a concise statement of the basis and purpose of the rule.

Informal rulemaking provides an efficient method for informing the public and reaching a prompt decision about a new rule. At times, however, informal rulemaking may produce inappropriate decisions because the agency's premises underlying the rule have not been examined in a public proceeding.

If rules produced through informal rulemaking procedures are later reviewed by a court, the reviewing court must first consider whether the statute that created the agency authorized it to make substantive rules. If the agency was not so authorized, any rules made by the agency are invalid. The court must also consider whether the statute requires that specific rulemaking procedures be used. If it does, the agency must have followed those procedures for the rule to be valid. The court must then consider whether the agency's analysis of the facts and information it received through the notice and comment procedure is reasonable. If the court finds the analysis is reasonable, it must uphold the rule. In other words, judicial review does not involve the court determining whether the agency's view is "correct" or whether the court agrees with the agency's position, only whether the agency's analysis is reasonable.

Formal Rulemaking

When the statute empowering an agency to act requires formal rulemaking or when the agency itself chooses formal rulemaking, a public hearing is required. A notice of the subject of the proposed rule is published in the *Federal Register* along with the date and location of the public hearing. All interested parties must be afforded an opportunity to participate in the hearing by giving testimony and cross-examining adverse witnesses. When numerous parties are involved, these procedures can be very cumbersome and time-consuming.

After the hearing has been completed, the agency must develop a rule based upon the evidence brought forth at the hearing. The Administrative Procedure Act requires that a rule promulgated through formal rulemaking procedures must be supported by "substantial evidence on the record as a whole." If such a rule is later subjected to judicial review, the court must consider whether there is "substantial" support for the rule based on all the evidence — both favorable and opposing — brought forth at the hearing. Again, the reviewing court is not to "second guess" the agency with regard to the wisdom of the rule. It is to consider only whether the evidence that supports the rule as adopted is substantial.

Hybrid Rulemaking

Because formal rulemaking is time-consuming and expensive, agencies are generally reluctant to resort to formal rulemaking unless it is required by statute. At the same time, informal rulemaking may not provide an adequate opportunity for public participation on some sensitive or contested issues. As a result, agencies often resort to **hybrid rulemaking,** a set of procedures that incorporates features of both formal and informal rulemaking.

When using the hybrid procedures, the agency publishes a notice of a proposed rule and invites public comment. If the comments indicate that some issues are contested or that some premises are seriously disputed, the agency will hold a hearing on those particular issues or premises. Thus, the public is afforded the opportunity to participate with respect to those matters of major concern, yet the scope of the hearing is restricted so that the delay and expense of formal rulemaking are reduced.

Choice of Rulemaking Procedures

In the absence of specific statutory requirements, the choice of which rulemaking procedures to use in a particular situation is generally left to the discretion of the agency. The Administrative Procedure Act does not require that particular procedures be used in specific situations. Rather, it describes the actions that must be followed when the agency chooses to use particular procedures.

The agency's choice of procedures must meet the due process requirements. That is, it must provide interested parties with notice of the proposed rule and with an opportunity to make their views known either through the submission of written comments or by participation in a public hearing.

In the following case, a party to an administrative proceeding argued that the procedures used by the agency were improper. The court had to consider the proper relationship of a reviewing court to an agency's choice of rulemaking procedures under the Administrative Procedure Act.

**VERMONT YANKEE NUCLEAR POWER CORPORATION v.
NATURAL RESOURCES DEFENSE COUNCIL**
435 U.S. 519 (U.S. Supreme Ct. 1978)

[The Atomic Energy Commission granted Vermont Yankee Nuclear Power Corporation (Vermont Yankee) a license to operate a nuclear power plant after proceedings before the Atomic Safety and Licensing Board, and the license grant was affirmed by the Atomic Safety and Licensing Appeal Board. Both of these boards are part of the Atomic Energy Commission (AEC). During the licensing proceedings, the Natural Resources Defense Council (NRDC) had argued that the Licensing Board should consider the environmental effects of the reprocessing and disposal of the plant's fuel. Both the Licensing Board and the Licensing Appeal Board refused to consider the issue.

The AEC then instituted informal rulemaking procedures to consider the environmental effects of the uranium fuel cycle. As a result of the informal rulemaking, the AEC issued a "fuel-cycle" rule. The AEC held, however, that it was unnecessary to apply this rule to the Vermont Yankee licensing proceeding, which had already been completed.

The NRDC sought judicial review of the AEC's adoption of the "fuel-cycle" rule and the decision to grant the operating license to Vermont Yankee. The Court of Appeals held that the rulemaking procedures employed were inadequate, and overturned the rule. It also remanded the licensing decision for reconsideration. Vermont Yankee then appealed to the Supreme Court.]

REHNQUIST, Justice
In 1946, Congress enacted the Administrative Procedure Act, which as we have noted elsewhere was not only "a new, basic and comprehensive regulation of procedures in many agencies," but was also a legis-

lative enactment which settled "long-continued and hard-fought contentions, and enacts a formula upon which opposing social and political forces have come to rest." Section 4 of the Act, dealing with rulemaking, requires . . . that "notice of proposed rulemaking shall be published in the Federal Register . . . ," describes the contents of that notice, and goes on to require that after the notice the agency

> shall give interested persons an opportunity to participate in the rulemaking through submission of written data, views or arguments with or without opportunity for oral presentation. After consideration of the relevant matter presented, the agency shall incorporate in the rules adopted a concise general statement of their basis and purpose.

Interpreting this provision of the Act, we held that generally speaking this section of the Act established the maximum procedural requirements which Congress was willing to have the courts impose upon agencies in conducting rulemaking procedures. Agencies are free to grant additional procedural rights in the exercise of their discretion, but reviewing courts are generally not free to impose them if the agencies have not chosen to grant them. This is not to say necessarily that there are no circumstances which would ever justify a court in overturning agency action because of a failure to employ procedures beyond those required by the statute. But such circumstances, if they exist, are extremely rare.

Even apart from the Administrative Procedure Act this Court has for more than four decades emphasized that the formulation of procedures was basically to be left within the discretion of the agencies to which Congress had confided the responsibility for substantive judgments. It is in the light of this background of statutory and decisional law that we [agreed] to review [the] judgment of the Court of Appeals because of our concern that they had seriously misread or misapplied this statutory and decisional law cautioning reviewing courts against engrafting their own notions of proper procedures upon agencies entrusted with substantive functions by Congress. We conclude that the Court of Appeals has done just that and we therefore remand for further proceedings.

We turn to the invalidation of the fuel cycle rule. After a thorough examination of the opinion itself, we conclude that while the matter is not entirely free from doubt, the majority of the Court of Appeals struck down the rule because of the perceived inadequacies of the procedures employed in the rulemaking proceedings. . . . The court concluded that absent extraordinary circumstances it is improper for a reviewing court to prescribe the procedural format an agency must follow, but it likewise clearly thought it entirely appropriate to "scrutinize the record as a whole to insure that genuine opportunities to participate in a meaningful way were provided. . . ." The court also refrained from actually ordering the agency to follow any specific procedures, but there is little doubt in our minds that the ineluctable mandate of the court's decision is that the procedures afforded during the hearings were inadequate. This conclusion is particularly buttressed by the fact that after the court examined the record and declared it insufficient, the court proceeded to discuss at some length the necessity for further procedural devices or a more "sensitive" application of those devices employed during the proceedings. The exploration of the record and the statement regarding its insufficiency might initially lead one to conclude that the court was only examining the sufficiency of the evidence, but the remaining portions of the opinion dispel any doubt that this was certainly not the sole or even the principal basis of the decision. Accordingly, we feel compelled to address the opinion on its own terms, and we conclude that it was wrong.

In prior opinions we have intimated that even in a rulemaking proceeding when an agency is making a "quasi-judicial" determination by which a very small number of persons are "exceptionally affected, in each case upon individual grounds," in some circumstances additional procedures may be required in order to afford the aggrieved individuals due process. It might also be true, although we do not think the issue is presented in this case and accordingly do not decide it, that a totally unjustified departure from well-settled agency procedures of long standing might require judicial correction. But this much is absolutely clear. Absent constitutional constraints or extremely compelling circumstances the "administrative agencies should be free to fashion their own rules of procedure and to pursue methods of inquiry capable of permitting them to discharge their multitudinous duties." Respondent NRDC argues that §4 of the Administrative Procedure Act merely established lower procedural bounds and that a court may routinely require more than the minimum when an agency's proposed rule addresses complex or technical factual issues or "Issues of Great Public Import." We have, however, previously shown that our decisions reject this view. We also think the legislative history does not bear out its contention. In short, all of this leaves little doubt that Congress intended that the discretion of the *agencies* and not that of the courts be exercised in determining when extra procedural devices should be employed.

There are compelling reasons for construing §4 in this manner. In the first place, if courts continually review agency proceedings to determine whether the agency employed procedures which were, in the court's opinion, perfectly tailored to reach what the court perceived to be the "best" or "correct" result, judicial review would be totally unpredictable. And the agencies operating under this vague injunction to employ the "best" procedures and facing the threat of reversal if they did not, would undoubtedly adopt full adjudicatory procedures in every instance. Not only would this totally disrupt the statutory scheme, through which Congress enacted "a formula upon which opposing social and political forces have come to rest," but all the inherent advantages of informal rulemaking would be totally lost.

Secondly, it is obvious that the court in these cases reviewed the agency's choice of procedures on the basis of the record actually produced at the hearing and not on the basis of the information available to the agency when it made the decision to structure the proceedings in a certain way. This sort of Monday morning quarterbacking not only encourages but almost compels the agency to conduct all rulemaking proceedings with the full panoply of procedural devices normally associated only with adjudicatory hearings.

Finally, and perhaps most importantly, this sort of review fundamentally misconceives the nature of the Standard for judicial review of an agency rule. The court below uncritically assumed that additional procedures will automatically result in a more adequate record because it will give interested parties more of an opportunity to participate in and contribute to the proceedings. But informal rulemaking need not be based solely on the transcript of a hearing held before an agency. Indeed, the agency need not even hold a formal hearing. Thus, the adequacy of the "record" in this type of proceeding is not correlated directly to the type of procedural devices employed, but rather turns on whether the agency has followed the statutory mandate of the Administrative Procedure Act or other relevant statutes. If the agency is compelled to support the rule which it ultimately adopts with the type of record produced only after a full adjudicatory hearing, it simply will have no choice but to conduct a full adjudicatory hearing prior to promulgating every rule. In sum, this sort of unwarranted judicial examination of perceived procedural shortcomings of a rulemaking proceeding can do nothing but seriously interfere with that process prescribed by Congress.

In short, nothing in the APA, . . . the circumstances of this case, the nature of the issues being considered, past agency practice, or the statutory mandate under which the Commission operates permitted the court to review and overturn the rulemaking proceeding on the basis of the procedural devices employed (or not employed) by the Commission so long as the Commission employed at least the statutory *minima,* a matter about which there is no doubt in this case. . . .

We accordingly remand so that the Court of Appeals may review the rule as the Administrative Procedure Act provides.

Reversed and remanded.

CASE REVIEW QUESTIONS

1. What procedures did the AEC employ to develop the "fuel-cycle" rule?
2. What was the Court of Appeals' view of the adequacy of these procedures? Why?
3. What was the Supreme Court's view of the adequacy of these procedures? Why?
4. What standard of judicial review is to be used by a court reviewing the procedures used by an agency to make a rule? Was this standard used by the Court of Appeals?

ADMINISTRATIVE ADJUDICATION

Besides having legislative power, an agency also has the power to adjudicate disputes arising under the statutes it enforces. This adjudicatory power carries with it the power to affect the rights of the parties involved and to impose sanctions. For example, the Federal Trade Commission Act, enforced by the Federal Trade Commission (FTC), prohibits false or deceptive advertising. In response to consumer complaints or as the result of an FTC investigation, the FTC may file charges against a firm allegedly engaging in false or deceptive advertising. The charges against the firm will be tried by an FTC adjudicator in an administrative hearing. If the FTC determines that the firm has violated the law, it will order the firm to cease the false advertising. If the firm does not comply with the FTC order, it can be fined up to $10,000 for each day the violation continues by the FTC.

In the course of exercising its judicial power, an agency may be called upon to apply and enforce one of its own substantive rules. Because the combination of executive and judicial functions within the agency may create the potential for bias in adjudication, several procedural safeguards are imposed upon agency adjudication. This section of the text examines federal agency procedures for adjudication and the requirements imposed upon agency adjudication to protect the rights of the parties involved. As was true with rulemaking procedures, state and local agencies follow similar processes for adjudication, and they are subject to similar safeguards.

Adjudicative Procedures

Because an administrative agency may act as prosecutor as well as adjudicator — that is, it may initiate a complaint against a party (its prosecutor function) and then decide whether to impose a sanction upon that party (its adjudicator function) — the organizational functions within agencies must be separated to ensure that adjudication is unbiased. The agency staff who, after an investigation, issue and prosecute a complaint are in a separate division of the agency from the hearing examiner, or **Administrative Law Judge** (ALJ), who decides whether to uphold the complaint.

In the National Labor Relations Board (NLRB), for example, complaints are issued and prosecuted by the staff members of the NLRB's regional offices, whereas the ALJs who decide the complaints are drawn from separate offices in New York, Atlanta, or San Francisco. Informal contacts between the regional office staff and the ALJs are prohibited, and the adjudicator is required to base his or her decision only on the information contained in the record of the hearing.

Agency adjudication must comply with the due process requirements of the Constitution. This means that, in addition to the measures outlined earlier to ensure unbiased decision making, the parties affected must be given timely notice of the proceedings and must be afforded an opportunity to participate in those proceedings.

The Administrative Procedure Act sets procedural requirements for adjudication by agencies when statutory provisions require that a hearing be held. The proceeding is initiated by the service of a timely notice to the affected parties. The notice must give the time and place of the hearing, the statutory authority upon which the agency relies in bringing the proceeding, and the issues of fact and law involved in the proceeding. During the hearing, the involved parties have the right to participate by offering evidence and cross-examining witnesses. The ALJ conducting the hearing is required to develop a full and adequate record of the hearing.

After the hearing, the Administrative Law Judge will decide the issues in question. The ALJ's decision must be based on the record of the hearing alone, and that decision must be supported by substantial evidence in the record when it is considered as a whole.

In most agencies, the ALJ's decision may be appealed to a commission or a board. For example, the National Labor Relations Board, a five-member commission, reviews ALJ decisions under the National Labor Relations Act. The Federal Trade Commission reviews decisions of the ALJ's acting under the Federal Trade Commission Act. An appeal results in a reconsideration of the issues. This means that the reviewing body, after considering the ALJ's decision, may make its own findings of fact and law. The reviewing body is not bound by the ALJ's findings. It may affirm, reverse, amend, or vary the findings of the ALJ. The reviewing body's decision is the final level of agency action. Any further action involving the decision must be taken to the courts.

Federal agency decisions are usually not self-enforcing; that is, an agency must normally go to a U.S. Courts of Appeals to have a decision enforced against the losing party. Also, any party adversely affected by an agency decision may seek judicial review of the decision in the courts. Judicial review and judicial enforcement proceedings are the major legal checks on administrative agency action. Because of its important role, judicial review will be discussed in some detail in the next section of the text.

JUDICIAL REVIEW OF AGENCY ACTION

Persons adversely affected by agency actions—whether rulemaking or adjudication—may seek judicial review of those actions to ensure that the agency has acted legally. Judicial review is the major legal check upon agency action. It serves to safeguard the rights of the parties affected by agency action and to prevent the abuse of informal agency procedures or agency functions.

Judicial review of agency action is not the same as an appeal of an agency decision. The reviewing court does not reconsider the issue that was before the agency in its entirety, nor does it substitute its judgment for that of the agency. The reviewing court simply ensures that the agency acted within its legal authority, followed the proper procedures, and reached a reasonable decision supported by substantial evidence.

Limits on Judicial Review

Only final agency actions are subject to judicial review. If opportunities for appeal or review are available within the agency, those opportunities must be exhausted before judicial review may be sought. For example, a ruling by an ALJ under the National Labor Relations Act must be appealed to the National Labor Relations Board before it can be subject to judicial review by the U.S. Courts of Appeal.

In addition, a person seeking judicial review must have legal standing to seek review. This normally means that the person must be able to demonstrate direct adverse effects because of the agency action. However, some regulatory statutes allow "any interested person," rather than just those who actually suffer some injury, to seek judicial review of agency actions.

Scope of Judicial Review

As already noted, the reviewing court does not substitute its own judgment for that of the agency. Such substitution would eliminate the benefits of the agency's technical expertise. Instead, the court ensures that the agency's decision was reached through fair and proper procedures.

Review of Agency Authority The first issue considered by the reviewing court is whether the agency was acting within the scope of the authority delegated to it by the legislature. The legislation creating the agency and empowering it to act — known as the agency's *organic act* or *enabling legislation* — usually sets some limitations upon the scope of agency actions. The agency may act only within these limits; actions that exceed them are invalid. The following case involves the judicial review of a decision by the Office of Federal Contract Compliance Programs, which was allegedly acting under authority granted to it by a presidential executive order.

LIBERTY MUTUAL INSURANCE COMPANY v. FRIEDMAN
639 F.2d 164 (4th Cir. 1981)

[Executive Order 11,246 is a presidential directive that requires all businesses that have contracts in excess of $10,000 with the federal government for construction or the supply of goods or services must agree not to discriminate in employment on the basis of race, color, religion, sex, or national origin. These businesses are also required to take affirmative action to ensure equal employment opportunity. The requirements also extend to any subcontractors under the firm's contract.

Liberty Mutual provides workers' compensation insurance for many companies doing business with the federal government. The Office of the Federal Contract Compliance Programs (OFCCP), the branch of the Labor Department that is responsible for enforcing Executive Order 11,246, held that Liberty Mutual was a subcontractor within the meaning of the executive order and was therefore subject to the affirmative action requirements.

Liberty Mutual brought suit to challenge the ruling that it was a subcontractor under the executive order. The defendant, Friedman, is an official responsible for the enforcement of the executive order. The District Court upheld the OFCCP determination that Liberty Mutual was covered. Liberty Mutual appealed.]

PHILLIPS, Circuit Judge

Liberty's . . . argument, that the broad definition of subcontractor, with its attendant consequences for meeting the recordkeeping and affirmative action requirements of Executive Order 11,246, is outside the scope of the Order or beyond any legislative grant of authority presents a . . . difficult question.

Executive Order 11,246, as amended, "charge[s] the Secretary of Labor with ensuring that corporations that benefit from government contracts provide equal employment opportunity regardless of race or sex." Although the Executive Order is written in broad terms, the prohibition against discrimination in employment is clearly intended to cover both government contractors and their subcontractors. Section 202(7) of the Order specifically requires contractors to include in all subcontracts the antidiscrimination, affirmative action, and recordkeeping provisions required by Executive Order 11,246. Subcontract is not defined within the Executive Order, but §201 provides that the Secretary of Labor "shall adopt such rules and regulations . . . as are deemed necessary and appropriate to achieve the purposes" of the Order. Those purposes, as declared by the Supreme Court "are an end to discrimination in employment by the Federal Government and those who deal with the Federal Government." Because Executive Order 11,246 is clearly intended to cover subcontractors and because the term "subcontractor" has no "single exact meaning," the Secretary had the power to define, by regulation, which subcontracts are covered so long as the definition is within the purposes of the Executive Order and the statutory grant of authority. Although the regulation's broad-ranging definition of subcontract is arguably consistent with the purposes of the Executive Order, we conclude that application of the Executive Order to plaintiffs is not reasonably within the contemplation of any statutory grant of authority.

The question before us is not whether Congress could require insurance companies providing workers' compensation insurance to federal contractors to comply with the affirmative action requirements of Executive Order 11,246, the question is "whether or to what extent Congress did grant . . . such authority" to the executive branch of the government. Determining whether defendants have the statutory authorization to require Liberty to comply with Executive Order 11,246 is rendered difficult because "[t]he origins of the congressional authority for Executive Order 11,246 are somewhat obscure and have been roundly debated by commentators and courts."

A congressional grant of legislative authority need not be specific in order to sustain the validity of regulations promulgated pursuant to the grant, but a court must "reasonably be able to conclude that the grant of authority contemplates the regulations issued." Our examination of the possible statutory sources of congressional authorization for Executive Order 11,246 convinces us that none of the statutes reasonably contemplates that Liberty, as a provider of workers' compensation insurance to government contractors, may be required to comply with Executive Order 11,245. We conclude therefore that none of the statutes authorize the action taken by defendants.

First, we consider as a possible source the general procurement power of Congress as delegated to the Executive by the Federal Property and Administrative Services Act (the Procurement Act). Congress has said of this Act that its purpose is to provide "an economical and efficient system" for, among other objectives, the procurement of personal property and services. The Act authorizes Executive Orders "necessary to effectuate [its] provisions," but does not mention employment discrimination.

The key point is that any application of the Order must be reasonably related to the Procurement Act's purpose of ensuring efficiency and economy in government procurement (whether direct or assisted) in order to lie within the statutory grant. This requirement of a reasonably close nexus [connection] between the efficiency and economy criteria of the Procurement Act and any exactions imposed upon federal contractors by Executive Orders promulgated under its authority has recently been highlighted by the District of Columbia Circuit in a closely related context. [In that case] . . . the court took great pains to emphasize that the court's holding was rested narrowly upon the manifestly close nexus between the Procurement Act's criteria of efficiency and economy and the Executive Order's predominant objective of containing procurement costs.

Assuming, without deciding, that the Procurement Act does provide constitutional authorization for some applications of Executive Order 11,246, we conclude that, in any event, the authorization could validly extend no further than to those applications satisfying the nexus test. Applying that test here, we are satisfied that it is not met. Liberty is not itself a federal contractor and there is, therefore, no direct connection to federal procurement. Instead, Liberty provides blanket workers' compensation insurance to employers that hold federal contracts. There are no findings that suggest what percentage of the total price of federal contracts may be attributed to the cost of this insurance.

Further, there is no suggestion that insurers have practiced the deliberate exclusion of minority employees. The connection between the cost of workers' compensation policies, for which employers purchase a single policy to cover employees working on both federal and nonfederal contracts without distinction between the two, and any increase in the cost of federal contracts that could be attributed to discrimination by these insurers is simply too attenuated to allow a reviewing court to find the requisite connection between procurement costs and social objective.

Defendants rely upon . . . decisions from other courts that can be read to reject the need for any such nexus between Procurement Act economy/efficiency criteria and Executive Order social objectives in order to uphold challenged applications of the Order. . . . The plain implication of such a rejection would be that regulations promulgated under an Executive Order that traces its lawmaking authority to a particular statute need bear no relation to the purposes of that authorizing statute so long as the regulations bear relation to national policies reflected in other sources — common

law, statutory, or constitutional. This would render meaningless the simple, fundamental separation of powers requirement, that such an "exercise of quasi-legislative authority by governmental departments and agencies must be rooted in a grant of [legislative] power by Congress . . ." and lie "reasonably within the contemplation of that grant of authority."

As indicated, we think that this fundamental requirement dictates application of the sort of nexus test we apply here, and that when applied to the regulations here in question and the Procurement Act it is plain that the former do not lie "reasonably within the contemplation of" the latter.

Defendants acted outside any grant of legislative authority when they sought to impose the requirements of Executive Order 11,246 upon plaintiffs. Without this critical connection to legislative authorization, defendants' action cannot be given effect. The decision of the district court is reversed.

Reversed.

CASE REVIEW QUESTIONS

1. What is the relationship of Liberty Mutual to firms performing services for the federal government?
2. What is the statutory source of authority for the imposition of affirmative-action requirements upon government contractors? What are the primary objectives of that statutory provision?
3. Why is the inclusion of Liberty Mutual as a subcontractor under the OFCCP requirements held to be invalid?

Review of Agency Procedure After determining whether an agency was acting within the scope of its statutory authority, the reviewing court must decide whether the agency followed proper procedures in making its decision. The agency procedures must meet the due process requirements already discussed — that is, they must provide for timely notice, an opportunity to participate, and unbiased adjudication. In addition, any statutory procedural requirements, such as the need for formal rulemaking through a hearing or for a formal evidentiary hearing in adjudication, must be met. As noted in the *Vermont Yankee* case, however, when an agency has met statutory procedural requirements, the reviewing court is not free to impose additional procedural requirements. When the agency's enabling legislation is silent as to the procedures required, the agency has discretion in choosing the procedures employed.

Review of Agency Reasonableness After considering whether the agency employed proper procedures, the reviewing court must consider whether the agency's action is reasonable and is supported by substantial evidence. When an agency rule is the product of formal rulemaking procedures or when agency adjudication involved a formal hearing, the reviewing court must consider whether the agency rule or decision is supported by substantial evidence when the entire record of the hearing is considered. When the agency has engaged in informal rulemaking, the court must consider whether the rule is reasonable in light of the information and comments submitted.

The reviewing court need not agree with the wisdom or the policy of the rule or decision. It may only consider whether the action is supported by the evidence and is reasonable.

When courts are reviewing state regulations or state agency decisions, they should not consider the need for or the wisdom of the regulation involved. As long as the state has acted with regard to a matter of legal concern, has not discriminated against or unduly burdened interstate commerce, is not in conflict with federal law, and is not dealing with a matter preempted by the federal government or requiring nationally uniform standards, the regulation should be held to be valid even if the court disagrees with the need for or the wisdom of the regulation.

The following case contains the classic legal explanation of the role of the reviewing court with regard to administrative agency action.

UNIVERSAL CAMERA CORPORATION v. NATIONAL LABOR RELATIONS BOARD
340 U.S. 474 (U.S. Supreme Ct. 1951)

[The National Labor Relations Board (NLRB) issued a decision ordering Universal Camera to reinstate an employee fired for giving testimony in another proceeding before the NLRB. The NLRB decision was reviewed and enforced by the Court of Appeals. Universal Camera appealed to the U.S. Supreme Court, arguing that the Court of Appeals had misapplied the legislative standard for judicial review of NLRB decisions.

The National Labor Relations Act, as amended by the Taft-Hartley Act, states that, upon judicial review, "[t]he findings of the Board (NLRB) with respect to questions of fact if supported by substantial evidence on the record considered as a whole shall be conclusive." The Administrative Procedure Act, which sets general procedures for judicial review of federal administrative agencies, requires a reviewing court to consider the record as a whole, and to "hold unlawful and set aside agency action, findings and conclusions . . . unsupported by substantial evidence. . . ." The Supreme Court considered the relationship between the two standards and the relationship of the reviewing court to the agency determination under review.]

FRANKFURTER, Justice

It would be mischievous word-playing to find that the scope of review under the Taft-Hartley Act is any different from that under the Administrative Procedure Act. The Senate Committee which reported the review clause of the Taft-Hartley Act expressly indicated that the two standards were to conform in this regard, and the working of the two Acts is for purposes of judicial administration identical. And so we hold that the standard of proof specifically required of the Labor Board by the Taft-Hartley Act is the same as that to be exacted by courts reviewing every administrative action subject to the Administrative Procedure Act. . . .

The substantiality of evidence must take into account whatever in the record fairly detracts from its weight. This is clearly the significance of the requirement in both statutes that courts consider the whole record. To be sure, the requirement for canvassing "the whole record" in order to ascertain substantiality does not furnish a calculus of value by which a reviewing court can assess the evidence. Nor was it intended to negative the function of the Labor Board as one of those agencies presumably equipped or informed by experience to deal with a specialized field of knowledge, whose findings within that field carry the authority of an expertness which courts do not possess and therefore must respect. Nor does it mean that even as to matters not requiring expertise a court may displace the Board's choice between two fairly conflicting views, even though the court would justifiably have made a different choice had the matter been before it *de novo.* Congress has merely made it clear that a reviewing court is not barred from setting aside a Board decision when it cannot conscientiously find

that the evidence supporting that decision is substantial, when viewed in the light that the record in its entirety furnished, including the body of evidence opposed to the Board's view. . . .

We conclude, therefore, that the Administrative Procedure Act and the Taft-Hartley Act direct that courts must now assume more fair responsibility for the reasonableness and fairness of Labor Board decisions than some courts have shown in the past. Reviewing courts must be influenced by a feeling that they are not to abdicate the conventional judicial function. Congress has imposed on them responsibility for assuring that the Board keeps within reasonable grounds. That responsibility is not less real because it is limited to enforcing the requirement that evidence appear substantial when viewed on the record as a whole, by courts invested with the authority and enjoying the prestige of the Courts of Appeals. The Board's findings are entitled to respect; but they must nonetheless be set aside when the record before a Court of Appeals clearly precludes the Board's decision from being justified by a fair estimate of the worth of the testimony of witnesses or its informed judgment on matters within its special competence or both. Whether on the record as a whole there is substantial evidence to support agency findings is a question which Congress has placed in the keeping of the Courts of Appeals. This Court will intervene only in what ought to be the rare instance when the standard appears to have been misapprehended or grossly misapplied.

[The Court remanded the case to the Court of Appeals for reconsideration.]

CASE REVIEW QUESTIONS

1. Why should a reviewing court defer to agency determinations of factual issues? Should the court also defer to agency determinations of points of law?
2. When, if ever, should a court substitute its view of the facts for that of the agency?
3. What should a reviewing court consider upon judicial review of a National Labor Relations Board decision?

OTHER CHECKS ON AGENCY ACTION

Although judicial review is the primary check upon administrative agency action, there are other checks as well. Both the executive and the legislative branches of government exercise some controls over agencies. Public opinion and the news media also have some effect upon agencies.

The legislative controls on agencies are relatively broad. Because the agency itself is a creature of the enabling legislation, Congress may control an agency by amending or repealing the statutes that empower it to act. Congress may also require that specific agency regulations be approved by the Congress before they become effective. Furthermore, Congress holds the "power of the purse strings" over agencies. Unpopular agency action may prompt Congress to reduce or eliminate an agency's appropriations for the coming fiscal year. Lastly, Congressional approval of the persons nominated by the president to fill the official posts of the various agencies is required.

Although Congressional control over administrative agencies is broad in scope, it is suited only for dealing with general issues. Congressional control does not operate on a day-to-day basis. It may occur only annually, as when the budget for the next fiscal year is adopted, or even less frequently, as with the approval of nominations. As a result, legislative controls are not as effective as judicial review for preventing the abuse of authority by an agency or for safeguarding the rights of persons involved in agency proceedings.

The president has some control over the persons who hold the high posts of the various federal agencies. The power to appoint and remove agency officials allows the president to influence the general policy positions taken by the various agencies. It does not, however, provide an effective means of controlling routine agency actions. The president also has the power to veto legislation affecting the agency. But again, this power does not provide control over specific agency actions, whereas judicial review does.

Public opinion and the news media also exert some influence upon agency action. Unfavorable publicity about a decision may create a negative public perception of an agency as being silly, petty, or unnecessarily harsh. Such perceptions are not very effective with regard to specific agency decisions, nor should they be. Still, since a poor public image could generate constituent pressure on Congress to control the agency by legislation, unfavorable publicity can sometimes influence an agency to change its general policies or procedures.

For example, in the early 1970s, the Occupational Safety and Health Administration (OSHA) adopted a large number of regulations that set standards for such things as the spacing of ladder rungs, the design of toilet seats for workplace restrooms, and the height at which fire extinguishers should be hung. Media emphasis on the "petty" nature of many of these regulations created a popular conception of OSHA as a "nit-picking, Mickey Mouse" agency. OSHA has since shifted its emphasis to more serious health and safety hazards, such as toxic substances in the workplace. The shift, while not entirely attributable to the negative public view of OSHA, was in some part a response to public opinion.

REGULATORY PROBLEMS —
CURRENT CONSIDERATIONS

Administrative agencies and the regulation of business activities will always be with us. Recent trends, however, indicate that some changes are occurring in the nature of agency regulation. There is an increasing awareness on the part of both industry and government of the costs of regulation. Agency procedures and judicial review are time-consuming. They cause delays, which result in increased operating costs for businesses. There are also substantial legal costs for the parties involved in agency actions. In the short run, these costs must be borne by the industries affected, but they are ultimately passed on to the consuming public. Moreover, the costs of operating the agencies are funded by tax dollars, which are again ultimately provided by the consuming public.

The presidential Executive Order 12,291 now requires agencies to prepare a "regulatory impact analysis" that assesses the costs and benefits expected of their major rules. These cost-benefit analyses are not subject to judicial review and do not create any rights enforceable against the federal government by litigation. They are simply an attempt to ensure that every agency action will only impose costs that are reasonable in relation to the benefits it creates.

Cost-benefit analyses are a step in the right direction, but they do have their limits. It is very easy to quantify certain costs associated with regulation, such as the cost of emission-control equipment for cars or protective devices for workers. Unfortunately, the benefits of the regulations themselves are not so easily quantified. How much are clean air and pure water worth? What is the value of reducing workplace deaths and injuries? Obviously, then, cost-benefit analysis can never be the *sole* determining factor of regulatory policy.

Another recent trend in the regulation of business has been the reduction or abolition of some regulatory schemes. Deregulation of the airline industry and the reduction of controls on the trucking industry are prime examples. This trend is the result of the realization that some regulatory schemes protect industries from competition instead of protecting the public interest. In such situations, deregulation allows the forces of the market to control business conduct. It also decreases costs and provides greater benefits to the consuming public. But competitive market forces may not ensure that firms take adequate precautions to protect their workers from occupational hazards, nor may market forces be sufficient to ensure that industries protect the quality of our air and water. As a result, deregulation is not the answer to all of the problems of regulation.

Nevertheless, by limiting regulation to those areas and activities where it can be most effective and by ensuring that the costs imposed by regulation do not greatly exceed the resulting benefits, regulatory policy can be greatly strengthened. These recent trends may herald the emergence of a more effective and more acceptable government regulatory policy. Regardless of the direction taken by regulatory policy, however, the regulation of business by government at all levels through administrative agencies will remain a prominent feature of the legal environment of business.

REVIEW QUESTIONS

1. What is the Administrative Procedure Act?
2. Why do agencies make rules?
3. What is informal rulemaking? What is formal rulemaking? What are the advantages and disadvantages of each? What is hybrid rulemaking?
4. What is the role of the courts in the judicial review of agency decisions? To what extent can a reviewing court substitute its judgment for that of the agency?
5. What is meant by "substantial evidence on the record considered as a whole"?
6. What are the advantages and disadvantages of using cost-benefit analyses to guide regulatory policy?
7. Can the marketplace be relied upon as a substitute for agency regulation? Could all agency regulation of business activity be eliminated? Should it be eliminated?

CASE PROBLEMS

1. The Consumer Product Safety Commission published a proposed rule requiring that mattresses be covered with fireproof materials. The Commission invited interested persons to submit written comments on the proposed rule. After considering all the comments submitted, the Commission adopted a rule requiring that at least one side of every mattress sold after January 1, 1986, be covered with fireproof material. Metzger Mattress Company opposes the rule. It files suit in federal court seeking to invalidate the rule because the Commission did not hold a public hearing before adopting the rule. Who will win the case? Explain.

2. The New York Human Rights Law, which applies to rental accommodations containing four or more units, prohibits discrimination on the basis of race, sex, or marital status. Collins owns a two-family house. His family resides on the first floor. Art Shaw and Tammy Wolfe have been roommates for several years. When they asked to rent the second floor of Collins' house, he refused because they were not married. They complained to the New York State Human Rights Division, which ordered Collins to rent to them. The order against Collins was affirmed by the Human Rights Appeals Board. If Collins seeks judicial review of the Appeals Board decision, who will win the case? Explain. Suppose Collins had sought judicial review of the Human Rights Division's decision rather than going to the Appeals Board. Would he have been successful?

3. During the oil shortages of the 1970s, independent gas station owners had difficulty getting sufficient supplies of gasoline from the major oil companies. The independent owners complained that the oil companies gave preference to company-owned stations, with whom the independent stations compete, when allocating gasoline supplies. In response to the independent dealers' plight, the state of Maryland passed a law prohibiting companies that own oil refineries from owning or operating gas stations in Maryland. Exxon owns both oil refineries and gas stations, and it owns a number of gas stations in Maryland. The law would force Exxon to sell those stations. Exxon filed suit in federal court to challenge the law. The trial court determines that the law will not solve the problem of gasoline shortages for independent dealers and, indeed, will only make the situation worse. The court therefore holds the law to be unconstitutional. Maryland appeals to the U.S. Court of Appeals. Will the Court of Appeals affirm the trial court's decision? Explain.

4. The National Labor Relations Act requires that the National Labor Relations Board include professional employees with nonprofessional employees in bargaining units only if a majority of the professionals vote to be included. The power to determine which groups of employees are to be included in a particular bargaining unit is left to the discretion of the regional directors of NLRB offices. Smith, the director of the Buffalo regional

office, approved a bargaining unit composed of 56 professional workers and three nonprofessionals at the Hooker Chemical Company. No vote by the professional employees was held. The chemical company has brought a legal action challenging the regional director's approval of the bargaining unit. Who will win the case? Explain.

5. The Occupational Safety and Health Administration (OSHA) adopted a regulation requiring that processors of cotton install extensive ventilation systems to protect workers from inhaling cotton dust fibers, which can cause a lung disease known as "brown lung." Karp Cotton Company, a leading cotton processor, opposes the regulation because of the excessive cost of such ventilation systems. Karp believes that OSHA severely underestimated these costs when considering the costs and benefits of the regulation. Karp files suit in federal court to invalidate the regulation, claiming that OSHA's regulatory impact analysis, required under Executive Order 12,291, was inadequate. Who will win the case? Explain.

47

ANTITRUST REGULATION OF BUSINESS STRUCTURE

The competitive behavior and structure of business firms are regulated by antitrust laws. The purpose of antitrust laws is to ensure that the marketplace in which business activity takes place remains a "free market" by eliminating threats to competition and by seeing to it that firms "play by the rules" of the market. Antitrust law in the United States consists of both state and federal statutes.

Federal antitrust laws apply to all business activity that takes place in interstate commerce. In some cases, they also apply to wholly intrastate activity that affects interstate commerce (see page 978 of Chapter 45). Wholly intrastate activity that does not affect interstate commerce is subject only to the various state antitrust laws (see page 984 of Chapter 45). The focus in this chapter will be on federal antitrust laws—the Sherman Act, the Clayton Act, the Robinson-Patman Act, and the Federal Trade Commission Act as they regulate business structure.

INTRODUCTION TO FEDERAL ANTITRUST LEGISLATION

The Sherman Act, passed by Congress in 1890, prohibits the monopolization of or any restraint of trade in or affecting interstate commerce. The Sherman Act was aimed at the concentrations of economic power that had developed in most industries through the use of cartels or voting trusts. (A voting trust allowed a few persons to control all the firms in an industry by giving them the voting rights of the firms' stockholders.) The term *antitrust* is derived from the Sherman Act's attack on voting trusts. The Sherman Act makes violations of its provisions criminal offenses and imposes fines or imprisonment as sanctions.

The Sherman Act was not very effective because of several problems with its enforcement. Because it is criminal legislation, its penalties are usually imposed only after harm to competition has already occurred. The criminal penalties available under the act are limited to fines or imprisonment and do nothing to restore competition that has been eliminated. The fines likely to be imposed are greatly exceeded by the financial gains resulting from anticompetitive activity. Lastly, several early court decisions held that manufacturing was not "commerce" within the meaning of the Sherman Act, so anticompetitive conduct by manufacturers was beyond its reach. (Those decisions have since been overruled.)

In response to the problems in enforcing the Sherman Act, Congress passed the Clayton Act in 1914. It prohibits specific kinds of activities that injure competition and provides for civil, rather than criminal, remedies. It also allows for civil remedies under the Sherman Act. The civil nature of the Clayton Act allows for more flexible and effective enforcement. For example, injunctions prohibiting conduct likely to injure competition can be granted by the courts before actual harm to competition occurs. However, in contrast to the Sherman Act, which applies to activities in or *affecting* interstate commerce, the Clayton Act applies only to activities actually *in* interstate commerce.

The Clayton Act provides that any person injured as the result of a violation of it can sue the violator for three times the amount of the harm suffered. In addition §4 of the Clayton Act extends the availability of treble damage suits to violations of the Sherman Act. These suits may be brought only by parties directly affected by the violations, such as customers who purchase directly from the violator. Indirect purchasers—those who purchase from the customers of the violator—may not bring damage suits. The federal government is also precluded from bringing treble damage suits against antitrust violators.

Congress also passed the Federal Trade Commission Act in 1914. This act created the Federal Trade Commission as an independent agency to administer and enforce antitrust laws. Section 5 of the act prohibits "unfair methods of competition in or affecting commerce and unfair or deceptive acts or practices in or affecting commerce. . . ."

In 1936, the Robinson-Patman Act was passed to strengthen the provisions of §2 of the Clayton Act, which prohibits price discrimination. Section 7 of the Clayton Act, which deals with mergers (a *merger* is the acquisition or take-over of one firm by another) that affect competition, was strengthened by the Celler-Kefauver Act of 1950. Premerger notification requirements were imposed under §7 of the Clayton Act by the Hart-Scott-Rodino Act of 1976. (See the appendix for the text of these various pieces of legislation.)

Enforcement and Administration of Antitrust Laws

The federal antitrust laws are enforced and administered by both the Justice Department and the Federal Trade Commission (FTC). The Antitrust Division of the Justice Department is responsible for the enforcement of the criminal provisions of the Sherman Act, which provide for fines of up to $1 million for corporations and fines of up to $100,000 and jail terms of up to three years for individuals. The Antitrust Division also enforces the merger provisions of §7 of the Clayton Act.

The FTC has no criminal jurisdiction. It is responsible for enforcing the Clayton Act and §5 of the Federal Trade Commission Act. Both the Antitrust Division and the FTC can file civil enforcement actions. Possible remedies include injunctions, **divestiture orders** (which are court orders that require merged firms to separate), and even **dissolution orders** (which are court orders that require single firms to split into separate firms). Other remedies, such as orders to make patents available to competitors or orders that prohibit firms from entering certain fields of business, are also available through civil actions.

Both the FTC and Justice Department can initiate legal action against alleged violators of the antitrust laws. The Justice Department can file criminal or civil suits in the federal courts. The FTC can hold administrative hearings on alleged violations. Both the Justice Department and the FTC are increasingly making use of pretrial (or prehearing) settlement agreements with firms alleged to have violated the law. These settlements, known as **consent decrees** or **consent orders,** allow a firm to agree to cease alleged antitrust violations without admitting guilt or liability under the laws. This device enables the enforcement agencies to stop alleged anticompetitive practices without having to resort to trials, which are both expensive and time-consuming.

In addition to the enforcement actions of the two government agencies, individuals or firms that have dealt directly with alleged antitrust violators may file civil suits seeking treble (triple) damages for injuries caused by the violations. For example, the price-fixing convictions of manufacturers of electrical equipment in the 1960s resulted in some 2,300 suits against the companies involved. The damages awarded amounted to over $400 million. These private actions have become an increasingly effective deterrent to anticompetitive activity. As of 1975, almost 1,400 suits of this type were being filed each year.

The Goals of Antitrust Policy

As mentioned earlier, the basic purpose of antitrust law is to ensure the free operation of the marketplace. The policy behind the enforcement and interpretation of these laws reflects two different sets of interests, however. These divergent interests result from the fact that antitrust policy is based on a mixture of social, political, and economic theories.

The economic goal of antitrust policy is efficiency through free competition in the marketplace. When competition is free, though, some firms may compete more effectively than others. According to the economic viewpoint, antitrust law should not penalize firms that become dominant in a market because they have competed successfully. The size of firms should be irrelevant as long as their activities result in efficiency.

In contrast to the economic goal, the social and political goals of antitrust policy emphasize concern for protecting competing firms as well as for promoting competition. From this viewpoint, small independent competitors should be protected to preserve economic freedom of choice, and the growth of businesses should be restricted to avoid the concentration of economic power and political influence in the hands of a few giant firms. The concern for protecting competitors means that the size of a firm may determine the legality of its conduct. Also, the protection of competitors should be pursued despite its costs in terms of efficiency.

Judicial interpretations and applications of the antitrust laws have reflected the tension between these competing goals. The *U.S.* v. *Aluminum Co. of America* monopoly case in 1945 and Supreme Court decisions in merger cases during the early 1960s emphasized the social and political goals of antitrust policy. More recent merger and monopoly decisions indicate an increasing emphasis on the economic goal. Despite this shift in emphasis, neither set of goals is ever completely dominant, and the courts usually consider both in determining the legality of business conduct or structure.

Judicial Analysis

When the legality of a business firm's conduct is challenged under the antitrust laws, a court must consider the impact of the firm's conduct on competition. The courts have adopted two different approaches for analyzing this impact—the rule of reason and the per se rule.

The **rule of reason** stems from the Supreme Court's *Standard Oil Company* v. *United States* decision of 1911, which held that some forms of activity are illegal only if they *unreasonably* restrict competition. The rule of reason is applied today when the conduct in question has a legitimate business purpose despite its anticompetitive effects. Under the rule of reason, the actual effects of the conduct upon competition must be considered. When the effects result in an undue or unreasonable lessening of competition, the court will prohibit the conduct.

Under the **per se rule,** which is derived from the rule of reason, some forms of conduct are considered to be so inherently anticompetitive that they are deemed to be illegal regardless of their actual effects on competition. When the per se rule is applied, the court will refuse to consider any justification for the anticompetitive conduct or any evidence of the impact of the conduct on competition.

The per se rule is generally applied to conduct that has no legitimate business justification. An example of such conduct, which is sometimes called "a naked restraint of trade," is price-fixing. The courts have adopted the per se rule in such cases because it eliminates the need to show actual harm to competition, which may be difficult to prove despite the blatantly anticompetitive nature of the conduct. The per se rule also provides a clear standard for predicting the legality of proposed business conduct.

Structural and Behavioral Antitrust

Antitrust law provisions can be categorized as either structural or behavioral in their focus. Structural provisions are concerned with the competitive structural organization of an industry—monopoly, oligopoly, or workable competition — and with such activities as mergers that are likely to affect structural organization. Behavioral provisions are concerned with anticompetitive practices by firms, such as price-fixing, group boycotts, price discrimination, or the imposing of restrictive terms as a condition of doing business.

Structural antitrust provisions generally involve the application of the rule of reason. Particular conduct or activities will be prohibited only if they are likely to have an unreasonable effect on the structure of competition in an industry. Behavioral provisions, on the other hand, may involve either the rule of reason or the per se rule; that is, some behavior may be illegal regardless of its effect on competition, whereas the legality of other practices may depend upon their effects on competition.

The balance of this chapter considers structural antitrust provisions. Behavioral antitrust provisions will be considered in the following chapter.

STRUCTURAL ANTITRUST PROVISIONS

Structural antitrust provisions are concerned with the structure of competition in an industry and with activities that may affect that structure. More specifically, structural antitrust policy is concerned with monopoly, oligopoly, and mergers. The legislative provisions involved are §2 of the Sherman Act and §7 of the Clayton Act.

Monopoly

From an economic standpoint, the concept of **monopoly** refers to a single firm that is the sole supplier of a unique product; that is, a product for which no substitutes exist. Buyers are forced to deal with the monopolist or with no one, and the monopolist has the power to set both price and output. The economic harm that results from monopoly is the restriction of output (too little of the product is produced) and the distortion of price (which is higher than it would be if the market were competitive). From a social standpoint, monopoly means the maldistribution of income (from the customers of the monopoly to its owners or shareholders) and the concentration of economic power in a single firm. It also creates the potential for undue political influence by the monopolist.

Monopoly and the Sherman Act Pure, "single-firm" monopoly is not likely to exist, but the possession of some monopoly power by the dominant firm in an industry is a cause for concern. Antitrust policy seeks to prevent any firm from gaining the power to set prices or to exclude competitors. The possession of such power may result in the imposition of antitrust sanctions under §2 of the Sherman Act, which states:

> Every person who shall monopolize, or attempt to monopolize, or conspire or combine with any other person . . . to monopolize any part of the trade or commerce among the several states . . . shall be deemed guilty of a felony. . . .

Notice that §2 outlaws the act of monopolizing, not the monopoly itself. This means that the rule of reason, not the per se rule, will be used by a court when it considers a charge under §2 because the court must look at the effects upon competition rather than simply at the existence of monopoly power. Any firm that introduces a completely new product has a monopoly of that product, but such a monopoly will only be in violation of §2 when the firm uses its power to restrict or to attempt to restrict competition unreasonably.

Judicial Analysis in Monopoly Cases In analyzing a charge of monopolizing under §2, a court must first consider whether the firm so charged actually possesses monopoly power. The first step in this process is the indentification of the product market and the geographic market in which the firm operates.

The **product market** has been defined by the courts as including all "commodities reasonably interchangeable by consumers for the same purposes." If substitutes for the product in question are available, then the firm producing the product may not be able to set price and determine output independently. Consumers will turn to the substitutes if the product is too expensive in relation to the substitutes or is unavailable. Thus, the firm producing the product faces competition from the substitutes and therefore does not possess monopoly power. The definition of the product market is crucial to the determination of whether or not monopoly power exists. The more narrowly the product market is defined, the less likely it is that substitutes will be available and the more likely it is that the firm producing the product will be held to have monopoly power.

The **geographic market** is that area of the country where a firm exercises its market power or where the effects of that power are felt. The definition of the geographic market depends on how far the consumer will go to obtain substitutes. If substitute products are available only at great distances from the consumer, the consumer may choose to deal with the monopolist rather than undergo the difficulty and expense of obtaining the substitutes.

If the consumer is likely to go a long way for substitutes, the geographic market will be broadly defined, and the market power of the alleged monopolist is likely to be diminished. If the consumer is unwilling to go very far in search of substitute products, however, the geographic market will be narrowly defined, and the market power of the alleged monopolist is likely to be enhanced.

After the relevant markets have been defined, the court must consider the market share held by the firm charged; that is, the court must determine whether the firm has a dominant position in that market. A dominant firm will be able to set the pricing and production conditions against which the other firms in the industry must compete. The nature of competition in the market must also be considered since the number and sizes of the other firms in the industry will determine the extent to which the alleged monopolist can control pricing and production conditions. If a market is populated by many small firms, a market share of 35 percent may be sufficient to find dominance. In a market populated by a few large firms, dominance requires a much larger market share.

Intent to Monopolize If a firm is found to have a substantial share of the relevant market, the court must then determine whether the firm has monopolized or attempted to monopolize that market before it can find the firm in violation of §2. The activity of the firm must be examined to determine whether the firm has displayed the intent to maintain or to extend its dominant position. According to the Supreme Court in *U.S.* v. *Aluminum Company of America* (Alcoa), the evidence need only be of the firm's general intention to maintain its position; that is, there needn't be specific evidence of an intention to exclude competitors or restrict competition. In *Alcoa,* the Court held that apparently normal business practices, such as stimulating demand, increasing capacity to meet anticipated demand, and controlling supplies of raw materials, constituted evidence of general intent to monopolize when engaged in by a dominant firm.

The emphasis on a firm's size in determining the legality of the firm's actions has been rejected in more recent decisions. Courts now consider whether the alleged activities are normal business practices available to any firm. Only if the activities are "predatory" in intent — that is, only if they are designed to exclude competitors or restrict competition — will they be considered evidence of intent to monopolize.

In the following case, CalComp, a maker of peripheral equipment for computer systems, alleged that IBM had violated §2 of the Sherman Act in its introduction of new products, its pricing and leasing policies, and its other marketing practices. The court considered whether these practices, viewed in light of IBM's dominant position in the computer industry, constituted evidence of intent to monopolize.

CALIFORNIA COMPUTER PRODUCTS, INC. v. INTERNATIONAL BUSINESS MACHINES CORPORATION
613 F.2d 727 (9th Circuit 1979)

[California Computer Products (CalComp) manufactured peripheral computer products, such a disk drives, that are used in connection with a computer's central processing unit (CPU). CalComp's equipment could be used with (i.e., was "plug compatible" with) the CPUs manufactured by International Business Machines Corporation (IBM) as well as those of other suppliers.

CalComp sued IBM for $306 million in damages for alleged violations of §2 of the Sherman Act. CalComp claimed that IBM violated §2 through the introduction of new CPUs and disk drives, through price cuts on disk products, and through its leasing and marketing practices. These practices, according to CalComp, prevented CalComp from competing effectively with IBM for disk product sales. The trial court directed the

jury to enter a verdict in favor of IBM on all counts. CalComp appealed.]

CHOY, Circuit Judge

CalComp contends that the evidence was sufficient to show that particular conduct on the part of IBM, detailed below, violated either or both the monopolization and attempt to monopolize clauses of §2 of the Sherman Act.

There are three essential elements to a successful claim of §2 monopolization:

(a) the possession of monopoly power in the relevant market;

(b) the willful acquisition or maintenance of that power, and

(c) causal "antitrust" injury.

The first two elements are derived from §2 itself. . . .

Monopoly power—the first element—"is the power to control prices or exclude competition." [This] definition of monopoly power has been applied principally with reference to the defendant's share of the relevant product and geographic markets.

The second element of a successful monopolization claim requires that the conceded monopolist have engaged in "willful" [intentional] acts directed at establishing or retaining its monopoly, "as distinguished from growth or development as a consequence of a superior product, business acumen, or historic accident."

The plaintiff need not show that the conceded monopolist's acts were of a kind that would be unlawful for an ordinary enterprise. Rather, the plaintiff must show that the defendant's acts "unnecessarily excluded competition" from the relevant market. Nor is it necessary to show a specific intent to eliminate a competitor. . . . [The] test is whether the defendant's acts, otherwise lawful, were *unreasonably* restrictive of competition.

There are four elements to a successful claim of §2 attempt to monopolize:

(a) specific intent to control prices or destroy competition with respect to a part of commerce;
(b) predatory or anticompetitive conduct directed to accomplishing the unlawful purpose;
(c) a dangerous probability of success; and
(d) causal "antitrust" injury.

While the completed offense of monopolization under §2 demands only a general intent to do the act . . . a specific intent to destroy competition or build monopoly is essential to guilt for the mere attempt.

The intent to "build monopoly" . . . is logically synonymous with the intent to control prices or exclude competition in the relevant market.

"Direct evidence" of specific intent to control prices or destroy competition, however, is not always necessary when the attempt claim is "founded upon a substantial claim of restraint of trade" . . . In these circumstances the requisite specific intent may be inferred.

The third element of a §2 attempt, the requirement that a defendant's demonstrated specific intent to control prices or destroy competition have a "dangerous probability of success," may be satisfied either by direct proof of market power, or by inference from the proven specific intent itself. Because this element may be inferred from the existence of a specific intent in proper cases, it is not an "essential" element of an attempt claim. For the same reason, neither is proof of any particular degree of market power necessarily an "independent" element of such a claim.

CalComp sought to define the relevant product markets as (a) a general purpose computer systems market; (b) an all disk drive and associated controller market; and (c) a plug-compatible disk drive and associated controller market (which excluded disk products for use with the CPU's of other manufacturers). [The geographic market was the U.S. as a whole.]

CalComp introduced the testimony of employees of IBM and other industry members concerning IBM's share of the loosely defined general purpose computer systems market: their estimates ranged from as low as 60% to as high as 80%, while IBM's proof was designed to show that none of these figures was even based on the particular market alleged. . . .

While the district judge expressly made no finding of the adequacy of proof of share of a relevant market, he noted "in passing" that he was not inclined to direct a verdict solely on that ground. For purposes of this decision, we assume that IBM possessed monopoly power in the [relevant] market during the period 1963 to 1972.

CalComp argued that IBM directly injured it in three ways. Principally, CalComp contends that IBM engaged in "predatory" pricing by cutting its peripheral equipment prices in response to competition from CalComp and other manufacturers. CalComp also attempted to show that IBM made design changes on certain of its CPUs, disk drives and controllers of no technological advantage and solely for the purpose of frustrating competition from plug-compatible manufacturers. Finally, it urged that IBM raised CPU prices in an effort to offset revenue losses caused by its price reductions on peripheral equipment, and that these price increases constituted impermissible conduct for a monopolist.

The test of reasonableness of the pricing actions, and the principal question facing us in this case, is whether IBM—which was the inventor and dominant supplier of the disk products in question—had the right to respond to the lower prices of its competitors with reduced, but still substantially profitable, prices on its own products. We conclude that it did.

CalComp's principal damages claim is for lost revenues as a result of price reductions made following IBM's announcements. But since these price reductions admittedly resulted from competition by IBM—and since, as both CalComp's and IBM's evidence clearly demonstrates, IBM's stimulus to price competition was in turn competition from peripheral equipment manufacturers such as CalComp—it is impossible to say that CalComp's losses represent compensable "injury" from acts of IBM unnecessarily *excluding or restricting* competition. Rather, IBM's price cuts were a part of the very competitive process the Sherman Act was designed to promote. To accept CalComp's position would be to hold that IBM could not compete if competition would result in injury to its competitors, an ill-advised reversal of the Supreme Court's pronouncement that the Sherman Act is meant to protect [the] competitive process, not competitors.

CalComp witnesses repeatedly testified that IBM's position and success were due to its capable management, technological leadership, market orientation and superior products. Particularly relevant is the fact that IBM invented the disk products that CalComp and other manufacturers copied. Granted that IBM's technological innovations resulted in "growth as a consequence of a superior product," it was entitled to maintain its consequent dominant position in the market it created through "business acumen," which we take to include shrewdness in profitable price competition. The Sherman Act does not draw a distinction between competition on the bases of price and of performance: the two are inseparable parts of any competitive offering. Where the opportunity exists to increase or protect market share profitably by offering equivalent or superior performance at a lower price, even a virtual monopolist may do so. CalComp has not only failed to produce evidence of pricing below marginal or average variable cost, but it has also failed as well to introduce any evidence to controvert IBM's substantial proof

that its price cuts were highly profitable. Moreover, the evidence of both parties established that IBM's disk price reductions were a response to lower-priced competition to which IBM was rapidly losing its disk business. The directed verdict as to CalComp's claims based on IBM's price competition was therefore proper.

[The Court then rejected the allegations that IBM's design changes constituted §2 violations. Its reasoning was as follows.]

IBM, assuming it was a monopolist, had the right to redesign its products to make them more attractive to buyers—whether by reason of lower manufacturing cost and price or improved performance. It was under no duty to help CalComp or other peripheral equipment manufacturers survive or expand. IBM need not have provided its rivals with disk products to examine and copy, nor have constricted its product development so as to facilitate sales of rival products. The reasonableness of IBM's conduct in this regard did not present a jury issue.

The complexity of a plaintiff's case does not entitle it to avoid a directed verdict if the evidence—no matter how much of it there may be—is weak. Having closely analyzed each of CalComp's arguments and the evidence on both sides in support thereof, drawing all reasonable inferences in CalComp's favor, we conclude that the district judge was correct.

Nor does viewing the various acts of IBM collectively change our conclusion. The number of legal and evidentiary issues has required us to consider each instance of IBM's alleged monopolizing conduct separately for purposes of analytical clarity. But there can be no synergistic result such as CalComp claims from a number of acts none of which show causal antitrust injury to CalComp.

Moreover, even assuming that IBM gained monopoly power in a relevant market, the acts constituted reasonable, pro-competitive conduct for a monopolist. CalComp suffered no "antitrust" injury from these, nor indeed any injury at all as that term is defined in §4 of the Clayton Act. [§4 grants the right to sue for treble damages to anyone injured by violations of the antitrust laws.]

Accordingly, the judgment of the district court entered on its directed verdict is affirmed.

CASE REVIEW QUESTIONS

1. What are the relevant product and geographic markets that IBM was alleged to have monopolized?
2. What activities of IBM were alleged to constitute evidence of intent to monopolize?
3. What caused a decline in IBM's market share in the relevant product market? How did IBM respond to that decline?
4. What was the effect of IBM's response to competition in the product market? What was the effect on CalComp specifically?

Oligopoly

The structure of competition in an industry is considered to be an **oligopoly** when a few large firms dominate the industry. Because each of the firms is likely to be able to anticipate the reaction of the others to any competitive action, the competitive decisions of all of the firms are likely to be similar. Such conduct, known as *conscious parallelism,* is beyond the reach of the antitrust laws as long as each firm reaches its decisions independently; that is, as long as there is no agreement or understanding among the firms. On the other hand, if the firms act according to a common understanding or agreement, they are in violation of §1 of the Sherman Act, which prohibits *concerted activity* (collective activity among competitors). The existence of an oligopoly may make it easier for concerted activity or collusion to take place. In the absence of such concerted activity, however, oligopoly itself is legal.

The economic effects of oligopoly may be similar to those of monopoly as a result of the lack of competition. Nevertheless, oligopoly is not subject to attack under §2 of the Sherman Act because no single firm possesses monopoly power. The legal approach to oligopoly is therefore purely behavioral—did the firms act pursuant to a common arrangement? Behavioral antitrust provisions will be discussed in detail in the following chapter.

Various attempts to pass legislation providing for a structural approach to oligopoly have been unsuccessful. The Federal Trade Commission at one time attempted to attack oligopolies as "shared monopolies" under §5 of the Federal Trade Commission Act, but it has now abandoned those attempts. As a result, legal challenges to oligopolies require the courts to search for some sort of agreement, either explicit or implicit, among the firms involved. In the absence of an agreement, even identical behavior by competing firms is legal.

Mergers

Section 7 of the Clayton Act prohibits mergers of firms in interstate commerce when the effects of the merger are likely to result in a substantial lessening of competition. **Mergers** are acquisitions or takeovers of one firm by another. Section 7 applies to mergers in which one firm purchases either the assets or the stock of another firm. Because the legality of any merger depends upon its effect on competition, the courts apply the rule of reason in merger cases. The effects of a merger upon competition depend upon the competitive relationship between merging firms and the conditions in the industry or industries in which the firms operate.

The judicial approach to merger cases under §7 involves the identification of the product market and geographic market affected by the merger. Just as in monopoly cases, the product market is defined according to the principles of substitutability (see the discussion on page 1016). The geographic market is the area or areas of the country likely to be affected by the merger. Again as in monopoly cases, the definitions of the markets are crucial. The more narrowly the markets are defined, the more likely it is that a merger will substantially affect competition in those markets.

After defining the relevant markets, the court must assess the probable results of the merger upon competition in those markets. Note that the court need concern itself only with the *probable* results of the merger; it needn't find any *actual* lessening of competition in order to prohibit or dissolve a merger. The assessment of the effects upon competition involves consideration of both structural and behavioral factors. The relative importance of these factors depends upon the relationship between the merging firms.

Horizontal Mergers When a merger involves firms that compete in the same market — which is called a **horizontal merger** — the court will consider whether the merged firms will be dominant in the market. If the resulting firm will have dominant share of a market in which there are few competitors or in which the competitors are significantly smaller, the merger will probably be held to violate §7. When two small firms merge in order to compete more effectively with a larger rival, the merger is likely to be allowed.

Until the mid-1970s, heavy emphasis was placed on the size of the resulting firm in most horizontal merger cases. When the new firm would have a significant market share in a concentrated industry, the merger would be held to be illegal. More recent cases have seen judicial consideration of the nature of the competition in the industry as well as of the merged firm's position in that industry. The following decision is an example of the present judicial approach to horizontal mergers.

UNITED STATES v. GENERAL DYNAMICS CORPORATION
415 U.S. 486 (U.S. Supreme Ct. 1974)

[Material Service Corporation was a large Midwest producer of concrete, limestone, and coal. Its coal production was from deep-shaft mines operated by Freeman Coal Mining Corporation, a wholly owned subsidiary of Material Service. Between 1954 and 1959, Material Service acquired all the stock of United Electric Coal Company, which operated strip mines and open-pit mines in Illinois and Kentucky. After Material Service completed the acquisition of United Electric, it was itself acquired by General Dynamics Corporation.

The United States alleged that the acquisition of United Electric by Material Service violated §7 of the

Clayton Act by substantially lessening competition in the sale and production of coal in either or both of two geographic markets. The United States argued that the relevant "section of the country" within the meaning of §7 was either the state of Illinois or the Eastern Interior Coal Province Sales Area (one of four major coal distribution areas recognized by the coal industry). The trial court held that the merger did not violate §7. The United States appealed to the Supreme Court.]

STEWART, Justice

The Government sought to prove a violation of §7 of the Clayton Act principally through statistics showing that within certain geographic markets the coal industry was concentrated among a small number of large producers; that this concentration was increasing; and that the acquisition of United Electric would materially enlarge the market share of the acquiring company and thereby contribute to the trend toward concentration.

[T]he question before us is whether the District Court was justified in finding that other pertinent factors affecting the coal industry and the business of the appellees mandated a conclusion that no substantial lessening of competition occurred or was threatened by the acquisition of United Electric. We are satisfied that the court's ultimate finding was not in error.

In this case, the District Court assessed the evidence of the "structure, history and probably future" of the coal industry, and on the basis of this assessment found no substantial probability of anticompetitive effects from the merger.

Much of the District Court's opinion was devoted to a description of the changes that have affected the coal industry since World War II. First, it found that coal had become increasingly less able to compete with other sources of energy in many segments of the energy market. Because of these changes in consumption patterns, coal's share of the energy resources consumed in this country fell from 78.4% in 1920 to 21.4% in 1968.

Second, the court found that to a growing extent since 1954, the electric utility industry has become the mainstay of coal consumption. While electric utilities consumed only 15.76% of the coal produced nationally in 1947, their share of total consumption increased every year thereafter, and in 1968 amounted to more than 59% of all the coal consumed throughout the Nation.

Third, and most significantly, the court found that to an increasing degree, nearly all coal sold to utilities is transferred under long-term requirements contracts, under which coal producers promise to meet utilities' coal consumption requirements for a fixed period of time, and at predetermined prices.

Because of these fundamental changes in the structure of the market for coal, the District Court was justified in viewing the statistics relied on by the Government as insufficient to sustain its case. Evidence of past production does not, as a matter of logic, necessarily give a proper picture of a company's future ability to compete. In most situations, of course, the unstated assumption is that a company that has maintained a certain share of a market in the recent past will be in a position to do so in the immediate future.

In the coal market, as analyzed by the District Court, however, statistical evidence of coal *production* was of considerably less significance. The bulk of the coal produced is delivered under long-term requirements contracts, and such sales thus do not represent the exercise of competitive power but rather the obligation to fulfill previously negotiated contracts at a previously fixed price. The focus of competition in a given time frame is not on the disposition of coal already produced but on the procurement of new long-term supply contracts. In this situation, a company's past ability to produce is of limited significance, since it is in a position to offer for sale neither its past production nor the bulk of the coal it is presently capable of producing, which is typically already committed under a long-term supply contract. A more significant indicator of a company's power effectively to compete with other companies lies in the state of a company's uncommitted reserves of recoverable coal. A company with relatively large supplies of coal which are not already under contract to a consumer will have a more important influence upon competition in the contemporaneous negotiation of supply contracts than a firm with small reserves, even though the latter may presently produce a greater tonnage of coal. In a market where the availability and price of coal are set by long-term contracts rather than immediate or short-term purchases and sales, reserves rather than past production are the best measure of a company's ability to compete.

The testimony and exhibits in the District Court revealed that United Electric's coal reserve prospects were "unpromising." United's relative position of strength in reserves was considerably weaker than its past and current ability to produce. While United ranked fifth among Illinois coal producers in terms of annual production, it was 10th in reserve holdings, and controlled less than 1% of the reserves held by coal producers in Illinois, Indiana, and Western Kentucky. United was found to be facing the future with relatively depleted resources at its disposal, and with the vast majority of those resources already committed under contracts allowing no further adjustment in price. In addition, the District Court found that "United Electric has neither the possibility of acquiring more [reserves] nor the ability to develop deep coal reserves," and thus was not in a position to increase its reserves to replace those already depleted or committed.

Viewed in terms of present and future reserve prospects — and in terms of probable future ability to compete — rather than in terms of past production, the District Court held that United Electric was a far less significant factor in the coal market than the Government contended or the production statistics seemed to indicate. While the company had been and remained a "highly profitable" and efficient producer of relatively large amounts of coal, its current and future power to compete for subsequent long-term contracts was severely limited by its scarce uncommitted resources. Irrespective of the company's size when viewed as a producer, its weakness as a competitor was properly analyzed by the District Court and fully substantiated that court's conclusion that its acquisition by Material Service would not "substantially . . . lessen competition. . . . "

The judgment of the District Court is affirmed.

CASE REVIEW QUESTIONS

1. Why was this merger a horizontal merger?
2. What are the relevant product and geographic markets in this case? Why are they so defined?
3. What is the nature of competition in the coal mining industry?
4. What evidence did the government use to support its attack on the merger? Did this evidence provide an accurate indication of the merger's effect on competition? Why?

Vertical Mergers When merging firms do not compete directly with each other but are at different levels in the production chain, the merger is called a **vertical merger.** Examples of vertical mergers would be the acquisition of a petroleum refining company by a firm that produces petrochemicals and the acquisition of a chain of gas stations by a petroleum refining company. In the first example, the acquired firm produces the raw materials for the product of the acquiring firm; in the second example, the acquired firm distributes (or retails) the product of the acquiring firm.

Because the merging firms do not operate in the same market, the analysis of the legality of a vertical merger under §7 of the Clayton Act involves the consideration of the size of each firm and its relative position in its respective market. The court must consider whether either firm occupies such a significant position in its market that the merger will foreclose a major source of supplies or a major distribution outlet from other competitors.

For example, if a chain of gas stations previously carried the products of a number of refiners, the court will consider whether the acquisition of the chain by one refiner will deny the other refiners access to the chain's sales outlets. If so and if the chain represents a significant share of the retail gasoline sales market, then the acquisition could violate §7 by substantially lessening competition in the distribution and retail sale of gasoline.

In addition to considering the size and position of each firm in its own market, the court will determine whether the merger will enable the resulting firm to engage in anticompetitive behavior in either market. When a merger creates significant opportunities for anticompetitive conduct, it will be held to violate §7.

As was the case with horizontal mergers, the courts in early vertical merger decisions emphasized the relative size of the merging firms in determining the merger's probable effect on competition. The courts also took the position that the sizes of the firms were directly related to the creation of opportunities for predatory conduct; that is, the larger the firms were, the more likely it was that such opportunities would be significant. More recent judicial analyses take the position that the sizes of the firms are not directly relevant to the creation of opportunities for predatory conduct. Rather, the courts now focus upon whether either firm is dominant or possesses monopoly power in its respective market. Much less emphasis is placed on the mere potential for anticompetitive behavior.

The following case, with its emphasis on possible predatory pricing, is representative of earlier judicial analyses. It does, however, reflect the concern about the relative size of each firm in its respective market. The case also represents one of the relatively few successful governmental challenges to a vertical merger.

REYNOLDS METALS COMPANY v. FEDERAL TRADE COMMISSION
309 F.2d 223 (D.C. Cir. 1962)

[Reynolds Metals Company (Reynolds), a producer of aluminum foil, sought judicial review of a Federal Trade Commission (FTC) determination that its acquisition of Arrow Brands, a company that converted aluminum foil into decorative foil for the florist industry, violated §7 of the Clayton Act. The FTC ordered Reynolds to divest itself of Arrow's stock and assets.

Reynolds specifically challenged the FTC's determination that the production and sale of decorative foil to the florist trade was a relevant line of commerce under §7 and its conclusion that the acquisition violated §7 by having the probable effect of substantially lessening competition in the relevant line of commerce.]

BURGER, Circuit Judge

This case is concerned chiefly with foil decorated in certain ways for use by the nation's approximately 700 wholesale florist outlets and 25,000 retail florists.

Reynolds is the largest producer of aluminum foil in the world. In 1957 its production capacity of 117 million pounds per year formed 40.5% of the total foil production capacity of all ten foil producers in the United States. The record indicates that the large foil producers such as Reynolds find it both impracticable and unprofitable to accept small orders from small buyers of foil to be used for specific and limited end purposes such as the decoration of flower pots or foodstuffs. Consequently, Reynolds and other major raw foil producers sell in quantity to intermediaries known in the trade as converters, who have come into existence precisely to meet the needs of these small foil markets, which individually do not require a sufficiently large amount of raw foil to purchase it in the minimum quantities sold by the manufacturers. These converters purchase large quantities of foil from the producers in so-called "jumbo" rolls, and after breaking these down and processing them with decorative or other features sought by the end users, sell in limited quantities to the several smaller markets.

Arrow, prior to and since its acquisition by Reynolds in 1956, has been engaged in converting "jumbo" rolls of raw foil into such limited quantities of a specialized kind which are then sold in decorated form almost exclusively to the florist trade. While roughly 200 foil converters are active in the United States, only eight, including Arrow, served the florist industry when this proceeding began. In 1956, these eight firms sold not more than an estimated 1,500,000 pounds of florist foil altogether, of which Arrow accounted for approximately 33%. Several of the firms competing with Arrow in converting foil for the florist industry purchased their plain or raw foil from Reynolds prior to the acquisition. Raw foil costs to an unintegrated florist foil converter, such as Arrow was, account for 70% of the total cost of production.

The remainder of the 200 converters process aluminum foil for all its many other uses, including usage as tape, candy box liners, covers for take-out foodstuffs [and] condensers. . . . The government concedes that theoretically all 200 converters could supply florist foil, but observes that in fact only the eight firms comprise the domestic *florist* foil converting industry. The problem of market definition in the present case centers only on the determination of the "line of commerce," since Reynolds does not disagree with the Commission's finding that the geographical area for measuring the competitive effects of this acquisition is the entire United States.

Until recently the established test for finding "patterns of trade" lay with measuring (1) the interchangeability of products from other markets with those in the market which the government was seeking to define and limit, and (2) the cross-elasticity of demand between the product itself and substitutes for it. It is now clear that mere potential interchangeability or cross-elasticity may be insufficient to mark the legally pertinent limits of a "relevant line of commerce." The "outer limits" of a general market may be thus determined, but sharply distinct submarkets can exist within these outer limits which may henceforth be the focal point of administrative and judicial inquiry under Section 7.

Analyzing the facts of the present case makes it abundantly clear that under these standards the production and sale of florist foil may rationally be defined by the Commission as comprising the relevant line of commerce in terms of (1) public and industrial recognition of it as a separate economic entity, (2) its distinct customers and (3) its distinct prices. . . . [T]he elements disclosed by the record are sufficient to support the Commission's determination that the florist foil market may be legitimately separated from aluminum foil markets generally and thus may be appropriately viewed as the area in which the activity allegedly prohibited by Sec. 7 occurred.

First, the identity of purchasers of florist foil is distinct and limited. With insignificant exception, the sole purchasers of florist foil are the nation's 700 wholesale florist outlets and, through these, the 25,000 retail florists throughout the country. Despite a clearly lower price for florist foil, other end users of decorative foil have not joined the identifiable mass of florist foil purchasers in noticeable numbers. As already noted, the identity of the florist foil converters who *alone* serve these florist purchasers is clearly limited to eight firms including Arrow, with some minor and as yet undefined competition from a few foreign firms indicated by the record. It is noteworthy that not only the number of firms thus serving the florists has remained fairly constant but up through the 1956 acquisition, now under review, the same individual firms comprised this number.

Secondly, both producer and consumer recognition of the florist foil submarket as a definite economic entity is clearly demonstrated by what appears to have been the election of other decorative foil converters not to serve the florist industry, by the habit and practice of the extensive florist industry itself in purchasing only from florist foil converters like Arrow and not from other decorative foil converters, and again, by the failure of decorative foil users other than florists to purchase the lower priced florist foil.

Pricing forms the final point. Substantial evidence discloses a markedly lower price for florist foil compared with the price of other colored or embossed aluminum foil sold in comparable weight units and gauged at approximately the same thickness. We think price differentials have an important if not decisive bearing in the quest to delimit a submarket.

It appears, therefore, that the florist foil market probably is a distinguishable product market, and therefore the production and sale of decorative aluminum foil to the florist trade is a "line of commerce" within the meaning of Sec. 7

The effect of the acquisition of Arrow on this line of commerce was therefore justifiably predicted as substantially anti-competitive. While as many as eight or more firms converted foil for the florist industry, we have observed that roughly 33% of this business had been captured by Arrow alone prior to the 1956 transaction tying Arrow into Reynolds. When Arrow was vertically integrated through the Reynolds' acquisition, one minor anti-competitive effect foreseeable was the exclusion of other manufacturers of raw foil (Reynolds' competitors) from selling to approximately 33% of the florist foil converting industry. However, neither

the examiner nor the Commission rested their conclusions that Sec. 7 had been violated on this basis, nor should we.

The truer picture of anti-competitive effect emerges from even the most cursory consideration of the post-acquisition competitive postures of the eight previously independent florist foil converters vis-a-vis one another. Arrow's assimilation into Reynolds' enormous capital structure and resources gave Arrow an immediate advantage over its competitors who were contending for a share of the market for florist foil. The power of the "deep pocket" or "rich parent" for one of the florist foil suppliers in a competitive group where previously no company was very large and all were relatively small opened the possibility and power to sell at prices approximating cost or below and thus to undercut and ravage the less affluent competition. The Commission is not required to establish that the Reynolds' acquisition of Arrow did in fact have anti-competitive consequences. It is sufficient if the Commission shows that acquisition had the capability or potentiality to lessen competition. That such a potential emerged from the combination of Reynolds and Arrow was enough to bring it within Sec. 7. But the Commission on substantial evidence has additionally provided us with a finding of *actual* anti-competitive effect, whereas an apparent consequence of retroactive price reductions for Arrow foil after the acquisition of florist foil sales of 5 of Arrow's 7 competitors had by 1957 dropped from 14% to 47% below 1955 sales. Arrow's sales over the same period increased by 18.9%.

The necessary probability of anti-competitive effect has thus been shown. In agreeing with the Commission, however, we do not, nor could we intimate, that the mere intrusion of "bigness" into a competitive economic community otherwise populated by commercial "pygmies" will per se invoke the Clayton Act.

Affirmed and order will be enforced.

CASE REVIEW QUESTIONS
1. Why was this a vertical merger?
2. Why was the product market defined as florist foil rather than as all decorative foil?

3. What was the effect of Reynolds' acquisition of Arrow upon Arrow's competitive position? What was its effect upon the competitors of Arrow?
4. What is the "deep pocket" or "rich parent" effect that the court refers to? How does it affect competition? Is the court protecting competitors or competition here? (More recent court decisions have held that potential "deep pocket" effects are not sufficient grounds to hold that a merger violates §7.)

Conglomerate Mergers The great majority of recent corporate mergers have involved conglomerate mergers. In **conglomerate mergers,** the merging firms are not competitors and are not involved in any production-supply relationship. Since the firms are not directly related, their sizes are not relevant to the merger's effect on competition. The courts must therefore consider whether the combination of the firms will create significant opportunities for anticompetitive behavior.

A court must determine whether the assets of the acquiring firm will enable the acquired firm to engage in predatory pricing or improve an already dominant position. The court must also consider whether the acquiring firm had contemplated entering the market in which the acquired firm operated. If so, the merger precludes that potential entry and prevents an increase in competition. The difficulty involved in proving that the probable effects of a potential merger will be the creation of significant opportunities for anticompetitive practices makes a legal challenge to a conglomerate merger a formidable task. It is not surprising, then, that antitrust enforcement authorities have not successfully challenged a conglomerate merger since 1974.

The case that follows deals with the doctrine of potential entrance by the acquiring firm. It also illustrates some of the difficulties involved in legal challenges to conglomerate mergers.

BOC INTERNATIONAL LTD. v. FTC
557 F.2d 24 (2nd Circuit 1977)

[BOC International Ltd. is the world's second largest producer of gases for industrial and medical use. BOC has never produced or sold any products in the United States. Airco is the third largest producer of industrial and medical gases in the United States, with 16 percent of the domestic market. The top two firms in the U.S. market have 26 and 18 percent market shares. BOC acquired a 35 percent interest in Airco in 1973.

The FTC challenged BOC's acquisition. The Commission, through its administrative proceedings, held that the acquisition violated §7 of the Clayton Act. BOC was ordered by the Commission to divest its share of Airco. BOC sought judicial review of the FTC ruling.]

OAKES, Circuit Judge

The theory on which the FTC based its holding in this case, the actual potential entrant theory, must be distinguished at the outset from the closely related theory, not here involved, addressed to the problem of the "perceived" or "recognized'" potential entrant. This latter theory is concerned with a present effect that a company not in an oligopolistic market is having on companies which are in that market. Because the insiders view the outsider as a likely entrant (a competitor "waiting in the wings"), they keep prices and profit margins lower than they would if there were no threat of the outsider entering the market either *de novo* (by starting a new firm) or via a toehold acquisition of a small firm, a threat that might be realized if prices and profits were higher. When the outsider acquires a large firm in the market, it no longer poses a threat, the "in the wings" effect on prices disappears, and competition is thereby lessened.

In the instant case, the FTC specifically found that there was no proof of any "wings" or "fringe" effect of BOC on the American industrial gases market or on prices therein. This finding, not challenged here, makes the instant case different from the typical one, in which there is both a perceived and an actual entrant concern. Here the FTC has in effect conceded that BOC as a potential entrant was having no *present* procompetitive effect on the relevant market; the Commission's order is instead grounded entirely on the belief that competition in the American industrial gases market would increase at some time in the *future* if BOC divests itself of Airco. All parties here are agreed that, had the acquisition not been blocked, competition in the American industrial gases market just after the acquisition would have been "exactly as it was [before the acquisition], neither hurt nor helped."

In determining whether an alleged future effect on competition by itself justifies blocking a present corporate acquisition under the actual potential entrant doctrine, two distinct questions looking to the future must be answered. First, would the firm in question enter de novo or by toehold acquisition if not permitted to enter by acquiring a large company? Second, would the de novo or toehold entry of the firm have procompetitive effects on the market in question? If there is no showing that the acquiring firm—and if the acquiring firm is exerting no present influence on the market as a perceived potential entrant, as is concededly the case here—then it cannot be said that the effect of the

acquisition "may be substantially to lessen competition," Clayton Act §7. In such situations, to the contrary, "there may even be a competitive gain to the extent that [the acquiring firm] strengthens the market position of the acquired firm."

In the instant case, with regard to the first of the two predictions, the FTC made a critical and controverted finding:

[A]s of December 1973, there was a "reasonable probability" that BOC would have eventually entered the U.S. industrial gases market by internal expansion or its equivalent, but for the acquisition of Airco. . . .

BOC challenges this finding . . . on the legal ground that the standard used—reasonable probability of *eventual* entry—places a lighter burden on the FTC than is justified by the statute and the purposes of the actual potential entrant doctrine. [W]e agree with BOC on the legal question and accordingly set aside the FTC's order.

The FTC was correct in using a "reasonable probability" test here, but its accompanying reference to "eventual entry" makes the overall FTC test, we believe, one based largely on "ephemeral possibilities."

There is no indication anywhere in the FTC opinion either as to what it meant in using the words "eventual entry," nor does the record indicate how long a period of time might elapse before BOC could be expected to enter the American industrial gases market de novo or by toehold acquisition. The Commission cited evidence indicating a BOC interest in entering the market since early 1970, but conceded that no entry had been attempted prior to the late 1973 acquisition of Airco:

Simply because no entry had been effectuated at the time the Airco opportunity presented itself did not mean that BOC would not have *eventually* realized its "*long-term* objectives" of entering the U.S. market—by growth rather than by this major acquisition.

In its brief to this court, the FTC entirely ignored BOC's argument that "[t]he degree of uncertainty in any economic prediction becomes unacceptably high as it is projected farther and farther into the future." And at oral argument counsel for the FTC all but conceded that the Commission's "eventually" standard contained no temporal estimate whatsoever, but rather involved "long range" considerations that might take "decades" to come to fruition.

These FTC statements, combined with what the Commission omitted to state, together establish the wholly speculative nature of the "eventual entry" test. We hold that such uncabined speculation cannot be the basis of a finding that Section 7 has been violated. While it is not clear—and we need not decide— whether the probable entry of the acquiring firm must be "imminent" in an actual potential entrant situation, it seems necessary under Section 7 that the finding of probable entry at least contain some reasonable temporal estimate related to the near future, with "near" defined in terms of the entry barriers and lead time necessary for entry in the particular industry, and that the finding be supported by substantial evidence in the record.

We emphasize that we are not requiring any exact, precisely calibrated assessment of time of entry. Such a requirement would be as inconsistent with Section 7's focus on "probabilities" as is the FTC's "eventual entry" standard. But here there was no finding regarding a reasonable probability of entry in the near future, nor is there any evidence in the record on which such a finding might be based.

The order of the FTC must accordingly be set aside.

CASE REVIEW QUESTIONS

1. Why is the merger a conglomerate merger?
2. What changes took place in the relevant market after BOC acquired Airco?
3. Upon what basis did the FTC find that BOC's acquisition substantially affected competition?
4. How does a "perceived potential entrant" differ from an "actual potential entrant"? What are the effects of each type of potential entrant upon competition?
5. What factors are considered to determine whether a firm is a potential entrant?

Premerger Notification Requirements The 1976 Amendments to §7 of the Clayton Act instituted a premerger notification requirement for mergers involving firms of certain sizes. The legislation added §7A, which requires that both the Antitrust Division of the Justice Department and the Federal Trade Commission be notified prior to any merger when the acquiring firm has assets or annual sales of over $100 million and the firm to be acquired has assets or annual sales of over $10 million. The notice must be given at least 15 days prior to the merger if it involves a cash purchase of securities. For mergers that involve an *exchange* of securities, the notice period is 30 days.

The purpose of the premerger notification requirement is to give the antitrust enforcement agencies the opportunity to analyze the effects of a proposed merger before it takes place. The notification requirement does not constitute a formal approval system; the merging firms need not get the permission of the enforcement authorities in order to consummate the merger. In practice, however, the requirement has allowed the authorities to raise legal concerns prior to some mergers. In most cases where concerns have been raised, the proposed merger has not taken place.

REVIEW QUESTIONS

1. What are the various goals suggested as the rationales for antitrust policy? Do these goals support or conflict with each other? What do you think the primary goal of antitrust policy should be?

2. What is the rule of reason? What is the per se rule? What is the rationale behind the use of each rule?

3. What elements are necessary for a violation of §2 of the Sherman Act? What is the significance of the statute's use of the word "monopolize" rather than the word "monopoly"?

4. What harmful effects on competition result from an oligopoly? Should antitrust policy regarding oligopoly be focused on the structural elements of the mere existence of an oligopoly rather than on the behavioral elements of concerted action among the firms?

5. Define a horizontal merger. How is it likely to affect competition? What is a vertical merger, and how does it affect competition? What is a conglomerate merger, and in what ways is it likely to affect competition?

6. When must firms proposing to merge give notification to the Justice Department and the Federal Trade Commission? What is the purpose of this notification requirement?

CASE PROBLEMS

1. Fields Manufacturing Company is the United States' leading producer of machines for manufacturing shoes. A number of different machines are required to complete the various steps of the shoe production process. There are 12 manufacturers of various shoe production machines, but only Fields produces machines for all the steps in the production process. Fields produces almost 70 percent of the machines used by U.S. shoe producers. Its dominant position is due in large part to its engineering and research skills. Fields developed most of the innovations in the manufacturing process. Unlike other manufacturers, Fields will not sell its machines; it leases them to shoe producers instead. The leases are for 10-year periods and cover service and repairs. There are substantial financial penalties for early termination of a lease. The rents charged by Fields for their machines reflect Fields' competitive position—rents are low for machines that are also produced by competitors and high for machines that only Fields produces. Garp Process Company is a small firm attempting to compete with Fields. Garp is having difficulty attracting customers because Fields' leasing system has tied up most of the potential customers. If Garp brings a legal action challenging Fields under §2 of the Sherman Act, who will win the case? If Garp wins, what remedies would it be entitled to? Explain.

2. The Kansas City Star Publishing Company publishes the only two major daily newspapers in the Kansas City area, the morning *Star* and the afternoon *Times*. The papers are distributed at the retail level by a group of independent distributors to whom Star Publishing awards exclusive distribution routes under one year contracts. The distributors purchase the papers at wholesale prices from Star Publishing and are free to set their own retail prices. Star Publishing decides to distribute the papers through its own distribution network in order to improve circulation and enhance advertising revenues. Star Publishing announces that it will not renew any distributor contracts when they expire and it will not sell the papers at wholesale prices anymore. If the distributors, who stand to lose their businesses, file a suit under §2 of the Sherman Act challenging Star Publishing's new policy, who will win the case? Explain.

3. Canco is the nation's second largest producer of metal containers, producing 33 percent of all metal containers sold in the United States. The largest can producer has 38 percent of the market, and the third largest producer accounts for 5 per-

cent of the market. The remaining 24 percent of the market is shared among 75 firms. Cans are used for packaging foods, beverages (primarily soda and beer), and other liquids such as motor oil products. Glassco manufactures glass containers and produces 9.6 percent of all the glass containers sold in the United States. It ranks third in the glass container industry. The two largest producers account for 34.2 and 11.6 percent of the market, respectively. Glass containers are used for foods, sauces, baby food, toiletries, and beverages. They have become increasingly popular as nonreturnable packaging for soda and beer. Canco had considered developing its own glass container division, but it decided to acquire Glassco instead. If the government brings a legal action challenging the Canco–Glassco merger under §7 of the Clayton Act, who will win the case? Explain.

4. GM is the leading producer of automobiles in the United States. While there are only three domestic car manufacturers, the auto companies face stiff competition from a number of foreign producers. The U.S. manufacturers dominate the large car market (luxury and full-size models); the foreign producers are superior in the production and sale of compact and subcompact models. Nippon Auto is the largest car producer in Japan. It accounts for the largest segment of the U.S. compact and subcompact car sales. Some Japanese producers are establishing plants in the United States in order to avoid the effects of import quota legislation limiting the importation of foreign cars. Rather than set up its own plant, Nippon agreed with GM to create a jointly owned firm to produce subcompact models in the United States. The newly created firm, General Nippon, Inc., is controlled entirely by the two parent firms, each owning 50 percent of the stock. If the government brings a legal action challenging this joint venture under §7 of the Clayton Act, who will win the case? Explain.

5. Family Shoe Stores, Inc., is a chain of discount shoe stores that sells low-priced men's, women's, and children's shoes. Family Shoe accounts for 1.2 percent of all shoe sales in the United States, but it

is the largest independent chain of shoe stores. Shoes are sold through shoe stores and through shoe departments in department stores. There are approximately 70,000 total retail outlets for shoes, but only 22,000 are classified as shoe stores (which are defined as deriving 50 percent or more of their gross receipts from the sale of shoes). Shoes are produced by almost 970 independent manufacturers. The largest producers account for 24 percent of all shoes produced. These large manufacturers are pursuing a policy of acquiring retail outlets for their shoes. Style-Line Shoe Company is the fourth largest shoe producer, with 4 percent of U.S. shoe production. Style-Line produces high quality, higher-cost shoes. Style-Line also controls a number of retail shoe outlets, which account for almost 2.7 percent of total shoe sales. Style-Line seeks to acquire Family Shoe Stores, Inc., in order to expand its retail market share. If the government brings a legal action under §7 of the Clayton Act challenging Style-Line's acquisition of Family Shoe Stores, who will win the case? Explain.

6. Wilson Corporation is the largest firm selling a general line of sporting goods equipment in the United States. Wilson sells golf clubs; football, basketball, and baseball equipment; sports uniforms; and gym mats. Wilson has annual sales of almost $150 million, and it has 18 percent of the general sporting goods market. Wilson has been seeking to broaden its product line by expanding into other markets such as fishing and gymnastics equipment. Nissen Company is the largest producer of gymnastics equipment in the United States. It has annual sales of $45 million, which account for 26 percent of the gymnastics equipment sold in the United States. There are eight other firms producing gymnastics equipment in the United States, but the top four firms account for 70 percent of all sales. The remaining five firms are small and sell regionally rather than nationally. Wilson had considered starting its own gymnastics division, but it decides to acquire Nissen instead. If the government brings a legal action challenging the merger, who will win the case? Explain.

48

ANTITRUST REGULATION OF BUSINESS BEHAVIOR

In addition to regulating the competitive *structure* of businesses, as was discussed in the previous chapter, the antitrust laws also regulate the competitive *behavior* of firms. Behavioral antitrust policies focus upon agreements or arrangements among firms and upon firms' pricing policies. Section 1 of the Sherman Act, which prohibits every "contract, combination . . . or conspiracy in restraint of trade or commerce," is the main provision of behavioral antitrust policies.

In determining the legality of an arrangement, it is usually necessary to determine whether the arrangement is horizontal — meaning that it involves competitors — or vertical — meaning that it involves firms at different levels of the production – distribution chain. The approach used to determine legality generally differs for horizontal and vertical arrangements. It may also be important to consider whether the arrangement involves prices or relates only to nonprice matters.

HORIZONTAL CONCERTED ACTIVITY

Horizontal arrangements, which are also called horizontal concerted activities, involve competing firms. Such arrangements may be pursuant to formal contracts or to tacit understandings, and they may involve pricing or nonprice competition. Because any agreement among competitors is likely to have an adverse effect on competition, the antitrust laws deal harshly with horizontal arrangements. Any concerted activity among competitors that restricts competition or that is intended to restrict competition is illegal per se. This means that the conduct is illegal regardless of its effect on competition (see page 1014 of the previous chapter).

The Per Se Rule

The per se rule approach to horizontal concerted activity was spelled out by the U.S. Supreme Court in its *United States* v. *Trenton Potteries* decision in 1927. This case involved a government challenge to a price-fixing arrangement among a number of firms manufacturing bathroom fixtures. The firms argued that the prices set under the arrangement were reasonable and that the arrangement should therefore be legal under the rule of reason. The Court rejected the argument and held that an agreement among competitors is illegal per se.

The impact of the per se rule is mainly evidentiary. A court will not consider any justification for concerted behavior. For instance, the fact that an agreement to set prices maintains them at a reasonable level or only specifies a ceiling price is irrelevant to the legality of the agreement. The rationale behind the per se approach, as articulated in *Trenton Potteries,* is as follows:

> The power to fix prices, whether reasonably exercised or not, involves power to control the market and to fix arbitrary and unreasonable prices. The reasonable price fixed today may through economic and business changes become the unreasonable price of tomorrow. Agreements which create such potential power may well be held to be in themselves unreasonable or unlawful restraints, without the necessity of minute inquiry whether a particular price is reasonable or unreasonable as fixed and without placing on the government . . . the burden of ascertaining from day to day whether it has become unreasonable through the mere variation of economic conditions.

The per se approach, under §1 of the Sherman Act, applies to a variety of horizontal concerted activities. Examples include territorial market divisions, agreements to restrict production or output, agreements not to deal with certain firms or customers, group boycotts, and agreements not to advertise prices.

Because concerted activity intended to restrict competition is illegal per se, it needn't achieve the desired results. It is illegal regardless of the actual effects on competition and regardless of the motives behind it. Firms acting independently may choose not to deal with certain customers or in certain areas or to charge certain prices. However, when such decisions are made in conjunction with competing firms, they are illegal. The crucial factor for determining the legality of particular behavior is whether the firms involved are acting jointly or independently.

Because of the per se rule, the judicial approach to cases of alleged horizontal concerted activity involves only the determination of whether the conduct was concerted rather than independent and whether the arrangement was indeed horizontal. If both questions are answered affirmatively, a court will refuse to consider any justification for the activity, as is illustrated by the following case.

UNITED STATES v. TOPCO ASSOCIATES, INC.
405 U.S. 596 (U.S. Supreme Ct. 1972)

[Topco Associates, Inc. (Topco) is a cooperative association of small, regional supermarket chains. Topco's main function is to serve as a purchasing agent for the member chains. It procures and distributes more than 1,000 products, which are marketed under brand names owned by Topco. The member supermarket chains operate independently. There is no pooling of profits or advertising efforts, and no grocery business is conducted under the Topco name. The member supermarket chains control all of the association's stock and voting rights, Topco's board of directors is composed of executives from the various member chains. As a result of these arrangements, the members have complete control over Topco's operations.

The United States challenged the legality of the association under §1 of the Sherman Act. The trial court held that the arrangement was legal. The United States appealed to the Supreme Court.]

MARSHALL, Justice

Topco was founded in the 1940s by a group of small, local grocery chains, independently owned and operated, that desired to cooperate to obtain high quality merchandise under private labels in order to compete more effectively with larger national and regional chains. By 1964, Topco's members had combined retail sales of more than $2 billion; by 1967, their sales totaled more than $2.3 billion, a figure exceeded by only three national grocery chains.

Members of the association vary in the degree of market share that they possess in their respective areas. [T]here is much evidence in the record that Topco members are frequently in as strong a competitive position in their respective areas as any other chain. The strength of this competitive position is due, in some measure, to the success of Topco-brand products. Although only 10% of the total goods sold by Topco members bear the association's brand names, the profit on these goods is substantial and their very

existence has improved the competitive potential of Topco members with respect to other large and powerful chains.

Section 1 of the Sherman Act provides, in relevant part:

> Every contract, combination in the form of trust or otherwise or conspiracy in restraint of trade or commerce among the several States, or with foreign nations is declared to be illegal. . . .

The United States charged that, beginning at least as early as 1960 and continuing up to the time that the complaint was filed, Topco has combined and conspired with its members to violate §1. . . . The Government alleged that there existed:

> a continuing agreement, understanding and concert of action among the co-conspirator member firms acting through Topco, the substantial terms of which have been and are that each co-conspirator member firm will sell Topco-controlled brands only within the marketing territory allocated to it, and will refrain from selling Topco-controlled brands outside such marketing territory.

The division of marketing territories to which the complaint refers consists of a number of practices by the association. When applying for membership [in Topco], a chain . . . must first be approved by the board of directors, and thereafter by an affirmative vote of 75% of the association's members. If, however, the member whose operations are closest to those of the applicant, or any member whose operations are located within 100 miles of the applicant, votes against approval, an affirmative vote of 85% of the members is required for approval. Because, as indicated by the record, members cooperate in accommodating each other's wishes, the procedure for approval provides, in essence, that members have a veto of sorts over actual or potential competition in the territorial areas in which they are concerned.

Following approval, each new member signs an agreement with Topco designating the territory in which that member may sell Topco-brand products.

No member may sell these products outside the territory in which it is licensed. Most licenses are exclusive, and even those denominated "coextensive" or "nonexclusive" prove to be *de facto* [as a practical matter] exclusive. When combined with each member's veto power over new members, provisions for exclusivity work effectively to insulate members from competition in Topco-brand goods. Should a member violate its license agreement and sell in areas other than those in which it is licensed, its membership can be terminated.

The Government maintains that this scheme of dividing markets violates the Sherman Act because it operates to prohibit competition in Topco-brand products among grocery chains engaged in retail operations.

From the inception of this lawsuit, Topco accepted as true most of the Government's allegations regarding territorial divisions . . . although it differed greatly with the Government on the conclusions, both factual and legal, to be drawn from these facts. . . .

Topco essentially maintains that it needs territorial divisions to compete with larger chains; that the association could not exist if the territorial divisions were anything but exclusive; and that by restricting competition in the sale of Topco-brand goods, the association actually increases competition by enabling its members to compete successfully with larger regional and national chains.

The District Court, considering all these things relevant to its decision, agreed with Topco. It recognized that the panoply of restraints that Topco imposed on its members worked to prevent competition in Topco-brand products, but concluded that

> [w]hatever anti-competitive effect these practices may have on competition in the sale of Topco private label brands is far outweighed by the increased ability of Topco members to compete both with the national chains and other supermarkets operating in their respective territories.

The court held that Topco's practices are procompetitive and, therefore, consistent with the purposes of the antitrust laws. But we conclude that the District Court used an improper analysis in reaching its result.

Whether or not we would decide this case the same way under the rule of reason used by the District Court is irrelevant to the issue before us. The fact is that courts are of limited utility in examining difficult economic problems. Our inability to weigh, in any meaningful sense, destruction of competition in one sector of the economy against promotion of competition in another sector is one important reason we have formulated per se rules.

The District Court determined that by limiting the freedom of its individual members to compete with each other, Topco was doing a greater good by fostering competition between members and other large supermarket chains. But, the fallacy in this is that Topco has no authority under the Sherman Act to determine the respective values of competition in various sectors of the economy. On the contrary, the Sherman Act gives to each Topco member and to each prospective member the right to ascertain for itself whether or not competition with other supermarket chains is more desirable than competition in the sale of Topco-brand products.

If a decision is to be made to sacrifice competition in one portion of the economy for greater competition in another portion, this is a decision that must be made by Congress and not by private forces or by the courts. Private forces are too keenly aware of their own interests in making such decisions and courts are ill-equipped and ill-situated for such decision-making. To analyze, interpret, and evaluate the myriad of competing interests and the endless data that would surely be brought to bear on such decisions, and to make the delicate judgment on the relative values to society of competitive areas of the economy, the judgment of the elected representatives of the people is required. For the reasons previously discussed, the arena in which Topco members compete must be left to their unfettered choice absent a contrary congressional determination.

We reverse the judgment of the District Court and remand the case for entry of an appropriate decree.

CASE REVIEW QUESTIONS

1. What was the purpose of Topco's restrictions upon the sales areas of its members?
2. What were the effects of Topco's restrictions on competition among large grocery

chains? What were the effects on competition among sellers of Topco brand products?

3. Did the trial court hold the Topco restrictions to be horizontal or vertical? Why did the trial court find the restrictions to be legal?

4. Did the Supreme Court characterize the Topco restrictions as horizontal or vertical? Why? Why did the Supreme Court refuse to consider the purpose of the restrictions when holding them to be illegal?

5. Had the member chains chosen to merge into a single firm in order to compete with the national chains rather than to purchase through Topco, would their conduct have been held to be illegal?

Trade Associations and Concerted Activity

Trade associations, which are organizations formed by the firms in a particular industry, must exercise caution in collecting and distributing information about that industry because of the potential for concerted activity based on such information. Gathering and publishing production and pricing information in aggregate form, with no individual firms or customers being identified, is legal. However, the distribution of current prices offered to specific customers is illegal when the effect of such information is to stabilize prices in an industry. Even an informal exchange of current price information, when the firms involved had no agreement to adhere to the prices quoted, has been held to be illegal. Since the effect of the exchange was to stabilize prices, it was in violation of §1 of the Sherman Act.

VERTICAL RESTRICTIONS

Restrictions imposed by a manufacturer or supplier of a product or service upon firms that distribute or retail that product or service are known as **vertical restrictions.** Such restrictions may involve territorial limits upon sales or agreements not to deal with competitors of the supplier.

Vertical restrictions may violate §1 of the Sherman Act or §3 of the Clayton Act. The judicial approach to such restrictions varies with the nature of the restriction. Considerations involve whether a restriction pertains to pricing or nonprice issues and whether it is a **tying arrangement** (which requires the purchaser of the product to take other products of the supplier as well) or an **exclusive dealing agreement** (which prohibits a retailer from dealing with other suppliers).

Vertical Price Restrictions

Attempts by suppliers or manufacturers to control the price at which their products are sold by a retailer or distributor may be illegal under §1 of the Sherman Act. Although a supplier may set the price for the sale of its products by retail outlets that it owns, it may not control the price at which independent outlets resell the product. The supplier is free to choose the retailers with which it will deal and to set the prices at which it will sell products to those retailers. It may even suggest a retail price to independent retailers, as long as the actual choice of the retail price is left to the retailer.

The supplier may not require the retailer to charge a certain price, nor may the retailer agree to charge a certain price. Such required prices or agreements involve concerted action, so they are illegal under §1 of the Sherman Act. An example of such an arrangement occurred in *U.S.* v. *Parke, Davis & Company.* In this case, a drug manufacturer had required both wholesalers and retailers to adhere to a price list in the resale of drugs. The retailers were also required to agree to refrain from advertising prices for the drugs. The Supreme Court held the arrangement to be in violation of §1 of the Sherman Act.

Recently, some commentators have questioned the application of the per se rule to vertical price restrictions. They argue that such restrictions affect only **intrabrand competition** (competition among the sellers of the supplier's products) and not **interbrand competition** (competition among the products of various suppliers). The courts, however, have refused to consider these arguments, and they continue to apply the per se rule to vertical price restrictions.

Vertical Nonprice Restrictions

Restrictions on Sales Efforts Vertical nonprice restrictions generally pertain to the right of a retailer or distributor to sell in certain areas or to certain types of customers. They usually involve the designation of certain retailers as the exclusive source of supply of a given product in a particular area. These restrictions benefit the retailer by giving it power in the particular product market through its status as a sole supplier. They benefit the manufacturer or distributor by ensuring that its retailers won't compete with each other.

Vertical nonprice restrictions affect both interbrand and intrabrand competition. Because they generally limit the source of supply for the manufacturer's product in a given area, they reduce or eliminate intrabrand competition. However, when a number of other firms manufacture and sell similar products, they may actually enhance interbrand competition. On the other hand, when only one or two firms manufacture a product, any restrictions on intrabrand competition will also reduce interbrand competition.

Because the effects of vertical nonprice restrictions depend upon the conditions in the particular industry, a court determining the legality of such restrictions must consider their actual effect upon competition in that industry. The court will therefore apply the rule of reason (see page 1014 of the previous chapter).

Prior to 1977, under a precedent set in the *United States* v. *Arnold Schwinn & Company* case, the legality of vertical territorial restrictions depended upon whether the distributor sold the products to the retailer or retained ownership of the products and used the retailer as a sales agent. The *Schwinn* approach involved a combination of the per se rule and the rule of reason. In the *Continental T.V.* v. *GTE Sylvania* case, which follows, the Supreme Court overruled *Schwinn.* As a result, a court must now consider the actual effects that intrabrand restictions have upon interbrand competition.

CONTINENTAL T.V., INC. v. GTE SYLVANIA, INC.
433 U.S. 36 (U.S. Supreme Ct. 1977)

[In response to declining sales, GTE Sylvania, Inc. (Sylvania) began to sell its televisions through franchised retailers. The number of these retailers in any given area was limited, and Sylvania required them to sell its products only from the locations for which franchises were granted. The franchises were not exclusive—that is, several might be granted for a given area. Sylvania retained the right to increase or decrease the number of franchises in an area, depending upon the success or failure of the retailers in that area.

Because of disappointing sales in San Francisco, Sylvania decided to award a new franchise to a retailer located approximately one mile from a store that held an existing franchise operated by Continental T.V., Inc. (Continental). Continental protested, but Sylvania proceeded to establish the new franchise. Continental also sought to open an outlet in Sacramento, but Sylvania refused to grant the franchise because it felt the market there was already adequately served. Continental then canceled an order from Sylvania and ordered from a competitor instead. It also notified Sylvania that is was opening a retail outlet in Sacramento.

Sylvania canceled Continental's franchise and initiated a suit for payments owed by Continental. Continental counter-sued, claiming that the Sylvania franchise agreements violated §1 of the Sherman Act. The trial court held for Continental, awarding treble damages of $1,7734,515 against Sylvania. The Court of Appeals reversed the trial verdict, and Continental appealed to the Supreme Court.]

POWELL, Justice

We turn first to Continental's contention that Sylvania's restriction on retail locations is a *per se* violation of §1 of the Sherman Act as interpreted in *Schwinn.*

Both Schwinn and Sylvania sought to reduce but not to eliminate competition among their respective retailers through the adoption of a franchise system. Although it was not one of the issues addressed by the District Court or presented on appeal by the Govern-

ment, the Schwinn franchise plan included a location restriction similar to one challenged here. These restrictions allowed Schwinn and Sylvania to regulate the amount of competition among their retailers by preventing a franchisee from selling franchised products from outlets other than one covered by the franchise agreement. To exactly the same end, the Schwinn franchise plan included a companion restriction, apparently not found in the Sylvania plan, that prohibited franchised retailers from selling Schwinn products to nonfranchised retailers. In *Schwinn* the Court expressly held that this restriction was impermissible under the broad principle stated there. In intent and competitive impact, the retail customer restriction in *Schwinn* is indistinguishable from the location restriction in the present case. In both cases the restrictions limited the freedom of the retailer to dispose of the purchased products as he desired. The fact that one restriction was addressed to territory and the other to customers is irrelevant to functional antitrust analysis, and indeed, to the language and broad thrust of the opinion in *Schwinn.*

Sylvania argues that if *Schwinn* cannot be distinguished, it should be reconsidered. [W]e are convinced that the need for clarification of the law in this area justifies reconsideration.

The market impact of vertical restrictions is complex because of their potential for a simultaneous reduction of intrabrand competition and stimulation of interbrand competition. Significantly, the Court in *Schwinn* did not distinguish among the challenged restrictions on the basis of their individual potential for intrabrand harm or interbrand benefit. Restrictions that completely eliminated intrabrand competition among Schwinn distributors were analyzed no differently than those that merely moderated intrabrand competition among retailers.

Vertical restrictions reduce intrabrand competition by limiting the number of sellers of a particular product competing for the business of a given group of buyers. Location restrictions have this effect because of practical constraints on the effective marketing area of retail outlets. Although intrabrand competition may be reduced, the ability of retailers to exploit the resulting market may be limited both by the ability of consumers to travel to other franchised locations, and perhaps more importantly, to purchase the competing products of other manufacturers. None of these key variables, however, is affected by the form of the transaction by which a manufacturer conveys his products to the retailers.

Vertical restrictions promote interbrand competition by allowing the manufacturer to achieve certain efficiencies in the distribution of his products. These "redeeming virtues" are implicit in every decision sustaining vertical restrictions under the rule of reason. Economists have identified a number of ways in which manufacturers can use such restrictions to compete more effectively against other manufacturers. For example, new manufacturers and manufacturers entering new markets can use the restrictions in order to induce competent and aggressive retailers to make the kind of investment of capital and labor that is often required in the distribution of products to the consumer. Established manufacturers can use them to induce retailers to engage in promotional activities or to provide service and repair facilities necessary to the efficient marketing of their products. Service and repair are vital for many products, such as automobiles and major household appliances. The availability and quality of such services affect a manufacturer's good will and the competitiveness of his product. Because of market imperfections such as the so-called "free rider" effect, these services might not be provided by retailers in a purely competitive situation, despite the fact that each retailer's benefit would be greater if all provided the services than if none did. . . .

Such [vertical] restrictions, in varying forms, are widely used in our free market economy. As indicated above, there is substantial scholarly and judicial authority supporting their economic utility. There is relatively little authority to the contrary. Certainly, there has been no showing in this case, either generally or with respect to Sylvania's agreements, that vertical restrictions have or are likely to have a "pernicious effect on competition" or that they "lack . . . any redeeming virtue." Accordingly, we conclude that the *per se* rule stated in *Schwinn* must be overruled.

In sum, we conclude that the appropriate decision is to return to the rule of reason that governed vertical restrictions before *Schwinn*. When competitive effects are shown to result from particular vertical restrictions they can be adequately policed under the rule of reason, the standard traditionally applied for the majority of anticompetitive practices challenged under §1 of the Act.

Accordingly, the decision of the Court of Appeals is affirmed.

CASE REVIEW QUESTIONS

1. Why did Sylvania impose restrictions on its retailers? What were the effects of these restrictions upon intrabrand competition and upon interbrand competition?
2. How do the Sylvania restrictions differ from the restrictions in the *Topco* case? Are the competitive effects different? Why are those in *Topco* illegal per se, whereas those in *Sylvania* are subject to the rule of reason?
3. What factors were considered in order to determine whether the Sylvania restrictions were legal or illegal?

Exclusive Dealing Requirements Vertical nonprice restrictions can also take the form of **exclusive dealing** or **requirements contracts.** These are agreements that require a retailer to deal only with a certain manufacturer or require a customer to purchase its supply of a certain product from a particular manufacturer or supplier. Exclusive dealing or requirements contracts benefit the retailer by ensuring a stable source of supply of a product. The manufacturer or supplier benefits because it has a guaranteed market for its product, and it can be certain that the retailer will devote its efforts to selling the manufacturer's product rather than that of a competitor.

Exclusive dealing or requirements contracts are subject to §1 of the Sherman Act and §3 of the Clayton Act when they involve goods or commodities. When they involve a service, such as advertising or maintenance work, they are subject only to §1 of the Sherman Act. Section 3 of the Clayton Act states:

> it shall be unlawful for any person engaged in commerce, in the course of such commerce, to lease or make a sale . . of goods, wares . . . or other commodities . . . on the condition, agreement or understanding that the lessee or purchaser . . . shall not use or deal in the goods . . . or other commodities of a competitor or competitors or the lessee or seller, where the effect of such lease, sale . . . or condition, agreement or understanding . . . may be to substantially lessen competition or tend to create a monopoly in any line of commerce.

Section 1 of the Sherman Act states:

> Every contract, combination . . . or conspiracy in restraint of trade or commerce . . . is hereby declared to be illegal.

Section 1 of the Sherman Act deals with any exclusive dealing requirement in or affecting commerce when actual harm to competition can be shown. On the other hand, §3 of the Clayton Act applies only to sales, leases, or contracts of sale involving goods or commodities actually in interstate commerce. Section 3 also provides that such arrangements are illegal if their effect may be to lessen competition substantially, so the showing of probable harm to competition, as opposed to having to show actual harm, suffices to invalidate the arrangements.

In determining the legality of exclusive dealing or requirements contracts, a court must consider their effect upon competition. This requires a definition of both the relevant product market and the geographic market. The approach is similar to that involving a vertical merger under §7 of the Clayton Act (see page 1023 of the previous chapter) because the degree of control over the customer acquired by the seller through such contracts has an effect on competition similar to that resulting from a vertical merger.

Because judicial analysis of exclusive dealing or requirements contracts involves a consideration of the effect of an arrangement upon competition in the relevant market, it uses the rule of reason approach. Early court decisions based on §3 of the Clayton Act held that such arrangements were illegal when they involved a substantial volume of commerce, regardless of their actual or probable consequence for competition. However, in the *Tampa Electric* v. *Nashville Coal* case, the Supreme Court held that the effect of the arrangement upon competition in the relevant market must be considered along with the volume of commerce affected. Today, exclusive dealing arrangements are illegal only when they foreclose competition in a substantial share of the relevant market.

Tying Arrangements The supplier of a particular product or service may condition the sale of that product upon the purchaser taking a different product as well. For example, the supplier of a copying machine may require that its customers agree to use its brand of paper in the copier. Such agreements "tie" the sale of one product—the copier—to the sale of another product—the paper—and, hence, are known as **tying arrangements.**

Tying arrangements are practical only when one of the supplier's products is highly desirable or when the supplier has some market power with respect to that product. For instance, if the supplier is the sole source of the copier or if the copier is superior to other copiers, then a customer desiring to purchase the copier will probably be willing to agree to purchase the paper also, even though the paper may be overpriced or inferior to other brands. Tying arrangements often reflect an attempt by the supplier to extend its market power with respect to one product (the *tying product*—the copier) to another product in which it does not have market power (the *tied product*—the paper).

Since tying arrangements are an attempt to give an advantage to the tied product that is unrelated to the qualities of the product itself, a court determining the legality of a tying arrangement must consider the effects of the arrangement upon competition in the tied product market. Section 3 of the Clayton Act and §1 of the Sherman Act apply when the arrangement involves goods or commodities. Section 1 of the Sherman Act applies when the arrangement involves services. If the supplier is dominant in the tying product market or possesses a legal monopoly of the product because of a patent or copyright, the use of a tying arrangement could also be challenged under §2 of the Sherman Act as an attempt to extend monopoly power into the tied product market.

Section 3 of the Clayton Act requires that the tying arrangement involve the sale or lease of the products or commodities involved and that the transaction actually be involved in interstate commerce. Section 1 of the Sherman Act applies to any contract in restraint of trade in or affecting interstate commerce. Whereas §1 requires that actual harm to competition result from the restrictive arrangement, §3 requires only the showing of probable substantial lessening of competition. Despite these differences in the statutory provisions, the judicial approach to tying arrangements is similar under either.

Court decisions involving tying arrangements have found such arrangements to be illegal per se when the supplier has sufficient power in the tying product market to restrain competition in the tied product market appreciably and the amount of commerce involved is "not insubstantial." However, the application of the per se rule to tying arrangements is not like its application in other situations because it *does* require the court to consider the effects of the arrangement upon competition in the tied product market. Because of this requirement, the judicial approach to tying arrangments resembles a rule of reason approach, despite its official designation as a per se approach. Tying arrangements are not automatically illegal; they must substantially restrict competition in the tied product market in order to be held illegal.

A court deciding the legality of a tying arrangement must first determine that two separate and distinct products—the tying product and the tied product—are involved. If so, the court must then consider whether the supplier possesses market power in the tying product market. This market power may be due to the supplier's dominance of the market, to the possession of exclusive rights because of a patent or copyright, or to the uniqueness of the product offered.

If the supplier is found to have power in the tying product market, the court must then determine whether the linking of that market power to the tied product has the effect of substantially reducing or restricting competition in the tied product market. When the effect is to reduce competition substantially, the tying arrangement is illegal if it involves a "not insubstantial" amount of commerce.

Because patents and copyrights create legal monopolies, they confer substantial market power. Any attempt to tie the sale of a different product to the sale of a patented or copyrighted product in a tying arrangement will be illegal because the arrangement will substantially lessen competition in the market of the product tied to the patented or copyrighted product. As well, attempts to use unique products as tying products will be illegal when the uniqueness of the product is the result of advantages not available to competitors. The uniqueness of the product creates market power sufficiently substantial to foreclose competition in the market of the tied product, making the tying arrangement illegal.

A number of recent cases dealing with tying arrangements have involved franchise agreements. The company granting the franchise agrees to allow the franchisee to use a particular system of doing business, to market products under the franchisor's well-recognized trademark, and to benefit from franchisor's promotional efforts. As a condition of being granted the franchise, the franchisee may also be required to purchase supplies from the franchisor. Does such an arrangement constitute a tying agreement? Can the franchise license be separated from the other requirements so that both a tying product and a tied product are involved? These questions are considered in the following case.

PRINCIPE v. MCDONALD'S CORPORATION
631 F.2d 303 (4th Circuit 1980)

[Frank Principe and his family operated two McDonald's restaurants in Virginia. When they acquired each franchise, they entered a 20-year franchise license agreement with McDonald's, and they leased the restaurant buildings from McDonald's for 20 years. The franchise and lease agreements required that the Principes pay a $12,500 license fee, a $15,000 security deposit, and 11.5 percent of their gross revenues to McDonald's (8.5 percent for rent and 3 percent for royalties on the franchise license). The Principes later sought a third franchise but were denied it.

The Principes then sued McDonald's, alleging that the franchise and lease agreements were illegal under §1 of the Sherman Act because they tied 20-year store leases and $15,000 security deposit notes to the franchise rights to operate a McDonald's restaurant.

The trial court held that since McDonald's sells only one product—the franchise package, which includes the lease and license contract—there was no illegal tying arrangement. The Principes appealed.]

PHILLIPS, Senior Circuit Judge

McDonald's is not primarily a fast food retailer.

While it does operate over a thousand stores itself, the vast majority of the stores in its system are operated by franchisees. Nor does McDonald's sell equipment or supplies to its licensees. Instead its primary business is developing and collecting royalties from limited menu fast food restaurants operated by independent business people.

McDonald's develops new restaurants according to master plans that originate at the regional level and must be approved by upper management. Once the decision is made to expand into a particular geographic area, specialists begin to search for appropriate restaurant sites.

McDonald's uses demographic data generated by the most recent census and its own research in evaluating potential sites. Based on a comparison of data for various available sites, the regional staffs select what they believe is the best site in each geographic area.

After the specifics of each proposed new restaurant are approved, McDonald's decides whether the store will be company operated or franchised. If the decision is to franchise the store, McDonald's begins the process of locating a franchisee. This involves offering the store either to an existing franchisee or to an applicant on the waiting list. . . . McDonald's often does not know who will operate a franchised store until it is nearly completed because a new restaurant may be offered to and rejected by several different applicants.

Meanwhile, Franchise Realty [a McDonald's subsidiary] acquires the land, either by purchase or long term lease and constructs the store. . . .

As constructed, McDonald's restaurants are finished shells; they contain no kitchen or dining room equipment. Furnishing store equipment is the responsibility of the operator. . . .

Having acquired the land, begun construction of the store and selected an operator, McDonald's enters into two contracts with the franchisee. Under the first, the franchise agreement, McDonald's grants the franchisee the rights to use McDonald's food preparation and to sell food products under the McDonald's name. The franchisee pays a $12,500 franchisee fee and agrees to remit three percent of his gross sales as a royalty in return. Under the second contract, the lease, McDonald's grants the franchisee the right to use the

particular store premises to which his franchise pertains. In return, the franchisee pays a $15,000 refundable security deposit (as evidence of which he receives a twenty year non-negotiable[,] non-interest bearing note) and agrees to pay eight and one half percent of his gross sales as rent. These payments under the franchise and lease agreements are McDonald's only sources of income from its franchised restaurants. Both the franchise agreement and the lease generally have twenty year durations, both provide that termination of one terminates the other, and neither is available separately.

The Principes argue McDonald's is selling not one but three distinct products, the franchise, the lease and the security deposit note. The alleged antitrust violation stems from the fact that a prospective franchisee must buy all three in order to obtain the franchise.

As evidence that this is an illegal tying arrangement, the Principes point to the unfavorable terms on which franchisees are required to lease their stores. Not only are franchisees denied the opportunity to build equity and depreciate their property, but they must maintain the building, pay for improvements and taxes, and remit eight and one half percent of their gross sales as rents. The Principes contend that the fact the store rents are so high proves that McDonald's cannot sell the [leases] on their own merits.

Nor has McDonald's shown any need to forbid its licensees to own their own stores, the Principes say. Appellants contend that McDonald's is the only fast food franchisor that requires its licensees not only to pay royalties but to lease their stores from the franchisor. McDonald's could maintain its desired level of uniformity by requiring franchisees to locate and construct stores according to company specifications. The Principes argue McDonald's has not shown that the success of its business or the integrity of its trademark depends on company ownership of all store premises.

A separate tied product is the note that evidences the lessee's security deposit, according to the appellants. The Principes argue the security deposit really is a mandatory contribution to McDonald's working capital, not security against damage to the store or breach of the lease contract. By tying the purchase of these $15,000 twenty year non-negotiable non-interest bearing notes to that of the franchise, McDonald's allegedly has generated a capital fund that totalled over $45 million in 1978. It is argued that no one would purchase such notes on their own merits. The Principes assert that only by requiring franchisees to purchase the notes as a condition of obtaining a franchise has McDonald's been able to sell them at all.

McDonald's responds that it is not in the business of licensing use of its name, improving real estate for lease or selling long term notes. Its only business is developing a system of hamburger restaurants and collecting royalties from their sales. The allegedly tied products are but parts of the overall bundle of franchise benefits and obligations. According to McDonald's the appellants are asking the court to invalidate the way McDonald's does business and to require it to adopt the licensing procedures of its less successful competitors. Federal antitrust laws do not compel such a result, McDonald's contends.

The Principes urge this court . . . to invalidate the McDonald's franchise lease note aggregation. They urge that McDonald's can protect the integrity of its trademarks by specifying how its franchisees shall operate, where they may locate their restaurants and what type of buildings they may erect. Customers do not and have no reason to connect the building's owner with the McDonald's operation conducted therein. Since company ownership of store premises is not an essential element of the trademark's goodwill, the Principes argue, the franchise, lease and note are separable products tied together in violation of the antitrust laws.

Far from merely licensing franchisees to sell products under its trade name, a modern franchisor such as McDonald's offers its franchisees a complete method of doing business. It takes people from all walks of life, sends them to its management school, and teaches them a variety of skills ranging from hamburger grilling to financial planning. It installs them in stores whose market has been researched and whose location has been selected by experts to maximize sales potential. Its regime pervades all facets of the business . . . nothing is left to chance. This pervasive franchisor supervision and control benefits the franchisee in turn. His business is identified with a network of stores whose very uniformity and predictability attracts cus-

tomers. In short, the modern franchisee pays not only for the right to use a trademark but for the right to become a part of a system whose business methods virtually guarantee his success. It is often unrealistic to view a franchise agreement as little more than a trademark license.

Given the realities of modern franchising, we think the proper inquiry is not whether the allegedly tied products are associated in the public mind with the franchisor's trademark, but whether they are integral components of the business method being franchised. Where the challenged aggregation is an essential ingredient of the franchised system's formula for success, there is but a single product and no tie in exists as a matter of law.

Applying this standard to the present case, we hold the lease is not separable from the McDonald's franchise to which it pertains. It is part of what makes a McDonald's franchise uniquely attractive to franchisees.

First, . . . McDonald's is able to obtain better sites than franchisees could select. Individual franchisees benefit from the McDonald's approach because their stores are located in areas McDonald's has determined will produce substantial fast food business. . . . Because McDonald's purposefully locates new stores where they will not undercut existing franchisees' business, McDonald's franchisees do not have to compete with each other, a substantial advantage in the highly competitive fast food industry.

Second, . . . McDonald's franchise arrangements are not static: franchisees retire or die; occasionally they do not live up to their franchise obligations and must be replaced; even if no such contingency intervenes, the agreements normally expire by their own terms after twenty years. If franchisees owned their own stores, any of these events could disrupt McDonald's business and have a negative effect on the system's goodwill. By owning its own stores, McDonald's assures its continued presence on the site, maintains the store's patronage even during management changes and avoids the negative publicity of having former McDonald's stores used for other purposes. By preserving the goodwill of the system in established markets, company store ownership produces attendant benefits for franchisees.

Third, because McDonald's acquires the sites and builds the stores itself, it can select franchisees based on their management potential rather than their real estate expertise or wealth. McDonald's policy of owning its own stores reduces a franchisee's initial investment, thereby broadening the applicant base and opening the door to persons who otherwise could not afford a McDonald's franchise.

Finally, because both McDonald's and the franchisee have a substantial financial stake in the success of the restaurant, their relationship becomes a sort of partnership that might be impossible under other circumstances. . . . Because its investment is on the line, the Company cannot allow its franchisees to lose money. This being so, McDonald's works with its franchisees to build their business, occasionally financing improvements at favorable rates or even accepting reduced royalty payments in order to provide franchisees more working capital.

All of these factors contribute significantly to the overall success of the McDonald's system. The formula that produced systemwide success, the formula that promises to make each new McDonald's store successful, that formula is what McDonald's sells its franchisees. To characterize the franchise as an unnecessary aggregation of separate products tied to the McDonald's name is to miss the point entirely. Among would[-]be franchisees, the McDonald's name has come to stand for the formula, including all that it entails. We decline to find that it is an illegal tie in.

Affirmed.

CASE REVIEW QUESTIONS

1. What were McDonald's reasons for imposing the challenged obligations upon franchisees?
2. What product(s) does McDonald's sell? How are the franchisee obligations related to that sale?
3. Why did the court refuse to find that the franchise arrangements constituted an illegal tie in?
4. Why was §1 of the Sherman Act, rather than §3 of the Clayton Act, used to challenge the franchise arrangements?

PRICE DISCRIMINATION

Price discrimination is simply the charging of different prices to different customers for the same product. When price discrimination occurs in interstate commerce and when its effects are "substantially to lessen competition or tend to create a monopoly . . . or to injure, destroy, or prevent competition," it is prohibited by the Robinson-Patman Act.

The Robinson-Patman Act is actually §2 of the Clayton Act. It was passed in 1936 to strengthen the Clayton Act prohibitions against price discrimination. Most commentators, however, refer to the prohibitions against price discrimination as the Robinson-Patman Act rather than as §2 of the Clayton Act.

The Robinson-Patman Act, passed during the Great Depression of the 1930s, reflects a concern that large retail chains could use the leverage of their purchasing power to obtain price concessions from their suppliers. With these price concessions, the chains would have a significant competitive advantage over smaller, independent retailers and could eventually drive them out of business. Congress therefore sought to prohibit sellers from discriminating in price among customers when the effect of such discrimination would be detrimental to competition. The Robinson-Patman Act's primary purpose then, is the protection of competitors rather than the protection of competition.

Price Discrimination under the Robinson-Patman Act
Section 2(a) of the Robinson-Patman Act prohibits

> discrimination in price between purchasers of commodities of like grade and quality, where either or any purchasers involved in such discrimination are in commerce . . . where the effect of such discrimination may be to substantially lessen competition or tend to create a monopoly in any line of commerce, or to injure, destroy or prevent competition with any person who either grants or knowingly receives the benefit of such discrimination, or with the customers of either of them. . . .

From the wording of §2(a), we can see that the protection of the act extends not only to firms in competition with the firm granting the discriminatory price (referred to as the *primary competitive effects*), but also to firms in competition with customers who receive the discriminatory price (referred to as the *secondary competitive effects*), and even to firms in competition with customers of the firms that receive the discriminatory price (referred to as the *tertiary competitive effects*). When price discrimination has the effect of substantially lessening any one of these forms of competition, it could be illegal.

Defenses to Price Discrimination Price discrimination may not be illegal if it falls under one of the defenses provided in §2(a) and (b) of the Robinson-Patman Act. When price differences apply to perishable or obsolete items or when they reflect actual differences in cost due to different methods of manufacture or delivery or because of the volume purchased, they are legal under §2(a). When a discriminatory price is offered by a seller in a good-faith attempt to meet the price of a competitor, it is legal under §2(b).

Other Provisions of the Robinson-Patman Act
Sections 2(c), (d) and (e) of the Robinson-Patman Act prohibit other potential abuses of large retail chains. Section 2(c) prohibits the granting of any allowance or discount as a commission or other compensation for promotional or brokerage services in connection with the sale of a product unless the services are actually performed by the firm receiving the allowance or discount. For example, a small company that manufactures toys may sell its products through a broker. The broker arranges the sale of the products to retailers and promotes and distributes the product for the manufacturer. In return for these services, the manufacturer pays the broker a commission on the sales. If the manufacturer decides to bypass the broker ("eliminate the middleman") and sell directly to a large retail chain, it saves the cost of the broker's commission. In this

situation, the manufacturer may grant the retail chain a discount reflecting its savings on the broker's commission only if the retail chain performs the distribution and promotion services normally performed by the broker. To grant the retailer a discount when it does not actually perform those services violates §2(c).

Sections 2(d) and (e) prohibit paying promotional fees or allowances or furnishing promotional facilities or services to only some customers. Such fees, allowances, facilities, or services must be provided to all customers on proportionately equal terms.

For example, if a food processing company pays large supermarket chains for advertising the food processor's products but does not pay for advertising by small, independent grocers, the food processor violates §2(d). Similarly, a company making sewing patterns that provides free display racks and cabinets to large department stores but requires small fabric stores to purchase the equipment violates §2(e).

Violations of §§2(c), (d), and (e) are per se offenses, which make the defenses in §2(a) and (b) unavailable. In other words, when fees, allowances facilities, or services furnished to some customers are not available to all customers on a proportionate basis or when allowances are granted for services not actually performed, the offense is a per se violation of the act and no defenses are available. In contrast to the per se approach of §§2(c), (d), and (e), §2(a) can only be violated when the effect of the price discrimination is to lessen competition substantially, which is a rule of reason approach.

Section 2(f) of the Act makes it a violation for a firm to "knowingly induce or receive" a discriminatory price that is prohibited by §2. Unlike the other provisions of the act, which are directed against the firm engaging in price discrimination, §2(f) is aimed at the customer who receives the discriminatory price. The relationship between §2(f) and §§2(a) and (b) and the question of whether a violation of §2(a) by the seller granting the price is necessary for a violation of §2(f) by the customer receiving the price to occur are dealt with in the following Supreme Court case.

GREAT ATLANTIC & PACIFIC TEA COMPANY, INC. v. FEDERAL TRADE COMMISSION
440 U.S. 69 (U.S. Supreme Ct. 1979)

[Great Atlantic & Pacific Tea Company, Inc. (A&P) asked Borden Company (Borden) to submit an offer for the right to supply milk and dairy products to the 200 A&P stores in the Chicago area. The products would be sold by A&P under its own label, called a "private label." After prolonged negotiations, Borden made an offer that would save A&P $410,000 a year for dairy products. A&P responded by telling Borden that it wasn't "even in the ballpark" compared to the bid of one of its competitors, Bowman Dairy.

Borden had just opened a new processing plant in the area, and the loss of the A&P account would have resulted in a drastic underutilization of the facility. Borden therefore submitted a new bid that doubled the savings to A&P, to $820,000 a year. In making the new bid, Borden emphasized that it needed to keep A&P's business and that it was trying to meet the competing bid. A&P accepted the Borden bid because it was significantly better than the Bowman bid.

The Federal Trade Commission filed a complaint against A&P, charging that it violated §2(f) of the Robinson-Patman Act by knowingly inducing or receiving price discrimination from Borden. In administrative proceedings, the FTC held that Borden had discriminated in price and that A&P knew or should have known that it had received unlawful price discrimination. The FTC also held that A&P could not claim the "meeting competition" defense under §2(b) or that the price discrimination was cost-justified. The Court of Appeals affirmed the FTC decision. A&P then appealed to the Supreme Court.]

STEWART, Justice

The Robinson-Patman Act was passed in response to the problem perceived in the increased market power and coercive practices of chain stores and other big buyers that threatened the existence of small independent retailers. Notwithstanding this concern with buyers, however, the emphasis of the Act is in §2(a), which prohibits price discrimination by sellers. Section 2(f) of the Act, making buyers liable for inducing or receiving price discriminations by sellers, was the product of a belated floor amendment near the conclusion of the Senate debates.

As finally enacted, §2(f) provides:

That it shall be unlawful for any person engaged in commerce, knowingly to induce or receive a discrimination in price *which is prohibited by this section.* [Emphasis added.]

Liability under §2(f) thus is limited to situations where the price discrimination is one "which is prohibited by this section." While the phrase "this section" refers to the entire §2 of the Act, only subsections (a) and (b) dealing with seller liability involve discriminations in price. Under the plain meaning of §2(f), therefore, a buyer cannot be liable if a prima facie case could not be established against a seller or if the seller has an affirmative defense. In either situation, there is no price discrimination "prohibited by this section." The legisla-

tive history of §2(f) fully confirms the conclusion that buyer liability under §2(f) is dependent on seller liability under §2(a).

[A&P] argues that it cannot be liable under §2(f) if Borden had a valid meeting competition defense. The [FTC], on the other hand, argues that the petitioner may be liable even assuming that Borden had such a defense. The meeting competition defense, the respondent contends, must in these circumstances be judged from the point of view of the buyer. Since A&P knew for a fact that the final Borden bid beat the Bowman bid, it was not entitled to assert the meeting competition defense even though Borden may have honestly believed that it was simply meeting competition. Recognition of a meeting competition defense for the buyer in this situation, the respondent argues, would be contrary to the basic purpose of the Robinson-Patman Act to curtail abuses by large buyers.

The short answer to these contentions of the respondent is that Congress did not provide in §2(f) that a buyer can be liable even if the seller had a valid defense. The clear language of §2(f) states that a buyer can be liable only if he receives a price discrimination "prohibited by this section." If a seller has a valid meeting competition defense, there is simply no prohibited price discrimination.

Accordingly, we hold that a buyer who has done no more than accept the lower of two prices competitively offered does not violate §2(f) provided the seller has a meeting competition defense.

Because both the Commission and the Court of Appeals proceeded on the assumption that a buyer who accepts the lower of two competitive bids can be liable under §2(f) even if the seller has a meeting competition defense, that was not a specific finding that Borden did in fact have such a defense. But it quite clearly did.

The test for determining when a seller has a valid meeting competition defense is whether a seller can show the existence of facts which would lead a reasonable and prudent person to believe that the granting of a lower price would in fact meet the equally low price of a competitor. A good faith belief, rather than absolute certainty, that a price concession is being offered to meet an equally low price offered by a competitor is sufficient to satisfy the Robinson-Patman's §2(b) defense. Since good faith, rather than absolute certainty, is the touchstone of the meeting competition defense, a seller can assert the defense even if it has unknowingly made a bid that in fact not only met but beat his competition.

Under the circumstances of this case, Borden did act reasonably and in good faith when it made its second bid.

Borden was informed that it was in danger of losing its A&P business in the Chicago area unless it came up with a better offer. Borden could justifiably conclude that A&P's statements were reliable and that it was necessary to make another bid offering substantial concessions to avoid losing its account with the petitioner.

Faced with a substantial loss of business and unable to find out the precise details of the competing bid, Borden made another offer stating that it was doing so in order to meet competition. Under these circumstances, the conclusion is virtually inescapable that in making that offer Borden acted in a reasonable and good-faith effort to meet its competition, and therefore was entitled to a meeting competition defense.

Since Borden had a meeting competition defense and thus could not be liable under §2(b), the petitioner who did no more than accept that offer cannot be liable under §2(f).

Accordingly, the judgment is reversed.

CASE REVIEW QUESTIONS

1. What is necessary for the court to find a violation of §2(f)? What is necessary for a court to find a violation of §2(a)?
2. Why was Borden's bid to A&P held not to violate §2(a)?
3. How does the purpose of the Robinson-Patman Act compare with that of the Sherman Act?

SECTION 5 OF THE FEDERAL TRADE COMMISSION ACT

In addition to the primary antitrust provisions of the Sherman Act and the Clayton Act, §5 of the Federal Trade Commission Act has also been used to attack anticompetitive business practices. Section 5 provides that "unfair methods of competition in or affecting commerce and unfair or deceptive acts or practices in or affecting commerce, are hereby declared unlawful." The Federal Trade Commission Act does not define the terms "unfair methods of competition" or "unfair or deceptive acts or practices." Congress wanted to avoid listing specific illegal practices because such a list would have to be updated continually to include new practices as they appeared. Congress therefore empowered the Federal Trade Commission (FTC) to determine what practices violated §5. The FTC, through its expertise, can adapt §5 to changing business practices.

Given the general wording of §5, its potential reach is very broad. The FTC has generally used §5 to attack deceptive advertising or high-pressure sales practices. It has also held that conduct violating the other antitrust laws violates

§5; for example, a violation of §1 of the Sherman Act or §3 of the Clayton Act also violates §5. Furthermore, in *Federal Trade Commission* v. *Cement Institute,* the Supreme Court held that §5 can be applied to conduct that the FTC has determined to be injurious to competition even though the conduct does not violate the other antitrust laws.

EXEMPTIONS FROM ANTITRUST

The coverage of the federal antitrust laws extends to all activities in or affecting interstate commerce. Several exceptions to that coverage have been judicially or legislatively created, however.

The Webb-Pomerene Act allows American firms to join together for the purpose of export trade. The results of such joint export activity must not, however, restrict trade within the United States or injure U.S. firms that do not join the concerted export activity. Similarly, the Capper-Volstead Act exempts agricultural marketing cooperatives from the antitrust laws.

Bona fide labor activities are also exempted from antitrust sanctions. Section 6 of the Clayton Act, which states that labor is not an article of commerce, was an early legislative attempt to exempt labor activities from the antitrust laws. It was not until the Supreme Court decision in *U.S.* v. *Hutcheson* in 1941, however, that conventional labor activity by a labor organization acting alone was held to be immune from antitrust law.

In *Meat Cutters Local 189* v. *Jewell Tea,* the Supreme Court held that a union may make agreements with a group of employers as long as the subject matter of the agreement is directly related to terms or conditions of employment and the agreement occurs within the context of a bona fide collective bargaining relationship. On the other hand, if unions join employers' groups in agreements about nonlabor matters, such as prices, or if unions make an agreement with one set of employers to demand concessions from a different set of employers, such agreements are not protected by the labor exemption.

Perhaps the broadest area of exemption falls under the **state action doctrine,** which deals with the anticompetitive effects of government regulations. Regulatory schemes may require some businesses to engage in conduct that is anticompetitive. For example, agricultural marketing regulations may limit the size of farmer's crops and may set the prices at which the farmers must sell those crops. Such an arrangement created by the farmers acting on their own would clearly be in violation of §1 of the Sherman Act. However, in *Parker* v. *Brown,* the Supreme Court held that such conduct is exempt from the antitrust laws when it is pursuant to a valid governmental regulatory scheme.

Subsequent court decisions have narrowed and more clearly defined the state action doctrine. The courts now hold that the government (whether state, federal, or local) must play an active role in the regulatory scheme, and the anticompetitive conduct *must* be required by the regulatory scheme in order for it to be exempt from the antitrust laws. The following case is a recent Supreme Court expression of the requirements for exemption under the state action doctrine.

CALIFORNIA RETAIL LIQUOR DEALERS ASSOCIATION v. MIDCAL ALUMINUM, INC.
445 U.S. 97 (U.S. Supreme Ct. 1980)

[California legislation required all wine producers or distributors to file "fair trade" contracts, which were price schedules, with the state. Once these fair trade contracts had been filed, no California wine merchant or wholesaler could sell wine to a retailer at a price other than the price set in the fair trade contract. The fair trade contract therefore allowed a wine producer or distributor to fix the price at which its wine would be sold, and the state of California would legally enforce the price-fixing contract under its regulations.

Prior to 1975, "fair trade" laws such as California's existed in a number of states and covered manufactured products as well as wines and liquor. They allowed the manufacturer or distributor of a product to set the price at which the product would be resold by retailers. The laws provided that when one retailer had agreed to resell at the fair trade price, then all retailers in the state could be required to resell at that price, even if they had not agreed to do so with the distributor. As with the California wine price regulations, the effect of fair trade laws was to legalize vertical price-fixing by the producer or distributor.

State fair trade laws were authorized by provisions in §1 of the Sherman Act that exempted such price-fixing from the antitrust laws. In 1975, however, those provisions in the Sherman Act were repealed, and fair trade laws were no longer exempt from the antitrust laws.

Midcal Aluminum, Inc. (Midcal), a California wine distributor, was charged by the state with selling wine at prices lower than those set in the price schedules filed by the wine producers. Midcal brought a legal action seeking an injunction to prohibit the state from enforcing the wine-pricing system, alleging that the scheme violated the Sherman Act. California was joined in defending the pricing system by the California Retail Liquor Dealers Association (CRLDA). They argued that the scheme was part of the state's regulation of alcoholic beverages and was protected under the state action doctrine. The trial held that the pricing system was illegal, and the California Court of Appeals affirmed the trial court decision. The California Su-

preme Court refused to hear an appeal, and CRLDA then appealed to the U.S. Supreme Court.]

POWELL, Justice

The Court of Appeals ruled that the wine pricing scheme restrained trade in violation of the Sherman Act. The court relied entirely on the reasoning in *Rice* v. *Alcoholic Beverage Control Appeals Bd.*, where the California Supreme Court struck down parallel restrictions on the sale of distilled liquors. In that case, the court held that because the State played only a passive part in liquor pricing, there was no *Parker* v. *Brown* [state action] immunity for the program.

The court determined that the national policy in favor of competition should prevail over the state interests in liquor price maintenance—the promotion of temperance and the preservation of small retail establishments. The court emphasized that the California system not only permitted vertical control of prices by producers, but also frequently resulted in horizontal price fixing. Under the program, many comparable brands of liquor were marketed at identical prices. Referring to congressional and state legislative studies, the court observed that resale price maintenance has little positive impact on either temperance or small retail stores.

In the instant case, the State Court of Appeals found the analysis in *Rice* squarely controlling. The court ordered the Department of Alcoholic Beverage Control not to enforce the resale price maintenance and price posting statutes for the wine trade. We . . . now affirm the decision of the state court.

The threshold question is whether California's plan for wine pricing violated the Sherman Act. This Court has ruled consistently that resale price maintenance illegally restrains trade.

California's system for wine pricing plainly constitutes resale price maintenance in violation of the Sherman Act.

Thus, we must consider whether the State's involvement in the price-setting program is sufficient to establish antitrust immunity under *Parker* v. *Brown.* That immunity for state regulatory programs is grounded in our federal structure.

> In a dual system of government in which, under the Constitution, the states are sovereign, save only as Congress may constitutionally subtract from their authority, an unexpressed purpose to nullify a state's control over its officers and agents is not lightly to be attributed to Congress.

In *Parker* v. *Brown,* this Court found in the Sherman Act no purpose to nullify state powers. Because the Act is directed against "individual and not state action," the Court concluded that state regulatory programs could not violate it.

Under the program challenged in *Parker,* the state Agricultural Prorate Advisory Commission authorized the organization of local cooperatives to develop marketing policies for the raisin crop. The Court emphasized that the Advisory Commission, which was specially appointed by the governor, had to approve cooperative policies following public hearings: "It is the state which has created the machinery for establishing the prorate program. . . . [I]t is the state, acting through the Commission, which adopts the program and enforces it. . . ." In view of this extensive official oversight, the Court wrote, the Sherman Act did not apply. Without such oversight, the result could have been different. The Court expressly noted, "a state does not give immunity to those who violate the Sherman Act by authorizing them to violate it, or by declaring that their action is lawful. . . ."

Only last term, this Court found antitrust immunity for a California program requiring state approval of the location of new automobile dealerships. That program provided that the State would hold a hearing if an automobile franchisee protested the establishment or relocation of a competing dealership. In view of the State's active role, the Court held, the program was not subject to the Sherman Act. The "clearly articulated and affirmatively expressed" goal of the state policy was to "displace unfettered business freedom in the matter of the establishment and relocation of automobile dealerships."

These decisions establish two standards for antitrust immunity under *Parker* v. *Brown.* First, the challenged restraint must be "one clearly articulated and affirmatively expressed as state policy"; second, the

policy must be "actively supervised" by the State itself. The California system for wine pricing satisfies the first standard. The legislative policy is forthrightly stated and clear in its purpose to permit resale price maintenance. The program, however, does not meet the second requirement for *Parker* immunity. The State simply authorized price-setting and enforces the prices established by private parties. The State neither establishes prices nor reviews the reasonableness of the price schedules; nor does it regulate the terms of fair trade contracts. The State does not monitor market conditions or engage in any "pointed reexamination" of the program. The national policy in favor of competition cannot be thwarted by casting such a gauzy cloak of state involvement over what is essentially a private price fixing arrangement. As *Parker* teaches, "a state does not give immunity to those who violate the Sherman Act by authorizing them to violate it, or by declaring that their action is lawful. . . ."

The state interests protected by California's resale price maintenance system were identified by the state courts in this case, and in *Rice* v. *Alcoholic Beverage Control Bd.*

In *Rice,* the State Supreme Court found two purposes behind liquor resale price maintenance: "to promote temperance and orderly market conditions." The court found little correlation between resale price maintenance and temperance. It cited a state study showing a 42% increase in per capita liquor consumption in California from 1950 to 1972, while resale price maintenance was in effect. Such studies, the court wrote, "at the very least raise a doubt regarding the justification for such laws on the ground that they promote temperance."

The *Rice* opinion identified the primary state interest in orderly market conditions as "protect[ing] small licensees from predatory pricing policies of large retailers." In gauging this interest, the court adopted the views of the Appeals Board of the Alcoholic Beverages Control Department, which first ruled on the claim in *Rice.* The state agency "rejected the argument that fair trade laws were necessary to the economic survival of small retailers. . . ." The agency relied on a congressional study of the impact on small retailers of fair trade laws. The study revealed that

> states with fair trade laws had a 55 percent higher rate of firm failures than free trade states, and the rate of

growth of small retail stores in free trade states between 1956 and 1972 was 32 percent higher than in states with fair trade laws.

[T]he State Supreme Court found no persuasive justification to continue "fair trade laws which eliminate price competition among retailers." The Court of Appeals came to the same conclusion with respect to the wholesale wine trade.

We have no basis for disagreeing with the view of the California courts that the asserted state interests are less substantial than the national policy in favor of competition. That evaluation of the resale price maintenance system for wine is reasonable, and is supported by the evidence cited by the State Supreme Court in *Rice*. Nothing in the record in this case suggests that the wine pricing system helps sustain small retail establishments. Neither the petitioner nor the State Attorney General . . . has demonstrated that the program inhibits the consumption of alcohol by Californians. We need not consider whether the legitimate state interests in temperance and the protection of small retailers ever could prevail against the undoubted federal interest in a competitive economy. The unsubstantiated state concerns put forward in this case simply are not of the same stature as the goals of the Sherman Act.

The judgment of the California Court of Appeals, Third Appellate District, is affirmed.

CASE REVIEW QUESTIONS

1. What are the required elements for an activity to be exempt under the state action doctrine?
2. What was the effect of the California wine-pricing program on competition? What were the justifications for the program?
3. Why was the wine-pricing program held not to be exempt under the state action doctrine?

Patents and Antitrust

Patents and copyrights are legally granted monopolies, for a limited period, for the production, reproduction, distribution, or use of the patented or copyrighted item. Patents are granted to the developers of products or production processes. They give the developers protection from competition for a limited time so that they can reap the benefits of their efforts. By so doing, patents encourage innovation. In the absence of patent protection, an invention could be copied by competitors who would thereby obtain a cost advantage over the developer since they were spared the costs of developing the invention.

Copyrights allow the creator of an artistic or intellectual work, such as a play or novel, to control its performance or reproduction. They prevent unauthorized use or sale of the work in order to allow its creator to enjoy the rewards of his or her creative efforts.

By encouraging invention and artistic creation, patents and copyrights promote the public interest. For that reason, the limited monopoly status that they grant is acceptable even though it may seem inconsistent with the antitrust policy of promoting competition.

Firms that hold patents or copyrights may license others to produce, use, or distribute the protected item. The extent to which these licenses may restrict competition or protect the position of the firm owning the patent or copyright has been the subject of a number of court decisions.

In the 1926 *General Electric* decision (*U.S.* v. *General Electric*), the Supreme Court upheld the right of a patent owner to impose a minimum resale price requirement upon another firm manufacturing the patented product under a license granted by that owner. Subsequent decisions have narrowed, but not overruled, the *General Electric* decision. Today, price-restrictive licenses may be granted only to a single firm by the patent owner. Imposing restrictions through licenses upon two or more firms creates a concerted price-fixing arrangement and is illegal.

Patent licenses may also be used to impose reasonable territorial restrictions upon the licensee's use or distribution of the protected product. However, when the primary purpose of these restrictions is to create a horizontal division of markets among competitors, they are illegal. Firms owning patent rights may not combine their rights or patents with those of competing firms in order to create a "patent pool" cartel where the competitors share the patents to the exclusion of all other firms. In addition, tying arrangements that use a patented or copyrighted item as the tying product are illegal.

REVIEW QUESTIONS

1. Why is the per se rule applied to horizontal concerted activity? What is the practical effect of the application of the per se rule?
2. Does the rule of reason or the per se rule apply to vertical price restrictions? Which rule applies to vertical territorial restrictions? Should both kinds of vertical restrictions be subject to the same rules or to different rules? Explain.
3. Are tying arrangements subject to the per se rule or the rule of reason? When are tying arrangements subject to §1 of the Sherman Act? When are they subject to §3 of the Clayton Act? Does the approach used by the courts under §3 differ from that used under §1? Explain.
4. When is price discrimination illegal under the Robinson-Patman Act? What defenses are available to firms alleged to have violated the Act?
5. What is the state action doctrine? When are labor activities exempt from the antitrust laws?

CASE PROBLEMS

1. "Holiday" Motels International (HMI) is a firm that grants franchises to persons wishing to operate "Holiday" Motels. At present, there are four "Holiday" Motels operating in the Fort Wayne area, but HMI feels that the area could probably support another franchise. After discussing the new franchise with the four existing franchisees, HMI agreed to award it only if none of the existing franchisees objected. They also agreed to give the existing franchisees priority if any of them wished to operate the new franchise. Smith, who is not presently a franchisee, wishes to operate the new franchise. However, one of the existing franchisees has objected, and no franchise has been awarded. If Smith sues under §1 of the Sherman Act, is his suit challenging the refusal to award the franchise likely to be successful? Explain.
2. The *Local Standard* is a daily newspaper published in Syracuse, New York, by Local Publishing Company. The paper is sold by numerous retail outlets and is delivered to homes by paper carriers. The carriers, usually boys and girls, are billed weekly by

Local for the papers they deliver. The prices Local charges the carriers are wholesale prices. The carriers charge their customers the "suggested retail price," which is printed on the front page of each paper.

   a. Is the pricing arrangement between Local and the carriers in violation of §1 of the Sherman Act? Why or why not?

   b. Local assigns each carrier a delivery route—a geographic area in which the carrier is the exclusive home-delivery outlet for the *Local Standard.* Is this territorial arrangement legal? Explain your answer.

   c. Local prohibits the carriers from charging a price greater than the suggested retail price, although carriers are free to charge less than the suggested retail price. Carriers who violate this policy have their routes taken away. Is this policy legal under §1? Explain your answer.

3. Local Publishing Company publishes both the *Local Standard,* a morning daily paper, and the *Post Herald,* an afternoon daily. Local requires advertisers wishing to place ads in either paper to purchase advertising space in both. Shaw's Shape-Up, a physical fitness club, wants to advertise in the *Local Standard* because it reaches a bigger audience than the *Post Herald.* Shaw's feels that ads in the afternoon daily are not cost effective. Local will only accept Shaw's ad if it appears in both papers. Shaw's files suit challenging Local's advertising policy.

   a. Which provision of the antitrust laws is applicable to the advertising policy? Explain.

   b. What arguments will Local use to support the policy? What arguments will Shaw's use to attack it?

   c. Who will win the case? Explain.

4. Balkan Burgers, Inc., licenses franchisees to operate Balkan Burger fast-food restaurants. In addition to agreeing to rent the restaurant building from Balkan Burger, Inc., franchisees are required to purchase all kitchen equipment, paper products, packaging materials, and food products from Balkan Burgers. Balkan Burgers maintains that this requirement is necessary to ensure the quality of the products to preserve Balkan Burgers' reputation and corporate image. Balkan Burgers also prohibits the franchisee from operating any fast-food restaurant other than those licensed by Balkan Burgers. Several franchisees have complained that the prices charged by Balkan Burger for kitchen equipment and food products are higher than those charged by other suppliers and that Balkan's products are of low quality. These franchisees would also like to operate other franchised fast-food restaurants. If they bring a legal action challenging Balkan Burger's policies, who will win the case? Explain.

5. Posner Paving is a small paving contractor that bids on municipal paving jobs in and around Chicago. Its operations are entirely within the state of Illinois. Posner is supplied with asphalt and other paving materials by Bork Products. Bork is a large building materials supply firm that operates throughout the Midwest. Posner has discovered that Bork has been supplying asphalt to the large contractors who work on the interstate highway system in Indiana and Illinois at $250 per truckload while it charges Posner $270 per truckload. Bork sells only in minimum units of at least one truckload and the costs of delivery per truckload are constant. If Posner brings a legal action challenging Bork's pricing policy under the Robinson-Patman Act, is the challenge likely to be successful? Explain.

6. The Sullivans desired to purchase a house in Arlington, Virginia. They contacted several lawyers about performing a title search. Each lawyer they contacted informed them that the fee for the search would be the fee set by the minimum-fee schedule of the Virginia State Bar Association. The minimum-fee schedule suggests the minimum fee that Virginia lawyers should charge for various kinds of legal services. Lawyers who wish to practice law in Virginia are required by law to join the Virginia State Bar Association and to abide by the association's Ethical Rules. The Ethical Rules include a prohibition on "habitually charging fees less than those in the minimum-fee schedule." No state laws require adherence to the fee schedule, and the state does not review or approve the fee schedule. The Sullivans have brought a legal action suit against the Virginia State Bar Association, alleging that the minimum fee schedule is illegal under §1 of the Sherman Act. What arguments can each party make to support its case? Who will win? Explain.

49

CONSUMER PROTECTION

Government regulates business activity in a number of areas. One prominent area of regulation is concerned with the protection of consumers and is known as consumer law. Statutes, regulations issued by administrative agencies, and court decisions make up the body of consumer law. Government regulation takes place at all levels of government: federal, state, and local. This chapter will concentrate on consumer laws at the federal level with occasional references to laws at the state level.

Although government regulation of business for the benefit of the consumer takes many forms and covers a variety of areas, this chapter will concentrate on regulations in the areas of marketing (advertising, labeling, and sales practices), safety, and credit. In it, we will follow consumer needs from the advertising phase of a transaction to the collection of any debt created. This chapter will examine a variety of the regulatory techniques used in each of these areas. Figure 49-1 lists a number of these techniques and gives an example for each. You should look for other examples. Also, you should be aware that, in addition to governmental regulation of business, business regulates itself through such groups as the Better Business Bureau and through the adoption of industry standards and procedures, such as those that provide for the arbitration of automobile disputes.

MARKETING

In 1962, President Kennedy described four basic consumer rights: (1) the right to choose, (2) the right to be informed, (3) the right to safety, and (4) the

Techniques for Consumer Protection

Techniques	Examples
1. Administrative agencies	Federal Trade Commission
2. Cease and Desist Orders and Consent Decrees	Federal Trade Commission orders ending unfair, deceptive, or false practices
3. Injunctions	Court order halting the publication of advertisements
4. Disclosure	Unit pricing in grocery stores
5. Corrective Advertisments	Federal Trade Commission remedy for unfair, deceptive, or false advertisements
6. Minimum Damages	Minimum penalties for violation of the Odometer Disclosure Act
7. Labels	Fabric content labels
8. Warnings	Warnings on cigarette packages
9. Quality Control	Silver and gold labeling
10. Notices	Notice of a buyers' rights in door-to-door sales
11. Cancellation of Contracts	Three-day cancellation period for health club contracts (N.Y. law)
12. Criminal Penalties	The crime of false advertising
13. Research	New drug research
14. Educational Requirements	Training of x-ray technicians
15. Prohibitions	Prohibition of interstate transportation of certain refrigerators
16. Bans	Ban of lead-containing paint
17. Inspections	Inspection of egg products
18. Seizure and Destruction	Treatment of misbranded or adulterated foods or drugs
19. Standards	Safety standards for walk-behind power lawn mowers
20. Limitation of Liability	$50 limit for unauthorized credit card use
21. Limiting Retaliation against Consumers	Creditors cannot discriminate against loan applicants who have exercised their rights under the Consumer Credit Protection Act
22. Civil Penalties	Awards to consumers for violations of the Fair Debt Collection Practices Act

FIGURE 49-1

Techniques for Consumer Protection

right to be heard. Marketing practices, especially advertising and labeling, are closely related to the first two of these rights. Information is necessary for consumers to be able to make effective choices in their selections of goods or services. A variety of techniques are used to control the information that is made available to consumers. One technique is to establish an administrative agency that has the authority to control the flow of this information. The principal governmental agency controlling the flow of information to consumers is the Federal Trade Commission.

The Federal Trade Commission

The Federal Trade Commission (FTC) was created in 1914, principally for the purpose of insuring fair competition in the market place (see Chapter 47). Over time, the FTC also took on the protection of the consumer. The essence of the power of the FTC comes from the Federal Trade Commission Act, which declares unlawful "unfair or deceptive acts or practices in or affecting commerce."

Like many administrative agencies, the FTC has quasi-legislative and quasi-judicial functions. In its legislative role, the FTC investigates areas where violations may occur and issues regulations and guidelines designed to assist businesses in avoiding unfair or deceptive acts or practices. It also has the power to propose legislation to Congress and to issue advisory opinions to businesses that seek its advice before undertaking a course of action about which they are unsure.

In its quasi-judicial role, the FTC has the power to investigate and to adjudicate violations of the law that fall within its jurisdiction. It issues complaints, holds hearings before administrative law judges, and issues cease and desist orders when a violation is found. Under a **cease and desist order,** a business must stop whatever practice was found to be in violation of the law. A decision of an administrative judge can be appealed to the full commission, which consists of four members and a chairman. A decision of the commission can be appealed to a federal district court.

The FTC can also enter a **consent decree,** which is an agreement between the FTC and a business specifying that the business will no longer perform certain actions, such as publishing a particular advertisement. However, a consent decree is not an admission by the business that it has violated the law. While the role of the FTC is primarily to prevent the occurrence of unfair and deceptive acts through cease and desist orders or consent decrees, it can also impose penalties for violations of its orders.

In certain cases, the FTC can seek an injunction from a federal district court prohibiting the continuation of an activity that may be a violation of the law while the matter is pending before the commission. In the following case, the FTC sought an injunction of this type. In its decision, the court discusses not only the standard for granting an injunction but also the false, unfair, and deceptive nature of the advertisement involved.

FTC v. PHARMTECH RESEARCH, INC.
576 F. Supp. 294 (D.C. 1983)

PARKER, District Judge

In this proceeding, the Federal Trade Commission ("FTC" or "Commission") challenges certain advertisements disseminated by the defendant Pharmtech Research, Inc. ("Pharmtech"). The advertisements are challenged on the grounds that they are false, misleading, and deceptive within the meaning of the Federal Trade Commission Act ("Act"). As provided by the statute, the FTC filed an administrative complaint . . . against the defendant. The FTC now seeks an injunction . . . restraining Pharmtech from disseminating the challenged advertisements, pending the outcome of the administrative proceedings before the Commission. . . .

Pharmtech, a California corporation, manufactures Daily Greens. . . . Since March 1983 Pharmtech has placed advertisements for Daily Greens in various magazines and newspapers. A typical print advertisement states:

> Cabbage, Brussel Sprouts, Carrots, Cauliflower, Spinach and Broccoli vs. Cancer. . . .
>
> According to the National Academy of Sciences, a regular diet of cruciferous (cabbage, brussel sprouts, broccoli, cauliflower) and carotene-rich (carrot and spinach) vegetables is associated with a reduction in the incidence of certain cancers.
>
> Of couse you may not really like these vegetables. Or you may not cook them quite right. . . . That's why there are Daily Greens. Daily Greens are concentrated servings of cruciferous and carotene-rich vegetables. Picked ripe. Carefully washed. And quickly dehydrated without cooking. . . . The National Academy of Sciences thinks a balanced diet may reduce your risk of cancer. Daily Greens were designed to be a part of that balanced diet. . . . Thanks to the process of dehydration, Daily Greens allows you to eat cruciferous vegetables regularly, with the convenience of a food supplement. . . .

Although the challenged advertisements differ in minor respects, each makes the claim that the consumption of Daily Greens is associated with a reduction in the risk of certain cancers. . . . In making these claims, defendant relies solely on a report published by the National Academy of Sciences. . . . The Committee [in its report] concluded that frequent consumption of certain fruits and vegetables is associated with a reduction in the incidence of cancer in human beings. . . . Thus it recommended that people consume carotene-rich and cruciferous vegetables daily. . . .

The Report, however, limited the application of its findings by several specific and cautionary warnings. First, the Committee stated that scientists have not identified the specific compounds responsible for the reduced incidence of cancer. . . . Second, the Report also warned that: *"[t]hese recommendations apply only to foods as sources of nutrients — not to dietary supplements of individual nutrients. . . ."* Lastly, the Report relied on the studies of the consumption of raw or whole vegetables. . . . The Committee admonished that dehydrated foods are "processed" foods which "produce significant structural and possible major chemical changes including nutrient loss. . . ."

An injunction may be issued for the violation of any provision of law enforced by the FTC. . . . A preliminary injunction under this section is proper if after "weighing the equities and considering the Commission's likelihood of ultimate success [the court determines that] such action would be in the public interest." The test employs a "public interest" standard for injunctive relief, rather than the more traditional equity standard. . . .

The public interest standard does not require the FTC to demonstrate irreparable harm or to show that the public interest will be served by provisional relief. The FTC must, however, make a showing of likelihood of success on the merits and the court must weigh both public and private equities. . . .

[The Federal Trade Commission Act] prohibits false advertising which is disseminated for the purpose of inducing the purchase of food, drugs and other products, or which is likely to induce the purchase of such products. An advertisement is false if it is "misleading in a material respect." In order to determine whether an advertisement is misleading:

> [a court] shall [take] into account (among other things) not only representations made or suggested by statement, word, design, device, sound, or any combination thereof, but also the extent to which the advertisement fails to reveal facts material in the light of such representations. . . .

Here, it is undisputed that Pharmtech's advertisements represent that the use of Daily Greens is associated with a reduction in cancer risk. . . . Thus, the relevant issue is whether the FTC has demonstrated a likelihood of ultimate success as to the falsity of this representation.

Here, the FTC has demonstrated that it is likely to prevail in its claim that Pharmtech's advertisements are false within the meaning of section 12. Pharmtech's advertisements are false both because they misstate the findings of the Report and fail to disclose certain material facts. The advertisements are false in the first respect because the report does not refer to a positive correlation between the use of a dietary or food supplement such as Daily Greens and a reduction in the risk of cancer. . . . On the contrary, the Report expressly denies that its findings apply to the consumption of dietary supplements. . . .

Second, . . . Pharmtech has omitted certain material facts in making these representations. For instance, Pharmtech should have revealed the Committee's substantial doubts concerning the application of its findings to processed foods such as Daily Greens. Pharmtech's failure to reveal these material facts . . . makes it highly likely that its representations are false in the second respect.

Section 12 of the Act also requires a showing that the challenged advertisement was disseminated "for the purpose of inducing" the purchase of Daily Greens, or was "likely to induce the purchase" of Daily Greens. . . . The FTC has shown that it can sufficiently establish this element. . . . Indeed, it is difficult to imagine that any manufacturer would sponsor an advertisement absent the purpose of influencing the purchase of its product.

Section 5 of the Act declares that unfair or deceptive acts or practices in or affecting commerce are un-

lawful. Under section 5, the capacity of an advertisement to deceive consumers is judged by the impression conveyed by the entire advertisement, and not by the impact of isolated words and phrases. . . . An advertisement may be deceptive if it has a tendency to convey a misleading impression, even if an alternative nonmisleading impression might also be conveyed. . . . The advertiser's good faith or absence of intent to deceive is irrelevant. . . .

Pharmtech's representations that the Report supports a finding that Daily Greens reduces the risk of cancer are unfair and deceptive because they convey a misleading impression. Pharmtech has played on the average consumer's well-founded fear of cancer as a vehicle for the sale of its product . . . and has used the findings of the Report to create the impression that Daily Greens will reduce the risk of cancer. . . .

Section 5 requires a manufacturer to have a "reasonable basis" for any affirmative performance claims for a product. . . . Absent such a reasonable basis, the advertisement is unfair. . . . The requirement of a reasonable basis for a product claim differs with the particular product at issue, and depends on the type of claim and product, the consequences of a false claim, and the degree to which consumers will rely on the claim. . . .

The FTC has also established that it is likely to prevail on its claims that the defendant lacks a reasonable basis for its claims that the use of Daily Greens reduces the risk of cancer. For its claims, Pharmtech relies solely on its interpretation of the Committee's findings . . . and a single affidavit prepared by Mr. William Vaughan. Mr. Vaughan is currently the Director of Research at . . . the laboratory which developed Daily Greens. The opinion that the Committee's findings can be applied to Daily Greens is flatly contradicted by the Report itself. . . . Moreover, Vaughan's conclusions are based on studies included in the Report and do not provide additional evidence which would support the defendant's claims.

Once the FTC has established a likelihood of ultimate success on the merits, the Court must weigh the equities in order to determine whether an injunction would be in the public interest. . . . The public equities on one side of the equation include possible harm to consumers, cost of the product, and the availability of alternate products, balanced against such private equities as the financial harm to the manufacturer. . . . A showing that the company will not realize an expected financial gain if a preliminary injunction is issued does not outweigh an FTC counter showing of likelihood of ultimate success. . . .

In this case, the FTC has clearly demonstrated that Pharmtech's representations that the use of Daily Greens reduces the risk of cancer are false, misleading and deceptive. This deception is especially harmful because it preys on consumers' fears about a health issue which has generated public concern. . . . In addition, people who use Daily Greens as a substitute for whole vegetables may more likely than not neglect to eat those vegetables. This is a very real harm in view of the Report's finding that the consumption of whole vegetables has a positive effect on the reduction of cancer in humans. The availability of whole vegetables also indicates that consumers do not have an overriding need for Daily Greens.

After weighing the equities, the Court determines that an injunction against these practices would be in the public interest. . . .

[Preliminary injunction ordered.]

CASE REVIEW QUESTIONS

1. How does the standard for an injunction under the Federal Trade Commission Act differ from the equity standard?
2. What elements must the FTC establish in order to obtain an injunction? Did they establish these elements? How?
3. What equities must the court balance in order to grant an injunction under the Federal Trade Commission Act? How did the court balance these equities?
4. What arguments can be made that the advertisements for Daily Greens are false, deceptive, and unfair?

Advertising and Disclosure

Statutes that control the disclosure of information are an important aspect of consumer law. Figure 49-2 lists some of these statutes. The techniques for control can be characterized as voluntary or compulsory. Control is voluntary if a business is not told what to say in an advertisement or other disclosure but is subject to sanctions if an advertisement or disclosure does not meet certain standards. Control is compulsory if the law requires that particular information be included in an advertisement or disclosure.

The FTC uses both techniques for control. It uses voluntary control when it controls advertising for the benefit of consumers primarily through its ability to declare an advertisement unfair, deceptive, or false. The FTC does not tell an advertiser what to say, but its standards place limitations on what an advertiser can say without having an advertisement challenged. For example, in *FTC v. Pharmtech Research, Inc.,* the FTC challenged the Daily Greens advertisement.

The FTC uses compulsory control when it orders a business to use corrective wording in future advertisements after it finds that an advertisement is unfair, deceptive, or false. For example, the FTC ordered the makers of Geritol affir-

Statutes Regulating Advertising and Disclosure

Law	Purpose
1. Federal Trade Commission Act (15 USCA* §41 et seq.)	To control unfair and deceptive acts and practices in commerce.
2. Plain Language Law (New York General Obligations Law §5–702)	To make contracts and other documents more readable and understandable.
3. Truth-in-Lending Act (15 USCA §1601)	To regulate the disclosure of information to consumers who are obtaining credit.
4. Unit Pricing (New York Agriculture & Markets Law §193–h)	To standardize the methods used for disclosing the prices of groceries.
5. Magnuson–Moss Warranty Act (15 USCA §2301 et seq.)	To describe the type of warranty given with a product.
6. Motor Vehicle Information and Cost Savings Act, Subchapter IV—Odometer Disclosure Act (15 USCA §1981 et seq.)	To disclose to buyers the actual mileage of motor vehicles.

FIGURE 49-2
Statutes Regulating Advertising and Disclosure

matively to disclose the fact that most people are not tired because of an iron deficiency despite what their previous advertisements had implied.

Plain language laws do not require the use of particular language, but they do establish standards for written agreements in consumer transactions. For example, New York's plain language law requires that consumer agreements must be

1. Written in a clear and coherent manner using words with common every day meanings.
2. Appropriately divided and captioned by its various sections.

Statutes that require specific disclosures are designed to insure that consumers are provided with important information so that they can use the information to make proper selections. An important feature of the Truth-in-Lending Act (commonly referred to simply as Truth in Lending) is the requirement that all interest rates be uniformly expressed as an annual percentage rate (APR) so that consumers can compare the cost of credit. Truth-in-Lending also requires that certain information be included in credit advertisements and that certain disclosures be made to a person who is receiving credit. Truth-in-Lending will be discussed in more detail later in this chapter.

Unit pricing laws, which have been enacted by many states, require grocers to post the price of items in standard measurements, such as the price per

---

* USCA is a reference to the United States Code Annotated, the Collection of laws enacted by Congress.

pound, when the items are sold in containers of different sizes. This allows the customers to compare the relative prices of products being sold.

The Magnuson–Moss Warranty Act requires that all warranties be designated as either "full" or "limited" so that consumers can make informed selections of warranted products. (For additional discussion of the Magnuson–Moss Warranty Act, see Chapter 22.)

Congress enacted Subchapter IV of the Motor Vehicle Information and Cost Savings Act (the Odometer Disclosure Act) because it found that buyers rely heavily on odometer readings as an index of the condition and value of a motor vehicle. The statute requires that a person transferring a motor vehicle must certify that the odometer reading is correct or that the correct reading is unknown. If a transferor violates the disclosure provision of the statute, a consumer can seek civil penalties in the form of damages. If there has been a violation, the statute requires that a minimum payment of $1,500 be made to the consumer even if there are few or no damages. In addition, law enforcement authorities can bring criminal charges against the transferor. In the following case, a consumer sued the seller of an automobile for violating the Odometer Disclosure Act.

TUSA v. OMAHA AUTO AUCTION INC.
712 F.2d 1248 (8th Cir. 1983)

[Omaha Auto Auction (OAA) operates an automobile auction that sells primarily to registered dealers. On July 12, 1979, the Tusas, who were not dealers, selected and purchased a 1974 Nova from OAA through T & M, which was a registered dealer.

Ownership to the Nova was transferred to OAA by Allan Studna who had acquired the Nova from Tracy Waton on July 6, 1979. When Waton received the car three weeks before selling it to Studna, the odometer statement showed 80,720 miles. When Studna delivered the Nova to OAA, however, the odometer read 60,239. Studna signed an odometer statement as transferror and gave it to OAA. Studna, however, did not list the mileage on the odometer statement. He left the space for mileage blank. OAA employees filled in the blank by copying the mileage figure from the odometer of the Nova. The certificate of title issued in the state of Kansas which Studna also delivered to OAA showed a mileage figure which had been obviously altered by someone. Using this certificate of title and the odometer statment signed by Studna and completed by its employees, OAA applied for a certificate of title in the state of Nebraska where the Tusas lived.

OAA then transferred the Nebraska certificate of title to T & M, who transferred it to the Tusas.

The district court found OAA liable under the Odometer Disclosure Act and awarded the Tusas damages of $1,500, the minimum allowed under the Act. OAA appealed.]

GIBSON, Senior Circuit Judge

Section 1988 of Title 15 requires a transferor of a car to disclose mileage information to a transferee. . . . Section 1988 reads:

(a) . . . [T]he Secretary [of Transportation] shall prescribe rules requiring any transferor to give the following written disclosure to the transferee in connection with the transfer of ownership of a motor vehicle:
  (1) Disclosure of the cumulative mileage registered on the odometer.
  (2) Disclosure that the actual mileage is unknown, if the odometer reading is known to the transferor to be different from the number of miles the vehicle has actually traveled. . . .

OAA contests its liability . . . on two points. First, OAA argues that [the act] only imposes duties on a "transferor" or a "transferee," and OAA was neither. Second, OAA argues that even if it did violate [the act], its liability . . . is limited to situations where the violation is committed with an "intent to defraud," and it had no such intent. We will treat each contention in turn.

Section 1988 requires that a "transferor" disclose mileage information to a "transferee." The regulations define those terms:

> "Transferor" means any person who *transfers his ownership in a motor vehicle* by sale, gift, or any means . . .

OAA argues that it was not a transferor . . . because it never was the owner; when it put itself in the chain of title it was simply acting as an agent for T & M. . . . Being in the chain of title is not conclusive evidence of ownership. OAA's lack of an ownership interest can be demonstrated by considering what would have happened if OAA had tried to transfer the title to someone other than T & M. No court would have considered OAA the owner had it tried that. . . . This analysis is correct to a limited extent, but it does not absolve OAA of liability.

We refuse to accept OAA's interpretation of the terms "transferor." . . . First, OAA was an owner of record. It had title to the car, and a "certificate of title of a motor vehicle is generally conclusive evidence in [Nebraska] of the ownership of the vehicle. . . ." There was other extremely persuasive evidence of OAA's ownership: OAA's own statements. . . . [W]hen OAA applied for a Nebraska title it stated under oath that it was the "lawful owner or purchaser" of the car.

Second, even if evidence of ownership under state law were not so overwhelming, we would be inclined to find out OAA was an owner *for purposes of the federal statute*. . . . We must examine the statute and its purpose to determine if OAA should be considered a transferor . . . under §1988. We believe that the purposes of the statute can be met only if a party in OAA's position is considered a transferor. . . . The legislative history . . . makes clear that the Act is intended to give car buyers accurate information about the number of miles the car has traveled. The Senate Report states:

> Because consumers rely upon odometer readings as an index of the condition and value of motor vehicles, title

IV mandates a national policy against the disconnecting of, or the setting back of, odometers in order to defraud purchasers of motor vehicles.

. . . Furthermore, the Act is intended to prohibit the giving of false odometer statements even by those who had nothing to do with changing the odometers. . . . The Senate Report to the original bill made clear that persons who, with reasonable care, can determine that an odometer reading is false, would have to verify that the true mileage is unknown. . . .

If OAA's argument that it cannot be liable under the Act were adopted, OAA could routinely process cars and give out mileage disclosure statements which, in the exercise of reasonable care, OAA knew were false. Such a practice would be at odds with the Act's purpose of getting as much information to the consumer as possible about a vehicle's mileage. . . .

In summary, the Act's intention of having each transferor give odometer information to the buyer, together with extremely strong documentary evidence of ownership which OAA voluntarily created, leads us to the conclusion that OAA's brief retention of title of the car makes it a transferor. . . .

Section 1989(a) . . . allows a civil action against "[a]ny person who, *with intent to defraud,* violates any requirement imposed under this subchapter. . . ." OAA argues that it did not give the inaccurate mileage information with an intent to defraud. . . .

The legislative history to that section makes it clear that a party must use "reasonable care" to assure the accuracy of odometer disclosure statements. The Senate Report states:

> [T]he auto dealer with expertise now would have an affirmative duty to mark "true mileage unknown" if, in the exercise of reasonable care, he would have reason to know that the mileage was more than that which the odometer recorded or which the previous owner had certified.

. . . The district court concluded that OAA did have an intent to defraud. . . .

The wrongdoer's intent to defraud is ordinarily proved by circumstantial evidence. . . . The district court inferred an intent to defraud on OAA's part because it evidenced a reckless disregard for preparing an accurate odometer statement. The court acknowledged that there was no evidence that OAA had actual knowledge the odometer reading on the Nova was wrong. However, the court found two items which led it to conclude that OAA was acting with a reckless disregard for the truth. First, OAA ignored the alteration of the mileage figure on the Kansas title. The district court said the erasure was clear and apparent. Our own examination of the title leads us to the same conclusion. The district court reasonably inferred that the failure to investigate in the face of an obvious change on the title was due to an intent on OAA's part to defraud the purchaser.

The district court's inference of a fraudulent intent is buttressed by the second item which the district court believed showed a reckless disregard for the

truth. . . . OAA filled in Studna's disclosure statement to OAA. Studna had signed the statement in blank and OAA filled in the mileage simply by looking at the odometer. OAA made no reasonable effort to obtain any previous disclosure statements. . . . Because a car buyer can read an odometer the way OAA did, a disclosure form based solely on reading the odometer does nothing to give the buyer additional information. OAA's method of compiling disclosure statements shows a total disregard for the purposes of the Act. The district court could reasonably find that OAA showed a reckless disregard for the truth.

[Judgment affirmed.]

CASE REVIEW QUESTIONS
1. What is the purpose of the Odometer Disclosure Act?
2. Why was OAA considered a transferor?
3. How did the court find an intent to defraud?
4. What could OAA have done to avoid liability?

Labeling

A number of laws require that specific labels be placed on certain products (see Figure 49-3). An important goal of labeling laws is to insure that consumers are provided with information in a readily identifiable format. For instance, the Automobile Information Disclosure Act and the Fair Packaging and Labeling Act both require that labels be affixed at specified locations and that they contain specific information.

The Automobile Information Disclosure Act requires that a label be affixed to the windshield or the side window of an automobile. The label must show a variety of things, such as identification numbers, prices, and the method of transportation used to deliver the automobile from its final assembly point to the point of delivery if the automobile was towed or driven.

The Fair Packaging and Labeling Act requires that the net quantity of the contents of a package be displayed in a uniform location upon the principal display panel of the label and that the contents be stated in both ounces and pounds or in gallons if the product weighs more than four pounds or is larger than one gallon. While manufacturers are not required to specify the number of servings in a package, a manufacturer that does provide this information must also state the quantity contained in each serving.

Statutes Regulating Labeling

Law	Purpose
1. Automobile Information Disclosure Act (15 USCA §1231)	To provide uniform information to purchasers of new automobiles.
2. Octane Disclosure (15 USCA §2821 et seq.)	To require a statement of the octane rating of gasoline.
3. Motor Vehicle Information and Cost Savings Act (15 USCA §2006)	To disclose automobile fuel economy and estimated fuel costs.
4. Fair Packaging and Labeling Act (15 USCA §1451 et seq.)	To standardize the labeling of products.
5. Wool Products Labeling Act (15 USCA §68)	To standardize the labeling of wool products.
6. Fur Products Labeling Act (15 USCA §69)	To standardize the labeling of fur products.
7. Textile Fiber Products Identification Act (15 USCA §70)	To provide for the disclosure of the types of fibers used in clothing.
8. Cigarette Labeling and Advertising Act (15 USCA §1331 et seq.)	To require specific warning labels on cigarettes and cigarette advertisements.
9. Hall Mark Act (Gold and Silver Articles) (15 USCA §291 et seq.)	To limit the use of quality labels, such as "sterling" on silver products.
10. Hobby Protection Act (15 USCA §2101 et seq.)	To require the identification of imitation political memorabilia.
11. Wholesome Meat Act (21 USCA §601 et seq.)	To require specific labels on meat products.

FIGURE 49-3
Statutes Regulating Labeling

Although a primary goal of labeling statutes is to provide information to the consumer, these laws can also serve other purposes. First, standards for goods can be imposed through the use of required labels. For example, the Wool Products Labeling Act specifies that an article of clothing must meet certain standards to be labeled "wool." If a product with a "wool" label does not meet these standards, the product is deemed to be misbranded and the manufacturer is subject to penalties.

Second, health can be promoted through the use of labels. The Cigarette Labeling and Advertising Act requires that packs of cigarettes bear certain warning labels, such as, "SURGEON GENERAL'S WARNING: Cigarette Smoke Contains Carbon Monoxide." There are several specified warning labels that must be used in rotation according to a plan approved by the Federal Trade Commission. In addition, the size of the type and the format of the label are specified by law.

Third, quality can be insured through the use of labels. For example, the Hall Mark Act prohibits the use of the word "sterling" on silver objects that are merely plated with silver. Similarly, the Hobby Protection Act requires that reproductions of political memorabilia must be labeled as reproductions to insure that the purchasers of these items are aware that they are buying copies and not originals.

In the following case, a consumer organization challenged a labeling regulation promulgated by the Secretary of Agriculture under the Wholesome Meat Act. First, the court had to determine whether the consumer organization had sufficient interest in the matter, which is referred to as **standing,** to allow it to sue. Then the court had to determine whether the secretary's regulation regarding the labeling of hot dogs conformed to the statute.

FEDERATION OF HOMEMAKERS v. HARDIN
328 F. Supp. 185 (D. Maryland 1971)

PARKER, District Judge

In this suit the Federation of Homemakers, a consumer organization dedicated to protecting the integrity of food products, challenges the use of "All Meat" labels [as well as "All Beef," "All Pork," and other "All *(species)*" labels] on frankfurters when such products actually contain up to 15 percent of non-meat ingredients. Such labels have been authorized for use by the defendants, the Secretary of Agriculture and the Assistant Secretary for the Consumer and Marketing Service and the Administrator of the Consumer and Marketing Service. [Regulations to this effect were promulgated pursuant to the standard rule-making procedures of the Department of Agriculture.] The Federation alleges that the defendants violated the Wholesome Meat Act . . . by causing misleading labels to be affixed to meat products. [I]njunctive relief is sought.

The cause has come before this court on plaintiff's motion for summary judgment. . . . There are no factual issues in dispute. . . . [P]laintiff's motion is granted. . . .

The defendants argued preliminarily that the plaintiff lacked standing to sue and that judicial review of this matter was precluded since determinations as to the labeling of meat food products were within the administrative discretion of the Secretary.

Plaintiff has standing if the defendant's actions have caused injury to its consumer constituents and if "the interest sought to be protected by the complainant is arguably within the zone of interest to be protected or regulated by the statute . . . in question. . . ."

The underlying statute in this case is the Wholesome Meat Act . . . enacted to protect the health and welfare of consumers by insuring that they have access to wholesome and properly marked meats. Incorrect or misleading labeling is recognized as an area of statutory concern:

> Misbranded . . . meat food products . . . are injurious to the public welfare [and] destroy markets for wholesome . . . properly labeled . . . meat food products.

The injuries of which plaintiff complains fall squarely within this area. Plaintiff alleges that consumers assume "All Meat" frankfurters are more nourishing than frankfurters not so labeled; however, frankfurters containing dried milk (which are precluded from using an "All Meat" label) are of higher nutritional value. Plaintiff reports that the "All Meat" frankfurters are destroying the market for wholesome products with dried milk and other nutritional additives. With a dwindling market, even those consumers who are aware of the food value of the latter products and would prefer to purchase them may be unable to do so. Thus, plaintiff's interest is "within the zone to be protected or regulated by the statute" and plaintiff has standing to prosecute this action. . . .

In reviewing the adoption of a regulation by an agency under its rule-making procedures, the Court is limited to considering whether the administrative action was "arbitrary, capricious, an abuse of discretion or otherwise not in accordance with law. . . ." In this matter, the Secretary's determination that "All Meat" labels were authorized for frankfurters which contained up to 15 percent of non-meat ingredients represented a codification of a term in common use in the meat industry. [The "All Meat" label distinguished frankfurters containing meat, water, corn syrup, spices, coloring, and flavorings from those containing such additional ingredients as meat byproducts, cereals, or dried milk.] However, there is nothing in the record to suggest that this "term of art" is understood by the general public.

The primary purpose of the Wholesome Meat Act is to benefit the consumer and to enable him to have a correct understanding of and confidence in meat products purchased. Prohibitions against mislabeling are an integral part of this purpose. Clearly, any rule-making procedure conducted under this Act which fails to primarily emphasize the understanding of the consumer is a procedure not conducted in accordance with [the Act]. . . .

The leading case in this jurisdiction on the problem of mislabeling is *Armour and Company v. Freeman.* There, a regulation promulgated by the Secretary required that hams with added moisture content be labeled "imitation." The court stated:

> To measure whether a label employing ordinary words of common usage is false or not, the words must be taken in their ordinary meaning. . . .

The Court itself construed the word "imitation" and rejected the "term of art" definition which had been adopted by the Secretary. It was noted that the determination of the Secretary had forced meat packers to violate the misbranding statute. The Court found the Secretary's action arbitrary and capricious.

This Court finds the *Armour* case controlling. In applying the "ordinary meaning" test to the word "all," it is clear when that adjective is used on a label with the word "meat," the common understanding is that it describes a substance that is *totally and entirely* meat. The application of the "All Meat" label to frankfurters that are 15 percent non-meat is a contradiction in terms and is misleading within the meaning of [the act]. The use of the term "All Meat" or "All *(species)*" as applied to frankfurters is invalid, and the defendant should be enjoined from permitting any frankfurter product to be so labeled.

Counsel for plaintiff shall present an appropriate order for an injunction within 10 days.

CASE REVIEW QUESTIONS

1. Why does the Federation of Homemakers have standing to sue?
2. What standard must the court apply in reviewing the adoption of a regulation?
3. What is the purpose of the Wholesome Meat Act?
4. Is the secretary's regulation in accordance with the act? Why?
5. What problems do "misbranded" foods present for the consumer?

Sales Practices

A variety of sales practices that can be detrimental to the consumer are the subject of regulations by both federal and state governments (see Figure 49-4). A number of statutes provide for **cooling-off periods,** which give a consumer an opportunity to rethink the wisdom of a particular transaction and an opportunity to avoid the contract in certain situations. For example, if a sale of goods or services with a purchase price of $25 or more is made at a place other than the seller's main or permanent branch office, FTC regulations and some state laws require that consumers be given the following or a similar notice.

> YOU, THE BUYER, MAY CANCEL THIS TRANSACTION AT ANY TIME PRIOR TO MIDNIGHT OF THE THIRD BUSINESS DAY AFTER THE DATE OF THIS TRANSACTION. SEE THE ATTACHED NOTICE OF CANCELLATION FORM FOR AN EXPLANATION OF THIS RIGHT.

This notice must appear in the immediate proximity of the space reserved for the buyer's signature on a contract or, if there is no contract, on the front page of any receipt given to the consumer. The accompanying notice spells out the consumer's rights concerning how cancellation can be made and the consumer's rights and obligations concerning any goods that may be part of the transaction. The seller must attach to the contract a form that the consumer can use to cancel the transaction. The contract, the notice, and the form must be in the same language as that used in the sales presentation. In other words, a salesperson cannot extoll the virtues of a product in Spanish and then use a contract written in English.

Even when a sale takes place at the seller's place of business, a cooling-off period may be allowed in situations in which overzealous salespeople have been known to take advantage of consumers. For example, the Health Club Services Act in New York requires that the following notice be included in all health club service contracts:

> CONSUMER'S RIGHT TO CANCELLATION. YOU MAY CANCEL THIS CONTRACT WITHOUT ANY PENALTY OR FURTHER OBLIGATION WITHIN THREE (3) DAYS FROM THIS DATE.

A consumer in New York can also avoid a health club contract if the contract is for services at a planned health club or one under construction and the services do not become available within one year from the date the contract is signed.

The mails have frequently been used to perpetrate schemes to the detriment of consumers. Consequently, there are laws prohibiting the use of the mails for fraudulent purposes. An FTC regulation specifies that merchandise ordered through the mail must be delivered within 30 days.

In the past, some sellers mailed unordered merchandise to consumers and then charged them for the products if they failed to return them. To combat this abuse, several states have enacted laws providing that unsolicited goods shall be deemed an unconditional gift that imposes no obligation on the recipient. Moreover, the seller can be enjoined from attempts to collect payment for these goods.

Abuses in the sale and development of real property are the subject of some federal legislation. The Real Estate Settlement Procedures Act provides for disclosure to home buyers of the costs involved in obtaining home mortgages prior to the time for the final settlement, for the elimination of kickbacks or referral fees, and for a limitation on the amounts home buyers are required to

Statutes Regulating Sales Practices

Law	Purpose
1. Cooling-Off	
A. FTC Door-to-Door Sales (16 CFR §429)	To allow consumers three days to cancel a contract made at other than the seller's usual place of business.
B. Health Club Services Law (New York General Business Law §620)	To allow consumers to cancel health club contracts within three days.
C. Truth-in-Lending Act (15 USCA §1625)	To allow consumers to cancel contracts that create a security interest in a home.
2. Mail	
A. Mail Fraud (18 USCA §1341 et seq.)	To prohibit the use of the mail for fraudulent purposes.
B. Unsolicited Goods (New York General Business Law §396(2))	To allow consumers to keep unordered goods with no obligation.
C. FTC Mail Order Rule (16 CFR §435)	To require businesses using the mails to ship ordered goods within 30 days.
3. Real Estate	
A. Real Estate Settlement Procedures Act (12 USCA §2601 et seq.)	To provide for the disclosure of information in the sales of real property.
B. Condominium and Cooperative Abuse Relief Act (15 USCA §3601 et seq.)	To protect consumers when apartment houses are converted to condominium or cooperative ownership.
C. Interstate Land Sales Full Disclosure Act (15 USCA §1701 et seq.)	To control sales practices in the sale of land using the mail or other means of interstate commerce.
4. Referral Sales and Leases	
(Iowa Code Ann. §537.3309)	To prohibit the use of discounts based on possible future sales to other customers.
5. Bait and Switch	
A. FTC Guides against Bait Advertising (16 CFR §238)	To declare bait and switch advertising to be an unfair or deceptive act.
B. Unlawful Selling Practices (New York General Business Law §396(1))	To prohibit bait and switch advertising.
C. False Advertising (New York Penal Law §190.20)	To make false advertising a criminal offense.

FIGURE 49-4
Statutes Regulating Sales Practices

place in escrow accounts for the payment of real estate taxes and insurance. The Condominium and Cooperative Abuse Relief Act was enacted to minimize the adverse impact of the conversion of apartment houses to condominiums or cooperative ownership plans. The promotion of sales of undesirable land to unsuspecting buyers through the use of the mails or other interstate advertisements is prohibited by the Interstate Land Sales Full Disclosure Act. A violation of this act is punishable as fraud.

A **referral or pyramid sale** occurs when a seller tells a prospective buyer that he or she can reduce the purchase price of goods or services by giving the seller the names of other prospective purchasers. Usually, the person referred by the consumer must also make a purchase for the consumer to benefit from a reduction in the purchase price. Sometimes, the prospective buyer is told that he or she can recoup the amount paid by making sales to other consumers. These schemes suggest to the consumer that he or she may be able to pay for the goods or services even though he or she may not have the money. But often, the consumer's referrals do not make purchases or the consumer is unable to make sales. Nevertheless, the consumer has signed a contract and must pay the contract price.

Figure 49-5 shows what happens in one of these schemes when a buyer is told that he or she will be able to reduce the purchase price of goods by $10 for each person who also purchases the goods. If the goods cost $120, the consumer in theory only has to find 12 buyers for the goods to be free. The first few people to try may succeed in finding 12 others who will buy, but by the time the fifth set of purchasers begins to look for people who will buy, everyone in a small city would have to purchase the goods in order for all of the fifth round buyers to recoup their costs.

General statutes that prohibit unfair or deceptive sales practices can be used to deal with referral or pyramid schemes. In addition, several states have enacted specific laws to deal with these types of sales. For example, the Iowa statute (see Figure 49-4) is part of Iowa's version of the Uniform Consumer Credit Code, which has been enacted by several states. It prohibits referral sales "if the earning of the rebate, discount or other value is contingent upon the occurrence of an event after the time the consumer agrees to buy or lease." The consumer who is induced to purchase through this type of referral scheme can rescind the agreement and keep the goods or the benefit of any services performed. In addition, the consumer has no obligation to pay for any of the goods or services.

Bait and switch advertising is an abusive sales practice that the FTC has defined as

> an alluring but insincere offer to sell a product or service which the advertiser in truth does not intend or want to sell. Its purpose is to switch consumers from buying the advertised merchandise, in order to sell something else, usually at a higher price or on a basis more advantageous to the advertiser.

The FTC's Guides Against Bait Advertising provide the basis for an FTC complaint that a merchant who fails to follow the guidelines is engaging in an

Pyramid and Referral Sales

1 Buyer Needs

12 Buyers Need

144 Buyers Need

1,728 Buyers Need

20,736 Buyers Need

248,832 Buyers Need

2,985,984 Buyers Need . . .

To Get the Goods for Free

FIGURE 49-5
Pyramid and Referral Sales

unfair or deceptive act or practice. A number of states have adopted statutes that declare bait and switch advertising to be an unlawful selling practice. New York State, for example, provides not only for injunctions prohibiting the continuance of the practice but also for a criminal penalty when a person intends to promote a sale by false or misleading advertising. In the following case, a seller was found guilty of the crime of false advertising.

PEOPLE v. BLOCK & KLEAVER, INC.
427 N.Y.S.2d 133 (Monroe County Court 1980)

MARK, Judge

. . . Section 190.20 of the Penal Law, insofar as it is applicable to this case, provides as follows:

A person is guilty of false advertising when, with intent to promote the sale or to increase the consumption of property or services, he makes or causes to be made a false or misleading statement in any advertisement. . . .

The defendant corporation was engaged in the business of selling retail bulk beef, which it advertised at unusually low prices in the local newspapers. Each customer who responded to the advertisement, regardless of what meat he indicated an interest in, was first shown the sale beef which was fatty, discolored, and unappetizing. An employee would disparage the sale beef, by advising the customer that the loss of fat and bone would make such a purchase unprofitable. After so discouraging the customer, the employee would show the customer much more appetizing meat at a higher price, but represent that there would be minimal loss from the pre-trimmed beef. . . . Except

in one instance, each customer was persuaded to purchase the more expensive beef.

Most customers never complained to the defendant corporation and became available to the prosecution only after a local television channel exposed the alleged fraudulent practices. Most customers were generally satisfied with the quality of the meat purchased. . . .

From June 1, 1978, until March 31, 1979, the defendant corporation consistently advertised the sale beef at a price per pound that was less than the price for which it purchased such meat and at a price that was less than two other retail bulk meat businesses were selling the meat for. For example, in June 1978, the defendant advertised bulk beef for sale at $.89 per pound at the same time it was purchasing such meat at $.94 per pound and at the same time the two businesses were selling the same at an average of $1.27 per pound. . . .

The various employees of the defendant corporation quoted the loss of sale beef from the minimum of 30 percent to a maximum of 90 percent to 21 customers. The average of the percentage of loss so quoted was 54 percent. The same employees represented the waste of pre-trimmed beef to 12 customers from a low of 0 percent to a high of [10-12 percent] the percentage most frequently mentioned being 10 percent.

As a result of the actions of the defendant corporation's employees, out of a total of 31 customers, 29 customers ultimately purchased the pre-trimmed beef; one customer could not be dissuaded from buying the sale beef and one imposter had no intention of making any purchase.

Section 190.20 of the Penal Law may be construed in conjunction with Section 396 of the General Business Law. . . . The latter section gave the Attorney General the right to seek a civil injunction against false advertising. . . . Both statutes proscribe the sale promotional practice known as "bait and switch advertising," "bait advertising" or "fictitious bargain claims." . . . This practice consists of advertising a product at a very low price; a pattern of conduct discouraging the purchase of the advertised article; and the resulting switch to the purchase of a product costing more than the one advertised. . . .

This is the exact factual predicate in the instant case. . . .

Accordingly, the defendant corporation is found guilty of the crime of False Advertising in violation of Section 190.20 of the Penal Law.

CASE REVIEW QUESTIONS

1. What was the pattern of conduct by the corporation's employees that established the violation of §190.20?
2. Could the attorney general have enjoined the defendant corporation from continuing the advertisements?
3. Is it relevant that the customers were satisfied with their purchases? Explain.

SAFETY

President Kennedy recognized that one of consumers' primary concerns is safety. A number of statutes deal with specific safety concerns (see Figure 49-6), and consumer safety is protected by a variety of techniques. One of these techniques is the use of standards. Government agencies, such as the Consumer Product Safety Commission, set standards that products must meet in order to be marketed, and they assist consumers in evaluating the safety of products. The Consumer Product Safety Commission also oversees the enforcement of and promulgates regulations for some statutes, such as the Hazardous Substances Act, the Flammable Fabrics Act, the Poison Prevention Packaging Act, and the Refrigerator Safety Act. (See Figure 49-7 for some of the Consumer Product Safety Commission regulations.)

Some statutes promote research to develop safer products. For example, the Cigarette Safety Act of 1984 calls for a study to determine the technical and commercial feasibility of developing cigarettes that will have a minimum abil-

Statutes Regulating Safety

Law	*Purpose*
1. Consumer Product Safety Act (15 USCA §2051 et. seq.)	To create an agency to regulate consumer safety.
A. Federal Hazardous Substances Act (15 USCA §1261 et seq.)	To regulate and ban dangerous products, including such things as radioactive devices and toys.
B. Flammable Fabrics Act (15 USCA §1191 et seq.)	To regulate fabrics used in certain products, especially children's sleepwear.
C. Poison Prevention Packaging Act (15 USCA §1471 et seq.)	To regulate the packaging and labeling of dangerous products, such as household cleaning products.
D. Refrigerator Safety Act (15 USCA §1211 et seq.)	To ban the interstate transportation of refrigerators that cannot be opened from the inside.
2. Motor Vehicle Information and Cost Safety Act, Subchapter 11 — Tire Safety (15 USCA §1421 et seq.)	To set standards for automobile tires.
3. Cigarette Safety Act of 1984 (98 STAT. §2925)	To promote research to develop a self-extinguishing cigarette.
4. Federal Food, Drug and Cosmetic Act (21 USCA §301 et seq.)	To regulate food, drugs, and cosmetics.
5. Consumer-Patient Radiation Health and Safety Act (42 USCA §10001 et seq.)	To provide educational standards for the operators of x-ray and radiation equipment.
6. Egg Products Inspection Act (21 USCA §1031)	To provide standards for and inspection of eggs and egg products.
7. Wholesome Poultry Products Act (21 USCA §451)	To provide standards for and inspection of products containing poultry.

FIGURE 49-6
Statutes Regulating Safety

ity to ignite mattresses or upholstered furniture. The Food and Drug Administration requires that extensive testing be conducted before new drugs can be marketed. Safety is also promoted through educational requirements. For example, the Consumer-Patient Radiation Health and Safety Act was enacted to establish minimum standards for the accreditation of educational programs and the certification of persons who administer radiological procedures such as x-rays or nuclear medicine procedures.

Products can be banned in order to protect the consumer. The Consumer Product Safety Commission has banned "lead-containing paint" on toys or

Some Consumer Product Safety Commission Regulations

1. Safety Standard for Walk-Behind Power Lawn Mowers (16 CFR §1207)

2. Ban on Lead-Containing Paint and Certain Consumer Products Bearing Lead-Containing Paint (16 CFR §1303)

3. Requirements for Bicycles (16 CFR §1512)

4. Poison Prevention Packaging (16 CFR §1700)

5. Standards for Devices to Permit the Opening of Household Refrigerator Doors from the Inside (16 CFR §1750)

FIGURE 49-7
Some Consumer Product Safety Commission Regulations

other articles used by children, for use on furniture, and for use in such places as homes, schools, and playgrounds where consumers have direct access to painted surfaces. By prohibiting the interstate transportation of refrigerators that are not equipped with a device that allows them to be opened from the inside, the Refrigerator Safety Act effectively bans such refrigerators.

Labeling statutes serve to promote safety in the area of food and drugs. If a food label does not meet certain standards, the food is considered to be "misbranded" and can be banned or seized. In addition, inspections are made by various agencies, such as the Department of Agriculture, to insure that products meet certain standards. In the following case, the Food and Drug Administration seized a quantity of eggs because they were adulterated. In its decision, the court discusses how the determinations of whether or not the eggs were adulterated must be made.

UNITED STATES v. 1,200 CANS, PASTEURIZED WHOLE EGGS, ETC.
339 F. Supp. 131 (N.D. Georgia 1972)

SMITH, Chief Judge

These . . . actions were brought . . . pursuant to . . . the Federal Food, Drug and Cosmetic Act . . . to condemn and destroy as adulterated various lots of pasteurized frozen whole eggs and sugar yolks processed . . . by the Golden Egg Products, Inc. ("Golden Egg"). Proceeding under the statute, the government contends that the lots were "adulterated" in one or more of the definitions prescribed by [the act]. . . .

Golden Egg is a so-called frozen egg breaking plant. . . . In the ideal process, wholesome clean cool eggs are broken by workers in antiseptic conditions, collected in buckets, strained, pasteurized, and sealed in sterile containers, quick frozen and stored at low temperatures until used. . . . Because of economic considerations, most plants must resort to the purchase of eggs of less than Grade A standard table eggs, which come in a variety of forms, grades and prices. . . . [Within the industry, these eggs are ascribed such descriptive terms as "smalls," "dirties," "moulds," "checks," "bloodies," "cracks," "mud balls," "rots," and the like.]

By way of enforcement, Food and Drug inspectors have administered the Act . . . [by] spot-checking of plants at one end and of shipped production at the other end. . . . [Effective as of June 29, 1972, the Department of Agriculture began continuous in-plant inspection services.]

I. Poisonous Substances under . . . §342(a)(1)

A food shall be deemed to be adulterated—if it bears or contains any poisonous or deleterious substances which may render it injurious to health.

Only one lot involved here (Can Code 1941) is claimed to be adulterated under this section. . . . In the course of the microbiological examination conducted in accordance with testing standards . . . one subsample was found to have Salmonella contamination. . . . Salmonella constitutes a serious threat to public health, particularly to the old, the young, and the sickly. . . . The presence of Salmonella in frozen eggs is a deleterious and poisonous additive which is dangerous to health within the meaning of [the act].

II. Decomposed Substances under . . . §342(a)(3)

A food shall be deemed to be adulterated—if it consists in whole or in part of any filthy, putrid, or decomposed substance.

[T]he question presented is not whether a particular lot "may" be filthy, putrid, or decomposed, but whether it actually is. [A] food substance may be condemned under the present statute . . . even though it is not unfit for food. . . . In any event, under the absolute language of the statute, there must exist actual filth, putridity, or decomposition. In this connection, the courts recognize that section (a)(3) sets a standard that if literally enforced would ban virtually all processed food from interstate commerce in that a scientist with a microscope could find filthy, putrid, and decomposed substances in almost any food we eat. To afford a practical application of the law, the Secretary has been granted the discretion . . . to adopt administrative working tolerances. . . . However, the Secretary has not seen fit to do so with egg products. . . . However, all agree that decomposition in-

volves a bacterial separation or breakdown in the elements of the food so as to produce an undesirable disintegration or rot. [The court discussed a variety of tests that might be used to determine decomposition, ranging from various types of scientific examinations to smelling the product, and concluded that the government had not established actual decomposition.]

III. Insanitary Conditions Under . . . §342(a)(4)

A food shall be deemed to be adulterated—if it has been prepared, packed, or held under insanitary conditions whereby it may have become contaminated with filth, or whereby it may have been rendered injurious to health.

While there are many similarities between (a)(3) and (a)(4) proceedings, the legislative thrust of the latter is entirely different. In essence, the (a)(3) section permits the seizure of foods which have actually decomposed regardless of processing conditions; even if they were completely sanitary. On the other hand, the (a)(4) section allows the condemnation of foods processed under insanitary conditions, whether they have actually decomposed or become dangerous to health or not. The objective of (a)(4) is to "require the observance of a reasonably decent standard of cleanliness in handling food products" and to insure "the observance of those precautions which consciousness of the obligation imposed upon producers of perishable food products should require in the preparation of food for consumption by human beings. . . ." It almost reaches the aim of removing from commerce those products produced under circumstances which would offend a consumer's basic sense of sanitation and which would cause him to refuse them had he been aware of the conditions under which they were prepared. . . .

Reviewing the evidence as a whole, the court must conclude that the conditions existing at the Golden Egg plant . . . were exactly those the Congress sought to prevent by the passage of (a)(4). . . . These problems lay primarily in a persistent use of inferior egg stock and very poor sanitizing procedures in the transfer room and breaking room. . . . Good practice only admits the entry into the breaking room of washed, clean sanitized eggs, either unmarked or "checks" (which are eggs with cracks, but the underlying protective membrane is unbroken). If proper procedures are utilized, a "crack" (wherein the membrane is broken) which occurs during washing and handling at the plant may also be processed. All other stock should be eliminated. In the breaking operation, extreme care must be exercised to eliminate unsuitable eggs by individual . . . examination, to prevent foreign matter from entering the stock. . . . Neither in stock, nor equipment, nor personal practices were these requirements met.

To the contrary, in varying degrees the following conditions existed at the times in question: improper refrigeration in the transportation and storage of breaking stock; . . . the regular failure to wash [and] sanitize . . . the breaking stock before it was sent to

the breaking room . . . the breaking of leaking eggs and eggs with maggots . . . and other foreign matter on the shells; . . . breakers with uncovered open sores breaking eggs; the breaking of eggs without even a sniff to detect rotten eggs; . . . failure to reject rotten eggs; . . . flies, in varying numbers, in the breaking and transfer rooms; . . . and improper cleanup and maintenance. . . .

That such practices are those demonstrating a reasonable possibility of the food becoming contaminated with filth or becoming injurious to health is beyond question. . . . Accordingly, the court finds that all lots are subject to condemnation under Section (a)(4). . . .

It is so ordered.

CASE REVIEW QUESTIONS

1. In what three ways can food be deemed to be adulterated?
2. What purposes are accomplished by §342(a)(3) and §342(a)(4) of the Food, Drug and Cosmetic Act?
3. What do you think will happen to the eggs as a result of the decision?
4. Do you agree with the decision? Explain.

CREDIT

Credit is important to many consumers who could not or would not purchase goods and services without it. A number of statutes have been enacted to protect consumers who use credit. Most of these statutes are part of the Consumer Credit Protection Act (see Figure 49-8).

Truth-in-Lending

The Truth-in-Lending Act, usually referred to simply as Truth-in-Lending, provides for the uniform disclosure of information about the costs of credit. For example, it requires that all interest rates must be stated in terms of an annual percentage rate (APR) that is determined by the actuarial method (interest on declining balances) rather than by an add-on method or a discount method. Figure 49-9 illustrates the differences in APR rates among the three methods based on the assumption that a person borrows $100 at a stated rate (not an annual percentage rate) of 12 percent and pays back the loan in equal monthly installments over a period of one year. Without the regulations provided by Truth-in-Lending, all three creditors could say that they were charging an

The Consumer Credit Protection Act

Law

1. Truth-in-Lending Act (15 USCA §1601 et seq.)

2. Federal Anti-Garnishment Act (15 USCA §1676 et seq.)

3. Fair Credit Reporting Act (15 USCA §1681 et seq.)

4. Equal Credit Opportunity Act (15 USCA §1691 et seq.)

5. Fair Debt Collection Practices Act (15 USCA §1692 et seq.)

6. Electronic Funds Transfer Act (15 USCA §1693 et seq.)

FIGURE 49-8

The Consumer Credit Protection Act

interest rate of 12 percent even though the APR can be much more, depending on the method of calculation and repayment used.

The FTC has general responsibility for enforcement of the act, but the Federal Reserve Board has the responsibility of issuing regulations and model disclosure forms. The regulations for Truth-in-Lending are known as Regulation Z. Figure 49-10 is a model form found in Regulation Z for a $5,000 loan at 12 percent interest payable over a two-year period.

Truth-In-Lending not only requires that uniform methods of disclosure be used at the time loans are made, but it also provides for the types of disclosures that must be made in advertising credit. The regulations are divided into those that govern *open-end creidt* — for example, a revolving charge account or a line of credit from which repeated borrowing is anticipated — and *closed-end credit* — for example, an installment loan under the terms of which no further borrowing is expected.

In addition to the provisions governing disclosure, open-end credit regulations also cover the use of periodic statements, the crediting of payments, and the handling of billing errors. Closed-end credit regulations provide for initial disclosures, the needs for subsequent disclosures, and the treatment of credit balances. Regulation Z also provides for a cooling-off period and cancellation of the contract if the creditor takes a security interest in or a mortgage on a person's principal residence in return for credit that is extended for purposes other than the purchase of the residence.

Credit Cards Truth-in-Lending has some specific provisions that deal with credit cards. The act prohibits the issuance of a credit card unless a person makes an oral or written application for it. If a person already has a credit card, however, a renewal or replacement card can be issued without reapplication. Prior to the enactment of this provision, some credit card companies issued cards to persons who had not applied for a card. Some consumers used these cards without understanding the obligations they were incurring or the repayment requirements.

Under Truth-in-Lending, a credit card holder has limited liability for the unauthorized use of his or her card. The act specifies that a credit card holder is

Comparison of Interest
Amount of Loan: $100
Stated Rate of Interest: 12%

Method	Monthly Payment	Finance Charge	APR
Actuarial	$8.88	$ 6.63	12.00%
Add-On	$9.33	$12.00	21.47%
Dis-count	$8.33	$12.00	24.29%

Actuarial Method   The interest due at the time of each payment is based upon the unpaid balance at that time. Each monthly payment is used, in part, to decrease the principle balance due; therefore, there is less interest due each month because more of the payment goes toward reducing the principle each month. Because the borrower pays some of the principle each month, he or she does not borrow the full $100 for a full year; therefore, the borrower pays less than $12.00 as a finance charge.

Add-On Method   To determine each monthly payment, the creditor computes the interest for the year, adds it to the amount lent, and divides the resulting figure — $112.00 — by the total number of payments. Because the borrower makes a payment each month, he or she does not enjoy the use of the $100 for a full year. The borrower also pays more in interest than he or she would if the interest were calculated on the balance due each month.

Discount Method   The creditor computes the interest for the year and deducts it from the amount lent. The borrower, therefore, gets only $88.00 but has to pay back $100. Because the borrower makes a payment each month, he or she does not enjoy the use of even the $88.00 for a full year. The interest rate paid by the borrower is higher than it would be if the actuarial method were used. It is also higher than it would be if the add-on method were used because the borrower is actually paying $12.00 to borrow $88 rather than $100.

NOTE: Computing the APR would not be easy for most consumers. In obtaining the APRs for this example, the author consulted a professor of mathematics. Aided by a calculator and several computer programs, he took nearly one hour to arrive at the APR for the Add-on and discount methods. Subsequently, the author discovered that her home computer had a program in its game package that did the computation in a matter of seconds.

FIGURE 49-9
Comparison of Interest

not liable for more than $50 of unauthorized charges prior to the time the credit card holder notifies the issuer of the unauthorized use. The credit card holder is not even liable for the $50 unless the issuer had provided adequate notice of the cardholder's liability and a means of notifying the issuer of the loss or theft of the card, such as by giving the credit cardholder the card issuer's phone number or address.

In the following case, a credit cardholder claims that the use of his credit card was unauthorized. In its decision, the court discusses what the credit card issuer must establish in order to recover more than the minimum $50 from the cardholder.

Model Truth-in-Lending Disclosure Form

Regulation Z

Friendly Bank & Trust Co.
700 East Street
Little Creek, USA

Lisa Stone
22-4859-22
300 Maple Avenue
Little Creek, USA

ANNUAL PERCENTAGE RATE The cost of your credit as a yearly rate.	FINANCE CHARGE The dollar amount the credit will cost you.	Amount Financed The amount of credit provided to you or on your behalf.	Total of Payments The amount you will have paid after you have made all payments as scheduled.
12 %	$ *675.31*	$ *5000 —*	$ *5675.31*

You have the right to receive at this time an itemization of the Amount Financed.
☐ I want an itemization.   ☐ I do not want an itemization.

Your payment schedule will be:

Number of Payments	Amount of Payments	When Payments Are Due
1	*$262.03* e	*6/1/81*
23	*$235.36*	*monthly beginning 7/1/81*

Late Charge: If a payment is late, you will be charged $5 or 10% of the payment, whichever is less.

Prepayment: If you pay off early, you ☒ may   ☐ will not   have to pay a penalty.

Required Deposit: The annual percentage rate does not take into account your required deposit.

See your contract documents for any additional information about nonpayment, default, any required repayment in full before the scheduled date, and prepayment refunds and penalties.

———
e means an estimate

FIGURE 49-10
Model Truth-in-Lending Disclosure Form

SOCIETY NATL. BANK v. KIENZLE
463 N.E.2d 1261 (Ohio App. 1983)

[Kienzle was issued a single MasterCard charge card. After incurring a large bill, Kienzle stopped using the card until his indebtedness could be paid off. Eight months later, he discovered an unauthorized cash advance on his monthly bill and immediately notified the credit card company of the apparent theft of his card. Prior to this discovery Kienzle had a balance due of $354.54. Evidence at the trial showed $4,057.76 as the amount charged to his account. Kienzle's testimony implicated his estranged wife as the unauthorized user of his card. The credit card issuer argued that her use was authorized and Kienzle was liable for the full amount due. The trial court awarded the Society National Bank the full amount. Kienzle appealed.]

STILLMAN, Judge

Defendant's alleged error asserts that at most, he was liable only to the extent mandated by the Federal Truth-in-Lending Act. . . . We agree.

Section 1643 . . . states:

(a)(1) A cardholder shall be liable for the unauthorized use of a credit card only if—
  (A) the card is an accepted credit card [which is a card that the cardholder has requested and received or has signed or used or authorized another to use for the purpose of obtaining money, property, labor, or services on credit];
  (B) the liability is not in excess of $50;
  (C) the card issuer gives adequate notice to the cardholder of the potential liability;
  (D) the card issuer has provided the cardholder with a description of a means by which the card issuer may be notified of loss or theft of the card, . . . ;
  (E) the unauthorized use occurs before the card issuer has been notified that an unauthorized use of the credit card has occurred or may occur as the result of loss, theft, or otherwise; and

  (F) the card issuer had provided a method whereby the user of such card can be identified as the person authorized to use it. . . .
(d) Except as provided in this section, a cardholder incurs no liability from the unauthorized use of a credit card.

Thus, a cardholder is liable for a limited amount if certain conditions are met and if the use of the credit card was unauthorized. . . .

[T]he burden of proof is upon the card issuer to show that the use was authorized or, if the use was unauthorized, then the burden of proof is upon the card issuer to show that the conditions of liability for the unauthorized use of a credit card, as set forth in subsection (a) of [§1643] have been met.

. . . Accordingly, the initial determination is whether the use of a credit card is unauthorized. . . .

The test for determining unauthorized use is agency, and State agency law must be used to resolve the issue.

In Ohio, a husband is not answerable for the acts of his wife unless the wife acts as his agent or he subsequently ratifies [approves] her acts. . . . In this case, there was no evidence introduced that defendant's wife acted as his agent, or that he ratified her conduct. Indeed, the transcript reveals that defendant notified plaintiff immediately after his discovery of someone else using his credit card. The transcript is devoid of any other evidence of agency or ratification. Thus, plaintiff failed in its burden of proof. . . . [W]e must reduce the judgment rendered to the maximum delineated . . . i.e., fifty dollars.

Judgment modified, and affirmed as modified.

CASE REVIEW QUESTIONS
1. What would the credit card issuer had to have proved in order to recover the $4,057.76?
2. How did the court determine that the use of the card was unauthorized?
3. How much does Kienzle owe the credit card issuer?

Electronic Funds Transfer Act Debit cards or bank cash cards are closely related but distinct from credit cards. With a credit card, a person "charges" the cost of goods or services, effectively promising to pay at a later date. With a **debit card,** funds are immediately withdrawn from the cardholder's account and transferred to the cardholder or to the account of a third person. The Electronic Funds Transfer Act was added to the Consumer Credit Protection Act because consumers' rights and liabilities in relation to debit cards were unclear. The act broadly defines an electronic transfer as

> any transfer of funds, other than a transaction originated by check, draft, or similar paper instrument, which is initiated through an electronic terminal, telephonic instrument, or computer or magnetic tape so as to order, instruct, or authorize a financial institution to debit or credit an account. Such term includes, but is not limited to, point-of-sale transfers, automated teller machine transactions, direct deposits or withdrawal of funds, and transfers initiated by telephone.

Certain transactions are not included under the act, such as a transfer of funds from a depositor's savings account to his or her checking account to cover an overdraft when the transfer is made by the bank in accordance with an agreement between the bank and the depositor.

The act requires that certain terms and conditions of electronic transfers involving a customer's account be disclosed and that periodic statements of transfers made be provided to the customer. It also establishes rules governing the preauthorization of transfers and the resolution of errors. Under the act, a customer's liability is limited to $50 if the customer notifies the issuer of a debit card of the loss or theft of either the card or the customer's access code (the customer's personal identification code) within two business days of the day the customer learns of the loss or theft. If a customer does not notify the issuer within two days, he or she is liable for a maximum of $500. However, if a customer fails to report any unauthorized transfers that appear on a periodic statement from the issuer within 60 days after the statement is mailed, he or she has unlimited liability for any unauthorized transfers made after the 60-day period has ended.

Obtaining Credit

Two parts of the Consumer Credit Protection Act, the Consumer Credit Reporting Act and the Equal Credit Opportunity Act, are designed to assist a consumer in obtaining credit. The basic technique used in these statutes is to require certain disclosures. Under the Consumer Credit Reporting Act, a creditor must disclose to a loan applicant the name and address of a credit reporting agency used to obtain information about the consumer if the creditor does not extend credit either wholly or partly because of information in a credit report.

Credit reporting agencies are regulated by the act. They may disclose information in their files only under certain conditions. For example, information can be disclosed only to persons who intend to use the information in connection with a credit transaction, for employment purposes, in connection with the underwriting of insurance, for determining license eligibility, or for other legitimate business needs. However, a court can order the release of information for other purposes, or a consumer can direct the release of his or her own file. Certain types of information cannot be disclosed. For example, a credit reporting agency cannot report a bankruptcy that occurred more than 10 years before the date of the report.

Under the act, consumers are given the right to obtain a disclosure of the information in their file. If a consumer so requests, a credit reporting agency must provide the consumer with a summary of the nature and substance of all information in his or her files and the sources of the information. The consumer can require a reinvestigation of any information that he or she deems to be in error. If the credit reporting agency does not revise the report after a reinvestigation, the consumer can file a brief statement setting forth his or her viewpoint. The credit agency can limit the statement to 100 words, but if it does so, it must assist the consumer in writing a statement that is clear. If a consumer files a statement, future reports must include either the consumer's statement or a clear and accurate codification or summary of it.

The Equal Credit Opportunity Act deals with discriminatory practices in the granting of credit. It makes it unlawful to discriminate against an applicant

(1) on the basis of race, color, religion, national origin, sex or marital status, or age (provided the applicant has the capacity to contract);
(2) because all or part of the applicant's income derives from any public assistance program; or
(3) because the applicant has in good faith exercised any right under the Consumer Credit Protection Act.

Provisions like (3) have been included in a number of consumer statutes in order to prevent retaliation against consumers who justifiably exercise their rights.

Under the Equal Credit Opportunity Act, a creditor who has denied credit to a loan applicant must notify the applicant of its action and disclose the reasons for its action. In this respect, the Equal Credit Opportunity Act differs from the Fair Credit Reporting Act. A creditor must give specific reason for denying credit under the Equal Credit Opportunity Act, whereas the creditor need only disclose the name and address of the credit reporting agency used under the Fair Credit Reporting Act. Although the Fair Credit Reporting Act allows the consumer to go to the credit reporting agency to find more specific information, merely knowing what is in an agency's files will not necessarily enlighten the consumer as to why a particular creditor chose not to extend credit. The Equal Credit Opportunity Act, however, requires the creditor to disclose its reasons for denying credit.

Debt Collection

After a consumer has obtained credit, he or she must repay the loan. Two parts of the Consumer Credit Protection Act, the Federal Anti-Garnishment Act and the Fair Debt Collection Practices Act, regulate business practices in the collection of debts.

The Federal Anti-Garnishment Act limits the amount of money that can be **garnished,** that is, withheld from a consumer's earnings by an employer for the purpose of repaying a debt. The act balances a debtor's need to support himself or herself and the creditor's need to be repaid by providing that no more than 25 percent of a debtor's disposable earnings (basically meaning take home pay) that are in excess of 30 times the minimum hourly wage can be withheld in any week. If a state's garnishment law is more generous in the amount that it allows a debtor to keep, the state law has priority over the federal law. The act also provides that an employer may not discharge an employee because his or her wages have been garnished. Congress enacted this provision because it found that garnishment frequently resulted in the loss of employment by debtors.

The Fair Debt Collection Practices Act was enacted because Congress found "abundant evidence of the use of abusive, deceptive and unfair debt collection practices by many debt collectors". Debt collection agencies are governed by the act, but neither creditors acting on their own behalf nor attorneys are considered debt collectors under the act.

The act prohibits a number of activities that might be used by debt collectors. Debt collectors are limited in the methods they can use to acquire information about a debtor. For example, a debt collector seeking information concerning the whereabouts of a debtor from a person other than the debtor must not state that a debtor owes a debt, communicate with a person more than once unless requested to do so by the person contacted by the debt collector (unless the debt collector has reason to believe that the person has new information), use a post card, or use any language or symbol on any envelope or in any other communication that indicates that he or she is in the debt collection business. If the debt collector knows that the debtor is represented by an attorney, the debt collector can communicate only with the attorney.

Harassment or abuse of debtors is also prohibited. For example, causing a telephone to ring repeatedly or continuously with the intent to abuse or annoy any person is considered harassment. Unfair or unconscionable means may not be used to collect debts. For example, debt collectors may not threaten to deposit a postdated check prior to the date on the check or to solicit a postdated check for the purpose of threatening a criminal prosecution. False or misleading representations are prohibited. For example, a representation that nonpayment of the debt will result in arrest or imprisonment is prohibited unless the debt collector can actually institute and intends to institute criminal procedures against the debtor.

In the following case, the court found a number of violations of the Fair Debt Collection Practices Act because of a letter sent to a debtor.

RUTYNA v. COLLECTION ACCOUNTS TERMINAL, INC.
478 F. Supp. 980 (N.D. Ill., E.D. 1979)

McMILLEN, District Judge

This is an action for violations of the Fair Debt Collection Practices Act . . . (the F.D.C.P.A.). The F.D.C.P.A. was enacted by Congress to eliminate abusive, deceptive, and unfair debt collection practices. . . .

The facts of this case are undisputed, except where noted herein. Plaintiff is a 60 year old widow and Social Security retiree. She suffers from high blood pressure and epilepsy. In December 1976 and January 1977, she incurred a debt for medical services performed by a doctor with Cabrini Hospital Medical Group. Her belief was that medicare or other, private, medical insurance had paid in full this debt for medical treatment. She contends that in July 1978, an agent of defendant telephoned her and informed her of an alleged outstanding debt for $56.00 to Cabrini Hospital Medical Group. When she denied the existence of this debt, the voice on the telephone responded, "you owe it, you don't want to pay, so we're going to have to do something about it." In its brief, defendant denies that it ever telephoned the plaintiff. . . . There is no evidentiary support in the record for defendant's contention.

On or about August 10, 1978, plaintiff received a letter from defendant which supplies the basis for her complaint. It stated:

> You have shown that you are unwilling to work out a friendly settlement with us to clear the above debt.

> Our field investigator has now been instructed to make an investigation in your neighborhood and to personally call on your employer.

> The immediate payment of the full amount, or a personal visit to this office will spare you this embarrassment. . . .

The envelope containing the letter presented a return address that included the defendant's full name: Collection Accounts Terminal, Inc.

Upon receiving this letter from defendant, plaintiff alleges that she became very nervous, upset, and worried, specifically that defendant would cause her embarrassment by informing her neighbors of the debt and about her medical problems.

(1) Harassment or Abuse (§1692d) The first sentence of §1692d provides: "A debt collector may not engage in any conduct the natural consequence of which is to harass, oppress, or abuse any person in connection with the collection of a debt." This section then lists six specifically prohibited types of conduct, without limiting the general application of the foregoing sentence. The legislative history makes clear that this generality was intended:

> In addition to these specific prohibitions, this bill prohibits in general terms any harassing, unfair or deceptive collection practice. This will enable the courts, where appropriate, to proscribe other improper conduct which is not specifically addressed. [Citation omitted.]

Plaintiff does not allege conduct which falls within one of the specific prohibitions contained in §1692d, but we find that defendant's letter to plaintiff does violate this general standard.

Without doubt defendant's letter has the natural (and intended) consequence of harassing, oppressing, and abusing the recipient. The tone of the letter is one of intimidation, and was intended as such in order to effect a collection. The threat of an investigation and resulting embarrassment to the alleged debtor is clear and the actual effect on the recipient is irrelevant. . . . Defendant's violation of §1692d is clear.

(2) Deception and Improper Threats (§1692e)

§1692e bars a debt collector from using any "false, deceptive, or misleading representation or means in connection with the collection of any debt." Sixteen specific practices are listed in this provision, without limiting the application of this general standard. §1692e(5) bars a threat "to take any action that cannot be legally taken or that is not intended to be taken." Defendant has violated this provision.

Defendant's letter threatened embarrassing contacts with plaintiff's employer and neighbors. This constitutes a false representation of the actions that defendant could legally take. §1692c(b) prohibits communication by the debt collector with third parties (with certain limited exceptions not here relevant). Plaintiff's neighbors and employer could not legally be contacted by defendant in connection with this debt. The letter falsely represents, or deceives the recipient, to the contrary. This is a deceptive means employed by defendant in connection with its debt collection. Defendant violated §1692e(5) in its threat to take such illegal action.

(3) Unfair Practice/Return Address (§1692f(8))

The envelope received by plaintiff bore a return address, which began "COLLECTION ACCOUNTS TERMINAL, INC." §1692f bars unfair or unconscionable means to collect or attempt to collect any debt. §1692f specifically bars:

> (8) Using any language or symbol, other than the debt collector's address, on any envelope when communicating with a consumer by use of the mails or by telegram, except that a debt collector may use his business name if such name does not indicate that he is in the debt collection business.

Defendant's return address violated this provision, because its business name does indicate that it is in the debt collection business. The purpose of this specific provision is apparently to prevent embarrassment resulting from a conspicuous name on the envelope, indicating that the contents pertain to debt collection. . . .

It is therefore ordered, adjudged and decreed that judgment is entered in favor of plaintiff on the issue of liability.

CASE REVIEW QUESTIONS

1. How did the debt collector violate the Fair Debt Collection Practices Act?
2. Why is it important that there be a general prohibition concerning certain types of debt collection practices?
3. How does the case demonstrate that both specific and general prohibitions are useful in controlling the behavior of debt collectors?

REVIEW QUESTIONS

1. What techniques are used by the Federal Trade Commission to control the disclosure of information to consumers?
2. How does the compulsory disclosure of information benefit consumers?
3. What functions are performed by labeling laws?
4. Describe nine abusive sales practices and the laws that have been enacted to control them.
5. Describe the techniques used to promote consumer safety.
6. How do the disclosure requirements of Truth-in-Lending assist consumers?
7. What are the liabilities of credit card holders and the users of debit cards?
8. What techniques do the Fair Credit Reporting Act and the Equal Credit Opportunity Act provide to assist consumers in obtaining credit?
9. What types of practices are prohibited by the Fair Debt Collection Practices Act?

CASE PROBLEMS

1. Colgate-Palmolive used a "sandpaper test" in a television commercial for Rapid Shave, an aerosol shave cream. The announcer informed the audience that "To prove Rapid Shave's super-moisturizing powers, we put it right from the can onto this tough, dry sandpaper. It was apply . . . soak . . . and off in a stroke." The commercial pictured Rapid Shave being applied to a surface that appeared to be sandpaper. Immediately thereafter, a razor was shown shaving the substance clean. In fact, the surface was not sandpaper but a pane of glass covered with sand. This simulated prop was used because the television camera would have made sandpaper look like nothing more than colored paper. Rapid Shave could shave sandpaper, but only after the sandpaper was soaked for a period of about 80 minutes. The Federal Trade Commission challenged the advertisement on the grounds that it was false and deceptive. Who will win the case? Explain.

2. Resort Car Rental System used a trade name "Dollar-A-Day" in conjunction with their advertising of rental automobiles. The Federal Trade Commission issued a cease and desist order prohibiting the use of the name. The company appealed on the grounds that the order destroyed valuable good will vested in the slogan. The FTC argued that the slogan carries strong psychological appeal and that the connotations of the name are obvious. It also argued that the use of qualifying language would merely result in a contradiction in terms. Who will win the case? Explain.

3. Grambo purchased a motorcycle from Loomis Cycle Sales, Inc. The odometer read 875 miles. Grambo later learned that the actual mileage on the motorcycle was over 14,000. Grambo sued, alleging a violation of the Odometer Disclosure Act. The statute defines a motor vehicle as any vehicle driven or drawn by mechanical power for use on public streets, roads, and highways. Who will win the case? Explain.

4. All-State Industries sold aluminum siding and storm windows, usually on credit. They had two grades of aluminum—"ADV" and "PRO." "ADV," the lower-cost grade, was featured in company advertisements. All-State's salespeople

contacted prospective customers in their homes and pressured them into signing a contract with the amount to be paid left blank. As soon as a contract was signed, the salesperson produced a sample of "ADV" and pointed out its deficiencies. A sample of "PRO" was then shown in contrast. The salesperson then negotiated for the highest price he or she could get from the consumer for the purchase of the "PRO" grade. Gimmicks were used to obtain the highest possible price, such as the promise of special discounts for sales made to prospective purchasers whose names had been supplied by the consumer. What violations of consumer law were committed by All-State's salespeople?

5. FoodScience Laboratories, Inc., manufactured and marketed tablets containing Aanagamik 15 under various names, such as "Calcium Pangamate," "Vitamin B–15," "Sport 15," or "the famous Russian formula." The tablets were marketed as a food. The Food and Drug Administration seized numerous cases of the tablets on the grounds that (1) they were adulterated food because they contained N,N–Dimethyglycine hydrochloride ("DMG"), which has been found to be unsafe; and (2) they contained calcium pangamate labeled "Vitamin B–15," which is not a vitamin nor is there any "accepted scientific evidence which establishes the nutritional properties of the substance or has identified a deficiency of calcium pangamate in men or animals." Who will win the case? Explain.

6. Ninety-eight percent of the people who purchased health club contracts from Norman Health Clubs, Inc., signed contracts whereby they paid $360 in 24 equal monthly installments of $15 each. The contracts did not disclose a finance charge. The contracts were sold to banks at a discount, that is, for less than $360. The people who paid cash to Norman were granted a 10 percent reduction in the $360 price. Patrons of the health clubs sued, alleging Truth-in-Lending violations. Norman argued that there was one basic price and that it was not extending credit. Who will win the case? Explain.

7. Mr. and Mrs. Donnelly, residents of New York State, entered into a contract for the construction of an in-ground swimming pool at their residence. The contract was signed at the Donnellys' home and contained a provision giving the seller a security interest in their home for any unpaid installments. The Donnellys had second thoughts about installing the pool, but the contract did not indicate that they could cancel the contract. The Donnellys sued to cancel the contract. Who will win the case? Explain.

8. Ann Eldridge used her MasterCharge credit card to make some purchases at a gift store and inadvertently left the card behind. She was notified by the store that she had left her card. Eldridge asked the store to hold her card until she could pick it up several days later. The card disappeared from the store, and $3,304.01 unauthorized purchases were made. The police later recovered the card. The bank that issued the card sued to recover the $3,304.01. Who will win the case? Explain.

9. Due to financial difficulties, Mr. and Mrs. Duty failed to make payments due on a loan. The debt collection agency made daily calls to the Dutys, awoke them from their sleep, called relatives and told them about the unpaid balance due, threatened to blacklist them with the Merchants Retail Credit Association, threatened to cause them to lose their jobs, and sent them postcards reading in part "Dear Customer: You received the loan because we thought you were honest . . ." The Dutys sued the collection agency. Who will win the case? Explain.

50

INSURANCE LAW

Life is full of economic risks. Many things can happen to a person that will cause economic loss. We do what we can to avoid these losses, such as driving carefully, buckling up our seat belts, locking the doors of our residences and offices, and installing smoke detectors. Nonetheless, losses sometimes occur despite our best attempts to prevent them.

When a loss occurs, a person can avoid its economic impact by having someone else indemnify (compensate) him or her for the loss. Much of the material discussed in this book concerns the circumstances in which one person is required by the law to compensate another person who has suffered an economic loss. Another of these situations occurs when a person has insured against the loss, in which case the insurer will indemnify him or her for the loss. In this way, the insured transfers the risk of loss to the insurer.

Insuring against risk is especially important for people who are engaged in business. A business firm that knows it is protected from the economic impact of particular losses that may occur can engage in long-range planning because it knows that it will remain financially stable even if those losses occur. In turn, the financial stability of a business firm encourages others to deal with it and to extend it credit, which contributes to the social goal of economic growth.

In this chapter, you will read about the way in which insurance transactions are regulated by the government and about the basic legal principles that affect insurance contracts. Also, you will read about the most common types of insurance, which are life insurance (protection of one person from loss caused by the death of another person), health insurance (protection from loss resulting from injury or illness), property insurance (protection from loss resulting from damage to property) and liability insurance (protection from loss resulting from liability to others).

GOVERNMENT REGULATION OF INSURANCE

Commercial transactions involving insurance comprise one of the most highly regulated areas of economic activity. This part of the book, which is about the regulatory environment of business, is primarily concerned with the regulation of economic activity by the federal government. The regulation of insurance, however, is carried out almost exclusively by the state governments because of the McCarran Act, enacted by Congress in 1945, which provides that the states may regulate the insurance industry.

The McCarran Act does reserve the right of the federal government to regulate insurance activity if Congress finds it necessary. Congress has exercised this right only to a very limited extent. Most of the federal involvement in insurance has involved providing insurance coverage that would be unavailable or very expensive through private insurance companies, such as crop and flood insurance.

State Regulation of Insurance

State regulation of insurance varies greatly from state to state, but the goal of regulation in every state is to protect the consumer of the insurance product in two ways. First, companies and people who are in the insurance business are regulated, and second, transactions between those in the insurance business and those who purchase insurance are regulated.

Regulation of the Insurance Business Any company that provides insurance protection in a state must register with and be licensed to do business by the office of the state official charged with regulating insurance, which is usually called the State Insurance Commission. The commission's primary concern with insurance companies is that they be financially sound so that they will be able to pay the claims of those who insure with them. State law requires that an insurance company have a specific minimum of capital and surplus, that it maintain required minimum reserves, and that it remain "solvent," as the state insurance law defines that term.

In addition, the people who sell insurance on behalf of insurance companies, who are called *insurance agents,* must be licensed by the state. To obtain a license, a person must satisfy specified educational and integrity requirements and must pass a licensing examination.

Regulation of Insurance Transactions One way in which insurance transactions are regulated is through the involvement of the State Insurance Commission in the determination of the terms that are included in insurance policies sold within the state. For some types of insurance, such as fire insurance, the commission prescribes uniform terms that must appear in all policies sold within the state. For other types of insurance, such as life insurance, the commission does not prescribe policy terms, but it must approve them before policies containing them can be sold within the state. The purpose of the insurance commission's role with regard to policy terms is to protect the insurance consumer, who is apt to be unable to understand the complex provisions of an insurance policy.

Some states have adopted statutes and regulations that require the use of plain language in insurance policies. This means that a policy must be written in a clear and cohesive manner, using common words in their everyday meanings, that can be understood by the average insurance purchaser.

Another way in which the states regulate insurance transactions is by controlling the premium rates that companies can charge. This is done not only to protect the insurance purchasers from paying too much for insurance but also to make sure that premium rates are adequate for the insurance companies to have sufficient funds to pay claims. Generally, rates for property insurance are regulated directly by the insurance commission whereas rates for life insurance are not. Life insurance rates are regulated indirectly, however, by the setting of minimum reserve requirements, as mentioned earlier. The need to maintain sufficient reserves affects the rates that a company can charge for its life insurance.

A third way in which the states regulate insurance transactions is by imposing time limits on the settlement of claims and penalties for negligent delays. The time allowed for settlement is intended to be long enough to allow the insurance companies to investigate the validity of claims but short enough for the claimants to receive indemnity for their losses without undue delay.

National Association of Insurance Commissioners

The diversity of state insurance statutes has presented complications for insurance companies that operate in more than one state and has complicated claims settlements in situations that involve more than one state. The National Association of Insurance Commissioners (NAIC) is an organization composed of the insurance commissioners of all the states. This organization devotes much of its effort to promoting uniform state insurance statutes and regulations. Although they have been successful in reducing some of the diversity among state laws, there is still a great lack of uniformity.

One very important ongoing activity of the NAIC is the cooperative examination of insurance companies that do business in more than one state. These examinations, which are usually the collective efforts of the insurance commissions of three of the states in which the company being examined conducts business, focus mainly on verifying compliance with the applicable state statutes concerning insurance company reserves and financial solvency.

The widespread use of computers in the insurance industry and the accompanying ease with which the personal records of individuals can be transferred from one institution to another have generated concern about the privacy of individuals. As a result, the issue of privacy in the insurance industry has been studied by both the federal government and the NAIC. The NAIC has drafted a model statute dealing with insurance information and the protection of privacy. To date, however, only a few states have enacted either the model statute or a variation of it.

THE INSURANCE CONTRACT

The primary purpose for purchasing insurance is to transfer risk from one party (either the policyholder or the beneficiary of the insurance) to another (the insurer, which is usually an insurance company). The risk is transferred when the purchaser and the insurer enter into a contract called an *insurance policy.* Because an insurance policy is a contract, it is subject to the rules of contract law that were discussed in Part II of this book.

In an insurance contract, the insurance company *promises* to pay money if a covered loss occurs. The policyholder does not promise anything in return, however. Instead, the policyholder *performs* the act of paying premiums, and the insurance contract continues only so long as the premiums continue to be paid. Since the policyholder has not promised to pay premiums, he or she can stop paying them at any time. State statutes usually provide for a grace period following the premium due date during which the policyholder can begin to pay premiums again and thereby keep the policy in effect. If he or she does not start paying the premiums again before the grace period elapses, the contract is terminated and the insurance company's promise is no longer binding. (Sometimes, a life insurance policy does not terminate completely because the policyholder stops paying premiums. This exception will be explained later in the chapter.)

In contract law terms, an insurance contract is *unilateral,* which means that one party makes a promise and the other party performs an act (see page 183). Performance of the act is the *consideration* that supports the enforcement of the promise (see Chapter 12).

The Insurable Interest Concept

An insurance contract is an **aleatory contract,** which means that the performance of at least one of the parties to the contract is contingent upon the occurrence of an event that may or may not occur. Wagering agreements are also aleatory contracts. For instance, if you wager that a certain team will win a particular game, the performance by the person you place the bet with — that is, his or her paying you your winnings — is contingent upon your team winning the game. A wagering contract is illegal because there are criminal statutes that prohibit gambling.

To determine whether an insurance contract is illegal and therefore unenforceable because it violates criminal laws that prohibit gambling, it is necessary to distinguish between legal risk-shifting and illegal wagering. A wager occurs when contracting parties agree that a payment will be made between them depending on the outcome of an uncertain event *in which they have no interest other than their agreement.* The lack of a legitimate interest is the reason a bet on a sports event is an illegal wager.

However, if a person is subject to an existing risk, it is not illegal for another person to agree to accept that risk. For example, an owner of a building is always subject to the risk that the building will be damaged or destroyed. Most building owners protect themselves from this risk by entering into contracts with insurance companies under which the insurance company agrees to accept the risk of damage to or destruction of the building in return for a premium payment. On the other hand, if a person without any financial interest in a building — that is, a person who is not subject to any risk because of damage to or destruction of the building — enters into an insurance contract covering the building, the agreement would be an illegal wager.

The financial relationship that is required between a policyholder and the person or property he or she is insuring is called an **insurable interest.** The purpose of the insurable interest requirement is to discourage people from intentionally causing losses. For instance, a policyholder who has no financial interest in a building that he or she has insured might be tempted to burn down the building in order to collect money from the insurance company. Therefore, an insurance company will not issue a policy to someone who does not have an insurable interest in whatever is being insured. If, by chance, a policy is issued to someone without an insurable interest and the contingent event occurs, the insurance company will not have to make payment.

With regard to life insurance, what constitutes an insurable interest varies among the states. Generally, though, one spouse has an insurable interest in the other spouse, as does a parent in a minor child, a minor child in a parent, and grandparents in minor grandchildren. Affectional relationships other than those between spouses do not constitute an insurable interest.

A business relationship can also constitute an insurable interest for life insurance purposes. For example, employers have an insurable interest in the lives of their key employees, and a partner has an insurable interest in the lives of his or her partners. Similarly, creditors have an insurable interest in the lives of their debtors.

With regard to property insurance, any interest or contract right that gives a person a financial interest in property can give him or her an insurable interest in that property. For example, a person who owns a house clearly has an insurable interest in the house. In addition, the bank that holds the mortgage on the house, the person who is renting the house, and the person who has a contract to buy the house also have insurable interests in the house.

The courts of the different states have disagreed over whether a person who purchases a stolen car without knowing that it is stolen has an insurable interest. This disagreement is reflected in the two opinions in the following case.

SCAROLA v. INSURANCE COMPANY OF NORTH AMERICA
292 N.E.2d 776 (N.Y. 1972)

[Scarola, the plaintiff, purchased a used Cadillac for $4,100. He registered the car in New York and obtained an automobile insurance policy from Insurance Company of North America (Company), the defendant. Three days later, the car was stolen from Scarola and was never recovered. When Company was processing Scarola's theft claim, it discovered that he had purchased a stolen car. At the time of the purchase, Scarola did not know that the car was stolen. Company refused to pay Scarola.

Scarola brought a legal action against Company to collect compensation for the theft of his car. Company argued that it didn't have to pay because Scarola did not have an insurable interest in the car. The trial court found for Scarola, and Company appealed. An intermediate appellate court affirmed, and Company appealed to the New York Court of Appeals, the highest court of New York State.]

BERGAN, Judge

Plaintiff had a right to possession of the car against any contrary assertion except that of the true owner. This right ought to be regarded as an insurable interest. The New York rule was laid down by Judge Finch. He noted that the [precedents]

> decide that [a legal] interest in the property burned is not necessary to support an insurance upon it; it is enough if the [insured] is so situated as to be liable to loss if it be destroyed by the peril insured against; that such an interest in property as will cause the insured to sustain a direct loss from its destruction is an insurable interest; that if there be a right in or against the property which some court will enforce upon the property, a right so closely connected with it and so much dependent for value upon the continued existence of it alone as that a loss of the property will cause pecuniary damage to the holder of the right against it, he has an insurable interest.

The general policy problem underlying the concept of "insurable interest" essentially is whether an insurer, having no real economic interest in the subject, is actually making a wagering contract.

> In general a person has an insurable interest in the subject matter insured where he has such a relation or

connection with, or concern in such subject matter that he will derive pecuniary benefit or advantage from its preservation, or will suffer pecuniary loss or damage from its destruction, termination or injury by the happening of the event insured against. Great liberality is indulged in determining whether a person has anything at hazard in the subject matter of the insurance, and any interest which would be recognized by a court is an insurable interest.

Two States have held under similar circumstances to those now here that the purchaser in good faith of a car has insurable interest. [In the State of Washington] the court observed:

> The car covered by the policy upon which the action is based was purchased by the respondent in good faith, used by him, the insurance policy issued to him and the premium paid. Even though the automobile may have been originally stolen from the rightful owner, the respondent had the title and the right of possession of it as against all the world, except the rightful owner, assuming that the car had been stolen from him.

The order should be affirmed.

BURKE, Judge (dissenting)

In this action to recover on an insurance policy, the issue presented is whether an innocent purchaser of stolen property has an insurable interest therein under section 148 of the Insurance Law.

The division of authority on this issue is widespread. While some jurisdictions have adopted the position taken by the courts below, others maintain the position that a purchaser of stolen property, having acquired no interest from the seller, has no insurable interest in the property. I am of the opinion that this latter position better represents the legislative intent underlying section 148 of the Insurance Law.

Under section 148, a contract of insurance is unenforceable absent an insurable interest in the person to be benefited. The section then defines an "insurable interest" as "any lawful and substantial economic interest in the safety or preservation of the property from loss, destruction or pecuniary damage." [S]uch interest . . . must be such that the loss or destruction of the property will result in liability or pecuniary damage to the insured. By statutory definition, the potential loss to the insured must be "substantial."

In my opinion, the insured innocent purchaser had no "substantial" economic interest in the stolen car. His monetary investment was lost at the time of purchase; and having purchased the vehicle from one without any interest therein, he acquired only a qualified possessory interest (as against all but the true owner) which was so tenuous that it might have been terminated at any moment by the true owner. As such, the value of the qualified possessory interest was highly speculative, and a loss thereof can hardly be considered "substantial."

Moreover, in thus holding the interest of the innocent purchaser of stolen property to be insurable, the courts are effectively expanding the liability exposure of insurance companies in this State. I submit that such is more properly a legislative function, which could be effected by a simple amendment of section 148 to include within its coverage the nonsubstantial interest of the innocent purchaser of stolen property.

Accordingly, the judgment below should be reversed.

CASE REVIEW QUESTIONS

1. In this case, who transferred an economic risk? To whom was that risk transferred? What transferred risk was the subject of the case?
2. In your own words, why did Judge Bergan and Judge Burke disagree on whether Scarola had an insurable interest in the car he purchased?

When Must the Insurable Interest Exist? The insurable interest required for property insurance need only exist at the time of the loss. The reason for this is the rapidity with which ownership of property may change. Policyholders often acquire insurance before they acquire ownership of the property that is the subject of the insurance. For example, a business may purchase insurance on an incoming shipment of goods before it takes title to or possession of the goods. Consequently, no insurable interest is required at the time the coverage is created. However, no benefits are payable under the policy unless the policyholder has an insurable interest in the property at the time of the loss.

Conversely, the insurable interest requirement for life insurance applies at the inception of the coverage; there need not be an insurable interest at the time of a death claim. One of the main justifications for this difference between life insurance and property insurance is the situation that is often presented when people divorce. Life insurance policies are frequently made payable to a spouse for the benefit of dependent minor children. Imposition of the insurable interest requirement at the time of death in situations in which the parents have divorced after the policy was purchased would undermine the purpose of the insurance and would place a hurdle in the way of protecting the children of divorced parents.

The Indemnity Concept

As discussed earlier, the purpose of an insurance contract is to transfer a risk of economic loss to an insurer. In the contract, the insurer promises to **indem-**

nify (compensate) the person subject to the risk if economic loss indeed occurs as a result of the risk.

Sometimes, however, people try to obtain payments from their insurers that exceed the amount necessary to indemnify them for the actual economic losses they have suffered. If people are successful in obtaining payment that is greater than the loss actually suffered, they and others will be encouraged to create losses. For example, if you know that you can collect $10,000 in insurance if your car that is worth $5,000 is destroyed in an accident, you will be tempted to destroy the car yourself and make it appear as though it were destroyed in an accident. Insurers therefore include provisions in insurance policies that attempt to prevent someone from collecting more than his or her actual economic loss.

Maximum Benefits Payable In property insurance policies, the *maximum benefits payable* for a loss is frequently stated to be the lesser of (1) the actual cash value of the damaged or stolen property or (2) the amount necessary to repair or replace the property. Actual cash value is calculated by first determining what replacing the damaged or stolen property with new property of a like kind and quality would cost and then subtracting the amount by which the actual property had depreciated prior to the loss. This amount is generally less than the cost of repairing or replacing the property. For instance, a house may have an actual cash value of $50,000, but replacing the house might cost $100,000. Thus, settlements of claims based on actual cash value do not encourage policyholders to create or welcome an insured loss. It is possible, however, to purchase property insurance that provides for indemnity on a replacement cost basis.

Coordination of Benefits Insurance contracts frequently contain provisions for the *coordination of benefits* between two or more concurrently valid policies that cover a single loss. A policy having this provision will limit the benefit it pays to a proportion of the total loss determined by dividing that policy's coverage limit for the loss by the sum of the coverage limits of all the valid policies that cover the loss. For instance, suppose that policy A provides up to $100,000 of coverage and policy B provides up to $200,000 of coverage for the same loss. With the coordination of benefits, policy A will pay only one-third of the loss, and policy B will pay two-thirds of the loss.

This type of limitation on benefits prevents the payment of more than full indemnity through the enforcement of more than one policy because the total settlement from all policies will not exceed the loss itself. Thus, the concept of indemnity is preserved by this type of policy provision. Because the concurrent coverage of multiple policies will not result in the overcompensation of losses in most situations, carrying multiple policies on the same property is justified only when insurance companies refuse to write coverage for the full amount of a risk in a single policy.

Subrogation Property and liability insurance policies generally contain a **subrogation** provision stating that if the insurer indemnifies the insured for a loss, the insurer is subrogated to the rights of the insured — that is the insurer stands in the place of the insured — against the party who is liable to the insured for the loss. For instance, suppose that Andretti negligently drives his car into Jackson's house. Since Jackson's damages were caused by Andretti's negligence, Andretti is liable to Jackson for the damages. Jackson, however, submits a claim to his insurance company under the property insurance provisions of his homeowner's policy. When the company pays the claim, it becomes subrogated to any rights that Jackson has against Andretti. Therefore, Andretti is then liable to the insurance company for the loss it incurred in indemnifying Jackson.

Subrogation supports the indemnity concept because it prevents an insured person from collecting for the same loss from both the insurance company and the party who caused the harm. If the insured could collect from both the insurer and the responsible party, he or she would collect an amount greater than the actual economic loss sustained.

In addition, subrogation helps to keep insurance premiums lower because insurance companies can sometimes recover for payments they have made to policyholders. The insured receives timely indemnification, but through subrogation, liability ultimately falls on the person who is legally responsible for the loss.

Indemnification and Life Insurance The preceding discussion of policy provisions that support the concept that the purpose of insurance is to indemnify people for their losses rather than to enrich them in excess of their losses generally applies only to health, property, and liability insurance. With regard to life insurance, the amount of insurance coverage need not relate to the economic worth of the person whose life is insured, a beneficiary may collect on more than one life insurance policy, and the insurance company is not subrogated to the rights of deceased when it pays the death benefits.

Other Insurance Contract Issues

Offer and Acceptance Generally, a person who wishes to purchase insurance submits an application, which is an offer to purchase, to the insurance company, and the company either accepts or rejects the offer by issuing or not issuing the policy. Sometimes, however, the agent of the insurance company selling the policy has the authority to accept the offer for the company by issuing a *binder*. This allows a person to obtain insurance on short notice and without delay. However, when an agent has the authority to issue a binder, the company usually still has the right to refuse to issue the policy. The agent's acceptance provides temporary insurance coverage until the company either issues the policy or notifies the applicant that it will not issue the policy or until a period of time stated in the binder or provided for by law elapses.

Misrepresentation When a person applies for insurance, he or she makes statements in the application that the insurance company considers in deciding whether or not to issue the policy. If the applicant makes a misrepresentation, which is a statement that is false when made or that becomes false to the applicant's knowledge before the policy is issued, and the company relies on the misrepresentation and is influenced by it in its decision to issue the policy — that is, if the misrepresentation is *material* — the company can rescind (avoid) the policy and treat it as void *ab initio* (from the beginning). This means that the company can return any premiums paid by the applicant and refuse to be bound by the policy. However, the insurance company must exercise its right to rescind within a reasonable time after it discovers the applicant's misrepresentation, or it will lose its right to do so.

In some cases, the courts have decided that an insurance company may only rescind an insurance policy if the misrepresentation in the application is related in some way to the loss later suffered by the insured. Suppose, for instance, that an applicant for property insurance covering both fire and theft represents that the insured building is equipped with smoke detectors when in fact it is not. Later, she submits a claim for a theft loss in the building. At that time, the insurance company discovers the misrepresentation about the smoke detectors. Many courts would not allow the company to rescind the contract and avoid indemnifying the insured for the theft loss because of the misrepresentation about the smoke detectors. Some courts, however, would permit the company to rescind. This is the kind of issue with which the court was confronted in the following case.

COUNTRYSIDE CASUALTY COMPANY v. ORR
523 F.2d 870 (Eighth Cir. 1975)

[Johnny Orr applied for an automobile insurance policy from Countryside Casualty Company (Countryside). In the application, Orr was asked whether he had ever been arrested, had ever been convicted of a moving traffic violation, or drank alcoholic beverages. He falsely answered "no" to each of these questions. On the basis of the application, Countryside issued the policy to Orr.

Later, Orr's automobile was involved in an accident with another automobile. One person in the other car was killed and two others were seriously injured. A friend of Orr was driving the car at the time of the accident. However, under the law of the state in which the accident occurred, the owner of a car is liable to anyone who dies or is injured in an accident caused by the negligence of an authorized driver of the car.

Orr notified Countryside of the accident. Upon investigation, Countryside discovered that Orr had made false statements in his policy application. Countryside then brought a legal action against Orr in a federal district court asking that Orr's policy be declared void *ab initio* because of Orr's misrepresentations in his application. The district court judge found that Orr had made material misrepresentations in the application and that Countryside had relied on them. He therefore declared the policy to be void *ab initio* and released Countryside from all obligations under it. Orr appealed. The basis of his appeal is discussed in the circuit court's opinion.]

WEBSTER, Circuit Judge

Orr contends that because he was not driving his car at the time of the accident the company should not be able to avoid liability for the accident. He argues that his misrepresentations bore no causal relation to the loss.

The only Arkansas case holding that a causal connection is necessary between a misrepresentation in an application for insurance and the ultimate loss before the policy can be voided is *National Old Line Insurance Co. v. People.* The court held that where a person had misrepresented the state of his health when applying for a credit life insurance policy upon his own life and later died on account of a cause not related to the misrepresentation, the company was not entitled to void the contract of insurance under [Arkansas Law]. The court said:

> It is our conclusion that, under the Code, the insurer must show a causal relation between the applicant's misrepresentation and the eventual loss.

National Old Line is a life insurance case. We think there are significant differences between life, disability, and accident insurance on the one hand, and property damage and personal injury liability insurance on the other. In the former, the risk is more apt to be measured in terms of physical propensities of the insured. The condition of an insured's legs, for example, may bear very little relationship to the risk of death by heart attack or injury by a falling object. Liability insurance, on the other hand, must take into account the negligence factor. The arrest and driving history of an insurance applicant may have no direct causal relationship to a subsequent injury to another person or his property, but, in actuarial [risk] terms, such prior conduct provides some measurable indication of the likelihood that the applicant will be associated in the future with activity or conduct which will expose the insurer to a greater risk of loss. This is no less true in evaluating the risk that the applicant will be more or less likely to permit negligence-prone friends to use his vehicle.

These differences are sufficient, we think, to warrant the conclusion that the Supreme Court of Arkansas would not extend to liability coverage the causal relationship requirement which it now applies in life insurance and disability cases.

The materiality of the misrepresentation goes to whether or not the insurer, with knowledge of the true facts, would have accepted the risk and issued the policy. In this case both Gary Wike, Underwriting Supervisor for Countryside Casualty Company, and agent Betty Handley Treadway testified that agents for Countryside Casualty do not have authority to accept applications from persons with prior criminal convictions. The finding of the District Court that the insurance company relied upon the misrepresentations and "would not have issued the policy had it known the true facts that existed at the time" is supported by substantial evidence.

Affirmed.

CASE REVIEW QUESTIONS

1. What things did Countryside have to prove in order to be able to rescind the policy?
2. Did the court decide that Countryside did not have to prove a causal relationship between the misrepresentation and the loss or that there was a causal relationship between the misrepresentation and the loss? Explain.

Concealment The case you just read concerned a misrepresentation by an insurance applicant. An insurance company may also rescind an insurance policy if an applicant intentionally *conceals* information that he or she knows or should know would be important to the insurer when it is deciding whether or not to issue the policy. For instance, a person applying for fire insurance on a warehouse has a duty to disclose to the insurer that there will be highly flammable material stored in the warehouse at some future time even if the application does not request such information.

Waiver and Estoppel Sometimes an insurance company is not allowed to rescind a policy on the basis of misrepresentation or concealment because it knew or should have known the true facts despite the lies or omissions of the applicant. Because the insurer knew or should have known the truth, it should not have *relied* on the applicant's lies or omissions. In cases dealing with this issue, some courts say that the insurer has *waived* (given up) its right to rescind whereas other courts say that the insurer is *estopped* (prohibited) from raising the issue of misrepresentation. Either way, the result is that the insurer cannot rescind the policy.

Determining whether an insurer knew or should have known the true facts despite the lies or omissions of the applicant is the difficult issue in these cases. Generally, if the insurer's selling agent knew the truth or if the company could easily have discovered the truth by referring to information it had on file, it may not rescind a policy on the grounds of lies or omissions by the applicant. On the other hand, if the insurer or its agent had only a vague clue that the applicant might be lying, it will not be held to have known the truth. However, if the clues that the applicant was lying were strong enough that a reasonable insurer would have tried to discover the truth and if the truth would have been discovered had it been sought out, the insurer will lose its right to rescind whether or not it actually discovered the truth.

Incontestability Clause Usually, life insurance contracts contain a provision called an **incontestability clause** that prohibits the insurance company from rescinding the policy on the grounds of misrepresentation or concealment after a specified period, often two years, from the date the policy is issued. Even if there is an incontestability clause, however, the company can raise the fact that an insured misrepresented his or her age. If the company is correct, it is allowed to reduce the insurance coverage under the policy to the amount that the premiums called for in the policy would have purchased had the company known the insured's correct age. The insurer may not rescind the policy, however.

Capacity to Contract When the law does not recognize the ability of a person to enter into a contract because the person is mentally incompetent or is a minor—a person under 18 in most states—that person is said to lack the capacity to contract. The general rules concerning capacity to contract, as discussed in Chapter 14, apply to insurance contracts. Most states, however, have adopted statutes that allow minors who have reached a certain age, usually 16, to obtain insurance.

Assignments of Insurance Policies Generally, health, property, and liability insurance policies cannot be assigned without the consent of the insurance company. The courts call these policies *personal contracts,* which means that the insurer's decision to issue them is based, in part, on the character and past behavior of the insured. Therefore, assignment to another person might materially increase the burden and risk of the insurer under the policy. For example, a person who sells a car cannot also sell and assign his or her automobile insurance policy to the purchaser without the consent of the insurance company because the factors considered in issuing the policy to the seller included his or her car-use pattern and driving record.

On the other hand, a life insurance policy can be assigned under some circumstances. While the insured is alive, a life insurance policy *cannot* be assigned if assignment is prohibited by the terms of the policy or if the designation of the beneficiary of the policy is irrevocable, which means that the policyholder does not have the right to change the beneficiary. If the designation of the beneficiary is irrevocable, assignment can only be made with the beneficiary's consent. Aside from these two situations, a policyholder can assign a life insurance policy while the insured is alive. Why such an assignment might be made by a policyholder and what contract rights can be assigned will be discussed later in this chapter.

After the death of the insured, a beneficiary who has not been paid the amount due under the policy becomes a creditor of the insurer. His or her right as a creditor — the right to the payment of money — can be assigned (meaning it can be sold, used as security for a loan, or given away) regardless of whether assignment is prohibited by the terms of the policy.

Duties of the Parties In an insurance contract, the primary duty of the insurer is to fully pay valid policy claims that are submitted to it. As noted earlier, state regulations of insurance companies provide for a maximum time within which claims must be paid. Failure to meet this requirement for timely payment can result in penalties to the insurer.

Conversely, people who make claims under an insurance policy have a duty to submit their claims promptly. This requirement helps to protect the insurer from having to pay invalid claims, because, the sooner a claim is submitted, the more likely it is that the insurer will be able to find evidence that will allow it to determine whether or not the claim is valid. The courts generally uphold policy provisions that require the submission of a claim within a specified amount of time as long as the period specified is reasonable.

Suppose, for instance, that the life insurance company that insures Mr. Smith's life is not required to pay under the terms of the policy if he commits suicide. Mr. Smith dies under circumstances that indicate he may have committed suicide. Mrs. Smith, the beneficiary named in the policy, does not submit a claim for 18 months, a period longer than that allowed in the policy for the submission of a claim. Because so much time has passed, it will be extremely difficult for the insurance company to determine whether Mr. Smith did or did not commit suicide. Thus, the insurer will probably be discharged from having to pay the claim because of Mrs. Smith's delay in submitting her claim.

Under a liability insurance contract, the insured has a duty to aid and cooperate with the insurer to a reasonable extent in defending against a legal claim brought by a third party that alleges the insured's liability. Similarly, when an insurer is subrogated to a claim of a policyholder, as discussed earlier, the insured has a duty to aid and cooperate with the insurer to a reasonable extent in the insurer's pursuit of that claim. The insured's breach of his or her duty to aid and cooperate with the insurer in legal proceedings such as these can result in the discharge of the insurer's duty to pay a claim under the policy.

You should recall that the policyholder does *not* promise to pay premiums in an insurance contract, so he or she has no legal duty to pay the premiums.

Policy Interpretation Generally, insurance policies are complicated printed documents that have been standardized as mandated or approved by the state insurance commissioner's office. An applicant for a policy may select such things as the kind of insurance and the amount of coverage, but he or she cannot otherwise negotiate or alter the provisions of a policy. Contracts such as this, in which one party's only options are either to accept the terms of the other party or not to contract, are called **contracts of adhesion.**

The courts interpret contracts of adhesion in the manner that is most beneficial to the party who did not write the contract, which in the case of an insurance contract, is the insured. It therefore behooves insurance companies to write policies in a clear manner so that they cannot be interpreted in more than one way.

LIFE INSURANCE

A life insurance policy usually provides that, as long as the premiums called for in the policy are paid, the insurer will pay a specified sum of money, called the **face value** of the policy, to the beneficiary designated in the policy when the person whose life is insured dies. Payment of the face value is made by the insured in a lump sum or in periodic payments, as provided for either by the terms of the policy or, if no provision is included in the policy, as desired by the beneficiary.

Types of Life Insurance Policies

Life insurance policies are categorized according to the period of time that the insurance remains in effect. The three basic types of life insurance are whole-life insurance, term life insurance, and endowment insurance.

Whole-Life Insurance Whole-life insurance remains in effect for the entire life of the insured, provided that the required premiums are paid. With an *ordinary whole-life* policy, premiums must be paid for the entire life of the insured. With a *limited payment whole-life* policy, however, premiums must be paid only for a specified period. A person may choose a limited payment policy in order to avoid having to pay premiums when he or she is elderly and less able to afford the payments.

Term Life Insurance Term life insurance remains in effect only for the period of time specified in the policy, provided that the required premiums are paid during the term of the policy. Term insurance is less expensive than whole-life because the company has to pay the face value on the policy only if the insured dies during the term of the policy and because term insurance is generally not available to anyone older than 70. Also, as will be explained later, a term life policy does not usually have any cash surrender value. A common provision found in term policies allows the policy to be renewed for an additional term at the option of the policyholder, regardless of the insured's health.

Endowment Insurance Endowment insurance remains in effect for the period of time, called the *endowment period,* specified in the policy or until the death of the insured, whichever occurs first. If the insured's death occurs first, the face value of the policy is paid to the designated beneficiary. If the insured survives the endowment period, payment of the face value is made to the policyholder. Endowment insurance is more expensive than either whole-life insurance or term insurance.

Cash Surrender Value

For most life insurance policies, each premium payment is the same amount throughout the period that premiums are to be paid. For instance, all the premiums for a limited payment whole-life policy might be $500 per year until the insured reaches age 65.

For a term life policy, the premium is calculated in such a way that the insured pays only for insurance protection. For whole-life and endowment policies, on the other hand, the premium is calculated in such a way that it exceeds the costs and risks of the policy to the insurer in the early years of the policy by an amount called the **cash surrender value** of the policy. Thus, each premium is partly a payment for insurance protection and partly a contribution to the cash surrender value of the policy.

Policyholder's Rights A policyholder may terminate a life insurance policy and stop paying the premiums called for in it at any time. If a policy is terminated, the insurer must either pay the cash surrender value to the policyholder or provide continued insurance coverage by using the cash surrender value as the source of future premium payments.

An insurer is required to make the cash surrender value available to the policyholder in the form of policy loans at a rate of interest provided in the policy. The policyholder need not repay the loan but may if he or she desires. If repayment is not made, the amount of the loan and any interest due will be deducted from the face value before payment of a death claim or from the cash surrender value if the policy is terminated. If the total amount of the loan plus the interest due is greater than the cash surrender value at any time, the policy automatically terminates.

The cash surrender value can also be used to pay premiums as they come due. Prolonged payment of premiums from the cash surrender value, however, will gradually reduce the death benefit protection because the advances from the cash surrender value and the interest due on them will be deducted from the face value of the policy before payment of a death claim. In time, the cash surrender value will be exhausted, and the policy will terminate.

Although life insurance companies are required to make loans on policies that have a cash value, they have been given some protection from the possibility of a runaway demand for policy loans. Life insurers are permitted to wait up to six months before honoring a policy loan request. This waiting period protects the insurer from the severe financial losses that could occur if a widespread demand for policy loans forced the insurer to liquidate its investments in order to make the requested loans. Insurance companies are extremely reluctant to delay granting policy loans, however, because policyholders might interpret the delays as a sign of financial difficulty. Indeed, a belief among policyholders that a life insurance company is having financial difficulty might trigger a widespread demand for policy loans.

Assignments of Life Insurance Earlier in this chapter, you read about assignments of insurance policies. You learned that a person who owns a life insurance policy frequently has the right to assign it. When someone wants to borrow money or receive credit, it is helpful if that person can provide security for the loan or the credit. One way for a debtor to provide security is to assign a life insurance policy to the creditor. If the debtor pays his or her debt, the creditor then reassigns the policy to the debtor. On the other hand, if the debtor fails to pay the debt, the creditor can obtain payment from either the cash surrender value or the face amount of the policy.

HEALTH INSURANCE

A health insurance policy usually provides that, as long as the premiums called for in the policy are paid, the insurer will indemnify the insured to the extent of the monetary limits of the policy for losses resulting from injury or illness. Although the details of health insurance policies vary greatly, the two basic types of loss that may be covered by health insurance are loss of income because the insured is unable to work and loss due to medical expenses.

Generally, health insurance excludes losses resulting from injuries sustained or illnesses contracted prior to the time the insurance takes effect and from injuries that are self-inflicted. Also, coverage is usually excluded if the insured is indemnified by worker's compensation insurance. Coordination of benefits, discussed earlier, also applies to health insurance.

Most employers are required to provide workers' compensation insurance for their employees. This kind of insurance provides compensation to employees for injuries that result from work-related accidents. Compensation is awarded regardless of whether the employee was in any way responsible for his or her own injuries. Indeed, workers' compensation is awarded for work-related injuries even if the employee deliberately causes his or her own injury.

In a *group* health insurance policy, which is provided by many companies, the organization to which the members of the group belong contracts with the insurance company, and the members of the group are covered by the policy without regard to the health of any individual member. On the other hand, a person who applies for *individual* health insurance must provide evidence concerning his or her health, and the insurer may decline to issue the insurance based on that evidence.

When a company has a group policy, it usually gives the employees written information about the policy. In the case that follows, the information given to an employee by an employer was incorrect. The court had to decide whether the insurer was subject to the terms of the policy with the employer or subject to the terms of the written document given to the employee by the employer.

MORRISON ASSURANCE COMPANY, INC. v. ARMSTRONG
264 S.E.2d 320 (Ga. 1980)

[Armstrong was injured during the course of her employment. She was entitled to recover payment under her employer's workers' compensation insurance. She also believed that she was entitled to recover under a group health insurance plan that her employer had contracted for with Morrison Assurance Company, Inc. (Morrison). To participate in the group policy, Armstrong had to make payments to her employer, which she did. She was given a certificate stating that she was covered by her employer's group policy and summarizing the terms of the policy. The summary of the policy terms provided that Armstrong could not recover for injuries incurred while working for an employer "other than the group policyholder" (Armstrong's employer) if the injuries were covered by workers' compensation. Since she had not been injured while working for an employer other than the group policyholder, she believed she was entitled to benefits under the group health policy.

When Armstrong submitted her claim to Morrison, it denied liability. Morrison pointed out that the master group policy — the contract between Armstrong's employer and Morrison — stated that an employee could not recover for injuries incurred while working for "an employer" if the injuries were covered by workers' compensation. In other words, the phrase "other than the group policyholder" that was included in the certificate that had been given to Armstrong did not appear

in the master group policy. Since she had been injured while working for an employer and since she had received workers' compensation, Morrison believed that Armstrong was not entitled to benefits under the group health policy.

Armstrong brought a legal action against Morrison to collect under the group policy. The trial court found for Armstrong, and Morrison appealed.]

CARLEY, Judge

The law is very clear that "[a] contract of group insurance is made up of the master group policy and the certificate, which must be construed together. The certificate holder is bound by the provisions of the group policy, the certificate being evidence of the coverage thereunder." [Citation omitted.] The reasoning behind this is that the contracting parties in group insurance are primarily the employer and the insurer.

Because of the long line of decisions upholding provisions of the master policy over conflicting terms of the certificate upon which the group insured has relied, we must reverse [the trial court's decision], albeit reluctantly. Justice is not well served by this rule of law. To insist, after a person has paid to secure benefits from an insurance company, that the document upon which she relied, and the only one in her possession, was merely "an instrument which contained a reference to another instrument in which were embodied the limitations'' [citation omitted] of her actual coverage is unreasonable. This rule applicable to group policy situations is inconsistent with the established general principle that insurance contracts are always to be construed in favor of the insured and against the insurer, particularly where exclusions are in issue. Certainly it violates the spirit of the trend toward consumer protection now recognized in all areas of the law. We

conclude that this court is powerless to provide the remedy. However, if this is a harsh rule, and if it does not have the approval of the people of the State, there is a definite way, a plain way, and a legal way, whereby it may be changed. A very simple and brief enactment of the legislature is all that is required.

Judgment reversed.

CASE REVIEW QUESTIONS
1. Explain in your own words why the court decided the case as it did.
2. Although it is not mentioned by the court, how does the indemnity concept discussed earlier in the chapter support the court's decision?
3. The court says that it is bound by ''the long line of decisions upholding provisions of the master policy over conflicting terms of the certificate upon which the group insured has relied.'' Suppose that the certificate given to Armstrong had been prepared by Morrison. Would you think that Morrison had *relied* on the ''long line of decisions'' referred to by the court in carelessly preparing a certificate that misrepresented the true terms of the policy? If not, would you think that Morrison's lack of reliance on those decisions should allow the court to overrule them rather than be bound by them? Explain.

PROPERTY INSURANCE

A property insurance policy provides that, as long as the premiums called for in the policy are paid, the insurer will indemnify the insured to the extent of the monetary limits of the policy for damage to specified property resulting from certain causes. In insurance terminology, those things that cause damage to property, like fire, flood, and theft, are called *perils*. In all-perils or all-risk contracts, the insured is indemnified for damage caused by any peril that is not expressly excluded from the policy. In a specified-perils contract, the insured is only indemnified for damage caused by those perils expressly specified in the policy.

It is very common for property insurance to include a *deductible* provision that states an amount of damage for which the insurer does not have to indemnify the insured, which means that damage up to that amount must be absorbed by the insured. For instance, if Andretti has property insurance on his car, which is called *collision insurance,* with a $100 deductible provision and if the car sustains $1,000 in damages, the insurer must indemnify Andretti for $900 of the damages and Andretti himself must absorb the remaining $100 of the damages.

Examples of property insurance include collision insurance on automobiles, fire insurance on buildings and their contents, crime insurance for losses caused by such things as burglary, and business interruption insurance for losses that occur when a business cannot continue to operate because of the occurrence of a covered peril such as vandalism or fire. Under all types of property insurance, however, the insurer need not indemnify the insured if the damage to the property is intentionally caused by the insured. For instance, a merchant who intentionally burns down his or her own store would not be indemnified under a fire insurance or a business interruption policy.

Co-Insurance

It is common for property insurance contracts to include **co-insurance** provisions, the purpose of which is to discourage people from insuring their property for less than its full value. Some people prefer to underinsure their property because it costs less than insuring their property for its full value, and the chance of partial destruction of the property is much greater than the chance of its full destruction.

For instance, suppose that Hubbard owns a building worth $200,000. To insure it for its full value for one year would require her to pay a premium of $500. If she believes that any claim she might make under the policy is not likely to exceed $100,000, she might decide to insure the building for only $100,000 so that she would only have to pay a premium of $250.

A co-insurance provision discourages people like Hubbard from underinsuring their property by penalizing them when they make a claim. It does this by reducing the indemnification to less than the full amount of the loss when the amount of insurance carried on the property is less than a specified percentage of the property's full value. In other words, maintaining coverage at an inadequate level will result in less than full indemnity for losses.

When the specified percentage of coverage is not maintained, the proportion of a loss that can be recovered is determined by multiplying the amount of the loss by the fraction that results when the total amount of insurance carried is divided by the proportion of the full value of the property that the policy specifies must be carried. For example, the recovery for $60,000 in damages to a building with a full value of $200,000 under a $120,000 policy with an 80 percent co-insurance clause would be $45,000.

$$\frac{\$120,000}{\$200,000 \times 0.80} \times \$60,000 = \$45,000$$

A property insurance policy will not pay more than the policy limits for a single loss. Thus, a total loss could result in partial recovery even when the co-insurance requirement is satisfied if the policy limit is less than the amount of the loss. The only way to assure full indemnity for total losses is to carry insurance for 100 percent of the property value.

LIABILITY INSURANCE

A liability insurance policy provides that, as long as the premiums called for in the policy are paid, the insurer will protect the insured from liability to third persons to the extent of the monetary limits of the policy. The insured is also protected from having to pay the costs of defending a lawsuit that is brought to establish his or her liability.

For example, suppose that Andretti, who has a $100,000 automobile liability insurance policy, causes an accident in which Allison is injured. If it is determined that Andretti was negligent and is therefore liable to Allison for his injuries, the insurance company will pay Allison the amount of his damages up to $100,000. If a lawsuit is required to establish Andretti's liability, the insurer will also pay the cost of Andretti's defense.

Types of Liability and Liability Insurance

Liability insurance generally protects the insured from tort liability to a third person. A tort is committed when one person breaches a noncontractual duty owed to another and the breach causes injury to the person or to the property of the person to whom the duty is owed (see Chapter 5). A person who commits a tort is called a *tortfeasor*. You should note that liability insurance does *not* protect a person from liability caused by poor business judgment or breach of contract.

Common situations in which a person is liable for a tort include the following:

1. When the person is the tortfeasor.
2. When the person is the employer of a tortfeasor who committed the tort in the course of his or her employment (see pages 695–704).
3. When the person is the manufacturer of a product that has caused injury to a consumer (see pages 105–131).
4. When the person is the owner of property on which the injury to the third person occurred.

Liability insurance can be purchased to cover each of these situations.

For instance, automobile insurance covers liability arising from the ownership, maintenance, or use of the insured automobile. In addition, it covers any person who is insured under the policy when he or she is driving an automobile owned by someone else. Another common form of liability coverage is found in a homeowner's policy. It covers liability arising from the use, occupancy, or maintenance of the insured premises. Professional malpractice insurance, which protects such people as doctors, lawyers, and accountants from liability based on their negligence, is still another form of liability insurance.

Generally, a liability insurance policy excludes coverage for intentional torts, such as assault (threatening harmful or offensive conduct) and battery (touching someone without his or her consent). If this were not so, people might feel free to cause personal injury or property damage to others intentionally because they would be protected by insurance from the liability that would arise. In the case that follows, for instance, the court determined that liability for assault and battery was not covered by a homeowner's liability policy.

HARTFORD FIRE INSURANCE CO. v. SPREEN
343 So.2d 649 (Fla. 1977)

[Donald Spreen was a guest at a party. Another guest, William King, made certain crude remarks about Spreen's wife that Spreen found to be insulting. Spreen walked over to where King was standing and swung his right fist at King, striking him in the left eye and causing a fracture of the orbital floor of the eye. King had two eye operations and suffered loss of vision and other problems with the eye. Spreen later said that he had intended to strike King but had not intended to damage King's face or eye.

King sued Spreen, basing his action on assault and battery. Spreen answered King's complaint and denied liability. He also filed a legal claim against two insurance companies with whom he had policies, arguing that if he were liable to King, the insurance companies had the duty to indemnify him under the policies. The two companies—Hartford Fire Insurance Company (Hartford) and St. Paul Fire and Marine Insurance Company (St. Paul)—denied liability on the grounds that liability for assault and battery was not covered by their respective policies. The trial court held for Spreen against the two insurance companies, and the companies appealed.]

HUBBART, Judge

The Hartford policy in this case is a homeowner's liability policy which covers the insured's legal obligation to pay damages for bodily injury and property damage caused by an "occurrence." The policy defines "occurrence" as an "accident"; it also excludes from coverage "bodily injury and property damage which is

either expected or intended from the standpoint of the insured. . . ."

As to this policy, the issue presented for review is whether bodily injury inflicted by the insured in an assault and battery is covered by a homeowner's liability policy which insures against damages caused by an "accident" and which specifically excludes damages which are "either expected or intended from the standpoint of the insured." We conclude that the assault and battery incident herein is not covered by the Hartford policy.

The Florida courts have consistently held that insurance policies covering liability for an "accident" apply to any bodily injury or property damage inflicted by the insured on a third party where the insured does not intend to cause any harm to the third party; this result obtains even though damages are caused by the insured's intentional acts and were reasonably foreseeable by the insured. Insurance coverage has accordingly been found under such policies where an insured unintentionally shoots himself while playing "Russian Roulette," or unintentionally shoots himself while attempting to disarm a person in a fight in which the insured is the aggressor, or unintentionally hits a person in a crowd of people with a car while slowly driving into the edge of the crowd intending to disperse them, or unintentionally injures a person in a car while intentionally pushing the car which was blocking a driveway. Running through all of these cases is an act of negligence by the insured, sometimes gross or even culpable negligence. But never has coverage been found under such policies where the insured's act was deliberately designed to cause harm to the injured party.

Indeed the law is well-settled that there can be no coverage under an insurance policy which insures against an "accident" where

the [insured's] wrongful act complained of is intentionally directed specifically toward the person injured by such act. [Citation omitted.] Early on it became the overwhelming consensus in those cases that since such a policy was in essence an indemnification contract public policy mandated that an intentional tort was not an "accident" within the coverage for the reason that one ought not to be permitted to indemnify himself against his intentional [torts]. [Citation omitted.]

Accordingly, an assault and battery committed by the insured has been held to be an intentional tort which is not covered by insurance policies which insure against an "accident."

In the instant case, the insured Donald Spreen committed an assault and battery upon William King. He reacted to deliberately hit King for a crude and insulting remark about his wife. In no sense, can this assault and battery be considered an "accident" which is covered under the Hartford policy.

[It is argued] that while Spreen intended to hit King he did so on the spur of the moment, did not foresee the extent of King's injuries, and therefore did not intend them. The argument is unpersuasive. Foreseeability is irrelevant to the coverage issue. The sole issue is whether Spreen intended to inflict any harm on King. This he clearly intended to do and the fact that he did not foresee or intend the extent of the harm inflicted does not convert the admitted assault and battery into an accident.

We are further supported in our conclusion by the specific exclusion from coverage under the Hartford policy for any damages "which are either expected or intended from a standpoint of the insured." "The courts have generally held that injury or damage is 'caused intentionally' within the meaning of an 'intentional injury exclusion clause' if the insured has acted with the specific intent to cause harm to a third party. . . ." [Citation omitted.] Spreen clearly acted to cause harm to King which thereby defeats coverage under the intentional injury exclusion clause.

We therefore hold that an injury caused by the insured in an intentional assault and battery is not covered under the Hartford homeowner's liability policy which provides coverage for damages caused by an "accident" and excludes from coverage damages "which are either expected or intended from the standpoint of the insured."

The St. Paul policy covers the insured's legal obligation to pay damages for "personal injuries." "Personal injuries" are defined as including but not limited to "bodily injury" as well as a number of intentional torts which do not include assault and battery.

As to this policy, the issue presented for review is whether bodily injury inflicted by the insured in an assault and battery is covered by a policy which insures against "personal injuries," or "bodily injury" but does not specifically mention the tort of assault and battery. We conclude that the assault and battery in the instant case is covered by the St. Paul policy and affirm.

Unlike Hartford, the St. Paul policy is not limited to coverage for damages arising from an "accident." It broadly covers damages which the insured is liable to pay on account of "personal injuries," or "bodily injury." There is no limitation in the coverage section of the policy which refers to an "accident." Nor is there a specific exclusion in the policy for damages which are intentionally caused by the insured.

The law is well-settled that "[a] contract of insurance, prepared and phrased by the insurer is to be construed liberally in favor of the insured and strictly against the insurer, where the meaning of the language is doubtful, uncertain or ambiguous." [Citation omitted.] In view of this canon of construction, we think the coverage of the St. Paul policy for "personal injuries" defined inter alia [among other things] as a "bodily injury" is broad enough to cover damages caused by an intentional assault and battery.

We, therefore, hold that an injury caused by the insured in an intentional assault and battery is covered under the St. Paul policy which provides coverage for damages legally incurred by the insured on account of "personal injuries" or "bodily injury."

Affirmed in part; reversed in part.

CASE REVIEW QUESTIONS

1. Explain in your own words why Spreen's claim was covered by the St. Paul liability insurance policy but not by the Hartford insurance policy.
2. If Spreen's claim had been covered by both policies, would King have been able to collect an amount greater than his damages by collecting from both companies? Explain.
3. If your answer to Question 2 was no, how would the liability for King's damages have been divided between Hartford and St. Paul if Spreen's claim had been covered by both policies?

No-Fault Insurance

Until recently, liability for an automobile accident in all states was determined by who was at fault, which was the party involved in the accident who was negligent. Suppose, for instance, that cars driven by Allen and Burns collide. If the accident was caused by Allen's negligence, Allen would be liable to Burns for Burns' damage. Burns' claim against Allen would be paid by Allen's insurer under the liability insurance coverage in Allen's automobile policy. Allen's damages would be paid by Allen's insurer under the property insurance coverage (collision insurance) in the same policy.

Today, about half the states have adopted some form of no-fault automobile insurance that changes the traditional method of determining liability in automobile accident cases. Under a no-fault system, liability is not based on fault. Instead, each party collects damages from his or her own insurer. In the example in the previous paragraph, for instance, both Allen and Burns would recover for their damages from their respective insurance companies, and Burns would probably not be able to sue Allen for damages.

The states that have changed from a fault to a no-fault system of insurance coverage for auto accidents have done so in order to make sure that all accident victims are compensated for their injuries and that they are compensated quickly. Under a fault system, only those victims who can prove that the other party was at fault will be compensated by the negligent person's liability insurer; the determination of fault and, therefore, the receipt of payment may take a number of years. It is hoped that the no-fault system of compensation will be simpler and more efficient than the fault system. If this is so, the expenses of insurers should be reduced, which should ultimately result in lower automobile insurance premiums.

REVIEW QUESTIONS

1. Why is insurance generally regulated by the state governments rather than by the federal government?

2. In what ways do the states regulate insurance?

3. Under what circumstances does a person have an insurable interest?

4. What provisions do insurance companies include in their policies in order to limit the recovery of insureds to indemnification of losses? Explain each of these provisions.

5. Under what circumstances may an insurer not be able to rescind a policy even though there has been a material misrepresentation in the application that the insurer relied on in issuing the policy?

6. What is the cash surrender value of a life insurance policy and what rights does a policyholder have in the cash surrender value?

7. What does a co-insurance clause in an insurance policy provide?

CASE PROBLEMS

1. Jack Secor was hired as general manager of Pioneer Foundry Company (Pioneer) in 1974. In March 1980, Pioneer applied for a whole-life insurance policy with a face value of $50,000 on the life of Secor. Under the terms of the policy, Pioneer was the policyholder and the beneficiary. Because of Secor's poor medical history, the annual premium was $5,625. Pioneer made the first premium payment when it purchased the policy and continued to pay the annual premium each March thereafter. When Secor quit his job with Pioneer in July 1983, Pioneer had paid $22,500 in premiums on the policy. When the March 1984, payment became due, Pioneer paid it. Secor died the next month. May the insurance company refuse to pay the death benefit to Pioneer on the grounds that Pioneer did not have an insurable interest in Secor? Explain.

2. Baum and Cook discussed the possibility of going into the advertising business together and incorporating under the name Media Sales, Inc. (Media). Cook had experience in advertising and Baum had funds to invest. After advancing some money to Cook so that the desirability of starting the business could be investigated further, Baum purchased insurance on Cook's life from New York Life Insurance Company (New York Life). Because Baum sold insurance for New York Life and the company did not allow its agents to be named as beneficiaries in the policies it issued, Media was designated beneficiary of the policy even though it did not yet exist. Unknown to Baum, Cook went into business with Cutler and they formed a corporation called Media Sales, Inc. Shortly thereafter, Cook died. Both Baum and Media claimed the

death benefit under the New York Life policy. Are either of them correct? Explain.

3. John and Fredericke Kludt, husband and wife, jointly owned their house. John purchased fire insurance on the house from German Mutual Fire Insurance Company (German). After he had purchased the policy, all of John's ownership interest in the house was transferred to Fredericke so that she was the sole owner. John and Fredericke continued to reside together in the house as husband and wife. When the house was destroyed by fire, John submitted a claim. On what grounds might German argue that it does not have to indemnify John for the loss of the house? Is German correct? Explain.

4. Urban Offices, Inc. (Urban) owns a 40-story building in San Francisco. Its property insurance policy contains an 80 percent co-insurance clause. The value of the building is $4 million. The amount of coverage provided by its property insurance policy is only $3 million, however. If an earthquake hits San Francisco and Urban's building is totally destroyed, how much will Urban be entitled to under its property insurance policy? Explain.

5. Schlusberg, an agent for Slocum Insurance Company (Slocum), took an application from Andretti for an automobile insurance policy. Andretti made no misrepresentations in the application and the information he gave included the fact that he had been involved in several serious car accidents. Schlusberg, who did not read the application, issued a binder to Andretti and told him that it would cover him until Slocum issued a policy. Schlusberg then mailed the application to Slocum,

which decided on the basis of the application not to issue the policy. However, the day before that decision was made, Andretti had an accident. Must Slocum indemnify Andretti for damages caused by the accident? Explain.

6. In 1981, Mattson's automobile liability policy was cancelled by State Farm Insurance Company (State Farm). Mattson applied for a new policy from Government Employees Insurance Company (GEICO). On GEICO's application, Mattson answered "no" to a question that asked whether any other insurance company had ever cancelled a policy belonging to him. GEICO issued a policy to Mattson. When Mattson made a claim under the policy in 1984, GEICO discovered the untrue statement in the application. It then returned the premiums that Mattson had paid and refused to pay the claim. Mattson sued GEICO to collect payment under the policy. GEICO defended on the grounds that it had the right to rescind the policy because of Mattson's misrepresentation. At the trial, an officer of State Farm testified that Mattson's policy with them had been cancelled for "general insurance reasons" but did not give any further explanation for the cancellation. On what grounds might Mattson argue that GEICO was not entitled to rescind the policy? Who will win the case? Explain.

7. Helen Marlowe discussed the possibility of purchasing hospital insurance with John Rouse, an agent of Reserve Life Insurance Company (Reserve). She told Rouse that she doubted she would qualify because she had been turned down by several other companies due to her very poor health. Rouse, however, said he would take her application. The application was filled out by Rouse, who asked Marlowe the questions in the application. When he asked her medical history, she said she could not remember it all and referred him to a doctor who knew her full medical history. When the application was completed, Rouse told Marlowe to sign it. Rouse never included Marlowe's medical history in the application. When Marlowe

received a policy from Reserve in the mail, she did not read it. Marlowe later submitted a claim for benefits under the policy, but Reserve refused to pay it. If Marlowe sues Reserve to collect her claim, on what grounds may Reserve defend? Who will win the case? Explain.

8. Nelson had an automobile accident in which the driver of the other car was negligent and Nelson was not. It turned out that the driver of the other car was Nelson's best friend, Jennings. Nelson told Jennings that he was not interested in holding him liable for the damages. To prove his friendship, Nelson signed a document releasing Jennings from any liability because of the accident. This release is legally binding. Nelson then submitted a claim to his own insurance company to collect for the damage done to his car. Jennings submitted a claim to his insurance company to collect for his liability to Nelson as a result of the accident. Are either Nelson or Jennings entitled to the payment of their respective claims? Explain.

9. Kenneth Poos works for Wild Animal Survival Center, Inc. (WASC), a not-for-profit corporation devoted to the preservation of wild animals. Poos' primary job is to present educational programs on behalf of WASC. As part of his job, he is required to care for Sophie, a wolf that is owned by WASC. Poos takes care of Sophie at his rural home. One day when Poos was not home, he left Sophie chained to a fence post inside his fence-enclosed yard. A child climbed into the yard and was bitten by the wolf. Poos notified North River Insurance Company (North River) of his possible liability. North River told Poos that liability for the wolf bite would not be covered by his policy because it excludes liability for injuries arising out of the insured's "business pursuits." However, the policy does include coverage for liability for injuries arising out of business pursuits that are "ordinarily incident to non-business pursuits." What arguments can North River and Poos make concerning whether Poos' liability for the wolf bite is covered by the policy?

51

SECURITIES REGULATION

Federal regulation of transactions in securities, such as stocks and bonds, began as a result of the stock market crash of 1929. Congress first enacted the Securities Act of 1933 (the 1933 Act), and in the following year, it enacted the Securities Exchange Act of 1934 (the 1934 Act). The objectives of these two laws are (1) to see to it that accurate and timely information is available to those who invest in securities and (2) to prevent deceptive and fraudulent practices by those engaged in securities transactions.

The 1934 Act created an administrative agency call the **Securities and Exchange Commission** (SEC) to administer the securities laws. The SEC has the authority to issue rules that carry out the objectives of the acts, to investigate complaints of alleged violations of those rules, and to prosecute those who violate the rules. The agency is headed by five commissioners who are nominated by the president and confirmed by the Senate for five-year terms. No more than three commissioners may belong to the same political party. The SEC has long enjoyed a good reputation for expertise, integrity, and political independence.

In this chapter, you will learn about various types of securities transactions and activities—issuance, insider trading, fraudulent disclosure, proxy solicitation, and tender offers—and the way in which they are regulated by the SEC. You will also learn about the ways in which the states regulate transactions in securities. We turn first, however, to the most basic question of securities regulation: What is a security?

WHAT IS A SECURITY?

The Securities Act of 1933, the Securities Exchange Act of 1934, and the SEC deal only with transactions and activities that involve securities. Stocks and bonds are examples of securities that you are probably familiar with. However, the legal definition of a security goes far beyond these common examples. According to §2(1) of the 1933 Act, a **security** is:

> Any note, stock, treasury stock, bond, debenture, evidence of indebtedness, certificate of interest or participation in any profit-sharing agreement, . . . investment contract, . . . voting trust certificate, . . . certificate of deposit for security, fractional undivided interest in oil, gas, or other mineral rights, or, in general any interest or instrument commonly known as a "security."

The 1934 Act's definition of a security is quite similar.

As you can see, the term *security* as it is used in securities regulation covers not only the common forms of securities but also many other forms of investment. Furthermore, in *SEC v. W.J. Howey Co.,* the Supreme Court said that the term *investment contract* in §2(1) includes any contract that "involves an investment of money in a common enterprise with profits to come solely from the efforts of others." This definition of an investment contract has resulted in many transactions that do not appear to involve securities being included under §2(1). For instance, in the *Howey* case, buyers purchased land on which orange trees were planted and the seller was required to cultivate, harvest, and market the orange crop. The contract involved was determined to be an investment contract and therefore a security. In the case that follows, the court had to decide whether a particular kind of contract was an investment contract under the Supreme Court's definition in the *Howey* case.

SEC v. GLENN W. TURNER ENTERPRISES, INC.
474 F.2d 476 (Ninth Cir. 1973)

[Dare To Be Great, Inc. (Dare), a wholly owned subsidiary of Glenn W. Turner Enterprises, Inc. (Turner), sells five courses of instruction ostensibly aimed at improving self-motivation and sales ability. The courses, which are called Adventures I, II, III, and IV and the $1,000 Plan, involve two elements. First, a person who purchases a course receives audio tapes and other materials and may attend seminars. Second, a purchaser of Adventure III or IV or the $1,000 Plan may sell the courses to others and receive a commission for the sales. The second element is more significant than the first.

The Securities and Exchange Commission brought a legal action against Turner seeking to have the court enjoin (stop) Turner from selling Adventures III and IV and the $1,000 Plan on the grounds that they were securities that had not been registered with the SEC as required by law. Turner defended on the grounds that the courses in question were not securities. The trial court found for the SEC, and Turner appealed.]

DUNIWAY, Circuit Judge
The trial court's findings, which are fully supported by the record, demonstrate that defendants' scheme is

a gigantic and successful fraud. The question presented is whether the "Adventures" or "Plan" enjoined are "securities" within the meaning of the federal securities laws.

It is apparent from the record that what is sold is not of the usual "business motivation" type of courses. Rather, the purchaser is really buying the possibility of deriving money from the sale of the plans by Dare to individuals whom the purchaser has brought to Dare. The promotional aspects of the plan, such as seminars, films, and records, are aimed at interesting others in the Plans. Their value for any other purpose is, to put it mildly, minimal.

Once an individual has purchased a Plan, he turns his efforts toward bringing others into the organization, for which he will receive a part of what they pay. His task is to bring prospective purchasers to "Adventure Meetings."

These meetings are like an old time revival meeting, but directed toward the joys of making easy money rather than salvation. Their purpose is to convince prospective purchasers, or "prospects," that Dare is a sure route to great riches. At the meetings are employees, officers, and speakers from Dare, as well as purchasers (now "salesmen") and their prospects. The Dare people, not the purchaser – "salesmen," run the meetings and do the selling. They exude great enthusiasm, cheering and chanting; there is exuberant handshaking, standing on chairs, shouting, and "money-humming." The Dare people dress in expensive, modern clothes; they display large sums of cash, flaunting it to those present, and even at times throwing it about; they drive new and expensive automobiles, which are conspicuously parked in large numbers outside the meeting place. Dare speakers describe, usually in a frenzied manner, the wealth that awaits the prospects if they will purchase one of the plans. Films are shown, usually involving the "rags-to-riches" story of Dare founder Glenn W. Turner. The goal of all of this is to persuade the prospect to purchase a plan, especially Adventure IV, so that he may become a "salesman," and thus grow wealthy as part of the Dare organization. It is intimated that as Glenn W. Turner Enterprises, Inc. expands, high positions in the organization, as well as lucrative opportunities to purchase stock, will be available. After the meeting, pressure is applied to the prospect by Dare people, in an effort to induce him to purchase one of the Adventures or the Plan.

In a scheme such as this, the possibility that a market will become "saturated" is a real one. Saturation has in fact occurred in some markets, but this is not mentioned at the meetings. Few, if any, purchasers of these plans have achieved any success remotely approaching that described by defendants and their agents.

The district [trial] court held that Adventures III and IV and the $1,000 Plan were securities under the Securities Act of 1933, and the Securities Exchange Act of 1934. The definitions of security that are found in each Act are almost identical. Both definitions include the terms "investment contract," "certificate of interest or participation in any profit-sharing agreement," and any "instrument commonly known as a 'security.'" The district court held that the plans in question fell into all three categories of securities. Because we find them to be investment contracts, we need not decide whether the other definitions are applicable as well.

The 1933 and 1934 Acts are remedial legislation, among the central purposes of which is full and fair disclosure relative to the issuance of securities. The Acts were designed to protect the American public from speculative or fraudulent schemes of promoters. For that reason Congress defined the term "security" broadly, and the Supreme Court in turn has construed the definition liberally. In *SEC v. W.J. Howey Co.*, the Court stated that the definition of a security "embodies a flexible rather than a static principle, one that is capable of adaptation to meet the countless and variable schemes devised by those who seek the use of the money of others on the promise of profits."

In *SEC v. W.J. Howey Co.*, the Supreme Court set out its by now familiar definition of an investment contract:

> The test is whether the scheme involves an investment of money in a common enterprise with profits to come solely from the efforts of others.

For purposes of the present case, the sticking point in the *Howey* definition is the word "solely," a qualification which of course exactly fitted the circumstances in *Howey*. All the other elements of the *Howey* test have been met here. There is an investment of money, a common enterprise, and the expectation of profits to come from the efforts of others. Here, however, the investor, or purchaser, must himself exert some efforts if he is to realize a return on his initial cash outlay. He must find prospects and persuade them to attend Dare Adventure Meetings, and at least some of them must then purchase a plan if he is to realize that return. Thus it can be said that the returns or profits are not coming "solely" from the efforts of others.

We hold, however, that in light of the remedial nature of the legislation, the statutory policy of affording broad protection to the public, and the Supreme Court's admonitions that the definition of securities should be a flexible one, the word "solely" should not be read as a strict or literal limitation on the definition of an investment contract, but rather must be construed realistically, so as to include within the definition those schemes which involve in substance, if not form, securities. Within this context, we hold that Adventures III and IV, and the $1,000 Plan, are investment contracts within the meaning of the 1933 and 1934 Acts.

In this case, Dare's source of income is from selling the Adventures and the Plan. The purchaser is sold the

idea that he will get a fixed part of the proceeds of the sales. In essence, to get that share, he invests three things: his money, his efforts to find prospects and bring them to the meetings, and whatever it costs him to create an illusion of his own affluence. He invests them in Dare's get-rich-quick scheme. What he buys is a share in the proceeds of the selling efforts of Dare. Those efforts are the *sine qua non* [essential element] of the scheme; those efforts are what keeps it going; those efforts are what produces the money which is to make him rich. In essence, it is the right to share in the proceeds of those efforts that he buys. In our view, the scheme is no less an investment contract merely because he contributes some effort as well as money to get into it.

We hold that the requirement that profits come "solely" from the efforts of others would in circumstances such as these, lead to unrealistic results if applied dogmatically, and that a more flexible approach is appropriate.

Affirmed.

CASE REVIEW QUESTIONS
1. Was Dare's scheme determined by the court to fall within the definition of a security because the court felt that it was "a gigantic and successful fraud"? Explain.
2. If your answer to Question 1 was no, why did the court determine that Dare's scheme fell within the definition of a security?
3. What do you think the court meant when it called the 1933 and 1934 Acts "remedial legislation"?

ISSUING SECURITIES

When a corporation wants to raise funds, it usually does so by issuing either equity securities, such as stocks, or debt securities, such as bonds and debentures. (Equity and debt securities are discussed at length in Chapter 38, pages 819–823.) Usually, a corporation will issue securities through an underwriter. For a fee, the **underwriter** agrees to advise and aid the corporation with regard to the legal requirements for issuing the securities, to purchase the securities from the corporation, and to resell them to securities *dealers*. (If the issue is a large one, the underwriter may join with other underwriters to form an underwriter syndicate.) The dealers, in turn, resell the securities to the public.

The legal requirements that must be met when securities are issued are found in the 1933 and 1934 Acts. The 1933 Act states that all securities, except for those that are exempt, must be registered with the SEC prior to the time that they are actually issued. In addition, the 1934 Act requires that any company whose securities are traded on a national stock exchange, such as the New York Stock Exchange, or whose assets exceed $3 million and who has more than 500 shareholders, register its securities with the SEC.

Exemptions

Being subject to the Securities Acts of 1933 and 1934 and to the rules of the Securities and Exchange Commission can be burdensome. For instance, the cost of issuing securities may be increased by hundreds of thousands of dollars if the securities are subject to federal regulation. In addition, the requirements for the public disclosure of information are greatly increased for companies that are subject to the federal securities laws. Therefore, if registration can be legally avoided, it is usually desirable to do so.

The issuance of securities is sometimes *exempt* from the registration requirements of the 1933 Act. Some of the exemptions provided for in the 1933 Act are based on the type of security being issued whereas others are based on the nature of the transaction involved.

Type of Security Issued The following types of securities are expressly exempt from registration under the 1933 Act:

1. Bank and government securities.
2. Notes, drafts, and some other negotiable instruments on which the maturity date (the time for repayment) does not exceed nine months.
3. Securities issued by charitable organizations.
4. Securities issued by savings and loan associations that are regulated by a state or by the federal government.
5. Securities issued by common carriers that are regulated by federal law.
6. Securities issued by a trustee in bankruptcy with the approval of the bankruptcy court.
7. Insurance, endowment, or annuity policies issued by companies regulated by a state government.

For the most part, these exemptions are given because the securities involved are regulated by other state or federal laws.

Nature of Transaction Involved The following types of transactions are expressly exempt from registration under the 1933 Act:

1. Transactions by individual investors. This exemption is given because securities regulation generally concerns only transactions by issuers, underwriters, and dealers.
2. Transactions involving small offerings. For instance, a corporation can issue up to $500,000 in shares in any 12-month period without registering the issue.

3. Transactions involving intrastate offerings. If the issuing corporation is incorporated in, does virtually all of its business in, and has its principal place of business in the same state in which all of the offerees reside, the issue will be regulated by state rather than federal law.

4. Transactions that are private offerings. A **private offering** is an offering in which no offer is made to the public, there are 35 or fewer purchasers, the offerees are knowledgeable and experienced investors or are able to bear the economic risk of the transaction, the information that would be included in a registration statement is otherwise available to the offerees, and the seller is careful to sell only to people who are purchasing for investment rather than for resale. It is believed that registering transactions such as these would serve no useful purpose. The majority of these transactions involve offers to institutional investors, such as insurance companies and pension funds; offers to key employees of the issuer; and offers to exchange stock as part of the purchase of closely-held companies.

The Registration Statement

When the issuance of securities must be registered with the SEC, the issuer is required to provide the following information in a **registration statement:**

1. A thorough picture of the financial status of the issuer, including a balance sheet dated not more than ninety days before filing and a profit and loss statement for at least the previous five years. Both of these documents must be certified by independent auditors who attest that the information presented complies with generally accepted accounting principles.

2. Information concerning the corporation's directors and officers; its organization, business, and property; its plan for the distribution of the securities; and the intended use of the proceeds received from the issuance.

3. Other *material* facts that might affect the price or value of the securities. The Supreme Court has said that a fact is material in this context "if there is a substantial likelihood that a reasonable shareholder would consider it important." This would include such matters as:

   a. The difference between the book value (the excess value of assets over all liabilities or the net assets) of the corporation's presently issued shares and the offering price of the new shares.

   b. Any substantial disparity between the public offering price and the cost of shares purchased by the officers, directors, or promoters of the corporation.

   c. If the issuer is a new company, the elements used to compute the offering price of the securities and other related financial information.

   d. Any facts that make the securities a high risk. These would include, for example, the fact that the corporation has no operating history or no history of earnings, the highly competitive nature of the industry, and any impending major lawsuits or governmental actions against the issuer.

   e. Facts regarding the financial status of the management of the issuer. This would include, for example, substantial loans by the issuer to management, pledges of the issuer's stock by management to secure loans to management, or any information relating to financial difficulties of key members of management.

Periodic Reporting

The 1934 Act requires that all corporations having securities registered under the 1933 or 1934 Acts file periodic reports with the SEC. These reports are to be submitted quarterly (on Form 10 – Q) and annually (on Form 10 – K). In addition, a report must be submitted on Form 8 – K in any month in which certain designated events occur.

Form 10 – Q contains a summary operating statement and a report on capital and shareholders' equity. None of the Form 10 – Q information need be audited before submission. *Form 10 – K,* on the other hand, is much more extensive; it is used to keep the information in the registration statement current. Form 10 – K requires the submission of an annual balance sheet and income statement and information concerning the operation of the corporation's business, its officers and directors, and its securities. *Form 8 – K* is used to submit information about such specific events as changes in capital structure, defaults in required payments to any security holders, and transfers of working control. More generally, Form 8 – K is used to report any important event that materially affects the corporation.

Until 1982, a corporation had to prepare a new registration statement providing all of the required information each time it issued new securities. However, much of the information disclosed in a registration statement is also disclosed in the periodic reports discussed in the previous paragraph. In 1982, the SEC integrated the disclosure requirements of the 1933 and 1934 Acts. Today, a corporation that wants to register a new issue of securities may incorporate much of the information contained in its periodic reports submitted under the 1934 Act in its registration statement simply by referring to those reports in the statement. This procedure can save a corporation substantial time and money in preparing a registration statement.

The Prospectus

The registration statement is filed with the SEC. Prospective purchasers do not have to go to the SEC to obtain the information contained in the registration statement, however. Instead, every person to whom a registered security is offered or sold must be provided with a **prospectus,** which is a document that contains a summary of the most important information in the registration statement. A prospectus provides the information that the investor needs to judge the value of the security being sold. It is illegal to sell a registered security without providing the purchaser with a prospectus before or at the time of the sale.

The Registration Process

It is illegal to sell a security that is subject to registration requirements unless a registration statement has been filed with the SEC and has become effective. If the SEC does nothing in response to a registration statement, it automatically becomes effective 20 days after it is filed. If the SEC determines that the information in the statement is insufficient or inaccurate and requires that the statement be amended, the twenty-day period starts over again once the required amendments are made. Shortly before the securities are to go on sale, an issuing corporation will generally amend the registration statement to reflect the actual price at which the securities will be sold. When this is done, the issuer usually does not have to wait an additional 20 days because the SEC normally allows the registration statement to become effective immediately.

Complete and accurate information is all an investor is entitled to. It is not the SEC's function to protect the investor from the risks inherent in the purchase of securities. Therefore, the SEC's review of the registration statement is limited to the completeness and accuracy of its information. The SEC does not have the power to approve or disapprove of either the securities or their price.

Regular Registration There are three important time periods in the regular registration process. The activities that an issuer can engage in with regard to the sale of securities vary with each period.

The Pre-Filing Period The activities in which an issuer can engage with regard to the sale of securities are strictly limited prior to the filing of a registration statement with the SEC. The issuer may not sell or even offer the securities for sale during this period. Any act by the issuer or its directors or officers that promotes the prospective issue in any way may be considered an offer to sell. Thus, the only activity the issuer is allowed during this period is preliminary negotiations with underwriters.

The Waiting Period The waiting period is the 20-day period between the date the registration statement is filed and the date it becomes effective. During this period, the issuer may not sell the securities. It may, however, make oral and written offers to sell the securities. Written offers, which you may have seen in financial newspapers and periodicals, are often called *tombstone advertisements* because they are usually surrounded by a black border. They may include only the name of the issuer, the kind of security being offered, the price of the security, the name of the underwriter, and where a prospectus can be obtained.

During the waiting period, the issuer may also distribute a preliminary prospectus, normally called a *red herring prospectus* because it must have a heading printed in red ink. The heading must state that the prospectus is a preliminary prospectus, that a registration statement has been filed with the SEC but has not yet become effective, that no final sale can be made until the registration statement does become effective, and that the preliminary prospectus is not an offer to sell.

Post-Effective Period After the registration statement has become effective, the securities may be sold. As noted earlier, every person to whom registered securities are offered or sold must be provided with a prospectus. This must be done until issuance of the security is completed. If the distribution of the issue takes longer than nine months, the prospectus must be brought up to date. Even within the nine-month period, the prospectus must be updated to reflect any important new developments that occur.

Shelf Registration In order to accelerate the registration process, the SEC has adopted a rule that allows a procedure called *shelf registration.* This method of registration allows a corporation to avoid filing a new registration statement for each new issue of securities by filing a single registration statement that discloses a plan to sell securities over a period of up to two years. The corporation must still update the registration statement as new information becomes available, but as long as this is done, the registration statement remains effective.

Shelf registration is controversial, however. Its opponents argue that it does not allow the time needed to form traditional underwriting syndicates. Consequently, only large brokerage and underwriting firms that have sufficient capital to absorb the risks and systems of retail dealers to sell the securities may be able to handle these issues. Opponents also question whether proper disclosure will be provided when an issue is shelf registered and is then quickly sold at a later date. Under these circumstances, they contend, underwriters and legal counsel may not be able to examine an issue with the due diligence required by law, and the investor may not be adequately alerted to corporate developments that occur subsequent to the registration.

Small brokerage and underwriting firms, which normally do not have systems of retail dealers, have vehemently opposed shelf registration because they fear it will cause a significant reduction in their business. Corporations have been using the procedure, however. For instance, in the first two months the rule was effective, Indianapolis Power & Light shelf registered 1.3 million shares of common stock, General Motors Acceptance placed $1 billion of debt securities on the shelf, and Exxon Finance shelf registered $500 million in debt securities.

Enforcement of Registration Requirements

SEC Enforcement When the SEC determines that a registration statement contains insufficient or inaccurate information, it issues a *refusal order.* A refusal order prevents the registration statement from becoming effective, which makes it illegal to issue the securities involved.

Even when a registration statement has become effective, the SEC may issue a *stop order* if it determines that the registration statement contains inaccurate information. A stop order suspends the effectiveness of the registration statement, which makes the further issuance of the securities involved illegal until the statement's effectiveness is reinstated.

The SEC may also obtain an *injunction,* which is a court order instructing a defendant to stop doing something, from a federal court against any issuer who is in violation of the 1933 Act. If that issuer violates the court's order, it may be held in contempt of court.

Criminal Enforcement The 1933 Act provides that any person who willfully violates the act or the SEC rules issued under it may be fined not more than $10,000 and imprisoned for not more than five years. These criminal penalties can only be imposed by a court after the offender has been prosecuted by the U.S. Justice Department. Securities cases are usually referred to the Justice Department by the SEC.

Private Enforcement The 1933 Act expressly provides for its enforcement by private individuals who have been damaged as a result of violations of its provisions. For instance, a purchaser of securities that have been issued without a required effective registration statement or that have been sold without being accompanied by a required prospectus may bring a legal action for damages against the party, usually the dealer, from whom he or she purchased the securities.

Another type of private enforcement of the 1933 Act occurs in cases in which a registration statement that has become effective contains a false material statement, an omission of a required material fact, or an omission of a material fact that is necessary to insure that statements made in the registration statement are not misleading. Any person who does not know of a material false statement or omission in an effective registration statement who acquires a security covered by it can recover damages from those parties who were required to sign the registration statement. The required signers would include the issuing corporation; its principal executive, financial, and accounting officers; and a majority of its board of directors. A suit for damages can also be brought against any expert — meaning a person such as an accountant, an underwriter, an appraiser, or a lawyer — who participated in the preparation of the registration statement if a material false statement or omission is found in that part of the statement the expert helped to prepare. As you can see, the number of potential defendants in this type of case is quite large.

If a registration statement does in fact contain a material false statement or omission, an individual defendant may escape liability by proving that he or she was not guilty of fraudulent intent or negligence by presenting evidence that he or she used *due diligence* in preparing the registration statement. To prove that he or she used due diligence, a defendant must show one of the following:

1. That with regard to any part of the registration statement prepared on the authority of someone else who is an expert — sometimes called the *expertised portion* of the registration statement — the defendant had no reasonable grounds to believe and indeed did not believe that there were any material false statements or omissions.
2. That with regard to other parts of the registration statement, the defendant made a reasonable investigation that revealed reasonable grounds for believing and based on which he or she did believe that there were no material false statements or omissions.

Note that a person sued as an expert could use only the second method of proving due diligence. The issuing corporation, however, is strictly liable for any material false statements or omissions in the registration statement, which means that it may not defend on the grounds of due diligence.

In the following case, a number of defendants were sued by private investors for violation of the 1933 Act. Each of the defendants defended on the grounds that he had used due diligence in executing his role in the preparation of the registration statement. As you read the case, note the various roles of the defendants in the preparation of the registration statement and how the test of due diligence is applied to each defendant.

ESCOTT v. BARCHRIS CONSTRUCTION CORPORATION
283 F. Supp. 643 (S.D.N.Y. 1968)

[BarChris Construction Corporation (BarChris) was in the business of constructing bowling alleys. In early 1961, BarChris sought to raise needed working capital by selling debentures. The registration statement for the debentures, which was prepared by Grant, BarChris' attorney, was filed with the SEC on March 30, 1961, and became effective on May 16. The underwriters, eight investment banking firms led by Drexel & Company (Drexel), sold the debentures and BarChris received the net proceeds on May 24. John Ballard was the attorney for the underwriters. BarChris defaulted on the payment of the interest due on the debentures on November 1, 1962.

Escott and other purchasers of the debentures issued by BarChris brought a legal action under the 1933 Act against BarChris, the signers of the registration statement, the underwriters, and BarChris' auditor, Peat, Marwick, Mitchell & Company (Peat, Marwick), for damages caused by material false statements and material omissions in the registration statement and in the prospectus. Among other things, the plaintiffs argued that the 1960 earnings statement of BarChris included the sale of a bowling alley called Heavenly Lanes. In fact, this bowling alley had not been sold and was operated by BarChris under the name Capitol Lanes. The earnings statement had been audited by Peat, Marwick.

The trial court found that there were material false statements and material omissions in the registration statement and in the prospectus. Nonetheless, each of the defendants, except BarChris, argued that he was not liable because he had used due diligence in preparing the registration statement and prospectus. In the excerpt from the trial court's opinion that follows, the court considers the due diligence defense of some of the signers of the registration statement, the underwriters, and the auditors.]

MCLEAN, District Judge

I turn now to the question of whether defendants have proved their due diligence defenses. The position of each defendant will be separately considered.

RUSSO

Russo was the chief executive officer of BarChris. He was a member of the executive committee. He was familiar with all aspects of the business.

In short, Russo knew all the relevant facts. He could not have believed that there were no untrue statements or material omissions in the prospectus. Russo has no due diligence defenses.

KIRCHER

Kircher was treasurer of BarChris and its chief financial officer. He is a certified public accountant and an intelligent man. He was thoroughly familiar with BarChris's financial affairs. Moreover, as a member of the executive committee, Kircher was kept informed as to those branches of the business of which he did not have direct charge. In brief, Kircher knew all the relevant facts.

Kircher worked on the preparation of the registration statement. He read the prospectus and understood it. He knew what it said and what it did not say. Kircher's contention is that he had never before dealt with a registration statement, that he did not know what it should contain, and that he relied wholly on Grant, Ballard and Peat, Marwick to guide him. He claims that it was their fault, not his, if there was anything wrong with it. He says that all the facts were recorded in BarChris's books where these "experts" could have seen them if they had looked. He says that he truthfully answered all their questions. In effect, he says that if they did not know enough to ask the right questions and to give him the proper instructions, that is not his responsibility.

There is an issue of credibility here. In fact, Kircher was not frank in dealing with Grant and Ballard. He withheld information from them. But even if he had told them all the facts, this would not have constituted the due diligence contemplated by the statute. Knowing the facts, Kircher had reason to believe that the expertised portion of the prospectus, i.e., the 1960 figures, was in part incorrect. He could not shut his eyes to the facts and rely on Peat, Marwick for that portion.

As to the rest of the prospectus, knowing the facts, he did not have a reasonable ground to believe it to be true. On the contrary, he must have known that in part it was untrue. Under these circumstances, he was not entitled to sit back and place the blame on the lawyers for not advising him about it. Kircher has not proved his due diligence defenses.

TRILLING

Trilling's position is somewhat different from Kircher's. He was BarChris's controller. He signed the registration statement in that capacity, although he was not a director.

Trilling entered BarChris's employ in October 1960. He was Kircher's subordinate. When Kircher asked him for information, he furnished it.

Trilling was not a member of the executive committee. He was a comparatively minor figure in BarChris. The description of BarChris's "management" on page 9 of the prospectus does not mention him. He was not considered to be an executive officer.

Trilling may well have been unaware of several of the inaccuracies in the prospectus. But he must have known of some of them. As a financial officer, he was familiar with BarChris's finances and with its books of account. I cannot find that Trilling believed the entire prospectus to be true.

But even if he did, he still did not establish his due diligence defenses. He did not prove that as to the parts of the prospectus expertised by Peat, Marwick he had no reasonable ground to believe that it was untrue. He also failed to prove, as to the parts of the prospectus not expertised by Peat, Marwick, that he made a reasonable investigation which afforded him a reasonable ground to believe that it was true. As far as appears, he made no investigation. He did what was asked of him and assumed that others would properly take care of supplying accurate data as to the other aspects of the company's business. This would have been well enough but for the fact that he signed the registration statement. As a signer, he could not avoid responsibility by leaving it up to others to make it accurate. Trilling did not sustain the burden of proving his due diligence defenses.

THE UNDERWRITERS

The underwriters other than Drexel made no investigation of the accuracy of the prospectus. They all relied upon Drexel as the "lead" underwriter.

Drexel did make an investigation. The work was in charge of Coleman, a partner of the firm, assisted by Casperson, an associate. Drexel's attorneys acted as attorneys for the entire group of underwriters. Ballard did the work.

Ballard, without checking, relied on the information which he got from Kircher. He also relied on Grant who, as company counsel, presumably was familiar with its affairs.

[I]t is clear that no effectual attempt at verification was made. The question is whether due diligence required that it be made. Stated another way, is it sufficient to ask questions, to obtain answers which, if true, would be thought satisfactory, and to let it go at that, without seeking to ascertain from the records whether the answers in fact are true and complete?

The purpose of Section 11 is to protect investors. To that end the underwriters are made responsible for the truth of the prospectus. If they may escape that responsibility by taking at face value representations made to them by the company's management, then the inclusion of underwriters among those liable under Section 11 affords the investors no additional protection. To effectuate the statute's purpose, the phrase "reasonable investigation" must be construed to require more effort on the part of the underwriters than the mere accurate reporting in the prospectus of data presented to them by the company. It should make no difference that this data is elicited by questions addressed to the company officers by the underwriters, or that the underwriters at the time believe that the company's officers are truthful and reliable. In order to make the underwriters' participation in this enterprise of any value to the investors, the underwriters must make some reasonable attempt to verify the data submitted to them. They may not rely solely on the company's officers or on the company's counsel. A prudent man in the management of his own property would not rely on them.

On the evidence of this case, I find that the underwriters' counsel did not make a reasonable investigation of the truth of those portions of the prospectus which were not made on the authority of Peat, Marwick as an expert. Drexel is bound by their failure. Drexel delegated to them, as its agent, the business of examining the corporate minutes and contracts. It must bear the consequences of their failure to make an adequate examination.

The other underwriters, who did nothing and relied solely on Drexel and on the lawyers, are also bound by it. It follows that although Drexel and the other underwriters believed that those portions of the prospectus were true, they had no reasonable ground for that belief, within the meaning of the statute. Hence, they have not established their due diligence defense, except as to the 1960 audited figures.

PEAT, MARWICK

The part of the registration statement purporting to be made upon the authority of Peat, Marwick as an expert was, as we have seen, the 1960 figures. But because the statute requires the court to determine Peat, Marwick's belief, and the grounds thereof, "at the time such part of the registration statement became effective," for the purposes of this defense, the matter must be viewed as of May 16, 1961, and the question is whether at that time Peat, Marwick, after reasonable investigation, had reasonable ground to believe and did believe that the 1960 figures were true and that no material fact had been omitted from the registration statement which should have been included in order to make the 1960 figures not misleading. In deciding this issue, the court must consider what Peat, Marwick did in its 1960 audit.

Peat, Marwick's work was in general charge of a member of the firm, Cummings, and more immediately in charge of Peat, Marwick's manager, Logan. Most of the actual work was performed by a senior accountant, Berardi, who had junior assistants.

Berardi was then about thirty years old. He was not yet a C.P.A. He had no previous experience with the bowling industry. This was his first job as a senior accountant. He could hardly have been given a more difficult assignment.

It is unnecessary to recount everything that Berardi did in the course of the audit. We are concerned only with the evidence relating to what Berardi did or did not do with respect to those items which I have found to have been incorrectly reported in the 1960 figures in the prospectus. More narrowly, we are directly concerned only with such of those items as I have found to be material.

First and foremost is Berardi's failure to discover that Capitol Lanes had not been sold. Fundamentally, the error stemmed from the fact that Berardi never realized that Heavenly Lanes and Capitol were two different names for the same alley.

The evidence is conflicting as to whether BarChris's officers expressly informed Berardi that Heavenly and Capitol were the same thing and that BarChris was operating Capitol and had not sold it. I find that they did not so inform him.

Berardi did become aware that there were references here and there in BarChris's records to something called Capitol Lanes. Berardi knew from various BarChris records that Capitol Lanes, Inc. was paying rentals. Also, a Peat, Marwick work paper recorded that Capitol Lanes, Inc. held certain insurance policies, including a fire insurance policy on "contents," a workmen's compensation and a public liability policy. Another Peat, Marwick work paper recorded that Capitol

Lanes, Inc. had $1,000 in a fund in Connecticut. A note on this paper read: "Traced to disbursements book — advanced for operation of alley."

Berardi testified that he inquired of Russo about Capitol Lanes and that Russo told him that Capitol Lanes, Inc. was going to operate an alley some day but as yet it had no alley. Berardi testified that he understood that the alley had not been built and that he believed that the rental payments were on vacant land.

I am not satisfied with this testimony. If Berardi did hold this belief, he should not have held it. The entries as to insurance and as to "operation of alley" should have alerted him to the fact that an alley existed. He should have made further inquiry on the subject. It is apparent that Berardi did not understand this transaction.

In any case, he never identified this mysterious Capitol with the Heavenly Lanes which he had included in his sales and profit figures. The vital question is whether he failed to make a reasonable investigation which, if he had made it, would have revealed the truth.

The burden of proof on this issue is on Peat, Marwick. Although the question is a rather close one, I find that Peat, Marwick has not sustained that burden. Peat, Marwick has not proved that Berardi made a reasonable investigation as far as Capitol Lanes was concerned and that his ignorance of the true facts was justified.

[The defendants are liable to the plaintiffs for violation of the 1933 Act.]

CASE REVIEW QUESTIONS

1. In what way did the defendants violate the Securities Act of 1933?
2. Why did the defendants want to prove that they had used due diligence in preparing the registration statement?
3. Explain in your own words what the defendants would have had to prove in order to show that they had used due diligence in preparing the registration statement.
4. Explain in your own words why each of the defendants failed to prove that he had used due diligence in preparing the registration statement.

INSIDER TRADING

Directors and officers of corporations can and do buy and sell the shares of their corporation. When they do this, they are said to be **insiders** engaged in insider trading. Ownership of shares of a corporation by its executives can be a good thing because it provides an incentive for them to work hard to make the corporation successful and thereby increase the value of their shares. On the other hand, is it fair to other investors when the executives of a corporation buy and sell its shares on the basis of information they obtain as a result of their positions that the other investors do not have?

For example, suppose that a corporate executive learns that an engineer who works for the company has made an improvement in the company's product that will probably cause sales of the product to increase dramatically. On the basis of this information, the executive purchases a large number of the company's shares on the New York Stock Exchange. When the corporation makes its product improvement public, investors decide that the company's sales and profits will increase, so the price at which the company's shares are traded increases. Naturally, the value of the shares purchased earlier by the executive also increases. But, should the executive be entitled to keep this profit? The law says no. Indeed, there are two provisions of the 1934 Act—§16 and §10(b)—that may be used to deny such profits to corporate executives.

Section 16

One approach to the problem of insider trading on the basis of inside information is found in §16 of the 1934 Act. Section 16(a) requires that a person who becomes a director, an officer, or an owner of 10 percent or more of any one class of shares of a corporation registered under the act must file a report disclosing the shares he or she owns. Then, additional reports must be filed whenever there is a transaction involving those shares.

Section 16(b) provides that those persons required to report under §16(a) may not sell short securities of the corporation. *Selling short* means selling shares that are not actually owned by the person selling them at the time of the sale. More significantly, §16(b) provides that any profit made by a person required to report under §16(a) from the purchase and sale or the sale and purchase of the corporation's shares within a six-month period belongs to the corporation.

For instance, if a director of XYZ, Inc., a corporation registered under the 1934 Act, purchases 100 shares of XYZ's stock on February 1 at $1.00 per share and sells 100 shares on May 2 at $2.00 per share, the $100 profit would belong to XYZ. Similarly, if the director sells 100 shares of XYZ's stock on February 1 at $2.00 per share and purchases 100 shares on May 2 at $1.00 per share, the $100 profit would again belong to XYZ. Profits made from transactions that occur within a six-month period are usually referred to as **short-swing profits.**

You should note that the actual use of inside information is not required for a violation of §16(b) to occur. In effect, this provision automatically presumes that any purchase and sale or sale and purchase by an insider that occurs within a six-month period is based on inside information. Thus, evidence presented by a defendant that his or her transactions were not based on inside information is generally not considered to be relevant by the courts. The Supreme Court has made one narrow exception to this general principle. It applies to cases that involve unorthodox transactions, such as the sale of shares by a corporation that was unsuccessful in an attempt to take over another corporation, in which the likelihood that inside information was used is extremely remote.

Enforcement of Section 16(b) Section 16(b) is not enforced by the SEC, nor does it give any legal rights to people who buy from or sell to insiders. Rather, it gives the right to recapture an insider's profit to the corporation involved. This right may be enforced by the corporation itself or by a shareholder who brings a derivative suit on behalf of the corporation (see page 876).

Contrary to the requirements for most derivative suits, the courts have held that a shareholder need not have owned his or her shares at the time that the insider's profit was made in order to bring a legal action on behalf of the corporation to recapture short-swing profits. Furthermore, if a shareholder's derivative suit is successful, the court is likely to award a substantial fee to the shareholder's attorney. These rulings, plus the method used by the courts to calculate short-swing profits discussed in the following section, have provided strong incentives for shareholders to enforce §16(b).

Calculation of Short-Swing Profit Although §16(b) expressly prohibits insiders from making short-swing profits, it does not define profit. The courts, however, have developed a very strict definition of profit in cases in which a series of transactions is involved by using a method of calculating the profit that maximizes it. This, in turn, maximizes the amount of money the insider must turn over to the corporation.

Consider the following transactions by a director subject to §16(b):

> Day 1: Purchases 10 shares at $7.00 per share
> Day 2: Sells 10 shares at $5.00 per share
> Day 3: Purchases 10 shares at $3.00 per share
> Day 4: Sells 10 shares at $1.00 per share

What is the director's profit from these four transactions? Common sense may suggest to you that the director bought 20 shares at a cost of $100 and sold 20 shares for only $60, thus losing $40. A court, however, would match the sale of 10 shares at $5.00 (for a total of $50.00) and the purchase of 10 shares at $3.00 (for a total of $30.00) and conclude that the director realized a profit of $20.00. It would not allow the director to use the loss from the other two transactions to offset the profit from the two matched transactions. The courts justify this method of calculating profit on the grounds that it contributes to achieving the purpose of §16(b), which is to discourage strongly attempts by insiders to make short-swing profits.

Section 10(b)

Another approach to the problem of insider trading is found in §10(b) of the 1934 Act, which makes it "unlawful for any person to use, in connection with the purchase or sale of any security . . . any manipulative or deceptive device or contrivance in contravention of such rules and regulations as the [Securities Exchange] Commission may prescribe. . . ." To carry out the objectives of §10(b), the SEC has prescribed Rule 10b–5, which provides:

It shall be unlawful for any person, directly or indirectly, by the use of any means or instrumentality of interstate commerce, or of the mails, or of any facility of any national securities exchange,

(1) to employ any device, scheme, or artifice to defraud,

(2) to make any untrue statement of a material fact or to omit to state a material fact necessary in order to make the statements made, in the light of the circumstances under which they were made, not misleading, or

(3) to engage in any act, practice, or course of business which operates or would

operate as a fraud or deceit upon any person, in connection with the purchase or sale of any security.

As you can see, Section 10(b) and Rule 10b–5 are very broad provisions. Their purpose is to protect investors by prohibiting fraud and by making sure that all investors have equal access to investment information. In fulfilling this purpose, they deal with many problems that arise in securities trading, some of which will be discussed later in this chapter. Here, however, our focus is on the application of §10(b) and Rule 10b–5 to insider trading situations.

Insider Trading Violations The courts have held that the purchase or sale of securities by an insider who possesses material information that is not generally available to the public is a violation of Rule 10b–5. As a result, insiders must "disclose or abstain," meaning that they must either disclose the inside information to the public or abstain from trading in the shares of their corporation.

Unlike §16(b), which was discussed earlier, Rule 10b–5 requires that the *actual use* of inside information must be shown in order to prove a violation of the rule. Thus, violations of this rule are more difficult to prove than are violations of §16(b).

In addition, a defense to a charge of having violated Rule 10b–5 is that the inside information was not *material*. This means that the information, if generally known, would most probably not have affected either the market price of the corporation's shares or the investment decision of a reasonable person. Information that probably would be material includes information about such things as a substantial increase or decrease in earnings, a proposed merger, or an important product development. In *SEC v. Texas Gulf Sulphur Co.,*the case that follows, the court had to determine whether very important but somewhat uncertain information was indeed material.

SEC v. TEXAS GULF SULPHUR CO.
401 F.2d 833 (Second Cir. 1968)

[On November 12, 1963, Texas Gulf Sulphur Company (TGS), a corporation, completed drilling hole K–55–1 on land it owned in Canada. TGS had drilled the hole to determine whether valuable minerals were present. Visual inspection of the core removed from the hole indicated that the land was rich in copper, zinc, and silver. TGS then decided to purchase land adjacent to that it already owned. In order to facilitate the purchase of the additional land, the president of TGS instructed the people involved in the drilling to stop drilling temporarily and to keep the results of K–55–1 confidential.

On November 8, 1963, the day the drilling of K–55–1 was begun, the price of TGS stock was just under $18.00 per share. During the period between the drilling of K–55–1 and the resumption of drilling, Charles Fogarty, executive vice president and director of TGS, purchased 3,100 shares of TGS. On March 31, 1964, drilling was resumed. The original findings were confirmed and made public. By May 15, 1964, the price of TGS stock had risen to $58.25 per share. (During this period, there were many additional transactions in TGS shares by others, but we are not concerned with them here.)

The SEC charged Fogarty with violating Rule 10b–5. Among Fogarty's defenses was the claim that the information he possessed when he purchased the TGS shares was not material. The trial court agreed and found for Fogarty. The SEC appealed.]

WATERMAN, Circuit Judge

An insider is not, of course, always foreclosed from investing in his own company merely because he may be more familiar with company operations than are outside investors. An insider's duty to disclose information or his duty to abstain from dealing in his company's securities arises only in "those situations which are essentially extraordinary in nature and which are reasonably certain to have a substantial effect on the market price of the security if [the] extraordinary situation is disclosed." [Citation omitted.]

The only regulatory objective is that access to material information be enjoyed equally, but this objective requires nothing more than the disclosure of basic facts so that outsiders may draw upon their own investment decisions with knowledge equal to that of the insiders. As we stated in *List v. Fashion Park, Inc.*:

> The basic test of materiality . . . is whether a reasonable man would attach importance . . . in determining his choice of action in the transaction in question. This, of course, encompasses any fact . . . which in reasonable and objective contemplation might affect the value of the corporation's stock of securities. . . .

Thus, material facts include not only information of a company but also those facts which affect the probable future of the company and those which may affect the desire of investors to buy, sell, or hold the company's securities.

In each case, then, whether facts are material within Rule 10b–5 when the facts relate to a particular event and are undisclosed by those persons who are knowledgeable thereof will depend at any given time upon a balancing of both the indicated probability that the event will occur and the anticipated magnitude of the event in light of the totality of the company activity.

[A] major factor in determining whether the K–55–1 discovery was a material fact is the importance attached to the drilling results by those who knew about it. In view of other unrelated recent developments favorably affecting TGS, participation by an informed person in a regular stock-purchase program or even sporadic trading by an informed person, might lend only minimal support to the inference of the materiality of the K–55–1 discovery; nevertheless, the timing by those who knew of it of their stock purchases virtually compels the inference that the insiders were influenced by the drilling results.

It was the intent of Congress that all members of the investing public should be subject to identical market risks, which market risks include, of course, the risk that one's evaluative capacity or one's capital available to put at risk may exceed another's capacity or capital. The insiders here were not trading on an equal footing with the outside investors. They alone were in a position to evaluate the probability and magnitude of what seemed from the outset to be a major ore strike; they alone could invest safely, secure in the expectation that the price of TGS stock would rise substantially in the event such a major strike should materialize, but would decline little, if at all, in the event of failure, for the public ignorant at the outset of the favorable probabilities would likewise be unaware of the unproductive exploration, and the additional exploration cost would not significantly affect TGS market prices. Such inequities based upon unequal access to knowledge should not be shrugged off as inevitable in our way of life, or, in view of the congressional concern in the area, remain uncorrected.

We hold, therefore, that all transactions in TGS stock . . . by individuals apprised of the drilling results of K–55–2 were made in violation of Rule 10b–5.

[Reversed.]

CASE REVIEW QUESTIONS

1. Charles Fogarty was an officer and director of TGS. Why do you think the SEC didn't charge him with a violation of §16(b) of the 1934 Act?

2.   What things did the SEC have to show to prove that Fogarty violated Rule 10b–5?
3.   Why was there any question about whether the information concerning K–55–1 was material?
4.   Why did the court decide that the information concerning K–55–1 was material?

Who Is an Insider? Rule 10b–5 expressly applies to *any* person who violates its provisions. This means that people who are beyond the reach of §16, which applies only to directors, officers, and owners of 10 percent or more of any one class of shares, are subject to Rule 10b–5. As a result, the courts have developed a much broader definition of who is an insider under Rule 10b–5. For instance, corporate employees and outsiders who perform services for a corporation who acquire material, nonpublic information are considered to be insiders under the rule.

A more difficult issue concerns whether a *tippee,* which is a person who is in no way connected with a corporation about which he or she has gained material, nonpublic information, can violate Rule 10b–5. The rule itself states that it applies to "any person," but the Supreme Court has held that a tippee can only violate the rule if the insider who provided the information to the tippee violated a fiduciary duty that he or she owed to the corporation.

All employees owe fiduciary duties to their employers. A *fiduciary* is a person who is vested with a special form of trust and who is required to display scrupulous good faith. As a result, an employee has a duty of loyalty to his or her employer that generally requires the employee not to disclose confidential information about the employer without the employer's consent. In the following case, the Supreme Court decided that if an employee — the tipper — has not violated his or her fiduciary duty of loyalty to the corporation by disclosing material inside information to the tippee, the tippee has not violated Rule 10b–5 by using the information in purchasing or selling the shares of the corporation.

DIRKS v. SEC
459 U.S. 1014 (Sup. Ct. 1983)

[The SEC charged Raymond Dirks with aiding and abetting violations of Rule 10b–5. Although Dirks himself had not traded in the shares of the corporation about which he had material, undisclosed information, he had given this information to investors who had traded in the shares of the corporation. The trial court held that Dirks had aided and abetted violations of Rule 10b–5 by giving the information to the investors. Dirks appealed.]

POWELL, Justice

In 1973, Dirks was an officer of a New York [securities dealer] firm who specialized in providing investment analysis of insurance company securities to institutional investors. On March 6, Dirks received information from Ronald Secrist, a former officer of Equity Funding of America. Secrist alleged that the assets of Equity Funding, a diversified corporation primarily engaged in selling life insurance and mutual funds, were vastly overstated as the result of fraudulent corporate practices. He urged Dirks to verify the fraud and disclose it publicly.

Dirks decided to investigate the allegations. He visited Equity Funding's headquarters in Los Angeles and interviewed several officers and employees of the corporation. The senior management denied any wrongdoing, but certain corporation employees corroborated the charges of fraud. Neither Dirks nor his firm owned or traded any Equity Funding stock, but throughout his investigation he openly discussed the information he had obtained with a number of clients and investors. Some of these persons sold their holdings of Equity Funding securities, including five investment advisers who liquidated holdings of more than $16 million.

While Dirks was in Los Angeles, he was in touch regularly with William Blundell, the Wall Street Journal's Los Angeles bureau chief. Dirks urged Blundell to write a story on the fraud allegations. Blundell did not believe, however, that such a massive fraud could go undetected and declined to write the story. He feared that publishing such damaging hearsay might be libelous.

During the two-week period in which Dirks pursued his investigation and spread word of Secrist's charges, the price of Equity Funding stock fell from $26 per share to less than $15 per share. This led the New York Stock Exchange to halt trading on March 27. Shortly thereafter California insurance authorities impounded Equity Funding's records and uncovered evidence of the fraud. Only then did the Securities and Exchange Commission (SEC) file a complaint against Equity Funding and only then, on April 2, did the Wall Street Journal publish a frontpage story based largely on information assembled by Dirks.

The SEC began an investigation into Dirks' role in the exposure of the fraud. After a hearing by an administrative law judge, the SEC found that Dirks had aided and abetted violations of Section 10(b) of the Securities Exchange Act of 1934 and SEC Rule 10b–5 by repeating the allegations of fraud to members of the investment community who later sold their Equity Funding stock.

In *Chiarella v. United States,* we accepted the two elements for establishing a Rule 10b–5 violation: "(i) the existence of a relationship affording access to inside information intended to be available only for a corporate purpose, and (ii) the unfairness of allowing a corporate insider to take advantage of that information by trading without disclosure." In examining whether Chiarella had an obligation to disclose or abstain, the Court found that there is no general duty to disclose before trading on material nonpublic information, and held that "a duty to disclose under Section 10(b) does not arise from the mere possession of nonpublic market information." Such a duty arises rather from the existence of a fiduciary relationship.

In effect, the SEC's theory of tippee liability appears rooted in the idea that the antifraud provisions require equal information among all traders. The trial court judge correctly read our opinion in *Chiarella* as repudiating any notion that all traders must enjoy equal information before trading: "[T]he 'information' theory is rejected. Because the disclosure-or-refrain duty is extraordinary, it attaches only when a party has legal obligations other than a mere duty to comply with the general antifraud proscriptions in the federal securities laws." We reaffirm today that "[a] duty [to disclose] arises from the relationship between parties . . . and not merely from one's ability to acquire information because of his position in the market."

Imposing a duty to disclose or abstain solely because a person knowingly receives material nonpublic information from an insider and trades on it could have an inhibiting influence on the role of market analysts, which the SEC itself recognizes is necessary to the preservation of a healthy market.

In determining whether a tippee is under an obligation to disclose or abstain, it thus is necessary to determine whether the insider's "tip" constituted a breach of the insider's fiduciary duty. Whether disclosure is a breach of duty depends in large part on the purpose of the disclosure. [T]he test is whether the insider personally will benefit, directly or indirectly, from his disclosure. Absent some personal gain, there has been no breach of duty to stockholders. And absent a breach by the insider, there is no breach [by the tippee].

Under the inside-trading and tipping rules set forth

above, we find that there was no violation by Dirks. It is undisputed that Dirks himself was a stranger to Equity Funding, with no pre-existing fiduciary duty to its shareholders. He took no action, directly or indirectly, that induced the shareholders or officers of Equity Funding to repose trust or confidence in him. There was no expectation by Dirk's sources that he would keep their information in confidence. Nor did Dirks misappropriate or illegally obtain the information about Equity Funding.

It is clear that neither Secrist nor the other Equity Funding employees violated their duty to the corporation's shareholders by providing information to Dirks.

The tippers received no monetary or personal benefit for revealing Equity Funding's secrets, nor was their purpose to make a gift of valuable information to Dirks. As the facts of this case clearly indicate, the tippers were motivated by a desire to expose the fraud. In the absence of a breach of duty to shareholders by the insiders, there was no breach by Dirks.

We conclude that Dirks, in the circumstances of this case, had no duty to abstain from the use of the inside information that he obtained.

Reversed.

CASE REVIEW QUESTIONS

1. Why do you think the SEC did not charge Dirks with a violation of §16 of the 1934 Act?
2. Explain in your own words why Dirks did not violate Rule 10b–5.
3. Suppose you are attending a football game and you overhear a person sitting behind you tell her companion that it's still a secret, but her company has been awarded a big government contract. Will you violate Rule 10b–5 if you purchase shares in the company before award of the contract is announced publicly? Explain.

Enforcement of Section 10(b) Section 10(b) may be enforced by the SEC, the U.S. Justice Department, and private individuals, as is explained in the following sections.

SEC Enforcement The SEC can impose a number of administrative sanctions on people and corporations it determines to have violated §10(b) of the 1934 Act. It can censure (publicly condemn), restrict the activities of, or bar activities by a regulated broker, dealer, or underwriter. It can also censure or restrict the activities of a registered corporation.

The SEC can also obtain an injunction from a federal court against any person or corporation that violates §10(b), and it can seek additional appropriate remedies from the court. For instance, it may ask the court to rescind (cancel) a prohibited transaction or to require the defendants to surrender their profits.

Criminal Enforcement The SEC can also refer violations of §10(b) to the U.S. Justice Department for criminal prosecution. If guilt is established, the defendant can be fined not more than $10,000 and imprisoned for not more than five years.

Private Enforcement Unlike the 1933 Act, the 1934 Act does not expressly provide for private enforcement by those who are damaged by violations of its provisions. Nonetheless, the courts have held that victims of §10(b) violations may sue the violators.

The courts have also held that the victims of §10(b) violations include not only those who have been damaged by the direct purchase of shares from or sale of shares to the violators but also anyone else who has been damaged by the purchase or sale of shares in the open market during the period in which material, nonpublic information was used by the violators. As a result, the damages to the victims who can bring lawsuits for violations of §10(b) can greatly exceed the profit made by the violator. At the present time, however, courts have not resolved the issue of whether a §10(b) violator's liability should be measured according to the damages to the victims or according to the profits made by the violator. For instance, in one case a §10(b) violator who made a profit of $13,000 was held liable by a court for damages of $361,000. Other courts, though, have limited a violator's liability to the amount of profit he or she made. The SEC's position is that limiting liability to the profits made by a §10(b) violator is not a sufficient deterrent to insider trading.

FRAUDULENT DISCLOSURE

In addition to cases of insider trading, §10(b) and Rule 10b–5 also apply to cases in which a corporation or a person fraudulently misstates or fails to disclose material information even though the corporation or the person has not traded on the basis of the information. For example, in a part of the decision that was not included in the excerpt of the *Texas Gulf Sulphur* case you read earlier in this chapter, the court held that the Texas Gulf Sulphur Company, which had not traded in its shares, violated §10(b) if a press release it issued concerning the discovery of copper, zinc, and silver deposits was false or misleading.

As you read earlier, §10(b) can be enforced by the SEC, the U.S. Justice Department, or private parties. In order to be successful in a suit for damages under §10(b), a private party must prove the same things that a plaintiff must prove in a case based on common-law contract fraud. As discussed in Chapter 11, a plaintiff asserting fraud must prove all three of the following:

1. There was intentional misrepresentation of a fact.
2. The fact was material.
3. There was justifiable reliance on the misrepresentation.

The special circumstances in which corporate disclosure fraud cases arise has led some courts to modify the common law fraud elements in §10(b) cases.

Intent At one time, some lower federal courts held that, in a §10(b) action brought by a private party, the plaintiff did not have to prove that the misrepresentation by the defendant had been intentional. This position was supported by the fact that neither §10(b) nor Rule 10b–5 uses the word *intent*.

In the case of *Ernst & Ernst v. Hochfelder,* however, the Supreme Court held that an accounting firm charged with a §10(b) violation could not be held liable if the plaintiff proved only that the accounting firm was negligent in performing an audit that resulted in false statements being made in a company's financial statement. The Court said there could be no violation "in the absence of any allegation of 'scienter'—[which means] an intent to deceive, manipulate, or defraud."

Since the *Hochfelder* case, some courts have held that although the requirement of scienter excludes merely negligent acts, it includes acts that are performed with a *reckless* disregard for the truth. Under this standard, an accounting firm would be held liable for the acts of accountants that resulted in false statements being made in a company's financial statement if those acts reflected a reckless disregard for the truth. For example, if an accountant verified the financial statement of a company without knowing whether the statement was correct or incorrect, the verification would be reckless. Whether the Supreme Court will accept this view of the scienter requirement or whether it will hold that actual intent to defraud is necessary is still a question, however.

Reliance Rule 10b–5(2) refers both to untrue statements and to omissions. When a plaintiff bases a Rule 10b–5 lawsuit on an omission, it is very difficult for the plaintiff to show that he or she would have relied on the omitted information had it been available. The courts have therefore held that the plaintiff does not have to prove reliance in such cases.

Even in lawsuits based on untrue statements, plaintiffs sometimes do not have to show direct reliance on the untrue statements. For instance, in a case in which a company's annual report contained false information, the court held that proof of reliance on a newspaper article based on the false information was sufficient to meet the reliance requirement. Another decision held that if an untrue statement inflated the price of shares traded on the open market, no proof of actual reliance on the untrue statement had to be shown by a person who purchased the shares at the inflated price.

Privity of Contract In contract cases, a party alleging fraud will only be successful if the misrepresentation was made by the other party to the contract; that is, the parties must be in privity of contract. In Rule 10b–5 cases, however, the courts have said that anyone violating the section is liable not only to those investors they bought shares from or sold shares to but also to all other investors who bought or sold the corporation's shares in reliance on the violator's untrue statements or omissions.

PROXY SOLICITATION

In Chapter 39, the annual meeting of shareholders was discussed. At the annual meeting, the shareholders elect directors, and they may also vote on matters concerning the corporation's bylaws and proposed extraordinary changes in the corporation. In fact, though, few shareholders actually attend the annual shareholders' meeting of a large, publicly held corporation. Nonetheless, a shareholder can have his or her shares counted toward a quorum and voted by appointing an agent to attend the meeting. The document authorizing an agent to vote a shareholder's shares is called a **proxy** (see Figure 51-1). Corporate management almost always solicits (requests) proxies from its shareholders prior to the annual meeting. Sometimes, others solicit proxies as well.

13733–085528231

GM PROXY

The Items shown below are described and page referenced in the Table of Contents (page i) to the Proxy Statement.
The Board of Directors Recommends a Vote AGAINST *the following Stockholder Proposals:*

	For	Against	Abstain
Item No. 4	☐	☐	☐
Item No. 5	☐	☐	☐
Item No. 6	☐	☐	☐

This proxy will be voted "AGAINST" Items 4 through 6 if no choice is specified.

FRED J NAFFZIGER & CAROL A
NAFFZIGER JT TEN
124 S GREENLAWN AVE
SOUTH BEND IND 46617

Dated: ____________________, 1982

____

____
Signature of Stockholder

Please add your title if you are signing as Attorney, Administrator, Executor, Guardian, Trustee, or in any other representative capacity.

PLEASE MARK, SIGN, DATE AND RETURN THIS PROXY CARD PROMPTLY USING THE ENCLOSED ENVELOPE.

GM PROXY

GENERAL MOTORS CORPORATION

Proxy Solicited by Board of Directors for Annual Meeting of Stockholders
Fisher Building, Detroit, Michigan, Friday, May 21, 1982, 9:00 A.M. Local Time

The undersigned authorizes Roger B. Smith, F. James McDonald, Howard H. Kehrl and F. Alan Smith, and each of them as the Proxy Committee, to vote the common stock of the undersigned upon the nominees for Director (A. L. Armstrong, C. B. Cleary, J. T. Connor, J. D. deButts, J. H. Evans, W. A. Fallon, C. T. Fisher, III, M. L. Goldberger, R. S. Hatfield, R. H. Herzog, J. J. Horan, R. R. Jensen, H. H. Kehrl, F. J. McDonald, W. E. McLaughlin, T. A. Murphy, E. C. Patterson, E. T. Pratt, Jr., G. P. Shultz, J. G. Smale, F. A. Smith, J. S. Smith, R. B. Smith, L. H. Sullivan, C. H. Townes), upon the other Items shown below and on the reverse side, *which are described and page referenced in the Table of Contents (page i) to the Proxy Statement,* and upon all other matters which may come before the 1982 Annual Meeting of Stockholders of General Motors Corporation, or any adjournment thereof.

You are encouraged to specify your choices by marking the appropriate boxes below, but you need not mark any boxes if you wish to vote in accordance with the Board of Directors' recommendations. The Proxy Committee cannot vote your shares unless you sign and return this card.

The Board of Directors Recommends a Vote FOR *the following Board of Directors Proposals:*

	For	Withheld
Item No. 1	☐	☐

For, except vote withheld from the following nominee(s):

____

	For	Against	Abstain
Item No. 2	☐	☐	☐
Item No. 3	☐	☐	☐

This proxy will be voted "FOR" Items 1 through 3 if no choice is specified.

SEE REVERSE SIDE

FIGURE 51-1
Proxy Authorizing Agent to Vote Shares

The Proxy Statement

Anyone who solicits a proxy for shares that are registered with the SEC is subject to §14(a) of the 1934 Act, which prohibits the solicitation of proxies in contravention of the rules and regulations prescribed by the SEC. Rule 14a–3 provides that proxies may not be solicited unless each shareholder solicited receives a **proxy statement** containing certain specified information about the corporation and the issues slated to be voted on at the shareholders' meeting. The purpose of this requirement is to provide shareholders with the information they need to make informed decisions as to how they want their shares to be voted. The proxy statement must be submitted to the SEC for approval before solicitation begins. Furthermore, even in those rare instances in which a corporation's management does not solicit proxies, SEC rules require the corporation to supply annual reports to its shareholders that contain information substantially equivalent to that required in a proxy statement.

Generally, a proxy statement must include the following information:

1. Who is soliciting the proxy; who is bearing the cost of the solicitation; the amount already spent on the solicitation; and an estimate of the total amount to be spent.
2. If directors are to be elected, the name and specified detailed information about the nominees of the party soliciting the proxy; the names of other directors whose terms of office continue beyond the meeting; and the names of the present officers of the corporation.
3. Other detailed information relating to any specific matter that is scheduled to come before the annual meeting for which the proxy is being solicited.

Rule 14a–9 provides that no proxy statement may contain any statement that is false or misleading with respect to any material fact at the time and in light of the circumstances under which the statement is made, nor may it omit any material fact that is necessary to make statements in the proxy statement not false or misleading. In determining liability under Rule 14a–9, a key consideration is whether a false, misleading, or omitted fact is material. The Supreme Court decision that follows explains what constitutes a material fact in a proxy statement.

TSC INDUSTRIES, INC. v. NORTHWAY, INC.
426 U.S. 438 (Sup. Ct. 1975)

MARSHALL, Justice

The proxy rules promulgated [adopted] by the Securities and Exchange Commission under the Securities Exchange Act of 1934 bar the use of proxy statements that are false or misleading with respect to the presentation or omission of material facts. We are called upon to consider the definition of a material fact under these rules.

The dispute in this case centers on the acquisition

of TSC Industries, Inc., by National Industries, Inc. In February 1969 National acquired 34% of TSC's voting securities by purchase from Charles E. Schmidt and his family. Schmidt, who had been TSC's founder and principal shareholder, promptly resigned along with his son from TSC's board of directors. Thereafter, five National nominees were placed on TSC's board; and Stanley R. Yarmuth, National's president and chief executive officer, became chairman of the TSC board, and Charles F. Simonelli, National's executive vice president, became chairman of the TSC executive committee. On October 16, 1969, the TSC board, with the attending National nominees abstaining, approved a proposal to liquidate and sell all of TSC's assets to National. On November 12, 1969, TSC and National issued a joint proxy statement to their shareholders, recommending approval of the proposal. The proxy solicitation was successful.

This is an action brought by Northway, a TSC shareholder, against TSC and National, claiming that their joint proxy statement was incomplete and materially misleading in violation of §14(a) of the Securities Exchange Act of 1934 and [SEC Rule 14a–9]. The Rule 14a–9 claim, is that TSC and National omitted from the proxy statement material facts relating to the degree of National's control over TSC.

Northway moved for summary judgment on the issue of TSC's and National's liability. The District Court denied the motion. [T]he Court of Appeals reversed the District Court's denial of summary judgment to Northway on its Rule 14a–9 [claim], holding that certain omissions of fact were material as a matter of law.

We granted certiorari because the standard applied by the Court of Appeals in resolving the question of materiality appeared to conflict with the standard applied by other Courts of Appeals. We now hold that the Court of Appeals erred in ordering that summary judgment be granted to Northway.

As we have noted on more than one occasion, §14(a) of the Securities Exchange Act was intended to promote "the free exercise of the voting rights of stockholders by ensuring that proxies would be solicited with 'explanation to the stockholder of the real nature of the questions for which authority to cast his vote is sought.'"

The question of materiality, it is universally agreed, is an objective one, involving the significance of an omitted or misrepresented fact to a reasonable investor. Variations in the formulation of a general test of materiality occur in the articulation of just how significant a fact must be or, put another way, how certain it must be that the fact would affect a reasonable investor's judgment.

The Court of Appeals in this case concluded that material facts include "all facts which a reasonable shareholder *might* consider important" (emphasis added). The formulation of the test of materiality has been explicitly rejected by at least two courts as setting too low a threshold for the imposition of liability under Rule 14a–9. In these cases, panels of the Second and Fifth Circuits opted for the conventional test of materiality—whether a reasonable man would attach importance to the fact misrepresented or omitted in determining his course of action.

In formulating a standard of materiality, we are guided, of course, by the Rule's broad remedial purpose. That purpose is not merely to ensure by judicial means that the transaction, when judged by its real terms, is fair and otherwise adequate, but to ensure disclosures by corporate management in order to enable the shareholders to make an informed choice. As an abstract proposition, the most desirable role for a court in a suit of this sort, coming after the consummation of the proposed transaction, would perhaps be to determine whether in fact the proposal would have been favored by the shareholders and consummated in the absence of any misstatement or omission. But such matters are not subject to determination with certainty. Doubts as to the critical nature of information misstated or omitted will be commonplace. And particularly in view of the purpose of the Rule and the fact that the content of the proxy statement is within management's control, it is appropriate that these doubts be resolved in favor of those the statute is designed to protect.

We are aware, however, that the disclosure policy embodied in the proxy regulations is not without limit. Some information is of such dubious significance that insistence on its disclosure may accomplish more harm than good. The potential liability for a Rule 14a–9 violation can be great indeed, and if the standard of materiality is unnecessarily low, not only may the corporation and its management be subjected to liability for insignificant omissions or misstatements, but also management's fear of exposing itself to substantial liability may cause it simply to bury the shareholders in an avalanche of trivial information—a result that is hardly conducive to informed decision-making. Precisely these dangers are presented, we think, by the definition of a material fact adopted by the Court of Appeals in this case—a fact which a reasonable shareholder *might* consider important.

The general standard of materiality that we think best comports with the policies of Rule 14a–9 is as follows: An omitted fact is material if there is a substantial likelihood that a reasonable shareholder would consider it important in deciding how to vote. It does not require proof of a substantial likelihood that disclosure of the omitted fact would have caused the reasonable investor to change his vote. What the standard does contemplate is a showing of a substantial likelihood that, under all the circumstances, the omitted fact would have assumed actual significance in the deliberations of the reasonable shareholder. Put another way, there must be a substantial likelihood that the disclosure of the omitted fact would have been viewed by the reasonable investor as having significantly altered the "total mix" of information made available.

The Court of Appeals concluded that two omitted facts relating to National's potential influence, or control, over the management of TSC were material as a matter of law. First, the proxy statement failed to state that at the time the statement was issued, the chairman of the TSC board of directors was Stanley Yarmuth, National's president and chief executive officer, and the chairman of the TSC executive committee was Charles Simonelli, National's executive vice president. [The second omitted fact has been deleted from this edited version of the case.] The Court of Appeals noted that TSC shareholders were relying on the TSC board of directors to negotiate on their behalf for the best possible rate of exchange with National. It then concluded that the omitted facts were material because they were "persuasive indicators that the TSC board was in fact under the control of National, and that National thus 'sat on both sides of the table' in setting the terms of the exchange."

We do not agree that the omission of these facts, when viewed against the disclosures contained in the proxy statements, warrants the entry of summary judgment against TSC and National on this record.

The proxy statement prominently displayed the facts that National owned 34% of the outstanding shares in TSC, and that no other person owned more than 10%. It also prominently revealed that 5 out of 10 TSC directors were National nominees, and it recited the positions of those National nominees with National—indicating, among other things, that Stanley Yarmuth was president and a director of National, and that Charles Simonelli was executive vice president and a director of National. These disclosures clearly revealed the nature of National's relationship with TSC and alerted the reasonable shareholder to the fact that National exercised a degree of influence over TSC. In view of these disclosures, we certainly cannot say that the additional facts that Yarmouth was chairman of the TSC board of directors and Simonelli chairman of its executive committee were, on this record, so obviously important that reasonable minds could not differ on their materiality.

[Reversed.]

CASE REVIEW QUESTIONS

1. What standard of materiality was used by the court of appeals?
2. On the basis of its standard of materiality, what decision did the court of appeals make? Explain.
3. What standard of materiality was used by the Supreme Court?
4. On the basis of its standard of materiality, what decision did the Supreme Court make? Explain.

Proxy Contests

Usually, only the current management of a corporation solicits proxies from shareholders. Sometimes, however, outsiders—often referred to as *insurgents* —oppose current management. The insurgents may be opposed to the election of management's nominees for the board of directors or to a specific management policy. To pursue their opposition, the insurgents will solicit proxies. The result is a proxy contest between the management and the insurgents.

The SEC has adopted rules for proxy contests. Under these rules, the insurgents must file a statement with the SEC that provides extensive specified information. In addition, the insurgents, like management, must supply a proxy statement to each shareholder when they solicit his or her proxy.

The SEC proxy contest rules require the corporation to provide the insurgents with a list of the corporation's shareholders or to mail the insurgent's proxy material to the shareholders. If the corporation chooses to mail the insurgent's proxy material itself, it may charge the insurgents for the cost of the mailing.

Another SEC rule prohibits either party in a proxy contest from using false or misleading statements in its solicitation. This rule may be enforced in a court in a legal action brought by either of the parties.

The expenses incurred in a proxy contest can be substantial. In addition to printing and mailing expenses, there will usually be large attorneys' and accountants' fees. Furthermore, both management and the insurgents will often hire professional proxy soliciting firms to handle their proxy solicitations. Generally, the costs of a proxy contest to management are paid for by the corporation whereas the insurgents must bear their own costs. For this reason, proxy contests usually involve battles to elect a majority of the board of directors. Only if the insurgents are successful in gaining control of the board will they be able to obtain reimbursement for their expenses from the corporation.

Shareholder Proposals

Because the costs of a proxy contest to insurgents can be substantial, shareholders who only want to influence corporate policy generally follow the simpler and far less costly course of making a shareholder proposal. Under SEC rules, if certain shareholders of a registered corporation give timely notice to the corporation of their intention to present a proposal for vote at the annual shareholders' meeting, management must include the proposal in its proxy statement. It may also include its own statement in opposition to the proposal if it so desires. Shareholders must be given the opportunity to vote for or against the proposal on management's proxy and at the annual meeting. As a result of these rules, a shareholder can present an issue for vote at the shareholders' meeting for no more than the cost of a letter and a stamp.

The Proposal Process SEC rules restrict the right to make proposals to shareholders who have owned $1,000 worth of shares or one percent of the total shares of the corporation, whichever is less, for at least one year. A qualified shareholder can only make one proposal per year. The notice to the corporation must be communicated in writing, and it must include a statement that the shareholder intends to present the proposal for action at the annual meeting. The notice must be received by the corporation substantially in advance of the meeting as specified in the SEC rules.

Proper Proposals Management must include a shareholder proposal in its proxy statement and proxy and allow a vote to be taken on it only if the proposal deals with a proper subject under SEC rules. Management can exclude a proposal if:

1. It is not a proper subject for shareholder action under the corporation law of the governing state.
2. It relates to a personal claim or grievance.
3. It is not significantly related to the company's business.
4. It is the same or substantially similar to a proposal that was submitted to the shareholders for vote at a recent annual meeting and that received few affirmative votes. (The exact requirements here are specified in the SEC rules.)
5. It is beyond the corporation's power to carry out the proposal.
6. It relates to the conduct of the corporation's ordinary business operations.

You may wonder why management can exclude shareholder proposals that relate to the conduct of the corporation's ordinary business operations. The reason is that under state corporation laws the shareholders have the power to elect directors, but they do not have the power to tell the directors they have elected how to operate the business. Instead, corporation law gives the *directors* the power to manage the business and affairs of the corporation (see Chapter 39). The SEC has therefore stated that a shareholder proposal is proper if it concerns corporate policy but not if it concerns the ordinary, day-to-day operations of the corporation.

TENDER OFFERS

Sometimes a conflict over control of a corporation is resolved by a proxy contest. At other times, those who want to wrest control of a corporation from management choose to do so by purchasing the necessary shares. In most instances, it is not necessary to own an actual majority of a corporation's shares in order to obtain working control of the corporation.

Purchasing shares to gain control of a corporation is normally accomplished through a **tender offer,** which is a public offer to purchase the shares of a corporation from its shareholders at a specified price during a specified period of time. The shareholders are *offered* the opportunity to *tender* (present for acceptance) their shares in return for cash, securities, or a combination of the two.

Tender offers are usually made by one corporation, called the *offeror,* that wants to take over another corporation, called the *target corporation.* Typically, the offeror offers to pay a price for the shares that is higher than the market price.

Hostile Takeovers

Frequently, the management of a target corporation will oppose an attempted takeover. In such a situation, the attempt to take over the corporation is called a *hostile takeover.* If a sufficient number of the target corporation's shares are tendered and purchased, the offeror elects its own candidates to the board of directors. The new board then approves a merger, the offeror votes its shares to obtain shareholder approval, and the merger is consummated.

One technique for resisting a takeover attempt is for the management of the target corporation to find a so-called "white knight," which is a corporation that will make a better offer for the shares than that of the original offeror. The target corporation eventually loses its independence to the white knight, but at least it has chosen the corporation with which it will be merged. Other techniques for resisting takeover attempts and questions about whether they violate the securities laws will be considered later in this section of the chapter.

Tender Offer Regulation

In the 1960s, tender offers became a very popular means of accomplishing corporate takeovers. As a result, Congress enacted amendments to the 1934 Act concerning tender offers in 1968. The purpose of the amendments is to protect investors by providing offerors, target corporations, and white knights the opportunity for timely communication with shareholders concerning tender offers for the shares of corporations registered with the SEC. The SEC has adopted rules that help to accomplish this purpose.

Five Percent Acquisition Report Regardless of how it is accomplished, any person or group that acquires ownership of more than five percent of a registered equity security must submit a report disclosing the acquisition to the SEC, to the corporation that issued the shares, and to each securities exchange on which the shares are traded within ten days of the acquisition. This report, made on Schedule 13D, must include a statement of the purpose for acquiring the shares. If the purpose is to acquire working control of the corporation, then any plan to liquidate, merge, sell the assets of, or make major changes in the business of the corporation must be disclosed.

Tender Offer Report Any person or group that intends to make a public tender offer must file a report with the SEC on or before the commencement date of the tender offer, which is the date of the first public announcement of the offer. The information in the report, which is made on Schedule 14D–1, is similar to that in Schedule 13D, including a statement of the purpose of the tender offer. Copies of all invitations for tenders and all advertisements that include the tender offer must also be filed with the SEC at or before the time they are published or sent. Copies of all information reported to the SEC must also be given to the corporation.

Schedule 14D–1 need be filed only when a *public* tender offer is made. The purchase of shares on a stock exchange or from an individual shareholder is not a public tender offer. Consequently, it does not have to be reported under the tender offer rule, although it might have to be reported under the five percent rule.

In some situations, it is unclear whether or not a tender offer is public. The courts have said that the solicitation of a large number of shareholders, the imposition of a strict time limit for tender, the payment of a premium price (an amount higher than the market price), the use of publicity, and an offer to pay a fixed and rigid price are all indications that a tender offer is public.

Tender Offer Process The target corporation's management must mail a tender offer to its shareholders, or it must provide a list of the shareholders to the offeror. Management must also inform the shareholders whether it supports, opposes, or is neutral about the tender offer within ten days of the effective date of the offer. If management or anyone else, such as another tender offeror, recommends to the shareholders that they either accept or reject the offer, a report of the recommendation, the reasons for it, and other information relevant to the tender offer must be filed with the SEC on Schedule 14D–9.

Opposing a Takeover Attempt Earlier you read that the management of a target corporation often opposes a takeover attempt. In its opposition, however, management must be careful not to engage in fraud or manipulation since the use of either to support or oppose a tender offer is prohibited by the 1968 amendments to the 1934 Act and by SEC rules.

Techniques of opposing takeovers that have been used successfully include (1) negotiating a large bank loan at an unfavorable interest rate that will become effective only if the takeover succeeds, (2) changing the corporation's state of incorporation to a state that has restrictive takeover laws, and (3) negotiating a union agreement that provides for a substantial increase in wages that will become effective only if the takeover succeeds. Generally, the courts have held that management has not been fraudulent or manipulative in resisting takeover attempts regardless of the techniques used. These decisions have been based on the business judgment rule, which is a legal principle that provides that business decisions made in good faith by corporate managers will not be second-guessed and overturned by the courts.

Nonetheless, in the case of *Mobil Corp. v. Marathon Oil Co.,* a court did decide that a target corporation's offer to sell a very valuable corporate asset to a white knight in order to make the target corporation much less attractive to a hostile tender offeror constituted manipulation that was prohibited by the tender offer amendments to the 1934 Act. About this technique, which is called a *lock-up option,* the court said:

> In our view, it is difficult to conceive of a more effective and manipulative device that the "lock-up" options employed here, options which not only artificially affect, but for all practical purposes completely block, normal healthy market activity and, in fact, could be construed as expressly designed solely for that purpose.

Tender Offer Terms A tender offer must remain open for acceptance by the tender of shares for at least 20 business days. During that time, the offeror may not purchase any of the shares that are tendered. Furthermore, a shareholder who tenders shares may withdraw the tender during the first 15 days of the offer, at any time after 60 days from the time the offer became effective, or within 10 days after a competing offer has been made.

If it appears that a tender offer is not going to be successful, the offeror may decide to increase the offer price. When this is done, all shareholders, including those who tendered their shares at the lower price, must be given the opportunity to tender their shares at the higher price.

When a tender offer is for less than all of the outstanding shares and more shares are tendered than the offeror has promised to buy, the offeror must purchase the shares on a *pro rata* basis. For instance, if the offer was for 40 percent of the shares and 80 percent were tendered, the offeror must purchase one-half of the shares tendered by each shareholder.

Enforcement of Tender Offer Regulations A tender offeror or the management of a target corporation may seek an injunction from a court for violations of the provisions of the amendments to the 1934 Act or the SEC rules regulating tender offers. In addition, a shareholder who suffers a loss as the result of reliance on fraudulent statements or omissions by one of the parties involved in the tender offer process may sue for damages.

State Regulation of Tender Offers

A number of states have adopted legislation regulating tender offers. Their purpose, however, has not been to protect investors but rather to protect the management of target corporations located in those states from hostile takeovers by making tender offer procedures burdensome for offerors. The states have done this so that local corporations will not become subject to the control of distant corporations that have accomplished successful tender offer takeovers. Control by distant corporations, these states believe, can result in less concern with local matters, reduced contributions to local charities, and even plant closings. In addition, states having this type of legislation will attract corporations that fear tender offer takeovers. In a recent case, however, the Supreme Court struck down the Illinois statute regulating tender offers, holding that it imposed an excessive burden on interstate commerce and was therefore unconstitutional. No doubt, similar statutes in other states are also unconstitutional.

STATE REGULATION OF SECURITIES

Prior to 1933, state statutes were the sole sources of securities regulation. Today, all the states except Delaware regulate securities through statutes called

blue sky laws. The phrase "blue sky laws" gained common acceptance after a judge stated that the purpose of state securities laws is to prevent "speculative schemes which have no more basis than so many feet of 'blue sky.'"

There is a great deal of variation among the states in the ways they regulate securities. Generally, however, there are three basic types of state regulation:

1. *Fraud Type Regulations.* These regulations usually prohibit the use of fraud in the issuance, promotion, distribution, sale, or purchase of securities. The term fraud is broadly defined, but it typically involves some form of deception or misrepresentation. Violations can lead to criminal prosecution for past activities and injunctions barring the future use of fraudulent practices.
2. *Dealer Type Regulations.* These regulations require that securities dealers and sales personnel located within a state to register with the state. Specific registration requirements vary from state to state.
3. *Registration Type Regulations.* These regulations require that securities must be registered or "qualified" before they can be traded. Again the specifics vary from state to state. They range from requiring that only minimal information be filed to requiring that all data a specified state official deems appropriate be disclosed. In some states, a state official may even judge the merits of registered securities. This is a power that the SEC does not have under federal law.

Some states use only the fraud type of securities regulation while other states may use two or all three types.

How effective are the blue sky laws within the regulatory scheme for securities? Generally, state regulation of securities transactions is regarded as less effective than federal regulation. Federal law has the advantage of being uniform and enforceable throughout the United States. Conversely, a state's power extends only to its geographical boundaries. Also, state regulations often receive only perfunctory execution, mainly because securities regulation is not usually a topic of great importance to state legislatures and appropriations to the agencies that enforce the laws may be small.

REVIEW QUESTIONS

1. Explain in your own words what an investment contract is.
2. What are the steps that must be taken by a corporation that issues a security?
3. What are the similarities and differences between §16 of the 1934 Act and SEC Rule 10b–5?
4. What must a private party prove to be successful in a legal action charging a defendant with a violation of §10(b) of the 1934 Act?
5. Under what circumstances would a shareholder prefer simply to have a proposal included in management's proxy rather than soliciting proxies?
6. What is a tender offer? When is a tender offer hostile? In what ways does the SEC regulate tender offers?
7. Name and explain the three types of state securities regulations.

CASE PROBLEMS

1. Gross is in the business of raising earthworms for sale to fishermen as bait. In order to raise enough worms to meet demand, Gross mailed out a promotional newsletter seeking people to purchase earthworms from him and then raise them. People who bought the worms were promised that the worms would double in quantity every 60 days and that Gross would purchase all worms raised at $2.25 a pound. Smith purchased worms, but his worms did not reproduce at anywhere near the rate promised by Gross, and Gross would not repurchase the worms for anywhere near the $2.25 promised. Smith brought a legal action against Gross claiming violations of federal securities laws. Gross defended on the grounds that he had not sold a security to Smith. Did Gross sell a security to Smith? Explain.

2. Daniel, who worked as a driver for a trucking company, was a member of the Teamsters Union. The union's contract with the trucking company included a pension plan for employees. All contributions to the plan were made by the company, so the company's contributions were the source of most of the assets in the pension fund. The rest of the assets were interest income from investments made by the managers of the pension fund. To be eligible for a pension, an employee was required to have 20 years of continuous service with the company. When Daniel retired, his application for a pension was denied on the grounds that, although he had worked for the company for 20 years, a break in his employment meant that he did not have 20 years of *continuous* service. Daniel brought a legal action against the union and the pension fund alleging that they had misrepresented and failed to disclose certain material facts regarding the plan and had thus violated the securities laws by committing fraud in connection with the sale of a security. The defendants argued that the pension fund was not a security. Who will win the case? Explain.

3. Issuer, Inc., a New York corporation engaged in retail sales within New York City, was interested in raising $1.6 million in capital. To this end, it approached 88 people in New York, New Jersey, and Connecticut through personal letters and then followed up with face-to-face negotiations where they seemed promising. After extensive efforts in which Issuer disclosed all the information that was requested, 19 of the people purchased Issuer's securities. Issuer did not limit its offer to insiders or their relatives or to wealthy or sophisticated investors. Did this constitute an exempt offering? Explain. [Adapted from CPA examination problem 1, question 15, *Business Law,* May, 1975.]

4. The directors of Clarion Corporation, their accountants, and their attorneys met to discuss the desirability of this highly successful corporation's going public. The discussion turned to the potential liability of the corporation and the parties involved in the preparation and signing of the registration statement under the Securities Act of 1933. Craft, Watkins, and Glenn are the largest shareholders. Craft is the chairman of the board, Watkins is the vice chairman, and Glenn is the chief executive officer. It has been decided that they will sign the registration statement. There are two other directors who are also executives and shareholders of the corporation. All of the board members are going to have a percentage of their shares included in the offering. Witherspoon & Friendly, CPAs, will issue an opinion as to the financial statements of the corporation, which will accompany the filing of the registration statement. Blackstone & Abernathy, attorneys-at-law, will render legal services.

   Discuss the types of potential liabilities and defenses that each of these parties or classes of parties may be subject to under the Securities Act of 1933 as a result of going public. [Adapted from CPA examination problem 2, question 36, *Business Law,* May, 1980.]

5. Whitworth was fired as president of Bonanza Corporation after the management of Bonanza lost a proxy contest. Bonanza then brought a legal action against Whitworth alleging that he had

violated the Securities Exchange Act of 1934 by making short-swing profits from the purchase and sale of Bonanza shares. Whitworth has raised the following defenses to Bonanza's allegations: (1) He is a New York resident, Bonanza is incorporated in New York, and the transactions were all made through the New York Stock Exchange. (2) He did not use any inside information in connection with any of the stock transactions in question. (3) All of his stock purchases were made during February, 1985, and all of his stock sales were made in September, 1985. (4) His motivation in selling the stock was solely the likelihood that he would be fired as president of Bonanza. Assuming that Whitworth will be able to prove all of his defenses, who will win the case? Explain. [Adapted from CPA examination problem 1, question 32, *Business Law,* May, 1979.]

6. Taylor is the executive vice president for marketing of Reflex Corporation and a member of the board of directors. On the basis of information obtained during the course of his duties, Taylor concluded that Reflex's profits would fall by 50 percent for the quarter and 30 percent for the year. He quietly contacted his broker and disposed of 10,000 shares of his Reflex stock at a profit, some of which he had acquired within the previous six months. In fact, Reflex's profits did not fall, but its stock price declined for unrelated reasons. Taylor had also advised a friend to sell her shares and repurchase the stock later. She followed Taylor's advice, sold her shares for $21, and subsequently repurchased an equal number of shares at $11. Reflex is considering bringing a lawsuit against Taylor and his friend to recover the profits each of them made. Against whom and on what basis should Reflex bring its lawsuit? Explain. [Adapted from CPA examination problem 1, question 27, *Business Law,* November, 1979.]

7. Taylor Corporation is a manufacturing company whose securities are registered on a national securities exchange. On February 6, 1985, one of Taylor's engineers disclosed to management that he had discovered a new product that he believed would be very profitable to the corporation. Messrs. Jackson and Wilson, the corporation's

president and treasurer and members of its board of directors, were very impressed with the prospects of the new product's profitability. Indeed, Wilson was so impressed that on February 12, 1985, he purchased 1,000 shares of the corporation's common stock on the open market at $10 per share. This was before news of the new product reached the public in late February and caused a rise in the market price of the stock to $30 per share. Jackson did not purchase any shares in February because he had already purchased 600 shares of the corporation's common stock for $10 per share on January 15, 1985.

Due to unexpected expenses arising from a fire in his home, Jackson sold the 600 shares of stock he purchased in January on the open market at $35 per share on April 16, 1985. Wilson continues to hold his 1,000 shares. To whom and on what bases can Wilson and Jackson be held liable for their purchases and sales of Taylor Corporation shares? [Adapted from CPA examination question 5b, *Business Law,* November, 1975.]

8. Androvette purchased 1,000 shares of Potash, Inc. She later learned that financial statements published by Potash a month before she purchased her shares had contained materially incorrect information and that Hurd & Zollers, the CPA firm that had audited Potash's financial statements, had been negligent in not discovering the incorrect information. However, Androvette had actually purchased the Potash shares because she had once had a friend named Potash. She had not read or even known about the tainted financial statements. If Androvette brings a lawsuit against Hurd & Zollers alleging a violation of SEC Rule 10(b)–5, on what basis may Hurd & Zollers defend? Explain.

9. Howe Chemical Corporation (Howe) recently received a letter from the president of the Medical Committee on Environmental Rights. The letter states that a proposal for an amendment to the corporation's articles of incorporation, which accompanied the letter, will be presented by the committee at the corporation's next annual shareholders' meeting. The proposed amend-

ment states that the corporation will not engage in the manufacture of products containing the chemical DTT because it is thought by some to be a cause of cancer. Howe holds an exclusive patent on DTT, and most of its products contain the chemical. The management of Howe believes that the corporation would go out of business if it could not use the chemical. Therefore, management does not wish to send the proposal to Howe's shareholders in the proxy material that will go out before the annual meeting. If you were called upon to advise Howe's management concerning possible ways they might be able to exclude the Medical Committee's proposal from the proxy material, what advice would you give? Explain.

10. Rubens Corporation has been steadily losing ground against its competitors, which has been reflected in a downward slide in the market price of its shares on the New York Stock Exchange. Mary Evans, a shareholder of Rubens, has been a vocal critic of Rubens' management team. Man-

agement recently learned that Evans has been purchasing large blocks of Rubens' stock and now owns about 4 percent of the outstanding shares. They calculate that, given her wealth and the depressed price of the stock, Evans can probably acquire at least 20 percent of the shares of Rubens, which will give her working control of the corporation. Because of the threat of a possible tender offer by Evans, management is considering two possible actions. First, they are considering repurchasing enough of the outstanding shares of Rubens to increase Evans' percentage of ownership to 5 percent, thus forcing her to divulge her intentions in a Schedule 13D report. Second, they are considering giving the officers of Rubens corporate contracts that guaranty very large salaries and benefits for a lengthy period if a takeover attempt by Evans is successful. If you were called upon by Rubens' management to give them your views concerning the legal effects of the two actions they are considering, what would you say?

52

LABOR-MANAGEMENT RELATIONS

In this chapter we will examine the major federal laws that regulate the employer-employee relationship. We will begin with a brief historical look at labor law. (It may come as a surprise to you that the first federal labor law was not enacted until 1926.) After this quick look back, we will discuss how labor–management relations are regulated today under the Wagner and Taft–Hartley Acts. The focus will then shift to occupational safety and health as we take a look at federal efforts to provide safe workplaces for American workers. The chapter will close with an explanation of the law that protects the pension benefits of employees.

THE HISTORICAL BACKGROUND OF LABOR LAW

Early American labor law was common law that was derived from British law. It emphasized the rights of the employer and was hostile to the concept of unions. Indeed, it viewed concerted union action as constituting a criminal conspiracy. Whereas one individual might ask an employer for improved wages and better working conditions, two or more workers joining together to make such a request was illegal. In 1806, for example, a jury convicted a group of bootmakers of criminal conspiracy for agreeing not to work for any employer who paid less than a specified wage. It was not until 1842 that the threat of criminal prosecution for engaging in union activities was removed. In that year, a court ruled that the formation of a union to achieve a closed shop through its member's refusal to work for an employer who would not agree to hire only union members was not criminal. The court ruled that the formation of the union did not have a criminal objective and that the union had not used criminal means to achieve its objective.

Civil law, however, continued to place many obstacles in the path of the union movement. Many employers required their employees to sign a **yellow dog contract,** which was a form of employment contract in which the employee agreed, as a condition of employment, not to join a union. If a union started an organizing attempt, the employer could fire any employee who joined the union and could seek an injunction against the union to prevent it from interfering with the contractual relationship between the employer and its employees. The threat to the employees' jobs combined with an injunction against the union usually resulted in the failure of the unionization attempt. Today, yellow dog contracts are against public policy and are not enforceable by a court.

The antitrust laws were also successfully wielded by employers to oppose unions. If a strike did not achieve a union's goal, the union would sometimes call for a boycott of an employer's product. The employer's response was often to bring an antitrust suit against the union under the Sherman and Clayton Acts in which the employer would seek to collect treble damages for losses caused by the boycott. The Supreme Court upheld the legality of these suits as recently as 1921. The Norris–LaGuardia Act, passed in 1932, limited the power of the federal courts to intervene in labor–management disputes. In 1935, Congress passed the Wagner Act, which will be discussed shortly. These two laws provide unions with substantial, but not complete, immunity from the antitrust laws. Generally, unions will not violate the antitrust statutes as long as they act in their own self-interest and do not combine their activities with those of a nonlabor group.

THE NATIONAL LABOR RELATIONS ACT

Congress provided labor with broad rights and significant protection when it passed the National Labor Relations Act, also known as the Wagner Act, in 1935. This act was the first comprehensive federal labor law, and it was decidedly "pro-labor." It gave workers the right to organize and to bargain collectively. To protect these rights, the act declared certain actions by an employer, called unfair labor practices, to be illegal. The act also created the National Labor Relations Board (NLRB) to administer the law. The NLRB fulfills two functions; (1) it administers the process whereby employees vote on whether or not they want a union to represent them in their dealings with their employer, and (2) it investigates and prevents unfair labor practices.

Employee Rights and Union Elections

Because employees frequently exercise their rights through a union, people often believe that it is the union that has these rights and that individuals who do not belong to the union lack these rights. This belief is incorrect. Labor law does not give rights to unions; it gives rights to employees. Therefore, employees have these rights whether they belong to a union or not. Under the law, employees have the right to form, join, or assist a labor organization; to bargain collectively through representatives of their own choosing; to engage in concerted activities, such as strikes, picketing, and handbilling, for the purpose of collective bargaining or mutual aid and protection; and to refrain from these activities in certain instances.

Notice that the law speaks of the rights of "employees." This is because there are two sides to the labor-management issue. Labor — the employees — makes up one side and management makes up the other. In labor-management relations, the two sides deal with each other at arms-length across the bargaining table. There is an adversary nature to the relationship under the law. If a person does not come within the law's definition of an employee, that person is not covered by the protections of the law. The law defines an **employee** as all workers except for agricultural workers; domestic servants; individuals employed by a parent or spouse; independent contractors; supervisors; people who work for employers that are subject to the Railway Labor Act (railroads and airlines); and all local, state, or federal government workers with the exception of the postal service workers.

The law defines a **supervisor** as a person who is given the authority by an employer to hire, transfer, suspend, lay off, recall, promote, discharge, assign, reward, or discipline employees or who has the responsibility to direct employees or adjust their grievances or effectively to recommend any of these actions if their exercise requires the use of independent judgment and not merely the carrying out of the actions in a routine manner or in a clerical capacity. Management personnel are considered to be supervisors.

Election Contests If an election petition is filed with the NLRB, it will conduct an election to determine whether or not the employees desire to have a union represent them. A petition can be filed by the employer, the employees, or a labor organization. If someone other than the employer files the petition, it must be supported by at least 30 percent of the employees. Once the NLRB determines that it has legal jurisdiction in the matter — that is, once it establishes that the workers are in fact employees and not supervisors under the law — it starts the election machinery. If all the parties agree upon the issues, as sometimes happens, the election will be a *consent election*. If they do not agree, the election will be a *contested election*. The NLRB holds hearings to determine the appropriate bargaining unit and the eligibility of various employees to vote. The NRLB will then conduct the election by secret ballot. The outcome is decided by a majority vote of those actually voting, not of those eligible to vote. See Figure 52-1 for examples of how the outcome of an election is determined.

The Duty of Fair Representation

If the employees select a union to represent them in collective bargaining, the union will be the exclusive representative of *all* the employees in the bargaining unit, not just those who voted for it or who became union members. Thus, any

Election Outcomes

Example 1

Employees eligible to vote: 100
Employees who actually voted: 80

>   **Vote Tally:**   No Union—43
>   United Auto Workers—37
>   **Result:**   No union representation of employees.

Example 2

Employees eligible to vote: 100
Employees who actually voted: 80

>   **Vote Tally:**   No union—30
>   United Auto Workers—30
>   Brotherhood of Electrical Workers—20
>   **Result:**   Runoff election between the options receiving the two highest
>   vote totals because no one choice received a majority.
>   **Runoff Tally:**   No Union—28
>   United Auto Workers—52
>   **Result:**   United Auto Workers will represent the employees.

FIGURE 52-1
Examples of Election Outcomes

contract that the union agrees upon with the employer with regard to wages, hours, and working conditions will apply to all the employees. An employee who disagrees with the union cannot obtain different terms from the employer. Because of this legally imposed doctrine of exclusivity, the law has also created a counterbalancing obligation—the duty of **fair representation**. This duty requires that the union represent everyone in the bargaining unit—union members, nonunion employees, or union members who belong to a dissident group, for example—with fairness and in good faith.

Fair representation and equal treatment are not the same thing, however. A union does not have to bargain for equal benefits for everyone. Differences that have a logical basis and a rational purpose are allowed. For instance, a union can negotiate a contract that provides higher wages for skilled workers than for nonskilled workers, longer vacations for workers with more years of employment, or a night-shift differential to provide higher pay for employees who work what is generally considered to be a less attractive shift. Such contractual terms are not unfair since they apply to everyone—men, women, blacks, whites, union members, nonunion employees, and so forth. Every employee will get the higher wages when they move into a skilled job or the longer vacation when they have the required years. A breach of the duty of fair representation would occur if a group, such as women or nonunion employees, were excluded from skilled jobs or the night shift.

Fair Representation and Employee Grievances Complaints by employees that they are not being treated properly or are not receiving what is due them under the terms of the collective bargaining agreement are called **grievances**. Most labor contracts include a mechanism for handling grievance disputes that may arise between the parties to the contract. The grievance process will have several steps in which mutual attempts are made to settle the dispute at successively higher levels in the union-management hierarchy. Often, the final step in the process involves bringing in an outside arbitrator who will make a final and binding decision. The operation of this grievance mechanism in a contract will frequently lead to fair representation disputes.

A union cannot casually refuse to take a worker's grievance to arbitration, nor can it take a grievance to arbitration without adequate investigation and preparation. To do either would be a breach of the duty of fair representation. Yet, a union need not take every grievance to arbitration. The union will have met its duty if, after a thorough review, it declines to arbitrate because a grievance lacks merit under the contract. A union that breaches this duty can be charged with unfair labor practices and may face a lawsuit for damages.

The following case involves a lawsuit that was brought against an employer, alleging wrongful discharge, and against a union, claiming a breach of the duty of fair representation. The union unsuccessfully attempted to avoid paying damages to the worker.

BOWEN v. U.S. POSTAL SERVICE
459 U.S. 212 (Sup. Ct. 1983)

[Bowen was discharged from his employment with the U.S. Postal Service after an altercation with a fellow employee. Bowen filed a grievance with his union, and at each step of the grievance process, the responsible union officer recommended that the grievance be pursued. For no apparent reason, however, the union's national office refused to take the matter to arbitration. Bowen brought a legal action against his employer and his union. A jury determined that Bowen had been wrongfully discharged and that the union had breached its duty of fair representation.

Bowen's lost benefits and wages totaled $52,954. The court determined that the employer should pay $22,954 and that the union should pay the remaining $30,000. The court reasoned that the union should pay for the period following the date that Bowen would have been reinstated if his grievance had been arbitrated. The union appealed, arguing that it should have no liability for Bowen's back pay since it was the employer who made the decision to discharge him. The

Intermediate Court of Appeals reversed the judgment against the union, and Bowen appealed to the U.S. Supreme Court.]

POWELL, Justice

Of paramount importance is the right of the employee, who has been injured by both the employer's and the union's breach, to be made whole. Were it not for the union's failure to represent the employee fairly, the employer's breach "could [have been] remedied through the grievance process to the employee-plaintiff's benefit."

It would indeed be unjust to prevent the employee from recovering in such a situation. It would be equally unjust to require the employer to bear the increase in the damages caused by the union's wrongful conduct. It is true that the employer discharged the employee wrongfully and remains liable for the employee's back-pay. The union's breach of its duty of fair representation, however, caused the grievance procedure to malfunction resulting in an increase in the employee's damages. Even though both the employer and the union have caused the damage suffered by the employee, the union is responsible for the increase in damages and, as between the two wrongdoers, should bear its portion of the damages.

Although each party participates in the grievance procedure, the union plays a pivotal role in the process since it assumes that responsibility of determining whether to press an employee's claims. The employer, for its part, must rely on the union's decision not to pursue an employee's grievance.

In the absence of damages apportionment where the default of both parties contributes to the employee's injury, incentives to comply with the grievance procedure will be diminished.

Reversed.

CASE REVIEW QUESTIONS

1. What legal duty owed to Bowen did the union breach? What did the union do that constituted a breach of that duty?
2. Does the decision in this case illustrate an anti-union bias on the part of the Supreme Court?
3. In deciding whether or not to take a grievance to arbitration, what factors do you think a union will take into consideration?

Right-to-Work Laws

As a general proposition, an employee is free to join or to refrain from joining a union. Under certain circumstances, though, the employer and the union can agree to a **union security clause.** Such a clause might require a worker to join the union within a certain number of days of becoming employed in order to remain employed. This type of requirement is called a **union shop** provision. (You should note, however, that requiring a person to belong to a union in order to be hired in the first place, which is called a **closed shop,** is illegal.) Alternatively, an employer and a union may agree to a provision that requires all workers to pay the union an amount equal to the union dues while leaving the workers free to join the union or not as they wish. This type of requirement is called an *agency shop* provision. Because a union must represent all the workers and because all the workers receive the benefits of the contract the union negotiates, union advocates believe that all the workers should contribute to the financial support of the union. Union opponents, on the other hand believe that they should not be forced to join the union or pay the equivalent of union dues if they do not want a union to represent them.

When Congress passed the Taft-Hartley Act in 1947, it included a right-to-work provision — Section 14(b) — that allows the states to outlaw union security clauses within their borders. Since then, 20 states have passed **right-to-work laws** that prohibit requiring union membership as a condition of employment. In these states, an employee can never be forced to join or to contribute to a union.

Employer Unfair Labor Practices

In order to protect the rights of workers, Congress has prohibited employers from engaging in certain types of conduct that constitute employer **unfair labor practices.** Thus, under the Wagner Act, an employer is not to do any of the following:

1. Interfere with, restrain, or coerce employees in the exercise of their rights.
2. Dominate or interfere with a labor organization.
3. Discriminate against an employee with the purpose of encouraging or discouraging his or her membership in a labor organization.
4. Discriminate against an employee who has participated in a NLRB proceeding.
5. Refuse to bargain with the union.

Frequently, a single act by an employer will violate more than one part of the law. For instance, if an employer fires an employee because the employee is trying to organize a union, the employer has violated both points 1 and 3. Indeed, threatening to fire a person for his or her union activity is just as illegal as actually firing the person.

Not only is penalizing an employee for certain activity illegal, but rewarding the person may be illegal also. Thus, if an employer who faces a campaign to organize a union suddenly grants wage increases and longer vacations, he or she has committed unfair labor practices in violation of points 1 and 3. The employer is interfering with the employees' free exercise of their rights and is attempting to discourage union membership just as much by granting benefits as he or she would be by voicing threats. An important point to remember here is that it is the individual employee that possesses the rights guaranteed by the Wagner Act and that employees have these rights whether they belong to a union or not.

In the following case, a woman signed a petition seeking to have a former employee rehired. Signing a petition is an activity that is protected by the labor law. It is concerted action by more than one person for the mutual aid and protection of them all in the event they ever found themselves in the same situation. The employer attempted to avoid the charge of committing an unfair labor practice by arguing that the woman, who was discharged for signing the petition, was not an employee. If the woman were management, she would not have the labor law rights, so her discharge would not violate the law. The employer lost the case.

NLRB v. HENDRICKS COUNTY RURAL ELECTRIC MEMBERSHIP CORPORATION
454 U.S. 170 (Sup. Ct. 1981)

BRENNAN, Justice

Mary Weatherman was the personal secretary to the general manager and chief executive officer of Hendricks County Rural Electric Membership Corp. (Hendricks), a rural electric membership cooperative.

In May 1977 she signed a petition seeking reinstatement of a close friend and fellow employee, who had lost his arm in the course of employment with Hendricks, and had been dismissed. Several days later she was discharged.

Weatherman filed an unfair labor practice charge with the National Labor Relations Board (NLRB or Board), alleging that the discharge violated the National Labor Relations Act (NLRA or Act). Hendricks' defense, *inter alia* [among others], was that Weatherman was denied the Act's protection because as a "confidential" secretary she was impliedly excluded from the Act's definition of "employee." The Administrative Law Judge (ALJ) rejected this argument. He noted that the Board's decisions had excluded from bargaining units only those "confidential employees . . . 'who assist and act in a confidential capacity to persons who formulate, determine, and effectuate management policies in the field of labor relations.' " Applying this "labor nexus" [labor relations connection] test, the ALJ found that Weatherman was not such a "confidential employee." He also determined that Hendricks had discharged Weatherman for activity — signing the petition — protected by the Act. The ALJ thus sustained Weatherman's unfair labor practice charge. The board affirmed "the rulings, findings, and conclusions of the Administrative Law Judge," and ordered that Weatherman be reinstated with backpay. (Hendricks appealed, and an intermediate appellate court overruled the ALJ on the grounds that all confidential employees, not just those with a labor nexus, were excluded as employees under the Act.]

The employees covered by the Act were defined in § 2(3):

> The term "employee" shall include any employee . . . but shall not include any individual employed as an agricultural laborer, or in the domestic sevice of any family or person at his home, or any individual employed by his parent or spouse.

Although the Act's express exclusions did not embrace confidential employees, the Board was soon faced with the argument that all individuals who had access to confidential information of their employers should be excluded, as a policy matter, from the definition of "employee." The Board rejected such an implied exclusion, finding it to have "no warrant under the Act." . . . But in fulfilling its statutory obligation to determine appropriate bargaining units, . . . for which broad discretion has been vested in the Board, . . . the Board adopted special treatment for the narrow group of employees with access to confidential, labor-relations information of the employer. The Board excluded these individuals from bargaining units composed of rank-and-file workers. . . . The Board's rationale was that management should not be required to handle labor relations matters through employees who are represented by the union with which the company is required to deal and who in the normal performance of their duties may obtain advance information of the company's position with regard to contract negotiations, the disposition of grievances, and other labor relations matters. . . .

The Court's ultimate task here is, of course, to determine whether the Board's "labor nexus" limitation on the class of confidential employees who, although within the definition of "employee," . . . may be denied inclusion in bargaining units has a reasonable basis in law. . . . Clearly the NLRB's longstanding practice of excluding from bargaining units only those confidential employees satisfying the Board's labor-nexus test, rooted firmly in the Board's understanding of the nature of the collective bargaining process, and Congress' acceptance of that practice, fairly demonstrates that the Board's treatment of confidential employees does indeed have a reasonable basis in law.

In this Court . . . Hendricks does not argue that Weatherman came within the labor-nexus test as formulated by the Board, but rather concedes that Weatherman did not have confidential duties with respect to labor policies. . . . Because there is therefore no dispute in this respect, and in any event no suggestion that the Board's finding regarding labor nexus was not supported by substantial evidence, we conclude that the Court of Appeals erred in holding that the record did not support the Board's determination that Weatherman was not a confidential employee with a labor nexus. We therefore reverse the judgment of the Court of Appeals . . . insofar as enforcement of the Board's order was denied, and remand with direction to enter an order enforcing the Board's order.

Reversed and remanded.

CASE REVIEW QUESTIONS

1. Which of the activities prohibited by the Wagner Act that are set out in the text prior to the case did Hendricks engage in?
2. Does the decision in this case reflect a realistic, common-sense method of determining which confidential employees enjoy the protection of labor law? Explain.
3. Mary Weatherman did not belong to a union. Does this case illustrate, therefore, the fact that the National Labor Relations Act protects all employees, regardless of whether or not they belong to an organized union? Explain.

NLRB Reinstatement Powers When an employer commits an unfair labor practice by discharging or otherwise penalizing an employee for the exercise of rights protected under the labor law, the NLRB has the power to remedy the situation. The employer can be ordered to cease the improper activity and to reinstate the individual, with backpay, to his or her previous position with the company. An NLRB order for reinstatement with backpay was upheld by the Supreme Court in the *Hendricks* case that you just read.

THE TAFT–HARTLEY ACT

In 1947, Congress passed the Taft–Hartley Act, officially titled the Labor Management Relations Act. This law significantly amended the National Labor Relations Act. It added union unfair labor practices to the law in an attempt to balance fairly the rights of employees and employers. In addition, it created the Federal Mediation and Conciliation Service, an agency that provides mediation, conciliation, and arbitration services to management and labor when they need assistance in settling particularly difficult labor disputes. The act created a mechanism for the President of the United States to enter any labor disputes that so imperil the health or safety of the nation that they constitute a national emergency. Lastly, the right-to-work provision, which allows the states to ban union security clauses, is also contained in the Taft–Hartley Act.

Union Unfair Labor Practices
The Taft–Hartley Act prohibits unions from engaging in certain types of conduct that constitute union unfair labor practices. Thus, under the act a labor organization is not to do any of the following:

1. Restrain or coerce employees in the exercise of their rights.
2. Cause or attempt to cause an employer to discriminate against an employee.
3. Refuse to bargain collectively with the employer.
4. Engage in secondary activities such as secondary strikes and boycotts.
5. Charge excessive or discriminatory membership fees.
6. Engage in certain types of featherbedding practices.

Because labor law gives certain rights to employees, it is just as illegal for the union to interfere with the exercise of those rights as it is for the employer. For example, a labor organization will commit an unfair labor practice if it uses violence or threats of violence against employees that oppose it. Union efforts to get an employer to fire an employee who belongs to another union or who engages in anti-union activity are also illegal. The issue of excessive membership fees is not usually a problem. Most unions realize that charging extremely high union dues would simply discourage membership in the union and would therefore be self-defeating.

A union engages in illegal featherbedding only when it causes an employer to pay for services that are not performed. Hence, many practices that might reasonably be regarded as featherbedding are not prohibited under the labor law. Consider, for example, a union that negotiates a contract with an employer that provides for an elevator operator in automatic elevators. Since the elevator is operated merely by pushing the button of the desired floor, an elevator operator might reasonably be considered unnecessary. However, though the operator may be of little value to the elevator's passengers, he or she is performing a service, so the union's insistence on there being an elevator operator is not illegal featherbedding.

The Obligation to Bargain

Both the employer and the union have the obligation to bargain in good faith. Both parties are therefore obligated to meet at reasonable times and to confer in good faith concerning wages, hours, other terms and conditions of employment, the negotiation of a collective bargaining agreement, or any questions that arise under a preexisting agreement. However, though the law provides that the parties must bargain in good faith, neither party is compelled to agree to a proposal of the other party, nor is either party required to make concessions.

Good-Faith Bargaining Good-faith bargaining is evidenced by a serious attempt to negotiate a contract or to settle a grievance. The parties must make a vigorous effort to reach an agreement. Although neither party is obligated to make concessions, total inflexibility, with no willingness to engage in the give-and-take of negotiations, will call the good faith of a party into question.

If the employer has information that is necessary for the bargaining process and the union requests it, the employer must supply that information to the union. For example, the employer's personnel office may have data on the racial, ethnic, or sexual makeup of the work force that the union needs to fulfill its duty of fair representation in an arbitration or bargaining context.

Bargaining Subjects Wages, hours, and working conditions are mandatory subjects of bargaining; the union and the employer must bargain with regard to them. Included within these very broad categories are such topics as pension and profit sharing plans, vacations, insurance coverage, seniority provisions, discipline procedures, safety regulations, and break time for meals.

There are also certain voluntary bargaining subjects. If the union and the employer wish to bargain these additional subjects, they may generally do so. One party cannot unilaterally force the other to bargain over these matters, however. For example, benefits paid to already retired employees are a frequent subject of voluntary bargaining.

Lastly, there are a very limited number of forbidden subjects about which it is illegal to bargain. The closed shop, which requires that a person belong to a union before he or she can be hired, is an example of such a forbidden subject. As we mentioned earlier in this chapter, the closed shop is illegal.

In the case that follows, the Supreme Court examines the difficult question of what employer decisions so directly affect employees that they constitute mandatory bargaining subjects and what decisions are a function of owning a business and therefore need not be bargained about despite their impact upon employees.

FIRST NATIONAL MAINTENANCE v. NLRB
452 U.S. 666 (Sup. Ct. 1981)

[First National Maintenance decided to cancel a maintenance contract with a Greenpark nursing home. The decision was purely a financial one. First National discharged the employees that were used to staff the Greenpark operation, and it refused to bargain about the decision with the union recently selected by those employees. The union charged that this refusal constituted a violation of the labor law, and the NLRB agreed. First National Maintenance appealed the decision of the NLRB to an intermediate appellate court that upheld the decision of the NLRB. First National Maintenance then appealed to the U.S. Supreme Court.]

BLACKMAN, Justice

Must an employer, under its duty to bargain in good faith "with respect to wages, hours, and other terms and conditions of employment," . . . negotiate with the certified representative of its employees over its decision to close part of its business?

A fundamental aim of the National Labor Relations Act is the establishment and maintenance of industrial peace to preserve the flow of interstate commerce. Central to achievement of this purpose is the promotion of collective bargaining as a method of defusing and channeling conflict between labor and manage-

ment. Congress ensured that collective bargaining would go forward by creating the National Labor Relations Board and giving it the power to condemn as unfair labor practices certain conduct by unions and employers that it deemed deleterious to the process, including the refusal "to bargain collectively."

Although parties are free to bargain about any legal subject, Congress has limited the mandate or duty to bargain to matters of "wages, hours, and other terms and conditions of employment." A unilateral change as to a subject within this category violates the statutory duty to bargain and is subject to the Board's remedial order. Conversely, both employer and union may bargain to impasse over these matters and use the economic weapons at their disposal to attempt to secure their respective aims. Congress deliberately left the words "wages, hours, and other terms and conditions of employment" without further definition, for it did not intend to deprive the Board of the power further to define those terms in light of specific industrial practices.

Nonetheless, in establishing what issues must be submitted to the process of bargaining, Congress had no expectation that the elected union representative would become an equal partner in the running of the business enterprise in which the union's members are employed. Despite the deliberate open-endedness of the statutory language, there is an undeniable limit to the subjects about which bargaining must take place. . . .

Some management decisions, such as choice of advertising and promotion, product type and design, and financing arrangements, have only an indirect and attenuated impact on the employment relationship. Other management decisions, such as the order of succession of layoffs and recalls, production quotas, and work rules, are almost exclusively "an aspect of the relationship" between employer and employee. The present case concerns a third type of managment decision, one that had a direct impact on employment, since jobs were inexorably eliminated by the termination, but had as its focus only the economic profitability of the contract with Greenpark, a concern under these facts wholly apart from the employment relationship. This decision, involving a change in the scope and direction of the enterprise, is akin to the decision whether to be in business at all, "not in [itself] primarily about conditions of employment, though the effect of the decision may be necessarily to terminate employment." At the same time, this decision touches on a matter of central and pressing concern to the union and its member employees; the possibility of continued employment and the retention of the employees' very jobs. Nonetheless, in view of an employer's need for unencumbered decision making, bargaining over management decisions that have a substantial impact on the continued availability of employment should be required only if the benefit, for labor-management relations and the collective bargaining process, outweighs the burden placed on the conduct of the business.

A union's interest in participating in the decision to close a particular facility or part of an employer's operation springs from its legitimate concern over job security. There is no dispute that the union must be given a significant opportunity to bargain about these matters of job security as a part of the "effects" bargaining mandated by § 8(a)(5). And, under § 8(a)(5), bargaining over the effects of a decision must be conducted in a meaningful manner and at a meaningful time, and the Board may impose sanctions to insure its adequacy.

Moreover, the union's legitimate interest in fair dealing is protected by § 8(a)(3) [of the NLRA], which prohibits partial closings motivated by anti-union animus, when done to gain an unfair advantage.

Management's interest in whether it should discuss a decision of this kind is much more complex and varies with the particular circumstances. If labor costs are an important factor in a failing operation and the decision to close, management will have an incentive to confer voluntarily with the union to seek concessions that may make continuing the business profitable. At other times, management may have great need for speed, flexibility, and secrecy in meeting business opportunities and exigencies. It may face significant tax or securities consequences that hinge on confidentiality, the timing of a plant closing, or a reorganization of the corporate structure. The publicity incident to the normal process of bargaining may injure the possibility of a successful transition or increase the economic damage to the business. The employer also may have no feasible alternative to the closing, and even good-faith bargaining over it may be both futile and cause the employer additional loss.

We conclude that the harm likely to be done to an employer's need to operate freely in deciding whether to shut down part of its business purely for economic reasons outweighs the incremental benefit that might be gained through the union's participation in making the decision, and we hold that the decision itself is *not* part of . . . "terms and conditions" . . . over which Congress has mandated bargaining.

Reversed and **remanded.**

BRENNAN with **MARSHALL,** Justices (dissenting)

The Court bases its decision on a balancing test. It states that "bargaining over management decisions that have a substantial impact on the continued availability of employment should be required only if the benefit, for labor-management relations and the collective-bargaining process, outweighs the burden placed on the conduct of the business."

I cannot agree with this test, because it takes into account only the interests of *management;* it fails to consider the legitimate employment interests of the workers and their Union. I therefore agree with the Court of Appeals that employers presumptively have a duty to bargain over a decision to close an operation, and that this presumption can be rebutted by a showing that bargaining would be futile, that the closing was due to emergency financial circumstances, or that, for some other reason, bargaining would not further the purposes of the National Labor Relations Act.

CASE REVIEW QUESTIONS

1. How powerful a hand will a union hold in its bargaining with an employer over the "effects" of a partial closure when the employer has already made the most significant decision, which is to terminate operations? Would a strike by the union be an effective threat against the employer during this "effects" bargaining? Explain.
2. Viewing this case from a labor-management perspective, does the decision enhance the collective bargaining process?
3. Is it illegal for a company to bargain with a union over the decision about the partial closure of a business?

Strikes and Lockouts

The strike and lockout are the economic weapons of labor and management, respectively. If the parties have bargained in good faith but have not been able to achieve an agreement, the workers are free to go on strike. A **strike** is simply the cessation of work by the employees. The striking employees have no legal right to reclaim their jobs, however. The employer may replace them with other workers, either temporarily or permanently.

Likewise, when bargaining has proved fruitless, the employer can lockout the employees in an effort to pressure them into a settlement. In a **lockout,** the employer prohibits the employees from entering the workplace and performing their jobs. The workplace will be literally locked to keep the employees out.

Because employers usually find it to be to their interest to maintain production while bargaining continues, lockouts are seldom used. In addition, employers seldom hire replacements for striking employees. Most strikes are of relatively brief duration. As a result, the problems and expenses of training a new group of employees are usually greater than the problems and expenses caused by a short strike.

Unfair Labor Practice Strikes If an unfair labor practice by the employer has either caused the strike or lengthened its duration, the legal situation is different. Such a strike is called an *unfair labor practice strike.* At the termination of the strike, the striking workers have the right to return to their jobs. If the employer has hired replacements, they cannot be retained in place of the striking workers.

Legal Strikes If the negotiating parties have met all their obligations under the law but a strike occurs because an agreement has not been reached, the strike is legal. The employees stop working and begin to picket outside their employer's place of business. The idea is to put economic pressure on the employer by halting the work at his or her facility and by preventing others from doing business with him or her through picketing. A picket line is intended, by its mere presence, to convince people that they should not cross the picket line in order to do business, make deliveries, or otherwise deal with the employer. Picketing is legal. However, it is not lawful for the pickets physically to prevent persons from crossing the picket line. The strikers' dispute, which is called a primary dispute, is with their employer, and their actions are aimed directly at their employer. The fact that others may be affected by the picket line is only incidental.

Secondary Activity

Secondary activity occurs when a union directly attempts to force a neutral third party to cease doing business with the employer. Engaging in secondary activity is an unfair labor practice on the part of the union. In a labor dispute, the rules of the game allow either party to exert directly whatever economic pressure they can on the other party. A disputing party may not, however, attempt to use an outside neutral party as a lever in the dispute. Suppose, for instance, that a striking union approaches an important supplier of the employer and informs the supplier that, unless deliveries to the employer are stopped, the supplier's place of business will be picketed. Such conduct by the union constitutes illegal secondary activity. Because the union has no direct labor dispute with the supplier, the supplier is neutral in the union's dispute with the employer. The supplier must therefore be allowed to make an independent decision whether or not to honor the picket line at the employer's place of business.

If another party is directly helping the employer to defeat the strike, that party is not neutral and can be legally picketed by the union. For example, when a company that was being struck arranged for some repair companies to do repair work that the struck company was legally obligated to perform for its customers, union picketing of the repair companies was held to be legal. The court held that these repair companies were allies of the struck company and were doing work that was normally performed by the striking workers. Thus, they were not true neutrals with regard to the labor dispute, and so they were not protected by the law written to protect neutrals.

Legal issues relating to secondary activities can easily flare up when there is more than one employer at a single physical location, which is called a *common situs*. For instance, suppose that Company A and Company B are working at the same construction site. If Company B's employees go on strike, may they picket the construction site? The answer is "Yes," so long as their employer is engaged in his or her normal business at the common situs and the picketers clearly indicate that their dispute is with Company B. Company A is not destined to have its operations at the common situs shut down by the picketers, however. Company A's rights can be protected by the "separate gate doctrine," which allows for the creation of an entrance for the exclusive use of nonstruck companies at the common situs. The union representing the striking employees of Company B cannot picket in front of this entrance. Thus, Company A's employees can come to work and deliveries can be made to Company A without anyone having to cross the picket line.

Consumer Boycotts

Sometimes, a union will attempt to increase the economic pressure on the employer by mounting a consumer boycott of the employer's product. An appeal to the public for a boycott is a primary activity and is therefore legal. Distributing handbills, placing newspaper ads, or conducting a rally to generate support for a consumer boycott constitute the exercise of the union's right of free speech. However, questions relating to secondary activities may arise if a campaign of this sort affects the place of business of a neutral party. Suppose, for instance, that a group of fruit packers strike their employer, who sells apples to retail stores. The union pickets the stores and passes out handbills in front of them. The signs and the literature request only that the stores' customers refrain from purchasing the struck employer's apples. The pickets are not in place when deliveries and pick-ups are made at the stores nor when the stores' employees come to and leave work. The picketing therefore does not prevent anyone from going to work or from doing business with the stores, except insofar as some people may not buy the specific apples. The Supreme Court has held that union action of this sort is legal. It does not constitute secondary activity because the union has merely followed the product of the struck employer, and it has closely confined its action to the primary dispute with the struck employer. The action would have been illegal, however, if the union had asked the public not to shop at the stores for any grocery products, which would have constituted an unlawful secondary boycott of the neutral retail stores.

OCCUPATIONAL SAFETY AND HEALTH

Job related injuries cost the work force and the economy staggering amounts, both financially and socially. Furthermore, the legal history of worker compensation for work-related injuries and of worker protection from unsafe working conditions is a sorry one. As the industrial revolution grew in this country and drew more and more people into the industrial work force, the law did not develop a corresponding duty for employers to furnish a safe workplace. Moreover, the early common law did not provide the injured worker much chance of receiving compensation. Indeed, an injured worker often put his or her job in jeopardy by suing or threatening to sue an employer who may have been negligent in providing faulty tools or an unsafe workplace. In addition, witnesses, who were often fellow workers, were usually hesitant to testify against the employer because of fear for their jobs.

The greatest barriers to compensation, however, were the legal defenses available to employers. The early common law had three established rules that were ordinarily used by employers to avoid paying compensation:

1. If an injury was caused by *another employee,* the common law held that the employer was not liable; this was called the Fellow-Servant Rule.

2. If the job were dangerous and had known risks, then the employer could defend on the basis of the employee's "assumption of the risks" when he or she took the job.

3. If the *employee's* lack of care played a part in the injury, then the employer could defend on the basis of "contributory negligence."

These defenses have been significantly limited today.

In response to growing public awareness of both the cost of work-related injuries to our society and the evidence that places of work once thought relatively safe — air-polluted factories, for example — actually pose substantial threats to human life, Congress passed the Williams–Steiger Occupational Safety and Health Act of 1970. This act, which became effective April 28, 1971, established the Occupational Safety and Health Administration. The public has adopted the abbreviation **OSHA** to refer to both the act and the administrative agency it created.

OSHA applies to all persons who are engaged in a business that affects commerce who have employees, though it does not apply to businesses already covered by the Coal Mine Health and Safety Act or the Atomic Energy Act. In addition, municipal, county, state, and federal government workers are not directly covered by OSHA. Many states, however, have their own occupational safety acts or plans that do include municipal, county, and state employees.

Duties of Employers

OSHA places two major duties on employers. First, employers must furnish employees with a workplace that is *free* from *recognized hazards* that are *likely* to cause *death* or *serious physical harm*. This requirement is referred to as the general duty clause of the act, but it applies *only* when no specific safety standard has been promulgated under the act. A second and related duty requires employers to comply with all appropriate standards for safety. The Department of Labor has promulgated literally thousands of safety standards that apply to employers, most of them derived from "national consensus standards" that had been developed earlier by such nationally recognized standards-producing organizations as the American National Standards Institute and the National Fire Protection Association. These safety standards are very specific and cover such subjects as the proper construction and maintenance of equipment, machine guarding, and fire and injury prevention procedures. They also specify the types of personal protective equipment that must be worn by employees and set training requirements to insure safe work practices.

In addition to complying with the two major duties just discussed, employers having more than 10 employees must keep detailed records and must file reports of all work-related injuries and deaths. You should note, at this point, that OSHA neither provides for compensation nor affects workers' compensation. Its concept is preventative, not compensatory.

Inspection by OSHA

To insure compliance with the standards promulgated by OSHA, the statute allows an inspector to enter any place of work in a reasonable manner at any reasonable time. In *Marshall v. Barlow's, Inc.,* however, the Supreme Court held this provision to be an unconstitutional violation of the Fourth Amendment's protection against unreasonable searches and seizures. The Court ruled that, if the owner of a business does not voluntarily consent to an inspection of the business premises, OSHA must obtain a search warrant before its inspector can enter those premises.

The requirement for a search warrant does not place a serious burden on OSHA. According to the Court's decision, OSHA need not show probable cause in the criminal law sense to obtain a search warrant from a federal judge. It need meet only a lesser standard. Thus, if OSHA can demonstrate a reasonable legislative or administrative justification for conducting the inspection of a particular business, a warrant will be issued. For example, a warrant will be issued if OSHA can show that the business has been chosen on the basis of a general administrative plan for the enforcement of the act derived from a study of injuries to employees in that type of industry in that geographical area. Of course, if OSHA has evidence of a specific violation by a business, that evidence alone will justify the issuance of a search warrant.

Penalties for Violations

If, upon inspection, a violation is found to exist, a citation will be issued. The employer is then given a reasonable time, not to exceed six months, to remedy the situation. If the employer believes that the citation or one of the safety standards used is unreasonable, he or she may appeal the citation or the standard to an administrative law judge. The appeal is an adversary one, with the appealing party being opposed by the Secretary of Labor. The decision of the judge is final unless a member of the Commission agrees to hear an appeal to the full Commission. If the Commission refuses to hear an appeal or if it rules against the employer, he or she may appeal the case to the U.S. Court of Appeals for the circuit in which the violation allegedly occured or in which the employer has his or her principal place of business.

Any employer who *willfully* and *repeatedly* violates the general duty clause may be assessed a civil penalty of not more than $10,000 for each violation. The fine for a simple violation is $1,000. Furthermore, any employer who fails to correct a violation may be assessed not over $1,000 for each day the failure continues.

OSHA takes cognizance of the lack of protection at common law afforded employees who wish to charge their employers with maintaining unsafe work areas. Under the act, an employee may report a violation of a standard to an OSHA area office on a complaint form that allows the employee to remain anonymous. If imminent danger is alleged or if the complaint appears to be valid, an inspection will be scheduled within a reasonable time. If the employee does not mind revealing his or her identity, he or she may accompany the inspector during the inspection of the work site. If an employee believes that he or she has been discriminated against because he or she reported a violation, the employee may file a complaint with OSHA. If the charges are proven, the employee may be compensated.

OSHA deals with hazards that are causing or are likely to cause death or serious harm to employees. The following case deals with two points. The first is the definition of a *recognized hazard*. The second is the fact that a violation may occur even though there has been no obvious permanent injury to an employee.

AMERICAN SMELTING & REFINING COMPANY v. OCCUPATIONAL SAFETY AND HEALTH REVIEW COMMISSION
501 F.2d 504 (Eighth Cir. 1974)

[The Steelworker's Union filed a complaint alleging unsafe working conditions caused by concentrations of airborne lead in American Smelting & Refining Company's plant. OSHA conducted an inspection and used an air-sampling pump to test for the presence of airborne lead. The refining company had supplied respirators to its employees to protect them from the lead. However, when OSHA conducted its inspection, all of the employees but one had their respirators hanging around their necks instead of properly wearing them.

After a hearing, the Occupational Safety and Health Review Commission ruled that the refining company had violated the law by allowing a recognized hazard that posed a threat to the workers to exist. The refining company appealed OSHA's decision.]

GIBSON, Circuit Judge

Relying on limited though express legislative history, the Petitioner argues that the general duty clause was not intended to cover hazards that can be detected only by testing devices. Since the airborne concentrations of lead in excess of .2mg/M3 were discovered by air sampling pumps instead of the human senses, Petitioner argues that no recognized hazard existed. In short, "recognized" only means recognized directly by human senses without the assistance of any technical instruments. . . .

We find [these] views unpersuasive. Looking to the words of the Act itself, "recognized hazards" was enacted instead of "readily apparent hazards." From the commonly understood meanings of the terms themselves, "recognized" denotes a broader meaning than "readily apparent."

We further think that the purpose and intent of the Act is to protect the health of the workers and that a narrow construction of the general duty clause would endanger this purpose in many cases. To expose workers to health dangers that may not be emergency situations and to limit the general duty clause to dangers only detectable by the human senses seems to us to be a folly. Our technological age depends on instrumentation to monitor many conditions of industrial operations and the environment. Where hazards are recognized but not detectable by the senses, common sense and prudence demand that instrumentation be utilized. Certain kinds of health hazards, such as carbon monoxide and asbestos poisoning, can only be detected by technical devices. . . . The Petitioner's contention, though advanced by arguable but loose legislative interpretation, would have us accept a result that would ignore the advances of industrial scientists, technologists, and hygienists, and also ignore the plain wording, purpose, and intent of this Act. The health of workers should not be subjected to such a narrow construction . . . .

Most important in the Petitioner's view is a reliance on a biological monitoring program, which involves the testing of each employee's blood and urine to determine the concentration of lead. Dr. Nelson, the Petitioner's Director of Environmental Sciences, stated that this testing is "a far more effective way of securing the safety of employees." Dr. Kehoe prefers biological monitoring, since air measurement "is not a standard which we regard as crucial in relation to the individual."

The biological monitoring . . . did not eliminate or even reduce the hazard, it merely disclosed it. Although testing of the blood and urine is the most important test for each individual, the use of air sampling tests is the most efficient and practical way for the Secretary to check for a hazard likely to cause death or serious physical harm to the workers as a group. We think it also the most efficient manner for the employer to check the existence of a hazard. . . . Workers should not be subjected to hazardous concentrations of airborne lead; biological monitoring should complement an industrial hygiene program for clean or at least safe air; it is not a substitute for a healthful working environment.

In addition, the Petitioner knew or should have known that the respirators would not reduce the likelihood of serious physical harm to the employees. During the unannounced tour of the plant by the Secretary's representatives, only one employee was properly wearing his respirator. The reasonable inference is that employees rarely used the awkward and uncomfortable respirators. It was reasonably foreseeable to the Petitioner that the respirators would not be properly worn. We hold that there was adequate evidence on the record considered as a whole that the biological monitoring program would not prevent a likelihood of harm to employees.

Affirmed.

CASE REVIEW QUESTIONS

1. Of what value was the biological monitoring system, seeing as how it did not eliminate the hazard?
2. What do you think the duties of an employer should be when it discovers that almost all of its employees do not use the safety devices it has provided?
3. What duty owed to employees under OSHA was breached by American Smelting & Refining Company?

Employees and Imminent Dangers

The case that follows demonstrates the right of self-protection enjoyed by employees when they face the imminent risk of serious injury and there is not sufficient time to apprise OSHA of the danger.

WHIRLPOOL v. MARSHALL
445 U.S. 1 (Sup. Ct. 1980)

[An overhead conveyor was used to transport components throughout a manufacturing plant owned and operated by Whirlpool. A wire mesh guard screen approximately 20 feet above the plant floor was used to protect employees from objects that occasionally fell from the conveyor. Maintenance employees spent several hours each week removing objects from the screen and performing work on the conveyors. Several employees had fallen through the screen, one to his death. About two weeks after the fatal accident, a foreman directed two men to perform their normal maintenance duties on the screen. The men refused, claiming that the screen was unsafe. They were sent home without being paid for the remaining six hours of their shift and written reprimands were placed in their employment files. Subsequently, Secretary of Labor Marshall filed suit against Whirlpool alleging that the action against the employees constituted discrimination in violation of the OSHA statute. The trial court ruled against the secretary, but the appellate court reversed that decision. Whirlpool then appealed the case to the Supreme Court.]

STEWART, Justice

The Occupational Safety and Health Act of 1970 (Act) prohibits an employer from discharging or discriminating against any employee who exercises "any right afforded by" the Act. The Secretary of Labor (Secretary) has promulgated a regulation providing that, among the rights that the Act so protects, is the right of an employee to choose not to perform his assigned task because of a reasonable apprehension of death or serious injury coupled with a reasonable belief that no less drastic alternative is available. The question presented in the case before us is whether this regulation is consistent with the Act.

The Act itself creates an express mechanism for protecting workers from employment conditions believed to pose an emergent threat of death or serious injury. Upon receipt of an employee inspection request stating reasonable grounds to believe that an imminent danger is present in a workplace, OSHA must conduct an inspection.

As this case illustrates, . . . circumstances may sometimes exist in which the employee justifiably believes that the express statutory arrangement does not sufficiently protect him from death or serious injury. Such circumstances will probably not often occur, but such a situation may arise when (1) the employee is ordered by his employer to work under conditions that the employee reasonably believes pose an imminent risk of death or serious bodily injury, and (2) the employee has reason to believe that there is not sufficient time or opportunity either to seek effective redress from his employer or to apprise OSHA of the danger.

The regulation clearly conforms to the fundamental objective of the Act—to prevent occupational deaths and serious injuries. The Act, in its preamble, declares

that its purpose and policy is "to assure so far as possible every working man and woman in the Nation safe and healthful working conditions and to *preserve* our human resources . . . ."

To accomplish this basic purpose, the legislation's remedial orientation is prophylactic in nature. . . . The Act does not wait for an employee to die or become injured. It authorizes the promulgation of health and safety standards and the issuance of citations in the hope that these will act to prevent deaths or injuries from ever occurring. It would seem anomalous to construe an Act so directed and constructed as prohibiting an employee, with no other reasonable alternative, the freedom to withdraw from a workplace environment that he reasonably believes is highly dangerous.

Moreover, the Secretary's regulation can be viewed as an appropriate aid to the full effectuation of the Act's "general duty" clause. That clause provides that "[e]ach employer . . . shall furnish to each of his employees employment and a place of employment which are free from recognized hazards that are causing or are likely to cause death or serious physical harm to his employees." . . . Since OSHA inspectors cannot be present around the clock in every workplace, the Secretary's regulation ensures that employees will in all circumstances enjoy the rights afforded them by the "general duty" clause.

The regulation thus on its face appears to further the overriding purpose of the Act, and rationally to complement its remedial scheme. In the absence of some contrary indication in the legislative history, the Secretary's regulation must, therefore, be upheld, particularly when it is remembered that safety legislation is to be liberally construed to effectuate the congressional purpose.

For these reasons we conclude that [the regulation] was promulgated by the Secretary in the valid exercise of his authority under the Act.

Affirmed.

CASE REVIEW QUESTION

1. If the company had repaired or replaced the screen after the man fell from it to his death, would it be difficult for an employee who was ordered to walk upon the screen to argue that he or she had reasonable fear for his or her safety? Explain.

THE EMPLOYMENT RETIREMENT INCOME SECURITY ACT OF 1974

The Employment Retirement Income Security Act of 1974 (**ERISA**) became law on Labor Day of 1974. It is a very complex piece of legislation and is so new that any statements about its value must be tenuous. Here, we present only a brief overview of the Act.

Retirement Programs

Most large corporations and many other employers provide retirement plans of some kind for their employees. Usually the employees and the employer both contribute to a fund that is administered for the benefit of the employees. Funds are invested conservatively, so slight growth in them can be expected. When an employee reaches retirement age, he or she typically can withdraw all or part of his or her share of the fund. However, at least three events could disasterously alter an employee's hopes for a secure retirement:

1. The employee could quit or be discharged before any legal right to a share of the retirement funds accrued.
2. The firm could fail and the retirement fund might be paid over to creditors.
3. Those in charge of administering the fund could abuse their position and either embezzle or squander the money in it.

ERISA attempts to preclude these unfortunate consequences or at least to minimize them. Primarily, the act assures the participants in a pension fund program that they will get what they had planned to get when they retire or quit. To achieve this end, the act emphasizes (1) the vesting of rights in the fund, (2) insurance against company collapse, and (3) strict duties for the administrators of the fund.

ERISA Requirements

Corporations are not required by law to have pension plans. For those that do, however, the following requirements apply.

Vesting First, the plan must cover all employees who are at least 25 years old and have at least one year of service. In certain instances, an employer may need three years of service to be eligible for plan benefits.

Employers may choose one of three ways to allow employees to gain vested or guaranteed rights in the fund, which become payable at the retirement age provided for in the plan or at age 65. The first way is for rights in the pension plan to become nonforfeitable after ten years of service, even if the employee quits. The second way is for the employee to become entitled to 25 percent of the accrued benefits after five years of service, 50 percent after 10 years, and 100 percent after fifteen years. The third way is to adopt the "rule of 45." This rule provides that an employee is vested in half of the benefits when his or her age plus years of service total forty-five after a minimum requirement of five years of service is met. The rule provides for full vesting after fifteen years of service for younger participants. The three methods of vesting just discussed provide employees with a measure of protection of their benefits in the event of discharge or circumstances that may compel them to quit.

Pension Plan Failures A study by the Labor and Treasury Departments revealed that 1,227 pension plans folded in 1972, resulting in the loss of almost $50 million in benefits to approximately 20,000 participants. The second objective of ERISA is to help prevent such losses to employees in the future by protecting their benefits in the event a corporation fails. The act creates a new Public Pension Benefit Guaranty Corporation, which through a scheme of insurance guarantees employees that they will receive the benefits that they are entitled to if the company they work for fails. The premiums for this insurance are about one dollar per worker per year (or 50 cents per worker per year for employees who come under more comprehensive multi-employer plans). The insurance provides maximum benefits of the lesser of $750 per month or 100 percent of an employee's average wage for his or her best paid five consecutive years of employment. The insurance corporation can also seek to recover up to 30 percent of the collapsed firm's net worth from the employer if the pension fund assets are not sufficient to pay benefits.

Pension Plan Administration In its third area of emphasis, some of ERISA's major provisions deal with the standards to be observed by the fiduciaries who administer the plan. These fiduciaries are barred from engaging in such transactions as buying property they own personally for the pension fund. In addition, pension funds that hold stock and real property of the employer cannot have these holdings exceed a maximum of 10 percent of the fund's total assets.

To insure compliance with the terms of the act, extensive reports to employees, the Labor and Treasury Departments, and the Pension Benefit Guaranty Corporation are required. These reporting requirements are designed to provide detailed information to the government as well as to pension-plan participants.

REVIEW QUESTIONS

1. List the rights given to employees by the National Labor Relations Act.
2. In your own words, explain what is required of a union by the duty of fair representation.
3. What is required of management and labor under their obligation to bargain with each other?
4. Discuss how the law protects neutral third parties from being unfairly caught in the middle of a strike by a union against an employer.
5. List the two major duties placed upon an employer by the federal occupational safety and health law.

CASE PROBLEMS

1. The NLRB conducts a representation election at a lumber company that has ten employees who are eligible to vote. Only eight persons vote. Three employees vote for union representation by the Oper-

ating Engineers, and five employees vote against unionization. Will the union represent the employees of this company? Explain.

2. The Machinists Union bargains its first contract with a metal fabricating company. Under the terms of the contract, the ten percent of the workforce that is composed of skilled workers will receive thirty percent more in hourly wages than will the unskilled workers. If an unskilled worker files a complaint with the NLRB arguing that the union has breached its duty of fair representation, will the unskilled worker win the case? Explain.

3. For the 14 years of its existence, ABC Electronics has always granted wage and benefit increases on April 1. However, this year when it does so, the Electrical Workers Union is engaged in an organizational campaign among the company's employees. If the Electrical Workers Union files unfair labor practice charges with the NLRB arguing that ABC Electronics' action is designed to interfere with the employees free exercise of their rights, on what basis can the employer defend? Who will win the case? Explain.

4. The Brotherhood of Railroad Trainpersons, negotiating a contract with a railroad, is calling for work crews that consist of five persons. Four are to perform the work, and the fifth is to watch for trains so that none of the work crew will be struck and injured by a locomotive or the cars that it is pulling. Frustrated by its inability to eliminate the fifth member of the work crew in its negotiations with the union, the railroad files an unfair labor practice complaint with the NLRB. The railroad argues that the union is engaging in illegal featherbedding. On what basis can the union defend? Who will win the case? Explain.

5. The Steelworkers Union represents the employees who perform the maintenance work at Fibreboard. As a cost saving measure, Fibreboard has decided to subcontract out the maintenance work to an independent corporation, which will result in the maintenance employees losing their jobs. Fibreboard has refused to bargain with the Steelworkers over the decision. Is this contracting out decision a mandatory subject of bargaining? If the NLRB charges Fibreboard with committing an unfair labor practice, who will win the case? Explain.

6. The Retail Clerks Union has called a legal strike against Safeco. Safeco underwrites title insurance that is sold by various independent title companies. In fact, these local companies derive 90 percent of their income from the sale of Safeco policies. The Retail Clerks Union is picketing the locations of these independent title companies and are asking the public not to purchase Safeco policies. The union pickets clearly indicate that their dispute is only with Safeco. If the independent title companies sue the Retail Clerks Union, on what basis can the union defend? Who will win the case? Explain.

7. Suppose an OSHA inspector appears at a plant to conduct an inspection, and the employer will not voluntarily consent to the inspection. Will OSHA be forced to cancel its planned inspection or is there another method in which it can gain entry to the premises? What is that method?

53

EMPLOYMENT DISCRIMINATION

The major employment discrimination legislation is contained in Title VII of the 1964 Civil Rights Act and the amendments to it in the 1972 Equal Employment Opportunity Act. Together, these statutes make it unlawful to discriminate in employment situations on the basis of race, color, religion, sex, or national origin. The law applies to employers in any industry that affects commerce who have 15 or more employees, to unions that have 15 or more members or that operate a hiring hall, to employment agencies, and to state and local governments and their political subdivisions.

Although employees of the federal government are not covered by these specific laws, each federal agency is required to exercise nondiscriminatory employment practices. Responsibility for the enforcement of equal opportunity in federal employment was transferred from the Civil Service Commission to the Equal Employment Opportunity Commission (EEOC) in 1979. It is EEOC that enforces the 1964 Civil Rights Act.

Under the statutes, it is an unlawful employment practice for an employer to fail to hire, to discharge, or otherwise to discriminate against any individual with respect to compensation, terms, conditions, or privileges of employment because of that individual's race, color, religion, sex, or national origin. Similarly, it is unlawful for a labor organization to exclude, to expel from its membership, or otherwise to discriminate against any individual because of race, color, religion, sex, or national origin. It is also unlawful for an employment agency to discriminate against an individual on any of these grounds. Furthermore, it is not enough for an organization simply to stop discriminatory practices. Rather, the organization must take affirmative action to remedy the effects of past illegal practices.

RELIGIOUS AND NATIONAL ORIGIN DISCRIMINATION

Individuals are guaranteed the free exercise of religion and the government is prohibited from establishing a religion by the First Amendment to the U.S. Constitution. Because of this right, the Civil Rights Act provides that it is not unlawful for a religious organization to hire employees of a particular religion to perform work connected with carrying on the organization's activities. In other words, it is legal for a religious organization to hire only its own members to teach in its schools.

The Civil Rights Act contains a provision that requires employers to reasonably accommodate the religious observances or practices of its employees. There is little protection, however, for individuals who, because of their religious beliefs, cannot work after sundown on Friday or on Saturday. Consider, for example, the case of an individual whose religion views Saturday as the Sabbath and forbids work on the Sabbath. Suppose further that this person does not have sufficient seniority to bid for a shift that has no Saturday work. What if the employee refuses to work on Saturday and is therefore discharged?

When a case like this actually occurred, the employee's union refused to allow any violation of its seniority system. The company, in turn, refused the employee's request that he be allowed to work a four-day week or that he be replaced with a supervisor or some other worker on the fifth day of his shift. It also refused to cover his position on Saturday by assigning overtime to another employee. Finally, because of the seniority provision in the collective bargaining agreement, the company refused to allow the employee to work out a swap with another employee on a different shift. When the employee filed suit, claiming that these actions constituted religious discrimination, the Supreme Court held that the employer had made a reasonable effort to accommodate the employee's religious practices. It further said that the adoption of any of the various alternatives proposed by the employee would have imposed an undue hardship on the employer.

It is also illegal for an individual to be discriminated against in employment because of his or her national origin. For instance, an employer could not legally refuse to hire a German-American because he or she dislikes people of German ancestry. However, it is not illegal to have a rule that only U.S. citizens will be hired. Though this is discrimination against aliens, it is based on citizenship and not national origin. For example, under such a rule an individual from Germany would be eligible for employment as long as he or she is a U.S. citizen.

SEX DISCRIMINATION

Although it is illegal to discriminate against a man because of his sex, most sex discrimination cases involve allegations that a company or union has discriminated against a woman because of her sex.

What the Civil Rights Act makes illegal is *disparate treatment,* which means unequal treatment, of men and women because of their sex. For example, an employer would violate the law if it required its female employees to be married while it allowed its male workers to be either married or single. What makes this treatment illegal is that one rule is applied to the members of one sex, whereas a different rule is applied to the members of the other sex.

Suppose that a company maintains sexually segregated seniority lists and women are only eligible for jobs that require lifting no more than 35 pounds. This practice is unlawful. All workers, regardless of their sex, must be afforded the opportunity to demonstrate their ability to perform strenuous jobs on a regular basis. If a woman demonstrates that she has the capability to perform a job that requires lifting items that weigh more than 35 pounds and if she desires that job, the job cannot be denied her because she is a woman.

Sometimes a company rule may appear to treat all groups the same but, in fact, does not. To be legal, rules must be neutral not only on their face but also in their effects. If they are neutral on their face but cause a disparate impact on a particular protected group, they are illegal. Minimum height and weight standards are good examples of such rules. For instance, Alabama required that its prison guards have a minimum height of 5′2″ and a minimum weight of 120 pounds. However, if one takes all the individuals in the United States between the ages of 18 and 79, these restrictions exclude 41.13 percent of the female population, but they exclude less than one percent of the male population. The Supreme Court struck down this requirement as unlawful discrimination because it so disproportionately excluded women from employment as prison guards.

The following case makes the important point that the discrimination laws not only prevent discriminatory conduct in hiring situations, but they also protect individuals after they have been hired. The case also presents a good example of disparate treatment of employees according to their sex.

EEOC v. BROWN & ROOT, INCORPORATED
688 F.2d 338 (Fifth Cir. 1982)

[EEOC brought a legal action against Brown & Root, Inc., on the basis of sex discrimination. Brown & Root moved for a summary judgment. The trial court granted the motion, and EEOC appealed.]

RUBIN, Circuit Judge

The following facts are undisputed: Sarah Joan Boyes was employed by Brown & Root as an electrician's helper. Brown & Root is a construction company and Ms. Boyes was assigned to work on an overhead steel beam that was part of a structure being erected at Escatawpa, Mississippi. She became paralyzed by fear and was unable to move, a condition known as "freezing." It was necessary physically to assist her to climb down. Brown & Root discharged Ms. Boyes from her job for the stated reason that she was "not capable of performing assigned work." After she was fired, another female worker was hired to fill the position of electrician's helper.

What is disputed is whether men who manifested the same acrophobia were also discharged. In opposition to the motion for summary judgement, the Equal Employment Opportunity Commission offered the affidavit of its investigator. To this were attached copies of statements taken from four male employees, each of whom stated that he or some other worker had at some prior time frozen on the beams, could not get down without help, and was not discharged. One statement referred also to a male worker who was kept on the ground because he was afraid of heights. There was also attached an "EEOC affidavit" from a male employee stating that he had "frozen" and had not been discharged.

[T]he disputed issue was not whether Ms. Boyes was unable to work at heights, a fact that was, indeed, undisputed, or whether she was replaced by a male, another fact that was not disputed, but whether, had she been a man, she would have suffered dismissal as a result of her phobia. When an employment discrimination claim contends that a person was discharged from employment because of sex, race, age or some other reprobated reason, a prima facie case of discrimination is made if it is shown that (1) the person was a member of a protected minority; (2) the person was qualified for the job from which discharged; (3) the person was discharged; and (4) after the discharge, their employer filled the position with a nonminority. This showing, however, is not the only way to establish a prima facie case of discriminatory discharge.

If an employee is discharged under circumstances in which an employee of another sex would not have been discharged, an inference of discrimination arises irrespective of the gender of the employee's replacement. Punitive action against employees for violating work rules must not differentiate on the basis of sex or any of the other criteria reprobated by Title VII.

The summary judgment is reversed and the case remanded for further proceedings consistent with this opinion.

CASE REVIEW QUESTIONS

1. Why might a company fire a woman for certain conduct when it did not fire men who engaged in the very same conduct?
2. If another female was hired to replace Ms. Boyes, can the company be viewed as discriminating against women? Explain.

Sexual Harrassment

What if a male supervisor conditions favorable job evaluations, working situations, or promotions for a subordinate female employee upon her grant of sexual favors. If the subordinate employee's job status depends upon a favorable response to the sexual demands, the employer must take prompt and appropriate remedial action as soon as it learns of the incident. If it does not, the employer will violate the law. The same rule would also apply in the case of a female supervisor who makes sexual demands upon a male subordinate.

Discrimination Against Homosexuals

The federal law does not prohibit discrimination against an individual on grounds of homosexuality. Some cities, however, do have ordinances that prohibit various forms of discrimination against homosexuals.

Pregnancy and Sex Discrimination

In 1976, the Supreme Court ruled that an employer did not violate Title VII's ban on sex discrimination when it denied benefits for pregnancy-related disabilities under its disability income protection plan. The Court said that the denial did not constitute discrimination against a particular gender of people; rather, it merely removed one physical condition — pregnancy — from the list of covered disabilities. The Court viewed pregnancy, which is of course confined to women, as significantly different from the typically covered disease or disability. It therefore held that excluding pregnancy from the coverage of a benefit plan should not be considered discrimination against women. This ruling is no longer in effect because Congress has amended the law. Let us now look at the situation as it is today.

The Pregnancy Disability Act The Pregnancy Disability Act of 1978 amends Title VII so as to forbid employment discrimination because of "pregnancy, childbirth, or related medical conditions." The law does not require an employer to have a fringe-benefit package or an insurance program for disabilities. It does, however, require that when an employer, including state and local governments, has an insurance program or benefits package, as most employers do, any woman unable to work for pregnancy-related reasons must receive the same disability benefits or sick leave as other employees receive when they are unable to work for other medical reasons. For instance, if the employer furnishes health insurance, that insurance must cover expenses for pregnancy-related conditions on the same basis as it covers expenses for other medical conditions.

Abortions are also covered by the law. Therefore, an employer cannot discriminate against a woman who has had an abortion. If fringe benefits, such as sick leave, are provided for other medical reasons, they must also be provided for abortions. However, health insurance coverage for abortions is required only when the life of the woman would be endangered if the fetus were carried to term or when medical complications arise from an abortion.

The idea of the law is to provide women with pregnancy-related disabilities with the same benefits that are received by employees with other types of medical disabilities. Thus, if an employer furnishes sick leaves, leaves without pay, alternate job assignments, and so forth to employees who are temporarily disabled by other medical problems, then the employer must furnish the same benefits to a woman who is temporarily disabled by a condition related to pregnancy. These benefits must be supplied to both married and unmarried employees. If an employer requires all employees to submit a doctor's statement verifying their inability to work as a condition for receiving sick leave benefits and so forth, then the employer can require similar verification from women who wish to qualify for those benefits for a pregnancy-related cause.

An employer cannot impose a higher deductible for pregnancy-related disabilities than for other medical conditions. When the employee is reimbursed for pregnancy-related expenses, the reimbursement must be figured on the same basis as are reimbursements for other medical costs. For instance, if the employer chooses to figure reimbursements on a fixed basis or as a percentage of customary charges, the same formula must be used in pregnancy situations.

Maternity Leaves On constitutional due process grounds, the Supreme Court has ruled that a woman cannot be forced by her employer to take maternity leave at some arbitrary cut-off point such as the fourth or fifth month of pregnancy. She is entitled to work for as long as her doctor believes it to be medically safe. Similarly, the EEOC interprets the Pregnancy Disability Act as permitting a woman and her doctor to determine when the woman can no longer work. In 1977, the Supreme Court held that the denial of accumulated seniority to employees returning from maternity leave constitutes illegal sex discrimination.

On a topic somewhat related to pregnancy, the Supreme Court has held that a company violates the Civil Rights Act by rejecting women job applicants who have preschool children if the company has no policy against hiring men who have preschool children.

RACE AND COLOR DISCRIMINATION

The law bars discrimination against an individual because of his or her color or race. This does not mean that the law guarantees every individual a job regardless of his or her qualifications. Rather, the law seeks to insure that all individuals have equal employment opportunities. It is therefore illegal to hire a lesser qualified white instead of a more qualified black. It is also illegal to hire a lighter-skinned black over a more qualified but darker-skinned black.

What was said earlier about facially neutral job qualifications—that is, qualifications that *appear* to be neutral but are in fact discriminatory—and sex discrimination also applies to race discrimination. The 1964 Civil Rights Act contains a provision that allows an employer to give and to act upon the results of any professionally developed ability test, provided that the test is not designed to or used to discriminate against an individual on the basis of his or her race, color, religion, sex, or national origin. However, the Supreme Court has ruled that such tests must be "job related."

Suppose, for instance, that a company requires that individuals pass an aptitude test before they can be hired or promoted. Also, suppose that the test does not measure an individual's ability to perform a particular job and that a markedly disproportionate number of blacks do not receive passing scores. The test, even though neutral on its face, is discriminatory and therefore violates the 1964 Civil Rights Act. Furthermore, the test is not job related because it does not bear a demonstrable relationship to the successful performance of a particular job.

In the next case, the court explores the issue of how an employer can prove that tests do measure the skills needed by job applicants to perform a job successfully. The Court also deals with the issue of backpay. When an individual is denied a job because of illegal discrimination, a court will normally order the employer to hire the individual and grant him or her backpay. Backpay is usually determined by taking the difference between the amount of money actually earned by the victim of the discriminatory practice and the amount the individual would have earned had he or she not been discriminated against.

ALBEMARLE PAPER CO. v. MOODY
422 U.S. 405 (Sup. Ct. 1975)

[A group of present and former black employees of the Albemarle Paper Company sued the company and their union for violations of the 1964 Civil Rights Act. They argued that the employer's testing program was not job related and that the union's seniority system illegally discriminated against blacks. After a trial, the judge ruled the seniority system to be improper but refused to order backpay. The judge held the testing program to be legal. The appellate court ruled that the testing should be halted and backpay awarded. The employer then appealed to the Supreme Court.]

STEWART, Justice

These consolidated cases raise two important questions under Title VII of the Civil Rights Act of 1964 . . . as amended by the Equal Employment Opportunity Act of 1972. . . . First: When employees or applicants for employment have lost the opportunity to earn wages because an employer has engaged in an unlawful discriminatory employment practice, what standards should a federal district court follow in deciding whether to award or deny backpay? Second: What must an employer show to establish that pre-employment tests racially discriminatory in effect, though not in intent, are sufficiently "job related" to survive challenge under Title VII?

The [trial] court refused . . . to award backpay to

the [plaintiffs] for losses suffered under the "job seniority" program. The court explained:

> In the instant case there was no evidence of bad faith non-compliance with the Act. . . .

It is true that backpay is not an automatic or mandatory remedy; like all other remedies under the Act, it is one which the courts "may" invoke. . . . The power to award backpay was bestowed by Congress, as part of a complex legislative design directed at an historic evil of national proportions. . . .

It is also the purpose of Title VII to make persons whole for injuries suffered on account of unlawful employment discrimination. . . . Title VII deals with legal injuries of an economic character occasioned by racial or other antiminority discrimination. . . .

The "make whole" purpose of Title VII is made evident by the legislative history. The backpay provision was expressly modeled on the backpay provision of the National Labor Relations Act. Under that Act, "[m]aking the workers whole for losses suffered on account of an unfair labor practice is part of the vindication of the public policy which the Board enforces." . . . We may assume that Congress was aware that the Board, since its inception, has awarded backpay as a matter of course—not randomly or in the exercise of a standardless discretion, and not merely where employer violations are peculiarly deliberate, egregious or inexcusable. . . .

It follows that, given a finding of unlawful discrimination, backpay should be denied only for reasons which, if applied generally, would not frustrate the central statutory purposes of eradicating discrimination throughout the economy and making persons whole for injuries suffered through past discrimination. . . .

If backpay were awardable only upon a showing of bad faith, the remedy would become a punishment for moral turpitude, rather than a compensation for workers' injuries. This would read the "make whole" purpose right out of Title VII, for a worker's injury is no less real simply because his employer did not inflict it in "bad faith." Title VII is not concerned with the employer's "good intent or absence of discriminatory intent" for "Congress directed the thrust of the Act to the consequences of employment practices, not simply the motivation."

In *Griggs v. Duke Power Co.,* . . . this Court unanimously held that Title VII forbids the use of employment tests that are discriminatory in effect unless the employer meets "the burden of showing that any given requirement [has] . . . a manifest relation to the employment in question." . . . This burden arises, of course, only after the complaining party or class has made out a prima facie case of discrimination — has shown that the tests in question select applicants for hire or promotion in a racial pattern significantly different from that of the pool of applicants. . . . If an employer does then meet the burden of proving that its tests are "job related," it remains open to the complaining party to show that other tests or selection devices, without a similarly undesirable racial effect, would also serve the employer's legitimate interest in "efficient and trustworthy workmanship." Such a showing would be evidence that the employer was using its tests merely as a "pretext" for discrimination. . . . In the present case, however, we are concerned only with the question whether Albemarle has shown its test to be job related.

Like the employer in *Griggs,* Albemarle uses two general tests, the Beta Examination, to test nonverbal intelligence, and the Wonderlic Test, . . . the purported measure of general verbal facility which was also involved in the *Griggs* case. . . .

Four months before this case went to trial, Albe-marle engaged an expert in industrial psychology to "validate" the job relatedness of its testing program. He spent a half day at the plant and devised a "concurrent validation" study, which was conducted by plant officials, without his supervision. The expert then subjected the results to statistical analysis. . . .

The EEOC has issued "Guidelines" for employers seeking to determine, through professional validation studies, whether their employment tests are job related. . . .

Measured against the Guidelines, Albemarle's validation study is materially defective in several respects:

1. Even if it had been otherwise adequate, the study would not have "validated" the Beta and Wonderlic test battery for all of the skilled lines of progression for which the two tests are, apparently, now required. The study showed significant correlations for the Beta Exam in only three of the eight lines. . . . The study . . . involved no analysis of the attributes of, or the particular skills needed in, the studied job groups. There is accordingly no basis for concluding that "no significant differences" exist among the lines of progression, or among distinct job groupings within the studied lines of progression. Indeed, the study's checkered results appear to compel the opposite conclusion.

2. The study compared test scores with subjective supervisorial rankings. While they allow the use of supervisorial rankings in test validation, the Guidelines quite plainly contemplate that the rankings will be elicited with far more care than was demonstrated here. Albemarle's supervisors were asked to rank employees by a "standard" that was extremely vague and fatally open to divergent interpretations. . . .

3. The company's study focused, in most cases, on job groups near the top of the various lines of progression. . . . The fact that the best of those employees working near the top of a line of progression score well on a test does not necessarily mean that that test, or some particular cutoff score on the test, is a permissible measure of the minimal qualifications of new workers, entering lower level jobs. . . .

4. Albemarle's validation study dealt only with job-

experienced, white workers; but the test themselves are given to new job applicants, who are younger, largely inexperienced, and in many instances nonwhite. . . .

Accordingly, the judgment is vacated, and these cases are remanded to the District Court for proceedings consistent with this opinion.

CASE COMMENT

The testing area is somewhat confused today. What if a sufficiently validated test has a racially disproportionate impact? In a case that involved the Due Process Clause of the Fifth Amendment rather than Title VII of the Civil Rights Act, the Supreme Court faced such an issue. It held that, so long as a racially discriminatory purpose was not proven, such a test was constitutional even though four times as many blacks as whites failed the test.

CASE REVIEW QUESTIONS

1. Why did the court that first heard the case refuse to award backpay to the plaintiffs?
2. Under what circumstances will a court award backpay to a class of employees who have been discriminated against?
3. Explain in your own words why Albemarle's validation study failed to demonstrate that its tests were job related.

BONA FIDE OCCUPATIONAL QUALIFICATIONS

It is not an unlawful employment practice for an employer, a union, or an employment agency to judge an individual on the basis of his or her religion, sex, or national origin in those particular situations where religion, sex, or national origin is a **bona fide occupation qualification (BFOQ),** which is defined as a qualification that is reasonably necessary for the normal operation of a particular enterprise. You should note, though, that it is *never* permissible to discriminate on the basis of a person's race or color!

But what constitutes a BFOQ? May an airline, for instance, restrict its cabin attendant jobs to females? Is being female a BFOQ if the passengers express an overwhelming preference for female cabin attendants? The answer to both of these questions is "No." Being female is not a BFOQ in this instance. Because a male can perform the tasks of a cabin attendant just as well as a female, refusal to hire a male for this position on the basis of his sex violates the Civil Rights Act.

Under guidelines on sex discrimination issued by the Equal Employment

Opportunity Commission (EEOC), BFOQ exceptions are interpreted narrowly. The occupation of actor or actress, for example, is given as a legitimate BFOQ. The guidelines say that it is unlawful to refuse to hire a woman on the assumption that the turnover rate for women is higher than that for men. It is also unlawful to refuse to hire an individual on the basis of stereotyped sexual characterizations—for example, that women are less capable of aggressive salesmanship or that men are less capable of assembling intricate equipment.

The Supreme Court has held that being male is a BFOQ for a job as prison guard under a specific set of circumstances. The particular case was the Alabama prison guard one discussed earlier in the section on sex discrimination. The unique circumstance involved a maximum security prison where violence was so rampant that a court had held that the conditions of the prison itself were unconstitutional. Twenty percent of the male inmates were sex offenders, and they were scattered throughout the general prison population. The institution was understaffed and, because of dormitory-type living arrangements, the prisoners had access to the guards. The Court said such a factual situation directly linked the sex of the prison guards to potential security problems.

Thus, the results of the decision in the case were twofold. First, an employer cannot use height and weight requirements to discriminate against job applicants. Second, being male is a BFOQ for guard positions in the unique circumstances of this one prison.

It is not unlawful for an employer to apply different standards of compensation or different terms, conditions, or privileges of employment pursuant to a bona fide seniority or merit system or to a system that measures earnings by quantity or quality of production or to employees who work in different locations, provided that the differences are not the net result of an intention to discriminate unlawfully.

AFFIRMATIVE-ACTION PLAN QUOTAS AND REVERSE DISCRIMINATION

Quota systems are extremely controversial. Some individuals claim that affirmative-action programs under the civil rights law constitute the imposition of a quota system. Others argue that remedial quotas are necessary to redress past discriminatory practices. The Civil Rights Act does not mandate a quota system. Indeed, the act states that a union, an employer, or an employment agency is *not* required to grant preferential treatment to any individual or group on the basis of the race, color, religion, sex, or national origin of that individual or group because of an existing imbalance in the percentage of such persons in the union, employed by the employer, or referred for employment by the agency.

The Fourteenth Amendment to the U.S. Constitution guarantees all persons equal protection under the laws. As jobs have become tight in times of economic stress and as women and minorities have begun to make some inroads in employment, some white males have come to believe that sex or color, rather than merit or ability, are being used to make hiring decisions. Because these hiring decisions are not necessarily going their way, these white males believe themselves to be the victims of reverse discrimination.

The first case concerning reverse discrimination to draw substantial publicity involved an educational institution. In 1973 and 1974 the University of California at Davis denied admission to its medical school to a white male by the name of Allan Bakke. Each year, 100 seats were available for the entering class of medical students. Eighty-four of the seats were filled by a normal admission process; the remaining 16 seats were filled by a special minority admissions process. Only members of minority races were eligible for consideration under the special admissions process. The two sets of applicants were rated separately, not against each other. As a result, some of the students admitted through the special process had ratings below Bakke. In 1978, the Supreme Court in a 5–4 decision ordered the medical school to admit Bakke. The Court held that, while race may be one of several factors considered in making admissions decisions, it cannot be the sole deciding factor.

Legal Affirmative-Action Plans

Some later decisions are very important with regard to the question of reverse discrimination in employment. In one, the United Steelworkers of America and the Kaiser Aluminum Company included an affirmative-action plan in their collective bargaining agreement. The plan established a program to train production workers to fill craft positions in order to eliminate a conspicuous racial imbalance in those positions. The program was to continue until the percentage of black craft workers in the plant was commensurate with the percentage of blacks in the local labor force. Trainees for the craft positions were to be selected on the basis of seniority with the proviso that at least 50 percent of the trainees were to be black.

During the plan's first year of operation, seven blacks and six whites were selected. The most junior black trainee had less seniority than several white production workers whose bids for admission were rejected. One of those whites, Brian Weber, filed suit, alleging that he had been illegally discriminated against because of his race.

The Supreme Court rejected Weber's argument in a 5–2 decision. The Court held that Title VII does not condemn all private, voluntary, race-conscious affirmative-action plans. The prohibition against race discrimination, it said, must be read against a legislative intent to open opportunities for blacks in occupations that had traditionally been closed to them.

Congress said that nothing in Title VII "shall be interpreted to *require* any employer . . . to grant preferential treatment . . . to any group because of race . . . on account of" a de facto racial imbalance in the employer's work force [emphasis added]. In the Court's view, this meant that although Congress did not *require* such action, it did *permit* such action. The Court therefore held that this particular type of affirmative-action plan was permissible. (By implication, some types of affirmative-action plans may not be permissible.) The court noted that the purpose of the plan was to break down old patterns of racial discrimination and to open employment opportunities in occupations that had traditionally been closed to blacks. (At the plant in question, only 1.83 percent of the craft positions were held by blacks.) The Court noted further that the plan did not require that white workers be discharged and replaced with newly-hired black workers. In addition, the program did not bar whites absolutely, since half of those admitted to the program could be white. Finally, the Court pointed out that the plan was temporary in nature and was intended simply to eliminate a manifest racial imbalance and not to maintain a racial balance.

In 1976, the Court did hold that Title VII prohibits racial discrimination against whites as well as nonwhites. In the particular case, an employer's cargo was stolen by three employees. Two of the employees involved, both of whom were white, were fired. However, the third employee involved, who was black, was not discharged. The white workers sued the employer and their union. They won reinstatement and backpay. The Court noted that while theft is a proper reason for which to discharge an employee, all employees must be judged by the same standards. It is improper to make discharge decisions on the basis of the race of the employee involved.

Equal Protection and Affirmative Action

Another case in which the Supreme Court faced an important reverse discrimination issue involved a challenge to a "ten percent set-aside" provision in a 1977 public works law. The law stated that at least 10 percent of the federal funds granted for local public works projects must be used to secure services or supplies from businesses owned by members of minority groups, which were defined as U.S. citizens "who are Negroes, Spanish-speaking, Orientals, Indians, Eskimos, and Aleuts." A group of nonminority contractors challenged the law, alleging that they had suffered economic injury from the enforcement of the law and arguing that the law violated the Equal Protection Clause of the Fourteenth Amendment and the equal protection component of the Due Process Clause of the Fifth Amendment.

The Supreme Court ruled that the law did not violate the Constitution. The Court said that the elimination of barriers to the access of minority firms to public contracts is a proper constitutional objective of Congress. Because the purpose of the program was remedial—that is, it was intended to redress the effects of prior discrimination—Congress was not required to act in a wholly "color-blind" fashion. Such a program is not defective, the Court said, even though it may deny contracting opportunities to nonminority firms who had not themselves discriminated in the past. In the Court's view, Congress had provided reasonable assurance that the application of the minority criteria would be narrowly limited to the accomplishment of proper remedial objectives. The Court further said that the law could be viewed as a pilot project that was appropriately limited in extent and duration and was subject to reassessment and reevaluation by Congress prior to any extension or reenactment.

SENIORITY SYSTEMS AND CIVIL RIGHTS

Seniority is a crucial matter in the workplace. The last hired – first fired formula, for instance, is traditionally used to determine layoffs. Seniority is also used in many other areas that are of importance to workers — job bids, order of recall, shift selection, bumping rights, and vacations, just to name a few.

Retroactive Seniority

What happens when an individual has low seniority because he or she was the target of illegal discrimination? The Supreme Court has ruled that retroactive seniority can be granted to an employee to cure the effects of prior discrimination. Backpay can also be granted to the employee, even when there has been no bad faith on the part of the employer. The Supreme Court has even gone so far as to rule that an individual who had not formally applied for a job can be granted retroactive seniority so long as he or she can prove that he or she would have applied for the job had it not been for the illegal discriminatory practices. Such a case might arise if an employer had a sign posted at the employment office saying "Whites Only" or if it were publicly known in the community that an employer never hired women and so women in the area knew there was no use in applying.

Seniority and Past Discrimination

What if an employer and a union discriminated against certain groups prior to the passage of the 1964 Civil Rights Act but then halted the discrimination once it became a violation of federal law? This question arises in the application of seniority provisions of collective bargaining agreements because the seniority system can carry forward the effects of past discrimination. Title VII provides that

> Notwithstanding any other provisions . . . it shall not be an unlawful employment practice for an employer to apply different standards of compensation, or different terms, conditions, or privileges of employment pursuant to a bona fide seniority . . . system. . . .

This issue was litigated against a company and a union that had discriminated against blacks and Spanish-surnamed individuals. The Supreme Court ruled that a bona fide seniority system does not become unlawful simply because it may perpetuate pre – Title VII discrimination. The Court said the provision quoted in the previous paragraph indicated that Congress did not intend to make it illegal for employees with vested seniority rights to continue to exercise those rights, even if they were exercised at the expense of pre – Civil Rights Act discrimination targets. In other words, the victim of discrimination that occurred prior to the effective date of the law is entitled to no seniority. However, a victim of discrimination that occurred after the law became effective is entitled to retroactive seniority to make him or her whole.

Bona Fide Seniority Systems

Notice that the law speaks of "bona fide" seniority systems. To be bona fide, a seniority system must apply equally to all racial, sexual, ethnic, and religious groups. It must also be negotiated and maintained free from any illegal purpose. If a seniority system meets these standards, it will be bona fide and will therefore not be rendered illegal by the mere fact that it does not extend retroactive seniority to victims of discrimination that occurred prior to the effective date of the act.

Another idea of what constitutes a bona fide seniority system is provided by a 1980 Supreme Court decision. A multi-employer brewery industry collective bargaining agreement provided greater benefits to "permanent" as opposed to "temporary" employees with respect to hiring and layoffs. To qualify as a permanent employee, a temporary employee had to work a minimum of 45 weeks in a single calendar year. A black challenged the provision, arguing that it had precluded him from a reasonable opportunity to gain permanent status and was not an acceptable provision of a bona fide seniority system.

The Supreme Court upheld the validity of the seniority system. It noted that the fact that two parallel seniority ladders were created, one allocating benefits for permanent employees and the other allocating benefits for temporary employees, did not prevent the seniority system from being proper. In the Court's view, the 45-week requirement served the needed function of determining eligibility for the permanent seniority ladder, and it focused on length of employment, as was appropriate in a seniority system. The Court also distinguished the requirement from such subjective criteria as educational standards, aptitude tests, or physical tests. Finally, the Court held that the system rewarded employment longevity with greater benefits and that the "temporary" seniority ladder generally operated in such a way that the more seniority a temporary employee gained, the greater was the likelihood that he or she would reach the 45-week requirement.

Seniority Systems and Affirmative-Action Plans

We have seen that persons who are victims of illegal job discrimination may be granted retroactive seniority under the 1964 Civil Rights Act. We have also seen that an employer may use a bona fide seniority system to determine eligibility for job assignments, fringe benefits, and so forth. However, we have not yet considered a very important issue that arises when the terms of an affirmative-action plan conflict with the seniority system in a collective bargaining agreement. The problem develops when an employee who has not been a direct victim of employment discrimination and therefore has not received retroactive seniority obtains a job pursuant to the terms of an affirmative action program. Such an employee will be vulnerable to any job layoffs under the seniority system while, at the same time, he or she may be protected from the layoffs by the affirmative-action program. What is the employer to do in such a situation? The Supreme Court provided an answer to this dilemma in the following case.

FIREFIGHTERS LOCAL UNION NO. 178 v. STOTTS
104 S.Ct. 2576 (Sup. Ct. 1984)

[To settle an employment discrimination lawsuit brought by Stotts against the city of Memphis fire department, the city adopted and a federal district court approved an affirmative-action plan. The plan increased the number of minority firefighters. Subsequent budget problems, however, necessitated the layoff of city workers. The court that had approved the affirmative-action plan ordered the city not to use its "last hired – first fired" seniority system to layoff firefighters. Instead, it required the city to maintain the existing percentage of blacks in the fire department. The city laid off 24 firefighters, three of whom were black. Six blacks would have been laid off under the seniority system. While complying with the court order, the city and the Firefighters Union appealed to an intermediate court of appeals, which affirmed the trial court's order. The city and the union then appealed to the U.S. Supreme Court.]

WHITE, Justice

Petitioners challenge the Court of Appeals' approval of an order enjoining the City of Memphis from following its seniority system in determining who must be laid off as a result of a budgetary shortfall. Respondents contend that the injunction was necessary to effectuate the terms of a Title VII consent decree in which the city agreed to undertake certain obligations in order to remedy past hiring and promotional practices.

The issue at the heart of this case is whether the District Court exceeded its powers in entering an injunction requiring white employees to be laid off, when the otherwise applicable seniority system would have called for the layoff of black employees with less seniority.

As our cases have made clear . . . Title VII protects bona fide seniority systems, and it is inappropriate to deny an innocent employee the benefits of his seniority in order to provide a remedy in a suit such as this.

Section 703(h) of Title VII provides that it is not an unlawful employment practice to apply different standards of compensation, or different terms, conditions, or privileges of employment pursuant to a bona fide seniority system, provided that such differences are not the result of an intention to discriminate because of race. . . . The District Court held that the City could not follow its seniority system in making its proposed layoffs because its proposal was discriminatory in effect and hence not a bona fide plan. Section 703(h), however, permits the routine application of a seniority system absent proof of an intention to discriminate.

If individual members of a plaintiff class demonstrate that they have been actual victims of the discriminatory practice, they may be awarded competitive seniority and given their rightful place on the seniority roster. This much is clear from *Franks v. Bowman Transportation* and *Teamsters v. United States.* . . . *Teamsters,* however, also made clear that mere membership in the disadvantaged class is insufficient to warrant a seniority award; each individual must prove that the discriminatory practice had an impact on him. Even when an individual shows that the discriminatory practice has had an impact on him, he is not automatically entitled to have a non-minority employee laid off to make room for him. He may have to wait until a vacancy occurs, and if there are non-minority employees on layoff, the Court must balance the equities in determining who is entitled to the job. . . . Here, there was no finding that any of the blacks protected from layoff had been a victim of discrimination and no award of competitive seniority to any of them. . . .

[T]he Court of Appeals was of the view that the District Court ordered no more than that which the City unilaterally could have done by way of adopting an affirmative action program. Whether the City, a public employer, could have taken this course without violating the law is an issue we need not decide. The fact is that in this case the City took no such action and that the modification of the decree was imposed over its objection.

We are thus unable to agree either that the order entered by the District Court was a justifiable effort to enforce the terms of the decree to which the City had agreed or that it was a legitimate modification of the decree that could be imposed on the City without its consent.

Accordingly, the judgment of the Court of Appeals is reversed.

CASE REVIEW QUESTIONS

1. If blacks, as a group of people, have been discriminated against, do you believe that the 1964 Civil Rights Act was written with the intention that blacks should receive the benefits of affirmative action to remedy the effects of past discrimination?

2. Did the Court decide whether the city could legally have made the unilateral decision to ignore its seniority system and thereby maintain its existing percentage of minority firefighters? Explain.

OTHER ANTIDISCRIMINATION PROVISIONS

Advertisements of a Discriminatory Nature

It is an unlawful employment practice for an employer, a union, or an employment agency to print or publish or to cause to be printed or published any notice or advertisement relating to employment that indicates any preference, limitation, specification, or discrimination on the basis of race, color, religion, sex, or national origin except when such a notice or advertisement indicates that a preference, limitation, specification, or discrimination based on religion, sex, or national origin is a bona fide occupational qualification for employment. For example, the Supreme Court has held that it is not a violation of the First Amendment to prohibit a newspaper from categorizing employment want ads by sex.

Reprisals Against Persons Filing Discrimination Complaints

It is also an unlawful employment practice for an employer, a union, or an employment agency to discriminate against any person because that person has opposed any practice made an unlawful employment practice by the civil rights law or because that person has made a charge, testified, assisted, or participated in any manner in an investigation, proceeding, or hearing under the law. In one case, the Supreme Court ordered a lower court to determine a company's motivation in refusing to rehire a properly discharged employee. If the refusal were based upon the former employee's impermissible activity, it would be legal. However, if it were based upon the former employee's civil rights activities against the company, the refusal to rehire the employee would be unlawful.

THE EQUAL EMPLOYMENT OPPORTUNITY COMMISSION

Compliance with the 1964 and 1972 antidiscrimination laws is enforced through the Equal Employment Opportunity Commission (EEOC), which consists of five members appointed to five-year terms by the President with the consent of the Senate. No more than three of the members can be from the same political party. There is, in addition, a General Counsel, who conducts any necessary litigation under the law. This position has a four-year term of office, and it is also filled by a Presidential appointment, again with the Senate's consent. Like the NLRB, the EEOC has numerous offices throughout the United States.

Charges of discrimination can be brought to the EEOC by an aggrieved individual, by a person or a party acting on behalf of an aggrieved individual (such as a union), or by a member of the commission. A charge must be filed within 180 days after the occurrence of the alleged discrimination. If a state or local government equivalent to the EEOC exists, the EEOC defers the charge to that agency for 60 days. If the case is not resolved within 60 days or if the state or local agency waives jurisdiction, the EEOC reassumes jurisdiction.

The organization charged with employment discrimination is notified within 10 days of the filing of the charge. Efforts are then made to resolve the problem informally. If these efforts fail, the EEOC decides whether a complete investigation and formal conciliation efforts are called for. If a full investigation is carried out, the EEOC will continue conciliation efforts. All of these activities are conducted confidentially. Should conciliation prove impossible, the EEOC may sue a charged party in the private sector in an effort to remedy the alleged unlawful practice. If the charged party is a government or any of its political subdivisions, the EEOC refers the case to the U.S. Justice Department, which can sue the governmental body. The EEOC can also bring class-action suits.

The person filing the charges, referred to as the *charging party,* is free to sue the charged party on his or her own behalf if (1) the EEOC dismisses the complaint; (2) more than 180 days have passed since the charge was filed; (3) the EEOC, or the Justice Department in cases involving governmental units, decides not to sue; or (4) a written request is made to the EEOC for a "right to sue letter" prior to the expiration of 180 days from the date the charge was filed and the EEOC sends the letter with a certification that it will be unable to complete its processing of the charge within 180 days of the date the charge was filed. Once the charging party receives the right to sue, the suit must be filed within 80 days.

Many persons who file charges end up having to sue. It is therefore important to know that if a lawsuit is brought and the charging party is successful in proving that illegal discrimination has occurred, the court can, and usually does, order the charged party to pay the reasonable attorney's fees of the charging party.

The EEOC now enforces both the Equal Pay Act and the Age Discrimination Act in addition to the 1964 and 1972 civil rights statutes. In the past, the Secretary of Labor enforced the equal pay and age discrimination laws. However, in 1978, President Carter shifted enforcement to the EEOC. Both of these laws encourage the voluntary settlement of disputes and both require that a voluntary settlement be attempted before a lawsuit may be filed. If the EEOC declines to bring a lawsuit, the private individual may do so. Again, if the suit is successful, the plaintiff can collect not only the amount of damages caused by the discrimination but also reasonable attorney's fees.

THE EQUAL PAY ACT

The Equal Pay Act was enacted in 1963. It amended Section 6 of the Fair Labor Standards Act, and it outlaws wage discrimination based upon an employee's sex. The act declares the concept that a man, because of his role in society, should be paid more than a woman for doing the same job to be unlawful. Every employee covered by the federal minimum wage law is protected by the Equal Pay Act. In 1972, the Act's protection was extended to executive, administrative, and professional employees and to outside sales personnel who had previously been exempt from coverage.

Provisions of the Equal Pay Act
The Equal Pay Act prohibits an employer from discriminating

> between employees on the basis of sex by paying wages to employees at a rate less than the rate at which he pays wages to employees of the opposite sex for equal work on jobs the performance of which requires equal skill, effort, and responsibility, and which are performed under similar working conditions.

The law also prohibits a union from causing or attempting to cause an employer to discriminate with regard to wage rates. Equal work does not mean that the jobs must be identical, only that they be substantially equal. Artificial job classifications that do not substantially differ from genuine classifications cannot be created to avoid the operation of the law. If unlawful wage differentials do exist, the employer cannot eliminate them by reducing wage rates. Instead, the employer must raise the wage rate of those being discriminated against to the higher wage rate of those performing equal work.

There are four exceptions to the mandate requiring equal pay for equal work. These occur when differential payment to employees of opposite sexes

> is made pursuant to (i) a seniority system; (ii) a merit system; (iii) a system which measures earnings by quantity or quality of production; or (iv) a differential based on any other factor other than sex.

Once it is shown that an employer pays workers of one sex more than workers of the opposite sex for equal work, the burden of showing that the differential is justified under one of these exceptions shifts to the employer.

Application of the Equal Pay Act
Litigation under the Equal Pay Act has been significant, and the amounts of money involved can be large. In one case, which will be discussed shortly, a court ordered an employer to pay $901,062 in backpay to women selector-packers. It is also worthwhile to note again that, in cases under the Equal Pay Act and the Age Discrimination Act, the court can order the company to pay the reasonable attorney's fees of the plaintiffs.

Let us take a brief look at three important cases to see how the courts are applying the equal pay law. In the case mentioned in the previous paragraph, an employer paid its female selector-packers $2.14 per hour while it paid its male selector-packers $2.355 per hour. The company denied that the men and women performed equal work. In any event, the company claimed, the pay differential was based on a factor other than sex. The company argued that, when there was no work for the selector-packers, the male workers could be assigned to perform the duties of "snap-up boys," who were paid $2.16 per hour. The court held that the company had failed to explain why the availability of men to perform work that paid two cents per hour more than women received should result in overall payment of 21.5 cents more to the men than to the women for the common work both performed. The court said that the jobs of male and female selector-packers were substantially equal and that the employer had therefore violated the Equal Pay Act.

What is a factor that can justify a wage differential between men and women? A court gave a helpful answer in a case involving the Robert Hall clothing company. Robert Hall had men staff its men's departments and women staff its women's departments. These sales personnel performed equal work, yet the salesmen received higher salaries than the saleswomen. Each received a base salary plus incentive payments based upon the profitability of the goods sold. Robert Hall claimed that the resulting wage differential was based not upon sex but upon economic factors, that is, the higher profitability of the men's departments. The court held that the economic benefit to Robert Hall could be used to justify the wage differential. It also held that Robert Hall had proved that it received the economic benefits upon which it based its salary differentials. Robert Hall showed that the men's departments were substantially more profitable than the women's departments for every year of the company's operation. The court pointed out that it may require equal effort to sell two different types of shoes for the same $10 price. However, if the employer receives a $4 profit on one type as opposed to a $2 profit on the other, the employer can pay a higher wage to the person selling the type of shoe that yields the higher profit.

Another factor that allows some individuals to receive a higher wage than others is participation in a bona fide training program. Of course, if the participants in the program are of only one sex, the legal issue of sex discrimination under Title VII will be raised and the program will immediately be suspect as to whether it is indeed a bona fide training program.

In the last case we will mention here, the Supreme Court held an employer in violation of the act for paying a higher base wage to male night shift inspectors than it paid to female inspectors who performed the same tasks on the day shift. The higher base wage was paid in addition to a night shift differential that was paid to all employees for night work.

Comparable Worth

The most recent issue to be raised in the area of equal pay concerns whether or not the law requires an employer to pay equal wages to employees of different sexes who do not perform equal work but whose jobs are of comparable worth. The phrase **comparable worth** represents the idea that if two different job classifications — for instance secretary and groundskeeper — contribute comparable economic benefits to an employer, the individuals holding those jobs should receive comparable pay. One court decision says that Title VII of the Civil Rights Act does not require equal pay for jobs of comparable worth. The language of the Equal Pay Act does not seem to require it either. However, the Supreme Court has held that if the male and female jobs are not equal, which therefore removes the case from the equal pay law, but the employer intentionally pays lower wages to women than to men, a case may be properly brought under the 1964 Civil Rights Law.

Finally, it is important to recognize that the Equal Pay Act mandates equal pay for men as well as for women. If a woman is being paid more money than a man who is performing the same job and the pay differential does not come under one of the law's exceptions, then the employer must raise the man's salary to the higher level of the woman's salary.

AGE DISCRIMINATION

Congress passed the Age Discrimination in Employment Act (ADEA) in 1967 and significant amendments to it in 1978. The ADEA prohibits discrimination against individuals who are at least 40 years of age but less than 70 years of age because of their age by employers, labor organizations, and employment agencies. Executive Order 11,141 forbids age discrimination by those holding federal contracts. These laws do not require that persons between the ages of 40 and 70 must be hired. Rather, they say that a refusal to hire them cannot be based upon their age.

The law applies to employers engaged in an industry that affects commerce who have 20 or more employees and to unions that either operate a hiring hall or have 25 or more members. Employment agencies are covered regardless of their size or the number of persons they place. If an employment agency regularly procures employees for an employer, it is covered, even if the agency is not paid for its services. Employees of state and local government agencies are covered, as are most, but not all, employees of the federal government. In fact, the 1978 amendments to the act eliminate the mandatory retirement age of 70 for most federal employees.

What Is Age Discrimination?

Under the 1967 Age Discrimination in Employment Act, it is unlawful for an employer to fail or refuse to hire, to discharge, or otherwise to discriminate against any individual with respect to his or her compensation, terms, conditions, or privileges of employment because of the individual's age. It is also unlawful to reduce the wage rate of any employee, irrespective of his or her age, in order to comply with the act. It is unlawful for a union to exclude, to expel from its membership, or otherwise to discriminate against any individual because of his or her age or to cause or attempt to cause an employer to discriminate against an individual in violation of the act. Finally, it is unlawful for an employment agency to fail or refuse to refer for employment or otherwise to discriminate against any individual because of the individual's age or to classify or refer for employment any individual on the basis of his or her age.

It is permissible to act on the basis of a person's age where age is a bona fide occupational qualification (BFOQ) reasonably necessary to the normal operation of the particular business or where the differentiation is based on reasonable factors other than age or on the terms of a bona fide seniority system. The original law allowed an employer to require the mandatory retirement of an individual under the age of 65 if such retirement were in accordance with the terms of a bona fide employment benefit plan—such as a retirement, a pension, or an insurance plan—that was not a subterfuge to evade the purpose of the act. The 1978 amendments removed this provision.

Exceptions to the Age Discrimination Law

We began this section with the comment that the age discrimination law prohibits discrimination against individuals between the ages of 40 and 70. Naturally, as with most laws, there are some exceptions. The law does permit an employer to require the retirement of certain executives at age 65. If a person was a bona fide executive or was in a high-level, policy-making position for the two year period immediately preceding retirement and is entitled to a pension of at least $27,000 a year, that person can be forced to retire at age 65.

Let us now look at the BFOQ exception to the law. The most important case in this area involves Greyhound Lines. Greyhound declined to consider applications for positions as intercity bus drivers from individuals 35 years of age or older. The Secretary of Labor alleged that this age limitation violated the ADEA. Greyhound argued that age was a BFOQ for intercity drivers. As it turned out, Greyhound won the case.

The court, greatly concerned for passenger safety, pointed out that more than the safety of the employee was involved. It held that for the age limitation to be valid, Greyhound had to demonstrate that the company in fact had a rational basis for believing that the elimination of its maximum hiring age would increase the risk of harm to its passengers. However, the court said that Greyhound need only show a minimal increase in risk of harm, namely that one additional person's safety would be jeopardized.

The government had argued that applicants 40 to 70 years of age should be judged on the basis of their "functional age"—that is, on their ability to perform the job—rather than on their chronological age. The Court rejected this argument, saying that it is not clear that functional age is readily determinable and that it was questionable whether Greyhound could practically scrutinize the continued fitness of older drivers on a frequent and regular basis. The Court ruled that Greyhound had proved its case by proving three things: (1) the rigors of extra-board assignments (the type of driving required of new employees); (2) the degenerative physical and sensory changes brought on by the aging process that begin in the late thirties; and (3) statistical evidence showing that the company's safest drivers had 16 to 20 years of experience and were between 50 and 55 years of age. This safety record could not be attained by hiring applicants 40 years of age or over.

In another case, this one involving a test pilot, a court ruled that age is not a BFOQ for test pilots. The employer's evidence was based on the changes that accompany the aging process in the general population, whereas the employee's evidence tended to show that the aging process occurs more slowly and to a lesser degree among pilots and that the accident rate actually decreased with age.

Age is not a BFOQ when it comes to jobs such as bank tellers, as is exemplified in the following factual situation. Between June 12, 1968, and July 14, 1969, an employer hired 35 tellers or teller trainees, none of whom was over 40 years of age. When two women, both of whom were over 40, applied for the jobs, the personnel manager wrote "too old for teller" and "wants teller, too old" in his notes. On December 3, 1968, the employer placed a request for teller trainees with an employment agency. The employer specified that the applicants were to be female, of moderate intelligence, with or without experience, and between the ages 21 and 24. A court concluded that the employer had violated the age discrimination law.

Job Advertisements

Because newspapers' classified want ads serve as a potential source for jobs, the Age Discrimination in Employment Act attends to such ads. It also attends to job referrals. In relevant part, the act provides that:

> It shall be unlawful for an employer, labor organization, or employment agency to print or publish, or cause to be printed or published, any notice or advertisement relating to employment by such an employer or membership in or any classification or referral for employment by such a labor organization, or relating to any classification or referral for employment by such an employment agency, indicating any preference, limitation, specification, or discrimination, based on age.

In developing guidelines for this portion of the act, the Department of Labor held such words and phrases as "young," "boy," "girl," "age 25 to 35," and "recent college graduate" to be illegal. Likewise, phrases such as "retired person" or "Social Security recipient" that indicate a preference for individuals over 70 are considered to be impermissible by the Department of Labor. The federal courts, however, do not regard all of these words and phrases to be automatic violations of the law. In one case, a federal appellate court decided that such phrases must be judged by reading them in context. An employment agency had used such terms in its job ads over a three and a half year period. The Secretary of Labor maintained that the terms were "trigger words" that constituted a per se violation when they were present in a job ad. The court concluded, though, that such terms as "junior executive" or "junior secretary" refer to the duties to be performed by the employee rather than to age in many contexts. On the other hand, the court ruled that such terms as "girl" or "career girl" implied youth and therefore violated the Act.

Early Retirement and State Laws

Before Congress amended the age discrimination law to include state and local government employees, there was a legal challenge to state laws that mandated early retirement. A Massachusetts state policeman argued that a state law requiring state police to retire at the age of 50 when other state employees could work beyond that age denied him equal protection under the law in violation of the Fourteenth Amendment. The Supreme Court, however, upheld the constitutionality of the Massachusetts law.

After Congress amended the law, various states challenged the constitutionality of the amendment. They argued that the Constitution does not grant Congress the power to regulate the states with regard to such matters. In the following case, the Supreme Court decided that Congress does have such power and that the states must abide by the age discrimination law.

EQUAL EMPLOYMENT OPPORTUNITY COMMISSION v. WYOMING
460 U.S. 226 (Sup. Ct. 1983)

[Bill Crump, a supervisor in the Wyoming Game and Fish Department, was involuntarily retired at age 55 under the provisions of Wyoming law. The EEOC challenged the retirement as being in violation of the Age Discrimination in Employment Act (ADEA). Wyoming argued that Congress had exceeded its constitutional powers when it attempted to regulate this aspect of state conduct. Wyoming supported its argument by pointing to the Supreme Court's decision in *National League of Cities v. Usery,* in which the Congressional extension of the wage and hour provisions of the Fair Labor Standards Act to the states was declared unconstitutional. The trial court dismissed the suit by the EEOC, and the EEOC appealed.]

BRENNAN, Justice

The question presented in this case is whether Congress acted constitutionally when, in 1974, it extended the definition of "employer" under §11(b) of Act to include state and local governments.

National League of Citizens v. Usery struck down Congress's attempt to extend the wage and hour provisions of the Fair Labor Standards Act to state and local governments.

The management of state parks is clearly a traditional state function. As we have already emphasized, however, the purpose of the doctrine of immunity articulated in *National League of Cities* was to protect States from federal intrusions that might threaten their "separate and independent existence." We conclude

that the degree of federal intrusion in this case is sufficiently less serious than it was in *National League of Cities* so as to make it unnecessary for us to override Congress's express choice to extend its regulatory authority to the States.

In this case, appellees claim no substantial stake in their retirement policy other than "assur[ing] the physical preparedness of Wyoming game wardens to perform their duties." Under the ADEA, however, the State may still, at the very least, assess the fitness of its game wardens and dismiss those wardens whom it reasonably finds to be unfit. Put another way, the Act requires the State to achieve its goals in a more individualized and careful manner than would otherwise be the case, but it does not require the State to abandon those goals, or to abandon the public policy decisions underlying them. Perhaps more important, appellees remain free under the ADEA to continue to do *precisely what they are doing now,* if they can demonstrate that age is a "bona fide occupational qualification" for the job of game warden. Thus, . . . even the State's discretion to achieve its goals *in the way it thinks best* is not being overridden entirely, but is merely being tested against a reasonable federal standard.

Finally, the Court's concern in *National League of Cities* was not only with the effect of the federal regulatory scheme on the particular decisions it was purporting to regulate, but also with the potential impact of that scheme on the States' ability to structure operations and set priorities over a wide range of decisions. In this case, we cannot conclude from the nature of the

ADEA that it will have either a direct or an obvious negative effect on state finances.

The extension of the ADEA to cover state and local governments, both on its face and as applied in this case, was a valid exercise of Congress's powers under the Commerce Clause.

Reversed.

CASE REVIEW QUESTIONS

1. Does this decision mean that Wyoming must retain all game wardens who are 55 years of age and older on the payroll?
2. Should Congress have the power to interfere in the employer-employee relationship between a state and one of its citizens?

Enforcement of the Age Discrimination in Employment Act

As noted earlier, the Secretary of Labor used to enforce the ADEA, but the EEOC enforces it today. The EEOC is empowered to make investigations and to require the keeping of records that are necessary for the administration of the act. Voluntary settlement of disputes is encouraged. In fact, before EEOC can sue, it must attempt to bring about the voluntary elimination of a discriminatory practice.

The 1978 amendments make it clear that an individual is entitled to a jury trial in age discrimination cases. An individual that has been the victim of illegal discrimination is entitled to monetary damages and equitable relief and a court *must* award him or her reasonable attorney's fees. Of course, if EEOC brings the lawsuit, the individual will have no legal fees.

DISCRIMINATION AGAINST THE HANDICAPPED

The Rehabilitation Act of 1973 was passed by Congress and signed by the President as part of the federal effort to remove discriminatory barriers to the employment of the handicapped. Section 504 of the act provides in pertinent part:

> No otherwise qualified handicapped individual in the United States . . . shall, solely by reason of his handicap, be excluded from participation in, be denied the benefits of, or be subjected to discrimination under any program or activity receiving Federal financial assistance. . . .

Section 503 of the act requires those receiving federal contracts in excess of $2,500 to take affirmative action to employ and to advance in employment qualified handicapped persons. Section 501 bars federal agencies from discriminating against handicapped individuals in the employment process. Handicapped can refer to either a physical or a mental impairment that substantially limits a person's activity.

The Office of Federal Contract Compliance Programs (OFCCP) in the U.S. Department of Labor enforces §503 through an administrative process. If the OFCCP determines that a violation has occurred, there are three sanctions that it can impose upon the federal contractor: (1) debarment from future federal contracts; (2) cancellation of a current contract; and (3) withholding progress payments due on current contracts. If the OFCCP decides to take no action even though it believes that a violation has occurred, can the aggrieved individual bring a private suit to collect damages? The answer is unclear. Originally the courts seemed to say "No." However, Congress amended the law in the Rehabilitation, Comprehensive Services & Developmental Disabilities Act of 1978. One of these amendments specifies that the prevailing party in a lawsuit, other than the United States, may be provided with reasonable attorney's fees by the court. If Congress is saying that the winner of a lawsuit can recover his or her legal fees, it seems only logical that Congress is saying that a private individual can bring a lawsuit in the first place. However, a 1980 court decision seems to indicate otherwise. It will take some time before we have a definitive answer to this question.

It should be noted that §504 does not speak in terms of employment. Instead, it speaks of those receiving federal financial assistance. This section of the law has also received mixed interpretations from the courts. More litigation must occur before we will be able to say definitely what the section means, to whom it applies, and who can bring a lawsuit for a violation under it.

THE OFFICE OF FEDERAL CONTRACT COMPLIANCE PROGRAMS

Executive Order 11,246 forbids discrimination by contractors and subcontractors that do business with the federal government. While this executive order resembles the provisions of the Civil Rights Act in many respects, there are some differences. An important difference is its requirement that those covered by the order take affirmative action to remove employment barriers to minorities and women. For example, in the famous "Philadelphia Plan," contractors were required to meet an affirmative-action plan that established goals for hiring minority workers based upon the percentage of representation of minorities in the construction industry in particular geographical areas. Any bidder on construction contracts in excess of $10,000 must certify that it will take the necessary affirmative action and that it will see to it that its subcontractors do likewise. Those who are not in the construction industry but who do business with the federal government are also covered by the order. If the employer has 50 or more employees and a contract in excess of $50,000, it must adopt a written affirmative-action plan. The plan must establish goals for hiring minorities and women as well as a timetable for achieving those goals.

The Office of Federal Contract Compliance Programs (OFCCP) in the U.S. Department of Labor enforces Executive Order 11,246. However, responsibility for compliance in some specific industries has been assigned to other federal agencies. The idea is that certain agencies will be more familiar with programs in certain industries. For example, the Defense Department has responsibility for the compliance of contractors who perform defense contracts. The OFCCP normally leaves the administration of cases within these industries to the federal agency assigned responsibility, but it can take over this responsibility if it so desires.

REVIEW QUESTIONS

1. What forms of discrimination are prohibited by the 1964 civil rights law?
2. Explain what is meant by the phrase "bona fide occupational qualification (BFOQ)." Give some examples of BFOQs.
3. Outline the role played by the EEOC in discrimination disputes.
4. Should Congress pass legislation mandating equal pay for persons who hold jobs of comparable worth to an employer? Is the position of police officer of comparable worth to that of a fire fighter? Why?
5. If a modeling agency rejected a 25-year-old job candidate as being too old and in her place selected a 19-year-old person, has the agency engaged in illegal age discrimination?

CASE PROBLEMS

1. As a devout member of the Sikh religion, Bhatia refused to shave. OSHA standards require employees whose duties involve potential exposure to toxic gases to wear a gas-tight respirator. Bhatia could not do this because of his beard. Chevron fired three other employees who refused to shave, but it transferred Bhatia to a lower-paying position that did not require a respirator. If Bhatia brings a legal action against Chevron on the grounds of religious discrimination, on what basis can Chevron defend? Who will win the case? Explain.

2. There was a job vacancy in a plant. Rodriguez, a Puerto Rican male of slight build, had the most seniority of all those in lower job classifications. The employer informed Rodriguez that the job was his if he could demonstrate the ability to perform each task of the job classification. He adequately performed each task except one. He was unable to dismantle a machine by grasping a major section of it, lowering it four feet to the ground, and then replacing it. The machine section weighs 200 pounds, and it must be removed twice a year for proper equipment maintenance. When he was denied the job, Rodriguez pointed out that, even

though the job description calls for the machine operator to perform the task, the former female operator was assisted by two or three coworkers whenever maintenance of the machine was necessary. Nonetheless, Rodriguez was denied the promotion. If Rodriguez sues his employer, what two types of discrimination could he allege? Who will win the case? Explain.

3. Jones Company, Inc., regards marriage as a sign of stability and therefore hires only married individuals. At Jones, singles need not apply, and divorced employees are discharged. Smith, a single person, was denied employment at Jones. If Smith brings a legal action against Jones, on what grounds may the company defend itself? Who will win the case? Explain.

4. A female vocational rehabilitation specialist in the District of Columbia Department of Corrections encountered frequent sexual propositions from her supervisors over a 30-month period of employment. When she complained to the top supervisor, he suggested that she have an affair with him. Her rejection of these repeated sexual advances did not result in her being denied any promotion. Has the

employer's toleration of this sexual harrassment violated the 1964 Civil Rights Law? Explain.

5. Mary, a black woman, is an operator in the rolling mill portion of a steel plant. She performs her job from the very small confines of a control booth high above the plant floor. Mary is pregnant. At the start of the eighth month of her pregnancy, she had become too large to enter the control booth. The employer therefore informed her that it would be necessary for her to begin her maternity leave. If the employer is sued by Mary, what argument will the employer make in its defense. Who will win the case? Would it affect the outcome of the case if there were proof that the employer had allowed overweight male operators to transfer to another job when they found it impossible to squeeze into the control booth? Explain.

6. A union is on strike against an employer. The union pays strike benefits to its members. However, to qualify for these benefits, each union member must perform picket duty a minimum of 10 hours per week. The employer's plant is located in a tough part of town. Consequently, the union leadership decrees that the women members will be exempt from night picket duty. If the male members of the union file sex discrimination charges with the EEOC, who will win the case? Explain.

7. Wynn Oil Company did not promote Ms. Fernandez to the position of Director of International Operations. She sued, claiming that she was the victim of sex discrimination. One of Wynn's legal defenses was that being male was a bona fide occupational qualification (BFOQ) for the job. Wynn claims that its South American clients would not, for cultural reasons, conduct business with a woman. Is being male a BFOQ for a position that involves dealing with customers who hold macho-male cultural attitudes? Is Wynn Oil guilty of sex discrimination? Explain.

8. A Pennsylvania county hospital pays its female beauticians $165 a month less than its male barbers. Both perform their work on hospital patients under similar working conditions. A barber spends 10 to 20 minutes cutting a patient's hair whereas a beautician spends 30 to 75 minutes on a female patient. The latter do more than simply cut hair; they also give shampoos and permanents and they file nails. Pennsylvania requires a separate course of study and a separate license for each occupation. Are the occupations of barber and beautician in this hospital substantially similar? Has the hospital violated the Equal Pay Act? Explain.

9. The personnel director of a company is faced with making a payroll cutback of approximately $70,000. Instead of discharging three employees in their late twenties who earn a total of $70,000, the director decides to eliminate the positions of two individuals in their fifties whose salaries total that amount. Is the director's action on safe legal ground? Explain.

54

ENVIRONMENTAL LAW

Environmental law as a separately recognizable body of the law is relatively new. Indeed, comprehensive environmental legislation did not begin to appear until 1969. Then, between 1969 and 1976, federal legislation aimed at most of the areas of environmental concern was passed. The decade of the seventies also saw the adoption of a wide variety of environmental laws by state and local governments. As a result, the inadequate laws addressing environmental problems that existed prior to 1969 were replaced by laws demanding environmental planning, the control of present and future sources of pollution, the rehabilitation of the environment, and the safe disposal of hazardous waste.

Environmental planning by the federal government was first mandated by the National Environmental Policy Act (1969). Present and future sources of pollution affecting basic, vital resources are regulated by the Clean Air Act (1970) and the Clean Water Act (1972). Rehabilitation of the environment is an important part of each pollution control measure, including the Resource Conservation and Recovery Act (1976), which deals with hazardous waste. These four pieces of federal legislation will be the focus of this chapter. They were selected to provide you with a sketch of the domain of environmental law and to give you a sense of the array of approaches chosen by Congress to protect the quality of the environment.

NATIONAL ENVIRONMENTAL POLICY ACT (1969)

The National Environmental Policy Act (NEPA) mandated that all federal agencies include a document called an **environmental impact statement (EIS)** in their recommendations or reports on proposals for legislation and on any other major federal actions that might significantly affect the quality of the human environment. Congress required that the EIS include a detailed statement of five elements:

1. The environmental impact of the proposed action.
2. The separate designation of any adverse environmental effects that cannot be avoided.
3. A discussion of the reasonable alternatives to the proposed action.
4. A description of the relationship between the local, short-term uses and the maintenance of long-term productivity.
5. A delineation of the irreversible and irretrievable commitment of resources to the proposed action.

Details pertaining to when an EIS had to be prepared and precisely what should be included in it were left unclear by Congress. Although the statute created the Council on Environmental Quality (CEQ) to advise the President on environmental matters, it did not directly delegate to the CEQ the function of clarifying the statutory language. Thus, for about ten years, the task of interpreting the meaning of NEPA fell mainly to the federal courts. After more than 1,000 cases had been decided by the courts, President Carter ordered the CEQ to draft a set of binding NEPA regulations in 1977. These regulations, which became effective in mid–1979, codified many of the judicial decisions made during the preceding decade, and they further clarified the EIS process.

Much of NEPA's history was made before the NEPA Regulations were adopted. From the start, many federal agencies were not enthusiastic about adapting to NEPA's rules. The new requirement that the agencies consider environmental factors imposed additional cost and time constraints on them. In addition, it was clear that NEPA was opening up agency decision making to increased public scrutiny. Neither of these changes was welcomed by the majority of agency administrators. As a result, some agencies attempted to minimize NEPA's impact on the status quo or even to circumvent it altogether. The federal courts, however, were not sympathetic to these attempts. The judicial reaction is illustrated by the landmark *Calvert Cliffs* case, excerpted here, in which the judge sternly reprimanded the Atomic Energy Commission and set the tenor for future court decisions in NEPA cases.

CALVERT CLIFFS COORDINATING COMMITTEE, INC. v. U.S. ATOMIC ENERGY COMMISSION
449 F.2d 1109 (D.C. Cir. 1971)

[The Atomic Energy Commission (AEC) adopted regulations aimed at implementing NEPA. The regulations were apparently geared initially to postpone and then to minimize the impact of NEPA on existing AEC procedures. Calvert Cliffs Coordinating Committee, Inc., sued the AEC, asking that several of these regulations be set aside because they were not consistent with the spirit of NEPA. Only one of the regulations is discussed in this edited version of the case. Basically, this regulation provided that the AEC did not have to consider environmental factors under NEPA during its public hearing stage unless these factors were raised by the public. The lasting importance of this case is not the courts' rulings on the individual regulations but Judge Wright's attitude toward both NEPA and the reluctant agency.]

WRIGHT, Judge

These cases are only the beginning of what promises to become a flood of new litigation—litigation seeking judicial assistance in protecting our natural environment. Several recently enacted statutes attest to the commitment of the Government to control, at long last, the destructive engine of material progress. But it remains to be seen whether the promise of this legislation will become a reality. Therein lies the judicial role. In these cases, we must for the first time interpret the broadest and perhaps most important of the recent statutes: the National Environmental Policy Act of 1969 (NEPA). We must assess claims that one of the agencies charged with its administration has failed to live up to the congressional mandate. Our duty, in short, is to see that important legislative purposes, heralded in the halls of Congress, are not lost or misdirected in the vast hallways of the federal bureaucracy.

NEPA, like so much other reform legislation of the last 40 years, is cast in terms of a general mandate and broad delegation of authority to new and old administrative agencies. It takes the major step of requiring all federal agencies to consider values of environmental preservation in their spheres of activity, and it prescribes certain procedural measures to ensure that those values are in fact fully respected. Petitioners argue that rules recently adopted by the Atomic Energy Commission to govern consideration of environmental matters fail to satisfy the rigor demanded by NEPA. The Commission, on the other hand, contends that the vagueness of the NEPA mandate and delegation leaves much room for discretion and that the rules challenged by petitioners fall well within the broad scope of the Act. We find the policies embodied in NEPA to be a good deal clearer and more demanding than does the Commission. We conclude that the Commission's procedural rules do not comply with the congressional policy.

NEPA, first of all, makes environmental protection a part of the mandate of every federal agency and department. The Atomic Energy Commission, for example, had continually asserted, prior to NEPA, that it had no statutory authority to concern itself with the adverse environmental effects of its actions. Now, however, its hands are no longer tied. It is not only permitted, but compelled, to take environmental values into account. Perhaps the greatest importance of NEPA is to require the Atomic Energy Commission and other agencies to consider environmental issues just as they consider other matters within their mandates. Beyond the "detailed statement," Section 102(2)(D) requires all agencies specifically to "study, develop, and describe appropriate alternatives to recommended courses of action in any proposal which involves unresolved conflicts concerning alternative uses of available resources." This requirement, like the "detailed statement" requirement, seeks to ensure that each agency decision maker has before him and takes into proper account all possible approaches to a particular project (including total abandonment of the project) which would alter the environmental impact and the cost-benefit balance. Only in that fashion is it likely that the most intelligent, optimally beneficial decision will ultimately be made. Moreover, by compelling a formal "detailed statement" and a description of alternatives, NEPA provides evidence that the mandated decision making process has in fact taken place and, most importantly, allows those removed from the initial process to evaluate and balance the factors on their own.

Of course, all of these Section 102 duties are qualified by the phrase "to the fullest extent possible." We must stress as forcefully as possible that this language does not provide an escape hatch for footdragging agencies; it does not make NEPA's procedural requirements somehow "discretionary." Congress did not intend the Act to be such a paper tiger. Indeed, the requirement of environmental consideration "to the fullest extent possible" sets a high standard for the agencies, a standard which must be rigorously enforced by the reviewing courts.

Thus the Section 102 duties are not inherently flexible. They must be complied with to the fullest extent, unless there is a clear conflict of statutory authority. Considerations of administrative difficulty, delay or economic cost will not suffice to strip the section of its fundamental importance.

In the cases before us now, we do not have to review a particular decision by the Atomic Energy Commission granting a construction permit or an operating license. Rather, we must review the Commission's recently promulgated rules which govern consideration of environmental values in all such individual decisions. The rules were devised strictly in order to comply with the NEPA procedural requirements — but petitioners argue that they fall far short of the congressional mandate.

Although environmental factors must be considered by the agency's regulatory staff under the rules, such factors need not be considered by the hearing board conducting an independent review of staff recommendations, unless affirmatively raised by outside parties or staff members.

The question here is whether the Commission is correct in thinking that its NEPA responsibilities may "be carried out in toto outside the hearing process" — whether it is enough that environmental data and evaluations merely "accompany" an application through the review process, but receive no consideration whatever from the hearing board.

We believe that the Commission's crabbed interpretation of NEPA makes a mockery of the Act. What possible purpose could there be in the Section 102(2)(C) requirement (that the "detailed statement" accompany proposals through agency review processes) if "accompany" means no more than physical proximity — mandating no more than the physical act of passing certain folders and papers, unopened, to reviewing officials along with other folders and papers? What possible purpose could there be in requiring the "detailed statement" to be before hearing boards, if the boards are free to ignore entirely the contents of the statement? NEPA was meant to do more than regulate the flow of papers in the federal bureaucracy. The word "accompany" in Section 102(2)(C) must not be read so narrowly as to make the Act ludicrous. It must, rather, be read to indicate a congressional intent that environmental factors, as compiled in the "detailed statement," be considered through agency review processes.

Beyond Section 102(2)(C), NEPA requires that agencies consider the environmental impact of their actions "to the fullest extent possible." The Act is addressed to agencies as a whole, not only to their professional staffs. Compliance to the "fullest" possible extent would seem to demand that environmental issues be considered at every important stage in the decision making process concerning a particular action — at every stage where an overall balancing of environmental and nonenvironmental factors is appropriate and where alterations might be made in the proposed action to minimize environmental costs. Of course, consideration which is entirely duplicative is not necessarily required. But independent review of staff proposals by hearing boards is hardly a duplicative function. A truly independent review provides a crucial check on the staff's recommendations. The Commission's hearing boards automatically consider nonenvironmental factors, even though they have been previously studied by the staff. Clearly, the review process is an appropriate stage at which to balance conflicting factors against one another. And, just as clearly, it provides an important opportunity to reject or significantly modify the staff's recommended action. Environmental factors, therefore, should not be singled out and excluded, at this stage, from the proper balance of values envisioned by NEPA.

The rationale of the Commission's limitation of environmental issues to hearings in which parties affirmatively raise those issues may have been one of economy. It may have been supposed that, whenever there are serious environmental costs overlooked or uncorrected by the staff, some party will intervene to bring those costs to the hearing board's attention. Such administrative costs are not enough to undercut the Act's requirement that environmental protection be considered "to the fullest extent possible." It is, moreover, unrealistic to assume that there will always be an intervenor with the information, energy and money required to challenge a staff recommendation which ignores environmental costs. NEPA establishes environmental protection as an integral part of the Atomic Energy Commission's basic mandate. The primary responsibility for fulfilling that mandate lies with the Commission. Its responsibility is not simply to sit back, like an umpire, and resolve adversary contentions at the hearing stage. Rather, it must itself take the initiative of considering environmental values at every distinctive and comprehensive stage of the process beyond the staff's evaluation and recommendation.

Strangely, the Commission has principally relied on more pragmatic arguments. It seems an unfortunate affliction of large organizations to resist new procedures and to envision massive roadblocks to their adoption. Hence the Commission's talk of the need for an "orderly transition" to the NEPA procedures.

In the end, the Commission's long delay seems based upon what it believes to be a pressing national power crisis. But the very purpose of NEPA was to tell federal agencies that environmental protection is as much a part of their responsibility as is protection and promotion of the industries they regulate. Whether or not the spectre of a national power crisis is as real as the Commission apparently believes, it must not be used to create a blackout of environmental consideration in the agency review process.

Remanded for proceedings consistent with this opinion.

CASE REVIEW QUESTIONS

1. Since the AEC's regulations required that the agency staff study environmental factors, why was it necessary for the hearing board to study them as well?
2. Why do you think large organizations "resist new procedures and . . . envision massive roadblocks" when new laws that affect them are passed?

The Threshold Decision

NEPA has an impact on decision making very early in an agency's proceedings. The NEPA Regulations state that environmental considerations must be integrated into regular agency planning at the earliest possible time. The purpose of this measure is to insure that the agency has adequately weighed the relevant environmental factors before making its final decision. For instance, if the agency is asked to resolve a flooding problem along a river, it must examine environmental factors along with economic and technical data during the early stages of its proceedings when it is deciding whether or not to resolve the problem.

When the agency begins to develop a proposal for action to resolve a problem, such as flooding, or is presented with a proposed course of action, such as building a dam, it must decide whether or not to prepare an EIS. This is referred to as the *threshold decision.* Each agency has a list of actions that "normally require" an EIS and a list of actions that "normally do not require" an EIS. If the action is found on either of these lists, the decision of whether to prepare an EIS is made accordingly.

If the action is not already listed, then the agency must prepare an environmental assessment to determine whether an EIS is necessary. The *environmental assessment* is a document that contains a brief discussion of the anticipated environmental impact of the proposed action and of any alternative actions the agency is studying. Its purpose is to help the agency decide whether or not the impact of the proposed action on the environment might be significant.

The significance of the impact of an action is determined by examining both its context and its intensity. Context means that the impact must be analyzed in several settings—national, regional, and local, for example. Intensity refers to the severity of the impact, which is determined by examining the degree to which the action may be controversial, the unique characteristics of the area involved, and some eight other broad criteria listed in the NEPA Regulations.

If the environmental assessment reveals that an EIS is not necessary, the agency prepares a "finding of no significant impact," which is a document that presents the reasons why the action will not have a significant effect on the environment. If the agency decides that the proposed action might have a significant impact on the environment, it will prepare an EIS.

Before initiating the preparation of the EIS, however, the agency is required to invite all interested parties, including the likely proponents and opponents of the action, to participate in determining the "scope" of the issues. The purpose of this *scoping process* is to ascertain the significant environmental issues related to the proposed action.

The lower federal courts have handled a large number of NEPA cases, but the U.S. Supreme Court has decided only a few. Two of these cases follow, both of which were decided in favor of the federal agency and against the party seeking to broaden the application of NEPA. However, despite the direct results of these cases, you should be alert for the expansive language used by the Court in its interpretations of NEPA.

KLEPPE v. SIERRA CLUB
427 U.S. 390 (USSC 1976)

[The federal government owns a large amount of coal-rich land in the western United States. These coal lands are divided into tracts and are leased to private companies for exploitation. The leasing program is administered by the Department of the Interior. When an individual tract is leased to a company, a "project" EIS is prepared. In addition, the department has done a "programmatic" EIS for its entire national coal leasing program. Although the department has not prepared an EIS for its regional coal leasing program, it has done several regional studies, including the Northern Great Plains Resources Program (NGPRP), which was devoted exclusively to environmental matters. The Sierra Club believed that an EIS should be prepared for the coal-rich Northern Great Plains region, which includes parts of the states of Wyoming, Montana, North Da-

kota, and South Dakota. The department refused to prepare this EIS.

The Sierra Club sued the Secretary of Interior (Kleppe) to enjoin further leasing until the agency had prepared a comprehensive EIS for the entire region. The Sierra Club argued that the individual project EISs did not show the combined effects of numerous leases on land in the region. The Department of the Interior contended that it had not proposed any regional level "action" that would trigger the EIS requirement of NEPA. The trial court, a district court, concluded that there was no plan for regional development and found for the department. An intermediate court of appeals reversed the decision, holding that the department was "contemplating" a regional plan or program and that the contemplation was adequate to trigger the regional EIS requirement. The department appealed the case to the U.S. Supreme Court.]

POWELL, Justice

The major issue remains the one with which the suit began: whether NEPA requires petitioners to prepare an environmental impact statement on the entire Northern Great Plains region. §102(2)(C) requires an impact statement "in every recommendation or report on proposals for legislation or other major Federal actions significantly affecting the quality of the human environment." Since no one has suggested that petitioners have proposed legislation on respondents' region, the controlling phrase in this section of the Act, for this case, is "major Federal actions." Respondents can prevail only if there has been a report or recommendation on a proposal for major federal action with respect to the Northern Great Plains region. Our statement of the relevant facts shows there has been none; instead, all proposals are for actions of either local or national scope.

The local actions are the decisions by the various petitioners to issue a lease, approve a mining plan, issue a right-of-way permit, or take other action to allow private activity at some point within the respondents' region. Several courts of appeals have held that an impact statement must be included in the report or recommendation on a proposal for such action if the private activity to be permitted is one "significantly affecting the quality of the human environment" within the meaning of §102(2)(C).

The petitioners do not dispute this requirement in this case, and indeed have prepared impact statements on several proposed actions of this type in the Northern Great Plains during the course of this litigation. Their admission is well made, for the new leasing program is a coherent plan of national scope, and its adoption surely has significant environmental consequences.

But there is no evidence in the record of an action or a proposal for an action of regional scope. The District Court, in fact, expressly found that there was no existing or proposed plan or program on the part of the Federal Government for the regional development of the area described in respondents' complaint. It found also that the three studies initiated by the Department

in areas either included within or inclusive of respondents' region were not parts of any plan or program to develop or encourage development of the Northern Great Plains. That court found no evidence that the individual coal development projects undertaken or proposed by private industry and public utilities in that part of the country are integrated into a plan or otherwise interrelated. These findings were not disturbed by the Court of Appeals, and they remain fully supported by the record in this Court.

Quite apart from the fact that the statutory language requires an impact statement only in the event of a proposed action, respondents' desire for a regional environmental impact statement cannot be met for practical reasons. In the absence of a proposal for a regional plan of development, there is nothing that could be the subject of the analysis envisioned by the statute for an impact statement.

We conclude that the Court of Appeals erred in both its factual assumption and its interpretation of NEPA. We think the court was mistaken in concluding, on the record before it, that the petitioners were "contemplating" a regional development plan or program.

Even had the record justified a finding that a regional program was contemplated by the petitioners, the legal conclusion drawn by the Court of Appeals cannot be squared with the Act. The court recognized that the mere "contemplation" of certain action is not sufficient to require an impact statement. But it believed the statute nevertheless empowers a court to require the preparation of an impact statement to begin at some point prior to the formal recommendation or report on a proposal. The Court of Appeals accordingly devised its own four-part "balancing" test for determining when, during the contemplation of a plan or other type of federal action, an agency must begin a statement. The factors to be considered were identified as the likelihood and imminence of the program's coming to fruition, the extent to which information is available on the effects of implementing the expected program and on alternatives thereto, the extent to which irretrievable commitments are being made and options precluded "as refinement of the proposal progresses," and the severity of the environmental effects should the action be implemented.

The Court's reasoning and action find no support in

the language or legislative history of NEPA. The statute clearly states when an impact statement is required, and mentions nothing about a balancing of factors. Rather, as we noted last term, under the first sentence of §102(2)(C) the moment at which an agency must have a final statement ready "is the time at which it makes a recommendation or report on a proposal for federal action." A court has no authority to depart from the statutory language and, by a balancing of court-devised factors, determine a point during the germination process of a potential proposal at which an impact statement should be prepared. Such an assertion of judicial authority would leave the agencies uncertain as to their procedural duties under NEPA, would invite judicial involvement in the day-to-day decision-making process of the agencies, and would invite litigation. As the contemplation of a project and the accompanying study thereof do not necessarily result in a proposal for major federal action, it may be assumed that the balancing process devised by the Court of Appeals also would result in the preparation of a good many unnecessary impact statements.

Respondents insist that, even without a comprehensive federal plan for the development of the Northern Great Plains, a "regional" impact statement nevertheless is required on all coal-related projects in the region because they are intimately related.

We begin by stating our general agreement with respondents' basic premise that §102(2)(C) may require a comprehensive impact statement in certain situations where several proposed actions are pending at the same time. NEPA announced a national policy of environmental protection and placed a responsibility upon the Federal Government to further specific environmental goals by "all practicable means, consistent with other essential considerations of national policy" [NEPA §101(b)]. Section 102(2)(C) is one of the "action-forcing" provisions intended as a directive to "all

agencies to assure consideration of the environmental impact of their action in decision-making." By requiring an impact statement Congress intended to assure such consideration during the development of a proposal or — as in this case — during the formulation of a position on a proposal submitted by private parties. A comprehensive impact statement may be necessary in some cases for an agency to meet this duty. Thus, when several proposals for coal-related actions that will have cumulative or synergistic environmental impact upon a region are pending concurrently before an agency, their environmental consequences must be considered together. Only through comprehensive consideration of pending proposals can the agency evaluate different courses of action.

Agreement to this extent with respondents' premise, however, does not require acceptance of their conclusion that all proposed coal-related actions in the Northern Great Plains region are so "related" as to require their analysis in a single comprehensive impact statement.

Respondents conceded at oral argument that to prevail they must show that petitioners have acted arbitrarily in refusing to prepare one comprehensive statement on this entire region, and we agree. The determination of the region, if any, with respect to which a comprehensive statement is necessary requires the weighing of a number of relevant factors, including the extent of the interrelationship among proposed actions and practical considerations of feasibility. Resolving these issues requires a high level of technical expertise and is properly left to the informed discretion of the responsible federal agencies. Absent a showing of arbitrary action, we must assume that the agencies have exercised this discretion appropriately. Respondents have made no showing to the contrary.

Reversed.

ANDRUS v. SIERRA CLUB
442 U.S. 347 (USSC 1979)

[The Office of Management and Budget (OMB) recommended that the budget of the Fish and Wildlife Service (FWS) of the Department of the Interior be substantially reduced. FWS manages some 350 wildlife refuges nationally. The Sierra Club believed that the budget cuts would interfere with the proper management of the National Wildlife Refuge System (NWRS).

The Sierra Club and two other environmental organizations sued the Director of OMB and the Secretary of Interior to enjoin the budget cuts until an EIS was prepared. The plaintiffs alleged that the budget cuts were a major federal action that might significantly affect the quality of the human environment. The trial court held that appropriation requests were "proposals for legislation" within the meaning of the statute and would clearly have a significant environmental effect. The court of appeals modified the trial court's ruling by stating that, although routine budget requests were not proposals for legislation, requests that would significantly change the status quo of an existing program were subject to the EIS requirements. An appeal was taken to the U.S. Supreme Court.]

BRENNAN, Justice

The question for decision is whether §102(2)(C) of the National Environmental Policy Act of 1969 (NEPA), requires federal agencies to prepare environmental impact statements (EISs) to accompany appropriation requests. We hold that it does not.

The thrust of §102(2)(C) is thus that environmental concerns be integrated into the very process of agency decision making. The "detailed statement" it requires is the outward sign that environmental values and consequences have been considered during the planning stage of agency actions. If environmental concerns are not interwoven into the fabric of agency planning, the "action-forcing" characteristics of §102(2)(C) would be lost.

> In the past, environmental factors have frequently been ignored and omitted from consideration in the early stages of planning. . . . As a result, unless the results of planning are radically reversed at the policy level— and this often means the Congress—environmental enhancement opportunities may be foregone and unnecessary degradation incurred.

For this reason the regulations of the Council on Environmental Quality (CEQ) require federal agencies to "integrate the NEPA process with other planning at the earliest possible time to insure that planning and decisions reflect environmental values. . . ."

NEPA requires EISs to be included in recommenda-

tions or reports on both "proposals for legislation . . . significantly affecting the quality of the human environment" and "proposals for . . . major Federal actions significantly affecting the quality of the human environment." Petitioners argue, however, that the requirements of §102(2)(C) have no application to the budget process. The contrary holding of the Court of Appeals rests on two alternative interpretations of §102(2)(C). The first is that appropriation requests which are the result of "an agency's painstaking review of an ongoing program," are "proposals for legislation" within the meaning of §102(2)(C). The second is that appropriation requests which are the reflection of "new" agency initiatives constituting "major Federal actions" under NEPA, are themselves "proposals for . . . major Federal actions" for purposes of §102(2)(C). We hold that neither interpretation is correct.

We note initially the NEPA makes no distinction between "proposals for legislation" that are the result of "painstaking review," and those that are merely "routine." When Congress has thus spoken "in the plainest of words," we will ordinarily decline to fracture the clear language of a statute, even for the purpose of fashioning from the resulting fragments a rule that "accords with 'common sense and the public weal.'" Therefore either all appropriation requests constitute "proposals for legislation," or none does.

There is no direct evidence in the legislative history of NEPA that enlightens whether Congress intended the phrase "proposals for legislation" to include requests for appropriations. At the time of the Court of Appeals' decision, however, CEQ guidelines provided that §102(2)(C) applied to "[r]ecommendations for favorable reports relating to legislation including requests for appropriations." At that time CEQ's guidelines were advisory in nature, and were for the purpose of assisting federal agencies in complying with NEPA.

In 1977, however, President Carter, in order to create a single set of uniform, mandatory regulations, ordered CEQ to "[i]ssue regulations to Federal agencies for the implementation of the procedural provisions" of NEPA. CEQ has since issued these regulations, and they reverse CEQ's prior interpretation of §102(2)(C). The regulations provide specifically that "'[l]egislation' includes a bill or legislative proposal to Congress . . . but does not include requests for appropriations." CEQ explained this reversal by noting that, on the basis of "traditional concepts relating to appropriations and the budget cycle, considerations of timing and confidentiality, and other factors, . . . the Council in its experience found that preparation of EISs is ill-suited to the budget preparation process."

It is true that in the past we have been somewhat less inclined to defer to "administrative guidelines" when they have "conflicted with earlier pronouncements of the agency." But CEQ's reversal of interpretation occurred during the detailed and comprehensive process, ordered by the President, of transforming advisory guidelines into mandatory regulations applicable to all federal agencies. A mandatory requirement that every federal agency submit EISs with its appropriation requests raises wholly different and more serious issues "of fair and prudent administration," than does nonbinding advice. This is particularly true in light of the Court of Appeal's correct observation that "[a] rule requiring preparation of an EIS on the annual budget request for virtually every ongoing program would trivialize NEPA." It would be absurd to require an EIS on every decision on the management of federal land, such as fluctuation in the number of forest fire spotters. Even respondents do not now contend that NEPA should be construed so that all appropriation requests constitute "proposals for legislation."

CEQ's interpretation of the phrase "proposals for legislation" is consistent with the traditional distinction which Congress has drawn between "legislation" and "appropriation." The rules of both Houses "prohibit 'legislation' from being added to an appropriation bill." The distinction is maintained "to assure that program and financial matters are considered independently of one another. This division of labor is intended to enable the Appropriations Committees to concentrate on financial issues and to prevent them from transpassing on substantive legislation." Since appropriations therefore "have the limited and specific purpose of providing funds for authorized programs," and since the "action-forcing" provisions of NEPA are directed precisely at the processes of "planning and . . . decisionmaking," which are associated with underlying legislation, we conclude that the distinction made by CEQ's regulations is correct and that "proposals for legislation" do not include appropriation requests.

The Court of Appeals' alternative interpretation of NEPA is that appropriation requests constitute "pro-

posals for . . . major Federal actions." But this interpretation distorts the language of the Act, since appropriation requests do not "propose" federal actions at all; they instead fund actions already proposed. Section 102(2)(C) is thus best interpreted as applying to those recommendations or reports that actually propose programmatic actions, rather than to those which merely suggest how such actions may be funded. Any other result would create unnecessary redundancy.

Even if changes in agency programs occur because of budgetary decisions, an EIS at the appropriation stage would only be repetitive. For example, respondents allege in their complaint that OMB required the Fish and Wildlife Service to decrease its appropriation request for the NWRS, and that this decrease would alter the operation of the NWRS in a manner that would significantly affect the quality of the human environment. But since the Fish and Wildlife Service could respond to OMB's budgetary curtailments in a variety of ways, it is impossible to predict whether or how any particular budget cut will in fact significantly affect the quality of the human environment. OMB's determination to cut the Service's budget is not a programmatic proposal, and therefore requiring OMB to include an EIS in its budgetary cuts would be premature. And since an EIS must be prepared if any of the revisions the Fish and Wildlife Service proposes in its ongoing programs in response to OMB's budget cuts would significantly affect the quality of the human environment, requiring the Fish and Wildlife Service to include an EIS with its revised appropriation request would merely be redundant. Moreover, this redundancy would have the deleterious effect of circumventing and eliminating the careful distinction Congress has maintained between appropriation and legislation. It would flood House and Senate Appropriations Committees with EISs focused on the policy issues raised by underlying authorization legislation thereby dismantling the "division of labor" so deliberately created by congressional rules.

We conclude therefore, for the reasons given above, that appropriation requests constitute neither "proposals for legislation" nor "proposals for . . . major Federal actions," and that therefore the procedural requirements of §102(2)(C) have no application to such requests.

The judgment of the Court of Appeals is reversed.

CASE REVIEW QUESTIONS

1. In the *Kleppe* case, does the Supreme Court conclude that regional or programmatic EISs are not required by NEPA?
2. In *Kleppe,* the Supreme Court determines the point in time at which an EIS must be completed. What important "timing" question is left unanswered by the Court?
3. In the *Andrus* case, the Supreme Court held that agencies need not prepare EISs for appropriation requests. Does this mean that agencies can circumvent NEPA by using reduced or increased budget requests to make significant changes in their programs?
4. Why do you think the CEQ changed its mind about the need for an EIS for an appropriation request between its 1971 advisory guidelines and its 1979 mandatory regulations?

The Comment Process

When an agency decides to prepare an EIS, the procedure it follows has two distinct phases. Initially, the agency will prepare a *draft EIS* (DEIS). The DEIS is circulated to all interested parties and is made available to the public. A comment period, lasting a minimum of 90 days, follows during which parties outside the agency have the opportunity to comment on the DEIS. After the comment period, the agency will issue a *final EIS* (FEIS). In it, the agency must respond to all reasonable comments made about the DEIS. The FEIS is then circulated. After 30 days have elapsed, the agency can make a decision on its proposed action.

An Adequate EIS

An EIS prepared by an agency must be an *adequate EIS.* The NEPA statute requires that an EIS contain the five elements mentioned earlier in this chapter (see page 1206). This requirement is clarified by the NEPA Regulations. Basically, the regulations state that the EIS must detail the proposed action, describe the existing environment, and depict and analyze the impact on the existing environment of both the proposed action *and* its reasonable alternatives.

The regulations note that the heart of an EIS is the "alternatives" section. An action proposed by an agency — to build a dam, for example — must be accompanied by reasonable alternative approaches to the problem — for example, to remove houses and other buildings from the floodplain or to take no action at all. Providing the decision makers with comparative presentations of the various alternatives helps to insure that the best decision will be made. Implicit within this approach is the concept of the EIS as a document designed to facilitate and enhance decision making. It is not intended to be merely a justification for a course of action already decided upon by the agency.

The following case was decided before the CEQ's regulations were formulated. However, it deals with the question of what constitutes an adequate EIS in a clear, straightforward manner. Although a court today might quote the regulations and thus use slightly different language, this decision remains valid.

NATIONAL HELIUM v. MORTON
486 F.2d 995 (10th Cir. 1973)

[The federal government had three contracts with National Helium for the supply of helium. Under the terms of the contracts, the government could terminate the contracts after it complied with certain procedures. The government terminated the contracts on the basis that the Department of the Interior, which administered the contracts, decided that no new helium was needed. Demand for helium was in decline, and the government estimated that it already had on hand six times as much helium as it would need by the year 2000.

National Helium sued to enjoin the termination of the contracts on the grounds that the EIS was inadequate. The district court ruled that the EIS was "appallingly deficient" and violated NEPA. The government appealed to the circuit court.]

DOYLE, [Judge]

The procedural requirements of NEPA impose specific procedural duties on federal agencies, one of which is the duty of preparing a detailed impact statement to accompany any recommendation for a major federal action significantly affecting the environment. The requirements of this impact statement include five specific areas to be covered in the impact statement:

(i) the environmental impact of the proposed action,
(ii) any adverse environmental effects which cannot be avoided should the proposed action be implemented,
(iii) alternatives to the proposed action,
(iv) the relationship between local short-term uses of man's environment and the maintenance and enhancement of long-term productivity, and
(v) any irreversible and irretrievable commitments of resources which would be involved in the proposed action should it be implemented.

The environmental impact statement should be placed in perspective. The relevant provisions bring environmental factors into the agency decisionmaking placing them on an equal footing with economic, technical and other considerations. Also this environmental impact statement serves as source material for the

head of the agency, the Congress, for the President and the public.

In summary, then, our view is that the review of [FEIS] is limited to the following:

(1) Whether [FEIS] discusses all of the five procedural requirements of NEPA.
(2) Whether the environmental impact statement constitutes an objective good faith compliance with the demands of NEPA.
(3) Whether the statement contains a reasonable discussion of the subject matter involved in the five required areas.

The remaining issue and the crucial one in the case pertains to the adequacy of the Final Environmental [Impact] Statement testing it by the five prescribed areas set forth [earlier].

We are of the opinion that consideration of the five subjects prescribed by the statute was sufficient.

(i) Environmental impact of the proposed action.

There is no contention that the loss of helium, should it be lost, will affect the environment. It is, after all, a colorless, odorless, nonflammable inert gas. Therefore, the matter to be weighed is the secondary effect, namely, loss of the resource. As we have noted above, the supply which the government has in storage is sufficient to the year 2000 and perhaps beyond. Continued purchases by the government would at best extend the inventory for a period of from four to fourteen years. Thus, it would not solve the problem of the future use of it. The Final Environmental [Impact] Statement considers the recovery of helium from the atmosphere. It considers the amount of electrical power which would be required and the effects of the generation of such power on air and thermal pollution. It notes that the extent of use of helium beyond the year 2000 is conjectural and speculative, and thus the effect on the atmosphere of recovering the helium is itself conjectural. For our purpose the statement took into consideration all of the possibilities and it was not required to do more than this.

(ii) Adverse environmental effects which are unavoidable.

The statement points out the future problems of recapturing the lost helium if it is necessary.

(iii) Alternatives to the proposed action.

The statement considers several alternatives, including reliance on the normal market process, expansion of the helium program by legislative action, use of leaner gases and recapture from the atmosphere. The discussion in our view satisfies the present requirement and the statement did not have to dwell on the imaginary horribles posed by the plaintiffs.

(iv) The relationship between local short-term use of man's environment and the maintenance and enhancement of long-term productivity.

That which appears in parts i, ii and iii above considers the present question. The statement took into account the known sources and supplies together with the possible uses such as generation and transmission of electrical power for nuclear reactors for the space program, for levitation systems of mass transportation and for cryogenics [branch of physics dealing in very low temperatures].

We disagree with the trial court's finding that the impact statement's failure to consider the alternative of making the helium purchase program financially self-sustaining was a fatal defect. Such an alternative is somewhat obvious in that it would be a continuation of the present purchase program. This alternative is discussed in the statement. The impact of this alternative is implicit in the discussion of the several alternatives contained in the Final Statement.

(v) Any irreversible and irretrievable commitments of resources which would be involved in the proposed action should it be implemented.

The termination which is involved in the proposed action is reversible by continuation of one or more of the contracts in modified form or by the negotiation of new contracts or by congressional action. Should the contracts be cancelled and should the company shut down their separation plants, the helium which is now preserved would, of course, be lost. Beyond this, hard and fast predictions about the effect of termination of helium purchases on the technology which we would have in the Twenty-First Century would be nothing more than speculation. We consider the subject matter sufficiently discussed in the Final Statement. There is enough there to alert the decision-makers and others concerned.

The courts should look for adequacy and completeness in an impact statement, not perfection.

Accordingly, the judgment of the district court is reversed and the cause is remanded with directions to dismiss the action.

CASE REVIEW QUESTIONS

1. Can a court expect an agency that specializes in building dams to be completely impartial when drafting an EIS to propose the construction of a dam? If not, what can a court reasonably demand from the agency?
2. Don't you find it strange that the district court found the EIS "appallingly deficient," whereas the Circuit Court found it completely satisfactory. How can this dramatic difference of opinion be explained?

Substantive Review

Procedurally, it is clear that an agency must prepare an adequate EIS whenever it is proposing legislation or an action that will significantly effect the quality of the human environment. If the agency performs this procedural task adequately, the question then arises as to whether the agency is then free to make any decision it desires on the proposed action irrespective of the environmental consequences. Conversely, can NEPA mandate a particular substantive result; for example, can it prevent the construction of a dam proposed by the agency?

The *Calvert Cliffs* case addressed this issue early in NEPA's history. Judge Wright stated:

> The reviewing courts probably cannot reverse a substantive decision on its merits, under §101, unless it be shown that the actual balance of costs and benefits that was struck was arbitrary or clearly gave insufficient weight to environmental values.

In this opinion, Judge Wright is saying that a court cannot order an agency to select a given course of action, such as to construct an environmentally less offensive over-flow lagoon rather than the dam proposed by the agency. However, NEPA gives the courts the authority to review an agency's substantive decision and to determine whether or not that decision is arbitrary with regard to the environmental concerns of NEPA. If the costs of a project, environmental and otherwise, clearly outweigh its benefits, NEPA allows a court to enjoin the project's implementation. For example, a court could prevent the agency from building an economically and technologically marginal dam that would be environmentally offensive.

Almost a decade after the *Calvert Cliffs* decision, the U.S. Supreme Court addressed the question of substantive review under NEPA. The facts of the case are complex and the opinion is brief and cursory. Substantive review under NEPA would appear to be alive. However, it is difficult to tell from the opinion whether the court was simply too brief to be clear or whether it reluctantly adopted substantive review. You should take special notice of the footnote in the majority opinion and Justice Marshall's dissenting opinion.

STRYCHER'S BAY NEIGHBORHOOD COUNCIL, INC. v. KARLEN
444 U.S. 223 (USSC 1980)

[In 1962, the New York City Planning Commission (Commission) in conjunction with the U.S. Department of Housing and Urban Development (HUD) began to formulate a redevelopment plan for housing on Manhattan's Upper West Side. The original plan called for a mix of 70 percent middle-income and 30 percent low-income housing. After a reassessment of needs in 1969, the Commission altered the plan to 100 percent low-income housing. HUD approved the revised plan in 1972.

Numerous parties became involved in multistage litigation concerning the redevelopment plan during the decade of the 1970s. The particular facet of the litigation in this case dealt with a section of NEPA other than the EIS requirement. The section mandates that an agency examine alternative courses of action where there are unresolved "conflicts regarding alternative uses of available resources." HUD prepared a "Special Environmental Clearance" to satisfy this requirement. The bottom-line of the HUD study was that the 100 percent low-income housing plan should remain intact on the original site because a change to another site would cause a two-year delay. The district court found HUD's report to be in compliance with NEPA. The circuit court disagreed and reversed. An appeal was then taken to the U.S. Supreme Court, which issued a per curiam—unsigned—opinion.]

PER CURIAM

The appellate court focused upon that part of HUD's report where the agency considered and rejected alternative sites, and in particular upon HUD's reliance on the delay such a relocation would entail. The Court of Appeals purported to recognize that its role in reviewing HUD's decision was defined by the Administrative Procedure Act (APA), which provides that agency actions should be set aside if found to be "arbitrary, capricious, an abuse of discretion or otherwise not in accordance with law." Additionally, however, the Court of Appeals looked to "[t]he provisions of NEPA" for "the substantive standards necessary to review the merits of agency decisions. . . ." The Court of Appeals conceded that HUD had "given 'consideration' to alternatives" to redesignating the site.

Nevertheless, the court believed that " 'consideration' is not an end in itself." Concentrating on HUD's finding that development of an alternative location would entail an unacceptable delay, the appellate court held that such delay could not be "an overriding factor" in HUD's decision to proceed with the development. According to the court, when HUD considers such projects, "environmental factors, such as crowding low-income housing into a concentrated area, should be given determinative weight."

In *Vermont Yankee Nuclear Power Corp. v. NRDC* we stated that NEPA, while establishing "significant substantive goals for the Nation," imposes upon agencies duties that are "essentially procedural."

As we stressed in that case, NEPA was designed "to insure a fully-informed and well-considered decision," but not necessarily "a decision the judges of the Court of Appeals or of this Court would have reached had they been members of the decision making unit of the agency." *Vermont Yankee* cuts sharply against the Court of Appeals' conclusion that an agency in selecting a course of action, must elevate environmental concerns over other appropriate considerations. On the contrary, once an agency has made a decision

subject to NEPA's procedural requirements, the only role for a court is to insure that the agency has considered the environmental consequences; it cannot "interject itself within the area of discretion of the executive as to the choice of the action to be taken."[1]

In the present case there is no doubt that HUD considered the environmental consequences of its decision to redesignate the proposed site for low-income housing. NEPA requires no more. The judgment of the Court of Appeals is therefore reversed.

Reversed.

MARSHALL, Justice (Dissenting)

The issue raised by these cases is far more difficult than the per curiam opinion suggests. The Court of Appeals held that the Secretary of Housing and Urban Development (HUD) had acted arbitrarily in concluding that prevention of a delay in the construction process justified the selection of a housing site which could produce adverse social environmental effects, including racial and economic concentration. Today the majority responds that "once an agency has made a decision subject to NEPA's procedural requirements, the only role for a court is to insure that the agency has considered the environmental consequences," and that in this case "there is no doubt that HUD considered the environmental consequences of its decision to redesignate the proposed site for low-income housing. NEPA requires no more." The majority finds support for this conclusion in the closing paragraph of our decision in *Vermont Yankee.*

Vermont Yankee does not stand for the broad proposition that the majority advances today. The relevant passage in that opinion was meant to be only a "further observation of some relevance to this case." That "observation" was a response to this Court's percep-

[1] If we could agree with the dissent that the Court of Appeals held that HUD had acted "arbitrarily" in redesignating the site for low-income housing, we might also agree that plenary review is warranted. But the District Court expressly concluded that HUD had not acted arbitrarily or capriciously and our reading of the opinion of the Court of Appeals satisfies us that it did not overturn that finding. Instead, the appellate court required HUD to elevate environmental concerns over other, admittedly legitimate, considerations. Neither NEPA nor the APA provides any support for such a reordering of priorities by a reviewing court.

tion that the Court of Appeals in that case was attempting "under the guise of judicial review of agency action" to assert its own policy judgment as to the desirability of developing nuclear energy as an energy source for this Nation, a judgment which is properly left to Congress. The Court of Appeals had remanded the case to the agency because of "a single alleged oversight on a peripheral issue, urged by parties who never fully cooperated or indeed raised the issue below." It was in this context that the Court remarked that "NEPA does set forth significant substantive goals for the Nation, but its mandate to the agencies is *essentially* procedural." Accordingly, "[a]dministrative decisions should be set aside in this context, as in every other, only for substantial procedural or substantive reasons as mandated by statute." Thus *Vermont Yankee* does not stand for the proposition that a court reviewing agency action under NEPA is limited solely to the factual issue of whether the agency "considered" environmental consequences. The agency's decision must still be set aside if it is "arbitrary, capricious, an abuse of discretion or otherwise not in accordance with law," and the reviewing court must still insure that the agency "has taken a 'hard look' at environmental consequences."

In the present case, the Court of Appeals did not "substitute its judgment for that of the agency as to the environmental consequences of its actions," for HUD in its Special Environmental Clearance Report acknowledged the adverse environmental consequences of its proposed action: "the choice of Site 30 for development as a 100 percent low-income project has raised valid questions about the potential social environmental impacts involved." These valid questions arise from the fact that 68% of all public housing units would be sited on only one crosstown axis in this area of New York City. As the Court of Appeals observed, the resulting high concentration of low-income housing would hardly further racial and economic integration. The environmental "impact on social fabric and community structures" was given a B rating in the Report; indicating that from this perspective the

project is "questionable" and ameliorative measures are "mandated." The Report lists 10 ameliorative measures necessary to make the project acceptable. The Report also discusses two alternatives, Sites 9 and 41, both of which are the appropriate size for the project and require "only minimal" amounts of relocation and clearance. Concerning Site 9 the Report explicitly concludes that "[f]rom the standpoint of social environmental impact, this location would be superior to Site 30 for the development of low-rent public housing." The sole reason for rejecting the environmentally superior site was the fact that if the location were shifted to Site 9, there would be a projected delay of two years in the construction of the housing.

The issue before the Court of Appeals, therefore, was whether HUD was free under NEPA to reject an alternative acknowledged to be environmentally preferable solely on the ground that any change in sites would cause delay. This was hardly a "peripheral issue" in the case. Whether NEPA, which sets forth "significant substantive goals," permits a projected two-year time difference to be controlling over environmental superiority is by no means clear. Resolution of the issue, however, is certainly within the normal scope of review of agency action to determine if it is arbitrary, capricious, or an abuse of discretion. The question whether HUD can make delay the paramount concern over environmental superiority is essentially a restatement of the question whether HUD in considering the environmental consequences of its proposed action gave those consequences a "hard look," which is exactly the proper question for the reviewing court to ask.

The issue of whether the Secretary's decision was arbitrary or capricious is sufficiently difficult and important to merit plenary consideration in this Court. Further, I do not subscribe to the Court's apparent suggestion that *Vermont Yankee* limits the reviewing court to the essentially mindless task of determining whether an agency "considered" environmental factors even if that agency may have effectively decided to ignore those factors in reaching its conclusion.

CASE REVIEW QUESTIONS

1. Summarize the basic difference between the majority opinion and Justice Marshall's dissent.

2.   In Justice Marshall's view, did HUD violate NEPA?

AIR AND WATER POLLUTION

Air and water are essential to the continuation of life as we know it on this planet. The twentieth century, though, has seen a marked decline in the quality of these two basic natural resources. Furthermore, as the quality of air and water has declined, medical research has discovered more and more links between this deterioration and major health problems such as cancer and heart disease.

One reason for the decline in the quality of the air and the water is that they were treated for too long a time as economically free resources. Industrial firms and urban residents alike used air and water for waste disposal. In the earth's natural system, reasonable amounts of wastes can be "treated" and rendered harmless through decomposition into basic nutrients. As the number of people and the amounts and concentrations of their wastes multiplied, however, the natural system was unable to deal with them adequately. In addition, new inorganic substances, such as plastics, were developed that were not susceptible to the natural decomposition process.

By 1970, concern over the impact of polluted air and water on health and social welfare had become so great that it triggered comprehensive national legislation. The Clean Air Act (CAA) was passed in 1970 and the Clean Water Act (CWA) was passed in 1972. These acts, along with their amendments, establish complex systems for maintaining and enhancing the quality of air and water in the United States. The statutes are several hundred pages in length, making a thorough examination of them impossible here. The purpose of the discussion of air and water pollution laws in this chapter is to give you an insight into several contrasting approaches for controlling pollution used in these statutes.

Dividing to Conquer

The control of air and water pollution cannot be efficiently accomplished through administration along traditional political boundaries. Polluted air is chiefly troublesome downwind of its origin, irrespective of city, county, or state lines. Likewise, water pollution victimizes those downstream from the pollution's source, regardless of the course of the stream.

The CAA divided the country into about 300 Air Quality Control Regions (AQCR). Though the designated regions are somewhat affected by state lines, the regions generally follow air-shed lines despite political subdivisions. In addition, the standards for controlling air pollution are measured and evaluated on an air-shed basis.

Standards for water pollution control are centered on bodies of water. Although streams cross state lines, water pollution control is confined within state boundaries for administrative convenience unless an interstate administrative body already exists.

Standards

The CAA and CWA establish two kinds of standards: source standards and ambient standards. **Source standards** control pollution at its source; for example, at the smoke stack or outfall pipe of the polluter. **Ambient standards** control the quality of the surrounding air and water that we might breathe or drink.

Under the CAA, *primary ambient standards* are set to protect public health. *Secondary ambient standards* are established to secure public welfare — for example to protect vegetation, visibility, and human-made structures. In order to meet ambient standards in many regions, source controls must be set on the emissions from individual stationary sources of pollution. In addition, national emissions limitations have been established for all new mobile pollution sources such as cars and trucks. The stringency of the source standards or emissions limitations for individual factories depend on the quality of the ambient air in the AQCR. If the ambient standards are being met when a law goes into effect, existing stationary sources will not be controlled. However, new stationary sources are subject to separate controls aimed at preventing significant deterioration of air quality in regions with clean air and at reaching ambient standards in regions with dirty air.

The CWA provides both ambient standards and source standards. The ambient standards are called *water quality standards*. The states determine the use that they intend to make of a stream or a portion thereof, such as for drinking water or for swimming. The designated use then determines the water quality standard that must be attained. Drinking water, for instance, is subject to stricter controls than is water used only for swimming.

The CWA's source standards are called *effluent standards*. These standards are set for various categories of industries — steel or inorganic chemicals, for example — and for various pollutants — mercury and cadmium, for instance. Unlike CAA source standards, the foremost goal of CWA source standards is not to meet ambient standards. The two standards operate separately, and the individual polluter is required to meet the stricter of the two. Each firm in a given category is required to meet the same effluent standard; however, the amount of effluent permitted firms by the water quality standard may vary, depending on such factors as the designated use of a stream or the number of similar polluters on a body of water.

There is another basic difference between CAA and CWA standards. The CAA's primary standards (though not its secondary standards) are technology forcing. This means that Congress initially required that these health-based standards be met within three years of a given time, irrespective of cost or technology. Congress did provide for variances for up to two years. However, at the end of any extra time allowed by the variances, failure to meet primary ambient standards would be a violation of the law.

In contrast, the CWA's effluent standards are technology based rather than technology forcing. Individual pollution sources were to adopt the "best practicable technology" (BPT) by 1977 and the "best available technology" (BAT) by 1983. The Environmental Protection Agency (EPA) was given the task of determining these standards, based upon the cost and the availability of technology.

Controls

Achieving the quality of air and water deemed necessary to protect public health and welfare requires control mechanisms. The form that these controls take under the CAA and the CWA vary, but the ultimate result is the same; that is, an emissions or effluent *limitation* is set. Another commonality between the CAA and the CWA is that the states play important roles in the control process. Under the CAA, the states must develop *state implementation plans* (SIPs) to meet ambient standards. The SIPs are a complex conglomeration of emissions limitations that are placed upon individual sources to insure that they do their part to meet the federal ambient standards. These SIPs are subject to the approval of the EPA.

Under the CWA, the control mechanism is a permit. Each major source that discharges a controlled pollutant into a regulated body of water must get a permit. The permit sets an effluent limitation that meets the water quality standard or the effluent standard, whichever is stricter. Initially, the EPA issued these permits, but now most states have assumed this function under the guidance of EPA.

Neither statute attempts to control all pollutants from all sources, nor are the administrators of the statutes likely to be equally successful in controlling all of the pollutants that they desire to regulate. Under the CAA, national ambient standards have been established for only six pollutants. Half of these are generic pollutants however, such as particulates, which include any particle within certain size parameters. Many other pollutants, such as odors, are unregulated. Under the CWA, specific substances from categories of major industries that are sources of pollution are controlled. Other substances and pollution sources that are not major are basically uncontrolled.

The CWA focuses most of its attention on "point sources"; that is, on pollution that comes from specific origins such as pipes and ditches. Nonpoint sources, like the runoff from a farmer's field or a timbering site, are not easy to control through permits. Although the statute recognizes nonpoint sources and attempts to regulate them, its success in this area has been limited.

Statutory Goals

The goals of the two statutes seem to be at variance. The CAA is concerned with cleaning the air only to the point that it is safe for health and welfare purposes. For instance, so long as the level of sulfur dioxide does not harm human health or, in changed chemical form, pockmark statues and monuments, the CAA will permit the air to be used for waste disposal.

The CWA's goals seem more uncertain. On one hand, the water quality standards seem to imply that certain levels of pollutants in the water are acceptable, provided that the designated use of the water is not affected. On the other hand, the effluent standards appear to have a more stringent goal. If the best practicable or best available technology allowed a firm to reduce its effluent to zero, it had to do so. The fact that the stream's designated use is not affected by existing levels of pollution is irrelevant. Thus, it would appear that the effluent standards are based on the idea that water should not be used for the disposal of wastes. This idea is reinforced by the statutory goal stated in the CWA that all discharges must cease by 1985. CWA's goals, then, seem to be a bit confused, but pragmatically speaking, they have proven to be overly ambitious. Perhaps Congress will make up its mind during the next round of amendments.

Interrelationships

The purpose of this section on air and water pollution has been to compare and contrast two distinct statutory frameworks. It is important to note, however, that the water and the air, like all natural systems, are intimately interrelated. Pollution cleansed from either the air or the water must still be disposed of in some fashion. Unless care is taken, one form of pollution may merely be exchanged for another, a result that would lead to little gain in social welfare.

A couple of examples will help to illustrate the extent to which air and water pollution are interrelated. The CWA fostered the massive construction of publicly-owned treatment works (POTWs) to remove pollution from municipal sewage. The POTWs removed the pollution from the sewage, but they then found themselves with mounds of sludge that had to be eliminated. If the sludge was dried and burned, care had to be taken not to create air pollution. If it was used for landfill, the site had to be made impermeable or the pollutants would leak from the sludge into the groundwater and ultimately back into the streams that had been cleaned up in the first place. If the sludge was buried at sea, the interment did not always prove to be permanent, as many visitors to beaches can attest.

The second example pertains to the CAA. To meet their SIP requirements, some large air-polluters, especially midwestern utilities, used a method they called a "dispersal enhancement technique." Simply put, they built tall smokestacks. Many of these stacks were over 500 feet high, and a few exceeded 1,000 feet. The stacks did not reduce pollutants. Instead, they merely dispersed the pollutants into the upper air where they were carried out of the range of monitoring stations on the ground.

Unfortunately, it was later learned that the pollutants did not stay aloft indefinitely. The sulfur dioxide and nitric oxide from the midwestern stacks changed into acids. These acids floated with the prevailing winds in an easterly direction. Then, when the winds collided with the mountains of the eastern United States and Canada, the pollutants were precipitated to earth as acid rain. Scientists agree that acid rain is harmful to lakes and other bodies of water and that it may be detrimental to forests and soils. The elimination of acid rain has thus become a new political problem. Who should pay for this Eastern pollution problem that was generated in the Midwest?

Wastes do not disappear. When they are removed from one medium, they may be merely transferred to another medium unless care is taken to plan thoughtfully for their disposal. The notion behind the word "ecology" is that all life systems are interrelated. To their chagrin, experts in the area of air and water pollution have rediscovered this basic idea the hard way.

The following two cases illustrate two issues under the air and water pollution control laws. More importantly, the judges' opinions will reinforce and add to the information about these statutes presented in the text material. Almost invariably, cases decided under these statutes are as complex as the statutes themselves. However, a close reading of the cases and the text should provide you with a thumbnail outline of the operation of the CAA and the CWA.

UNION ELECTRIC CO. v. EPA
427 U.S. 246 (Sup. Ct. 1976)

[In April of 1971, the Environmental Protection Agency (EPA) promulgated national primary and secondary ambient standards for six pollutants found to have an adverse effect on the public health and welfare. Subsequently, Missouri's state implementation plan (SIP) was approved by EPA. This SIP concentrated on the St. Louis Air Quality Control Region, which exceeded national standards for sulfur dioxide. Union Electric Company was an electric utility firm servicing the St. Louis area. Its coal-fired generating plants were subjected to sulfur dioxide reduction restrictions under the SIP.

Union Electric had received variances from these restrictions. When the variances ended in 1974, EPA notified Union Electric that it was in violation of the SIP. The utility petitioned the court of appeals for review of the SIP approved in 1972. The utility argued that although it was well beyond the 30-day period permitted for challenging SIP approvals, new information regarding the economic and technological infeasibility of the SIP had arisen since the 30-day period had expired. The statute allows review based on new information after the 30-day challenging period.

The issue in the case is whether the economic and technological infeasibility of a plan or part of a plan can provide a basis for the EPA to refuse to approve an SIP. The various appellate courts were split on this issue. In this case, the court of appeals rejected the relevance of the new information about the infeasibility of the SIP. Union Electric appealed to the U.S. Supreme Court.]

MARSHALL, Justice

After the Administrator of the Environmental Pro-

tection Agency (EPA) approves a state implementation plan under the Clean Air Act, the plan may be challenged in a court of appeals within 30 days, or after 30 days have run if newly discovered or available information justifies subsequent review. We must decide whether the operator of a regulated emission source, in a petition for review of an EPA-approved state plan filed after the original 30-day appeal period, can raise the claim that it is economically or technologically infeasible to comply with the plan.

The heart of the [statute] is the requirement that each State formulate, subject to EPA approval, an implementation plan designed to achieve national primary ambient air quality standards — those necessary to protect the public health — "as expeditiously as practicable but . . . in no case later than three years from the date of approval of such plan." The plan must also provide for the attainment of national secondary ambient air quality standards — those necessary to protect the public welfare — within a "reasonable time." Each State is given wide discretion in formulating its plan, and the Act provides that the Administrator "shall approve" the proposed plan if it has been adopted after public notice and hearing and if it meets eight specified criteria [§110(a)(2)].

Since a reviewing court — regardless of when the petition for review is filed — may consider claims of economic and technological infeasibility only if the Administrator may consider such claims in approving or rejecting a state implementation plan, we must address ourselves to the scope of the Administrator's responsibility. The Administrator's position is that he has no power whatsoever to reject a state implementation plan on the ground that it is economically or technologically infeasible, and we have previously accorded great deference to the Administrator's construction of the Clean Air Act. After surveying the relevant provisions of the Clean Air Act Amendments of 1970 and their legislative history, we agree that Congress intended claims of economic and technological infeasibility to be wholly foreign to the Administrator's consideration of a state implementation plan.

As we have previously recognized, the 1970 Amendments to the Clean Air Act were a drastic remedy to what was perceived as a serious and otherwise uncheckable problem of air pollution. The Amendments place the primary responsibility for formulating pollution control strategies on the States, but nonetheless subject the States to strict minimum compliance requirements. These requirements are of a "technology-forcing character," and are expressly designed to force regulated sources to develop pollution control devices that might at the time appear to be economically or technologically infeasible.

This approach is apparent on the face of §110 (a)(2). The provision sets out eight criteria that an implementation plan must satisfy, and provides that if these criteria are met and if the plan was adopted after reasonable notice and hearing, the Administrator "shall approve" the proposed state plan. The mandatory "shall" makes it quite clear that the Administrator is not to be concerned with factors other than those specified and none of the eight factors appears to permit consideration of technological or economic infeasibility. Nonetheless, if a basis is to be found for allowing the Administrator to consider such claims, it must be among the eight criteria, and so it is here that the argument is focused.

It is suggested that consideration of claims of technological and economic infeasibility is required by the first criterion—that the primary air quality standards be met "as expeditiously as practicable but . . . in no case later than three years . . ." and that the secondary air quality standards be met within a "reasonable time" [§110(a)(2)(A)]. The argument is that what is "practicable" or "reasonable" cannot be determined without assessing whether what is proposed is possible. This argument does not survive analysis.

Section 110(a)(2)(A)'s three-year deadline for achieving primary air quality standards is central to the Amendments' regulatory scheme and, as both the lan-

guage and the legislative history of the requirement make clear, it leaves no room for claims of technological or economic infeasibility. The 1970 congressional debate on the Amendments centered on whether technology forcing was necessary and desirable in framing and attaining air quality standards sufficient to protect the public health standards, later termed primary standards. The House version of the Amendments was quite moderate in approach, requiring only that health-related standards be met "within a reasonable time." The Senate bill, on the other hand, flatly required that, possible or not, health-related standards be met "within three years."

The Conference Committee and, ultimately, the entire Congress accepted the Senate's three-year mandate for the achievement of primary air quality standards, and the clear import of that decision is that the Administrator must approve a plan that attains the primary standards in three years even if attainment does not appear feasible. In rejecting the House's standard of reasonableness, however, the conferees strengthened the Senate standard. The Conference Committee made clear that the States could not malinger until the deadline approached. Rather, the primary standards must be met in less than three years if possible; they must be met "as expeditiously as practicable" [§110(a)(2)(A)]. Whatever room there is for considering claims of infeasibility in the attainment of primary standards must lie in this phrase, which is, of course, relevant only in evaluating those implementation plans that attempt to achieve the primary standard in less than three years.

Our conclusion is bolstered by recognition that the Amendments do allow claims of technological and economic infeasibility to be raised in situations where consideration of such claims will not substantially interfere with the primary congressional purpose of prompt attainment of the national air quality standards. Thus, we do not hold that claims of infeasibility are never of relevance in the formulation of an implementation plan or that sources unable to comply with emission limitations must inevitably be shut down.

Perhaps the most important forum for consideration of claims of economic and technological infeasibility is before the state agency formulating the implementation plan. So long as the national standards are met, the State may select whatever mix of control devices it desires, and industries with particular economic or technological problems may seek special treatment in the plan itself. Moreover, if the industry is not exempted from, or accommodated by, the original plan, it may obtain a variance, as petitioner did in this case; and the variance, if granted after notice and a hearing, may be submitted to the EPA as a revision of the plan.

While the State has virtually absolute power in allocating emission limitations so long as the national standards are met, if the state plan cannot meet the national standards, the EPA is implicated in any postponement procedure. There are two ways that a State can secure relief from the EPA for individual emission sources, or classes of sources, that cannot meet the national standards. First, if the Governor of the State so requests at the time the original implementation plan is submitted, and if the State provides reasonable interim controls, the Administrator may allow a two-year extension of the three-year deadline for attainment of primary air quality standards if he finds, *inter alia* [among other things] that it is technologically infeasible for the source to comply [§110(c)]. Second, again upon application of the Governor of the

State, the Administrator may allow a one-year postponement of any compliance date in an implementation plan if he finds, *inter alia,* that compliance is technologically infeasible and that "the continued operation of [the emission source] is essential to national security or to the public health or welfare. . . ."

Even if the State does not intervene on behalf of an emission source, technological and economic factors may be considered in at least one other circumstance. When a source is found to be in violation of the state implementation plan, the Administrator may, after a conference with the operator, issue a compliance order rather than seek civil or criminal enforcement. Such an order must specify a "reasonable" time for compliance with the relevant standard, taking into account the seriousness of the violation and "any good faith efforts to comply with applicable requirements." Claims of technological or economic infeasibility, the Administrator agrees, are relevant to fashioning an appropriate compliance order under §113(a)(4).

Affirmed.

WEYERHAEUSER CO. v. COSTLE
590 F.2d 1011 (D.C. Cir. 1978)

[Pursuant to the Clean Water Act, the EPA issued effluent standards for each category of industry that is a major source of water pollution. One of these industries, pulp and paper manufacturers, brought action against the Administrator of the EPA challenging the validity of the EPA's regulations setting effluent standards for the "best practicable technology" (BPT) for 1977 and the "best available technology" (BAT) for 1983. In part, the challenges were based upon the EPA's refusal to consider the quality of the receiving waters in setting the effluent standards. In addition, some members of the industry attacked the way in which cost and nonwater environmental impacts were considered by the agency. The case was heard by the circuit court of appeals.]

MCGOWAN, [Judge]
Some of the paper mills that must meet the effluent limitations under review discharge their effluent into the Pacific Ocean. Petitioners contend that the ocean can dilute or naturally treat effluent, and that EPA must take this capacity of the ocean ("receiving water capacity") into account in a variety of ways. They urge what they term "common sense," i.e., that because the amounts of pollutant involved are small in comparison to bodies of water as vast as Puget Sound or the Pacific Ocean, they should not have to spend heavily on treatment equipment, or to increase their energy requirements and sludge levels, in order to treat wastes that the ocean could dilute or absorb.

EPA's secondary response to this claim was that

pollution is far from harmless, even when disposed of in the largest bodies of water. As congressional testimony indicated, the Great Lakes, Puget Sound, and even areas of the Atlantic Ocean have been seriously injured by water pollution. Even if the ocean can handle ordinary wastes, ocean life may be vulnerable to toxic compounds that typically accompany those wastes. In the main, however, EPA simply asserted that the issue of receiving water capacity could not be raised in setting effluent limitations because Congress had ruled it out. We have examined the previous legislation in this area, and the 1972 Act's wording, legislative history, and policies, as underscored by its 1977 amendments. These sources . . . fully support EPA's construction of the Act. They make clear that based on long experience, and aware of the limits of technological knowledge and administrative flexibility, Congress made the deliberate decision to rule out arguments based on receiving water capacity.

The earliest version of the Federal Water Pollution Control Act was passed in 1948 and amended five times before 1972. Throughout that 24 year period, Congress attempted to use receiving water quality as a basis for setting pollution standards. At the end of that period, Congress realized not only that its water pollution efforts until then had failed, but also that reliance on receiving water capacity as a crucial test for permissible pollution levels had contributed greatly to that failure.

Based on this experience, Congress adopted a new approach in 1972. Under the Act, "a discharger's performance is . . . measured against strict technology-based effluent limitations—specified levels of treatment—to which it must conform, rather than against limitations derived from water quality standards to which it and other polluters must collectively conform."

Moreover, by eliminating the issue of the capacity of particular bodies of receiving water, Congress made nationwide uniformity in effluent regulation possible. Congress considered uniformity vital to free the states from the temptation of relaxing local limitations in order to woo or keep industrial facilities. In addition, national uniformity made pollution cleanup possible without engaging in the divisive task of favoring some regions of the country over others.

More fundamentally, the new approach implemented changing views as to the relative rights of the public and of industrial polluters. Hitherto, the right of the polluter was pre-eminent, unless the damage caused by pollution could be proven. Henceforth, the right of the public to a clean environment would be pre-eminent, unless pollution treatment was impractical or unachievable.

The Act reflects the new approach in a number of provisions. As noted, its goal was zero discharge of pollutants by 1985, not discharges at acceptable or tolerable levels for receiving water. The rest of the statute "authorize[s] a series of steps to be taken to achieve [that] goal." It defines "pollution," "pollutant," "discharge of a pollutant," and "effluent limitation" in terms of any addition to water that alters its "chemical, physical, biological, [or] radiological integrity"; it does not specify additions that diminish the quality of the receiving water. In only one limited instance, thermal pollution, is receiving water capacity to be considered in relaxing standards, and the section allowing such consideration was drafted as a clear exception. Otherwise, receiving water quality was to be considered only in setting "more stringent" standards than effluent limitations otherwise would prescribe.

The Act was passed with an expectation of "midcourse corrections," and in 1977 Congress amended the Act, although generally holding to the same tack set five years earlier. Notably, during those five years, representatives of the paper industry had appeared before Congress and urged it to change the Act and to incorporate receiving water capacity as a consideration. . . . Except for a provision specifically aimed at discharges from "publicly owned treatment plants," Congress resolved in the recent amendments to continue regulating discharges into all receiving waters alike.

Petitioners also challenge EPA's manner of assessing two factors that all parties agree must be considered: cost and non-water quality environmental impacts. They contend that the Agency should have more carefully balanced costs versus the effluent reduction benefits of the regulations, and that it should have also balanced those benefits against the non-water quality environmental impacts to arrive at a "net" environmental benefit conclusion.

In order to discuss petitioners' challenges, we must first identify the relevant statutory standard. Section 304(b)(1)(B) identifies the factors bearing on [BPT] in two groups. First, the factors shall

> include consideration of the total cost of application of technology in relation to the effluent reduction benefits to be achieved from such application,

and second, they

> shall also take into account the age of equipment and facilities involved, the process employed, the engineering aspects of the application of various types of control techniques, process changes, non-water quality environmental impact (including energy requirements), and such other factors as the Administrator deems appropriate.

The first group consists of two factors that EPA must compare: total cost versus effluent reduction benefits. We shall call these the "comparison factors." The other group is a list of many factors that EPA must "take into account": age, process, engineering aspects, process changes, environmental impacts (including energy), and any others EPA deems appropriate. We shall call these the "consideration factors." Notably, section 304(b)(2)(B), which delineates the factors relevant to setting 1983 [BAT] limitations, tracks the 1977 [BPT] provision before us except in one regard: in the 1983 section, all factors, including costs and benefits, are consideration factors, and no factors are separated out for comparison.

Based on our examination of the statutory language and the legislative history, we conclude that Congress mandated a particular structure and weight for the 1977 comparison factors, that is to say, a "limited" balancing test. In contrast, Congress did not mandate any particular structure or weight for the many consideration factors. Rather, it left EPA with discretion to decide how to account for the consideration factors, and how much weight to give each factor. In response to these divergent congressional approaches, we conclude that, on the one hand, we should examine EPA's treatment of cost and benefit under the 1977 standard to assure that the Agency complied with Congress' "limited" balancing directive. On the other hand, our scrutiny of the Agency's treatment of the several consideration factors seeks to assure that the Agency informed itself as to their magni-

tude, and reached its own express and considered conclusion about their bearing. More particularly, we do not believe that EPA is required to use any specific structure such as a balancing test in assessing the consideration factors, nor do we believe that EPA is required to give each consideration factor any specific weight.

Our conclusions are based initially on the section's wording and apparent logic. By singling out two factors (the comparison factors) for separate treatment, and by requiring that they be considered "in relation to" each other, Congress elevated them to a level of greater attention and rigor. Moreover, the comparison factors are a closed set of two, making it possible to have a definite structure and weight in considering them and preventing extraneous factors from intruding on the balance.

By contrast, the statute directs the Agency only to "take into account" the consideration factors, without prescribing any structure for EPA's deliberations. As to this latter group of factors, the section cannot logically be interpreted to impose on EPA a specific structure of consideration or set of weights because it gave EPA authority to "upset" any such structure by exercising its discretion to add new factors to the mix. Instead, the listing of factors seems aimed at noting all of the matters that Congress considered worthy of study before making limitation decisions, without preventing EPA from identifying other factors that it considers worthy of study. So long as EPA pays some attention to the congressionally specified factors, the section on its face lets EPA relate the various factors as it deems necessary.

The legislative history reveals that clear congressional policies support the section's facial structure. The original House and Senate versions of the section differed significantly. A major point of contention between the two versions involved the House's stronger concern over the economic effects of imposing stringent effluent limitations. Ultimately a compromise was reached at Conference and accepted by both houses. It provided, first, that the Agency must use "limited" cost–benefit balancing in deriving 1977 standards, but not in arriving at the 1983 standards. A "mid-course" evaluation was then to occur in the mid- to late-1970s, after the Act had been in effect for several years but before full implementation of the 1983 standards. The latter step was designed to allow Congress to rewrite the 1983 standards in order to continue the cost–benefit balancing during that period as well, if Congress found after early experience that such a course was necessary.

Thus the fact that Congress indicated its greater concern for cost–benefit calculation in the short run by making cost and benefit "comparison factors" for 1977, but only "consideration factors" for 1983, dem-

onstrates the more relaxed view it took of EPA's treatment of consideration factors relevant to both the 1977 and 1983 standards. Indeed, after studying the need for mid-course correction, Congress decided to retain the 1972 arrangement, which, except for limited modifications not germane here, gives the Agency more complete discretion in considering the relevant factors in the future.

[Judgment for the defendant.]

CASE REVIEW QUESTIONS

1. Is economic or technological infeasibility a relevant matter to a state administrator in formulating an SIP? Is it relevant to the EPA in approving or disapproving an SIP submitted to it?
2. In formulating the CAA, why do you think Congress rejected, under some circumstances, the relevance of vital criteria like feasibility?
3. One reason Congress omitted consideration of the quality of the receiving waters as a criterion for setting effluent standards was the desire to have uniform standards. Why is uniformity desirable?
4. What is the difference between "comparison factors" and "consideration factors"?

HAZARDOUS WASTE

The disposal of hazardous waste is probably the most important environmental issue of the 1980s. Approximately 51 million tons of hazardous waste are produced annually. About 90 percent of this waste is disposed of in inadequate ways. The unsafe disposal of hazardous waste can lead to the contamination of private and public water supplies and the environment in general.

Legal control of hazardous or toxic materials is spread over several statutes. The Toxic Substances Control Act of 1976 deals with screening new and existing substances for their impact on public health and the environment. The Clean Air Act, the Clean Water Act, the Safe Drinking Water Act, and the Federal Insecticide, Fungicide and Rodenticide Act all regulate toxics in so far as they are relevant to the subject matter of the particular statute. The statute that deals primarily with hazardous or toxic waste is the Resource Conservation and Recovery Act of 1976 (RCRA). RCRA is concerned with the land disposal of hazardous waste into active sites. The cleanup of inactive sites is controlled by the so-called "Superfund" legislation of 1981.

Congress has put together a regulatory system that traces hazardous waste from "the cradle to the grave." Each party who handles large amounts of these wastes is subject to the regulatory scheme. The scheme begins with the EPA developing criteria for identifying hazardous waste. In order for a waste to be classified as hazardous, it must be determined to cause an increase in mortality or illness or to pose a substantial threat to public health or the environment. In addition, its characteristics must be measurable by test methods that are reasonably within the capability of the waste generator. Under these guidelines, EPA has developed four criteria: **ignitability, corrosivity, reactivity, and toxicity.**

The EPA's second chore was to identify the wastes that met these criteria of hazardousness. The EPA's initial list contained about 400 substances that are to be treated as presumptively hazardous. Even if a waste is not on the EPA's list, the generator of that waste is responsible for determining whether it meets the hazardousness criteria.

If a firm produces a hazardous waste, it must prepare a manifest describing the kind of waste and designating the ultimate disposal site. This document must follow the waste from its creation to its final disposal. Shipment of the waste must be made in a Department of Transportation approved container, and the transporter must be registered with EPA.

When the waste generator passes the waste and the manifest to a transporter for delivery to the disposal site, the generator retains one copy of the manifest. The other copies travel with the waste. The transporter delivers the waste and the manifest to the owner of the disposal site designated in the manifest. Anyone who owns a treatment, storage, or disposal facility for hazardous waste must obtain a permit from EPA. The site must be lined with an impermeable material, such as clay or plastic, so that the waste cannot migrate from the site. The disposal-site owner returns a copy of the manifest to the generator, thereby declaring that the waste has been disposed of in an approved fashion. If the generator does not receive a copy of the manifest from the disposal-site owner within 45 days of delivery of the waste to the transporter, it must notify EPA. This is to make sure that waste does not simply disappear from the system. When the disposal site is filled to capacity, it must be sealed with an impermeable material and monitored for a period of twenty years.

The generator itself may dispose of the waste. In such instances, the generator must obtain a permit like any other disposal-site owner. If hazardous waste is stored on the generator's site for more than 90 days, the generator automatically becomes an owner of a disposal site. To begin the 90-day clock, each container holding hazardous waste must be dated when the first waste is deposited in it.

The case that follows is one of the few decided under the Resource Conservation and Recovery Act. It illustrates the difficulty of dealing legally with situations in which the scientific data are inconclusive.

U.S. v. VERTAC CHEMICAL CORP.
489 F. Supp. 870 (E.D. Ark. 1980)

[Vertac runs a chemical manufacturing plant located on a 98-acre site. Rocky Branch Creek, a tributary of Bayou Meto, flows through the site. Since the mid-1950s Vertac and its predecessors have manufactured phenoxy herbicides — 2,4-D; 2,4,5-T; and 2,4,5-TP. Two waste-water streams emanated from the plant. One contained acids and phenols, and the other contained dioxin. These substances are classified as hazardous wastes under RCRA. Indeed, dioxin is referred to as the most dangerous substance known to humans. Vertac and its predecessor have been involved in the pretreatment and on-site storage of these wastes for over fifteen years. The government was concerned that the dioxin stored on the Vertac site was escaping and would continue to escape into the environment unless prompt action was taken.

The United States sued Vertac in a federal district court, asking the court to impose civil penalties and to issue an injunction ordering Vertac to stop the discharge of hazardous wastes into navigable waters, soil, atmosphere, and ground water in violation of RCRA.]

WOODS, [Judge]

Although the [clean-up] efforts of Vertac thus far have been extensive, it is clear that dioxin is present in the parts per billion (ppb) level in soil and sediment on the plant site and in the low parts per trillion range at isolated points off site. The significance of these levels of dioxin depends upon two factors, the toxicity of such small concentrations of dioxin and the likelihood that there will be human or environmental exposure.

It is undisputed that dioxin is the most acutely toxic substance yet synthesized by man. The acute toxicity of dioxin is not directly relevant to this proceeding, however, because the concentrations on and off the plant site are far below the threshold for acute or single-dose toxic effects. The chronic toxicity of dioxin (i.e., the effects of repeated, low-level exposure over a long period of time) is the real focus of this proceeding. The chronic toxicity of dioxin has been the subject of

lengthy scientific debate, and the expert testimony in this proceeding reflects the nature of that debate. There is evidence that dioxin has produced mutagenic, teratogenic, fetotoxic, and possibly carcinogenic results in low-dose levels in various laboratory animals and cell culture tests. The EPA . . . experts testified that in their opinion no level of dioxin exposure, other than zero, had been proven to be safe.

The second factor in determining the significance of the levels of dioxin reported is the likelihood of human or environmental exposure. The highest sample readings were found, not surprisingly, in the toluene [liquid hydrocarbon] stillbottoms [residue after distillation of toluene]. These readings are high, but they pose no present threat to health or the environment because the parties all agree that storage of the stillbottoms in the new roofed facility provides adequate interim protection against human or environmental exposure until suitable permanent disposal is decided upon.

The evidence regarding dioxin levels off the plant site contrasts sharply with the evidence regarding samples taken on site. The evidence indicates that there is no dioxin in the water in Rocky Branch Creek, Bayou Meto, or the effluent from the Jacksonville sewage treatment plant. There is evidence that dioxin is present in the low parts per trillion (''ppt'') level in sediment in Rocky Branch Creek in Bayou Meto, and in sludge in the Jacksonville sewage treatment plant. This evidence is consistent with the expert testimony that dioxin is highly insoluble in water and binds tightly to clay. There is also evidence that some fish and other aquatic life in Bayou Meto have bioaccumulated dioxin to levels up to 600 parts per trillion.

The parties vigorously dispute the significance of the dioxin levels observed off site, as well as the issue of where the dioxin originated. The government parties presented expert witnesses who theorized about means by which the dioxin found off site could have been transported from the Vertac site, namely by storm water run off, airborne dust particles, and volatilization [evaporation]. The main thrust of this testimony was to suggest that all dioxin presently found on the Vertac plant site was likely to escape into the environment rapidly if action was not taken immediately.

We need look no further than our own Court of Appeals to find the guidelines for the issuance of a preliminary injunction in this case. *Reserve Mining Co. v. Environmental Protection Agency* is one of the most significant decisions in the field of environmental law. In that case the court reversed some aspects of a preliminary injunction issued by Judge Miles Lord closing Reserve's plant located on the shores of Lake Superior, because of the discharge of taconite "tailings" into the lake and ambient air.

> The trial court, not having any proof of actual harm, was faced with a consideration of (1) the probabilities of any health harm and (2) the consequence, if any, should the harm actually occur.

Just as in *Reserve* there exists in the present case no proof of actual harm sustained from the escape of dioxin from the premises of Vertac. There is proof that a number of Vertac employees did develop chloracne, a skin pathology, after a "blowout" at the plant several years ago. It has been conceded that Vertac has installed modifications to prevent a recurrence of such an event in the future. The question presented here is whether dioxin is now escaping from the Vertac premises in sufficient quantities to justify an injunction. On the record, the best that can be said is that the existence of dioxin in the sediment of Bayou Meto, the equalization pond, the cooling pond, and Jacksonville sewage treatment plant, and in the soil of the Vertac site gives rise to a reasonable medical concern for the public health. The public exposure to dioxin creates some health risk. As much as humanly possible this risk must be removed. We adhere to the view in *Reserve* that "the existence of this risk to the public justifies an injunctive decree requiring abatement of the health hazard on reasonable terms as a precautionary and preventive measure to protect the public health."

In so doing we are not unmindful that the proof with respect to the harmful effect of dioxin on humans is far from conclusive. Its potential effect on humans has necessarily been extrapolated from extensive animal testing. Unquestionably, acute dosage fed to animals has shown dioxin to be a killer of unprecedented effectiveness. However, we are here concerned with chronic exposure to dioxin in the most minute quantities. The expert testimony in this case spoke to concentrations of dioxin in order of parts per million, billion, trillion, and even quadrillion range. Such minute quantities baffle the imagination. One expert said that the existence of one part per trillion was analogous to comparing the width of a hair to the distance between the earth and the moon or comparing the size of a grain of sand to a concrete wall a foot thick, eight feet high and a mile long.

Nevertheless, even in such minute quantities dioxin has been a source of concern to the scientific community since the late 1960s, principally because of two events—the use of a mixture of 2,4-D and 2,4,5-T known as "Agent Orange" as a defoliate in Vietnam and a study in the Bionetics Research Laboratories indicating that dioxin caused teratogenic effects (birth defects) in mice and rats.

Because of the language of the Resource Conservation and Recovery Act, the parties have focused their attention on whether discharges from the Vertac site constitute "imminent and substantial endangerment." The medical and scientific opinions and testing adduced in this case clearly lie "on the frontiers of scientific knowledge." While there may be a low probability of harm from dioxin as defendants contend, there is a serious and dire risk from exposure to dioxin should the hypotheses advanced by the plaintiffs prove to be valid.

> These concepts of potential harm, whether they be assessed as "probabilities and consequences" or "risk and harm," necessarily must apply in a determination of whether any relief should be given in cases of this kind in which proof with certainty is impossible.

As in *Reserve* we must determine whether "endangerment" encompasses the potential of harm to public health in the degree shown here. As to the meaning of this term, the court in *Reserve* quoted with approval the following language of Judge Skelly Wright in *Ethyl Corporation v. Environmental Protection Agency*:

> The meaning of "endanger" is [I hope, beyond dispute]. Case law and dictionary definition agree that endanger means something less than actual harm. When one is endangered, harm is threatened; no actual injury need ever occur. . . . "Endanger" . . . is not a standard prone to factual proof alone. Danger is a risk, and so must be decided by assessment of risk.

In the context of the term "endangerment"as defined in *Reserve,* the record shows that dioxin is escaping from the Vertac plant site in quantities that under an acceptable but unproved theory may be considered as teratogenic, mutagenic, fetotoxic, and carcinogenic. Such gives rise to a reasonable medical concern over the public health. We therefore hold that the escape of dioxin into Rocky Branch Creek and Bayou Meto from the plant site constitutes "an imminent and substantial endangerment to the health of persons" and is subject to abatement.

In devising a remedy . . . we again follow the guidelines set forth in *Reserve.* We must strike a proper balance between the benefits conferred and the hazards created by Vertac's facility.

The United States has asked that Vertac stop discharging its present waste into the equalization pond. This would have the effect of immediately closing the facility. At present the discharged wastes do not contain dioxin since Vertac is not manufacturing 2,4,5-T. The United States postulates that a residue of dioxin may remain in the 2,4-D waste since the same facilities are utilized in the manufacture of 2,4-D as were utilized in the manufacture of 2,4,5-T a year ago. Such has not been proved in these proceedings. Furthermore, Vertac has substantially completed the necessary engineering plans for a proposed new system for the equa-lization pond. The injunction will contain appropriate orders concerning this system. The court will order that those areas where the soil samples contain dioxin are to be covered with a clay topping and sodded with grass. These measures Vertac has agreed to take. Vertac will also be ordered to construct an underground clay barrier to the north and east of the Reasor-Hill landfill, which it has also agreed to do. Vertac will also be required to institute systematic sampling procedures from each of the monitoring wells presently on the property. The court may in the future require additional monitoring wells after the assessment of the results from the measures now being ordered.

None of these measures are beyond the financial ability of Vertac to undertake. Indeed it has agreed on the record to move forward immediately with regard to all of them. The Court is not disposed to order closure of a facility employing about seventy-five people and producing a herbicide which is of great value to the rice farmers of this state. Testimony was adduced indicating that Vertac manufactures a substantial portion of the total U.S. supply of this product and that its closure would entail foreign imports at a higher cost to rice farmers. Vertac has not been recalcitrant in its dealings with either the State or the United States.

[The injunction is denied.]

CASE REVIEW QUESTIONS

1. Since the court concludes that there is a low probability of harm, how can it also conclude that the Vertac site constitutes an "imminent and substantial endangerment" under the statute?
2. In devising a remedy in the Vertac case, with what formula does the court begin?

REVIEW QUESTIONS

1. Discuss the accuracy of the following statement: "The primary goal of NEPA is to eliminate environmentally bad federal projects."
2. What is scoping under NEPA? What purpose does it serve?
3. What information must be included in an EIS?
4. What advantages and disadvantages do you see emanating from using technology-forcing standards rather than technology-based standards?
5. Distinguish effluent standards from water quality standards under the CWA.
6. Distinguish ambient standards and source standards under the CAA.
7. One problem that existed with the disposal of haz-

ardous waste was that the transporters of the waste sometimes dumped it into the sewer system or along country roads at night. How does RCRA attempt to halt this practice?

CASE PROBLEMS

1. The Nuclear Regulatory Commission (NRC) and its predecessor, the Atomic Energy Commission, have been engaged in developing the liquid-metal fast-breeder nuclear reactor. This technology, if it proves to be commercially feasible, will develop reactors that "breed" their own fuel. Not needing the scarce fuel resource that nuclear power plants now require would greatly enhance the desirability of nuclear generated electricity. The NRC has been developing this technology for over 20 years, and the government's investment has reached several billion dollars. If a national environmental group brings an action against the NRC requesting that they prepare a "programmatic EIS," who will win the case? Explain.

2. The Federal Department of Transportation (DOT) is funding the construction of the final leg of the Pan-American Highway through the Darien Gap between Panama and Colombia. The highway will link North America with South America by road. One of the environmental impacts that could occur upon the completion of the highway is that foot and mouth disease (FMD), a devastating livestock disease, could spread by road from Colombia to the United States. In an EIS, the DOT indicates that the loss in domestic livestock should the disease spread to this country would be $10 billion the first year. However, the EIS points out that FMD is under control in Panama, and though it is not under control in Colombia, the federal government is helping Colombia work out a control program. DOT therefore concludes the threat of an outbreak of FMD in the United States is insignificant. If an environmental group brings an action against DOT contending that the EIS is inadequate, who will win the case? Explain.

3. Soul-American Steel Company has become aware that the EPA is going to announce national ambient air quality standards for the substance cadmium. The company emits cadmium. At a meeting of corporate officers, you are asked to advise them as to how and when to act to minimize the impact of these standards on the company. What would you suggest?

4. Flimsy Plastic Company is planning to construct a new facility on Black Creek in New York State. Derek Beau, Flimsy's Vice-President for External Affairs, outlined the water-pollution requirements in a memo to the other officers. As to its petroleum-based effluents, he stated that Flimsy will be limited to 0.13 units per day. The industry-based effluent standard is 0.20 units per day, and the water quality standard for Flimsy's Philadelphia plant is 0.13 units. Beau stated that Flimsy would be required to adopt the stricter of the two standards for its New York facility. The Philadelphia plant is located on the Delaware River. Discuss the accuracy of Beau's memo.

5. At a recent hearing on RCRA procedures, a representative from Dumont Chemical Company testified that the administrative provision making waste generators ultimately responsible for the legal disposal of hazardous waste even after the transporter or site owner had possession of the waste was unfair. The EPA representative argued that holding the generator liable was the administratively efficient approach. Elaborate on the arguments that each side might make on the issue of the final responsibility for hazardous waste disposal resting with the generator.

55

REGULATION OF LAND USE

A popular cliché maintains that "a man's home is his castle." The connotation of this saying is that a person attains a certain royal stature on his or her own land and has an absolute right to use it as he or she sees fit. William Pitt echoed this idea when he stated that "the poorest man may in his cottage bid defiance to all the forces of the Crown."

Despite the romantic appeal of this notion, it has never been an accurate portrayal of American law. There have always been some restrictions on a landowner's use of land. Moreover, during the twentieth century, the rights of landowners have gradually given way to substantial public and, to a lesser extent, private constraints on land use.

PRIVATE RESTRICTIONS ON LAND USE

Restrictive Covenants

A **restrictive covenant** is a restriction placed on the use of land by the seller of the land. Usually, such restrictions are included in the deed. Furthermore, unless they have a specific expiration date, they are effective indefinitely. Thus, once placed in a deed, restrictive covenants may constrain all future owners of the land; they are therefore said to "run with the land."

For example, a deed conveying Greenacre to Wormly may contain a restriction declaring that the land cannot be used for the sale of alcoholic beverages. When Wormly later decides to sell the land to Geist, the restriction on the sale of alcoholic beverages continues to limit Geist and all future owners of the land, regardless of whether the restriction is contained in the deed Wormly gives to Geist. A restrictive covenant need not be repeated in future deeds to continue to run with the land.

Because restrictive covenants restrain the free transferability of land indefinitely, the courts have never been enthusiastic about them. As a result, the courts tend to require that clear language be used by the *covenantor,* that is, the person creating the restriction. If a covenant's language is unclear as to meaning or duration, the courts will generally refuse to enforce the restriction.

Restrictive covenants are popular with residential subdividers; that is, persons who divide a parcel of land into multiple lots for the purpose of constructing houses on each lot. Normally, subdividers attach a sizeable list of restrictions either to the individual deeds given to the homeowners or to the subdivision plan that is recorded as part of the subdivision process. Typical restrictions include limitations on the construction of sheds and other detached buildings and constraints against keeping farm animals on the premises. These covenants are means of controlling future land use within the subdivision, thereby maintaining the economic value of the homes for the benefit of all the homeowners.

When a seller attaches restrictive covenants to a conveyance of land, he or she has the right to sue to enforce the restrictions. When a subdivider is the author of the covenants, the other landowners in the subdivisions have the right to sue to enforce the constraints. A mechanism used by many subdividers is to provide a committee with the power to enforce the covenants and to grant exceptions to them.

Common Law Limits to Land Use

The common law offers a landowner several causes of action against a neighbor's use of land even when there are no contractual limits imposed by a restrictive covenant. One common law cause of action that may be available to a landowner is **trespass,** which is a wrongful physical invasion of the property of another. For example, when a neighbor's fence encroaches on your land, a trespass is committed by the neighbor. When trespass occurs, a landowner may be able to enjoin future encroachments and to recover damages caused by past invasions.

Another cause of action is called a **private nuisance,** which is the unreasonable interference by one landowner with another landowner's use and enjoyment of his or her land. An action for nuisance does not require proof of actual entry onto the complainant's land. The nuisance may be caused by noise, dust, odors, and other types of unreasonable interference.

The complainant may seek money damages and perhaps an injunction, that is, a court order requiring that the neighbor stop doing those things that are causing the nuisance. Prior to granting a request for an injunction, a court normally weighs the benefits that would result to the complainant against the detriment that would result to the defendant if the injunction were granted. Such economically based analyses often prevent small landowners from obtaining injunctions against larger commercial and industrial enterprises. However, the small landowner is entitled to recover money for any damages that can be proven.

Because the law of nuisance prohibits "unreasonable" interference with a neighbor's land, it has some inherent flexibility. The following case illustrates that what is considered to be an unreasonable use of land may change as the needs of society change.

PRAH v. MARETTI
321 N.W.2d 182 (Wis. 1982)

[In 1978 and 1979, Glenn Prah, the plaintiff, constructed a residence in a subdivision. He installed a solar system, including roof collectors, to supply the energy to heat water and the house itself. Sometime later, Richard Maretti, the defendant, purchased the adjoining lot to the south. He got approval from the Planning Commission and the subdivision's Architectural Control Committee to construct a residence on the lot. Prah requested that Maretti change his plans and move the house further south on the lot so that the new house would not obstruct the sunlight needed to operate Prah's solar collectors. Maretti refused and began construction.

Prah filed a complaint in the circuit court, alleging that he was entitled to unrestricted access to the sun to obtain solar power under the doctrine of private nuisance. He requested an injunction to halt Maretti's construction. Maretti moved for summary judgment, arguing that Prah had failed to state a cause of action for which relief could be granted. The trial court granted the summary judgment. Prah appealed to the Wisconsin Supreme Court.]

ABRAHAMSON, Justice

We consider whether the complaint states a claim for relief based on common law private nuisance. This state has long recognized that an owner of land does not have an absolute or unlimited right to use the land in a way which injures the rights of others. The rights of neighboring landowners are relative; the uses by one must not unreasonably impair the uses or enjoyment of the other. When one landowner's use of his or her property unreasonably interferes with another's enjoyment of his or her property, that use is said to be a private nuisance.

The private nuisance doctrine has traditionally been employed in this state to balance the conflicting rights of landowners, and this court has recently adopted the analysis of private nuisance set forth in the Restatement (Second) of Torts. The Restatement defines private nuisance as "a nontrespassory invasion of another's interest in the private use and enjoyment of land." The phrase "interest in the private use and enjoyment of land" is broadly defined to include any disturbance of the enjoyment of property.

Although the defendant's obstruction of the plaintiff's access to sunlight appears to fall within the Restatement's broad concept of a private nuisance as a nontrespassory invasion of another's interest in the private use and enjoyment of land, the defendant asserts that he has a right to develop his property in compliance with statutes, ordinances and private covenants without regard to the effect of such development upon the plaintiff's access to sunlight. In essence, the defendant is asking this court to hold that the private nuisance doctrine is not applicable in the instant case and that his right to develop his land is a right which is *per se* superior to his neighbor's interest in access to sunlight. This position is expressed in the maxim *"cujus est solum, ejus est usque ad coelum et ad infernos,"* that is, the owner of land owns up to the sky and down to the center of the earth. The rights of the surface owner are, however, not unlimited.

The defendant is not completely correct in asserting

that the common law did not protect a landowner's access to sunlight across adjoining property. At English common law a landowner could acquire a right to receive sunlight across adjoining land by both express agreement and under the judge-made doctrine of "ancient lights." Under the doctrine of ancient lights if the landowner had received sunlight across adjoining property for a specified period of time, the landowner was entitled to continue to receive unobstructed access to sunlight across the adjoining property. Under the doctrine the landowner . . . could prevent the adjoining landowner from obstructing access to light.

Although American courts have not been as receptive to protecting a landowner's access to sunlight as the English courts, American courts have afforded some protection to a landowner's interest in access to sunlight. American courts honor express easements to sunlight. American courts initially enforced the English common law doctrine of ancient lights, but later every state which considered the doctrine repudiated it as inconsistent with the needs of a developing country. Indeed, for just that reason this court concluded that an easement to light and air over adjacent property could not be created or acquired and has been unwilling to recognize such an easement.

Many jurisdictions in this country have protected a landowner from malicious obstruction of access to light (the spite fence cases) under the common law private nuisance doctrine. If an activity is motivated by malice it lacks utility and the harm it causes others outweighs any social value. This court was reluctant to protect a landowner's interest in sunlight even against a spite fence, only to be overruled by the legislature. Shortly after this court upheld a landowner's right to erect a useless and unsightly sixteen-foot spite fence four feet from his neighbor's windows, the legislature enacted a law specifically defining a spite fence as an actionable private nuisance. Thus a landowner's interest in sunlight has been protected in this country by common law private nuisance law at least in the narrow context of the modern American rule invalidating spite fences.

This court's reluctance in the nineteenth and early part of the twentieth century to provide broader protection for a landowner's access to sunlight was premised on three policy considerations. First, the right of landowners to use their property as they wished, as

long as they did not cause physical damage to a neighbor, was jealously guarded.

Second, sunlight was valued only for aesthetic enjoyment or as illumination. Since artificial light could be used for illumination, loss of sunlight was at most a personal annoyance which was given little, if any, weight by society.

Third, society had a significant interest in not restricting or impeding land development. This court repeatedly emphasized that in the growth period of the nineteenth and early twentieth centuries change is to be expected and is essential to property and that recognition of a right to sunlight would hinder property development.

Considering these three policies, this court concluded that in the absence of an express agreement granting access to sunlight, a landowner's obstruction of another's access to sunlight was not actionable. These three policies are no longer fully accepted or applicable. They reflect factual circumstances and social priorities that are now obsolete.

First, society has increasingly regulated the use of land by the landowner for the general welfare.

Second, access to sunlight has taken on a new significance in recent years. In this case the plaintiff seeks to protect access to sunlight, not for aesthetic reasons or as a source of illumination but as a source of energy. Access to sunlight as an energy source is of significance both to the landowner who invests in solar collectors and to a society which has an interest in developing alternative sources of energy.

Third, the policy of favoring unhindered private development in an expanding economy is no longer in harmony with the realities of our society. The need for easy and rapid development is not as great today as it once was, while our perception of the value of sunlight as a source of energy has increased significantly.

Courts should not implement obsolete policies that have lost their vigor over the course of the years. The law of private nuisance is better suited to resolve landowners' disputes about property development in the 1980s than is a rigid rule which does not recognize a landowner's interest in access to sunlight. "What is regarded in law as constituting a nuisance in modern times would no doubt have been tolerated without question in former times."

Yet the defendant would have us ignore the flexible

private nuisance law as a means of resolving the dispute between the landowners in this case and would have us adopt an approach favoring the unrestricted development of land and of applying a rigid and inflexible rule protecting his right to build on his land and disregarding any interest of the plaintiff in the use and enjoyment of his land. This we refuse to do.

Private nuisance law, the law traditionally used to adjudicate conflicts between private landowners, has the flexibility to protect both a landowner's right of access to sunlight and another landowner's right to develop land. Private nuisance law is better suited to regulate access to sunlight in modern society and is more in harmony with legislative policy and the prior decisions of this court than is an inflexible doctrine of non-recognition of any interest in access to sunlight across adjoining land.

We therefore hold that private nuisance law, that is, the reasonable use doctrine as set forth in the Restatement, is applicable to the instant case. Recognition of a nuisance claim for unreasonable obstruction of access to sunlight will not prevent land development or unduly hinder the use of adjoining land. It will promote the reasonable use and enjoyment of land in a manner suitable to the 1980s. That obstruction of access to light might be found to constitute a nuisance in certain circumstances does not mean that it will be or must be found to constitute a nuisance under all circumstances. The result in each case depends on whether the conduct complained of is unreasonable.

Accordingly we hold that the plaintiff in this case has stated a claim under which relief can be granted. Nonetheless we do not determine whether the plaintiff in this case is entitled to relief. In order to be entitled to relief the plaintiff must prove the elements required to establish actionable nuisance, and the conduct of the defendant herein must be judged by the reasonable use doctrine.

Reversed.

CASE REVIEW QUESTIONS

1. Did the court conclude that Maretti's construction constituted a private nuisance? Explain.
2. What will Prah have to prove in the trial court in order to establish that Maretti's conduct constitutes a nuisance?
3. Why is the Wisconsin Supreme Court abandoning its original rule that held that interference with sunlight does not constitute a nuisance? Given the court's reasoning, will such interference necessarily provide a basis for nuisance actions in the future? Explain.

PUBLIC RESTRICTIONS ON LAND USE

Governmental regulation of land use takes two distinct forms. First, governmental bodies have the power of **eminent domain.** This means that they may take land away from private owners provided that the taking, or **condemnation,** is for a public use and that just — that is, reasonable — compensation is paid. Land for public highways, utility lines, and recreational facilities is often taken by government in this way. Eminent domain is the ultimate in regulation because it physically takes the land away from its owner.

The second form of governmental land-use regulation is carried out under the police power of state governments. A state's **police power** is its inherent regulatory power for the purpose of protecting the public health, safety, and welfare. This power gives state governments a great deal of latitude in adopting regulations that restrict land use. Police-power regulations must be based upon a public purpose—that is, to promote health, safety, or welfare—but no payment need be made to the landowner, and there is no physical appropriation of the land by the government. A classic form of police-power regulation, zoning, will be discussed later in this chapter.

The "Taking" Issue

Drawing the line between those situations in which the government should condemn and pay for land and those in which police-power regulation will suffice gives rise to the so-called "taking" issue. If a regulation under the government's police power is overly restrictive of a property owner's right to use the land, the government must condemn the land under its power of eminent domain and pay for it. No uniform rule has been established for differentiating between a legitimate use of the police power and an overreaching restriction, but the most commonly used test is whether or not the regulation takes all reasonable use of the land away from its owner.

If a regulation is challenged in court and the court determines that the government has taken all reasonable use of the land away from the owner, the regulation is labeled a "taking without due process of law," and the owner is no longer constrained by the regulation. For example, suppose a town adopted a regulation designating Blackburn's land as a park that must be open to the public for its use. A court would find this regulation to be a taking of all reasonable use of Blackburn's land. Therefore, if the town wants Blackburn's land for a park, it must condemn the land under its power of eminent domain and pay Blackburn just compensation for it.

The difficult problem in cases of this sort is determining whether or not the landowner has been deprived of "all reasonable use" of his or her property. The courts have disagreed over the circumstances in which such deprivation occurs. For instance, courts have held that regulations prohibiting development in wetlands—that is, swamps and marshes—and confining their uses to those consistent with maintaining the wetlands deprives the owner of all reasonable use. Other courts have upheld such regulations, contending that wetlands are different from other areas and that development is not a reasonable use of wetlands.

In addition, what is considered to be a reasonable use of a given type of land is something that will change over time. For instance, the status of wetlands has changed from "wasteland" to "valuable natural resource" in the last 15 years. The only thing that is definite about most determinations of whether a landowner has been deprived of all reasonable use of his or her land is that they involve a great deal of subjectivity.

Euclidian Zoning

Zoning is a type of police-power regulation that places restrictions on the use of land and on the structures erected on the land. Zoning laws are authorized by state legislation and are generally administered by municipal or county governments. **Euclidian zoning** obtains its name from *Euclid v. Ambler,* the 1926 Supreme Court case that held zoning to be legal.

In its simplest form, Euclidian zoning has three categories of land use: residential, commercial, and industrial. Today, most growing communities have further subdivided these three categories. For instance, a zoning ordinance may specify a number of different residential use districts, distinguished by the size of the lot required and by the type of residential units that may be constructed on a lot. As a result, certain residential zoning districts may require a minimum of one acre per lot; others may require at least one-half acre; and still others, one-fourth acre or less. In addition, special zones may be established for garden apartments, condominiums, and high-rise apartment buildings. Commercial and industrial zones may also have subcategories.

Because each zoning district has distinct rules controlling development, subcategorizing provides zoning administrators with additional control over land development. Thus, a zoning code may regulate such things as bulk, height, and building location as well as maximum floor space, number of stories, and the extent of front, rear, and side-yard setbacks.

Comprehensive Plan The courts have made it very clear that the basis of any zoning code must be a comprehensive plan. A **comprehensive plan** provides a set of standards to guide the decisions of the zoning administrator. In addition, a comprehensive plan gives the courts, which are often called upon to review zoning decisions, criteria for determining whether a zoning administrator has made a reasonable decision (i.e., one that conforms to the plan) or an arbitrary decision (i.e., one that does not conform to the plan). For example, if a comprehensive plan designates an area for residential development, a decision to approve a proposal for a residential subdivision would conform to the plan, whereas a decision to approve a plan for an industrial plant would not.

There is little clarity, however, with regard to the legal minimums required for a comprehensive plan. At one extreme, a plan may be an extensive written document that is the product of an in-depth study of how the community should develop. Such a document is often referred to as a master plan. At the other extreme, a plan may consist of little more than a zoning map and a zoning code. Both extremes have been accepted by courts as adequate comprehensive plans.

It is inaccurate, though, to think of a comprehensive plan as a specific document. In reality, a comprehensive plan is a process. Generally, it consists of an initial document such as a master plan plus the day-to-day decisions and modifications made by the zoning administrators. For example, if subsequent to the adoption of the initial plan the legislative body decides that the zoning for a portion of the town should be changed from residential to commercial, that change becomes part of the comprehensive plan.

Whenever a legislative or administrative body wishes to make changes in the plan, it is required to consider the needs of the entire community, not just those of the applicant or the immediate neighbors. In addition, the changes must be a product of a deliberative process. Procedurally, this means that notice of the proposed change must be given and a hearing on it must be held. Substantively, it means that reasonable alternative uses for the land in question must be considered.

Departures from Zoning Codes The failure to act in accordance with the comprehensive plan is called **spot zoning** and is illegal. However, not all uses that are contrary to those designated in the zoning code are instances of spot zoning. The term is used only for those uses that are "unplanned." Some departures from the comprehensive plan fall within the scheme of the zoning code. These will be discussed in the following sections of this chapter.

Nonconforming Use A **nonconforming use** is a use that is inconsistent with the use designated in the zoning code that predates either the zoning code or subsequent amendments to it. Nonconforming uses are legal and are allowed. Otherwise the nonconforming users could sue on the basis that the zoning code has effected a taking of their land without due process of law.

Although nonconforming uses must be allowed to continue, they are not favored. The user will not be allowed to expand the use beyond its scope at the time it became nonconforming. If the landowner discontinues the nonconforming use or if buildings necessary for that use are destroyed, the right to use the land inconsistent with the zoning code terminates. The nonconforming use does, however, run with the land; that is, subsequent buyers of the land have the right to continue the nonconformity.

Despite unfavorable treatment by courts and administrators, nonconforming uses do not always fade away as desired. For example, a nonconforming grocery store in a residential zone may thrive. As a result, some municipalities have put time limits on nonconforming uses. When the time limit lapses, the nonconforming use must end. Generally, the courts apply a test of reasonableness in reviewing these time limits. Given the uncertainty in getting judicial approval under a reasonableness test, however, many municipalities are reluctant to place time constraints on nonconforming uses.

Special Use Permit The **special use permit** is employed by municipalities to maintain control over the location of certain types of development. For instance, a zoning code might not provide zone designations that allow cemeteries, churches, or schools. A special use permit must therefore be obtained from the planning administrator or planning board in order to locate one of these uses in the municipality.

The failure to provide for these uses in the zoning code is not an indication that they are undesirable. Instead, it reflects recognition of the fact that additional administrative control is needed to locate them appropriately. For instance, schools can be an acceptable use of land in some residential zones. In other residential zones, however, schools may be an inappropriate use of land because of traffic, congestion, or the age of the residents.

Variance If an applicant requests a modest deviation from the zoning code, he or she is asking for a **variance.** The granting of a variance by the appropriate administrative body does not involve a change in the zone's designated use. Instead, it permits a deviation from one of the restrictions imposed by the code on the designated use. For example, a variance might be granted if an applicant requests the zoning board to reduce the zoning code's 20-foot front yard setback requirement to a 15-foot set-back for a particular parcel of land.

In order to obtain a variance, the applicant must prove that unnecessary hardship will occur without it, that the change will not reduce property values in the vicinity, and that the granting of the variance will be consistent with both the public interest and the spirit of the zoning code.

Zone Change An amendment or zone change can be made by the municipalities' legislative body. A designated use or other zoning restriction may be altered to reflect changed conditions. As mentioned earlier, the zoning code is created to implement the comprehensive plan. Because the plan is a dynamic process, its implementating tool must be capable of change.

Usually, a request for a zone change is initiated by a landowner rather than by municipal officials. The applicant for the zone change must prove that conditions have been significantly altered since the zoning code was adopted and that the proposed zone change makes sense in light of these altered conditions. For instance, a landowner may contend that, because of significantly increased traffic flow and other recent development in the vicinity of his or her land, residential zoning is no longer appropriate and that rezoning the area for commercial use would make good planning sense.

As is illustrated in the following case, it is not sufficient for a developer merely to show that he or she will lose money if the zone change is not granted. The case is also noteworthy because the court, under a contention of an unconstitutional taking, upholds a very restrictive zoning classification.

CHOKECHERRY HILLS ESTATES v. DEUEL COUNTY
294 N.W.2d 654 (S.D. 1980)

[Chokecherry Hills Estates (Chokecherry) purchased 223 acres of land in Deuel County, situated on the north shore of Lake Oliver. The purpose of the acquisition was to develop homesites on the 13 acres of land fronting on the lake. The remainder of the acreage was to continue to be used for agricultural purposes. The land involved is zoned as a Natural Resource District, which restricts it to wildlife and open-space uses. Chokecherry was aware at the time of purchase that the existing zoning would not allow the construction of the proposed single-family houses.

Chokecherry applied for a zone change to the Lake-Park District that would allow the building of single-family houses. After public hearings, both the Deuel County Planning and Zoning Commission and the county commissioner denied the zone change request. The basis for the denial was that the applicant knew about the zoning restriction at the time of purchase, that agriculture and natural resource uses were the highest and best uses, and that the land was unsuitable for development because of the impact development would have on the natural resource and ecological values of the lake and its shore line.

Chokecherry brought a legal action against Deuel County, attacking the legality and constitutionality of the zoning designation. The trial court found for the county. Chokecherry appealed to the South Dakota Supreme Court.]

DUNN, Justice

Appellant advances two theories to attack the zoning ordinance. In Count One it is alleged that the classification of this land as a natural resource district constitutes a taking. Appellant asks for compensation based upon the alleged taking. In Count Two it is alleged that the classification as applied to this property is unconstitutional and should be declared null and void, thus allowing appellant to develop the property pursuant to a Lake-Park District classification.

Appellant purchased this property fully aware that the land was zoned as a natural resources area. Kalhoff [President of Chokecherry] testified that he bought the land at a price that reflected the farmland value. Evidence indicates he had been using the land for agricultural purposes at the time of this lawsuit. On the whole, the evidence paints a picture of Mr. Kalhoff taking a gamble that he could succeed in changing the existing zoning law so that he could realize a higher profit.

In *State Theatre Co. v. Smith,* we held that a zoning law, like all legislative enactments, is presumed to be reasonable, valid, and constitutional. Appellant has not met the heavy burden placed upon it in challenging the zoning law. There was no evidence that it could not obtain reasonable income on the property by continuing to use it for agricultural purposes. Kalhoff testified

that he had not investigated the possibilities of leasing the land for pasturing or building a public hunting area. In response to the reasons given by the zoning commission and the county board for denying the change, Kalhoff merely stated that it was his opinion that residential development was the highest and best use of the land and would not create the problems cited by the commissions. The trial court was not convinced, and neither are we.

We agree wholeheartedly that county commissioners may not effectuate a taking without compensation by the manipulation of the zoning laws. "Spot zoning" is a prime example of such an improper taking. There is no evidence of spot zoning in this case. The zoning map of Deuel County shows that the great majority of the lakes in the county have been zoned into the natural resource district. There is no evidence that this property has been singled out for improper or unusual treatment.

We agree with the county commission that the only reason that the change was requested was for the convenience and pecuniary gain of appellant. These are not proper grounds upon which to rezone property or declare a zoning law unconstitutional.

In *Just v. Marinette County,* the Supreme Court of Wisconsin stated that the police power was properly exercised in preventing a public harm by protecting the natural environment of shorelands. No taking was found and no compensation given in *Just,* despite the fact that the landowners had purchased the land before it was restrictively zoned for natural uses. Appellant in the instant case is in a weaker position than the landowner in *Just,* due to the lack of evidence to counter the reasons set forth by the commissioners and the fact that he purchased the land with full knowledge of the zoning restrictions.

The order of the trial court is affirmed.

CASE REVIEW QUESTIONS

1. Would the court have reached the same conclusion if Chokecherry had not been aware at the time of purchase that the land was zoned as a Natural Resources District, which prohibited residential development?

2. Assuming that the Natural Resources District Zone is constitutional, what would Chokecherry have to prove in order to get a zone change?

Subdivision Regulations

The subdivision of land means that the land is divided into two or more lots for the purpose of developing each lot, usually with the intention of reselling the developed lots. For instance, in a residential development, the land is subdivided into individual house lots. In most municipalities, the process of subdivision is regulated by a special law.

Zoning, you will recall, controls the use and location of structures on the lots. Subdivision regulations impose requirements concerning the location of streets, sewer lines, and water lines; the contours necessary for proper drainage; the location of parks; and other matters affecting the public health, safety, and welfare. Subdivision regulations are administered by a planning board. The developer must present a plan that describes how the development will meet requirements of the subdivision regulations; the plan must be approved by the planning board.

The right of the municipality to regulate the details of subdivision development is based on the state's police power; that is, on the state's right to regulate for the protection of the public health, safety, and welfare. In exchange for compliance with the detailed requirements of the subdivision regulations, the developer can expect the municipality to accept title to and maintenance responsibilities for the subdivision's infrastructure. The infrastructure includes roads, sewer lines, parks, and the like. The municipality gets a development that meets its specifications, and the developer is relieved of the responsibility for owning and maintaining the subdivision's infrastructure.

Planned Unit Development

The exact meaning of the term **planned unit development (PUD)** is difficult to pinpoint. Generally, a PUD is a development that is larger than the traditional subdivision and that encompasses different types of land use. For instance, a PUD may include various kinds of residential housing, some commercial usage, and perhaps even some light industrial usage in the same development. The PUD zone is provided for in the zoning code. It may be a traditional fixed Euclidian-type zone, or it may be a floating zone that can be affixed to any large tract of land in the municipality upon the approval of the planning board.

Whichever form a PUD takes, it has several advantages. First of all, it allows more flexibility for integrated uses than is likely to be available under traditional zoning. Because of increased energy costs, general inconvenience, and the decline in a sense of community, planners have begun to recognize that the wide separation of uses caused by zoning is sometimes counterproductive.

These planners have come to believe that a better living arrangement may be achieved if uses can be blended without creating such hazards as congestion, traffic problems, and unreasonable noise levels. It therefore becomes the duty of the body that must approve the PUD, usually a planning board, to make sure that safety and health hazards that are undesirable in residential neighborhoods are avoided.

Another advantage of a PUD zone is the maximization of open space. The PUD will generally authorize houses to be built on smaller lots than are required in other residential zones. This clustering of residential units can reduce the developer's costs by reducing the amount of infrastructure that is necessary; for example, closer houses may allow roads, sewer lines, and water lines to be short. In return for allowing the clustering of houses, the planning board will often require that a substantial amount of open space be retained. For example, if a normal single-family development of 100 houses has one house per acre, clustering the 100 houses on one-half-acre lots will allow 50 acres to be designated as open space for the benefit of the residents and the community at large.

Generally, PUDs are approved in several stages. The planning board will first approve an overall conceptual plan. However, the size of the PUD usually requires that the actual development be spread over several years. Therefore, each part of the PUD must be given specific approval as its development is begun. The series of approvals allow both the planning board and the developer to make changes in the original proposal in response to altered needs or demands. Over time, these changes can lead to something quite different from the initial concept, unless the planning board demands reasonable consistency. For example, if the original PUD plan called for a variety of housing to accommodate all economic segments of the community, the planning board must carefully monitor the individual approvals so that the developer does not change the PUD into predominantly single-family houses on large lots in an attempt to maximize his or her profits. If the community needs a variety of housing, the planning board must insist upon conformity to the original PUD plan.

Performance Standards Zoning

One specialized zoning technique that is growing in popularity is **performance standards zoning,** which establishes certain standards that must be met by any user of land within the zone. Performance standards have been set for such things as noise, vibrations, odors, toxic wastes, signs, and heat emanating from a site. For instance, a standard may provide that no odor is allowed beyond the property line. Most of these standards have been established for industrial operations to insure that they do not interfere with surrounding land uses.

Performance standards are especially appropriate for multiple-use situations, such as exist in PUD developments. The concept of performance standards may also be useful for controlling adverse impacts in traditional commercial and residential zones. For instance, they can be used to regulate impacts on drainage, visual sensitivity, and traffic congestion.

In the following case, performance standards were set within an industrial zone. The type of use proposed by the applicant in the case already existed on other land within the zone, but it predated the performance standards zoning. The question that arose was whether the city was bound to permit the applicant's similar use in spite of the subsequently adopted performance standards.

DeCOALS, INC. v. BOARD OF ZONING APPEALS
284 S.E.2d 856 (W.V. 1981)

[DeCoals, Inc., applied for a building permit from the city of Westover to construct a coal tipple on property in an industrial zone. There was another coal tipple operating in the industrial zone. The mayor granted the building permit. DeCoals received permits from four other local, state, and federal agencies. Neighboring residents appealed the mayor's decision to the Board of Zoning Appeals, which had the authority to review these decisions. The board voted 3 to 2 to rescind the building permit because DeCoals would not be able to conform to certain performance standards for users in the industrial zone. Specifically, the board concluded that the performance standard for dust, which prohibited any "dust" from escaping the site, and the standard for "noise and sound," which limited noise to a maximum of 70 decibels at the property line but not louder than street traffic noise in the vicinity, were legal.

DeCoals appealed the board's decision. The circuit court affirmed the board's decision. DeCoals appealed to the Supreme Court of West Virginia.]

HARSHBARGER, Chief Justice

Local governments have a right to zone as an exercise of police power.

[A] municipality may enact a zoning ordinance which restricts the use of property in designated districts within the municipality if the restrictions imposed by the ordinance are not arbitrary or unreasonable and bear a substantial relation to the public health, safety, morals, or the general welfare of the municipality.

Substantive due process considerations require legislation to be reasonable — to be substantially related to a legitimate goal. One of government's primary purposes is protecting its constituency.

Legislation designed to free from pollution the very air that people breathe clearly falls within the exercise of even the most traditional concept of what is known as the police power.

If the end is legitimate, our inquiry is limited to whether the means are substantially related to that end. It is not ours to judge the wisdom or efficacy of those chosen means.

This is not to say that there are not serious questions raised as to the wisdom and the practicality of the undoubtedly rigorous measures required by the ordinance. But the ultimate conclusion must be that these are questions within the domain of legislative and executive discretion because they involve choices among alternative reasonable courses of action based on the presently limited knowledge of the extent of the pollution evil and methods of cure. So long as there is reasonable basis in available information, and rationality in chosen courses of conduct to alleviate an accepted evil, there is no constitutional infirmity.

Whether a no-dust standard is the best way to protect public health, welfare, safety and morals is a legislative judgment.

[T]he most important current trend in industrial zoning is the gradual movement towards zoning by performance standards. Since a primary purpose of industrial zoning is to regulate those establishments which result in substantial amounts of nuisance, it is clear that performance standards zoning . . . is a . . . sensitively attuned instrument for carrying out those purposes. . . .

Is it, then, reasonable to prohibit escape of *any* dust? Are private property rights unreasonably sacrificed for public good? A community's sensible decisions protecting its health and welfare must prevail over any individual property rights; but is prohibition of any dust production sensible? This individual [property] right is not unqualified. It does have to yield to the higher and greater right of the best interest of the people. This holds true though a proper exercise of the police power brings about a material financial loss, for that cannot stand in the way of public welfare, the latter not being susceptible to being impeded or thwarted by a private loss which is incident to the exercise of that power. The justification for a zoning ordinance reducing the value of some individual rights is the greater benefit accruing to the public as a whole; and this includes the limitation of the potential value of a particular parcel of property. When the legislature has determined what is a proper exercise of the police power, this court has no right to question legislative policy. When the legislature has determined what is a proper exercise of the police power, this court does have the right to determine whether the means employed in a particular matter have a real and substantial relation to the public health, comfort, morals, safety or welfare, or are unreasonable and arbitrary. In the use of his property acording to his desires, the owner must not endanger or threaten the safety, health, comfort or general welfare of the people. A zoning ordinance passed in the exercise of a delegated police power is clothed with a presumption in favor of its validity. The party attacking it as an unreasonable and oppressive exercise of that power has the burden of showing affirmatively and clearly its unreasonableness. This court will not hold such ordinance unreasonable where there is room for a fair difference of opinion on the question.

If people jointly resolve that no more dust or noise inspired by industry in their community is acceptable, we should not interfere. They live there; they breathe the air; their lifestyles are affected by the noise and traffic; and they suffer whatever economic loss that results from regulations that eliminate certain potential industries that might there be put but for strict performance zoning rules. Any city is entitled to that choice.

Alleged technical infeasibility or economic hardship need not be considered. "Technology-forcing" pollution regulations have been approved.

It is a fairly debatable issue whether an absolute prohibition against dust is unreasonable or arbitrary, and "[c]ourts are not disposed to declare an ordinance invalid in whole or in part where it is fairly debatable as to whether the action of the municipality is arbitrary or unreasonable."

Courts have written that a no-dust standard does not preclude development of any industry in an industrial zone. If it did, there might be a different issue. We find that this ordinance does not deny due process rights under federal or state constitutions.

We recognize a substantial problem caused by grandfather performance standard zoning clauses. Nonetheless, Westover is entitled to determine that "enough is enough," choosing not to interfere with property uses in existence when its zoning or ordinance was enacted, but to prevent further intrusion upon air and noise quality by yet to be developed industries.

Affirmed.

CASE REVIEW QUESTIONS
1. Describe the court's role in reviewing a legislative action like the setting of a performance standard for dust.
2. Since a small amount of dust escaping from an industrial site may not be harmful to health or to the living environment, why did the city adopt an absolute ban on dust leaving the premises?

REVIEW QUESTIONS

1. Contrast private restrictions with public restrictions on land use as to their origins and purposes.

2. Why are courts reluctant to enforce restrictive covenants?

3. Discuss the following statement: "Nonconforming uses are legal, but they cannot be expanded. This limit on expansion will assure their eventual discontinuance."

4. Compare the role played by zoning ordinances with that played by subdivision regulations.

5. On its face, the concept of a planned unit development is a reversion to the prezoning days of mixed land uses. What are the similarities and dissimilarities between a properly executed planned unit development and the unregulated growth of the prezoning period?

CASE PROBLEMS

1. Potts owned a six-acre tract in the city of Franklin. He maintained a barn on the tract in which he stored lumber and other building materials. Outside the barn, he stored bricks to a height of about five feet. The land is now zoned residential, but Potts' use preceded that zoning and is considered a legal nonconforming use. Subsequently, Potts had the rear of the tract leveled and he began to store logs behind the barn. The city brought a legal action against Potts, claiming that the storage of the logs is an illegal expansion of the nonconforming use. Who will win the case? Explain.

2. The town of Weston is located on the edge of an area of population growth spilling into Connecticut from metropolitan New York City and is zoned entirely for residential development. The only existing commercial development in the town is on a six-acre parcel and operates as a nonconforming use. Cadoux applied for a zone change to permit him to construct a shopping center within the town. The town denied the application. If Cadoux brings a legal action, on what grounds can the town argue that zoning itself entirely for residential use is justified? Who will win the case? Explain.

3. Suppose you are a member of the board of directors of a church. The congregation is proposing to build a new church and is seeking a site for it. At a board meeting, the president reports that he can find no zone designation in the city's new zoning code that permits a church as a valid use. He concludes that the congregation will have to look elsewhere for a site. Though you have not read the zoning code yourself and cannot speak with certainty, how might you explain to the board why the president's conclusion may not be accurate?

4. Auld MacDonald owns a hamburger stand in a zone that permits only fast-food retail businesses. MacDonald is discouraged because of the intense competition from national hamburger franchises in the area and has decided to change the hamburger stand into a bar. He applies to the zoning board for a variance. Will he be successful?

5. DuPage applied to the city for a zone change from single-family residential to multifamily residential. The city denied the application, and DuPage sued, claiming that the ordinance was unconstitutional. DuPage was able to prove that the present zoning would cause it significant economic hardship. Under state law, the burden of proof then shifted to the city to prove that the zoning was reasonably related to the public health, safety, and welfare. As a representative of the city, what arguments would you make in support of the ordinance?

56

THE RECENT EVOLUTION OF LAND-USE REGULATIONS

When used for their stated purpose, the zoning-type regulations discussed in the previous chapter have traditionally been attempts to steer growth to appropriate locations in a community and to insure that the growth is inoffensive. However, the decade of the seventies saw an increasing interest in public regulations with different goals. These new regulations were aimed primarily at limiting growth and protecting natural resources. Communities were beginning to take the stance that there was no intrinsic right to develop every parcel of land. Naturally, the courts were soon called upon to determine the legal limits of these new land-use controls.

This chapter will be divided into two sections. The first will take up regulations that attempt to control the rate or extent of urban sprawl. The second section will focus on regulations aimed at protecting the natural resource value of land. Neither section will cover all of the methods used by communities to accomplish these goals. Instead, the material in this chapter is intended to provide an introduction to the types of approaches used and to the reaction of courts to these approaches.

CONTROL OF URBAN SPRAWL

The post–World War II period saw rapid changes in the living habits of Americans. People spilled from the cities into the newly developed suburbs in the nearby countryside. Their main reason for abandoning the cities was to avoid the ills of city life. They were fleeing noise and traffic congestion, closely clustered and aging housing, and increasing crime and pollution.

As the suburbs continued to expand during the 1950s and 1960s, the urban ills people had fled the cities to avoid began to follow them into their new communities. In response, suburban communities began to adopt regulations designed to stop the decline in the quality of suburban life by limiting the rate of growth. Specific reasons for limiting growth included insuring that sewer and water systems remained adequate, maintaining property values, and preventing an array of urban maladies. The regulations used to accomplish these ends were justified as legitimate expressions of the communities' police power.

Despite their laudatory purpose, regulations aimed at limiting growth have received mixed reviews by the courts. In this section, you will read about some of the techniques that have been used to limit growth and the reactions of the courts to them.

Large-Lot Zoning

Large-lot zoning refers to a technique of limiting growth by requiring that houses be built on lots of an unnecessarily large minimum size. The term large lot is imprecise, however. What constitutes a large lot may vary depending on the location of the lot.

Generally, it would seem that a lot of more than one acre would be a large lot. Still, residential zoning classifications that require lots larger than one acre may be justifiable because of soil and other geological conditions. For example, some soils cannot handle the waste water from a septic system for more than one housing unit per two acres. In addition, large, esthetically pleasing lots help to maintain local property values.

One of the side effects of large-lot zoning, whether intended or not, is discrimination. If a zoning code requires relatively large lots throughout the community, housing that is affordable to people with low and moderate incomes cannot be constructed. Some state courts, concerned about the shortage of moderately priced housing and the growing trend toward large-lot zoning, have decided that this type of zoning is illegal prima facie under state law. Pennsylvania is a leader in this judicial movement. The following case is one of a series of Pennsylvania decisions that have prompted negative responses to large-lot zoning in several other states.

IN RE KIT MAR
268 A.2d 765 (Pa. 1970)

[Kit Mar Builders, Inc., agreed to purchase 140 acres of land in Concord Township. The agreement was contingent upon the ability of the applicant to get a rezoning changing the required size of lots from two and three acre per lot to one acre per lot. The rezoning application was denied by the township. The denial was upheld on appeal by the Zoning Board of Adjustment because the applicant had failed to prove the necessary hardship to secure a variance. The term variance is used broadly in Pennsylvania and includes a zone change. The board was reversed by the Court of Common Pleas, and Concord Township appealed to the Pennsylvania Supreme Court.]

ROBERTS, [Judge]

We conclude that, even accepting the findings of the zoning board, the ordinance here in question is unconstitutional under the test set forth in our decision in *National Land and Investment Company v. Easttown Township Board of Adjustment.*

We decided in *National Land* that a scheme of zoning that has an exclusionary purpose or result is not acceptable in Pennsylvania. We do not intend to say, of course, that minimum lot size requirements are inherently unreasonable. Planning considerations and other interests can justify reasonably varying minimum lot sizes in given areas of a community. At some point along the spectrum, however, the size of lots ceases to be a concern requiring public regulation and becomes simply a matter of private preference. The two- and three-acre minimums imposed in this case are no more reasonable than the four-acre requirements struck down in *National Land.* As we pointed out in *National Land,* there are obvious advantages to the residents of a community in having houses built on four- or three-acre lots. However, minimum lot sizes of the magnitude required by this ordinance are a great deal larger than what should be considered as a necessary size for the building of a house, and are therefore not the proper subjects of public regulation. As a matter of fact, a house can fit quite comfortably on a one-acre lot without being the least bit cramped. Absent some extraordinary justification, a zoning ordinance with minimum lot sizes such as those in this case is completely unreasonable.

As the primary justification for the zoning ordinance now before us the township contends that lots of a smaller size will create a potential sewage problem. It was on this question that the zoning board and the trial court made conflicting findings of fact. Whether a potential sewage problem exists or not is irrelevant, however, since we explicitly rejected the argument that sewage problems could excuse exclusionary zoning in *National Land.* We in effect held in *National Land* that because there were alternative methods for dealing

with nearly all the problems that attend a growth in population, including sewage problems, zoning which had an exclusive purpose or effect could not be allowed. This is not to say that the village may not, pursuant to its other and general police powers (i.e., not zoning power), impose other restrictions or conditions on the granting of a building permit to plaintiff, such as a general assessment for reconstruction of the sewage system, granting of building permit . . . in stages, or perhaps even a moratorium on the issuance of any building permits, reasonably limited as to time. But whatever the right of a municipality to impose "a . . . temporary restraint of beneficial enjoyment . . . where the interference is necessary to promote the ultimate good of either the municipality as a whole or of the immediate neighborhood." Such restraint must be kept within the limits of necessity, and may not prevent permanently the reasonable use of private property for the only purposes to which it is practically adapted.

We once again reaffirm our past authority and refuse to allow the township to do precisely what we have never permitted — keep out people, rather than make community improvements.

The implication of our decision in *National Land* is that communities must deal with the problems of population growth. They may not refuse to confront the future by adopting zoning regulations that effectively restrict population to near present levels. It is not for any given township to say who may or may not live within its confines, while disregarding the interests of the entire area. If Concord Township is successful in unnaturally limiting its population growth through use of exclusive zoning regulations, the people who would normally live there will inevitably have to live in another community, and the requirement that they do so is not a decision that Concord Township should alone be able to make.

While our decision in *National Land* requires municipalities to meet the challenge of population growth without closing their doors to it, we have indicated our willingness to give communities the ability to respond with great flexibility to the problems caused by suburban expansion.

New and exciting techniques are available to the local governing bodies of this Commonwealth for dealing with the problems of population growth. Neither

Concord Township nor Easttown Township nor any other local governing unit may retreat behind a cover of exclusive zoning. We fully realize that the overall solution to these problems lies with greater regional planning; but until the time comes that we have such a system we must confront the situation as it is. The power currently resides in the hands of each local governing unit, and we will not tolerate their abusing that power in attempting to zone out growth at the expense of neighboring communities.

Finally, we cannot ignore the fact that in the narrow confines of the case before us, Concord Township's argument that three-acre minimum zoning is necessary for adequate on-site sewage is patently ridiculous. The Township does not argue that on-site sewage is impossible for the lots in question; instead it maintains that if houses are built on lots of one acre, as envisioned by appellee, not on lots of three acres, on-site sewerage will become unfeasible. This argument assumes that all of the lot where the house is not is necessary for waste effluence, which simply is not what happens. The difference in size between a three-acre lot and a one-acre lot is irrelevant to the problem of sewage disposal, absent the construction of a house of an unimaginably enormous magnitude.

Decree affirmed.

CASE REVIEW QUESTIONS

1. What is Concord Township's rationale for large-lot zoning?
2. Why does the court find large-lot zoning unconstitutional?
3. Does the court require municipalities to use a regional approach in its land-use regulating? Why?
4. May large-lot zoning ever be legal in Pennsylvania? If so, under what circumstances?

Regional "Fair Share" Zoning

In the *Kit Mar* case, the Pennsylvania Supreme Court was concerned with the failure to plan for land use regionally. In most areas of the country, land use is regulated at the municipal level, often without the conditions and regulations in surrounding communities being taken into account. This approach causes unnecessary inefficiencies in planning and in development. Adequate provisions within a region for various types of housing, shopping centers, and industrial parks are more apt to be the product of chance than the result of regional planning. Furthermore, existing political boundaries inhibit integrated regional planning by most states and localities.

Concern about the failure to plan land use regionally has been discussed by the courts for a considerable length of time. However, like the Pennsylvania Supreme Court, the courts have generally been reluctant to do anything about it. They tend to believe that creation and implementation of regional planning is the job of the legislature, not the courts. According to this view, the most that the courts can do is strike down individual municipal regulations that violate specific legislative or constitutional provisions.

In 1975, the New Jersey Supreme Court rejected judicial reticence in this area and attacked municipal zoning that discriminated against the financially disadvantaged through the use of large lots and large holding zones. The court did not confine itself to the single offending municipality in the lawsuit; it also established rules for municipal land-use regulation throughout the state. The comprehensive and innovative approach of the New Jersey Supreme Court has inspired a great deal of comment among legal writers and other courts and no small amount of confusion and litigation in New Jersey. As a result, the *Mount Laurel* decision, whatever its shortcomings, is one of the most important of this era.

SOUTHERN BURLINGTON COUNTY N.A.A.C.P. v. TOWNSHIP OF MT. LAUREL
336 A.2d 713 (N.J. 1975)

[The township of Mt. Laurel is on the edge of the urban sprawl from the Philadelphia, Pennsylvania – Camden, New Jersey metropolitan area. Sixty-five percent of the township is vacant or in agricultural use. Approximately 30 percent of Mt. Laurel is zoned industrial; 1 percent is zoned commercial; and 70 percent is zoned for single-family residential use. Of the 4,121 acres zoned industrial, only 100 acres are occupied by industrial development, and it is clear that no where near 4,000 acres will be needed in the foreseeable future. With very few exceptions, the single-family housing available in the town is affordable only to middle- and upper-income buyers.

The South Burlington County N.A.A.C.P., a civil rights organization, brought suit to have the Mt. Laurel zoning ordinance declared illegal for discriminating against poor minorities. The trial judge concluded that Mt. Laurel had acted affirmatively over the years through its zoning code to achieve a selected type of growth. This policy, the court held, constituted economic discrimination against the poor and was illegal under New Jersey law. Mt. Laurel appealed to the New Jersey Supreme Court.]

HALL, [Judge]

There cannot be the slightest doubt that the reason for this course of conduct has been to keep down local taxes on property and that the policy was carried out without regard for non-fiscal considerations with respect to people, either within or without its boundaries.

This conclusion is demonstrated not only by what was done and what happened, as we have related, but also by innumerable direct statements of municipal officials at public meetings over the years which are found in the exhibits.

This policy of land use regulation for a fiscal end derives from New Jersey's tax structure, which has imposed on local real estate most of the cost of municipal and county government and of the primary and secondary education of the municipality's children. The latter expense is much the largest, so, basically, the fewer the school children, the lower the tax rate. Sizeable industrial and commercial ratables are eagerly sought and homes and the lots on which they are situate are required to be large enough, through minimum lot sizes and minimum floor areas, to have substantial value in order to produce greater tax revenues to meet school costs. Large families who cannot afford to buy large houses and must live in cheaper rental accommodations are definitely not wanted, so we find drastic bedroom restrictions for, or complete prohibition of, multifamily or other feasible housing for those of lesser income.

This pattern of land use regulation has been adopted for the same purpose in developing municipality after developing municipality. Almost every one acts solely in its own selfish and parochial interest and in effect builds a wall around itself to keep out those people or entities not adding favorably to the tax base, despite the location of the municipality or the demand for varied kinds of housing. There has been no effective intermunicipal or area planning or land use regulation. One incongruous result is the picture of developing municipalities rendering it impossible for lower paid employees in industries they have eagerly sought and welcomed with open arms (and, in Mount Laurel's case, even some of its own lower paid municipal employees) to live in the community where they work.

The legal question before us is whether a developing municipality like Mount Laurel may validly, by a system of land use regulation, make it physically and economically impossible to provide low and moderate income housing in the municipality for the various categories of persons who need and want it and thereby as Mount Laurel has, exclude such people from living within its confines because of the limited extent of their income and resources. Necessarily implicated are the broader questions of the right of such municipalities to limit the kinds of available housing and of any obligation to make possible a variety and choice of types of living accommodations.

We conclude that every such municipality must, by its land use regulations, presumptively make realistically possible an appropriate variety and choice of housing. More specifically, presumptively it cannot foreclose the opportunity of the classes of people mentioned for low and moderate income housing and in its regulations must affirmatively afford that opportunity, at least to the extent of the municipality's fair share of the present and prospective regional need therefor. These obligations must be met unless the particular municipality can sustain the heavy burden of demonstrating peculiar circumstances, which dictate that it should not be required so to do.

It is plain beyond dispute that proper provision for adequate housing of all categories of people is certainly an absolute essential in promotion of the general welfare required in all local land use regulation. Further, the universal and constant need for such housing is so important and of such broad public interest that the general welfare which developing municipalities like Mount Laurel must consider extends beyond their boundaries and cannot be parochially confined to the claimed good of the particular municipality. It has to follow that, broadly speaking, the presumptive obliga-

tion arises for each such municipality affirmatively to plan and provide, by its land use regulations the reasonable opportunity for an appropriate variety and choice of housing, including of course, low and moderate cost housing, to meet the needs, desires and resources of all categories of people who may desire to live within its boundaries. Negatively, it may not adopt regulations or policies which thwart or preclude that opportunity.

As a developing municipality, Mount Laurel must, by its land use regulations, make realistically possible the opportunity for an appropriate variety and choice of housing for all categories of people who may desire to live there, of course including those of low and moderate income. It must permit multifamily housing, without bedroom or similar restrictions, as well as small dwellings on very small lots, low cost housing of other types and in general, high density zoning, without artificial and unjustifiable minimum requirements as to lot size, building size and the like, to meet the full panoply of these needs. Certainly when a municipality zones for industry and commerce for local tax benefit purposes, it without question must zone to permit adequate housing within the means of the employees involved in such uses. The amount of land removed from residential use by allocation to industrial and commercial purposes must be reasonably related to the present and future potential for such purposes. In other words, such municipalities must zone primarily for the living welfare of people and not for the benefit of the local tax rate.

The composition of the applicable region will necessarily vary from situation to situation and probably no hard and fast rule will serve to furnish the answer in every case. Confinement to or within a certain county appears not to be realistic, but restriction within the boundaries of the state seem practical and advisable. (This is not to say that a developing municipality can ignore a demand for housing within its boundaries on the part of people who commute to work in another state.) Here we have already defined the region at present as "those portions of Camden, Burlington and Gloucester Counties within a semicircle having a radius of 20 miles or so from the heart of Camden City." The concept of "fair share" is coming into more general use and, through the expertise of the municipal planning adviser, the county planning boards and the state planning agency, a reasonable figure for Mount Laurel can be determined, which can then be trans-lated to the allocation of sufficient land therefor on the zoning map.

The judgment of the Law Division is modified as set forth herein.

CASE REVIEW QUESTIONS

1. What difficulties do you foresee for municipalities that try to apply the *Mt. Laurel* decision in their communities?
2. Under what circumstances can a community legally not provide for its fair share of low and moderate income housing?

Timed-Growth Schemes

Some communities have attacked the problems of urban sprawl by adopting comprehensive timed-growth regulations. These controls dictate when and where growth will take place, and their implementation can take such forms as limiting the number of houses that can be built each year, placing a cap on population in the community, or timing growth so that it is compatible with the municipality's ability to provide adequate community services. The impact of a **timed-growth scheme** is to limit growth. The avowed purpose of this type of regulation is to avoid development when and where the community is unable to provide adequate services.

Some restrictions on growth may be only temporary, as when only a limited number of housing starts are allowed each year. Theoretically, the same total amount of growth is simply being spread out over a longer period of time. On the other hand, when the scheme takes the form of a population cap—for example, an ordinance that allows no more than 30,000 housing units to be built within a city—the limitation is permanent.

The courts that have reviewed timed-growth schemes have generally reacted positively. For example, in the developing community of Petaluma, California, a court approved a plan that limited housing starts to 500 units per year, which was considerably under existing demand. In a case involving the Florida community of Boca Raton, a court rejected a population cap of 40,000 residential units. However, the court clearly stated that the problem was not with the notion of a population cap; rather, it was that the community had offered no reasonable basis for selecting the number 40,000.

In a third case originating in Ramapo, New York, the state's highest court approved a complex scheme that limited growth to those sections of the community that were provided with adequate public services—that is, sewers, drainage facilities, public parks and schools, roads, and firehouses. The scheme was upheld despite the fact that public services would not be provided for some sections of the community for up to 18 years, which thereby limited the development of those sections for that period of time. The court expressed some concern about limiting growth in this fashion, but it noted that municipalities must be free to devise reasonable methods for controlling the negative impact of rapid growth.

The courts have expressed several common concerns in timed-growth cases. Basically, they have indicated that a successful timed-growth scheme should include the following:

1. Evidence that the community leaders are dealing with and not avoiding the problems of large scale growth. The evidence looked for is that substantial study and planning precede the regulations.
2. Provisions for low- and moderate-income housing.
3. A safety valve provision that permits small-scale, unobtrusive development over and above the scheme's limitations. For instance, an individual should be allowed to build a house on his or her lot even when it would exceed a scheme's 500 units per year housing-start limit.

Timed-growth schemes have been sharply criticized by some land-use experts. They object to the fact that, even though zoning is provided for low- and moderate-income housing, as a practical matter very little of it actually gets built. This is due, in part, to the fact that timed-growth schemes tend to escalate land values, thereby making the development of less expensive housing uneconomical. As a result, the burden of constructing low- and moderate-income housing unfairly falls on neighboring municipalities where land values have not escalated.

REGULATION OF SPECIAL ENVIRONMENTS

Recognition of the fact that land is a valuable natural resource as well as a commodity for barter is a recent development in the United States. As certain types of lands have become in short supply, an awareness has arisen that the value of land as a commodity may sometimes be outweighed by its value as a natural resource. Under some conditions, wetlands, floodplains, agricultural lands, forests, and historic buildings have more social value if they are preserved than if they are developed or destroyed.

Although some regulation of special environments has existed for many years, it was not until the 1970s that such regulations were widely adopted. The remainder of the chapter will discuss some of these special environments and the typical regulations devised to protect them. The concept of special environments is an expanding one that will continue to increase as certain types of land are further diminished and as the awareness of the importance of special environments permeates society.

Wetlands

Wetlands are lands that have groundwater levels at or near the surface for a substantial part of the year or that are vegetated by aquatic plants. Wetlands have traditionally been viewed as wastelands without much social utility and as breeding areas for mosquitos and other pests. The general attitude has been that the best thing that can happen to a wetland is for someone to fill it, thereby turning it into a useful commodity.

Whether tree-filled swamps or grassy marshlands, wetlands have an improved public image of late. Wetlands have come to be recognized as important flood-control areas because they retain storm water and return it slowly, safely, and inexpensively to the ground water supply and the air. Hunters, trappers, fishermen, bird-watchers, and other "nature lovers" have found that wetlands are crucial breeding and resting areas for wildlife. In addition, these areas can provide fruitful study areas for scientists and their students. In short, wetlands have been discovered to be important natural resources.

Despite the realization by many of their significance, wetlands continue to be destroyed at the rate of about 400,000 acres annually. Governments have responded by attempting to limit this destruction through a variety of methods. Some localities have used zoning to limit the uses of wetlands to those that are consistent with maintaining them. However, the predominant form of regulation has been permitting. States such as Connecticut, Florida, Massachusetts, New Jersey, New York, and Wisconsin have adopted permitting statutes. In addition, the Clean Water Act of 1972 includes a federal permit system for wetlands. It requires that dredging and filling activities must be authorized by a permit issued by the Corps of Engineers.

Some of the early attempts at regulating development in wetlands, and a few of the later ones, have been declared illegal by the courts. These courts have held that limited-use zoning and restrictive permitting regulations for wetland areas constitutes an unconstitutional taking of all reasonable use of the land. However, in most of the recent cases, the courts have held that the concept of reasonable use must be related to the type of land involved and to currently recognized social needs. The following case is one that acknowledges the fact that an owner's expectation of developing a wetland may be unreasonable.

JUST v. MARINETTE COUNTY
201 N.W.2d 769 (Wis. 1973)

[The Wisconsin legislature adopted a law designed to protect the state's navigable waters and shorelands from uncontrolled development. Under the law, the Department of Natural Resources set up standards and criteria to guide counties in creating their own ordinances to effect this protection. If a county failed to pass such an ordinance, one would be imposed by the Department of Natural Resources.

Marinette County's shorelands zoning ordinance designated a "conservancy district" that included all the swamps and marshes in the county. Anyone seeking to dredge or fill in these areas was required to get a permit from the county. Prior to passage of the ordinance, Ronald and Kathryn Just purchased 36.4 acres of swamp and marshland along the shore of a navigable lake. The Justs began to fill the land without obtaining a permit.

When ordered by county officials to discontinue the

filling activities, the Justs brought a legal action against the county seeking to have the ordinance declared unconstitutional. The trial court entered a judgment for the county, and the Justs appealed to the Wisconsin Supreme Court.]

HALLOWS, [Judge]

The real issue is whether the conservancy district provisions and the wetlands-filling restrictions are unconstitutional because they amount to a constructive taking of the Justs' land without compensation. Marinette County and the state of Wisconsin argue the restrictions of the conservancy district and wetlands provisions constitute a proper exercise of the police power of the state and do not so severely limit the use or depreciate the value of the land as to constitute a taking without compensation.

To state the issue in more meaningful terms, it is a conflict between the public interest in stopping the despoilation of natural resources, which our citizens until recently have taken as inevitable and for granted, and an owner's asserted right to use his property as he wishes. The protection of public rights may be accomplished by the exercise of the police power unless the damage to the property owner is too great and amounts to a confiscation. The securing or taking of a benefit not presently enjoyed by the public for its use is obtained by the government through its power of eminent domain. The distinction between the exercise of the police power and condemnation has been said to be a matter of degree of damage to the property owner. In the valid exercise of the police power reasonably restricting the use of property, the damage suffered by the owner is said to be incidental. However, where the restriction is so great the landowner ought not to bear such a burden for the public good, the restriction has been held to be a constructive taking even though the actual use or forbidden use has not been transferred to the government so as to be a taking in the traditional sense. Whether a taking has occurred depends upon whether "the restriction practically or substantially renders the land useless for all reasonable purposes." The loss caused the individual must be weighted to determine if it is more than he should bear.

Many years ago, Professor Freund stated in his work on The Police Power, "It may be said that the state takes property by eminent domain because it is useful to the public, and under the police power because it is harmful. . . . From this results the difference between the power of eminent domain and the police power, that the former recognizes a right to compensation, while the latter on principle does not." Thus the necessity for monetary compensation for loss suffered to an owner by police power restriction arises when restrictions are placed on property in order to create a public benefit rather than to prevent a public harm.

This case causes us to re-examine the concepts of public benefit in contrast to public harm and the scope of an owner's right to the use of his property. In the instant case we have a restriction on the use of a citizens' property, not to secure a benefit for the public, but to prevent a harm from the change in the natural character of the citizens' property. We start with the premise that lakes and rivers in their natural state are unpolluted and the pollution which now exists is man made. The state of Wisconsin has a duty to eradicate the present pollution and to prevent further pollution in its navigable waters. This is not, in a legal sense, a gain or a securing of a benefit by the maintaining of the natural status quo of the environment. What makes this case different from most condemnation or police power zoning cases is the interrelationship of the wetlands, the swamps and the natural environment of shorelands to the purity of the water and to such natural resources as navigation, fishing, and scenic beauty. Swamps and wetlands were once considered wasteland, undesirable, and not picturesque. But as the people became more sophisticated, an appreciation was acquired that swamps and wetlands serve a vital role in nature, are part of the balance of nature and are essential to the purity of the water in our lakes and streams. Swamps and wetlands are a necessary part of the ecological creation and now, even to the uninitiated, possess their own beauty in nature.

Is the ownership of a parcel of land so absolute that man can change its nature to suit any of his purposes? The great forests of our state were stripped on the theory man's ownership was unlimited. But in forestry, the land at least was used naturally, only the natural fruit of the land (the trees) were taken. The despoilage was in the failure to look to the future and provide for the reforestation of the land. An owner of land has no absolute and unlimited right to change the essential natural character of his land so as (1) to use it for a purpose for which it was unsuited in its natural state and (2) which injures the rights of others. The exercise of the police power in zoning must be reasonable and we think it is not an unreasonable exercise of that power to prevent harm to public rights by limiting the use of private property to its natural uses.

This is not a case where an owner is prevented from using his land for natural and indigenous uses. The uses consistent with the nature of the land are allowed and other uses recognized and still others permitted by special permit. The shoreland zoning ordinance prevents to some extent the changing of the natural character of the land within 1,000 feet of a navigable river because of such land's interrelation to the contiguous water. The changing of wetlands and swamps to the damage of the general public by upsetting the natural environment and the natural relationship is not a reasonable use of that land which is protected from police power regulation . . . but nothing this court has said or held in prior cases indicates the destroying the natural character of a swamp or a wetland so as to make that location available for human habitation is a reasonable use of that land when the new use, although of a more economical value to the owner, causes a harm to the general public.

Wisconsin has long held that laws and regulations to prevent pollution and to protect the waters of this state from degradation are valid police-power enactments. The duty of the state of Wisconsin in respect to navigable waters requires the state not only to promote navigation but also to protect and preserve those waters for fishing, recreation, and scenic beauty.

The Justs rely on several cases from other jurisdictions which have held zoning regulations involving flood plain districts, flood basins and wetlands to be so confiscatory as to amount to a taking because the owners of the land were prevented from improving such property for residential or commercial purposes. While some of these cases may be distinguished on their facts, it is doubtful whether these differences go to the basic rationale which permeates the decision that an owner has a right to use his property in any way and for any purpose he sees fit.

It seems to us that filling a swamp not otherwise commercially usable is not in and of itself an existing use, which is prevented, but rather is the preparation for some future use which is not indigenous to a swamp. Too much stress is laid on the right of an owner to change commercially valueless land when that change does damage to the rights of the public.

The Justs argue their property has been severely depreciated in value. But this depreciation of value is not based on the use of the land in its natural state but on what the land would be worth if it could be filled and used for the location of a dwelling. While loss of value is to be considered in determining whether a restriction is a constructive taking, value based upon changing the character of the land at the expense of harm to public rights is not an essential factor or controlling.

We are not unmindful of the warning in *Pennsylvania Coal Co. v. Mahon* (1922), ''. . . We are in danger of forgetting that a strong public desire to improve the public condition is not enough to warrant achieving the desire by a shorter cut than the constitutional way of paying for the change.'' This observation refers to the improvement of the public condition, the securing of a benefit not presently enjoyed and to which the public is not entitled. The shoreland zoning ordinance preserves nature, the environment, and natural resources as they were created and to which the people have a present right. The ordinance does not create or improve the public condition but only preserves nature from the despoilage and harm resulting from the unrestricted activities of humans.

Affirmed.

CASE REVIEW QUESTIONS

1. In assessing the validity of the regulation, the court used a rule that drew a distinction between laws that confer a public benefit and ones that prevent a public harm. Do you see any difficulty in using this rule? Explain.

2. The Justs did not apply for a permit. If they had applied and had been denied a permit to fill the land, would the result of this case have been different? Explain.

Floodplains

Floodplains are lands near waterways that are prone to flooding. Because waterways provide a means of transportation, a source of food, and a pleasant living environment, people have tended to settle near them. Waterways are naturally apt to flood adjacent lands periodically. This propensity is worsened by the activities of people living on the flood-prone lands. For example, trees and other vegetation that absorb water may be removed, and water permeable surfaces may be covered with impermeable ones. The result is extensive flooding.

Removing people from floodplains is not practical because it is too costly. Therefore, the main thrust of current land-use regulations is to prohibit a worsening of the problem. Some communities have used zoning to minimize future floodplain development. As with wetlands zoning, the legality of floodplain zoning depends upon a court's interpretation of "reasonable use."

The chief regulatory device for floodplain protection emanates from the federal government. The National Flood Insurance Program (1968) and succeeding legislation and amendments have encouraged floodplain management. For instance, flood insurance can only be obtained in communities that have adopted land-use regulations protecting the floodplain. Moreover, banks and other financial institutions are prohibited from lending money for construction on floodplains, or flood hazard areas as they are now called. In addition, communities cannot permit any development in more restricted areas called floodways.

It is anticipated that these measures will eventually reduce the social costs related to floods. Specifically, people unaware of the dangers of the floodplain will be discouraged from moving onto it, people already on the floodplain will not have their flood prone situation worsened by additional development, and the general public will pay less in flood disaster relief.

Historic Preservation

Historic building and sites have a present and future role to play in our culture, so historic preservation regulations have been developed to protect them. Where an entire area is of historical significance — Williamsburg, Virginia, for example — zoning is an appropriate tool to accomplish protection. However, where historic or landmark buildings are interspersed with other buildings, zoning is less useful. Adding to the problems in this area is the fact that the economic burden of preservation and upkeep falls solely on the owner of a landmark building.

An alternative approach to zoning that has been adopted by some communities to protect landmarks is the use of transferable development rights (TDRs).

A simplified version of a TDR scheme is as follows: The community designates two distinct zones—a transfer zone and a preservation zone. *Each zone* is assigned a number of TDRs on some basis, for example, two per acre. The number of TDRs assigned in the transfer zone is less than the number needed to develop the land to the maximum allowed under the zoning code. For instance, if the land in the transfer zone is zoned for residential development that allows four houses per acre, it may be assigned two TDRs per acre, which will allow the construction of only two houses per acre. In order to fully develop the land, the owner must purchase two additional TDRs. The preservation zone is zoned for nondevelopment, and the owner cannot use the TDRs assigned to his or her land. The owner can, however, sell the TDRs to a landowner in the transfer zone and thereby recover some economic value for the land despite his or her inability to develop it.

TDR arrangements can be devised to protect landmarks, agricultural lands, wetlands, open space, or any other type of special environment. New York City's Landmark Preservation Law, which includes a TDR scheme, is the subject of the case that follows. In deciding this case, the U.S. Supreme Court had the opportunity to rule on the legality of this relatively new concept.

PENN CENTRAL TRANSPORTATION COMPANY v. NEW YORK CITY
438 U.S. 104 (U.S.S.C. 1978)

[In 1965, New York City adopted the Landmark Preservation Law. The law created a commission that was to establish criteria for identifying landmarks and then designate specific buildings that met the criteria as landmarks. Designation of a building as a landmark requires the owner to keep the exterior in good repair and to obtain the commission's approval prior to altering the exterior architectural features of the building. However, an owner of a landmark building may seek a permit to change the building's appearance. In addition, the owners of parcels not developed to the fullest extent legally permissible can sell TDRs to the owners of contiguous parcels on the same city block.

Penn Central, the owner of Grand Central Terminal, a designated landmark, applied to the Landmark Commission for a permit to add more than 50 stories of offices atop the existing terminal. The commission denied the application. Penn Central sued in a New York State court to have the Landmark Preservation Law declared an unconstitutional taking as it applied to the terminal and for damages for the "temporary taking"

that resulted from the commission's denial of the application.

The trial court found for Penn Central, the plaintiff. An intermediate appellate court reversed the decision, and the reversal was affirmed by New York's highest court. Penn Central then appealed to the U.S. Supreme Court.]

BRENNAN, Justice

The issues presented by appellants are (1) whether the restrictions imposed by New York City's law upon appellants' exploitation of the Terminal site effect a "taking" of appellants' property for a public use within the meaning of the Fifth Amendment, which of course is made applicable to the States through the Fourteenth Amendment, and, (2) if so, whether the transferable development rights afforded appellants constitute "just compensation" within the meaning of the Fifth Amendment. We need only address the question whether a "taking" has occurred.

In contending that the New York City law has

"taken" their property in violation of the Fifth and Fourteenth Amendments, appellants make a series of arguments, which while tailored to the facts of this case, essentially urge that any substantial restriction imposed pursuant to a landmark law must be accompanied by just compensation if it is to be constitutional.

They first observe that the air space above the Terminal is a valuable property interest. They urge that the Landmark Law has deprived them of any gainful use of their "air rights" above the Terminal and that, irrespective of the value of the remainder of their parcel, the city has "taken" their right to this superadjacent air space, thus entitling them to "just compensation" measured by the fair market value of these air rights.

Apart from our own disagreement with appellants' characterization of the effect of the New York law, the submission that appellants may establish a "taking" simply by showing that they have been denied the ability to exploit a property interest that they heretofore had believed was available for development is quite simply untenable. "Taking" jurisprudence does not divide a single parcel into discrete segments and attempt to determine whether rights in a particular segment have been entirely abrogated. In deciding whether a particular governmental action has effected a taking, this Court focuses rather both on the character of the action and on the nature and extent of the interference with rights in the parcel as a whole, here, the city tax block designated as the "landmark site."

Secondly, appellants, focusing on the character and impact of the New York City law, argue that it effects a "taking" because its operation has significantly diminished the value of the Terminal site. Appellants concede that the decisions sustaining other land use regulations, which, like the New York law, are reasonably related to the promotion of the general welfare, uniformly reject the proposition that diminution in property value, standing alone, can establish a taking, but appellants argue that New York City's regulation of individual landmarks is fundamentally different from zoning or from historic district legislation because the controls imposed by New York City's law apply only to individuals who own selected properties.

Stated baldly, appellants' position appears to be that the only means of ensuring that selected owners are not singled out to endure financial hardship for no reason is to hold that any restriction imposed on individual landmarks pursuant to the New York scheme is a "taking" requiring the payment of "just compensation." Agreement with this argument would of course invalidate not just New York City's law, but all comparable landmark legislation in the Nation. We find no merit in it.

It is true, as appellants emphasize, that both historic district legislation and zoning laws regulate all properties within given physical communities whereas landmark laws apply only to selected parcels. But, contrary to appellants' suggestions, landmark laws are not like discriminatory, or "reverse spot," zoning: that is, a land use decision which arbitrarily singles out a particular parcel for different, less favorable treatment than the neighboring ones. In contrast to discriminatory zoning, which is the antithesis of land use control as part of some comprehensive plan, the New York City law embodies a comprehensive plan to preserve structures of historic or aesthetic interest wherever they might be found in the city, and as noted, over 400 landmarks and 31 historic districts have been designated pursuant to this plan.

Next, appellants observe that New York City's law differs from zoning laws and historic district ordinances in that the Landmark Law does not impose identical or similar restrictions on all structures located in particular physical communities. Legislation designed to promote the general welfare commonly burdens some more than others.

In any event, appellants' repeated suggestions that they are solely burdened and unbenefited is factually inaccurate. This contention overlooks the fact that the New York City law applies to vast numbers of structures in the city in addition to the Terminal—all the structures contained in the 31 historic districts and over 400 individual landmarks, many of which are close to the Terminal. Unless we are to reject the judgment of the New York City Council that the preservation of landmarks benefits all New York citizens and all structures, both economically and by improving the quality of life in the city as a whole—which we are unwilling to do—we cannot conclude that the owners of the Terminal have in no sense been benefited by the Landmark Law.

Rejection of appellants' broad arguments is not

however the end of our inquiry, for all we thus far have established is that the New York law is not rendered invalid by its failure to provide "just compensation" whenever a landmark owner is restricted in the exploitation of property interests, such as air rights, to a greater extent than provided for under applicable zoning laws. We now must consider whether the interference with appellants' property is of such a magnitude that "there must be an exercise of eminent domain and compensation to sustain [it]." That inquiry may be narrowed to the question of the severity of the impact of the law on appellants' parcel, and its resolution in turn requires a careful assessment of the impact of the regulation on the Terminal site.

[T]he New York City law does not interfere in any way with the present uses of the Terminal. Its designation as a landmark not only permits but contemplates that appellants may continue to use the property precisely as it has for the past 65 years: as a railroad terminal containing office space and concessions. So the law does not interfere with what must be regarded as Penn Central's primary expectation concerning the use of the parcel. More importantly, on this record, we must regard the New York City law as permitting Penn Central not only to profit from the Terminal but to obtain a "reasonable return" on its investment.

Appellants, moreover, exaggerate the effect of the Act on its ability to make use of the air rights above the Terminal in two respects. First, it simply cannot be maintained, on this record, that appellants have been prohibited from occupying any portion of the airspace above the Terminal. While the Commission's actions in denying applications to construct an office building in excess of 50 stories above the Terminal may indicate that it will refuse to issue a certificate of appropriateness for any comparably sized structure, nothing the Commission has said or done suggests an intention to prohibit any construction above the Terminal.

Second, to the extent appellants have been denied the right to build above the Terminal, it is not literally accurate to say that they have been denied all use of even those preexisting air rights. Their ability to use these rights has not been abrogated; they are made transferable to at least eight parcels in the vicinity of the Terminal, one or two of which have been found suitable for the construction of new office buildings. Although appellants and others have argued that New York City's transferable development rights program is far from ideal, the New York courts here supportably found that, at least in the case of the Terminal, the rights afforded are valuable. While these rights may well not have constituted "just compensation" if a "taking" had occurred, the rights nevertheless undoubtedly mitigate whatever financial burdens the law has imposed on appellants and, for that reason, are to be taken into account in considering the impact of regulation.

The restrictions imposed are substantially related to the promotion of the general welfare and not only permit reasonable beneficial use of the landmark site but afford appellants opportunities further to enhance not only the Terminal site proper but also other properties.

Affirmed.

CASE REVIEW QUESTIONS

1. Is it safe to say that New York City's Landmark Preservation Law is constitutional with respect to all designated landmarks so long as appropriate procedures are followed? Explain.
2. Do TDRs constitute "just compensation" sufficient to satisfy the Fifth Amendment? Explain.
3. Some people have stated that the U.S. Supreme Court upheld the legality of "transferable development rights" in the *Penn Central* case. Discuss the accuracy of this statement.

Open Space

The retention of open space within developed areas has long been recognized as beneficial to a community. Environmentally sensitive people have argued that the maintenance of open-space areas is necessary to sustain the ecological balance, to maximize public well-being, and to preserve esthetically pleasing living places. Others have argued more pragmatically that the retention of open space increases property values and reduces the cost of community services. Indeed, studies have shown that the old assertion that land left undeveloped reduces tax revenues is only half true. When land is developed, gross tax revenues are increased, but net tax revenues (revenues minus the cost of public services for the additional development) are very often decreased.

Certain specific open-space areas have greater natural resource value than real estate commodity value. A virgin forest, a cattail marsh, a cypress swamp, or a woodland with numerous species of wildflowers may be extremely valuable to the local community or even to the nation. Development of such an area into a housing subdivision or a shopping center would have a negative impact on a community's social well-being.

Some areas need to be protected from development entirely. Generally, however, open-space areas can be preserved within the context of a development plan. For instance, a residential subdivision can be planned around open space for recreational use, and beautiful vistas can be retained if development is sufficiently unobtrusive. Similarly, the quality of a lake's water can be maintained despite development through provisions for adequate sewage treatment and through setback provisions.

Communities have devised an array of techniques for protecting open space. They have used limited-density zoning, permits, conservation and scenic easements, and outright acquisition to retain open space. One technique that has been broadly adopted is subdivision exactions. Here, a municipality provides in its regulations that approval of a proposed subdivision is contingent upon the developer dedicating a certain percentage of the land to the town for park or other open-space purposes. Alternatively, the municipality may require a cash payment in lieu of land. If the municipality does not want a park within a particular subdivider's development, the cash payment can be used to purchase land for parks in more appropriate locations.

Subdivision exactions are justified on the basis that a park or open-space area is necessary to satisfy the needs of the people who will buy the subdivider's houses. So long as there is a need for a park or open-space area for the subdivision and the amount of land or money required is reasonable, most courts will approve subdivision exactions.

The U.S. Supreme Court has encouraged municipalities to experiment with techniques for protecting open space. The court's flexibility is illustrated by its approval of the limited-density zoning used by the city of Tiburon, California, in the following case.

AGINS v. CITY OF TIBURON
447 U.S. 255 (U.S.S.C. 1980)

[Agins purchased five acres of unimproved land in the city of Tiburon for the purpose of residential development. Subsequently, the state ordered all cities to prepare plans governing land use and the development of open-space land. Pursuant to this order, the city modified its zoning ordinance. The new ordinance placed Agins' land in a restricted Residential Planned Development and Open Space Zone (RPD-1). Property in the RPD-1 zone could be used for single-family residential and open-space use. In addition, housing density was limited to one to five dwellings per five acre parcel.

Agins did not submit a development plan. Instead, it sued the city, requesting that the court declare the ordinance unconstitutional and asking that it be awarded $2 million in damages for inverse condemnation. A claim based on inverse condemnation contends that the plaintiff's property has de facto been taken without the payment of just compensation. Agins alleged that the land in question had had the highest market value of all lands in Tiburon because it provided a magnificent view of San Francisco Bay but that its value had been "completely destroyed" by the rezoning. The city claimed that the complaint failed to state a cause of action. The trial court found for the city and the state Supreme Court affirmed. Agins appealed to the U.S. Supreme Court.]

POWELL, Justice

The Fifth Amendment guarantees that private property shall not "be taken for public use, without just compensation." The appellants' complaint framed the question as whether a zoning ordinance that prohibits all development of their land effects a taking under the Fifth and Fourteenth Amendments. The California Supreme Court rejected the appellants' characterization of the issue by holding as a matter of state law, that the terms of the challenged ordinances allow the appel-

lants to construct between one and five residences on their property. The court did not consider whether the zoning ordinances would be unconstitutional if applied to prevent appellants from building five homes. Because the appellants have not submitted a plan for development of their property as the ordinances permit, there is as yet no concrete controversy regarding the application of the specific zoning provisions. Thus, the only question properly before us is whether the mere enactment of the zoning ordinances constitutes a taking.

The application of a general zoning law to particular property effects a taking if the ordinance does not substantially advance legitimate state interests, or denies an owner economically viable use of his land. The determination that governmental action constitutes a taking is, in essence, a determination that the public at large, rather than a single owner, must bear the burden of an exercise of state power in the public interest. Although no precise rule determines when property has been taken, the question necessarily requires a weighing of private and public interests. The seminal decision in *Euclid v. Ambler Co.* is illustrative. In that case, the landowner challenged the constitutionality of a municipal ordinance that restricted commercial development of his property. Despite alleged diminution in value of the owner's land, the Court held that the zoning laws were facially constitutional. They bore a substantial relationship to the public welfare, and their enactment inflicted no irreparable injury upon the landowner.

In this case, the zoning ordinances substantially advance legitimate governmental goals. The State of California has determined that the development of local open-space plans will discourage the "premature and unnecessary conversion of open-space land to urban uses." The specific zoning regulations at issue are exercises of the city's police power to protect the residents of Tiburon from the ill effects of urbanization. Such governmental purposes long have been recognized as legitimate.

The ordinances place appellants' land in a zone limited to single-family dwellings, accessory buildings, and open-space uses. Construction is not permitted until the builder submits a plan compatible with "adjoining patterns of development and open space." In passing upon a plan, the city also will consider how well the proposed development would preserve the surrounding environment and whether the density of new construction will be offset by adjoining open spaces. The zoning ordinances benefit the appellants as well as the public by serving the city's interest in assuring careful and orderly development of residential property with provision for open-space areas. There is no indication that the appellants' 5-acre tract is the only property affected by the ordinances. Appellants therefore will share with other owners the benefits and burdens of the city's exercise of its police power. In assessing the fairness of the zoning ordinances, these benefits must be considered along with any diminution in market value that the appellants might suffer.

Although the ordinances limit development, they neither prevent the best use of appellants' land, nor extinguish a fundamental attribute of ownership. The appellants have alleged that they wish to develop the land for residential purposes, that the land is the most expensive suburban property in the State, and that the best possible use of the land is residential. The California Supreme Court has decided, as a matter of state law, that appellants may be permitted to build as many as five houses on their five acres of prime residential property. At this juncture, the appellants are free to pursue their reasonable investment expectations by submitting a development plan to local officials. Thus, it cannot be said that the impact of general land-use regulations has denied appellants the "justice and fairness" guaranteed by the Fifth and Fourteenth Amendments.

Affirmed.

CASE REVIEW QUESTIONS

1. What is the city's justification for severely limiting development on the land of Agins and other area owners?
2. What specific things would Agins have to prove in order to have the court declare the amended zoning ordinance unconstitutional?

REVIEW QUESTIONS

1. In states like Pennsylvania that make large-lot zoning presumptively illegal, are developers prohibited from utilizing large lots to satisfy wealthy customers? Explain.
2. Courts have long recognized the need for regional planning. Why have they been so reluctant to require communities to do it?
3. What is the basic difference in terms of impact between adopting a timed-growth scheme and establishing a population cap?
4. At a recent town meeting, there was a discussion of the pros and cons of adopting a floodplain zoning ordinance. A man in the back of the meeting room

rose and quoted this passage from *A Sand County Almanac* by Aldo Leopold:

> I once knew an educated lady, lauded by Phi Beta Kappa, who told me that she had never heard or seen the geese that twice a year proclaim the revolving seasons to her well-insulated roof. Is education possibly a process of trading awareness for things of lesser worth? The goose who trades his is soon a pile of feathers.

What does this quote have to do with floodplain zoning?

CASE PROBLEMS

1. Salamar Builders purchased 70 acres of land for residential development. The existing zoning allowed one house per acre. Before Salamar could get its subdivision plan approved, the town changed the zoning to require one and a half acres per house. Salamar sued the town, seeking to have the rezoning declared unconstitutional. The town justified the change on the basis that topography, soil conditions, and drainage difficulties made the larger lots necessary. Salamar argued that there was no public welfare justification for the rezoning. Who will win the case? Explain.

2. The town of Raymond attempted to limit growth by adopting an ordinance that prohibited the issuance of more than four building permits per year to any one party. Beck, a developer, applied for a fifth permit and was refused because of the ordinance. Beck sued the town, challenging the legality of the ordinance as unconstitutionally limiting the natural growth of the area. Who will win the case? Explain.

3. Washington Township in New Jersey is a "bedroom community" of single-family residences. The township is fully developed. A civil rights group sued the township to have a court require it to provide space for apartment houses for low- and moderate-income families. Using the Mt. Laurel case as a guide, what might a representative of the township argue?

4. The town of Clay needs a regional park. Grimaldi Builders proposed to subdivide a 200-acre parcel of land that included the 30 acres the town had in mind for its regional park. The town agreed to approve the subdivision provided that Grimaldi dedicate the 30 acres for parkland. Grimaldi refused and the town denied approval of the subdivision. Grimaldi brought a legal action against the town, contending that 30 acres was more land than was necessary to meet the needs of people in his subdivision. Who will win the case? Explain.

5. The town of Hastings has recently adopted a zoning code in which they have designated the northern half of the community A-1 for agricultural use. The town's justification for the zoning is that the area is prime agricultural land, it is predominantly in agricultural use at the present time, and the farm products produced on the land are required to supply the needs of the city of Sparta to the south of Hastings. Dustin, a nonfarming landowner in the northern portion of the town, has sued the town, claiming that the zoning ordinance is an unconstitutional taking of her land without just compensation. Dustin argues that the agricultural designation denies her "a reasonable return on her investment-backed expectations." Who will win the case? Explain.

GLOSSARY

ab initio From the beginning.

abandoned property Property in which the owner has intentionally surrendered his or her interests.

abstention The act dismissing a debtor's petition in a bankruptcy proceeding when a judge determines that the best interest of the debtor or creditors is served by a dismissal.

acceleration The advancement of time for performance in a contract or a negotiable instrument upon the occurrence of a stated event.

acceptance In contract law, the meeting of an offeror's demand by an offeree; in sales law, the act that can only occur after an inspection of the goods by which a buyer becomes obligated to pay the price for the goods; in negotiable instruments law, the act by which the person on whom a draft is drawn promises by signing the draft to pay the draft when it becomes due.

acceptor A person who accepts a negotiable instrument.

accession An increase in the value of personal property through the use of labor or materials.

accommodation party A person who signs a negotiable instrument, without receiving any consideration, for the purpose of benefitting or accommodating another party to the instrument.

account In the law of secured transactions, a right to receive payment for the sale of goods or services that is not evidenced by chattel paper or a negotiable instrument.

accounting See *formal account.*

acknowledgment A written declaration made before a public official, usually a notary public, assuring that a document is genuine and has been executed voluntarily.

act of God Any injury or damage that happens by the direct and exclusive operation of natural forces in the absence of human intervention and that could not have been prevented or escaped from through any reasonable degree of care.

action for waste A legal action that may be brought by a fee simple owner against a life tenant who has used the owner's land in such a way as to reduce permanently its market value.

actual authority Authority that a principal either expressly confers on an agent or allows the agent reasonably to believe he or she possesses.

adaptation The use of an item in a way particularly suited to the real property on which the item is used so that the item becomes a fixture.

ademption A failure of a specific devise or bequest because the property devised or bequeathed is not owned by the deceased at the time of his or her death.

adequate assurance An act that gives sufficient certainty that a performance promised under a sales contract will occur.

administrative law judge An administrative agency's staff examiner who, after a hearing, decides whether or not to uphold a complaint against an alleged violator of the agency's rules.

Administrative Procedure Act A federal law setting procedural requirements for federal administrative agency action.

administrator A man appointed by a court to administer the estate of a person who has died without leaving a valid will.

administratrix A woman appointed by a court to administer the estate of a person who has died without leaving a valid will.

adversary process The procedure by which the parties to a lawsuit are allowed to present their view of the case to a passive and neutral court.

adverse possession Wrongful possession of another's land that is actual, exclusive, continuous, open and notorious, and hostile and adverse that leads in time to the ownership of the land by the wrongful possessor.

advisory opinion A decision that will generally not be given by a court because a real conflict does not exist between the parties to the legal action.

after-acquired property In the law of secured transactions, property obtained by a debtor subsequent to the signing of a security agreement that is nevertheless subject to the security agreement.

agency A fiduciary relation that results from the manifestation of consent by one person to another that the other shall act on his or her behalf and subject to his or her control and consent by the other party so to act.

agency coupled with an interest An agency relationship in which the authority of the agent cannot be revoked by the principal because it was created to benefit the agent by securing the performance of a duty owed to the agent by the principal.

agent The person who acts for another in an agency relationship.

aggrieved party The party to a contract who has been wronged.

aleatory contract A contract in which the performance of at least one of the parties is contingent upon the happening of an event that may or may not occur.

allonge A paper attached to a negotiable instrument that provides additional space for indorsements.

ambient standards Standards set to control the quality of the surrounding air or water.

annexation Attachment of an item to land or other realty in such a way that it becomes a fixture.

answer A pleading made by a defendant in response to the plaintiff's complaint.

anticipatory breach An express statement by a party to a contract of his or her intent to breach the contract or circumstances in which an intent to breach can be implied from a party's actions.

apparent authority An agent's power to affect the legal relations of the principal by transactions with a third party that arises from the principal's manifestations to the third party.

appellant A person who brings an appeal from a judgment of a lower court.

appellee A person against whom an appeal is brought from a judgment of a lower court.

appraisal right A right that shareholders who dissent from an extraordinary corporate change sometimes have to have their shares valued and purchased by the corporation that is making the extraordinary change.

appurtenant An easement directly benefitting a nearby parcel of land.

arrangement An agreement between a debtor and creditors for the payment of debts according to a different schedule as to the amounts of the payments and the times that they are due.

arson The intentional damaging of a building by fire or explosion.

articles of incorporation The document that is filed with the secretary of state of the state of incorporation when a corporation is formed; also called *certificate of incorporation* or *corporate charter.*

assault A threat to inflict injury upon another person.

assignee One to whom an assignment is made.

assignment In contract law, a transfer of rights under a contract from the contract promisee to a third party; in real estate law, a transfer by a tenant of all of his or her leasehold interest to a third party.

assignment for the benefit of creditors The transfer of property of a debtor to an assignee for the purpose of liquidating the debtor's property and paying his or her creditors.

assignor One who makes an assignment.

assumption of the risk A defense to negligence that consists of showing that the plaintiff voluntarily exposed himself or herself to a known and appreciated danger.

attachment A legal process by which a creditor acquires a security interest in goods.

authorized shares The number of shares that a corporation is authorized to issue by its articles of incorporation.

bailee The person to whom goods are delivered in a bailment.

bailment A delivery of goods by one person (the bailor) to another (the bailee) under an express or implied contract for the accomplishment of a specific objective involving the goods (e.g., repair) and the subsequent return of the goods to the bailor.

bailor The person who delivers goods to another under a bailment.

banking day A day on which a bank is open to the public for carrying on substantially all of its banking functions.

battery An intentional touching that is not consented to by the person touched.

bearer instrument A negotiable instrument payable to the bearer or indorsed in blank.

beneficiary A person designated to receive a benefit, such as a trust beneficiary, an estate beneficiary, or an insurance beneficiary.

bequest A disposition of personal property in a will.

bilateral contract A contract in which the parties exchange promises.

bill of exchange A draft.

bill of lading A document issued by a carrier that serves as a receipt and as a contract for the carriage of goods.

blank indorsement An indorsement of a negotiable instrument that does not name the person to whom the instrument is transferred.

blue sky laws State securities laws.

bona fide occupational qualification (bfoq) A limited situation in which a certain religion, sex, or national origin is reasonably necessary for the performance of a job.

bond A form of corporate debt financing in which the debt is secured by a mortgage on corporate assets.

borrowed servant A servant who is directed or permitted by the master to perform services for another.

burden of proof A duty owed by a party to a lawsuit to prove the truth of that party's allegations.

burglary Entering or unlawfully remaining in a building with the intent to commit a crime while in the building.

business judgment rule A concept in corporation law providing that a decision made in good faith by a corporate executive will not subject the executive to liability even though the decision was negligently made.

bylaws Rules of governance adopted by a corporation or a similar association.

C&F Cost and freight; a term meaning that the price of goods includes cost of the goods and the cost of freight (transportation) to a named destination.

CIF Cost, insurance, and freight; a term meaning that the price of goods includes cost of the goods, the cost of insurance, and the cost of freight (transportation) to a named destination.

COD Cash on delivery; a sales contract term meaning that goods must be paid for in cash at the time they are delivered.

capacity The legally recognized ability to act; legal competence.

cash surrender value The amount by which the premiums paid on a whole-life or endowment life insurance policy exceed the cost of insurance protection and in which the policyowner has certain rights.

cashier's check A check drawn by a bank on itself and for which the bank is primarily liable.

caveat emptor Buyer beware.

cease and desist order An order from an administrative agency telling a business to stop doing something.

certificate of deposit A negotiable instrument that acknowledges that the person named has deposited a specified sum of money in the issuing bank and that the bank will repay the money to the named individual, or to his or her order, or to some other person named in the instrument as payee.

certificate of incorporation See *articles of incorporation.*

certificate of title A document issued by a state to show who is the owner of a motor vehicle.

certified check A check that has been accepted by the drawee bank.

certiorari See *writ of certiorari.*

challenge for cause A request to a trial court judge by a party to a lawsuit that a juror be dismissed because the juror is biased.

charge The explanation that a judge gives to a jury concerning how the jury is to carry out its tasks.

charging order A court order directing that a partner's profits and surplus be paid to the creditor who has obtained the order.

charitable trust A trust created for a purpose that is beneficial to society.

chattel An article of personal property.

chattel paper A writing that is evidence of a debt and a security interest in specific goods.

check A negotiable instrument that is a draft drawn on a deposit of funds in a bank and that is payable on demand.

chose in action A right to personal property that is not in the owner's possession but to which the owner has a right of action for possession of the property.

claim A demand asserting a right to something.

class action A legal action brought by a member of a group on his or her own behalf and on behalf of all of the members of the group.

clean hands A legal concept that requires that a person seeking an equitable remedy must have acted properly in the transaction involved in the case.

close corporation A corporation that has a small number of shareholders whose shares are not publicly traded and who are subject to restrictions on the transfer of their shares.

closed shop An agreement by which an employer agrees to hire only union members.

codicil An amendment to a will.

co-insurance A property insurance provision that reduces the amount paid to an insured to less than the full amount of a loss if the amount of insurance on the property is less than a specified percentage of the property's full value.

collateral Property that is used as security for the repayment of a debt.

collateral contract A contract whereby one person promises to pay another person's debts.

collecting bank A bank in the bank collection chain that handles an item for the purpose of collecting the money due on it.

collusive suit A legal action in which the parties attempt to concoct a conflict in order to obtain an advisory opinion that a court would normally refuse to provide.

commercial frustration A legal excuse that discharges a promisor from performance of a contract because of the occurrence of an unforeseen event that has caused much greater than anticipated cost of performance; also called *commercial impracticability.*

commercial impracticability See *commercial frustration.*

commercial paper Negotiable instruments.

common carrier A transporter of persons or property for the general public for a price.

common law The body of law initially developed from the case decisions of judges in England that continues to evolve today; distinguished from statutory law.

comparable worth The idea that individuals holding different jobs should receive the same pay when the jobs require equal skill, effort, and training and are of comparable value to the employer.

comparative negligence A defense to negligence in which the plaintiff's damages are reduced by the proportion which his or her fault bears to the total harm suffered by him or her.

compensatory damages A legal remedy by which a court orders one person to pay damages that will compensate another person for the harm suffered by the other person.

competent evidence Evidence that a witness can provide as a result of his or her personal knowledge.

complaint A pleading made by a plaintiff that begins a lawsuit and that contains the basis of the court's jurisdiction, the remedy sought by the plaintiff, and the plaintiff's legal claim.

composition An agreement between a debtor and his or her creditors for the payment of less than the full amount of the debt due either in one payment or over a period of time followed by the discharge of the debtor from any additional obligations to his or her creditors.

comprehensive plan A set of standards formulated to guide the decisions of a zoning administrator.

concurrent conditions Contract performances that are to occur at the same time.

concurring opinion A written decision in which an appellate judge states his or her agreement with the result of a case but in which the judge separately states his or her views concerning the case.

condemnation A government's taking of private land for public use.

condition precedent An event that must occur before certain acts or promises become legally operative.

condition subsequent An event that discharges a duty that has previously arisen.

conditional indorsement An indorsement that depends for its effectiveness upon the happening of an event or the performance of a stated act.

confusion The mingling of similar types of personal property belonging to different owners in such a way that each individual's property cannot be separately identified.

conglomerate merger The merger of firms that do not have any production or supply relationship and that do not compete in the same market.

consent decree A decree entered by the consent of the parties whereby the defendant agrees to cease alleged illegal activities without admitting guilt or legal liability.

consent order See *consent decree.*

consequential damages Damages that do not arise naturally from a breach of contract but that are foreseeable by the party committing the breach; in sales law, damages that result from a seller's breach, including any losses resulting from general or particular requirements that the seller had reason to know would occur in the event of a breach and damages due to injury to persons or property caused by a breach of warranty.

consideration Value that is requested from and given by one party to a contract in exchange for the promise of the other party; payment.

consignment A situation in which a seller (consignor) keeps title to goods but transfers possession to a distributor (consignee) who agrees to resell them.

consolidation A method of combining corporations in which two or more corporations combine and form a new corporation.

constitution A document that sets forth the basic principles of a government, such as the authority of the government, the division of authority within the government, and the rights of the people.

constructive conditions Conditions imposed by law on the parties to a contract that are not dependent on the intent of the parties.

constructive eviction A defense asserted by a tenant in an action for unpaid rent that seeks to establish that the premises have become uninhabitable because of the landlord's failure to keep them repaired.

constructive trust An implied trust imposed by law in order to prevent unjust enrichment.

consumer goods Goods purchased primarily for personal, family, or household purposes.

contempt An act of disrespect toward a court, such as failing to obey an order of the court.

contract of adhesion A contract the terms of which are required by one party and not subject to negotiation by the other party.

contributory negligence Conduct on the part of a plaintiff that falls below the standard of care that the plaintiff must exercise for his or her own protection and that contributes as a legal cause of plaintiff's harm.

conversion The unauthorized assumption of ownership of goods belonging to another.

cooling-off period A period of time during which a consumer purchaser

of goods or services can rescind a contract.

copyright The right granted by statute to the author or originator of a literary or artistic work giving him or her the exclusive privilege of copying and selling the work for a limited period of time.

corporate charter See *articles of incorporation.*

corporation de facto A corporation that has not been formed in substantial compliance with the requirements for incorporation but is nonetheless legally recognized as a corporation except when its existence is challenged by the state.

corporation de jure A corporation that has been formed fully or substantially in compliance with the requirements for incorporation.

corpus In the law of trusts, property that is held in trust.

corrosivity The quality of having the power to corrode or eat away.

counterclaim A legal claim by a defendant that is made in response to the plaintiff's complaint.

counter-offer An offer made by an offeree to the offeror that deals with the same subject matter as the offeror's original offer but demands new terms.

course of dealing Conduct of parties in previous transactions indicating that they have a common understanding concerning the terms of their current sales agreement.

course of performance Conduct by parties after a contract is formed that indicates a particular interpretation of the contract.

covenant not to compete An agreement by an employee or a seller of a business not to enter into the same business as the employer or the buyer of the business.

cover The purchase of substitute goods by an aggrieved buyer.

creditor beneficiary A person who is not a party to a contract but who is intended to receive benefit from the contract as a means of discharging an obligation of the promisee of the contract.

crime A violation of a duty that an individual owes to the community.

cumulative voting A method of voting that is sometimes used at corporate shareholders' meetings in which a shareholder is allowed to multiply the number of shares he or she has by the number of directors to be elected and then to cast the resulting votes for one or more director candidates; the purpose of this voting method is to allow for minority shareholder representation on the board of directors.

cure The right of a seller to correct any errors in the delivery of goods or any defects in the goods themselves.

curtesy A common law life estate given to a husband in his wife's property, commencing upon the wife's death; similar to dower.

de minimus non curat lex The law does not concern itself with trifles; a legal doctrine by which a slight deviation in the performance of a contractual duty is excused.

debenture A form of corporate debt financing in which the debt is unsecured.

debit card A card issued by a bank that allows the holder of the card to debit (withdraw from) his or her account directly through the use of automated tellers or other electronic means.

debtor A person who owes money or other value to another person.

debtor in possession In bankruptcy law, a debtor in a Chapter 11 (reorganization or arrangement) proceeding who continues to operate the business in place of a trustee.

declaratory judgment A judgment given by a court in a case that is not fully ripe but in which a real conflict between adverse parties exists and the risks and costs to the parties if the conflict is allowed to fully ripen are very great.

deed A written instrument through which a grantor (seller) conveys real property to a grantee (buyer).

defamation The unprivileged publication of false statements that results in injury to another.

default A failure to perform.

defendant The person against whom a legal action is brought.

defense A reason or argument for not doing or being responsible for something.

delegate A person to whom a delegation is made.

delegation A transfer of duties under a contract from the contract promisor to a third party.

delegator A person who makes a delegation.

delivery A voluntary transfer of possession.

depositary bank The first bank in the bank collection chain to which an item is transferred for the purpose of collecting the money due on it.

derivative suit A lawsuit in which a corporate shareholder brings the suit not on his or her own behalf but rather on behalf of the corporation.

destination contract A contract requiring a seller to deliver the goods to a specific destination.

devise A disposition of real property in a will.

dicta Those statements of law in a court's written decision that go beyond what is necessary to decide the case.

directed verdict A verdict granted by a judge on the grounds that the jury could reasonably come to only one conclusion on the basis of the evidence presented during the trial.

disaffirmance A legally recognized refusal by a person to be bound by his or her past acts.

discharge An act or an agreement relieving a party from his or her obligations.

disclaimer of warranty A denial of the existence of a promise concerning the nature of goods or of an instrument.

disclosed principal A principal whose identity and existence are known or should be known by a person who transacts business with the principal's agent.

dishonor A refusal to accept or to pay a negotiable instrument.

dissenting opinion A written decision in which an appellate judge explains his or her disagreement with the result reached by a majority of the court.

dissolution In corporation law, the legal process by which a corporation's status as a legal entity is terminated; in partnership law, the change in the relation of partners caused by any partner ceasing to be associated with the others in the carrying on of the business.

dissolution order A court order that a firm be split into separate firms.

diversity of citizenship A situation in which the opposing parties in a case are citizens of different states.

divestiture order A court order that merged firms be separated.

dividend In corporate finance, the distribution of a corporation's assets to its shareholders with respect to the number of shares each shareholder owns; in bankruptcy proceedings, a payment made to a creditor who has filed a claim.

document of title A paper, such as a bill of lading or a warehouse receipt, that is evidence that the holder of it is entitled to receive, hold, and dispose of the goods it describes.

domestic corporation A corporation operating within the state of its incorporation.

dominant tenement The parcel of land benefitted by an easement.

donee beneficiary A person who is not a party to a contract but who is intended to receive benefit from the contract as a gift.

donor A person who creates a trust.

double jeopardy The fifth amendment prohibition against a second prosecution after a first trial for the same offense.

dower A life estate for a widow in one third of all the real property owned by her husband, commencing immediately upon the husband's death.

draft A written order signed by one person directing another person to pay money held for the benefit of the directing person.

drawee A person to whom a draft is addressed and who is ordered to pay the sum of money in the draft.

drawer A person who draws a draft.

duress A wrongful use of acts or threats by one person to force another

person to do something that he or she would not otherwise do.

easement A nonpossessory interest in real property.

easement by necessity An easement created by law when both the dominant and the servient tenements were once part of the same parcel and no other access to the dominant tenement exists.

easement by prescription An easement created by open, notorious, continuous, hostile, and adverse use of the servient tenement by the party claiming the easement.

emancipated minor An independent minor who is free from parental care and custody.

eminent domain A government's power to take land away from private owners for public use that is conditioned upon reasonable compensation being paid for the land.

employee A specialized term in labor law that refers to those workers who are not part of management or who are not agricultural workers, domestic servants, employed by the railroads or airlines, working for a parent or spouse, or government workers.

employee at will An employee who does not have a contract that states the duration of the employment and who may thus be discharged at any time for almost any reason.

enabling legislation Legislation creating an administrative agency and empowering it to act; also known as the *organic act.*

encumbrance A claim or lien affecting title.

entrapment The act of officers or agents of the government in inducing a person to commit a crime not contemplated by him or her.

entrusting In sales law, any acquiescence or retention of possession by a merchant of goods of the type in which the merchant deals.

environmental impact statement A detailed analytical report that describes the existing physical environment, the proposed project or action, and the impact the proposed project or action will have on the existing physical environment.

equipment In a secured transaction, goods used or bought for use primarily in a business that are not inventory, farm products, or consumer goods.

ERISA The Employment Retirement Income Security Act of 1974, which attempts to protect workers' pension benefits.

escheat The passing to the state of property that has no legal owner; this occurs when a person dies without a will and is not survived by anyone who is entitled to receive the deceased's property under the intestacy laws.

escrow The holding of property or documents by one party for the safe keeping of a second party with the obligation to deliver it to a third party upon the fulfillment of a condition.

estate in land Property rights in real property held by one or more individuals.

estoppel A rule of law designed to prevent a person from denying a fact that his or her conduct influenced others to believe was true.

Euclidian zoning Zoning based on categories of land use.

eviction A legal action brought by a landlord seeking to have a tenant removed because of a breach of duty by the tenant.

ex post facto An ex post facto law is one that imposes criminal sanctions upon a person for an act that, when committed, was not criminal.

ex ship A contract term that requires a seller to deliver the goods being sold from a ship at a named port of destination where goods of the kind are usually unloaded.

exclusionary rule The rule by which evidence that has been obtained in violation of an individual's constitutional rights may not be admitted against him or her at trial.

exclusive dealing agreement A contract in which a buyer promises to buy a particular product from no one but the seller or the seller promises to sell a particular product to no one but the buyer.

exculpatory clause A provision in a contract by which one party agrees not to hold the other party liable for damages.

executor A man appointed by a court to administer the estate of a person who has died leaving a valid will.

executory Not yet performed.

executrix A woman appointed by a court to administer the estate of a person who has died leaving a valid will.

exemption A privilege allowed by law to a debtor by which he or she may hold certain types or amounts of property free from seizure or sale by court order or from the claims of creditors.

express authority Authority that a principal expressly confers on an agent.

express warranty An express promise made by a seller about the goods that is based upon statements of fact made by the seller about the nature and quality of the goods.

extrinsic evidence External evidence, that is, evidence not contained in the body of a document itself.

FAS Free alongside; a term meaning that the seller must deliver goods alongside a vessel at his or her own expense or risk in the manner usual at that port and obtain a receipt for the goods.

FOB Free on board; a term meaning that a seller will deliver the goods on board a railroad car or ship at the place named without charge to the buyer.

face value The amount of money specified in a life insurance policy that is to be paid when the person whose life is insured dies.

fair representation A duty imposed on a union to represent everyone in the bargaining unit fairly.

false imprisonment The wrongful confinement or restraint of another.

farm products In a secured transaction, goods that are crops, livestock, or supplies used or produced in farming operations or that are products of crops or livestock in their unmanufactured states (such as ginned cotton, maple syrup, milk, and eggs) provided that they are in the possession

of a debtor engaged in raising, fattening, grazing, or other farming operations.

federal question A legal issue that is resolved by application of the Constitution, laws, or treaties of the United States.

Federal Register A daily federal government publication that chronicles all federal regulatory activity.

fee simple An estate in land that gives the owner the right to possess and use the property, to exclude others from it, and to dispose of it.

feigned controversy See *collusive suit.*

felony A serious crime, usually punishable by imprisonment for more than a year.

fictitious payee A name of a payee on a negotiable instrument that is a made up name or a name taken from some list, such as a telephone book, with no intent that the person named will actually receive any money from the instrument.

fiduciary A person who is vested with a special form of trust and is required to use care and to display scrupulous loyalty in carrying out his or her duties.

final payment What occurs when a payor bank has paid an item in cash, has settled with a collecting bank without reserving a right to revoke the settlement, has completed the process of posting an item to a drawer's account, or has made a provisional settlement and has failed to revoke the provisional settlement in the time and manner allowed by law.

final settlement See *final payment.*

financing statement In the law of secured transactions, a document that in many situations must be filed in order to perfect a security interest.

firm offer An irrevocable offer.

fixture An object intentionally attached to real property and adapted to the use to which the real property is being put; considered part of the realty.

floodplain Real property located near waterways and prone to flooding.

foreign corporation A corporation operating in a state other than the state of its incorporation or in a foreign country.

forged signature A fraudulent or un-authorized signing of an instrument.

forgery The unauthorized imitation or alteration of a writing with the intent to defraud.

formal account A legal remedy sought by a party associated with a partnership in which the court orders a comprehensive investigation of the transactions of the partnership and a complete statement of the partnership accounts.

formal rulemaking Developing substantive federal administrative agency rules through the hearing process.

forum non conveniens Inconvenient forum; on occasion, a state court will refuse jurisdiction in a case on the grounds of forum non conveniens because it would be too expensive to bring the evidence and witnesses to that state and it would be more convenient to bring the legal action in another state that also has jurisdiction over the defendant.

fraud An intentional misrepresentation of a material fact upon which there is justifiable reliance and that causes damage.

fraud in the execution Fraud related to the signing of a document or instrument.

fraud in the factum See *fraud in the execution.*

fraud in the inducement A fraud committed in the means used to attract a person to enter into a contract.

fraudulent conveyance A transfer made by a debtor to hinder, delay, or defraud his or her creditors.

fungible goods Goods of a class in which any unit is the equivalent of any other unit.

future goods Goods that either do not yet exist or are not yet identified to a contract for sale.

garnish To use the process of garnishment.

garnishment A legal process by which a creditor obtains property of a debtor held by a third party, such as an employer who holds the employee debtor's wages.

general agent A person employed as a permanent employee to carry out a series of transactions.

general damages Damages arising naturally from the breach of a contract.

general warranty deed An instrument that conveys title to real property in which the grantor promises that the title is clear of any encumbrances anywhere in the chain of title.

geographic market The area of the country in which a firm exercises market power or where the effects of the firm's market power are felt.

gift A transfer of ownership of property for no consideration requiring delivery of the property with donative intent.

gift inter vivos A gift made by a person while he or she is still alive.

good faith Honest intention, sincerity, and lack of deceit; under the Uniform Commercial Code, the observance of reasonable commercial standards of fair dealing in the trade.

goods In sales law, all things (including unborn animals and crops) that are moveable at the time they are identified to the contract, except for investment securities, choses (things) in action, and money that is the price of the goods.

grand jury A group of citizens selected to determine whether there is probable cause to believe that a crime has been committed and whether a specified person should be charged with the crime.

grievance A formal complaint by an employee that he or she is not being treated properly under the terms of a collective bargaining agreement.

guardian A person appointed to act for one who is legally incompetent.

heir A person who receives the property of a person who dies without leaving a will.

holder A person in possession of a document of title, a negotiable instrument, or an investment security that by its terms indicates that the person in possession of the instrument is the owner of the instrument.

holder in due course A holder who takes a negotiable instrument for value, in good faith, and without notice of any claim or defense or that the instrument is overdue or has been dishonored.

holding The essential part of a court's written decision that resolves the conflict before the court.

holographic will A will that is written and signed entirely in the handwriting of the person who made the will.

homestead exemption A debtor's right to keep creditors from taking all or a part of the debtor's ownership in his or her principal residence.

horizontal arrangements Arrangements or activities involving firms that are competitors; also called *horizontal concerted activities.*

horizontal merger The merger of two firms that compete in the same market.

hornbook A book that provides a basic explanation of a science or branch of knowledge such as law.

hybrid rulemaking A substantive rulemaking procedure used by federal administrative agencies that incorporates features of both formal and informal rulemaking procedures.

identification In sales law, marking, shipping, or otherwise designating goods as the goods belonging to the contract.

ignitability The quality of being combustible.

illusory Something that appears to be real or valid but is not.

implied authority Authority that an agent reasonably believes he or she has.

implied warranty A promise that concerns the quality or other characteristic of something that is sold that is not actually made by the seller but is imposed by law.

imposter A person masquerading as another person.

in pari delicto Equally guilty.

incidental authority See *implied authority.*

incidental beneficiary A person who is not a party to a contract but who receives benefit from the contract that is neither intended as a gift nor intended to discharge an obligation of the promisee of the contract.

incidental damages Damages resulting from a buyer's breach of contract, such as the costs of stopping delivery and reselling the goods; damages resulting from a seller's breach, including the expenses incurred in returning rightfully rejected goods and procuring replacements.

incontestability clause A provision in an insurance policy that prohibits the insurance company from cancelling the policy on the grounds of misrepresentation or concealment after a specified period has passed from the time the policy is issued.

indemnify Compensate.

independent contractor A person who is employed by another to perform a task but who is not subject to the control of the other in the physical activities involved in performing the task.

indictment A written accusation presented by a grand jury charging an individual with having committed a crime.

indorsee A person named in an indorsement as the new holder.

indorsement The signature of the holder on a negotiable instrument for the purpose of transferring the instrument.

informal rulemaking The notice and comment procedure used by federal administrative agencies to develop substantive rules.

inherent agency power Power a general agent has to bind a principal by acts that similar agents are authorized to perform, even though such acts have been forbidden by the principal.

injunction An order issued by a court directing a person or a group to refrain from doing a specific act.

insider An executive or other person who has inside corporate information that affects the value of the corporations' securities.

insider trading Trading in the securities of a corporation by executives or others who possess inside corporate information that affects the value of the corporation's securities.

insolvent The condition when a debtor's debts and liabilities exceed his or her assets.

installment contract A contract requiring or authorizing the delivery of goods in separate lots to be separately accepted.

instructions See *charge*.

insurable interest In insurance law, the relationship between a policyholder and the person or property insured that must exist in order for an insurance contract to be legal; in sales law, a property right that the buyer receives when the goods are identified to the contract.

intangible Something that has value but not intrinsic value in its own right, such as a promissory note.

integration A document that is intended as a complete and final expression of an agreement.

intentional infliction of mental distress Extreme and outrageous conduct calculated to cause and actually causing very serious mental distress.

intentional tort The intentional invasion of a protected interest that causes injury.

interbrand competition Competition among the different available brands of a product.

interlocking directorate A situation in which corporations share one or more directors.

intermediary bank A bank in the bank collection chain to which an item is transferred that is not a depositary or payor bank.

interpretive rules Rules designed to guide the administration and interpretation of statutes enforced by a regulatory agency.

interstate commerce Trade activities between the states; commerce that crosses state lines.

intestate A person who dies without leaving a valid will.

intra vires Within the power of; a term used to indicate that a particular corporate action is within the power of the corporation.

intrabrand competition Competition among retailers selling a particular brand of product.

intrastate commerce Trade activity wholly within a single state's boundaries.

invasion of privacy The violation of one's right to be left alone.

inventory Goods that are held by a person for sale or lease or raw materials that are used or consumed in a business.

involuntary bankruptcy A bankruptcy proceeding initiated by a debtor's creditors.

issued shares Shares that a corporation has sold to shareholders.

item Any instrument for the payment of money other than money.

joint adventure A business association that is essentially a partnership but that is formed for a single undertaking or a series of related undertakings of fairly short duration that do not require the complete attention of the associates.

joint and several liability Liability that a person has either together with others who are also liable or individually without the others; procedurally, the person to whom such liability is owed may sue either all of those who are liable or any of the individuals who are liable.

joint liability Liability that is owed by two or more persons together; procedurally, the person to whom such liability is owed must sue all of those who are liable in a single lawsuit.

joint tenancy Co-ownership of real property created when the co-owners receive their interests at the same time and in the same instrument, acquire a similar estate, and have an undivided right to possession.

joint venture See *joint adventure*.

judgment The official declaration of a court that states the winner of a case and the remedies, if any, to which the parties are entitled.

judgment lien A claim or lien obtained through a court proceeding as the result of a judgment in favor of the party having the lien.

judgment n.o.v. (non obstante verdicto) A judgment notwithstanding the verdict; a judgment granted by a judge after a jury returns a verdict on the grounds that the jury could reasonably have given a verdict only to the party to whom they did not give their verdict on the basis of the evidence presented during the trial.

judicial lien creditor A creditor with a judgment lien.

justiciable Capable of being properly decided by a court.

L.S. See *locus sigilli*.

laches Unreasonable delay in bringing a legal claim.

larceny The unprivileged taking of the personal property of another.

large-lot zoning A method of limiting community growth by requiring houses to be built on unnecessarily large lots.

leasehold estate The conveyance of a possessory interest in real property in exchange for rent.

legal tender A medium of exchange that the law forces a creditor to accept in payment of a debt when it is legally offered to him or her by the debtor.

legislative rules Administrative agency rules that specify standards of conduct and may impose sanctions for violations; also known as *substantive rules.*

letter of credit An engagement by a bank or other person made at the request of a customer providing that the bank or other person will honor drafts or other demands for payment made according to the terms of the letter.

libel False and unprivileged publication in writing of material that is injurious to the reputation of another.

lien A claim against property.

lien creditor A creditor with a lien against property belonging to a debtor.

life estate An estate in land, the duration of which is measured by the span of the life of the life tenant or other person.

limited partner A partner in a limited partnership whose liability from partnership transactions is limited to the amount of his or her contribution of capital to the partnership.

limited partnership A partnership formed by two or more persons having one or more general partners and one or more limited partners.

liquidated damages Damages expressly agreed to by the parties to a contract as a term of the agreement as being the amount due as compensation for a loss suffered in the event of a breach.

liquidated debt A debt about which the existence and amount of the debt are not in dispute.

liquidation In corporation law, the process by which a corporation's uncompleted contracts are performed or terminated, all the corporate assets are collected and reduced to cash, creditors are paid, and the remaining funds are distributed to shareholders according to their liquidation preferences; in bankruptcy proceedings, the collection and sale of all of a debtor's property except exempt property for the purpose of paying the creditors.

lockout A temporary closure of a business by an employer in order to put economic pressure on the employees and their union.

locus poenitentiae Withdrawal from an illegal agreement in time to prevent the illegal aspect of the agreement from occurring.

locus sigilli A term designating the authenticity of a document in place of a seal; sometimes abbreviated "L.S."

lost property Property with which the owner has involuntarily or unconsciously parted possession.

majority opinion A written decision by an appellate court with which a majority of the judges deciding the case agree.

maker One who executes a two-party negotiable instrument.

mala in se Acts wrong in themselves.

mala prohibita Acts that are made wrong by legislation.

master A principal that engages another, called a servant, to perform service on his or her behalf and who exercises control over the physical acts of the servant in the performance of the service.

material alteration A change in a negotiable instrument that alters the duty of a party in any respect.

mechanic's lien A claim created by statute for the benefit of a person supplying labor or materials for the construction or repair of a building giving him or her a lien on the building.

merchant In sales law, a person who deals in goods of the kind being sold.

merger A method of combining corporations in which one or more corporations merge into another existing corporation.

merger clause An express statement in a written contract that the writing contains the parties' complete agreement.

midnight deadline In bank collection, midnight on the next banking day following the banking day on which a bank receives an item for processing.

mining partnership A partnership in which the partners co-own land, jointly operate a mining claim on the land, and share in the operation's profits and losses.

misdemeanor A crime that is less serious than a felony, usually punishable by imprisonment for a year or less.

mislaid property Property that has intentionally been placed somewhere and then unintentionally left or forgotten.

misrepresentation An assertion that is unintentionally not in accordance with the facts; a legal defense to a claim of breach of contract.

mistrial A trial that ends because of a defect or error in the proceedings.

modify a warranty To qualify or limit a promise made about the nature or quality of something.

monopoly An industry in which a single firm is the sole supplier of a unique product.

moot Already resolved; a court will not decide a case that is moot.

moral turpitude Depraved behavior, morally unacceptable to society.

mutual mistake A mistake of fact made by both parties to a contract.

mutual rescission A mutual agreement between the parties to a contract to terminate the contract.

necessaries Goods and services essential to the survival of a minor for which a contract for sale between the seller and the minor purchaser is legally binding.

negligence The failure to use such care as a reasonably prudent and careful person would use under similar circumstances.

negligence per se The unexcused violation of an applicable statute.

negotiability A legal theory that makes certain pieces of paper acceptable means of payment or substitutes for goods.

negotiable document of title A document of title that serves as a substitute for goods and allows a holder to have title to the document and to the goods.

negotiable instrument Any two- or three-party instruments, such as drafts, checks, trade acceptances, promissory notes, and certificates of deposit, that contain an obligation for the payment of a sum of money, the legal title to which may be transferred from one person to another by indorsement and delivery by the holder if it is an order instrument or by delivery alone if it is a bearer instrument.

negotiation The effective transfer of a negotiable instrument to a new holder.

nominal damages Very small damages awarded when one person violates the rights of another person but there is no loss or injury or the amount of loss or injury is not proved.

nonacceptance remedy In sales law, a seller's remedy for a buyer's breach.

nonconforming use A use of land predating the zoning code or zoning code amendments that is inconsistent with the zoning code or zoning code amendments.

nondelivery In sales law, a buyer's remedy for a seller's breach.

nonnegotiable document of title A document of title that serves as a receipt for goods but does not give the owner title to the goods.

non-servant agent An agent who is employed to perform nonphysical tasks, such as securing orders or contracting.

note In the law of commercial paper, a two-party negotiable instrument containing a promise to pay.

notice of dishonor In the law of commercial paper, a notice that must be given in the event of a dishonor in order to preserve the liability of secondary parties.

novation The substitution of a new contract in place of an old contract.

nuncupative will An oral will that is spoken to witnesses.

obligor A person who owes a duty.

offer A promise that is conditional upon receiving something that is demanded in return.

offeree A person to whom an offer is made.

offeror A person who makes an offer.

oligopoly An industry dominated by a few large firms.

open terms Terms that have not been decided in a contract.

option An offer that is irrevocable because the offeree has paid the offeror to keep the offer open.

opt-out statute A statute enacted by a state that allows a debtor to exempt in a bankruptcy only that property specified by the state's law.

oral deposition A pretrial discovery device by which an attorney of a party to a lawsuit can question someone prior to trial in a manner similar to the questioning of a witness at trial.

order instrument A negotiable instrument payable to the order of a named payee or indorsed to a named indorsee.

organic act Legislation creating an administrative agency and empowering the agency to act; also known as the *enabling legislation.*

OSHA The Occupational Safety and Health Act of 1970, which attempts to provide a safe work environment for employees; also, the Occupational Safety and Health Administration.

output contract A contract in which one party agrees to sell its entire output of a product to the other party.

overdraft A draft for an amount in excess of the amount in a depositor's account.

overdue Beyond the proper time for payment.

par value shares Shares of a corporation that have a stated money value placed on them in the articles of incorporation; also called *par shares.*

parent corporation A corporation that owns a majority of the stock of another corporation.

parol evidence rule A rule stating that a written document intended by the parties to be a complete and final expression of their agreement cannot be contradicted or supplemented by evidence of an oral agreement between the parties made prior to or at the same time as the written contract or by other extrinsic evidence.

partially disclosed principal A principal whose existence is known or should be known by a person who transacts business with the principal's agent but whose actual identity is not known by that person.

partner A member of a partnership.

partner by estoppel A person who represents himself or herself to be a partner in a partnership and is therefore held liable to anyone to whom such representation has been made and who has given credit to the partnership.

partnership An association of two or more persons to carry on as co-owners a business for profit.

partnership by estoppel Persons who consent to representations by another that he or she is a partner and are thus liable as though the other were in fact a partner to those who rely on the representations.

partnership interest A partner's share of the partnership's profits and surplus.

partnership property All property contributed to a partnership when it is created and all property subsequently contributed to or acquired by the partnership.

patent The governmental grant of the right to the exclusive manufacture and sale of an invention.

payable at a definite time A negotiable instrument is payable at a definite time if it meets certain statutory requirements, such as being payable on or before a stated date.

payable on demand A negotiable instrument is payable on demand if it is payable at sight or upon presentation or when no time for payment is stated or indicated.

payee The person to whom a negotiable instrument is made or drawn.

payor bank A bank in the bank collection chain on which the item is payable as drawn or accepted.

per curiam By the court; a term signifying that a court's decision is from the court as a whole and was not written by a particular judge.

per se rule A rule formulated by the

courts providing that some activities are inherently so anticompetitive that they are deemed illegal regardless of the actual effect of the activities on competitors.

peremptory challenge A request by a party to a lawsuit, which must be granted by a trial court judge, that a juror be dismissed.

perfect tender rule In sales law, the right of a buyer to reject goods for any contractual nonconformity in the goods or in the manner of delivery.

perfection The process by which a creditor makes a public filing of a security agreement or a financing statement; also the process whereby a creditor's claim in certain property of a debtor is given priority over certain other creditors' claims in the same property.

performance standards zoning A specialized zoning technique that establishes standards for such things as noise, odor, vibrations, and signs that must be met by any user of land within the zone.

periodic tenancy A leasehold estate continuing over a set span of time unless terminated by timely notice by either the landlord or tenant.

personal defense A defense that cannot be raised against a holder in due course, such as failure of consideration.

personal property All forms of property other than land and those things affixed permanently to land.

plaintiff The person who brings a legal action.

planned unit development A development generally defined to be larger than the traditional subdivision that integrates different types of land use.

pleadings The formal written statements made by the parties to a lawsuit, such as the complaint and the answer.

pledge A bailment of goods as security for a debt.

police power The state's inherent regulatory power to protect the public health, safety, and welfare.

possession Having physical control over property with the intent to control that property to the exclusion of others.

posting The process followed by a bank in paying an item and recording the payment.

power of attorney A written statement that another person is authorized to act for and in the place of the person signing the statement.

precedent A court decision that affects a subsequent court decision.

preemptive right The right of a corporate shareholder to purchase a pro rata share of any newly authorized and issued shares so that he or she can maintain a proportionate interest in the corporation.

preference The payment of money or the transfer of property to a creditor that gives the creditor a benefit or priority over other creditors.

present sale A sale that is accomplished by the making of a contract.

presenting bank A bank in the bank collection chain that presents an item, except for a payor bank.

presentment A demand for payment or acceptance of a negotiable instrument made upon the maker, acceptor, drawer, or other payor.

pretermission The unintentional omission of a person, usually a child, from a will.

pre-trial discovery The uncovering of evidence prior to trial through the use of various procedural devices that are intended for that purpose.

price discrimination Charging different prices to different customers for the same product.

prima facie At first sight; evidence that makes a fact presumptively true unless it is disproved by contrary evidence.

prima facie tort A general principle of intentional tort liability.

primary party A maker or an acceptor who is liable on a negotiable instrument regardless of whether certain procedural steps are followed, such as the giving of a notice of dishonor.

principal The person for whom action is taken in an agency relationship.

private nuisance Unreasonable interference by one landowner with another landowner's use and enjoyment of his or her land.

private offering An offer to sell securi-

ties that meets certain requirements so as to be exempt from registration under the 1933 Securities Act.

privity of contract A term used to describe a situation in which a contractual relationship exists.

probate The legal process by which the validity of a will is determined, a person is appointed to administer the deceased's estate, and the estate is administered.

procedural rules Rules guiding the methods and procedures used in carrying out the tasks of an organization such as an administrative agency.

proceeds In the law of secured transactions, whatever is received upon the sale, exchange, collection, or other disposition of collateral.

product market In antitrust law, one of the considerations in the determination of market power in which a court determines the product over which the firm exercises power; the product market includes all commodities reasonably interchangeable by consumers with the firm's product.

promisee A person to whom a promise is made.

promisor A person who makes a promise.

promissory estoppel A basis for enforcing a promise that is not supported by consideration that is used to avoid injustice when a promisor should expect the promisee to act in reliance on the promise and the promisee does take such action.

promissory note A two-party negotiable instrument containing a promise to pay.

promoter A person who takes the preliminary steps in the organization of a corporation.

prospectus A document that provides information concerning securities being issued by a corporation.

protest A formalized notice of dishonor signed by a United States consul or vice consul or by a notary public.

provisional credit A term indicating that a payor bank has reserved a right to revoke a settlement made with a collecting bank.

provisional settlement See *provisional credit.*

proximate cause The primary cause of an injury without which the injury would not have resulted.

proxy A document signed by a corporate shareholder authorizing an agent to vote his or her shares at a shareholders' meeting; an agent who is authorized to vote the shares of a shareholder.

proxy statement A document that a corporation sends to shareholders in advance of a shareholders' meeting that contains information about the corporation and the issues to be voted on at the meeting.

public policy The policy reflected by a society's laws, customs, and public opinion.

puffing A seller's opinion that is not a misrepresentation concerning that which is being sold.

punitive damages Money awarded to a plaintiff above and beyond compensatory damages to penalize the defendant for malicious conduct.

purchase money Money that is lent or credit that is advanced to allow a person to make a purchase.

pyramid sale A sale of goods or services to a buyer who is induced to make the purchase by the claim that the buyer can get the goods or services for less than the full purchase price by making similar sales to other persons.

qualified drawer A person who draws a negotiable instrument using the words "without recourse" or words of similar effect, evidencing the drawer's intent not to be bound should the primary party fail to pay.

qualified indorsement An indorsement containing the words "without recourse" or words of similar effect, evidencing the indorser's intent not to be bound should the primary party fail to pay.

qualified indorser A person who uses a qualified indorsement.

quasi-contract An obligation between parties that is similar to a contract obligation but that arises out of the relationship between or actions of the parties rather than from their agreement.

quasi-judicial action An administrative action involving factual determinations and the discretionary application of rules and regulations.

quasi-legislative action An administrative action involving the creation of rules and regulations.

quitclaim deed An instrument that conveys whatever interest in real property the grantor has and in which the grantor makes no promise that he or she actually has title to the property.

quo warranto proceeding A legal action brought by a state that challenges the existence of a corporation.

quorum The number of people or votes that must be present or represented at a meeting before business can be validly transacted.

ratification A person's informed approval of a prior act that was performed either by the person or on his or her behalf but was not binding on him or her when performed that results in the act being treated as if it were originally authorized.

reactivity The quality of having a tendency to enter into chemical reactions.

real defense A defense that is good against a holder in due course, such as fraud in the execution.

real estate See *real property.*

real property Land and things permanently affixed to the land.

receivership The collection of rents and profits from land or the transaction of other business by a person called a receiver who is appointed by a court to preserve a person's property.

recourse The right to seek recovery from another party when a person is required to pay.

referral sale A sale of goods or services to a buyer who is induced to make the purchase by the claim that the buyer can get the goods or services for less than the full purchase price by referring other persons to the seller; similar to a pyramid sale.

reformation A legal remedy requiring that a document be rewritten to conform with the actual agreement of the parties.

registration statement In securities regulation, a statement filed with the SEC by a corporation when it issues securities.

regulation A rule made by an administrative agency.

reject In sales law, to refuse to accept goods that do not conform to the contract or were not properly delivered.

rejection Notification to an offeror by an offeree that the offeree does not intend to accept the offer.

release Discharge of one party's duties under a contract by the other party to the contract.

relevant evidence Evidence that tends to prove or disprove a fact about which the parties to a lawsuit are in dispute.

remand An order by an appellate court sending a case back to a lower court.

remitting bank A bank in the bank collection chain that sends or transmits money for an item; any payor or intermediary bank.

renunciation A legally recognized refusal by a person to be bound by his or her past acts.

replevin A legal action to recover possession of goods.

reply A pleading made by a plaintiff in response to a defendant's answer when the answer contains a counterclaim.

repossess In the law of secured transactions, the taking by a creditor of goods in which the creditor has a security interest.

repudiation A breach of a contract prior to the time that performance is due.

request for admission A pretrial discovery device by which one party to a lawsuit can request another party to admit either the genuineness of documents or the truth of facts.

requirements contract A contract in which one party agrees to purchase all of its requirements for a product from the other party.

res In the law of trusts, property that is held in trust.

res ipsa loquitur The thing speaks for itself; the rebuttable presumption that the defendant was negligent.

res judicata A matter settled by judgment; a case in which there has been a final judgment so that the plaintiff may not bring another legal action against the defendant based on the same claim.

resale remedy In sales law, a seller's remedy for a buyer's breach.

rescind To cancel a contract and return the parties to their original positions.

rescission The legal annulment of a contract by agreement of the parties or by judicial order.

respondeat superior Let the master answer; a doctrine that makes a master liable for the torts of a servant committed while the servant is acting in the scope of employment.

restitution A legal remedy that requires the payment of damages in order to prevent unjust enrichment.

restraint of trade Interference with normal competition.

restrictive covenant A restriction on the use of land created by a seller, normally included in the deed conveying the land.

restrictive indorsement An indorsement that is conditional or attempts to prohibit further transfer of a negotiable instrument or includes words such as "for deposit" or states that it is for the benefit of the indorser or another person.

resulting trust An implied trust imposed by law to carry out the apparent intent of a person to create a trust even though that intent has not been made expressly clear.

revocation Notification by an offeror to an offeree that the offer is no longer open for acceptance.

revoke acceptance In sales law, the withdrawal of a buyer's acceptance.

right-to-work law A state law that prohibits union security agreements.

ripe Fully developed; a court will not decide a case unless it is ripe.

risk of loss In sales law, the hazard of loss if goods are damaged or destroyed.

robbery Forcible stealing of property.

rule of reason A test applied by the courts in antitrust cases that holds some forms of activity illegal only when the activity unreasonably restricts competition; applied when the activity has a legitimate business purpose despite anticompetitive effects.

sale The passage of title for a price.

sale on approval A sale in which a buyer who has purchased goods primarily for use has the option of returning the goods to the seller even though the goods conform to the contract.

sale or return A sale in which a buyer who has purchased goods primarily for resale has the option of returning the goods to the seller even though the goods conform to the contract.

scintilla A very small particle.

scope of employment The ambit or range of a servant's job or task.

seal An official symbol affixed to a document to certify its authenticity.

secondary activity Illegal action taken by a union against a neutral party in an effort to force the neutral party to cease doing business with another party, usually the employer with whom the union is having a labor dispute.

secondary party A drawer or indorser who is liable on a negotiable instrument in the event of dishonor provided certain procedural steps are followed, such as the giving of a notice of dishonor.

secured transaction A transaction that creates a security interest.

Securities and Exchange Commission (SEC) The administrative agency that administers the federal securities laws.

security In securities regulation, a document that represents an investment in a corporation.

security agreement An agreement between a debtor and a creditor creating a security interest.

security interest An interest held by a creditor in personal property or fixtures belonging to a debtor that secures payment or performance of an obligation and allows the property to be sold in the event of the debtor's default in order to satisfy the indebtedness.

self-defense An excuse for a person's use of force in resisting an attack on his or her person or property.

servant An agent who is employed by a master to perform service on the master's behalf and whose physical conduct in the performance of the service is controlled by the master.

servient tenement Real property subject to an easement.

setoff The right of a claimant to deduct a claim from property held by the claimant for a person against whom the claimant has the claim.

settlor A person who creates a trust.

shelter rule A legal rule that gives a holder who acquires his or her interest in a negotiable instrument from a holder in due course the same rights as a holder in due course even if the new holder is not a holder in due course.

shipment contract A contract that requires a seller to deliver the goods sold to a carrier and to make proper arrangement for their carriage.

short-swing profits Profits made from trading in a corporation's shares within a six-month period.

sight draft A draft that is payable when presented to the drawer.

slander The speaking of false and unprivileged material that is injurious to the reputation of another.

source standards Standards set to control pollution from such discrete or specific sources as a stack or an outfall pipe.

special agent A person employed by a principal to carry out a specific task.

special damages Damages that do not arise naturally from a breach of contract but are foreseeable by the party committing the breach.

special indorsement An indorsement of a negotiable instrument that names the person to whom the instrument is transferred.

special property In sales law, a property right that a buyer receives when the goods sold are identified to the contract.

special use permit An authorization allowing land uses not provided for in the zoning code.

special warranty deed An instrument that conveys title to real property in which the grantor promises only that the title is free of any encumbrances arising during the grantor's ownership.

specific performance A legal remedy by which a court orders someone to perform a specified act.

speculative bargaining agreement An agreement whereby a party agrees to accept a risk to which another party is subject; an insurance policy, for example.

spendthrift trust A trust containing a clause that prevents the beneficiary from voluntarily or involuntarily assigning his or her rights in the trust.

spot zoning An unplanned land use that fails to conform to the comprehensive plan.

stale In negotiable instruments law, a check that is more than six months old.

standing The capacity of a person to bring a legal action because he or she is asserting his or her own rights.

stare decisis Let the decision stand; the tendency of courts to apply legal principles found in precedents to later cases.

state action doctrine An exemption from federal antitrust laws of anti-competitive conduct that is required by government regulation.

statute A law enacted by a legislature.

Statute of Frauds A statute requiring that certain promises, to be enforceable, must be in a writing that was signed by the party against whom the promises are to be enforced.

statute of limitations A statute providing that a legal claim must be brought within a specified period of time or the right to bring it is lost.

stock dividend A distribution by a corporation of shares of its own stock to its shareholders; technically, a stock dividend is not a dividend.

stop payment order An order directing a bank not to pay an item drawn on a depositor's account.

straight bill of lading A nonnegotiable document of title.

straight warehouse receipt A nonnegotiable document of title.

strict liability Liability without fault.

strict liability crime An act declared unlawful by statute that does not require a criminal state of mind.

strike A cessation of work by employees that is designed to put economic pressure on an employer.

strike suit A derivative suit that is not brought by a corporate shareholder with the intent to correct or obtain compensation for a wrong done to the corporation but rather to obtain a settlement that is personally profitable to the shareholder and his or her attorney.

subagent A person appointed by an agent to perform acts undertaken by the agent for the principal but for whose conduct the agent is primarily responsible.

subpoena An order by a court that a person appear at a trial and give testimony.

subpoena duces tecum An order by a court that a person appear at a trial and produce a document that is in his or her possession.

subrogate To substitute one party in the place of another party in order to enforce the other party's claim against a third party.

subrogation The substitution of one person for another in a claim against a third person.

subsidiary corporation A corporation that has a majority of its stock owned by another corporation.

substantial performance Performance of a contract in such a way that the promisee's expectations under the contract are substantially fulfilled by the promisor's good faith attempt at full performance under the contract.

substantive rules Rules formulated by regulatory agencies that have the force of law, that may require specific standards of conduct, and that may impose sanctions upon violators.

summary judgment A determination made by a trial court judge prior to trial that judgment should be given to one of the parties because there is no genuine issue of fact between the parties.

summons A notice that a legal action has been begun.

Sunday laws Laws prohibiting the formation of contracts on a Sunday.

supervisor In labor law, a person who belongs to management because he or she has the power on behalf of management to direct employees in the performance of their jobs.

takeover A process in which one corporation buys enough shares of another corporation to gain working control of it and then merges the acquired corporation into the acquiring corporation.

tenancy at sufferance A leasehold estate created when a tenant who originally gained possession of real property legally continues to possess that property wrongfully.

tenancy at will A leasehold estate that has no fixed term of existence.

tenancy by the entirety A joint tenancy existing between husband and wife that cannot be terminated by one without the other's consent.

tenancy in common Co-ownership of real property that gives each owner an undivided interest in the property but includes no right of survivorship.

tender An offer of payment, combined with intent and ability to perform; an offer to perform in accord with a contract.

tender of delivery In sales law, a seller's offer to deliver conforming goods.

tender offer A conditional offer to purchase shares of a corporation that are tendered at a specified price for a specified time.

term tenancy A leasehold estate created by agreement that has specific beginning and ending dates.

termination In partnership law, that which occurs to a partnership when it has been dissolved and its business has been wound up.

testator A man who makes a will.

testatrix A woman who makes a will.

theft of services The obtaining of services, such as gas, water, electricity, and telecommunications services, with the intent to avoid payment.

things in action See *chose in action.*

third-party beneficiary contract A contract that benefits a third person who is not a party to the contract.

time draft A draft that is payable at a specific time.

timed-growth scheme Regulations formulated by communities to dictate when and where community growth will occur through such means as limitations on houses constructed per year, population caps, or the timing of community growth to match the growth of services.

title Legal evidence of ownership.

title search An examination of the records of conveyance concerning a parcel of land that is made to obtain the chain of title.

tort A civil wrong other than a breach of contract.

tortfeasor One who commits a tort.

totten trust A revocable trust that is created when a person deposits money in a bank account and names himself or herself as trustee for the benefit of another person.

toxicity The quality of being poisonous.

trace To identify property or money that has been converted into different property or money.

trade secret A formula, pattern, device, or compilation of information that is used in a business and gives that business an advantage over competitors who do not know or use it.

trade usage A regular practice or method of dealing in a particular trade or industry that indicates a particular interpretation of a contract.

trademark A distinctive mark through which the products of a particular manufacturer may be distinguished from those of other manufacturers.

treasury shares Shares of a corporation that have been issued and subsequently reacquired by the corporation.

trespass An unlawful interference with a person's property.

trespass to chattels An unlawful interference with the possessory rights of another to personal property.

trespass to land An unlawful interference with another's real property.

trust A legal device by which a person with legal title to property holds it for the benefit of another person, who is said to have equitable title to the property.

trustee A person who administers a trust; a person in whom an estate, in-

terest, or power is vested under an agreement or a court order that provides for the administration of the property or the exercise of the power for the benefit or use of another.

trustee in bankruptcy A trustee who administers the property of the debtor in a bankruptcy proceeding.

tying arrangement An agreement conditioning the purchase of a particular product or service upon the purchase of a different product or service.

UCC See *Uniform Commercial Code.*

ultra vires Beyond the power of; a term used to indicate that a particular corporate action is not within the power of the corporation.

unauthorized signature A fraudulent or unpermitted signing of an instrument.

unclean hands A legal concept signifying that a person seeking a remedy from a court has himself or herself engaged in improper conduct.

unconscionable Something that is so improper that it is shocking to the conscience.

underwriter An organization that aids and advises a corporation that issues securities and that may also purchase the securities and resell them to dealers.

undisclosed principal A principal who a person transacting business with an agent has no notice of.

undue influence A wrongful use of power by a person in a dominant position of trust for the purpose of persuading the dependent person to do something he or she would not otherwise do.

unfair labor practice An activity prohibited by federal labor law.

Uniform Commercial Code A statute proposed by the National Commissioners on Uniform State Laws that modernizes and unifies commercial law and that has been adopted by all the states except Louisiana.

unilateral contract A contract in which the offeror makes a promise that is conditional upon receiving something other than a promise (usually an act) from the promisee.

unilateral mistake A mistake of fact by one of the parties to a contract.

union security clause A provision in a collective bargaining agreement that requires employees to join or financially support the union that represents them.

union shop An arrangement whereby an employee must join the union that represents all employees who work for the employer or be discharged.

unliquidated debt A debt about which the existence of the debt, the amount of the debt, or both are in dispute.

unqualified indorsement An indorsement that is not qualified.

usage of trade A practice or method of dealing that is so common that it can be expected to be part of an agreement even though it is not expressly included in the agreement.

usury The charging of an interest rate in excess of that permitted by statute.

value Consideration sufficient to support a simple contract.

variance A modest deviation from a zoning code's restrictions that is granted to a landowner by the zoning administrator.

verdict A declaration made by a jury of who wins a lawsuit.

vertical merger A merger of firms that are at different levels in the same production chain.

vertical restrictions Restrictions imposed by a manufacturer or a supplier of a product or service upon the firms that retail or distribute that product or service.

vicarious liability Liability that the law imposes upon one person for the illegal acts of another.

violation Prohibited conduct that is less serious than a crime.

void Of no legal effect.

voidable Capable of being set aside.

voidable contract A contract that has come into existence but that may be set aside by one of the parties.

voidable title A title that a seller has transferred but that can be reclaimed by him or her.

voluntary bankruptcy A bankruptcy proceeding initiated by a debtor.

wagering agreement An agreement in which payment depends on the occurrence of an uncertain event.

waiver The giving up of a right.

waiver-of-defense clause A clause in an agreement providing that a party will not use against an assignee of the agreement any defense that arose out of the original transaction.

warehouse receipt A document issued by a warehouseman that serves as a receipt for the goods and expresses the terms for storage.

warranty A promise made by a seller concerning the quality or other characteristic of something that is sold.

warranty deed An instrument that conveys title to real property in which the grantor promises that the title is free from any encumbrances.

warranty of authority An implied promise, made by an agent when he or she purports to make a contract on behalf of a principal, that he or she has the power to bind the principal to the contract.

warranty of fitness A promise implied in a sale of goods that the goods are fit for a particular purpose that arises when the buyer is relying on the seller's skill and judgment to select suitable goods and the seller knows of the buyer's particular purpose.

warranty of habitability A landlord's implied promise that residential property that he or she leases is safe, sanitary, and fit for living during the entire period of the tenancy.

warranty of merchantability A promise implied in a sale of goods by a merchant that the goods are reasonably suited for the general purpose for which they are sold.

warranty of title An implied promise by a transferor that he or she has title or the right to transfer title.

wetlands Real property that has groundwater levels at or near the surface for a substantial part of the year or that is vegetated by aquatic plants.

will A declaration by a person of the way in which his or her property is to be distributed when he or she dies.

winding up In partnership law, selling the partnership's assets, paying off the firms obligations to third parties, and distributing the amounts remaining to the partners.

workers' compensation Payments made to employees or their dependents under a statute that provides for fixed awards in the event of an employment-related accident or disease.

writ of certiorari A formal request to an appellate court that it voluntarily hear an appeal in a case in which there is no right of appeal.

written interrogatories A pretrial discovery device by which a party to a lawsuit can submit to another person written questions to be answered.

wrongful dishonor A refusal by a bank to pay an item drawn on a depositor's account that was properly payable.

yellow dog contract An employment contract in which an employee promises not to join or remain in a union; such a contract is illegal.

zoning Regulations that promote the public health, safety, or welfare by placing restrictions on the use of land and on the structures that can be erected on the land.

CASE INDEX

INDEX